Natural Resource and Environmental Economics

Third Edition

Roger Perman
Yue Ma
James McGilvray
Michael Common

PEARSON

Addison
Wesley

Harlow, England • London • New York • Boston • San Francisco • Toronto
Sydney • Tokyo • Singapore • Hong Kong • Seoul • Taipei • New Delhi
Cape Town • Madrid • Mexico City • Amsterdam • Munich • Paris • Milan

Pearson Education Limited
Edinburgh Gate
Harlow
Essex CM20 2JE

and Associated Companies throughout the world

Visit us on the World Wide Web at:
www.pearsoned.co.uk

First published 1996 Longman Group Limited
Second edition 1999 Addison Wesley Longman Limited
Third edition 2003 Pearson Education Limited

ISBN: 978-0-273-65559-6

British Library Cataloguing-in-Publication Data
A catalogue record for this book is available from the British Library

Library of Congress Cataloging-in-Publication Data
Natural resource and environmental economics / Roger Perman . . . [et al.].—3rd ed.
   p. cm.
   Rev. ed. of: Natural resource and environmental economics / Roger Perman,
Yue Ma, James McGilvray. 1996.
   Includes bibliographical references and index.
   ISBN 0-273-65559-0 (pbk.)
   1. Environmental economics.   2. Natural resources—Management.
3. Sustainable development.   I. Perman, Roger, 1949– Natural resource and
environmental economics.

HC79.E5 P446 2003
333.7—dc21   2002042567

10   9
09

Typeset in 9.75/12pt Times by 35
Printed and bound in Malaysia   (CTP - VVP)

Contents

Preface to the Third Edition

As we wrote in a previous preface, there are two main reasons for producing a new edition of a textbook. First, the subject may have moved on – this has certainly been true in the area of natural resource and environmental economics. Second, experience in using the text may suggest areas for improvement. Both reasons warrant a third edition now.

We will say nothing here about the ways in which the subject area has 'moved on' except to note that it has and that you will find those changes reflected in this new edition. As far as experience in the use of this text is concerned, some more comment is warranted.

First, we have received much feedback from users of the text. Much of this has been highly favourable. Indeed, the authors are very pleased to note that its readership has become very broad, particularly since the appearance of a Chinese translation of the second edition of the text. Negotiations have just started for a Russian translation of the third edition. User feedback – formal and informal – has provided us with many ideas for ways of making the text better. We are particularly grateful to those individuals who provided solicited reviews of the first and second editions, and to the many readers who made unsolicited comments. Many of the changes you will find here reflect that body of advice.

Some of the main changes that have taken place between the second and third editions are as follows. There is substantial change to the organisation of the text, principally involving a division into Parts that reflect clusters of themes. Details of this change are given in the Introduction. There are three new chapters: pollution policy with imperfect information, cost–benefit analysis, and stock pollution problems. Most of the chapters that are retained from the second edition have been very substantially changed. Of the many changes that could be listed, we mention just four. We pay greater attention to game theory (especially in considering international environmental problems); the consequences of decision making under uncertainty are treated more widely throughout the text; and our use of mathematics has been changed significantly. Much of the formal treatment has been pulled into appendices, leaving the main body of the chapters to emphasise intuition and verbal or diagrammatic explanation. However, despite this, the exposition and application is more strongly based in economic theory than before, rather than less. Finally, considerably more attention has been given to the spatial dimension of pollution problems and abatement programmes.

The other major area of change we have made to the text lies in the development of the accompanying website for the text, and in the additional resources it contains. We will leave you to peruse the *Additional Resources* section a few pages below this point to find out what this set of resources comprises.

There are several friends and colleagues the authors would like to thank. Our thanks go to Alison Wilson for her assistance in preparation of the indexes. We remain grateful to Jack Pezzey for writing an appendix to what is now Chapter 19, and for giving comments on drafts of the relevant parts of the chapter in its second edition counterpart. Mick Common, Yue Ma and Roger Perman would like to express their gratitude to Alison McGilvray for her continued support and encouragement throughout this revision process. The genesis, early editions, and current form of the book owe much to her late husband, Jim. We hope that she would agree that this new edition is one of which Jim would feel proud.

Roger, Yue and Mick have succeeded in remaining permanent partners with their wives – Val Perman, Hong Lin and Branwen Common – despite the increasing burdens of academic life and textbook preparation. Once again, we are grateful to our wives for their help and encouragement.

It would be wrong of us not to express once again our debt to Chris Harrison (now at Cambridge University Press) for his excellence in all aspects of commissioning, editing and providing general support for the two previous editions. We know he remains interested in its success. Michael Fitch has edited the manuscript with diligence and professionalism, correcting many of our errors and improving the transparency and readability of the text. For this we are very grateful. The staff at Pearson Higher Education, particularly Paula Harris, Catherine Newman and Ellen Morgan have, as always, been helpful, enthusiastic and professional.[1]

ROGER PERMAN

YUE MA

MICHAEL COMMON

JULY 2002

---

[1] The individuals responsible for typesetting made a superb job of translating the copy-edited manuscript into pages for the book.

Acknowledgements

It is impossible to fully acknowledge our debt to the many individuals who have developed, and fostered awareness of, the discipline of natural resource and environmental economics. We hope that this debt becomes clear to the reader of this text. What will not be evident to the reader is the debt which the authors owe to those teachers who have cultivated our interests in this area of study.

Wherever the authors have drawn heavily on expositions, in written or other form, of particular individuals or organisations, care was taken to ensure that proper acknowledgement was made at the appropriate places in the text. As noted in the Preface to the Second Edition, Jack Pezzey wrote the first of the appendices to Chapter 19.

We are grateful to the following for permission to reproduce copyright material:

Figure 2.13 from *The Limits to Growth: A Report for The Club of Rome's Project on the Predicament of Mankind* (Meadows, D.H., *et al.* 1972); Figures 6.1 and 6.2 from *Externalities of Energy, Vol. 4, Oil and Gas*, by permission of the Office for Official Publications of the European Communities. Unite 'Services auteurs' Copyright Bureau JMO C5-129 (ExternE, 1995); Tables 6.5 and 10.8 and Figures 10.16 and 10.17 from *Climate Change 2001: Mitigation. Third Assessment Report of Working Group III of the IPCC* by permission of the Intergovernmental Panel on Climate Exchange (IPCC, 2001); Table 7.4 from Economic foundations of the current regulatory reform efforts, *Journal of Economic Perspectives* **10**(3), 124–5 (Viscusi, W.K. 1996); Table 7.7 from T.H. Tietenberg, Economic Instruments for Environmental Regulation, *Oxford Review of Policy* **6**(1), 17–34, by permission of Oxford University Press and the author (Tietenberg, T.H. 1990); Figure 10.13 from EUR report 16523 reproduced by permission of the Publishers, the Office for Official Publications of the European Communities © European Communities; Table 18.2 from *FRA 2000 Main Report*, Table 49-1, page 334, by permission of the Food and Agriculture Organization of the United Nations (FRA, 2000); Figure 19.1 from Data from Environmental Indicators: OECD Core Set, Copyright OECD, 1995; Tables 19.1 and 19.2 from *Environmental Measures*, Environmental Challenge Group; Figure 19.3 from Index of sustainable economic welfare for the UK, *Index of Sustainable Economic Welfare – a Pilot Index: 1959–1990* (Jackson and Marks, 1994); Extracts on p. 345 from 'Global warming won't cost the earth' (F.C. Ind, 1995), *The Independent*.

In some instances we have been unable to trace the owners of copyright material, and we would appreciate any information that would enable us to do so.

Notation

List of variables

As far as possible, in using letters or symbols to denote variables or other quantities of interest, we have tried to use each character consistently to refer to one variable or quantity. This has not always been possible or desirable, however, because of the large number of variables used in the book. In the following listing, we state the meaning that is usually attached to each letter or symbol used in this way. On the few occasions where a symbol is used in two ways, this is also indicated. Where usage differs from those given below, this is made clear in the text.

A = Pollution stock (or ambient pollution level)

B = Gross benefit of an activity

C = Consumption flow *or* total cost of production of a good

D = Damage flow

E = An index of environmental pressure

e = Natural exponent

F = Reduction in pollution stock brought about by clean-up

G = Total extraction cost of a resource *or* biological growth of a resource

H = Renewable resource harvest rate

I = Investment flow

i = Market rate of interest

K = Capital stock (human-made)

L = Labour service flow

M = Emissions (pollution) flow

MP_K = Marginal product of capital

MP_L = Marginal product of labour

MP_R = Marginal product of resource

MU = Marginal utility

MU_X = Marginal utility of good X

NB = Net benefit of an activity

P = Unit price of resource (usually upper-case for gross and lower-case for net)

Q = Aggregate output flow

R = Resource extraction or use flow

r = Consumption rate of interest

S = Resource stock

T = Terminal time of a planning period

t	= A period or instant of time
U	= Utility flow
V	= Environmental clean-up expenditure
W	= Social welfare flow
Z	= Pollution abatement flow
δ	= Social rate of return on capital
α	= Pollution stock decay rate
ρ	= Rate of utility time preference (utility discount rate)

The Greek characters μ, χ and ω are used for shadow prices deriving from optimisation problems.

The symbols X and Y are used in a variety of different ways in the text, depending on the context in question.

Mathematical notation

Where we are considering a function of a single variable such as

$$Y = Y(X)$$

then we write the first derivative in one of the following four ways:

$$\frac{dY}{dX} = \frac{dY(X)}{dX} = Y'(X) = Y_X$$

Each of these denotes the first derivative of Y with respect to X. In any particular exposition, we choose the form that seems best to convey meaning.

Where we are considering a function of several variables such as the following function of two variables:

$$Z = Z(P, Q)$$

we write first partial derivatives in one of the following ways:

$$\frac{\partial Z}{\partial P} = \frac{\partial Z(P, Q)}{\partial P} = Z_P$$

each of which is the partial derivative of Z with respect to the variable P.

We frequently use derivatives of variables with respect to time. For example, in the case of the variable S being a function of time, t, the derivative is written in one of the following forms:

$$\frac{dS}{dt} = \frac{dS(t)}{dt} = \dot{S}$$

Our most common usage is that of dot notation, as in the last term in the equalities above.

Finally, much (but not all) of the mathematical analysis in this text is set in terms of continuous time (rather than discrete time). For reasons of compactness and brevity, we chose in the first and second editions to avoid using the more conventional continuous-time notation $x(t)$ and to use instead the form x_t. That convention is continued here. This does, of course, run the risk of ambiguity. However, we have made every effort in the text to make explicit when discrete-time (rather than continuous-time) arguments are being used.

Introduction

Who is this book for?

This book is directed at students of economics, undertaking a specialist course in resource and/or environmental economics. Its primary use is expected to be as a principal textbook in upper-level undergraduate (final year) and taught masters-level postgraduate programmes. However, it will also serve as a main or supporting text for second-year courses (or third-year courses on four-year degree programmes) that have a substantial environmental economics component.

This third edition of the text is intended to be comprehensive and contemporary. It deals with all major areas of natural resource and environmental economics. The subject is presented in a way that gives a more rigorous grounding in economic analysis than is common in existing texts at this level. It has been structured to achieve a balance of theory, applications and examples, which is appropriate to a text of this level, and which will be, for most readers, their first systematic analysis of resource and environmental economics.

Assumptions we make about the readers of this text

We assume that the reader has a firm grasp of the economic principles covered in the first year of a typical undergraduate economics programme. In particular, it is expected that the reader has a reasonable grounding in microeconomics. However, little knowledge of macroeconomics is necessary for using this textbook. We make extensive use throughout the book of welfare economics. This is often covered in second-year micro courses, and those readers who

have previously studied this will find it useful. However, the authors have written the text so that relevant welfare economics theory is developed and explained as the reader goes through the early chapters.

The authors have also assumed that the reader will have a basic knowledge of algebra. The text has been organised so that Parts I to III inclusive (Chapters 1 to 13) make use of calculus only to an elementary level. Part IV (Chapters 14 to 19) deals with the use of environmental resources over time, and so necessarily makes use of some more advanced techniques associated with dynamic optimisation. However, we have been careful to make the text generally accessible, and not to put impediments in the way of those students without substantial mathematics training. To this end, the main presentations of arguments are verbal and intuitive, using graphs as appropriate. Proofs and derivations, where these are thought necessary, are placed in appendices. These can be omitted without loss of continuity, or can be revisited in a later reading.

Nevertheless, the authors believe that some mathematical techniques are sufficiently important to an economic analysis of environmental issues at this level to warrant a brief 'first-principles' exposition in the text. We have included, as separate appendices, sections explaining the Lagrange multiplier technique of solving constrained optimisation problems, an exposition of optimal control theory, and a brief primer on elementary matrix algebra.

Contents

A novel feature of this third edition is the division of the text into four parts; these parts cluster together the principal areas of interest, research and learning in natural resource and environmental economics.

Part I deals with the foundations of resource and environmental economics

The first chapter provides a background to the study of resource and environmental economics by putting the field in its context in the history of economics, and by briefly outlining the fundamental characteristics of an economics approach to environmental analysis. The text then, in Chapter 2, considers the origins of the sustainability problem by discussing economy–environment interdependence, introducing some principles from environmental science, and by investigating the drivers of environmental impact. Sustainable development is intrinsically related to the quality of human existence, and we review here some of the salient features on the current state of human development. Chapter 3 examines the ethical underpinnings of resource and environmental economics, while Chapter 4 considers conceptualisations of the sustainability problem. Part I finishes, in Chapter 5, with a comprehensive review of the theory of static welfare economics, and provides the fundamental economic tools that will be used throughout the rest of the book.

Part II covers what is usually thought to be 'environmental economics'

A principal focus of the five chapters in Part II is the analysis of pollution. We deal here with pollution targets, in Chapter 6, and with methods of attaining pollution targets (that is, instruments), in Chapter 7. We are careful to pay proper attention to the limits of economic analysis in these areas. Pollution policy is beset by problems of limited information and uncertainty, and Chapter 8 is entirely devoted to this matter. Many environmental problems spill over national boundaries, and can only be successfully dealt with by means of international cooperation. Again, we regard this topic of sufficient importance to warrant a chapter, 10, devoted to it. A central feature of this chapter is our use of game theory as the principal tool by which we study the extent and evolution of international cooperation on environmental problems. Finally, the authors stress the limits of partial equilibrium analysis. In Chapter 9 we take the reader through the two principal tools of economy-wide economy–environment modelling, input–output analysis and computable general equilibrium modelling. The ways in which general equilibrium – as opposed to partial equilibrium – modelling can enhance our understanding of resource and environmental issues and provide a rich basis for policy analysis is demonstrated here.

Part III is concerned with the principles and practice of project appraisal

Many practitioners will find that their work involves making recommendations about the desirability of particular projects. Cost–benefit analysis is the central tool developed by economists to support this activity. We provide, in Chapter 11, a careful summary of that technique, paying close attention to its theoretical foundations in intertemporal welfare economics. Our exposition also addresses the limits – in principle and in practice – of cost–benefit analysis, and outlines some other approaches to project appraisal, including multi-criteria analysis. A distinguishing characteristic of the economic approach to project appraisal is its insistence on the evaluation of environmental impacts on a basis that allows comparability with the other costs and benefits of the project. In Chapter 12 we examine the economic theory and practice of valuing environmental (and other non-marketed) services, giving examples of the application of each of the more commonly used methods. Inevitably, decisions are made within a setting of risk and uncertainty, and in which actions will often entail irreversible consequences. Chapter 13 examines how these considerations might shape the ways in which projects should be appraised.

Part IV covers what is commonly known as resource economics

The basic economic approach to natural resource exploitation is set out in Chapter 14. In Chapter 15 we focus on non-renewable resources, while Chapter 17 is about the economics of renewable resource harvesting and management, focusing especially on ocean fisheries. Forest resources have some special characteristics, and are the subject of Chapter 18. Chapter 16 revisits the analysis of pollution problems, but this time focusing on stock pollutants, where the analytical methods used to study resources are applicable. In this chapter pollution generation is linked to the extraction and use of natural resources, as is necessary in order to develop a sound understanding of many environmental problems, in particular that of the enhanced greenhouse effect. Finally, Chapter 19 returns to the question of sustainability in the context of a discussion of the theory and practice of environmental accounting.

Perspectives

All books look at their subject matter through one or more 'lenses' and this one is no exception.

- It adopts an *economics* perspective, while nevertheless recognising the limits of a purely economic analysis and the contributions played by other disciplines.
- It is an *environmental* economics (as opposed to an *ecological* economics) text, although the reader will discover something here of what an ecological economics perspective entails.
- The authors have oriented the text around the organising principles of *efficiency* and *sustainability*.
- Many textbook expositions fail to distinguish properly between the notions of efficiency and optimality; it is important to use these related, but nevertheless separate, ideas properly.
- Although the partitioning of the text might be taken to imply a separation of resource economics from environmental economics, our treatment of topics has made every effort to avoid this.
- Some topics and ideas appear at several points in the book, and so are examined from different perspectives and in various contexts. Examples include the Hartwick rule and the safe minimum standard principle.
- Substantial attention is given to the consequences of limited information (or uncertainty) for policy making.

The textbook as a learning resource

The authors are aware that students need a variety of resources for effective learning. We have tried to move this third edition of the text closer to providing a full set of such resources. This has been done mainly through the development of an accompanying website.

The content of that site is described at length in the section on *Additional Resources*. At this point it is sufficient just to note that these consist (principally but not exclusively) of

- a set of web links, carefully structured to facilitate further reading and research;
- specimen answers for the Discussion Questions and Problems that appear at the end of the chapters in the book;
- many additional online Word documents, examining at greater length some topics that had relatively brief coverage in the main text (such as biodiversity, agriculture, traffic);
- a large number of Excel files that use simulation techniques to explore environmental issues, problems, or policies. These can be used by the reader to enhance understanding through exploring a topic further; and teachers may work them up into problems that give powerful insight.

Other pedagogical features

We have gone to some trouble to use, as far as is possible, consistent notation throughout the book. A list of the main symbols used and their usual meanings is given on page xvi. However, given the range of material covered it has not been possible to maintain a one-to-one correspondence between symbols and referents throughout the book. Some symbols do have different meanings in different places. Wherever there is the possibility of confusion we have made explicit what the symbols used mean at that point in the text.

Secondly, each chapter begins with learning objectives and concludes with a chapter summary. While these are relatively modest in extent, we hope the reader will nevertheless find them useful. Finally, each chapter also contains a guide to further reading. Several of these are very extensive. Combined with the website-based links and bibliographies, the reader will find many pointers on where to go next.

Course designs

The authors do, of course, hope that this text will be used for a full course of study involving the material in all 19 chapters. However, we are aware that this would be time-consuming and may not fit with all institutional structures. We therefore offer the following three suggestions as to how the text might be used for shorter courses. Suggestions A and B avoid the chapters where dynamic optimisation techniques need to be used, but still include material on sustainability and the principles and application of cost–benefit analysis. In all cases, courses could be further shortened for students with a strong economics background by treating some parts, at least, of Chapters 5 and 11 as revision material. We do not recommend that this material be completely dropped for any course. Obviously, other permutations are also possible.

A: An environmental economics course

Part I Foundations

Chapter 1 An introduction to natural resource and environmental economics
Chapter 2 The origins of the sustainability problem
Chapter 3 Ethics, economics and the environment
Chapter 4 Concepts of sustainability
Chapter 5 Welfare economics and the environment

Part II Environmental Pollution

Chapter 6 Pollution control: targets
Chapter 7 Pollution control: instruments
Chapter 10 International environmental problems

Part III Project Appraisal

Chapter 11 Cost–benefit analysis
Chapter 12 Valuing the environment

B: An environmental policy course

Part I Foundations

Chapter 2 The origins of the sustainability problem
Chapter 3 Ethics, economics and the environment

Chapter 4 Concepts of sustainability
Chapter 5 Welfare economics and the environment

Part II Environmental Pollution

Chapter 6 Pollution control: targets
Chapter 7 Pollution control: instruments
Chapter 8 Pollution policy with imperfect information
Chapter 9 Economy-wide modelling
Chapter 10 International environmental problems

Part III Project Appraisal

Chapter 11 Cost–benefit analysis
Chapter 12 Valuing the environment
Chapter 13 Irreversibility, risk and uncertainty

C: A resource economics and policy course

Part I Foundations

Chapter 2 The origins of the sustainability problem
Chapter 4 Concepts of sustainability
Chapter 5 Welfare economics and the environment

Part III Project Appraisal

Chapter 11 Cost–benefit analysis
Chapter 12 Valuing the environment
Chapter 13 Irreversibility, risk and uncertainty

Part IV Natural Resource Exploitation

Chapter 14 The efficient and optimal use of natural resources
Chapter 15 The theory of optimal resource extraction: non-renewable resources
Chapter 16 Stock pollution problems
Chapter 17 Renewable resources
Chapter 18 Forest resources
Chapter 19 Accounting for the environment

Additional resources

On the back cover of this textbook, you will find the URL (website address) of a site that is available to accompany the text. For convenience, we reproduce the web address again here; it is www.booksites.net/perman.

Clicking on this hyperlink will take you to the top page of the Natural Resource and Environmental Economics website maintained by one of the authors. A screenshot of what this web page looks like is shown below.

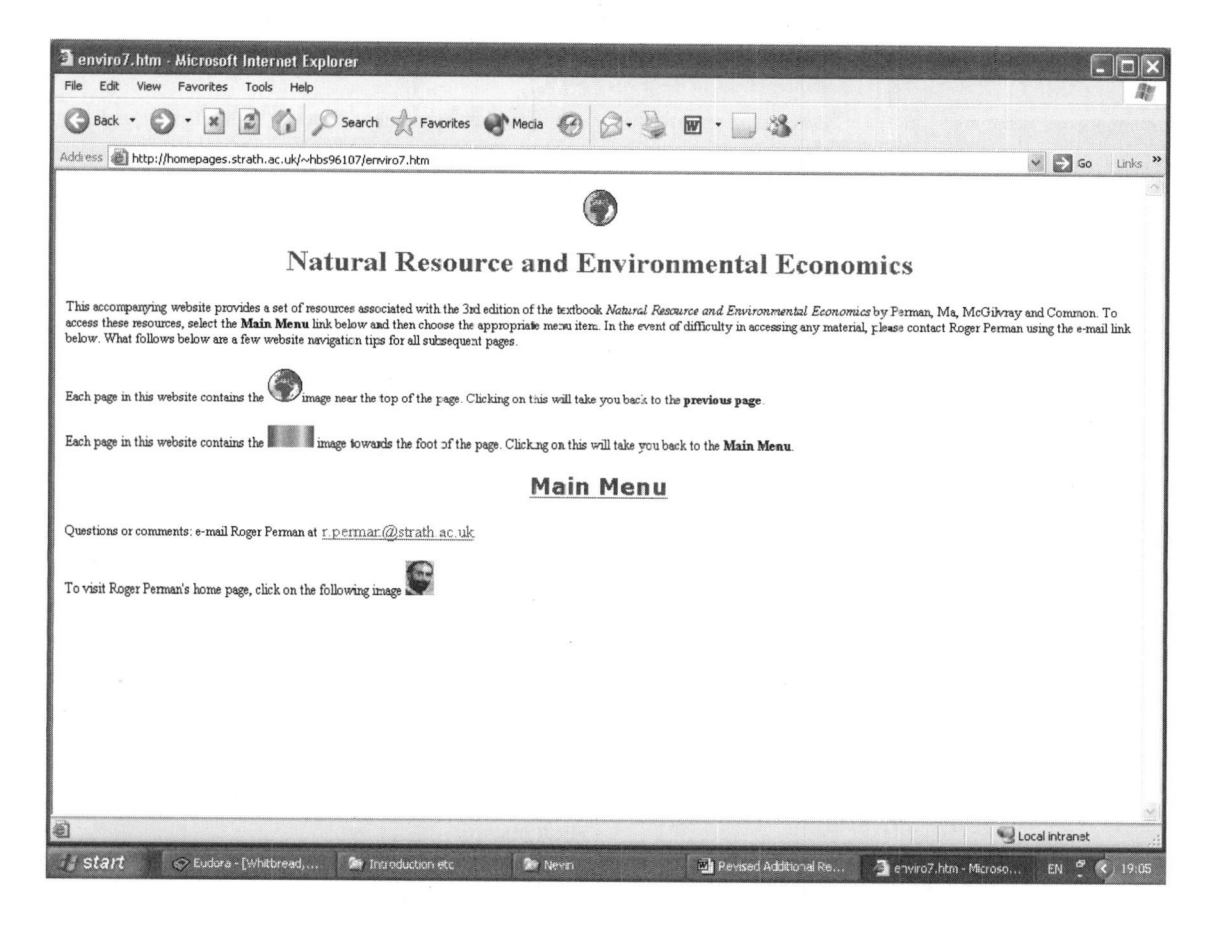

This web page contains, among other things, some navigation tips to help you find your way around this site. When you are ready to move on, please click on the link indicated by **Main Menu**. This takes you to the main menu of resources available on the accompanying website.

The Main Menu contains eight choices. The four on the left are directly related to the textbook. The four on the right are of associated interest. In the table overleaf, a brief description is given of the resources available from each of these menu items. Fuller descriptions of some of these menu items are given later in this Introduction.

This accompanying website will undergo a process of evolution throughout the life of the textbook. Periodically, the content of the web pages will be reviewed and updated where necessary or desirable. Some of the menu items which are relatively 'sparsely populated' right now (such as Miscellaneous Items, and Courses: Outlines and Details) are likely to become more heavily populated as time goes by. As errata become known to us, the relevant web pages will be periodically updated.

The authors welcome suggestions for further items to include on these web pages. If you would like to make any such suggestion, or if you have a particular 'ready-made' item that you feel would be a useful addition, please e-mail Roger Perman at r.perman@strath.ac.uk. The authors will consider these suggestions carefully and, wherever possible and desirable, incorporate them (with proper attribution) in these web pages.

Additional Materials for the Text	Selecting this page gives the reader access to all the *Additional Materials* referred to throughout the text and to many others not mentioned explicitly in the text.
Images from the Text	Here you will find downloadable copies of the images used in the textbook.
Errors in the Third Edition	This page lists all errors in the text currently known to the authors.
Answers to Questions in the Text	Selecting this page takes the reader to a page that gives access to answers to all questions and problems in the text.
Environmental Economics Links	Provides an extensive annotated set of web page links of interest to the resource and environmental economist.
A variety of Bibliographies	Here you will find several large bibliographies of readings compiled by various individuals and organisations.
Courses: Outlines and Details	A compendium of resource and environmental courses available throughout the world.
Miscellaneous Items	As the name implies, contains a collection of items that are difficult to classify but may be of interest to you.

We now give a little more information about some of these menu items.

Additional Materials for the Text

This is intended by the authors to be the main resource available on this accompanying website. It is important to be clear that all the materials here are entirely optional and genuinely additional. It is not necessary for the reader to read, study, or work through any of them. It is not required that you use any of these materials to follow any of the arguments and/or examples used in the text. The textbook has been written in such a way that it stands alone, and does not intrinsically depend on these additional materials. (Where we felt something was necessary, it was included in the main text.)

However, the fact that we have included these materials does imply that the authors think you may find some of them useful. Some materials are designed to broaden knowledge (by giving, in Word files, additional commentary on related matters). Others are aimed at deepening understanding by using standard software packages (such as Excel) to show how numerical examples used in the text were obtained, and to allow the reader to experiment a little, perhaps by changing parameter values from those used in the text and observing what happens. Occasionally we use the symbolic mathematical package Maple for some of the items in *Additional Materials*. Many readers will be unfamiliar with this pakage, and you should not worry if they are not,

therefore, useful to you. But please note that Maple is increasingly being used in higher education, is not difficult to learn, and it can be a very powerful tool to have at your disposal. You may wish to follow some of our suggestions about how this package can be learned. Finally, we also anticipate that some lecturers and instructors will wish to adapt some of these materials for class use (much as many of the files you will find here benefit from other writers' earlier work). The authors believe that much useful learning can take place if instructors adapt some of the spreadsheet exercises as exploratory problems and set them as individual or group tasks for their students.

Accessing the Additional Materials

Most of the chapters in the textbook refer to one or more files that are called *Additional Materials*, plus a specific file name. To find, and then open/download these files, go to the 'Additional Materials for the Text' link in the Main Menu. Then select the appropriate chapter from the table you will see there. The page you will then see contains a hyperlinked listing of all *Additional Materials* for that chapter. The first item in the list for each chapter is a *Readme* file that briefly summarises all of these.

Please note that we do not place a comprehensive listing of all *Additional Materials* referred to in any particular chapter at the end of that chapter. Such a listing can only be found on the appropriate *Readme* file that we mentioned above.

Answers to Questions in the Text

All chapters in this textbook (except the first) contain a small number of Discussion Questions and Problems. Answers are available to most of these. Those answers are collated chapter-by-chapter, and can be accessed through the main table that you will find on this web page.

However, the authors must admit to being in something of a quandary about how those answers should be made available. One principle that we regard as eminently reasonable is that all readers of this text should have free access to the answers. But we are also aware that some instructors may wish to set some of the Questions or Problems for their students, possibly with the intention of assessing answer quality. This seems to be in conflict with the desire to give open access.

At the time of writing, we are inclined to provide open access to the answers. However, the authors reserve the right to change this policy, particularly if instructors inform us that a password-protected answer set would be of particular value to them. Therefore, we may at some point in the future ask Pearson Education Limited to password-protect this site. Those wishing to be given a password would, in that event, need to apply through the relevant form that would be provided in the 'Answers to Questions in the Text' pages on the website. All requests from instructors and any other 'reasonable request' for a password would be met in the affirmative.

Environmental Economics Links

As we remarked in the second edition, a huge volume of information of interest to the environmental economist can now be found on the Internet. This can be read online, printed for future reference or saved to disk. It is hardly a novel idea to compile a set of 'Useful links' and to place this on one's own website. We have also done that.

However, we have reasons for believing you may find this one more useful than most. The main reason for this belief lies in its structure. Actually, these links are structured in two different ways:

- by chapter topic
- by the provider type

For example, suppose that you have just read Chapter 17 (on renewable resources) and wish to be pointed to a set of web links that are particularly useful in relation to the content of that chapter. Then go to the chapter-by-chapter menu option, select 17 from the table, and the links will be provided. We do not claim that our classification is always uncontentious; but the authors have tried to be helpful. Some of the web links contain brief annotated commentary that may help you select more efficiently.

The 'By organisation link' structure is more conventional but still very useful, given that so much of value comes from a relatively small set of organisations. You will find that we have further sub-classified this set in various ways to help your searching. It will be too cumbersome to explain the classification structure here. It will be much simpler for you to follow the appropriate link from the Main Menu and view it directly. You will no doubt know already many incredibly good Internet sites maintained by organisations with an interest in the environment (such as those of the US EPA, various United Nations bodies, and many environmental ministries). You may be less aware of the existence of a large number of excellent university or research group sites, or those of various individuals and NGOs.

Note also that the main menu has one specific item labelled as 'A variety of Bibliographies'. Listed here are not only links to some excellent printed book and/or article bibliographies but also links to a small number of other exceptionally good website compilations. You do not have to rely only on us, therefore!

We are always looking for new suggestions for links to be included in our lists. Please e-mail suggestions to Roger Perman (address given earlier).

Site availability

Although the URL for the accompanying website is www.booksites.net/perman, the server location used is actually at the University of Strathclyde. The site can also be accessed via the URL http://homepages.strath.ac.uk/~hbs96107/enviro7.htm. In common with web addresses at many university servers, this address may change at some time in the future. In the event of such a change, a link to the revised address will be given on the accompanying website.

Foundations

CHAPTER 1 · An introduction to natural resource and environmental economics

Contemplation of the world's disappearing supplies of minerals, forests, and other exhaustible assets has led to demands for regulation of their exploitation. The feeling that these products are now too cheap for the good of future generations, that they are being selfishly exploited at too rapid a rate, and that in consequence of their excessive cheapness they are being produced and consumed wastefully has given rise to the conservation movement.

Hotelling (1931)

Learning objectives

In this chapter you will
- be introduced to the concepts of efficiency, optimality and sustainability
- learn about the history of natural resource and environmental economics
- have the main issues of modern resource and environmental economics identified
- see an overview and outline of the structure of this text

Introduction

The three themes that run through this book are efficiency, optimality and sustainability. In this chapter we briefly explain these themes, and then look at the emergence of the field of study which is the economic analysis of natural resources and the environment. We then identify some of the key features of that field of study, and indicate where, later in the book, the matters raised here are discussed more fully.

1.1　Three themes

The concepts of efficiency and optimality are used in specific ways in economic analysis. We will be discussing this at some length in Chapter 5. However, a brief intuitive account here will be useful. One way of thinking about efficiency is in terms of missed opportunities. If resource use is wasteful in some way then opportunities are being squandered; eliminating that waste (or inefficiency) can bring net benefits to some group of people. An example is energy inefficiency. It is often argued that much energy is produced or used inefficiently, and that if different techniques were employed significant resource savings could be gained with no loss in terms of final output.

This kind of argument usually refers to some kind of technical or physical inefficiency. Economists usually assume away this kind of inefficiency, and focus on allocative inefficiencies. Even where resources are used in technically efficient ways, net benefits are sometimes squandered. For example, suppose that electricity can be, in technically efficient ways, generated by the burning of either some heavily polluting fossil fuel, such as coal, or a less polluting alternative fossil fuel, such as gas. Because of a lower price for the former fuel, it is chosen by profit-maximising electricity producers. However, the pollution results in damages which necessitate expenditure on health care and clean-up operations. These expenditures, not borne by the electricity supplier, may exceed the cost saving that electricity producers obtain from using coal.

If this happens there is an inefficiency that results from resource allocation choices even where there are no technical inefficiencies. Society as a whole would obtain positive net benefits if the less polluting alternative were used. We show throughout the book that such allocative inefficiencies will be pervasive in the use of natural and environmental resources in pure market economies. A substantial part of environmental economics is concerned with how economies might avoid inefficiencies in the allocation and use of natural and environmental resources.

The second concept – optimality – is related to efficiency, but is distinct from it. To understand the idea of optimality we need to have in mind:

1. a group of people taken to be the relevant 'society';
2. some overall objective that this society has, and in terms of which we can measure the extent to which some resource-use decision is desirable from that society's point of view.

Then a resource-use choice is socially optimal if it maximises that objective given any relevant constraints that may be operating.

As we shall see (particularly in Chapter 5), the reason efficiency and optimality are related is that it turns out to be the case that a resource allocation cannot be optimal unless it is efficient. That is, efficiency is a necessary condition for optimality. This should be intuitively obvious: if society squanders opportunities, then it cannot be maximising its objective (whatever that might be). However, efficiency is not a sufficient condition for optimality; in other words, even if a resource allocation is efficient, it may not be socially optimal. This arises because there will almost always be a multiplicity of different efficient resource allocations, but only one of those will be 'best' from a social point of view. Not surprisingly, the idea of optimality also plays a role in economic analysis.

The third theme is sustainability. For the moment we can say that sustainability involves taking care of posterity. Why this is something that we need to consider in the context of resource and environmental economics is something that we will discuss in the next chapter. Exactly what 'taking care of posterity' might mean is discussed in Chapter 4. On first thinking about this, you might suspect that, given optimality, a concept such as sustainability is redundant. If an allocation of resources is socially optimal, then surely it must also be sustainable? If sustainability matters, then presumably it would enter into the list of society's objectives and would get taken care of in achieving optimality. Things are not quite so straightforward. The pursuit of optimality as usually considered in economics will not necessarily take adequate care of posterity. If taking care of posterity is seen as a moral obligation, then the pursuit of optimality as economists usually specify it will need to be constrained by a sustainability requirement.

1.2 The emergence of resource and environmental economics

We now briefly examine the development of resource and environmental economics from the time of the industrial revolution in Europe.

1.2.1 Classical economics: the contributions of Smith, Malthus, Ricardo and Mill to the development of natural resource economics

While the emergence of natural resource and environmental economics as a distinct sub-discipline has been a relatively recent event, concern with the substance of natural resource and environmental issues has much earlier antecedents. It is evident, for example, in the writings of the classical economists, for whom it was a major concern. The label 'classical' identifies a number of economists writing in the eighteenth and nineteenth centuries, a period during which the industrial revolution was taking place (at least in much of Europe and North America) and agricultural productivity was growing rapidly. A recurring theme of political–economic debate concerned the appropriate institutional arrangements for the development of trade and growth.

These issues are central to the work of Adam Smith (1723–1790). Smith was the first writer to systematise the argument for the importance of markets in allocating resources, although his emphasis was placed on what we would now call the dynamic effects of markets. His major work, *An Inquiry into the Nature and Causes of the Wealth of Nations* (1776), contains the famous statement of the role of the 'invisible hand':

> But it is only for the sake of profit that any man employs a capital in the support of industry; and he will always, therefore, endeavour to employ it in the support of that industry of which the produce is likely to be of the greatest value, or to exchange for the greatest quantity, either of money or of other goods.
>
> As every individual, therefore, endeavours as much as he can both to employ his capital in the support of domestic industry, and so to direct that industry that its produce may be of the greatest value; every individual necessarily labours to render the annual revenue of the society as great as he can. He generally, indeed, neither intends to promote the public interest, nor knows how much he is promoting it. . . . he is, in this as in many other cases, led by an invisible hand to promote an end which was no part of his intention . . .
>
> . . . By pursuing his own interest he frequently promotes that of society more effectively than when he really intends to promote it.
>
> *Smith ([1776] 1961), Book IV, Ch. 2, p. 477*

This belief in the efficacy of the market mechanism is a fundamental organising principle of the policy prescriptions of modern economics, including resource and environmental economics, as will be seen in our account of it in the rest of the book.

A central interest of the classical economists was the question of what determined standards of living and economic growth. Natural resources were seen as important determinants of national wealth and its growth. Land (sometimes used to refer to natural resources in general) was viewed as limited in its availability. When to this were added the assumptions that land was a necessary input to production and that it exhibited diminishing returns, the early classical economists came to the conclusion that economic progress would be a transient feature of history. They saw the inevitability of an eventual stationary state, in which the prospects for the living standard of the majority of people were bleak.

This thesis is most strongly associated with Thomas Malthus (1766–1834), who argued it most forcefully in his *Essay on the Principle of Population* (1798), giving rise to the practice of describing those who now question the feasibility of continuing long-run economic growth as 'neo-Malthusian'. For Malthus, a fixed land quantity, an assumed tendency for continual positive population growth, and diminishing returns in agriculture implied a tendency for output per capita to fall over time. There was, according to Malthus, a long-run tendency for the living standards of the mass of people to be driven down to a subsistence level. At the subsistence wage level, living standards would be such that the population could just reproduce itself, and the economy would attain a steady state with a constant population size and constant, subsistence-level, living standards.

This notion of a steady state was formalised and extended by David Ricardo (1772–1823), particularly in his *Principles of Political Economy and Taxation* (1817). Malthus's assumption of a fixed stock of land was replaced by a conception in which land was available in parcels of varying quality. Agricultural output could be expanded by increasing the intensive margin (exploiting a given parcel of land more intensively) or by increasing the extensive margin (bringing previously uncultivated land into productive use). However, in either case, returns to the land input were taken to be diminishing. Economic development then proceeds in such a way that the 'economic surplus' is appropriated increasingly in the form of rent, the return to land, and development again converges toward a Malthusian stationary state.

In the writings of John Stuart Mill (1806–1873) (see in particular Mill (1857)) one finds a full statement of classical economics at its culmination. Mill's work utilises the idea of diminishing returns, but recognises the countervailing influence of the growth of knowledge and technical progress in agriculture and in production more generally. Writing in Britain when output per person was apparently rising, not falling, he placed less emphasis on diminishing returns, reflecting the relaxation of the constraints of the extensive margin as colonial exploitation opened up new tranches of land, as fossil fuels were increasingly exploited, and as innovation rapidly increased agricultural productivity. The concept of a stationary state was not abandoned, but it was thought to be one in which a relatively high level of material prosperity would be attained.

Foreshadowing later developments in environmental economics, and the thinking of conservationists, Mill adopted a broader view of the roles played by natural resources than his predecessors. In addition to agricultural and extractive uses of land, Mill saw it as a source of amenity values (such as the intrinsic beauty of countryside) that would become of increasing relative importance as material conditions improved. We discuss a modern version of this idea in Chapter 11.

Mill's views are clearly revealed in the following extract from his major work.

> Those who do not accept the present very early stage of human improvement as its ultimate type may be excused for being comparatively indifferent to the kind of economic progress which excites the congratulations of ordinary politicians: the mere increase of production . . . It is only in the backward countries of the world that increased production is still an important object; in those most advanced, what is needed is a better distribution . . . There is room in the world, no doubt, and even in old countries, for a great increase in population, supposing the arts of life to go on improving, and capital to increase. But even if innocuous, I confess I see very little reason for desiring it. The density of population necessary to enable mankind to obtain, in the greatest degree, all of the advantages both of cooperation and of social intercourse, has, in all the most populous countries, been attained. A population may be too crowded, though all be amply supplied with food and raiment. It is not good for man to be kept perforce at all times in the presence of his species . . . Nor is there much satisfaction in contemplating the world with nothing left to the spontaneous activity of nature: with every rood of land brought into cultivation, which is capable of growing food for human beings; every flowery waste or natural pasture ploughed up, all quadrupeds or birds which are not domesticated for man's use exterminated as his rivals for food, every hedgerow or superfluous tree rooted out, and scarcely a place left where a wild shrub or flower could grow without being eradicated as a weed in the name of improved agriculture. If the earth must lose that great portion of its pleasantness which it owes to things that the unlimited increase of wealth and population would extirpate from it, for the mere purpose of enabling

> it to support a larger, but not a happier or better population, I sincerely hope, for the sake of posterity, that they will be content to be stationary long before necessity compels them to it.
>
> *Mill (1857), Book IV*

1.2.2 Neoclassical economics: marginal theory and value

A series of major works published in the 1870s began the replacement of classical economics by what subsequently became known as 'neoclassical economics'. One outcome of this was a change in the manner in which value was explained. Classical economics saw value as arising from the labour power embodied (directly and indirectly) in output, a view which found its fullest embodiment in the work of Karl Marx. Neoclassical economists explained value as being determined in exchange, so reflecting preferences and costs of production. The concepts of price and value ceased to be distinct. Moreover, previous notions of absolute scarcity and value were replaced by a concept of relative scarcity, with relative values (prices) determined by the forces of supply and demand. This change in emphasis paved the way for the development of welfare economics, to be discussed shortly.

At the methodological level, the technique of marginal analysis was adopted, allowing earlier notions of diminishing returns to be given a formal basis in terms of diminishing marginal productivity in the context of an explicit production function. Jevons (1835–1882) and Menger (1840–1921) formalised the theory of consumer preferences in terms of utility and demand theory. The evolution of neoclassical economic analysis led to an emphasis on the structure of economic activity, and its allocative efficiency, rather than on the aggregate level of economic activity. Concern with the prospects for continuing economic growth receded, perhaps reflecting the apparent inevitability of growth in Western Europe at this time. Leon Walras (1834–1910) developed neoclassical General Equilibrium Theory, and in so doing provided a rigorous foundation for the concepts of efficiency and optimality that we employ extensively in this text. Alfred Marshall (1842–1924) (see *Principles of Economics*, 1890) was responsible for elaboration of the partial equilibrium supply-and-demand-based analysis of price determination so familiar to students of modern microeconomics. A substantial part of modern environmental economics continues to use these techniques as tools of exposition, as do we at many points throughout the book.

We remarked earlier that concern with the level (and the growth) of economic activity had been largely ignored in the period during which neoclassical economics was being developed. Economic depression in the industrialised economies in the inter-war years provided the backcloth against which John Maynard Keynes (1883–1946) developed his theory of income and output determination. The Keynesian agenda switched attention to aggregate supply and demand, and the reasons why market economies may fail to achieve aggregate levels of activity that involve the use of all of the available inputs to production. Keynes was concerned to explain, and provide remedies for, the problem of persistent high levels of unemployment, or recession.

This direction of development in mainstream economics had little direct impact on the emergence of resource and environmental economics. However, Keynesian 'macroeconomics', as opposed to the microeconomics of neoclassical economics, was of indirect importance in stimulating a resurgence of interest in growth theory in the middle of the twentieth century, and the development of a neoclassical theory of economic growth. What is noticeable in early neoclassical growth models is the absence of land, or any natural resources, from the production function used in such models. Classical limits-to-growth arguments, based on a fixed land input, did not have any place in early neoclassical growth modelling.

The introduction of natural resources into neoclassical models of economic growth occurred in the 1970s, when some neoclassical economists first systematically investigated the efficient and optimal depletion of resources. This body of work, and the developments that have followed from it, is natural resource economics. The models of efficient and optimal exploitation of natural resources that we present and discuss in Chapters 14, 15, 17 and 18 are based on the writings of those authors. We will also have call to look at such models in Chapter 19, where we discuss the theory of accounting for the environment as it relates to the question of sustainability.

1.2.3 Welfare economics

The final development in mainstream economic theory that needs to be briefly addressed here is the development of a rigorous theory of welfare economics. Welfare economics, as you will see in Chapter 5, attempts to provide a framework in which normative judgements can be made about alternative configurations of economic activity. In particular, it attempts to identify circumstances under which it can be claimed that one allocation of resources is better (in some sense) than another.

Not surprisingly, it turns out to be the case that such rankings are only possible if one is prepared to accept some ethical criterion. The most commonly used ethical criterion adopted by classical and neoclassical economists derives from the utilitarian moral philosophy, developed by David Hume, Jeremy Bentham and John Stuart Mill. We explore this ethical structure in Chapter 3. Suffice to say now that utilitarianism has social welfare consisting of some weighted average of the total utility levels enjoyed by all individuals in the society.

Economists have attempted to find a method of ranking different states of the world which does not require the use of a social welfare function, and makes little use of ethical principles, but is nevertheless useful in making prescriptions about resource allocation. The notion of economic efficiency, also known as allocative efficiency or Pareto optimality (because it was developed by Vilfredo Pareto (1897)) is what they have come up with. These ideas are examined at length in Chapter 5. It can be shown that, given certain rather stringent conditions, an economy organised as a competitive market economy will attain a state of economic efficiency. This is the modern, and rigorous, version of Adam Smith's story about the benign influence of the invisible hand.

Where the conditions do not hold, markets do not attain efficiency in allocation, and a state of 'market failure' is said to exist. One manifestation of market failure is the phenomenon of 'externalities'. These are situations where, because of the structure of property rights, relationships between economic agents are not all mediated through markets. Market failure and the means for its correction will be discussed in Chapter 5.

The problem of pollution is a major concern of environmental economics. It first attracted the attention of economists as a particular example of the general class of externalities. Important early work in the analysis of externalities and market failure is to be found in Marshall (1890). The first systematic analysis of pollution as an externality is to be found in Pigou (1920). However, environmental economics did not really 'take off' until the 1970s. The modern economic treatment of problems of environmental pollution is covered in Chapters 6, 7 and 8, and in Chapter 16.

Environmental economics is also concerned with the natural environment as a source of recreational and amenity services, which role for the environment can be analysed using concepts and methods similar to those used in looking at pollution problems. This branch of modern environmental economics is covered in Chapters 11, 12 and 13. Like pollution economics, it makes extensive use of the technique of cost–benefit analysis, which emerged in the 1950s and 1960s as a practical vehicle for applied welfare economics and policy advice. The basic structure and methodology of cost–benefit analysis is dealt with in Chapter 11, building on the discussion of market failure and public policy in Chapter 5.

The modern sub-disciplines of natural resource economics and environmental economics have largely distinct roots in the core of modern mainstream economics. The former emerged mainly out of neoclassical growth economics, the latter out of welfare economics and the study of market failure. Both can be said to effectively date from the early 1970s, though of course earlier contributions can be identified.

1.2.4 Ecological economics

Ecological economics is a relatively new, interdisciplinary, field. In the 1980s a number of economists and natural scientists came to the conclusion that if progress was to be made in understanding and addressing environmental problems it was necessary to study them in an interdisciplinary way. The International Society for Ecological Economics was set up in 1989. The precise choice of name for this society may have been influenced by the fact that a majority of the natural scientists involved were ecologists, but more important was the fact that economics and ecology were seen as the two disciplines most directly concerned with what was seen as the central problem – sustainability.

Ecology is the study of the distribution and abundance of animals and plants. A central focus is an ecosystem, which is an interacting set of plant and animal populations and their abiotic, non-living, environment. The Greek word 'oikos' is the common root for the 'eco' in both economics and ecology. Oikos means 'household', and it could be said that ecology is the study of nature's housekeeping, while economics is the study of human housekeeping. Ecological economics could then be said to be the study of how these two sets of housekeeping are related to one another. Earlier in this chapter we said that sustainability involves taking care of posterity. Most of those who would wish to be known as ecological economists are concerned that the scale of human housekeeping is now such that it threatens the viability of nature's housekeeping in ways which will adversely affect future generations of humans.

The distinguishing characteristic of ecological economics is that it takes as its starting point and its central organising principle the fact that the economic system is part of the larger system that is planet earth. It starts from the recognition that the economic and environmental systems are interdependent, and studies the joint economy–environment system in the light of principles from the natural sciences, particularly thermodynamics and ecology. We shall briefly discuss these matters in the next chapter, which has the title 'The origins of the sustainability problem', as it is the interdependence of economic and natural systems that gives rise to the sustainability problem.

Kenneth Boulding is widely regarded as one of the 'founding fathers' of ecological economics. Box 1.1 summarises a paper that he wrote in 1966 which uses vivid metaphors to indicate the change in ways of thinking that he saw as necessary, given the laws of nature and their implications for economic activity. As we have seen, the dependence of economic activity on its material base – the natural environment – was a central concern of classical economics, but not of neoclassical economics. Boulding was one of a few scholars, including some economists,

Box 1.1 Economics of 'Spaceship Earth'

In a classic paper written in 1966, 'The economics of the coming Spaceship Earth', Kenneth Boulding discusses a change in orientation that is required if mankind is to achieve a perpetually sustainable economy. He begins by describing the prevailing image which man has of himself and his environment. The 'cowboy economy' describes a state of affairs in which the typical perception of the natural environment is that of a virtually limitless plane, on which a frontier exists that can be pushed back indefinitely. This economy is an open system, involved in interchanges with the world outside. It can draw upon inputs from the outside environment, and send outputs (in the form of waste residuals and so on) to the outside. In the cowboy economy perception, no limits exist on the capacity of the outside to supply or receive energy and material flows.

Boulding points out that, in such an economy, the measures of economic success are defined in terms of flows of materials being processed or transformed. Roughly speaking, income measures such as GDP or GNP reflect the magnitudes of these flows – the cowboy perception regards it as desirable that these flows should be as large as possible.

However, Boulding argues, this economy is built around a flawed understanding of what is physically possible in the long run. A change in our perception is therefore required to one in which the earth is recognised as being a closed system or, more precisely, a system closed in all but one respect – energy inputs are received from the outside (such as solar energy flows) and energy can be lost to the outside (through radiative flows, for example). In material terms, though, planet earth is a closed system: matter cannot be created or destroyed, and the residuals from extraction, production and consumption activities will always remain with us, in one form or another.

Boulding refers to this revised perception as that of the 'spaceman economy'. Here, the earth is viewed as a single spaceship, without unlimited reserves of anything. Beyond the frontier of the spaceship itself, there exist no reserves from which the spaceship's inhabitants can draw resources nor sinks into which they can dispose of unwanted residuals. On the contrary, the spaceship is a closed material system, and energy inputs from the outside are limited to those perpetual but limited flows that can be harnessed from the outside, such as solar radiation.

Within this spaceship, if mankind is to survive indefinitely, man must find his place

in a perpetually reproduced ecological cycle. Materials usage is limited to that which can be recycled in each time period; that, in turn, is limited by the quantity of solar and other external energy flows received by the spaceship.

What is an appropriate measure of economic performance in spaceship earth? It is not the magnitude of material flows, as measured by GNP or the like. On the contrary, it is desirable that the spaceship maintain such flows of material and energy throughput at low levels. Instead, the well-being of the spaceship is best measured by the state – in terms of quality and quantity – of its capital stock, including the state of human minds and bodies.

So, for Boulding, a 'good' state to be in is one in which certain stocks are at high levels – the stock of knowledge, the state of human health, and the stock of capital capable of yielding human satisfaction. Ideally we should aim to make material and energy flows as small as possible to achieve any chosen level of the spaceship's capital stock, maintained over indefinite time.

Boulding is, of course, arguing for a change in our perceptions of the nature of economy–environment interactions, and of what it is that constitutes economic success. He states that

> The shadow of the future spaceship, indeed, is already falling over our spendthrift merriment. Oddly enough, it seems to be in pollution rather than exhaustion, that the problem is first becoming salient. Los Angeles has run out of air, Lake Erie has become a cesspool, the oceans are getting full of lead and DDT, and the atmosphere may become man's major problem in another generation, at the rate at which we are filling it up with junk.

Boulding concludes his paper by considering the extent to which the price mechanism, used in a way to put prices on external diseconomies, can deal with the transition to spaceship earth. He accepts the need for market-based incentive schemes to correct such diseconomies, but argues that these instruments can only deal with a small proportion of the matters which he raises. Boulding concludes:

> The problems which I have been raising in this paper are of larger scale and perhaps much harder to solve . . . One can hope, therefore, that as a succession of mounting crises, especially in pollution, arouse public opinion and mobilize support for the solution of the immediate problems, a learning process will be set in motion which will eventually lead to an appreciation of and perhaps solutions for the larger ones.

Source: Boulding (1966)

who continued, during the ascendancy of neoclass-ical economics, to insist on the central importance of studying economics in a way which takes on board what is known about the laws of nature as they affect the material basis for economic activity. As is made clear in Box 1.1, Boulding did not, and ecological economics does not, take the view that everything that resource and environmental economics has to say, for example, about using price incentives to deal with environmental problems is wrong. Rather, the point is that what it has to say needs to be put in the proper context, one where the economic system is seen as a subsystem of a larger system.

To date, the impact of ecological economics on the approach to the natural environment that emerged from mainstream economics has been somewhat limited, and this book will largely reflect that. We will be dealing mainly with mainstream resource and environmental economics, though the next two chapters do directly address the problem of sus-tainability. While the theme of sustainability runs through the book, it is not obviously at the forefront in Chapters 5 to 18 which are, mainly, about the mainstream approach. We do, however, at some points in those chapters briefly consider how adopt-ing an ecological economics perspective would affect analysis and policy. In the final chapter of the book, Chapter 19, sustainability returns to the fore-front in the context of a discussion of the prospects for promoting sustainability by better economic accounting.

1.3   Fundamental issues in the economic approach to resource and environmental issues

Here we provide a brief anticipatory sketch of four features of the economic approach to resource and environmental issues that will be covered in this book.

1.3.1   Property rights, efficiency and government intervention

We have already stated that a central question in resource and environmental economics concerns allocative efficiency. The role of markets and prices is central to the analysis of this question. As we have noted, a central idea in modern economics is that, given the necessary conditions, markets will bring about efficiency in allocation. Well-defined and enforceable private property rights are one of the necessary conditions. Because property rights do not exist, or are not clearly defined, for many envir-onmental resources, markets fail to allocate those resources efficiently. In such circumstances, price signals fail to reflect true social costs and benefits, and a prima facie case exists for government policy intervention to seek efficiency gains.

Deciding where a case for intervention exists, and what form it should take, is central in all of resource and environmental economics, as we shall see throughout the rest of this book. The foundations for the economic approach to policy analysis are set out in Chapter 5, and the approach is applied in the subsequent chapters. Some environmental problems cross the boundaries of nation states and are pro-perly treated as global problems. In such cases there is no global government with the authority to act on the problem in the same way as the government of a nation state might be expected to deal with a prob-lem within its borders. The special features of inter-national environmental problems are considered in Chapter 10.

1.3.2   The role, and the limits, of valuation, in achieving efficiency

As just observed, many environmental resources – or the services yielded by those resources – do not have well-defined property rights. Clean air is one example of such a resource. Such resources are used, but without being traded through markets, and so will not have market prices. A special case of this general situation is external effects, or externalities. As shown in Chapter 5, an externality exists where a consumption or production activity has unintended effects on others for which no compensation is paid. Here, the external effect is an untraded – and unpriced – product arising because the victim has no property rights that can be exploited to obtain com-pensation for the external effect. Sulphur emissions from a coal-burning power station might be an example of this kind of effect.

However, the absence of a price for a resource or an external effect does not mean that it has no value. Clearly, if well-being is affected, there is a value that is either positive or negative depending on whether well-being is increased or decreased. In order to make allocatively efficient decisions, these values need to be estimated in some way. Returning to the power station example, government might wish to impose a tax on sulphur emissions so that the polluters pay for their environmental damage and, hence, reduce the amount of it to the level that goes with allocative efficiency. But this cannot be done unless the proper value can be put on the otherwise unpriced emissions.

There are various ways of doing this – collectively called valuation techniques – which will be explored at some length in Chapter 12. Such techniques are somewhat controversial. There is disagreement between economists over the extent to which the techniques can be expected to produce accurate valuations for unpriced environmental services. These are discussed in Chapter 12. Many non-economists with an interest in how social decisions that affect the environment are made raise rather more fundamental problems about the techniques and their use. Their objection is not, or at least not just, that the techniques may provide the wrong valuations. Rather, they claim that making decisions about environmental services on the basis of monetary valuations of those services is simply the wrong way for society to make such decisions. These objections, and some alternative ways proposed for society to make decisions about the environment, are considered in Chapter 11.

1.3.3 The time dimension of economic decisions

Natural resource stocks can be classified in various ways. A useful first cut is to distinguish between 'stock' and 'flow' resources. Whereas stock resources, plant and animal populations and mineral deposits, have the characteristic that today's use has implications for tomorrow's availability, this is not the case with flow resources. Examples of flow resource are solar radiation, and the power of the wind, of tides and of flowing water. Using more solar radiation today does not itself have any implications for the

availability of solar radiation tomorrow. In the case of stock resources, the level of use today does have implications for availability tomorrow.

Within the stock resources category there is an important distinction between 'renewable' and 'non-renewable' resources. Renewable resources are biotic, plant and animal populations, and have the capacity to grow in size over time, through biological reproduction. Non-renewable resources are abiotic, stocks of minerals, and do not have that capacity to grow over time. What are here called non-renewable resources are sometimes referred to as 'exhaustible', or 'depletable', resources. This is because there is no positive constant rate of use that can be sustained indefinitely – eventually the resource stock must be exhausted. This is not actually a useful terminology. Renewable resources are exhaustible if harvested for too long at a rate exceeding their regeneration capacities.

From an economic perspective, stock resources are assets yielding flows of environmental services over time. In considering the efficiency and optimality of their use, we must take account not only of use at a point in time but also of the pattern of use over time. Efficiency and optimality have, that is, an intertemporal, or dynamic, dimension, as well as an intratemporal, or static, dimension. Chapter 11 sets out the basics of intertemporal welfare economics. In thinking about the intertemporal dimension of the use of environmental resources, attention must be given to the productiveness of the capital that is accumulated as a result of saving and investment. If, by means of saving and investment, consumption is deferred to a later period, the increment to future consumption that follows from such investment will generally exceed the initial consumption quantity deferred. The size of the pay-off to deferred consumption is reflected in the rate of return to investment.

Environmental resource stocks similarly have rates of return associated with their deferred use. The relations between rates of return to capital as normally understood in economics and the rates of return on environmental assets must be taken into account in trying to identify efficient and optimal paths of environmental resource use over time. The arising theory of the efficient and optimal use of natural and environmental resources over time is examined in Chapters 14, 15, 17 and 18, and is drawn on in Chapter 19. As discussed in Chapter 16, many pollution problems also have an intertemporal dimension, and it turns out that the analysis developed for thinking about the intertemporal problems of resource use can be used to analyse those problems.

1.3.4   Substitutability and irreversibility

Substitutability and irreversibility are important, and related, issues in thinking about policy in relation to the natural environment. If the depletion of a resource stock is irreversible, and there is no close substitute for the services that it provides, then clearly the rate at which the resource is depleted has major implications for sustainability. To the extent that depletion is not irreversible and close substitutes exist, there is less cause for concern about the rate at which the resource is used.

There are two main dimensions to substitutability issues. First, there is the question of the extent to which one natural resource can be replaced by another. Can, for example, solar power substitute for the fossil fuels on a large scale? This is, as we shall see, an especially important question given that the combustion of fossil fuels not only involves the depletion of non-renewable resources, but also is a source of some major environmental pollution problems, such as the so-called greenhouse effect which entails the prospect of global climate change, as discussed in Chapter 10.

Second, there is the question of the degree to which an environmental resource can be replaced by other inputs, especially the human-made capital resulting from saving and investment. As we shall see, in Chapters 2, 3, 4, 14 and 19 particularly, this question is of particular significance when we address questions concerning long-run economy–environment interactions, and the problem of sustainability.

Human-made capital is sometimes referred to as reproducible capital, identifying an important difference between stocks of it and stocks of non-renewable resources. The latter are not reproducible, and their exploitation is irreversible in a way that the use of human-made capital is not. We shall discuss this further in the next chapter, and some arising implications in later chapters, especially 14 and 19.

With renewable resource stocks, depletion is reversible to the extent that harvesting is at rates that allow regeneration. Some of the implications are discussed in Chapter 17. Some pollution problems may involve irreversible effects, and the extinction of a species of plant or animal is certainly irreversible.

Some assemblages of environmental resources are of interest for the amenity services, recreation and aesthetic enjoyment that they provide, as well as for their potential use as inputs to production. A wilderness area, for example, could be conserved as a national park or developed for mining. Some would also argue that there are no close substitutes for the services of wilderness. A decision to develop such an area would be effectively irreversible, whereas a decision to conserve would be reversible. We show in Chapter 13 that under plausible conditions this asymmetry implies a stronger preference for non-development than would be the case where all decisions are reversible, and that this is strengthened when it is recognised that the future is not known with certainty. Imperfect knowledge of the future is, of course, the general condition, but it is especially relevant to decision making about many environmental problems, and has implications for how we think about making such decisions.

1.4   Reader's guide

We have already noted in which chapters various topics are covered. Now we will briefly set out the structure of this text, and explain the motivation for that structure.

In Part I we deal with 'Foundations' of two kinds. First, in Chapter 2, we explain why many people think that there is a sustainability problem. We consider the interdependence of the economy and the environment, look at the current state of human development, and at some views on future prospects. Second, in the next three chapters, we work through the conceptual basis and the analytical tools with which economists approach environmental problems. Chapter 3 looks at the ethical basis for policy analysis in economics. Chapter 4 reviews several conceptualisations of what sustainability could be. Chapter 5 is about welfare economics and markets – what they achieve when they work properly, why they do not always work properly, and what can be done about it when they do not work properly.

Throughout the book we have put as much of the mathematics as is possible in appendices, of which extensive use is made. Readers who have learned the essentials of the calculus of constrained optimisation will have no problems with the mathematics used in the appendices in Part I. Appendix 3.1 provides a brief account of the mathematics of constrained optimisation. The arguments of Part I can be followed without using the mathematics in the appendices, but readers who work through them will obtain a deeper understanding of the arguments and their foundations.

Part II is about 'Environmental pollution'. It turns out that much, but not all, of what economists have to say about pollution problems relates to the question of intratemporal allocative efficiency and does not essentially involve a time dimension. The static analysis of pollution problems is the focus of Part II. Static, as opposed to dynamic, analysis follows naturally from the material covered most intensively in Chapter 5, and, subject to an exception to be noted shortly, the mathematics used in the appendices in Part II is of the same kind as used in the appendices in Part I.

Chapter 6 considers the setting of targets for pollution control, and Chapter 7 looks at the analysis of the policy instruments that could be used to meet those targets. In these chapters it is assumed that the government agency responsible for pollution control has complete information about all aspects of the pollution problem to be addressed. This is a patently unrealistic assumption, and Chapter 8 examines the consequences of its relaxation. The analysis in these three chapters is partial, analysing the control of a particular pollutant as if it were the only such problem, and as if what were done about it had no implications for the rest of the economy. Chapter 9, in contrast, takes an approach which looks at the economy as a whole, using input–output analysis and introducing applied general equilibrium modelling. This chapter includes an appendix that provides a brief review of the matrix algebra which facilitates the understanding and application of these methods. Part II finishes with Chapter 10, which deals with

the special issues that arise when the impacts of a pollution problem cross the boundaries of nation states.

Part III has the title 'Project appraisal'. Its focus is on the rationale for, and application of, the methods and techniques that economists have developed for evaluating whether going ahead with some discrete investment project, or policy innovation, is in the public interest. Of particular concern here, of course, are projects and policies with environmental impacts. Also, the focus is on projects and policies which have consequences stretching out over time. Chapter 11 deals with the principles of intertemporal welfare economics and their application in cost–benefit analysis. Chapter 11 also looks at some alternative methods for project appraisal that have been advocated, especially by those who have ethical objections to the use of cost–benefit analysis where the natural environment is involved. A necessary input to a cost–benefit analysis of a project with effects on the natural environment is a monetary evaluation of those effects. The methods that economists have devised for monetary evaluation of non-marketed environmental services are explained in Chapter 12. Chapter 13 looks at the implications for project appraisal of recognition of the facts that when looking at projects with environmental impacts, we are often dealing with impacts that are irreversible, and always considering future effects about which our knowledge is incomplete.

In Part III the arguments and analysis are developed mainly in the context of the recreation and amenity services that the natural environment provides, though they are, of course, also relevant to the problem of environmental pollution, the focus of Part II. In Part IV we turn to a focus on the issues associated with the extraction of natural resources from the environment for use as inputs to production. The problems that have most interested economists here are essentially dynamic in nature, that is, are problems in intertemporal allocation. In addressing these problems, economists typically use the mathematics of 'optimal control'. We have minimised the explicit use of this mathematics in the body of the text, but we do make extensive use of it in the appendices in Part IV. For readers not familiar with this sort of mathematics, Appendix 14.1 provides a brief account of it, treating it as an extension of the ideas involved in ordinary constrained optimisation developed in Appendix 3.1.

Chapter 14 introduces the application of the basic ideas about intertemporal optimality and efficiency, developed in Chapter 11, to the question of natural resource extraction. Chapter 15 looks specifically at the extraction of non-renewable resources, that is, stocks of minerals and fossil fuels. The case of renewable resources – populations of plants and animals harvested for use in production and consumption – is dealt with in Chapter 17. Trees are plants with some special characteristics, and Chapter 18 reviews the major elements of forestry economics. Many important pollution problems have the characteristic that the pollutant involved accumulates in the environment as a stock, which may decay naturally over time. Analysis of such pollution problems has much in common with the analysis of natural resource extraction, and is dealt with in Chapter 16. Finally in Part IV we return to the sustainability issue. Chapter 19 is about modifying standard accounting procedures so as to have economic performance indicators reflect environmental impacts, and particularly so as to measure sustainable national income.

Summary

There is not a single methodology used by all economists working on matters related to natural resources and the environment. Ecological economists have argued the need to work towards a more holistic discipline that would integrate natural-scientific and economic paradigms. Some ecological economists argue further that the sustainability problem requires nothing less than a fundamental change in social values, as well as a scientific reorientation. While some movement has been made in the direction of interdisciplinary cooperation, most analysis is still some way from having achieved integration. At the other end of a spectrum of methodologies are economists who see no need to go beyond the application of neoclassical techniques to environmental problems, and stress the importance of constructing a more complete set of quasi-market incentives to induce efficient behaviour. Such economists would reject the idea that existing social values need to be questioned, and many have great faith in the ability of continuing technical progress to ameliorate problems of resource scarcity and promote sustainability. Ecological economists tend to be more sceptical about the extent to which technical progress can overcome the problems that follow from the interdependence of economic and environmental systems.

However, there is a lot of common ground between economists working in the area, and it is this that we mainly focus upon in this text. Nobody who has seriously studied the issues believes that the economy's relationship to the natural environment can be left entirely to market forces. Hardly anybody now argues that market-like incentives have no role to play in that relationship. In terms of policy, the arguments are about how much governments need to do, and the relative effectiveness of different kinds of policy instruments. Our aim in this book is to work through the economic analysis relevant to these kinds of questions, and to provide information on the resource and environmental problems that they arise from. We begin, in the next chapter, by discussing the general interdependence of the economic and environmental systems, and the concerns about sustainability that this has given rise to.

Further reading

As all save one of the topics and issues discussed in this chapter will be dealt with more comprehensively in subsequent chapters, we shall not make any suggestions for further reading here other than for that one topic – the history of economics. Blaug (1985), *Economic Theory in Retrospect*, is essential reading for anybody who wants to study the history of economic ideas in detail. For those who do not require a comprehensive treatment, useful alternatives are Barber (1967) and Heilbronner (1991). Crocker (1999) is a short overview of the history of environmental and resource economics, providing references to seminal contributions.

The leading specialist journals, in order of date of first issue, are: *Land Economics*, *Journal of Environmental Economics and Management*, *Ecological Economics*, *Environmental and Resource Economics*, *Environment and Development Economics*. The first issue of *Ecological Economics*, February 1989, contains several articles on the nature of ecological economics. The May 2000 issue, Vol. 39, number 3, of the *Journal of Environmental Economics and Management* marks the journal's 25th anniversary and contains articles reviewing the major developments in environmental and resource economics over its lifetime.

The *Journal of Environmental Economics and Management* is run by the Association of Environmental and Resource Economists, whose web site at www.aere.org has useful information and links. The equivalent European association is the European Association of Environmental and Resource Economists – www.vwl.unimannheim.de/conrad/eaere/ – which runs the journal *Environmental and Resource Economics*. The journal *Ecological Economics* is run by the International Society for Ecological Economics – http://pangaea.esci.keele.ac.uk/kudis/isee/.

CHAPTER 2

The origins of the sustainability problem

Certainly it is a problem to sustain many billions of people, a problem for each human to sustain himself and his/her own family. But the growth in numbers over the millennia from a few thousands or millions of humans living at low subsistence, to billions living well above subsistence, is a most positive assurance that the problem of sustenance has eased rather than grown more difficult with the years. The trend in population size by itself should suggest cheer rather than gloom.

Mark Perlman, in Simon and Kahn (1984), p. 63

Learning objectives

In this chapter you will
- learn how economic activity depends upon and affects the natural environment
- be introduced to some basic material from the environmental sciences
- learn about the proximate drivers of the economy's impact on the environment – population, affluence and technology
- review the current state of human economic development
- consider the argument that the environment sets limits to economic growth
- learn about the emergence of the idea of sustainable development

---

Introduction

We inhabit a world in which the human population has risen dramatically over the past century and may almost double during the next. The material demands being made by the average individual have been increasing rapidly, though many human beings now alive are desperately poor. Since the 1950s and 1960s economic growth has been generally seen as *the* solution to the problem of poverty. Without eco-

nomic growth, poverty alleviation involves redistribution from the better-off to the poor, which encounters resistance from the better-off. In any case, there may be so many poor in relation to the size of the better-off group, that the redistributive solution to the problem of poverty is simply impossible – the cake is not big enough to provide for all, however thinly the slices are cut. Economic growth increases the size of the cake. With enough of it, it may be possible to give everybody at least a decent slice, without having to reduce the size of the larger slices.

However, the world's resource base is limited, and contains a complex, and interrelated, set of ecosystems that are currently exhibiting signs of fragility. It is increasingly questioned whether the global economic system can continue to grow without undermining the natural systems which are its ultimate foundation.

This set of issues we call 'the sustainability problem' – how to alleviate poverty in ways that do not affect the natural environment such that future economic prospects suffer. In this chapter we set out the basis for the belief that such a problem exists.

This chapter is organised as follows. We first look at the interdependence of the economy and the environment, and give a brief overview of some environmental science basics that are relevant to this. In the second section the proximate drivers of the economy's impact on the environment are considered. The third section of the chapter presents data on the current state of human development in relation to the problems of poverty and inequality. In this section we note the attachment of economists to economic growth as the solution to the poverty problem. In the next section we consider limits to growth. The chapter ends by looking at the emergence in the 1980s of the idea of sustainable development – growth that does not damage the environment – and progress toward its realisation.

2.1   Economy–environment interdependence

Economic activity takes place within, and is part of, the system which is the earth and its atmosphere. This system we call 'the natural environment', or more briefly 'the environment'. This system itself has an environment, which is the rest of the universe. Figure 2.1 is a schematic representation of the two-way relationships between, the interdependence of, the economy and the environment.[1]

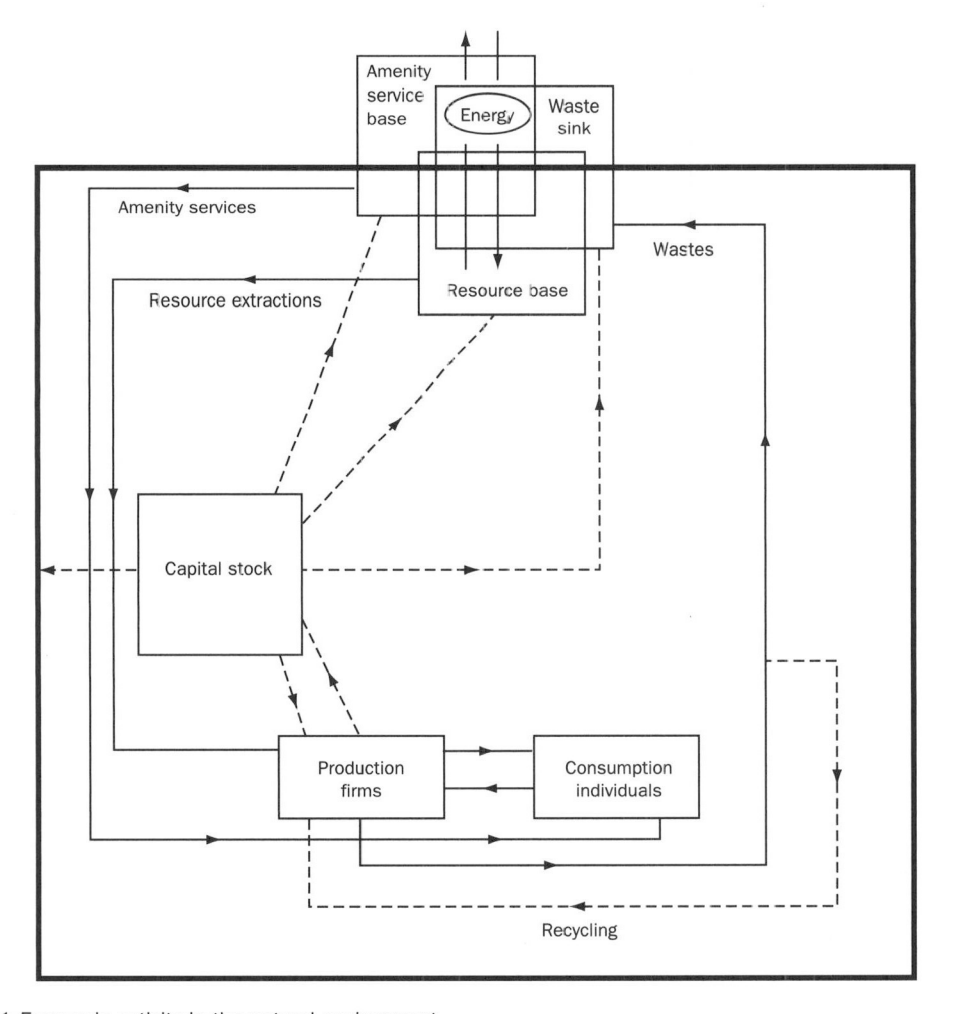

Figure 2.1 Economic activity in the natural environment

---

[1] Figure 2.1 is taken from Common (1995), where economy–environment interdependence is discussed at greater length than here. References to works which deal more fully, and rigorously, with the natural science matters briefly reviewed here are provided in the Further Reading section at the end of the chapter.

The outer heavy black lined box represents the environment, which is a thermodynamically closed system, in that it exchanges energy but not matter with its environment. The environment receives inputs of solar radiation. Some of that radiation is absorbed and drives environmental processes. Some is reflected back into space. This is represented by the arrows crossing the heavy black line at the top of the figure. Matter does not cross the heavy black line. The balance between energy absorption and reflection determines the way the global climate system functions. The energy in and out arrows are shown passing through three boxes, which represent three of the functions that the environment performs in relation to economic activity. The fourth function, represented by the heavy black lined box itself, is the provision of the life-support services and those services which hold the whole functioning system together. Note that the three boxes intersect one with another and that the heavy black line passes through them. This is to indicate that the four functions interact with one another, as discussed below.

Figure 2.1 shows economic activity located within the environment and involving production and consumption, both of which draw upon environmental services, as shown by the solid lines inside the heavy lined box. Not all of production is consumed. Some of the output from production is added to the human-made, reproducible, capital stock, the services of which are used, together with labour services, in production. Figure 2.1 shows production using a third type of input, resources extracted from the environment. Production gives rise to wastes inserted into the environment. So does consumption. Consumption also uses directly a flow of amenity services from the environment to individuals without the intermediation of productive activity.

We now discuss these four environmental functions, and the interactions between them, in more detail.

2.1.1 The services that the environment provides

As noted in the previous chapter, natural resources used in production are of several types. One distinguishing characteristic is whether the resource exists as a stock or a flow. The difference lies in whether the level of current use affects future availability. In the case of flow resources there is no link between current use and future availability. The prime example of a flow resource is solar radiation – if a roof has a solar water heater on it, the amount of water heating done today has no implications for the amount that can be done tomorrow. Wave and wind power are also flow resources. Stock resources are defined by the fact that the level of current use does affect future availability.

Within the class of stock resources, a second standard distinction concerns the nature of the link between current use and future availability. Renewable resources are biotic populations – flora and fauna. Non-renewable resources are minerals, including the fossil fuels. In the former case, the stock existing at a point in time has the potential to grow by means of natural reproduction. If in any period use of the resource is less than natural growth, stock size grows. If use, or harvest, is always the same as natural growth, the resource can be used indefinitely. Such a harvest rate is often referred to as a 'sustainable yield'. Harvest rates in excess of sustainable yield imply declining stock size. For non-renewable resources there is no natural reproduction, except on geological timescales. Consequently, more use now necessarily implies less future use.

Within the class of non-renewables the distinction between fossil fuels and the other minerals is important. First, the use of fossil fuels is pervasive in industrial economies, and could be said to be one of their essential distinguishing characteristics. Second, fossil fuel combustion is an irreversible process in that there is no way in which the input fuel can be even partially recovered after combustion. In so far as coal, oil and gas are used to produce heat, rather than as inputs to chemical processes, they cannot be recycled. Minerals used as inputs to production can be recycled. This means that whereas in the case of minerals there exists the possibility of delaying, for a given use rate, the date of exhaustion of a given initial stock, in the case of fossil fuels there does not. Third, fossil fuel combustion is a major source of a number of waste emissions, especially into the atmosphere.

Many of the activities involved in production and consumption give rise to waste products, or residuals, to be discharged into the natural environment. Indeed, as we shall see when we discuss the materials balance principle, such insertions into the environment are the necessary corollary of the extraction of material resources from it. In economics, questions relating to the consequences of waste discharge into the environment are generally discussed under the heading of 'pollution'. To the extent, and only to the extent, that waste discharge gives rise to problems perceived by humans economists say that there is a pollution problem. Pollution problems can be conceptualised in two ways. One, which finds favour with economists, sees pollution as a stock of material resident in the natural environment. The other, which finds favour more with ecologists, sees pollution as a flow which affects the natural environment.

In the former case, pollution is treated in the same way as a stock resource, save that the stock has negative value. Residual flows into the environment add to the stock; natural decay processes subtract from it. We will look at pollution modelled this way in Chapter 16. The flow model treats the environment as having an 'assimilative capacity', defined in terms of a rate of residual flow. Pollution is then the result of a residual flow rate in excess of assimilative capacity. There is no pollution if the residual flow rate is equal to, or less than, assimilative capacity. If the residual flow rate is persistently in excess of assimilative capacity, the latter declines over time, and may eventually go to zero.

In Figure 2.1 amenity services flow directly from the environment to individuals. The biosphere provides humans with recreational facilities and other sources of pleasure and stimulation. Swimming from an ocean beach does not require productive activity to transform an environmental resource into a source of human satisfaction, for example. Wilderness recreation is defined by the absence of other human activity. Some people like simply lying out of doors in sunshine. The role of the natural environment in regard to amenity services can be appreciated by imagining its absence, as would be the case for the occupants of a space vehicle. In many cases the flow to individuals of amenity services does not directly involve any consumptive material flow. Wilderness recreation, for example, is not primarily about exploiting resources in the wilderness area, though it may involve this in the use of wood for fires, the

capture of game for food and so on. A day on the beach does not involve any consumption of the beach in the way that the use of oil involves its consumption. This is not to say that flows of amenity services never impact physically on the natural environment. Excessive use of a beach area can lead to changes in its character, as with the erosion of sand dunes following vegetation loss caused by human visitation.

The fourth environmental function, shown in Figure 2.1 as the heavy box, is difficult to represent in a simple and concise way. Over and above serving as resource base, waste sink and amenity base, the biosphere currently provides the basic life-support functions for humans. While the range of environmental conditions that humans are biologically equipped to cope with is greater than for most other species, there are limits to the tolerable. We have, for example, quite specific requirements in terms of breathable air. The range of temperatures that we can exist in is wide in relation to conditions on earth, but narrow in relation to the range on other planets in the solar system. Humans have minimum requirements for water input. And so on. The environment functions now in such a manner that humans can exist in it. An example will illustrate what is involved.

Consider solar radiation. It is one element of the resource base, and for some people sunbathing is an environmental amenity service. In fact, solar radiation as it arrives at the earth's atmosphere is harmful to humans. There it includes the ultraviolet wavelength UV-B, which causes skin cancer, adversely affects the immune system, and can cause eye cataracts. UV-B radiation affects other living things as well. Very small organisms are likely to be particularly affected, as UV-B can only penetrate a few layers of cells. This could be a serious problem for marine systems, where the base of the food chain consists of very small organisms living in the surface layers of the ocean, which UV-B reaches. UV-B radiation also affects photosynthesis in green plants adversely.

Solar radiation arriving at the surface of the earth has much less UV-B than it does arriving at the atmosphere. Ozone in the stratosphere absorbs UV-B, performing a life-support function by filtering solar radiation. In the absence of stratospheric ozone, it is questionable whether human life could exist.

Currently, stratospheric ozone is being depleted by the release into the atmosphere of chlorofluorocarbons (CFCs), compounds which exist only by virtue of human economic activity. They have been in use since the 1940s. Their ozone-depleting properties were recognised in the 1980s, and, as discussed in Chapter 10, policy to reduce this form of pollution is now in place.

The interdependencies between economic activity and the environment are pervasive and complex. The complexity is increased by the existence of processes in the environment that mean that the four classes of environmental services each interact one with another. In Figure 2.1 this is indicated by having the three boxes intersect one with another, and jointly with the heavy black line representing the life-support function. What is involved can be illustrated with the following example.

Consider a river estuary. It serves as resource base for the local economy in that a commercial fishery operates in it. It serves as waste sink in that urban sewage is discharged into it. It serves as the source of amenity services, being used for recreational purposes such as swimming and boating. It contributes to life-support functions in so far as it is a breeding ground for marine species which are not commercially exploited, but which play a role in the operation of the marine ecosystem. At rates of sewage discharge equal to or below the assimilative capacity of the estuary, all four functions can coexist. If, however, the rate of sewage discharge exceeds assimilative capacity, not only does a pollution problem emerge, but the other estuarine functions are impaired. Pollution will interfere with the reproductive capacity of the commercially exploited fish stocks, and may lead to the closure of the fishery. This does not necessarily mean its biological extinction. The fishery may be closed on the grounds of danger to public health. Pollution will reduce the capacity of the estuary to support recreational activity, and in some respects, such as swimming, may drive it to zero. Pollution will also impact on the non-commercial marine species, and may lead to their extinction, with implications for marine ecosystem function.

An example at the global level of the interconnections between the environmental services arising from interacting environmental processes affected by economic activity is provided by the problem of global climate change, which is discussed below and, at greater length, in Chapter 10.

2.1.2 Substituting for environmental services

One feature of Figure 2.1 remains to be considered. We have so far discussed the solid lines. There are also some dashed lines. These represent possibilities of substitutions for environmental services.

Consider first recycling. This involves interception of the waste stream prior to its reaching the natural environment, and the return of some part of it to production. Recycling substitutes for environmental functions in two ways. First, it reduces the demands made upon the waste sink function. Second, it reduces the demands made upon the resource base function, in so far as recycled materials are substituted for extractions from the environment.

Also shown in Figure 2.1 are four dashed lines from the box for capital running to the three boxes and the heavy black line representing environmental functions. These lines are to represent possibilities for substituting the services of reproducible capital for environmental services. Some economists think of the environment in terms of assets that provide flows of services, and call the collectivity of environmental assets 'natural capital'. In that terminology, the dashed lines refer to possibilities for substituting reproducible capital services for natural capital services.

In relation to the waste sink function consider again, as an example, the discharge of sewage into a river estuary. Various levels of treatment of the sewage prior to its discharge into the river are possible. According to the level of treatment, the demand made upon the assimilative capacity of the estuary is reduced for a given level of sewage. Capital in the form of a sewage treatment plant substitutes for the natural environmental function of waste sink to an extent dependent on the level of treatment that the plant provides.

An example from the field of energy conservation illustrates the substitution of capital for resource base functions. For a given level of human comfort, the energy use of a house can be reduced by the installation of insulation and control systems. These add to that part of the total stock of capital equipment which is the house and all of its fittings, and thus to the total capital stock. Note, however, that the insulation and control systems are themselves material structures, the production of which involves extractions, including energy, from the environment. Similar fuel-saving substitution possibilities exist in productive activities.

Consider next some examples in the context of amenity services. An individual who likes swimming can do this in a river or lake, or from an ocean beach, or in a manufactured swimming pool. The experiences involved are not identical, but they are close substitutes in some dimensions. Similarly, it is not now necessary to actually go into a natural environment to derive pleasure from seeing it. The capital equipment in the entertainment industry means that it is possible to see wild flora and fauna without leaving an urban environment. Apparently it is envisaged that computer technology will, via virtual reality devices, make it possible to experience many of the sensations involved in being in a natural environment without actually being in it.

It appears that it is in the context of the life support function that many scientists regard the substitution possibilities as most limited. However, from a purely technical point of view, it is not clear that this is the case. Artificial environments capable of supporting human life have already been created, and in the form of space vehicles and associated equipment have already enabled humans to live outside the biosphere, albeit in small numbers and for limited periods. It would apparently be possible, if expensive, to create conditions capable of sustaining human life on the moon, given some suitable energy source. However, the quantity of human life that could be sustained in the absence of natural life-support functions would appear to be quite small. It is not that those functions are absolutely irreplaceable, but that they are irreplaceable on the scale that they operate. A second point concerns the quality of life. One might reasonably take the view that while human life on an otherwise biologically dead earth is feasible, it would not be in the least desirable.

The possibilities for substituting for the services of natural capital have been discussed in terms of capital equipment. Capital is accumulated when output from current production is not used for current consumption. Current production is not solely of material structures, and reproducible capital does not only comprise equipment – machines, buildings, roads and so on. 'Human capital' is increased when current production is used to add to the stock of knowledge, and is what forms the basis for technical change. However, while the accumulation of human capital is clearly of great importance in regard to environmental problems, in order for technical change to impact on economic activity, it generally requires embodiment in new equipment. Knowledge that could reduce the demands made upon environmental functions does not actually do so until it is incorporated into equipment that substitutes for environmental functions.

Capital for environmental service substitution is not the only form of substitution that is relevant to economy–environment interconnections. In Figure 2.1 flows between the economy and the environment are shown as single lines. Of course, each single line represents what is in fact a whole range of different flows. With respect to each of the aggregate flows shown in Figure 2.1, substitutions as between components of the flow are possible and affect the demands made upon environmental services. The implications of any given substitution may extend beyond the environmental function directly affected. For example, a switch from fossil fuel use to hydro-electric power reduces fossil fuel depletion and waste generation in fossil fuel combustion, and also impacts on the amenity service flow in so far as a natural recreation area is flooded.

2.1.3 Some environmental science

We now briefly review those elements of the environmental sciences which are most important to an understanding of the implications of economy–environment interdependence. The review is necessarily very selective; references to useful supplementary reading are provided at the end of the chapter.

2.1.3.1 Thermodynamics

Thermodynamics is the science of energy. Energy is the potential to do work or supply heat. It is a characteristic of things, rather than a thing itself. Work is involved when matter is changed in structure, in physical or chemical nature, or in location. In thermodynamics it is necessary to be clear about the nature of the system under consideration. An 'open' system is one which exchanges energy and matter with its environment. An individual organism – a human being for example – is an open system. A 'closed' system exchanges energy, but not matter, with its environment. Planet earth and its atmosphere are a closed system. An 'isolated' system exchanges neither energy nor matter with its environment. Apart from the entire universe, an isolated system is an ideal, an abstraction.

The first law of thermodynamics says that energy can neither be created nor destroyed – it can only be converted from one form to another. Many of those who are concerned about the environment want to encourage people to go in for 'energy conservation'. But, the first law says that there is always 100% energy conservation whatever people do. There is no real contradiction here, just an imprecise use of language on the part of those seeking to promote 'energy conservation'. What they actually want to encourage is people doing the things that they do now but in ways that require less heat and/or less work, and therefore less energy conversion.

The second law of thermodynamics is also known as 'the entropy law'. It says that heat flows spontaneously from a hotter to a colder body, and that heat cannot be transformed into work with 100% efficiency. It follows that all conversions of energy from one form to another are less than 100% efficient. This appears to contradict the first law, but does not. The point is that not all of the energy of some store, such as a fossil fuel, is available for conversion. Energy stores vary in the proportion of their energy that is available for conversion. 'Entropy' is a measure of unavailable energy. All energy conversions increase the entropy of an isolated system. All energy conversions are irreversible, since the fact that the conversion is less than 100% efficient means that the work required to restore the original state is not available in the new state. Fossil fuel combustion is irreversible, and of itself implies an increase in the entropy of the system which is the environment in which economic activity takes place. However, that environment is a closed, not an isolated, system, and is continually receiving energy inputs

from its environment, in the form of solar radiation. This is what makes life possible.

Thermodynamics is difficult for non-specialists to understand. Even within physics it has a history involving controversy, and disagreements persist, as will be noted below. There exist some popular myths about thermodynamics and its implications. It is, for example, often said that entropy always increases. This is true only for an isolated system. Classical thermodynamics involved the study of equilibrium systems, but the systems directly relevant to economic activity are open and closed systems which are far from equilibrium. Such systems receive energy from their environment. As noted above, a living organism is an open system, which is far from equilibrium. Some energy input is necessary for it to maintain its structure and not become disordered – in other words, dead.

The relevance of thermodynamics to the origins of the problem of sustainability is clear. The economist who did most to try to make his colleagues aware of the laws of thermodynamics and their implications, Nicholas Georgescu-Roegen (who started academic life as a physicist), described the second law as the 'taproot of economic scarcity' (Georgescu-Roegen, 1979). His point was, to put it graphically, that if energy conversion processes were 100% efficient, one lump of coal would last for ever. Material transformations involve work, and thus require energy. Given a fixed rate of receipt of solar energy, there is an upper limit to the amount of work that can be done on the basis of it. For most of human history, human numbers and material consumption levels were subject to this constraint. The exploitation of fossil fuels removes this constraint. The fossil fuels are accumulated past solar energy receipts, initially transformed into living tissue, and stored by geological processes. Given this origin, there is necessarily a finite amount of the fossil fuels in existence. It follows that in the absence of an abundant substitute energy source with similar qualities to the fossil fuels, such as nuclear fusion, there would eventually be a reversion to the energetic situation of the pre-industrial phase of human history, which involved total reliance on solar radiation and other flow sources of energy. Of course, the technology deployed in such a situation would be different from that available in the pre-industrial phase. It is now possible, for example, to use solar energy to generate electricity.

2.1.3.1.1 Recycling

The laws of thermodynamics are generally taken to mean that, given enough available energy, all transformations of matter are possible, at least in principle. On the basis of that understanding it has generally been further understood that, at least in principle, complete material recycling is possible. On this basis, given the energy, there is no necessity that shortage of minerals constrain economic activity. Past extractions could be recovered by recycling. It is in this sense that the second law of thermodynamics is the ultimate source of scarcity. Given available energy, there need be no scarcity of minerals. This is what drives the interest in nuclear power, and especially nuclear fusion, which might offer the prospect of a clean and effectively infinite energy resource.

Nicholas Georgescu-Roegen, noted above as the economist who introduced the idea of the second law as the ultimate basis for economic scarcity, subsequently attacked the view just sketched as 'the energetic dogma', and insisted that 'matter matters' as well (Georgescu-Roegen, 1979). He argued that even given enough energy, the complete recycling of matter is, in principle, impossible. This has been dubbed 'the fourth law of thermodynamics' and its validity has been denied: e.g. 'complete recycling is physically possible if a sufficient amount of energy is available' (Biancardi et al., 1993). The basis for this denial is that the fourth law would be inconsistent with the second. This disagreement over what is a very basic scientific issue is interesting for two reasons. First, if qualified scientists can disagree over so fundamental a point, then it is clear that many issues relevant to sustainability involve uncertainty. Secondly, both sides to this dispute would agree, that as a practical matter, complete recycling is impossible however much energy is available. Thus, the statement above rebutting the fourth law is immediately followed by: 'The problem is that such expenditure of energy would involve a tremendous increase in the entropy of the environment, which would not be sustainable for the biosphere' (Biancardi et al., 1993). Neither party to the dispute is suggest-

ing that policy should be determined on the basis of an understanding that matter can actually be completely recycled.

2.1.3.2 The materials balance principle

'The materials balance principle' is the term that economists tend to use to refer to the law of conservation of mass, which states that matter can neither be created nor destroyed. An early exposition of the principle as it applies to economic activity is found in Kneese et al. (1970). As far as economics goes, the most fundamental implication of the materials balance principle is that economic activity essentially involves transforming matter extracted from the environment. Economic activity cannot, in a material sense, create anything. It does, of course, involve transforming material extracted from the environment so that it is more valuable to humans. But, another implication is that all of the material extracted from the environment must, eventually, be returned to it, albeit in a transformed state. The 'eventually' is necessary because some of the extracted material stays in the economy for a long time – in buildings, roads, machinery and so on.

Figure 2.2 shows the physical relationships implied by the materials balance principle. It abstracts from the lags in the circular flow of matter due to capital accumulation in the economy. It amplifies the picture of material extractions from and insertions into the environment provided in Figure 2.1. Primary inputs (ores, liquids and gases) are taken from the environment and converted into useful products (basic fuel, food and raw materials) by 'environmental' firms. These outputs become inputs into subsequent production processes (shown as a product flow to non-environmental firms) or to households directly. Households also receive final products from the non-environmental firms sector.

The materials balance principle states an identity between the mass of materials flow from the environment (flow A) and the mass of residual material discharge flows to the environment (flows $B + C + D$). So, in terms of mass, we have $A \equiv B + C + D$. In fact several identities are implied by Figure 2.2. Each of the four sectors shown by rectangular boxes receives an equal mass of inputs to the mass of its outputs. So we have the following four identities:

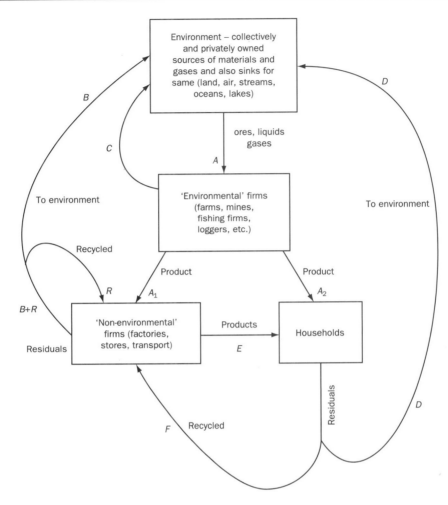

Figure 2.2 A materials balance model of economy–environment interactions
Source: Adapted from Herfindahl & Kneese (1974)

The environment:	$A \equiv B + C + D$ as above
Environmental firms:	$A \equiv A_1 + A_2 + C$
Non-environmental firms:	$B + R + E \equiv R + A_1 + F$
Households:	$A_2 + E \equiv D + F$

Several insights can be derived from this model. First, in a materially closed economy in which no net stock accumulation takes place (that is, physical assets do not change in magnitude) the mass of residuals into the environment ($B + C + D$) must be equal to the mass of fuels, foods and raw materials extracted from the environment and oxygen taken from the atmosphere (flow A). Secondly, the treat-ment of residuals from economic activity does not reduce their mass although it alters their form. Never-theless, while waste treatment does not 'get rid of' residuals, waste management can be useful by trans-forming residuals to a more benign form (or by changing their location).

Thirdly, the extent of recycling is important. To see how, look again at the identity $B + R + E \equiv R + A_1 + F$. For any fixed magnitude of final output, E, if the amount of recycling of household residuals, F, can be increased, then the quantity of inputs into final production, A_1, can be decreased. This in turn implies that less primary extraction of environmental resources, A, need take place. So the total amount of material throughput in the system (the magnitude A)

can be decreased for any given level of production and consumption if the efficiency of materials utilisation is increased through recycling processes.

2.1.3.2.1 Production function specification

In most of microeconomics, production is taken to involve inputs of capital and labour. For the ith firm, the production function is written as

$$Q_i = f_i(L_i, K_i) \qquad (2.1)$$

where Q represents output, L labour input and K capital input. According to the materials balance principle, this cannot be an adequate general representation of what production involves. If Q_i has some material embodiment, then there must be some material input to production – matter cannot be created.

If we let R represent some natural resource extracted from the environment, then the production function could be written as:

$$Q_i = f_i(L_i, K_i, R_i) \qquad (2.2)$$

Production functions with these arguments are widely used in the resource economics literature. In contrast, the environmental economics literature tends to stress insertions into the environment – wastes arising in production and consumption wastes – and often uses a production function of the form

$$Q_i = f_i(L_i, K_i, M_i) \qquad (2.3)$$

where M_i is the flow of waste arising from the ith firm's activity. Equation 2.3 may appear strange at first sight as it treats waste flows as an input into production. However, this is a reasonable way of proceeding given that reductions in wastes will mean reductions in output for given levels of the other inputs, as other inputs have to be diverted to the task of reducing wastes.

A more general version of equation 2.3 is given by

$$Q_i = f_i\left(L_i, K_i, M_i, A\left[\sum_i M_i\right]\right) \qquad (2.4)$$

in which A denotes the ambient concentration level of some pollutant, which depends on the total of waste emissions across all firms. Thus, equation 2.4 recognises that ambient pollution can affect production possibilities.

However, as it stands equation 2.4 conflicts with the materials balance principle. Now, matter in the form of waste is being created by economic activity alone, which is not possible. A synthesis of resource and environmental economics production functions is desirable, which recognises that material inputs (in the form of environmental resources) enter the production function and material outputs (in the form of waste as well as output) emanate from production. This yields a production function such as

$$Q_i = f_i\left(L_i, K_i, R_i, M_i[R_i], A\left[\sum_i M_i\right]\right) \qquad (2.5)$$

Where some modelling procedure requires the use of a production function, the use of a form such as equation 2.5 has the attractive property of recognising that, in general, production must have a material base, and that waste emissions necessarily arise from that base. It is consistent, that is, with one of the fundamental laws of nature. This production function also includes possible feedback effects of wastes on production, arising through the ambient levels of pollutants. It is, however, relatively uncommon for such a fully specified production function to be used in either theoretical or empirical work in economics. In particular cases, this could be justified by argument that for the purpose at hand – examining the implications of resource depletion, say – nothing essential is lost by an incomplete specification, and the analysis is simplified and clarified. We shall implicitly use this argument ourselves at various points in the remainder of the book, and work with specialised versions of equation 2.5. However, it is important to keep in mind that it is equation 2.5 itself that is the correct specification of a production process that has a material output.

2.1.3.3 Ecology

Ecology is the study of the distribution and abundance of plants and animals. A fundamental concept in ecology is the ecosystem, which is an interacting set of plant and animal populations, together with their abiotic, i.e. non-living, environment. An ecosystem can be defined at various scales from the small and local – a pond or field – through to the large and global – the biosphere as a whole.

2.1.3.3.1 Stability and resilience

Two concepts of fundamental importance in ecology are stability and resilience. The ecologist Holling (1973, 1986) distinguishes between stability as a property attaching to the populations comprised by an ecosystem, and resilience as a property of the ecosystem. Stability is the propensity of a population to return to some kind of equilibrium following a disturbance. Resilience is the propensity of an ecosystem to retain its functional and organisational structure following a disturbance. The fact that an ecosystem is resilient does not necessarily imply that all of its component populations are stable. It is possible for a disturbance to result in a population disappearing from an ecosystem, while the ecosystem as a whole continues to function in broadly the same way, so exhibiting resilience.

Common and Perrings (1992) put these matters in a slightly different way. Stability is a property that relates to the levels of the variables in the system. Cod populations in North Atlantic waters would be stable, for example, if their numbers returned to prior levels after a brief period of heavy fishing was brought to an end. Resilience relates to the sizes of the parameters of the relationships determining ecosystem structure and function in terms, say, of energy flows through the system. An ecosystem is resilient if those parameters tend to remain unchanged following shocks to the system, which will mean that it maintains its organisation in the face of shocks to it, without undergoing catastrophic, discontinuous, change.

Some economic activities appear to reduce resilience, so that the level of disturbance to which the ecosystem can be subjected without parametric change taking place is reduced. Expressed another way, the threshold levels of some system variable, beyond which major changes in a wider system take place, can be reduced as a consequence of economic behaviour. Safety margins become tightened, and the integrity and stability of the ecosystem is put into greater jeopardy. This aligns with the understanding, noted above, of pollution as that which occurs when a waste flow exceeds the assimilative capacity of the receiving system, and that which if it occurs itself reduces the system's assimilative capacity.

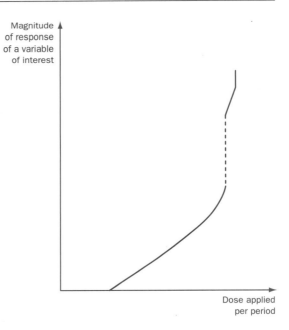

Figure 2.3 Non-linearities and discontinuities in dose–response relationships

When such changes takes place, dose–response relationships may exhibit very significant non-linearities and discontinuities. Another way of putting this is to say that dose–response relationships may involve thresholds. Pollution of a water system, for example, may have relatively small and proportional effects at low pollution levels, but at higher pollutant levels, responses may increase sharply and possibly jump discontinuously to much greater magnitudes. Such a dose–response relationship is illustrated in Figure 2.3.

2.1.3.3.2 Biodiversity

A definition of biodiversity is:

the number, variety and variability of all living organisms in terrestrial, marine and other aquatic ecosystems and the ecological complexes of which they are parts.[2]

It is evident from this definition that biodiversity is intended to capture two dimensions: first, the number of biological organisms and, secondly, their

---

[2]   This definition is taken from the Convention on Biological Diversity adopted at the UNCED conference in Rio de Janeiro in 1992: see 2.5.2 below.

variability. There are three levels at which biodiversity can be considered:

1. Population: genetic diversity within the populations that constitute a species is important as it affects evolutionary and adaptive potential of the species, and so we might measure biodiversity in terms of the number of populations.
2. Species: we might wish to measure biodiversity in terms of the numbers of distinct species in particular locations, the extent to which a species is endemic (unique to a specific location), or in terms of the diversity (rather than the number) of species.
3. Ecosystems: in many ways, the diversity of ecosystems is the most important measure of biodiversity; unfortunately, there is no universally agreed criterion for either defining or measuring biodiversity at this level.

For the purposes of this classification of levels, a species can be taken to be a set of individual organisms which have the capacity to reproduce, while a population is a set that actually do reproduce. A population is, that is, a reproductively isolated subset of a species.

Biodiversity is usually considered in terms of species, and the number of distinct species is often used as the indicator of biodiversity. There are problems with this measure. For example, within one population of any species there will be considerable genetic variation. Suppose a harvesting programme targets individuals within that population with a particular characteristic (such as large size). The target individuals are likely to possess genetic material favouring that characteristic, and so the harvesting programme reduces the diversity of the gene pool in the remaining population. Managed harvesting programmes, therefore, may result in loss of biodiversity even though the number of extant species shows no change.

Biodiversity is important in the provision of environmental services to economic activity in a number of ways. In regard to life-support services, diverse ecological systems facilitate environmental functions, such as carbon cycling, soil fertility maintenance, climate and surface temperature regulation, and watershed flows. The diversity of flora and fauna in ecosystems contributes to the amenity services that

we derive from the environment. In relation to inputs to production, those flora and fauna are the source of many useful products, particularly pharmaceuticals, foods and fibres; the genes that they contain also constitute the materials on which future developments in biotechnology will depend. In terms of agriculture, biodiversity is the basis for crop and livestock variability and the development of new varieties.

Ecologists see the greatest long-term importance of biodiversity in terms of ecosystem resilience and evolutionary potential. Diverse gene pools represent a form of insurance against ecological collapse: the greater is the extent of diversity, the greater is the capacity for adaptation to stresses and the maintenance of the ecosystem's organisational and functional structure.

We have very poor information about the current extent of biodiversity. The number of species that currently exist is not known even to within an order of magnitude. Estimates that can be found in the literature range from 3–10 million (May, 1988) to 50–100 million (Wilson, 1992). A current best guess of the actual number of species is 12.5 million (Groombridge, 1992). Even the currently known number of species is subject to some dispute, with a representative figure being 1.7 million species described to date (Groombridge, 1992). About 13 000 new species are described each year. Table 2.1 reports current knowledge about species

Table 2.1 Numbers of described species and estimates of actual numbers for selected taxa (thousands)

Taxa	Species described	Estimated number of species: High	Estimated number of species: low	Working figure
Viruses	4	1 000	50	400
Bacteria	4	3 000	50	1 000
Fungi	72	2 700	200	1 500
Protozoa and algae	80	1 200	210	600
Plants	270	500	300	320
Nematodes (worms)	25	1 000	100	400
Insects	950	100 000	2 000	8 000
Molluscs	70	200	100	200
Chordates	45[a]	55	50	50

Source: Jeffries (1997, p. 88), based in turn on Groombridge (1992) and Heywood (1995)

[a] Of the 45 000 chordates (vertebrate animals), there are about 4500 mammals, 9700 birds, 4000 amphibians and 6550 reptiles

numbers for a variety of important taxonomic classes.

2.2 The drivers of environmental impact

The environmental impact of economic activity can be looked at in terms of extractions from or insertions into the environment. In either case, for any particular instance the immediate determinants of the total level of impact are the size of the human population and the per capita impact. The per capita impact depends on how much each individual consumes, and on the technology of production. This is a very simple but useful way to start thinking about what drives the sizes of the economy's impacts on the environment. It can be formalised as the IPAT identity.

Box 2.1 reports estimates of a measure of global impact that is relevant to biodiversity and reductions in it.

Box 2.1 Human appropriation of the products of photosynthesis

The basis for life on earth is the capture by plants of radiant solar energy, and its conversion to organic material by the process of photosynthesis. The rate at which plants produce plant tissue is primary productivity, measured in terms of energy per unit area per unit time – calories per square metre per year say. Gross primary productivity is the total amount of solar energy that is fixed by photosynthesis, whereas net primary productivity is that less the amount of energy lost to the environment as respiration, and so the amount that is actually stored in the plant tissue. Net primary productivity is the measure of the energy that is potentially available to the animals that eat the plants.

Table 2.2 shows estimates of the proportion of net primary productivity that is appropriated by humanity. About 70% of the earth's surface is covered by water. The aquatic zone produces about 40% of total global net primary productivity. The terrestrial zone, although accounting for only 30% of the surface area, accounts for about 60% of total primary productivity.

For each zone, and for both zones together, Table 2.2 shows estimates of human appropriation on three different bases:

- Low – for this estimate what is counted is what humans and their domesticated animals directly use as food, fuel and fibre.
- Intermediate – this counts the current net primary productivity of land modified by humans. Thus, for example, whereas the low estimate relates to food eaten, the intermediate estimate is of the net primary productivity of the agricultural land on which the food is produced.
- High – this also counts potential net primary productivity that is lost as a result of human activity. Thus, with regard to agriculture, this estimate includes what is lost as a result, for example, of transforming forested land into grassland pasture for domesticated animals. It also includes losses due to desertification and urbanisation.

For the aquatic zone, it makes no difference which basis for estimation is used. This reflects the fact that human exploitation of the oceans is much less than it is of land-based ecosystems, and that the former is still essentially in the nature of hunter–gatherer activity rather than agricultural activity. It also reflects that what are reported are rounded numbers, to reflect the fact that we are looking at – for both zones – approximations rather than precise estimates.

For the terrestrial zone, the basis on which the human appropriation of net primary productivity is measured makes a lot of difference. If we look at what humans and their domesticates actually consume – the low basis – it is 4%. If we look at the net primary productivity of land managed in human interests – the intermediate basis – it is 31%. Commenting on the high terrestrial figure, the scientists responsible for these estimates remark:

Table 2.2 Human appropriation of net primary productivity

	Percentages		
	Low	Intermediate	High
Terrestrial	4	31	39
Aquatic	2	2	2
Total	3	19	25

Source: Vitousek *et al.* (1986)

Box 2.1 *continued*

An equivalent concentration of resources into one species and its satellites has probably not occurred since land plants first diversified.

(Vitousek *et al.*, 1986, p. 372)

For ecologists, this is the most fundamental human impact on the natural environment, and is the major driver of the current high rate of biodiversity loss. In a speech at the Natural History Museum on 28 November 2001, the ecologist Lord Robert May, President of the Royal Society and fomerly the UK government's chief scientist, stated that:

There is little doubt that we are standing on the breaking tip of the sixth great wave of extinction in the history of life on earth. It is different from the others in that it is caused not by external events, but by us – by the fact that we consume somewhere between a quarter and a half of all the plants grown last year.

(Quoted in *The Guardian*, 29 November 2001)

Just how fast is the stock of genetic resources being depleted? Given that the number of species existing is not known, statements about rates of extinction are necessarily imprecise, and there are disagreements about estimates. Table 2.3 shows data for *known* extinctions since 1600. The actual number of extinctions would certainly be equal to or exceed this. The recorded number of extinctions of mammal species since 1900 is 20. It is estimated from the fossil record that the normal, long-run average, rate of extinction for mammals is one every two centuries. In that case, for mammals the known current rate of extinction is 40 times the background rate.

To quote Lord Robert May again:

If mammals and birds are typical, then the documented extinction rate over the past century has been running 100 to more like 1000 times above the average background rate in the fossil record. And if we look into the coming century it's going to increase. An extinction rate 1000 times above the background rate puts us in the

Table 2.3 Known extinctions up to 1995

Group	Extinctions
Mammals	58
Birds	115
Molluscs	191
Other animals	120
Higher plants	517

Source: Groombridge (1992)

ballpark of the acceleration of extinction rates that characterised the five big mass extinctions in the fossil records, such as the thing that killed the dinosaurs.

(*The Guardian*, 29 November 2001)

According to Wilson (1992) there could be a loss of half of all extant birds and mammals within 200–500 years. For all biological species, various predictions suggest an overall loss of between 1% and 10% of all species over the next 25 years, and between 2% and 25% of tropical forest species (UNEP, 1995). In the longer term it is thought that 50% of all species will be lost over the next 70 to 700 years (Smith *et al.*, 1995; May, 1988).

Lomborg (2001) disputes many of the claims made about the severity of the impacts of man's economic activity on the natural environment. He takes issue, for example, with most of the estimates of current rates of species loss made by biologists. His preferred estimate for the loss of animal species is 0.7% per 50 years, which is smaller than many of those produced by biologists. It is, however, in Lomborg's own words: 'a rate about 1500 times higher than the natural background extinction' (p. 255). There really is no disagreement about the proposition that we are experiencing a wave of mass extinctions, and that it is due to the human impact on the environment.

2.2.1 The IPAT identity

The IPAT identity is

$$I \equiv P \times A \times T \tag{2.6}$$

where

I is impact, measured as mass or volume
P is population size

A is per capita affluence, measured in currency units
T is technology, as the amount of the resource used or waste generated per unit production

Let us look at impact in terms of mass, and use GDP for national income. Then *T* is resource or waste per unit GDP. Then for the resource extraction case, the right-hand side of (2.6) is

$$\text{Population} \times \frac{\text{GDP}}{\text{Population}} \times \frac{\text{Resource use}}{\text{GDP}}$$

where cancelling the two population terms and the two GDP terms leaves Resource use, so that (2.6) is an identity. If mass in measured in tonnes, GDP in $, and population is n, we have

$$\text{tonnes} \equiv n \times \frac{\$}{n} \times \frac{\text{tonnes}}{\$}$$

where on the right-hand side the ns and the $s cancel to leave tonnes.

The IPAT identity decomposes total impact into three multiplicative components – population, affluence and technology. To illustrate the way in which IPAT can be used, consider global carbon dioxide emissions. The first row of Table 2.4 shows the current situation. The first-row figures for P, A as 1999 world GDP per capita in 1999 PPP US$, and I as 1996 global carbon dioxide emissions are taken from the indicated sources: the figure for T is calculated from these, dividing I by P times A to give tonnes of carbon dioxide per $ of GDP.[3] The second row uses the T figure from the first to show the implications for I of a 50% increase in world population, for constant affluence and technology. The third row also uses the T figure from the first to show the implications of that increase in population together with a doubling of per capita GDP. A 50% increase in world population is considered because that is a conservative round number for the likely increase to 2100 (see below), and a doubling of per capita GDP is used as a round-number conservative estimate of what would be necessary to eliminate poverty (see below). As will be discussed in Chapter 10, many climate experts take the view that the current level of carbon dioxide emissions is dangerously high. The fourth row in Table 2.4 solves IPAT for T when I is set equal to its level in the first row, and P and A are

Table 2.4 Global carbon dioxide scenarios

	P (billions)	A (PPP US$)	T (tonnes per $)	I (billions of tonnes)
Current	5.8627	6948	0.0005862	23.881952
$P \times 1.5$	8.8005	6948	0.0005862	35.843711
$P \times 1.5$ and $A \times 2$	8.8005	13896	0.0005862	71.687417
$P \times 1.5$ and $A \times 2$ with I at current	8.8005	13896	0.0001952	23.881952

Sources: UNDP (2001), WRI (2000)

as in the third row – compared with the first-row figure for T, it shows that carbon dioxide emissions per unit GDP would have to be reduced to one third of their current level in order to keep total emissions at their current level given a 50% population increase and a doubling of affluence.

We now look briefly at the current situation, a little history, and future prospects in regard to each of P, A and T.

2.2.2 Population

Past, current and estimated future levels of human population are shown in Figure 2.4. At the time that this chapter was being written, early 2002, the most recent year for which data on global population size was available was 1999. In that year the estimated human population was 5.8627 billion. The estimated growth rate for 1975–1999 was 1.6% per year. Applying this to the figure for 1999 gives 5.9565 billion for 2000. The appropriate way to state the size of the human population in 2000 is as 6 billion. The staggering increase in human population in the second half of the twentieth century can be gauged by the fact that in 1950 world population was less than half that size, 2.5 billion. United Nations Population

---

[3] PPP stands for purchasing power parity. In making international GDP comparisons, and aggregating GDP across countries, using market exchange rates overlooks the fact that average price levels differ across countries, and are generally lower in poor countries. Using market exchange rates exaggerates differences in real income levels. Purchasing Power Parity exchange rates, relative to the US$, are calculated by the International Comparison Programme in order to overcome this problem, and PPP US$ GDP data convert local-currency GDP at these exchange rates: see UN

Statistical Division (1992). The difference between the market exchange-rate GDP figure and the PPP exchange-rate figure can be large – for China in 1999, for example, the latter was more than four times the former. Whereas on the former basis the US economy was nine times as big as the Chinese economy, on the latter basis it was twice as big. In terms of carbon dioxide emissions per unit GDP, on the market exchange-rate measure of GDP the Chinese figure for T is more than five times that for the US; on the PPP exchange-rate basis of GDP measurement it was just 25% bigger.

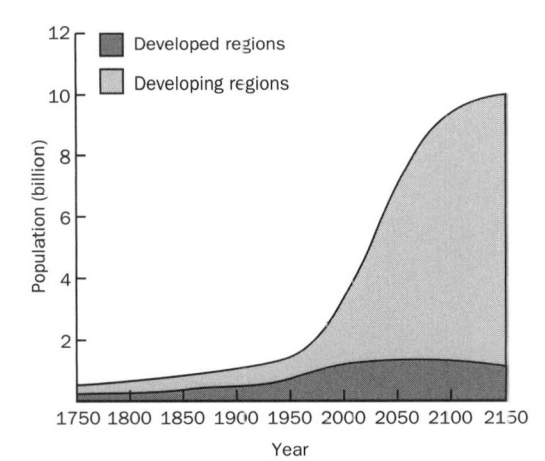

Figure 2.4 Trends and projections in world population growth, 1750–2150
Source: Figure 8.1, *World Resources 1996–97*

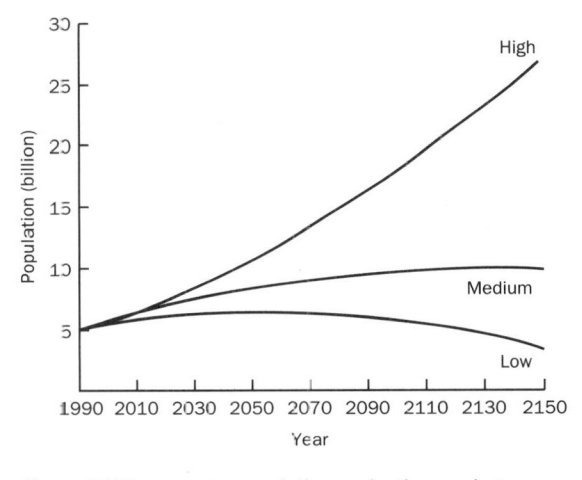

Figure 2.5 Long-range population projections using alternative fertility rate assumptions
Source: Derived from *World Resources 1996–97*

Division forecasts suggest that the world population will grow to about 8.3 billion by the year 2025, reaching 10.4 billion by 2100, before stabilising at just under 11 billion by around 2200. These forecasts are dependent on an assumption of 'average' levels of the fertility rate being maintained (slightly above two children per woman, the population replacement ratio).[4]

As shown by the documents on which Figure 2.4 is based, population outcomes are very sensitive to trends in the fertility rate. This is illustrated in Figure 2.5. Under baseline assumptions about fertility rates, world population stabilises by 2200 at a level roughly twice its 1990 size. However, under high rates of fertility (an additional half child per woman compared with the 'average' case), no such plateau is reached, with population rising at an increasing rate to 30 billion and beyond. But under low-fertility-rate assumptions (one half child less per woman relative to the average case) an end to population growth is in sight: population would peak at just under 8 billion by 2050, and would fall rapidly thereafter. As discussed below, policies aimed at reducing fertility rates can be designed and they offer the prospect of eliminating overpopulation as a contribution to the sustainability problem.

In fact, the percentage rate of increase of global population is already well below its historical peak, having decreased in recent years in all regions of the world. Growth rates are currently less than 0.5% per year in developed countries and just over 2% in developing countries. Several countries now have falling populations (for example, Germany, Austria, Denmark and Sweden), and many others are expected to move into this category in the near future. In many countries (including all industrialised countries and China), fertility rates are below the replacement rates that are required for a population size to be stationary in the long run. For these countries, population is destined to fall at some point in the future even though the momentum of population dynamics implies that population will continue to rise for some time to come. For example, although the Chinese birth-rate fell below the replacement rate in 1992, population is committed to rise from 1.2 billion in 1995 to 2 billion by 2050, and subsequently increase further. However, if the fertility rate were to fall slightly, the population could peak at 1.5 billion in 2050, and then decline. Once again, we see that very small changes in fertility rates can have major effects upon the level to which population eventually grows.

---

[4]   The figures for world population in 1999 and its growth rate for 1975–1999 are taken from UNDP (2001). The other data and estimates here come from UNPD (1998).

2.2.3 Affluence

As shown in Table 2.4, the 1999 world average for GDP per capita, in round numbers of 1999 PPP US$, was 7000. To get some sense of what this means, note the following figures (also from UNDP, 2001) for 1999 GDP per capita in 1999 PPP US$ for a few selected individual nations:

USA	31 872
Germany	23 742
UK	22 093
Portugal	16 064
Czech Republic	13 018
Hungary	11 430
China	3 617
India	2 248
Sierra Leone	448

The world average is about twice that for China, and about 20% of that for the USA.

Over the period 1975 to 1999, world average GDP per capita grew at 1.3% per annum. At that rate of growth, over 50 years the level of world average GDP would just about double, taking it to about the current level for the Czech Republic. A longer-term perspective is provided in Maddison (1995), where per capita GDP, in 1990 PPP $s, is estimated for 57 countries from 1820 through to 1992. For this sample of countries, which currently account for over 90% of world population, mean estimated per capita GDP grew from about $1000 in 1820 to about $8500 in 1992. Notwithstanding the necessary imprecision in estimates of this kind, it is clear that over the last two centuries, average global affluence has increased hugely. It is also clear that it is currently distributed very unevenly – a matter to which we return below.

2.2.4 Technology

Given the range of things that we extract from and insert into the environment, even a summary documentation of values for T as mass extracted, or inserted, per $ of economic activity would be very long, and well beyond the scope of this book. One way of giving some summary sense of the role of technology in environmental impact is to look at energy use. There are three reasons for this. First, energy is the potential to do work and energy use increases with work done. Moving and transforming matter requires work, and the amount of energy used directly reflects the amount of movement and transformation. It is the levels of extractions and insertions by the economy that determine its environmental impact, and those levels, which are linked by the law of conservation of mass, are measured by the level of energy use. While it is true that some extractions and insertions are more damaging than others, the level of its energy use is a good first approximation to the level of an economy's environmental impact.

The second and third reasons both follow from the fact that in the modern industrial economies that now dominate the global economy, about 90% of energy use is based on the combustion of the fossil fuels – coal, oil, gas. These are non-renewable resources where recycling is impossible. Hence the second reason for looking at energy – the more we use now, the less fossil fuel resources are available to future generations. The third reason is that fossil fuel combustion is directly a major source of insertions into the environment, and especially the atmosphere. Particularly, about 80% of carbon dioxide emissions originate in fossil fuel combustion, and carbon dioxide is the most important of the greenhouse gases involved in the enhanced greenhouse effect.

The energy that an animal acquires in its food, and which is converted into work, growth and heat, is called somatic energy. When the human animal learned how to control fire, about 500 000 years ago, it began the exploitation of extrasomatic energy. It began, that is, to be able to exert more power than was available from its own muscles. The human energy equivalent, HEE, is a unit of measure which is the amount of somatic energy required by a human individual. This amount varies across individuals and with circumstances. A convenient amount to use for the HEE is 10 megajoules per day, which is a round-number version of what is required by an adult leading a moderately active life in favourable climatic conditions.

Human history can be divided into three main phases, the distinguishing characteristics of which are technological. The first two phases are distinguished according to the technology for food production. The first is the hunter–gatherer phase, which lasted from the beginning of human history until about 12 000 years ago – it accounts for most of human history. During this phase food production involved gathering wild plants and hunting wild animals. It is estimated that the use of fire by an individual in hunter–gatherer societies was, on average and approximately, equivalent to the use of 1 HEE – per capita the use of fire was about equivalent to the amount of energy flowing through a human body. The total per capita use of energy was, that is, about 2 HEE.[5]

The agricultural phase of human history lasted about 12 000 years, and ended about 200 years ago. Agriculture involves producing food by domesticating some plant and animal species, and managing the environment so as to favour those species as against wild species. The technology of energy use was evolving throughout the agricultural phase of history. By its end the average human being was deploying some 3–4 HEE, so that in addition to her own muscle power she was using extrasomatic energy at the rate of 2–3 HEE. In addition to fire, almost entirely based on biomass (mainly wood) combustion, the sources of extrasomatic energy were animal muscles, the wind, and water. Animals – horses, oxen, donkeys – were used mainly for motive power in transport and agriculture. The wind was used to propel boats, to drive pumps for lifting water, and to drive mills for grinding corn. Water mills were also used for grinding corn, as well as powering early machinery for producing textiles and the like.

Comparing the situation at the end of the agricultural phase of human history with that of the hunter–gatherer phase, the per capita use of energy had approximately doubled, and the population size had increased by a factor of about 200, so that total energy use by humans had increased by a factor of about 400.

The industrial phase of human history began about 200 years ago, around 1800. Its distinguishing characteristic has been the systematic and pervasive use of the fossil fuels. In the first instance this was mainly about the use of coal in manufacturing, and then in transport. In the twentieth century oil use became much more important, as did the use of it, as well as coal, to produce electricity. In the twentieth century, the use of fossil fuels and electricity became standard, in the more advanced economies, in the domestic household sector, and in agricultural production. In a modern economy, nothing is produced that does not involve the use of extrasomatic energy, and most of what is used is based on fossil fuel combustion.

By 1900 the average human used about 14 extrasomatic HEE. By the end of the twentieth century the average human used about 19 extrasomatic HEE – the equivalent of 19 human slaves. This global average for 1997 comes from a wide range for individual nations. In 1997, per capita extrasomatic energy use in the USA was 93 HEE, while in Bangladesh it was 4 (mainly from biomass). Comparing the situation at the end of the twentieth century with that at the end of the eighteenth, the human population had increased in size by a factor of approximately 6, while extrasomatic energy use per capita had also increased by a factor of approximately 6. In 200 years total global extrasomatic energy use had increased by a factor of about 35. As noted above, this implies that the work done in moving and transforming matter – the scale of economic activity and its impact on the environment – had increased by a factor of 35.

2.2.5 Behavioural relationships

IPAT is an accounting identity. Given the way that P, A and T are defined and measured, it must always be the case that I is equal to PAT. As we saw, IPAT can be useful for figuring the implications of certain assumptions, for producing scenarios. In Table 2.4 we used it, for example, to calculate I on the assumption that P increased by 50%, A increased by 100%, and T remained the same. P, A and T are the proximate drivers of I. But we could ask, what

---

[5] The estimates for HEE for hunter–gatherers, agriculturalists and 1900 are taken from Boyden (1987). The figures for 1997 are from WRI (2000).

drives *P*, *A* and *T*? Apart from being an interesting question, this is important if we want to consider policies to drive some *I*, such as carbon dioxide emissions for example, in a particular direction. We could, that is, look to build a model which incorporates the behavioural relationships that we think determine what happens to *P*, *A* and *T*, and other variables, over time. In such a model we would very likely have relationships between *P*, *A* and *T*, as well as between them and other variables.

There are many behavioural relationships that affect, and are affected by, movements in *P*, *A* and *T*. Economists are particularly interested, for example, in supply and demand functions for inputs to production. These determine the relative prices of those inputs, and hence affect *T* – a high price for fossil fuels will reduce their use, and hence reduce carbon dioxide emissions. Much of the rest of the book will be concerned with the role of the price mechanism in relation to the determination of the level of extractions from and insertions into the natural environment. Here we will look at two examples of behavioural relationships where affluence is the driver.

2.2.5.1 Affluence and population growth: the demographic transition

A statistical relationship that is often remarked upon is the negative correlation between income level and population growth rate. Several attempts have been made to explain this observed relationship, the most well-known of which is the theory of demographic transition (Todaro, 1989). The theory postulates four stages through which population dynamics progress, shown in Figure 2.6. In the first stage, populations are characterised by high birth-rates and high death-rates. In some cases, the death-rates reflect intentions to keep populations stable, and so include infanticide, infant neglect and senilicide (see Harris and Ross, 1987). In the second stage, rising real incomes result in improved nutrition and developments in public health which lead to declines in death-rates and rapidly rising population levels. In the third stage of the demographic transition, economic forces lead to reduced fertility rates. These forces include increasing costs of childbearing and family care, reduced benefits of large family size,

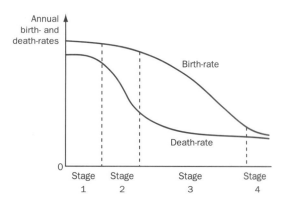

Figure 2.6 The theory of demographic transition

higher opportunity costs of employment in the home, and changes in the economic roles and status of women. In the final stage, economies with relatively high income per person will be characterised by low, and approximately equal, birth- and death-rates, and so stable population sizes.

The theory of demographic transition succeeds in describing the observed population dynamics of many developed countries quite well. If the theory were of general applicability, it would lead to the conclusions that rising population is a transient episode, and that programmes which increase rates of income growth in developing countries would lower the time profile of world population levels. But it remains unclear whether the theory does have general applicability. For many developing countries the second stage was reached not as a consequence of rising real income but rather as a consequence of knowledge and technological transfer. In particular, public health measures and disease control techniques were introduced from overseas at a very rapid rate. The adoption of such measures was compressed into a far shorter period of time than had occurred in the early industrialising countries, and mortality rates fell at unprecedented speed. During the nineteenth century, the higher-income countries typically experienced falls in birth-rates relatively soon after falls in mortality rates. However, while birth-rates are falling in most developing countries, these falls are lagging behind drops in the mortality levels, challenging the relevance of the theory of demographic transition. Dasgupta (1992) argues that the accompanying population explosions created the potential for a vicious

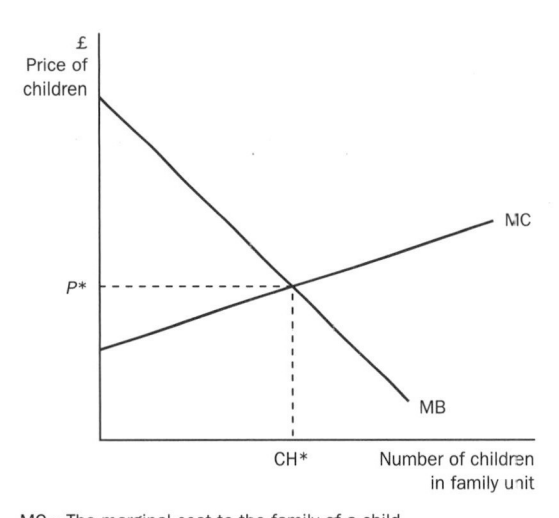

MC = The marginal cost to the family of a child
MB = The marginal benefit to the family of a child
   = (the demand curve for children)

Figure 2.7 The microeconomics of fertility

cycle of poverty, in which the resources required for economic development (and so for a movement to the third stage of the demographic transition) were crowded out by rapid population expansion.

Two important determinants of the rate at which a population changes over time are the number of children born to each female of reproductive age, and the life expectancy of each child. There have been dramatic increases in life expectancy throughout the world, attributed to improved medical and public health services. The number of children born into each household is primarily the outcome of a choice made by (potential) parents. Family size is the choice-variable; contraceptive and other family planning practices are the means by which that choice is effected. Microeconomic theory suggests that the marginal costs and the marginal benefits of children within the family (see Figure 2.7) determine family size. The marginal costs of children depend on the costs of childbearing, child rearing and education, including the opportunity costs of parental time in these activities. Marginal benefits of children to the family include the psychic benefits of children, the contribution of children to family income, and the extent to which old age security is enhanced by larger family size.

An important advantage of this line of analysis is that it offers the prospect of deriving guidelines for

population policy: attempts to alter desired family size should operate by shifting the marginal cost of bearing and raising children, or the marginal benefits derived from children within the family. What measures might governments take, or what intermediate goals might they pursue, to reduce the desired family size? Several suggest themselves:

- Increased levels of education, particularly education of women. This could affect fertility through three related routes. First, education enhances the effectiveness of family planning programmes: families become more proficient at having the number of children that they choose. Secondly, greater participation in education increases the status of women: it is now widely agreed that where females have low-status roles in the culture of a society, fertility rates are likely to be high. Thirdly, greater education decreases labour-market sex discrimination, allows females to earn market incomes, and raises real wage rates in the labour market. These changes increase the opportunity cost of children, and may well also reduce the marginal benefits of children (for example, by salaried workers being able to provide for old age through pension schemes).
- Financial incentives can be used to influence desired family size. Financial penalties may be imposed upon families with large numbers of children. Alternatively, where the existing fiscal and welfare state provisions create financial compensation for families with children, those compensations could be reduced or restructured. There are many avenues through which such incentives can operate, including systems of tax allowances and child benefits, subsidised food, and the costs of access to health and educational facilities. There may well be serious conflicts with equity if financial incentives to small family size are pushed very far, but the experiences of China suggest that if government is determined, and can obtain sufficient political support, financial arrangements that increase the marginal cost of children or reduce the marginal benefits of children can be very powerful instruments.
- Provision of care for and financial support of the elderly, financed by taxation on younger groups

in the population. If the perceived marginal benefits of children to parents in old age were to be reduced (by being substituted for in this case), the desired number of children per family would fall. As the tax instrument merely redistributes income, its effect on welfare can be neutral. But by reducing the private marginal benefits of children it can succeed (at little or no social cost) in reducing desired family size.

■ The most powerful means of reducing desired family size is almost certainly economic development, including the replacement of subsistence agriculture by modern farming practices, giving farm workers the chance of earning labour market incomes. There may, of course, be significant cultural losses involved in such transition processes, and these should be weighed against any benefits that agricultural and economic development brings. Nevertheless, to the extent that subsistence and non-market farming dominates an economy's agricultural sector, there will be powerful incentives for large family size. Additional children are valuable assets to the family, ensuring that the perceived marginal benefits of children are relatively high. Furthermore, market incomes are not being lost, so the marginal cost of child-rearing labour time is low. Important steps in the direction of creating markets for labour (and reducing desired family size) can be taken by defining property rights more clearly, giving communities greater control over the use of local resources, and creating financial incentives to manage and market resources in a sustainable way.

2.2.5.2 Affluence and technology: the EKC

The *World Development Report 1992* (World Bank, 1992) was subtitled 'Development and the environment'. It noted that 'The view that greater economic activity inevitably hurts the environment is based on static assumptions about technology, tastes and environmental investments'. If we consider, for example, the per capita emissions, e, of some pollutant into the environment, and per capita income, y, then the view that is being referred to can be represented as

$$e = \alpha y \tag{2.7}$$

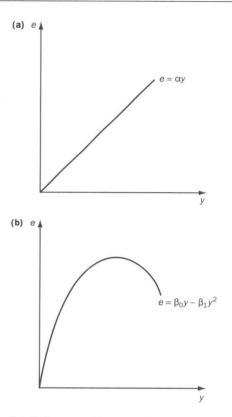

Figure 2.8 Environmental impact and income
Source: Adapted from Common (1996)

so that e increases linearly with y, as shown in Figure 2.8(a). Suppose, alternatively, that the coefficient α is itself a linear function of y:

$$\alpha = \beta_0 - \beta_1 y \tag{2.8}$$

Then, substituting Equation 2.8 into Equation 2.7 gives the relationship between e and y as:

$$e = \beta_0 y - \beta_1 y^2 \tag{2.9}$$

For β_1 sufficiently small in relation to β_0, the e/y relationship takes the form of an inverted U, as shown in Figure 2.8(b). With this form of relationship, economic growth means higher emissions per capita until per capita income reaches the turning point, and thereafter actually reduces emissions per capita.

It has been hypothesised that a relationship like that shown in Figure 2.8(b) holds for many forms of environmental degradation. Such a relationship is called an 'environmental Kuznets curve' (EKC) after Kuznets (1955), who hypothesised an inverted U for the relationship between a measure of inequality in the distribution of income and the level of income. If the EKC hypothesis held generally, it would imply that instead of being a threat to the environment as is often argued (see the discussion of *The Limits to Growth* below), economic growth is the means to environmental improvement. That is, as countries develop economically, moving from lower to higher levels of per capita income, overall levels of environmental degradation will eventually fall.

The argument for an EKC hypothesis has been succinctly put as follows:

> At low levels of development both the quantity
> and intensity of environmental degradation is limited
> to the impacts of subsistence economic activity
> on the resource base and to limited quantities of
> biodegradable wastes. As economic development
> accelerates with the intensification of agriculture
> and other resource extraction and the takeoff of
> industrialisation, the rates of resource depletion begin
> to exceed the rates of resource regeneration, and waste
> generation increases in quantity and toxicity. At higher
> levels of development, structural change towards
> information-intensive industries and services, coupled
> with increased environmental awareness, enforcement
> of environmental regulations, better technology and
> higher environmental expenditures, result in levelling
> off and gradual decline of environmental degradation.
> *Panayotou (1993)*

Clearly, the empirical status of the EKC hypothesis is a matter of great importance. If economic growth is actually and generally good for the environment, then it would seem that there is no need to curtail growth in the world economy in order to protect the global environment. In recent years there have been a number of studies using econometric techniques to test the EKC hypothesis against the data. Some of the results arising are discussed below. According to one economist, the results support the conclusion that

> there is clear evidence that, although economic
> growth usually leads to environmental degradation
> in the early stages of the process, in the end the best
> – and probably the only – way to attain a decent
> environment in most countries is to become rich.
> *Beckerman (1992)*

Assessing the validity of this conclusion involves two questions. First, are the data generally consistent with the EKC hypothesis? Second, if the EKC hypothesis holds, does the implication that growth is good for the global environment follow? We now consider each of these questions.

2.2.5.2.1 Evidence on the EKC hypothesis

In one of the earliest empirical studies, Shafik and Bandyopadhyay (1992) estimated the coefficients of relationships between environmental degradation and per capita income for ten different environmental indicators as part of a background study for the *World Development Report 1992* (IBRD, 1992). The indicators are lack of clean water, lack of urban sanitation, ambient levels of suspended particulate matter in urban areas, urban concentrations of sulphur dioxide, change in forest area between 1961 and 1986, the annual rate of deforestation between 1961 and 1986, dissolved oxygen in rivers, faecal coliforms in rivers, municipal waste per capita, and carbon dioxide emissions per capita. Some of their results, in terms of the relationship fitted to the raw data, are shown in Figure 2.9. Lack of clean water and lack of urban sanitation were found to decline uniformly with increasing income. The two measures of deforestation were found not to depend on income. River quality tends to worsen with increasing income. As shown in Figure 2.9, two of the air pollutants were found to conform to the EKC hypothesis. Note, however, that CO_2 emissions, a major contributor to the 'greenhouse gases' to be discussed in relation to global climate change in Chapter 10, do not fit the EKC hypothesis, rising continuously with income, as do municipal wastes. Shafik and Bandyopadhyay summarise the implications of their results by stating:

> It is possible to 'grow out of' some environmental
> problems, but there is nothing automatic about
> doing so. Action tends to be taken where there are
> generalised local costs and substantial private and
> social benefits.

Panayotou (1993) investigated the EKC hypothesis for: sulphur dioxide (SO_2), nitrogen oxide (NO_x) suspended particulate matter (SPM) and deforestation. The three pollutants are measured in terms of emissions per capita on a national basis. Deforestation

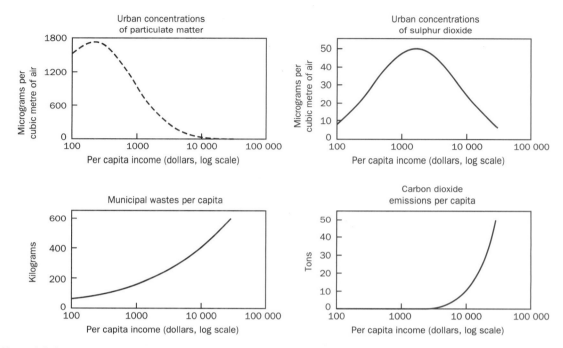

Figure 2.9 Some evidence on the EKC. Estimates are based on cross-country regression analysis of data from the 1980s
Source: Adapted from IBRD (1992)

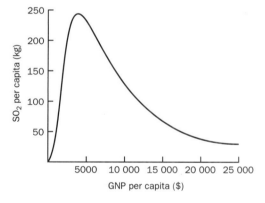

Figure 2.10 An EKC for SO_2
Source: Adapted from Panayotou (1993)

is measured as the mean annual rate of deforestation in the mid-1980s. All the fitted relationships are inverted Us, consistent with the EKC hypothesis. The result for SO_2 is shown in Figure 2.10, where the turning point is around $3000 per capita.

There is now an extensive literature investigating the empirical status of the EKC hypothesis. The Further Reading section at the end of the chapter provides points of entry to this literature, and the key references. Some economists take the results in the literature as supporting the EKC for local and regional impacts, such as sulphur for example, but not for global impacts, such as carbon dioxide for example. However, Stern and Common (2001) present results that are not consistent with the existence of an EKC for sulphur. The EKC hypothesis may hold for some environmental impacts, but it does not hold for all.

2.2.5.2.2 Implications of the EKC

If the EKC hypothesis were confirmed, what would it mean? Relationships such as that shown in Figure 2.10 might lead one to believe that, given likely future levels of income per capita, the global environmental impact concerned would decline in the medium-term future. In Figure 2.10 the turning point is near world mean income. In fact, because of the highly skewed distribution for per capita incomes, with many more countries – including some with very large populations – below rather than above the mean, this may not be what such a relationship implies.

This is explored by Stern *et al.* (1996), who also critically review the literature on the existence of meaningful EKC relationships. Stern *et al.* use the projections of world economic growth and world population growth published in the *World Development Report 1992* (IBRD, 1992), together with Panayotou's EKC estimates for deforestation and SO_2 emissions, to produce global projections of these variables for the period 1990–2025. These are important cases from a sustainable development perspective. SO_2 emissions are a factor in the acid rain problem: deforestation, especially in the tropics, is considered a major source of biodiversity loss. Stern *et al.* projected population and economic growth for every country in the world with a population greater than 1 million in 1990. The aggregated projections give world population growing from 5265 million in 1990 to 8322 million in 2025, and mean world per capita income rising from $3957 in 1990 to $7127 in 2025. They then forecast deforestation and SO_2 emissions for each country individually using the coefficients estimated by Panayotou. These forecasts were aggregated to give global projections for forest cover and SO_2 emissions. Notwithstanding the EKC relationship shown in Figure 2.10, total global SO_2 emissions rise from 383 million tonnes in 1990 to 1181 million tonnes in 2025; emissions of SO_2 per capita rise from 73 kg to 142 kg from 1990 to 2025. Forest cover declines from 40.4 million km^2 in 1990 to a minimum of 37.2 million km^2 in 2016, and then increases to 37.6 million km^2 in 2025. Biodiversity loss on account of deforestation is an irreversible environmental impact, except on evolutionary timescales, so that even in this case the implications of the fitted EKC are not reassuring.

Generally, the work of Stern *et al.* shows that the answer to the second question is that even if the data appear to confirm that the EKC fits the experience of individual countries, it does not follow that further growth is good for the global environment. Arrow *et al.* (1995) reach a similar position on the relevance of the EKC hypothesis for policy in relation to sustainability. They note that

> The general proposition that economic growth is good for the environment has been justified by the claim that there exists an empirical relation between per capita income and some measures of environmental quality.

They then note that the EKC relationship has been 'shown to apply to a selected set of pollutants only', but that some economists 'have conjectured that the curve applies to environmental quality generally'. Arrow *et al.* conclude that

> Economic growth is not a panacea for environmental quality; indeed it is not even the main issue

and that

> policies that promote gross national product growth are not substitutes for environmental policy.

In Box 2.2 we report some simulation results that indicate that even if an EKC relationship between income and environmental impact is generally applicable, given continuing exponential income growth, it is only in very special circumstances that there will not, in the long run, be a positive relationship between income and environmental impact.

Box 2.2 The environmental Kuznets curve and environmental impacts in the very long run

The environmental Kuznets curve (EKC) implies that the magnitude of environmental impacts of economic activity will fall as income rises above some threshold level, when both these variables are measured in per capita terms. Here we assume for the sake of argument that the EKC hypothesis is correct. Common (1995) examines the implications of the EKC hypothesis for the long-run relationship between environmental impact and income. To do this he examines two special cases of the EKC, shown in Figure 2.11.

In case **a** environmental impacts per unit of income eventually fall to zero as the level of income rises. Case **b** is characterised by environmental impacts per unit income falling to some minimum level, k, at a high level of income, and thereafter remaining constant at that level as income continues to increase. Both of these cases embody the basic principle of the EKC, the only difference being whether environmental impacts per unit income fall to zero or just to some (low) minimum level.

Box 2.2 continued

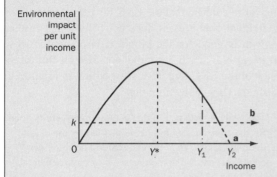

Figure 2.11 Two possible shapes of the environmental Kuznets curve in the very long run
Source: Adapted from Common (1995)

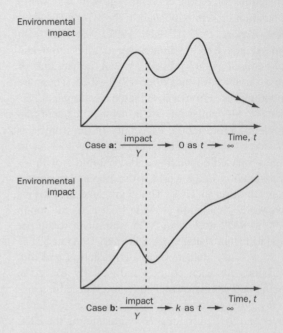

Figure 2.12 Two scenarios for the time profile of environmental impacts
Source: Adapted from Common (1995)

Suppose that the world consists of two countries that we call 'developed' and 'developing' which are growing at the same constant rate of growth, g. However, the growth process began at an earlier date in the developed country and so at any point in time its per capita income level is higher than in the developing country. Common investigates what would happen in the long run if case **a**, the highly optimistic version of the EKC, is true. He demonstrates that the time path of environmental impacts one would observe would be similar to that shown in the upper part of Figure 2.12. Why should there be a dip in the central part of the curve? For some period of time, income levels in the two countries will be such that the developed country is on the downward-sloping portion of its EKC while the developing country is still on the upward-sloping part of its EKC. However, as time passes and growth continues, both countries will be at income levels where the EKC curves have a negative slope; together with the assumption in case a that impacts per unit income fall to zero, this implies that the total level of impacts will itself converge to zero as time becomes increasingly large.

But now consider case **b**. No matter how large income becomes the ratio of environmental impacts to income can never fall below some fixed level, k. Of course, k may be large or small, but this is not critical to the argument at this point; what matters is that k is some constant positive number. As time passes, and both countries reach high income levels, the average of the impacts-to-income ratio for the two countries must converge on that constant value, k. However, since we are assuming that each

country is growing at a fixed rate, g, the total level of impacts (as opposed to impacts per unit income) must itself eventually be increasing over time at the rate g. This is shown in the lower part of Figure 2.12.

What is interesting about this story is that we obtain two paths over time of environmental impacts which are entirely different from one another in qualitative terms for very small differences in initial assumptions. In case a, k is in effect zero, whereas in case b, k is greater than zero. Even if environmental impacts per unit of income eventually fell to a tiny level, the total level of impacts would eventually grow in line with income.

Which of these two possibilities – case **a** or case **b** – is the more plausible? Common argues that the laws of thermodynamics imply that k must be greater than zero. If so, the very-long-run relationship between total environmental impacts and the level of world income would be of the linear form shown (for per capita income) in panel a of Figure 2.8. The inference from the inverted U shape of the EKC that growth will reduce environmental damage in the very long run would be incorrect.

2.3   Poverty and inequality

Each year the United Nations Development Programme (UNDP) produces a *Human Development
Report*, which draws on reports and data collections
from a wide range of United Nations and other international agencies, and is the most useful single
source of data and analysis on the current global
state of humanity. This section draws heavily on
these reports, and especially that for 2001 (UNDP,
2001) from which the following quotation is taken:

> Human development challenges remain large in
> the new millennium . . . Across the world we see
> unacceptable levels of deprivation in people's lives.
> Of the 4.6 billion people in developing countries, more
> than 850 million are illiterate, nearly a billion lack
> access to improved water sources, and 2.4 billion lack
> access to basic sanitation. Nearly 325 million boys
> and girls are out of school. And 11 million children
> under age five die each year from preventable causes
> – equivalent to more than 30 000 a day. Around 1.2
> billion people live on less than $1 a day (1993 PPP
> US$), and 2.8 billion live on less than $2 a day.

In its report for 1998 (UNDP, 1998), the UNDP
had additionally noted that of the population of
the developing nations: 1.1 billion lacked adequate
housing; 0.9 billion were undernourished; 0.9 billion
had no access to modern health services.

Against this background, the report for 2001 comments that:

The magnitude of these challenges appears daunting.
Yet too few people recognize that the impressive
gains in the developing world in the last 30 years
demonstrate the possibility of eradicating poverty. A
child born today can expect to live eight years longer
than one born 30 years ago. Many more people can
read and write, with the adult literacy rate having
increased from an estimated 47% in 1970 to 73% in
1999. The share of rural families with access to safe
water has grown more than fivefold. Many more
people can enjoy a decent standard of living, with
average incomes in developing countries having
almost doubled in real terms between 1975 and 1998,
from $1300 to $2500 (1985 PPP US$).

We now examine the current situation and recent
trends in a little more detail. For a fuller version of
what is a complex story, the reader should consult
the *Human Development Report 2001* (UNDP,
2001) and other references provided in the Further
Reading section at the end of the chapter.

2.3.1   The current state of human development

Table 2.5 gives data on a number of indicators taken
from recent issues of the *Human Development
Report*. The data cover 162 nations. There are 29
members of the UN that are not included in these
data on the grounds that reliable information for
them is not available. The excluded nations have an
aggregate population of about 100 million out of a

Table 2.5 International comparisons at the end of the twentieth century

	Life expectancy[a]	Infant mortality[b]	Calories per day[c]	GDP per capita[d]	Electricity per capita[e]
World	66.7	56	2791	6 980	2 074
OECD	76.6	13	3380	22 020	6 969
USA	76.8	7	3699	31 872	11 832
Turkey	69.5	40	3525	6 380	1 353
EE and CIS	68.5	25	2907	6 290	2 893
Hungary	71.1	9	3313	11 430	2 888
Uzbekistan	68.7	45	2433	2 251	1 618
Developing	64.5	61	2663	3 530	757
Least developed	51.7	100	2099	1 170	76
Sub-Saharan	48.8	107	2237	1 640	480

[a] Years at birth, 1999, Table 1, UNDP (2001)
[b] Per 1000 live births, 1999, Table 8, UNDP (2001)
[c] 1997, Table 23, UNDP (2000)
[d] 1999, PPP US$, Table 1, UNDP (2001)
[e] Kilowatt hours, 1998, Table 18, UNDP (2001)

total world population of about 6 billion. The largest excluded nations are: Afghanistan, Cuba, Democratic Republic of Korea, Iraq and Yugoslavia.

The nations of the world are grouped in different ways in different contexts. The three groupings in Table 2.5 are one of the classifications used in the *Human Development Report*. OECD stands for 'Organisation for Economic Co-operation and Development'. This organisation has 30 members, and corresponds roughly to the set of advanced industrial nations sometimes referred to as the 'developed world' or 'the North'. As indicated, Turkey is a member, as is Mexico. 'EE and CIS' is short for 'Eastern Europe and the Commonwealth of Independent States', which is the former Soviet Union and its satellites. This grouping includes countries at very different levels of development, as illustrated by Hungary and Uzbekistan. All of the nations that are covered by the data but in neither the OECD nor EE and CIS are classified as 'developing'. For most indicators the *Human Development Report* provides data for several subsets of this classification, two of which are included in Table 2.5. Many of the 'least developed' nations are located in Sub-Saharan Africa; non-African members of the least developed nations set include Bangladesh, Cambodia, Haiti, Lao People's Democratic Republic, Myanmar and Nepal. The 1999 population sizes for the three groups of nations are: OECD 1122 million; EE and CIS 398 million; developing 4610 million. The population of the set of least developed is 609 million, and for Sub-Saharan Africa it is 591 million.

On average, people in the OECD can expect to live 12 years longer than people in the developing world. OECD infant mortality is about one quarter the rate in the developing world. A moderately active adult requires about 2500 calories per day. On this basis nutrition in the developing world as a whole is adequate on average, but less than adequate in the least developed nations and in Sub-Saharan Africa. On average, people in the OECD get 35% more daily calories than is required. In round number terms, the *Human Development Report* follows the World Bank and defines poverty as an annual income of less than PPP US$600 in terms of current PPP $s – this corresponds to $1 per day in terms of 1993 PPP US$. On that basis, according to

Table 2.5, even for the least developed nations average income is above the poverty line. However, as quoted above, looking behind the average, it is estimated that 1.2 billion people are below the poverty line. In terms of averages, GDP per capita in the OECD is more than six times that in the developing world, and almost 19 times that in the least developed nations. For electricity consumption per capita, the relativities are broadly the same as for income per capita.

The data in Table 2.5 are for just a small sample of the possible indicators of human development. The picture that they show is broadly the same across all indicators – many human beings currently experience poverty and deprivation, and there are massive inequalities. In regard to income inequality, the *Human Development Report 2001* cites (UNDP, 2001) some results from a study that is based on household survey data rather than national income data. The study relates to the period 1988–1993 and covers 91 countries with 84% of world population. According to this study:

- The income of the poorest 10% was 1.6% of that of the richest 10%
- The richest 1% of the world population received as much income in total as the poorest 57%
- Around 25% of the population received 75% of total income

2.3.2 Recent trends

An important question is whether things have been getting better in recent history. Table 2.6 shows the ratio of the values taken by the Table 2.5 indicators to their values as near to a quarter of a century ago as the data allow.

Life expectancy increased proportionately more in the developing world than in the OECD. It actually decreased for EE and the CIS as a whole, though in some of its constituent nations it did increase a little. In the Russian Federation, life expectancy decreased from 69.7 for 1970–75 to 66.1 in 1999. This is associated with economic collapse and a major breakdown in preventive health care. Also culpable may be the cumulative effects of serious environmental contamination over many years in the Soviet Union, especially toxic wastes from chemical

Table 2.6 Ratios for change in the last quarter of the twentieth century

	Life expectancy[a]	Infant mortality[b]	Calories per day[c]	GDP per capita[d]	Electricity per capita[e]
OECD	1.09	0.33	1.11	1.61	1.42
USA	1.07	0.35	1.25	1.61	1.33
Turkey	1.20	0.27	1.15	1.65	3.08
EE and CIS	0.99	0.68	..	..	..
Hungary	1.03	0.25	0.99	1.21	1.21
Uzbekistan	1.07	0.68	..	0.48	..
Developing	1.16	0.56	1.24	1.73	2.28
Least Developed	1.17	0.67	1.00	1.05	1.31
Sub-Saharan	1.08	0.78	0.99	0.79	1.04

[a] Base is 1970–75, Table 8, UNDP (2001)
[b] Base is 1970, Table 8, UNDP (2001)
[c] Base is 1970, Table 23, UNDP (2000) (.. means not available)
[d] Base is 1975, calculated from annual growth rates, Table 11, UNDP (2001)
[e] Base is 1980, Table 18, UNDP (2001)

plants, pesticides from agriculture and nuclear radiation from various sources. For infant mortality a ratio of less than one indicates improvement over the period. Considering the three groupings, the improvement was least in EE and the CIS. Looking at nutrition, we see that while the situation improved for the developing world as a whole, for the least developed nations there was no change, and for Sub-Saharan Africa things actually got slightly worse. A figure for daily calories for EE and the CIS as a whole in 1970 is not available; for Hungary average daily calorie intake fell very slightly from 1970 to 1997, while for the Russian Federation it fell by 25%.

In the developing world as a whole GDP per capita grew by more than it did in the OECD. However, here again, there is much variation within the developing world. For the least developed nations, per capita income increased by just 5% over 24 years, and for Sub-Saharan Africa it actually fell by about 20%. There was also a lot of variation within EE and the CIS, for which a figure for the base year of 1975 is not available. Over the 1990s the total number of people living below the poverty line as defined above was more or less constant at 1.2 billion. Given that the world population grew over this period, the proportion of the world's population living in poverty so defined fell slightly.

What about inequality? The *Human Development Report 2001* (Box 1.3) reports calculations based on GDP per capita data which show that from 1970 to 1997 the ratio of the income of the richest 10% to

Table 2.7 GDP per capita relativities to the USA

	1975	1999
OECD	0.69	0.69
USA	1.00	1.00
Turkey	0.20	0.20
EE and CIS	..	0.20
Hungary	0.48	0.36
Uzbekistan	..	0.07
Developing	0.10	0.11
Least developed	0.06	0.04
Sub-Saharan	0.11	0.05

Calculated from 1999 $s and annual growth rates, Table 11, UNDP (2001)

the poorest 10% increased from 19.4 to 26.9, indicating increasing inequality. On the other hand, if the ratio is calculated for the top and bottom 20% it falls from 14.9 to 13.1, indicating decreasing inequality.

Table 2.7 is based on the GDP per capita data used for Tables 2.5 and 2.6. It shows the ratio of GDP per capita for a group or nation to that of the USA for the same year. Thus, for the OECD as a whole GDP per capita was 69% of that of the USA in 1975 and 1999 – the OECD and the USA grew at the same rate, so that relative to the latter the former became neither better off nor worse off – the inequality remained constant. This is also the case for Turkey. There is no 1975 figure for EE and the CIS as a whole, nor is there one for Uzbekistan. For Hungary the ratio fell from 0.48 to 0.36, so that inequality between Hungary and the USA increased. One would guess this to be the case for the whole of EE and the CIS – for its largest member, the Russian

Federation, the ratio fell from 0.50 in 1975 to 0.24 in 1999.

For the developing world as a whole, inequality in relation to the USA decreased a little, in that the ratio increases from 0.10 to 0.11. However, for the least developed nations and Sub-Saharan Africa, in relation to the USA and – given the above observations on the USA and the OECD – the OECD as a whole, income inequality increased. In the case of Sub-Saharan Africa, per capita GDP fell by about 20% while USA per capita GDP increased by about 60% (Table 2.6), and the ratio of the former to the latter fell by over 50%.

2.3.3 Growth as the solution

Economists have a very strong attachment to economic growth as a major policy objective. A major reason for this is that they see it as the only feasible way to solve the problem of poverty. The argument is that with economic growth, the lot of the poor can be improved without taking anything away from the better-off. Generally the better-off will resist attempts to redistribute from them to the poor, so that this route to poverty alleviation will involve social tension and possibly violent conflict. Further, over and above such considerations, poverty alleviation via redistribution may not work even if it is politically and socially feasible. The problem is that typically the poor are much more numerous than the rich, so that there is simply not enough to take from the rich to raise the poor above the poverty line. When, in the years following the Second World War, economists thought that they understood how to bring about economic growth they came to think that they could solve an age-old problem of the human condition – they came to think that the poor need not always be with us.

Indeed, perhaps the most famous economist of the twentieth century, J.M. Keynes, saw in economic growth the prospect that the very problem that was taken to be the essential economic problem – scarcity – would be abolished, so that economists would become largely redundant. In an essay (Keynes, 1931), written in the early 1930s, on the economic prospects for the grandchildren of adults then alive, Keynes was concerned to put in perspect-

ive the waste entailed in the then-prevalent underuse of available resources, especially labour. If the means to avoid such waste could be found and adopted, Keynes argued, economic growth, i.e. increasing per capita GDP, at 2% per year would easily be attained and sustained. This, he pointed out, would mean that in one hundred years output would increase sevenfold. Scarcity would be abolished, and a situation arise in which economics and economists were no longer important. In the years after the Second World War, most economists thought that Keynesian macroeconomics was the means to achieving full employment and sustained growth throughout the world.

The arithmetic of compound growth – growth at a constant proportional rate – is indeed striking. And, there is no doubt that historically economic growth has raised the consumption levels of the mass of the population in the rich industrial world to levels that could scarcely have been conceived of at the start of the industrial revolution, 200 years ago. There is also no doubt that for the developing world as a whole, economic growth in the latter part of the twentieth century reduced the extent of poverty. The arithmetic of economic growth does not, however, necessarily imply any reduction in economic inequality. If the incomes of the rich and the poor grow at the same rates, the proportionate difference between them stays the same, and the absolute difference – in dollars per year – actually increases. The original Kuznets curve hypothesis was that, with growth, income inequality first increased then decreased. The evidence on this hypothesis is mixed. As noted above, global income inequalities have not generally decreased in recent years. Within some advanced economies inequality has increased.

2.4   Limits to growth?

An important event in the emergence in the last decades of the perception that there is a sustainability problem was the publication in 1972 of a book, *The Limits to Growth* (Meadows *et al.*, 1972), which was widely understood to claim that environmental limits would cause the collapse of the world economic system in the middle of the twenty-first century.

The book was roundly condemned by most economists, but influenced many other people. It is arguable that it was a stimulus to the re-emergence of interest in natural resources on the part of economists in the early 1970s noted in Chapter 1. One economist argued, at around the same time, that the limits to growth were social rather than environmental.

2.4.1   Environmental limits

The Limits to Growth reported the results of a study in which a computer model of the world system, World3, was used to simulate its future. World3 represented the world economy as a single economy, and included interconnections between that economy and its environment. According to its creators, World3

> was built to investigate five major trends of global concern – accelerating industrialization, rapid population growth, widespread malnutrition, depletion of non-renewable resources, and a deteriorating environment. These trends are all interconnected in many ways, and their development is measured in decades or centuries, rather than in months or years. With the model we are seeking to understand the causes of these trends, their interrelationships, and their implications as much as one hundred years in the future.
>
> *(Meadows et al., 1972, p. 21)*

It incorporated:

(a) a limit to the amount of land available for agriculture;

(b) a limit to the amount of agricultural output producible per unit of land in use;

(c) a limit to the amounts of non-renewable resources available for extraction;

(d) a limit to the ability of the environment to assimilate wastes arising in production and consumption, which limit falls as the level of pollution increases.

The behaviour of the economic system was represented as a continuation of past trends in key variables, subject to those trends being influenced by the relationships between the variables represented in the model. These relationships were represented in terms of positive and negative feedback effects. Thus, for example, population growth is determined by birth- and death-rates, which are determined by fertility and mortality, which are in turn influenced by such variables as industrial output per capita, the extent of family planning and education – for fertility – and food availability per capita, industrial output per capita, pollution, and the availability of health care – for mortality. The behaviour over time in the model of each of these variables, depends in turn on that of others, and affects that of others.

On the basis of a number of simulations using World3, the conclusions reached by the modelling team were as follows:

> 1. If the present growth trends in world population, industrialization, pollution, food production and resource depletion continue unchanged, the limits to growth on this planet will be reached sometime within the next 100 years. The most probable result will be a sudden and uncontrollable decline in both population and industrial capacity.
> 2. It is possible to alter these trends and to establish a condition of ecological and economic stability that is sustainable far into the future. The state of global equilibrium could be designed so that the basic material needs of each person on earth are satisfied and each person has an equal opportunity to realize his or her individual human potential.
> 3. If the world's people decide to strive for this second outcome rather than the first, the sooner they begin working to attain it, the greater will be their chances of success.
>
> *(Meadows et al., 1992)*

What *The Limits to Growth* actually said was widely misrepresented. It was widely reported that it was an unconditional forecast of disaster sometime in the next century, consequent upon the world running out of non-renewable resources. In fact, as the quotation above indicates, what was involved was conditional upon the continuation of some existing trends. Further, this conditional prediction was not based upon running out of resources.

The first model run reported did show collapse as the consequence of resource depletion. Figure 2.13 is a reproduction of the figure in *The Limits to Growth* that reports the results for 'World Model Standard Run'. This run assumes no major changes in social, economic or physical relationships. Variables follow

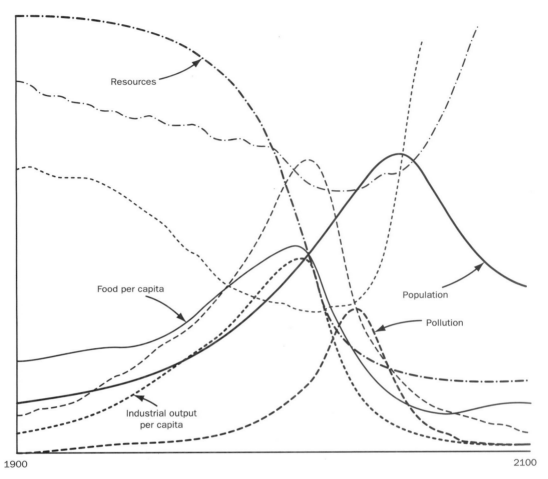

Figure 2.13 Base run projections of the 'limits to growth' model
Source: Meadows *et al.* (1972), page 124

actual historical values until the year 1970. Thereafter, food, industrial output and population grow exponentially until the rapidly diminishing resource base causes a slowdown in industrial growth. System lags result in pollution and population continuing to grow for some time after industrial output has peaked. Population growth is finally halted by a rise in the mortality rate, as a result of reduced flows of food and medical services.

However, the next reported run involved the model modified by an increase in the resource availability limit such that depletion did not give rise to problems for the economic system. In this run, the proximate source of disaster was the level of pollution consequent upon the exploitation of the increased amount of resources available, following from the

materials balance principle. A number of variant model runs were reported, each relaxing some constraint. The conclusions reached were based on consideration of all of the variant model runs. Successive runs of the model were used to ascertain those changes to the standard configuration that were necessary to get the model to a sustainable state, rather than to collapse mode.

It was widely reported that the World3 results said that there were limits to 'economic growth'. In fact, what they said, as the conclusions quoted above indicate, is that there were limits to the growth of material throughput for the world economic system. As economic growth is measured it includes the consumption of the output of the service sector, as well as the agricultural and industrial sectors.

The origins of the sustainability problem **47**

A sequel (Meadows *et al.*, 1992) to *The Limits to Growth*, written by the same team and entitled *Beyond the Limits*, was published in 1992 to coincide with the UNCED conference held in Rio de Janeiro. To date, the publication of the sequel appears to have generated much less controversy than the original did. This might suggest some major change in analysis and conclusions as between original and sequel. In fact there is very little substantive difference in the conclusions, and apart from updating of numerical values used, the model is stated to be modified in only minor ways from the original World3. The position on this as stated in the sequel is:

> As far as we can tell from the global data, from the World3 model, and from all we have learned in the past twenty years, the three conclusions we drew in *The Limits to Growth* are still valid, but they need to be strengthened.

2.4.2 Economists on environmental limits

The response by economists to *The Limits to Growth* was almost entirely hostile. Given their commitment to economic growth as the solution to the problem of poverty and the widespread existence of the problem, noted in the previous section, this was hardly surprising. Prominent among the critical responses from economists were those by Page (1973), Nordhaus (1972), Beckerman (1972, 1974), Cole *et al.* (1973) and Lecomber (1975). According to one eminent economist it was 'a brazen, impudent piece of nonsense that nobody could possibly take seriously' (Beckerman, 1972). As noted above, economists have had much less to say, and much less critical things to say, about the sequel, *Beyond the Limits*. In a foreword to it, a Nobel laureate in economics, Jan Tinbergen, says of it: 'We can all learn something from this book, especially we economists'.

The main line of the criticism of the original by economists was that the feedback loops in World3 were poorly specified in that they failed to take account of behavioural adjustments operating through the price mechanism. In particular, it was argued that changing patterns of relative scarcity would alter the structure of prices, inducing behavioural changes in resource-use patterns. Given a well-functioning

market mechanism, it was argued, limits to growth would not operate in the way reported by the modelling team. It was conceded by some of the economist critics that the force of this argument was weakened by the fact that for many environmental resources and services, markets did not exist, or functioned badly where they did. However, it was also argued that such 'market failure' could be corrected by the proper policy responses to emerging problems. This presumes that the sorts of substitutions for environmental services that we discussed above can be made, given properly functioning markets or policy-created surrogates for such, to the extent that will overcome limits that would otherwise exist. A major, and largely unresolved, question in the debates about the existence of a sustainability problem is the existence and effectiveness of substitutes for environmental services.

2.4.3 Social limits to growth

Daly (1987) argues that there are two classes of limits to growth. First, there are the biophysical limits arising from the laws of thermodynamics and from the fragility of ecosystems. The second class relates to the desirability of growth, rather than its feasibility. Daly states four propositions about the desirability of growth:

1. The desirability of growth financed by running down resources is limited by the cost imposed on future generations.
2. The extinction or reduction in the number of sentient non-human species whose habitat disappears limits the desirability of growth financed by takeover.
3. The self-cancelling effects on welfare limit the desirability of aggregate growth.
4. The desirability of growth is limited by the corrosive effects on moral standards of the very attitudes that foster growth, such as glorification of self-interest and a scientific–technocratic worldview.

The last two of these propositions concern what have been called 'social limits to growth'.

The argument for 'social limits to growth' was explicitly advanced in a book with that title (Hirsch,

1977), published five years after *The Limits to Growth*. Hirsch argued that the process of economic growth becomes increasingly unable to yield the satisfaction which individuals expect from it, once the general level of material affluence has satisfied the main biological needs for life-sustaining food, shelter and clothing. As the average level of consumption rises, an increasing portion of consumption takes on a social as well as an individual aspect, so that

> the satisfaction that individuals derive from goods and services depends in increasing measure not only on their own consumption but on consumption by others as well.
>
> *(Hirsch, 1977, p. 2)*

The satisfaction a person gets from the use of a car, for example, depends on how many other people do the same. The greater the number of others who use cars, the greater is the amount of air pollution and the extent of congestion, and so the lower is the satisfaction one individual's car use will yield. However, Hirsch's main focus was on what he calls 'positional goods', the satisfaction from which depends upon the individual's consumption relative to that of others, rather than the absolute level of consumption. Consider, as an example, expenditure on education in an attempt to raise one's chances of securing sought-after jobs. The utility to a person of a given level of educational expenditure will decline as an increasing number of others also attain that level of education. Each person purchasing education seeks to gain individual advantage, but the simultaneous actions of others frustrate these objectives for each individual. As the average level of education rises, individuals will not receive the gains they expect from higher qualifications.

Once basic material needs are satisfied, further economic growth is associated with an increasing proportion of income being spent on such positional goods. As a consequence, growth is a much less socially desirable objective than economists have usually thought. It does not deliver the increased personal satisfactions that it is supposed to. Traditional utilitarian conceptions of social welfare (see Chapters 3 and 5) may be misleading in such circumstances, as utilities are interdependent. Using

terminology to be introduced and explained in Chapter 5, we can say that given the external effects arising due to the consumption of others affecting the utility that an individual derives from his or her own consumption, the simple summation of individual consumption levels overstates collective welfare.

2.5   The pursuit of sustainable development

Many people now live in conditions such that basic material needs are not satisfied. This is particularly true for people living in the poor nations of the world, but is by no means restricted to them. Even in the richest countries, income and wealth inequalities are such that many people live in conditions of material and social deprivation. For many years, it was thought that the eradication of poverty required well-designed development programmes that were largely independent of considerations relating to the natural environment. The goal of economic and political debate was to identify growth processes that could allow continually rising living standards. Economic development and 'nature conservation' were seen as quite distinct and separate problems. For some commentators, concern for the natural environment was a rather selfish form of self-indulgence on the part of the better-off.

Perspectives have changed significantly since the 1970s. While the pursuit of economic growth and development continues, it is recognised that the maintenance of growth has an important environmental dimension. During the 1970s, a concern for sustainability began to appear on the international political agenda, most visibly in the proceedings of a series of international conferences. The common theme of these debates was the interrelationship between poverty, economic development and the state of the natural environment.

Perhaps the best-known statement of the sustainability problem derives from the 1987 report of the World Commission on Environment and Development, which set the agenda for much of the subsequent discussion of sustainability.

2.5.1 The World Commission on Environment and Development

The World Commission on Environment and Development, WCED, was established in 1983 by the United Nations. Its mandate was:

1. to re-examine the critical environment and development issues and to formulate realistic proposals for dealing with them;
2. to propose new forms of international cooperation on these issues that will influence policies and events in the direction of needed changes;
3. to raise the levels of understanding and commitment to action of individuals, voluntary organisations, businesses, institutes and governments.

WCED comprised 23 commissioners from 21 different countries. The chairperson was Gro Harlem Brundtland, who had previously been both Minister for the Environment and Prime Minister of Norway. Over a period of two years, the commissioners held public meetings in eight countries, at which people could submit their views on WCED's work. In regard to analysis and awareness-raising, WCED focused on population growth, food security, biodiversity loss, energy, resource depletion and pollution, and urbanisation.

2.5.1.1 The Brundtland Report

The report that WCED produced in 1987 – *Our Common Future* (WCED, 1987) – is often referred to as 'the Brundtland report' after the name of the WCED chairperson. It advanced, with great effect, the concept of 'sustainable development', which is now on political agendas, at least at the level of rhetoric, around the world. The Brundtland report was, in political terms, an outstanding and influential piece of work.

It provides much information about what we have called here the sustainability problem, setting out the nature of economy–environment interdependence, identifying a number of potential environmental constraints on future economic growth, and arguing that current trends cannot be continued far

into the future. Thus, according to the Brundtland report,

> Environment and development are not separate challenges: they are inexorably linked. Development cannot subsist on a deteriorating environmental base; the environment cannot be protected when growth leaves out of account the costs of environmental protection.
>
> *(p. 37)*

while

> The next few decades are crucial. The time has come to break out of past patterns. Attempts to maintain social and ecological stability through old approaches to development and environmental protection will increase instability.
>
> *(p. 22)*

The Brundtland report does not conclude that future economic growth is either infeasible or undesirable. Having defined sustainable development as development that

> seeks to meet the needs and aspirations of the present without compromising the ability to meet those of the future.
>
> *(p. 43)*

it states that:

> Far from requiring the cessation of economic growth, it [sustainable development] recognizes that the problems of poverty and underdevelopment cannot be solved unless we have a new era of growth in which developing countries play a large role and reap large benefits.
>
> *(p. 40)*

Nor does it require that those nations already developed cease to pursue economic growth:

> Growth must be revived in developing countries because that is where the links between economic growth, the alleviation of poverty, and environmental conditions operate most directly. Yet developing countries are part of an interdependent world economy; their prospects also depend on the levels and patterns of growth in industrialized nations. The medium term prospects for industrial countries are for growth of 3–4 per cent, the minimum that international financial institutions consider necessary if these countries are going to play a part in expanding

the world economy. Such growth rates could be environmentally sustainable if industrialized nations can continue the recent shifts in the content of their growth towards less material- and energy-intensive activities and the improvement of their efficiency in using materials and energy.

(p. 51)

In the light of an appreciation of the economy–environment interdependence and the current level of global economic activity, some environmentalists have expressed the view that 'sustainable development' is an oxymoron. It is their assessment that the current situation is such that we already are at the limits of what the environment can tolerate, so that growth will inevitably damage the environment, and cannot, therefore, be sustainable. It is the assessment of the Brundtland report that environmental limits to growth can be avoided, given the adoption, world-wide, of policies to affect the form that economic growth takes. To make growth sustainable, those policies would have to involve reducing, at the global level, the material content of economic activity, economising in the use of resources as the value of output increases, and substituting the services of reproducible capital for the services of natural capital. Much of resource and environmental economics is about the policy instruments for doing that, as we shall see in later chapters.

Given the nature of the WCED, it is not surprising that the Brundtland report is not strong on detailed and specific policy proposals that would facilitate the move from 'past patterns' to sustainable development. It urges, for example, that national governments merge environmental and economic considerations in their decision making. It did make a specific recommendation regarding item 2 from its mandate. This was that the UN General Assembly convene an international conference

to review progress made and promote follow-up arrangements that will be needed over time to set benchmarks and to maintain human progress within the guidelines of human needs and natural laws.

(p. 343)

This recommendation was acted upon, and the result was the United Nations Conference on Environment and Development, UNCED, which took place in Rio de Janeiro in June 1992.

2.5.2 UNCED: Rio de Janeiro 1992

The conference itself was preceded by over two years of preparatory international negotiations. Delegations were sent from 178 nations and the meeting was attended by 107 heads of government (or state). During UNCED several parallel and related conferences took place in Rio de Janeiro; the meeting for 'non-governmental organisations', mainly pro-environment pressure groups, involved more participants than UNCED itself. It has been estimated that, in total, over 30 000 people went to Rio de Janeiro in June 1992.

The preparatory negotiations dealt with four main areas: draft conventions on biodiversity conservation, global climate change, forest management, and the preparation of two documents for adoption at UNCED. The main UNCED outcomes were as follows. There was complete agreement on the non-binding adoption of the *Rio Declaration* and *Agenda 21*. The first of these comprises 27 statements of principle in regard to global sustainable development. The second is an 800-page document covering over 100 specific programmes for the attainment of global sustainable development: many of these programmes involve resource transfers from the industrial to the developing nations. UNCED also agreed on the creation of a new UN agency, a Commission for Sustainable Development, to oversee the implementation of *Agenda 21*. Agreement was also reached on the, non-binding, adoption of a set of principles for forest management. The industrial nations reaffirmed their previous non-binding commitments to a target for development aid of 0.7% of their GNP. It should be noted that it is still true that only a few of the industrial nations actually attain this target.

Two conventions were adopted, by some 150 nations in each case, which would be binding on signatories when ratified by them. These covered global climate change and biodiversity conservation: the latter was not signed by the USA at the Rio meeting, but the USA did sign in 1993 after a change of administration. Although binding, these conventions did not commit individual nations to much in the way of specific actions. The *Convention on Biological Diversity* deals with two main issues – the exploitation of genetic material and biodiversity conservation. In regard to the latter, signatories agree to create systems of protected areas, for example, but undertake no commitments regarding their extent. The *Framework Convention on Climate Change* was mainly about the principles according to which future negotiations – known as Conferences of the Parties, COPS – were to try to establish commitments and rules. A major principle was that commitments would be limited to the developed nations.

Many environmental activists, as well as many concerned to promote economic development in poor nations, regarded the actual achievements at UNCED as disappointing, but it did confirm that sustainable development was, and would remain, firmly on the world political agenda. While specific commitments were not a major feature of the outcomes, there were agreements with the potential to lead to further developments. The creation of the Commission for Sustainable Development is clearly an important institutional innovation at the international level.

The convening of, and the outcomes at, UNCED suggest that the need to address the economic and environmental problems arising from economy–environment linkages is widely accepted. Equally, UNCED and subsequent events suggest that even when the existence of a problem is widely agreed by national governments, agreement on the nature of appropriate policy responses is limited. Further, there is clearly reluctance on the part of national governments to incur costs associated with policy responses, and agreed action is even more difficult to realise than agreement about what should be done. The difficulties involved in achieving international action on environmental problems are discussed in Chapter 10, along with progress that has been made since 1987.

2.5.3 World Summit on Sustainable Development: Johannesburg 2002

The United Nations Commission on Sustainable Development, established as a result of UNCED in 1992, organised the 2002 World Summit on Sustainable Development, WSSD, in Johannesburg to build upon the achievements of UNCED. This chapter is being written in June 2002, and WSSD is to take place from 26 August to 4 September, so a report on WSSD is impossible! However, a great deal of the preparatory work that has already been done for WSSD can be accessed at http://www.johannesburgsummit.org/index.html. It is clear that the hope is that WSSD will move things further in the direction of actions for sustainable development, as opposed to declarations in favour of it.

There is already a huge amount of documentation at the above web site, including a Draft Plan of Implementation, adoption of which would move signatories in the direction of specific commitments. There is also the text of a lecture given at the London School of Economics on 25 February 2002 by the United Nations Secretary-General, Kofi Annan. The title of the lecture is 'From Doha to Johannesburg by way of Monterrey: how to achieve, and sustain, development in the 21st century'. The following quotations from the lecture give the sense of the Secretary-General's assessment of progress since UNCED in 1992, and of his hopes for WSSD in 2002.

Much was achieved at Rio. Agenda 21, adopted there, remains as visionary today as it was then – and local authorities and civil society in almost every part of the world have been working to implement it. Moreover, legally binding conventions on climate change, biodiversity and desertification have been added since then.

Prevailing approaches to development remain fragmented and piecemeal; funding is woefully inadequate; and production and consumption patterns continue to overburden the world's natural life support systems.

Agenda 21 and all that flowed from it can be said to have given us the 'what' – what the problem is, what principles must guide our response.

Johannesburg must give us the 'how' – how to bring about the necessary changes in state policy; how to use policy and tax incentives to send the right signals to business and industry; how to offer better choices to individual consumers and producers; how, in the end, *to get things done*.

Summary

Our objectives in this chapter have been to describe some aspects of the current state of human development, and of the fundamental material and biological conditions within which future development must take place. We have also examined some of the consequences that human activity currently has, and may have in the future, on the natural environment. While our discussion has not been comprehensive, it has demonstrated that the natural environment and the human economy are not independent systems. On the contrary, they are intimately related through a complex set of interactions. Economic activity affects the environment, which affects the economy. Whatever 'sustainability' might mean, it is clear from our analysis here that a necessary condition for an economy to be sustainable is that its natural environment should be maintained so as to continue to deliver a diverse set of services.

Further reading

Data on the topics dealt with in this chapter can be found in the publications of agencies such as the United Nations (UN), the Food and Agriculture Organization of the United Nations (FAO), the United Nations Environment Programme (UNEP), the United Nations Development Programme (UNDP), the World Bank, the Organisation for Economic Co-operation and Development (OECD), the International Energy Agency (IEA), and the World Conservation Union (WCN, formerly the International Union for the Conservation of Nature, IUCN). Each year the World Resources Institute (WRI) collates data from these and other sources in a series of tables in its publication *World Resources*. This is jointly produced by WRI, UNEP, the World Bank and UNDP. Each year this publication also focuses on some particular aspect of economy–environment interdependence – for example, at the time of writing the latest available report was *World Resources 2000–2001: People and Ecosystems*. Some data are available from the web sites of these organisations:

UN – www.un.org
FAO – www.fao.org/default.htm
UNEP – www.unep.org
UNDP – www.undp.org
World Bank – www.worldbank.org
OECD – www.oecd.org
IEA – www.iea.org

WRI – www.wri.org
WCN – www.iucn.org

Lomborg (2001) is a useful point of entry to the vast array of statistical materials on the current state of the environment and human development. The appearance of Lomborg's book in English generated a great deal of interest and controversy, as he argues that what the statistics show is that those 'environmentalists' who claim that the human condition is deteriorating and that the ability of the environment to support economic activity is decreasing are, overall, quite wrong. Many of those environmentalists have, in turn, claimed that Lomborg is both wrong and irresponsible. Lomborg treats each potential environmental problem in isolation, rather than as the set of linked phenomena that they are. Lomborg has a web site, www.lomborg.com, which provides links to various contributions to the controversy.

There are a number of well-documented examples of unsustainable societies in human history, where collapse followed resource exhaustion. Ponting (1992) is an environmental history of humanity and provides brief accounts of some examples, and references to more detailed works; see also Diamond (1993).

Jackson and Jackson (2000) and Park (2001) are two standard texts that deal at greater length with the environmental science topics covered in this chapter. Both are at an introductory level: Jackson and

Jackson assumes some prior knowledge of chemistry. Krebs (2001) is a successful ecology text that is comprehensive but assumes no prior knowledge of the subject. Folke (1999) is a brief overview of ecological principles as they relate to ecological economics, and provides useful references to the literature. As it is set out here, the idea of resilience as a property of an ecosystem is developed in Holling (1986). The paper by Ludwig *et al.* (1997) is a clear, but technical, exposition of the basic mathematics of Holling resilience and how it relates to another concept of resilience that appears in the ecology literature.

There is no uniquely correct way to classify the services that the environment provides to the economy. Barbier *et al.* (1994), in Table 3.1, provide a four-way classification of what they call the 'life support functions of ecosystems' into regulation, production, carrier and information functions. Costanza *et al.* (1997) distinguish 17 classes of 'ecosystem service'. Common (1995), Dasgupta (1982) and Perrings (1987) consider economy–environment interdependence and some of its implications from an economics perspective. D'Arge and Kogiku (1972) is an early contribution to the resource and environmental economics literature that contains a growth model which obeys the law of conservation of matter. As noted in the body of the chapter, the economist who did most to draw the attention of economists to the laws of thermodynamics and their implications for economics was Nicholas Georgescu-Roegen; various assessments of his contribution are presented in a special issue of the journal *Ecological Economics*, Vol. 22, no 3, September 1997.

Barbier *et al.* (1994) is a good introduction to biodiversity issues. Wilson's classic work (Wilson, 1988) on biodiversity has been updated as *Biodiversity II* (Reaka-Kudla *et al.*, 1996). UNEP (1995) is the definitive reference work in this field, dealing primarily with definition and measurement of biodiversity loss, but also containing good chapters on economics and policy. See also Groombridge (1992) and Jeffries (1997) for excellent accounts of biodiversity from an ecological perspective. Measurement and estimation of biodiversity are examined in depth in Hawksworth (1995), and regular updated accounts are provided in the annual publication *World Resources*. The extent of human domination of global ecosystems is considered in Vitousek *et al.* (1997); for the range of uncertainty attending such estimates see Field (2001).

The IPAT identity was introduced in Ehrlich and Holdren (1971); see also Ehrlich and Ehrlich (1990). It was originally set out as $I \equiv PCT$ where C stands for consumption, but IPAT is a better acronym than IPCT, and it is income per capita rather than consumption that matters and is most easily measured. The identity indicates the scale of technological change that is necessary to hold impact constant for any given change in population and/or affluence. The feasible prospects for technological change are discussed in von Weizsäcker *et al.* (1997) – it is claimed that T could be reduced by a factor of four, so that affluence could double and impact be cut by 50%, for constant population. Lovins *et al.* (2000) is even more optimistic about technological possibilities.

Becker (1960) is the classic original source of the literature on the economics of population. Easterlin (1978) provides a comprehensive and non-mathematical survey of the economic theory of fertility, and his 1980 volume provides an excellent collection of readings. The EKC hypothesis was the subject of a special issue of the journal *Environment and Development Economics* in October 1997 (Vol. 2, part 4), and also of the journal *Ecological Economics* in May 1998 (Vol. 25, no 2). See also de Bruyn and Heintz (1999).

The UNDP's annual *Human Development Report* is the best single source of data and commentary on the global situation in regard to affluence, poverty and inequality. As well as basic data, each year it reports country performance against a series of indices intended to capture several dimensions of human development. Arndt (1978) is a very interesting account of the rise to the top of the policy agenda of the growth objective in the 1950s and 1960s, and of reaction to claims that continuing economic growth was infeasible due to environmental limits. Useful accounts of debates over limits to growth are to be found in Simon (1981), Simon and Kahn (1984) and Repetto (1985). The October 1998 issue (Vol. 3, part 4) of the journal *Environment and Development Economics* included several papers which revisited the debate over *The Limits to Growth* in response to an article in *The Economist* with the title 'Environmental scares: plenty of gloom'.

McCormick (1989) provides a useful account of the modern history of environmental concerns and their impact on politics, and traces the evolution of the development versus environment debate through the various international conferences which preceded the publication of the Brundtland report. That report (WCED, 1987) is essential reading on sustainable development.

One very important dimension of the sustainability problem, where many particular issues come together and interact, is the matter of feeding the human population. We have not been able to cover this here because of space limitations. The Companion Web Site discusses some of the issues, and provides lots of pointers to further reading.

Discussion questions

1. Many economists accept that a 'Spaceship Earth' characterisation of the global economy is valid in the final analysis, but would dispute a claim that we are currently close to a point at which it is necessary to manage the economy according to strict principles of physical sustainability. On the contrary, they would argue that urgent problems of malnutrition and poverty dominate our current agenda, and the solution to these is more worthy of being our immediate objective. The objective of physically sustainable management must be attained eventually, but is not an immediate objective that should be pursued to the exclusion of all else.

   To what extent do you regard this as being a valid argument?

2. How effective are measures designed to increase the use of contraception in reducing the rate of population growth?

3. How may the role and status of women affect the rate of population growth? What measures might be taken to change that role and status in directions that reduce the rate of population growth?

4. Does economic growth inevitably lead to environmental degradation?

Problems

1. Use the microeconomic theory of fertility to explain how increasing affluence may be associated with a reduction in the fertility rate.

2. Suppose that families paid substantial dowry at marriage. What effect would this have on desired family size?

3. What effect would one predict for desired family size if family members were to cease undertaking unpaid household labour and undertake instead marketed labour?

4. Take the following data as referring to 2000 (they come from UNDP (2001), P and A are for 1999 and T uses CO_2 data for 1997), and the world as being the sum of these three groups of nations.

	P (millions)	A (PPP US$)	T (tonnes)
Rich OECD	848	26 050	0.0004837
EE and CIS	398	6 290	0.0011924
Developing	4610	3 530	0.0005382

   a. Calculate total world CO_2 emissions in 2000.
   b. Work out the 2000 group shares of total population and CO_2 emissions.
   c. Assume population growth at 0.5% per year in Rich OECD and EE and CIS and at 1.5% per year in Developing, out to 2050. Assume

per capita income growth at 1.5% per year in Rich OECD, at 2.5% per year in EE and CIS, and at 3.0% in Developing, out to 2050. Work out total world emissions and group shares of the total for 2050, and also group shares of world population.

By what factor does total world emissions increase over the 50-year period?

d. For the same population growth and per capita income growth assumptions, by how much would T have to fall in Rich OECD for that group's 2050 emissions to be the same as in 2000? With Rich OECD emissions at their 2000 level in 2050, assume that T for EE and CIS in 2050 is the same as T for Rich OECD in 2000 (which would be 2050 T for EE and CIS, being about half of its 2000 level) and work out what total world CO_2 emissions would then be.

CHAPTER 3

Ethics, economics and the environment

And God said, Let us make man in our image, after our likeness: and let them have dominion over the fish of the sea, and over the fowl of the air, and over the earth, and over every creeping thing that creepeth upon the earth.

Genesis 1:24–8

Learning objectives

In this chapter you will
- learn about utilitarianism as the ethical basis for welfare economics
- see how it differs from some other ethical systems
- be introduced to some of the criticisms of utilitarianism
- take a first look at the vexed question of discounting
- be introduced to optimal growth analysis where production uses a non-renewable natural resource

---

Introduction

Environmental and resource economics is concerned with the allocation, distribution and use of environmental resources. To some extent, these matters can be analysed in a framework that does not require the adoption of any particular ethical viewpoint. We can focus our attention on answering questions of the form 'If X happens in a particular set of circumstances, what are the implications for Y?' Analyses of this form constitute what is sometimes described as 'positive' economics.

However, limiting our scope to answering questions of this form is restrictive. Many economists wish also to do 'normative' economics, to address questions about what *should* be done in a particular set of circumstances. To do this it is necessary to use ethical criteria derived from theories about how persons ought to behave. In doing normative economics, generally referred to as 'welfare economics', economists usually employ criteria derived from utilitarian ethical theory. Normative resource and environmental economics is predominantly founded in utilitarian ethics.

The main purpose of this chapter is to provide an introduction to and overview of the nature of the utilitarian approach to ethics, and to show how it informs normative economics. Welfare economics as such is dealt with in Chapters 5 and 11, and gets applied throughout Parts II, III and IV of the book. This chapter begins by looking briefly, in the first two sections, at other approaches to ethics, so as to provide some context. The chapter then, in the third section, sets out the basic elements of utilitarianism as a general approach to the question of how we should behave, and the particular ways in which welfare economics uses that general approach. Some of the criticisms of utilitarianism and its use in welfare economics are then reviewed in the fourth section of the chapter.

In the context of economic activity and the natural environment, the question of how we should behave with respect to future generations is important. As we saw in the previous chapter, there is, for many, a concern that current economic activity is affecting the environment so as to entail damage to future generations. The fifth section of the chapter looks at the utilitarian approach to the question of intertemporal distribution, focusing particularly on the sustainability issue. The next chapter considers a number of possible concepts of sustainability.

A fundamental distinction can be drawn between two broad families of ethical systems: humanist and naturalist moral philosophies. In humanist philosophies, rights and duties are accorded exclusively to human beings, either as individuals or as communities – while humans may be willing to give them consideration, non-human things have no rights or responsibilities in themselves. A naturalist ethic denies this primacy or exclusivity to human beings. In this ethical framework, values do not derive exclusively from human beings. Rather, rights can be defined only with respect to some natural system. A classic exposition of this ethic is to be found in Aldo Leopold's 'A Sand County Almanac' (1970, p. 262): 'A thing is right when it tends to preserve the integrity, stability and beauty of the biotic community. It is wrong when it tends otherwise.'

Peter Singer (1993) describes this position as a 'deep ecology' ethic. When a development is proposed, a deep ecologist might argue that the project would not be right if significant disturbances to ecosystems are likely to occur. Given that a large part of human behaviour does have significant ecological implications, strict adherence to a naturalist philosophy would prohibit much current and future human activity. The implications of a thoroughgoing adherence to such a moral philosophy seem to be quite profound, although much depends upon what constitutes a *significant* impact.

A weak form of naturalist ethic – roughly speaking, the notion that behaviour which has potentially large impacts on those parts of the biosphere that are deserving of safeguard, because of their unusualness or scarcity, should be prohibited – has had some impact on public policy in many countries. Examples

include the designation of Sites of Special Scientific Interest and the consequent special provisions for management of these sites in the United Kingdom, the system of National Parks in the USA, and the designation of Internationally Important Sites by the Worldwide Fund for Nature.

In the period since 1970, a number of important works have emerged which attempt to establish the nature of mankind's obligation to non-human beings. Much of this writing has made use of Kant's categorical imperative, according to which an action is morally just only if it is performed out of a sense of duty and is based upon a valid ethical rule. Justice is not to be assessed in terms of the consequence of an action.

But what is a valid rule? According to Kant, a valid rule is a universal rule. Universality here means that such a rule can be applied consistently to every individual. He writes: 'I ought never to act except in such a way that I can also will that my maxim [rule] should become a universal law.' This principle is Kant's categorical imperative. The basis of ethical behaviour is found in the creation of rules of conduct that each person believes should be universalised. For example, I might legitimately argue that the rule 'No person should steal another's property' is an ethical rule if I believe that everyone should be bound by that rule.

One categorical imperative suggested by Kant is the principle of respect for persons: no person should treat another exclusively as a means to his or her end. It is important to stress the qualifying adverb *exclusively*. In many circumstances we do treat people as means to an end; an employer, for example, regards members of his or her workforce as means of producing goods, to serve the end of achieving profits for the owner of the firm. This is not wrong in itself. What is imperative, and is wrong if it is not followed, is that all persons should be treated with the respect and moral dignity to which any person is entitled.

Kant was a philosopher in the humanist tradition. His categorical imperatives belong only to humans, and respect for persons is similarly restricted. However, naturalists deny that such respect should be accorded only to humans. Richard Watson (1979) begins from this Kantian imperative of respect for persons, but amends it to the principle of respect for others. In discussing who is to count as 'others', Watson makes use of the principle of reciprocity, the capacity to knowingly act with regard to the welfare of others. He denies that only humans have the capacity for reciprocal behaviour, arguing that it is also evident in some other species of higher animal, including chimpanzees, dolphins and dogs. Such animals, Watson argues, should be attributed moral rights and obligations: at a minimum, these should include intrinsic rights to life and to relief from unnecessary suffering.

But many writers believe that human obligations extend to a far broader class of 'others'. The philosopher G.J. Warnock (1971) grappled with the concept of consideration, the circumstances that imply that something has a right for its interests to be taken into account in the conscious choices of others. Warnock concluded that all sentient beings – beings which have the capacity to experience pleasure or pain – deserve to be considered by any moral agent. So, for Warnock, when you and I make economic decisions, we have a moral obligation to give some weight to the effects that our actions might have on any sentient being.

Some other naturalist philosophers argue that the condition of sentience is too narrow. Our obligations to others extend beyond the class of other animals that can experience pain and pleasure. Kenneth Goodpaster (1978) concludes that all living beings have rights to be considered by any moral agent. W. Murray Hunt (1980) adopts an even stronger position. He concludes that 'being in existence', rather than being alive, confers a right to be considered by others. For Hunt, all things that exist, living or dead, animate or inanimate, have intrinsic rights.

Although our summary of naturalistic philosophies has been brief, it does demonstrate that the typical humanist philosophy adopted by most economists has not gone unchallenged. It seems to be the case that the moral foundations of some ecological and environmentalist arguments owe much to naturalistic ethics. This may account for why conventional economists and some environmentalists have found it difficult to agree. Readers who wish to explore naturalistic moral philosophy in more depth than has been possible here should consult the Further Reading section at the end of the chapter.

3.2   Libertarian moral philosophy

Libertarianism is a humanist moral philosophy. It takes as its central axiom the fundamental inviolability of individual human rights. There are no rights other than the rights of human individuals, and economic and social behaviour is assessed in terms of whether or not it respects those rights. Actions that infringe individual rights cannot be justified by appealing to some supposed improvement in the level of social well-being. Libertarianism asserts the primacy of processes, procedures and mechanisms for ensuring that fundamental liberties and rights of individual human beings are respected and sustained. Rights are inherent in persons as individuals, and concepts such as community or social rights are not meaningful.

We will discuss the work of one influential libertarian philosopher, Robert Nozick (1974). Nozick's intellectual foundations are in the philosophy of John Locke, and in particular his principle of just acquisition. Locke argued that acquisition is just when that which is acquired has not been previously owned and when an individual mixes their labour power with it. For Locke, this is the source of original and just property rights.

Nozick extends this argument. He asks: when is someone entitled to hold (that is, own) something? His answer is: 'Whoever makes something, having bought or contracted for all other held resources used in the process (transferring some of his holdings for these co-operating factors), is entitled to it.' So any holding is a just holding if it was obtained by a contract between freely consenting individuals, provided that the seller was entitled to dispose of the object of the contract. (Some people will not be entitled to their holdings because they were obtained by theft or deception.) The key point in all of this is free action. Distributions are just if they are entirely the consequence of free choices, but not otherwise.

Libertarians are entirely opposed to concepts of justice based on the consequences or outcomes. An outcome cannot in itself be morally good or bad. Libertarian moral philosophy is likely to drastically limit the scope of what government may legitimately do. For example, policy to redistribute income and wealth (between people, between countries or between generations) in favour of the poor at the expense of the rich requires taxation that is coercive, and so unjust unless every affected person consents to it. Government action would be limited to maintaining the institutions required to support free contract and exchange. Those who believe in a limited role for government have adopted libertarianism enthusiastically. However, it by no means clear that a laissez-faire approach is necessarily implied by libertarianism, as can be seen by considering the following three questions that arise from the notion of just acquisition:

1. What should government do about unjust holdings?
2. How are open access resources to be dealt with?
3. How do external effects and public goods relate to the concept of just acquisition?

If you are unfamiliar with them, the terms 'open access', 'external effects' and 'public goods' are explained in Chapter 5. You may want to come back to questions 2 and 3 after reading that chapter.

3.3   Utilitarianism

Utilitarianism originated in the writings of David Hume (1711–1776) and Jeremy Bentham (1748–1832), and found its most complete expression in the work of John Stuart Mill (1806–1873), particularly in his *Utilitarianism* (1863). The ethical basis for modern normative economics is a particular variety of utilitarianism, as we shall explain. 'Utility' is the term introduced by early utilitarian writers for the individual's pleasure or happiness. Modern economics still uses this term in that way. The term 'welfare' is used to refer to the social good, which in utilitarianism, and hence welfare economics, is some aggregation of individual utilities. For utilitarians actions which increase welfare are right and actions that decrease it are wrong.

Utilitarianism is a consequentialist theory of moral philosophy – it is solely the consequences or outcomes of an action that determine its moral worth. In this it differs from motivist theory, according to which an action is to be judged according to

its motivation (Kant was a motivist), and from deontological theory, according to which it is an action's inherent nature that makes it right or wrong. For a utilitarian an action may be considered morally justified even if it is undertaken for unworthy reasons and has a nature that might in some circumstances be considered bad. For a utilitarian, the ends might justify the means.

3.3.1   Anthropocentric utilitarianism

In order to make a utilitarian judgement we have, among other things, to decide on the composition of the set of entities over whom consequences count. We have to decide who is to be considered in deciding whether an action is right or wrong. The founding fathers of utilitarianism took it as self-evident that only individual humans were morally considerable, that the set of entities over whom consequences should count comprised only human beings. Modern economists adopt the same anthropocentric position. Indeed, in doing applied welfare economics they often restrict the morally considerable set further, and consider only the consequences for the human citizens of a particular nation state.

The restriction to human beings is not a logical necessity. We mentioned earlier a conclusion reached by the philosopher Peter Singer. In his book *Practical Ethics* (1993), Singer adopts what he regards as being a utilitarian position. He argues that utility is derived from gaining pleasure and avoiding pain, and that since all sentient beings (by definition) can experience pleasure or pain, all can be regarded as capable of enjoying utility. Utility, that is, is a characteristic of sentience, not only of humanity. Singer concludes that the principle of judging actions on the basis of their implications for utilities, and hence welfare, is morally valid, but asserts that weight should be given to non-human as well as human utilities.

It needs to be noted here that the rejection of Singer's arguments for the extension of moral considerability need not imply that the interests of non-human entities are ignored. There are two ways in which non-human interests could influence decisions, notwithstanding that only human utilities count. First, some humans suffer on account of what they regard as the suffering of non-human, mainly animal, entities. Within the framework of anthropocentric utilitarianism this kind of altruism would entail that what the humans thought the interests of the relevant entities were would be accounted for. Second, humans use some renewable resources – plants and animals – as inputs to production, and prudent resource management would then imply that some consideration be given to, at least, the future availability of such. For both of these sorts of reasons, some species of plants and animals 'have value' to the humans who are directly morally considerable. As we shall see throughout this book, it is often the case that the values arising are not made manifest in markets. An important area of resource and environmental economics is about inducing market systems of economic organisation to take proper account of the ways – direct in the case of altruism, indirect in the case of production use – that what happens to these plants and animals affects human utilities.

3.3.2   Preference-satisfaction utilitarianism

Given that we have decided that what is right and wrong is to be decided by the consequences for human individuals, there remains the question of how we should decide which consequences are good, i.e. utility-enhancing, and which are bad, i.e. utility-diminishing. How should we decide, that is, what is good for people? For the utilitarianism that is the basis of normative economics, the answer is that the affected people decide. If individual A prefers a state of affairs identified by I to a state of affairs identified by II, then according to the preference-satisfaction utilitarianism of welfare economics, I confers more utility on A than does II. This is also known as 'the doctrine of consumer sovereignty' – the economy should be ruled by the wants of consumers.

Anthropocentric utilitarianism does not logically entail consumer sovereignty. One could identify individual utility with physical and mental health rather than preference satisfaction. While this is logically true, as a matter of terminological fact most people take utilitarianism to mean self-assessment according to preference. It is precisely because this

usage is so widespread that it is important to be clear that an anthropocentric consequentialist theory of ethics does not have to imply consumer sovereignty. What is true is that the preference satisfaction/consumer sovereignty version that economists employ does, as we shall see, lend itself to formalisation and quantification. It is also true, as we shall also see, that it aligns well with the form of economic organisation that has come to dominate human society – the market. It is not, however, without critics, some of whom are economists. We shall look at some of the criticism of (preference-satisfaction) utilitarianism after considering how it deals with social welfare.

3.3.3   From utilities to welfare

In utilitarianism, and hence welfare economics, social welfare is some aggregation of individual utilities. For utilitarians actions which increase welfare are right and actions that decrease it are wrong. We now need to consider precisely how to get from utilities to welfare.

3.3.3.1 Cardinal and ordinal utility functions

One thing that is agreed by all utilitarians is that social well-being, i.e. welfare, is some function of the utilities of all relevant persons. We shall examine shortly what form or forms this function might take. But whatever the answer to this, we can only obtain such an aggregate measure if individual utilities are regarded as comparable across persons.

For an individual, a utility function maps states of the world into a single number for utility. In economics, states of the world are usually represented in terms of levels of the individual's consumption of various goods and services. In that case, we have

$$U = U(X_1, X_2, \ldots, X_i, \ldots, X_N)$$

where U is the utility measure and the arguments of the function X_i are the levels of consumption of the $1, 2, \ldots, N$ goods and services. The arguments of a utility function can, however, include, for example, consumptions by other human economic agents, or states of the environment. We shall be looking at the latter of these in some detail in Chapter 12. For the present, we will work with situations where the arguments are just own levels of consumptions.

We now need to make the distinction between a cardinal and an ordinal measure of utility. Cardinal data are numerical observations where all the standard operations of arithmetic – addition, subtraction, multiplication and division – make sense. Examples of cardinal data are observations on height, weight and length. If John weighs 100 kg and Jane weighs 70 kg, it makes sense to say that John is 30 kg heavier than Jane, and weighs 1.4286 times as much. Ordinal data are numerical observations where ranking is possible, but the standard operations of arithmetic do not apply. Street numbers are an example – from number 10, number 30 is known to be further away than number 20, but it is not known to be twice as far away. Note that we could multiply street numbers by a constant and this would not change their information content – it is only the ordering by number that means anything.

If we want to aggregate meaningfully over individual measures of utility, those measures must be cardinal. Suppose that we have two individuals A and B, that A's utility is 10 and B's is 5, and that it is agreed that simple addition is the way to aggregate. In that case, welfare is 15 utils. But, if the measures are ordinal, we could just as well say that B's utility is 50, in which case welfare is 60 utils. More to the point, it is then 5 times that of A, whereas formerly it was 0.5 times that of A. It is as if we were using the highest street numbers used in each case to determine the lengths of two streets.

In doing positive economics, economists have established that preference orderings can be represented by ordinal utility functions, from which the standard propositions of demand theory can be derived. Put this the other way round. Demand theory does not need cardinal measurement of utility – it only needs ordinal measurement. There is, then, no basis for interpersonal utility comparisons. We cannot observe the circumstances and behaviour of A and B and properly say that A is experiencing more utility than B, or vice versa.

Given this, economists would prefer not to have to make interpersonal comparisons when doing normative economics, and have spent some time trying to devise ways of avoiding the need to do so. This area of welfare economics, referred to as compensation tests, is discussed fully in Chapter 5 below. Here we just sketch the essentials. Suppose that we are considering some change to economic arrangements such that the consumption levels for A and B change. If both get to consume more of everything, the standard assumptions of positive demand theory have both better off, and we do not need to make interpersonal comparisons to conclude that welfare is improved by the change. Changes such as this are not typical.

Typically, any proposed change will make one of A or B better off, increase A or B's utility, while making the other worse off, experience lower utility. How now do we decide whether the change is desirable? The obvious thing to do is to add the utility changes, possibly using weights, and see if the answer is positive or negative, concluding that the change is desirable if we get a positive answer. But, given that interpersonal utility comparisons are inadmissible, this we cannot do. A way round this is to say that the change is desirable – is welfare-improving – if it is such that, according to her evaluation, the gainer from the change would be better off after it and fully compensating the loser, according to his evaluation, for the change. This would be what is known as a 'Pareto improvement' – a change where at least one person gains and nobody loses.

Now, while this way of proceeding does avoid the need for interpersonal comparisons, it is not of much actual use. If economists restricted themselves to advising on policy on the basis of the Pareto improvement test, they would not have a lot to say. They would only be able to say anything about changes where either everybody was a winner, or the winners had to compensate the losers. Compulsory compensation is not a feature of many policy changes that governments seek advice on. In order to widen the scope for giving advice, economists came up with the idea of the 'potential Pareto improvement' test. According to this, a change is desirable if the gainers could compensate the losers and still be better off. Actual compensation is not required. As shown in Chapter 5, although widely used in applied welfare economics, potential compensation tests do not solve the problem. If economists want to identify changes that are welfare-improving then they need to aggregate over individual utilities, making interpersonal comparisons, and that requires cardinal utility functions. There are basically two ways that economists have responded to this fundamental problem for the practice of normative economics. The first is to opt for a more limited basis on which to offer advice. As discussed in Chapter 5, much of the advice that economists do offer is based on efficiency rather than welfare criteria. The second is to treat utility functions as if they were cardinal and go ahead and work with functions, known as social welfare functions, that aggregate over utilities to produce welfare measures. It is this second approach that we now explore.

3.3.3.2 Social welfare functions and distribution

Consider a hypothetical society consisting of two individuals, A and B, living at some particular point in time. One good (X) exists, the consumption of which is the only source of utility. Let U^A denote the total utility enjoyed by A, and U^B the total utility enjoyed by B, so we have

$$U^A = U^A(X^A)$$
$$U^B = U^B(X^B)$$
(3.1)

where X^A and X^B denote the quantities of the good consumed by A and B respectively. We assume diminishing marginal utility, so that

$$U_X^A = dU^A/dX^A > 0 \text{ and } U_{XX}^A = d^2U^A/dX^{A^2} < 0$$

and

$$U_X^B = dU^B/dX^B > 0 \text{ and } U_{XX}^B = d^2U^B/dX^{B^2} < 0$$

In general, utilitarianism as such does not carry any particular implication for the way output should be distributed between individuals in a society. Generally, social welfare, W, is determined by a function of the form

$$W = W(U^A, U^B)$$
(3.2)

where $W_A = \partial W/\partial U^A > 0$ and $W_B = \partial W/\partial U^B > 0$ so that social welfare is increasing in both of the individual utility arguments. Here, welfare depends in some particular (but unspecified) way on the levels of utility enjoyed by each person in the relevant community. This social welfare function allows us to rank different configurations of individual utilities in terms of their social worth.

Assume, to make things simple and concentrate on the essentials here, that there is a fixed total

quantity of the good, denoted $\bar{X}$. (Analysis of cases where the total quantities of two consumption goods are variable are considered in Chapter 5.) Consumption, and hence utility levels, for A and B are chosen so as to maximise welfare. X^A and X^B are chosen, that is, to maximise

$$W = W(U^A, U^B)$$

given U^A and U^B determined according to equations (3.1) and subject to the constraint that

$$X^A + X^B = \bar{X}$$

It is shown in Appendix 3.2 (using the Lagrange method outlined in Appendix 3.1) that the solution to this problem requires that

$$W_A U_X^A = W_B U_X^B$$
(3.3)

This is the condition that the marginal contributions to social welfare from each individual's consumption be equal. What this means is that the consumption levels for each individual will vary with the utility function for each individual and with the nature of the social welfare function 3.2.

A widely used particular form for the function 3.2 has W as a weighted sum of the individual utilities, as in

$$W = w_A U^A(X^A) + w_B U^B(X^B)$$
(3.4)

where w_A and w_B are the, fixed, weights. These weights reflect society's judgement of the relative worth of each person's utility. In this case the condition for the maximisation of social welfare is

$$w_A U_X^A = w_B U_X^B$$

A further specialisation is to make the weights equal to one, so that social welfare is a simple sum of utilities of all individuals. For this special case we have

$$W = U^A + U^B$$
(3.5)

Figure 3.1 illustrates one indifference curve, drawn in utility space, for such a welfare function. The social welfare indifference curve is a locus of combinations of individual utilities that yield a constant amount of social welfare, $\bar{W}$. The assumption that the welfare function is additive implies that the indifference curve, when drawn in utility space, is linear. In the case of equal welfare weights the condition for the maximisation of social welfare, equation 3.3, becomes

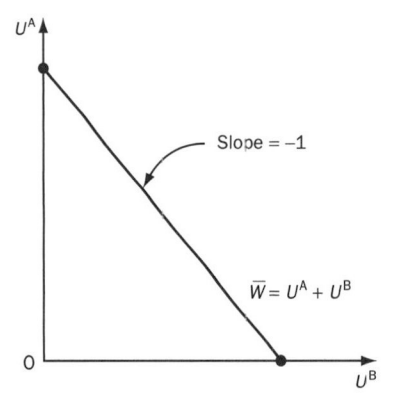

Figure 3.1 An indifference curve from a linear form of social welfare function

$$U_X^A = U_X^B \qquad (3.6)$$

which is the equality of the individuals' marginal utilities. This still does not tell us how goods should be distributed. To find this, we need some information about the utility function of each individual. Consider the case where each person has the same utility function. That is,

$$U^A = U^A(X^A) = U(X^A)$$
$$U^B = U^B(X^B) = U(X^B) \qquad (3.7)$$

It is then easy to see that in order for marginal utility to be equal for each person, the consumption level must be equal for each person. An additive welfare function, with equal weights on each person's utility, and identical utility functions for each person, implies that, at a social welfare maximum, individuals have equal consumption levels.

The solution to the problem with equal weights and identical utility functions is illustrated in Figure 3.2. Notice carefully that the diagram is now drawn in commodity space, not utility space. Under the common assumption of diminishing marginal utility, the linear indifference curves in utility space in Figure 3.1 map into welfare indifference curves that are convex from below in commodity space. The curves labelled W_1, W_2 and W_3 are social welfare indifference curves, with $W_1 < W_2 < W_3$. Remember that we assume that there is a fixed quantity $\bar{X}$ of the good available to be distributed between the two individuals. Maximum social welfare, W_2, is attained at the point Z where the consumption levels

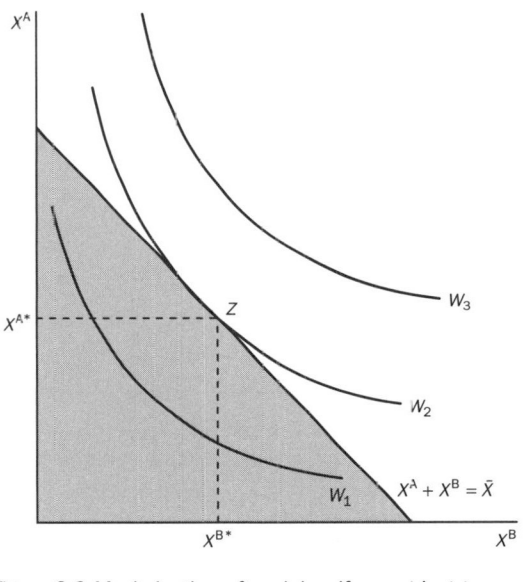

Figure 3.2 Maximisation of social welfare subject to a constraint on the total quantity of goods available

enjoyed by each person are X^{A*} and X^{B*}. The maximised level of social welfare will, of course, depend on the magnitude of $\bar{X}$. But irrespective of the level of maximised welfare, the two consumption levels will be equal.

In the example we have just looked at, the result that consumption levels will be the same for both individuals was a consequence of the particular assumptions that were made. But utilitarianism does not necessarily imply equal distributions of goods. An unequal distribution at a welfare maximum may occur under any of the following conditions:

1. The SWF is not of the additive form specified in equation 3.4.
2. The weights attached to individual utilities are not equal.
3. Utility functions differ between individuals.

To illustrate the third condition, suppose that the utility functions of two persons, A and B, are as shown in Figure 3.3. The individuals have different utility functions in that A enjoys a higher level of utility than individual B for any given level of consumption. We still assume that the social welfare function is additive with equal weights, so that equal marginal utilities are required for welfare maximisation. Because of that difference in the utility functions,

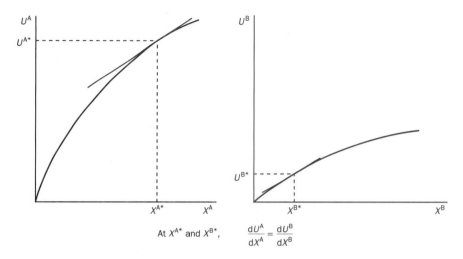

At X^{A*} and X^{B*}, $\dfrac{\mathrm{d}U^A}{\mathrm{d}X^A} = \dfrac{\mathrm{d}U^B}{\mathrm{d}X^B}$

Figure 3.3 Maximisation of social welfare for two individuals with different utility functions

the marginal utilities of the two individuals can only be equal at different levels of consumption. In interpreting the diagram recall that the value of marginal utility at a particular level of consumption is indicated by the slope of the (total) utility function at that point.

The outcome shown in Figure 3.3 illustrates something of a paradox. Individual B is less efficient at turning consumption into utility than individual A. The result then of using a simple addition of utilities is that she gets less allocated to her. Suppose that B is that way because she suffers from depression. Would we then want to say that utilitarianism with equal weights is fair? This illustrates an important general point about ethical theorising. As well as considering the apparent desirability of the adopted principles as such, it is also necessary to consider explicitly what the principles imply in different circumstances.

3.4 Criticisms of utilitarianism

There is, of course, much criticism of the utilitarian approach to ethical theory. As noted already, there are other, non-consequentialist, theories of ethics, which criticise utilitarianism if only by implication. In this section we look first at one influential recent contribution to moral philosophy which is concerned

with utilitarianism generally, and then at some criticisms directed primarily at the preference-satisfaction utilitarianism that is the basis for modern welfare economics.

3.4.1 Rawls: a theory of justice

The work of John Rawls in *A Theory of Justice* (1971) has influenced the consideration given by economists to ethical issues. Rawls's work challenges classical utilitarianism, where welfare is the simple sum of individual utilities. His objection is grounded in the following assertion. Being indifferent to the distribution of satisfaction between individuals (and only being concerned with the sum of utilities), a distribution of resources produced by maximising welfare could violate fundamental freedoms and rights that are inherently worthy of protection.

In common with many moral philosophers, Rawls seeks to establish the principles of a just society. Rawls adopts an approach that owes much to the ideas of Kant. Valid principles of justice are those which would be agreed by everyone if we could freely, rationally and impartially consider just arrangements. In order to ascertain the nature of these principles of justice, Rawls employs the device of imagining a hypothetical state of affairs (the 'original position') prior to any agreement about

principles of justice, the organisation of social institutions, and the distribution of material rewards and
endowments. In this original position, individuals
exist behind a 'veil of ignorance'; each person has
no knowledge of his or her inherited characteristics
(such as intelligence, race and gender), nor of the
position he or she would take in any agreed social
structure. Additionally, individuals are assumed to be
free of any attitudes that they would have acquired
through having lived in particular sets of circumstances. The veil of ignorance device would, according to Rawls, guarantee impartiality and fairness in
the discussions leading to the establishment of a social
contract. Rawls then seeks to establish the nature of
the social contract that would be created by freely
consenting individuals in such an original position.

He reasons that, under these circumstances, people would unanimously agree on two fundamental
principles of justice. These are

> First: each person is to have an equal right to the
> most extensive basic liberty compatible with a
> similar liberty for others.

> Second: social and economic inequalities are to
> be arranged so that they are both (a) reasonably
> expected to be to everyone's advantage, and (b)
> attached to positions and offices and open to all.

It is the second principle, the Difference Principle,
that is of interest here. The Difference Principle
asserts that inequalities are only justified if they
enhance the position of everyone in society (if
they lead to Pareto improvements).[1] The Difference
Principle has been interpreted as a presumption in
favour of equality of position; deviations from an
equal position are unjust except in the special cases
where all persons would benefit (or perhaps where
the least advantaged benefit). Economists have tried
to infer what a Rawlsian position would imply for
the nature of a social welfare function (SWF).[2]

One approach has been to argue that a Rawlsian
position can, for the case of two individuals, be represented by an SWF of the form:

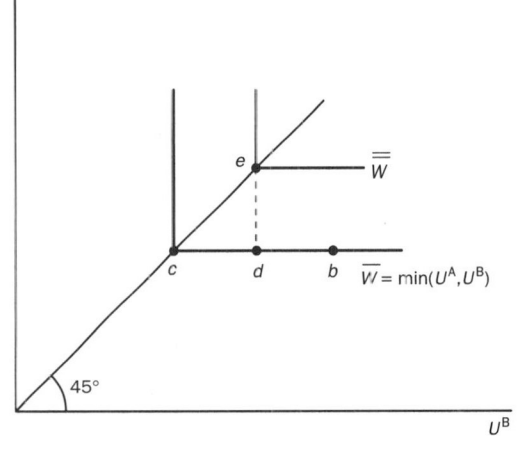

Figure 3.4 Rawlsian social welfare function indifference curve

$$W = \min(U^A, U^B) \tag{3.8}$$

This says that W is equal to whichever is the smaller
of U^A and U^B, that W is the minimum of U^A and U^B.
Two SWF indifference curves from such a function
are illustrated in Figure 3.4. As the utility level of
the least advantaged person determines welfare, a
Rawlsian SWF implies that raising the utility of
the person with the lowest utility level will increase
welfare. Compare the two points labelled b and c in
Figure 3.4, which by virtue of lying on one indifference curve generate identical levels of social welfare. Starting from point b, reallocate utility between
persons, by subtracting $(b - d)$ utility from person B
and adding this to person A. The point labelled e
will have been attained on another indifference
curve with a higher level of social welfare. It is clear
that the only combinations of utility for which
higher welfare levels are not possible through interpersonal transfers of utility are those which lie along
the 45° ray from the origin. Along this locus, utility
is allocated equally between individuals. So, for any

---

[1]   Rawls sometimes seems to advocate a rather different position, however, arguing that inequalities are justified in particular when they maximally enhance the position of the least advantaged person in society.

[2]   However, one could argue that such an attempt forces Rawls's theory into a utilitarian framework – something of which he would probably strongly disapprove.

Table 3.1 Consumption welfare weights

α	$X^A = 10, X^B = 1$		$X^A = 100, X^B = 1$	
	W_{XA}	W_{XB}	W_{XA}	W_{XB}
$^1/_2$	0.3612	1	0.1	1
$^1/_4$	0.1778	1	0.0316	1
0	0.1	1	0.01	1
$-^1/_2$	0.0316	1	0.001	1
-1	0.01	1	0.0001	1
-2	0.001	1	0.000001	1

given total amount of utility, a Rawlsian social welfare function implies that, whenever utility levels differ between individuals, it is possible to increase social welfare by redistributing utility from individuals with higher utility to those with lower utility. An egalitarian distribution is implied by this logic.

Another approach to representing a Rawlsian concern for the worst-off within a utilitarian framework retains the simple additive welfare function, but specifies the utility functions in a particular way. If all individuals have the same utility function,

$$U = \frac{1}{\alpha}X^\alpha \quad \text{with } \alpha < 1 \quad \text{and} \quad \alpha \neq 0$$

so that marginal utility is positive, including cases for which $\alpha < 0$, and declining with increasing consumption. For the two-person case, with this utility function the simple additive welfare function becomes

$$W = \frac{1}{\alpha}(X^A)^\alpha + \frac{1}{\alpha}(X^B)^\alpha \tag{3.9}$$

and the consumption of the worse-off individual gets a larger weight. The relative weight accorded to increases in consumption for the worse-off individual increases as the degree of inequality between the individuals increases, and as $\alpha \to -\infty$. For B as the worse-off individual this is shown mathematically in Appendix 3.2, and illustrated in Table 3.1 where $W_{XA} = \partial W/\partial X^A$ and $W_{XB} = \partial W/\partial X^B$.

3.4.2 Criticisms of preference-based utilitarianism

The basic idea involved in the version of utilitarianism that is the basis for welfare economics is that individuals' preferences are the measure of social welfare. Subject to the constraints given by the availability of resources and technological possibilities, people should get what they want. Social welfare improves when people get more of what they want. Economics does not inquire into the determinants of individuals' preferences, which are taken as given. Economics does not involve questions about what is good for people. The answer implicit in economics to such questions is that individuals are the best judge of what is good for themselves, so that their preferences tell us what is good for them.

Criticism of this, consumer sovereignty, approach to social welfare has come from some economists, as well as many non-economists. Not all of the criticism is well founded. One frequently finds non-economists claiming that economics assumes that individuals only care about their own consumption of produced goods and services. This claim is wrong, though some introductory economics texts do not do very much to counter the impression that supports it. In fact, the utility functions used in welfare economic analysis can, and do, include, for example, arguments which are indicators of the state of the environment. What is true is that market systems do not work very well where individuals have preferences over things other than produced goods and services. But, as we shall be working through in many subsequent chapters, one of the major concerns of welfare economics is to devise policies to make market systems work better in such circumstances. In regard to preferences over the state of the environment, economists have devised a whole range of policies and techniques which they claim can make market systems perform better according to consumer sovereignty criteria.

Critics of consumer sovereignty are on firmer ground when, on informational grounds, they question the assumption that people always know what is good for them, that their preferences reflect their true interests. The questions raised can be broadly classified as being of two kinds. First, taking preferences as given and truly reflecting interests, is it reasonable to assume that people generally have enough information to properly assess the consequences for their own utility of the various alternatives open to them? Second, is it reasonable to assume generally that, in a world where socialisation processes and advertising are pervasive, people's preferences do truly reflect their interests? Here, all that space permits is that we raise these questions. Readers interested in answers should follow some of the suggestions in the Further Reading section at the end of the chapter. Some aspects of these questions as they arise in the particular context of applying welfare economics to environmental issues will be covered in Chapters 11 and 12.

One economist who has written extensively about the utilitarian basis for economics is the Nobel laureate Armatya Sen – see especially Sen (1987). According to Sen, persons have a fundamental dualism, being concerned with the satisfaction of their own preferences and also pursuing objectives which are not exclusively self-interested. Individuals exist, that is, as both 'consumers' and 'citizens'. In regard to concern for others, altruism, for example, Sen distinguishes between 'sympathy' and 'commitment'. Sympathy is where my concern is reflected in the arguments of my utility function, so that if some change improves the lot of the relevant other(s) my own utility increases. Commitment is where my concern is based on my ethical principles, and to the extent that I am committed to other(s) I may approve of some change even though it reduces my own utility. For some people, that is, activity may be directed to pursuing goals that do not affect the arguments of their utility functions. This does not in itself imply that utilitarianism should be abandoned, but rather that its practice is more problematic than many economists recognise. We shall return to this sort of argument in relation to social decisions about the environment in Chapter 11.

3.5 Intertemporal distribution

Many of the issues with which we deal in this text involve choices with consequences that extend over time. Such choices are said to have an 'intertemporal' dimension. Where we deal only with current consequences we are doing an 'intratemporal' analysis. Thus far in this chapter we have been looking at

utilitarianism as the ethical basis for intratemporal normative economics. Most economists also approach normative intertemporal issues on the basis of utilitarianism, in the manner to be considered in this section. It should be noted, however, that while there is fairly general agreement about the general framework for analysis, there is considerable disagreement about what exactly its implications are for policy. Chapter 11 is also largely about intertemporal welfare economics, and we shall make reference here to results that will be established in that chapter. The treatment here is in the nature of an introductory overview of intertemporal distribution issues.

In order to keep the analysis reasonably simple, and to focus clearly on intertemporal ethics, we will adopt a practice widely followed in this area of economics. We will think about time in terms of successive generations of humans. We will assume that the size of the human population is constant over time, and that we can consider each generation in terms of a single representative individual from it.[3] What we are then thinking about is how the current generation would behave with respect to future generations if it followed the prescriptions that derive from a particular ethical position, in this case utilitarianism, on how to make choices with consequences for future generations.

3.5.1 The utilitarian intertemporal social welfare function

In the intertemporal case, as in the intratemporal case, the implications of utilitarianism are examined by looking at the maximisation, subject to the appropriate constraints, of the function that maps utilities into welfare. We begin, therefore, with the specification of the intertemporal social welfare function.

Initially, we consider just two generations. This will allow us to use the same general form of notation as when looking at two individuals at a point in time. Generation 0 is the present generation; generation 1 represents the one which follows. Then U_0 and

[3] An alternative interpretation of the formal analysis that follows could be that we are looking at a single representative individual who lives through successive time periods. This interpretation becomes less appealing as the number of periods being considered increases. Individuals are definitely mortal (lifespan currently of the order of 100 years), whereas human society may persist for such a long time (of the order of 1 000 000 years) that its end could effectively be indefinitely far into the future.

U_1 denote the utility enjoyed by (the representative individual from) generations 0 and 1, respectively. W now denotes *intertemporal* social welfare (or, alternatively, intergenerational social welfare). In general terms an intertemporal social welfare function can then be written as[4]

$$W = W(U_0, U_1)$$

The specific functional form usually employed by utilitarianism is

$$W = \phi_0 U_0 + \phi_1 U_1 \tag{3.10}$$

so that W is a weighted average of the utilities for each generation, where ϕ_0 and ϕ_1 are the weights used in summing utility over generations to obtain a measure of social welfare. The utilitarian approach to intertemporal questions is typically further specialised by having the weights in equation 3.10 take a particular form. It is usual to set $\phi_0 = 1$ and $\phi_1 = 1/(1 + \rho)$, where ρ is the utility discount rate. Equation 3.10 then becomes

$$W = U_0 + \frac{U_1}{1 + \rho} \tag{3.11}$$

Time discounting, for $\rho > 0$ as generally assumed, means that future utility 'counts for less' than the same quantity of present utility in obtaining a measure of intertemporal welfare. In this formulation, the value of a small increment of utility falls as its date of receipt is delayed. Thus if one unit of utility received by the next generation were regarded as less valuable by a proportion of 0.1 (i.e. 10%) than one unit of utility received this period, then $1/(1 + \rho) = 0.9$.

Before looking at the justification for this kind of discounting, it will be useful to note some generalisations and modifications of the foregoing widely encountered in the literature and subsequently used in this book. First, write

$$W = \frac{1}{(1 + \rho)^0} U_0 + \frac{1}{(1 + \rho)^1} U_1 + \ldots + \frac{1}{(1 + \rho)^T} U_T$$

$$= \sum_{t=0}^{t=T} \frac{1}{(1 + \rho)^t} U_t \tag{3.12}$$

This is equivalent to equation 3.11 but for the fact that welfare is being summed not over two periods but over $T + 1$ periods (i.e. period 0, the present period, through to period T). In many problems we shall be investigating an infinite time horizon will be used, in which case equation 3.12 will become

$$W = \sum_{t=0}^{t=\infty} \frac{1}{(1 + \rho)^t} U_t \tag{3.13}$$

It will often be convenient to work with the continuous time version of equation 3.13, which is

$$W = \int_{t=0}^{t=\infty} U_t e^{-\rho t} dt \tag{3.14}$$

3.5.1.1 Why discount future utility?

What is the ethical basis for discounting future utility? Some economists argue it is necessarily implied by the logic of the preference satisfaction variant of utilitarianism. Individuals as consumers are observed to exhibit positive time preference in that they require an incentive, in the form of the payment of interest, to postpone consumption, and hence utility, by saving. It follows from consumer sovereignty, it is argued, that in thinking about how society should make intertemporal choices, we should work with positive time preference in the form of $\rho > 0$.

Other economists argue that society should not adopt the preferences of individuals in this way. One version of this argument is a special case of a more general argument of the same nature. We noted above Sen's distinction between the individual's roles as consumer and citizen. This can be applied in the intertemporal context. As citizens exhibiting commitment toward others, future generations in this case, individuals would not necessarily wish to discount the future at the same rate as they do when considering the distribution of their own utility over time. Another version of the argument is specific to the intertemporal context. Pigou (1920), for example, argued that individuals suffer from a 'defective telescopic faculty', taking decisions now on the basis of

---

[4]   Note that we are ignoring the intratemporal distribution of utility. This is fairly standard in the literature, but see Broome (1992).

an underestimate of the utility of future consumption. There is, the argument goes, no reason to carry this myopia into social decision making.

Many people argue that in comparing utilities over successive generations, the only ethically defensible position is that utilities attaching to each generation should be treated equally, implying a zero rate of utility discounting, $\rho = 0$.

One argument that has been used to justify a positive utility discount rate is that there is, for every point in time in the future, a positive probability that the human species will become extinct. Presumably this probability is very small, but one would expect it to increase as the length of time into the future extends. One may take the view that future generations should be given less weight than the present, given that we cannot be certain of the existence of any future generation.

Another argument for a positive utility discount rate is based on our observation above that in considering ethical prescriptions one needs to examine their consequences in varying circumstances. As we shall see below when we look at optimal growth models, the prescription of a zero utility discount rate could have consequences that are the opposite of what would correspond to most people's notion of intergenerational equity.

3.5.1.2 The arithmetic of discounting

Discounting is controversial. As just discussed, there are disagreements at a fundamental level about how the utility discount rate should be determined, and particularly about whether it should be zero or some positive number. Another reason for the existence of controversy lies in the arithmetic of discounting. Given that intergenerational distribution is to be determined by the maximisation of W, utility discounting might be described as discriminating against future generations, by giving their utility levels less weight in the maximisation exercise. It is this feature of discounting which leads many to regard any positive discount rate as ethically indefensible.

Table 3.2 provides some numbers that indicate what is involved. The rows refer to the futurity of a generation, the columns to values for the utility discount rate ρ. The entries in the body of the table give the present value of utility of 100 for the given

Table 3.2 The arithmetic of discounting

Generation	Discount rates			
	0.10	0.25	0.50	1.00
1	90.91	80.00	66.67	50.00
2	82.65	64.00	44.44	25.00
3	75.13	51.20	29.63	12.5
4	68.30	40.96	19.75	6.25
5	62.09	32.77	13.17	3.13
10	38.55	10.73	1.73	0.10
50	0.85	0.001	0.0000002	0.0000000000001

generation at the given discount rate. The present value is

$$\frac{U_t}{(1 + \rho)^t}$$

that is what the tth generation's utility counts for in a simple summation across generations. It is what future utility is treated as being worth in welfare terms now. Thus, in Table 3.2 we see that at $\rho = 0.10$, 100 for the next generation contributes 90.91 to the current assessment of welfare, while 100 for the fiftieth of future generations contributes just 0.85, approximately one-hundredth of what the next generation's utility counts for. For $\rho = 0.5$, 100 for the fifth of future generations has a present value of just 13.17, 100 for the tenth has a present value of less than 2, and the fiftieth generation is effectively totally ignored. For $\rho = 1.0$, the present value of 100 for the fifth future generation is 3.13.

Now, these discount rates refer to generations. Most discussion, including our own below, of numerical values for discount rates is actually about rates which refer to periods of one year. Suppose that a generation spans 35 years, so that looking a century ahead is equivalent to thinking in terms of the next three generations. Then Table 3.3 shows the annual discount rates corresponding to the generational discount rates shown in Table 3.2, together with the generational rates implied by some other annual rates. The entries in Table 3.3 are calculated by solving

$$\frac{U}{(1 + x)^{35}} = \frac{U}{1 + y}$$

for the annual rate x with y as the given generational rate, or for y as the generational rate with x as the

Table 3.3 Generational and annual discount rates

Discount rates	
Generational	Annual
0.10	0.0027
0.25	0.0064
0.50	0.0116
1.00	0.0200
1.81	0.03
2.95	0.04
4.52	0.05
27.10	0.10

given annual rate. Note that $\rho = 0.0116$ per annum, for example, is otherwise stated as 1.16% per year. Taking Tables 3.2 and 3.3 together, it is clear that even at low annual rates of discount little weight is given to the utility of future generations. An annual rate of 2% means that the present value of 100 of utility for the first future generation is 50, for example, that the present value of 100 for the third generation is 12.5, and that the utility of the tenth generation is almost completely ignored, or discounted.

3.5.1.3 Utility and consumption discount rates

In order to produce reasonably simple models for the analysis of intertemporal distribution, economists typically assume that the representative individual's utility depends only on her aggregate consumption, denoted by C, as in

$$U_t = U(C_t) \tag{3.15}$$

As regards the form of equation 3.15, the standard assumption is diminishing marginal utility, as shown in Figure 3.5. For

$$W = W(U_0, U_1, \ldots, U_t, \ldots) \tag{3.16}$$

equation 3.15 means that W is a function of C at different dates, as in

$$W = F(C_0, C_1, \ldots, C_t, \ldots) \tag{3.17}$$

Now, if equation 3.16 involves discounting and takes the form that we have been using here, i.e. equation 3.14, which is

$$W = \int_{t=0}^{t=\infty} U_t e^{-\rho t} dt$$

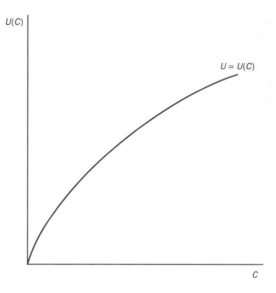

Figure 3.5 Utility as a function of aggregate consumption

then clearly the function 3.17 is also going to involve discounting, but of future consumption rather than future utility.

The relationship between the utility discount rate and the rate at which consumption is discounted is explored in Chapter 11. It is conventional to use r as the symbol for the consumption discount rate. It is important to note that, despite the use of this notation, the consumption discount rate is not, as the utility discount rate is, a constant. In Chapter 11 it is shown that

$$r = \rho + \eta g \tag{3.18}$$

where η is the elasticity of the marginal utility of consumption and g is the proportional growth rate of consumption, i.e.

$$\eta = -\frac{(\partial^2 U / \partial C^2) C}{\partial U / \partial C}$$

and

$$g = \frac{\dot{C}}{C}$$

For ρ constant, r varies with the level of C and its growth rate. Note that for diminishing marginal utility, as is assumed, $\partial^2 U / \partial C^2 < 0$, so that η is positive.

In fact, in the application of welfare economics, discounting is most often discussed in terms of consumption-discounting – see Chapter 11 here, on cost–benefit analysis, for example. As equation 3.18 shows, discounting the value of future consumption – treating X of next period consumption as worth $X/(1 + r)$ now when thinking about intertemporal distribution – need not entail utility-discounting. Unless η and/or g is equal to zero, r exceeds ρ so that $\rho = 0$ is consistent with $r > 0$. Equation 3.18 indicates that there are two reasons for discounting future consumption:

- because future utility is treated as being worth less than current utility, the first term;
- because it is believed that consumption will be higher in the future, the second term.

Even if one were to accept that ρ should be zero, this does not necessarily imply that the consumption discount rate will necessarily be zero – the term $\eta \dot{C}/C$ may be non-zero. To many people, this is an intuitively reasonable conclusion. It seems reasonable, that is, to think about intertemporal distribution on the basis that if an economy is experiencing growth in income and consumption through time, then an additional unit of consumption will be worth less to a typical person in the future than to such a person now, as the former will be more affluent. This has nothing to do with discounting future utility.

3.5.1.4 What numbers should be used?

The arithmetic of discounting applies to both consumption and utility discount rates. As we have seen, the arithmetic is very powerful in reducing the weight given to the future in making current decisions. As Tables 3.2 and 3.3 indicate, the current worth given to utility of 100 one century ahead varies from 75.13 for an annual discount rate of 0.27% to 12.5 for 2.0%. The choice of a value to use as the discount rate is very important when thinking about intertemporal distribution.

For applied economics, as we have noted, discussion of discounting is mainly in terms of the annual consumption discount rate. There are basically two approaches to deciding what number should be used for the consumption discount rate. The prescriptive approach starts from first principles, and equation 3.18. The descriptive approach, in the spirit of preference-satisfaction utilitarianism, starts from observations of what people actually do.[5]

In order to follow the prescriptive approach, we need numbers for ρ, η and g. None of these are readily observable. The utility discount is not observable even in principle – the value to be assigned to it is a purely ethical question. An approximation to the elasticity of marginal utility could, in principle, be estimated from data on behaviour, but the widespread view that η should be taken as lying in the range 1 to 2 is based on guesstimation rather than estimation. Since g is the consumption growth rate of the economy over the relevant planning horizon, a value for it is an estimate, or guesstimate, of future economic performance. Suppose we take the view that utility should not be discounted, that η is 1.5 and that the economy will grow at the rate 0.04, i.e. 4% per annum. Then, according to equation 3.18, we should discount consumption at 0.06 or 6% per annum. For the same $\rho = 0$ and $\eta = 1.5$, $g = 0.02$ gives $r = 0.03$. If we were agreed that future utility should be discounted at $\rho = 0.02$, then $\eta = 1.5$ and $g = 0.02$ gives $r = 0.05$. Clearly, reasonable economists could reasonably disagree on the question of the value for r that emerges from the prescriptive approach.

About all that can be said is that advocates of the prescriptive approach (who tend to argue for $\rho = 0$) tend to come up with smaller numbers for the consumption discount rate than do those who follow the descriptive approach. The basic idea in the descriptive approach is that there are markets in which individuals' intertemporal consumption preferences are revealed. These are the markets through which borrowing and lending are effected, in which interest rates are observed. Such markets will be considered in a little detail in Chapter 11. For present purposes, the important point is that in an ideal world we could observe a rate of interest that would correspond both to individuals' consumption rate of discount and to the marginal rate of return on investment. According to the descriptive approach, this is the rate which we should use as the consumption discount rate for social decision making.

---

[5] The prescriptive/descriptive distinction is made in Arrow et al. (1996).

A major problem that the descriptive approach faces is that investment rates of return are, in fact, generally higher, in some cases considerably higher, than market rates of interest which are assumed to reflect individuals' consumption discount rate. The question arising is: which to use? Economists are divided on this. The main issues are discussed in Chapter 11. Most would agree that in principle the lower market rate of interest should be used, but many argue that in practice it is necessary to use the higher rate of return on investment. In that case one is looking at a rate perhaps as high as 8%.

This is one of the more controversial areas of economics. Within economics there are disagreements about fundamentals, as well as about details arising in practical application. Many non-economists take the view, especially where the environment is involved, that using a positive discount rate is simply wrong because of the way in which it attaches less weight to the interests of future generations. In fact, as we have seen, one could legitimately argue for a positive rate of consumption discount even if one did not attach less weight to the utility of future generations. As we shall see in the following section, it is not even completely clear that it is obviously wrong to discount future utility.

3.5.2 Optimal growth

Thus far in considering the utilitarian, and hence the economic (in the most part), approach to matters intertemporal, we have looked at things from the consumption and utility perspective, in which the big thing is impatience. For preference-satisfaction utilitarianism, the reason for discounting is that individuals prefer consumption now to consumption in the future. There is another perspective to matters intertemporal, that of production, and the shifting of consumption, and hence utility, over time by the accumulation and use of capital. Just as economists take it as a major given, or stylised fact, that people are impatient, so they take it as a stylised fact that capital accumulation is productive in the sense that a unit of consumption forgone now for capital

accumulation will pay off with more than one unit of future consumption. The study of optimal growth is the study of the interaction between impatience and productivity.

3.5.2.1 The basic model

The simplest exercise in optimal growth modelling is to find the path for consumption over time that results in

$$W = \int_{t=0}^{t=\infty} U(C_t)\,e^{-\rho t}\mathrm{d}t \tag{3.19}$$

taking the maximum value that is feasible, given the constraint that

$$\dot{K} = Q(K_t) - C_t \tag{3.20}$$

Equation 3.19 is just the utilitarian social welfare function that we have already spent some time looking at, and exhibits impatience. In the constraint 3.20, K stands for capital and $\dot{K}$ is the time derivative of K, i.e. the rate of investment. In this simple model, output is produced using just capital according to $Q(K_t)$.[6] The marginal product of capital is positive but declining, i.e.

$$Q_K = \frac{\partial Q_t}{\partial K_t} > 0 \text{ and } Q_{KK} = \frac{\partial^2 Q_t}{\partial K_t^2} < 0$$

Output can be either consumed or invested. The pay-off to investment follows from the positive marginal product of capital – a small amount of output invested today carries a cost in terms of current consumption of dC, but adds an amount larger than dC to future consumption possibilities.

This model is examined in some detail in Chapters 11 and 14. Here we just state one of the conditions that describes the optimal path for C_t, and briefly discuss its intuition and implications. The condition is

$$\frac{\dot{U}_C}{U_C} = \rho - Q_K \tag{3.21}$$

The left-hand side here is the proportional rate of change of marginal utility, and along the optimal

---

[6] Having output depend on just capital input, rather than on inputs of capital and labour, simplifies the analysis and exposition without losing anything essential. Recall that we are assuming that the population size is constant.

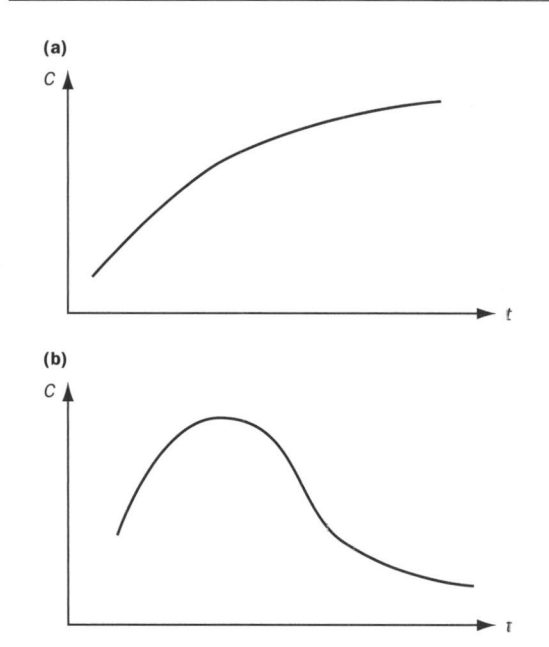

Figure 3.6 Optimal consumption growth paths

consumption path this is equal to the difference between the utility discount rate and the marginal product of capital. The former is a constant parameter, while the marginal product of capital falls as the size of the capital stock increases.

Panel a of Figure 3.6 shows the nature of the optimal consumption path that equation 3.21 characterises, given the standard assumptions. Initially the capital stock is small and its marginal product is high. So long as $Q_K > \rho$, the right-hand side of equation 3.21 is negative, and given diminishing marginal utility $\dot{U}_C/U_C < 0$ implies that consumption is increasing. This makes sense as the pay-off to deferring consumption, Q_K, is more than the cost of deferring it, ρ, so capital is accumulated, increasing output and consumption. As the size of the capital stock increases, so Q_K falls. For $Q_K = \rho$ the left-hand side of equation 3.21 is zero, so that growth and capital accumulation cease. Panel a of Figure 3.6 shows consumption going asymptotically to a level which is determined by the size of ρ and the properties of the production function.

Following an intertemporal consumption/savings plan derived from this model, early generations would be saving for the benefit of later generations who will be richer even though there is positive

utility-discounting. If planning were based on $\rho = 0$, savings at every point in time would be higher, and the accumulation of capital would continue until its marginal product was driven to zero. Given the productivity of savings and investment, zero discounting of utility could lead to poor early generations doing lots of saving for the benefit of rich later generations. On the other hand, with ρ relatively high, early generations would do relatively little saving and accumulation, and the society might remain relatively poor despite the fact that it could become rich.

The main point here is to again illustrate that the consequences of an ethical position – in this case 'discounting future utility is wrong' – depend on the circumstances in which it is acted upon. What appears to be an intrinsically sound ethical position may turn out in some circumstances to lead to outcomes that are not obviously sensible.

3.5.2.2 Optimal growth with non-renewable resources used in production

Now consider an exercise in optimal growth modelling that differs from the foregoing in just one respect – production uses inputs of a non-renewable natural resource as well as capital. The path for consumption, and hence savings and capital accumulation, is determined as that which maximises

$$W = \int_{t=0}^{t=\infty} U(C_t)\,e^{-\rho t}dt \qquad (3.22)$$

subject to the constraints

$$\dot{K} = Q(K_t, R_t) - C_t \qquad (3.23a)$$

$$\dot{S} = -R_t \qquad (3.23b)$$

$$\bar{S} = \int_{t=0}^{t=\infty} R_t dt \qquad (3.23c)$$

The first of the constraints says, as before, that output, Q, can either be used for consumption, C, or investment, $\dot{K}$. It differs from equation 3.20 in that the production of output now involves two inputs, capital, K, and some natural resource, R. The standard assumption is that the marginal product of the resource input is positive and diminishing. In equation 3.23b, S stands for stock, and this constraint says that the natural resource being used is non-renewable in that the stock size decreases by the amount used. $\bar{S}$ is the initial finite stock of the resource, and equation 3.23c says that total cumulative use of the resource cannot exceed the initial stock.

This problem will be considered in some detail in Chapter 14, and analysis of it and variants of it – such as for the case of a renewable resource – will take up much of Part 4. For present purposes we simply want to note that the optimal consumption path that this model produces is as shown in panel b of Figure 3.6. Given $\rho > 0$, it is optimal for consumption first to increase, but eventually to start to decrease and to go asymptotically toward zero. Further, this is the case even when production technology is such that there is a constant level of consumption that could be maintained for ever. It needs to be noted here that the production function $Q(K_t, R_t)$ may be such that constant consumption for ever may simply be impossible; we return to this in the next chapter.

As between panels a and b of Figure 3.6, the intertemporal social welfare functions are identical. What changes is the situation in regard to production. The morality of a positive rate of utility discount looks very different as between panels a and b in Figure 3.6.

3.5.3 Sustainability

The lesson drawn from panel b of Figure 3.6 is that if we live in a world where non-renewable resources are an essential input to production, then following utilitarianism with discounting makes generations in the near future better off than we are, but makes many generations in the more distant future worse off, possibly very much worse off. And, this is the case even though it is technologically possible to have constant consumption and utility for ever.

Many people take it as self-evident that it is wrong to act so as to make future generations worse off than we are. Also, many people take it that the essential stylised facts about production and consumption possibilities are pretty much like those of the model that leads, with positive utility-discounting, to the panel b of Figure 3.6 outcome. While nobody would argue that equations 3.23 are a literal description of actual production possibilities – there is, for example, no use of renewable resources, nor any technological innovation – many would argue that they are the 'canonical' model, that is the simplest model that captures the essential features of the situation. Certainly, this model puts the sustainability problem in its starkest form.

As we will consider in the next chapter, there are a number of concepts of sustainability. For the moment, however, we will simply take it that sustainability means that consumption is constant, that future generations enjoy the same level of consumption as the current generation. Adopting sustainability as an objective follows from an ethical view that it is wrong to make future generations worse off. Arguing that sustainability as an objective requires particular kinds of current behaviour follows from that ethical objective plus a particular appreciation of the stylised facts. If we think, perhaps because of faith in technical progress, that ultimately the big picture is in essence that of equation 3.20 – resource inputs are not a constraint on production possibilities – and we want future generations to be no worse off, it does not matter if we plan and act along the lines of utilitarianism with positive discounting as captured in equation 3.19. If we think it wrong for future generations to be worse off and that the big picture is in essence that of equations 3.23, then it does matter if we plan our behaviour according to equation 3.22, which is the same as equation 3.19.

Supposing that the stylised facts about production possibilities are equations 3.23, an ethical position for intergenerational equality can be expressed analytically in two ways. Either utilitarianism can be abandoned or modified so that the intertemporal social welfare function leads to intergenerational equality, or additional constraints on the maximisation of a utilitarian welfare function can be adopted.

An example of the first approach would be the adoption of a Rawlsian intertemporal social welfare function. Considering just two generations, 0 and 1, this would take the form:

$$W = \min(U_0, U_1) \tag{3.24}$$

With generations substituted for individuals, the previous discussion of this type of social welfare function applies. Generalising equation 3.24 for many generations and assuming production possibilities as per equations 3.23 and such that constant consumption for ever is feasible, maximising such a welfare function leads to constant consumption for ever. Solow (1974a) considers the conditions under which constant consumption for ever is possible in the circumstances of equations 3.23, and shows that it will be the optimal consumption path if a Rawlsian intertemporal welfare function is maximised.

An example of the second approach would be the adoption of some constraint on savings and investment behaviour, such as the Hartwick rule (Hartwick, 1977). We shall discuss this rule more fully in the next chapter, and at several points in Part IV of the book. What matters here is that the rule says that at every point in time the amount saved and added to the capital stock should be equal to the rent arising in the extraction of the resource. If this rule is followed where production conditions are as in equations 3.23 and constant consumption for ever is feasible, then the result is constant consumption for ever.

Summary

Economists make recommendations concerning environmental policy objectives, such as, for example, the level of pollution to be allowed. Such recommendations are derived from welfare economics, the ethical basis for which is a form of utilitarianism where the criterion of what is good for a human individual is that individual's own tastes. Many of those who are concerned about the natural environment have different ethical positions. Some want, for example, to confer moral standing on non-human individuals. In the preference-based utilitarianism that underpins welfare economics, the interests of non-humans get taken into account only in so far as some humans care about those interests.

Many of the decisions that have to be taken regarding the use of the services that the natural environment provides have implications for human interests that stretch out over time. The question that then arises is whether future effects should be given the same weight as current effects in current decision making. This is the question of discounting. In thinking about this question, it is important to keep clear the distinction between discounting future utility and discounting future consumption. It is also important to be clear that the implications of discounting vary with the terms on which consumption and utility can be shifted over time. We shall return to the analysis of intertemporal allocation in Chapter 11.

Further reading

A good introduction to ethics, including environmental applications, may be found in Singer (1993). Sen (1987) looks at ethics in relation to economics. Beauchamp and Bowie (1988) give a good presentation, especially in Chapters 1 and 9; the book contains an interesting analysis of the business implications of ethical principles. Penz (1986) and Scitovsky (1986) consider consumer sovereignty and its problems.

Kneese and Schulze (1985) and Glasser (1999) are survey articles dealing specifically with ethics in relation to environmental economics and policy analysis, both of which provide extensive references to the literature. The journal *Environmental Values* aims to bring together contributions from philosophy, law, economics and other disciplines concerning the ethical basis for our treatment of the natural environment. The February/March 1998 issue (Vol. 24, nos 2, 3) of *Ecological Economics* was a special issue on 'Economics, ethics and environment'.

References on intertemporal allocation and related matters will be provided with Chapter 11.

Discussion questions

1. We argued in the text that Rawls's Difference Principle asserts that it is only just to have an unequal distribution of wealth if all persons benefit from that allocation, relative to the situation of an equal distribution. But we also argued that the total level of utility attainable might depend on the distribution of wealth, as utility could be higher in an unequal position if incentive effects enhance productive efficiency. Discuss the implications of these comments for a morally just distribution of resources within and between countries.

2. In discussing the work of Robert Nozick, it was argued that libertarian ethics have been adopted most enthusiastically by those who believe in a limited role for government. But we also noted that it is by no means clear that a laissez-faire approach is necessarily implied. Three difficult issues arise in connection with the principle of just acquisition:

   What should government do about unjust holdings?

   How are open access or common property resources to be dealt with?

   How do external effects and public goods relate to the concept of just acquisition?

   Sketch out reasoned answers to these three questions.

3. If society deemed it to be correct that some animals or plants have intrinsic rights (such as rights to be left undisturbed or rights to be reasonably protected), then such rights can be protected by imposing them as constraints on human behaviour so that the scope of legitimate activity is reduced. Do humans appear to regard whales as having intrinsic rights, and if so, what rights are these? In what ways, if at all, do humans defend these rights by imposing constraints on human behaviour?

4. *A river tumbles through forested ravines and rocky gorges towards the sea. The state hydro-electricity commission sees the falling water as untapped energy. Building a dam across one of the gorges would provide three years of employment for a thousand people, and provide longer-term employment for twenty or thirty. The dam would store enough water to ensure that the state could economically meet its energy needs for the next decade. This would encourage the establishment of energy-intensive industry thus further contributing to employment and economic growth.*

   The rough terrain of the river valley makes it accessible only to the reasonably fit, but it is nevertheless a favoured spot for bush-walking. The river itself attracts the more daring whitewater rafters. Deep in the sheltered valleys are stands of rare Huon Pine, many of the trees being over a thousand years old. The valleys and gorges are home to many birds and animals, including an endangered species of marsupial mouse that has seldom been found outside the valley. There may be other rare plants and animals as well, but no one knows, for scientists are yet to investigate the region fully.

   (Singer, 1993, p. 264)

   Peter Singer's discussion of ethics and the environment begins with this scenario. His description is loosely based on a proposed dam on the Franklin River in Tasmania. Singer notes that this is an example of a situation in which we must choose between very different sets of values. Please answer the following question, as put by Singer: Should the dam be built? (Note: in Chapters 11, 12 and 13 we shall work through the way that economists would deal with this question and some of the criticisms that have been made of their approach – you may want to come back to Singer's question after reading those chapters.)

Problems

1. Suppose that one believed that each generation should have the same level of well-being as every other one. Demonstrate that we could not ensure the attainment of this merely by the choice of a particular discount rate, zero or otherwise.

2. Prove that, under the assumption of diminishing marginal utility, the linear indifference curves in utility space in Figure 3.1 map into indifference curves that are convex from below in commodity space, as illustrated in Figure 3.2.

3. Demonstrate that an unequal distribution of goods at a welfare maximum may occur when the weights attached to individual utilities are not equal, and/or when individuals have different utility functions.

Appendix 3.1 The Lagrange multiplier method of solving constrained optimisation problems

Suppose we have the following problem in which a function of three variables is to be maximised subject to two constraints:

$$\max \quad f(x_1, x_2, x_3)$$

subject to

$$g(x_1, x_2, x_3) = 0$$

$$h(x_1, x_2, x_3) = 0$$

To obtain a solution to this problem, we begin by writing the Lagrangian (L) for the problem. The Lagrangian consists of two components. The first of these is the function to be maximised. The second contains the constraint functions (but without being set equal to zero), with each constraint being preceded by a separate Lagrange multiplier variable. The Lagrangian is the sum of all these terms.

So in this case the Lagrangian, L, is

$$L(x_1, x_2, x_3, \lambda_1, \lambda_2) = f(x_1, x_2, x_3) + \lambda_1 g(x_1, x_2, x_3) + \lambda_2 h(x_1, x_2, x_3) \quad (3.25)$$

in which λ_1 and λ_2 are two Lagrange multipliers (one for each constraint) and the term $L(x_1, x_2, x_3, \lambda_1, \lambda_2)$ signifies that we are now to regard the Lagrangian as a function of the original choice variables of the problem and of the two Lagrange multiplier variables.

We now proceed by using the standard method of unconstrained optimisation to find a maximum of the Lagrangian with respect to x_1, x_2, x_3, λ_1 and λ_2.

The necessary first-order conditions for a maximum are

$$\frac{\partial L}{\partial x_1} = f_1 + \lambda_1 g_1 + \lambda_2 h_1 = 0$$

$$\frac{\partial L}{\partial x_2} = f_2 + \lambda_1 g_2 + \lambda_2 h_2 = 0$$

$$\frac{\partial L}{\partial x_3} = f_3 + \lambda_1 g_3 + \lambda_2 h_3 = 0$$

$$\frac{\partial L}{\partial \lambda_1} = g(x_1, x_2, x_3) = 0$$

$$\frac{\partial L}{\partial \lambda_2} = h(x_1, x_2, x_3) = 0$$

where

$$f_i = \frac{\partial f}{\partial x_i}, \ g_i = \frac{\partial g}{\partial x_i}, \ h_i = \frac{\partial h}{\partial x_i} \text{ for } i = 1, 2, 3$$

These are solved simultaneously to obtain solution values for the choice variables.

The second-order conditions for a maximum require that the following determinant be positive:

$$\begin{vmatrix} L_{11} & L_{12} & L_{13} & g_1 & h_1 \\ L_{21} & L_{22} & L_{23} & g_2 & h_2 \\ L_{31} & L_{32} & L_{33} & g_3 & h_3 \\ g_1 & g_2 & g_3 & 0 & 0 \\ h_1 & h_2 & h_3 & 0 & 0 \end{vmatrix}$$

where

$$L_{ij} = \frac{\partial^2 L}{\partial x_i \partial x_j}$$

For a constrained maximum, a sufficient second-order condition can be stated in terms of the signs of the bordered principal minors of the Hessian matrix. Details of this condition are beyond the scope of this appendix, but can be found on page 386 of Chiang (1984).

The Lagrange multiplier method is widely used in economic analysis generally, and in resource and environmental economics particularly. This is because the Lagrange multipliers have a very useful interpretation in analysis. They are 'shadow prices' on the constraints. In the case of a constrained maximisation problem as considered above, this means that the value of a Lagrange multiplier tells us what the effect on the maximised value of the objective function would be for a small – strictly an infinitesimal (or vanishingly small) – relaxation of the corresponding constraint. The same interpretation arises in constrained minimisation problems. Clearly, this is very useful information. We now illustrate this interpretation using a simple example from an environmental economics context. We consider the problem of the least-cost allocation across sources of a reduction in total emissions, which problem will be discussed at length in Chapter 6.

Suppose that there are two firms, 1 and 2, where production gives rise to emissions M_1 and M_2. In the absence of any regulation of their activities, the firms' profit-maximising emissions levels are 1000 and 7500 tonnes respectively. The firms can cut back, or abate, emissions, but so doing reduces profits and is costly. Further, abatement costs as a function of the level of abatement vary as between the two firms. The abatement cost functions are

$$C_1 = 10A_1 + 0.01A_1^2 = 10(1000 - M_1) \\ + 0.01(1000 - M_1)^2 \quad (3.26a)$$

$$C_2 = 5A_2 + 0.001A_2^2 = 5(7500 - M_2) \\ + 0.001(7500 - M_2)^2 \quad (3.26b)$$

where A_1 and A_2 are the levels of abatement, the amount by which emissions in some regulated situation are less than they would be in the absence of regulation.

The regulatory authority's problem is to determine how a reduction in total emissions from 8500 $= (1000 + 7500)$ to 750 tonnes should be allocated as between the two firms. Its criterion is the minimisation of the total cost of abatement. The problem is, that is, to find the levels of A_1 and A_2, or equivalently of M_1 and M_2, which minimise C_1 plus C_2 given that M_1 plus M_2 is to equal 750. Formally, using M_1 and M_2 as the control or choice variables, the problem is

$$\min(C_1 + C_2)$$

subject to

$$M_1 + M_2 = 750$$

Substituting for C_1 and C_2 from equations 3.26, and writing the Lagrangian, we have

$$L = 113\,750 - 30M_1 - 20M_2 + 0.01M_1^2 + \\ 0.001M_2^2 + \lambda[750 - M_1 - M_2] \quad (3.27)$$

where the necessary conditions are

$$\frac{\partial L}{\partial M_1} = -30 + 0.02M_1 - \lambda = 0 \quad (3.28a)$$

$$\frac{\partial L}{\partial M_2} = -20 + 0.02M_2 - \lambda = 0 \quad (3.28b)$$

$$\frac{\partial L}{\partial \lambda} = 750 - M_1 - M_2 = 0 \quad (3.28c)$$

Eliminating λ from equations 3.28a and 3.28b gives

$$-30 + 0.02M_1 = -20 + 0.002M_2 \quad (3.29)$$

and solving equation 3.28c for M_1 gives

$$M_1 = 750 - M_2 \quad (3.30)$$

so that substituting equation 3.30 into equation 3.29 and solving leads to M_2 equal to 227.2727, and then using equation 3.30 leads to M_1 equal to 522.7272. The corresponding abatement levels are A_1 equal to 477.2728 and A_2 equal to 7272.7273. Note that firm 2, where abatement costs are much lower than in firm 1, does proportionately more abatement.

Now, in order to get the allocation of abatement across the firms we eliminated λ from equations 3.28a and 3.28b. Now that we know M_1 and M_2 we can use one of these equations to calculate the value of λ as -19.5455. This is the shadow price of pollution, in the units of the objective function, which are here £s, when it is constrained to be a total emissions level of 750 tonnes. This shadow price gives what the impact on the minimised total cost of abatement would be for a small relaxation of the constraint that is the target regulated level of total emissions. To see this, we can compare the minimised total cost for 750 tonnes and 751 tonnes. To get the former, simply substitute $M_1 = 522.7272$ and $M_2 = 227.2727$ into

$$C = 113\,750 - 30M_1 - 20M_2 + 0.01M_1^2 + 0.001M_2^2 \tag{3.31}$$

to get 96 306.819. To get the latter, replace 750 by 751 in equation 3.28c, and then solve equations 3.28a, 3.28b and 3.28c as before to get $M_1 = 522.8181$ and $M_2 = 228.1818$, which on substitution into equation 3.31 for C gives the total cost of abatement to 751 tonnes as 96 287.272. Subtracting 96 306.819 from 96 287.272 gives -19.547, to be compared with the value for λ calculated above as -19.5455. The two results do not agree exactly because strictly the value for λ is for an infinitesimally small relaxation of the constraint, whereas we actually relaxed it by one tonne.

Note that the shadow price is in £s per tonne, so that the Lagrangian is in the same units as the objective function, £s.

It is not always necessary to use the method of Lagrange multipliers to solve constrained optimisation problems. Sometimes the problem can be solved by substituting the constraint(s) into the objective function. This is the case in our example here. We want to find the values for M_1 and M_2 which minimise C as given by equation 3.31, given that $M_1 + M_2 = 750$. That means that $M_1 = 750 - M_2$, and if we use this to eliminate M_1 from equation 3.31, after collecting terms we get

$$C = 96\,875 - 5M_2 + 0.011M_2^2 \tag{3.32}$$

where the necessary condition for a minimum is

$$\frac{\partial C}{\partial M_2} = -5 + 0.022M_2$$

which solves for $M_2 = 227.2727$, and from $M_1 = 750 - M_2$ we then get M_1 as 522.7273.

Even where solution by the substitution method is possible, using the method of Lagrange multipliers is generally preferable in that it provides extra information on shadow prices, with the interpretation set out above. In fact, these shadow prices are often useful in a further way, in that they have a natural interpretation as the prices that could be used to actually achieve a solution to the problem under consideration. Again, this can be illustrated with the emissions control example. If the regulatory authority had the information on the abatement cost functions for the two firms, it could do the calculations as above to find that for the least-cost attainment of a reduction to 750 tonnes firm 1 should be emitting 522.7272 tonnes and firm 2 emitting 227.2727 tonnes. It could then simply instruct the two firms that these were their permissible levels of emissions.

Given that it can also calculate the shadow price of pollution at its desired level, it can achieve the same outcome by imposing on each firm a tax per unit emission at a rate which is the shadow price. A cost-minimising firm facing a tax on emissions will abate to the point where its marginal abatement cost is equal to the tax rate. With t for the tax rate, and M^* for the emissions level in the absence of any regulation or taxation, total costs are

$$C(A) + tM = C(A) + t(M^* - A)$$

so that total cost minimisation implies

$$\frac{\partial C}{\partial A} - t = 0$$

or

$$\frac{\partial C}{\partial A} = t \tag{3.33}$$

For firm 1, the abatement cost function written with A_1 as argument is

$$C_1 = 10A_1 + 0.01A_1^2 \tag{3.34}$$

so that marginal abatement costs are given by

$$\frac{\partial C_1}{\partial A_1} = 10 + 0.02A_1 \tag{3.35}$$

Using the general condition, which is equation 3.33 with equation 3.35, we get

$$10 + 0.02A_1 = t$$

and substituting for t equal to the shadow price of pollution, 19.5455, and solving yields A_1 equal to 477.275, which is, rounding errors apart, the result that we got when considering what level of emissions the authority should regulate for in firm 1. Proceeding in the same way for firm 2, it will be found that it will do as required for the least-cost allocation of total abatement if it also faces a tax of £19.5455 per tonne of emissions.

When we return to the analysis of instruments for pollution control in Chapter 6 we shall see that the regulatory authority could reduce emissions to 750 by issuing tradable permits in that amount. Given the foregoing, it should be intuitive that the equilibrium price of those permits would be £19.5455.

Appendix 3.2 Social welfare maximisation

For two persons and a fixed amount of the consumption good, the problem is to choose X^A and X^B so as to maximise

$$W = W\{U^A(X^A), U^B(X^B)\}$$

subject to the constraint

$$X^A + X^B = \bar{X}$$

The Lagrangian for this problem is

$$L = W\{U^A(X^A), U^B(X^B)\} + \lambda[\bar{X} - X^A - X^B]$$

and the necessary conditions include

$$\frac{\partial L}{\partial X^A} = W_A U_X^A - \lambda = 0 \qquad (3.36a)$$

$$\frac{\partial L}{\partial X^B} = W_B U_X^B - \lambda = 0 \qquad (3.36b)$$

where we are using the notation for derivatives introduced in the chapter – W_A for $\partial W/\partial U^A$ and U_X^A for $\partial U^A/\partial X^A$ etc. – and making the same assumptions – $W_A > 0$, $U_X^A > 0$, $U_{XX}^A < 0$ etc. From equations 3.36 here we get the condition stated as equation 3.3 in the chapter:

$$W_A U_X^A = W_B U_X^B \qquad (3.37)$$

For $W = W\{U^A, U^B\} = w_A U^A + w_B U^B$, $W_A = w_A$ and $W_B = w_B$ so that the necessary condition (3.37) here becomes

$$w_A U_X^A = w_B U_X^B \qquad (3.38)$$

and for $w_A = w_B$ this is

$$U_X^A = U_X^B \qquad (3.39)$$

which is equation 3.6 in the chapter text.

Now consider a case where the social welfare function is

$$W = U^A + U^B$$

and where the two individuals have identical utility functions. Specifically, suppose that

$$U^A(X^A) = 2(X^A)^{1/2} \text{ and } U^B(X^B) = 2(X^B)^{1/2}$$

so that

$$U_X^A = (X^A)^{-1/2} \text{ and } U_X^B = (X^B)^{-1/2}$$

and

$$U_{XX}^A = -\frac{1}{2}(X^A)^{-3/2} \text{ and } U_{XX}^B = -\frac{1}{2}(X^B)^{-3/2}$$

Then equation 3.39 becomes

$$(X^A)^{-1/2} = (X^B)^{-1/2}$$

so that

$$X^A = X^B = 0.5\bar{X}$$

and each individual gets half of the available X.

Now consider a case where the social welfare function is again

$$W = U^A + U^B$$

but the two individuals have different utility functions. Specifically, suppose that

$$U^A(X^A) = 2(X^A)^{1/2} \text{ and } U^B(X^B) = (X^B)^{1/2}$$

so that

$$U_X^A = (X^A)^{-1/2} \text{ and } U_X^B = 0.5(X^B)^{-1/2}$$

In this case, the condition which is equation 3.39 still applies, but now it gives

$$X^B = \frac{X^A}{4}$$

The numerically specified utility functions just used are particular versions of

$$U = \frac{1}{\alpha}X^{\alpha} \quad \text{with } \alpha < 1 \tag{3.40}$$

which was used in the text when discussing utilitarian formulations of Rawlsian differentiation in favour of the worst off. It was stated there that the relative weight accorded to increases in consumption for the worse-off individual increases as the degree of inequality between the individuals increases, and as $\alpha \to -\infty$. To see this, we proceed as follows. For

$$W = U^{A} + U^{B}$$

with the Us given by equation 3.40 we have

$$W_{A} = \frac{\partial W}{\partial X^{A}} = (X^{A})^{\alpha-1} \text{ and } W_{B} = \frac{\partial W}{\partial X^{B}} = (X^{B})^{\alpha-1}$$

so that

$$\frac{W_{A}}{W_{B}} = \frac{(X^{A})^{\alpha-1}}{(X^{B})^{\alpha-1}} = \left(\frac{X^{A}}{X^{B}}\right)^{\alpha-1} = r^{\alpha-1} \tag{3.41}$$

where r is the ratio of X_{A} to X_{B} and $r > 1$ for B the worse-off person.

From equation 3.41

$$\frac{\partial\left(\dfrac{W_{A}}{W_{B}}\right)}{\partial r} = (\alpha - 1)r^{\alpha-2} < 0 \quad \text{for } \alpha < 1$$

and

$$\frac{\partial\left(\dfrac{W_{A}}{W_{B}}\right)}{\partial \alpha} = r^{\alpha-1}\ln r > 0$$

CHAPTER 4

Concepts of sustainability

But we can be fairly certain that no new technology will abolish absolute scarcity because the laws of thermodynamics apply to all possible technologies. No one can be absolutely certain that we will not some day discover perpetual motion and how to create and destroy matter and energy. But the reasonable assumption for economists is that this is an unlikely prospect and that while technology will continue to pull rabbits out of hats, it will not pull an elephant out of a hat – much less an infinite series of ever-larger elephants!

Daly (1974), p. 19

Learning objectives

In this chapter you will
- be introduced to concepts of sustainability
- learn about the importance of substitution possibilities in considerations of whether constant consumption is feasible
- have the distinction between 'weak' and 'strong' sustainability explained
- find out when and how the Hartwick rule works
- learn about incentives and information in relation to sustainability

---

Introduction

The principal purpose of this chapter is to show how economists think about sustainability. We also consider the way in which ecologists think about sustainability. We will not be considering whether or not sustainability should be a policy objective. That is the sort of ethical question that the previous chapter addressed. Here we will take it as given that sustainability is desirable, that it is agreed that the current human generation should take account of the interests of future human generations. The first

question that then arises is: what are the interests of future generations? The next question then is: how do we look after those interests? This second question itself involves two stages. First, the identification of current policy objectives that look after future interests. Second, devising policy instruments to achieve those objectives. This chapter is concerned mainly with mapping the interests of future generations into current policy objectives. It addresses questions about instruments only in a very general way: much of the rest of the book is concerned with more detailed analysis of such questions.

In the first section of the chapter we identify interests as consumption levels, and consider comparisons of different time paths for consumption so as to discuss how the idea of sustainability as stated above might be made more precise. For economists this is the obvious way to proceed with the analysis of the sustainability problem. In this section of the chapter we also introduce, for later discussion, other ways of conceptualising the sustainability problem. The next two sections then look, respectively, at economic and ecological approaches to sustainability. We then discuss an approach which sees the problem primarily in terms of social processes and institutions. These different ways of conceptualising sustainability should not be seen as competitive or mutually exclusive. Rather, they are complementary; and the last section of the chapter attempts to draw, at a general level, some policy lessons.

Throughout this chapter, analysis will assume that the size of the human population is constant. This assumption greatly simplifies exposition without the loss of any essential insights.[1] For example, if we take sustainability to be constant consumption, then clearly if we are really looking out for the interests of future generations we must be thinking about per capita consumption. The assumption of a constant population size means that when we talk about consumption going up, or down, or being constant, we are referring to the nature of the time path for both per capita and aggregate consumption. As in the previous chapter, we can treat the consumption/utility that we refer to as that of some representative individual, where all individuals are the same in all relevant respects.

4.1   Concepts and constraints

Even if we restrict attention to the economics literature, there is no universally agreed definition of the concept of sustainability. On the contrary, in that literature, one finds a variety of definitions, meanings and interpretations. In one recent paper, Jack Pezzey wrote: 'So I see little point in expanding the collection of fifty sustainability definitions which I made in 1989, to the five thousand definitions that one could readily find today' (Pezzey, 1997, p. 448). A more useful exercise than providing an exhaustive list of the definitions that have appeared in the economics literature is to give just three that can illuminate the difficulties of coming up with a single all-embracing definition. This will help in understanding the various approaches to sustainability that can be taken, and in identifying the major issues addressed.

Pezzey (1997) distinguishes between 'sustainable' development, 'sustained' development and 'survivable' development. These are defined in Box 4.1, which you should now read.

---

[1] The feasibility of sustainability as constant per capita consumption where the population is increasing is analysed in, for example, Solow (1974a).

Box 4.1 Sustainable, sustained and survivable development

The following notation is used:

U_t = the utility level at time t

$\dot{U}_t$ = the rate of change of utility at time t

U_t^{MAX} = the maximum utility which can be held constant for ever from time t onwards, given production opportunities available at time t

U^{SURV} = the minimum utility level consistent with survival of the given population

Development is *sustainable* if $U_t \le U_t^{MAX}$ always
Development is *sustained* if $\dot{U}_t \ge 0$ always
Development is *survivable* if $U_t > U^{SURV}$ always

If utility is a function of consumption alone, the usual assumption in intertemporal economic analysis (see previous chapter), then it is possible to replace the word 'utility' by 'consumption' in each of these criteria (and to change symbols from U to C commensurably) and thereby to define them in terms of consumption rather than utility. Doing this we obtain:

Development is *sustainable* if $C_t \le C_t^{MAX}$ always
Development is *sustained* if $\dot{C}_t \ge 0$ always
Development is *survivable* if $C_t > C^{SURV}$ always

Note that the level of utility (or consumption) corresponding to survivability is taken to be constant over time (hence C^{SURV} carries no time subscript). But C_t^{MAX} does (and must) include a time subscript. The highest level of constant, sustainable consumption an economy can obtain from any point of time onwards does depend on which point in time we consider. For example, at the end of a prolonged and major war, in which large stocks of resources have been consumed or irretrievably degraded, the maximum feasible level of sustainable consumption is likely to be smaller than it was before the war broke out.

4.1.1   Consumption time paths

We will use some hypothetical time paths of consumption to illustrate some notions of sustainability. As noted in Box 4.1, and following on from the previous chapter, it is standard when thinking about intertemporal distribution issues such as sustainability for economists to work with utility functions where consumption is the only argument, and where utility increases with consumption. In that case we can look at things in terms of either utility or consumption. The consumption time paths that we want to consider are shown in Figure 4.1. The vertical axis measures the level of consumption at any point in time. The passage of time from the present ($t = 0$) onwards corresponds to movement from left to right along the horizontal axis. Six alternative time paths of consumption are shown, labelled $C(1)$ to $C(6)$. In addition, the heavy horizontal line denoted C^{MIN} represents the level of consumption which is the minimum that society deems as being socially and morally acceptable, while the dotted line, C^{SURV}, represents the biophysical minimum consumption level.

We suggest that you now try to rank the six alternative time paths. Put yourself in the position of a social planner aiming to do the best for society over many generations. How would you then rank the alternatives?

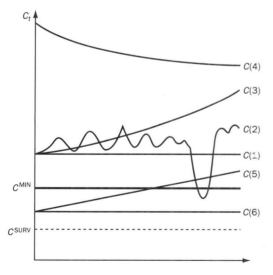

Figure 4.1 Consumption paths over time

4.1.2   Comparing consumption time paths

Consider the idea of sustainability as non-declining consumption, which is the concept of sustainability that is most widely used in economic analysis. In Figure 4.1, four of the paths – $C(1)$, $C(3)$, $C(5)$ and $C(6)$ – satisfy the criteria of non-declining consumption. Can we rank them? Only if we adopt some kind of social welfare function. We saw in the previous chapter that we could incorporate sustainability considerations into intertemporal welfare maximisation by adopting them as constraints. That kind of approach would identify one of $C(1)$, $C(2)$, $C(3)$ or $C(4)$ as 'best'. Given that along $C(3)$ consumption is at every point in time higher than on any of the other three paths, and is nowhere declining, that kind of approach with a utilitarian social welfare function of the sort considered in the previous chapter would identify $C(3)$ as the best path. Although $C(4)$ has higher consumption at every point in time, it is ruled out by the non-declining consumption constraint.

We saw in the previous chapter that an apparently sound ethical principle could in some circumstances lead to outcomes that are not obviously sensible. The same point can, and needs to, be made here. Consider path $C(2)$ in Figure 4.1. It clearly does not have the non-declining consumption property. Suppose a choice has to be made between $C(2)$ and $C(6)$. Strict adherence to the non-declining consumption criterion as a constraint on choice would, for any social welfare function, mean selecting $C(6)$ rather than $C(2)$ despite the fact that at every point in time consumption is higher on the former than on the latter path.

A serious objection to the non-declining consumption criterion is that it does not impose any requirements on how large the non-declining level of consumption should be. On this criterion, an economy is sustainable even if living standards are abysmally low and remain so, provided they do not get any lower over time. One can imagine a poor economy which could become considerably less poor in the medium future by the sacrifice of some consumption in the near future. Planning for such an economy with the non-declining consumption criterion as a constraint would rule out such a development path.

So, the adoption of a simple constraint such as non-declining consumption is not problem-free. What about alternative constraints that might be placed on the conventional maximisation of an inter-temporal social welfare function so as to capture the spirit of an ethical concern for future generations? As noted above, Pezzey (1997) introduced the idea of survivable development. In Figure 4.1 the broken line labelled C^{SURV} shows some minimum level of consumption consistent with biophysical survival requirements. One could maximise subject to the constraint that consumption does not fall below such a level. That would avoid the problems with the non-declining consumption constraint noted above. It would not, for example, rule out $C(2)$ or $C(4)$.

But one might feel that such a constraint is not really 'fair' to future generations. In discussions of poverty, it is now widely agreed that the poverty line should be culturally rather than biologically determined. In this spirit, we might argue that consumption should not fall below some minimum, decent, culturally determined level over time. Let us assume that such a level can be defined, and suppose that it corresponds to the horizontal line labelled C^{MIN} in Figure 4.1. We can use the term 'minimum condition' to describe the constraint on the choice of optimal consumption path that consumption should never fall below C^{MIN}. Such a constraint would rule out $C(2)$ but not $C(4)$.

Table 4.1 summarises how the six consumption paths of Figure 4.1 fare against the three constraints considered here. All of the six consumption paths satisfy the survivable development criterion (although we have noted that this is a relatively undemanding requirement). Three of them – paths $C(1)$, $C(3)$ and $C(4)$ – also satisfy the minimum condition. Which paths satisfy all of the three criteria we have examined? Just two, $C(1)$ and $C(3)$. Clearly, given that both satisfy all of the constraints considered, maximising a conventional utilitarian intertemporal social welfare function would mean the choice of $C(3)$ over $C(1)$ whichever sustainability constraint were adopted. $C(4)$ would be the chosen path with either the survivability or the minimum condition constraint, but would be eliminated if the non-declining consumption constraint were adopted.

Table 4.1 Various sustainability criteria applied to the hypothetical consumption paths

	Criterion		
	Non-declining consumption	Survivability	Minimum condition
Consumption path			
C(1)	S	S	S
C(2)	NS	S	NS
C(3)	S	S	S
C(4)	NS	S	S
C(5)	S	S	NS
C(6)	S	S	NS

KEY:
S = Satisfied
NS = Not satisfied

4.1.3 Concepts of sustainability

A concern for sustainability derives from an ethical concern for future generations together with an appreciation of the facts which implies that such concern needs to be incorporated into current decision making – because, for example, of the use of non-renewable resources in production. If we did not care about future generations, then the use of non-renewable resources in production would not require any particular attention in current decision making. Equally, if nothing that we did now had any implications for future generations, then notwithstanding an ethical concern for them there would be no need to think about them in current planning and decision making.

What we have seen so far here is that even if we restrict attention to consumption, a 'concern for future generations' can take a variety of expressions, and does not translate into a single simple constraint on current planning. It should also be noted that in explaining this using Figure 4.1 we implicitly assumed that the various alternative consumption paths are feasible, could actually be followed if chosen. This, of course, need not be the case in fact. Given, for example, the use of non-renewable resources in production, some would argue that constant consumption for ever, at any rate other than zero, is not feasible. We look at this and related matters below.

Table 4.2 Six concepts of sustainability

1. A sustainable state is one in which utility (or consumption) is non-declining through time.
2. A sustainable state is one in which resources are managed so as to maintain production opportunities for the future.
3. A sustainable state is one in which the natural capital stock is non-declining through time.
4. A sustainable state is one in which resources are managed so as to maintain a sustainable yield of resource services.
5. A sustainable state is one which satisfies minimum conditions for ecosystem resilience through time.
6. Sustainable development as consensus-building and institutional development.

Before doing that we need to note that constant consumption (or utility) is not the only possible conceptualisation of sustainability. Table 4.2 lists six concepts that are widely used and discussed in the sustainability literature.

We will be discussing each of the concepts listed in Table 4.2 in some detail in the rest of the chapter. Concepts 1, 2 and 3 are basically economic in nature, and will be discussed in the next section 'Economists on sustainability'. Concepts 4 and 5 originate with ecologists, and are covered in Section 4.3 below, 'Ecologists on sustainability'.[2] As we shall see, while the third concept is expressed in economic terminology, it reflects a position, on substitution possibilities, that is more commonly found among ecologists than among economists. The final concept, really a group of concepts, sees sustainability as being essentially a problem of governance in the broadest sense.

Note that the concepts should not be seen as mutually exclusive. The first, for example, largely entails the second, because if utility or consumption is not to decline, resources must be managed so that productive opportunities are maintained for subsequent generations. The fourth is a particular case of the second. Again, the first seems to require the fifth if we take the view that production and consumption cannot be maintained over time in the face of ecosystem collapse.

None of these concepts explicitly specifies the duration of time over which sustainability is to operate. Presumably one must have in mind very long horizons for the idea of sustainability to have substance. But this merely begs the question of what is meant by a long period of time. Some writers choose to think of indefinitely long (or infinite) time horizons: a state is sustainable if it is capable of being reproduced in perpetuity. Others conceive of millennia or the like: periods of time over which human populations are approximately genetically constant. However, it is not necessary to decide upon any particular span of time: we could define a sustainable state as one in which some relevant magnitude is bequeathed to the following period in at least as good a state as it is in the initial period. Provided no finite terminal time is set, this implies that one is thinking about unlimited time spans.

4.2   Economists on sustainability

In this section we provide an overview and preview of the way that economists approach the analysis of sustainability issues. We will come to a more detailed and rigorous account of many of the issues considered here later in the book, and especially in Part IV.

4.2.1   Economic concepts of sustainability

In the previous section of this chapter we noted two economic concepts of sustainability:

1. A sustainable state is one in which utility/ consumption is non-declining through time.
2. A sustainable state is one in which resources are managed so as to maintain production opportunities for the future.

An example of a definition relating to the first concept is

> Sustainability is defined as . . . non-declining utility of a representative member of society for millennia into the future.
>
> *(Pezzey, 1992, p. 323)*

---

[2] Here, as elsewhere, we use the term 'ecologist' rather loosely to refer to natural scientists interested in matters environmental.

Note that in terms of the terminology of Box 4.1 (taken from Pezzey (1997)) this relates to 'sustained' rather than 'sustainable' development. In fact, in his 1997 *Land Economics* paper, Pezzey states that he now regards 'sustainable' rather than 'sustained' development as the appropriate criterion of sustainability. However, most economists would still opt for what the 1997 Pezzey calls 'sustained' as the definition of sustainability that focuses on the behaviour of utility/consumption over time.

An example of a definition relating to the second of the above concepts is that sustainability involves

> Preserving opportunities for future generations as a common sense minimal notion of intergenerational justice.
>
> *(Page, 1977, p. 202, 1982, p. 205)*

In thus defining sustainability, Page is appealing to John Locke's concept of just acquisition which was noted in the previous chapter, and the idea is that the present generation does not have the right to deplete the opportunities afforded by the resource base since it does not properly 'own' it.

Another version of the opportunities-based view underpins the most well-known definition of sustainability, that due to the Brundtland Report:

> Sustainable development is development that meets the needs of the present without compromising the ability of future generations to meet their own needs.
>
> *(WCED, 1987, p. 43)*

While the utility/consumption-based and opportunities-based concepts start from different places, where they end up in terms of formal analysis is very much the same place. This is because for economists the opportunities that matter are consumption opportunities, so that to say that A has the same opportunities as B but consumes differently is to say that A has different preferences from B. However, in the context of the single-commodity representative-consumer models that are mostly used for the analysis of intertemporal distribution, and hence sustainability, issues, it is explicitly assumed that the utility function is the same over generations. In that kind of simple model, as we shall see when discussing the Hartwick rule later in this section (and in Chapter 19), it turns out that constant consumption and equal opportunities are inextricably linked.

4.2.2 Is sustainability feasible? Substitution possibilities

We have already noted that the clearest setting for the analysis of the sustainability problem is a model where a non-renewable resource, of which there is necessarily a finite amount in existence, is used in production. With such a characterisation of the problem in mind, the Nobel laureate economist Robert Solow has criticised those environmentalists who urge that we should conserve resources for future generations. This

> is a damagingly narrow way to pose the question. We have no obligation to our successors to bequeath a share of this or that resource. Our obligation refers to generalized productive capacity or, even wider, to certain standards of consumption/living possibilities over time.
>
> *(Solow, 1986)*

What our successors will be interested in, Solow is in effect saying, is not the amount of 'oil' in the ground that they inherit from us, but rather whether they inherit the capability to do the things that we now do using 'oil'. They will be interested in the consumption opportunities that they inherit, not the stocks of resources that they inherit.

To make the distinction that Solow makes it is necessary to believe that we can bequeath to our successors something that is a substitute for non-renewable resources. If we cannot bequeath a substitute, then, to honour our ethical commitment, which Solow accepts, to leave them with the same consumption opportunities as ourselves, we do have an obligation 'to bequeath a share of this or that resource'.

The basic issues can be explored within the framework of the simple optimal growth model, where production uses a non-renewable resource, that was introduced in the previous chapter. That model's welfare function is

$$W = \int_{t=0}^{t=\infty} U(C_t)e^{-\rho t}dt \tag{4.1}$$

to be maximised subject to the constraints

$$\dot{K} = Q(K_t, R_t) - C_t \tag{4.2}$$

$$\dot{S} = -R_t \tag{4.3}$$

$$\bar{S} = \int_{t=0}^{t=\infty} R_t dt \qquad (4.4)$$

When discussing the optimal consumption path arising in the previous chapter, it was noted that 'the production function $Q(K_t, R_t)$ may be such that constant consumption for ever may simply be impossible'. We were then interested in whether the standard utilitarian approach would, in circumstances where sustainability as constant consumption for ever was feasible, indicate sustainability. We saw that it would not. What we are now interested in is the question of feasibility – under what conditions is constant consumption for ever possible, notwithstanding that production uses inputs of a non-renewable resource available only in finite total amount?

Figure 4.2 shows the isoquants for three specifications of the production function $Q_t = Q(K_t, R_t)$ that identify the possibilities. Panel a corresponds to:

$$Q_t = \alpha K_t + \beta R_t \qquad (4.5)$$

In this case, the resource is non-essential in production. For $R_t = 0$, $Q_t = \alpha K_t$, and any level of output can be produced if there is enough capital. The use of a non-renewable resource in production does not, in this case, mean that sustainability as constant consumption is infeasible. Capital is a perfect substitute for the non-renewable resource.

Panel c of Figure 4.2 corresponds to

$$Q_t = \min(\alpha K_t, \beta R_t) \qquad (4.6)$$

In this case, Q is equal to whichever is the smaller of αK_t and βR_t. In panel c, given resource input R_1, for example, Q_1 is the maximum feasible output, however much capital input is used. In this case, the resource is essential in production, and substitution possibilities are non-existent. If there is no resource input, there is no output. Given the production function 4.6, the initial stock of the resource sets an upper limit to the amount that can be produced and consumed – total production over all time cannot exceed $\beta \bar{S}$. The intertemporal distribution problem is now that of sharing out use of the resource over time.

This is often called the 'cake-eating' problem. If the production function is 4.6, then clearly in the model where production possibilities are given by

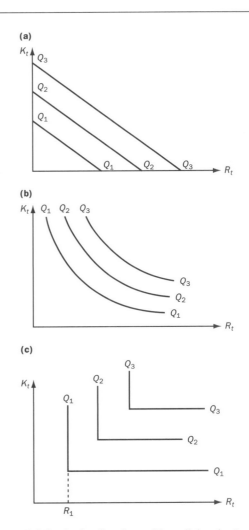

Figure 4.2 Production functions with capital and natural resource inputs

equations 4.2 to 4.4, the size of $\bar{S}$ sets an upper limit to the total amount that can be produced over all time. In this model there are no substitution possibilities, and there is no technical progress – when the resource runs out, production, and hence consumption, goes to zero. Basically, the intertemporal problem reduces to optimally sharing the stock of the resource as between those alive at different points in time. The problem with the obviously 'fair' solution of equal shares is that $\bar{S}$ is finite, so that the infinite planning horizon embodied in equation 4.1 would mean that the equal shares are of size zero – a finite cake cannot be divided into an infinite number of pieces. If there is a resource that is always an essential input to production, and if there are no substitution possibilities for that resource, then the intertemporal problem reduces to making the resource last as long as possible by consuming, at each point in time, as little as is possible consistent with survival.

With equation 4.5 as production function, the case shown in panel a of Figure 4.2, the intertemporal problem posed by the use of a non-renewable resource in production is trivial – constant consumption for ever requires no special attention to the rate at which the resource is used. With equation 4.6 as production function, the case shown in panel c of Figure 4.2, the problem is insoluble – there is no pattern of resource use over time that can make constant consumption for ever feasible. The remark by Solow quoted above does not apply to either of these situations – in the former case conservation is unnecessary, in the latter case future generations would be interested in how much of the resource stock we left for them to use. In making this remark, Solow, like most economists, is assuming that substitution possibilities are somewhere between those of equations 4.5 and 4.6, so that the intertemporal distribution problem is non-trivial but soluble. He is assuming, that is, that while non-zero output requires non-zero resource input, capital can substitute for the resource in production.

Panel b in Figure 4.2 shows the isoquants for such a production function. They are drawn for

$$Q_t = K_t^\alpha R_t^\beta \quad \text{with } \alpha + \beta = 1 \qquad (4.7)$$

which is a Cobb–Douglas production function with constant returns to scale. For this production function it can be shown that if $\alpha > \beta$ then constant consumption for ever is feasible. Clearly, if in equation 4.7 R_t is set at 0, then Q_t is 0 – the resource is essential in production. However, given enough K, and $\alpha > \beta$, very high levels of output can be produced with very small levels of resource input, and there exists a programme of capital accumulation such that R_t never actually becomes 0 (it goes asymptotically to zero) and consumption can be maintained constant for ever.

The nature of this capital accumulation programme, which results from following the Hartwick

rule, is discussed in the next subsection. The important point from that subsection is that the Hartwick rule is necessary but not sufficient for sustainability as constant consumption where production essentially uses a non-renewable resource input. If the production function is equation 4.6, for example, following the Hartwick rule will not result in constant consumption for ever. Nor will it if the production function is equation 4.7 with $\alpha < \beta$. Most economists follow Solow in taking the view that, in fact, substitution possibilities are such that sustainability as constant consumption for ever (or at least for a very long time) is feasible, so that the Hartwick rule is of great practical policy relevance.

4.2.3   The Hartwick rule

John Hartwick (1977, 1978) sought to identify conditions under which constant consumption could be maintained indefinitely, given the essential use in production of input from a finite stock of a non-renewable resource. He assumed that production conditions were as in equations 4.2 to 4.4 here, with the production function taking the form of equation 4.7 with $\alpha > \beta$. In such conditions, he showed that constant consumption would be the outcome if a particular savings/investment rule, now known as 'the Hartwick rule', were followed in an economy where depletion of the resource satisfied the conditions for intertemporal efficiency. It has since been shown that the Hartwick rule 'works', i.e. leads to constant consumption, in more general settings where, for example, several types of non-renewable resource are being used in production, provided that all are being depleted efficiently. It needs to be emphasised that in all cases the Hartwick rule is necessary but not sufficient – following it will realise constant consumption only if intertemporal efficiency conditions are satisfied, and if sustainability as constant consumption is feasible, i.e. if the substitution possibilities as between capital and resources are great enough.

Here we discuss the Hartwick rule for the case where just one non-renewable resource is used in production. We assume that the intertemporal efficiency conditions are satisfied. The general nature of these conditions is introduced and explained in

Chapter 11, and Part IV deals at length with the way they apply to the exploitation of natural resources. For now we can say that assuming that they are satisfied in relation to our setting – use of a single non-renewable resource in production – is equivalent to assuming that the resource is extracted by perfectly competitive firms with perfect foresight, and that the economy as a whole is also perfectly competitive.

The Hartwick rule is that at every point in time the total rent arising in the resource extraction industry be saved and invested in reproducible capital. In terms of the model which is equations 4.2 to 4.4, the rule is that $\dot{K}$ must be equal to the total rents arising in the resource extraction industry. The unit rent is the difference between the price at which an extracted unit of the resource sells and the marginal cost of extraction. It is, essentially, the scarcity value of the resource, which as will be considered at length in Part IV, rises as the resource is depleted according to an efficient programme. Total rent is simply unit rent times the number of units extracted. As will be discussed in Chapter 19, it turns out that following the Hartwick rule means that the total value of the economy's stock of reproducible capital together with its stock of the non-renewable resource is held constant over time – as the value of the remaining stock of the resource declines, so the value of the stock of reproducible capital increases in compensating amount. The constant consumption level that goes with following the Hartwick rule can be thought of as being like the interest on this constant stock of total wealth.

4.2.4   Weak and strong sustainability

In some economic contributions to the sustainability literature a distinction is made between 'weak sustainability' and 'strong sustainability'. In fact, the point being made concerns differing views about the conditions that need to be met for the realisation of sustainability as constant consumption (or utility), rather than different conceptions or definitions of sustainability. 'Weak' is not a different kind of sustainability from 'strong'. Proponents of both weak and strong sustainability take constant consumption (or utility) to be what sustainability is. They differ

over what is necessary for its realisation, and the difference is actually about substitution possibilities. In terms of the production functions just considered, 'weak sustainabilists' judge that the state of the world is effectively captured by equation 4.7 with $\alpha > \beta$ (or equation 4.5 even), while 'strong sustainabilists' see equation 4.6 as being more relevant.

As developed in the literature, the weak versus strong sustainability debate makes extensive use of the notion of 'natural capital', which we now explain. Production potential at any point in time depends on the stock of productive assets available for use. This stock can be classified into human labour and all other productive resources. Now let us define the term 'capital' in a very broad sense, to include any economically useful stock, other than raw labour power. In this broad sense capital consists of:

(a) Natural capital: any naturally provided stock, such as aquifers and water systems, fertile land, crude oil and gas, forests, fisheries and other stocks of biomass, genetic material, and the earth's atmosphere itself. We have previously discussed, in Chapter 2, the services that the natural environment provides to the economy. Talking of 'natural capital' is a way of referring to the collectivity of the environmental assets from which all such services flow.

(b) Physical capital: plant, equipment, buildings and other infrastructure, accumulated by devoting part of current production to capital investment.

(c) Human capital: stocks of learned skills, embodied in particular individuals, which enhances the productive potential of those people.

(d) Intellectual capital: disembodied skills and knowledge. This comprises the stock of useful knowledge, which we might otherwise call the state of technology. These skills are disembodied in that they do not reside in particular individuals, but are part of the culture of a society. They reside in books and other cultural constructs, and are transmitted and developed through time by social learning processes.

If human-made capital is defined to be the sum of physical, human and intellectual capital, then the total stock of capital stock can be seen as consisting of two parts: natural and human-made capital. The latter is sometimes referred to as reproducible capital.

This way of classifying production inputs leads to writing the economy's production function in summary representative form as

$$Q = Q(L, K_N, K_H) \qquad (4.8)$$

where L represents labour, K_N natural capital and K_H human-made capital. Note that we have defined technology as part of K_H so that our formulation does not allow the function itself to change with changing technology. Within this framework, the difference between weak and strong sustainabilists turns on what they judge to be the extent of the substitution possibilities between K_N and K_H.

The operational difference is that proponents of strong sustainability argue that sustainability requires that the level of K_N be non-declining, while proponents of weak sustainability argue that it requires that it is the sum of K_N and K_H that must be non-declining. Clearly, going back to the previous subsection, Solow and Hartwick are weak sustainabilists. Most, but not all, economists are weak sustainabilists. Sustainability as non-declining K_N is the third concept distinguished in Table 4.2. In so far as their arguments can be cast within this framework, most, but not all, ecologists are strong sustainabilists – in effect, they judge the possibilities for substituting K_H for K_N to be rather limited.

Economists have tended to think about threats to sustainability as constant consumption mainly in terms of natural resource inputs to production and the possible exhaustion of the stocks of natural resources. It is in that context that their judgement that K_H can be substituted for K_N has to be understood. Historical experience does tend to support the idea that physical, human and intellectual capital accumulation can offset any problems arising as stocks of natural resources are depleted. It is also true that there are many opportunities for substitution as between particulars of the general class of natural resources – bauxite for copper, for example.

It is in regard to the life-support and amenity services that natural capital provides, as discussed in Chapter 2, that there appears to less ground for optimism about the extent to which human-made capital can be substituted for natural capital. As spacecraft have already demonstrated, it is possible to use K_H to provide necessary life-support services such as temperature control, breathable air, etc., but only on a small scale. It has yet to be demonstrated, or even seriously argued, that human-made capital could replace natural capital in providing life-support services for several billions of humans. In regard to amenity services, some take the view that a lack of contact with the natural environment is dehumanising, and would argue that in this context we should, as an ethical matter, regard the possibilities of K_H for K_N substitution as limited.

Clearly, the weak versus strong sustainability question is multi-faceted, and does not permit of firm precise answers, except in particular contexts. There is no answer to the general question: how far is K_H substitutable for K_N? And, in some particulars, the answer is as much a matter of taste and/or ethics as it is a matter of science and technology.

In terms of simple high-level policy advice, weak sustainabilists say do not let the size of the total stock of capital fall, while strong sustainabilists say do not let the size of the natural capital stock fall. In order to do either, it is necessary to be able to measure the size of the natural capital stock. It is not a homogeneous thing, but consists of many qualitatively different components. How, then, does one define a single-valued measure of the natural capital stock? How do we add two lakes and one forest into a single value for natural capital, for example? Anyone familiar with national income accounting will recognise this difficulty. National income accounts do have a single-valued measure of the quantity of output. To obtain this, weights are employed. For example, 2 cars plus 3 televisions would correspond to an output of 26 if we agreed to give each car a weight of 10 and each television a weight of 2 in the summation. For output of goods, an obvious weight to use is relative prices, and this is what is done in the national accounts.

But there are no obvious weights to use for aggregating individual items of natural capital. Prices do not exist for many items of natural capital and even where they do, there are many reasons why one would not be willing to accept them as correct reflections of 'true' values. If prices are to be used as weights, these prices will have to be imputed somehow or other. We will leave a discussion of how this might be done until Chapter 12 (on valuation of environmental goods and services) and Chapter 19 (on environmental accounting). However, to anticipate some conclusions we reach in those chapters, most economists would agree that no fully satisfactory method yet exists for valuing environmental resources, and some would argue that none could ever exist. This means that a criterion which says that the total stock of natural capital should not be allowed to fall comes up against the fundamental problem that there is no satisfactory method of measuring the total stock of natural capital. If the stock of natural capital cannot be measured, then the total capital stock cannot be measured.

Some strong sustainabilists argue for maintaining individually subsets of K_N. For example, a very strong version of the non-declining natural capital stock criterion is implied by UNESCO in its assertion that

> Every generation should leave water, air and soil resources as pure and unpolluted as when it came on earth. Each generation should leave undiminished all the species of animals it found on earth.

Such a criterion appears to be completely infeasible. Almost every form of human activity will have some adverse impact on the environment. For example, human impacts will lead to the loss of some species no matter how cautious and environmentally conscious is our behaviour. Advocates of the UNESCO position might respond by arguing that this criterion should not be taken too literally. It is not meant to imply that every single species, or that every particular narrowly defined category of natural capital, should suffer no loss in terms of quality or quality. Rather, the requirement applies to wider classes. Thus, some moist tropical forests might be allowed to decline if that is compensated for by an extension of natural temperate forest cover. But this form of defence is unsatisfactory: once some kind of substitutability is permitted between subsets of natural capital, why not just accept that the relevant object of interest – the thing to be defended, if you like – is the total stock of natural capital.

4.3   Ecologists on sustainability

Table 4.2 identified, as numbers 4 and 5, two concepts of sustainability that originated with ecologists. In this section we shall look at those two concepts, and at the related idea of the steady-state economy. We shall also make some observations on the general approach to policy that is frequently advocated by ecologists.

4.3.1   Sustainable yields

As discussed in Chapter 2, renewable resources are biotic populations – flora and fauna – where the stock existing at a point in time has the potential to grow by means of natural reproduction. If in any period the harvest of the resource taken into the economy is less than natural growth, stock size grows. If the harvest is larger than natural growth, stock size declines. If harvest is kept larger than natural growth over successive periods, the stock size will continuously fall and it may be harvested to extinction – renewable resources are 'exhaustible'. If the harvest is the same size as natural growth, stock size is constant and if harvest is always the same as natural growth, the resource can be used indefinitely at a constant rate. Such a harvest rate is often referred to as a 'sustainable yield', as, in the absence of exogenous shocks, it can be maintained, or sustained, indefinitely.

For many of those who come to natural resource management from an ecological background, it is obvious that the correct rate of harvest is a sustainable yield. It is generally understood that, other things being equal, natural growth varies with the size of the stock. The basic idea, to be explained in more detail in Chapter 17, is as follows. When the population is small it is underexploiting its environment and can grow quickly. As the population grows, so the growth rate declines, and goes to zero when the population is fully exploiting its environment. The absolute amount of growth – numbers of individuals, or mass – first increases, then levels off, then declines to zero. This is shown in Figure 4.3, where stock size, S, is measured along the horizontal axis and absolute growth, $G(S)$, is measured on the vertical axis. The curve for $G(S)$ is both the

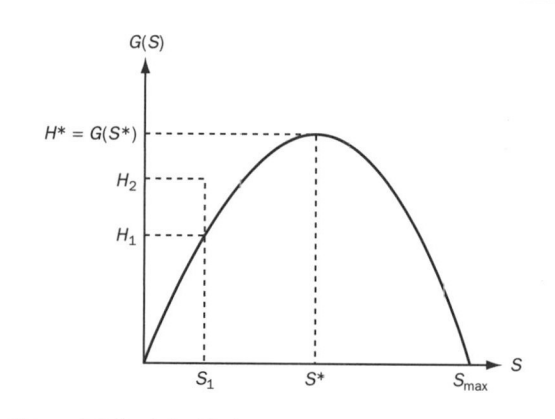

Figure 4.3 Sustainable harvests

graph for absolute growth and for sustainable harvests. Thus, for example, given stock size S_1, H_1 is the corresponding sustainable yield, while H_2 is larger than that and would reduce the stock size.

The maximum amount of growth, $G(S^*)$, occurs when the stock size is S^*, and the harvest that just takes the maximum amount of growth, H^*, is known as the 'maximum sustainable yield'. H^* is the largest harvest that is consistent with non-declining stock size and, hence, can be maintained indefinitely. For many ecologists, it is self-evident that the ideal rate of harvest for a renewable resource would be the maximum sustainable yield. As we shall see in Chapter 17, this is not necessarily the conclusion to which economic analysis leads, and, in fact, maximum-sustainable-yield harvesting is economically efficient only in very special circumstances. In some circumstances, it may not even be desirable, according to economic criteria, to harvest on a sustainable-yield basis.

Some ecologists take the view that sustainability is to be defined as a situation where all of the resource stocks exploited by the economy are harvested sustainably. Note that if this were done, the sizes of each of the resource stocks would be constant over time, and, in the language introduced in the previous section, natural capital would be being maintained intact. Note further that in such circumstances, the fact that it was being maintained intact would be unambiguous because each stock would itself be constant in size – there would be no need to use weights to aggregate across declining and increasing stocks.

Where an economy exploits non-renewable natural resources, as all modern economies do, this conceptualisation of sustainability runs into a major difficulty. For non-renewable resources, natural growth is zero, so that the only sustainable rate of harvest for a non-renewable resource is zero. One way round this difficulty that has been suggested is to require that as the stock of a non-renewable resource is run down, some of the proceeds arising are used to generate the capacity to provide substitutes for the resource. Thus, for example, the argument would be that as oil stocks are being depleted, some of the rent arising should be spent on research and development to make solar power available at low cost. If all renewables were being exploited on a sustainable-yield basis, and if the capacity to deliver a constant flow of the services based on non-renewable exploitation were being maintained, then, on this view, we could say that we were in a sustainable state. Note the similarities here with the economic conceptualisation that is sometimes referred to as 'weak sustainability' – feasibility requires sufficient substitutability, and realisation requires the appropriate savings and investment behaviour.

4.3.2　Resilience

Ecological science looks at its subject matter within a systems perspective. The whole system – the biosphere – consists of an interlocking set of ecological subsystems or ecosystems. Systems analysts are concerned with organisational characteristics and structure, and with systems dynamics – processes of evolution and change.

Ecologists look at sustainability from the point of view of an ecological system of which humans are just one part. Sustainability is assessed in terms of the extent to which the prevailing structure and properties of the ecosystem can be maintained. Human interests are not regarded as paramount; rather, they are identified with the continuing existence and functioning of the biosphere in a form more or less similar to that which exists at present. Thus:

> Sustainability is a relationship between human
> economic systems and larger dynamic, but normally
> slower-changing, ecological systems in which 1)

human life can continue indefinitely, 2) human individuals can flourish, and 3) human cultures can develop; but in which effects of human activities remain within bounds, so as not to destroy the diversity, complexity, and function of the ecological life support system.

(Costanza et al., *1991, p. 8)*

Ecological views are often more human-centred, anthropocentric, than is made explicit in their advocacy. There is generally a presumption, often implicit, that the present system structure, including the important place in it occupied by humans, is to be preferred to others. To confirm that this is so, consider the attitude an ecologist might take to the threat of global warming. If large-scale global warming were to occur, there is a high probability that major ecosystem change would occur. The biosphere would not cease to operate, of course – it would just operate in a different way. We guess that nearly all ecologists would take a stand against global warming, and most would do so on the grounds that human life is more threatened in a changed ecosystem than in the present one. Some non-human species would be much more favoured in a biosphere operating in substantially different ways from that which it currently does.

In this spirit, Common and Perrings (1992) argue that ecological sustainability is a prerequisite for the sustainability of the joint environment–economy system, and that ecological sustainability requires resilience. The concept of resilience was introduced in Chapter 2. We can say that an ecosystem is resilient if it maintains its functional integrity in the face of exogenous disturbance. Common and Perrings show that satisfying the conditions for intertemporal economic efficiency (which are set out in detail in Chapter 11 here) and following the Hartwick rule is neither necessary nor sufficient for sustainability as resilience. An economy–environment system could, that is, be sustainable in their sense without satisfying those conditions, and, on the other hand, an economy which satisfied those conditions could be unsustainable in their sense. Basically, the problem is that the economic conditions reflect individuals' preferences – they derive from consumer sovereignty – and there is no reason to suppose that those preferences reflect the requirements of resilience.

As noted in Chapter 2, while we are able to observe whether a system is resilient after a disturbance has taken place, *ex ante* we cannot know whether a system will be resilient in the face of future shocks that it will be subject to. Further, we do not know what form those future shocks will take. We do know that a system could be resilient in the face of a shock of one sort, but not in the face of one of a different sort. Uncertainty pervades the behaviour of ecological systems, ensuring that we cannot know in advance whether some system is or is not resilient.

Some authors have suggested that some indicators are useful as monitoring devices: they can be used to make inferences about potential changes in the degree of resilience of ecosystems in which we are interested. Schaeffer *et al.* (1988) propose a set of indicators, including:

- changes in the number of native species;
- changes in standing crop biomass;
- changes in mineral micronutrient stocks;
- changes in the mechanisms of and capacity for damping oscillations.

Suggestive as these and other indicators might be, none can ever be a completely reliable instrument in the sense that a satisfactory rating can be taken as a guarantee of resilience. We return to the question of sustainability indicators, mainly from an economic perspective, in Chapter 19.

4.3.3 The steady-state economy

Writing in the early 1970s, prior to the emergence of the concepts of 'sustainability' and 'sustainable development', Herman Daly argued for the idea of the 'steady-state economy' (see, for example, Daly, 1973, 1974). Daly's arguments are based on the laws of thermodynamics, and his steady-state economy has much in common with Boulding's 'Spaceship Earth', considered in Box 1.1 in Chapter 1.

Recall that in Boulding's spaceship economy, perpetual reproducibility of the economic–physical system (the spaceship) requires that a steady state be achieved in which the waste flows from production and consumption are equated with the system's recycling capacity. Reproducibility of the spaceship

Box 4.2 Herman Daly: the steady-state economy

In his article 'The economics of the steady state' (1974), Daly begins by defining his concept of a steady-state economy:

> A steady-state economy is defined by constant stocks of physical wealth (artifacts) and a constant population, each maintained at some chosen, desirable level by a low rate of throughput – i.e., by low birth rates equal to low death rates and by low physical production rates equal to low physical depreciation rates, so that longevity of people and durability of physical stocks are high. The throughput flow, viewed as the cost of maintaining the stocks, begins with the extraction (depletion) of low entropy resources at the input end, and terminates with an equal quantity of high entropy waste (pollution) at the output end. The throughput is the inevitable cost of maintaining the stocks of people and artifacts and should be minimized subject to the maintenance of a chosen level of stocks.
>
> Daly (1974), p. 15

The ultimate benefit of economic activity is the services (want satisfaction) yielded by the stocks of artefacts and people. Conventional indicators of economic performance measure the wrong thing: instead of measuring service flows, GDP and the like measure throughputs. But there is no longer any reason to believe that these two will be closely correlated, or have a stable relationship over time.

It is possible to make progress in the steady state through two types of efficiency improvement: either by maintaining a given stock level with less throughput, or by obtaining more services per unit of time from the same stock. Unfortunately, the fundamental laws of thermodynamics imply that these two forms of efficiency gain are likely to be unobtainable in the long term; we are condemned to efficiency losses, not gains. The main reason for this arises from the fact that

> as better grade (lower entropy) sources of raw materials are used up, it will be necessary to process ever larger amounts of materials using ever more energy and capital equipment to get the same quantity of needed mineral.

Daly notes that a choice must be made about the level of stocks in the steady state. Selecting from the large number of feasible stock levels is a difficult choice problem, involving economic, ecological and ethical principles. We will never be able to identify an optimal stock level and so, as a matter of practice, should learn to be stable at or near to existing stock levels.

Ultimately there is no real choice over whether to seek a steady state. If the economic subsystem is not to eventually disrupt the functioning of the larger system of which it is a part, then at some point the economy will have to be run in a steady state. Daly does not claim that the steady state is infinitely sustainable. Indeed, his view is quite the opposite:

> Thus a steady state is simply a strategy for good stewardship, for maintaining our spaceship and permitting it to die of old age rather than from the cancer of growthmania.

The necessary ultimate demise of the system arises from the irresistible force of increasing entropy. Daly pours particular scorn upon those economists who see substitution as the salvation of perpetual growth. Conventional economists envisage a sequence of substitution effects; as one input becomes relatively scarce, it will be replaced by another that is less relatively scarce. The possibility of absolute scarcity is assumed away in this approach. But, for Daly,

> Substitution is always of one form of low entropy matter–energy for another. There is no substitute for low entropy itself, and low entropy is scarce, both in its terrestrial source (finite stocks of concentrated fossil fuels and minerals) and in its solar source (a fixed rate of inflow of solar energy).

Technology does not offer the solution to perpetual economic growth that is often claimed. All technologies obey the logic of thermodynamics, and so we cannot appeal to any technology to wrench us from the grasp of the entropy principle. (See the epigraph at the start of this chapter.)

as a functioning system over time implies that waste flows cannot be ejected into outer space through the air lock, as that would lead to a gradual depletion of the material resource base upon which the space-ship is reliant. As the maximum recycling capacity of the system is determined by the (constant) flow of incoming energy that can be harnessed from extra-terrestrial sources, so there must be in this steady state a maximum rate of sustainable materials usage in the economy.

Daly's steady-state economy, described in Box 4.2, is similar, and he sometimes refers to it as a 'spaceship'. Although included in this section about ecologists, Daly was trained – as was Boulding – as an economist. Daly was greatly influenced by Georgescu-Roegen (see Chapter 2), who started has academic career as a physicist before becoming an economist and introducing his new colleagues to the laws of thermodynamics and their economic implications. Boulding, Georgescu-Roegen and Daly could all be regarded as ecological economists, in that their main concern is with the implications for economics of the fact that the economy and the environment are interdependent systems, the joint behaviour of which is subject to the laws of nature. This determines the conceptions of sustainability that emerge from their work. Note that, as indicated in Box 4.2, Daly explicitly addresses the substitution question. Like most of those who approach substitutability from an ecological perspective, and in contrast to most economists, Daly sees limited prospects for the substitution of human for natural capital. Hence the argument for the preservation of the latter. The ecological approach to sustainability is basically of the 'strong' variety.

4.3.4   A cautious approach

As well as taking it that the ability of human-made capital to substitute for natural capital is limited, the ecological approach to sustainability is characterised by an insistence that, as noted above in discussing sustainability as resilience, our ability to predict the ecological consequences of our behaviour is highly imperfect. Our understanding of how natural systems function is very incomplete, and in thinking about how to manage them in our interests we have to recognise that there is great uncertainty. Given this, ecologists generally argue for a cautious approach to environmental policy. It is not that the economic approach ignores the fact of imperfect knowledge about the future consequences of current action. It does not. As we shall see later, and in Chapter 13 especially, economists have spent a lot of time thinking about how to deal with the problem of imperfect future knowledge.

However, in conceptualising the sustainability problem and considering policy responses to it, ecologists have tended to give uncertainty a more

central role than have most economists. Ecologists – again using the term widely for those coming at the problem from a natural science rather than an economics perspective – have, for example, advocated the precautionary principle. According to it, there should be a presumption against any action which may have adverse environmental impacts, and it should be necessary to show convincingly that such impacts will not occur before the action is permitted. A closely related idea is that of the safe minimum standard. According to it, actions that may entail irreversible adverse environmental impacts should not be undertaken unless it can be shown that this, not undertaking the action, would give rise to unacceptably large social costs. We shall discuss the precautionary principle and the safe minimum standard, and other matters relating to uncertainty, in Chapter 13.

4.4   The institutional conception

The sixth concept of sustainability listed in Table 4.2 involved consensus building and institutional development. This sort of view of sustainability is found mainly in the writings of political scientists and sociologists, though, of course, economists and ecologists do recognise that sustainability is a problem with social, political and cultural dimensions. This view focuses on processes, rather than looking at outcomes or constraints as do the economic and ecological approaches.

A good example of this school of thought is to be found in a recent paper by de Graaf *et al.* (1996, p. 214). In this paper, sustainable development is defined in two ways. First, as

> development of a socio-environmental system with a high potential for continuity because it is kept within economic, social, cultural, ecological and physical constraints.

and second, as

> development on which the people involved have reached consensus.

The first definition is described by the authors as 'formal but not operational', the second as 'procedural, but does not guarantee stability'. De Graaf *et al.* begin from the premise that one cannot separate environmental objectives – such as avoiding environmental catastrophes – from other social and political objectives, such as the elimination of poverty. It is therefore very much in the spirit of the Brundtland report (WCED, 1987), discussed in Chapter 2. The authors consider that conventional approaches to sustainable development are fundamentally flawed by information problems and by their failure to address issues of political will and feasibility.

They classify conventional approaches as:

1. recognising that human societies are parts of ecosystems, determining the carrying capacity of those ecosystems, and then legislating to prevent human activity exceeding carrying capacities;
2. conceptualising environmental decline as external costs, evaluating these costs in monetary terms, and then using a price mechanism to internalise these costs.

They argue that the first strategy is not sufficient because its success is dependent on persuading citizens, especially in their role as voters, of the need to respect carrying capacities. It is also flawed because carrying capacities are unknown (and are probably unknowable – see our earlier remarks on uncertainty). Further, carrying capacities are not technical data but depend on human choices. To quote de Graaf *et al.* on this:

> Summing up, it is difficult or impossible to prove that environmental limits exist and, if they do, what they are. It is perhaps even more difficult to convince people to respect those limits and to provide strategies for doing so. One could say that this strategy overestimates our knowledge of human carrying capacity and underestimates the importance of socio-economic factors.
>
> *(de Graaf* et al.*, 1996, p. 208)*

They argue that the second of the conventional approaches, which is basically that of economists, is also of limited usefulness for similar reasons, and ultimately because it 'overestimates the possibilities of pricing under difficult social circumstances' (p. 209). In arriving at this claim, they argue that some values are unpriceable, giving as examples cultural development, nature conservation and landscape

planning. We will be discussing the issues that this argument raises in Chapters 11 and 12.

In proposing a new strategy, de Graaf *et al.* urge that we do not view the attainment of sustainability as simply a technical problem. Fundamental limits to our ability to know the consequences of human behaviour mean that it is futile to look for necessary or sufficient conditions for sustainability. De Graaf *et al.* take a different tack altogether, proposing consensus-building through negotiations. It is our success in building a consensus about what should and should not be done that is their criterion of sustainability. The notion of negotiation that they have in mind is very broad, referring to an institutional process of social choice that involves people as widely as possible, and involves a process of trade-offs in which all benefit from the avoidance of environmental disturbances. It is not yet clear, however, exactly what this negotiation process will consist of. According to de Graaf *et al.*, research should be focused on the structure and management of these negotiations, and on the supply of relevant information about preventable problems and steerable development.

4.5   Sustainability and policy

The different conceptualisations of sustainability discussed in the previous section should not be seen as mutually exclusive. Rather, we have a situation where people from differing academic disciplines are trying to state what they see as the essence of a very complicated problem. The problem involves the subject matter of the natural as well as the social sciences. The various conceptions should be regarded as complementary rather than competitive. In this final section of the chapter, we will briefly review some of the general lessons about policy that such a synthetic approach yields. The rest of the book is mainly about working through the economic approach to dealing with the interdependencies between humans and nature which are the origin of the sustainability problem.

Our particular observations on policy can be conveniently classified as relating to incentives, information and irreversibility. Before looking at each of these in turn, it will be useful to make some general observations on the role of the models of economic theory in relation to policy analysis. Similar observations could be made about ecological theory and models, but this is primarily a book about economics.

4.5.1 Economic models and policy prescription

In order to illustrate the role of abstract modelling let us consider again the derivation of the Hartwick rule. The starkest setting for the sustainability problem is one where an economy has a fixed quantity of some non-renewable resource, the recycling of which is impossible. Suppose that consuming this resource directly is the only source of human utility. What is the largest constant rate of consumption of this stock that is feasible over indefinite time? The answer must be zero, because of the finiteness of the stock. The situation here is the same as that discussed above – the cake-eating model – where the resource is essential in production and cannot be substituted for at all.

Now suppose that the resource stock is not consumed directly, but is an input, together with human-made capital, into the production process: the output of this production process can be either consumed or accumulated as capital. Let us now re-pose the question: what is the largest constant rate of consumption in this economy that is feasible over indefinite time? The analysis of this model shows that under certain conditions, the answer is no longer zero; some positive amount of consumption can be maintained in perpetuity. What conditions are required to obtain this result?

The first condition concerns, as discussed above, substitutability between the resource and human capital: these two inputs must be substitutable for one another in a particular way. What is required is that as the resource is depleted, so the physical capital stock can be accumulated so as to substitute for the resource in the production process in such a way that there is always enough output to hold consumption constant and provide the necessary investment.

The second condition is that the resource be extracted according to an efficient programme. We shall define and explain exactly what is meant by an efficient programme in Chapters 11 and 14. Basically it means a programme which is such that there is no waste in the sense that the use over time of the resource could be changed so as to increase output at one time without decreasing it at another time.

The third condition is the Hartwick rule, which concerns the rate at which capital is accumulated. This rule requires that the rents arising in resource extraction should be saved and invested. If constant consumption indefinitely is feasible – condition 1 – and if the extraction programme is efficient – condition 2 – then following the Hartwick rule will mean that consumption is constant indefinitely. Lying behind this result is a very simple idea: given substitutability and efficiency, the savings rule implies that a compensating increase in the stock of reproducible capital is taking place. The Hartwick rule ensures that an aggregate measure of capital is being maintained at a constant level.

Clearly, strong assumptions are required for the Hartwick rule to 'work'. Since not all of these conditions will be met in practice, one might argue that the practical usefulness of this rule is very limited. However, this is not really the way in which to appraise the value of this model. On the contrary, its value lies in forcing us to think about the important roles that substitutability and efficiency play.

In practice in an economy that exploits a non-renewable resource there is no guarantee that following the Hartwick rule will ensure that consumption will not decline over time, because the actual economy is not identical to the economy in Hartwick's model. However, there are very good grounds for believing that if the rule were adopted sustainable outcomes would be more likely than if the rule were not adopted. What is clear is that if sustainability as constant consumption is feasible, and the Hartwick rule is not followed – with the rent used for consumption rather than investment – then sustainability as constant consumption will not be realised and eventually consumption must decline. It does make sense to argue as a practical matter that as the resource is depleted, human-made capital should be accumulated to compensate for the diminishing resource base. Once the model has been used to derive the rule, it is clear that it is an intuitively appealing practical guide to prudent behaviour; this is explored further in Chapter 19.

How could the Hartwick rule be implemented? The required level of accumulation of capital would only be forthcoming in a market economy if all decision makers used a particular socially optimal discount rate. As this will almost certainly not happen in any actual market economy, another mechanism would be required. To bring forth the optimal amount of savings over time, government could tax resource rents, and invest the proceeds in human-made capital. Taxing resource rents turns out to be fairly difficult, as they are often not easily identified. Devising the tax regime which would do the job is a matter for those with detailed knowledge of the extraction industry, not for economic theorists concerned about sustainability. However, it is also the case that without the work of economic theorists such as John Hartwick, it would not have been known what task those specialist tax designers should be set.

The economic models used to analyse sustainability issues are generally abstract analytical constructs. Herein lie both the strength and the weakness of much of the conventional economics contribution to sustainability. Analytical models can sharpen our insights, and force us to think about what is crucial in any problem. Beginning with a set of assumptions, we can often deduce very powerful general conclusions. But these rarely take a form that is immediately applicable to detailed policy prescription. The case of the Hartwick rule also illustrates another important point. The deductions from a model are dependent on the particular assumptions built into it. These assumptions are not usually based on concrete descriptions of conditions that actually prevail, but are idealised mental constructs, and may be inappropriate as such. Following the savings and investment policy that is the Hartwick rule will only produce sustainability as constant consumption if that is feasible. As we have noted, some argue that it is not generally appropriate to assume that kind of substitutability. The modelling that leads to the Hartwick rule identifies substitutability as a key issue, but it does not resolve the issue.

4.5.2 Incentives

One way in which economists have used abstract analytical models is to show that, given certain conditions, selfish individual behaviour operating through a system of markets will, in some sense, serve the general social interest. The point of this kind of economic theorising is not to argue that everything should be left to market forces. On the contrary, the point is to identify precisely the conditions which need to be satisfied if markets are to work properly, and on the basis of that to map out, in general terms, the sorts of policy interventions necessary to improve their performance where those conditions are not satisfied. Chapter 5 sets out the conditions under which markets work to serve the general interest, and explains the sense in which they do that.

The sense in which they serve the general interest is that, given ideal circumstances, they bring about efficient outcomes. An efficient outcome is a situation where no individual can be made better off except at the cost of making some other individual(s) worse off. It is in this sense that efficiency means that there is no waste. However, markets do not, even given ideal circumstances, necessarily bring about outcomes that are fair. An efficient market outcome could involve major inequalities between individuals. To appreciate this point imagine two individuals sharing a fixed amount of something. So long as the two shares exhaust the supply, any allocation is efficient, including, for example, one where A gets 99% and B gets 1%.

As we shall see in Chapter 5, and subsequently, as regards many of the services provided by the natural environment, the ideal circumstances necessary for market incentives to lead to efficient outcomes are not satisfied. With regard to environmental services, we often get 'market failure' – in the absence of corrective policy, market-based incentives send the wrong signals to firms and individuals. Much of environmental and resource economics, and hence of the rest of this book, is about the analysis of market failure and of corrective policies. It is important to be clear, and we shall spend some time on this in what follows, that policy to correct market failure will, if successful, bring about efficiency, but will not, unless accompanied by other measures, necessarily bring about fairness.

Chapter 5 looks at these matters in terms of allocations at a point in time – it is concerned with intratemporal efficiency and fairness. Chapter 11 is concerned with allocations over time – with intertemporal efficiency and fairness. As we shall see in Chapter 11, the point just made about markets and intratemporal allocation carries over to markets and intertemporal allocation. We can, that is, postulate circumstances in which markets promote intertemporal efficiency, but there is no reason to suppose that they serve the cause of intertemporal fairness. Actually, we have already encountered some analysis which illustrates this point when looking at a model where a non-renewable resource is used in production. In the previous chapter we saw, see panel b of Figure 3.6, that 'optimal growth' in such a model would involve consumption declining in the long term. Given various assumptions, it can be shown that a market system would follow this optimal-growth path. In this chapter, we have seen that in this kind of model it is necessary to impose a constraint – the Hartwick rule – on behaviour to achieve intertemporal justice as constant consumption. Efficiency here is necessary but not sufficient for the fairness that is embodied in the concept of sustainability as constant consumption.

As we shall see, most economic analysis leads to the conclusion that this is generally the case – sustainability requires that market failure is corrected (using the sorts of instruments that we shall be discussing in detail in what follows), but correcting market failure does not in itself ensure sustainability. Purely self-interested behaviour driven by market forces will not succeed in moving economies very far towards sustainability unless additional incentives are provided to steer that behaviour in appropriate directions. Attempts to show that 'green' behaviour can be privately profitable tend to rely on evidence that is both anecdotal and selective. As we show repeatedly in later chapters, there are strong grounds for believing that, in the absence of policy interventions, financial incentives typically work in the opposite direction: environmentally responsible behaviour is costly, and individuals have incentives to pass costs on to others. It is often, for example, in the interests of individual harvesters of renewable resources to maximise current rates of harvest rather than to manage the resource on a sustainable basis. The fishing industry throughout the world provides one clear example of the last-mentioned point. This is discussed in Chapter 17.

As will be explained in Chapter 5, a necessary condition for an uncontrolled system of markets to properly promote social welfare is that all of the things that affect it are the subject of private property rights. This is because in the absence of such rights economic agents will not be made to face all of the costs that their actions entail, so that they do not face the proper incentives. Many of the services that the natural environment provides are such that they are not privately owned. In that case, government can seek to alter individuals' incentives by direct regulation or by taxes/subsidies. This is equivalent to establishing collective ownership, or property rights. Many economists argue that an alternative, and superior, approach is to legislate private property rights, and then let the market work to control the use of the environmental services at issue. In some cases this alternative is feasible, but in others it is not, in which case there is a need for ongoing governmental intervention in the market system. The creation of the necessary incentives for the proper use of environmental services under common ownership, will have an important part to play in any programme for sustainable development.

4.5.3 Information

The prospects for sustainable development will be enhanced if pollution flows are reduced, recycling is encouraged, and more attention is given to the regulation, management and disposal of waste. How can this be achieved? One school of thought argues that information is of central importance. Businesses sometimes seem able to increase profitability by behaving in environmentally friendly ways, and consumers sometimes appear to give preference to sellers with good environmental credentials. It is easy to find examples to support such claims. Consider the Dow Chemical Corporation: this organisation, by refining its method of synthesising agricultural chemicals at its Pittsburg (California) plant, reduced its demand for a key reactant by 80%, eliminated 1000 tons of waste annually, and reduced costs by $8 million per year (Schmidheiny, 1992, p. 268). Much has also been made of the power that the green consumer can have in altering producer behaviour (see Smart, 1992, for one example).

Proponents of the view that self-interest will stimulate environmentally friendly behaviour sometimes argue that the potential of this is limited only by the amount of relevant information that consumers and producers possess. On this view, environmental problems largely reflect ignorance; if that ignorance were to be overcome by improving the quality of information flows, much progress could be made towards sustainable economic behaviour.

An example of the role that can be played by information is given by the US Toxics Release Inventory (TRI). In 1986, the US government enacted legislation which required businesses to quantify their emissions of any of the 313 toxic substances covered by the TRI. The public exhibition of this information, no doubt linked with fears of possible future control, has served as a powerful incentive on firms to revise their production processes, and many large firms have voluntarily committed themselves to very demanding clean-up targets. Similar disclosure schemes are planned or are in operation in the European Union, Canada, Australia and India (Sarokin, 1992; WWF, 1993; *Business Week*, 1991).

While the provision of better information may assist environmental protection, there is no guarantee that it will do so. As already noted, private incentives are not necessarily consistent with environmentally friendly behaviour, and improved information flows will be of no help if private interests conflict with the promotion of social welfare. In the absence of the right incentives, the argument that better information will lead decision makers to behave in more socially responsive ways may be wishful thinking.

A major vehicle for the dissemination of information is education. One often comes across arguments that government should educate its young citizens to be more aware of the impacts of human activities on the environment. Much the same kind of comments we made about the role of information apply to this argument. There is, however, one important difference. Education is not only about the dissemination of information. It is also one of the ways in which cultural values are developed and transmitted. One may believe that education should teach people to behave in certain ways, but if so, it is sensible to be clear that the role that education is being expected to play is one of socialisation rather than the provision of information *per se*.

A strong case can be made that generous funding and promotion of pure and applied research by the public sector will assist in the pursuit of sustainability goals. There are two points to be made here. First, the products of research are often what are known in economics as 'public goods'. This terminology is fully explained in Chapter 5. Here we can say that public goods have the characteristic that once provided they are available to all and that the provider cannot capture the full value of provision. The arising incentive structure is, as discussed in Chapter 5, such that public goods will tend to be under-provided (or not provided at all) by profit-seeking organisations operating in markets.

The second point is that research is likely to be valuable where environmental preservation is concerned. It can, for example, generate new pollution abatement technologies, contribute to economically viable methods of harnessing renewable energy flow resources, lead to organic substitutes for materials such as plastics currently derived from crude oil, and produce crop varieties that can more easily tolerate environmental stresses. The public provision of many kinds of research activity is likely to be important in the pursuit of sustainability.

4.5.3.1 Environmental accounting

If sustainability is a social goal, then it would seem necessary to have in place a system for collecting and publishing information about whether or not the goal is being achieved. Currently, such systems are not generally in place, and the sustainability literature contains many contributions suggesting 'sustainability indicators' of various kinds. Chapter 19 is an extended discussion of the nature and role of various kinds of sustainability indicators. Here we can just note the two basic approaches.

The first is based upon the idea of modifying national income accounting conventions and practices so that what gets measured is sustainable national income, which is the highest level of consumption that can be maintained indefinitely. A variant of this approach involves measuring and reporting 'genuine saving' as conventionally defined saving and investment minus the monetary value of the depletion of the stock of natural resources. Since that monetary value is to be measured as the size of the rents arising in extraction in the relevant period, negative genuine saving indicates that the Hartwick rule – save and invest an amount equal to depletion rents – is not being followed, so that it follows that behaviour is not consistent with sustainability requirements.

The second approach involves looking for indicators that directly and closely relate to whatever criteria of sustainability have been adopted. An example of this approach is the work of Schaeffer *et al.* (1988) noted above, which adopts a concept of sustainability based on ideas about resilience and proposes a set of indicators including:

- changes in the number of native species;
- changes in standing crop biomass;
- changes in mineral micronutrient stocks;
- changes in the mechanisms of and capacity for damping oscillations.

It needs to be noted again here that presenting new information does not in itself alter the incentives facing individual decision makers. However, it is widely argued that by drawing attention to the consequences of activities, or by putting these in sharper relief, requiring firms to provide the information on which national sustainability indicator measurements would be based may encourage behavioural changes. For example, many firms appear to have very poor procedures for recording quantities of waste flows, where they originate, how much cost is associated with waste controls and to which activity these costs can be attributed. More generally, environmental impacts and the costs of environmental management within firms are not usually adequately represented in a cost-accounting framework. Similarly, when legislative or administrative controls impose costs of environmental control on firms, these costs are not usually attributed to particular production processes, but are treated as general environmental management expenses. This hides the true costs of particular products and processes from managers, and undervalues the benefits to the firm of pollution-control programmes. An implication is that firms should be encouraged to develop cost-accounting procedures so that pollution-control costs and benefits can be evaluated at the level of

individual products and processes within the firm. Not only will this create correct signals for resource allocation decisions within the firm, but it will create a recording framework that will enable the government to more easily and accurately compile national accounts that pay due attention to environmental impacts of economic activity. As noted, the final chapter, 19, of this book will examine such national accounting procedures.

The pursuit of sustainability can also be helped by encouraging firms to adopt what are sometimes called 'green design principles', which would build on better information. The objective of green design is to minimise the environmental impact of a product though its life cycle without compromising the product's performance or quality. Green design can be assisted by life-cycle assessment, a process which attempts to measure the total environmental impact of a product from its conception through to any effects that result from its final disposal (in whole or in parts) to the environment. Government can encourage firms to adopt green design by extending the legal liability of firms to all damages over the life cycle of the products that they sell (see Chapter 7 for a discussion of this policy instrument).

4.5.4   Irreversibility

If all resource-use decisions were reversible, then much of the force behind sustainability arguments would be lost. If we were to discover that present behaviour is unsustainable, then our decisions could be changed in whatever way and at whatever time was deemed appropriate. Reversibility implies that nothing would have been irretrievably lost.

But many decisions about the use of environmental services cannot be reversed, particularly those that involve the extraction of resources or the development of undisturbed ecosystems. When irreversibility is combined with imperfect knowledge of the future then optimal decision rules can change significantly. In these circumstances, there are good reasons for keeping options open and behaving in a relatively cautious manner (with a presumption against development built into each choice). Clearly, this has important implications for policy appraisal methods and rules, as we demonstrate in Chapter 13.

Summary

Economists typically conceptualise sustainability as constant, or non-declining, consumption (or utility). Given the use of a model where there is a single commodity, this is equivalent to sustainability as maintaining productive potential through time. Ecologists are more inclined to focus explicitly on the properties of the biosphere, such as resilience, than on human welfare. However, in effect, their approach is also anthropocentric and at the level of general objectives the approaches should be seen as complementary rather than competitive. Ecologists tend to be less optimistic than economists about the possibilities of substituting human-made for natural capital, so that at the level of particular objectives they tend to favour some variant of 'keep natural capital intact' whereas economists tend to favour 'keep total capital intact'. Ecologists tend, that is, to be 'strong sustainabilists' whereas economists tend to be 'weak sustainabilists'. Ecologists are more inclined to urge a cautious approach to policy objectives, and less inclined to rely on price incentives as policy instruments.

Further reading

Redclift (1992) examines a number of the dimensions within which the idea of sustainable development can be explored, as do Pezzey (1992, 1997), Barbier and Markandya (1990), Common (1995) and Lele (1991). Farmer and Randall (1997) present an overlapping generations model in which sustainability issues are examined. Van den Bergh and Hofkes (1999) review economic models of sustainable development, while Faucheux *et al.* (1996) contains a number of models representing differing disciplinary approaches. Good general surveys are presented in Barbier (1989a), Klassen and Opschoor (1991), Markandya and Richardson (1992), Toman *et al.* (1993), and Neumayer (1999) which has a very comprehensive bibliography. Beckerman (1994) argues that the concept of sustainability is not useful. The argument that policy should be directed towards maintaining a non-declining natural capital stock appears to have first been developed in Pearce and Turner (1990).

The ecological economics approach to sustainability is explored in various contributions to Köhn *et al.* (1999); see also Pearce (1987), Costanza (1991), Common and Perrings (1992), Goodland (1999) and Söderbaum (2000). Page (1997) compares two approaches to the problem of achieving the goals of sustainability and intergenerational efficiency.

Seminal economic contributions in the framework of the neoclassical growth model, are to be found in Solow (1974b, 1986) and Hartwick (1977, 1978); further references in this area will be given in Chapter 19. Historically interesting contributions from a more ecological perspective are Boulding (1966) and Daly (1974, 1977, 1987). Daly (1999) is a recent restatement of his position as set out in Box 4.2 here. An interesting assessment of the contribution of scientific understanding to the debate is to be found in Ludwig *et al.* (1993).

The original contribution arguing for a cautious approach to environmental conservation is Ciriacy-Wantrup (1968). As noted, we deal with issues of uncertainty and irreversibility in Chapter 13, where further references will be provided.

Discussion questions

1. To what extent are the ecologist's and the economist's concepts of sustainable behaviour mutually consistent?

2. Given that the question of the substitution possibilities as between human-made and natural capital is so important, how can the fact that we do not know the answer be explained?

3. Can you think of any incentives that you face that encourage you to behave in ways consistent with sustainability? Can you think of any that have the opposite effects? How could the latter be changed?

Problems

1. Find the marginal and average products of K and R for $Q = K^{\alpha} R^{\beta}$ with $\alpha + \beta = 1$. This is the Cobb–Douglas production function 4.7 for which panel b of Figure 4.2 is drawn. How do your results for the average and marginal products relate to the feasibility of indefinite constant consumption despite the fact that $Q = 0$ for $R = 0$?

2. Show that the equation

$$G(S) = g(1 - \{S/S_{max}\})S$$

gives the density-dependent growth shown in Figure 4.3, and that then S^* is equal to $\dfrac{S_{max}}{2}$, and express the maximum sustainable yield in terms of the parameters of the equation.

CHAPTER 5

Welfare economics and the environment

Welfare economics is the branch of economic theory which has investigated the nature of the policy recommendations that the economist is entitled to make.   **Baumol (1977), p. 496**

Learning objectives

In this chapter you will
- learn about the concepts of efficiency and optimality in allocation
- derive the conditions that are necessary for the realisation of an efficient allocation
- find out about the circumstances in which a system of markets will allocate efficiently
- learn about market failure and the basis for government intervention to correct it
- find out what a public good is, and how to determine how much of it the government should supply
- learn about pollution as an external effect, and the means for dealing with pollution problems of different kinds
- encounter the second-best problem

Introduction

When economists consider policy questions relating to the environment they draw upon the basic results of welfare economics. The purpose of this chapter is to consider those results from welfare economics that are most relevant to environmental policy problems. Efficiency and optimality are the two basic concepts of welfare economics, and this chapter explains these concepts as they relate to problems of allocation. There are two classes of allocation problem: static and intertemporal. Efficiency and optim-

ality are central to both. In this chapter we confine attention to the static problem – the allocation of inputs across firms and of outputs across individuals at a point in time. The intertemporal problem – allocation over time – is dealt with in Chapter 11. If you have previously studied a course in welfare economics, you should be able to read through the material of this chapter rather quickly. If not, the chapter will fill that gap.

There are three parts to this chapter. The first states and explains the conditions required for an allocation to be (a) efficient and (b) optimal. These conditions are derived without regard to any particular institutional setting. In the second part of the chapter, we consider how an efficient allocation would be brought about in a market economy characterised by particular institutions. The third part of the chapter looks at the matter of 'market failure' – situations where the institutional conditions required for the operation of pure market forces to achieve efficiency in allocation are not met – in relation to the environment.

PART 1 EFFICIENCY AND OPTIMALITY

In this part, and the next, of this chapter we will, following the usage in the welfare economics literature, use 'resources' to refer generally to inputs to production rather than specifically to extractions from the natural environment for use in production. In fact, in these parts of the chapter, when we talk about resources, or 'productive resources' we will have in mind, as we will often make explicit, inputs of capital and labour to production.

At any point in time, an economy will have access to particular quantities of productive resources. Individuals have preferences about the various goods that it is feasible to produce using the available resources. An 'allocation of resources', or just an 'allocation', describes what goods are produced and in what quantities they are produced, which combinations of resource inputs are used in producing those goods, and how the outputs of those goods are distributed between persons.

In this section, and the next, we make two assumptions that will be relaxed in the third part of this chapter. First, that no externalities exist in either consumption or production; roughly speaking, this means that consumption and production activities do not have unintended and uncompensated effects upon others. Second, that all produced goods and services are private (not public) goods; roughly speaking, this means that all outputs have characteristics that permit of exclusive individual consumption on the part of the owner.

In the interests of simplicity, but with no loss of generality, we strip the problem down to its barest essentials. Our economy consists of two persons (A and B); two goods (X and Y) are produced; and production of each good uses two inputs (K for capital and L for labour) each of which is available in a fixed quantity.

Let U denote an individual's total utility, which depends only on the quantities of the two goods that he or she consumes. Then we can write the utility functions for A and B in the form shown in equations 5.1:

$$U^A = U^A(X^A, Y^A)$$
$$U^B = U^B(X^B, Y^B)$$

(5.1)

The total utility enjoyed by individual A, denoted U^A, depends upon the quantities, X^A and Y^A, he or she consumes of the two goods. An equivalent statement can be made about B's utility.

Next, we suppose that the quantity produced of good X depends only on the quantities of the two inputs K and L used in producing X, and the quantity

produced of good Y depends only on the quantities of the two inputs K and L used in producing Y. Thus, we can write the two production functions in the form shown in 5.2:

$$X = X(K^X, L^X)$$
$$Y = Y(K^Y, L^Y)$$

(5.2)

Each production function specifies how the output level varies as the amounts of the two inputs are varied. In doing that, it assumes technical efficiency in production. The production function describes, that is, how output depends on input combinations, given that inputs are not simply wasted. Consider a particular input combination K_1^X and L_1^X with X_1 given by the production function. Technical efficiency means that in order to produce more of X it is necessary to use more of K^X and/or L^X.

The marginal utility that A derives from the consumption of good X is denoted U_X^A; that is, $U_X^A = \partial U^A/\partial X^A$. The marginal product of the input L in the production of good Y is denoted as MP_L^Y; that is, $MP_L^Y = \partial Y/\partial L^Y$. Equivalent notation applies for the other three marginal products.

The marginal rate of utility substitution for A is the rate at which X can be substituted for Y at the margin, or vice versa, while holding the level of A's utility constant. It varies with the levels of consumption of X and Y and is given by the slope of the indifference curve. We denote A's marginal rate of substitution as $MRUS^A$, and similarly for B.

The marginal rate of technical substitution as between K and L in the production of X is the rate at which K can be substituted for L at the margin, or vice versa, while holding the level output of X constant. It varies with the input levels for K and L and is given by the slope of the isoquant. We denote the marginal rate of substitution in the production of X as $MRTS_X$, and similarly for Y.

The marginal rates of transformation for the commodities X and Y are the rates at which the output of one can be transformed into the other by marginally shifting capital or labour from one line of production to the other. Thus, MRT_L is the increase in the output of Y obtained by shifting a small, strictly an infinitesimally small, amount of labour from use in the production of X to use in the production of Y, or vice versa. Similarly, MRT_K is the increase in the output of Y obtained by shifting a small, strictly an infinitesimally small, amount of capital from use in the production of X to use in the production of Y, or vice versa.

With this notation we can now state, and provide intuitive explanations for, the conditions that characterise efficient and optimal allocations. Appendix 5.1 uses the calculus of constrained optimisation (which was reviewed in Appendix 3.1) to derive these conditions formally.

5.1   Economic efficiency

An allocation of resources is said to be efficient if it is not possible to make one or more persons better off without making at least one other person worse off. Conversely, an allocation is inefficient if it is possible to improve someone's position without worsening the position of anyone else. A gain by one or more persons without anyone else suffering is known as a Pareto improvement. When all such gains have been made, the resulting allocation is sometimes referred to as Pareto optimal, or Pareto efficient. A state in which there is no possibility of Pareto improvements is sometimes referred to as being allocatively efficient, rather than just efficient, so as to differentiate the question of efficiency in allocation from the matter of technical efficiency in production.

Efficiency in allocation requires that three efficiency conditions are fulfilled – efficiency in consumption, efficiency in production, and product-mix efficiency.

5.1.1   Efficiency in consumption

Consumption efficiency requires that the marginal rates of utility substitution for the two individuals are equal:

$$MRUS^A = MRUS^B \qquad (5.3)$$

If this condition were not satisfied, it would be possible to rearrange the allocation as between A and B of whatever is being produced so as to make one better

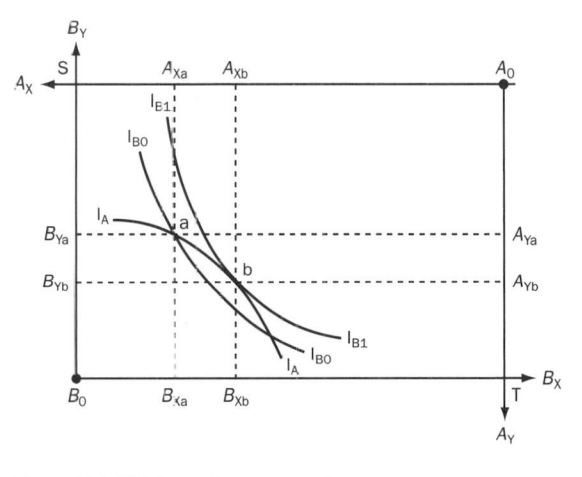

Figure 5.1 Efficiency in consumption

off without making the other worse off. Figure 5.1 shows what is involved by considering possible allocations of fixed amounts of X and Y between A and B.[1] The top right-hand corner, labelled A_0, refers to the situation where A gets nothing of the available X or Y, and B gets all of both commodities. The bottom left-hand corner, B_0, refers to the situation where B gets nothing and A gets everything. Starting from A_0 moving horizontally left measures A's consumption of X, and moving vertically downwards measures A's consumption of Y. As A's consumption of a commodity increases, so B's must decrease. Starting from B_0 moving horizontally right measures B's consumption of X, and moving vertically upwards measures B's consumption of Y. Any allocation of X and Y as between A and B is uniquely identified by a point in the box SA_0TB_0. At the point a, for example, A is consuming A_0A_{Xa} of X and A_0A_{Ya} of Y, and B is consuming B_0B_{Xa} of X and B_0B_{Ya} of Y.

The point a is shown as lying on I_AI_A, which is an indifference curve for individual A. I_AI_A may look odd for an indifference curve, but remember that it is drawn with reference to the origin for A which is the point A_0. Also shown are two indifference curves for B, $I_{B0}I_{B0}$ and $I_{B1}I_{B1}$. Consider a reallocation as between A and B, starting from point a and moving along I_AI_A, such that A is giving up X and gaining Y, while B is gaining X and giving up Y. Initially, this means increasing utility for B, movement onto a

---

[1]   This figure is an 'Edgeworth box'.

higher indifference curve, and constant utility for A. However, beyond point b any further such reallocations will involve decreasing utility for B. Point b identifies a situation where it is not possible to make individual B better off while maintaining A's utility constant – it represents an efficient allocation of the given amounts of X and Y as between A and B. At b, the slopes of $I_A I_A$ and $I_{B1} I_{B1}$ are equal – A and B have equal marginal rates of utility substitution.

5.1.2 Efficiency in production

Turning now to the production side of the economy, recall that we are considering an economy with two inputs, L and K, which can be used (via the production functions of equations 5.2) to produce the goods X and Y. Efficiency in production requires that the marginal rate of technical substitution be the same in the production of both commodities. That is,

$$\text{MRTS}_X = \text{MRTS}_Y \qquad (5.4)$$

If this condition were not satisfied, it would be possible to reallocate inputs to production so as to produce more of one of the commodities without producing less of the other. Figure 5.2 shows why this condition is necessary. It is constructed in a similar manner to Figure 5.1, but points in the box refer

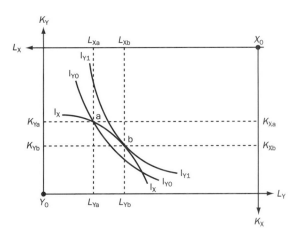

Figure 5.2 Efficiency in production

to allocations of capital and labour to the production of the two commodities rather than to allocations of the commodities between individuals.[2] At X_0 no capital or labour is devoted to the production of commodity X – all of both resources is used in the production of Y. Moving horizontally to the left from X_0 measures increasing use of labour in the production of X, moving vertically down from X_0 measures increasing use of capital in the production of X. The corresponding variations in the use of inputs in the production of Y – any increase/decrease in use for X production must involve a decrease/increase in use for Y production – are measured in the opposite directions starting from origin Y_0.

$I_X I_X$ is an isoquant for the production of commodity X. Consider movements along it to the 'southeast' from point a, so that in the production of X capital is being substituted for labour, holding output constant. Correspondingly, given the full employment of the resources available to the economy, labour is being substituted for capital in the production of Y. $I_{Y0} I_{Y0}$ and $I_{Y1} I_{Y1}$ are isoquants for the production of Y. Moving along $I_X I_X$ from a toward b means moving onto a higher isoquant for Y – more Y is being produced with the production of X constant. Movement along $I_X I_X$ beyond point b will mean moving back to a lower isoquant for Y. The point b identifies the highest level of production of Y that is possible, given that the production of X is held at the level corresponding to $I_X I_X$ and that there are fixed amounts of capital and labour to be allocated as between production of the two commodities. At point b the slopes of the isoquants in each line of production are equal – the marginal rates of technical substitution are equal. If these rates are not equal, then clearly it would be possible to reallocate inputs as between the two lines of production so as to produce more of one commodity without producing any less of the other.

5.1.3 Product-mix efficiency

The final condition necessary for economic efficiency is product-mix efficiency. This requires that

---

[2]   Appendix 5.1 establishes that all firms producing a given commodity are required to operate with the same marginal rate of technical substitution. Here we are assuming that one firm produces all of each commodity.

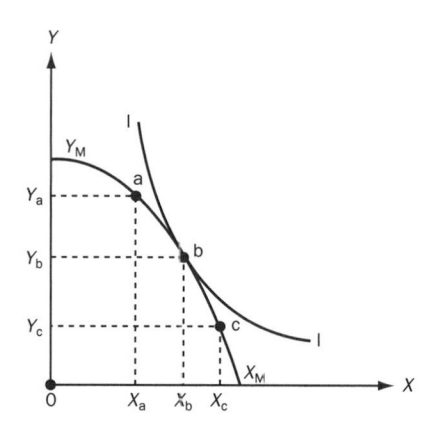

Figure 5.3 Product-mix efficiency

$$\text{MRT}_L = \text{MRT}_K = \text{MRUS}^A = \text{MRUS}^B \qquad (5.5)$$

This condition can be understood using Figure 5.3. Given that equation 5.3 holds, so that the two individuals have equal marginal rates of utility substitution and $\text{MRUS}^A = \text{MRUS}^B$, we can proceed as if they had the same utility functions, for which II in Figure 5.1 is an indifference curve with slope MRUS. The individuals do not, of course, actually have the same utility functions. But, given the equality of the MRUS, their indifference curves have the same slope at an allocation that satisfies the consumption efficiency condition, so we can simplify, without any real loss, by assuming the same utility functions and drawing a single indifference curve that refers to all consumers. Given that Equation 5.4 holds, when we think about the rate at which the economy can trade off production of X for Y and vice versa, it does not matter whether the changed composition of consumption is realised by switching labour or capital between the two lines of production. Consequently, in Figure 5.3 we show a single production possibility frontier, $Y_M X_M$, showing the output combinations that the economy could produce using all of its available resources. The slope of $Y_M X_M$ is MRT.

In Figure 5.3 the point a must be on a lower indifference curve than II. Moving along $Y_M X_M$ from point a toward b must mean shifting to a point on a higher indifference curve. The same goes for movement along $Y_M X_M$ from c toward b. On the other hand, moving away from b, in the direction of either a or c, must mean moving to a point on a lower

indifference curve. We conclude that a point like b, where the slopes of the indifference curve and the production possibility frontier are equal, corresponds to a product mix – output levels for X and Y – such that the utility of the representative individual is maximised, given the resources available to the economy and the terms on which they can be used to produce commodities. We conclude, that is, that the equality of MRUS and MRT is necessary for efficiency in allocation. At a combination of X and Y where this condition does not hold, some adjustment in the levels of X and Y is possible which would make the representative individual better off.

An economy attains a fully efficient static allocation of resources if the conditions given by equations 5.3, 5.4 and 5.5 are satisfied simultaneously. Moreover, it does not matter that we have been dealing with an economy with just two persons and two goods. The results readily generalise to economies with many inputs, many goods and many individuals. The only difference will be that the three efficiency conditions will have to hold for each possible pairwise comparison that one could make, and so would be far more tedious to write out.

5.2   An efficient allocation of resources is not unique

For an economy with given quantities of available resources, production functions and utility functions, there will be many efficient allocations of resources. The criterion of efficiency in allocation does not, that is, serve to identify a particular allocation.

To see this, suppose first that the quantities of X and Y to be produced are somehow given and fixed. We are then interested in how the given quantities of X and Y are allocated as between A and B, and the criterion of allocative efficiency says that this should be such that A/B cannot be made better off except by making B/A worse off. This was what we considered in Figure 5.1 to derive equation 5.3, which says that an efficient allocation of fixed quantities of X and Y will be such that the slopes of the indifference curves for A and B will be the same. In Figure 5.1 we showed just one indifference curve for A and

Box 5.1 Productive inefficiency in ocean fisheries

The total world marine fish catch increased steadily from the 1950s through to the late 1980s, rising by 32% between the periods 1976–1978 and 1986–1988 (UNEP, 1991). However, the rate of increase was slowing toward the end of this period, and the early 1990s witnessed downturns in global harvests. The harvest size increased again in the mid-1990s, was at a new peak in 1996, and then levelled off again in the late 1990s. It is estimated that the global maximum sustainable harvest is about 10% larger than harvest size in the late 1990s.

The steady increase in total catch until 1989 masked significant changes in the composition of that catch; as larger, higher-valued stocks became depleted, effort was redirected to smaller-sized and lower-valued species. This does sometimes allow depleted stocks to recover, as happened with North Atlantic herring, which recovered in the mid-1980s after being overfished in the late 1970s. However, many fishery scientists believe that these cycles of recovery have been modified, and that species dominance has shifted permanently towards smaller species.

Rising catch levels have put great pressure on some fisheries, particularly those in coastal areas, but also including some pelagic fisheries. Among the species whose catch declined over the period 1976–1988 are Atlantic cod and herring, haddock, South African pilchard and Peruvian anchovy. Falls in catches of these species have been compensated for by much increased harvests of other species, including Japanese pilchard in the north-west Pacific.

Where do inefficiencies enter into this picture? We can answer this question in two ways. First, a strong argument can be made to the effect that the total amount of resources devoted to marine fishing is excessive, probably massively so. We shall defer giving evidence to support this claim until Chapter 17 (on renewable resources), but you will see there that a smaller total fishing fleet would be able to catch at least as many fish as the present fleet does. Furthermore, if fishing effort were temporarily reduced so that stocks were allowed to recover, a greater steady-state harvest would be possible, even with a far smaller world fleet of fishing vessels. There is clearly an inefficiency here.

A second insight into inefficiency in marine fishing can be gained by recognising that two important forms of negative external effect operate in marine fisheries, both largely attributable to the fact that marine fisheries are predominantly open-access resources. One type is a so-called crowding externality, arising from the fact that each boat's harvesting effort increases the fishing costs that others must bear. The second type may be called an 'intertemporal externality': as fisheries are often subject to very weak (or even zero) access restrictions, no individual fisherman has an incentive to conserve stocks for the future, even if all would benefit if the decision were taken jointly.

As the concepts of externalities and open access will be explained and analysed in the third part of this chapter, and applied to fisheries in Chapter 17, we shall not explain these ideas any further now. Suffice it to say that production in market economies will, in general, be inefficient in the presence of external effects.

Sources: WRI (2000), WRI web site www.wri.org, FAO web site www.fao.org

---

two for B. But, these are just a small subset of the indifference curves for each individual that fill the box SA_0TB_0. In Figure 5.4 we show a larger subset for each individual. Clearly, there will be a whole family of points, like b in Figure 5.1, at which the slopes of the indifference curves for A and B are equal, at which they have equal marginal rates of utility substitution. At any point along CC in Figure 5.4, the consumption efficiency condition is satisfied. In fact, for given available quantities of X and Y there are an indefinitely large number of allocations as between A and B that satisfy $MRUS^A = MRUS^B$.

Now consider the efficiency in production condition, and Figure 5.2. Here we are looking at variations in the amounts of X and Y that are produced. Clearly, in the same way as for Figures 5.1 and 5.4, we could introduce larger subsets of all the possible isoquants for the production of X and Y to show that there are many X and Y combinations that satisfy equation 5.4, combinations representing uses of capital and labour in each line of production such that the slopes of the isoquants are equal, $MRTS_X = MRTS_Y$.

So, there are many combinations of X and Y output levels that are consistent with allocative efficiency,

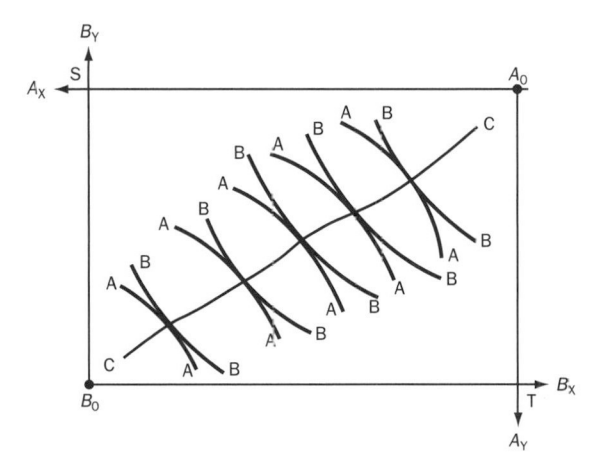

Figure 5.4 The set of allocations for consumption efficiency

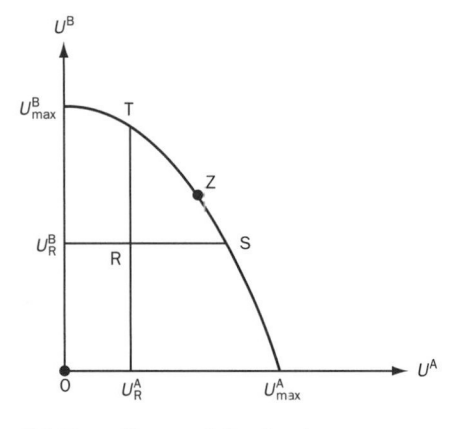

Figure 5.5 The utility possibility frontier

and for any particular combination there are many allocations as between A and B that are consistent with allocative efficiency. These two considerations can be brought together in a single diagram, as in Figure 5.5, where the vertical axis measures A's utility and the horizontal B's. Consider a particular allocation of capital and labour as between X and Y production which implies particular output levels for X and Y, and take a particular allocation of these output levels as between A and B – there will correspond a particular level of utility for A and for B, which can be represented as a point in U^A/U^B space, such as R in Figure 5.5. Given fixed amounts of capital and labour, not all points in U^A/U^B space are feasible. Suppose that all available resources were

used to produce commodities solely for consumption by A, and that the combination of X and Y then produced was such as to maximise A's utility. Then, the corresponding point in utility space would be U^A_{max} in Figure 5.5. With all production serving the interests of B, the corresponding point would be U^B_{max}. The area bounded by $U^A_{max}0U^B_{max}$ is the utility possibility set – given its resources, production technologies and preferences, the economy can deliver all combinations of U^A and U^B lying in that area. The line $U^A_{max}U^B_{max}$ is the utility possibility frontier – the economy cannot deliver combinations of U^A and U^B lying outside that line. The shape of the utility possibility frontier depends on the particular forms of the utility and production functions, so the way in which it is represented in Figure 5.5 is merely one possibility. However, for the usual assumptions about utility and production functions, it would be generally bowed outwards in the manner shown in Figure 5.5.

The utility possibility frontier is the locus of all possible combinations of U^A and U^B that correspond to efficiency in allocation. Consider the point R in Figure 5.5, which is inside the utility possibility frontier. At such a point, there are possible reallocations that could mean higher utility for both A and B. By securing allocative efficiency, the economy could, for example, move to a point on the frontier, such as Z. But, given its endowments of capital and labour, and the production and utility functions, it could not continue northeast beyond the frontier. Only U^A/U^B combinations lying along the frontier are feasible. The move from R to Z would be a Pareto improvement. So would be a move from R to T, or to S, or to any point along the frontier between T and S.

The utility possibility frontier shows the U^A/U^B combinations that correspond to efficiency in allocation – situations where there is no scope for a Pareto improvement. There are many such combinations. Is it possible, using the information available, to say which of the points on the frontier is best from the point of view of society? It is not possible, for the simple reason that the criterion of economic efficiency does not provide any basis for making interpersonal comparisons. Put another way, efficiency does not give us a criterion for judging which allocation is best from a social point of view. Choosing a point along the utility possibility frontier is about making moves that must involve making one individual worse off in order to make the other better off. Efficiency criteria do not cover such choices.

5.3   The social welfare function and optimality

In order to consider such choices we need the concept of a social welfare function, SWF, which was introduced in Chapter 3. A SWF can be used to rank alternative allocations. For the two-person economy that we are examining, a SWF will be of the general form:

$$W = W(U^A, U^B) \tag{5.6}$$

The only assumption that we make here regarding the form of the SWF is that welfare is non-decreasing in U^A and U^B. That is, for any given level of U^A welfare cannot decrease if U^B were to rise and for any given level of U^B welfare cannot decrease if U^A were to rise. In other words, we assume that $W_A = \partial W/\partial U^A$ and $W_B = \partial W/\partial U^B$ are both positive. Given this, the SWF is formally of the same nature as a utility function. Whereas the latter associates numbers for utility with combinations of consumption levels X and Y, a SWF associates numbers for social welfare with combinations of utility levels U^A and U^B. Just as we can depict a utility function in terms of indifference curves, so we can depict a SWF in terms of social welfare indifference curves. Figure 5.6 shows a social welfare indifference curve WW that has the same slope as the utility possibility frontier at b, which point identifies the combination of U^A and U^B that maximises the SWF.

The reasoning which establishes that b corresponds to the maximum of social welfare that is attainable should be familiar by now – points to the left or the right of b on the utility possibility frontier, such as a and c, must be on a lower social welfare indifference curve, and points outside of the utility possibility frontier are not attainable. The fact that the optimum lies on the utility possibility frontier means that all of the necessary conditions for efficiency must hold at the optimum. Conditions 5.3, 5.4 and 5.5 must be satisfied for the maximisation of

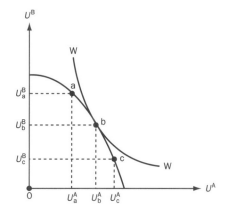

Figure 5.6 Maximised social welfare

welfare. Also, an additional condition, the equality of the slopes of a social indifference curve and the utility possibility frontier, must be satisfied. This condition can be stated, as established in Appendix 5.1, as

$$\frac{W_A}{W_B} = \frac{U_X^B}{U_X^A} = \frac{U_Y^B}{U_Y^A} \tag{5.7}$$

The left-hand side here is the slope of the social welfare indifference curve. The two other terms are alternative expressions for the slope of the utility possibility frontier. At a social welfare maximum, the slopes of the indifference curve and the frontier must be equal, so that it is not possible to increase social welfare by transferring goods, and hence utility, between persons.

While allocative efficiency is a necessary condition for optimality, it is not generally true that moving from an allocation that is not efficient to one that is efficient must represent a welfare improvement. Such a move might result in a lower level of social welfare. This possibility is illustrated in Figure 5.7. At C the allocation is not efficient, at D it is. However, the allocation at C gives a higher level of social welfare than does that at D. Having made this point, it should also be said that whenever there is an inefficient allocation, there is always some other allocation which is both efficient and superior in welfare terms. For example, compare points C and E. The latter is allocatively efficient while C is not, and E is on a higher social welfare indifference curve. The move from C to E is a Pareto improvement

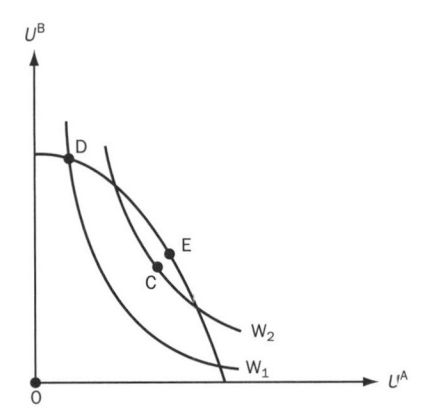

Figure 5.7 Welfare and efficiency

where both A and B gain, and hence involves higher social welfare. On the other hand, going from C to D replaces an inefficient allocation with an efficient one, but the change is not a Pareto improvement – B gains, but A suffers – and involves a reduction in social welfare. Clearly, any change which is a Pareto improvement must increase social welfare as defined here. Given that the SWF is non-decreasing in U^A and U^B, increasing U^A/U^B without reducing U^B/U^A must increase social welfare. For the kind of SWF employed here, a Pareto improvement is an unambiguously good thing (subject to the possible objections to preference-based utilitarianism noted in Chapter 3, of course). It is also clear that allocative efficiency is a good thing (subject to the same qualification) if it involves an allocation of commodities as between individuals that can be regarded as fair. Judgements about fairness, or equity, are embodied in the SWF in the analysis here. If these are acceptable, then optimality is an unambiguously good thing. In Part 2 of this chapter we look at the way markets allocate resources and commodities. To anticipate, we shall see that what can be claimed for markets is that, given ideal institutional arrangements and certain modes of behaviour, they achieve allocative efficiency. It cannot be claimed that, alone, markets, even given ideal institutional arrangements, achieve what might generally or reasonably be regarded as fair allocations. Before looking at the way markets allocate resources, we shall look at economists' attempts to devise criteria for evaluating alternative allocations that do not involve explicit reference to a social welfare function.

5.4   Compensation tests

If there were a generally agreed SWF, there would be no problem, in principle, in ranking alternative allocations. One would simply compute the value taken by the SWF for the allocations of interest, and rank by the computed values. An allocation with a higher SWF value would be ranked above one with a lower value. There is not, however, an agreed SWF. The relative weights to be assigned to the utilities of different individuals are an ethical matter. Economists prefer to avoid specifying the SWF if they can. Precisely the appeal of the Pareto improvement criterion – a reallocation is desirable if it increases somebody's utility without reducing anybody else's utility – is that it avoids the need to refer to the SWF to decide on whether or not to recommend that reallocation. However, there are two problems, at the level of principle, with this criterion. First, as we have seen, the recommendation that all reallocations satisfying this condition be undertaken does not fix a unique allocation. Second, in considering policy issues there will be very few proposed reallocations that do not involve some individuals gaining and some losing. It is only rarely, that is, that the welfare economist will be asked for advice about a reallocation that improves somebody's lot without damaging somebody else's. Most reallocations that require analysis involve winners and losers and are, therefore, outside of the terms of the Pareto improvement criterion.

Given this, welfare economists have tried to devise ways, which do not require the use of a SWF, of comparing allocations where there are winners and losers. These are compensation tests. The basic idea is simple. Suppose there are two allocations, denoted 1 and 2, to be compared. As previously, the essential ideas are covered if we consider a two-person, two-commodity world. Moving from allocation 1 to allocation 2 involves one individual gaining and the other losing. The Kaldor compensation test, named after its originator, Nicholas Kaldor, says that allocation 2 is superior to allocation 1 if the winner could compensate the loser and still be better off. Table 5.1 provides a numerical illustration of a situation where the Kaldor test has 2 superior to 1. In this, constructed, example, both individuals have

Table 5.1 Two tests, two answers

	Allocation 1			Allocation 2		
	X	Y	U	X	Y	U
A	10	5	50	20	5	100
B	5	20	100	5	10	50

Table 5.2 Two tests, one answer

	Allocation 1			Allocation 2		
	X	Y	U	X	Y	U
A	10	5	50	20	10	200
B	5	20	100	5	10	50

utility functions that are $U = XY$, and A is the winner for a move from 1 to 2, while B loses from such a move. According to the Kaldor test, 2 is superior because at 2 A could restore B to the level of utility that he enjoyed at 1 and still be better off than at 1. Starting from allocation 2, suppose that 5 units of X were shifted from A to B. This would increase B's utility to 100 (10×10), and reduce A's utility to 75 (15×5) – B would be as well off as at 1 and A would still be better off than at 1. Hence, the argument is: allocation 2 must be superior to 1, as, if such a reallocation were undertaken, the benefits as assessed by the winner would exceed the losses as assessed by the loser. Note carefully that this test does not require that the winner actually does compensate the loser. It requires only that the winner could compensate the loser, and still be better off. For this reason, the Kaldor test, and the others to be discussed below, are sometimes referred to as 'potential compensation tests'. If the loser was actually fully compensated by the winner, and the winner was still better off, then we would be looking at a situation where there was a Pareto improvement.

The numbers in Table 5.1 have been constructed so as to illustrate a problem with the Kaldor test. This is that it may sanction a move from one allocation to another, but that it may also sanction a move from the new allocation back to the original allocation. Put another way, the problem is that if we use the Kaldor test to ask whether 2 is superior to 1 we may get a 'yes', and we may also get a 'yes' if we ask if 1 is superior to 2. Starting from 2 and considering a move to 1, B is the winner and A is the loser. Looking at 1 in this way, we see that if 5 units of Y were transferred from B to A, B would have U equal to 75, higher than in 2, and A would have U equal to 100, the same as in 2. So, according to the Kaldor test done this way, 1 is superior to 2.

This problem with the Kaldor test was noted by J.R. Hicks, who actually put things in a slightly different way. He proposed a different (potential) compensation test for considering whether the move from 1 to 2 could be sanctioned. The question in the Hicks test is: could the loser compensate the winner for forgoing the move and be no worse off than if the move took place. If the answer is 'yes', the reallocation is not sanctioned, otherwise it is on this test. In Table 5.1, suppose at allocation 1 that 5 units of Y are transferred from B, the loser from a move to 2, to A. Now A's utility would then go up to 100 (10 $\times$ 10), the same as in allocation 2, while B's would go down to 75 (5 $\times$ 15), higher than in allocation 2. The loser in a reallocation from 1 to 2 could, that is, compensate the individual who would benefit from such a move for its not actually taking place, and still be better off than if the move had taken place. On this test, allocation 1 is superior to allocation 2.

In the example of Table 5.1, the Kaldor and Hicks (potential) compensation tests give different answers about the rankings of the two allocations under consideration. This will not be the case for all reallocations that might be considered. Table 5.2 is a, constructed, example where both tests give the same answer. For the Kaldor test, looking at 2, the winner A could give the loser B 5 units of X and still be better off than at 1 ($U = 150$), while B would then be fully compensated for the loss involved in going from 1 to 2 ($U = 10 \times 10 = 100$). On this test, 2 is superior to 1. For the Hicks test, looking at 1, the most that the loser B could transfer to the winner A so as not to be worse off than in allocation 2 is 10 units of Y. But, with 10 of X and 15 of Y, A would have $U = 150$, which is less than A's utility at 2, namely 200. The loser could not compensate the winner for forgoing the move and be no worse off than if the move took place, so again 2 is superior to 1.

For an unambiguous result from a (potential) compensation test, it is necessary to use both the Kaldor and the Hicks criteria. The Kaldor–Hicks–Scitovsky test – known as such because

Table 5.3 Compensation may not produce fairness

	Allocation 1			Allocation 2		
	X	Y	U	X	Y	U
A	10	5	50	10	4	40
B	5	20	100	15	16	240

Tibor Scitovsky pointed out that both criteria are required – says that a reallocation is desirable if:

(i)   the winners could compensate the losers and still be better off
and
(ii) the losers could not compensate the winners for the reallocation not occurring and still be as well off as they would have been if it did occur.

In the example of Table 5.2 the move from 1 to 2 passes this test; in that of Table 5.1 it does not.

As we shall see, especially in Chapters 11 and 12 on cost–benefit analysis and environmental valuation respectively, compensation tests inform much of the application of welfare economics to environmental problems. Given that utility functions are not observable, the practical use of compensation tests does not take the form worked through here, of course. Rather, as we shall see, welfare economists work with monetary measures which are intended to measure utility changes. As noted above, the attraction of compensation tests is that they do not require reference to a SWF. However, while they do not require reference to a SWF, it is not the case that they solve the problem that the use of a SWF addresses. Rather, compensation tests simply ignore the problem. As indicated in the examples above, compensation tests treat winners and losers equally. No account is taken of the fairness of the distribution of well-being.

Consider the example in Table 5.3. Considering a move from 1 to 2, A is the loser and B is the winner. As regards (i), at 2 moving one unit of Y from B to A would make A as well off as she was at 1, and would leave B better off ($U = 225$) than at 1. As regards (ii), at 1 moving either two of X or one of Y from A to B would leave A as well off as at 2, but in neither case would this be sufficient to compensate B for being at 1 rather than 2 (for B after such trans-

fers $U = 140$ or $U = 105$). According to both (i) and (ii) 2 is superior to 1, and such a reallocation passes the Kaldor–Hicks–Scitovsky test. Note, however, that A is the poorer of the two individuals, and that the reallocation sanctioned by the compensation test makes A worse off, and makes B better off. In sanctioning such a reallocation, the compensation test is either saying that fairness is irrelevant or there is an implicit SWF such that the reallocation is consistent with the notion of fairness that it embodies. If, for example, the SWF was

$$W = 0.5U^A + 0.5U^B$$

then at 1 welfare would be 75 and at 2 it would be 140. Weighting A's losses equally with B's gains means that 2 is superior to 1 in welfare terms. If it were thought appropriate to weight A's losses much more heavily than B's gains, given that A is relatively poor, then using, say

$$W = 0.95U^A + 0.05U^B$$

gives welfare at 1 as 52.5 and at 2 as 50, so that 1 is superior to 2 in welfare terms, notwithstanding that the move from 1 to 2 is sanctioned by the (potential) compensation test.

In the practical use of compensation tests in applied welfare economics, welfare, or distributional, issues are usually ignored. The monetary measures of winners' gains (benefits) and losers' losses (costs) are usually given equal weights irrespective of the income and wealth levels of those to whom they accrue. In part, this is because it is often difficult to identify winners and losers sufficiently closely to be able to say what their relative income and wealth levels are. But, even in those cases where it is clear that, say, costs fall mainly on the relatively poor and benefits mainly on the better off, economists are reluctant to apply welfare weights when applying a compensation test by comparing total gains and total losses – they simply report on whether or not £s of gain exceed £s of loss. Various justifications are offered for this practice. First, at the level of principle, that there is no generally agreed SWF for them to use, and it would be inappropriate for economists to themselves specify a SWF. Second, that, as a practical matter, it aids clear thinking to separate matters of efficiency from matters of equity, with the question of the relative sizes of gains and losses being treated as an efficiency issue, while the question of their incidence across poor and rich is an equity issue. On this view, when considering some policy intended to effect a reallocation the job of the economic analyst is to ascertain whether the gains exceed the losses. If they do, the policy can be recommended on efficiency grounds, and it is known that the beneficiaries could compensate the losers. It is a separate matter, for government, to decide whether compensation should actually occur, and to arrange for it to occur if it is thought desirable. These matters are usually considered in the context of a market economy, and we shall return to them in that context at the end of Part 2 of the chapter.

PART 2 ALLOCATION IN A MARKET ECONOMY

5.5 Efficiency given ideal conditions

A variety of institutional arrangements might be employed to allocate resources, such as dictatorship, central planning and free markets. Any of these can, in principle, achieve an efficient allocation of resources. Here, we are particularly interested in the consequences of free-market resource allocation decisions. This is for three, related, reasons. First, for dictatorship and central planning to achieve allocative efficiency it is necessary that the dictator or central planner know all of the economy's production and utility functions. This is clearly infeasible, and is one of the reasons that attempts to run economies in these ways have been unsuccessful. The great attraction of free markets as a way of organising economic activity is that they do not require that any institution or agent have such knowledge. That is the second reason for our concentration on markets – they are decentralised information-processing systems of great power. The third reason is that the modern welfare economics

that is the basis for environmental and resource economics takes it that markets are the way economies are mainly organised. Environmental and resource issues are studied, that is, as they arise in an economy where markets are the dominant social institution for organising production and consumption. The market economy is now the dominant mode of organising production and consumption in human societies.

Welfare economics theory points to a set of circumstances such that a system of free markets would sustain an efficient allocation of resources. The 'institutional arrangements', as we shall call them, include the following:

1. Markets exist for all goods and services produced and consumed.
2. All markets are perfectly competitive.
3. All transactors have perfect information.
4. Private property rights are fully assigned in all resources and commodities.
5. No externalities exist.
6. All goods and services are private goods. That is, there are no public goods.
7. All utility and production functions are 'well behaved'.[3]

In addition to these institutional arrangements, it is necessary to assume that the actors in such a system – firms and individuals, often referred to jointly as 'economic agents' or just 'agents' – behave in certain ways. It is assumed that agents always strive to do the best for themselves that they can in the circumstances that they find themselves in. Firms are assumed to maximise profits, individuals to maximise utility. A shorthand way of saying this is to say that all agents are maximisers.

An efficient allocation would be the outcome in a market economy populated entirely by maximisers and where all of these institutional arrangements were in place. Before explaining why and how this is so, a few brief comments are in order on these conditions required for a market system to be capable of realising allocative efficiency. First, note that,

---

[3] For a full account of what 'well behaved' means the reader is referred to one of the welfare economics texts cited in the Further Reading section at the end of the chapter. Roughly, in regard to utility it means that indifference curves are continuous and have the bowed-toward-the-origin shape that they are usually drawn with in the textbooks. In regard to production, the main point is that increasing returns to scale are ruled out.

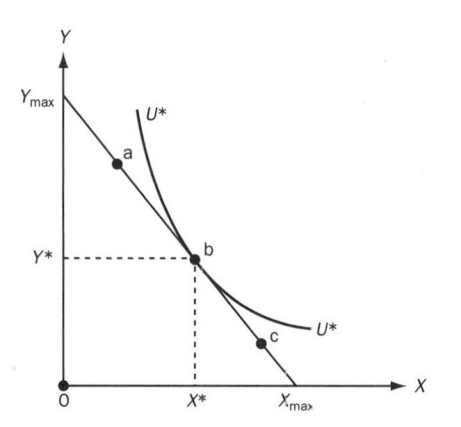

Figure 5.8 Utility maximisation

as we shall see in later sections of this chapter where we discuss public goods and externalities, arrangements 5 and 6 are really particulars of 4. Second, note that 4 is necessary for 1 – markets can only work where there are private property rights and a justice system to enforce and protect such rights. Third, that an important implication of 2 is that buyers and sellers act as 'price-takers', believing that the prices that they face cannot be influenced by their own behaviour. No agent, that is, acts in the belief that they have any power in the market. Finally, note that these are a very stringent set of conditions, which do not accurately describe any actual market economy. The economy that they do describe is an ideal type, to be used in the welfare analysis of actual economies as a benchmark against which to assess performance, and to be used to devise policies to improve the performance, in regard to efficiency criteria, of such actual economies.

We now explain why a market allocation of resources would be an efficient allocation in such ideal circumstances. A more formal treatment is provided in Appendix 5.2.

Consider, first, individuals and their consumption of produced commodities. Any one individual seeks to maximise utility given income and the, fixed, prices of commodities. Figure 5.8, familiar from introductory microeconomics, refers to an individual in a two-commodity economy. The line $Y_{max}X_{max}$ is the budget constraint. Y_{max} is the amount of Y available if all income is spent on Y, X_{max} is consumption if all income is spent on X. The slope of the budget constraint gives the price ratio P_X/P_Y. Utility max-

imisation requires consumption X^* and Y^* corresponding to point b on the indifference curve U^*U^*. Consumption at points on $Y_{max}X_{max}$ to the left or right of b, such as a and c, would mean being on a lower indifference curve than U^*U^*. Consumption patterns corresponding to points to the northeast of $Y_{max}X_{max}$ are not attainable with the given income and prices. The essential characteristic of b is that the budget line is tangential to an indifference curve. This means that the slope of the indifference curve is equal to the price ratio. Given that the slope of the indifference curve is the MRUS, we have:

$$MRUS = \frac{P_X}{P_Y}$$

In the ideal conditions under consideration, all individuals face the same prices. So, for the two-individual, two-commodity market economy, we have

$$MRUS^A = MRUS^B = \frac{P_X}{P_Y} \tag{5.8}$$

Comparison of equation 5.8 with equation 5.3 shows that the consumption efficiency condition is satisfied in this ideal market system. Clearly, the argument here generalises to many-person, multi-commodity contexts.

Now consider firms. To begin, instead of assuming that they maximise profits, we will assume that they minimise the costs of producing a given level of output. The cost-minimisation assumption is in no way in conflict with the assumption of profit maximisation. On the contrary, it is implied by the profit-maximisation assumption, as, clearly, a firm could not be maximising its profits if it were producing whatever level of output that involved at anything other than the lowest possible cost. We are leaving aside, for the moment, the question of the determination of the profit-maximising level of output, and focusing instead on the prior question of cost minimisation for a given level of output. This question is examined in Figure 5.9, where X^*X^* is the isoquant corresponding to some given output level X^*. The straight lines K_1L_1, K_2L_2, and K_3L_3 are isocost lines. For given prices for inputs, P_K and P_L, an isocost line shows the combinations of input levels for K and L that can be purchased for a given total expenditure on inputs. K_3L_3 represents, for example,

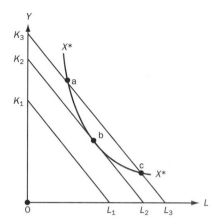

Figure 5.9 Cost minimisation

a higher level of expenditure on inputs, greater cost, than K_2L_2. The slope of an isocost line is the ratio of input prices, P_K/P_L. Given production of X^*, the cost-minimising firm will choose the input combination given by the point b. Any other combination, such as a or c, lying along X^*X^* would mean higher total costs. Combinations represented by points lying inside K_2L_2 would not permit of the production of X^*. The essential characteristic of b is that an isocost line is tangential to, has the same slope as, an isoquant. The slope of an isoquant is the MRTS so that cost-minimising choices of input levels must be characterised by:

$$\text{MRTS} = \frac{P_K}{P_L}$$

In the ideal circumstances under consideration, all firms, in all lines of production, face the same P_K and P_L, which means that

$$\text{MRTS}_X = \text{MRTS}_Y \qquad (5.9)$$

which is the same as equation 5.4, the production efficiency condition for allocative efficiency – cost-minimising firms satisfy this condition.

The remaining condition that needs to be satisfied for allocative efficiency to exist is the product mix condition, equation 5.5, which involves both individuals and firms. In explaining how this condition is satisfied in an ideal market system we will also see how the profit-maximising levels of production are determined. Rather than look directly at the profit-

maximising output choice, we look at the choice of input levels that gives maximum profit. Once the input levels are chosen, the output level follows from the production function. Consider the input of labour to the production of X, with marginal product X_L. Choosing the level of X_L to maximise profit involves balancing the gain from using an extra unit of labour against the cost of so doing. The gain here is just the marginal product of labour multiplied by the price of output, i.e. $P_X X_L$. The cost is the price of labour, i.e. P_L. If P_L is greater than $P_X X_L$, increasing labour use will reduce profit. If P_L is less than $P_X X_L$, increasing labour use will increase profit. Clearly, profit is maximised where $P_L = P_X X_L$.

The same argument applies to the capital input, and holds in both lines of production. Hence, profit maximisation will be characterised by

$$P_X X_L = P_L$$
$$P_X X_K = P_K$$
$$P_Y Y_L = P_L$$
$$P_Y Y_K = P_K$$

which imply

$$P_X X_L = P_Y Y_L = P_L$$

and

$$P_X X_K = P_Y Y_K = P_K$$

Using the left-hand equalities here, and rearranging, this is

$$\frac{P_X}{P_Y} = \frac{Y_L}{X_L} \qquad (5.10a)$$

and

$$\frac{P_X}{P_Y} = \frac{Y_K}{X_K} \qquad (5.10b)$$

Now, the right-hand sides here are MRT_L and MRT_K, as they are the ratios of marginal products in the two lines of production and hence give the terms on which the outputs change as labour and capital are shifted between industries. Given that the left-hand sides in equations 5.10a and 5.10b are the same we can write

$$\text{MRT}_L = \text{MRT}_K = \frac{P_X}{P_Y} \qquad (5.11)$$

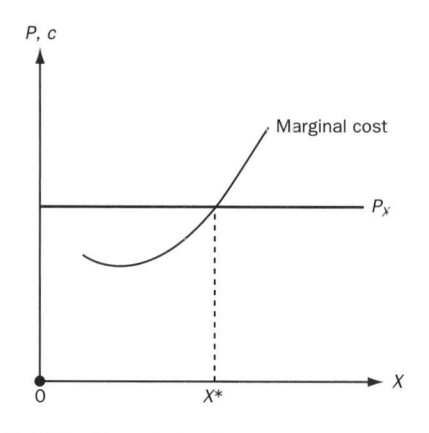

Figure 5.10 Profit maximisation

showing that the marginal rate of transformation is the same for labour shifting as for capital shifting. Referring back to equation 5.8, we can now write

$$\text{MRT}_L = \text{MRT}_K = \frac{P_X}{P_Y} = \text{MRUS}^A = \text{MRUS}^B$$

$$(5.12)$$

showing that the profit-maximising output levels in the ideal market economy satisfy the product mix condition for allocative efficiency, equation 5.5.

This completes the demonstration that in an ideal market system the conditions necessary for allocative efficiency will be satisfied. We conclude this section by looking briefly at profit-maximising behaviour from a perspective that will be familiar from an introductory microeconomics course. There, students learn that in order to maximise profit, a firm which is a price-taker will expand output up to the level at which price equals marginal cost. Figure 5.10 refers. For output levels below X^*, price exceeds marginal cost so that increasing output will add more to receipts than to costs, so increasing profit as the difference between receipts and costs. For output levels greater than X^*, marginal cost exceeds price, and reducing output would increase profit. This is in no way inconsistent with the discussion above of choosing input levels so as to maximise profit. It is just a different way of telling the same story. In order to increase output, assuming technical efficiency, more of at least one input must be used. In thinking about whether or not to increase output the firm considers increasing the input of capital or labour, in the manner described above.

For the case of labour in the production of X, for example, the profit-maximising condition was seen to be $P_L = P_X X_L$, which can be written as

$$\frac{P_L}{X_L} = P_X$$

which is just marginal cost equals price, because the left-hand side is the price of an additional unit of labour divided by the amount of output produced by that additional unit. Thus if the wage rate is £5 per hour, and one hour's extra labour produces 1 tonne of output, the left-hand side here is £5 per tonne, so the marginal cost of expanding output by one tonne is £5. If the price that one tonne sells for is greater(less) than £5 it will pay in terms of profit to increase(decrease) output by one tonne by increasing the use of labour. If the equality holds and the output price is £5, profit is being maximised. The same argument goes through in the case of capital, and the marginal cost equals price condition for profit maximisation can also be written as

$$\frac{P_K}{X_K} = P_X$$

5.6 Partial equilibrium analysis of market efficiency

In examining the concepts of efficiency and optimality, we have used a general equilibrium approach. This looks at all sectors of the economy simultaneously. Even if we were only interested in one part of the economy – such as the production and consumption of cola drinks – the general equilibrium approach requires that we look at all sectors. In finding the allocatively efficient quantity of cola, for example, the solution we get from this kind of exercise would give us the efficient quantities of all goods, not just cola.

There are several very attractive properties of proceeding in this way. Perhaps the most important of these is the theoretical rigour it imposes. In developing economic theory, it is often best to use general equilibrium analysis. Much (although by no means all) of the huge body of theory that makes up resource and environmental economics analysis has such a general approach at its foundation.

But there are penalties to pay for this rigour. Doing applied work in this way can be expensive and time-consuming. And in some cases data limitations make it impossible. The exercise may not be quite as daunting as it sounds, however. We could define categories in such a way that there are just two goods in the economy: cola and a composite good that is everything except cola. Indeed, this kind of 'trick' is commonly used in economic analysis. But even with this type of simplification, a general equilibrium approach is likely to be difficult and costly, and may be out of all proportion to the demands of some problem for which we seek an approximate solution.

Given the cost and difficulty of using this approach for many practical purposes, many applications use a different framework that is much easier to operationalise. This involves looking at only the part of the economy of direct relevance to the problem being studied. Let us return to the cola example, in which our interest lies in trying to estimate the efficient amount of cola to be produced. The partial approach examines the production and consumption of cola, ignoring the rest of the economy. It begins by identifying the benefits and costs to society of using resources to make cola. Then, defining *net* benefit as total benefit minus total cost, an efficient output level of cola would be one that maximises net benefit.

Let X be the level of cola produced and consumed. Figure 5.11(a) shows the total benefits of cola (labelled B) and the total costs of cola (labelled C) for various possible levels of cola production. The reason we have labelled the curves $B(X)$ and $C(X)$, not just B and C, is to make it clear that benefits and costs each depend on, are functions of, X. Benefits and costs are measured in money units. The shapes and relative positions of the curves we have drawn for B and C are, of course, just stylised representations of what we expect them to look like. A researcher trying to answer the question we posed above would have to estimate the shapes and positions of these functions from whatever evidence is available, and they may differ from those drawn in the diagram. However, the reasoning that follows is not conditional on the particular shapes and positions that we have used, which are chosen mainly to make the exposition straightforward.

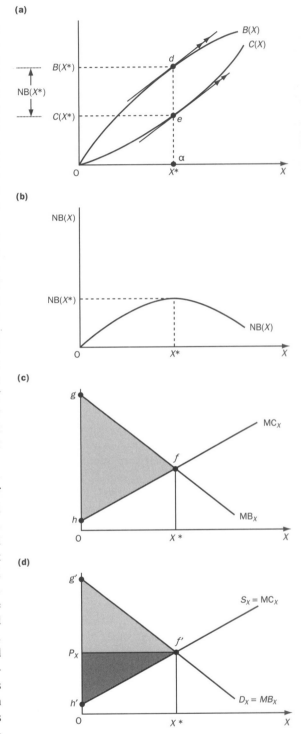

Figure 5.11 A partial equilibrium interpretation of economic efficiency

Given that we call an outcome that maximises net benefits 'efficient', it is clear from Figure 5.11(a) that X^* is the efficient level of cola production. Net benefits (indicated by the distance de) are at their maximum at that level of output. This is also shown in Figure 5.11(b), which plots the *net* benefits for various levels of X. Observe the following points:

- At the efficient output level X^* the total benefit and total cost curves are parallel to one another (Figure 5.11(a)).

- The net benefit function is horizontal at the efficient output level (Figure 5.11(b)).

The distance de, or equivalently the magnitude $NB(X^*)$, where NB is net benefit, can be interpreted in efficiency terms. It is a measure, in money units, of the efficiency gain that would come about from producing X^* cola compared with a situation in which no cola was made.

These ideas are often expressed in a different, but exactly equivalent, way, using marginal rather than total functions. As much of the environmental economics literature uses this way of presenting ideas (and we shall do so also in several parts of this book), let us see how it is done. We use MC_X to denote the marginal cost of X, and MB_X denotes the marginal benefit of X. In Figure 5.11(c), we have drawn the marginal functions which correspond to the total functions in Figure 5.11(a). We drew the curves for $B(X)$ and $C(X)$ in Figure 5.11(a) so that the corresponding marginal functions are straight lines, a practice that is often adopted in partial equilibrium treatments of welfare economics. This is convenient and simplifies exposition of the subsequent analysis. But, the conclusions do not depend on the marginal functions being straight lines. The results to be stated hold so long as marginal benefits are positive and declining with X and marginal costs are positive and increasing with X – as they are in Figure 5.11(c).

In Figure 5.11(c) we show X^*, the cola output level that maximises net benefit, as being the level of X at which MC_X is equal to MB_X. Why is this so? Consider some level of X below X^*. This would involve MB_X greater than MC_X, from which it follows that increasing X would increase benefit by more than cost. Now consider some level of X greater than X^*, with MC_X greater than MB_X, from

which it follows that reducing X would reduce cost by more than benefit, i.e. increase net benefit. Clearly, considering X levels above or below X^* in this way, it is X^* that maximises net benefit.

Can we obtain a measure of maximised net benefits from Figure 5.11(c) that corresponds to the distance de in Figure 5.11(a)? Such a measure is available; it is the area of the triangle gfh. The area beneath a marginal function over some range gives the value of the change in the total function for a move over that range. So the area beneath MB_X over the range $X = 0$ to $X = X^*$ gives us the total benefits of X^* cola (i.e. B^*), which is equal to the distance ad in Figure 5.11(a). Similarly, the area beneath MC_X over the range $X = 0$ to $X = X^*$ gives us the total cost of X^* (i.e. C^*), which is the same as the distance ae in Figure 5.11(a). By subtraction we find that the area gfh in Figure 5.11(c) is equal to the distance de in Figure 5.11(a).

Now we turn to the partial equilibrium version of the demonstration that an ideal market system maximises net benefit and secures allocative efficiency. We assume that all of the institutional arrangements listed in the previous section apply, and that all agents are maximisers. Then all those who wish to drink cola will obtain it from the market, and pay the going market price. The market demand curve, D_X, for cola will be identical to the MB_X curve, as that describes consumers' *willingness to pay* for additional units of the good – and that is exactly what we mean by a demand curve. Under our assumptions, cola is produced by a large number of price-taking firms in a competitive market. The market supply curve, S_X, is identical to the curve MC_X in Figure 5.11(c) because, given that firms produce where price equals marginal cost, the supply curve is just the marginal cost curve – each point on the supply curve is a point where price equals marginal cost. S_X shows the cost of producing additional (or marginal) cans of cola at various output levels.

The market demand and supply curves are drawn in Figure 5.11(d). When all mutually beneficial transactions have taken price, the equilibrium market price of the good will be P_X, equal at the margin to both

- consumers' subjective valuations of additional units of the good (expressed in money terms); and

- the costs of producing an additional unit of the good.

Put another way, all consumers face a common market price P_X, and each will adjust their consumption until their marginal utility (in money units) is equal to that price. Each firm faces that same fixed market price, and adjusts its output so that its marginal cost of production equals that price. So we have:

$$P_X = MC_X = MB_X \qquad (5.13)$$

The equality at the margin of costs and benefits shows that cola is being produced in the amount consistent with the requirements of allocative efficiency. We must emphasise here something that it is sometimes possible to forget when using partial equilibrium analysis. The fact that equation 5.13 holds for the cola, or whatever, market means that the quantity of cola, or whatever, produced and consumed is consistent with allocative efficiency only if *all* the institutional arrangements listed at the start of this section are in place. It is necessary, for example, not only that the cola market be perfectly competitive, but also that all markets be perfectly competitive. And, it is necessary, for example, that all inputs to and outputs from production be traded in such markets. If such requirements are not met elsewhere in the economy, the supply and demand curves in the cola market will not properly reflect the costs and benefits associated with different levels of cola production. Some of the issues arising from these remarks will be dealt with in section 5.11 under the heading of 'the second-best problem'.

Finally here, we can use Figure 5.11(d) to introduce the concepts of *consumers' surplus* and *producers' surplus*, which are widely used in welfare economics and its application to environmental and natural resource issues. The area beneath the demand curve between zero and X^* units of the good shows the total consumers' willingness to pay, WTP, for X^* cans of cola per period. To see this, imagine a situation in which cans of cola are auctioned, one at a time. The price that the first can offered would fetch is given by the intercept of the demand curve. $0g'$. As successive cans are offered so the price that they fetch falls, as shown by the demand curve. If we add up all the prices paid until we get to X^*, and recognising that X^* is a very large

number of cans, we see that the total revenue raised by the auction process which stops at X^* will be the area under the demand curve over $0X^*$, i.e. $0g'f'X^*$. But this is not the way the market works. Instead of each can being auctioned, a price is set and all cans of cola demanded are sold at that price. So, the individual who would have been willing to pay $0g'$ for a can actually gets it for P_X. Similarly, the individual who would have been willing to pay just a little less than $0g'$ actually pays P_X. And so on and so on, until we get to the individual whose WTP is P_X, and who also actually pays P_X. All individuals whose WTP is greater than P_X are, when all cans sell at P_X, getting a surplus which is the excess of their WTP over P_X. Consumers' surplus is the total of these individual surpluses, the area between the demand curve and the price line over $0X^*$, i.e. $P_X g'f'$. Another way of putting this is that consumers' surplus is the difference between total willingness to pay and total actual expenditure, which is the difference between area $0g'f'X^*$ and area $0P_X f'X^*$, which is the area of the triangle $P_X g'f'$.

Producers' surplus in Figure 5.11(d) is the area of the triangle $h'P_X f'$. The reasoning to this is very similar to that for consumers' surplus. As noted above, the supply curve is, given the ideal conditions being assumed here, just the marginal cost curve. The first can of cola costs $0h'$ to produce, but sells in the market for P_X, so there is a surplus of $h'P_X$. The surplus on the production of each further can is given by the vertical distance from the price line to the supply curve. The sum of all these vertical distances is total producers' surplus, the area $h'P_X f'$. An alternative way of putting this is that total revenue is the area $0P_X f'X^*$, while total cost is $0h'f'X^*$, so that producers' surplus is revenue minus costs, i.e. $h'P_X f'X^*$.

5.7 Market allocations are not necessarily equitable

The previous sections have shown that, provided certain conditions are satisfied, a system of free markets will produce allocations that are efficient in the sense that nobody can be made better off except at the cost of making at least one other person worse off. It has not been shown that a system of free markets will produce an optimal allocation according to any particular social welfare function.

The basic intuition of both the positive – the attainment of efficiency – and the negative – no necessary attainment of equity – here is really rather simple. The essential characteristic of markets is voluntary exchange. Think of two individuals who meet, each carrying a box containing an assortment of commodities. The two assortments are different. The two individuals lay out the contents of their boxes, and swap items until there are no further swaps that both see as advantageous. Then, considering just these two individuals and the collection of commodities jointly involved, the allocation of that collection at the end of the swapping is efficient in the sense that if somebody else came along and forced them to make a further swap, one individual would feel better off but the other worse off, whereas prior to the enforced swap both felt better off than they did with their initial bundles. The attainment of efficiency is simply the exhaustion of the possibilities for mutually beneficial exchange. Clearly, if one individual's box had been several times as large as the other's, if one individual had a much larger initial endowment, we would not expect the voluntary trade process to lead to equal endowments. Voluntary trade on the basis of self-interest is not going to equalise wealth. Further, it is also clear that as the initial endowments of the two individuals – the sizes of their boxes and their contents – vary, so will the positions reached when all voluntary swaps have been made.

The formal foundations for modern welfare economics and its application to policy analysis in market economies are two fundamental theorems. These theorems take it that all agents are maximisers, and that the ideal institutional conditions stated at the start of this section hold. The first states that a competitive market equilibrium is an efficient allocation. Basically, this is saying that equilibrium is when there are no more voluntary exchanges, and that when there are no more voluntary exchanges all the gains from trade have been exhausted, so the situation must be one of efficiency – one where nobody can be made better off save at the cost of making somebody else worse off. The second theorem states that to every efficient allocation there corresponds a competitive market equilibrium based on a particu-

lar distribution of initial endowments. An alternative statement of this theorem, of particular relevance to policy analysis, is that any efficient allocation can be realised as a competitive market equilibrium given the appropriate set of lump-sum taxes on and transfers to individual agents. The point of the second theorem is that the efficient allocation realised by a competitive equilibrium is conditioned on the distribution of initial endowments, and that if those initial endowments are such that the resulting efficient allocation is considered inequitable, altering them by lump-sum taxes and transfers will produce another efficient allocation. If the taxes/transfers redistribute from the better to the worse off, the new efficient allocation will be more equitable.

The implication of these two theorems, which has enormous influence on the way that economists approach policy analysis in an economy mainly run by markets, is that there are two essentially separable dimensions to the economic problem. These are the problems of efficiency and equity. The theorems are taken to mean that, in effect, society can, via government, take a view on equity and achieve what it wants there by a system of redistributive taxes and payments, and then leave it to markets to achieve efficiency in allocation given the distribution of endowments after the tax/transfer. This can be put the other way round. The theorems are taken to mean that the government should not intervene in markets directly to pursue any equity objectives. It should not, for example, subsidise a commodity that figures largely in the consumption of the poor. To do so would prevent the market system attaining an efficient allocation. Anyway, it is unnecessary. The interests of the poor are to be looked after by redistributive taxes and transfers.

These theorems hold only in the ideal conditions being assumed in this part of the chapter. It will already have occurred to the reader that these conditions are not fully satisfied in any actual economy – we consider some violations and their policy implications in the next part of the chapter. It is also required that the government's redistribution be in the form of lump-sum taxes and transfers. By 'lump-sum' is meant taxes and transfers that do not directly affect the incentives facing agents – in the case of taxes, for example, liability must not depend on behaviour, so that income taxes are not lump-sum taxes. Lump-sum taxes and transfers are not, in fact, widely used by governments as they are generally seen as politically infeasible.

Notwithstanding that the conditions under which the two theorems hold are not fully satisfied in any actual economy, the overwhelming majority of economists do approach practical policy analysis on the basis that the problems of efficiency and equity can be dealt with independently.

PART 3 MARKET FAILURE, PUBLIC POLICY AND THE ENVIRONMENT

In Part 1 of this chapter, we laid out the conditions that characterise an efficient allocation. In Part 2, we showed that, given 'ideal' circumstances concerning institutions and behaviour, a system of markets would produce an efficient allocation. We noted that the ideal circumstances are truly ideal, in that they do not describe any actual economy. Actual market economies depart from the ideal circumstances in a variety of ways, and the allocations that they produce are not efficient. Economists use welfare economics to identify 'market failures' – situations where actual circumstances depart from the ideal – and to recommend policies to correct them so that actual economies perform better in relation to the objective of efficiency. Much of environmental and resource economics is welfare economics of this sort. It is concerned with identifying and correcting market failure in relation to the services that the environment provides to the economy. In this part of the chapter, we introduce some of the basic ideas involved here. In Part II of the book, we apply the basic ideas to the problem of environmental pollution. Part III extends the basic ideas to cover intertemporal allocation problems, and then looks, mainly, at the welfare economics of the amenity services that the environment provides. Part IV of the book then deals, mainly, with the economics of natural resources as inputs to production.

5.8 The existence of markets for environmental services

To recapitulate, we have seen that for markets to produce efficient allocations, it is necessary that:

1. Markets exist for all goods and services produced and consumed.
2. All markets are perfectly competitive.
3. All transactors have perfect information.
4. Private property rights are fully assigned in all resources and commodities.
5. No externalities exist.
6. All goods and services are private goods. That is, there are no public goods.
7. All utility and production functions are 'well behaved'.
8. All agents are maximisers.

Clearly, 1 here is fundamental. If there are goods and services for which markets do not exist, then the market system cannot produce an efficient allocation, as that concept applies to all goods and services that are of interest to any agent, either as utility or production function arguments. Further, 4 is necessary for 1 – a market in a resource or commodity can only exist where there are private property rights in that resource or commodity.

We can define a property right as: a bundle of characteristics that convey certain powers to the owner of the right.[4] These characteristics concern conditions of appropriability of returns, the ability to divide or transfer the right, the degree of exclusiveness of the right, and the duration and enforceability of the right. Where a right is exclusive to one person or corporation, a private property right is said to exist.

In Chapter 2 we provided a classification of the services that the natural environment provides to economic activity, using Figure 2.1. Let us now briefly consider the different classes of service distinguished there in relation to the question of the existence of private property rights. Where these do not exist, market forces cannot allocate efficiently. If efficiency is the objective, some kind of public

---

[4]   This definition is taken from Hartwick and Olewiler (1986).

policy intervention is required. Our remarks here are intended only to provide a general overview, as a guide to what follows in the rest of this book. The details of any particular case can be quite complicated.

In regard to the provision of inputs to production, natural resources, we made two major distinctions – between flow and stock resources, and, for the latter, between renewables and non-renewables. Generally, there are no private property rights in flow resources as such. Individuals or corporations do not, for example, have property rights in flows of solar radiation. They may, however, have property rights in land, and, hence, in the ability to capture the solar radiation falling on that land.[5] Deposits of non-renewable natural resources are, generally, subject to private property rights. Often these reside ultimately with the government, but are sold or leased by it to individuals and/or corporations. The problems arising from the non-existence of private property rights are not central to the economics of non-renewable resources.

They do, on the other hand, feature large in the renewable resource economics literature. Many, but not all, of the biotic populations exploited by humans as hunter–gatherers, rather than agriculturists, are not subject to private property rights. The standard example of the case where they are not is the ocean fishery. Where private property rights are absent, two sorts of situation may obtain. In the case of 'open-access resources' exploitation is uncontrolled. The term 'common-property resources' is used whenever some legal or customary conventions, other than private property rights, regulate exploitation of the resource. Whereas an open-access regime definitely will not promote exploitation that corresponds to efficiency, a common property regime may do so given the appropriate conventions and regulation. Much of the modern fisheries economics literature, as will be seen in Chapter 17, is concerned with the design of systems of government regulation of common property that will promote behaviour consistent with efficiency on the part of the private agents actually exploiting the fishery.

The second class of environmental service that was distinguished was that of receptacle for the wastes arising in economic activity. Generally, for most of history and for many wastes, the environment as waste sink has not been subject to private property rights, and has been, in effect, an open-access resource. With increasing awareness of the problems of pollution arising, states have moved to legislate so as to convert many waste sinks from open-access resources to common-property resources. Much of Part II of the book is about the economic analysis that is relevant to the public-policy questions arising. What is the level of pollution that goes with efficiency? How should the behaviour of waste dischargers be regulated? We shall introduce the basic ideas involved here later in this chapter, when discussing 'externalities'.

The case of the amenity services that the environment provides is rather like that of flow resources, in that the service itself will not generally be subject to private property rights, though the means of accessing it may be. Thus, for example, nobody can own a beautiful view, but the land that it is necessary to visit in order to see it may be privately owned. Private property rights in a wilderness area would allow the owner to, say, develop it for agriculture or extractive resource use, thus reducing the amenity services flow from the area, or to preserve the wilderness. While in principle the owner could charge for access to a wilderness area, in practice this is often infeasible. Further, some of the amenity services that the area delivers do not require access, and cannot be charged for by the owner. The revenue stream that is available under the preservation option is likely to understate the true value to society of that option. This is not true of the development option. In this case, a decision as between the options based on market revenues will be biased in favour of the development option, and the operative question in terms of market failure is whether the existing private property rights need to be attenuated, so as to secure the proper, efficient, balance between preservation and development. This sort of issue is dealt with in Part III of the book.

---

[5] To see the complexities that can arise, note that in some jurisdictions a householder may be able to prevent others taking action which reduces the light reaching her property, though this may depend on the nature and purpose of the action.

The life-support services provided by the natural environment are not subject to private property rights. Consider, as an example, the global atmosphere, the carbon cycle and the climate system. Historically, the global atmosphere has been a free-access resource. As briefly discussed in Chapter 2, and to be revisited at several places in the rest of the book (especially Chapter 10), anthropogenic emissions of carbon dioxide have increased atmospheric concentrations of that greenhouse gas. The consensus of expert judgement is that this has affected the way that the global climate system works, and that unless action is taken to reduce the rate of growth of anthropogenic carbon dioxide emissions, further change, on balance harmful to human interests, will occur. Given this, most nations are now parties to an international agreement to act to curb the rate of growth of carbon dioxide and other greenhouse gas emissions. This agreement is discussed in Chapter 10. It can be seen as a first step in a process of transforming the global atmosphere from a free-access to a common-property resource.

5.9 Public goods

One of the circumstances, 6 in the listing above, required for it to be true that a pure market system could support an efficient allocation is that there be no public goods. Some of the services that the natural environment provides to economic activity have the characteristics of public goods, and cannot be handled properly by a pure market system of economic organisation. So we need to explain what public goods are, the problems that they give rise to for markets, and what can be done about these problems.

5.9.1 What are public goods?

This turns out to be a question to which there is no simple short answer. Public goods have been defined in different ways by different economists. At one time it was thought that there were just private goods and public goods. Now it is recognised that pure private and pure public goods are polar cases, and that a complete classification has to include intermediate cases. It turns out that thinking about these matters helps to clarify some other issues relevant to resource and environmental economics.

There are two characteristics of goods and services that are relevant to the public/private question. These are rivalry and excludability. What we call rivalry is sometimes referred to in the literature as divisibility. Table 5.4 shows the fourfold classification of goods and services that these two characteristics give rise to, and provides an example of each type. Rivalry refers to whether one agent's consumption is at the expense of another's consumption. Excludability refers to whether agents can be prevented from consuming. We use the term 'agent' here as public goods may be things that individuals consume and/or things that firms use as inputs to production. In what follows here we shall generally discuss public goods in terms of things that are of interest to individuals, and it should be kept in mind that similar considerations can arise with some inputs to production.

Pure private goods exhibit both rivalry and excludability. These are 'ordinary' goods and services, the example being ice cream. For a given amount of ice cream available, any increase in consumption by A must be at the expense of consumption by others, is rival. Any individual can be excluded from ice cream consumption. Ice cream comes in discrete units, for each of which a con-

Table 5.4 Characteristics of private and public goods

	Excludable	Non-excludable
Rivalrous	**Pure private good** Ice cream	**Open-access resource** Ocean fishery (outside territorial waters)
Non-rivalrous	**Congestible resource** Wilderness area	**Pure public good** Defence

sumption entitlement can be identified and traded (or gifted). Pure public goods exhibit neither rivalry nor excludability. The example given is the services of the national defence force. Whatever level that it is provided at is the same for all citizens of the nation. There are no discrete units, entitlement to which can be traded (or gifted). One citizen's consumption is not rival to, at the cost of, that of others, and no citizen can be excluded from consumption.

Open-access natural resources exhibit rivalry but not excludability. The example given is an ocean fishery that lies outside of the territorial waters of any nation. In that case, no fishing boat can be prevented from exploiting the fishery, since it is not subject to private property rights and there is no government that has the power to treat it as common property and regulate its exploitation. However, exploitation is definitely rivalrous. An increase in the catch by one fishing boat means that there is less for other boats to take.

Congestible resources exhibit excludability but not, up to the point at which congestion sets in, rivalry. The example given is the services to visitors provided by a wilderness area. If one person visits a wilderness area and consumes its services – recreation, wildlife experiences and solitude, for example – that does not prevent others from consuming those services as well. There is no rivalry between the consumption of different individuals, provided that the overall rate of usage is not beyond a threshold level at which congestion occurs in the sense that one individual's visit reduces another's enjoyment of theirs. In principle, excludability is possible if the area is either in private ownership or subject to common-property management. In practice, of course, enforcing excludability might be difficult, but, often, given limited points of access to vehicles it is not.

The question of excludability is a matter of law and convention, as well as physical characteristics. We have already noted that as the result of an international agreement that extended states' territorial waters, some ocean fisheries that were open access have become common property. We also noted above that a similar process may be beginning in respect to the global atmosphere, at least in regard to emissions into it of greenhouse gases. In some countries beaches cannot be privately owned, and in some such cases while beaches actually have the

legal status of common property they are generally used on a free-access basis. This can lead to congestion. In other countries private ownership is the rule, and private owners do restrict access. In some cases where the law enables excludability, either on the basis of private ownership or common property, it is infeasible to enforce it. However, the feasibility of exclusion is a function of technology. The invention of barbed wire and its use in the grazing lands of North America is a historical example. Satellite surveillance could be used to monitor unauthorised use of wilderness areas, though clearly this would be expensive, and presumably at present it is not considered that the benefit from so doing is sufficient to warrant meeting the cost.

In the rest of this section we shall consider pure public goods, which we will refer to simply as 'public goods'. As noted, we will be returning to a detailed consideration of open-access resources, and common-property resources, at several places later in the book. Box 5.2 considers some examples of public goods. Box 5.3 looks at property rights in relation to biodiversity, and the arising implications for incentives regarding conservation and medicinal exploitation.

5.9.2 Public goods and economic efficiency

For our economy with two persons and two private goods, we found that the top-level, product-mix, condition for allocative efficiency was

$$MRUS^A = MRUS^B = MRT \qquad (5.14)$$

which is equation 5.8 written slightly differently. As shown in Appendix 5.3, for a two-person economy where X is a public good and Y is a private good, the corresponding top-level condition is:

$$MRUS^A + MRUS^B = MRT \qquad (5.15)$$

We have shown that, given certain circumstances, the first of these will be satisfied in a market economy. It follows that the condition which is equation 5.15 will not be satisfied in a market economy. A pure market economy cannot supply a public good at the level required by allocative efficiency criteria.

A simple numerical example can provide the rationale for the condition that is equation 5.15.

Box 5.2 Examples of public goods

The classic textbook examples of public goods are lighthouses and national defence systems. These both possess the properties of being non-excludable and non-rival. If you or I choose not to pay for defence or lighthouse services, we cannot be excluded from the benefits of the service, once it is provided to anyone. Moreover, our consumption of the service does not diminish the amount available to others. Bridges also share the property of being non-rival (provided they are not used beyond a point at which congestion effects begin), although they are not typically non-excludable.

Many environmental resources are public goods, as can be seen from the following examples. You should check, in each case, that the key criterion of non-rivalry is satisfied. The benefits from biological diversity, the services of wilderness resources, the climate regulation mechanisms of the earth's atmosphere, and the waste disposal and reprocessing services of environmental sinks all constitute public goods, provided the use made of them is not excessive.

Indeed, much public policy towards such environmental resources can be interpreted in terms of regulations or incentives designed to prevent use breaking through such threshold levels.

Some naturally renewing resource systems also share public goods properties. Examples include water resource systems and the composition of the earth's atmosphere. Although in these cases consumption by one person does potentially reduce the amount of the resource available to others (so the resource could be 'scarce' in an economic sense), this will not be relevant in practice as long as consumption rates are low relative to the system's regenerative capacity.

Finally, note that many public health measures, including inoculation and vaccination against infectious diseases, have public goods characteristics, by reducing the probability of any person (whether or not he or she is inoculated or vaccinated) contracting the disease. Similarly, educational and research expenditures are, to some extent, public goods.

Box 5.3 Property rights and biodiversity

Among the many sources of value that humans derive from biological diversity is the contribution it makes to the pharmaceutical industry. This is examined in a volume which brings together a collection of papers on the theme of property rights and biological diversity (Swanson, 1995a). In this box we summarise some of the central issues raised there.

Swanson begins by noting that the biological characteristics of plants (and, to a lesser extent, animals) can be classified into primary and secondary forms. Primary characteristics concern the efficiency with which an organism directly draws upon its environment. For example, plant growth – and the survivability of a population of that plant over time – depends upon its rate of photosynthesis, by which solar energy is converted into the biological material of the plant itself. The success of a species depends on such primary characteristics; indeed, the ecological dominance of humans can be described largely in terms of the massive increases in primary productivity attained through modern agriculture.

But another set of characteristics – secondary characteristics – are also of great importance in the survivability of an organism within its environment. To survive in a particular ecological complex, an organism must be compatible with other living components of its environment. The secondary metabolites which plants develop are crucial in this respect. Some plants develop attractors (such as fruits and aromas) which increase the spread of their reproductive materials. Acorns, for example, are transported and eaten by small animals, thereby encouraging the spread of oak woodlands. Other plants develop repellents in the form of (unattractive) aromas or toxins, which give defence against predatory organisms.

A diverse ecosystem will be characterised by a large variety of biological organisms in which evolutionary processes generate a rich mix of these secondary metabolites. Many of these will be highly context-specific. That is, even within one fairly narrow class of plants, there can be a large variety of these secondary metabolites that function to give relative fitness in a particular

Box 5.3 *continued*

location. These secondary characteristics are helpful to plants and animals not only in aiding current survival but also in terms of long-term evolutionary sustainability. The presence of a diverse collection of secondary metabolites provides resources to help organisms survive environmental disruptions.

But these secondary characteristics are also of immense value to humans, and have been for much of recorded history. Let us look at a few examples discussed by Swanson. Lemons have been used to avoid scurvy in humans for hundreds of years, without any knowledge about how this beneficial effect was taking place. We now know that the active ingredient is vitamin C, one of the secondary metabolites of citrus fruits. Similarly, the bark of the willow tree was used for pain relief for centuries before the active substance (salicylic acid) was identified; its current form is the drug aspirin. More recently, the plant sweetclover was found to be causing severe internal bleeding in cattle. Trials showed that it served as an anti-coagulant across a wide variety of animals. Subsequent developments led to its use in warfarin (the major rodent poison in the world) and in drugs to treat victims of strokes (to reduce blood clotting).

Until recently, almost all medicines were derived more or less directly from natural sources. Even today, in the modern pharmaceuticals industry, a large proportion of the drugs in use throughout the world are derived from natural sources. Much work within the pharmaceuticals industry is concerned with identifying medicinal uses of secondary metabolites within plant, animal and microbial communities. The first step in this process is to develop chemicals from these organisms that have demonstrable biological effects within humans. Possible uses of the chemicals can then be found. What is interesting is that even today, the drugs developed in this way (such as those used in general anaesthesia) are often used without good understanding of their mechanism.

Two things are virtually certain. First, a large number of substances are being, or have been, used in specific cultural contexts without their usefulness having become generally known. Secondly, we have only begun to scratch the surface of the range of possible uses that the biosphere permits. Our collective knowledge encompasses only a small part of what there is to know.

All of this suggests that the conservation of biological diversity is of enormous value. This was recognised in the 1992 Rio Convention on Biological Diversity, which stated that biological diversity must be conserved and cultural/institutional diversity respected. Yet the institutional arrangements we have in place are poorly designed to conserve that diversity.

Swanson focuses on the role that property rights plays. The nub of the problem is that the system of property rights which has been built up over the past 100 years rewards the creators of information in very different ways. Consider a drug company that extracts biological specimens from various parts of the world and screens these for potential beneficial effects. Intellectual property rights will be awarded to the first individual or organisation that can demonstrate a novel use of information in a product or process. There is nothing wrong with this, of course. A system which rewards people who create useful information by granting them exclusive rights to market products that incorporate that information is of immense value. Intellectual property rights, in the form of patents and the like, give market value to information, and create incentives to search for and exploit more information.

However, Swanson points out that not all forms of information have such market value. In particular, the existence of biologically diverse ecosystems creates a reservoir of potentially useful information, but no system of property rights exists which rewards those who build up or sustain biodiversity. He writes (1995a, p. 6):

> Internationally-recognised property rights systems must be flexible enough to recognise and reward the contributions to the pharmaceutical industry of each people, irrespective of the nature of the source of that contribution. In particular, if one society generates information useful in the pharmaceutical industry by means of investing in natural capital (non-conversion of forests etc.) whereas another generates such information by investing in human capital (laboratory-based research and school-based training) each is equally entitled to an institution that recognises that contribution.

What is needed, therefore, is a property rights system that brings the value of biodiversity back into human decision-making. So-called 'intellectual' property rights should be generalised to include not only intellectual but natural sources of information. Put another

---

Box 5.3 *continued*

way, it is *information* property rights rather than just *intellectual* property rights that should be protected and rewarded. An ideal system would reward any investment that generates information, including that which is produced naturally.

It is ironic that the 'success' of modern scientific systems of medicine may be contributing to a loss of potentially useful information. Swanson points to the fact that knowledge which is used with demonstrable success in particular cultural contexts often fails to be widely recognised and rewarded. The difficulty has to do with the fact that this knowledge is not codified in ways that satisfy conventional scientific standards. Publication in academic and professional journals, for example, tends to require analysis in a standard form of each link in the chain running from chemical input to accomplished objective. Unconventional or alternative forms of medicine that cannot fit this pattern struggle to survive, even when they have demonstrable value and where no orthodox substitute exists (such as in the treatment of eczema). Reading the collection of papers in full will show you what Swanson and his co-authors recommend to rectify these shortcomings.

Source: Swanson (1995a, b)

Suppose that an allocation exists such that $MRT = 1$, $MRUS^A = 1/5$ and $MRUS^B = 2/5$, so that $MRUS^A + MRUS^B < MRT$. The fact that the MRT is 1 means that, at the margin, the private and public commodities can be exchanged in production on a one-for-one basis – the marginal cost of an extra unit of X is a unit of Y, and vice versa. The fact that $MRUS^A$ is 1/5 means that A could suffer a loss of 1 unit of X, and still be as well off if she received 1/5th of a unit of Y by way of compensation. Similarly, the fact that $MRUS^B$ is 2/5 means that B could suffer a loss of 1 unit of X, and still be as well off if he received 2/5 of a unit of Y by way of compensation. Now, consider a reduction in the production of X by 1 unit. Since X is a public good, this means that the consumption of X by both A and B will fall by 1 unit. Given the MRT of 1, the resources released by this reduction in the production of X will produce an extra unit of Y. To remain as well off as initially, A requires 1/5 of a unit of Y and B requires 2/5 of a unit. The total compensation required for both to be as well off as they were initially is $1/5 + 2/5 = 3/5$ units of Y, whereas there is available 1 unit of Y. So, at least one of them could actually be made better off than initially, with neither being worse off. This would then be a Pareto improvement. Hence, the initial situation with $MRUS^A + MRUS^B < MRT$ could not have been Pareto optimal, efficient.

Now consider an initial allocation where $MRT = 1$, $MRUS^A = 2/5$ and $MRUS^B = 4/5$ so that $MRUS^A$ + $MRUS^B > MRT$. Consider an increase of 1 unit in the supply of the public good, so that the consumption of X by both A and B increases by 1 unit. Given $MRT = 1$, the supply of Y falls by 1 unit. Given $MRUS^A = 2/5$, A could forgo 2/5 units of Y and remain as well off as initially, given X^A increased by 1. Given $MRUS^B = 4/5$, B could forgo 4/5 units of Y and remain as well off as initially, given X^B increased by 1. So, with an increase in the supply of X of 1 unit, the supply of Y could be reduced by $2/5 + 4/5 = 6/5$ without making either A or B worse off. But, in production the Y cost of an extra unit of X is just 1, which is less than 6/5. So, either A or B could actually be made better off using the 'surplus' Y. For $MRUS^A + MRUS^B > MRT$ there is the possibility of a Pareto improvement, so the initial allocation could not have been efficient.

Since both $MRUS^A + MRUS^B < MRT$ and $MRUS^A + MRUS^B > MRT$ are situations where Pareto improvements are possible, it follows that $MRUS^A + MRUS^B = MRT$ characterises situations where they are not, so it is a necessary condition for allocative efficiency.

In the case of a private good, each individual can consume a different amount. Efficiency requires, however, that all individuals must, at the margin, value it equally. It also requires, see equation 5.14, that the common valuation, at the margin, on the part of individuals is equal to the cost, at the margin, of the good. In the case of a public good, each individual must, by virtue of non-rivalry, consume the same amount of the good. Efficiency does not require that they all value it equally at the margin. It does require, see equation 5.15, that the sum of their marginal valuations be equal to the cost, at the margin, of the good.

Markets cannot provide public goods in the amounts that go with allocative efficiency. In fact, markets cannot supply public goods at all. This follows from their non-excludability characteristic. A market in widgets works on the basis that widget makers exchange the rights to exclusive control over defined bundles of widgets for the rights to exclusive control over defined bundles of something else. Usually, the exchange takes the form of the exchange of widgets for money. This can only work if the widget maker can deny access to widgets to those who do not pay, as is the case with private goods. Where access to widgets is not conditional on payment, a private firm cannot function as it cannot derive revenue from widget production. Given that the direct link between payment and access is broken by non-excludability, goods and services that have that characteristic have to be supplied by some entity that can get the revenue required to cover the costs of production from some source other than the sale of such goods and services. Such an entity is government, which has the power to levy taxes so as to raise revenue. The supply of public goods is (part of) the business of government. The existence of public goods is one of the reasons why all economists see a role for government in economic activity.

Given that it is the government that must supply a public good, the question which naturally arises for an economist is: what rule should government follow so as to supply it in amounts that correspond to efficiency? In principle, the answer to this question follows from equation 5.15. In a two-person, two-commodity economy, the efficient level of supply for the public good is the level at which the sum of two MRUSs is equal to the MRT between it and the private good. Actual economies have many individuals and many private commodities. The first point here presents no difficulty, as it is clear that we simply need to extend the summation over all MRUSs, however many there are. As regards the second, it is simply a matter of noting that the MRT is the

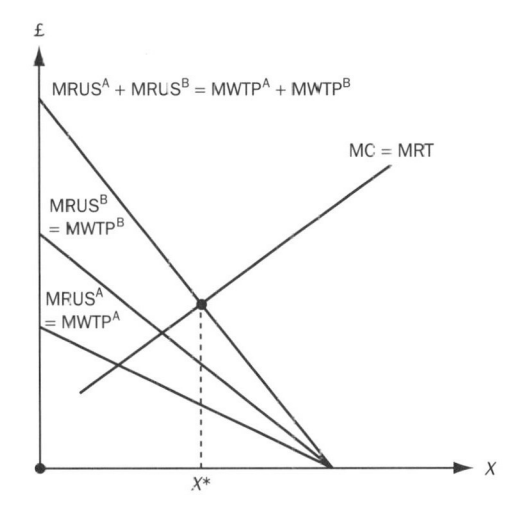

Figure 5.12 The efficient level of supply for a public good

marginal cost in terms of forgone private goods consumption, so that the rule becomes: supply the public good at the level where the sum of all the MRUSs is equal to the marginal cost. Now, it follows from its definition that the MRUS is the same as marginal willingness to pay, MWTP, so this rule can be stated as: supply the public good at the level where aggregate marginal willingness to pay is equal to marginal cost. The determination of the efficient amount of a public good, for two individuals for convenience, is illustrated in Figure 5.12.

5.9.3 Preference revelation and the free-rider problem

While the rule for the efficient supply of a public good is simple enough at the level of principle, its practical application faces a major difficulty. In order to apply the rule, the government needs to know the preferences, in terms of marginal willingness to pay, of all relevant individuals. It is in the nature of the case that those preferences are not revealed in markets. Further, if the government tries to find out what they are in some other way, then individuals have (on the standard assumptions about their motivations and behaviour) incentives not to truthfully reveal their preferences. Given that all consume equal amounts of a public good, and that exclusion from consumption on account of non-payment is impossible, individuals will try to 'free-ride' with respect to public goods provision.

To bring out the basic ideas here in a simple way we shall consider an example where the problem is to decide whether or not to provide a discrete amount of a public good, rather than to decide how much of a public good to supply. The nature of the problem is the same in either case, but is easier to state and understand in the 'yes/no' case than in the 'how much?' case. At issue is the question of whether or not to install street lighting. We will first look at this when there is no government. There are two individuals A and B. Both have an endowment of private goods worth £1000. Installing the street lighting will cost £100. The two individuals both have preferences such that they would be willing to pay £60 for the installation of street lighting. The analysis that follows is not dependent on the two individuals being equally well off and having the same preferences, that just makes the story easier to tell initially. An obvious modification of the rule derived for the efficient level of provision of a public good derived above for the 'yes/no' situation is that the decision should be 'yes' if the sum of individuals' willingness to pay is equal to or greater than the cost. In this case it is greater: £60 + £60 = £120.

Now, suppose that A and B agree to proceed in the following way. Each will independently write down on a piece of paper either 'Buy' or 'Don't buy'. If when the two pieces of paper are brought together, both have said 'Buy', they buy the street lighting jointly and share the cost equally. For two 'Don't buy' responses, the street lighting is not bought and installed. In the event of one 'Buy' and one 'Don't buy', the street lighting is bought and the individual who voted 'Buy' pays the entire cost. The four possible outcomes are shown in the cells of Table 5.5 in terms of the monetary valuations on the part of each individual, that of A to the left of the slash, that of B to the right.[6]

Table 5.5 The preference revelation problem

		B	
		Buy	Don't buy
A	Buy	1010/1010	960/1060
	Don't buy	1060/960	1000/1000

In the bottom right cell, the decision is not to go ahead. Neither incurs any cost in regard to street lighting and neither gets any benefit, so both are in their initial situations with £1000. Suppose both responded 'Buy'. Then with the street lighting installed, as shown in the top left cell, the situation for both can be expressed in monetary terms as £1010. Each has paid £50, half of the total of £100, for something valued at £60, so gaining by £10 as compared with the no street lighting situation. Suppose A wrote 'Buy' and B wrote 'Don't buy'. The lighting goes in, A pays the whole cost and B pays nothing. A pays £100 for something she values at £60, and goes from £1000 to £960. B pays nothing for something he values at £60, and goes from £1000 to £1060. This is shown in the top right cell. The bottom left cell has the entries of that cell reversed, because B pays the whole cost.

Now, clearly both are better off if both write 'Buy' and the street lighting is bought. But, either will be even better off if, as in the bottom left or top right cell, they can 'free-ride'. For each individual thinking about what to write on their piece of paper, writing 'Don't buy' is the dominant strategy. Consider individual B. If A goes for 'Buy', B gets to £1010 for 'Buy' and to £1060 for 'Don't buy'. If A goes for 'Don't buy', B gets to £960 for 'Buy' and to £1000 for 'Don't buy'. Whatever A does, B is better off going for 'Don't buy'. And the same is true for A, as can readily be checked. So, while installing the lighting and sharing the cost equally is a Pareto improvement, it will not come about where both

---

[6] This is a 'game' with the structure often referred to as 'the prisoner's dilemma' because of the setting in which the structure is often articulated. A 'game' is a situation in which agents have to take decisions the consequences of which depend on the decisions of other agents. We shall come back to looking at some game structures in Chapter 10. In the prisoner's dilemma setting, the agents are two individuals arrested for a crime and subsequently kept apart so that they cannot communicate with one another. The evidence against them is weak, and the police offer each a deal – confess to the crime and get a much lighter sentence than if you are convicted without confessing. Confession by one implicates the other. If neither confesses both go free. If both confess, both get lighter sentences. If only one confesses, the confessor gets a light sentence while the other gets a heavy sentence. The dominant strategy is confession, though both would be better off not confessing.

individuals act independently to serve their own self-interest. What is needed is some kind of co-ordination, so as to bring about the Pareto improvement which is going ahead with the street lighting.

Given what we have already said about public goods, government would seem the obvious way to bring about the required coordination. It can, in principle, ascertain whether the installation of street lighting is justified on efficiency grounds, and if it is install it and cover the cost by taxing each individual according to their willingness to pay. However, in practice, given self-seeking individuals, the free-rider problem also attends this programme. The problem comes up in trying to get the individuals to reveal their true preferences for the public good.

Suppose now that a government does exist, and that it wants to follow efficiency criteria. It knows that installing the street lighting will cost £100, and that it should install it if total willingness to pay is equal to or greater than that. It does not know the preferences, in terms of willingness to pay, of the two individuals who, in this simple example, constitute the citizenry. The obvious thing for it to do is to ask them about it. It does that, stating that the cost of installation will be met by a tax on each individual which is proportional to their willingness to pay and such that the total tax raised is equal to the cost of installation. If each individual truly reports willingness to pay £60, the street lighting will go ahead and each will pay £50 in tax. This represents a Pareto improvement – see the top left cell in Table 5.5. The problem is that the incentives facing each individual are not such as to guarantee truthful preference revelation. Given that tax liability will be proportional to stated willingness to pay, there is an incentive to understate it so as to reduce the tax liability if the street lighting goes ahead, and to get something of a free ride. In the example of Table 5.5, if B states willingness to pay as £40 and A tells the truth, the street lighting will go ahead – stated aggregate willingness to pay £100 – and B will pay 40%, rather than 50%, of £100. If A also understates willingness to pay by £20, the government's estimate of aggregate willingness to pay will mean that it does not go ahead with the lighting. The attempt to free-ride may fail if many make it.

The problem of securing truthful preference revelation in regard to the supply of public goods

has been the subject of a lot of investigation by economists. It turns out to be very difficult to come up with systems that provide the incentives for truthful revelation, and are feasible. The interested reader will find references to work in this area in the Further Reading section at the end of the chapter. Here we will, in order to indicate the nature of the difficulties, simply note one idea that is intended to overcome the free-riding incentives generated by the system just discussed. There the problem was that an individual's tax liability depended on stated willingness to pay. This could be avoided by the government's asking about willingness to pay on the understanding that each individual would, if the installation went ahead, pay a fixed sum. Suppose that the government divided the cost by the number of individuals, and stated that the fixed sum was £50 per individual. For both individuals, true willingness to pay is £60. Both have an incentive now to overstate their willingness to pay. Both value the street lighting at more than it is going to cost them so they want to see it installed. Both know that this is more likely the higher they say that their willingness to pay is, and that however much in excess of £60 they report they will only pay £50.

In this case overstating willingness to pay produces the right decision. The street lighting should be installed on the basis of true aggregate willingness to pay, and will be installed on the basis of reported willingness to pay. If the lighting is installed, each individual is better off, there is a Pareto improvement. Suppose, however, that A's willingness to pay is £55 and B's is £40. In that case, aggregate willingness to pay is £95, less than the cost of £100, and the street lighting should not be installed. In this case, on the understanding that each would pay a tax of £50 if the lighting is installed, A would have an incentive to overstate her willingness to pay as before, but B would have an incentive to understate his. In fact, it would make sense for B to report willingness to pay as £0 – if the lighting goes ahead he pays £50 for something worth just £40 to him, so he will want to do the most he can to stop it going ahead. Whether it does go ahead or not depends on how much A overstates her willingness to pay by. If A reports £200 or more, despite B reporting £0, the street lighting will be installed when on efficiency grounds it should not be.

Finally, this simple example can be used to show that even if the government could secure the truthful revelation of preferences, public goods supply is still a difficult problem. Suppose that A's true willingness to pay is £60 and B's is £41, and that somehow or other the government knows this without needing to ask the individuals. The government has to decide how to cover the cost. It could tax each in proportion to willingness to pay, but given that A and B are initially equally wealthy in terms of private goods, this is in practice unlikely as it would be regarded as unfair. Taxing each at equal shares of the cost would be likely to be seen as the 'fair' thing to do. In that case, A would pay £50 for a benefit worth £60, and B would pay £50 for a benefit worth £41. In monetary terms, as the result of installing the lighting, A would go from £1000 to £1010 and B would go from £1000 to £991. Since there is a loser this is not a Pareto improvement, though it is a potential Pareto improvement – we are into the domain of the Kaldor–Hicks–Scitovsky test. By looking at equally wealthy individuals, we avoided the problem that efficiency gains are not necessarily welfare gains. Suppose that the gainer A were much richer than the loser B. Then, the question arises as to whether gains and losses should be given equal weight in coming to a decision.

For a government to make decisions about the supply and financing of public goods according to the criteria recommended by economists requires that it have lots of difficult-to-acquire information, and can involve equity questions as well as efficiency questions.

5.10   Externalities

An external effect, or an externality, is said to occur when the production or consumption decisions of one agent have an impact on the utility or profit of another agent in an unintended way, and when no compensation/payment is made by the generator of the impact to the affected party.[7] In our analysis thus far in this chapter, we have excluded the existence of externalities by the assumptions that were made about the utility and production functions. But in practice consumption and production behaviour by some agents does affect, in uncompensated/unpaid-for ways, the utility gained by other consumers and the output produced, and profit realised, by other producers. Economic behaviour does, in fact, involve external effects.

The stated definition of an external effect is not perhaps very illuminating as to what exactly is involved. Things will become clearer as we work through the analysis. The two key things to keep in mind are that we are interested in effects from one agent to another which are unintended, and where there is no compensation, in respect of a harmful effect, or payment, in respect of a beneficial effect. We begin our analysis of externalities by discussing the forms that externalities can take.

5.10.1 Classification of externalities

In our two-person, two-(private)-commodity, two-input economy we have worked with

$$U^A = U^A(X^A, Y^A)$$

$$U^B = U^B(X^B, Y^B)$$

as utility functions, and

$$X = X(K^X, L^X)$$

$$Y = Y(K^Y, L^Y)$$

as production functions. Note that here the only things that affect an individual's utility are her own consumption levels, and that the only things that affect a firm's output are the levels of inputs that it uses. There are, that is, no external effects.

---

7   Some authors leave out from the definition of an externality the condition that the effect is not paid or compensated for, on the grounds that if there were payment or compensation then there would be no lack of intention involved, so that the lack of compensation/payment part of the definition as given in the text here is redundant. As we shall see, there is something in this. However, we prefer the definition given here as it calls attention to the fact that lack of compensation/payment is a key feature of externality as a policy problem. Policy solutions to externality problems always involve introducing some kind of compensation/payment so as to remove the unintentionality, though it has to be said that the compensation/payment does not necessarily go to/come from the affected agent.

Table 5.6 Externality classification

Arising in	Affecting	Utility/production function
Consumption	Consumption	$U^A(X^A, Y^A, X^B)$
Consumption	Production	$X(K^X, L^X, Y^A)$
Consumption	Consumption and production	$U^A(X^A, Y^A, X^B)$ and $Y(K^Y, L^Y, X^B)$
Production	Consumption	$U^A(X^A, Y^A, X)$
Production	Production	$X(K^X, L^X, Y)$
Production	Consumption and production	$U^A(X^A, Y^A, Y)$ and $X(K^X, L^X, Y)$

External effects can, first, be classified according to what sort of economic activity they originate in and what sort of economic activity they impact on. Given two sorts of economic activity, consumption and production, this gives rise to the sixfold classification shown in Table 5.6. The first column shows whether the originating agent is a consumer or producer, the second whether the affected agent is a consumer or producer, and the third provides an illustrative utility or production function for the affected agent. In Table 5.6, we are concerned only to set out the forms that unintended interdependence between agents could take. Some examples will be provided shortly.

In the first row in Table 5.6, an example of a consumption externality is where agent B's consumption of commodity X is an argument in A's utility function – B's consumption of X affects the utility that A derives from given levels of consumption of X and Y. In the second row, A's consumption of Y is shown as affecting the production of X, for given levels of capital and labour input. Row 3 has B's consumption of X affecting both A's utility and the production of Y. In row 4, the amount of X produced, as well as A's consumption of X, affects A's utility. Row 5 has the production of Y determining, for given capital and labour inputs, the amount of X produced. Finally, in row 6 we have a situation where the level of Y affects both A's utility and the production of X.

The unintended impact that an external effect involves may be harmful or beneficial. Table 5.7 provides examples of both kinds. If an individual has a vaccination that protects them, which is their intention, it also has the unintended effect of reducing the probability that others will contract the disease. An individual playing their radio loudly in the park inflicts suffering on others, though that is not their intention. In these two cases, the external effect originates in consumption and affects individuals. A beneficial externality originating in production, and impacting on production, is the case where a honey producer's bees pollinate a nearby fruit orchard. Pollution, in the bottom right cell, is a harmful externality which most usually originates in production activities. It can affect consumers, or producers, or both.

Another dimension according to which external effects can be classified is in terms of whether they have, or do not have, the public goods characteristics of non-rivalry and non-excludability. While external effects can have the characteristics of private goods, those that are most relevant for policy analysis exhibit non-rivalry and non-excludability. This is especially the case with external effects that involve the natural environment, which mainly involve pollution problems. Why this is the case will become clear in the analysis that follows here. All of the examples in Table 5.7 involve non-rivalry and non-excludability.

5.10.2 Externalities and economic efficiency

Externalities are a source of market failure. Given that all of the other institutional conditions for a pure market system to realise an efficient allocation hold, if there is a beneficial externality the market will produce too little of it in relation to the

Table 5.7 Beneficial and harmful externalities

Effect on others	Originating in consumption	Originating in production
Beneficial	Vaccination against an infectious disease	Pollination of blossom arising from proximity to apiary
Adverse	Noise pollution from radio playing in park	Chemical factory discharge of contaminated water into water systems

---

Box 5.4 Atmospheric ozone and market failure

Evidence now suggests that the accumulation of tropospheric ozone in urban areas poses serious threats to human health, and also leads to agricultural crop damage in surrounding areas.[8] A major source of tropospheric ozone is road vehicle exhaust emissions. Because vehicle emissions have real effects on well-being through our utility and production functions, these emissions can be termed 'goods' (although it may be preferable to label them as 'bads' as the effects on utility are adverse). However, with no individual private property rights in clean air, in the absence of government intervention, no charge is made for such emissions. With no charges being made for damaging emissions, resources will not be allocated efficiently. An efficient allocation would involve lower exhaust emissions, implying one or more of: lower traffic volumes, change in fuel type used, increased

engine efficiency, enhanced exhaust control. How such objectives might be achieved is considered in this chapter, and in more detail in Chapter 7, but it should be clear at this stage that one method would be through the use of a tax on the emissions that cause ozone accumulation. An efficient emissions tax would impose a tax rate equal to the value of the marginal damage that would occur at the efficient level of emissions.

In arriving at this conclusion, we do not explicitly consider the time dimension of pollution. But note that if ozone accumulates over time, and damage is dependent on the stock of ozone rather than the flow of emissions in any particular period, then we need to consider the accumulation of the pollutant over time. As Chapter 16 shows, where emission flows lead to accumulating stocks of pollutants, it may be efficient to impose a tax rate that rises over time.

---

[8] Note that this accumulation of ozone in lower layers of the atmosphere is completely distinct from the destruction of the ozone layer in the earth's upper atmosphere (the stratosphere). The latter phenomenon – often known as 'holes in the ozone layer' – causes different problems, as is explained in Chapter 10.

---

requirements of allocative efficiency, while in the case of a harmful externality the market will produce more of it than efficiency requires. Since we are concerned with the application of welfare economics to environmental problems, and the main relevance of externalities there is in regard to environmental pollution, we shall look in any detail only at harmful externalities here. Box 5.4 concerns an important example of a harmful externality pollution problem. We will demonstrate that the market, in the absence of corrective policy, will 'over-supply' pollution by looking at three sorts of pollution problem – a consumer-to-consumer case, a producer-to-producer case, and a case where the unintended effect is from a producer to consumers. These three cases bring out all of the essential features of pollution as a market failure problem. In the text we shall use diagrams and partial equilibrium analysis to make the essential points – the reader may find it useful to review our exposition of this method of analysis in an earlier part of this chapter. In Appendix 5.3 we cover the same ground using general equilibrium analysis.

Before getting into these cases in a little detail, we can make a general intuitive point that covers both beneficial and harmful externalities. The basic problem with external effects follows directly from the definition in regard to unintendedness and lack of payment/compensation. These two features of the externality problem are directly related. The lack of intentionality follows from the fact that the impact involved does not carry with it any recompense, in the case of a beneficial effect, or penalty, in the case of a harmful effect. External effects arise where an agent's actions affecting other agents do not involve any feedback – benefit is conferred which is not rewarded, or harm is done which is not punished. Given the lack of reward/punishment, which in a market system would be signalled by monetary payment, an agent will not take any account of the effect concerned. It will be unintended and 'external' to their decision making. Where it is a beneficial effect, it will not be encouraged sufficiently, and there will not be enough of it. Where it is a harmful effect, it will not be discouraged sufficiently, and there will be too much of it. The key to dealing with the market failure that external effects give rise to is to put in place the missing feedbacks, to create a system which does reward/punish the generation of beneficial/harmful effects, so that they are no longer unintentional.

5.10.3 Consumption–consumption externality

Suppose that A and B live in adjacent flats (apartments). A is a saxophone player, who enjoys practising a lot. B does not like music, and can hear A practising. The utility functions are

$$U^A = U^A(M^A, S^A)$$

$$U^B = U^B(M^B, S^A)$$

where M represents wealth and S^A is the hours that A plays the saxophone each week, with $\partial U^A/\partial M^A > 0$, $\partial U^B/\partial M^B > 0$, $\partial U^A/\partial S^A > 0$ and $\partial U^B/\partial S^A < 0$. In Figure 5.13 we show, as MB, the marginal benefit of playing to A, and, as MEC for marginal external cost, the marginal cost of playing to B. Marginal benefit is the amount that A would pay, if it were necessary, to play a little more. Conversely, MB is the amount of compensation that would be required to leave A as well off given a small reduction in playing. Marginal external cost is the amount that B would be willing to pay for a little less playing. Conversely, MEC is the amount of compensation that would be required to leave B as well off given a small increase in M (hours of A's saxophone playing).

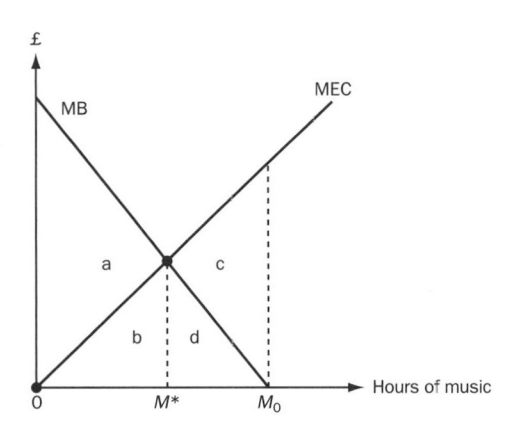

Figure 5.13 The bargaining solution to an externality problem

Given that A does not in fact have to pay anything to play her saxophone in her flat, she will increase her hours of playing up to the level M_0, where MB is equal to zero. At that level, A's total benefit from playing is given by the sum of the areas of the triangles a, b and d, and B's total suffering is measured in money terms by the sum of the areas b, d and c.

This is not an efficient outcome, because at M_0, MEC > MB. The efficient outcome is at M^* where MEC = MB. At any M to the left of M^*, MB > MEC, so that for a small increase in M, A would be willing to pay more than would compensate B for that increase. At any M to the right of M^*, MEC > MB so that for a small decrease in M, B would be willing to pay more for a small decrease in M than would be required to compensate A for that decrease. The inefficient level of saxophone playing at M_0 comes about because there are no payments in respect of variations in M, no market in M, so that the effect on B is unintentional on the part of A.

At the level of principle, the solution to this problem of inefficiency is fairly obvious. The problem is that A does not compensate B because B does not have any legal right to such compensation, does not have a property right in a domestic environment unpolluted by saxophone music. So, the solution is to establish such a property right, to give B the legal right to a domestic environment that is not noise-polluted. Such legal arrangements would support bargaining which would lead to M^* as the level of M. The argument that establishes that M^* would be the outcome under a legal regime where B can claim compensation from A exactly parallels the argument that establishes that M^* is the efficient outcome. To the left of M^*, with MB > MEC, A will be willing to pay more in compensation for a small increase in M than B requires, so will pay and play more. A will not increase M beyond M^* because the compensation that it would be necessary to pay B would be greater than the worth to A of the small increase thereby attained.

5.10.3.1 The Coase theorem

The idea that, given a suitable assignment of property rights, private bargaining between individuals can correct externality problems and lead to efficient outcomes is generally attributed to the Nobel prize winning economist Ronald Coase, and the result discussed above is often referred to as the 'Coase theorem' (the seminal paper is Coase, 1960). In fact, the result discussed above is only half of the Coase theorem. The other half says that an efficient outcome can also be attained by vesting the property right in the generator of the external effect. In that case, the generator would have the legal right to play, for this example, as much saxophone as she liked. The point is that given that right, it could be in the interests of the victim to offer money to the generator not to exercise their right to the full. Just as the absence of a clear property right vested in the victim inhibits one kind of bargaining, so does the absence of a clear property right vested in the generator inhibit another kind of bargaining.

Suppose then, that in our saxophone-playing example a law is passed saying that all saxophone players have an absolute right to practise up to the limits of their physical endurance. Legally A can play as much as she wants. But, a legal right can be traded. So, the opportunity now exists for A and B to bargain to a contract specifying the amount that A will actually play. That amount will be M^* in Figure 5.13. To the right of M^*, MEC > MB, so B's willingness to pay for a small reduction is greater than the compensation that A requires for that small reduction. Starting at M_0 and considering successive small reductions, B will be offering more than A requires until M^* is reached where B's offer will exactly match the least that A would accept. A and B would not be able to agree on a level of M to the left of M^*, since there B's willingness to pay is less than A requires by way of compensation.

So, what the Coase theorem actually says is that given this kind of externality situation, due to incomplete private property rights, one solution involves creating property rights for either the victim or the generator, and that either assignment will lead to an efficient outcome. It needs to be explicitly and carefully noted here that there are two things that are not being claimed. First, that it is not being said that the outcome will be the same in both cases. Second, that it is not being said that either way of assigning property rights necessarily promotes equity.

In regard to the first point here, note that considering the move from M_0 to M^* in our saxophone music example consequent upon the establishment of the property right and the ensuing bargaining we have:

(a) For the case where B gets the property right – there is an M reduction of $(M_0 - M^*)$ and A pays B an amount equal to the area of triangle b, the money value of B's suffering at the efficient outcome M^*.

(b) For the case where A gets the property right – there is an M reduction of $(M_0 - M^*)$ and B pays A an amount equal to the area of triangle d, the money value of A's loss as compared with the no-property-rights situation.

Clearly, which way the property right is assigned affects the wealth of A or B. To be granted a new property right is to have one's potential monetary wealth increased. In case (a), B experiences less saxophone hours and an increase in wealth by virtue of a payment from A, so that A's wealth goes down with her pleasure from playing. In case (b), B experiences less saxophone hours and a decrease in wealth by virtue of a payment to A, who gets less pleasure from playing. As we have drawn Figure 5.13, in neither (a) nor (b) does the increase in wealth affect the receiving individual's tastes. In case (a), that is, B's willingness to pay for less music hours is not affected by becoming wealthier – the slope of the MEC line does not change. In case (b), A's willingness to pay for more music hours is not affected by becoming wealthier – the slope and position of the MB line do not change. While these assumptions may be plausible in this example, they clearly are not generally appropriate. They were imposed here to produce a simple and clear graphical representation. If the assumption that tastes are unaffected by wealth increases is dropped, then with the case (a) assignment MEC would shift and with the case (b) assignment MB would shift. In neither case then would M^* as shown in Figure 5.13 be the bargaining outcome, and the outcomes would be different in the two cases. Both outcomes would be efficient, because in both cases we would have MB = MEC, but they would involve different levels of M.

So, the first point is that the Coase theorem properly understood says that there will be an efficient outcome under either assignment of property rights, not that there will be the same efficient outcome under either assignment. The second point, concerning equity, is simply that there is no implication that either assignment will have any desirable implications in terms of equity. This follows directly from our earlier discussions of the relationship between optimality and efficiency. In the case of our saxophone example, we have said nothing about the initial wealth/income situations of the two individuals. Clearly, our views on which way the property right should be assigned will, unless we are totally uninterested in equity, be affected by the wealth/income of the two individuals. Given that efficiency criteria do not discriminate between the two possible assignments of property rights, it might seem natural to take the view that the assignment should be on the basis of equity considerations. Unfortunately, this does not lead to any generally applicable rules. It is not always the case that externality sufferers are relatively poor and generators relatively rich, or vice versa. Even if we confine attention to a particular class of nuisance, such as saxophone playing in flats, it cannot be presumed that sufferers deserve, on equity grounds, to get the property right – some may be poor in relation to their neighbour and some rich.

Given the simple and compelling logic of the arguments of the Coase theorem, the question arises as to why uncorrected externalities are a problem. If they exist by virtue of poorly defined property rights and can be solved by the assignment of clearly defined property rights, why have legislatures not acted to deal with externality problems by assigning property rights? A full answer to this question would be well beyond the scope of this book, but the following points are worthy of note. First, as we have seen, the case for property rights solutions is entirely an efficiency case. Legislators do not give efficiency criteria the weight that economists do – they are interested in all sorts of other criteria. Second, even given clearly defined property rights, bargaining is costly. The costs increase with the number of par-

ticipants. While expositions of the Coase theorem deal with small numbers of generators and sufferers, typically one of each, externality problems that are matters for serious policy concern generally involve many generators and/or many sufferers, and are often such that it is difficult and expensive to relate one particular agent's suffering to another particular agent's action. This makes bargaining expensive, even if the necessary property rights exist in law. The costs of bargaining, or more generally 'transactions costs', may be so great as to make bargaining infeasible. Third, even leaving aside the large numbers problem, in many cases of interest the externality has public bad characteristics which preclude bargaining as a solution.[9] We shall discuss this last point in the context of producer-to-consumer externalities.

5.10.4 Production–production externality

For situations where numbers are small, this case can be dealt with rather quickly. Consider two firms with production functions

$$X = X(K^X, L^X, S)$$

$$Y = Y(K^Y, L^Y, S)$$

where S stands for pollutant emissions arising in the production of Y, which emissions affect the output of X for given levels of K and L input there. As an example, Y is paper produced in a mill which discharges effluent S into a river upstream from a laundry which extracts water from the river to produce clean linen, X. Then, the assumption is that $\partial Y/\partial S > 0$, so that for given levels of K^Y and L^Y lower S emissions means lower Y output, and that $\partial X/\partial S < 0$, so that for given levels of K^X and L^X higher S means lower X.[10]

This externality situation is amenable to exactly the same kind of treatment as the consumer-to-consumer case just considered. Property rights could be assigned to the downstream sufferer or to the

---

[9] 'Public bad' is a term often used for a public good that confers negative, rather than positive, utility on those who consume it.
[10] Note that we are guilty here of something that we cautioned against in Chapter 2 in our discussion of the materials balance principle – writing a production function in which there is a material

output, S, for which no material input basis is given. We do this in the interests of simplicity. A more appropriate production function specification is given in Appendix 5.3, where it is shown that the essential point for present purposes is not affected by our shortcut in the interests of simplicity.

upstream generator. Bargaining could then, in either case, produce an efficient outcome. To see this simply requires the reinterpretation and relabelling of the horizontal axis in Figure 5.13 so that it refers to S, with S_0 replacing M_0 and S^* replacing M^*. For profits in the production of X we have

$$\pi^X = P_X X(K^X, L^X, S) - P_K K^X - P_L L^X$$

where $\partial \pi^X / \partial S < 0$. The impact of a small increase in S on profits in the production of X is, in the terminology of Figure 5.13, marginal external cost, MEC. For profits in the production of Y we have

$$\pi^Y = P_X Y(K^Y, L^Y, S) - P_K K^Y - P_L L^Y$$

where $\partial \pi^Y / \partial S > 0$. The impact of a small increase in S on profits in the production of Y is, in the terminology of Figure 5.13, marginal benefit, MB. With these reinterpretations, the previous analysis using Figure 5.13 applies to the producer-to-producer case – in the absence of a well-defined property right S will be too large for efficiency, while an efficient outcome can result from bargaining based on a property right assigned to either the producer of X or the producer of Y.

An alternative way of internalising the externality would be to have the firms collude so as to maximise their joint profits. That this would produce an efficient outcome is proved in Appendix 5.3. The matter is, however, quite intuitive. The externality arises because the Y producer does not take account of the effects of its actions on the output for given inputs of the X producer. If the Y producer chooses its levels of K^Y, L^Y and S in the light of the consequences for the output of X for given K^X and L^X, and hence on the profits arising in the production of X, then those consequences will not be unintended. On the contrary, the two firms will be operated as if they were a single firm producing two commodities. We know that a single firm producing a single commodity will behave as required for efficiency, given all of the ideal conditions. All that is being said now is that this result carries over to a firm producing two commodities. For the firm that is producing both X and Y the ideal conditions do apply, as there is no impact on its activities the level of which is unintentionally set by others.

While joint profit maximisation can internalise an externality as required for efficiency, there appear to be few, if any, recorded instances of firms colluding, or merging, so as to internalise a pollution externality. Collusion to maximise joint profits will only occur if both firms believe that their share of maximised joint profits will be larger than the profits earned separately. There is, in general, no reason to suppose that cases where there is the prospect of both firms making higher profits with collusion will coincide with circumstances where there is a recognised inter-firm pollution externality.

5.10.5 Production–consumption externality

The key feature of the case to be considered now is that the external effect impact on two agents, and with respect to them is non-rival and non-excludable in consumption. As is the case generally in this chapter, 'two' is a convenient way of looking at 'many' – the two case brings out all the essential features of the many case while simplifying the notation and the analysis. Putting this key feature in the context of the production-to-consumption case aligns with the perceived nature of the pollution problems seen as most relevant to policy determination. These are typically seen as being situations where emissions arising in production adversely affect individuals in ways that are non-rival and non-excludable.

So, in terms of our two-person, two-commodity economy we assume that:

$$U^A = U^A(X^A, Y^A, S) \text{ with } \partial U^A / \partial S < 0$$

$$U^B = U^B(X^B, Y^B, S) \text{ with } \partial U^B / \partial S < 0$$

$$X = X(K^X, L^X)$$

$$Y = Y(K^Y, L^Y, S) \text{ with } \partial Y / \partial S > 0$$

Emissions arise in the production of Y and adversely affect the utilities of A and B. The pollution experienced by A and B is non-rival and non-excludable. A concrete example, bearing in mind that 'two' stands for 'many', would be a fossil-fuel-burning electricity plant located in an urban area. Its emissions pollute the urban airshed, and, to a first

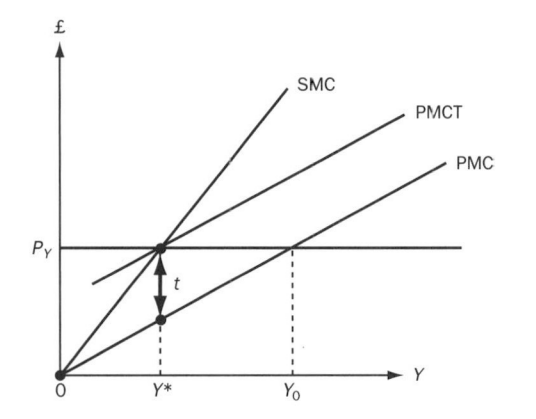

Figure 5.14 Taxation for externality correction

approximation, all who live within the affected area experience the same level of atmospheric pollution.

Given our earlier discussion of the supply of public goods, we can immediately conclude here that private bargaining based on some assignment of property rights will not deal with the externality problem. And, the joint profit maximisation solution is not relevant. In this kind of situation, correcting the market failure requires some kind of ongoing intervention in the workings of the market by some government agency. As we shall consider at some length and in some detail in Part II of the book, there is a range of means of intervention that the government agency, call it an environmental protection agency or EPA, could use. Here, we shall just look at the use of taxation by the EPA, so as to bring out the essential features of the situation where the externality has the characteristics of a public bad. A formal general equilibrium analysis is sketched in Appendix 5.3. Here we shall use partial equilibrium analysis based on Figure 5.14.

It introduces some new terminology. PMC stands for private marginal cost. Private costs are the input costs that the Y producer actually takes account of in determining its profit-maximising output level, i.e.

$$C = P_K K^Y + P_L L^Y = C(Y)$$

so that PMC $= \partial C/\partial Y$. We introduced the idea of MEC (marginal external cost) in considering the consumer-to-consumer case, as the amount that the sufferer would be willing to pay to reduce suffering by a small amount. In the present case there are two

sufferers and MEC is the sum of the willingness to pay of each of them, as consumption of suffering is non-rival and non-excludable. We define social marginal cost as:

SMC = PMC + MEC

Figure 5.14 shows PMC increasing with Y in the usual way. The SMC line has a steeper slope than the PMC line, so that MEC is increasing with Y – as Y production increases, S output increases.

To maximise profit, the Y firm will produce at Y_0, where PMC is equal to the output price P_Y. This is not the Y output that goes with efficiency, as in balancing costs and benefits at the margin it is ignoring the costs borne by A and B. Efficiency requires the balancing at the margin of benefits and costs which include the external costs borne by A and B. The efficient output level for Y is, that is, Y^* where SMC equals P_Y. In the absence of any correction of the market failure that is the external costs imposed on A and B, the market-determined level of Y output will be too high for efficiency, as will the corresponding level of S.

To correct this market failure the EPA can tax S at a suitable rate. In Figure 5.14, we show a line labelled PMCT, which stands for private marginal cost with the tax in place. This line shows how the Y firm's marginal costs behave given that the EPA is taxing S at the appropriate rate. As shown in Figure 5.14, the appropriate tax rate is

$$t = \text{SMC}^* - \text{PMC}^* = \text{MEC}^* \tag{5.16}$$

that is, the tax needs to be equal to marginal external cost at the efficient levels of Y and S. In Appendix 5.3 we show that another way of stating this is:

$$t = P_X \lfloor \text{MRUS}^A_{XS} + \text{MRUS}^B_{XS} \rfloor \tag{5.17}$$

Comparing equations 5.16 and 5.17, we are saying that

$$\text{MEC}^* = P_X \lfloor \text{MRUS}^A_{XS} + \text{MRUS}^B_{XS} \rfloor \tag{5.18}$$

This makes a lot of sense. Recall that MRUS stands for marginal rate of utility substitution. The XS subscripts indicate that it is the MRUS for commodity X and pollution S that is involved here. Recall also that the MRUS gives the amount of the increase in, in this case, X that would keep utility constant in the face of a small increase in S. Equation 5.18 says that

MEC* is the monetary value of the extra consumption of commodity X by A and B that would be required to compensate them both for a small increase in S, from the efficient level of S. In saying this we are choosing to use the commodity X as the compensation vehicle. We could equally well have chosen the commodity Y for this purpose and derived

$$t = P_Y \lfloor \text{MRUS}_{YS}^A + \text{MRUS}_{YS}^B \rfloor \qquad (5.19a)$$

and

$$\text{MEC*} = P_Y \lfloor \text{MRUS}_{YS}^A + \text{MRUS}_{YS}^B \rfloor \qquad (5.19b)$$

Taxation at the rate MEC* is required to bring about efficiency. Note that the tax rate required is not MEC at Y_0, is not MEC in the uncorrected situation. In order to be able to impose taxation of emissions at the required rate, the EPA would need to be able to identify Y^*. Given that prior to EPA intervention what is actually happening is Y_0, identification of Y^* and calculation of the corresponding MEC* would require that the EPA knew how MEC varied with S, i.e. knew the utility functions of A and B. It is in the nature of the case that this information is not revealed in markets. The problems of preference revelation in regard to public goods were discussed above. Clearly, those problems carry over to public bads such as pollution. The implications of this for feasible policy in respect of pollution control by taxation are discussed in Part II of the book.

Finally here we should note that the basic nature of the result derived here for the case where just one production activity gives rise to the emissions of concern carries over to the case where the emissions arise in more than one production activity. Consider a two-person, two-commodity economy where

$$U^A = U^A(X^A, Y^A, S) \text{ with } \partial U^A/\partial S < 0$$

$$U^B = U^B(X^B, Y^B, S) \text{ with } \partial U^B/\partial S < 0$$

$$X = X(K^X, L^X, S^X) \text{ with } \partial S/\partial S^X > 0$$

$$Y = Y(K^Y, L^Y, S^Y) \text{ with } \partial Y/\partial S^Y > 0$$

$$S = S^X + S^Y$$

Both production activities involve emissions of S, and both individuals are adversely affected by the total amount of S emissions. In this case, efficiency requires that emissions from both sources be taxed at the same rate, $t = \text{MEC*}$.

5.11 The second-best problem

In our discussion of market failure thus far we have assumed that just one of the ideal conditions required for markets to achieve efficiency is not satisfied. Comparing our list of the institutional arrangements required for markets to achieve efficiency with the characteristics of actual economies indicates that the latter typically depart from the former in several ways rather than just in one way. In discussing harmful externalities generated by firms, we have, for example, assumed that the firms concerned sell their outputs into perfectly competitive markets, are price-takers. In fact, very few of the industries in a modern economy are made up of firms that act as price-takers.

An important result in welfare economics is the second-best theorem. This demonstrates that if there are two or more sources of market failure, correcting just one of them as indicated by the analysis of it as if it were the only source of market failure will not necessarily improve matters in efficiency terms. It may make things worse. What is required is an analysis that takes account of multiple sources of market failure, and of the fact that not all of them can be corrected, and derives, as 'the second-best policy', a package of government interventions that do the best that can be done given that not all sources of market failure can be corrected.

To show what is involved, we consider in Figure 5.15 an extreme case of the problem mentioned above, where the polluting firm is a monopolist. As

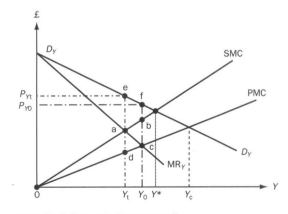

Figure 5.15 The polluting monopolist

above, we assume that the pollution arises in the production of Y. The profit-maximising monopolist faces a downward-sloping demand function, $D_Y D_Y$, and produces at the level where marginal cost equals marginal revenue, MR_Y. Given an uncorrected externality, the monopolist will use PMC here, and the corresponding output level will be Y_0. From the point of view of efficiency, there are two problems about the output level Y_0. It is too low on account of the monopolist setting marginal cost equal to marginal revenue rather than price: Y_c is the output level that goes with PMC $= P_Y$. It is too high on account of the monopolist ignoring the external costs generated and working with PMC rather than SMC: Y_t is the output level that goes with SMC $= MR_Y$. What efficiency requires is SMC $= P_Y$, with corresponding output level Y^*.

Now suppose that there is an EPA empowered to tax firms' emissions and that it does this so that for this monopolist producer of Y, SMC becomes the marginal cost on which it bases its decisions. As a result of the EPA action, Y output will go from Y_0 down to Y_t, with the price of Y increasing from P_{Y0} to P_{Yt}. The imposition of the tax gives rise to gains and losses. As intended, there is a gain in so far as pollution damage is reduced – the monetary value of this reduction is given by the area abcd in Figure 5.15. However, as a result of the price increase, there is a loss of consumers' surplus, given by the area $P_{Yt}efP_{Y0}$. It cannot be presumed generally that the gain will be larger than the loss. The outcome depends on the slopes and positions of PMC, SMC and $D_Y D_Y$, and in any particular case the EPA would have to have all that information in order to figure out whether imposing the tax would involve a net gain or a net loss.

When dealing with polluting firms that face downward-sloping demand functions, in order to secure efficiency in allocation the EPA needs two instruments – one to internalise the externality and another to correct under-production due to the firms' setting MC $=$ MR rather than MC $= P$. With two such instruments, the EPA could induce the firm to operate at Y^* where SMC $= P_Y$. However, EPAs are not given the kinds of powers that this would

require. They can tax emissions, but they cannot regulate monopoly. It can be shown that, given complete information on the cost and demand functions, and on how damages vary with the firm's behaviour, the EPA could figure out a second-best tax rate to be levied on emissions.[11] The second-best tax rate is one that guarantees that the gains from its imposition will exceed the losses. It does not move the firm to Y^* in Figure 5.15, but it does guarantee that the equivalent to abcd that it induces will be larger than the corresponding equivalent to $P_{Yt}efP_{Y0}$. The level of the second-best tax rate depends on the damage done by the pollutant, the firm's costs, and the elasticity of demand for its output. With many polluting monopolies to deal with, the EPA would be looking at imposing different tax rates on each, even where all produce the same emissions, on account of the different elasticities of demand that they would face in their output markets. It needs to be noted that charging different firms different rates of tax on emissions of the same stuff is unlikely to be politically feasible, even if the EPA had the information required to calculate the different rates.

5.12 Imperfect information

Given that all of the other ideal institutional arrangements are in place, the attainment of efficient outcomes through unregulated market behaviour presupposes that all transactors are perfectly informed about the implications for themselves of any possible transaction. This is clearly a strong requirement, not always satisfied in actual market economies. The requirement carries over to the analysis of the correction of market failure. Consider, to illustrate the point here, a case of consumption-to-consumption external effect where two individuals share a flat and where A is a smoker but B is not. Suppose that B does not find cigarette smoke unpleasant, and is unaware of the dangers of passive smoking. Then, notwithstanding that the government has legislated for property rights in domestic air unpolluted with cigarette smoke, B will not seek to reduce A's

[11] See Chapter 6 of Baumol and Oates (1988).

smoking. Given B's ignorance, the fact that bargaining is possible is irrelevant. The level of smoke that B endures will be higher than it would be if B were not ignorant. Given that B does not, when legally he could, bargain down A's level of smoking, we could describe the situation as one of 'conditional efficiency'. But this is not really very helpful. Rather, we recognise B's ignorance and consider it to be the source of an uncorrected externality. The nature of the corrective policy in the case of imperfect information is clear – the provision of information. In many cases, the information involved will have the characteristics of a public good, and there is a role for government in the provision of accurate information.

In some cases the government cannot fulfil this role because it does not have accurate and unambiguous information. Particularly where it is the future consequences of current actions that are at issue – as for example in the case of global warming – it may be simply impossible for anybody to have complete and accurate information. We all, as they say, live in an uncertain world. Imperfect information about the future consequences of current actions becomes particularly important in circumstances where those actions have irreversible consequences. It does appear to be the case that many of the consequences of decisions about environmental resource use are irreversible. Global warming may be a case in point. Again, it is arguable that, once developed, a natural wilderness area cannot be returned to its natural state. We take up some of the issues arising from such considerations in Parts III and IV of the book.

5.13 Government failure

We have shown that government intervention offers the possibility of realising efficiency gains, by eliminating or mitigating situations of market failure. First, many environmental resources are not subject to well-defined and clearly established property rights. As we have seen, efficiency gains may be obtained if government can create and maintain appropriate institutional arrangements for establishing and supporting property rights as the basis for

bargaining. However, we have also seen that the scope of this kind of government action to correct market failure is limited to cases where non-rivalry and non-excludability are absent. Many environmental problems do involve non-rivalry and non-excludability. In such cases, possible government interventions to correct market failure are often classified into two groups. So-called command-and-control instruments take the form of rules and regulations prohibiting, limiting or requiring certain forms of behaviour. Fiscal instruments – tax and subsidy systems, and marketable permits – are designed to create appropriate patterns of incentives on private behaviour. We have looked at taxation briefly in this chapter, and we shall explore all of these instruments in depth in Chapter 7. As noted immediately above, another form that government intervention to correct market failure could take is providing information, or funding research activity that can increase the stock of knowledge. The arguments we have used so far in this chapter have all pointed to the possibility of efficiency gains arising from public-sector intervention in the economy. But actual government intervention does not always or necessarily realise such gains, and may entail losses. It would be wrong to conclude from an analysis of 'market failure' that all government intervention in the functioning of a market economy is either desirable or effective.

First, the removal of one cause of market failure does not necessarily result in a more efficient allocation of resources if there remain other sources of market failure. We discussed this above, using the case of the polluting monopolist as an illustration. A second consideration is that government intervention may itself induce economic inefficiency. Poorly designed tax and subsidy schemes, for example, may distort the allocation of resources in unintended ways. Any such distortions need to be offset against the intended efficiency gains when the worth of intervention is being assessed.

In some cases, the chosen policy instruments may simply fail to achieve desired outcomes. This is particularly likely in the case of instruments that take the form of quantity controls or direct regulation. One example of this is the attempt by the Greek government to reduce car usage, and hence congestion and pollution, in Athens. Regulations prohibiting entry into the city by cars with particular letters on their licence plates on particular days has served to promote the purchase of additional cars by households wishing to maintain freedom of mobility in the city. Similarly, the use of quantity controls in fisheries policy (such as determining minimum mesh sizes for nets, maximum number of days of permitted fishing, required days in port for vessels, and so on), intended to address the free-access problem of overexploitation, have met with very little success. Fishermen have responded to the regulations by making behavioural adjustments to minimise their impact. The limited success of quantitative controls in fishing is explored at length in Chapter 17.

It is not the case that actual government interventions are always motivated by efficiency, or even equity, considerations. It has been argued that the way government actually works in democracies can best be understood by applying to the political process the assumption of self-interested behaviour that economists use in analysing market processes. Four classes of political agent are distinguished: voters, elected members of the legislature, workers in the bureaucracy, and pressure groups. Voters are assumed to vote for candidates they believe will serve their own interests. Legislators are assumed to maximise their chances of re-election. Bureaucrats are assumed to seek to enlarge the size of the bureaucracy, so improving their own career prospects. Pressure groups push special interests with politicians and bureaucrats. The argument is that, given these motivations and circumstances, the outcome is not going to be a set of enacted policies that promote either efficiency or equity.

Politicians lack accurate information about voters' preferences. Voters lack reliable information about politicians' intentions. It is relatively easy for pressure groups to get their message across to politicians precisely because they focus on particular concerns arising from the strongly held views of a relatively small number of individuals or firms. Pressure groups access politicians directly, and via the bureaucracy. Bureaucrats, given their self-interest, amplify for politicians the messages from pressure groups that appear to call for a larger bureaucracy. They also control the flow of technical information to the politicians. The outcome of all this is, it is argued, an excessively large government doing, largely, things which keep, at least some, pressure groups happy, rather than things that reflect the preferences of the majority of voters.

Summary

In this chapter, we have defined and explained the terms 'efficiency' and 'optimality' as they are used in welfare economics. We have also demonstrated that a perfectly functioning 'ideal' market economy would bring about an efficient outcome, but not necessarily an optimal one.

However, it is clear that economies in practice do not satisfy the conditions of the ideal competitive economy that we described above. Markets are incomplete – there are many things that concern economic agents that are not traded in markets. Where they exist, markets are often not perfectly competitive. Many producers and consumers operate with information that is not perfect. Government must exist and raise revenue for the supply of public goods. Often, consumption and production behaviour generates uncompensated external effects upon others. These 'failures' will result in inefficient allocations of resources.

Many of the services that the environment provides involve some kind of market failure, and hence the levels of provision in a market system will not be those corresponding to allocative efficiency. Much of resource and environmental economics is about devising ways to intervene in the market system so as to promote efficiency in the use of environmental services. In the next Part of the book we look at the problem of pollution, building on our preliminary discussion of that problem in this chapter under the externality rubric.

Further reading

For a thorough general coverage of welfare economics principles, see Bator (1957), Baumol (1977), Just *et al.* (1982), Kreps (1990), Varian (1987) or Layard and Walters (1978, chapter 1). Cornes and Sandler (1996) is an excellent advanced treatment of the welfare economics of public goods and externalities. Baumol and Oates (1988) develops the theory of environmental economics, with special attention to policy, from the welfare economics of public goods and externalities; see also Dasgupta (1990), Fisher (1981), Johansson (1987), Mäler (1985), and McInerney (1976). Verhoef (1999) is a recent survey of externality theory in relation to environmental economics, and Proost (1999) surveys contributions from public-sector economics. Classic early articles on environmental externalities include Ayres and Kneese (1969) and D'Arge and Kogiku (1972).

The analysis of democratic governance in terms of self-interested behaviour by politicians, voters, bureaucrats and pressure groups was systematically developed by Buchanan: see, for example, Buchanan and Tullock (1980). Renner (1999) derives some implications for sustainability policy from the work of the 'Virginia school' associated with Buchanan. Everret in Dietz *et al.* (1993) considers the history of environmental legislation in the USA in the period 1970 to 1990 within this framework.

Discussion questions

1. 'If the market puts a lower value on trees as preserved resources than as sources of timber for construction, then those trees should be felled for timber.' Discuss.

2. Do you think that individuals typically have enough information for it to make sense to have their preferences determine environmental policy?

3. How is the level of provision of national defence services, a public good, actually determined? Suggest a practical method for determining the level of provision that would satisfy an economist.

4. Economists see pollution problems as examples of the class of adverse externality phenomena. An adverse externality is said to occur when the decisions of one agent harm another in an unintended way, and when no compensation occurs. Does this mean that if a pollution source, such as a power station, compensates those affected by its emissions, then there is no pollution problem?

5. While some economists argue for the creation of private property rights to protect the environment, many of those concerned for the environment find this approach abhorrent. What are the essential issues in this dispute?

Problems

1. Suppose that a wood pulp mill is situated on a bank of the River Tay. The private marginal cost (MC) of producing wood pulp (in £ per ton) is given by the function

$$MC = 10 + 0.5Y$$

where Y is tons of wood pulp produced. In addition to this private marginal cost, an external cost is incurred. Each ton of wood pulp produces pollutant flows into the river which cause damage valued at £10. This is an external cost, as it is borne by the wider community but not by the polluting firm itself. The marginal benefit (MB) to society of each ton of produced pulp, in £, is given by

$$MB = 30 - 0.5Y$$

a. Draw a diagram illustrating the marginal cost (MC), marginal benefit (MB), external marginal cost (EMC) and social marginal cost (SMC) functions.

b. Find the profit-maximising output of wood pulp, assuming the seller can obtain marginal revenue equal to the marginal benefit to society derived from wood pulp.

c. Find the pulp output which maximises social net benefits.

d. Explain why the socially efficient output of wood pulp is lower than the private profit-maximising output level.

e. How large would marginal external cost have to be in order for it to be socially desirable that no wood pulp is produced?

2. Demonstrate that equations 5.1 and 5.2 embody an assumption that there are no externalities in either consumption or production. Suppose that B's consumption of Y had a positive effect upon A's utility, and that the use of K by firm X adversely affects the output of firm Y. Show how the utility and production functions would need to be amended to take account of these effects.

3. In the chapter and in Appendix 5.3 we consider the two-person consumption-to-consumption externality. As invited in the Appendix, show that an efficient outcome could be realised if a planner required the sufferer to bribe the generator at the appropriate rate, and work out what that rate is.

4. In considering producer-to-consumer externalities in Appendix 5.3, it is stated that where there are multiple sources of emissions, and where only individuals suffer from pollution, each source should be taxed at the same rate. Prove this, and derive the tax rate.

5. Repeat Problem 4 for the case where pollution affects both lines of production as well as both individuals' utility.

Appendix 5.1 Conditions for efficiency and optimality

A5.1.1 Marginal rates of substitution and transformation

For an individual consumer the marginal rate of utility substitution, MRUS, between two commodities is defined as the rate at which one commodity can be substituted for the other, holding utility constant. For marginal changes in consumption levels, for $U = U(X, Y)$

$$dU = U_X dX + U_Y dY$$

where dU, dX and dY are differentials, and we are using U_X for $\partial U/\partial X$ and U_Y for $\partial U/\partial Y$, the marginal utilities. Setting $dU = 0$,

$$0 = U_X dX + U_Y dY$$

so that

$$-U_Y dY = U_X dX$$

and

$$-dY/dX = U_X/U_Y$$

gives the MRUS as the ratio of the marginal utilities:

$$MRUS = U_X/U_Y \qquad (5.20)$$

The MRUS is the slope of the indifference curve at the relevant (X, Y) combination times -1. Since the slope is negative, the MRUS itself is positive, as it must be here given positive marginal utilities.

The marginal rate of technical substitution, MRTS, between two inputs to production is the rate at which one can be substituted for the other holding output constant. For marginal changes in input levels, for $X = X(K, L)$

$$dX = X_K dK + X_L dL$$

where dX, dK and dL are differentials, and where $X_K = \partial X/\partial K$ and $X_L = \partial X/\partial L$ are the marginal products of capital and labour. Setting

$$dX = 0$$

$$0 = X_K dK + X_L dL$$

$$-X_K dK = X_L dL$$

and

$$-dK/dL = X_L/X_K$$

gives the MRTS as the ratio of the marginal products of the labour and capital inputs:

$$\text{MRTS} = X_L/X_K \qquad (5.21)$$

The MRTS is the slope of the isoquant at the relevant (K, L) combination times -1. Since the slope is negative, the MRTS itself is positive, as it must be here given positive marginal products.

The marginal rate of transformation, MRT, refers to the rate at which one commodity can be transformed into the other by means of marginal reallocations of one of the inputs to production. Thus MRT_K refers the effect on the output of Y when capital is, at the margin, shifted from use in the production of X to the production of Y, and MRT_L refers the effect on the output of Y when labour is, at the margin, shifted from use in the production of X to the production of Y. Consider shifting capital at the margin. For $X = X(K^X, L^X)$ and $Y = Y(K^Y, L^Y)$

$$dX = X_K dK^X + X_L dL^X \text{ and } dY = Y_K dK^Y + Y_L dL^Y$$

where dK^X, for example, is a marginal increase/decrease in the use of capital in the production of X. The definition of the marginal rate of transformation for capital is

$$\text{MRT}_K \equiv -dY/dX$$

when there is no reallocation of labour. Note the use of the three-bar identity sign here to indicate a matter of definition. Then

$$\text{MRT}_K = -\left[\frac{Y_K dK^Y + Y_L dL^Y}{X_K dK^X + X_L dL^X}\right]$$

which for $dL^Y = dL^X = 0$ is

$$\text{MRT}_K = -\left[\frac{Y_K dK^Y}{X_K dK^X}\right]$$

and $dK^Y = -dK^X$, so

$$\text{MRT}_K = -\left[\frac{Y_K(-dK^X)}{X_K dK^X}\right]$$

where the dK^X's cancel, and taking account of the two minus signs we have

$$\text{MRT}_K = Y_K/X_K \qquad (5.22a)$$

so that the marginal rate of transformation for capital is the ratio of the marginal products of capital in each line of production. A similar derivation, for $dK^Y = dK^X = 0$ and $dL^Y = -dL^X$, establishes that

$$\text{MRT}_L = Y_L/X_L \qquad (5.22b)$$

A5.1.2 Efficiency conditions

Allocative efficiency exists when it is impossible to make one individual better off without making some other individual(s) worse off. We consider an economy with two individuals each consuming two commodities, where each commodity is produced by an industry comprising two firms, each of which uses two inputs – capital and labour.[12] For such an economy, the conditions characterising allocative efficiency can be derived by considering the following constrained maximisation problem:

$$\text{Max } U^A(X^A, Y^A)$$

subject to

$$U^B(X^B, Y^B) = Z$$

$$X_1(K_1^X, L_1^X) + X_2(K_2^X, L_2^X) = X^A + X^B$$

$$Y_1(K_1^Y, L_1^Y) + Y_2(K_2^Y, L_2^Y) = Y^A + Y^B$$

$$K^T = K_1^X + K_2^X + K_1^Y + K_2^Y$$

$$L^T = L_1^X + L_2^X + L_1^Y + L_2^Y$$

We are looking for the conditions under which A's utility will be maximised, given that B's is held at some arbitrary level Z. The other constraints are that the total consumption of each commodity is equal to the amount produced, and that the sum of the capital and labour inputs across all firms is equal to the economy's respective endowments, K^T and L^T.

---

[12] Using two individuals, two commodities and two firms in each industry does not really involve any loss of generality. Exactly the same qualitative conditions in terms of marginal rates of substitution and transformation would emerge if we used h individuals, n commodities and m firms in each industry. Our analysis could be generalised by having individual utility depend also on labour sup-plied, so that the total amount of labour available to the economy would be a variable rather than a constraint. This would introduce additional conditions, but would not alter those derived here. Another direction of generalisation would be over time so that the availability of capital is a matter of choice rather than a constraint – Chapter 11 looks at intertemporal efficiency and optimality.

This problem can be dealt with using the Lagrangian method reviewed in Appendix 3.1. Here the Lagrangian is

$$
\begin{aligned}
L = \; & U^A(X^A, Y^A) + \lambda_1[U^B(X^B, Y^B) - Z] \\
& + \lambda_2[X_1(K_1^X, L_1^X) + X_2(K_2^X, L_2^X) - X^A - X^B] \\
& + \lambda_3[Y_1(K_1^Y, L_1^Y) + Y_2(K_2^Y, L_2^Y) - Y^A - Y^B] \\
& + \lambda_4[K^T - K_1^X - K_2^X - K_1^Y - K_2^Y] \\
& + \lambda_5[L^T - L_1^X - L_2^X - L_1^Y - L_2^Y]
\end{aligned}
$$

We now need a way of indicating the marginal product of an input to the production of a commodity in a particular firm. A straightforward extension of the notation already introduced here is to use, for example, X_K^1 for $\partial X_1/\partial K_1^X$, the marginal product of capital in the production of commodity X in firm 1 in the industry producing X.

In this notation, the first-order conditions are:

$$
\frac{\partial L}{\partial X^A} = U_X^A - \lambda_2 = 0 \tag{5.23a}
$$

$$
\frac{\partial L}{\partial Y^A} = U_Y^A - \lambda_3 = 0 \tag{5.23b}
$$

$$
\frac{\partial L}{\partial X^B} = \lambda_1 U_X^B - \lambda_2 = 0 \tag{5.23c}
$$

$$
\frac{\partial L}{\partial Y^B} = \lambda_1 U_Y^B - \lambda_3 = 0 \tag{5.23d}
$$

$$
\frac{\partial L}{\partial K_1^X} = \lambda_2 X_K^1 - \lambda_4 = 0 \tag{5.23e}
$$

$$
\frac{\partial L}{\partial K_2^X} = \lambda_2 X_K^2 - \lambda_4 = 0 \tag{5.23f}
$$

$$
\frac{\partial L}{\partial L_1^X} = \lambda_2 X_L^1 - \lambda_5 = 0 \tag{5.23g}
$$

$$
\frac{\partial L}{\partial L_2^X} = \lambda_2 X_L^2 - \lambda_5 = 0 \tag{5.23h}
$$

$$
\frac{\partial L}{\partial K_1^Y} = \lambda_3 Y_K^1 - \lambda_4 = 0 \tag{5.23i}
$$

$$
\frac{\partial L}{\partial K_2^Y} = \lambda_3 Y_K^2 - \lambda_4 = 0 \tag{5.23j}
$$

$$
\frac{\partial L}{\partial L_1^Y} = \lambda_3 Y_L^1 - \lambda_5 = 0 \tag{5.23k}
$$

$$
\frac{\partial L}{\partial L_2^Y} = \lambda_3 Y_L^2 - \lambda_5 = 0 \tag{5.23l}
$$

From equations a and b here

$$
\frac{U_X^A}{U_Y^A} = \frac{\lambda_2}{\lambda_3} \tag{5.23m}
$$

and from c and d

$$
\frac{U_X^B}{U_Y^B} = \frac{\lambda_2/\lambda_1}{\lambda_3/\lambda_1} = \frac{\lambda_2}{\lambda_3} \tag{5.23n}
$$

so that

$$
\frac{U_X^A}{U_Y^A} = \frac{U_X^B}{U_Y^B}
$$

which from equation 5.20 in Section A5.1.1 above is

$$
\text{MRUS}^A = \text{MRUS}^B \tag{5.24}
$$

which is the consumption efficiency condition stated as equation 5.3 in the text of the chapter.

Now, from equations 5.23e and 5.23f we have

$$
X_K^1 = X_K^2 = \lambda_4/\lambda_2 \tag{5.23o}
$$

from equations 5.23g and 5.23h

$$
X_L^1 = X_L^2 = \lambda_5/\lambda_2 \tag{5.23p}
$$

from equations 5.23i and 5.23j

$$
Y_K^1 = Y_K^2 = \lambda_4/\lambda_3 \tag{5.23q}
$$

and from equations 5.23k and 5.23l

$$
Y_L^1 = Y_L^2 = \lambda_5/\lambda_3 \tag{5.23r}
$$

From equations 5.23o and 5.23p

$$
\frac{X_L^1}{X_K^1} = \frac{X_L^2}{X_K^2} = \frac{\lambda_5/\lambda_2}{\lambda_4/\lambda_2} = \frac{\lambda_5}{\lambda_4}
$$

and from equations 5.23q and 5.23r

$$
\frac{Y_L^1}{Y_K^1} = \frac{Y_L^2}{Y_K^2} = \frac{\lambda_5/\lambda_3}{\lambda_4/\lambda_3} = \frac{\lambda_5}{\lambda_4}
$$

so that

$$
\frac{X_L^1}{X_K^1} = \frac{X_L^2}{X_K^2} = \frac{Y_L^1}{Y_K^1} = \frac{Y_L^2}{Y_K^2} \tag{5.23s}
$$

Recall from equation 5.21 in Section A5.1.1 above that for $X = X(K, L)$, $\text{MRTS} = X_L/X_K$. Hence, equation 5.23s here can be written as

$$\text{MRTS}_X^1 = \text{MRTS}_X^2 = \text{MRTS}_Y^1 = \text{MRTS}_Y^2 \quad (5.25)$$

where MRTS_X^1, for example, is the marginal rate of technical substitution for capital and labour in the production of commodity X by firm 1 in the X industry. What equation 5.25 says is (a) that all firms in an industry must have the same MRTS and (b) that the MRTS must be the same in all industries. The interpretation in the sense given by (b) means that equation 5.25 is equivalent to the production efficiency condition, equation 5.4, the intuition for which is found in the text of this chapter. It is (a) here that makes it legitimate to consider, as we did in the text, each industry as comprising a single firm.

Given that firms in the same industry operate with the same marginal products, we can write equations 5.23o to 5.23r as

$$X_K = \lambda_4/\lambda_2 \quad (5.23t)$$

$$X_L = \lambda_5/\lambda_2 \quad (5.23u)$$

$$Y_K = \lambda_4/\lambda_3 \quad (5.23v)$$

and

$$Y_L = \lambda_5/\lambda_3 \quad (5.23w)$$

Then, from equations 5.23v and 5.23t

$$\frac{Y_K}{X_K} = \frac{\lambda_4/\lambda_3}{\lambda_4/\lambda_2} = \frac{\lambda_2}{\lambda_3}$$

and from equations 5.23w and 5.23u

$$\frac{Y_L}{X_L} = \frac{\lambda_5/\lambda_3}{\lambda_5/\lambda_2} = \frac{\lambda_2}{\lambda_3}$$

so that

$$\frac{Y_K}{X_K} = \frac{Y_L}{X_L} = \frac{\lambda_2}{\lambda_3}$$

which from equations 5.22a and 5.22b in Section A5.1.1 above can be written as

$$\text{MRT}_L = \text{MRT}_K = \lambda_2/\lambda_3 \quad (5.23x)$$

At equations 5.23m and 5.23n we obtained

$$\frac{U_X^A}{U_Y^A} = \frac{U_X^B}{U_Y^B} = \frac{\lambda_2}{\lambda_3}$$

which, by equation 5.20 from Section A5.1.1, is

$$\text{MRUS}^A = \text{MRUS}^B = \lambda_2/\lambda_3 \quad (5.23y)$$

From equations 5.23x and 5.23y we get

$$\text{MRUS}^A = \text{MRUS}^B = \text{MRT}_L = \text{MRT}_K \quad (5.26)$$

which is the product-mix efficiency condition stated as equation 5.5 in the chapter.

A5.1.3 Optimality conditions

We now introduce a social welfare function, so as to derive the conditions that characterise an optimal allocation. Using the same assumptions about utility and production as in Section A5.1.2, the problem to be considered here is:

Max $W\{U^A(X^A, Y^A), U^B(X^B, Y^B)\}$

subject to

$$X_1(K_1^X, L_1^X) + X_2(K_2^X, L_2^X) = X^A + X^B$$

$$Y_1(K_1^Y, L_1^Y) + Y_2(K_2^Y, L_2^Y) = Y^A + Y^B$$

$$K^T = K_1^X + K_2^X + K_1^Y + K_2^Y$$

$$L^T = L_1^X + L_2^X + L_1^Y + L_2^Y$$

Here the Lagrangian is

$$\begin{aligned}
L = {}& W\{U^A(X^A, Y^A), U^B(X^B, Y^B)\} \\
&+ \lambda_2[X_1(K_1^X, L_1^X) + X_2(K_2^X, L_2^X) - X^A - X^B] \\
&+ \lambda_3[Y_1(K_1^Y, L_1^Y) + Y_2(K_2^Y, L_2^Y) - Y^A - Y^B] \\
&+ \lambda_4[K^T - K_1^X - K_2^X - K_1^Y - K_2^Y] \\
&+ \lambda_5[L^T - L_1^X - L_2^X - L_1^Y - L_2^Y]
\end{aligned}$$

where we have started numbering the multipliers at 2 so as to bring out more transparently the correspondences between the necessary conditions for efficiency and optimality – the fact that we use the same symbols and numbers in both cases does not, of course, mean that the multipliers take the same values in both cases.

The first-order conditions for this welfare maximisation problem are:

$$\frac{\partial L}{\partial X^A} = W_A U_X^A - \lambda_2 = 0 \quad (5.27a)$$

$$\frac{\partial L}{\partial Y^A} = W_A U_Y^A - \lambda_3 = 0 \quad (5.27b)$$

$$\frac{\partial L}{\partial X^B} = W_B U_X^B - \lambda_2 = 0 \quad (5.27c)$$

$$\frac{\partial L}{\partial Y^B} = W_B U_Y^B - \lambda_3 = 0 \qquad (5.27d)$$

$$\frac{\partial L}{\partial K_1^X} = \lambda_2 X_K^1 - \lambda_4 = 0 \qquad (5.27e)$$

$$\frac{\partial L}{\partial K_2^X} = \lambda_2 X_K^2 - \lambda_4 = 0 \qquad (5.27f)$$

$$\frac{\partial L}{\partial L_1^X} = \lambda_2 X_L^1 - \lambda_5 = 0 \qquad (5.27g)$$

$$\frac{\partial L}{\partial L_2^X} = \lambda_2 X_L^2 - \lambda_5 = 0 \qquad (5.27h)$$

$$\frac{\partial L}{\partial K_1^Y} = \lambda_3 Y_K^1 - \lambda_4 = 0 \qquad (5.27i)$$

$$\frac{\partial L}{\partial K_2^Y} = \lambda_3 Y_K^2 - \lambda_4 = 0 \qquad (5.27j)$$

$$\frac{\partial L}{\partial L_1^Y} = \lambda_3 Y_L^1 - \lambda_5 = 0 \qquad (5.27k)$$

$$\frac{\partial L}{\partial L_2^Y} = \lambda_3 Y_L^2 - \lambda_5 = 0 \qquad (5.27l)$$

where $W_A = \partial W/\partial U^A$ and $W_B = \partial W/\partial U^B$.

Note that equations e through to l in the set 5.27 are the same as e through to l in the set 5.23. It follows that optimality requires the efficiency in production condition, equation 5.25, rewritten here as

$$MRTS_X^1 = MRTS_X^2 = MRTS_Y^1 = MRTS_Y^2 \qquad (5.28)$$

From a and b in set 5.27

$$\frac{U_X^A}{U_Y^A} = \frac{\lambda_2}{\lambda_3}$$

as W_A cancels. Similarly, from c and d in set 5.27,

$$\frac{U_X^B}{U_Y^B} = \frac{\lambda_2}{\lambda_3}$$

so that optimality requires

$$\frac{U_X^A}{U_Y^A} = \frac{U_X^B}{U_Y^B}$$

or

$$MRUS^A = MRUS^B = \lambda_2/\lambda_3 \qquad (5.29)$$

which is the same as the consumption efficiency condition, 5.24, in the previous section.

From equations 5.27e through to 5.27l we can, as in the previous section, derive

$$MRT_L = MRT_K = \lambda_2/\lambda_3 \qquad (5.30)$$

and from 5.29 and 5.30 we have

$$MRUS^A = MRUS^B = MRT_L = MRT_K \qquad (5.31)$$

which is the same product mix condition as is required for efficiency.

Optimality requires the fulfilment of all of the efficiency conditions. In deriving the efficiency conditions, the utility of B is set at some arbitrary level. The maximisation problem considered there, as well as producing the conditions that any efficient allocation must satisfy, identifies the maximum level for A's utility conditional on the selected level of B's utility. In the welfare maximisation problem the function $W\{U^A, U^B\}$ selects the utility levels for A and B. As discussed in the text, only combinations of U^A and U^B that lie along the utility possibility frontier are relevant for welfare maximisation. All such combinations satisfy the efficiency conditions, and hence welfare maximisation entails satisfying the efficiency conditions as shown above. It also entails the condition stated as equation 5.7 in the chapter, which condition fixes the utility levels for A and B using the social welfare function.

From equations 5.27a through to 5.27d we have

$$W_A = \frac{\lambda_2}{U_X^A} \qquad (5.32a)$$

$$W_A = \frac{\lambda_3}{U_Y^A} \qquad (5.32b)$$

$$W_B = \frac{\lambda_2}{U_X^B} \qquad (5.32c)$$

$$W_B = \frac{\lambda_3}{U_Y^B} \qquad (5.32d)$$

From a and c here we get

$$\frac{W_A}{W_B} = \frac{U_X^B}{U_X^A}$$

and from b and d we get

$$\frac{W_A}{W_B} = \frac{U_Y^B}{U_Y^A}$$

so that

$$\frac{W_A}{W_B} = \frac{U_X^B}{U_X^A} = \frac{U_Y^B}{U_Y^A} \qquad (5.33)$$

which is equation 5.7 in the chapter.

The SWF is $W = W(U^A, U^B)$ so that

$$dW = W_A dU^A + W_B dU^B$$

Setting the left-hand side here equal to zero so as to consider small movements along a social welfare indifference curve, and rearranging, gives

$$-\frac{dU^B}{dU^A} = \frac{W_A}{W_B}$$

for the slope of a social welfare indifference curve. The slope of the utility possibility frontier is $-dU^B/dU^A$ which is equal to U_X^B/U_X^A and to U_Y^B/U_Y^A.

Appendix 5.2 Market outcomes

In this appendix we establish that, given the 'ideal' institutional conditions set out in the text of the chapter, a system of markets will bring about the satisfaction of the necessary conditions for efficiency in allocation – the consumption efficiency condition, the production efficiency condition and the product-mix condition.

A5.2.1 Individuals: utility maximisation

Consider an individual consumer, with a fixed money income M and gaining utility from the consumption of two goods, X and Y. The prices of these goods are determined in competitive markets, at the levels P_X and P_Y, and are taken as given by all individuals. With this individual's utility function given by

$$U = U(X, Y)$$

we can express the problem of maximising utility subject to a budget constraint as

Max $U(X, Y)$

subject to

$$P_X X + P_Y Y = M$$

The Lagrangian for this problem is

$$L = U(X, Y) + \lambda[P_X X + P_Y Y - M]$$

and, using the same notation for the derivatives (the marginal utilities) as previously, the first-order conditions for a maximum are:

$$\frac{\partial L}{\partial X} = U_X + \lambda P_X = 0 \qquad (5.34a)$$

$$\frac{\partial L}{\partial X} = U_Y + \lambda P_Y = 0 \qquad (5.34b)$$

From these equations we get

$$U_X = -\lambda P_X$$

$$U_Y = -\lambda P_Y$$

so that

$$\frac{U_X}{U_Y} = \frac{P_X}{P_Y} \qquad (5.35)$$

Equation 5.35 holds for all consumers, all of whom face the same P_X and P_Y, and the left-hand side is the marginal rate of utility substitution. So, for any two consumers A and B, we have:

$$\mathrm{MRUS}^A = \mathrm{MRUS}^B = \frac{P_X}{P_Y} \qquad (5.36)$$

The consumption efficiency condition is satisfied, see equation 5.3 in the chapter and equation 5.24 in the previous appendix, and the marginal rate of utility substitution common to all individuals is equal to the price ratio, as stated in the chapter at equation 5.8.

A5.2.2 Firms: profit maximisation

Consider the production of X by firms $i = 1, 2, \ldots, m$. All firms face the same selling price, P_X, and all pay the same fixed prices for capital and labour inputs, P_K and P_L. The objective of every firm is to maximise profit, so to ascertain the conditions characterising the behaviour of the ith firm we consider

$$\text{Max} \quad P_X X_i(K_i^X, L_i^X) - P_K K_i^X - P_L L_i^X$$

where the necessary conditions are

$$P_X X_K^i - P_K = 0 \tag{5.37a}$$

$$P_X X_L^i - P_L = 0 \tag{5.37b}$$

or

$$X_K^i = \frac{P_K}{P_X} \tag{5.38a}$$

$$X_L^i = \frac{P_L}{P_X} \tag{5.38b}$$

from which

$$\frac{X_K^i}{X_L^i} = \frac{P_K}{P_L} \tag{5.39}$$

Equation 5.39 holds for all i, and the left-hand side is the expression for the marginal rate of technical substitution. Hence, all firms producing X operate with the same MRTS. Further, it is obvious that considering profit maximisation by the jth firm in the industry producing the commodity Y will lead to

$$\frac{Y_K^j}{Y_L^j} = \frac{P_K}{P_L} \tag{5.40}$$

which with equation 5.39 implies

$$\text{MRTS}_X^i = \text{MRTS}_Y^j \tag{5.41}$$

for $i = 1, 2, \ldots, m$ and $j = 1, 2, \ldots, n$. The production efficiency condition, equation 5.4 in the chapter, is satisfied.

Recall that

$$\text{MRT}_K = \frac{Y_K}{X_K} \tag{5.42a}$$

and

$$\text{MRT}_L = \frac{Y_L}{X_L} \tag{5.42b}$$

From equations 5.38a and 5.38b, and the corresponding conditions from profit maximisation in the production of Y, omitting the superscripts for firms we have

$$X_K = \frac{P_K}{P_X}, \ X_L = \frac{P_L}{P_X}, \ Y_K = \frac{P_K}{P_Y}, \ Y_L = \frac{P_L}{P_Y}$$

and substituting and cancelling in equations 5.42a and 5.42b,

$$\text{MRT}_K = \frac{P_X}{P_Y} = \text{MRT}_L$$

and bringing this together with equation 5.36 gives

$$\text{MRUS}^A = \text{MRUS}^B = \text{MRT}_K = \text{MRT}_L \tag{5.43}$$

which shows that the product-mix condition, equation 5.5 in the chapter and 5.26 in the previous appendix, is satisfied.

In the chapter it was stated that the necessary condition for profit maximisation was the equality of marginal cost with the output price. To establish this let $C(X^i)$ be the firm's cost function and write the profits for the ith firm in the industry producing X as

$$\pi_X^i = P_X X^i - C(X^i)$$

from which the necessary condition for maximisation is

$$\partial \pi_X^i / \partial X^i = P_X - \partial C / \partial X^i = 0$$

which is

$$P_X = \partial C / \partial X^i$$

i.e. price equals marginal cost.

Appendix 5.3 Market failure

A5.3.1 Public goods

In the two-person, two-commodity, two-resource economy considered in the preceding appendix, now let X be a public good and Y a private good. Given the results established there regarding the conditions for efficiency in relation to firms in the same industry, we can simplify here without loss by assuming that each commodity is produced in an industry which has just one firm. Given that we are taking the defining characteristic of a public good to be that it is consumed in the same quantity by all, we can state the problem from which the necessary conditions for efficiency are to be derived as:

Max $U^A(X, Y^A)$

subject to

$U^B(X, Y^B) = Z$

$X(K^X, L^X) = X$

$Y(K^Y, L^Y) = Y^A + Y^B$

$K^T = K^X + K^Y$

$L^T = L^X + L^Y$

The Lagrangian for this problem is

$$L = U^A(X, Y^A) + \lambda_1[U^B(X, Y^B) - Z]$$
$$+ \lambda_2[X(K^X, L^X) - X]$$
$$+ \lambda_3[Y(K^Y, L^Y) - Y^A - Y^B]$$
$$+ \lambda_4[K^T - K^X - K^Y]$$
$$+ \lambda_5[L^T - L^X - L^Y]$$

from which the necessary conditions for maximisation are:

$$\frac{\partial L}{\partial X} = U_X^A + \lambda_1 U_X^B - \lambda_2 = 0 \tag{5.44a}$$

$$\frac{\partial L}{\partial Y^A} = U_Y^A - \lambda_3 = 0 \tag{5.44b}$$

$$\frac{\partial L}{\partial Y^B} = \lambda_1 U_Y^B - \lambda_3 = 0 \tag{5.44c}$$

$$\frac{\partial L}{\partial K^X} = \lambda_2 X_K - \lambda_4 = 0 \tag{5.44d}$$

$$\frac{\partial L}{\partial L^X} = \lambda_2 X_L - \lambda_5 = 0 \tag{5.44e}$$

$$\frac{\partial L}{\partial K^Y} = \lambda_3 Y_K - \lambda_4 = 0 \tag{5.44f}$$

$$\frac{\partial L}{\partial L^Y} = \lambda_3 Y_L - \lambda_5 = 0 \tag{5.44g}$$

Consider first equations 5.44d to 5.44g, which relate to production. They imply

$$\frac{X_L}{X_K} = \frac{\lambda_5}{\lambda_4} = \frac{Y_L}{Y_K}$$

which is

$MRTS_X = MRTS_Y$

so that production efficiency is required. They also imply

$$\frac{Y_K}{X_K} = \frac{\lambda_2}{\lambda_3} = \frac{Y_L}{X_L}$$

which is

$$MRT_K = MRT_L = \frac{\lambda_2}{\lambda_3} \tag{5.45}$$

so that as regards production activities, the conditions in the presence of a public good are the same as in the standard case, see Appendix 5.1, where there are no public goods.

Now consider equations 5.44a to 5.44c, which relate to consumption. From equations a and b there

$$\frac{U_X^A}{U_Y^A} = \frac{\lambda_2}{\lambda_3} - \frac{\lambda_1 U_X^B}{\lambda_3} \tag{5.46a}$$

and using equation 5.44c we can write

$$\frac{U_X^B}{U_Y^B} = \frac{U_X^B}{\lambda_3/\lambda_1} = \frac{\lambda_1 U_X^B}{\lambda_3} \tag{5.46b}$$

and adding 5.46a and 5.46b gives:

$$\frac{U_X^A}{U_Y^A} + \frac{U_X^B}{U_Y^B} = \frac{\lambda_2}{\lambda_3} - \frac{\lambda_1 U_X^B}{\lambda_3} + \frac{\lambda_1 U_X^B}{\lambda_3} = \frac{\lambda_2}{\lambda_3} \tag{5.47}$$

Using the definition for MRUS, equation 5.47 is

$$MRUS^A + MRUS^B = \frac{\lambda_2}{\lambda_3}$$

so that from equation 5.45 we have the condition

$$MRUS^A + MRUS^B = MRT \tag{5.48}$$

stated as equation 5.15 in the chapter.

A5.3.2 Externalities: consumer to consumer

As in the text, we ignore production in looking at this case. Given that we have not previously looked at a pure exchange economy, it will be convenient first to look at such an economy where there is no external effect.

To identify the necessary conditions for efficiency, we look at

Max $U^A(X^A, Y^A)$

subject to

$$U^B(X^B, Y^B) = Z$$

$$X^T = X^A + X^B$$

$$Y^T = Y^A + Y^B$$

where X^T and Y^T are the total amounts of the two commodities to be allocated as between A and B. The Lagrangian for this problem is

$$L = U^A(X, Y^A) + \lambda_1[U^B(X, Y^B) - Z]$$
$$+ \lambda_2[X^T - X^A - X^B]$$
$$+ \lambda_3[Y^T - Y^A - Y^B]$$

and the necessary conditions are

$$\frac{\partial L}{\partial X^A} = U_X^A - \lambda_2 = 0$$

$$\frac{\partial L}{\partial Y^A} = U_Y^A - \lambda_3 = 0$$

$$\frac{\partial L}{\partial X^B} = \lambda_1 U_X^B - \lambda_2 = 0$$

$$\frac{\partial L}{\partial Y^B} = \lambda_1 U_Y^B - \lambda_3 = 0$$

from which we get

$$\frac{U_X^A}{U_Y^A} = \frac{U_X^B}{U_Y^B} = \frac{\lambda_2}{\lambda_3}$$

which is the same consumption efficiency condition as for the economy with production, i.e. $\text{MRUS}^A = \text{MRUS}^B$. We already know, from Appendix 5.2, that consumers facing given and fixed prices P_X and P_Y and maximising utility subject to a budget constraint will satisfy this condition.

Now, suppose that B's consumption of Y is an argument in A's utility function. We are assuming that Y^B is a source of disutility to A. Then the maximisation problem to be considered is

Max $U^A(X^A, Y^A, Y^B)$

subject to

$$U^B(X^B, Y^B) = Z$$

$$X^T = X^A + X^B$$

$$Y^T = Y^A + Y^B$$

for which the Lagrangian is

$$L = U^A(X^A, Y^A, Y^B) + \lambda_1[U^B(X^B, Y^B) - Z]$$
$$+ \lambda_2[X^T - X^A - X^B]$$
$$+ \lambda_3[Y^T - Y^A - Y^B]$$

with necessary conditions

$$\frac{\partial L}{\partial X^A} = U_X^A - \lambda_2 = 0 \tag{5.49a}$$

$$\frac{\partial L}{\partial Y^A} = U_Y^A - \lambda_3 = 0 \tag{5.49b}$$

$$\frac{\partial L}{\partial X^B} = \lambda_1 U_X^B - \lambda_2 = 0 \tag{5.49c}$$

$$\frac{\partial L}{\partial Y^B} = U_{YB}^A \lambda_1 U_Y^B - \lambda_3 = 0 \tag{5.49d}$$

where $U_{YB}^A = \partial U^A / \partial Y^B$. Note that Y^B is a source of disutility to A so that $U_{YB}^A < 0$. From 5.49a and 5.49b we get

$$\frac{U_X^A}{U_Y^A} = \frac{\lambda_2}{\lambda_3} \tag{5.50a}$$

from 5.49c

$$U_X^B = \frac{\lambda_2}{\lambda_1} \tag{5.50b}$$

and from 5.49d

$$U_Y^B = \frac{\lambda_3}{\lambda_1} - \frac{U_{YB}^A}{\lambda_1} \tag{5.50c}$$

so that, using 5.50b and 5.50c,

$$\frac{U_X^B}{U_Y^B} = \frac{\lambda_3}{\lambda_3 - U_{BY}^A} \tag{5.50d}$$

Looking at 5.50a and 5.50d we see that with the externality, efficiency does not require the condition $\text{MRUS}^A = \text{MRUS}^3$. But we have just seen that, facing just the prices P_X and P_Y, market trading between A and B will give $\text{MRUS}^A = \text{MRUS}^B$. So, given the existence of this externality, market exchange will not satisfy the conditions, 5.50a and 5.50d, for efficiency.

Suppose now that there exists a central planner who knows the two agents' utility functions and the quantities of X and Y available. The planner's objective is an efficient allocation, to be realised by the two agents individually maximising utility on terms set by the planner, rather by the planner telling the agents at what levels to consume. The planner declares prices P_X and P_Y, and also requires B to compensate A for her Y^B suffering at the rate c per unit of Y^B. In that case, A's utility maximisation problem is

Max $U^A(X^A, Y^A, Y^B)$

subject to

$P_X X^A + P_Y Y^A = M^A + c Y^B$

where M^A is A's income before the receipt of any compensation from B. The Lagrangian for this problem is:

$L = U^A(X^A, Y^A, Y^B)$
$\quad + \lambda_A[P_X X^A + P_Y Y^A - M^A - c Y^B]$

Note that Y^B is not a choice variable for A. The level of Y^B is chosen by B. The necessary conditions for A's maximisation problem are

$$\frac{\partial L}{\partial X^A} = U_X^A + \lambda_A P_X = 0$$

$$\frac{\partial L}{\partial Y^A} = U_Y^A + \lambda_A P_Y = 0$$

from which

$$\frac{U_X^A}{U_Y^A} = \frac{P_X}{P_Y} \tag{5.51a}$$

B's utility maximisation problem is

Max $U^B(X^B, Y^B)$

subject to

$P_X X^B + P_Y Y^B = M^B - c Y^B$

the Lagrangian for which is

$L = U^B(X^B, Y^B) + \lambda_B[P_X X^B + P_Y Y^B - M^B + c Y^B]$

with necessary conditions

$$\frac{\partial L}{\partial X^B} = U_X^B + \lambda_B P_X = 0$$

$$\frac{\partial L}{\partial Y^B} = U_Y^B + \lambda_B P_Y + \lambda_B c = 0$$

from which

$$\frac{U_X^B}{U_Y^B} = \frac{P_X}{P_Y + c} \tag{5.51b}$$

So, we have 5.50a and 5.50d as the efficiency conditions and 5.51a and 5.51b as the individual utility-maximising conditions. Comparing 5.50a and 5.50d with 5.51a and 5.51b, it will be seen that they are the same for:

$\lambda_2 = P_X$, $\lambda_3 = P_Y$ and $c = -U_{YB}^A$

If, that is, the planner solves the appropriate maximisation problem and sets P_X and P_Y at the shadow prices of the commodities, and requires B to compensate A at a rate which is equal to, but of opposite sign to, A's marginal disutility in respect of the external effect, then A and B individually maximising utility given those prices and that compensation rate will bring about an efficient allocation. The planner is putting a price on the external effect, and the required price is A's marginal disutility.

However, as shown in the discussion of the Coase theorem in the body of the chapter, it is not actually necessary to have this kind of intervention by the planner. If A had the legal right to extract full compensation from B, had a property right in an unpolluted environment, then the right price for efficiency would emerge as the result of bargaining between A and B.

In considering the consumption-to-consumption case in the chapter we argued that the liability/property right could be assigned the other way round and still bring about an efficient outcome. The corresponding procedure with a planner setting the terms on which the two agents maximised utility would be to have the planner work out what Y^B would be with the externality uncorrected, say Y^{B*}, and then require A to compensate B for reducing Y^B below that level. In that case, A's maximisation problem would be

Max $U^A(X^A, Y^A, Y^B)$

subject to

$P_X X^A + P_Y Y_A = M^A - b(Y^{B*} - Y^B)$

and B's would be

Max $U^B(X^B, Y^B)$

subject to

$$P_X X^B + P_Y Y^B = M^B + b(Y^{B*} - Y^B)$$

where we use b for 'bribe'. It is left as an exercise to confirm that this arrangement would, given suitable P_X, P_Y and b, produce an efficient outcome.

The situation considered in the chapter actually differed from that considered here in a couple of respects. First, in that example the external effect involved A doing something – playing a musical instrument – which did not have a price attached to it, and which B did not do. In the uncorrected externality situation there, A pursued the 'polluting' activity up to the level where its marginal utility was zero. In the chapter, we considered things in terms of monetary costs and benefits in a partial equilibrium context, rather than utility maximisation in a general equilibrium context. Thinking about that noise pollution example in the following way may help to make the connections, and make a further point.

Let Y^A be the number of hours that A plays her instrument. Consider each individual's utility to depend on income and Y^A, so that $U^A = U^A(M^A, Y^A)$ and $U^B = U^B(M^B, Y^A)$, where $\partial U^A / \partial Y^A > 0$ and $\partial U^B / \partial Y^A < 0$. Consider welfare maximisation for given M^A and M^B. The problem is

Max $W\{U^A(M^A, Y^A), U^B(M^B, Y^A)\}$

where the only choice variable is Y^A, so that the necessary condition is:

$$W_A U_{YA}^A = -W_B U_{YA}^B$$

For equal welfare weights, this is

$$U_{YA}^A = -U_{YB}^B$$

or

Marginal benefit of music to A = Marginal cost of music to B

which is the condition as stated in the chapter. The further point that the derivation of this condition here makes is that the standard simple story about the Coase theorem implicitly assigns equal welfare weights to the two individuals.

A5.3.3 Externalities: producer to producer

To begin here, we suppose that the production function for Y is

$$Y = Y(K^Y, L^Y, S) \text{ with } Y_S = \partial Y / \partial S > 0$$

and for X is

$$X = X(K^X, L^X, S) \text{ with } X_S = \partial X / \partial S < 0$$

where S is pollutant emissions arising in the production of Y and adversely affecting the production of X. The Lagrangian from which the conditions for efficiency are to be derived is:

$$
\begin{aligned}
L = U^A(X^A, Y^A) &+ \lambda_1 [U^B(X^B, Y^B) - Z] \\
&+ \lambda_2 [X(K^X, L^X, S) - X^A - X^B] \\
&+ \lambda_3 [Y(K^Y, L^Y, S) - Y^A - Y^B] \\
&+ \lambda_4 [K^T - K^X - K^Y] \\
&+ \lambda_5 [L^T - L^X - L^Y]
\end{aligned}
$$

The reader can readily check that in this case, taking derivates of L with respect to X^A, Y^A, X^B, Y^B, K^X, L^X, K^Y and L^Y gives, allowing for the fact that there is just one firm in each industry, the consumption, production and product-mix conditions derived in Section A5.1.2 and stated in the chapter. Taking the derivative of L with respect to S gives the additional condition

$$\frac{\partial L}{\partial S} = \lambda_2 X_S + \lambda_3 Y_S = 0$$

or

$$\frac{\lambda_2}{\lambda_3} = -\frac{Y_S}{X_S} \tag{5.52}$$

Now, suppose that a central planner declares prices $P_X = \lambda_2$, $P_Y = \lambda_3$, $P_K = \lambda_4$, $P_L = \lambda_5$, and requires that the firm producing Y pay compensation to the firm affected by its emissions at the rate c per unit S. Then, the Y firm's problem is

Max $P_Y Y(K^Y, L^Y, S) - P_K K^Y - P_L L^Y - cS$

with the usual necessary conditions

$$P_Y Y_K - P_K = 0$$

$$P_Y Y_L - P_L = 0$$

plus

$$P_Y Y_S - c = 0 \tag{5.53}$$

Compare equation 5.52 with 5.53. If we set $c = -P_X X_S$ then the latter becomes

$$P_Y Y_S = -P_X X_S$$

or

$$\frac{P_X}{P_Y} = -\frac{Y_S}{X_S} \qquad (5.54)$$

which, for $P_X = \lambda_2$ and $P_Y = \lambda_3$, is the same as equation 5.52. With this compensation requirement in place, the profit-maximising behaviour of the Y firm will be as required for efficiency. Note that the rate of compensation makes sense. $P_X X_S$ is the reduction in X's profit for a given level of output when Y increases S. Note also that while we have called this charge on emissions of S by the Y firm 'compensation', we have not shown that efficiency requires that the X firm actually receives such compensation. The charge c, that is, might equally well be collected by the planner, in which case we would call it a tax on emissions.[13]

In the chapter we noted that one way of internalising a producer-to-producer externality could be for the firms to merge, or to enter into an agreement to maximise joint profits. A proof of this claim is as follows. The problem then is

Max $P_X X(K^X, L^X, S) + P_Y(K^Y, L^Y, S)$
$- P_K(K^X + K^Y) - P_L(L^X + L^Y)$

for which the necessary conditions are

$$P_X X_K - P_K = 0$$
$$P_X X_L - P_L = 0$$
$$P_Y Y_K - P_K = 0$$
$$P_Y Y_L - P_L = 0$$

which, given $P_X = \lambda_2$, $P_K = \lambda_4$ etc., satisfy the standard (no externality) efficiency conditions, plus

$$P_X X_S + P_Y Y_S = 0$$

This last condition for joint profit maximisation can be written as

$$\frac{P_X}{P_Y} = -\frac{Y_S}{X_S}$$

which is just equation 5.54, previously shown to be necessary, in addition to the standard conditions, for efficiency in the presence of this kind of externality.

In Chapter 2 we noted that the fact that matter can neither be created nor destroyed is sometimes overlooked in the specification of economic models. We have just been guilty in that way ourselves – writing

$$Y = Y(K^Y, L^Y, S)$$

with S as some kind of pollutant emission, has matter, S, appearing from nowhere, when, in fact, it must have a material origin in some input to the production process. A more satisfactory production function for the polluting firm would be

$$Y = Y(K^Y, L^Y, R^Y, S\{R^Y\})$$

where R^Y is the input of some material, say tonnes of coal, and $S\{R^Y\}$ maps coal burned into emissions, of say smoke, and $\partial Y/\partial R^Y = Y_R > 0$, $\partial Y/\partial S = Y_S > 0$ and $\partial S/\partial R^Y = S_{RY} > 0$. We shall now show that while this more plausible model specification complicates the story a little, it does not alter the essential message.

To maintain consistency with the producer-to-producer case as analysed above, and in the chapter, we will assume that in the production of X the use of R does not give rise to emissions of smoke. Then, the Lagrangian for deriving the efficiency conditions is:

$$\begin{aligned} L = {}& U^A(X^A, Y^A) + \lambda_1[U^B(X^B, Y^B) - Z] \\ & + \lambda_2[X(K^X, L^X, R^X, S\{R^Y\}) - X^A - X^B] \\ & + \lambda_3[Y(K^Y, L^Y, R^Y, S\{R^Y\}) - Y^A - Y^B] \\ & + \lambda_4[K^T - K^X - K^Y] \\ & + \lambda_5[L^T - L^X - L^Y] \\ & + \lambda_6[R^T - R^X - R^Y] \end{aligned}$$

In the production function for X, $\partial X/\partial R^X = X_R > 0$ and $\partial X/\partial S = X_S < 0$. The reader can confirm that taking derivatives here with respect to all the choice variables except R^X and R^Y gives all of the standard conditions. Then, with respect to R^X and R^Y, we get

[13] However, if c takes the form of a tax rather than compensation paid to the X firm, the question arises as to what happens to the tax revenue. It cannot remain with the planner, otherwise the government, as the planner does not count as an agent. If the planner/government has unspent revenues, it would be possible to make some agent better off without making any other agent(s) worse off. Given the simple model specification here, where, for example, there is no tax/welfare system and no public goods supply, we cannot explore this question further. It is considered, for example, in Chapter 4 of Baumol and Oates (1988), and the 'double dividend' literature reviewed in Chapter 10 below is also relevant.

$$\frac{\partial L}{\partial R^X} = \lambda_2 X_R - \lambda_6 = 0 \qquad (5.55a)$$

$$\frac{\partial L}{\partial R^Y} = \lambda_2 X_S S_{RY} + \lambda_3 Y_R + \lambda_3 Y_S S_{RY} - \lambda_6 = 0 \qquad (5.55b)$$

As before, suppose a planner sets $P_X = \lambda_2, \ldots, P_L = \lambda_5$ plus $P_R = \lambda_6$ and a tax on the use of R in the production of Y at the rate t. Then the profit maximisation problem for the firm producing Y is

Max $P_Y Y(K^Y, L^Y, R^Y, S\{R^Y\}) - P_K K^Y - P_L L^Y$
$- P_R R^Y - tR^Y$

and for the firm producing X it is

Max $P_X X(K^X, L^X, R^X, S\{R^Y\}) - P_K K^X - P_L L^X$
$- P_R R^X$

If the reader derives the necessary conditions here, which include

$$P_Y Y_R + P_Y Y_S S_{RY} - P_R - t = 0 \qquad (5.56)$$

you can verify that for $P_X = \lambda_2, \ldots, P_L = \lambda_5$ and $P_R = \lambda_6$ with

$$t = -P_X X_S S_{RY} \qquad (5.57)$$

independent profit maximisation by both firms satisfies the standard efficiency conditions plus the externality correction conditions stated above as equations 5.55a and 5.55b. The rationale for this rate of tax should also be apparent: S_{RY} is the increase in smoke for an increase in Y's use of R, X_S gives the effect of more smoke on the output of X for given K^X and L^X, and P_X is the price of X.

Now consider joint profit maximisation. From

Max $P_X X(K^X, L^X, R^X, S\{R^Y\}) + P_Y(K^Y, L^Y, R^Y,$
$S\{R^Y\}) - P_K(K^X + K^Y) - P_L(L^X + L^Y) - P_R(R^X + R^Y)$

the necessary conditions are

$P_X X_K - P_K = 0$

$P_X X_L - P_L = 0$

$P_Y Y_K - P_K = 0$

$P_Y Y_L - P_L = 0$

$P_X X_R - P_R = 0$

$P_Y Y_R + P_Y Y_S S_{RY} + P_X X_S S_{RY} - P_R = 0$

Substituting from equation 5.57 into 5.56 for t gives the last of these equations, showing that the outcome under joint profit maximisation is the same as with the tax on the use of R in the production of Y.

A5.3.4 Externalities: producer to consumers

The main point to be made for this case concerns the implications of non-rivalry and non-excludability. These are not peculiar to the producer-to-consumers case, but are conveniently demonstrated using it. To simplify the notation, we revert to having emissions in production occur without any explicit representation of their material origin. As noted in the analysis of the producer-to-producer case, this simplifies without, for present purposes, missing anything essential. We assume that the production of Y involves pollutant emissions which affect both A and B equally, though, of course, A and B might have different preferences over pollution and commodities. Pollution is, that is, in the nature of a public bad – A/B's consumption is non-rival with respect to B/A's consumption, and neither can escape, be excluded from, consumption.

The Lagrangian for the derivation of the efficiency conditions is

$$\begin{aligned}
L = U^A(X^A, Y^A, S) &+ \lambda_1[U^B(X^B, Y^B, S) - Z] \\
&+ \lambda_2[X(K^X, L^X) - X^A - X^B] \\
&+ \lambda_3[Y(K^Y, L^Y, S) - Y^A - Y^B] \\
&+ \lambda_4[K^T - K^X - K^Y] \\
&+ \lambda_5[L^T - L^X - L^Y]
\end{aligned}$$

where $\partial U^A/\partial S = U_S^A < 0$, $\partial U^B/\partial S = U_S^B < 0$ and $\partial Y/\partial S = Y_S > 0$. The necessary conditions are:

$$\frac{\partial L}{\partial X^A} = U_X^A - \lambda_2 = 0 \qquad (5.58a)$$

$$\frac{\partial L}{\partial Y^A} = U_Y^A - \lambda_2 = 0 \qquad (5.58b)$$

$$\frac{\partial L}{\partial X^B} = \lambda_1 U_X^B - \lambda_2 = 0 \qquad (5.58c)$$

$$\frac{\partial L}{\partial Y^B} = \lambda_1 U_Y^B - \lambda_3 = 0 \qquad (5.58d)$$

$$\frac{\partial L}{\partial S} = U_S^A + \lambda_1 U_S^B + \lambda_3 Y_S = 0 \qquad (5.58e)$$

$$\frac{\partial L}{\partial K^X} = \lambda_2 X_K - \lambda_4 = 0 \qquad (5.58\text{f})$$

$$\frac{\partial L}{\partial L^X} = \lambda_2 X_L - \lambda_5 = 0 \qquad (5.58\text{g})$$

$$\frac{\partial L}{\partial K^Y} = \lambda_3 Y_K - \lambda_4 = 0 \qquad (5.58\text{h})$$

$$\frac{\partial L}{\partial L^Y} = \lambda_3 Y_L - \lambda_5 = 0 \qquad (5.58\text{i})$$

The reader can check that these can be expressed as the standard consumption, production and product-mix conditions plus

$$U_S^A + \lambda_1 U_S^B = -\lambda_3 Y_S \qquad (5.59)$$

from equation 5.58e.

Now suppose that a central planner declares prices $P_X = \lambda_2$, $P_Y = \lambda_3$, $P_K = \lambda_4$ and $P_Y = \lambda_5$. Proceeding as done previously in this appendix, the reader can check that utility and profit maximisation at these prices will satisfy all of the standard conditions, but not equation 5.59. Suppose then that the planner also requires the producer of Y to pay a tax at the rate t on emissions of S. Considering

$$\text{Max } P_Y Y(K^Y, L^Y, S) - P_K K^Y - P_L L^Y - tS$$

gives the standard conditions

$$P_Y Y_K - P_K = 0$$

$$P_L L_Y - P_L = 0$$

plus

$$P_Y Y_S - t = 0$$

which can be written as

$$t = \lambda_3 Y_S \qquad (5.60)$$

Comparing equations 5.59 and 5.60, we have the result that, in this case, achieving efficiency as the result of individual utility and profit maximisation requires, in addition to the usual 'ideal' institutional arrangements, that the producer of Y faces an emissions tax at the rate:

$$t = -[U_S^A + \lambda_1 U_S^B] \qquad (5.61)$$

Note that since U_S^A and U_S^B are both negative, the tax rate required is positive.

In the chapter, we stated that the correction of this kind of externality required that the tax rate be set equal to the marginal external cost at the efficient allocation. We will now show that this is exactly what the result 5.61 requires. From equation 5.58c

$$\lambda_1 = \frac{\lambda_2}{U_X^B}$$

and from equation 5.58a

$$1 = \frac{\lambda_2}{U_X^A}$$

so that equation 5.61 can be written

$$t = -\left[\frac{\lambda_2}{U_X^A} U_S^A + \frac{\lambda_2}{U_X^B} U_S^B\right]$$

which, using $P_X = \lambda_2$, is

$$t = -P_X \left[\frac{U_S^A}{U_X^A} + \frac{U_S^B}{U_X^B}\right]$$

or

$$t = P_X \lfloor \text{MRUS}_{XS}^A + \text{MRUS}_{XS}^B \rfloor \qquad (5.62)$$

as stated at equation 5.17 in the chapter.[14] The tax rate is the monetary value of the increases in X consumption that would be required to hold each individual's utility constant in the face of a marginal increase in S. We could, of course, have derived the marginal external cost in terms of Y, rather than X, compensation.

In this case, the joint profit maximisation solution is clearly not, even in principle, available for the correction of the market failure problem. Nor, given the public good characteristic of the suffering of A and B, is the property rights/legal liability solution. The way to correct this kind of market failure is to tax the emissions at a rate which is equal to the marginal

---

[14] To recapitulate, the marginal rate of substitution here is derived as follows. For $U(X, Y, S)$

$$dU = U_X dX + U_Y dY + U_S dS$$

so for dU and $dY = 0$

$$0 = U_X dX + U_S dS$$

and

$$\frac{U_S}{U_X} = -\frac{dX}{dS}$$

external cost arising at the efficient allocation. It can be shown that where there is more than one source of the emissions, all sources are to be taxed at the same rate. The checking of this statement by considering

$$
\begin{aligned}
L = U^A(X^A, Y^A, S) &+ \lambda_1 [U^B(X^B, Y^B, S) - Z] \\
&+ \lambda_2 [X(K^X, L^X, S^X) - X^A - X^B] \\
&+ \lambda_3 [Y(K^Y, L^Y, S^Y) - Y^A - Y^B] \\
&+ \lambda_4 [K^T - K^X - K^Y] \\
&+ \lambda_5 [L^T - L^X - L^Y] \\
&+ \lambda_6 [S - S^X - S^Y]
\end{aligned}
$$

is left to the reader as an exercise. The result also applies where total emissions adversely affect production as well as having utility impacts – consider

$$
\begin{aligned}
L = U^A(X^A, Y^A, S) &+ \lambda_1 [U^B(X^B, Y^B, S) - Z] \\
&+ \lambda_2 [X(K^X, L^X, S^X, S) - X^A - X^3] \\
&+ \lambda_3 [Y(K^Y, L^Y, S^Y, S) - Y^A - Y^B] \\
&+ \lambda_4 [K^T - K^X - K^Y] \\
&+ \lambda_5 [L^T - L^X - L^Y] \\
&+ \lambda_6 [S - S^X - S^Y]
\end{aligned}
$$

where $\partial X/\partial S < 0$ and $\partial Y/\partial S < 0$.

PART II   Environmental pollution

CHAPTER 6

Pollution control: targets

The use of coal was prohibited in London in 1273, and at least one person was put to death for this offense around 1300. Why did it take economists so long to recognize and analyze the problem?

Fisher (1981), p. 164

Learning objectives

At the end of this chapter, the reader should be able to

- understand the concept of a pollution target
- appreciate that many different criteria can be used to determine pollution targets
- understand that alternative policy objectives usually imply different pollution targets
- understand how in principle targets may be constructed using an economic efficiency criterion
- understand the difference between flow and stock pollutants
- analyse efficient levels of flow pollutants and stock pollutants
- appreciate the importance of the degree of mixing of a pollutant stock
- recognise and understand the role of spatial differentiation for emissions targets

Introduction

In thinking about pollution policy, the economist is interested in two major questions. How much pollution should there be? And, given that some target level has been chosen, what is the best method of achieving that level? In this chapter we deal with the first of these questions; the second is addressed in the next chapter.

How much pollution there should be depends on the objective that is being sought. Many economists regard economic optimality as the ideal objective. This requires that resources should be allocated so as to maximise social welfare. Associated with that allocation will be the optimal level of pollution. However, the information required to establish the optimal pollution level is likely to be unobtainable, and so that criterion is not feasible in practice.[1] As a result, the weaker yardstick of economic efficiency is often proposed as a way of setting pollution targets.[2]

---

[1] In Chapter 5 we showed that identification of an optimal allocation requires, among other things, knowledge of an appropriate social welfare function, and of production technologies and individual preferences throughout the whole economy. Moreover, even if such an allocation could be identified, attaining it might involve substantial redistributions of wealth.

[2] If you are unclear about the difference between optimality and efficiency it might be sensible to look again at Chapter 5. It is worth

recalling that the efficiency criterion has an ethical underpinning that not all would subscribe to, as it implicitly accepts the prevailing distribution of wealth. We established in Chapter 5 that efficient outcomes are not necessarily optimal ones. Moreover, moving from an inefficient to an efficient outcome does not necessarily lead to an improvement in social well-being.

The use of efficiency as a way of thinking about how much pollution there should be dates back to the work of Pigou, and arose from his development of the concept of externalities (Pigou, 1920). Subsequently, after the theory of externalities had been extended and developed, it became the main organising principle used by economists when analysing pollution problems.

In practice, much of the work done by economists within an externalities framework has used a partial equilibrium perspective, looking at a single activity (and its associated pollution) in isolation from the rest of the system in which the activity is embedded. There is, of course, no reason why externalities cannot be viewed in a general equilibrium framework, and some of the seminal works in environmental economics have done so. (See, for example, Baumol and Oates, 1988, and Cornes and Sandler, 1996.)

This raises the question of what we mean by the 'system' in which pollution-generating activities are embedded. The development of environmental economics and of ecological economics as distinct disciplines led some writers to take a comprehensive view of that system. This involved bringing the material and biological subsystems into the picture, and taking account of the constraints on economy–environment interactions.

One step in this direction came with incorporating natural resources into economic growth models. Then pollution can be associated with resource extraction and use, and best levels of pollution emerge in the solution to the optimal growth problem. Pollution problems are thereby given a firm material grounding and policies concerning pollution levels and natural resource uses are linked. Much of the work done in this area has been abstract, at a high level of aggregation, and is technically difficult. Nevertheless, we feel it is of sufficient importance to warrant study, and have devoted Chapter 16 to it.[3]

There have been more ambitious attempts to use the material balance principle (which was explained in Chapter 2) as a vehicle for investigating pollution problems. These try to systematically model interactions between the economy and the environment. Production and consumption activities draw upon materials and energy from the environment. Residuals from economic processes are returned to various environmental receptors (air, soils, biota and water systems). There may be significant delays in the timing of residual flows from and to the environment. In a growing economy, a significant part of the materials taken from the environment is assembled in long-lasting structures, such as roads, buildings and machines. Thus flows back to the natural environment may be substantially less than extraction from it over some interval of time. However, in the long run the materials balance principle points to equality between outflows and inflows. If we defined the environment broadly (to include human-made structures as well as the natural environment) the equality would hold perfectly at all times. While the masses of flows to and from the environment are identical, the return flows are in different physical forms and to different places from those of the original, extracted materials. A full development of this approach goes beyond what we are able to cover in this book, and so we do not discuss it further (beyond pointing you to some additional reading).

Economic efficiency is one way of thinking about pollution targets, but it is certainly not the only way. For example, we might adopt sustainability as the policy objective, or as a constraint that must be satisfied in pursuing other objectives. Then pollution levels (or trajectories of those through time) would be assessed in terms of whether they are compatible with sustainable development. Optimal growth models with natural resources, and the materials balance approach just outlined, lend themselves well to developing pollution targets using a sustainability criterion. We will show later (in Chapters 14, 16 and 19) that efficiency and sustainability criteria do not usually lead to similar recommendations about pollution targets.

Pollution targets may be, and in practice often are, determined on grounds other than economic efficiency or sustainability. They may be based on what risk to health is deemed reasonable, or on what is acceptable to public opinion. They may be based on what is politically feasible. In outlining the political economy of regulation in Chapter 8, we demonstrate

---

[3] Our reason for placing this material so late in the text is pedagogical. The treatment is technically difficult, and is best dealt with after first developing the relevant tools in Chapters 14 and 15.

that policy is influenced, sometimes very strongly, by the interplay of pressure groups and sectional interests. Moreover, in a world in which the perceived importance of international or global pollution problems is increasing, policy makers find themselves setting targets within a network of obligations and pressures from various national governments and coalitions. Pollution policy making within this international milieu is the subject of Chapter 10.

In the final analysis, pollution targets are rarely, if ever, set entirely on purely economic grounds. Standards setting is usually a matter of trying to attain multiple objectives within a complex institutional environment. Nevertheless, the principal objective of this chapter is to explain what economics has to say about determining pollution targets.

6.1   Modelling pollution mechanisms

Before going further, it will be instructive to develop a framework for thinking about how pollution emissions and stocks are linked, and how these relate to any induced damage. An example is used to help fix ideas. Box 6.1 outlines the stages, and some characteristics, of the oil fuel cycle. It illustrates the material and energy flows associated with the extraction and transportation of oil, its refining and burning for energy generation, and the subsequent transportation and chemical changes of the residuals in this process.

The contents of Box 6.1 lead one to consider several important ideas that will be developed in this

---

Box 6.1 The oil-to-electricity fuel cycle

Figure 6.1 describes the process steps of the oil-to-electricity fuel cycle. At each of these steps, some material transformation occurs, with potential for environmental, health and other damage.

The task given to the ExternE research team was, among other things, to estimate the external effects of power generation in Europe. A standard methodology framework – called the Impact Pathway Methodology – was devised for this task. The stages of the impact pathway are shown on the left-hand side of Figure 6.2. Each form of pollutant emission associated with each fuel cycle was investigated in this standard framework. One example of this, for one pollutant and one kind of impact of that pollutant, is shown on the right-hand side of Figure 6.2; coal use results in sulphur dioxide emissions, which contribute to acidification of air, ground and water systems.

An indication of the pervasiveness of impacts and forms of damage is shown in Table 6.1, which lists the major categories of damages arising from the oil-to-electricity fuel cycle. In fact, ExternE identified 82 sub-categories of the items listed in Table 6.1. It attempted to measure each of these 82 impacts for typical oil-fired power stations in Europe, and place a monetary value on each sub-category.

ExternE (1995) compiled a detailed summary of its estimates of the annual total damage impacts of one example of an oil fuel cycle

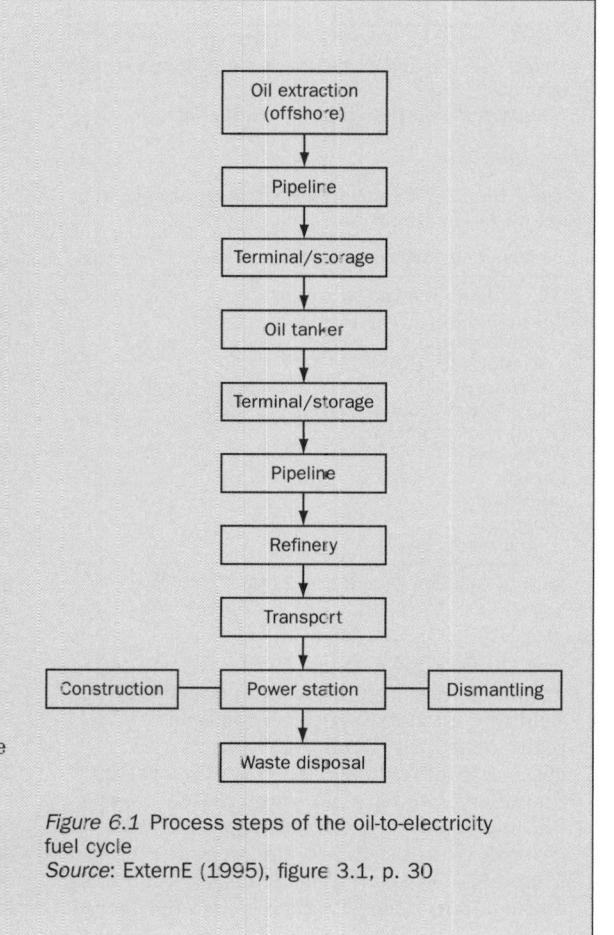

Figure 6.1 Process steps of the oil-to-electricity fuel cycle
Source: ExternE (1995), figure 3.1, p. 30

Box 6.1 *continued*

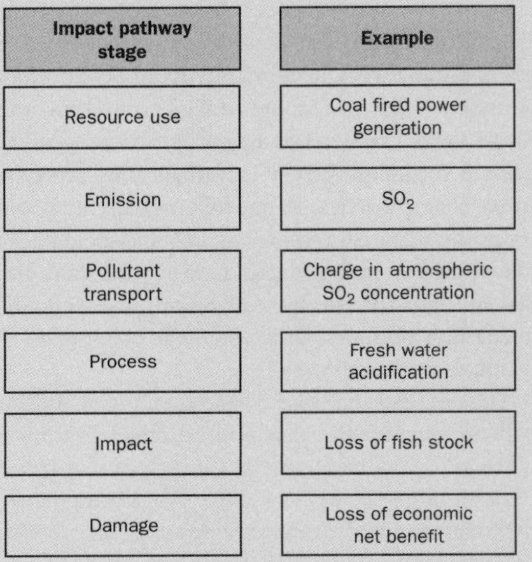

Impact pathway stage	Example
Resource use	Coal fired power generation
Emission	SO_2
Pollutant transport	Charge in atmospheric SO_2 concentration
Process	Fresh water acidification
Impact	Loss of fish stock
Damage	Loss of economic net benefit

Figure 6.2 The impact pathways methodology and one example
Source: Adapted from ExternE (1995), figure 1, p. iii

Table 6.1 Major categories of damage arising from the oil-to-electricity fuel cycle

Damage category
Oil spills on marine ecosystems
Public health:
Acute mortality
Acute morbidity
Ozone
Chronic morbidity
Occupational health
Agriculture
Forests
Materials
Noise
Global warming

Source: Adapted from ExternE (1995)

(the Lauffen power plant, Germany, employing a peak-load gas turbine plant operated with light fuel-oil and a base load combined cycle plant using heavy fuel-oil). Given its size – about 100 individual categories of impact are identified – we have chosen to present these findings separately, in the Excel workbook *ExternE.xls* in the *Additional Materials* for Chapter 6. For convenience, the Excel table also contains damage estimates for one example

Table 6.2 ExternE estimates of the damage impacts of two power stations

Category	Total
All Other	0.7826
Death	18.4362
Other human health	4.30331
Grand Total	23.5221

Category	Total
All Other	3.33%
Death	78.38%
Other human health	18.29%
Grand Total	100.00%

Source: ExternE (1995), as compiled in the Excel workbook *ExternE.xls*. Full definitions of units and variables are given there

of a natural gas fuel cycle (the West Burton power station, a 652 MW Combined Cycle Gas Turbine Plant in the East Midlands of the UK). Data is shown in currency units of mecu (milli-ecu, or 0.001 ecu; at 1992 exchange rates $US 1.25 ≈ 1 ecu).

It is useful to study this material for two reasons. First, it shows the huge breadth of types of pollution impact, and the great attention to detail given in well-funded research studies. Second, as Table 6.2 demonstrates, estimates of pollution damages are often dominated by values attributed to human mortality impacts. The data in Table 6.2 shows the sums of annual combined impacts of the two example power stations (expressed in units of mecu/kWh) for three very broad impact categories, and then in terms of percentages of total impact. Impacts on human mortality constitute over 78% of the identified and quantified impacts. It should be pointed out that the figures shown were arrived at when the ExternE analysis was incomplete; in particular, little attention had been given to greenhouse warming impacts of CO_2 emissions. Nevertheless, the figures here illustrate one property that is common to many impact studies: human health impacts account for a large proportion of the total damage values. Given that valuation of human life is by no means straightforward (as we shall indicate in Chapter 12), estimates produced by valuation studies can often be highly contentious.

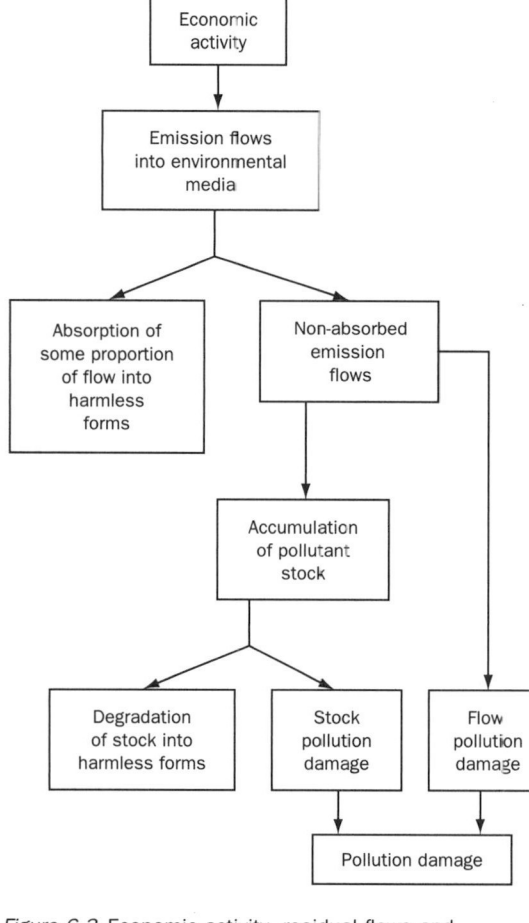

Figure 6.3 Economic activity, residual flows and environmental damage

chapter. In particular, residual flows impose loads upon environmental systems. The extent to which these waste loads generate impacts that are associated with subsequent damage depends upon several things, including:

- the assimilative (or absorptive) capacity of the receptor environmental media;
- the existing loads on the receptor environmental media;
- the location of the environmental receptor media, and so the number of people living there and the characteristics of the affected ecosystems;
- tastes and preferences of affected people.

Figure 6.3 illustrates some of these ideas schematically for pollution problems in general. Some pro-

portion of the emission flows from economic activity is quickly absorbed and transformed by environmental media into harmless forms. The assimilative capacity of the environment will in many circumstances be sufficient to absorb and transform into harmless forms some amount of wastes. However, carrying capacities will often be insufficient to deal with all wastes in this way, and in extreme cases carrying capacities will become zero when burdens become excessive. Furthermore, physical and chemical processes take time to operate. Some greenhouse gases, for example, require decades to be fully absorbed in water systems or chemically changed into non-warming substances (see Table 6.3).

This implies that some proportion of wastes will, in any time interval, remain unabsorbed or untransformed. These may cause damage at the time of their emission, and may also, by accumulating as pollutant stocks, cause additional future damage. Stocks of pollutants will usually decay into harmless forms but the rate of decay is often very slow. The half-lives of some radioactive substances are thousands of years, and for some highly persistent pollutants, such as the heavy metals, the rate of decay is approximately zero.

6.2 Pollution flows, pollution stocks and pollution damage

Pollution can be classified in terms of its damage mechanism. This has important implications for how pollution targets are set and for the way in which pollution is most appropriately controlled. The distinction here concerns whether damage arises from the flow of the pollutant (that is, the rate of emissions) or from the stock (or concentration rate) of pollution in the relevant environmental medium. We define the following two classes of pollution: flow-damage pollution and stock-damage pollution (but recognise that there may also be mixed cases).

Flow-damage pollution occurs when damage results only from the flow of residuals: that is, the rate at which they are being discharged into the environmental system. This corresponds to the right-hand side branch in Figure 6.3. By definition, for pure cases of flow-damage pollution, the damage will instantaneously drop to zero if the emissions flow becomes zero. This can only be exactly true when the pollutant exists in an energy form such as noise or light so that when the energy emission is terminated no residuals remain in existence. However, this characterisation of damages may be approximately true in a wider variety of cases, particularly when the residuals have very short lifespans before being transformed into benign forms.

Stock-damage pollution describes the case in which damages depend only on the stock of the pollutant in the relevant environmental system at any point in time. This corresponds to the central branch in Figure 6.3. For a stock of the pollutant to accumulate, it is necessary that the residuals have a positive lifespan and that emissions are being produced at a rate which exceeds the assimilative capacity of the environment. An extreme case is that in which the assimilative capacity is zero, as seems to be approximately the case for some synthetic chemicals and a number of heavy metals. (The left-hand branch in Figure 6.3 does not then exist.) Metals such as mercury or lead accumulate in soils, aquifers and biological stocks, and subsequently in the human body, causing major damage to human health. Persistent synthetic chemicals, such as PCBs (polychlorinated biphenyls), DDT and dioxins, have similar cycles and effects. Rubbish which cannot biodegrade is another case. So are, for all practical purposes, strongly radioactive elements such as plutonium with extremely long radiation half-lives.

Most important pollution problems have the attribute of a stock-damage pollution effect being present. The most prominent are those which affect human health and life expectancy. But the phenomenon is more pervasive than this. Pollution stocks are harmful to built structures (buildings, works of art and so on) and they may adversely affect production potential, particularly in agriculture. Stock pollution levels influence plant and timber growth, and the size of marine animal populations. Less direct effects operate through damages to environmental resources and ecological systems. There is another way in which stock effects operate. The assimilative capacity of the environment often depends on the emissions load to which relevant environmental media are exposed. This is particularly true when the natural cleaning mechanism operates biologically. In water systems, for example, bacterial decomposition of pollutants is the principal cleaning agency. But where critical loads are exceeded, this biological conversion process breaks down, and the water system can effectively become dead. Its assimilative capacity has fallen to zero.

Mixed cases, where pollution damage arises from both flow and stock effects, also exist. Waste emissions into water systems are sometimes modelled as mixed stock-flow pollutants. So too are damages arising from the emissions of compounds of carbon, sulphur and nitrogen. However, in these mixed cases, it may often be preferable to view the problem as one of a pure stock pollutant.

Using M to denote the pollution flow, A to denote the pollution stock and D to denote pollution damage, we therefore have two variants of damage function:

Flow-damage pollution: $D = D(M)$ (6.1a)

Stock-damage pollution: $D = D(A)$ (6.1b)

For simplicity of notation, we shall from this point on call these 'flow pollution' and 'stock pollution'.

6.3   The efficient level of pollution

We now investigate how pollution targets can be set using an efficiency criterion. Given that pollution is harmful, some would argue that only a zero level of pollution is desirable. But, as we shall see, pollution can also be beneficial. Therefore, zero pollution is not economically efficient except in particular special circumstances. In what sense is pollution beneficial? One answer comes from the fact that producing some goods and services that we do find useful may not be possible without generating some pollution, even if only a small amount. More generally, goods might only be producible in non-polluting ways at large additional expense. Thus, relaxing a pollution abatement constraint allows the production of goods that could not otherwise have been made, or to produce those goods at less direct cost. This is the sense in which pollution could be described as beneficial.

With both benefits and costs, economic decisions about the appropriate level of pollution involve the evaluation of a trade-off. Thinking about pollution as an externality arising from production or consumption activities makes this trade-off clear. The efficient level of an externality is not, in general, zero as the marginal costs of reducing the external effect will, beyond a certain point, exceed its marginal benefits.

The discussion of efficient pollution targets which follows is divided into several parts. In the first two (Sections 6.4 and 6.5) a static modelling framework is used to study efficient emissions of a flow pollutant. This explains the key principles involved in dealing with the trade-off. We next, in Section 6.6, investigate the more common – and important – case of stock-damage pollution. Two variants of stock damage are considered. Sections 6.7 and 6.8 deal with those stock pollutants for which the location of the emission source matters as far as the pollutant stock, and so the extent of damages, is concerned. Our emphasis here will be on the *spatial* dimension of pollution problems. Section 6.9 focuses on the *time* dimension of pollution problems. It studies long-lived pollutants, such as greenhouse gases, which can accumulate over time. At this stage, our treatment of persistent stock pollutants will be relatively simple. Later, in Chapter 16, a richer dynamic modelling framework will be used to identify emission targets where pollution is modelled as arising from the depletion of natural resources.

6.4 A static model of efficient flow pollution

A simple static model – one in which time plays no role – can be used to identify the efficient level of a flow pollutant. In this model, emissions have both benefits and costs. In common with much of the pollution literature, the costs of emissions are called damages. Using a concept introduced in Chapter 5, these damages can be thought of as a negative (adverse) externality. Production entails joint products: the intended good or service, *and* the associated pollutant emissions. In an unregulated economic environment, the costs associated with production of the intended good or service are paid by the producer, and so are internalised. But the costs of pollution damage are not met by the firm, are not taken into account in its decisions, and so are externalities. Moreover, in many cases of interest to us, it is also the case that the externality in question is what Chapter 5 called a public bad (as opposed to a private bad), in that once it has been generated, no one can be excluded from suffering its adverse effects.

For simplicity, we suppose that damage is independent of the time or source of the emissions and that emissions have no effect outside the economy being studied. We shall relax these two assumptions later, the first in Section 6.6 and in Chapter 7, and the second in Chapter 10.

An efficient level of emissions is one that maximises the net benefits from pollution, where net benefits are defined as pollution benefits minus pollution costs (or damages). The level of emissions at which net benefits are maximised is equivalent to the outcome that would prevail if the pollution externality were fully internalised. Therefore, the identification of the efficient level of an adverse externality in Figure 5.14, and the discussion surrounding it, is apposite in this case with an appropriate change of context.

In the case of flow pollution, damage (D) is dependent only on the magnitude of the emissions flow (M), so the damage function can be specified as

$$D = D(M) \qquad (6.2)$$

Matters are a little less obvious with regard to the benefits of pollution. Let us expand a little on the earlier remarks we made about interpreting these benefits. Suppose for the sake of argument that firms were required to produce their intended final output without generating any pollution. This would, in general, be extremely costly (and perhaps even impossible in that limiting case). Now consider what will happen if that requirement is gradually relaxed. As the amount of allowable emissions rises, firms can increasingly avoid the pollution abatement costs that would otherwise be incurred. Therefore, firms make cost savings (and so profit increases) if they are allowed to generate emissions in producing their goods. The larger is the amount of emissions generated (for any given level of goods output), the greater will be those cost savings.

A sharper, but equivalent, interpretation of the benefits function runs as follows. Consider a representative firm. For any particular level of output it chooses to make, there will be an unconstrained emissions level that would arise from the cost-minimising method of production. If it were required to reduce emissions below that unconstrained level, and did so in the profit-maximising way, the total of production and control costs would exceed the total production costs in the unconstrained situation. So there are additional costs associated with emissions reduction. Equivalently, there are savings (or benefits) associated with emissions increases. It is these cost savings that we regard as the benefits of pollution.

Symbolically, we can represent this relationship by the function

$$B = B(M) \qquad (6.3)$$

in which B denotes the benefits from emissions.[4] The social net benefits (NB) from a given level of emissions are defined by

$$NB = B(M) - D(M) \qquad (6.4)$$

It will be convenient to work with marginal, rather than total, functions. Thus dB/dM (or $B'(M)$ in an alternative notation) is the marginal benefit of pollution and dD/dM (or $D'(M)$) is the marginal damage of pollution. Economists often assume that the total and marginal damage and benefit functions have the general forms shown in Figure 6.4. Total damage is thought to rise at an increasing rate with the size of the pollution flow, and so the marginal damage will be increasing in M. In contrast, total benefits will rise at a decreasing rate as emissions increase (because per-unit pollution abatement costs will be more expensive at greater levels of emissions *reduction*). Therefore, the marginal benefit of pollution would fall as pollution flows increase.

It is important to understand that damage or benefit functions (or both) will not necessarily have these general shapes. For some kinds of pollutants, in particular circumstances, the functions can have very different properties, as our discussions in Section 6.11 will illustrate. There is also an issue

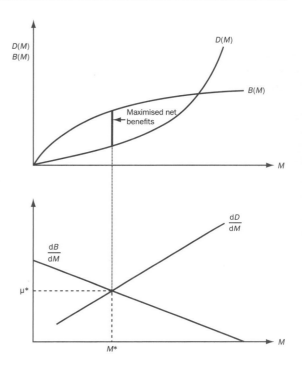

Figure 6.4 Total and marginal damage and benefit functions, and the efficient level of flow pollution emissions

about whether the benefit function correctly describes the social benefits of emissions. Under some circumstances, emissions abatement can generate a so-called double dividend. If it does, the marginal benefit function as defined in this chapter will overstate the true value of emissions benefits. For some explanation of the double dividend idea, see Box 6.3. Nevertheless, except where it is stated otherwise, our presentation will assume that the general shapes shown in Figure 6.4 are valid.

To maximise the net benefits of economic activity, we require that the pollution flow, M, be chosen so that

$$\frac{dNB(M)}{dM} = \frac{dB(M)}{dM} - \frac{dD(M)}{dM} = 0 \qquad (6.5a)$$

or, equivalently, that

---

[4] Given our interpretation of the emissions benefit function (which involves optimised emissions abatement costs at any level of emissions below the unconstrained level), it will not be an easy matter to quantify this relationship numerically. However, there are various ways in which emissions abatement cost functions can be estimated, as you will see in Section 6.12. And with a suitable change of label (again, as we shall see later) abatement cost functions are identical to the benefit function we are referring to here.

$$\frac{\mathrm{d}B(M)}{\mathrm{d}M} = \frac{\mathrm{d}D(M)}{\mathrm{d}M} \qquad (6.5b)$$

which states that the net benefits of pollution can be maximised only where the marginal benefits of pollution equal the marginal damage of pollution.[5] This is a special case of the efficiency condition for an externality stated in Chapter 5.

The efficient level of pollution is M^* (see Figure 6.4 again). If pollution is less than M^* the marginal benefits of pollution are greater than the marginal damage from pollution, so higher pollution will yield additional net benefits. Conversely, if pollution is greater than M^*, the marginal benefits of pollution are less than the marginal damage from pollution, so less pollution will yield more net benefits.

The value of marginal damage and marginal benefit functions at their intersection is labelled μ^* in Figure 6.4. We can think of this as the equilibrium 'price' of pollution. This price has a particular significance in terms of an efficient rate of emissions tax or subsidy, as we shall discover in the following chapter. However, as there is no market for pollution, μ^* is a hypothetical or shadow price rather than one which is actually revealed in market transactions. More specifically, a shadow price emerges as part of the solution to an optimisation problem (in this case the problem of choosing M to maximise net benefits). We could also describe μ^* as the shadow price of the pollution externality. If a market were, somehow or other, to exist for the pollutant itself (thereby internalising the externality) so that firms had to purchase rights to emit units of the pollutant, μ^* would be the efficient market price. Indeed, Chapter 7 will demonstrate that μ^* is the equilibrium price of tradable permits if an amount M^* of such permits were to be issued.

Another interpretation of the emissions efficiency condition (equation 6.5b) is obtained by inspection of Figure 6.5. The efficient level of pollution is

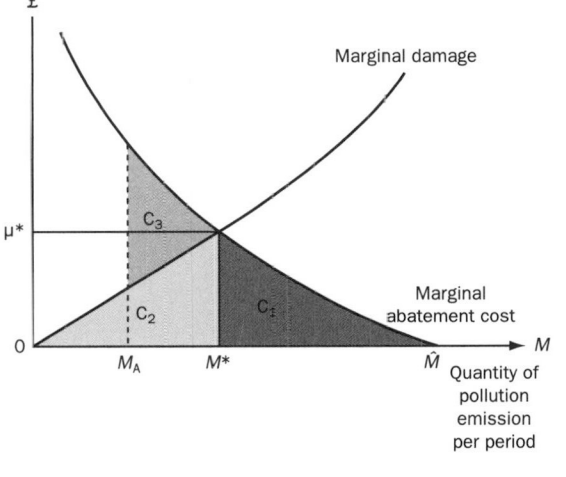

Figure 6.5 The economically efficient level of pollution minimises the sum of abatement and damage costs

the one that minimises the sum of total abatement costs plus total damage costs. Notice that in the diagram we have relabelled the curve previously called marginal benefit as marginal abatement cost. The logic here should be clear given our earlier discussion about the derivation of the benefits of pollution function.[6]

To confirm this cost-minimising result, note that at the efficient pollution level, M^*, the sum of total damage costs (the area C_2) and total abatement costs (the area C_1) is $C_2 + C_1$. Any other level of emissions yields higher total costs. If too little pollution is produced (or too much abatement is undertaken) with a pollution flow restricted to M_A, it can be deduced that total costs rise to $C_1 + C_2 + C_3$, so C_3 is the efficiency loss arising from the excessive abatement. If you cannot see how this conclusion is reached, look now at Problem 2 at the end of this chapter. You should also convince yourself that too much pollution (too little abatement) results in higher costs than $C_1 + C_2$.

---

[5] This marginal equality applies when the optimum is at an interior point (does not fall at either extreme of the domain of the function). A sufficient second-order condition for this solution to be a net benefit maximum is that $\mathrm{d}^2NB/\mathrm{d}M^2 = \mathrm{d}^2B/\mathrm{d}M^2 - \mathrm{d}^2D/\mathrm{d}M^2 < 0$. Both an interior solution and the second-order condition are satisfied given the slopes and relative positions of the functions assumed in the text and shown in Figure 6.4 (see Chiang, 1984).

[6] The reinterpretation follows from the fact that reducing emissions incurs abatement costs. By construction, these (marginal) abatement costs are equal to the marginal benefits that will be lost if emissions fall. So, in Figure 6.5, if we start at the unconstrained emissions level, denoted as $\hat{M}$ in the diagram, then moving leftwards towards the origin corresponds to rising amounts of pollution abatement. Marginal abatement costs are low at small levels of abatement, and rise at an increasing rate as the abatement level becomes larger.

Box 6.2 Efficient solution for a flow pollutant: a numerical example

Suppose that the total damage and total benefits functions have the following particular forms:

$$D = M^2 \text{ for } M \geq 0$$

$$B = \begin{cases} 96M - 0.2M^2 & \text{for } 0 \leq M \leq 240 \\ 11\,520 & \text{for } M > 240 \end{cases}$$

What is M^*?

If M is less than or equal to 240, then we have $B = 96M - 0.2M^2$ and so $dB/dM = 96 - 0.4M$. For any positive value of M we also have $D = M^2$ which implies that $dD/dM = 2M$, Now setting $dB/dM = dD/dM$ we obtain $96 - 0.4M = 2M$, implying that $M^* = 40$.

Substituting $M^* = 40$ into the benefit and damage functions gives us the result that $B^* = 3520$ and $D^* = 1600$, and so maximised total net benefits (NB^*) are 1920. Note also that at M^* marginal benefit and marginal damage are equalised at 80 and so the shadow price μ^* – the value of value of marginal pollution damage at the efficient outcome – is 80.

You should now verify that $M^* = 40$ is a global optimum. This can be done by sketching the respective marginal functions and showing that net benefits are necessarily lower than 1920 for any (positive) level of M other than 40.

Additional materials

It can be useful to write a spreadsheet to do the kind of calculations we have just gone through. Moreover, if the spreadsheet is constructed appropriately, it can also serve as a template by means of which similar calculations can be quickly implemented as required. Alternatively, we could use such a spreadsheet to carry out comparative statics; that is, to see how the solution changes as parameter values are altered.

We have provided an Excel workbook *Targets examples.xls* that can be used in these ways in the *Additional Materials* available on the textbook's web pages. That spreadsheet also shows how one of Excel's tools – 'Solver' – can be used to obtain the efficient level of M directly, by finding the level of M which maximises the net benefit function $NB = B - D = (96M - 0.2M^2) - (M^2)$.

It can also be deduced from Figures 6.4 and 6.5 that the efficient level of pollution will not, in general, be zero. (By implication, the efficient level of pollution abatement will not, in general, correspond to complete elimination of pollution.) Problem 1 examines this matter.

We round off this section with a simple numerical example, given in Box 6.2. Functional forms used in the example are consistent with the general forms of marginal benefit and marginal damage functions shown in Figure 6.4. We solve for the values of M^*, B^*, D^* and μ^* for one set of parameter values. Also provided, in the *Additional Materials* that are linked to this text, is an Excel spreadsheet (*Targets examples.xls*) that reproduces these calculations. The Excel workbook is set up so that comparative statics analysis can be done easily by the reader. That is, the effects on M^*, B^*, D^* and μ^* of changes in parameter values from those used in Box 6.2 can be obtained.

6.5 Modified efficiency targets

Our notion of efficiency to this point has been a comprehensive one; it involves maximising the difference between *all* the benefits of pollution and *all* the costs of pollution. But, sometimes, one particular kind of pollution cost (or damage) is regarded as being of such importance that pollution costs should be defined in terms of that cost alone. In this case we can imagine a revised or modified efficiency criterion in which the goal is to maximise the difference between all the benefits of pollution and this particular kind of pollution damage.

Policy makers sometimes appear to treat risks to human health in this way. So let us assume policy makers operate by making risks to human health the only damage that counts (in setting targets). How would this affect pollution targets? The answer depends on the relationship between emissions and

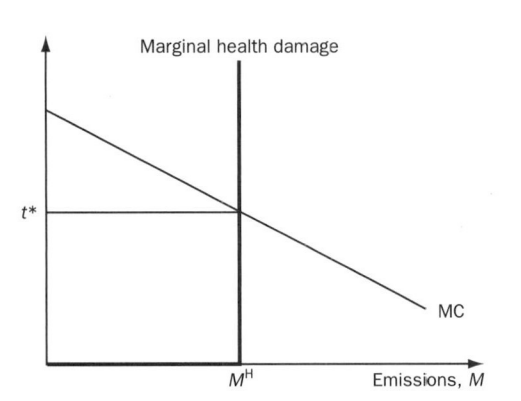

Figure 6.6 Setting targets according to an absolute health criterion

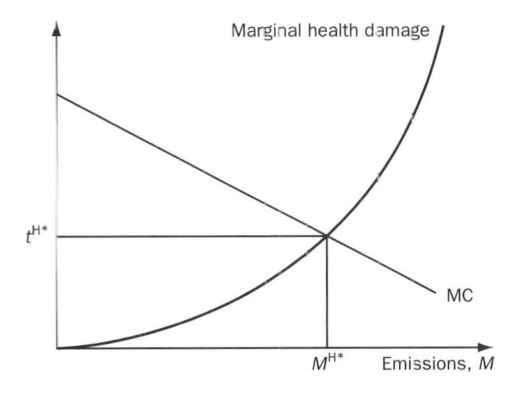

Figure 6.7 A 'modified efficiency-based' health standard

health risks. One possible relationship is that illustrated by the ⌐-shaped relationship in Figure 6.6. Total (and marginal) health risks are zero below the threshold, but at the threshold itself risks to human health become intolerably large. It is easy to see that the value of marginal benefits is irrelevant here. A modified efficiency criterion would, in effect, lead to the emissions target being set by the damage threshold alone. Target setting is simple in this case because of the strong discontinuity we have assumed about human health risks. It is easy to see

why an absolute maximum emission standard is appropriate.

But now suppose that marginal health damage is a rising and continuous function of emissions, as in Figure 6.7. A trade-off now exists in which lower health risks can be obtained at the cost of some loss of pollution benefits (or, if you prefer lower health risks involve higher emission abatement costs). It is now clear that with such a trade-off, both benefits and costs matter. A 'modified efficiency target' would correspond to emissions level $M^{H}*$.

Box 6.3 No regrets and a double dividend from environmental control?

It is sometimes possible to achieve environmental objectives at no cost or, better still, at 'negative' cost. Not surprisingly, ways of doing things that have such effects are known as 'no regrets' policies. There are several reasons why these may arise:

- double dividends;
- elimination of technical and economic inefficiencies in the energy-using or energy-producing sectors;
- induced technical change;
- achievement of additional ancillary benefits, such as improved health or visual amenity.

We will explain these ideas in the context of one potential example: reducing the emissions of carbon dioxide to reduce global climate change. First, the 'double dividend' hypothesis is explained.

The double dividend hypothesis

The double dividend idea arises from the possibility that the revenues from an emissions tax (or a system of permits sold by auction) could be earmarked to reduce marginal rates of other taxes in the economy. If those other taxes have distortionary (i.e. inefficiency-generating) effects, then reducing their rate will create efficiency gains. Thus an environmental tax with revenues ring-fenced for reducing distortionary taxes has a double benefit (dividend); the environment is improved *and* efficiency gains accrue to the economy as whole.

There are other reasons why 'no regret' options may be available. The existence of market imperfections can cause firms to be producing away from the frontier of what is technically and/or economically possible. Firms may be unaware of new techniques, or poorly informed

Box 6.3 *continued*

about waste recycling mechanisms. Companies may have old, technologically obsolete capital, but are unable because of credit market imperfections to update even when that would generate positive net present value. An environmental programme that requires firms to use new, less polluting techniques, or which provides incentives to do so, can generate a different kind of double benefit. Pollution is reduced and productive efficiency gains are made.

One special case of this is dynamic efficiency gains, arising through induced technical change. It has long been recognised (see, for example, Porter, 1991) that some forms of regulatory constraint may induce firms to be more innovative. If a pollution control mechanism can be devised that accelerates the rate of technical change, then the mechanism may more than pay for itself over the long run. One area where this may be very important is in policy towards the greenhouse effect. Grubb (2000) argues persuasively that the provisions of the Kyoto Protocol will have beneficial induced effects on technical change. He writes:

> general economic processes of international investment and the dissemination of technologies and ideas – accelerated by the provisions on technology transfer and other processes under the Convention and the Protocol – could contribute to global dissemination of cleaner technologies

and practices. In doing so, they will also yield multiplicative returns upon industrialised country actions.

Grubb (2000), p. 124

More generally, there is a large set of possible ancillary benefits to environmental reforms. Perhaps the most important type is health benefits. Reductions of greenhouse gases tend to go hand in hand with reductions in emissions of secondary pollutants (such as particulates, sulphur dioxide, nitrogen dioxide and carbon monoxide), which can have important health impacts.

Some writers distinguish between a 'weak form' and a 'strong form' of the double dividend hypothesis. For a revenue-neutral environmental reform, the weak form refers to the case where total real resource costs are lower for a scheme where revenues are used to reduce marginal rates of distortionary taxes than where the revenues are used to finance lump-sum payments to households or firms. There is almost universal agreement that this hypothesis is valid. The strong form asserts that the real resource costs of a revenue-neutral environmental tax reform are zero or negative. Not surprisingly, this hypothesis is far more contentious.

For a more thorough examination of the double dividend hypothesis, and some empirical results, see the Word file *Double Dividend* in *Additional Materials*, Chapter 6.

Box 6.4 Measures of stocks and flows for a variety of pollutants

Pollutant emissions are measured (like all flows) in rates of output per period of time. For example, it is estimated that worldwide anthropogenic emissions of carbon dioxide, the most important greenhouse gas, were 6.9 gigatonnes of carbon equivalent per year (6.9 GtC/yr) as of 1990.[7] These flows accumulate through time as pollutant stocks, measured either in quantities in existence at some point in time, or in terms of some measure of concentration in an environmental medium of interest to us. Carbon dioxide atmospheric concentrations have

risen from about 280 ppmv (parts per million by volume) in 1750 (the start of the industrial era) to 367 ppmv in 1999 (an increase of 31%). The current rate of change of the CO_2 concentration rate is estimated to be 1.5 ppmv per year (a growth rate of 0.4% per year). IPCC scenarios suggest that by 2100, concentrations will be in the range 549 to 970 ppm (90 to 250% above pre-industrial levels).

Sources: Technical Summary of the Working Group 1 Report (IPCC(1), 2001), particularly Figure 8, p. 36

---

[7]   A metric tonne is equal to 1000 kilograms (kg). Commonly used units for large masses are (i) a gigatonne (Gt) which is 10^9 tonnes, (ii) a megatonne (Mt) which is 10^6 tonnes, and (iii) a petragram (Pg) which is equal to 1 Gt. Finally, 1 GtC = 3.7 Gt carbon dioxide.

Table 6.3 Expected lifetimes for several pollutants

	Pre-industrial concentration	Concentration in 1998	Rate of concentration change	Atmospheric lifetime
CO_2 (carbon dioxide)	about 280 ppm	365 ppm	1.5 ppm/yr	5 to 200 yr[1]
CH_4 (methane)	about 700 ppb	1745 ppb	7.0 ppb/yr	12 yr
N_2O (nitrous oxide)	about 270 ppb	314 ppb	0.8 ppb/yr	114 yr
CFC-11 (chlorofluorocarbon-11)	zero	268 ppt	−1.4 ppt/yr	45 yr
HFC-23 (hydrofluorocarbon-23)	zero	14 ppt	0.55 ppt/yr	260 yr
CF_4 (perfluoromethane)	40 ppt	80 ppt	1 ppt/yr	>50 000 yr
Sulphur	Spatially variable	Spatially variable	Spatially variable	0.01 to 7 days
NO_X	Spatially variable	Spatially variable	Spatially variable	2 to 8 days

Note:
1. No single lifetime can be defined for CO_2 because of the different rates of uptake by different removal processes
Sources: Technical Summary of the IPCC Working Group 1 Report, IPCC(1) (2001), Table 1, p. 38

6.6 Efficient levels of emission of stock pollutants

The analysis of pollution in Section 6.4 dealt with the case of flow pollution, in which pollution damage depends directly on the level of emissions. In doing so, there were two reasons why it was unnecessary to distinguish between flows and stocks of the pollutant. First, both benefits and damages depended on emissions alone, so as far as the objective of net benefit maximisation was concerned, stocks – even if they existed – were irrelevant. But we also argued that, strictly speaking, stocks do not exist for pure flow pollutants (such as noise or light).

How do we need to change the analysis in the case of stock pollutants where damage depends on the stock level of the pollutant? It turns out to be the case – as we shall see below – that the flow pollution model also provides correct answers in the special (but highly unlikely) case where the pollutant stock in question degrades into a harmless form more-or-less instantaneously. In that case, the stock dimension is distinguishable from the flow only by some constant of proportionality, and so we can work just as before entirely in flow units. But in all other cases of stock pollutants, the flow pollution model is invalid.

The majority of important pollution problems are associated with stock pollutants. Pollution stocks derive from the accumulation of emissions that have a finite life (or residence time). The distinction between flows and stocks now becomes crucial for two reasons. First, without it understanding of the science lying behind the pollution problem is impos-

sible. Second, the distinction is important for policy purposes. While the damage is associated with the pollution stock, that stock is outside the direct control of policy makers. Environmental protection agencies may, however, be able to control the rate of emission flows. Even where they cannot control such flows directly, the regulator may find it more convenient to target emissions rather than stocks. Given that what we seek to achieve depends on stocks but what is controlled or regulated are typically flows, it is necessary to understand the linkage between the two.

As we shall now demonstrate, the analysis of stock pollution necessitates taking account of space and time. For clarity of presentation it will be convenient to deal with these two dimensions separately. To do so, we draw a distinction between pollutants with a relatively short residence time (of the order of a day or so) and those with considerably longer lifetimes (years rather than days, let us say). Table 6.3 provides some idea of the active life expectancy of a range of pollutants under normal conditions.

6.7 Pollution control where damages depend on location of the emissions

In this section and the next we deal with stock pollutants which have relatively short residence times in the environmental media into which they are dumped. To help fix ideas, consider the graphic in Figure 6.8 which represents two polluting 'sources',

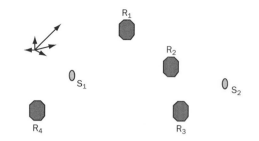

Figure 6.8 A spatially differentiated airshed

S_1 and S_2, that are located near four urban areas, R_1, R_2, R_3 and R_4. These areas contain populations whose health is adversely affected by local ambient concentrations of the pollutant. Our interest lies in the amount of pollution these areas – called 'receptors' – receive from the emission sources. We assume that emissions from the two sources persist for at most a few days; atmospheric processes break up and degrade concentrations rather quickly, so that on any one day pollutant concentrations are determined purely by emissions of the last few days. There is no long-term accumulation effect taking place.

Now consider the extent of pollutant dispersion and mixing. Mixing of a pollutant refers to the extent to which physical processes cause the pollutant to be dispersed or spread out. One possibility is that emissions are 'uniformly mixing' (UM). A pollutant is uniformly mixing if physical processes operate so that the pollutant quickly becomes dispersed to the point where its spatial distribution is uniform. That is, the measured concentration rate of the pollutant does not vary from place to place. This property is satisfied, for example, by most greenhouse gases.

By definition, the location of the emission source of a UM pollutant is irrelevant as far as the spatial distribution of pollutant concentrations is concerned. Irrespective of the source location, pollutant stocks become evenly distributed across the whole spatial area of interest – in our picture over the whole rectangle depicted. All that matters, as far as concentration rates at any receptor are concerned, is the total amount of those emissions.

What can be said about the efficient level of emissions with the twin properties of short residence time

(whose accumulation is therefore negligible) and uniform mixing? Intuition suggests that the simple flow pollution model developed in Section 6.4 can be used with only minor modification. To see why, note that there will be a one-to-one relationship between the level of emissions of the pollutant (M) and the pollutant stock size (A). Specifically, M and k are related by a fixed coefficient relationship of the form $A = kM$, with k fixed for any particular kind of pollution. Therefore, while damage is a function of the stock, and benefit is a function of flow, the damage function can be translated into an equivalent flow function using the $A = kM$ relationship, permitting use of the flow pollution model. A simple numerical example is given in Box 6.5. This has been reproduced as an Excel spreadsheet in Sheet 2 of the workbook *Targets examples.xls*. As was the case for the numerical example in Box 6.2, the Excel workbook has been set up to allow comparative static analysis to be carried out, and shows the use of Solver to obtain a direct solution to the optimisation problem.

As we will now see, the flow pollution model cannot be used where the pollutant is not uniformly mixing nor where it has a relatively long lifespan. (Can you explain why?) Most air, water and ground pollutants are not uniformly mixing. Look at Figure 6.8 again. Suppose that the principal determinants of the spatial distribution of the pollutant are wind direction and velocity. In the diagram, the length and direction of the arrow vectors in the multiple arrow symbol represent the relative frequency of these two components. Clearly, emissions from S_1 are going to matter much more for the four receptor areas than emissions from S_2. Furthermore, looking at emissions from S1 alone, these are likely to raise pollutant concentration levels to a greater amount in R1 than in the other three receptors. R4 is likely to suffer the least from emissions by either source.

Other factors will, of course, come into play too. For example, suppose R1 is at high elevation, whereas R2 is situated in a depression surrounded by a ring of hills. Then R2 may experience the highest concentrations, both on average and at peak times. All of this amounts to saying that where pollutants are not uniformly mixing, location

---

Box 6.5 Efficient solution for a uniformly mixed and short-lived stock pollutant: a numerical example

As in Box 6.2 we suppose that total benefits function is given by:

$$B = \begin{cases} 96M - 0.2M^2 & \text{for} \quad 0 \le M \le 240 \\ 11\,520 & \text{for} \quad M > 240 \end{cases}$$

Our total damage, however, now needs to be specified appropriately for a stock pollutant and is taken to be:

$$D = 0.2A^2 \text{ for } A \ge 0$$

and in steady state we assume that $A = 2M$

What are M^* and A^*?

We first consider the case in which there is an interior solution with M positive but less than 240. The relevant first derivatives are:

$$dB/dM = 96 - 0.4M$$

$$dD/dM = 1.6M$$

(as $D = 0.2A^2$ implies $D = 0.2 \times (2M)^2 = 0.8M^2$ which implies $dD/dM = 1.6M$).

Now setting $dB/dM = dD/dM$ we obtain:

$$96 - 0.4M = 1.6M \rightarrow M^* = 48 \text{ and so } A^* = 96$$

Additional materials

As we remarked at the end of Box 6.2, a spreadsheet can be used for obtaining solutions to problems of this kind, or for carrying out comparative statics. Sheet 2 of the Excel workbook *Targets examples.xls* sets up a template for simple stock pollution models of this form. The interested reader may find it helpful to explore that sheet.

---

matters. There will not be a single relationship between emissions and concentration over all space. A given total value of M will in general lead to differentiated values of A across receptors. Moreover, if M remained constant but its source distribution changed then the spatial configuration of A would also change.

Non-uniform mixing is of great importance as many types of pollution fall into this category. Examples include ozone accumulation in the lower atmosphere, oxides of nitrogen and sulphur in urban airsheds, particulate pollutants from diesel engines and trace metal emissions. Many water and ground pollutants also do not uniformly mix. An environmental protection agency (EPA) may attempt to handle these spatial issues by controlling *ex ante* the location of pollution creators and victims. This approach, implemented primarily by zoning and other forms of planning control, forms a substantial part of the longer-term way of dealing with spatial aspects of pollution. However, in the next section we focus on the situation in which the location of polluters and people is already determined, and moving either is not a feasible option. Our interest must then lie in how targets for emissions from the various sources can be calculated

(and, in the next chapter, on what instruments can be used).

6.8 Ambient pollution standards

It will be convenient to use a little elementary matrix algebra for the exposition of the arguments that follow. For the reader unfamiliar with matrix algebra, or who needs a quick refresher, a brief appendix is provided at the end of this chapter (Appendix 6.1) explaining the notation used in matrix algebra and stating some simple results. It would be sensible to read that now.

Some additional notation is now required. Using earlier terminology, we regard the environment as a series of spatially distinct pollution 'reception' areas (or receptors). Suppose that there are J distinct receptors, each being indexed by the subscript j (so $j = 1, 2, \ldots, J$) and N distinct pollution sources, each being indexed by the subscript i (so $i = 1, 2, \ldots, N$). Various physical and chemical processes determine the impact on pollutant concentration in any particular receptor from any particular source. For simplicity, we assume that the relationships are linear. In that case, a set of constant 'transfer coefficients' can be defined. The transfer coefficient d_{ji} describes the impact on pollutant concentration at receptor j attributable to source i.[8] The total level, or concentration rate, of pollution at location j, A_j, will be the sum of the contributions to pollution at that location from all N emission sources. This can be written as

$$A_j = \sum_{i=1}^{N} d_{ji} M_i \qquad (6.6)$$

where M_i denotes the total emissions from source i.

A numerical example will help. In the case shown in Figure 6.8, we have $N = 2$ sources and $J = 4$ receptors. Then we have four equations corresponding to equation 6.6. These are

$$A_1 = d_{11}M_1 + d_{12}M_2 \qquad (6.7a)$$

$$A_2 = d_{21}M_1 + d_{22}M_2 \qquad (6.7b)$$

$$A_3 = d_{31}M_1 + d_{32}M_2 \qquad (6.7c)$$

$$A_4 = d_{41}M_1 + d_{42}M_2 \qquad (6.7d)$$

We can collect all eight d_{ji} coefficients into a $J \times N$ matrix, **D**. Denoting the vector of emissions from the two sources as **M** and the vector of ambient pollution levels in the four receptors as **A** we have

$$\mathbf{A} = \mathbf{DM} \qquad (6.8)$$

or

$$\begin{bmatrix} A_1 \\ A_2 \\ A_3 \\ A_4 \end{bmatrix} = \begin{bmatrix} d_{11} & d_{12} \\ d_{21} & d_{22} \\ d_{31} & d_{32} \\ d_{41} & d_{42} \end{bmatrix} \begin{bmatrix} M_1 \\ M_2 \end{bmatrix} \qquad (6.9)$$

Knowledge of the **M** vector and the **D** matrix allows us to calculate ambient pollution levels at each receptor. If, for example, **D** and **M** are

$$\mathbf{D} = \begin{bmatrix} 0.7 & 0.1 \\ 0.9 & 0.2 \\ 0.3 & 0.2 \\ 0.1 & 0.0 \end{bmatrix} \text{ and } \mathbf{M} = \begin{bmatrix} 10 \\ 20 \end{bmatrix}$$

then $A_1 = 9$, $A_2 = 13$, $A_3 = 7$ and $A_4 = 1$. The Excel workbook *Matrix.xls* and Word file *Matrix.doc* in *Additional Materials*, Chapter 6, illustrate how this – and other similar – matrix calculations can be done using a spreadsheet program.

Armed with this terminology, we now answer the following question in a general way: what is the socially efficient level of emissions from each source? As in all previous cases in this chapter, it will be the set of emission levels that maximises net benefits. To see how this works here, note that there are N emission sources, and so our solution will consist of N values of M_i, one for each source. Benefits consist of the sum over all N sources of each firm's pollution benefits. So we have

$$B = \sum_{i=1}^{N} B_i(M_i)$$

Damages consist of the sum over all J receptor areas of the damage incurred in that area. That is,

$$D = \sum_{j=1}^{J} D_j(A_j)$$

Hence the net benefits function to be maximised (by appropriate choice of M_i, $i = 1, \ldots, N$) is

$$NB = \sum_{i=1}^{N} B_i(M_i) - \sum_{j=1}^{J} D_j(A_j) \qquad (6.10)$$

By substitution of equation 6.6 into 6.10, the latter can be written as

$$NB = \sum_{i=1}^{N} B_i(M_i) - \sum_{j=1}^{J} D_j\left(\sum_{i=1}^{N} d_{ji} M_i \right) \qquad (6.11)$$

A necessary condition for a maximum is that

$$\frac{\partial NB}{\partial M_i} = B_i'(M_i) - \sum_{j=1}^{J} D_j'(A_j)\frac{dA_j}{dM_i} = 0$$

$$\text{for } i = 1, \ldots, N$$

$$= B_i'(M_i) - \sum_{j=1}^{J} D_j'(A_j)d_{ji} = 0 \text{ for } i = 1, \ldots, N$$

$$(6.12)$$

---

[8] The linearity assumption is a very good approximation for most pollutants of interest. (Low-level ozone accumulation is one significant exception.) Each coefficient d_{ji} will, in practice, vary over time, depending on such things as climate and wind conditions. However, if we measure average values of these coefficients over some period of time, they can be regarded as constant coefficients for the purposes of our analysis.

which, after rearranging, yields the set of N marginal conditions

$$B_i'(M_i) = \sum_{j=1}^{J} D_j'(A_j)d_{ji} \text{ for } i = 1, \ldots, N$$

Where

$$D_j'(A_j) = \frac{\partial D_j}{\partial A_j} \qquad (6.13)$$

The intuition behind this result is straightforward. The emissions target (or standard) for each firm should be set so that the private marginal benefit of its emissions (the left-hand side of the equation) is equal to the marginal damage of its emissions (the right-hand side of the equation). Note that because the ith firm's emissions are transferred to some or all of the receptors, the marginal damage attributable to the ith firm is obtained by summing its contribution to damage over each of the J receptors.

An interesting property of the solution to equation set 6.13 is that not only will the efficient emission level differ from firm to firm, but also the efficient ambient pollution level will differ among receptors. It is easy to see why efficient emission levels should vary. Firms located at different sources have different pollution impacts: other things being equal, those sources with the highest pollution impact should emit the least. But what lies behind the result that efficient levels of pollution will vary from place to place? Receptors at different spatial locations will experience different pollution levels: other things being equal, those receptors which would (in an unconstrained world) experience the highest pollution-stock level should have the highest efficient ambient pollution level. Of course, these two considerations have to be met jointly; NB = $B - D$ is being maximised, and so we are searching for the best trade-off between the benefits reduction and damages reduction. Appendix 6.2 provides a worked numerical example of efficient emissions that illustrates this point.

In practice, environmental regulators might deem that it is unethical for A to vary from place to place. So, they might impose an additional constraint on the problem to reflect this ethical position. One form of constraint is that the pollution level in no area should exceed some maximum level A^* (that is $A_j^* \leq A^*$ for all j). Another, stricter, version would be

the requirement that A should be the same over all areas (that is $A_j^* = A^*$ for all j). In the latter case, the net benefit function to be maximised is

$$L = \sum_{i=1}^{N} B_i(M_i) - \sum_{j=1}^{J} D_j(A^*) \qquad (6.14)$$

By imposing additional constraints, maximised net benefit is lower in equation 6.14 than in equation 6.10. An efficiency loss has been made in return for achieving an equity goal.

6.9 Intertemporal analysis of stock pollution

We now consider the case of stock pollutants that have a relatively long active (i.e. damaging) lifespan but which are uniformly mixing. Doing so has two implications. First, the uniformly mixing assumption implies that pollutant concentrations will not differ from place to place, and so the spatial dimension of emissions control is no longer of direct relevance. Second, persistence of pollution stocks over time means that the temporal dimension is of central importance. As we shall see, an efficient pollution control programme will need to take account of the trajectory of emissions over time, rather than just at a single point in time.

The model we use to examine pollution targets is the simplest possible one that can deal with the intertemporal choices involved. Damage at time t is determined by the contemporaneous stock size or concentration rate of the pollutant in a relevant environmental medium. Gross benefits depend on the flow of emissions. Hence our damage and (gross) benefit functions have the general forms

$$D_t = D(A_t) \qquad (6.15)$$

$$B_t = B(M_t) \qquad (6.16)$$

The variables A and M in equations 6.15 and 6.16 are, of course, not independent of one another. With relatively long-lived pollutants, emissions add to existing stocks and those stocks accumulate over time. However, except in the special case where pollutants are infinitely long-lived, part of the existing stock will decay or degrade into a harmless form over time, thereby having a negative impact on stock accumulation. A convenient way of representing this stock–flow relationship is by assuming that the rate of change of the pollutant stock over time is governed by the differential equation

$$\dot{A}_t = M_t - \alpha A_t \qquad (6.17)$$

where a dot over a variable indicates its derivative with respect to time, so that $\dot{A}_t = dA/dt$. To interpret this equation, it will be helpful to have an example in mind. Consider atmospheric carbon dioxide (CO_2), one source of which is emissions from the combustion of fossil fuels. Current emissions (M_t) add to CO_2 stocks, and so the concentration level rises; that is, $\dot{A}_t$ is positive. However, offsetting factors are at work too. Some of the existing CO_2 stock will be transformed into harmless substances by physical or chemical processes, or will be absorbed into oceans or other sinks where it has no damaging effect. In other words, part of the pollution stock decays. The amount of pollution decay is captured by the term $-\alpha A_t$.

The net effect on A (and so whether $\dot{A}_t$ is positive or negative overall) depends on the magnitudes of the two terms on the right-hand side of equation 6.17.[9] The parameter α is a proportion that must lie in the interval zero to one. A pollutant for which $\alpha = 0$ exhibits no decay, and so the second term on the right-hand side of equation 6.17 is zero. This is known as a perfectly persistent pollutant. In this special case, integration of equation 6.17 shows that the stock at any time is the sum of all previous emissions. Notice that the absence of decay means that damages arising from current emissions will last indefinitely. This is approximately true for some synthetic chemicals, such as heavy metal residuals, and toxins such as DDT and dioxin. Moreover, the pollution stock and pollution damages will increase without bounds through time as long as M is positive.

More generally, we expect to find $0 < \alpha < 1$, and denote this as an imperfectly persistent pollutant. Here, the pollutant stock decays gradually over time, being converted into relatively harmless elements or compounds. Greenhouse gases provide one example, but (as we show in Chapter 10) with slow or very slow rates of decay. The second limiting case, where $\alpha = 1$, implies instantaneous decay, and so the pollutant can be regarded as a flow rather than a stock pollutant. We need deal with this special case no further here.

The specification given in equation 6.17 imposes the restriction that the parameter α is constant; a constant *proportion* of the pollution stock decays over any given interval of time. This may be invalid in practice. If the restriction is approximately true equation 6.17 might still be used for reasons of convenience and simplicity. But if it is grossly inaccurate, and the decay rate (or assimilation rate as it is often called) changes substantially over time, or varies with changes in either A or M, then it is not an appropriate basis for modelling. We will return to this matter later.

We mentioned earlier that, unlike in the previous cases investigated in this chapter, the relationship between M and A is not independent of time. By integrating equation 6.17 over time we obtain

$$A_t = \int_{\tau=t_0}^{\tau=t} \left(M_t - \alpha A_t \right) d\tau$$

where t_0 denotes the first point in time at which the pollutant in question was emitted. Thus the pollution stock level at any time t, A_t, depends on the entire history of emissions up to that point in time. Even if emissions had been at a constant level in the past and were to remain so in the future, A would not be constant throughout time. Put another way, as emissions

---

[9] In this chapter, we are working principally with economic models specified in continuous time terms. However, sometimes it is convenient to work in a discrete time framework. Doing this requires defining the meaning to be attached to time subscripts for stock variables. A convention that we follow throughout this text is that for any stock variable the subscript t denotes the *end* of period t. Then the discrete time counterpart of equation 6.17 would be:

$$A_t - A_{t-1} = M_t - \alpha A_{t-1}$$

Notice that the last term on the right-hand side now has the time subscript $t - 1$, as compared with t in equation 6.17. Given our convention, A_{t-1} refers to the pollution stock at the end of period $t - 1$ (or, equivalently, start of period t). The discrete time counterpart of equation 6.17 would then say that the inflow (new emissions) is taking place contemporaneously with the outflow (stock decay), and that it is the difference between inflow and outflow during period t that determines whether stock will rise, fall or remain constant between the end of period $t - 1$ and the end of period t. This is intuitively sensible.

at time t add to pollution stocks at that time *and* in future time periods, there is no one-to-one relationship between A and M. It is because time matters here in a fundamental way that the variables in equations 6.15 and 6.16 are time-dated.[10]

As time periods are linked together through a stock–flow relationship, efficient pollution targets and policies must be derived from an intertemporal analysis. We proceed by assuming that the policy maker aims to maximise discounted net benefits over some suitable time horizon. For simplicity, the horizon is taken to be of infinite span. Using $t = 0$ to denote the current period of time, and defining the net benefits of pollution as gross benefits minus damages (specified respectively by equations 6.15 and 6.16) the policy maker's objective is to select M_t for $t = 0$ to $t = \infty$ to maximise

$$\int_{t=0}^{t=\infty} (B(M_t) - D(A_t))e^{-rt}dt \qquad (6.18)$$

where r is the social (consumption) discount rate.

A complete description of efficient stock pollution will, therefore, consist not of a single number for, but a *trajectory* (or time path) of, emission levels through time. In general, this optimal trajectory will be one in which emission levels vary throughout time. However, in many circumstances, the trajectory will consist of two phases. One of these phases is a so-called *steady state* in which emissions (and concentration levels) remain constant indefinitely at some level. The other is an adjustment phase; the trajectory describes a path by which emissions (and concentrations) move from current levels to their efficient, steady-state levels. This adjustment process may be quick, or it may take place over a long period of time.

Even with complete information, obtaining such a trajectory is technically difficult, involving the calculus of optimal control. We will explain this

technique in Chapter 14, and apply it to the pollution model being examined here in Chapter 16. In this chapter, we consider only the second of the two phases described above: the efficient *steady-state* pollution level.[11] In a steady state, by definition, the pollution flow and the pollution stock are each at a constant, unchanging level.[12] Hence the time subscripts we have attached to variables become redundant and can be dropped. Moreover, with an unchanging stock $\dot{A}_t = 0$ and so equation 6.17 simplifies to $M = \alpha A$. The intuition that lies behind this is straightforward: for a pollutant that accumulates over time, the pollution stock can only be constant if emission inflows to the stock (M) are equal to the amount of stock which decays each period (αA). It then follows that in a steady state, the stock–flow relationship between A and M can be written as

$$A = \frac{M}{\alpha} \qquad (6.19)$$

This shows that, in a steady state, the smaller is the value of α the larger will be the pollution stock for any given level of emissions.

The full derivation of the steady-state solution to this problem is presented in Chapter 16. You may wish to return to, and reread, this section after studying that later chapter. Here, we just state one major result from that solution, interpret it intuitively, and discuss some of its characteristics. If you are prepared to take this result on trust, little will be lost by not going through its derivation.

The key result we draw upon from Chapter 16 is that an efficient steady-state level of pollution emissions requires that the following condition be satisfied:

$$\frac{dB}{dM} = \frac{dD}{dA}\left(\frac{1}{r + \alpha}\right) \qquad (6.20)$$

Equation 6.20 is a variant of the familiar marginal condition for efficiency. The marginal benefit and

[10] In the last section, the relationship between stocks and flows of the pollutant was complicated because *space* mattered; the effect of M on A depended on the respective locations of the pollution source and recipient. There we used i and j terminology to denote that dependence on location. Here the relationship is complicated by the fact that *time* matters, hence the use of t terminology.

[11] Doing this assumes that the problem is one in which a steady-state solution exists, which is not always true. Chapter 16 will briefly examine the adjustment process to a steady state, and whether such a state exists.

[12] There is a second sense in which the term *steady state* is sometimes used: as a state in which all variables of interest in some system are growing at a constant rate. We do not use this alternative meaning in this text.

the marginal cost of the chosen emissions level should be equal. More precisely, it can be read as an equality between the present value of the gross benefit of a marginal unit of pollution (the left-hand side of 6.20) and the present value of the damage that arises from the marginal unit of pollution (the right-hand side of 6.20). Note that a marginal emission today has benefits only today, and so the present value of that marginal emission is identical to its current marginal benefit. In contrast, the damage arising from the marginal emission takes place today and in future periods. The 'discount factor' $1/(r + \alpha)$ has the effect of transforming the single period damage into its present-value equivalent. (A fuller explanation of this interpretation is given in Chapter 16.) At the level of M that satisfies equation 6.20, the value taken by the expression on each side of the equation is known as the shadow price of a unit of emission. It is labelled as μ in several of the diagrams in this chapter and will figure prominently in our discussions in the next chapter.[13]

Examination of equation 6.20 shows two very important results:

1. Other things being equal, the faster is the decay rate, the higher will be the efficient level of steady-state emissions. Reasoning: For any given value of dD/dA, a rise in α implies that the value of dB/dM would have to fall to satisfy the marginal equality. A lower value of dB/dM implies higher emissions. Intuition: The greater is the rate of decay the larger is the 'effective' discount rate applied to the marginal stock damage term and so the smaller is its present value. A higher discount rate means we attach less weight to damages in the future, and so the emission level can be raised accordingly.
2. Other things being equal, the larger is the consumption discount rate, the higher will be the efficient level of steady-state emissions. Reasoning: For any given value of dD/dA,

Table 6.4 Special cases of equation 6.21

	Imperfectly persistent pollutant $\alpha > 0$	Perfectly persistent pollutant $\alpha = 0$
$r = 0$	A	D
$r > 0$	B	C

a rise in r implies that the value of dB/dM would have to fall to satisfy the marginal equality. A lower value of dB/dM implies higher emissions. Intuition: The greater is the consumption discount rate r, the larger is the discount rate applied to the stock damage term and so the smaller is its present value. A higher discount rate means we attach less weight to damages in the future, and so the emission level can be raised accordingly.

Problem 4 at the end of this chapter asks the reader to explore these and other results from the stock pollution model. The model is simulated in the Excel workbook *Stock1.xls*.

For the purpose of looking at some special cases of equation 6.20, it will be convenient to rearrange that expression as follows (the full derivation is given in Chapter 16):

$$\frac{dD}{dM} = \frac{dB}{dM}\left(1 + \frac{r}{\alpha}\right) \quad (6.21)$$

Four special cases of equation 6.21 can be obtained, depending on whether $r = 0$ or $r > 0$, and on whether $\alpha = 0$ or $\alpha > 0$. We portray these combinations in Table 6.4.

Case A: $r = 0$, $\alpha > 0$

In this case the pollutant is imperfectly persistent and so eventually decays to a harmless form. With $r = 0$, no discounting of costs and benefits is being undertaken. Equation 6.21 collapses to:[14]

---

[13] In some of the economics literature, the shadow price of emissions is constructed to be a negative quantity (and would correspond here to the negative of μ). This arises because some authors choose to attach a different interpretation to the shadow price. Whenever a different interpretation is being used in our text, that will be made clear to the reader explicitly.

[14] Notice that equation 6.23 appears to be identical to the efficiency condition for a flow pollutant. But it is necessary to be careful here, as 6.23 holds only in a steady state, and is not valid outside those states for a stock pollutant.

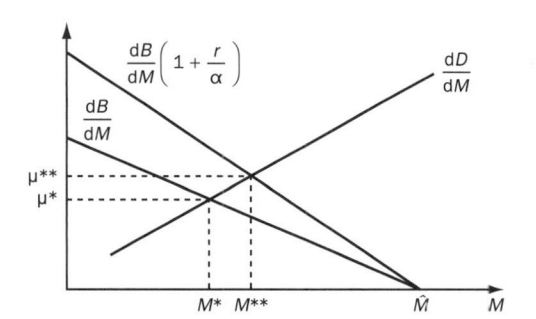

Figure 6.9 Efficient steady-state emission level for an imperfectly persistent stock pollutant. Two cases: $\{r = 0$ and $\alpha > 0\}$ and $\{r > 0$ and $\alpha > 0\}$

$$\frac{\mathrm{d}D}{\mathrm{d}M} = \frac{\mathrm{d}B}{\mathrm{d}M} \tag{6.22}$$

This has a straightforward interpretation. An efficient steady-state rate of emissions for a stock pollutant requires that the contribution to benefits from a marginal unit of pollution flow be equal to the contribution to damage from a marginal unit of pollution flow. The steady-state equilibrium is shown in Figure 6.9 (by the intersection of the functions $\mathrm{d}D/\mathrm{d}M$ and $\mathrm{d}B/\mathrm{d}M$). Net benefits are maximised at the steady-state pollution flow M^*. In the steady state, A^* will be at the level at which $\alpha A^* = M^*$, and both the pollution stock and emissions track along through time at constant levels. You may find it useful to look at Box 6.6 at this point; this goes through a simple numerical example to illustrate the nature of the equilibrium.

Case B: $r > 0$, $\alpha > 0$

With r and α being positive numbers, the equilibrium condition is given by equation 6.21 in unchanged form. The marginal equality in this case incorporates the additional term $1/(r + \alpha)$ to reflect the presence of discounting at a positive rate. This is shown diagrammatically in Figure 6.9, with M^{**} denoting the equilibrium emission level. It is instructive to compare this equilibrium with that obtained in Case A. As r increases above zero, the marginal benefits function rotates clockwise about the point $\hat{M}$. Discounting, therefore, increases the steady-state level of emissions. Moreover, the larger is the discount rate, the larger is the amount by which efficient steady-state emissions rise. Intuitively, a larger value

---

Box 6.6 Steady-state efficient solution for a stock pollutant: a numerical example

No discounting, $r = 0$ (Case A: $r = 0$, $\alpha > 0$)

Let $\alpha = 0.5$, $D = A^2$, $B = 96M - 2M^2$. What are M^* and A^*?

$$B = 96M - 2M^2 \rightarrow \mathrm{d}B/\mathrm{d}M = 96 - 4M$$

$$D = A^2 = (M/\alpha)^2 = (1/0.5)^2 M^2$$
$$= 4M^2 \rightarrow \mathrm{d}D/\mathrm{d}M = 8M$$

Now setting $\mathrm{d}B/\mathrm{d}M = \mathrm{d}D/\mathrm{d}M$ we obtain:

$$96 - 4M = 8M \rightarrow M^* = 8$$

Therefore $A = (M/\alpha) \rightarrow A^* = 16$

This result is obtained by inspection and by use of Solver in Sheet 1, and shown graphically in Chart 1, of Excel workbook *Stock1.xls* in the *Additional Materials* for Chapter 6.

Positive discounting, $r > 0$ (Case B: $r > 0$, $\alpha > 0$)

Let $\alpha = 0.5$, $r = 0.1$, $D = A^2$, $B = 96M - 2M^2$. What are M^* and A^*?

$$B = 96M - 2M^2 \Rightarrow \mathrm{d}B/\mathrm{d}M = 96 - 4M$$

$$D = A^2 = (M/\alpha)^2 = (1/0.5)^2 M^2$$
$$= 4M^2 \rightarrow \mathrm{d}D/\mathrm{d}M = 8M$$

Now setting $\dfrac{\mathrm{d}D}{\mathrm{d}M} = \dfrac{\mathrm{d}B}{\mathrm{d}M}\left(1 + \dfrac{r}{\alpha}\right)$ we obtain:

$$8M = (96 - 4M)(1 + \{0.1/0.5\}) \rightarrow M^* = 9$$

Therefore $A = (M/\alpha) \rightarrow A^* = 18$

This result is obtained by inspection and by use of Solver in Sheet 2, and shown graphically in Chart 2, of Excel workbook *Stock1.xls*. Note that we use Solver there to find the value of M that sets marginal net benefits (expressed in terms of emissions) equal to zero.

---

of r reduces the present value of the future damages that are associated with the pollutant stock. In effect, higher weighting is given to present benefits relative to future costs the larger is r. However, notice that the shadow price of one unit of the pollutant emissions becomes larger as r increases.

Cases C ($r > 0$, $\alpha = 0$) and D ($r = 0$, $\alpha = 0$)

In both Cases C and D the pollutant is perfectly persistent, and so never decays to a harmless form. One might guess that something unusual is happening here by noting that equation 6.21 is undefined when $\alpha = 0$; division by zero is not a legitimate mathematical operation. The intuition that lies behind this is straightforward. No steady state exists except for the case in which M is zero. A steady state cannot exist for any positive value of M as A would rise without bound. But then pollution damage would also rise to infinity.

It follows that, at some point in time, the environmental protection agency would have to require that emissions be permanently set to zero to avoid the prospect of intolerable damage. The pollution stock level would remain at whatever level A had risen to by that time. Pollution damage would also continue indefinitely at some constant level, but no additional damage would be generated. The zero-emissions steady-state solution turns out to be perfectly in accord with good sense.

One caveat to this conclusion should be noted. Although a perfectly persistent pollutant has a zero natural decay rate, policy makers may be able to find some technique by which the pollutant stock may be artificially reduced. This is known as clean-up expenditure. If such a method can be found, and can be implemented at reasonable cost, it allows the possibility of some perpetual level of emissions. We examine this possibility further in Chapter 16.

Of course, even if the EPA accepted that emissions would have to be set to zero at some date (and remain zero thereafter), the question remains of which date the switch to zero should be made. Steady-state analysis is unable to answer this question. To obtain that answer, another technique (or another criterion than economic efficiency) is required. Chapter 16 shows how optimal control can be used to find both the efficient steady-state solution and the optimal adjustment path to it.

6.10 Variable decay

The stock pollution models used in this chapter have assumed that the proportionate rate of natural decay of the stock, α, is constant. This assumption is commonly employed in environmental economics analysis, but will not always be valid. In many situations,

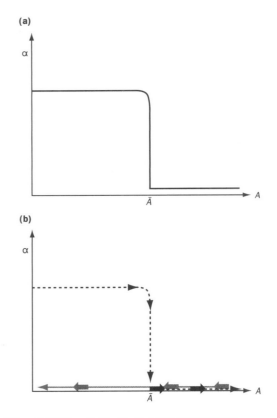

Figure 6.10 Threshold effects and irreversibilities

one would expect that the rate of decay depend on the size of the pollution stock, or on some other associated variable. For example, it is thought that the decay rate of greenhouse gases alters (in quite complex ways) as mean temperature levels change. Of particular importance are the existence of threshold effects (where the decay rate changes in a sudden, discontinuous way) and irreversibilities (where the nature of a relationship changes depending on the direction in which a variable is moving). One example of a threshold effect is illustrated in the top panel of Figure 6.10. Here the decay rate of a waterborne pollutant collapses towards zero as some threshold level of biological oxygen demand (BOD) on a river is reached. This critical level of BOD is reached when the pollution stock is at $\bar{A}$. The lower panel illustrates a threshold effect combined with an irreversibility. The arrows denote the direction in which A is changing. As the pollution stock rises from a low level, α collapses suddenly at the threshold $\bar{A}$ and remains close to zero as A continues to rise. At high levels of pollution, the biological ability of the river to break down harmful pollutants might be largely destroyed. So if the change is reversed, and *A* falls from a high value, the value of α would remain very low (as shown by the path with left-pointing arrows). This path dependence is also known as hysteresis; in this example, the history of pollutant flows matters, and reversing pollution pressures does not bring one back to the *status quo ex ante*.

Another way of thinking about this issue is in terms of carrying capacities (or assimilative capacities, as they are sometimes called) of environmental media. In the case of water pollution, for example, we can think of a water system as having some capacity to transform pollutants into harmless forms. The stock pollution model of Section 6.8 has in effect assumed unlimited carrying capacities: no matter how large the load on the system, more can always be carried and transformed at a constant proportionate rate.

Whether this assumption is plausible is, in the last resort, an empirical question. Where it is not, modelling procedures need to reflect limits to carrying capacity. The suggestions for further reading point you to some literature that explores models with variable pollution decay rates.

6.11 Convexity and non-convexity in damage and abatement cost functions

When benefit and damage functions were first presented in Section 6.4, a number of assumptions were made about their shapes. Those assumptions relate to the concept of convexity of a function. After explaining what is meant by a convex function, this section gives some examples of why the relevant functions may not be convex, and then shows some consequences of non-convexity.

Consider a function, *f(x)*, of a single variable *x*. The function is *strictly convex* if the line segment connecting any two distinct points on the function

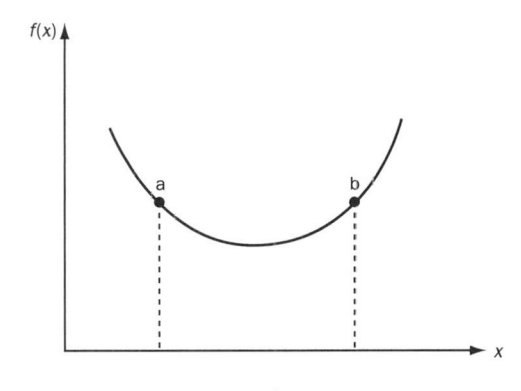

Figure 6.11 A strictly convex function

lies everywhere above the function *f(x)*, except at the two points themselves. A function is convex (as opposed to strictly convex) if the line segment lies everywhere above or on the function *f(x)*, but not below it. As an example, the function graphed in Figure 6.11 is strictly convex.

Looking back at Figure 6.4, it is clear that the damage function *D(M)* is convex.[15] This is not true for the benefits function *B(M)* as that is drawn in Figure 6.4. However, suppose that we reinterpret benefits as avoided abatement costs, as suggested earlier. Now construct the horizontal image of *B(M)*, so that moving to the right on this mirror image corresponds to more pollution abatement. Then the abatement cost function will be convex.

Actually, this terminological contortion is not really necessary. What really matters, as we shall see, is whether the functions describing the problem being investigated are smooth, continuous, and lead to unique marginal efficient conditions. All of these properties are satisfied by the benefit and damage functions used in Figure 6.4. It is clear from the lower panel of Figure 6.4 that there is just one level of pollution at which the marginal efficiency condition is satisfied: the marginal benefit of pollution (or equivalently marginal cost of abatement) is equal to the marginal damage of pollution. This implies that marginal analysis alone is sufficient for identifying the efficient level of pollution.[16]

---

[15] In fact, as drawn it is strictly convex. But what matters is whether the weaker property of convexity is satisfied. So we shall use the word 'convex' from now on to cover strict as well as (weak) convexity.

[13] Mathematically, the efficient pollution level is obtained from the first-order conditions for optimisation; second-order conditions will automatically be satisfied (and so do not need to be checked).

6.11.1 Non-convexity of the damage function and its implications

There are many reasons why the damage function and the abatement cost function may be non-convex. Here we restrict attention to the more commonly discussed case of non-convex damages. So what might cause a pollution damage function to not be of the smooth, continuously increasing form that we have assumed so far? One example was given implicitly in Section 6.10 where we introduced the ideas of threshold effects and irreversibility. A closely related example to that is acidic pollution of rivers and lakes. Here, pollution may reach a threshold point at which the lake become biologically dead, unable to support animal or plant life. No further damage is done as pollution levels rise beyond that point. The total and marginal damages function in this case will be of the form shown in Figure 6.12.

Another example, discussed in Fisher (1981), is non-convexity of damages arising from averting behaviour by an individual. Suppose a factory emits particulate emissions that create external damages for an individual living in the neighbourhood of the factory. The marginal damage initially rises with the amount of the pollution. However, at some critical level of pollution flow, the affected individual can no longer tolerate living in the neighbourhood of the factory, and moves to live somewhere else where the damage to him or her becomes zero. As far as this particular individual is concerned, their marginal damage function is also of the form shown in Figure 6.12. However, if there are many individuals living in the neighbourhood, with varying tolerance levels, many of whom are prepared to move at some level of pollution, the aggregate marginal pollution damage function will be the sum of a set of individual functions, each of which has the same general form but with differing pollution tolerance levels. The aggregate damage function will be of the non-convex form shown in the top panel of Figure 6.13, with its marginal counterpart being shown by the curve labelled MD in the central panel.

Now combine the marginal damage function for the averting behaviour example with a marginal benefit function of conventional shape. This is shown in the central panel of Figure 6.13. Marginal damage and benefits are equalised here at three emission levels. To ascertain which of these, if any, is the efficient level of pollution, it is necessary to inspect the level of total net benefits at these three points, *and* at all other levels of emission (as net benefits will not necessarily even correspond to a marginal equality when one or more function is not convex). The two points labelled A and B are 'local optima', as they satisfy the second-order conditions for a local maximum of net benefits, as shown in the lower panel of Figure 6.13. In this case it can be seen by inspection of the NB curve that M_3 is a 'global' net benefits-maximising pollution level. Note that in moving from M_1 to M_3, net benefits at first fall (by the area labelled **a**) and then rise (by the area labelled **b**).

Why does non-convexity matter? There are two major reasons why this is a matter of concern. The first could be described as a 'practical' matter: calculating the efficient level of emissions (or pollution stock) is likely to be more complicated than where all functions are convex. This is partly a matter of computational difficulty. But more importantly, it is to do with the fact that the information required to identify the (non-convex) functions may be immense and very costly to obtain. Obtaining

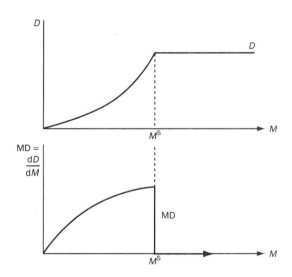

Figure 6.12 A non-convex damage function arising from pollution reaching a saturation point

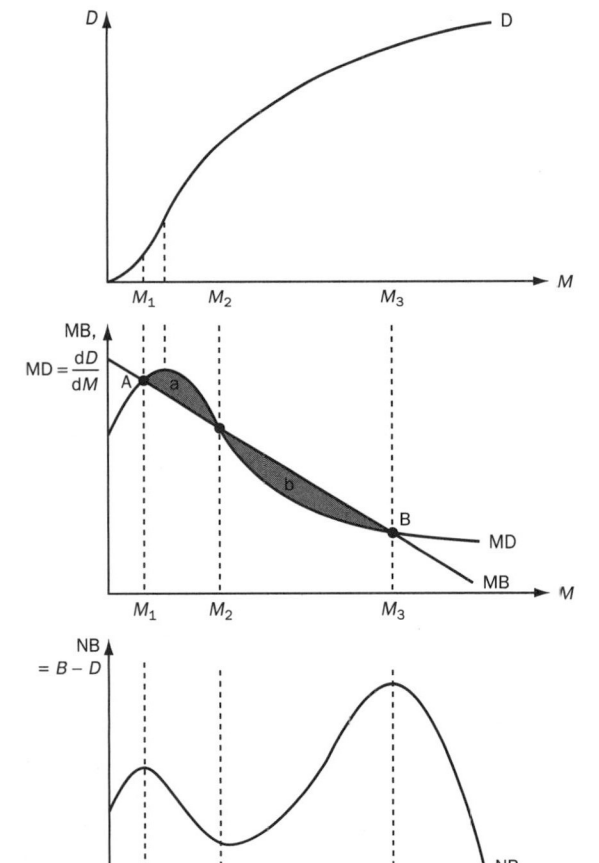

Figure 6.13 Multiple marginal equalities arising from a non-convex damage function: the case of behavioural adjustments of individuals

cost–benefit analysis completely wrong. (One example is explored in Problem 5 at the end of this chapter.)

One reason why policy makers may fail to recognise non-convexity is to do with the way information is acquired. We often find out about things by exploring a relevant 'local neighbourhood'. For example, cross-section sampling techniques may generate data on emissions and damage that are relatively closely clustered around current levels, and tell us little or nothing about properties of the function outside the current sample range. Inspection of that data may suggest convexity when in fact the function is only convex over part of its range. This becomes important – and potentially dangerous – if the policy maker falsely projects the apparently convex function outside this current range.

6.12 Estimating the costs of abating pollution[17]

There are many ways in which estimates can be made of the costs of pollution abatement. Two broad classes can be identified:

- engineering models;
- economic models.

In practice, most studies have used linked engineering–economic models, but the relative attention paid to each component varies widely.

6.12.1 Engineering models

These typically use what is called a 'bottom-up' approach. An emissions abatement objective is defined. Then all the techniques by which this target could be achieved are listed. For each technique, the researcher calculates the expected expenditures by firms on pollution abatement equipment and other investments, fuel, operation, maintenance and other labour costs. The costs incurred by each firm are

reliable estimates of functions will be particularly difficult where information is limited or uncertain.

The second reason for concern is more fundamental. Non-convexity may be important because it exists but we do not recognise that it exists. In that case, some commonly advocated tools could give seriously misleading results. For example, a failure to recognise the existence of threshold effects or irreversibilities could render project appraisal using

---

[17] For a more extensive version of the material in this section, see *Additional Materials*: Chapter 6 '*Abatement costs*'.

then added up to arrive at the total economy-wide abatement cost. Hence the name 'bottom-up'. For a complete accounting of control costs, expenditures incurred by regulatory agencies should be added in. Best achievable abatement costs are those which are the minimum among those techniques studied. A more modest variant of this approach would involve the researcher obtaining cost estimates of one technique rather than all available. This requires making assumptions about the form of responses of firms to the controls they face.

There are some desirable properties in estimating abatement costs in this way. They are simple to understand, and simple (at least in principle) to undertake. Engineering models are typically highly disaggregated. They consider technology options in a rich, detailed way, providing large amounts of information at the micro-production level. This technology-rich property means that engineering models are very well suited to costing specific projects, such as using wind power to generate 25% of a country's electricity. They are also capable of dealing in a careful way with some kinds of 'no-regret' or 'free-lunch' possibilities arising from technical and economic inefficiencies in existing method of production. (See Box 6.3 for more details.)

But this approach also has some serious limitations. Each technology is assessed independently via an accounting of its costs and savings, but possible interdependencies (or linkages and feedback) between the elements being studied and the economy as a whole are not taken into account. This leads to biased estimates of the true costs of abatement. Some examples of important linkages that matter – but which are typically ignored by engineering models – are:

- productivity changes induced by regulatory control;
- changes in unemployment;
- change in overall industrial structure of the economy.

The most fundamental problem is that engineering models ignore changes in relative prices, and the associated impacts on factor substitution and the behaviour of firms and individuals. Results can be seriously misleading because of this, particularly when long-term effects are being investigated.

6.12.2 Economic models

These are typically 'top-down' models.[18] They are constructed around a set of aggregate economic variables, the relationships among which are determined by (micro or macro) economic theory and equilibrium principles. These relationships are estimated econometrically, using time-series data. Alternatively, relationships are calibrated to match with data for one chosen base year. To obtain cost estimates, some project of interest such as the introduction of a carbon tax is taken as an exogenous shock. The model is solved for equilibrium before and after the shock. By comparing the values of relevant variables in the baseline and shocked case, cost estimates are obtained.

The top-down nature of these models means that they tend to be highly aggregated, and that they do not have the richness of detail (particularly about energy technology options) that can be captured in engineering models. The strength of economic models lies in their ability to deal with supply and demand relationships, and to capture behavioural changes and substitution effects that are important for making inferences about long-term consequences. In addition, they are good for the analysis of distributional effects, and for simulating the use of economic instruments.

But economic models alone treat the energy sector as a relatively undifferentiated whole, and so are of limited use for answering questions that involve changes within the energy sector. Aggregate output–energy use relationships tend to be relatively inflexible, and so economic models are not well suited to examining possible decoupling effects. One major practical limitation of economic models is their assumption that resource allocation in the baseline case is already fully efficient. As a result, they can say nothing about negative cost potential from removing existing inefficiencies.

---

[18] See IPCC(3) (2001) for further analysis of bottom-up and top-down models.

Economic models typically yield higher abatement cost estimates than engineering models. This arises because (a) they do not consider existing inefficiencies and (b) they take account of losses of consumer surplus arising from price increases as regulated firms attempt to pass additional costs on to consumers.

6.12.3 Linked or integrated engineering–economic models

Ideally, one would like to base cost estimates on models that combine the advantages of economic and engineering models. This might be done by linking the two, or by more systematically developing an integrated modelling approach. Among the many attempts that have been made to do this, we find the following types.

6.12.3.1 Input–output (IO) models

IO models (see Chapter 9 for a more developed account) partition the economy into a number of sectors, and then represent the economy mathematically by a set of simultaneous linear equations. These equations embody the input–output relationships between those sectors. IO models, therefore, capture sectoral interdependences and spillovers. So, for example, if the use of coal were to be reduced, IO models could explore the ramifications of this for the economy as a whole, and so give some idea about the likely costs. However, the fixed coefficients in the IO equations preclude modelling of behavioural changes and factor substitution effects as relative prices change. Hence, they will tend to overestimate abatement costs. IO models are useful for short-run modelling where disaggregated sectoral detail is required.

6.12.3.2 Macroeconomic models

Macroeconomic models give a key role to changes in effective demand and investigate the resulting quantity changes. More sophisticated models also incorporate overall wage and price-level changes, and describe the dynamics of, and adjustment to,

new equilibria as a result of shocks. When these models are linked with others that deal more richly with the energy sector, they can be useful for investigating the short-run and medium-term cost implications of environmental policy changes.

6.12.3.3 Computable general equilibrium (CGE) models

CGE models (see Chapter 9 for more details) simulate the behaviour of agents based on optimising microeconomic theory. The models are solved for sets of prices and wages that generate general equilibrium. CGE models are typically static models, and do not analyse adjustment processes from one equilibrium state to another. They are widely used to simulate the consequences of emissions taxes.

6.12.3.4 Dynamic energy optimisation models

These are 'bottom-up', technology rich, partial equilibrium energy-sector models. They are used to minimise cost of the energy sector over a long-term horizon, yielding a partial equilibrium for energy markets. Sophisticated versions allow energy demand to respond to price, and examine the dynamics of changes in the energy sector (and so can trace out the evolution through time of changes in the size and type of capital stock used in the energy sector. Energy optimisation models are often linked with macro models.

6.12.3.5 Purpose-built integrated energy–economic system simulation (E–E) models

E–E models are usually purpose-built to estimate abatement costs in one particular context (such as the costs of abatement required to attain Kyoto Protocol targets for greenhouse gases). They are bottom-up representations of energy demand and supply technologies, and as such typically have a very rich specification of technologies at a highly disaggregated level. A purpose-built economic component is constructed that is consistent with the energy structure of the model. E–E models are often used to simulate the consequences (and costs) of various scenarios.

In practice, most E–E models are hybrids, with problems of inconsistency between components. For

Box 6.7 IPCC estimates of the costs of CO_2 abatement to reach Kyoto Protocol targets

The *gross* abatement costs to attain Kyoto targets for carbon dioxide reduction depend on several factors:

1. The magnitude of emissions reduction required to meet the target. Assumptions made about marginal sources of supply (cost and availability of carbon-based and carbon-free technologies)
2. Short- and long-run price elasticities
3. Whether or not there is emissions trading (and how extensive this is)

Point 1 implies that the emissions 'baseline' is critical to the magnitude of total abatement costs. The larger emissions growth would be in the absence of control, the higher will be total abatement costs required to attain the Kyoto target. Emissions baseline growth rate of CO_2 depends on GDP growth, the rate of decline of energy per unit output, and the rate of decline of CO_2 emissions per unit energy.

The *net* costs depend on the gross costs and also on

1. Availability of no-regrets efficiency gains (e.g. can revenues be used to reduce marginal rates on other distortionary taxes – such as income, sales, or employment taxes – or reduce other technical/economic inefficiencies?)

2. Whether abatement will generate other ancillary benefits
3. The magnitude of any induced technical progress. Of importance here, in terms of the timing of costs, is whether the innovation route is via R&D or learning-by-doing.

Working Group III of the Intergovernmental Panel on Climate Change (IPCC) of the United Nations commissioned a number of independent modelling groups to simulate emissions reductions achieved by carbon taxes. Each of these groups employed some variant of energy–economy model. Tax revenues were recycled via lump-sum payments to the whole economy. The value of the tax rate required to achieve an emissions target indicates the marginal abatement cost in that model. With each team using different assumptions about baseline emissions and different model structures and/or parameter values, the exercise allows multi-model comparisons to be made, and the sensitivity of findings to variations in assumptions can be explored.

The estimated marginal abatement costs from these various models for attaining Kyoto Protocol targets by 2010 are shown in Table 6.5. Figures are given for three scenarios. The first scenario is one in which no trading of allowances is allowed

Table 6.5 Marginal abatement costs (1990 US$/tC) for attainment of Kyoto target by 2010

Model	No trading				Annex 1 trading	Global trading
	US	OECD-Europe	Japan	CANZ		
ABARE-GTEM	322	665	645	425	106	23
AIM	153	198	234	147	65	38
CETA	168				46	26
Fund					14	10
G-Cubed	76	227	97	157	53	20
GRAPE		204	304		70	44
MERGE3	264	218	500	250	135	86
MIT-EPPA	193	276	501	247	76	
MS-MRT	236	179	402	213	77	27
RICE	132	159	251	145	62	18
SGM	188	407	357	201	84	22
WorldScan	85	20	122	46	20	5
Administration	154				43	18
EIA	251				110	57
POLES	135.8	135.3	194.6	131.4	52.9	18.4

Source: IPCC(III) 2001, Table TS.4, p. 56
One set of results (Oxford) has been omitted from this table, as it had not been fully reviewed at the time of writing, and relied on early 1980s data for initial parameterisation.
Models do not take account of induced technical progress, Clean Development Mechanism, sinks, negative cost options, targeted recycling of revenues, ancillary benefits, inclusion of non-CO_2 gases, or inefficiencies in implementation.
Models here are typically general equilibrium rather than bottom-up technology-rich models.

Box 6.7 *continued*

between countries – each country must independently achieve the emission target for it specified in the Protocol (see Chapter 10 for details of these targets). In this case, marginal abatement costs are shown for four 'blocs' of countries. It is evident that the marginal abatement costs vary considerably over countries, implying that the total global emissions reduction is not being achieved at least cost.

A second scenario allows trading of allowances (permits) among the Annex 1 countries (roughly speaking, the industrialised economies). Notice how partial trading dramatically reduces marginal (and so total) abatement costs. This is even more evident in results for the third scenario in which trading can take place between any countries. The efficiency gains that this generates mean that marginal costs are reduced by around an order of magnitude (a tenfold reduction) in some cases.

---

example, one may have as its basis a sophisticated engineering model that can be used to calculate direct technical costs. Linked to this might be a module which uses observed market behaviour to estimate technology adaptations. Further components estimate welfare losses due to demand reductions, and the revenue gains and losses due to trade changes.

6.13 Choosing pollution targets on grounds other than economic efficiency

This chapter has been largely concerned with pollution targets set in terms of an economic efficiency criterion. But there are (at least) two reasons why this focus is unduly restrictive. First, in the context of limited or imperfect information, there may be immense difficulties in identifying economically efficient targets.[19] In that case, efficiency-based targets may be of theoretical interest only and have little practical significance. We examine this issue at some length in Chapter 8.

Second, policy makers are likely to have multiple objectives. Efficiency matters, but it is not the only thing that matters. It is not surprising, therefore, that

targets (or 'environmental standards' as they are sometimes called) are often chosen in practice on the basis of a mix of objectives. The mix may include health or safety considerations, equity, and perceptions of what is technically feasible (usually subject to some 'reasonable cost' qualification). In recent years, sustainability has taken its place as another stated goal of policy. As we show in Chapter 8, sustainability in conjunction with imperfect information and uncertainty may also point to some form of precautionary principle being incorporated in the set of objectives pursued by policy makers.

National and international policy is also determined in the context of a network of pressures and influences. It is not surprising, therefore, that political feasibility plays a significant role. This has been particularly important in the area of international environmental agreements over such things as ozone depletion, acid rain and the greenhouse effect, as we show in Chapter 10.

Tables 6.6 and 6.7 list some existing environmental standards and the criteria that appear to have been used in their selection. In the next chapter we investigate which instruments are available to an environmental protection agency for attaining a given pollution target, however that target may have been determined.

---

[19] Many of the problems posed by imperfect information also apply to targets set on the basis of sustainability, health, or indeed any other criterion. Nevertheless, they apply particularly strongly to efficiency-based targets. However, as we shall see in the following chapter, several of the alternative criteria can be interpreted as appropriate for target setting precisely when information is imperfect. They should then be thought of as responses to uncertainty rather than as being weakened or limited by it.

Table 6.6 Environmental targets

Pollutant	Target	Relevant criterion
United Kingdom		
Grains emitted in cement production	0.1–0.2 grains per cubic foot	Best practicable means
Sewage concentration	Max. 30 mg/litre suspended solids Max. BOD 20 mg/litre	1976 National Water Council: precautionary principle, perceived health risks
Cadmium/lead	Discharges into North Sea to fall by 70% between 1985 and 1995	Health criterion
PCBs	Phase out by 1999	Strict precautionary principle – health risks
Waste recycling	50% domestic waste to be recycled	Political target?
United States		
Criteria air pollutants	See Table 6.7	Health risks
International		
CFCs	CFC production to fall to 80% and 50% of 1986 levels by 1994 and 1999 respectively	Political feasibility, with final targets set in terms of critical load

Key: BOD = biochemical oxygen demand. The concepts of 'Best practicable means', 'Critical load', and 'Precautionary principle' are explained elsewhere in the chapter

Table 6.7 Primary NAAQS for Criteria Air Pollutants, 1997

Pollutant	Averaging time	Concentration level	
		ppm	$\mu g/m^3$
Particulate matter (PM10)	Annual	–	50
	24-hour	–	150
Particulate matter (PM2.5)	Annual	–	15
	24-hour	–	65
Sulphur dioxide	Annual	0.030	80
	24-hour	0.140	365
Carbon monoxide	8-hour	9.000	10
	1-hour	35.000	40
Nitrogen oxide	Annual	0.053	100
Ozone	8-hour	0.008	–
Lead	Max. quarterly	–	1.5

Summary

- We do not expect pure market economies to deliver efficient outcomes in terms of pollution. Pollution tends to be an externality to the market process and as a result is not adequately reflected in private market decisions. Put another way, while firms would meet the costs of controlling or abating pollution, the benefits of abatement would not be received by firms (although they would by society). Hence, in considering pollution abatement, the control level that maximises net benefits to firms is different from the level that maximises social net benefits.
- Economists often recommend that pollution targets should be set using an economic efficiency criterion. This can be thought of as selecting pollution targets so as to maximise social net benefits
- Economic efficiency is not the only relevant criterion for pollution target setting. Several others were discussed in the chapter. Which criteria are important to policy makers will tend to reflect their policy objectives and the constraints under which they operate.

- There are important differences between flow pollutants and stock pollutants in terms of the mechanisms by which damage is generated. This distinction has implications for the way in which targets are derived using an economic efficiency criterion. For stock pollutants, persistence implies that attention must be given to the accumulation (and decay) of pollutants over time, and so an intertemporal analysis is required. This is not necessary for the analysis of flow pollutants.
- For long-lived stock pollutants, pollution targets are best thought of in terms of emissions paths over time. Efficient pollution paths will not in general imply the same level of control at all points in time. However, it is often useful to think of steady-state outcomes and to investigate what (constant) level of pollution control would be efficient in an equilibrium steady state.
- Where a stock pollutant is not uniformly mixing, the spatial distribution of emissions sources becomes relevant. If targets are set in terms of pollutant concentrations, then the allowable emissions of any particular source will depend on its location.

Further reading

Excellent and extensive presentations of the economics of pollution are to be found in Fisher (1981, chapters 5 and 6), Anderson (1985, 1991), Hartwick and Olewiler (1986, 1998) and Kolstad (2000). Baumol and Oates (1988) is a classic source in this area, although the analysis is formal and quite difficult. Cornes and Sandler (1996) provides a powerful theoretical underpinning in terms of the theory of public goods.

Tietenberg (1992) gives very extensive, descriptive coverage of several specific types of pollution. Other useful treatments which complement the discussion in this chapter are Dasgupta (1982, chapter 8), and two survey articles by Fisher and Peterson (1976) and Cropper and Oates (1992). Smith (1972) gives a mathematical presentation of the theory of waste accumulation. Several excellent articles can be found in the edited volume by Bromley (1995).

In this chapter we have taken a 'normative' approach to the setting of pollution targets, analysing what such targets should be in terms of some criterion of the public interest. An alternative literature considers targets in 'positive' terms, dealing with how targets are actually set. This approach focuses on the behaviour of interest groups, attempting to gain rents by manipulating government policy to their advantage. Good introductory accounts of this 'political economy' of regulation can be found in Goodstein (1995, 1999) and Kolstad (2000), par-

ticularly chapter 8. More advanced references are Laffont and Tirole (1993) which discusses theories of regulation, and Stigler (1971) and Peltzman (1976); these last two references are seminal works on the interest group theory of regulation.

Grubb (1998) provides a very interesting account of greenhouse gas policy, focusing on technological responses to the Kyoto Protocol. Ulph (1997) considers the relationship between environmental policy and innovation. Porter (1991) articulates the argument that strict environmental policy may be a factor which stimulates the rate of technological innovation. The double dividend hypothesis is discussed by Bovenberg (1997). The collection of readings edited by Carraro and Siniscalco (1997) focuses on the application of game theory to environmental problems. This is a particularly useful tool in the analysis of international pollution problems, as we shall see in Chapter 10, but has interesting applications too for domestic pollution policy. One of the first studies about the difficulties in designing optimal taxes (and still an excellent read) is Rose-Ackerman (1973).

Some journals provide regular applications of the economic theory of pollution. Of particular interest are the *Journal of Environmental Economics and Management, Ambio, Environmental and Resource Economics, Land Economics, Ecological Modelling, Marine Pollution Bulletin, Ecological Economics* and *Natural Resources Journal*.

1. 'Only the highest standards of environmental purity will do.' Discuss.

2. 'A clean environment is a public good whose benefits cannot be privately appropriated. Therefore private industry which is run for

   private gain will always be the enemy of a clean environment.' Examine this proposition.

3. Discuss the relevance and application of the concept of externalities in environmental economics.

Problems

1. Under which circumstances will the economically optimal level of pollution be zero? Under which circumstances will it be optimal to undertake zero pollution abatement?

2. We have seen that the efficient level of pollution is the one that minimises the sum of total abatement costs plus total damage costs. Refer now to Figure 6.5. Show that if pollution abatement takes place to the extent $\hat{M} - M_A$ the sum of total damage costs and total abatement costs is $C_1 + C_2 + C_3$. Prove that 'too little' abatement (relative to the optimal quantity) results in higher costs than $C_1 + C_2$.

3. Explain the concept of the 'efficient level of pollution'. What information is required in order to identify such an efficient quantity?

4. Using equation 6.20 or 6.21, deduce the effect of (i) a decrease in α and (ii) an increase in r (*ceteris paribus*) on:
   (a) M^*
   (b) A^*
   (c) μ^*

   Note that you could answer this question analytically. Alternatively, you could explore the issue numerically using the Excel file

Stock1.xls (found in the *Additional Materials* for Chapter 6).

5. This problem illustrates how marginal analysis might give misleading results in the presence of non-convexity. It is based on an example from Goodstein (1995). Nitrogen oxides (NO_x), in combination with some volatile organic compounds and sunlight, can produce damaging lower-atmosphere ozone smog. Initially, the damage rises at an increasing rate with NO_x emissions. However, high levels of NO_x act as ozone inhibitors, and so beyond some critical level of emissions, higher levels of NO_x reduce ozone damage.
   (i) Sketch a marginal damage (MD) function that is consistent with these properties.
   (ii) Add to your diagram a conventionally shaped marginal benefits function (or marginal abatement cost function) that intersects the MD function in more than one place.
   (iii) By an appropriate choice of some initial level of emissions, demonstrate that the following rule may give misleading results. Rule: emissions should be increased (decreased) if a small increase in emissions increases (decreases) net benefits.

Appendix 6.1 Matrix algebra

A6.1.1 Introduction

In this chapter, and in a few of the later ones (particularly Chapter 9 and the appendix to Chapter 14), some use is made of matrix algebra notation and ele-

mentary matrix operations. This appendix provides, for the reader who is unfamiliar with matrix algebra, a brief explanation of the notation and an exposition of a few of its fundamental operations. We deal here only with those parts of matrix algebra that are necessary to understand the use made of it in this text. The reader who would like a more extensive account should go to any good first-year university-level mathematics text. For example, chapter 4 of Chiang (1984) provides a relatively full account of introductory-level matrix algebra in an accessible form.

A6.1.2 Matrices and vectors

A *matrix* is a set of elements laid out in the form of an array occupying a number of rows and columns. Consider an example where the elements are numbers. Thus, the array of numbers

> 0.7   0.1
> 0.9   0.2
> 0.3   0.2
> 0.1   0.0

can be called a matrix. In such an array, the relative positions of the elements *do* matter. Two matrices are identical if the elements are not only the same but also occupy the same positions in each matrix. If the positions of two or more elements were interchanged, then a different matrix would result (unless the interchanged elements were themselves identical).

It is conventional, for presentational purposes, to place such an array within square brackets, and to label the matrix by a single bold letter (usually upper-case).[20] So in the following expression, **A** is the name we have given to this particular matrix of eight numbers.

$$\mathbf{A} = \begin{bmatrix} 0.7 & 0.1 \\ 0.9 & 0.2 \\ 0.3 & 0.2 \\ 0.1 & 0.0 \end{bmatrix}$$

It is also conventional to define the *dimension* of a matrix by the notation $m \times n$ where m is the number of rows occupied by the elements of the matrix and n is the number of columns occupied by elements of the matrix. So, for our example, **A** is of dimension 4×2 as its elements span four rows and two columns.

Notice that because elements of matrices span rows and columns, they can be handled very conveniently within spreadsheet programs.

Sometimes we want to define a matrix in a more general way, such that its elements are numbers, but those numbers are as yet unspecified. To do this we could write **A** in the more general form

$$\mathbf{A} = \begin{bmatrix} a_{11} & a_{12} \\ a_{21} & a_{22} \\ a_{31} & a_{32} \\ a_{41} & a_{42} \end{bmatrix}$$

Notice the way in which each of the elements of this matrix has been labelled. Any one of them is a_{ij} where i denotes the row in which it is found and j denotes its column. With this convention, the bottom right element of the matrix – here a_{42} – will necessarily have a subscript identical to the dimension of the matrix, here 4×2.

It is convenient to have another shorthand notation for the matrix array. This is given by

$$\mathbf{A} = [a_{ij}] \quad \begin{aligned} i &= 1, \ldots, m \\ j &= 1, \ldots, n \end{aligned}$$

The bracketed term here lets the reader know that what is being referred to is a matrix with $m \times n$ elements a_{ij}.

A6.1.2.1 A special form of matrix: the identity matrix

A matrix is said to be *square* if its row and column dimensions are equal (it has the same number of rows and columns). Thus, the matrix

$$\mathbf{B} = \begin{bmatrix} 3 & 2 \\ 4 & 1 \end{bmatrix}$$

is a 2×2 square matrix. Furthermore, if the coefficients of a square matrix satisfy the restrictions that each element along the leading (top left to bottom right) diagonal is 1 and every other coefficient is zero, then that matrix is called an *identity matrix*. Thus the matrix

$$\mathbf{I} = \begin{bmatrix} 1 & 0 \\ 0 & 1 \end{bmatrix}$$

is a 2×2 identity matrix. An identity matrix is often denoted by the symbol **I**, or sometimes by $\mathbf{I}_n$

---

[20] The use of square brackets is not universal; some authors prefer round brackets or braces.

where the n serves to indicate the row (and column) dimension of the identity matrix in question. In our example, it would be $\mathbf{I}_2$.

A6.1.2.2 Vectors

A vector is a special case of a matrix in which all elements are located in a single row (in which case it is known as a row vector) or in a single column (known as a column vector). Looking at the various rows and columns in the 4×2 matrix $\mathbf{A}$ above, it is evident that we could make up six such vectors from that matrix. We could construct four row vectors from the elements in each of the four rows of the matrix. And we could make up two column vectors from the elements in each of the two columns.[21] The four row vectors constructed in this way are

$$[a_{11} \quad a_{12}] \quad [a_{21} \quad a_{22}] \quad [a_{31} \quad a_{32}] \quad \text{and} \quad [a_{41} \quad a_{42}]$$

each of which is of dimension 1×2, while the two column vectors, each of dimension 4×1, are given by

$$\begin{bmatrix} a_{11} \\ a_{21} \\ a_{31} \\ a_{41} \end{bmatrix} \text{ and } \begin{bmatrix} a_{12} \\ a_{22} \\ a_{32} \\ a_{42} \end{bmatrix}$$

A6.1.2.3 The transpose of a matrix or a vector

Various 'operations' can be performed on matrices.[22] One of the most important – and commonly used – is the operation of forming the 'transpose' of a matrix. The transpose of a matrix is obtained by interchanging its rows and columns, so that the first column of the original matrix becomes the first row of the transpose matrix, and so on. Doing this implies that if the original matrix $\mathbf{A}$ were of dimension $m \times n$, its transpose will be of dimension $n \times m$. The transpose of $\mathbf{A}$ is denoted as $\mathbf{A}'$, or sometimes as $\mathbf{A}^T$.

Consider two examples. First, let $\mathbf{a}$ be the 4×1 column vector

$$\mathbf{a} = \begin{bmatrix} a_{11} \\ a_{21} \\ a_{31} \\ a_{41} \end{bmatrix}$$

then its transpose, $\mathbf{a}'$ is given by the row vector $\mathbf{a}' = [a_{11} \ a_{21} \ a_{31} \ a_{41}]$.

As a second example, consider the first array that we introduced in this appendix. That matrix and its transpose are given by

$$\mathbf{A} = \begin{bmatrix} 0.7 & 0.1 \\ 0.9 & 0.2 \\ 0.3 & 0.2 \\ 0.1 & 0.0 \end{bmatrix} \quad \mathbf{A}' = \begin{bmatrix} 0.7 & 0.9 & 0.3 & 0.1 \\ 0.1 & 0.2 & 0.2 & 0.0 \end{bmatrix}$$

A6.1.2.4 Bold notation for vectors and matrices

As we mentioned earlier, it is conventional to use the **bold** font to denote vectors or matrices, and to use an ordinary (non-bold) font to denote a scalar (single number) term. Hence, in the following expression, we can deduce from the context and the notation employed that each of $\mathbf{a_1}$ and $\mathbf{a_2}$ is a column vector consisting respectively of the first column of scalars and the second column of scalars. We know that the element a_{21}, for example, is a scalar because it is not written in bold font.

$$\mathbf{A} = \begin{bmatrix} a_{11} & a_{12} \\ a_{21} & a_{22} \\ a_{31} & a_{32} \\ a_{41} & a_{42} \end{bmatrix} = [\mathbf{a_1} \quad \mathbf{a_2}]$$

A6.1.3 Other operations on matrices

As with algebra more generally, several operations such as addition and multiplication can, under some conditions, be performed on matrices.

A6.1.3.1 Addition and subtraction

Two matrices can be added (or subtracted) if they have the same dimension. Essentially, these operations

---

[21] One could also, of course, make up other vectors as mixtures of elements from different rows or columns.

[22] From this point on in this appendix, we shall use the term matrix to include both vectors and matrices, unless the context requires that we distinguish between the two.

involve adding (or subtracting) comparably positioned elements in the two individual matrices. Suppose that we wish to add the two $(m \times n)$ matrices $\mathbf{A} = [a_{ij}]$ and $\mathbf{B} = [b_{ij}]$. The sum, $\mathbf{C} = [c_{ij}]$ is defined by

$$\mathbf{C} = [c_{ij}] = [a_{ij}] + [b_{ij}] \quad \text{where } c_{ij} = a_{ij} + b_{ij}$$

Example:

$$\begin{bmatrix} 7 & 1 \\ 9 & 2 \\ 3 & 2 \\ 1 & 0 \end{bmatrix} + \begin{bmatrix} 3 & 0 \\ 9 & 1 \\ 0 & 4 \\ 2 & 3 \end{bmatrix} = \begin{bmatrix} 7+3 & 1+0 \\ 9+9 & 2+1 \\ 3+0 & 2+4 \\ 1+2 & 0+3 \end{bmatrix} = \begin{bmatrix} 10 & 1 \\ 18 & 3 \\ 3 & 6 \\ 3 & 3 \end{bmatrix}$$

Matrix subtraction is equivalent, but with the addition operation replaced by the subtraction operation in the previous expression.

A6.1.3.2 Scalar multiplication

Scalar multiplication involves the multiplication of a matrix by a single number (a scalar). To implement this, one merely multiplies every element of the matrix by that scalar.

Example:

$$\text{If } \mathbf{A} = \begin{bmatrix} 0.7 & 0.1 \\ 0.9 & 0.2 \\ 0.3 & 0.2 \\ 0.1 & 0.0 \end{bmatrix} \text{ then } 2\mathbf{A} = \begin{bmatrix} 1.4 & 0.2 \\ 1.8 & 0.4 \\ 0.6 & 0.4 \\ 0.2 & 0.0 \end{bmatrix}$$

A6.1.3.3 Multiplication of matrices

Suppose that we have two matrices, $\mathbf{A}$ and $\mathbf{B}$. Can these be multiplied by one another? The first thing to note is that here (unlike with ordinary algebra) the order of multiplication matters. Call $\mathbf{A}$ the lead matrix and $\mathbf{B}$ the lag matrix. For the matrix multiplication to be possible (or even meaningful) the following condition on the dimensions of the two matrices must be satisfied:

Number of columns in $\mathbf{A}$ = Number of rows in $\mathbf{B}$

If this condition is satisfied, then the matrices are said to be 'conformable' and a new matrix $\mathbf{C}$ can be obtained which is the matrix product $\mathbf{AB}$. The matrix $\mathbf{C}$ will have the same number of rows as $\mathbf{A}$ and the same number of columns as $\mathbf{B}$.

How are the elements of $\mathbf{C}$ obtained? The following rule is used.

$$c_{ij} = \sum_{k=1}^{n} a_{ik}b_{kj} \text{ for } i = 1 \text{ to } m \text{ and } j = 1 \text{ to } n$$

Example:

$$\mathbf{A} = \begin{bmatrix} 2 & 1 \\ 0 & 3 \\ 1 & 2 \end{bmatrix} \quad \mathbf{B} = \begin{bmatrix} 3 & 2 \\ 4 & 1 \end{bmatrix} = \mathbf{AB} =$$

$$\begin{bmatrix} (2 \times 3) + (1 \times 4) & (2 \times 2) + (1 \times 1) \\ (0 \times 3) + (3 \times 4) & (0 \times 2) + (3 \times 1) \\ (1 \times 3) + (2 \times 4) & (1 \times 2) + (2 \times 1) \end{bmatrix} = \begin{bmatrix} 10 & 5 \\ 12 & 3 \\ 11 & 4 \end{bmatrix}$$

An intuitive way of thinking about this is as follows. Suppose we want to find element c_{ij} of the product matrix $\mathbf{C}$ (the element in the cell corresponding to row i and column j). To obtain this, we do the following:

- multiply the first element in row i by the first element in column j
- multiply the second element in row i by the second element in column j

.

.

and so on up to
- multiply the final element in row i by the final element in column j

The sum of all these multiplications gives us the number required for c_{ij}. (Note that this process requires the dimension condition that we stated earlier to be satisfied.) This process is then repeated for all combinations of i and j.

Doing this kind of exercise by hand for even quite small matrices can be very time-consuming, and prone to error. It is better to use a spreadsheet for this purpose. To see how this is done – and to try it out for yourself with an Excel spreadsheet, *Matrix.xls* – read the file *Matrix.doc* in the *Additional Materials* for Chapter 6.

However, we suggest you calculate the products $\mathbf{AB}$ and $\mathbf{BA}$ of the following two 2×2 matrices $\mathbf{A}$ and $\mathbf{B}$ to convince yourself that $\mathbf{AB}$ does not equal $\mathbf{BA}$.

$$\mathbf{A} = \begin{bmatrix} 3 & 2 \\ 1 & 0 \end{bmatrix} \quad \mathbf{B} = \begin{bmatrix} 3 & 2 \\ 4 & 1 \end{bmatrix}$$

A6.1.3.4 Division

Whereas obtaining the product of two matrices is a meaningful operation in matrix algebra, and can be done providing the two matrices are 'conformable', the same cannot be said of matrix division. Indeed, the division of one matrix by another is not a meaningful operation.

A6.1.3.5 The inverse matrix

However, a related concept – matrix inversion – does exist and is fundamental to much that is done in matrix algebra. To motivate this concept, think of ordinary algebra. If a and b are two numbers then the division of a by b (i.e. a/b) can be done, provided that b is non-zero. But notice that a/b can also be written as ab^{-1}, where b^{-1} is the inverse (or reciprocal of b).

Where $\mathbf{B}$ is a matrix, we can under some conditions obtain its inverse matrix, $\mathbf{B}^{-1}$. And if we have a second matrix, say $\mathbf{A}$, which has the same number of rows as $\mathbf{B}^{-1}$ has columns, then the product $\mathbf{B}^{-1}\mathbf{A}$ can be obtained.

How is the inverse of B defined? The matrix inverse must satisfy the following equality:

$$\mathbf{BB}^{-1} = \mathbf{B}^{-1}\mathbf{B} = \mathbf{I}$$

That is, the product of a matrix and its inverse matrix is the identity matrix. Inspecting the dimension conditions implied by this definition shows that a matrix can only have an inverse if it is a square matrix.

Let us look at an example. The inverse of the matrix

$$\mathbf{A} = \begin{bmatrix} 3 & 2 \\ 1 & 0 \end{bmatrix}$$

is given by

$$\mathbf{A}^{-1} = \begin{bmatrix} 0 & 1 \\ 0.5 & -1.5 \end{bmatrix}$$

as

$$\begin{bmatrix} 0 & 1 \\ 0.5 & -1.5 \end{bmatrix}\begin{bmatrix} 3 & 2 \\ 1 & 0 \end{bmatrix} = \begin{bmatrix} 3 & 2 \\ 1 & 0 \end{bmatrix}\begin{bmatrix} 0 & 1 \\ 0.5 & -1.5 \end{bmatrix} = \begin{bmatrix} 1 & 0 \\ 0 & 1 \end{bmatrix}$$

We will not give any methods here by which an inverse can be obtained. There are many such rules, all of which are tedious or difficult to implement once the matrix has more than 3 rows. Instead, we just report that a modern spreadsheet package can obtain inverse matrices by one simple operation, even for matrices of up to about 70 rows in size. There is clearly no need to bother about deriving an inverse by hand! And, of course, it is always possible to verify that the inverse is correct by checking that its product with the original matrix is $\mathbf{I}$.

Once again, to see how this is done, see *Matrix.doc* and *Matrix.xls*.

A6.1.4 The uses of matrix algebra

The two main uses we make of matrix algebra in this text are

- to describe a system of linear equations in a compact way;
- to solve systems of equations or to carry out related computations.

Each of these is used in this chapter (in Section 6.8, where we discuss ambient pollution standards) and in Chapter 9. As an example of the first use, it is evident that the system of equations used in our ambient pollution example,

$$A_1 = d_{11}M_1 + d_{12}M_2$$

$$A_2 = d_{21}M_1 + d_{22}M_2$$

$$A_3 = d_{31}M_1 + d_{32}M_2$$

$$A_4 = d_{41}M_1 + d_{42}M_2$$

can be more compactly written as $\mathbf{A} = \mathbf{DM}$

where

$$\mathbf{D} = \begin{bmatrix} d_{11} & d_{12} \\ d_{21} & d_{22} \\ d_{31} & d_{32} \\ d_{41} & d_{42} \end{bmatrix} \quad \mathbf{M} = \begin{bmatrix} M_1 \\ M_2 \end{bmatrix} \quad \mathbf{A} = \begin{bmatrix} A_1 \\ A_2 \\ A_3 \\ A_4 \end{bmatrix}$$

Check for yourself that, after the matrix multiplication $\mathbf{DM}$, this reproduces the original system of four equations.

The potential power of matrix algebra as a computational or solution device is illustrated in our analysis of input–output analysis in Chapter 9. We will leave you to follow the exposition there. As you will see, it is in this context that the inverse of a matrix is useful.

Appendix 6.2 Spatially differentiated stock pollution: a numerical example

This appendix provides a numerical example of a spatially differentiated ambient pollution problem. We obtain the efficient level of M for each source and A for each receptor. Some of the material below is copied from the output of a Maple file *ambient.mws*. The interested reader can find the Maple file itself in the *Additional Materials* for Chapter 6.

The problem is one in which in the relevant spatial area ('airshed') there are two emissions sources, and two pollution receptors. The **D** matrix of transition coefficients is, therefore of the following form:

$$D_{ij} = \begin{bmatrix} d_{11} & d_{12} \\ d_{21} & d_{22} \end{bmatrix}$$

for which we use below the specific values

$$\begin{bmatrix} 2 & 4 \\ 3 & 2 \end{bmatrix}$$

Assumptions used:

1. The marginal damage of pollution function is $MD(A) = A$ (a very simple special case), and is identical everywhere.
2. The marginal benefit of emissions function, $MB(M)$, is identical for each firm, and is given by

$$MB(M_i) = a - bM_i$$

where we assume $a = 344$ and $b = 7$.

As shown in the text, an efficient solution requires that for each i, $i = 1,2$

$$MB(M_i) = \sum_{j=1}^{N} \left(\frac{\partial}{\partial A_j} D(A_j) \right) d_{ji}$$

which under Assumption (1) is

$$MB(M_i) = \sum_{j=1}^{N} A_j d_{ji}$$

This is here a two-equation linear system:

$$a - bM_1 = d_{11}A_1 + d_{21}A_2$$

$$a - bM_2 = d_{12}A_1 + d_{22}A_2$$

which gives:

$$a - bM_1 = d_{11}(d_{11}M_1 + d_{12}M_2) + d_{21}(d_{21}M_1 + d_{22}M_2)$$

$$a - bM_2 = d_{12}(d_{11}M_1 + d_{12}M_2) + d_{22}(d_{21}M_1 + d_{22}M_2)$$

We next define an expression (called sys1) that consists of these two equations:

$$sys1 := \{a - bM_2 = d_{12}(d_{11}M_1 + d_{12}M_2)$$
$$+ d_{22}(d_{21}M_1 + d_{22}M_2),$$
$$a - bM_1 = d_{11}(d_{11}M_1 + d_{12}M_2)$$
$$+ d_{21}(d_{21}M_1 + d_{22}M_2)\}$$

This can be solved (using the 'solve' command in Maple) to obtain solutions for M_1 and M_2 in terms of the parameters, a, b and the components of the **D** matrix.

The solutions are given by

$$M_1 = \frac{(b - d_{11}d_{12} - d_{21}d_{22} + d_{12}^2 + d_{22}^2)a}{\left(\begin{array}{c} b^2 + bd_{12}^2 + bd_{22}^2 + d_{11}^2 b + d_{11}^2 d_{22}^2 + \\ d_{21}^2 b + d_{21}^2 d_{12}^2 - 2d_{11}d_{12}d_{21}d_{22} \end{array} \right)}$$

$$M_2 = \frac{a(b - d_{11}d_{12} + d_{21}^2 + d_{11}^2 - d_{21}d_{22})}{\left(\begin{array}{c} b^2 + bd_{12}^2 + bd_{22}^2 + d_{11}^2 b + d_{11}^2 d_{22}^2 + \\ d_{21}^2 b + d_{21}^2 d_{12}^2 - 2d_{11}d_{12}d_2 d_{22} \end{array} \right)}$$

To obtain specific values for the solutions, we now substitute the particular values $a = 344$, $b = 7$, $d_{11} = 2$, $d_{12} = 4$, $d_{21} = 3$ and $d_{22} = 2$ for the parameters, giving the solution:

$$\{M_1 = 13, M_2 = 6\}$$

We next find the efficient ambient pollution levels in the two receptor areas. First define a new system of equations:

$$sys11 := \{A_1 = d_{11}M_1 + d_{12}M_2, A_2 = d_{21}M_1 + d_{22}M_2\}$$

This can be solved (using the 'solve' command) to obtain solutions for A_1 and A_2 in terms of the components of the **D** matrix and the emission levels, M_1 and M_2:

$$sols22 := \{A_1 = d_{11}M_1 + d_{12}M_2, A_2 = d_{21}M_1 + d_{22}M_2\}$$

To obtain specific values for the solutions, we now substitute our assumed particular values for the parameters, giving

$$\{A_1 = 50, A_2 = 51\}$$

CHAPTER 7

Pollution control: instruments

Economists can only repeat, without quite understanding, what geologists, ecologists, public health experts, and others say about physical and physiological facts. Their craft is to perceive how economies and people in general will respond to those facts.   **Dorfman (1985), p. 67**

Learning objectives

After reading this chapter, the reader should understand

- how bargaining processes might bring about efficient resource allocations (and so might lead to the attainment of efficient pollution outcomes without regulatory intervention)
- the conditions which limit the likelihood of bargaining solutions to pollution problems being achieved
- the instruments available to attain a pollution target
- the mechanisms by which pollution instruments operate in attaining targets
- the comparative merits of alternative instruments
- the significance, in instrument choice, of whether a pollutant is uniformly mixing

---

Introduction

The previous chapter dealt with pollution targets. Here we consider how an environmental protection agency (EPA) could attain a predetermined pollution target by investigating the instruments that could be used.

In some circumstances no intervention would be required. Perhaps fortuitously, the prevailing level of pollution is not different from the target. Or interven-

tion may be unnecessary because of the existence of voluntary bargaining. We show in Section 7.3 that bargaining between generators and victims of pollution could lead to an outcome in which the unregulated amount of pollution is equal to the pollution target. But we also show that such an outcome is unlikely for most important types of pollution problem. Where bargaining fails to reduce pollution to its targeted level, intervention of some form is called for.

This chapter is organised around three main themes. First, we describe the instruments that are available, and how each operates. Second, we provide a comparative assessment of those instruments. Finally, we consider whether there are particular circumstances – or particular types of pollution problems – which tend to favour the use of specific instruments. Of decisive importance is a matter raised in the previous chapter: whether or not the pollutant being targeted is uniformly mixing.

For the most part, our *analysis* will be quite general. That is, we will be thinking about instruments in the context of 'pollution problems' in general, rather than separately for air pollution, water pollution, soil contamination, and so on. However, the generality of the analysis will be limited in one important way. We will focus on pollution problems that are national (or sub-national) in scope, rather than on ones which are international. Control and regulation of *international* pollution problems will be addressed specifically in Chapter 10. The reason for segmenting the material in this way has nothing to do with the relative importance of different pollution problems. It is because dealing with international pollution issues brings another dimension into the picture: developing, coordinating and monitoring control across sovereign states. At this stage, we wish to keep this dimension out of our treatment.[1]

Although the analysis in this chapter is general in its scope, the examples and applications deal with specific contexts and case studies. Several applications not covered in this chapter – specifically instruments for conserving biological diversity, mobile source (transport) pollution, and agricultural pollution – are examined in the Word files *Biodiversity*, *Transport* and *Agriculture* in the *Additional Materials* for Chapter 7.

<table>
<tr><td>7.1</td><td>Criteria for choice of pollution control instruments</td></tr>
</table>

There are many instruments available to an EPA charged with attaining some pollution target. How should it choose from among these? If attaining the target were all that mattered, instrument choice would be relatively simple. The best instrument would be the one which meets the target with greatest reliability. But the EPA is unlikely to have only this objective. Government typically has multiple objectives, and the terms of reference that policy makers impose on their agents will tend to reflect that diversity of objectives. Even where these terms of reference are not explicit, the network of influences and pressures within which the EPA operates will lead it to adopt multiple goals *de facto*.

Instrument choice can be envisaged in the following way. Each available instrument can be characterised by a set of attributes, relating to such things as impacts on income and wealth distribution, the structure of incentives generated, and the costs imposed in abating pollution. A score can be given to each instrument, dependent on how well its attributes match with the set of objectives sought by the EPA. (A hypothetical example of this is explored in Problem 1 at the end of this chapter.) This perspective is useful as it draws attention to what kinds of attributes a 'good' instrument might have. Table 7.1 lays out a set of criteria in terms of which the relative merits of instruments can be assessed.

The brief descriptions in the right-hand column of the table should be sufficient to convey what the various criteria mean. Fuller definitions and explanations of the first five items will be given later in the chapter. The remaining four all relate, in some way or other, to decision making under conditions of limited information or uncertainty, and will be investigated in the next chapter. However, three observations about these criteria warrant mention now (and will be developed later).

Table 7.1 Criteria for selection of pollution control instruments

Criterion	Brief description
Cost-effectiveness	Does the instrument attain the target at least cost?
Long-run effects	Does the influence of the instrument strengthen, weaken or remain constant over time?
Dynamic efficiency	Does the instrument create continual incentives to improve products or production processes in pollution-reducing ways?
Ancillary benefits	Does the use of the instrument allow for a 'double dividend' to be achieved?
Equity	What implications does the use of an instrument have for the distribution of income or wealth?
Dependability	To what extent can the instrument be relied upon to achieve the target?
Flexibility	Is the instrument capable of being adapted quickly and cheaply as new information arises, as conditions change, or as targets are altered?
Costs of use under uncertainty	How large are the efficiency losses when the instrument is used with incorrect information?
Information requirements	How much information does the instrument require that the control authority possess, and what are the costs of acquiring it?

---

[1] As you will see, our attempt to avoid dealing with the international dimension in this chapter will be compromised as soon as we get to grips with biodiversity. For that reason, it is taken up again in Chapter 10.

First, the use of any instrument is likely to involve conflicts or trade-offs between alternative criteria. Instrument choice will, therefore, depend on the relative weights attached to the criteria by the EPA. Second, it is likely that the weights (and so the choice of instrument) will vary over different types of pollution. For example, where a dangerous and persistent toxin is concerned, the EPA may regard cost efficiency as being of low importance relative to the long-run effect of the chosen instrument. Third, no single instrument is best for dealing with all types of pollution in all circumstances. We shall see in the next chapter that this is true *a fortiori* where instrument choice takes place under conditions of uncertainty. One particular criterion – cost efficiency – has received so much attention in the environmental economics literature that it warrants special attention now.

7.2   Cost efficiency and cost-effective pollution abatement instruments

Suppose a list is available of all instruments which are capable of achieving some predetermined pollution abatement target.[2] If one particular instrument can attain that target at lower real cost than any other can then that instrument is cost-effective.[3] Cost-effectiveness is clearly a desirable attribute of an instrument. Using a cost-effective instrument involves allocating the smallest amount of resources to pollution control, conditional on a given target being achieved. It has the minimum opportunity cost. Hence, the use of cost-effective instruments is a prerequisite for achieving an economically efficient allocation of resources.[4]

Let us explore some ramifications of the cost-effectiveness criterion. There will (usually) be many sources of an emission, and so many potential abaters. This raises the question of how the overall target should be shared among the sources. The principle of cost efficiency provides a very clear answer: a necessary condition for abatement at least cost is that the marginal cost of abatement be equalised over all abaters. This result is known as the least-cost theorem of pollution control. It is derived algebraically in the first part of Appendix 7.1. You will find it useful to read that now.

The intuition behind this result is easily found. Consider a situation in which marginal abatement costs were not equalised. For example, suppose that at present abatement levels two firms, A and B, have marginal abatement costs of 60 and 100 respectively. Clearly if B did one unit less abatement and A did one more (so that total abatement is unchanged) there would be a cost reduction of 40. Cost savings will accrue for further switches in abatement effort from B to A as long as it is more expensive for B to abate pollution at the margin than it is for A.

Let us examine these ideas a little further.[5] Suppose government wishes to reduce the total emission of a particular pollutant from the current, uncontrolled, level $\hat{M}$ (say, 90 units per period) to a target level M^* (say, 50 units). This implies that the abatement target is 40 units of emission per period. Emissions arise from the activities of two firms, A and B. Firm A currently emits 40 units and B 50 units.

The following notation is used. The subscript i indexes one firm (so here i = A or B). M_i is the actual level of the ith firm's emissions, which will depend on what control regime is in place. Two particular levels are of special interest. $\hat{M}_i$ is the profit-maximising level of emissions by firm i in the absence of any controls set by government and in the absence of any pollution charges. M_i^* is an emission ceiling (upper limit) set for the firm by the EPA. The quantity of pollution abatement by the ith firm is Z_i, given by $Z_i = \hat{M}_i - M_i^*$. Hence we assume that

---

[2] You will notice that we refer here to a pollution reduction (or abatement) target, rather than to a target level of pollution itself. This conforms to conventional usage in the literature on instruments. In this chapter, the context should make it clear whether the target being referred to relates to pollution or pollution abatement.

[3] Strictly speaking an instrument is cost-effective if its real resource cost is no greater than that of any other instrument available. This means that a cost-effective instrument may not be unique. For example, suppose that two instruments each incur costs of £10m to bring sulphur dioxide pollution down to some target level, while all others cost more than £10m. Then those two instruments are cost-effective.

[4] It is this which explains why the cost-effectiveness criterion has figured so prominently in the economics literature.

[5] The following problem is replicated in the Excel workbook *Leastcost.xls*, found in the *Additional Materials* for Chapter 7.

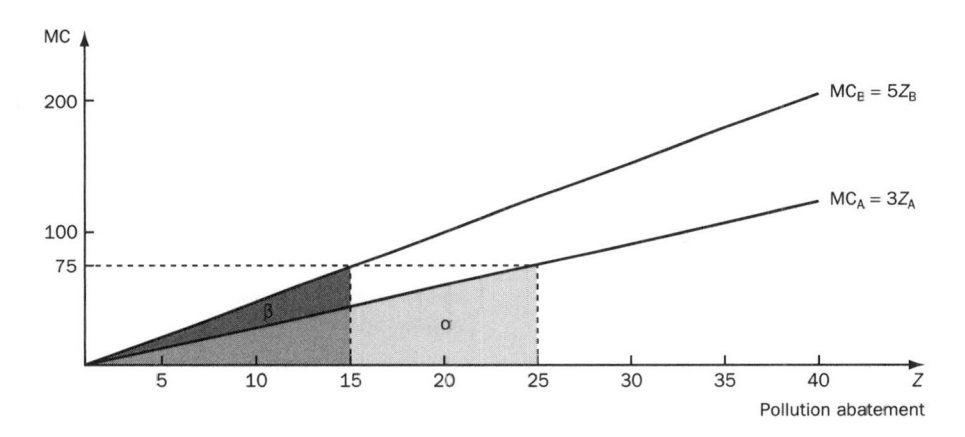

Figure 7.1 Marginal abatement cost functions for the two firms

whenever an emissions regulation is in operation the amount of emissions the firm actually produces is that set by the EPA. C_i is the total abatement cost of the ith firm.

Suppose that the total abatement cost functions of the two firms are $C_A = 100 + 1.5Z_A^2$ and $C_B = 100 + 2.5Z_B^2$. Therefore, the marginal abatement cost functions are $MC_A = 3Z_A$ and $MC_B = 5Z_B$. These are sketched in Figure 7.1. The least-cost solution is obtained by finding levels of Z_A and Z_B which add up to the overall abatement target $Z = 40$ *and* which satisfy the least-cost condition that $MC_A = MC_B$. This gives the answer $Z_A = 25$ and $Z_B = 15$. Figure 7.1 shows this least cost solution. At those respective abatement levels both firms have marginal abatement costs of 75. Minimised total abatement costs (1700) can be read from the diagram. The darker shaded area denoted β shows B's total abatement costs (662.5), while the lighter area denoted α represents A's total abatement costs (1037.5).

To verify this result, you could use the Lagrange multiplier technique, obtain the necessary first-order conditions, and solve these for the two firms' abatement levels. This was explained in the appendix to Chapter 4, where this problem – albeit with different numbers – was solved to show how the technique works. A convenient alternative, taking only a couple of minutes, is to use Excel's Solver routine to do this task for us. The mechanics of doing so are given in *Leastcost.xls* (in *Additional Materials, Chapter 7*) and you are recommended to study this Excel workbook now.

It is instructive to compare this solution with two others. First, one might think that as firm A has a lower marginal abatement cost schedule than B it should undertake all 40 units of abatement. It is easy to verify that this results in higher costs (2500) than those found in the least-cost solution (1700). Second, an equity argument might be invoked to justify sharing the abatement burden equally between the two firms. But it is easy to show (for example by looking at *Sheet1* of *Leastcost.xls*) that this also leads to higher costs (1800 in fact). If the regulator wanted such an equitable outcome, it would come at an additional real cost to the economy of 100 units (1800 − 1700). Note that the greater the difference in the firms' abatement cost functions, the greater would be the cost penalty from not pursuing the least-cost outcome. (See Problem 2.)

Some important conclusions emerge from this analysis:

- A least-cost control regime implies that the marginal cost of abatement is equalised over all firms undertaking pollution control.
- A least-cost solution will in general not involve equal abatement effort by all polluters.
- Where abatement costs differ, cost efficiency implies that relatively low-cost abaters will undertake most of the total abatement effort, but not all of it.

We shall use these results later in this chapter to establish whether particular kinds of pollution control instrument are cost-effective.

In this section, we describe and explain the instruments available for pollution control. For convenience, the most common are listed in Table 7.2. Our emphasis is on the method of operation of each instrument and whether the instrument is cost-efficient. A more complete examination of the relative advantages of the instruments is left until later in the chapter.

7.3.1   Institutional approaches which facilitate internalisation of externalities

The various approaches to environmental policy that we consider in this section are best thought of not as pollution control instruments as such but rather as institutions which may avert the need to use pollution control instruments. Each shares the characteristic of potentially preventing the emergence of externalities, or internalising externalities which have arisen. In doing so, it is possible that decentralised behaviour by consumers and producers may generate efficient outcomes and so obviate the need for the regulatory intervention, at least if targets are set on efficiency grounds.

7.3.1.1 Bargaining solutions and the limitations on bargaining solutions to environmental problems

The way in which bargaining can internalise externalities and so achieve efficient outcomes was explained in Chapter 5. There we considered an example of a musician disturbing a single neighbour, and how bargaining between those two parties could generate an efficient quantity of music playing. However, our discussion also demonstrated that efficient bargaining outcomes are often hard to obtain, and are sometimes impossible. These limitations are particularly likely for many kinds of environmental problem. We now briefly review why this should be so.

First, the likelihood of bargaining taking place is low unless enforceable property rights exist. For many environmental resources, well-defined and enforceable property rights do not exist. Second, bargaining is facilitated by the existence of a relatively small number of affected parties, and by all such parties being easily identifiable. Again, many environmental problems fail to satisfy either of those properties. Typically, environmental degradation affects many people and in many cases, as with vehicle pollution, is attributable to a large number of sources. It is often difficult to identify all affected parties, and the transactions costs associated with undertaking a bargaining exercise can be enormous. Hence where the number of affected individuals is large, the scope for efficient bargaining behaviour is very restricted.

Another pertinent issue relates to the possibility of intertemporal bargaining, including bargaining between current and future generations. Many environmental externalities cut across generations – our behaviour today imposes externalities on future persons. While bargaining between affected individuals at one point in time seems feasible, it is difficult to imagine that this could happen between representatives of the present generation and those not yet living. One would not, therefore, expect that bargaining between directly affected individuals and firms would offer much prospect of bringing about an efficient response to global climate change, involving as it does many generations.

Finally, bargaining solutions are extremely unlikely to be able to bring about socially efficient provision or conservation of public goods. Given that a substantial proportion of natural resources – or the services that they yield – have public good characteristics, this is a profound limitation.

What do these observations imply about the role for government? If, despite these limitations, bargaining does offer the prospect of substantial efficiency gains, then government should facilitate it wherever that is cost-effective. It could do so by clearly defining and explicitly allocating property rights wherever that is practicable (and ethically acceptable). Government might also seek to develop and sustain an institutional structure that maximises the scope for bargaining behaviour, as is sometimes done for employment disputes. Gains may derive from government's taking some responsibility for environmental monitoring so as to identify pollution producers and recipients, and disclosing information from this to affected parties. Finally, access to the judicial system should be easy and cheap. This will

Table 7.2 Classification of pollution control instruments

Instrument	Description	Examples
Institutional approaches to facilitate internalisation of externalities		
Facilitation of bargaining	Cost of, or impediments to, bargaining are reduced	Polluter information placed in the public domain
Specification of liability	Codification of liability for environmental damage	Respiratory damage in Japan
Development of social responsibility	Education and socialisation programmes promoting citizenship	Energy-conservation media campaigns Environmental labelling
Command and control instruments		
Input controls over quantity and/or mix of inputs	Requirements to use particular inputs, or prohibitions/restrictions on use of others	Bans on use of toxic cleansing agents
Technology controls	Requirements to use particular methods or standards	Requirement to install catalytic converters in exhausts. BATNEEC
Output controls: Output quotas or prohibitions	Non-transferable ceilings on product outputs	Ban on use of DDT Singapore: vehicle quotas Effluent discharge licences
Emissions licences	Non-transferable ceilings on emission quantities	
Location controls (zoning, planning controls, relocation)	Regulations relating to admissible location of activities	Heavy industry zoning regulations
Economic incentive (market-based) instruments		
Emissions charges/taxes	Direct charges based on quantity and/or quality of a pollutant	Air pollution charges (e.g. NO_x charges in France and Sweden; SO_2 charges in France and Japan) Carbon/energy taxes Water effluent charges (evidence of effectiveness in Germany, Netherlands and Malaysia) Noise pollution charges (Belgium, France, Germany, Japan, Netherlands, Norway, Switzerland) Fertiliser and pesticide taxes (Austria, Belgium, Scandinavian countries)
User charges/fees/natural resource taxes	Payment for cost of collective services (charges), or for use of a natural resource (fees or resource taxes)	User charges on municipal waste collection, treatment or disposal Hazardous waste, wastewater user, and aircraft noise charges Water extraction charges (thought to be effective in several Asian countries) Congestion pricing (France, Norway, Singapore, USA)
Product charges/taxes	Applied to polluting products	Hungary: vehicle tyres Finland: nuclear waste Italy: plastic bags Belgium: disposables tax
Emissions abatement and resource management subsidies	Financial payments designed to reduce damaging emissions or conserve scarce resources	Quebec: subsidy for energy generated from waste Norway: grants to ecological farming
Marketable (transferable, marketable) emissions permits	Two systems: those based on emissions reduction credits (ERCs) or cap-and-trade	Denmark: CO_2 emissions from power plants
Deposit-refund systems	A fully or partially reimbursable payment incurred at purchase of a product	Austria: refillable plastic bottles Quebec: one-way beer and soft-drink bottles Also used in Korea, Greece, Norway and Sweden
Non-compliance fees	Payments made by polluters or resource users for non-compliance, usually proportional to damage or to profit gains	Greece: car emissions Sweden: sea dumping of oil from ships
Performance bonds	A deposit paid, repayable on achieving compliance	Australia: mine sites US: open pits
Liability payments	Payments in compensation for damage	Japan: waste – restoration of sites polluted by illegal dumping

Notes to table:
1. Many of the examples in the table are drawn from OECD (1999) and EPA (1999). These references are available online, the first via the OECD web site www.oecd.org, the second at http://yosemite1.epa.gov/ee/epalib/incent.nsf. They provide extensive accounts of incentive-based environmental controls used in OECD countries.
2. Particular countries are mentioned purely as examples. Listings are not exhaustive.

also facilitate use of the liability principle that we shall discuss in the next section.

Nevertheless, the limitations to bargaining that we have described do appear to be very substantial, and it would be inappropriate to place too much reliance on such a mechanism. There is one important exception to this conclusion, however. When it comes to dealing with pollution, or other environmental, problems that spill over national boundaries, the absence of supra-national sovereign institutions means that there is often little or no alternative to bargaining solutions. These are unlikely, of course, to take place directly between affected individuals or firms. Rather, international policy coordination and cooperation is negotiated between representatives of affected national governments.

Discussions about greenhouse gas emissions or about the maintenance of biological diversity are two of the more well-known examples of such international bargaining processes, and have the potential to generate massive collective benefits. As international policy cooperation about environmental problems is the subject of a separate chapter (Chapter 10), we shall postpone further consideration of this matter until then.

7.3.1.2 Liability

The role that may be played by the judicial system in helping to bring about efficient outcomes has been implicit in our discussion of bargaining. But that role can be taken a step further. Suppose that a general legal principle is established which makes any person or organisation liable for the adverse external effects of their actions. Then any polluter knows that there is some probability, say p, of being identified and successfully prosecuted, and so made to pay for that pollution. One variant of this scheme has the prosecuted polluter paying p times the value of the damages, so that the expected value of the liability equals the value of pollution damage.[6]

The liability principle is related to property rights. Where pollution is a private good, the liability is equivalent to a statement of enforceable property rights vested in the victims, and enforcement would be done through civil law. But where the pollutant is a public good, this way of making the polluter pay is not usually feasible. In that case, the EPA acts as an agent of the public interest, enforcing the liability principle on behalf of affected parties. An interesting question is whether any damages obtained in this way should be returned to individuals as compensation. We explore this matter in Discussion Question 1.

Using the liability principle is not without its problems. One difficulty arises where damage only becomes apparent a long time after the relevant pollutants were discharged. Tracking down those who are liable may be a substantial undertaking, and those responsible – individuals or firms – may no longer exist. An interesting development is the process of establishing legal liability throughout the life cycle of a product, using the principle that producers are responsible for damage from 'cradle to grave'.

7.3.1.3 Development of social responsibility

Pollution problems happen, in the final analysis, because of self-interested but uncoordinated, or sometimes thoughtless, behaviour. Encouraging people to behave as responsible citizens can help to attain environmental goals. Clearly, the government of the day has limited influence over the cultural context of human behaviour. But it would be wrong to ignore the opportunities that exist for using educational institutions and the mass communications media to help achieve specific targets and to promote ethical behaviour.

The evidence that individuals do not exclusively act in a narrowly utilitarian way suggests that this objective may be more than just wishful thinking. Among the very many examples that could be cited are support for green parties and the increasing importance being given to environmental issues by voters, the success of some ethical investment funds, our willingness to support charities. Perhaps the strongest evidence is to be found in our family and social lives, where much of what we think and do has a social – rather than purely self-interested – basis. Although we write little about 'cultural' instruments in this text, the authors recognise that they may be the most powerful ways of achieving general environmental goals.

---

[6] It is important to note, however, that damages may be assessed differently by a court from the way we have in mind, and so the liability principle may generate different outcomes from the 'efficient outcomes' achieved through bargaining.

Box 7.1 Liability for environmental damage

An important example of the liability for damage principle can be found in the regulations relating to hazardous waste disposal in the USA. Under the terms of the Resource Conservation and Recovery Act, a 'cradle-to-grave' tracking and liability principle has been adopted.

The *Superfund* concerns abandoned waste dumps. The fund is built up from various sources including damages settlements. The principle of 'strict, joint and several liability' establishes a special form of retrospective liability, in which parties that have dumped waste (legally or illegally) can be sued for the whole costs of clean-up, even though they were only partial contributors to the dump. The sued party may then attempt to identify others responsible to recover some of the damages. Moreover, liability lies with the generators of waste as well as those who subsequently reprocess or dispose along the waste cycle.

The use of liability payment schemes is now widespread, with examples to be found in Quebec, Denmark, Finland, Germany, Japan,

Sweden and Turkey. Several countries have instituted general liability schemes (e.g. Denmark, Finland, Sweden and Turkey), in some cases requiring compulsory environmental damage insurance for large polluters (e.g. Finland). Other governments have specified liability schemes for particular categories of polluter (Quebec – tioxide (titanium dioxide) pollution; Germany – noise; USA – hazardous waste).

Since the 1970, Japanese courts have developed an extensive liability case law, relating primarily to waste, air and water pollution. Japanese businesses contribute to a compensation fund. Until 1988, persons with bronchial asthma and other respiratory diseases were entitled to compensation from the fund without judicial procedure. After 1988, new sufferers were no longer entitled to automatic compensation, as air pollution was no longer unequivocally accepted as the principal contributory factor to respiratory illnesses.

Source: OECD (1999)

One particular policy mechanism which could be said to be in the 'social responsibility' category is environmental labelling, used in virtually all industrialised economies and in many developing countries. This has been credited with reducing VOC (volatile organic compound) emissions in Germany, and with increasing paper recycling in Korea (EPA, 1999).

7.3.2   Command and control instruments

The dominant method of reducing pollution in most countries has been the use of direct controls over polluters. This set of controls is commonly known as *command and control* instruments. Figure 7.2 provides a schema by which these instruments can be classified. There we see that the regulations can be classified in terms of what is being targeted.

The first panel (Figure 7.2a) represents the various relationships that link production to pollution levels. Emissions are by-products in the production of intended final output. The amount (and type) of emissions will depend on which goods are being produced, and in what quantities. It will also depend on the production techniques being employed, and

on the amount (and mix) of inputs being used. For uniformly mixing pollutants (UMPs), pollution levels will depend only on total emissions levels. In the case of non-uniformly-mixing pollutants (indicated in the diagram by the dotted lines in the branch to the right) the spatial distribution of ambient pollution levels will also depend on the location of emission sources.

Command and control instruments can be designed to intervene at any of these stages. So, as the second panel (Figure 7.2b) illustrates, regulations may apply to outputs of emissions themselves, to the quantity of final production, to production techniques used, or to the level and/or mix of productive inputs. For non-UMPs, controls may also apply to location of emission sources.

In general, there should be advantages in directing the controls at points closest (in this sequence of linkages) to what is ultimately being targeted: that is, ambient pollution levels. This allows polluters the most flexibility in how a pollution reduction is to be achieved. But it may not always be feasible – or desirable on other grounds – to set regulations in that way.

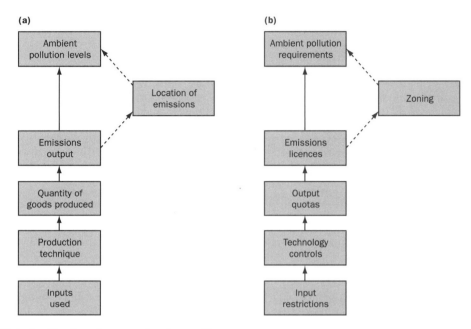

Figure 7.2 A classification of command and control instruments

There is huge variation from place to place in the detail of regulatory systems. It would be of little use – and probably impossible – to list the plethora of command and control regulations. Our coverage of command and control instruments will be limited, therefore, to some general comments on the main categories shown in Figure 7.2b, together with some illustrative examples in boxes. For further detail, the reader should visit the text's Accompanying Website www.booksites.net/perman, which provides links to many sites that provide regularly updated accounts of regulatory regimes in various countries.

Some examples of the use of command and control in the USA are given in Box 7.2. The material

---

Box 7.2 Environmental protection in the USA

The United States system of environmental controls is one of the most comprehensive to be found. A set of Congressional statutes provides the legal framework for the regulatory system, and give responsibility to the United States Environmental Protection Agency (US EPA) for implementing and administering the system. A comprehensive, and well-indexed, account of US environmental policy can be found on the 'Laws & regulations' section of the US EPA web site (www.epa.gov/epahome/lawreg.htm). Here we focus on a small, but important, part of that system.

Table 7.3 outlines the regulatory framework in six particular areas: air and water pollution, hazardous waste disposal, agricultural chemicals, toxic substances, and species protection. It identifies the regulatory area in each case, and

states the criteria that must be considered by US EPA in setting standards.

Air quality

The *Clean Air Act* defines ambient air quality standards for all parts of the USA for two types of pollutant: criteria (common) and hazardous air pollutants. *Criteria* air pollutants consist of particulates, SO_2, CO, NO_2, low-level ozone and lead. Each of these is given a *primary NAAQS* (National Ambient Air Quality Standard), set to protect human health. Some are also given a *secondary* NAAQS to protect wildlife, visibility and ecological systems. The levels of NAAQS for the criteria pollutants were listed in Table 6.7 in Chapter 6.

The system for *criteria* air pollutants is as follows. For *stationary sources* of air pollutants,

Box 7.2 continued

the principal control instrument is technology-based regulation. This is supported by maximum allowable emissions rates in some cases. *Existing pollution sources* must satisfy 'reasonably available control technology' (RACT). *New pollution sources* must meet more restrictive 'new source performance standards' (NSPS), based on the criterion of commercially available 'best technological system of emissions reduction'. Where NAAQS have not been met, stricter criteria may be used, such as 'lowest achievable emissions rate' (LAER), or in Class 1 (unspoilt) areas 'best available control technology' (BACT). What counts as satisfying these requirements is often laid out in great detail by US EPA after thorough study of particular production processes. Firms may be required to use particular techniques to recover fumes or waste products, or they may be prohibited from using certain production processes. Not surprisingly, the interpretation of these different criteria and the particular requirements that US EPA mandates for firms,

are contentious, and lead to significant amounts of judicial action.

For *mobile source* air pollution, control is largely directed at vehicle manufacturers, again in the form of required technology controls. Stricter controls are used in some non-attainment areas (such as mandated use of low-polluting fuels).

Although air pollution is mainly controlled by technology-based regulation, there are some exceptions. A flexible incentive-based system has been developed for acid-rain-inducing pollutants, and will be examined in Chapter 10. Individual states may also, if they wish pursue higher than national standards. Some states are experimenting with various market-based controls, such as those being used in the Los Angeles basin area.

In the cases of *hazardous air pollutants* (about 200 air toxins listed by US EPA other than the criteria pollutants), 'large' stationary sources must use 'maximum achievable control technology' (MACT). Additional control

Table 7.3 Factors to be considered by the US EPA in setting standards and regulations

Statute	Coverage	Factors to be considered in setting standards
Clean Air Act (CAA) (as amended 1990) www.epa.gov/oar/oaqps/ peg_caa/pegcaain.html	Ambient air quality standards	Standards to be set on safety grounds (to achieve an 'adequate margin of safety') US EPA must consider benefits of regulation but *not* costs
Clean Water Act (CWA) 1987 (in conjunction with Federal Water Pollution Control Act) www.epa.gov/region5/ defs/html/cwa.htm	Effluent emissions, from stationary point sources and non-point sources	Standards to be set on safety grounds Waters required to be at least 'swimmable and fishable' US EPA must consider benefits and costs of regulation (but balancing is not required)
The Resource Conservation and Recovery Act (RCRA) Comprehensive Environmental Response, Compensation, and Liability Act (Superfund) The Superfund Amendments and Reauthorization Act (SARA) www.epa.gov/superfund	Hazardous waste disposal on land, both current disposal (RCRA) and abandoned waste dumps (Superfund)	Standards to be set on safety grounds US EPA must consider benefits of regulation but *not* costs
The Endangered Species Act (ESA)		Ecological sustainability standard Protection of species at any cost
Federal Insecticide, Fungicide and Rodenticide Act (FIFRA) Toxic Substances Control Act (TSCA) Emergency Planning and Right-to-Know Act	Restricting the use of dangerous substances FIFRA: agricultural chemicals TSCA: toxic substances	Targets to be set on efficiency grounds Benefits and costs of regulation to be balanced in both cases

Box 7.2 *continued*

measures, and/or new listed pollutants, may be added by the US EPA if risk analysis suggests that this is warranted. With the passage of time, US EPA has gone some way along the process of defining acceptable risk in operational terms. For example, 'ample margin of safety' is now defined to mean that cancer risks to the most exposed population do not exceed 1 in 10 000. (The long-term target has been specified as 1 in 1 million for the population at large.)[7] Note from Table 7.3 that the Clean Air Act requires the US EPA to only take account of the benefits of control in setting regulations over toxic air emissions. However, in 1987 a Court of Appeals ruling found that US EPA has been (unlawfully) considering both benefits and costs in setting ambient standards. As a result, US EPA tightened its standards (so that control was extended to cover emissions for which it previously felt that the cost-to-benefit ratio was too high to justify control).

Clean water

Water standards are again typically based on technology controls. In the initial control phase, this required the use of 'best *practical* technology' (BPT). Later control phases mandated the more stringent 'best *available* technology' (BAT). In addition to BAT, dischargers must acquire (non-marketable) effluent emissions licences, often containing very detailed plans about how discharges are treated as well as the amounts that may be discharged. What counts as 'best' is defined by US EPA (although, again, not without much judicial challenge). Technology controls ('best-management practices' are also employed to reduce runoff from non-point sources (industrial and agricultural sites).

Hazardous waste disposal

Under the terms of the Resource Conservation and Recovery Act, the US EPA has developed a list of about 450 hazardous substances. Disposal is controlled through location restrictions, required staff training, groundwater monitoring by disposing firms, and the requirement to construct detailed plans for site closure and post-

closure practice. Operators must also undertake sufficient insurance cover. These, and other, restrictions are supported by a licence system. An interesting innovation here is the adoption of a 'cradle-to-grave' tracking and liability principle (see Box 7.1). The Superfund has provided a mechanism for dealing with abandoned waste dumps. The fund is built up from general taxation and from taxes on the petroleum and chemical industries. The principle of 'strict, joint and several liability' (see Box 7.1) establishes strong incentives throughout the waste cycle to minimise the amount of waste produced.

Toxic substances

The TSCA requires US EPA to review all new chemicals, and gives it authority to restrict use of, or ban, existing chemicals. Unlike most areas of environmental regulation, the TSCA requires balancing of the costs of regulation (in money terms) and the benefits of regulation (in terms of cancer or other serious health impacts avoided). A study by Van Houtven and Cropper (1996) investigated US EPA bans on the use of asbestos in particular uses under the provisions of the TSCA. Of the 39 uses of asbestos it investigated, Van Houtven and Cropper found that US EPA was able to measure costs and benefits in 31 cases. Of these, 21 products were banned.

Agricultural chemicals

FIFRA imposes a duty of registration of all new pesticides. New ingredients in agricultural chemicals cannot be introduced until the US EPA is satisfied, after cost–benefit analysis, that the product will generate positive net benefits. As an input to this study, manufacturers must submit a detailed scientific study of the ingredient. US EPA may also carry out Special Reviews on existing pesticides. As with TSCA, FIFRA requires that the EPA 'balance' benefits against costs in arriving at its decisions about bans or other restrictions. The Van Houtven and Cropper study investigated 245 food crop applications of 19 pesticide active ingredients. Of these, 96 applications were banned after US EPA Special Reviews.

---

[7]   Actual risks have often been very much higher. A US EPA study in the late 1980s revealed that risks were worse than 1 in 1000 in 205 communities around the country.

there shows that the administration of instruments is not entirely separate from the setting of targets (or 'standards' as they are also known). In the examples, the 'goal' passed on to the US Environmental Protection Agency (USEPA) is given in the form of a general principle regarding the criterion that should be used in setting standards, together with some direction about what information should be used in its deliberations. The USEPA is then required to translate that goal into specific targets and/or regulations and to administer their implementation.

In the sections that follow, we describe in a little more detail the three most commonly used types of command and control instrument, and then investigate instruments that use the price mechanism to create incentives for pollution abatement. In doing so, the likely cost-efficiency of each instrument will be discussed. A more complete appraisal of the relative merits of each instrument using the criteria listed in Table 7.1 will be left until Section 7.6.

7.3.2.1 Non-transferable emissions licences

Suppose that the EPA is committed to attaining some overall emissions target for a particular kind of pollutant. It then creates licences (also called permits or quotas) for that total allowable quantity. After adopting some criterion for apportioning licences among the individual sources, the EPA distributes licences to emissions sources. We use the term *non-transferable licences* to refer to a system where the licences cannot be transferred (exchanged) between firms: each firm's initial allocation of pollution licences sets the maximum amount of emissions that it is allowed.[8] Successful operation of licence schemes is unlikely if polluters believe their actions are not observed, or if the penalties on polluters not meeting licence restrictions are low relative to the cost of abatement. Licence schemes will have to be supported, therefore, by pollution monitoring systems and by sufficiently harsh penalties for non-compliance.

Under special conditions, the use of such emissions licences will achieve an overall target at least

cost (that is, be cost-efficient). But it is highly unlikely that these conditions would be satisfied. We know (see the first part of Appendix 7.1) that cost-efficiency requires the marginal cost of emissions abatement to be equal over all abaters. If the EPA knew each polluter's abatement cost function, it could calculate which level of emissions of each firm (and so which number of licences for each firm) would generate this equality *and* meet the overall target.

It is very unlikely that the EPA would possess, or could acquire, sufficient information to set standards for each polluter in this way. The costs of collecting that information could be prohibitive, and may outweigh the potential efficiency gains arising from intervention. Moreover, there is a problem of information asymmetries; those who possess the necessary information about abatement costs at the firm level (the polluters) do not have incentives to provide it in unbiased form to those who do not have it (the regulator).[9] We examine these incentives in a little more detail in Section 7.6. A system of long-term relationships between regulator and regulated may overcome these asymmetries to some extent, but might bring other problems (such as high administrative cost and regulatory capture – to be defined and explained in Chapter 8) in its wake. Given all this, it seems likely that arbitrary methods will be used to allocate licences, and so the controls will not be cost-efficient. Box 7.10 gives some indication of how great this cost-inefficiency is in practice.

7.3.2.2 Instruments which impose minimum technology requirements

Another command and control approach involves specifying required characteristics of production processes or capital equipment used. In other words, minimum technology requirements are imposed upon potential polluters. Examples of this approach have been variously known as *best practicable means* (BPM), *best available technology* (BAT) and *best available technology not entailing excessive cost* (BATNEEC). Some further information on technology controls is given in Box 7.3.

---

[8] We use the term 'licence' to denote non-transferable emissions quotas. Later in the chapter, transferable quotas will be discussed. To avoid confusion, we call these 'permits'.

[9] Another possibility is that firms themselves may also be unaware of their abatement costs.

Box 7.3 Required technology controls

Regulations mandating the use of particular technologies are common forms of pollution control instrument in Europe, North America and the other OECD countries. In the UK, a criterion underlying required technology standards has been 'best practicable means'. The adjective *practicable* has never been given a precise legal definition, but the 1956 Clean Air Act stated that

> Practicable means reasonably practicable having regard, amongst other things, to local conditions and circumstances, to the financial implications and the current state of technology.

Despite an element of tautology in this statement, it can be interpreted as meaning that a practicable control technology should be technologically effective, subject to the constraint that it is not excessively costly. In recent years, the cost qualification has been given greater priority, and has been enshrined in the principle of BATNEEC: the best available technology not entailing excessive cost. This puts the instrument closer to the kind advocated by economists, as the 'excessive cost' condition implies a quasi-cost–benefit calculation in the administration of the instrument.

However, while the cost of control is often measured by the regulator in money terms (for example, the additional money cost of one technique over another), the benefits are not usually measured in money terms; instead, benefits are seen in terms of reduced probabilities of death or serious damage to health. In this sense, although some balancing of costs against benefits does often take place, the approach being used is not 'cost–benefit analysis' in the economics sense of that term. Rather than using the public's estimate of benefits (in terms of willingness to pay) the regulator has to come to a view as to what cost is reasonable to save a life or reduce a health risk. Some information on this is provided in Box 7.3a. Equivalent kinds of money-cost relative to health-benefit comparisons are also made in the US regulatory system.

The manner in which technology-based instruments have been implemented varies considerably between countries. In the UK, officials of the Inspectorate of Pollution negotiate controls with plant managers, but have the right, in the last instance, to require the adoption of certain control technologies. The United States Environmental Protection Agency administers a rather more uniform control programme: in 1990, Congress required the EPA to establish technology-based standards for about 200 specific pollutants.

Box 7.3a The value of life, as revealed by actions of the United States Environmental Protection Agency

A series of recent papers have attempted to deduce what value the United States Environmental Protection Agency (US EPA) places on saving lives. In one of these papers, Van Houtven and Cropper (1996) examined four particular areas over which the US EPA has sought to achieve regulation. We noted in Box 7.2 that the US EPA can issue bans on particular uses of asbestos. Van Houtven and Cropper investigated 39 applications for asbestos use. From data on the costs of regulation and the number of lives expected to be saved in each application, the authors were able to estimate the value of a statistical life that is implied by US EPA decisions. By definition, if an action results in the expected level of deaths falling by one person over some relevant time period, that

action has saved one statistical life. Van Houtven and Cropper found that, on average, products were banned when the cost of saving one life was below $49 million (in 1989 US dollar prices).

Van Houtven and Cropper obtain a very similar implied value ($51.51) million for a fatal cancer avoided in their study of 245 pesticide applications (of which 96 were banned). Decisions here were taken under the auspices of FIFRA agricultural chemicals legislation, which also requires cost and benefit balancing to be used by the US EPA. Van Houtven and Cropper also investigated controls of toxic air pollutants – specifically benzene, arsenic, asbestos and mercury – under the provisions of the Clean Air Act. Prior to 1987, the implied value of a fatal

Box 7.3a *continued*

cancer avoided was about $16 million. As we remarked earlier, a 1987 Court of Appeals ruling found that EPA has been unlawfully considering the costs of regulation in making its decisions. In so doing, some emissions had been allowed where the US EPA had estimated the cost-to-benefit ratio to be too high to justify control. The tighter standards the US EPA subsequently imposed (based only on the benefits of control) implied a value of a statistical life after 1987 of $194 million.

These values are considerably higher than the values which people seem to be willing to pay to reduce the risk of death. For example, Viscusi (1992, 1993) estimated the compensating wage differential required by workers to take on high-risk jobs. Observed wage differentials imply a value of a statistical life of $5 million, just one-tenth of that implied by US EPA regulations that required balancing.

In the previous edition of this text, we remarked that the US EPA appeared to be using the principle of cost-effectiveness in making decisions. For example, that would entail that, for any given sized health benefit, those products with the lower control costs are banned while those with higher costs are not banned. But other research suggests that this is questionable. For example, Viscusi (1996) examines a number of command and control regulations designed to save lives and protect health. Table 7.4 shows the costs of a statistical life saved for each category of regulation. Huge variability is evident, although some of this reflects differences in what the US EPA is required to consider in making decisions (that is: just benefits, benefits and costs but without balancing, or benefits and costs with balancing).

Another example of widely varying marginal costs is given in a study by Magat *et al.* (1986) of the marginal treatment cost of biological oxygen demand (BOD) from US rivers and lakes. The authors estimated that marginal costs of attaining regulatory standards varied from as little as $0.10 per kilogram of BOD removal to as much as $3.15.

In the case of both BOD removal and reduction of the risk of death, there appear to be very large efficiency gains possible from reallocating control (and so control expenditures) from high-cost to low-cost areas.

Table 7.4 The statistical value of a life as revealed by US EPA command and control regulations

Regulation	Initial annual risk	Expect annual lives saved	Cost per expected life saved ($US 1984)
Unvented space heaters	2.7 in 10^5	63.000	0.10
Airplane cabin fire protection	6.5 in 10^8	15.000	0.20
Auto passive restraints/belts	9.1 in 10^5	1850.000	0.30
Underground construction	1.6 in 10^3	8.100	0.30
Servicing wheel rims	1.4 in 10^5	2.300	0.50
Aircraft seat cushion flammability	1.6 in 10^7	37.000	0.60
Aircraft floor emergency lighting	2.2 in 10^8	5.000	0.70
Crane suspended personnel platform	1.8 in 10^3	5.000	1.20
Concrete and masonry construction	1.4 in 10^5	6.500	1.40
Benzene/fugitive emissions	2.1 in 10^5	0.310	2.80
Grain dust	2.1 in 10^4	4.000	5.30
Radionuclides/uranium mines	1.4 in 10^4	1.100	6.90
Benzene in workplace	8.8 in 10^4	3.800	17.10
Ethylene oxide in workplace	4.4 in 10^5	2.800	25.60
Arsenic/copper smelter	9.0 in 10^4	0.060	26.50
Uranium mill tailings, active	4.3 in 10^4	2.100	53.00
Asbestos in workplace	6.7 in 10^5	74.700	89.30
Arsenic/glass manufacturing	3.8 in 10^5	0.250	142.00
Radionuclides/DOE facilities	4.3 in 10^6	0.001	210.00
Benzene/ethylbenzenol styrene	2.0 in 10^6	0.006	483.00
Formaldehyde in workplace	6.8 in 10^7	0.010	72000.00

Source: Viscusi (1996), pp. 124–125

In some variants of this approach, specific techniques are mandated, such as requirements to use flue-gas desulphurisation equipment in power generation, designation of minimum stack heights, the installation of catalytic converters in vehicle exhaust systems, and maximum permitted lead content in engine fuels. In other variants, production must employ the (technically) best technique available (sometimes subject to a reasonable cost qualification). The specific technique adopted is sometimes negotiated between the EPA and the regulated parties on an individual basis.

Much the same comments about cost-effectiveness can be made for technology controls as for licences. They are usually not cost-efficient, because the instrument does not intrinsically focus abatement effort on polluters that can abate at least cost. Moreover, there is an additional inefficiency here that also involves information asymmetries, and which relates back to a point made earlier about Figure 7.2. Technology requirements restrict the choice set allowed to firms to reduce emissions. Decisions about emissions reduction are effectively being centralised (to the EPA) when they may be better left to the firms (who will choose this method of reducing emissions rather than any other only if it is least-cost for them to do so).

Required technology controls blur the pollution target/pollution instrument distinction we have been drawing in this and the previous chapter. The target actually achieved tends to emerge jointly with the administration of the instrument. We need to be a little careful here. Sometimes government sets a general target (such as the reduction of particulates from diesel engines by 25% over the next 5 years) and then pursues that target using a variety of instruments applied at varying rates of intensity over time. In this case, no single instrument need necessarily have a particular target quantity associated with it. Nevertheless, it does matter (as far as cost-efficiency is concerned) if the actual operation of any particular component of this programme does not involve any comparison of the benefits and costs of that component (because then the wrong mix of components will be used). There are many examples of technology control where it appears to be the case that emphasis is given almost exclusively to the costs of pollution reduction technologies, and in particular to

what kind of cost premium is involved in using the technically best method as compared with its lower-ranked alternatives. (See Box 7.10, for example. And think about saving lives via safety regulations.)

Although technology-based instruments may be lacking in cost-effectiveness terms, they can be very powerful; they are sometimes capable of achieving large reductions in emissions quickly, particularly when technological 'fixes' are available but not widely adopted. Technology controls have almost certainly resulted in huge reductions in pollution levels compared with what would be expected in their absence.

7.3.2.3 Location

Pollution control objectives, in so far as they are concerned only with reducing human exposure to pollutants, could be met by moving affected persons to areas away from pollution sources. This is only relevant where the pollutant is not uniformly mixing, so that its effects are spatially differentiated. Implementing this *ex ante*, by zoning or planning decision, is relatively common. *Ex post* relocation decisions are rarer because of their draconian nature. There have been examples of people being removed from heavily contaminated areas, including movements away from irradiated sites such as Chernobyl, Times Beach (Missouri) and Love Canal (New York). However, it has been far more common to move pollution sources away from areas where people will be affected, or to use planning regulations to ensure separation. Planning controls and other forms of direct regulation directed at location have a large role to play in the control of pollution with localised impacts and for mobile source pollution. They are also used to prevent harmful spatial clustering of emission sources.

Location decisions of this kind will not be appropriate in many circumstances. Moving people away from a pollution source cannot, for example, reduce impacts on ecosystems. Relocating (or planning the location of new) emission sources has wider applicability, but will be of no use in cases where pollution is uniformly mixing. In Section 7.5 we shall consider a number of incentive-based instruments that are designed, among other things, to influence the spatial location of emissions sources. These are not, however, examples of command and control instruments.

7.4   Economic incentive (quasi-market) instruments

Command and control instruments operate by imposing mandatory obligations or restrictions on the behaviour of firms and individuals. Incentive-based instruments work by creating incentives for individuals or firms to voluntarily change their behaviour. These instruments alter the structure of pay-offs that agents face.

Employing incentives to make behaviour less polluting can be thought about in terms of prices and markets. Taxes, subsidies and transferable permits create markets (or quasi-markets, something equivalent to markets) for the pollution externality.[10] In these markets, prices exist which generate opportunity costs that profit-maximising firms will take account of in their behaviour.

7.4.1   Emissions taxes and pollution abatement subsidies

In this section, we examine tax and subsidy instruments used to alter the rate of emissions of uniformly mixed pollutants, for which the value of the damage created by an emission is independent of the location of its source. It is shown later that the results also apply, with minor amendment, to non-uniformly mixing pollutants. Given that taxes on emissions are equivalent to subsidies (negative taxes) on emissions abatement, it will be convenient to deal explicitly with tax instruments, and refer to subsidy schemes only when there is a difference that matters.

Looking again at Figure 7.2, it is evident that there are several points at which a tax could be applied (just as there were several points of intervention for command and control regulations). We focus here on taxation of emissions. It is important to note that taxes on output of the final product, or on the levels of particular inputs (such as coal), will not have the same effect as emissions taxes, and will generally be less efficient in attaining pollution targets. This matter is examined in Problem 9 at the end of the chapter.

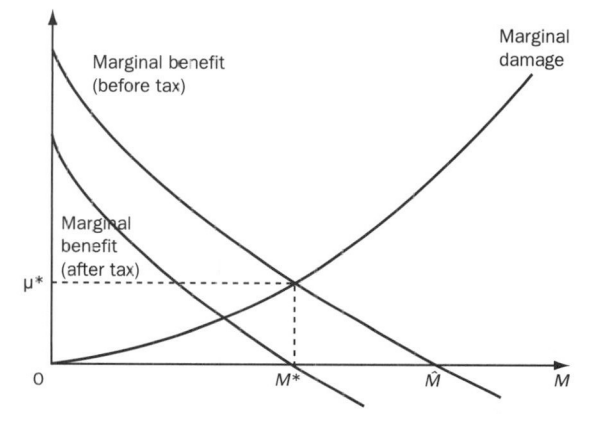

Figure 7.3 An economically efficient emissions tax

A tax on pollutant emissions has for long been the instrument advocated by economists to achieve a pollution target. It is useful to distinguish between three cases:

1. the pollution target is the economically efficient level of pollution (the level which maximises social net benefits);
2. a specific target is sought, but it is set according to some criterion other than economic efficiency;
3. an emission reduction of some unspecified amount is sought.

We deal with each of these cases in turn. To attain the *efficient* level of pollution, it is necessary to have solved the net benefit maximisation problem discussed in the previous chapter. You should recall from that analysis that a shadow price implicitly emerges from that exercise, this price being equal to the monetary value of marginal damage at the efficient level of pollution. This is the rate at which the tax (or subsidy) should be applied per unit of emissions.

Figure 7.3 illustrates the working of an emissions tax. Note that the diagram uses aggregate, economy-wide marginal benefit and marginal damage functions (not those of individuals or single firms). If firms behave without regard to the pollution they generate, and in the absence of an emissions tax,

---

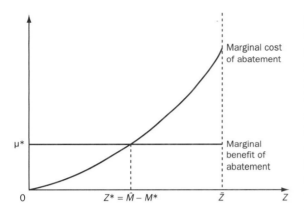

Figure 7.4 The economically efficient level of emissions abatement

emissions will be produced to the point where the private marginal benefit of emissions is zero. This is shown as $\hat{M}$, the pre-tax level of emissions.

Now suppose an emissions tax was introduced at the constant rate μ^* per unit emission, the value of marginal damage at the efficient pollution level. Given this, the post-tax marginal benefit schedule differs from its pre-tax counterpart by that value of marginal damage. Once the tax is operative, profit-maximising behaviour by firms leads to a pollution choice of M^* (where the post-tax marginal benefits of additional pollution are zero) rather than $\hat{M}$ as was the case before the tax. Note that levying an emissions tax at the rate μ^* creates just the right amount of incentive to bring about the targeted efficient emission level, M^*.[11]

It is sometimes more convenient to view the problem in terms of abatement, Z, rather than the level of pollution itself. This can be done by reinterpreting Figure 7.3. Viewed in this new light, the emission tax causes abatement to increase from zero (at $\hat{M}$) to its efficient level $Z^* = \hat{M} - M^*$ at the point M^* on the horizontal axis. Alternatively, we can map the relevant parts of Figure 7.3 into abatement space, from which we obtain Figure 7.4. It is important to be clear about the relationships between these two diagrams. First, the curve labelled 'marginal cost of abatement' is just the mirror image of the (before-tax) marginal benefit curve in Figure 7.3; what firms

privately forgo when they abate emissions is, of course, identical to the benefits they receive from emissions. The 'marginal benefit of abatement' to a representative firm is the tax rate applied, μ^*. Each unit of abated emissions reduces the firm's total tax bill by that amount. As the tax rate is constant, the marginal benefit of abatement curve is horizontal. Secondly, note that we have truncated the two curves in Figure 7.4 at $Z = \bar{Z}$, where $\bar{Z}$ is identical in magnitude to $\hat{M}$. Confirm for yourself the reason for doing this. Finally, note that $Z^* = \hat{M} - M^*$, and so the distance from the origin to Z^* in Figure 7.4 is equal to the horizontal distance between $\hat{M}$ and M^* along the emissions axis in Figure 7.3.

In the absence of an emissions tax (or an abatement subsidy), firms have no economic incentive to abate pollution. (In terms of Figure 7.4, the marginal benefit of abatement lies at zero along the Z axis.) Profit-maximising behaviour implies that firms would then undertake zero abatement, corresponding to emissions $\hat{M}$. However, when an emissions tax is levied (or, equivalently, when an abatement subsidy is available) an incentive to abate exists in the form of tax avoided (or subsidy gained). It will be profitable for firms to reduce pollution as long as their marginal abatement costs are less than the value of the tax rate per unit of pollution (or less than the subsidy per unit of emission abated). If the tax/subsidy is levied at the level μ^* the efficient pollution level is attained without coercion, purely as a result of the altered structure of incentives facing firms.

In the language of externalities theory, the tax eliminates the wedge (created by pollution damage) between private and socially efficient prices; the tax brings private prices of emissions (zero) into line with social prices (μ^*). The tax 'internalises the externality' by inducing the pollution generator to behave as if pollution costs entered its private cost functions. Decisions will then reflect all relevant costs, rather than just the producer's private costs, and so the profit-maximising pollution level will coincide with the socially efficient level. Not only will the tax instrument (at rate μ^*) bring about an efficient level of pollution but it will also achieve

---

[11] As shown in Appendix 7.1, a subsidy at the rate μ^* on units of pollution abated would have an equal short-run effect on emissions to a pollution tax at the rate μ^* on unabated units of pollution.

that target in a cost-effective way. Remember that cost-efficiency requires that the marginal abatement cost be equal over all abaters. Under the tax regime all firms adjust their firm-specific abatement levels to equate their marginal abatement cost with the tax rate. But as the tax rate is identical for all firms, so are their marginal costs.

Our discussion in this section so far has dealt with the case in which the EPA wishes to attain the economically efficient level of emissions, M^*. However, we saw in the previous chapter that the EPA may not have sufficient information for this to be feasible. Suppose that the EPA does have an emissions target, $\tilde{M}$, set perhaps on health grounds. To attain this (or indeed any other specific) emissions target, knowledge of the aggregate (economy-wide) marginal emissions abatement cost function would be sufficient. This should be clear by looking at Figure 7.4 again. For any target $\tilde{M}$, knowledge of the aggregate marginal cost of abatement function allows the EPA to identify the tax rate, say $\tilde{\mu}$, that would create the right incentive to bring about that outcome. Even though the target is not an efficient target, the argument used above about cost-efficiency remains true here: the emissions tax, levied at $\tilde{\mu}$, attains the target $\tilde{M}$ at least total cost, and so is cost-efficient. This result is rather powerful. Not only does the EPA not need to know the aggregate marginal pollution damage function, it does not need to know the abatement cost function of each firm. Knowledge of the aggregate abatement cost function alone is sufficient for achieving any arbitrary target at least cost. Compare this result with the case of command and control instruments; there, knowledge of every firm's marginal abatement cost function is required – a much more demanding information requirement.

Finally, let us deal with the third of the listed cases where an emission reduction of some unspecified amount is sought. Without knowledge of anything about abatement costs and benefits, the EPA could select some arbitrary level of emissions tax, say $\tilde{\mu}$. Faced with this tax rate, profit-maximising firms will reduce emissions up to the point where marginal abatement costs are brought into equality with this tax rate. As all firms do this the emissions reduction is achieved at least cost, once again. Although the government cannot know in advance how much pollution reduction will take place, it can be confident that whatever level of abatement is generated would be attained at minimum feasible cost. Taxes (and subsidies by an equivalent argument) are, therefore, cost-efficient policy instruments. These results are demonstrated formally in Appendix 7.1, Parts 4 and 5.

We stated earlier that an emissions tax and an emissions abatement subsidy (at the same rate) have an identical effect in terms of pollution outcome in the short term (see Part 6 of Appendix 7.1). However, the two instruments do have some very important differences. Most importantly, the distribution of gains and losses will differ. Taxes involve net transfers of income from polluters to government, while subsidies lead to net transfers in the other direction (see Problem 4). This has important implications for the political acceptability and the political feasibility of the instruments. It also could affect the long-run level of pollution abatement under some circumstances. Some more discussion on this matter is given in Box 7.4.

To reinforce your understanding of this material in this section, you are recommended to work through Problem 10 at the end of this chapter. This uses an Excel workbook to simulate emissions reduction using command and control techniques, tax and subsidy instruments, and (to be discussed in the next section) transferable permits. Some information on practical experience with pollution taxes and abatement subsidies is given in Box 7.5.

7.4.2 Marketable emissions permits

As with command and control and tax/subsidy instruments, marketable permits (also known as tradable or transferable permits) can be applied at many points in the production-to-pollution process represented in Figure 7.2. Here we consider only one form: permits on the quantity of *emissions*. Marketable permit systems are based on the principle than any increase in emissions must be offset by an equivalent decrease elsewhere. There is a limit set on the total quantity of emissions allowed, but the regulator does not attempt to determine how that total allowed quantity is allocated among individual sources.

Box 7.4 Are pollution taxes and emissions abatement subsidies equivalent?

For an industry of a given size, an emission tax and an abatement subsidy levied or paid at the same rate are equivalent in terms of units of emissions abated. Thus, looking at Figure 7.3 again, a subsidy or a tax at the rate μ^* would reduce emissions from $\hat{M}$ to M^* for a single firm with a given capital structure. As the industry is simply the sum of all firms, if the number of firms remains constant and the capital structure of each firm is unchanged, then the effects of taxes and subsidies are identical.

However, the two instruments are different in their effects on income distribution. A firm gains additional income from an abatement subsidy, as it will undertake abatement only when the unit abatement subsidy exceeds its marginal abatement cost. A tax on the other hand results in a loss of income to the firm as it pays the tax on all its emissions. To make this comparison more precise, look at Figure 7.5, the functions in which reproduce those in Figure 7.3.

An abatement subsidy will result in a payment to the firm equal to the areas $S_1 + S_2$, that is, μ^* multiplied by ($\hat{M} - M^*$). However, by reducing emissions from $\hat{M}$ to M^* the firm loses S_2 in profit on final output. The net gain to the firm is equal, therefore, to the area S_1. A tax levied at the rate μ^* on emissions M^* will cost the firm μ^*M^*, that is, the sum of the areas S_3, S_4, S_5 and S_6.

However, by reducing emissions from $\hat{M}$ to M^* the firm also loses profit on reduced output, the area S_2. So the income effects are entirely different.

Let us explore this difference a little further. Recall that the tax paid is equal in value to μ^*M^*, while the subsidy received is $\mu^*(\hat{M} - M^*)$. But $\mu^*(\hat{M} - M^*) = \mu^*\hat{M} - \mu^*M^*$. The second term on the right-hand side is the tax paid, and will depend on the amount of abatement undertaken. It is this second component which gives the firm an incentive to abate emissions. Recalling that μ is an outflow in a tax scheme and an inflow in a subsidy scheme, an outflow of μ^*M^* (with a tax) is identical to an inflow of $-\mu^*M^*$ (with a subsidy). The two incentive effects are identical, and it is this that forms the basis for the claim that the instruments are equivalent. However, the subsidy differs from the tax by the presence of the additional term, $\mu^*\hat{M}$, a fixed or lump-sum payment, independent of the amount of abatement the firm actually undertakes. In the long run such payments may alter industry profitability, and so alter the size of the industry itself. This lump-sum payment component of the subsidy may destroy the equivalence between the two instruments in terms of their effects on emissions abatement.

We are faced with the possibility that a subsidy might enlarge the industry, partially or wholly offsetting the short-run emissions reduction. It is not possible to be more precise about the final outcome, as that depends on several other factors, including whether or not government introduces other fiscal changes to counteract the income effects we have just described. A general equilibrium analysis would be necessary to obtain clear results. This is beyond our scope in this text, so we just note that the equivalence asserted above is not valid in all cases.

Finally, note another aspect of an abatement subsidy scheme. As one component of the subsidy payment depends on the uncontrolled level of emissions (that is, the component $\mu^*\hat{M}$), a firm has an incentive to misrepresent the uncontrolled level of emissions in order to obtain a favourable benchmark in terms of which the subsidy payments are calculated.

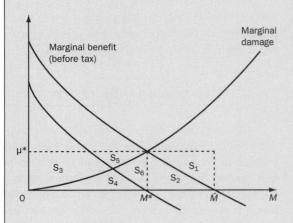

Figure 7.5 Emissions tax and abatement subsidy schemes: a comparison

Box 7.5 The use of economic instruments in OECD countries

The use of economic instruments to achieve environmental goals has increased markedly since the 1970s. The number of applications has increased, as has the variety of instruments used. Revenues from environmentally related taxes in 2000 constituted about 7% of total OECD tax revenue, a figure that is growing steadily and which had accelerated at the end of the 1990s.

User charges and subsidies were being applied in the 1970s. Since then, emissions charges and taxes have become widespread, subsidies to encourage the installation or use of environmentally friendly capital equipment have become common, and several other incentive-based instruments have appeared for the first time, including deposit-refund systems and performance bonds. The use of marketable permits has began to appear, although it is as yet not widely spread. Table 7.5 lists the main categories of economic instruments and their usage in OECD economies. Box 7.6 considers several examples of the use of emissions taxes and emissions abatement subsidies.

Economic instruments are also widely used for natural resource management. Common applications are in the management of water quantity (typically abstraction charges or taxes), fisheries (taxes, fees and transferable quotas), forestry (charges and subsidies) and wetlands (financial assistance to owners). Economic instruments are also used to preserve soil and land quality, and to preserve species and wildlife (typically fees and permits). Several examples of resource management or conservation instruments are given in the resource harvesting chapters (17 and 18) later in the text.

Table 7.5 Economic instruments used in OECD countries

Country	Fees, charges and taxes	Tradable permits	Deposit-refund systems	Non-compliance fees	Performance bonds	Liability payments	Subsidies
Australia	•	•	•		•		•
Austria	•		•				•
Belgium	•						
Canada	•	•	•	•	•	•	•
Czech Republic	•		•	•			•
Denmark	•	•	•			•	•
Finland	•		•			•	•
France	•	•					•
Germany	•					•	
Greece	•			•			•
Hungary	•		•	•			
Iceland	•		•				
Ireland	•						
Italy	•		•				
Japan	•					•	•
Korea	•		•	•			
Mexico	•		•				
Netherlands	•		•				•
New Zealand	•						
Norway	•		•	•			•
Poland	•	•	•	•			•
Portugal	•						
Spain	•						
Sweden	•		•	•		•	•
Switzerland	•	•					•
Turkey	•		•	•		•	•
UK	•						
USA	•	•	•		•	•	•

Source: OECD (1999)

Notes to Table 7.5:

1. Entries marked by • denote that the instrument category was stated to be used (or to have been used) by the country in question in response to a questionnaire-based survey of all (29) OECD economies in 1999. 24 countries responded. Non-respondent countries are those for which there are no entries in this table in any column except that labelled 'Fees, charges and taxes'

2. 'Charges' refer to requited emissions charges, user charges and product charges

Box 7.6 Emissions tax and abatement subsidies in practice[12]

The majority of emissions taxes in current use apply to the transport and energy sectors. A third important application is to waste management. Emissions fees were used in at least 20 OECD countries in 1999, and their use has been growing steadily since 1985. The OECD now lists approximately 200 examples of fees or taxes in the areas of air, water and noise pollution, and waste disposal. In some cases, tax revenues are earmarked for purposes of environmental improvement. In Germany and Italy, charges are used in conjunction with effluent standards: those firms which meet or better the standards are taxed at a lower rate per unit effluent than others.

Air-pollutant emissions charges are being used predominantly in Japan and a number of European countries. France has used charges as an incentive to install pollution abatement technology, with charges being repaid in the form of capital subsidies to firms adopting recommended control technologies. In 1998, France integrated several existing charges into a unified 'General Tax on Polluting Activities' (TGAP); the environmental agency is allocated a share of TGAP revenues for environmental improvement programmes. Sweden charges combustion plants for NO_X emissions, with revenue being distributed among emitters in proportion to their share in total energy output. Hence the total cost of the system to emitters is zero, but each plant has an incentive to reduce its emissions-to-energy-output ratio. The regime appears to have led to significant falls in NO_X emissions and to have spurred innovation in combustion technology. In Japan emissions levies are earmarked as a compensation fund for victims of air pollution; charge levels are dependent upon amounts of compensation paid out in previous years.

Several countries – including Australia, the Czech Republic, Hungary and Iceland – have systems of charges for ozone-depleting substances. Differential tax rates on leaded and unleaded petrol in the United Kingdom serve as an indirect charge on lead emissions, and Sweden has used differential charges and subsidies on cars and heavy vehicles to encourage the purchase of low-pollution engines and the adoption of catalytic converters. There are relatively high rates of tax on electricity and

primary energy sources throughout Western Europe; while not being pollution taxes as such, they do have similar incentive effects by encouraging energy conservation and enhancing energy efficiency.

Although the European Union has abandoned plans for a common carbon tax, Denmark, Finland, Italy, the Netherlands, Norway, Sweden and the UK all currently use some form of energy tax which, to varying degrees, reflects the carbon content of fuels. However, in the great majority of countries where CO_2 (or other environmental) taxes have been implemented, some sectors have been exempted from the tax, or the tax rate is differentiated across sectors. This reduces the cost-effectiveness, and so raises the real cost, of the tax.

Water effluent charges are used in Australia, Belgium, Canada, the Czech Republic, France, Italy, Germany, Mexico, the Netherlands, Poland and several US states. Charge rates vary according to the quantity and quality of waste water. The UK has a landfill tax; this is examined in Box 7.7.

The USA makes little use of emissions taxes or charges. Exceptions include a tax on chlorofluorocarbons to help in the phasing out of these chemicals, and fees on sewage and solid and hazardous waste at landfills. Households typically pay by the gallon for sewage disposal, and waste haulage firms pay by the ton for solid waste disposal. However, household and business enterprises have traditionally paid *lump-sum* charges for solid waste disposal, and so *marginal* disposal costs are not passed on to the initial producers of waste, leading to significant efficiency losses. As more states move to volume-related charges (37 states now do this), volumes discarded have fallen and recycling rates have risen significantly (Anderson *et al.*, 1997). The United States has, though, made more extensive use of marketable emission permit instruments than have European economies (see Box 7.8).

Tax rates are typically set at levels insufficient to fully internalise external costs (EEA, 2000). Low rates of tax or subsidy imply correspondingly low levels of impact. In some cases charges have been high enough to have large incentive effects. The Netherlands, with relatively high rates, has shown large

---

[12] In this box we do not distinguish between taxes and fees or charges, using the terms interchangeably.

Box 7.6 *continued*

improvements in water quality. Sweden's use of differential taxes and subsidies, and the differential tax on unleaded petrol in the UK have been very effective in causing substitution in the intended directions. In some instances, the revenues from specific charges are earmarked for particular forms of environmental defence or clean-up expenditure – one example is the use of taxes on new paint purchases in British Columbia to support reprocessing and safe disposal of used paint.

Subsidies for attainment of environmental improvements are used widely. A few countries use subsidies that are proportionately related to quantities of air emissions or water effluent. It is far more common, though, for subsidies to be paid in the form of grants, tax allowances or preferential loans for capital projects that are expected to lead to environmental improvements (such as low-emissions vehicles, cleaner waste-treatment plants or the development of environmentally friendly products). These schemes are often financed from earmarked environmental funds. A comprehensive listing of such schemes can be found on the web page of OECD (1999).

Sources: Tietenberg (1990),
Goodstein (1995), OECD (1999)

Box 7.7 Landfill tax example

A landfill tax was introduced in the UK in 1996. The tax, paid by landfill operators, is set at different rates for inactive waste such as bricks (£2 per tonne) and other waste (£7 per tonne). An element of tax neutrality is imposed by reducing employers' national insurance contributions to offset the costs of the landfill tax.

The tax is designed so that incentives exist to reduce waste flows. However, since its inception, operation of the tax has been plagued by concerns that waste has been disposed of illegally to avoid landfill tax charges. This illustrates the point that incentive-based instruments for environmental control may be ineffective unless there is careful monitoring and methods for ensuring compliance.

Charges levied on landfill operators are also found in the Czech Republic (since 1992). The tax is in two parts, the first being imposed on all landfill operators [with revenues recycled to municipal authorities for environmental protection activities). The second component – strictly speaking, a non-compliance fee – charges operators who fail to attain specified standards. Evidence suggests that the tax has markedly increased the proportion of sites attaining specified standards. A similar system operates in the Slovak Republic. It is more common for charges to be placed on generators of waste (rather than disposers of it), with applications in China, Estonia, Hungary, Poland and Russia.

There are two broad types of marketable emission permit systems – the 'cap-and-trade' system and the emission reduction credit (ERC) system. We shall analyse the cap-and-trade approach in some depth, and briefly consider the ERC system in Section 7.4.2.4 below.

A cap-and-trade marketable emission permits scheme *for a uniformly mixing pollutant* involves:[13]

- A decision as to the total quantity of emissions that is to be allowed (the 'cap'). The total amount of permits issued (measured in units of pollution) should be equal to that target level of emissions.
- A rule which states that no firm is allowed to emit pollution (of the designated type) beyond the quantity of emission permits it possesses.
- A system whereby actual emissions are monitored, and penalties – of sufficient deterrent power – are applied to sources which emit in excess of the quantity of permits they hold.
- A choice by the control authority over how the total quantity of emission permits is to be initially allocated between potential polluters.
- A guarantee that emission permits can be freely traded between firms at whichever price is agreed for that trade.

---

[13] We deal with marketable permits for non-uniformly-mixing pollutants in Section 7.5.3.

Marketable permit schemes differ from tax or subsidy schemes by working in terms of quantities rather than prices. But this feature is also true for command and control instruments such as quotas, licences and standards. The distinguishing feature is the transferability of permits between individual sources in the marketable permits case. Permit trading is not allowed in command and control licence systems.

It is the exchange process that generates the attractive qualities of the marketable permit system. In effect, tradability creates a market in the right to pollute. In that market, the right to pollute will have a value, given by the prevailing market price. So the decision to pollute generates an opportunity cost. By emitting an extra unit of the pollutant, one unit of permit is used up and so cannot be sold to another firm. The firm incurs a cost in emitting each unit of the pollutant, that cost being the current market permit price. Intuitively, this suggests that a marketable permit system should be equivalent (at least in some ways) to a tax or subsidy system, provided the permit price is equal to the tax or subsidy rate. As we shall see, this intuition is correct.

Let us consider how an equilibrium price might emerge in the market for permits. Suppose that permits have been allocated at no charge to firms in some arbitrary way. Once this initial allocation has taken place, firms – both those holding permits in sufficient number to cover their desired emission levels and those not holding sufficient for that purpose – will evaluate the marginal worth of permits to themselves. These valuations will differ over firms.

Some firms hold more permits than the quantity of their desired emissions (in the absence of any control). The value of a marginal permit to these firms is zero.[14] Others hold permits in quantities insufficient for the emissions that they would have chosen in the absence of the permit system. The marginal valuations of permits to these firms will depend upon their emission abatement costs. Some will have high marginal abatement costs, and so are willing to pay high prices to purchase emissions permits. Others can abate cheaply, so that they are

willing to pay only small sums to purchase permits; their marginal permit valuation is low.

Indeed, it is not necessarily the case that a firm which holds fewer permits than its desired emissions level will *buy* permits. It always has the option available to reduce its emissions to its permitted level by undertaking extra abatement. The firm may find it preferable to sell permits (rather than buy them) if the price at which they could be sold exceeds its marginal abatement cost.

In any situation where many units of a homogeneous product are held by individuals with substantially differing marginal valuations, a market for that product will emerge. In this case, the product is tradable permits, and the valuations differ because of marginal abatement cost differences between firms. Therefore, a market will become established for permits, and a single, equilibrium market price will emerge, say μ. Notice that trading does not alter the quantity of permits in existence, it merely redistributes that fixed amount between firms.

In equilibrium marginal abatement costs will be equal over all firms. It is this property of the system which ensures that transferable marketable permits, like taxes and subsidies, achieve any given target at least cost. Moreover, another equivalence arises. If the total quantity of permits issued is M^* *and* that quantity is identical to the level of emissions which would emerge from an emissions tax (or an abatement subsidy) at the rate μ^* then a marketable permit scheme will generate an equilibrium permit price μ^*. In effect, the marketable permit system is an equivalent instrument to either emissions taxes or emissions abatement subsidies. We demonstrate this result algebraically in Part 7 of Appendix 7.1.

7.4.2.1 The initial allocation of permits

The implementation of a marketable permits system requires that the EPA select a method by which the total allowable quantity of permits (the cap) is initially allocated among sources. Simplifying matters somewhat, we can envisage that it must choose one of the following:

---

[14] If permits were storable or 'bankable' so that they could be used in the future, their worth would be positive (rather than zero) as there will be some positive probability that they could be used later when the firm would otherwise have insufficient permits to cover desired emissions. But we shall leave this complication to one side for now.

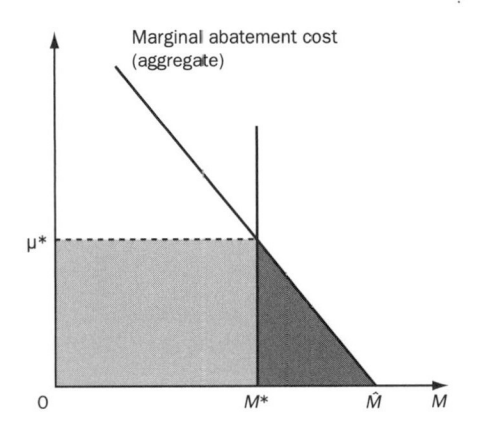

Figure 7.6 The determination of the market price of emissions permits

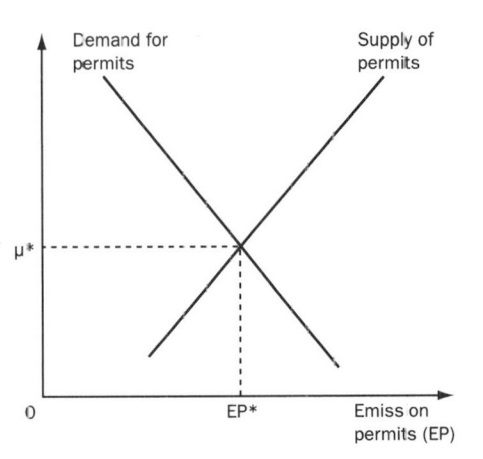

Figure 7.7 The determination of the market price of emissions permits: free initial allocation case

■ the EPA sells all permits by auction;
■ the EPA allocates all permits at no charge (which in turn requires that a distribution rule be chosen).

We shall now investigate how the market price of permits is determined in each of these two cases.

7.4.2.2 Determination of the equilibrium market price of permits

Case 1: Auctioned permits

Suppose that the permits are initially allocated through a competitive auction market. Individual firms submit bids to the EPA. When ranked in descending order of bid price, the resulting schedule can be interpreted as a market demand curve for permits. Assuming that no strategic behaviour takes place in the bidding process, this demand curve will be identical to the aggregate marginal abatement cost function.

The market equilibrium permit price is determined by the value of the aggregate marginal abatement cost at the level of abatement implied by the total number of issued permits.[15] This is illustrated in Figure 7.6. The demand curve for permits is the aggregate marginal abatement cost function for all polluting firms. The total number of permits (allowed emissions) is M^*. Given this quantity of permits, the

market price for permits will be μ^*. Firms collectively are required to reduce emissions from $\hat{M}$ to M^*.

Case 2: Free initial allocation of permits on an arbitrary basis

Alternatively, the EPA may distribute the permits at no charge, and allow them to be subsequently traded in a free market. The initial allocation is unlikely to correspond to the desired (that is, profit-maximising) holdings of permits (and in aggregate, of course, is likely to be less than total desired emissions). Some firms will try to buy additional permits from others, while others will try to sell some of their initial holding. Buyers will typically be firms with relatively high marginal abatement costs, who hope to purchase additional quantities at a price less than their marginal abatement cost. Sellers will be those in an opposite position, hoping to sell some permits at a price greater than their marginal abatement cost.

In a well-functioning competitive market, the market price that would emerge in this case would be identical to that which would be established if permits were sold at a competitive auction. This is portrayed in Figure 7.7. Note that the quantity traded, EP*, is less than the number of permits issued by the EPA (M^*), because trades only take place as holdings are adjusted to desired levels.

---

[15] It is assumed here that all permits are sold at one price (the highest single price consistent with selling all permits).

It is clear that the method by which permits are initially allocated has no bearing on the amount of abatement that takes place; that depends only on the total number of permits issued. What is, perhaps, less evident is that the method of initial allocation also has no effect on the equilibrium permit price.

There is one important qualification to these remarks about permit price determination. We have assumed that the market behaves as if it were perfectly competitive. But if the polluting industry in question is dominated by a small number of firms, or if for any reason the quantity of trading is small, strategic behaviour may take place. This could happen both in permit auctions and where firms are adjusting permit holdings from their initial allocations to their profit-maximising levels. Strategic behaviour may cause the market price of permits to diverge from its competitive level.

A simple numerical illustration (which extends an example used earlier in the chapter) will help to strengthen understanding about the way that this instrument operates. Consider the information shown in Table 7.6. We suppose that the EPA selects an emissions cap – and so a total permit allocation – of 50 units. The pollutant is emitted by just two firms, A and B, and emissions abatement can only be undertaken by these firms. The EPA decides arbitrarily to allocate half of total permits to each firm, so prior to trading A and B are each allowed to emit 25 units of the pollutant. As in our earlier discussion, we assume that in the absence of any control system A would choose to emit 40 units and B 50 units.

Table 7.6 Emissions abatement data for firms A and B

	A	B	A + B
Uncontrolled emissions	40	50	90
Uncontrolled abatement	0	0	0
Efficient emissions	15	35	50
Efficient abatement	25	15	40
Initial permit allocation	25	25	50
Final permit allocation	15	35	50

Given the initial permit allocations, A must reduce emissions by 15 units and B by 25 units. It can be seen from Figure 7.8 (which reproduces exactly the abatement cost functions used previously in Figure 7.1) that A has a marginal abatement cost of 45 and B a marginal abatement cost of 125.

The fact that firm A has lower marginal abatement cost than firm B after the initial permit allocation implies that the total abatement of 40 units of emission is not being achieved at least cost. Moreover, B places a much higher value on an incremental permit than does A (125 as compared with 40). Thus the two will find it mutually beneficial to trade with one another in permits. What will be the outcome of this trade? If the market behaved as if it were a competitive market, an equilibrium market price of 75 would emerge. At that price, firm B (the high-cost abater) would buy permits and A (the low-cost abater) would sell permits. In fact, A would buy 10 permits from A at 75 each, because for each of those

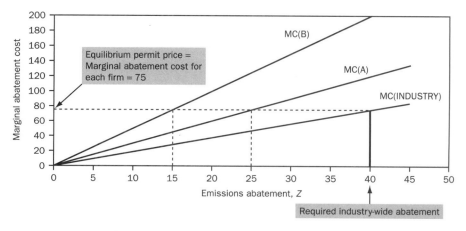

Figure 7.8 Efficient abatement with two firms and marketable permits

10 permits, it would be paying less than it would cost the firm to abate the emissions instead. Conversely, B would sell 10 permits to A at 75 each, because for each of those 10 permits, it would be receiving more than it would cost the firm to abate the emissions instead.

Trading finishes at the point where A has 15 permits (10 less than its initial allocation) and B has 35 (10 more than its initial allocation). Marginal control costs are equalised across polluters, and the total cost of abating emissions by 40 units has thereby been minimised. The permit system will, therefore, have identical effects on output and emissions as an optimal tax or subsidy system, and will be identical in terms of its cost-effectiveness property.

One other feature shown in Figure 7.8 should be noted. The line labelled MC(Industry) is the industry-wide (or aggregate) marginal cost of abatement schedule. It is obtained by summing horizontally the two firm's marginal abatement cost functions, and is given by[16]

$$\text{MC(Industry)} = \frac{15}{8}Z$$

The equilibrium permit price is found as the industry marginal cost (75) at the required level of industry abatement (40). Note that as the required abatement rises, so will the equilibrium permit price.

7.4.2.3 Marketable permit systems and the distribution of income and wealth

In a perfectly functioning marketable permit system the method of initial allocation of permits has no effect on the short-run distribution of *emissions* between firms. But it does have significant effects on the distribution of *income and wealth* between firms. If the permits are sold by competitive auction, each permit purchased will involve a payment by the acquiring firm to the EPA equal to the equilibrium permit price. A sum of money equal to μ^* multiplied by M^* will thus be transferred from businesses to government. This is shown by the lighter shaded area in Figure 7.6.

In addition to this, the emissions restrictions will impose a real resource cost (rather than a financial transfer) on firms. In terms of Figure 7.6 again, firms collectively are required to reduce emissions from $\hat{M}$ to M^* and so the real resource costs of the abatement are given by the area of the shaded triangle to the right of M^*; that is, the sum of marginal abatement costs over the interval $\hat{M}$ to M^*. If firms must initially buy the permits from the government at the price μ^* then they will collectively face a further financial burden shown by the lighter shaded area in the diagram.

Note that the transfer of income from the business sector to the government when successful bids are paid for is not a real resource cost to the economy. No resources are being used, there is simply a transfer of income between sectors of the economy. Whenever we discuss least-cost methods of abatement in this chapter, you should note that it is the real resource costs that are being minimised, not any transfer costs such as those just referred to.

If, on the other hand, the EPA distributes permits at no charge, there is no transfer of income from businesses to government. However, there will be transfers between firms. Some will buy from others and some will sell to others. So some firms will gain financially while others lose. The pattern and magnitude of these within-industry transfers will depend on the formula used to make the initial permit allocation.

But even here there is still a real resource cost to the business sector, equal once again to the triangular shaded area in Figure 7.6. That burden is the same whatever initial allocation system is used. Taking all these remarks together, it is clear that the free allocation system is more attractive to polluting firms than the auction sale of permits.

The fact that there are different net income effects means that we must introduce the same qualification we made earlier (in comparing taxes with subsidies) about long-run effects. An industry may contract in the long run if permits must be initially purchased; this effect will not be present when they are distributed at no charge.

---

[16] To obtain this, first invert the two firm's functions, giving $Z_A = (1/3)\text{MC}$ and $Z_B = (1/5)\text{MC}$. Next sum the two inverted equations to give $Z = (1/3) + (1/5))\text{MC} = (8/15)\text{MC}$. Finally, invert this summed expression to obtain $\text{MC} = (15/8)Z$.

7.4.2.4 The emission reduction credit (ERC) form of marketable permit system

Previous paragraphs have referred to a cap-and-trade permit system. A few comments are in order about the alternative ERC system. In an ERC approach, a 'business-as-usual' scenario is taken to estimate a baseline profile of relevant emissions. Emissions by any particular source above its anticipated baseline volume are subject to some non-compliance penalty. However, if a source emits less than its calculated baseline level, it earns a corresponding amount of emission reduction credits. Such credits can be sold to other sources that anticipate exceeding their baseline emission level.[17] The purchased ERCs constitute an entitlement to exceed baseline emissions without penalty.

The US emission permits scheme is a modified form of this ERC system. There, marketable permits operate in conjunction with more conventional standards or licence schemes. The United States Environmental Protection Agency (US EPA) establishes national ambient air quality or permissible water pollutant concentration standards. To attain these standards, controls – required abatement technologies or ceilings on emissions flows – are imposed on individual polluting sources. This is the conventional command and control approach that has characterised pollution control in most countries in the twentieth century. The novelty arises in the next component of the programme.

If any polluter succeeds in reducing emissions by a greater amount than is required by the standard it must satisfy, it obtains emission reduction credits of that quantity. The firm which acquires these emission reduction credits can engage in trades, selling some or all of its ERC to other firms, which then obtain a legal entitlement to emit pollutants beyond the standard which the USEPA has imposed on them. Put another way, each firm is legally entitled to emit a quantity of pollutants up to the sum of its standard entitlement plus any ERC it has acquired. Each ERC is, thus, in effect, a transferable or marketable emissions permit.

The American ERC trading system has a number of other distinctive features:

The *offset policy* allows existing firms to expand, or new firms to enter, areas in which emission standards have not been met in the aggregate provided that they acquire sufficient quantities of ERC. In other words, growth can take place provided corresponding emissions reductions take place by existing firms within that area.

The *bubble policy* treats an aggregate of firms as one polluting source (as if they were enclosed in a single bubble) and requires that the bubble as a whole meets a specified standard. If that is achieved, it does not matter whether an individual source within the bubble fails to meet the firm-specific standard imposed on it.

Emissions banking allows firms to store ERC for subsequent use or sale to others.

Some additional information on the complexities of marketable permit schemes that have been used in practice is given in Box 7.8. The examples considered there also include permit schemes in which what is being 'permitted' is something other than pollution emissions.

7.5 Pollution control where damages depend on location of the emissions

We now consider instruments designed to attain pollution stock (rather than emission) targets for non-uniformly-mixing stock pollutants (non-UMP). Previous analysis has shown that in this case the spatial location of emissions is of central importance. It will be convenient to deal with the particular example of air pollution in an 'airshed' that contains several spatially distinct receptor areas and many emission sources. However, our results will apply, with suitable change of terminology, to any non-UMP.

We saw earlier that one way in which the EPA may handle these issues is by controlling *ex ante* the location of polluters and people affected by pollution. Indeed, in the very long run, the best way of dealing with this problem is likely to be zoning: prohibiting

---

[17] If banking is allowed, they may also be used by the source at a later date.

Box 7.8 Marketable permits in practice

The United States seems to have been the first country to adopt the use of marketable permits to attain environmental goals. In the case of *emissions* control, these have covered SO_2 and ozone-depleting substances (ODS), mobile-source pollutants (HC and NO_X), lead in petrol, and water quality (BOD). Marketable permit systems can now also be found in Australia (saline discharges into rivers), Canada (ODS, and pilot schemes for NO_X and VOC in Ontario), Denmark (CO_2 power plant emissions), Poland (VOC), Switzerland (NO_X and VOC) and several individual US states (NO_X and SO_2 and the use of woodstoves and fireplaces in mountainous areas).

There are also examples of marketable permit schemes for purposes other than emissions control. Often, these consist of marketable extraction, harvesting or development rights for a variety of natural resources. Examples include the Australian system of water abstraction rights, construction or development permits for land management in the USA, France (housing in the Alps) and New Zealand (housing density), and a large variety of permit systems for the harvesting of renewable resources (e.g. transferable fishing or logging quotas; several of these are described in Chapters 17 and 18).

The actual extent to which marketable emissions permit programmes have been used is limited, but has undergone considerable growth in recent years. It has been used to reduce the lead content in petrol, to control production and use of chlorofluorocarbon ozone-depleting substances, and in the 'Emissions Trading Program' for the control of volatile organic compounds, carbon monoxide, sulphur dioxide, particulates and nitrogen oxide. Details of these programmes can be found in surveys by Cropper and Oates (1992), Tietenberg (1990), Hahn (1989, 1995), Hahn and Hester (1989a, b), Opschoor and Vos (1989) and Goodstein (1995). The passage of the 1990 Amendments to the Clean Air Act has seen the United States introduce a major system of marketable permits to control sulphur emissions.

Most economists expect emissions trading to confer large efficiency gains relative to the use of command and control instruments alone. These gains arise from the reductions in overall abatement costs that trading permits. Recall from our previous discussions that high-cost abaters do less abatement and low-cost abaters do more abatement when trading of permits or ERC is allowed. Tietenberg's assessment of the performance of the emissions permit trading schemes is

- The programme has unquestionably and substantially reduced the costs of complying with the Clean Air Act. Most estimates place the accumulated capital savings for all components of the programme at over $10 billion. This does not include the recurrent savings in operating costs. On the other hand the programme has not produced the magnitude of cost savings that was anticipated by its strongest proponents at its inception.
- The level of compliance with the basic provisions of the Clean Air Act has increased. The emissions trading programme increased the possible means for compliance and sources have responded accordingly.
- The vast majority of emissions trading transactions have involved large pollution sources.
- Though air quality has certainly improved for most of the covered pollutants, it is virtually impossible to say how much of the improvement can be attributed to the emissions trading programme.

Tietenberg, in Markandya and Richardson (1992), pp. 269–270

A survey by Cropper and Oates confirms the view that the use of transferable permit programmes, and other market incentive schemes based on taxes or subsidies, has been limited in scale, but they assess that interest in and acceptability of market-based incentive instruments is growing:

effluent charges and marketable permit programs are few in number and often bear only a modest resemblance to the pure programs of economic incentives supported by economists. . . . As we move into the 1990's, the general political and policy setting is one that is genuinely receptive to market approaches to solving our social problems. Not only in the United States but in other countries as well, the prevailing atmosphere is a conservative one with a strong predisposition towards the use of market incentives wherever possible, for the attainment of our social objectives.

Cropper and Oates (1992), pp. 729, 730

An important new development was initiated at Kyoto, Japan in 1997. The industrialised countries, in agreeing to a programme of greenhouse gas emissions limits, decided that the rights to emit pollutants could be traded between nations. This scheme, which is still in the process of being implemented, is discussed at length in Chapter 10.

Sources: Tietenberg (1990), Goodstein (1995), OECD (1999)

new sources from being set up in, or near to, the air-shed, and requiring existing sources to move away from the receptor areas. But what should the EPA do when the location of polluters and people is already determined, and moving either is not a feasible option?

When the location of sources is regarded as being fixed, pollution control must work by regulating in some way the emissions from those sources so as to meet the relevant air quality standards.[18] As we have been doing throughout this chapter, it is assumed here that targets have already been set. In this case, standards will consist of maximum allowable concentration rates of the stock pollutant in each of the relevant receptor areas. These targets may be 'efficient' targets (those we analysed in Chapter 6) or they may not. To the authors' knowledge, no targets for non-UMP have ever been set in terms of economic efficiency. So it will be sensible to deal with the case of arbitrary specific targets. For simplicity, we take the target to be the same for all receptors. Finally, we assume that in pursuit of its objectives the EPA seeks to reach targets at least cost.

Let us consider each of the following three instruments in turn:

1. non-transferable emissions licences allocated to each source (a command and control approach);
2. emissions taxes or emissions abatement subsidies;
3. marketable emissions permits.

7.5.1 Using non-transferable emissions licences

The use of non-transferable emissions licences is simple in principle. All that is required is for the EPA to calculate the maximum allowable emissions from each source so that the pollution target is reached in every receptor area, *and* at minimum possible overall cost. That is, the EPA needs to solve a cost-minimisation problem. Licences can then be allocated to each source in the quantities that emerge from the solution to that problem.

In order to obtain clear, analytical results, it is necessary to take the reader through the maths of this problem. That is done in Appendix 7.1. In the main text here, we just indicate the way in which the problem is set up, and interpret the main results obtained in Appendix 7.1. An Excel workbook (*Ambient instruments.xls*) provides a worked numerical example of the problem we are investigating.

As a prelude to doing this, it will be convenient to recap the notation we use for non-UMP. The airshed being considered contains J spatially distinct pollution receptors (indexed $j = 1, 2, \ldots, J$) and N distinct pollution sources (indexed $i = 1, 2, \ldots, N$). The transfer coefficient d_{ji} describes the impact on pollutant concentration from source i in receptor j. Pollution at location j, A_j, is the sum of the contributions to pollution at that location from all N emission sources:

$$A_j = \sum_{i=1}^{N} d_{ji} M_i \tag{7.1}$$

where M_i is emissions from source i. Section 6.6 provided much of the theoretical background for the case of non-UMP, but there is one major difference of emphasis between the approach we took there and the approach we adopt here. In Chapter 6, our interest was in target choice. To find the efficient emissions target, we maximised a net benefit function. Therefore, the solutions to that exercise give us the net benefit maximising level of emissions (for each source).

However, in this chapter our interest is not in target choice but rather in instrument choice. It is assumed that targets (for pollutant stocks in each receptor area) have already been set. As far as licences are concerned, our task is to find the level of emissions from each source that minimises the overall cost of reaching those targets. For tax (subsidy) instruments, our goal is to find the tax (subsidy) rate or rates that will reach those targets at least cost. We shall also be interested in how a marketable permit system could be designed in this case.

Let A_j^* denote the EPA's target pollutant concentration at receptor j. (The symbol A can be thought

---

[18] The terms 'targets' and 'standards' are being used synonymously here.

of as ambient air quality, another expression for the concentration rate of some relevant air pollutant.) For simplicity we suppose that the target for each receptor area is the same, so that $A_j^* = A^*$ for all j. The overall goal of the EPA is that in no area should the pollutant concentration exceed A^*. That is,

$$A_j = \sum_{i=1}^{N} d_{ji}M_i \leq A^* \quad \text{for } j = 1, \ldots, J \qquad (7.2)$$

Next suppose that the EPA adopts one single criterion in pursuing its objective. It wishes to achieve the overall target (given in equation 7.2) at least cost. The solution (as we show in Part 8 of Appendix 7.1) requires that

$$MC_i = \mu_1^* d_{1i} + \mu_2^* d_{2i} + \ldots + \mu_J^* d_{Ji}, \, i = 1, 2, \ldots, N \qquad (7.3)$$

where MC_i denotes the marginal abatement cost of firm i. We shall interpret equation 7.3 in a moment. Meanwhile, note that the systems 7.2 and 7.3 constitute $N + J$ equations which can be solved for the cost-minimising values of the $N + J$ unknowns (N emissions levels and J shadow prices).

To implement a non-transferable licence system to achieve the pollution targets at least cost, the N values of M_i^* need to be calculated, and licences allocated to firms accordingly. Note that even if firms have identical marginal abatement cost functions, they will *not* do equal amounts of emission abatement. This can be seen from the fact that the transfer coefficients on the right-hand side of 7.3 will vary from firm to firm. Hence the value of the whole expression on the right-hand side of 7.3 will differ between firms, and so their marginal abatement costs must differ too. That implies doing different amounts of abatement.

This may be compared with the condition that we found earlier for a uniformly mixing pollutant,

$$MC_i = \mu^*, \, i = 1, 2, \ldots, N$$

which means that the marginal cost of emissions abatement is equal over all pollution sources. Hence, if firms had identical abatement cost functions they would do identical amounts of abatement. The intuition behind the result that firms will abate to different amounts where they emit non-UMP is simple. Emissions from some sources have more damaging

consequences than emissions from others, because of the way in which emissions become distributed over the area of concern. Those sources whose emissions lead to relatively high damage should have relatively low emissions.

7.5.2 Using emissions taxes or emissions abatement subsidies

We now turn to consider a tax (or subsidy) instrument. This requires a bit more care in interpreting equation system 7.3. The μ_j^* terms that appear in each of the N equations are shadow prices. There is one of these for each receptor area. Each denotes the monetary value of a worsening of the pollution stock by one unit in that area. The d_{ij} coefficients tell us how many units pollution increases by in receptor j if emissions from source i rise by one unit. So for example $\mu_2^* d_{2i}$ gives the monetary value of damage that accrues in area 2 from an additional unit of emissions in source i. By summing these values over all source areas (that is, $\mu_1^* d_{1i} + \mu_2^* d_{2i} + \ldots + \mu_J^* d_{Ji}$) we find the total value of damage caused in all receptor areas by an additional unit of emission from i. Cost-efficiency requires that each firm pays a tax on each unit of emission, t_i, (or receives a subsidy on each unit abated, s_i) equal to the value of that damage, so we have

$$t_i = s_i = \mu_1^* d_{1i} + \mu_2^* d_{2i} + \ldots + \mu_J^* d_{Ji}$$

Note that the tax (subsidy) rate will now not be the same for each firm. This is just what we would expect for non-UMP as damage varies according to the location of emission source.

There is one important corollary of this. As tax or subsidy instruments require that rates are unique to each pollution source, one of the attractive features of these instruments (that a single rate can be applied over all polluters) no longer applies. Indeed, a single tax rate would *not* lead to a cost-effective abatement programme in this case.

If the EPA were determined to use a tax instrument, nonetheless, and tried to calculate the source-specific tax rates, it would require exactly the same amount of information as a command and control system does. In particular, it would need to know the marginal abatement cost function for every firm.

Hence a second desirable property of a tax instrument – that it does not need knowledge of an individual firm's costs – also disappears. All in all, one would expect much less use to be made of pollution tax or subsidy instruments in the case of non-uniformly-mixing air, water or ground pollution than with a uniformly mixing pollutant.

7.5.3 Using marketable emissions permits

How would marketable permits work in this case? The system – known as an ambient marketable permits or spatially differentiated system – would operate as follows:

1. Each receptor site will have a pollution concentration target. As before, we assume that this is the same for all receptors, A^*.
2. For each receptor site, the EPA must calculate how many units of emission can be allowed to arrive at that site before the pollution target is breached. More formally, it must calculate how many 'emissions permits' there can be that will allow firms to decrement (that is, worsen) ambient concentrations at that site.
3. These permits are issued to pollution sources, either by competitive auction or by free initial allocation ('grandfathering' if this is done proportionally to previous unregulated emission levels).
4. A pollution source is prohibited from making an emission to any receptor site above the quantity of permits it holds for emissions to that site. Each firm will, therefore, be required to hold a portfolio of permits to worsen concentrations at specific receptor areas.
5. A market for permits will emerge *for each receptor area*. Each polluting source will trade in many of these markets simultaneously. The results of these trades will determine a unique equilibrium price in each market.
6. Permits for each receptor area are freely marketable on a one-to-one basis, but this does not apply to permits for different receptors.

Note that 'emissions permits' have a special meaning in this context. They are not unrestricted rights to emit. Rather, they are rights to emit such that pollutant concentrations will worsen by a particular amount at a particular place. So, for example, if I want to emit one unit, and that will worsen pollution by 3 units at receptor 1 and by 4 units at receptor 2, I must buy a permit to worsen pollution (by those amounts) in each of the two markets.

How does this relate to equation 7.3? The J shadow prices μ_j^* correspond to the equilibrium permit prices in each market. At the least-cost solution, a firm will equate the marginal cost of emissions abatement with the marginal cost of not abating the emission. The right-hand side of equation 7.3 gives this latter cost, which is a weighted sum of these permit prices. The weights attached to the permit price for receptor j will be the impact that one unit of emissions has on pollutant concentration at site j. Thus the right-hand side gives the cost to the firm, in permit prices paid, for one unit of its emissions.

Clearly, the administration of an ideal least-cost marketable permit system is hugely demanding. However, it does have one major advantage over both command-and-control and tax/subsidy instruments: the EPA does not have to know the marginal abatement cost function of each firm in order to achieve the pollution targets at least cost. This is the major reason why emissions permits have attracted so much attention from economists, and why they are being introduced in practice in a form similar to that outlined above.

There are as yet no actual examples of systems that match this ideal form exactly. Existing permit systems are only approximations to the ideal type. The most important departure in practice is the absence of separate markets for permits for each receptor. (Systems in practice tend, instead, to have markets for each type of pollution generator.) You should be able to see that the absence of separate receptor markets may substantially increase the true cost of achieving pollution targets.

The extent to which an ideal least-cost marketable permit scheme would attain ambient standards at lower cost than some alternative instruments has been analysed by several authors. We outline one of these studies (Krupnick, 1986) in Box 7.9. Krupnick's study also highlights another matter of considerable importance: abatement costs can rise very sharply as the desired targets are progressively tightened.

Box 7.9 Costs of alternative policies for the control of nitrogen dioxide in Baltimore

Nitrogen dioxide (NO_2) is a good example of a non-uniformly-mixing pollutant. Alan Krupnick (1986) investigated the cost of meeting alternative one-hour NO_2 standards in the Baltimore area of the United States. He compared a variety of control programmes applied to 200 large emission point sources in the area. He identified 404 separate receptor areas in the region. Krupnick considered three alternative standards applied for each receptor area: 250, 375 and 500 µg/m³ control.

Simulation techniques are used to estimate total abatement costs for each of several different policy instruments. We deal here with four of the cases that Krupnick investigated:

- the least-cost instrument: a spatially differentiated ambient-pollution marketable permits scheme of the type discussed in the text;
- a type-specific fee: an effluent charge with charges differentiated by source type (but not by receptor areas impacted);
- a uniform fee: an effluent charge not differentiated by source type (nor location of impact);
- a hybrid instrument, labelled RACT/least-cost: a mixture of command and control and incentive instruments. The RACT part takes the form of a technology standard ('Reasonably Available Control Technology') which is imposed on all firms. For firms that fail to meet (weaker) national air-quality standards, market incentives are used to induce further emissions reductions (the least-cost part).

The results of Krupnick's simulations (for two ambient targets) are shown in Table 7.7. Numbers not in parentheses refer to the stricter target of 250 µg/m³, those in parentheses the weaker target of 500 µg/m³. These targets were selected in view of the fact that uncontrolled emissions led to high ambient pollution levels of around 700–800 µg/m³ at several receptor sites, and technology studies suggest that targets stricter than around 190 µg/m³ are unobtainable given the presence of the existing point sources.

Comparing first the costs of attaining different targets, Krupnick notes that 'compliance costs rise steeply as the standard is tightened, regardless of the policy simulated. In the least-cost case, costs rise by a factor of 25 (from $66 000 to $1.633 million) when standards are halved (from 500 to 250 µg/m³.' The smaller proportionate increase in the hybrid case

(RACT/least-cost) is due to the fact that the technology controls imposed by RACT give the firms little additional room for manoeuvre for further cost reductions when the standard is made stricter.

Notice that the emissions reduction is relatively small for the least-cost control compared with others. This happens because the target being sought is not a given total emissions reduction but a maximum ambient pollution standard over the whole area. Several of the instruments are inefficient (in abatement cost terms) because they operate in a more uniform manner than the spatially differentiated least-cost permit method. In so doing, the optimal distribution of abatement effort is not being applied, and excessive amounts of control are being adopted on many pollution sources.

For the type-specific fee, control costs are not much larger than for the least-cost method (and are identical for the weaker control). A fee that distinguishes between different types of polluter does seem able to mimic fairly well a proper spatially differentiated permit (or tax) approach. This is reassuring, as type-specific fees are likely to be used in practice instead of least-cost ambient permit methods as a result of their much greater simplicity. In contrast, note that when a uniform fee is imposed to achieve the stricter ambient standard (and where uniformity means that no effort is made to relate the charge to impact of emissions on ambient levels at various places) control costs increase very dramatically. A uniform fee can result in the largest emission reduction, but without doing any better in terms of ambient standards, and at hugely additional cost. Note, finally, that a single market emissions permit system would have an identical effect to that of a uniform fee. Spatially differentiating permit markets offers huge cost savings in principle.

Table 7.7 Simulation results for the cost of meeting two ambient targets

	Emissions reduction (%)		Abatement costs $US millions/year	
Least cost (ambient permits)	32	(6)	1.663	(0.066)
Type-specific fee	34	(6)	1.719	(0.066)
RACT/least cost	42	(36)	2.200	(1.521)
Uniform fee	73	(21)	14.423	(0.224)

Source: Adapted from Krupnik (1986), Tables II and III

7.6 A comparison of the relative advantages of command and control, emissions tax, emission abatement subsidy and marketable permit instruments

In this section, we bring together a set of results obtained earlier in the chapter, and introduce a few additional results; all these are of benefit in assessing the relative merits of alternative pollution control instruments.

7.6.1 Cost-efficiency

We established earlier several results relating to cost-efficiency. To summarise, an emissions tax, emissions abatement subsidy or marketable permit system can achieve any emissions target at least cost. A command and control (CAC) regulation instrument may, but will not usually, be cost-efficient. In order to be cost-efficient, the EPA must know each polluter's marginal cost of abatement function so that an emission control can be calculated for each firm that will equalise marginal abatement costs. It is very unlikely that this requirement will be met. The conclusion we draw from this is that a command and control quantity regulation approach is inefficient relative to a tax, subsidy or marketable permit scheme, and so will achieve any specified target at a higher real cost. Some empirical evidence on this is presented in Box 7.10.

For a non-UMP, the remarks above need to be qualified. Cost-effective command and control systems, as before, require knowledge of individual firms' marginal cost of abatement functions. But so too do tax and subsidy instruments in this case. In general, only transferable permit schemes do not require that knowledge. This accords permit systems great potential advantages over others.

7.6.2 Monitoring, administering and enforcing compliance costs

Little or nothing has been said so far about the costs associated with monitoring, administering and enforcing compliance for each instrument. Yet these

---

Box 7.10 The costs of emissions abatement using command and control and market-based instruments

A substantial literature now exists on the comparative costs of attaining emissions abatement targets using traditional quantity or technology regulations – what we call command and control (CAC) instruments – and so-called market instruments (particularly emissions taxes, abatement subsidies and marketable/transferable emissions permits). Much of this literature derives from experience in the USA with these two categories of instrument. Tietenberg (1990) provides an admirable account of recent evidence on these costs. Table 7.8 reproduces one of Tietenberg's tables, showing the ratio of costs under CAC approaches to the least-cost controls (using market instruments) for air pollution control in the United States. We have examined one of these studies – that by Krupnick (1986) – in more detail in Box 7.9.

Although they can be 'best' instruments in some circumstances, such direct controls are often extremely costly. Tietenberg (1984) finds that the CAC approach costs from twice to 22 times the least-cost alternative for given degrees of control. These ratios suggest that massive cost savings might be available if market instruments were to be used in place of CAC. In his 1990 paper, Tietenberg reports estimates that compliance with the US Clean Air Act through market instruments has led to accumulated capital savings of over $10 billion. It should be pointed out, however, that most studies compare actual CAC costs with those theoretically expected under least-cost market-based instruments. In practice, one would not expect market instruments to operate at these theoretical minimum costs, and so the ratios we quoted above overstate the cost savings that would be obtained in practice by switching from CAC techniques.

Three arguments underlie the tenet that market-based incentive approaches are likely to be more efficient than regulation and control. First, markets are effective in processing information; second, market instruments tend

Box 7.10 *continued*

to result in pollution control being undertaken where that control is least costly in real terms; and third, market-based approaches generate dynamic gains through responses over time to their patterns of incentives.

However, stringent conditions are necessary for markets to guarantee efficient outcomes. Policy instrument choice takes place in a 'second-best' world, where results are much less clear. The absence of markets (including those for externalities and public goods), asymmetric information, moral hazard and other instances of market failure, all point to possible benefits of CAC-based public intervention or to the inappropriateness of complete reliance on

markets and market instruments. (See Fisher and Rothkopf (1989) for an excellent survey.)

A European example is given in the file *Agriculture.doc* in the *Additional Materials* for Chapter 7. A study by Andreasson (1990) examines the real resource costs of three different policies for reducing nitrate fertiliser use on the Swedish island of Gotland: non-marketable quotas on fertiliser use, a tax on nitrogenous fertiliser and a marketable permit system. Some additional references to studies which attempt to quantify the costs of attaining pollution standards using various instruments are given in the recommendations for further reading.

Table 7.8 Empirical studies of air pollution control

Study	Pollutants covered	Geographic area	CAC benchmark	Ratio of CAC cost to least cost
Atkinson and Lewis	Particulates	St Louis	SIP regulations	6.00[a]
Roach *et al.*	Sulphur dioxide	Four corners in Utah	SIP regulations Colorado, Arizona, and New Mexico	4.25
Hahn and Noll	Sulphates standards	Los Angeles	California emission	1.07
Krupnick	Nitrogen dioxide regulations	Baltimore	Proposed RACT	5.96[b]
Seskin *et al.*	Nitrogen dioxide regulations	Chicago	Proposed RACT	14.40[b]
McGartland	Particulates	Baltimore	SIP regulations	4.18
Spofford	Sulphur dioxide	Lower Delaware Valley	Uniform percentage regulations	1.78
	Particulates	Lower Delaware Valley	Uniform percentage regulations	22.0
Harrison	Airport noise	United States	Mandatory retrofit	1.72[c]
Maloney and Yandle	Hydrocarbons	All domestic DuPont plants	Uniform percentage reduction	4.15[d]
Palmer *et al.*	CFC emissions from non-aerosol applications	United States	Proposed standards	1.96

Notes:
CAC = command and control, the traditional regulatory approach.
SIP = state implementation plan.
RACT = reasonably available control technologies, a set of standards imposed on existing sources in non-attainment areas.
[a] Based on a 40 µg/m³ at worst receptor.
[b] Based on a short-term, one-hour average of 250 µg/m³.
[c] Because it is a benefit–cost study instead of a cost-effectiveness study the Harrison comparison of the command and control approach with the least-cost allocation involves different benefit levels. Specifically, the benefit levels associated with the least-cost allocation are only 82% of those associated with the command-and-control allocation. To produce cost estimates based on more comparable benefits, as a first approximation the least-cost allocation was divided by 0.82 and the resulting number was compared with the command-and-control cost.
[d] Based on 85% reduction of emissions from all sources.
Source: Tietenberg (1990), Table 1

costs could be quite substantial. If they are large, and if they differ significantly between instruments, these costs are likely to have an important bearing on which type of instrument is least-cost for achieving some target. One reason for the prevalence of minimum technology requirements as a pollution control instrument may be that these costs are low relative to those of instruments that try to regulate emissions output levels.

7.6.3 Long-run effects

From the point of view of the EPA, instrument selection will depend on the degree to which the amount of pollution control varies with the passage of time for any particular instrument. An important consideration concerns whether or not the long-run effect is markedly different from the short-run effect. The long-run effect of an instrument depends mainly on two things: net income effects and technological innovation effects. We consider each of these in turn.

Net income effects

Changes in net income arising from the operation of a pollution control instrument can affect the long-run industry size. We noted earlier that subsidy schemes may have the (environmentally) undesirable property of increasing the long-run size of the targeted industry through positive income effects. Similar issues were raised when we were comparing alternative methods of initially allocating marketable permits.

Of course, it is possible in principle to design control regimes that are revenue-neutral. For example, firms in a subsidised industry may be required to make lump-sum payments which sum to the total value of subsidies. This would preserve the incentive effects of subsidy systems without allowing long-run effects arising from income changes. However, it may be politically difficult to implement such a scheme, and there may be reasons why government does not wish to match receipts and payments in such a way.

Technology effects

A second route through which long-run effects may transmit is via induced impacts on the rate of tech-

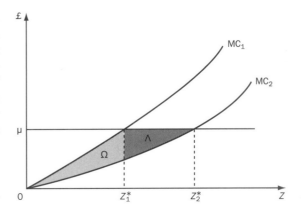

Figure 7.9 Dynamic incentives under emissions tax controls

nological innovation. There are two aspects to this. One concerns what are sometimes called *dynamic efficiency* effects. These arise from the pattern of incentives to innovate generated by a pollution control instrument. A common argument in this regard is that command and control instruments have poor long-run properties because they generate weak incentives for innovation (see, for example, Jaffe and Stavins, 1994). The binary nature of many such instruments (you reach the target or you do not reach it) creates a discrete switch in behaviour: once a required target has been obtained there is no longer any incentive to go further.

In contrast (it is argued) an emissions tax (or abatement subsidy) will generate a dynamically efficient pattern of incentives on corporate (and consumer) behaviour. The incentive structure operates to continually reward successful environmentally friendly innovation. In a market-based scheme, every unit of emissions reduction is rewarded by a tax saving. The key issue here is what incentives firms face in developing pollution-saving technology or developing new, environmentally cleaner products. Under a emissions tax scheme, these incentives may be strong, as we show in Figure 7.9.

Area Ω is the saving that would result if marginal costs were lowered from MC_1 to MC_2 and the emissions level were unchanged. But if marginal cost were lowered in this way, the firm's profit-maximising emissions abatement level would rise from Z_1^* to Z_2^*, and so an additional saving of Λ would accrue to the firm. The firm has an incentive to develop new technology to abate emission if the total costs of developing and applying the technology are less than the present value of the savings $\Omega + \Lambda$ accumulated over the life of the firm.[19] In contrast, in a CAC regulatory system, dynamic incentives are weaker or non-existent. As we said above, if a target is set in (non-marketable) quantitative terms, then once that target has been met there is little or no further incentive on the polluter to reduce emissions.

But there is a second aspect that weakens the force of these arguments. Some researchers believe that technological change can be driven from above. Suppose that the EPA identifies best-practice environmentally friendly technology, and imposes this as a requirement on firms through minimum acceptable technology regulations. Not only will this have a direct effect on spreading technology diffusion, but the indirect effects may be powerful too. Barriers due to frictions, lack of information, and other market imperfections that may lead firms to be overcautious or unable to act voluntarily no longer bite in the face of imposed requirements. Moreover, these changes have catalytic effects which set in motion spurts of innovation as learning effects occur. These kinds of arguments are likely to have most relevance for technological innovation and diffusion in developing economies.

It is difficult to arrive at unequivocal conclusions from all this. However, a reasonable conclusion must be that, in some circumstances at least, technology-based controls and other command and control instruments will have superior long-run properties to market-based instruments.

7.6.4 Double dividend

In the previous chapter, we noted the possibility that some environmental regulation schemes may generate a so-called double dividend. It seems likely that the availability and size of a double dividend will vary from one circumstance to another, and on which instrument is being used. A sensible choice of instrument should consider these matters.

7.6.5 Equity/distribution

Finally, we note that the distributional consequences of a pollution control policy instrument will be very important in determining which instruments are selected in practice. Different instruments for pollution control have different implications for the distribution of income within an economy. We have already examined the direct business financial gains and losses (which are, of course, exactly mirrored by offsetting government financial losses or gains). It is also necessary to think about the consequences for income and wealth distribution in society as a whole. For example, an emissions tax imposed upon fossil fuels will indirectly affect final consumers who purchase goods that have large energy input. Individuals for whom heating comprises a large proportion of their budget may well experience quite large falls in real income. Indeed, many kinds of 'green taxes' are likely to have regressive effects upon income distribution.

It is important to distinguish between income shifts that are merely redistributive and do not correspond to any real resource gains and losses to the economy, and real income changes which do imply real resource changes for the economy as a whole. The latter arise because pollution control does involve real costs. Of course, by having less pollution, there are benefits to be had as well, which in a well-designed pollution control programme should outweigh these real costs. Nevertheless, the beneficiaries and losers will not be the same individuals, and it is this that one is concerned with when discussing the equity or fairness of an instrument.

It should also be noted that emissions taxes (and other environmental controls) have important implications for the relative competitiveness of national economies. (See Chapter 10 for more on this.) Some analysts have advocated a switch from taxes on labour and capital to taxes on emissions to avoid excessive tax burdens, and schemes have been proposed to penalise nations that attempt to gain competitive advantage by not introducing emissions taxes. Good discussions of these issues are to be

---

[19] Note that the optimal tax rate would change as new technology lowers control costs, so matters are a little more complicated.

found in Bertram *et al.* (1989), Brown (1989), Grubb (1989a), Hansen (1990), Kosmo (1989) and Weizsäcker (1989).

As we noted earlier, where a particular instrument has an adverse financial effect on one sector of the economy, it is open to the government to use compensating fiscal changes to offset those changes so that the distribution of income and wealth between individuals is not systematically changed. For example, the financial transfers implied by a emissions tax scheme could be compensated by lump-sum payments to firms or by abatement subsidy payments. And income transfers from poorer groups facing higher energy bills, for example, could be compensated for by other fiscal changes.

The main point here is that additional tax revenues received by government could be distributed to groups adversely affected by the initial policy change. However, the difficulties in designing distributionally neutral packages are immense. Where compensation is paid to individuals or groups for whom the tax incidence is considered excessive, the form of compensation should be designed not to alter behaviour, otherwise the efficiency properties of the instrument will be adversely affected. This implies lump-sum compensation should be used where possible. Compensation schemes of this form rarely happen in practice. Nevertheless, decision makers do have this option; whether they choose to exercise it is another matter.

Summary

- An instrument that attains a pollution target at least cost is known as a cost-effective instrument.
- A least-cost control regime implies that the marginal cost of abatement is equalised over all firms undertaking pollution control.
- Bargaining processes might bring about efficient outcomes (and so might lead to the attainment of targets without regulatory intervention).
- The likelihood of efficient bargaining solutions to pollution problems being achieved is reduced by the presence of bargaining costs, and if bargaining would take place over a public (as opposed to a private) good.
- Pollution control instruments can be classified into a set of broad classes, the most important of which are command and control instruments and economic incentive-based instruments.
- In many – but not all – circumstances, economic incentive-based instruments are more cost-effective than command and control instruments.
- The long-run effects of pollution control instruments can be very different from their short-run effects, because of net income effects and impacts on the rate and direction of technological change.
- Where a pollutant is not uniformly mixing, the relative advantages of incentive-based instruments are considerably reduced. Some forms of marketable permit systems appear to offer the best prospect of attaining ambient pollution targets cost-effectively.
- Our discussion of the properties and relative advantages of various instruments that could be used to attain environmental policy targets has taken place under the implicit assumption that some single authority has the ability to implement and administer a control programme. But many pollution problems spill over national boundaries. Given that the world does not have a single government, how can policy targets and instruments be devised, introduced, administered and monitored for global or international pollution problems? This question warrants separate attention in Chapter 10.

Further reading

Where a reference is underlined below, it is available online; the URL is given in the References.

Baumol and Oates (1988) is a classic source in the area of environmental regulation. The whole book is relevant but it is quite difficult and formal. The theoretical basis for a political economy of environmental regulation is investigated in Boyer and Laffont (1999). Tietenberg (1992, chapters 14 to 20) provides an extensive and primarily descriptive coverage of specific types of pollution and the control techniques applied to each. Other good general accounts of pollution control policy are to be found in Fisher (1981, chapter 12), which discusses the work of Ronald Coase and the roles of wealth and bargaining power, Common (1995), Hartwick and Olewiler (1986) and Goodstein (1995). Fisher and Rothkopf (1989) consider the justification for public policy in terms of market failure. A possibility, that we touch upon in the next chapter, is that public intervention itself generates substantial costs. These costs may be sufficiently large to prevent intervention delivering positive net benefits. This notion of 'government failure' is analysed in Weimer and Vining (1992). Laffont and Tirole (1993, 1996) discuss the innovation incentive effects of permits when number is limited.

There are several national and international agencies that produce periodic surveys of environmental protection instruments and their effectiveness. Among these are various parts of the United Nations Organisation, the European Union, the United States EPA and the OECD. An extensive listing can be found on the Chapter 7 Links web page. References that the reader may find useful include OECD (1995), which surveys the use of environmental taxes and other charges used for environmental protection in the OECD countries; Anderson *et al.* (1997), US experience with economic incentives instruments; OECD (1997d), evaluating economic instruments for environmental policy; OECD (1999) for a detailed account of instruments used – and their effectiveness – in OECD countries; EPA (1999), economic incentives for pollution control in the USA; EPA (2001), US experience with economic incentives; EEA (2001), which considers ways of improving official environmental reporting; and

EEA (2000), an online survey of environmental taxes in the EU.

Pearce and Brisson (1993) discuss the use of command and control instruments in the UK. Bohm (1981) considers deposit refund systems. Helm (1993, 1998) discusses possible reform of environmental regulation in the UK. Smith (1998) investigates taxation of energy. Portney (1990) analyses air pollution policy in the USA, and Portney (1989) assesses the US Clean Air Act. Crandall (1992) provides an interesting analysis of the relative inefficiency of a standards-based approach to fuel efficiency in the United States. Kolstad (1987) examines the inefficiency losses associated with using undifferentiated taxes or other charges when economic efficiency requires that charges be differentiated across sources. Krupnick's (1986) paper on nitrogen dioxide control in Baltimore, discussed in the chapter, repays reading in the original.

Dales (1968) is the paper generally credited with having established the notion that marketable permits may be used for pollution control, and Montgomery (1972) derived the efficiency properties of marketable permits. For accounts of the use of market-based pollution control instruments see Hahn (1984, 1989), Hahn and Hester (1989a, b), Opschoor and Vos (1989) and Tietenberg (1990, 1992). Jorgensen and Wilcoxen (1990a, b, c) analyse the impact of environmental regulation upon economic growth in the United States (but note that these papers are relatively difficult).

The following references deal with air pollution emissions trading programmes in developing countries: Ellerman (2001), SO_2 emissions in China; Blackman and Harrington (1999); Benkovic and Kruger (2001); Montero *et al.* (2000), Chile; and several papers in the *Journal of Economic Perspectives* (Summer 1998, Vol. 12, no 3). Some general accounts of air emissions problems and policies in India are found in Bose *et al.* (1997, 1998). Cowan (1998) considers the use of economic instruments for water pollution and abstraction.

Enforcement issues and incentive compatibility (to be discussed in the next chapter) are analysed in Heyes (1998) and Laplante and Rilstone (1996). For a detailed analysis of issues concerning compensation in connection with distribution effects of tax changes, see Hartwick and Olewiler (1986, chapter 12), who also analyse the consequences of subsidies and taxes in the short run and the long run. The role and importance of non-convexities are discussed in Fisher (1981, p. 177), Portes (1970) and Baumol and Oates (1988). Second-best aspects of taxation, and possible double dividends from environmental policy, are discussed in Cremer and Gahvani (2001) and Parry *et al.* (1999).

The seminal text on non-point pollution is Russell and Shogren (1993). Others on this topic include Dosi and Tomasi (1994), Braden and Segerson (1993), Laffont (1994), Millock *et al.* (1997), Romstad *et al.* (1997), Segerson (1988) and Shogren (1993). For water pollution see Segerson (1990) and Ribaudo *et al.* (1999), and for non-point pollution from agriculture Vatn *et al.* (1997).

Useful accounts of instruments used in fisheries management include OECD (1997c) and the regular OECD publication *Review of Fisheries*, which covers changes in fishery management systems. Discussion of the idea of a safe minimum standard of conservation can be found in Bishop (1978) and Randall and Farmer (1995). The 'Blueprint' series (see, for example, Pearce, 1991a) provides a clear and simple account of the new environmental economics policy stance, in a rather ideological style. Finally, a number of texts provide collections of papers, several of which are relevant to pollution control policy: these include Bromley (1995) and, at a more rigorous level, the three 'Handbooks' edited by Kneese and Sweeney (1985a, b, 1993).

Discussion questions

1. Suppose that the EPA obtains damages from polluting firms in recompense for the damage caused by the pollution. Should the EPA distribute the moneys recovered from such damage settlements to the pollution victims? (Hint: consider, among other things, possible changes in victim behaviour in anticipation of such compensation.)

2. Consider a good whose production generates pollution damage. In what way will the effects of a tax on the output of the good differ from that of a tax on the pollutant emissions themselves? Which of the two is likely to be economically efficient? (Hint: think about substitution effects on the demand side and on the supply side.)

3. Evaluate the arguments for the use of market or incentive-based instruments versus 'command and control' instruments in the regulation of environmental externalities under conditions of certainty.

4. Discuss the scope for the allocation of private property rights to bring the privately and socially optimal levels of soil pollution into line.

5. Discuss the distributional implications of different possible methods by which marketable permits may be initially allocated.

6. Distinguish between private and public goods externalities. Discuss the likelihood of bargaining leading to an efficient allocation of resources in each case.

7. Use diagrams to contrast pollution tax instruments with marketable emission permit systems, paying particular attention to the distributional consequences of the two forms of instrument. (Assume a given, target level of pollution abatement, and that permits are initially distributed through sale in a competitive market.)

8. Discuss the efficiency properties of a pollution tax where the tax revenues are earmarked in advance for the provision of subsidies for the installation of pollution abatement equipment.

9. Suppose that a municipal authority hires a firm to collect and dispose of household waste. The firm is paid a variable fee, proportional to the quantity of waste it collects, and is charged a

fee per unit of waste disposed at a municipal waste landfill site. Households are not charged a variable fee for the amount of waste they leave for collection, instead they pay an annual fixed charge. Comment on the economic efficiency of these arrangements and suggest how efficiency gains might be obtained.

10. An interesting example of a regulatory failure relates to electricity generating stations in the UK. Several thermal power stations in the UK were required to install flue-gas desulphurisation (FGD) plant in order to meet a national standard for sulphur emissions. The power stations fitted with FGD plant are not compensated for sulphur abatement. Electricity is purchased for the national grid on a competitive bidding system. The stations fitted with FGD are unable to compete on cost with other stations without that equipment, and as a result are withdrawn entirely from the grid at some times and operate below capacity at others.

   Explain why this situation is socially inefficient, and suggest a means by which this inefficiency could be avoided.

Problems

1. Suppose that an EPA must select one instrument from two available. Two criteria matter: (a) P, the probability of the instrument attaining its target; (b) C, the proportionate saving in abatement cost incurred in using that instrument (relative to the cost using the highest-cost instrument). The EPA calculates a weighted sum (score) for each instrument, and chooses that with the highest score. Assume that the instruments have the following values for P and C:

   Instrument 1: $P = 0.9$, $C = 0.0$

   Instrument 2: $P = 0.7$, $C = 0.2$

   (i) Write an Excel spreadsheet to illustrate how the instrument choice varies with changes in the relative weights (between zero and one) attached to the two criteria. Also explore how instrument choice varies as the magnitudes of P and C for each instrument vary.

   (ii) Use an algebraic formulation of this problem to obtain expressions that allow these results to be shown analytically.

2. Using the Excel workbook *Leastcost.xls*, demonstrate that the cost penalty from sharing abatement equally between the two firms rather than using the least-cost distribution of abatement is larger the greater is the difference in the firms' abatement cost functions (as measured by the value of the slope parameter in the abatement cost functions).

3. The Coase theorem claims that a unique and efficient allocation of resources would follow from rational bargaining, irrespective of how property rights were initially allocated. Demonstrate that the distribution of net gains between bargaining parties will, in general, depend upon the initial distribution of property rights.

4. Show that a pollution tax on emissions and a subsidy to output producers for each unit of pollution reduction would, if the rates of subsidy were identical to the pollution tax rate, lead to identical outcomes in terms of the levels of output and pollution for a given sized industry. Explain why the distribution of gains and losses will usually differ, and why the long-run level of pollution abatement may differ when the industry size may change.

5. In all discussions of pollution abatement costs in this chapter, the fixed costs of pollution abatement were implicitly taken to be zero. Do any conclusions change if fixed costs are non-zero?

6. Demonstrate that in the simple special case of a uniformly mixing flow pollutant, in which the value of the damage created by the

emission is independent of the location of the emission source or the time of the emission, the tax rate should be uniform over all polluters for the tax to be an efficient instrument (that is, it will be applied at the same rate per unit of pollution on all units of the pollutant).

7. Our discussion in this chapter has shown that if the control authority does not know the marginal damage function, it will not be able to identify the economically efficient level of pollution abatement, nor the efficient tax or subsidy level. Demonstrate that
   (a) knowledge of the pollution abatement schedule alone means that it can calculate the required rate of tax to achieve any target level it wishes,
   (b) if it knew neither the marginal damage nor the marginal abatement cost schedules, then it could arbitrarily set a tax rate, confident in the knowledge that whatever level of abatement this would generate would be attained at minimum feasible cost.

8. You are given the following information:
   (a) A programme of air pollution control would reduce deaths from cancer from 1 in 8000 to 1 in 10 000 of the population.
   (b) The cost of the programme is expected to lie in the interval £2 billion (£2000 million) to £3 billion annually.
   (c) The size of the relevant population is 50 million persons.
   (d) The 'statistical value' of a human life is agreed to lie in the interval £300 000 to £5 million.

If the only benefit from the programme is the reduced risk of death from cancer, can the adoption of the programme be justified using an economic efficiency criterion?

9. In controlling emissions, there is an important difference between a command and control instrument and a tax instrument. Both require that the polluter pay the cost of attaining the emission reduction target. However, the tax instrument imposes an additional charge (on the emissions which remain at the target level of pollutions); this is not paid under a command and control regime. The failure to incorporate damage costs into the price of the product can generate distortions or inefficiencies in the economy. Kolstad (2000), from which this problem is drawn, gives an example in the paper manufacturing industry. Suppose that paper can be produced using pulp either from recycled paper (which is non-polluting) or from virgin timber (which is polluting). Compare the operation of a CAC instrument with a tax instrument applied to the manufacture of pulp from virgin timber, and show how this distorts (creates an inefficiency) in paper production.

10. This exercise involves using an Excel file to undertake some simulations regarding the relative costs of alternative instruments, and to interpret and comment on your results. Instructions for the exercise are given in *Pollution2.doc*; the Excel file is *Pollution2.xls*. Both of these can be found in the *Additional Materials* for Chapter 7.

Appendix 7.1 The least-cost theorem and pollution control instruments

This appendix is structured as follows. In Part 1, we define the notation used and set the scene for what follows. Then in Part 2 we derive a necessary condition for pollution control to be cost-effective: that is, to attain any given target at least cost. An EPA has several instruments available for attaining a pollution (or pollution abatement) target. Here we con-sider three classes of instrument: quantitative regulations (a variant of command and control) in Part 3; an emissions tax (Parts 4 and 5); an emissions abatement subsidy (Part 6); and transferable emissions permits (Part 7). Collectively, Parts 3 to 7 take the reader through what an EPA would need to know, and how it could operate each of those instruments, in order to achieve a target at least cost. Finally in Part 8, we generalise previous results to the case of a non-uniformly-mixing pollutant.

Part 1 Introduction

There are N polluting firms, indexed $i = 1, \ldots, N$. Each firm faces a fixed output price and fixed input prices, and maximises profits by an appropriate choice of output level (Q_i) and emission level (M_i). Emissions consist of a uniformly mixing pollutant, so that the source of the emission is irrelevant as far as the pollution damage is concerned.

Let $\hat{\Pi}_i$ be the maximised profit of the ith firm in the absence of any control over its emission level and in the absence of any charge for its emissions. This is its unconstrained maximum profit level. At this unconstrained profit maximum the firm's emission level is $\hat{M}_i$.

Let Π_i^* be the maximised profit of the ith firm when it is required to attain a level of emissions $M_i^* < \hat{M}_i$. This is its constrained maximum level of profits. To reduce emissions, some additional costs will have to be incurred or the firm's output level must change (or both). The constrained profit level will, therefore, be less than the unconstrained profit level. That is, $\Pi_i^* < \hat{\Pi}_i$.

We next define the firm's abatement costs, C, as constrained minus unconstrained profits:

$$C_i = \hat{\Pi}_i - \Pi_i^*$$

Abatement costs will be a function of the severity of the emissions limit the firm faces; the lower is this limit, the greater will be the firm's abatement costs. Let us suppose that this abatement cost function is quadratic. That is

$$C_i = \alpha_i - \beta_i M_i^* + \delta_i M_i^{*2} \qquad (7.4)$$

We illustrate this abatement cost function in Figure 7.10. Note that that the abatement cost function is defined only over part of the range of the quadratic function. Abatement costs are zero when the emission limit is set at $\hat{M}_i$, the level the firm would have itself chosen to emit in the absence of control. Abatement costs are maximised when $M_i^* = 0$, and so the firm is prohibited from producing any emissions.

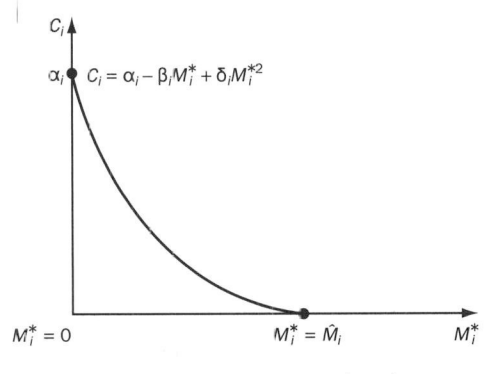

Figure 7.10 The firm's abatement cost function

Two things should be said about equation 7.4. First, as each parameter is indexed by i, abatement costs are allowed to vary over firms. Second, the arguments that follow do not depend on the abatement cost function being quadratic. We have chosen that functional form for expositional simplicity only.

Part 2 The least-cost theorem

We now consider the problem of an environmental protection agency (EPA) meeting some standard for total emissions (from all N firms) at the least cost. Let M^* denote the predetermined total emission target. In the expressions that follow, the M_i^* variables are to be interpreted as endogenous, the values for which are not predetermined but emerge from the optimising exercise being undertaken. The problem can be stated as

$$\text{Min} \sum_{i=1}^{N} C_i \text{ subject to } M^* = \sum_{i=1}^{N} M_i^* \qquad (7.5)$$

The Lagrangian for this problem is

$$L = \sum_{i=1}^{N} C_i + \mu \left(M^* - \sum_{i=1}^{N} M_i^* \right)$$

$$= \sum_{i=1}^{N} (\alpha_i - \beta_i M_i^* + \delta_i M_i^{*2}) - \mu \left(M^* - \sum_{i=1}^{N} M_i^* \right) \qquad (7.6)$$

The necessary conditions for a least-cost solution are

$$\frac{\partial L}{\partial M_i^*} = -\beta_i + 2\delta_i M_i^* + \mu^* = 0, \quad i = 1, 2, \ldots, N \qquad (7.7)$$

and

$$\frac{\partial L}{\partial \mu} = -M^* + \sum_{i=1}^{N} M_i^* = 0 \qquad (7.8)$$

Equations 7.7 and 7.8 give $N + 1$ equations in $N + 1$ unknowns. Solving these simultaneously gives each firm's emission limit, M_i^* (which now should be regarded as the *optimised* emissions limit for the firm), and the optimised shadow price of the pollution constraint (the Lagrange multiplier) μ^*. Since μ^* is constant over all firms, it can be seen from equation 7.7 that a least-cost pollution abatement programme requires that the marginal cost of abatement be equal over all firms.

There is a tricky issue relating to signs in equation 7.7. Notice that an increase in M_i^* corresponds to a relaxation of a pollution target (a decrease in required abatement) so the term $(-\beta_i + 2\delta_i M_i^*)$ is the marginal cost of a *reduction in pollution abatement* being required of firm i. It will therefore be a negative quantity. This can be verified by looking at the slope of the C_i function in Figure 7.10.

By multiplying equation 7.7 through by minus one, we obtain

$$\beta_i - 2\delta_i M_i^* = \mu^* \qquad (7.7')$$

Here the term on the left-hand side $(\beta_i - 2\delta_i M_i^*)$ is the firm's marginal cost of an increase in pollution abatement, a positive quantity. It follows from 7.7′ that μ^* is also a positive quantity. This is consistent with the text of this chapter and the previous one, and matches, for example, the graphic in Figure 7.4.

Part 3 Least-cost pollution control using quantitative regulation

If the EPA knew each firm's abatement cost function (that is, it knew C_i for $i = 1, \dots, N$), then for any total emission standard it seeks, M^*, the system of equations 7.7 and 7.8 could be solved for M_i^* for each firm. The EPA could then tell each firm how much it could emit. The total quantity of emissions would, from equation 7.8, be reached exactly, and the target would, as the above theorem shows, be attained at least cost.

Part 4 Least-cost pollution control using an emissions tax

As an alternative to setting quantitative emissions controls on each firm, an emission tax could be used. If the EPA knew each firm's abatement cost function, then for any total emission standard it seeks, M^*, the system of equations 7.7 and 7.8 could be solved for the value of the shadow price of the pollution constraint, μ^*. Note that, unlike M_i^*, this shadow price is constant for each firm. The EPA could then set a tax at a rate of t^* per unit of emissions and charge each firm this tax on each unit of pollution it emitted. Profit-maximising behaviour would then lead each firm to produce M_i^* emissions, the least-cost solution.

To see why this should be so, note that in the absence of any quantity constraint on emissions, profit-maximising behaviour in the face of an emissions tax implies that the firm will minimise the sum of its abatement costs and pollution tax costs. That is, the firm chooses M_i to minimise CT_i, the total of its abatement and tax costs:

$$CT_i = C_i + tM_i = \alpha_i - \beta_i M_i + \delta_i M_i^2 + t^* M_i$$

The necessary condition is

$$\frac{\partial CT_i}{\partial M_i} = -\beta_i + 2\delta_i M_i^* + t^* = 0, \quad i = 1, 2, \dots, N$$

$$(7.9)$$

Clearly, if t^* in equation 7.9 is set equal to μ^* in equation 7.7, the necessary conditions 7.7 and 7.9 are identical, and so the tax instrument achieves the total emissions target at least cost.

Part 5 What role is there for a tax instrument where each firm's abatement cost functions are not known?

In general, the EPA will not know abatement costs. However, if an arbitrarily chosen tax rate, say $\bar{t}$, is selected, and each firm is charged that rate on each unit of emission, then *some* total quantity of emissions, say $\bar{M}$, will be realised at least cost. Of course, that amount $\bar{M}$ will in general be different from M^*. Only if $\bar{t} = t^*$ will $\bar{M}$ be identical to M^*. An iterative, trial-and-error process of tax rate change may enable the EPA to find the necessary tax rate to achieve a specific target.

Part 6 Least-cost pollution control using an emissions-abatement subsidy

Another method of obtaining a least-cost solution to an emissions target is by use of abatement subsidies. Suppose a subsidy of s^* is paid to each firm on each unit of emissions reduction below its unconstrained profit-maximising level, $\hat{M}_i$. Then profit-maximising behaviour implies that the firm will maximise total subsidy receipts less abatement costs. That is, the firm maximises

$$CS_i = s(\hat{M}_i - M_i) - C_i = s(\hat{M}_i - M_i)$$
$$- (\alpha_i - \beta_i M_i + \delta_i M_i^2)$$

The necessary condition is

$$\frac{\partial CS_i}{\partial M_i} = \beta_i - 2\delta_i M_i^* - s = 0, \quad i = 1, 2, \ldots, N \tag{7.10}$$

which, after multiplying through by -1, is identical to equation 7.9 if $s = t$. So, once again, if s in equation 7.10 is set equal to μ^* in equation 7.7, the necessary conditions 7.7 and 7.10 are identical, and so the subsidy instrument achieves the total emissions target at least cost. Moreover, this result demonstrates that in terms of their effects on emissions, a tax rate of t per unit of emissions is identical to a subsidy rate of s per unit of emissions abatement, provided $s = t$.

Part 7 Least-cost pollution control using transferable emissions permits

Suppose that the EPA issues to each firm licences permitting L_i^0 units of emissions. Firms are allowed to trade with one another in permits. The ith firm will trade in permits so as to minimise the sum of abatement costs and trade-acquired permits:

$$CL_i = C_i + P(L_i - L_i^0)$$
$$= \alpha_i + \beta_i M_i + \delta_i M_i^2 + P(L_i - L_i^0) \tag{7.11}$$

where P is the market price of one emission permit. Given that L_i is the quantity of emissions the firm will produce after trade we can write this as

$$CL_i = C_i + P(L_i - L_i^0)$$
$$= \alpha_i - \beta_i L_i + \delta_i L_i^2 + P(L_i - L_i^0) \tag{7.12}$$

The necessary condition for minimisation is

$$\frac{\partial CL_i}{\partial L_i} = -\beta_i + 2\delta_i L_i^* + P = 0, \quad i = 1, 2, \ldots, N \tag{7.13}$$

which can be interpreted as the firm's demand function for permits.

If the EPA sets a total emissions target of M^* then M^* is the total supply of permits and

$$M^* = \sum_{i=1}^{N} L_i^0 = \frac{\partial L}{\partial \mu} = \sum_{i=1}^{N} L_i \tag{7.14}$$

Now compare equations 7.13 and 7.14 with equations 7.7 and 7.8. These are identical if $P = \mu^*$ (remembering that $L_i = M_i^*$). Moreover, comparison of equation 7.13 with equations 7.11 and 7.12 shows that $P = t = s$. So by an initial issue of permits (distributed in any way) equal to the emissions target, the EPA can realise the target at least cost. Moreover, it can do so without knowledge of individual firms' abatement cost functions.

Part 8 Least-cost abatement for a non-uniformly-mixing pollutant

The target of the EPA is now in terms of ambient pollution levels rather than emission flows. Specifically the EPA requires that

$$A_j = \sum_{i=1}^{N} d_{ji} M_i \le A_j^* \quad \text{for } j = 1, \ldots, J \tag{7.15}$$

The problem for the EPA is to attain this target at least cost. We deal with the case where the same ambient target is set for each receptor area. This problem can be stated as

$$\text{Min} \sum_{i=1}^{N} C_i \text{ subject to } A_j = \sum_{i=1}^{N} d_{ji} M_i \le A^*$$
$$\text{for } j = 1, \ldots, J \tag{7.16}$$

The Lagrangian for this problem is

$$L = \sum_{i=1}^{N} C_i - \mu_1 \left(A^* - \sum_{i=1}^{N} d_{1i} M_i \right) - \cdots$$

$$- \mu_J \left(A^* - \sum_{i=1}^{N} d_{Ji} M_i \right) \tag{7.17}$$

where $C_i = \alpha_i - \beta_i M_i + \delta_i M_i^2$

The necessary conditions for a least-cost solution are

$$\frac{\partial L}{\partial M_i^*} = -\beta_i + 2\delta_i M_i + \sum_{j=1}^{j=J} (\mu_j^* d_{ji}) = 0,$$
$$i = 1, 2, \ldots, N \tag{7.18}$$

and

$$\frac{\partial L}{\partial \mu_j} = -A^* + \sum_{i=1}^{N} d_{ji} M_i = 0 \quad \text{for } j = 1, \ldots, J \tag{7.19}$$

The system of equations 7.18 and 7.19 consists of $N + J$ equations which can be solved for the $N + J$ unknowns ($M_i^*, i = 1, \ldots, N$ and $\mu_j^*, j = 1, \ldots, J$).

Equation 7.18 can be written as

$$-\beta_i + 2\delta_i M_i = -\sum_{j=1}^{j=J} (\mu_j^* d_{ji}), \quad i = 1, 2, \ldots, N \tag{7.20}$$

Then after multiplying through by -1, using MC_i to denote the ith firm's marginal cost of abatement, and expanding the sum on the right-hand side, we obtain

$$MC_i = \mu_1^* d_{1i} + \mu_2^* d_{2i} + \ldots + \mu_J^* d_{Ji},$$
$$i = 1, 2, \ldots, N \tag{7.21}$$

The pair of equations 7.20 and 7.21 can be compared with the solution for the uniformly mixing pollution case, equation 7.7 multiplied by -1.

CHAPTER 8

Pollution policy with imperfect information

It surely goes without saying that the real world of resource and environmental economics is an uncertain one.

Conrad and Clark, 1987, p. 176

Learning objectives

Having read this chapter, the reader should be able to

- distinguish between uncertainty about pollution abatement costs and pollution damages
- understand the concept of efficiency losses arising from making decisions under conditions of uncertainty
- appreciate why all types of pollution control instrument will, in general, generate efficiency losses under uncertainty
- analyse how the choice of pollution control instrument might depend on the relative slopes of control cost and damage functions, and so discuss the comparative merits of alternative instruments
- appreciate some of the implications of non-linearity or threshold effects in emissions damage functions for pollution control programmes
- recognise the conceptual difference between an efficiency loss arising from pursuit of an inefficient target, and an inefficiency loss from not achieving pollution reductions at least cost
- understand some consequences of asymmetry of information between the EPA, as regulator, and the regulated parties
- explain how, at least in principle, an EPA may elicit private ('inside') information about emissions abatement costs from regulated businesses
- understand the idea of the precautionary principle, and how it might be applied in the case of pollution control policy

Introduction

An environmental protection agency (EPA) will, in practice, find itself in the position of having to make choices with only limited information. In this chapter we cluster together a set of issues that are all relevant to making choices about pollution control under conditions of imperfect information.

The words *risk* and *uncertainty* are often used to characterise various situations in which less than complete information is available. Risk is usually taken to mean situations in which some chance process is taking place in which the set of possible outcomes is known and probabilities can be attached to each possible outcome. However, it is not known which possible outcome will occur. Alternatively, all that may be known is what could occur (but not probabilities), a situation often described as uncertainty. A more extreme case – sometimes called radical uncertainty – concerns circumstances in which it would not be possible even to enumerate all the possible outcomes.

It will not be necessary in this chapter to differentiate sharply between these (and other possible) types of limited information. We shall often refer to them all by the generic term 'uncertainty'. Later in the text, in Chapter 13, it will be necessary to be more precise in the language used, and so more complete definitions will be given for the various forms of uncertainty.

In this chapter we shall be concerned with *choices* that the EPA has to make. Those choices may concern what kinds of pollution to control and by how much to reduce pollution (pollution targets) or they may be about how to achieve those goals (pollution instruments). In particular, it is the consequences of making those choices under conditions of uncertainty that is of central focus here. Our presentation follows the sequence of topics in the previous two chapters: Sections 8.1 and 8.2 largely concern target choices, while the following section is mainly about instrument choices. However, as you will see, the independence of targets and instruments – where it is legitimate to first establish a target *without* regard to the instrument or instruments available for its implementation and *then* select an instrument to attain that target – is difficult to maintain where information is imperfect.

More specifically, Section 8.1 looks at the difficulties faced by an EPA in setting standards exclusively on the basis of economic efficiency in a world of imperfect information and uncertainty. Partly in response to this, but also because of concepts developed in other disciplines, we then (in Section 8.2) discuss the use of some form of precautionary principle as a basis for pollution control policy. The importance of the precautionary principle is such that we shall not complete our analysis of it in this chapter; we shall return to consider this matter further at several points later in the book, particularly in Chapters 13 and 17.

Section 8.3 will have something to say about each of the following:

- the choice of pollution instrument where there is uncertainty about either pollution abatement costs or pollution damages (or both);
- implications of non-linearity or threshold effects in emissions damage functions;
- asymmetric information: where distinct groups of actors (here the EPA, as regulator, and the various regulated parties) have different sets of information available to them;
- how the EPA may improve the flows of information available to it, and in particular how it may elicit inside information about emissions abatement costs from regulated businesses.

Finally, Section 8.4 investigates the causes and consequences of regulatory failure. This is a situation in which public policy that is intended to bring about efficiency gains or achieve other stated objectives either fails to realise those gains to any large extent or, in extreme cases, leads to outcomes which are worse than the pre-regulation state of affairs.

8.1 Difficulties in identifying pollution targets in the context of limited information and uncertainty

In discussing efficiency-based pollution targets in Chapter 6, we implicitly assumed that the policy maker was well informed, and so either knew – or by an investment of resources could discover – the relevant cost and benefit functions. Is this assumption reasonable? To try and answer this question, it is useful to begin by listing what the policy maker needs to know (or have reliable estimates of) in order to identify economically efficient emission or pollution targets.

The environmental agency must know the functional forms, and parameter values, of all the relevant functions for the pollution problem being considered. In particular, knowledge of the benefits and damages of pollution (or the costs and benefits of pollution abatement) is required. Moreover, as we showed in our treatment of convexity, it is not sufficient to know the values of such things near the current position; they have to be known across the whole range of possibilities.

Further, while it is pedagogically convenient to write about 'pollution' as if it were a single, homogeneous thing, it is clear that 'pollution problems' come in many distinct forms. Even for one type of pollutant, we have seen (in Chapter 6) that stock effects and spatial considerations imply that the appropriate functions vary from place to place and from time to time. Clearly, knowledge is required about a large number of functions, and it is not evident that knowledge about one case can easily be transferred to other cases.

Where does information about marginal costs and benefits of pollution abatement come from? Section 6.12 outlined some of the ways in which the marginal costs of pollution abatement can be estimated. In a world of certainty, the word 'estimation' is not really appropriate: identification of marginal costs would be a simple matter of collating and processing known information, and the standard error of the resulting quantities would be zero. Estimation *per se* only becomes necessary where the information available to the regulator is imperfect. This, of course, is the normal state of affairs. Relevant information is decentralised, and those who possess it may have incentives not to truthfully reveal it. (We discuss these incentives later in the chapter.) There are costs in acquiring, collating, validating and processing information, and these costs imply that it will not be efficient to search for information until all uncertainties are resolved.

The benefits of pollution abatement are principally avoided damages. Identifying abatement benefits typically involves a two-step process. First, the impacts of abatement have to be established. Second, monetary valuations are put on those impacts. Two chapters of this book are devoted to the issue of valuation of environmental damage under conditions of certainty (Chapter 12) and uncertainty (Chapter 13), and so we shall not investigate the topic of marginal abatement benefit estimation here.

These processes are, once again, normally done in the context of imperfect information. This is most evident in the first stage. Scientific knowledge about pollution impacts is far from complete, and arguably can never be complete because of the stochastic, complex nature of ecosystem functioning. Hence we cannot be sure about the biological, ecological, health, physical and other impacts of a pollutant. Knowledge of those impacts is not sufficient for an EPA to establish efficiency-based targets: these 'physical' units need to be given monetary values. The available evaluation procedures yield statistical estimates; point estimates are intrinsically uncertain. Moreover, as we show in Chapters 12 and 13, valuation of environmental services is beset by a host of theoretical and practical problems, and there is no consensus about the validity of current valuation techniques.

Three further complications beset policy makers. First, the relevant costs and prices (on both benefit and cost estimation sides) needed for evaluation should be those that correspond to a socially efficient outcome; these may bear little relation to observed costs and prices where the economy is a

long way from that optimum. Second, difficulties are compounded by 'second-best' considerations. If the economy suffers from other forms of market failure too, then the 'first-best' outcomes we investigated earlier are not efficient. Finally, limited information and uncertainty do not simply mean that decisions should be taken in the same way (but have less 'accuracy') as under conditions of full information. As we show in Chapter 13, there can be profound implications for appropriate decision making under conditions of risk or uncertainty.

8.2 Sustainability-based approaches to target setting and the precautionary principle

Even taking the perspective of an economist, one would be very reluctant to rely exclusively on efficiency-based targets given the difficulties identified in the last section. It seems sensible to at least give some weight to alternative approaches to pollution policy that explicit address limited information and uncertainty.

Non-economists are generally suspicious of driving policy on what are perceived as narrowly economic grounds and are critical of the importance that is often attached to efficiency by economists in thinking about pollution targets. Natural scientists, environmentalists and ecologists typically regard stability and resilience – defined in the ways we outlined in Chapters 2 and 4 – as being more fundamental objectives.

However, these objectives – on the one hand, population stability and/or ecosystem resilience, and on the other hand, maximisation of net economic benefits – are not necessarily mutually contradictory. Much of environmental economics (and, more so, ecological economics) consists of an attempted synthesis of the two. There are many ways in which that synthesis might be pursued. Several are explained in Common (2004).

Two directions that have been espoused as general guides, and which could be interpreted as being part of such an attempted synthesis, are to target policy at achieving sustainability, and to adopt some form of precautionary principle. In many respects, a sustainability approach is implied by the precautionary principle, and so we shall not address it separately here. In this section, we consider an approach to setting environmental targets or 'standards' which places less weight on economic efficiency and gives high weight to security and sustainability as policy objectives.

In a world of certainty (and so complete predictability) taking precautions would be unnecessary. But in a stochastic environment where outcomes are not certain, where processes are incompletely understood, or where non-linearities of various kinds are thought to exist, some form of 'playing safe' is sensible. The precautionary principle – in some of its guises at least – can be thought of as a hybrid criterion. It tries to bring together efficiency, sustainability, ethical and ecological principles, into a bundle that can inform target setting. Of course, in trying to do several things at the same time, it runs the risk of not doing any of them particularly well. But the approach is now being widely advocated, and we will review it later in the chapter.

Suppose, for example, that unregulated pollution levels pose threats to the quality or availability of some natural resource (such as European marine fisheries or tropical forests) or jeopardise a more broadly defined environmental or ecological system (such as a wilderness area characterised by extensive biodiversity). In such circumstances, sustainability might be regarded as of greater importance than efficiency. Of course, if efficiency and sustainability criteria yielded identical policy recommendations, their relative importance would not matter. But as our analysis in Chapter 4 suggested, and as we demonstrate more thoroughly in Chapters 14 to 18, they do not. In general, the efficiency criterion is not sufficient to guarantee the survival of a renewable resource stock or environmental system in perpetuity.

The precautionary principle can be thought of as proposing a lexicographic approach to setting targets. We regard one criterion (in this case sustainability) as being of overriding significance, and require that any target do as well as possible in terms

of this measure. If this leaves us with more than one option, then other desirable criteria can be employed (perhaps in a hierarchical way too) to choose among this restricted choice set. Alternatively, a constraint approach could be adopted: pollution policy should in general be determined using an efficiency criterion, but subject to an overriding sustainability constraint.[1]

An example of the latter kind is given in Chapter 13, where we explain the notion of a safe minimum standard (SMS) of conservation. When applied to pollution policy, the adoption of an SMS approach entails that threats to survival of valuable resource systems from pollution flows are eliminated. This is a strict interpretation of SMS. A modified SMS would eliminate the pollution flow, provided that so doing does not entail 'excessive cost'. It remains, of course, to determine what is an 'excessive cost'. This formulation of pollution policy recognises the importance of economic efficiency but accords it a lower priority than conservation when the two conflict, provided that the opportunity costs of conservation are not excessive.

This compromise between efficiency and conservation criteria implies that 'correct' levels of pollution cannot be worked out analytically. Instead, judgements will need to be made about what is reasonable uncertainty, what constitutes excessive costs, and which resources are deemed sufficiently valuable for application of the SMS criterion.

SMS is one example of a wider set of concepts that all embody some form of precautionary principle. Most statements of the precautionary principle begin with an explicit recognition of the presence of uncertainty. In most circumstances where environmental policy choices have to be made, we do not and cannot have full information. Outcomes of choices cannot be known with certainty. This is more than simply about risk; not only do we not know which outcome will occur, but also we may not know the full set of possible outcomes.[2] Given that possible outcomes may include ones which are catastrophic, in such circumstances the policy maker may choose to play safe, adopting a presumption

---

[1] The difference is that the lexicographic approach entails maximising objectives sequentially, whereas constraints only need to be satisfied.

[2] See Chapter 13 for more on the distinction between risk and uncertainty.

about not changing conditions too much from the *status quo ex ante*. This is explored at more length in Chapter 13.

8.3 The relative merits of pollution control instruments under conditions of uncertainty

Table 7.1 listed a set of criteria that could be used to appraise the relative advantages of alternative types of pollution control instruments. Five of these – cost-effectiveness, long-run effects, dynamic efficiency, ancillary benefits, and equity – were discussed in Chapter 7. We listed, but did not discuss, four others, noting that they all relate in some way to the issue of instrument choice under conditions of uncertainty.

Before we take up this thread, note that one particular kind of uncertainty did play an important role in the conclusions reached in Chapter 7. There, we recognised that the EPA is unlikely to know the marginal abatement cost functions of individual firms. Indeed, it was precisely this which allowed us to argue that economic incentive-based instruments have an important advantage over command and control regulations. Incentive-based instruments are often able to attain targets at least cost even where the regulator has no information about individual firms' abatement costs. This is not true when the EPA uses a command and control technique.

Important as that matter may be, it only deals with one, relatively narrow, facet of uncertainty. It is now time to broaden the discussion. To do so, we begin by bringing into consideration the four criteria listed in Table 7.1 that were not examined earlier. For convenience, these are restated in Table 8.1. We now examine each of them in turn.

8.3.1 Dependability of the control instrument

An instrument is dependable if it can be relied upon to achieve a predetermined target. Where the EPA has full information, each of the instruments discussed in the previous chapter has this property.

Table 8.1 Additional criteria for selection of pollution control instruments

Criterion	Brief description
Dependability	To what extent can the instrument be relied upon to achieve the target?
Flexibility	Is the instrument capable of being adapted quickly and cheaply as new information arises, as conditions change, or as targets are altered?
Costs of use under uncertainty	How large are the efficiency losses when the instrument is used with incorrect information?
Information requirements	How much information does the instrument require that the control authority possess, and what are the costs of acquiring it?

Emissions quantity controls – whether or not they are marketable – can be set directly to the targeted emissions. Price controls (emissions taxes and abatement subsidies) will also have known quantity outcomes, and so can be set at whatever level is necessary to achieve the relevant objective. For example, with full knowledge of the aggregate abatement cost function, the EPA can determine what emissions tax rate (or emissions abatement subsidy) is needed to achieve any given level of abatement. Once that tax rate is introduced, abatement takes place at the desired level, as shown in the top half of Figure 8.1. Moreover, the aggregate target would be achieved at least cost.

But now consider one particular form of imperfect information: the EPA does not know the position (location) of the aggregate emission abatement cost function with certainty. Then price-based instruments (taxes and subsidies) and quantity-based instruments (licences and marketable permits) differ. With an emissions tax the amount of abatement that results from any given rate of tax will not be certainly known, as it will depend upon the unknown position of the abatement cost function. Licences and marketable permits are dependable in terms of abatement (although there will be uncertainty about the size of abatement costs and, with marketability, the price of emissions permits).

The differing way in which abatement cost uncertainty affects taxes and marketable permits is illustrated in Figure 8.1. In the upper half of the figure, a

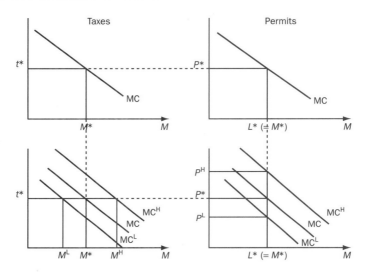

Figure 8.1 A comparison of emissions taxes and marketable emissions permits when abatement costs are uncertain

single aggregate marginal abatement cost function (MC) is drawn, assumed to be known by the authority.[3] Tax and permit regimes are identical in outcomes. Abatement cost uncertainty is represented in the lower half of the diagram by showing three different realisations of marginal abatement costs. These three curves can be thought of as three drawings from a probability distribution that describes the whole set of possible outcomes. It is evident that quantity-based controls can have very different impacts from price-based controls. In general, uncertainty about abatement costs translates into uncertainty about the quantity of abatement in a price system (such as emissions taxes or emissions abatement subsidies). It translates into uncertainties about prices or costs under a quantity-control system. For example, the aggregate marginal abatement cost and the marginal abatement costs for individual firms will be uncertain under a non-tradable permits system, or the equilibrium permit price, P, and aggregate marginal abatement cost will be uncertain under a marketable permits system.

It is sometimes claimed that command and control instruments – or more specifically emissions quotas and non-tradable licences – allow the EPA to control pollution outcomes more dependably than other instruments in situations of uncertainty. However, the preceding comments suggest that they do not have that property to any greater extent than tradable permits.[4] Moreover, some command and control instruments are clearly not dependable. The emissions outcomes from using technology requirements, for example, cannot be known *a priori*. It is evident that only emission quotas/licences or tradable permit systems can achieve emissions targets dependably in conditions of uncertainty.

8.3.2   Flexibility

Where decisions are made with perfect information, flexibility of an instrument is of little or no value. But with uncertainty, the EPA might need to learn adaptively by trial-and-error methods, and to change the rates or levels at which instruments are applied as new information arrives. Other things being equal, the more flexible an instrument is the better.

It is difficult to find any general conclusions about the relative flexibility of different instruments, as

---

[3]   As in previous chapters, we can think of a marginal abatement cost function as the profits forgone from various levels of emissions abatement. There is an opportunity cost to firms if they are required, or induced, to abate emissions, hence the use of our 'MC' terminology. Note that abatement becomes greater as we move from right to left (that is, less emissions) in the diagrams used in this chapter.

[4]   Licences may be more dependable than permits for a non-UMP pollutant where location matters, as the consequences of trading may then be unpredictable in terms of pollution concentrations.

much depends on the specific circumstances that prevail. The literature contains a number of observations, some of which we outline in this section. However, their validity, or practical usefulness, remains unclear. One common assertion is that price-based incentive instruments (that is, tax or subsidy schemes) are inflexible as there is inherently strong resistance to changes in rates. Changes in licences or permits do not seem to engender such strong resistance. Command and control regulation might also be more flexible relative to schemes that are theoretically more attractive in economic terms (such as the ambient permit system described in Chapter 7). The latter schemes might be very difficult or costly to design and, once established, will not easily admit piecemeal changes that could be done using command and control. Whether or not these assertions are empirically valid is, however, a moot point.

Another way of thinking about flexibility is in terms of whether price changes or quantity changes, brought about by new information, are socially less desirable. If the EPA judges that quantity variations are worse than price changes (perhaps because the former incur much larger transactions or adjustment costs), then instruments directed at quantities have an advantage.

Technology regulations can be inflexible in a particular way. They direct producers to do things in certain ways, and so impose large capital costs that are regulation-specific. Changes in those regulations lead to (potentially large) re-equipping or re-engineering investments. So technology requirements may be inadequate where new information is continually being obtained. Finally, we note that flexibility of an instrument is related to the transactions costs associated with its use. The greater are these costs, the less will the EPA wish to change the instrument setting. Transactions costs are discussed in Section 8.4.

8.3.3 Costs associated with uncertainty

Making choices in circumstances where everything is known or perfectly predictable is fundamentally different from making choices where that is not the case. In the former situation mistakes are avoidable, and are generated only by computational error or by limits to computational capacity. Pollution abatement will, of course, involve real resource costs as resources have to be devoted to pollution control, or techniques have to be used that would not otherwise be selected. These costs make up the abatement cost functions we have been referring to throughout this book. The regulator will also incur costs: those associated with processing information, and implementing, monitoring and enforcing the pollution control programmes.

However, in an uncertain world, decisions may have to be made before all information that is relevant to that choice is known. Not only may computational mistakes be made, but also a second class of 'error' can be made. Choices made today using available information will sometimes turn out – with the benefit of hindsight – to be less good than some other choice would have been.[5] This kind of error is unavoidable in situations of uncertainty, and is conceptually distinct from avoidable 'mistakes'. Nevertheless such errors will generate costs that are additional to those already described.

Two of these additional 'uncertainty' costs are relevant to our present discussion:

1. costs incurred as a result of the selection of incorrect targets;
2. costs incurred by failing to attain aggregate targets at least cost.

For instrument choice, it is important to have some idea about how large the costs associated with these errors might be using one instrument rather than another. If one instrument turned out to always carry greater cost-penalties from making these errors than any other instrument would, that would create a strong presumption against its use.

We begin by investigating the costs associated with (unknowingly) selecting the wrong target. These costs are known as 'efficiency losses' or 'welfare losses'. It is important to be clear about what kind of loss we have in mind here. To help understand

---

[5] There are circumstances in which it will never be known whether the choices that have been made were the best ones (or at least not until an avoidable catastrophe takes place which reveals that the choices made were not wise).

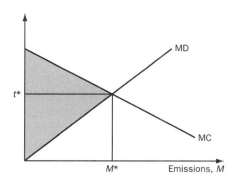

Figure 8.2 Target setting under perfect information

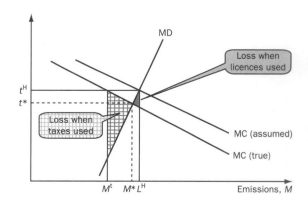

Figure 8.3 Uncertainty about abatement costs – costs overestimated

this, look at Figure 8.2. This establishes a 'baseline' against which the efficiency losses from errors due to uncertainty can be measured. The efficient target, $M*$, is that level of emissions which equates the marginal cost of emissions abatement (MC) and the marginal damage of emissions (MD). The shaded area in Figure 8.2 represents the total net social benefit that would be generated at that level of emissions. This is the maximum net benefit available. The efficiency losses we have in mind are those in which emissions are at any level other than $M*$, and so attained net benefits fall short of their maximum level.

8.3.3.1 Uncertainty about abatement costs

Uncertainty about abatement costs may result in an efficiency loss of this kind. Suppose that the EPA knows the pollution marginal damage function (MD) but has to estimate the marginal emissions abatement cost function (MC), and will often make errors in doing so. Overestimation and underestimation of abatement costs will each lead the EPA to wrongly identify the efficient level of emissions, and so to an efficiency loss. But, as we shall see, the magnitude of that loss will differ depending on which instrument the EPA chooses to use. In this section, we investigate the relative magnitudes of efficiency loss under an emission tax system and an emission licence scheme.

Figure 8.3 shows the case in which the marginal cost of abatement is overestimated. Consider first an emissions fee. On the (incorrect) assumption that the marginal abatement cost curve is the one labelled

'MC (assumed)', the EPA imposes a tax at the rate t^H (as opposed to its true efficiency level, $t*$). Firms will abate emissions as long as their actual (true) marginal abatement costs are below the tax, and so will emit at M^t, a rate less than the efficient level. The resulting efficiency loss is defined by the shortfall of net benefits at M^t compared with the maximum obtainable level at $M*$; this is indicated by the hatched area in the diagram.

Compare this efficiency loss with that which results from using an emissions licence system. Using incorrect information, the EPA believes the efficient target is L^H (when in fact it should be $M*$). Incorrect information has led the regulator to pursue an insufficiently tight control. The efficiency loss is indicated by the solidly shaded area (corresponding to the surplus of marginal damages over marginal abatement costs for the excessive units of emissions).

Of course, errors may also take the form of underestimation of abatement costs. This is represented in Figure 8.4, in which the shapes and positions of the 'true' functions are identical to those in Figure 8.3 to allow direct comparison of the two diagrams. Now the assumed marginal abatement cost curve lies below its true position. Using similar reasoning to that given above, it can be seen that an emissions tax results in a loss (shown by the hatched area) that is greater than the loss associated with licences (the solidly shaded triangle).

An incorrectly estimated abatement cost function results in an efficiency loss. In the case we have

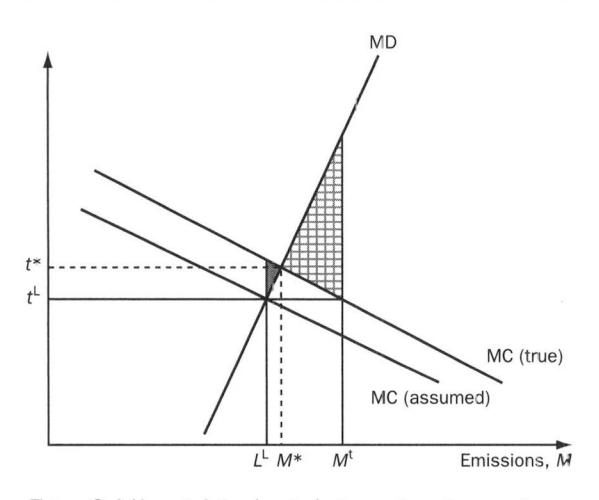

Figure 8.4 Uncertainty about abatement costs – costs underestimated

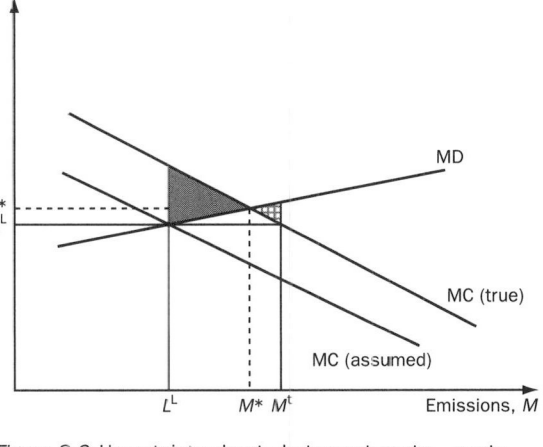

Figure 8.6 Uncertainty about abatement costs – costs underestimated

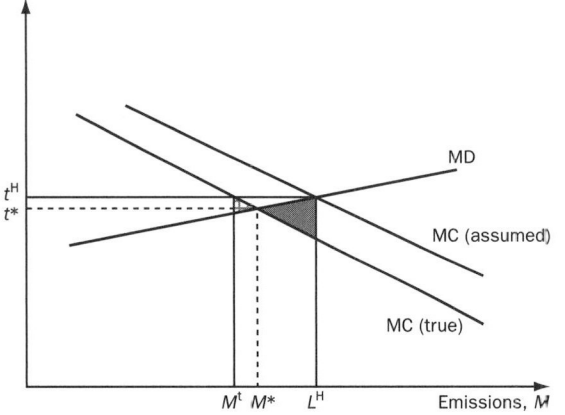

Figure 8.5 Uncertainty about abatement costs – costs overestimated

investigated, irrespective of whether the error is one of over- or underestimation, the loss from using taxes exceeds that from using licences. However, this result depends on the manner in which we constructed the functions in Figures 8.3 and 8.4. Compare these with the cases shown in Figures 8.5 and 8.6. These are analogues of the two situations just investigated, but are drawn with a substantially flatter marginal damage curve. Once again, both instruments generate efficiency losses when mistakes are made about abatement costs. But the ranking of the two instruments is now reversed: the loss is larger with licences than with a tax.

It turns out to be the case that what differentiates these two pairs of cases is the relative slopes of the MC and MD functions. We obtain the following general results:

- When the (absolute value of the) slope of the MC curve is less than the slope of the MD curve, licences are preferred to taxes (as they lead to smaller efficiency losses).
- When the (absolute value of the) slope of the MC curve is greater than the slope of the MD curve, taxes are preferred to licences (as they lead to smaller efficiency losses).

8.3.3.2 Uncertainty about pollution damages

The arguments so far have been conducted in the context of uncertainty about abatement costs. The conclusions we reached do not carry over to uncertainty about damage costs. In this case, the choice of quantity- or price-based instruments has no bearing on the magnitude of the efficiency loss arising from errors in estimating damage costs. The size of that loss is the same in each case, and so knowledge about the relative slopes of functions can give no information that would minimise such losses. This result is illustrated in Figure 8.7.

Given the estimated marginal damage function and the marginal cost function (assumed here to be correctly estimated), an EPA might set a tax at the rate t or a quantity control at the amount L. In either

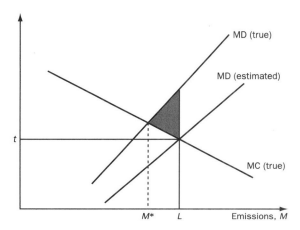

Figure 8.7 Uncertainty about damage costs – damages underestimated

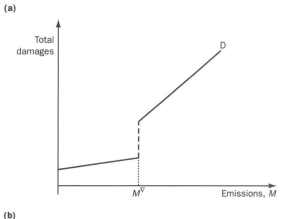

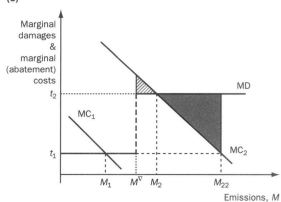

Figure 8.8 Consequences of a threshold in the damages function

case, the level of realised emissions exceeds the efficient level $M*$ and the efficiency loss associated with the erroneous target is shown by the shaded area in Figure 8.7.

The reason why errors in damage estimation and errors in abatement cost estimation have different implications concerns the behaviour of abating firms. Where errors are made on the damage side, a tax scheme and a quantity control are coincident in their effects on abatement. But where errors relate to abatement costs, the divergence between estimated costs (which determine the level of regulation imposed by the EPA) and true costs (which determine behaviour of polluting firms) drives a wedge between the realised emissions of firms under price- and quantity-based regulation.

It is important to note that the results we have derived so far relate only to a particular – and very limited – form of uncertainty, in which the general form of the damage function is known, but its position cannot be estimated with certainty. Where uncertainty about damages is of a more profound, radical form, an entirely different approach to setting targets (and choosing instruments) may be warranted, as we suggested in Section 8.2.

8.3.3.3 The consequences of a threshold effect in the pollution damage function

In this section we continue to assume that there is uncertainty about the location of the MC function,

but now assume that the pollution damage function is known to contain a threshold effect. Can any conclusions be obtained about the best choice of instrument in the case? We go through an argument used in Hartwick and Olewiler (1998) that generates some interesting insights into this question. Hartwick and Olewiler present the situation shown in Figure 8.8. The total damage function contains two linear segments, with a discontinuity ('threshold') at emission level M^∇. This total damage function corresponds to the marginal damage function portrayed in panel (b) of the diagram. As with the total function, marginal damages again exhibit a discontinuity, although they are constant above and below that discontinuity (because of the linearity of the two segments of the total damage function).

The case we investigate is one in which the EPA knows the shape and position of the marginal damage function, and so is aware that a threshold exists at $M = M^{\nabla}$. However, as in Section 8.3.3.1, the EPA is uncertain of the location of the marginal abatement cost function. Two of the many possible locations of the marginal abatement cost curve are labelled as MC_1 and MC_2. Suppose that the EPA estimates that marginal costs are given by the curve MC_1, and sets an emissions tax at the rate t_1. If the EPA's estimate of MC were true, this would yield the efficient level of emissions, M_1. Even if that estimate were incorrect by a relatively small amount that tax rate would still generate an efficient level of emissions.[6] More precisely, provided that the true value of MC is such that its intersection with MD is somewhere between $M = 0$ and $M = M^{\nabla}$, the tax rate t_1 would induce an efficient emission. Note, in contrast, that a quantity control would not have this attractive property.

However, suppose that the EPA had grossly underestimated marginal abatement costs, with the true function actually being MC_2. Inspection of the diagram makes it clear that a tax rate set at the value t_1 would lead to substantially excessive emissions. Efficient emissions would be M_2 but realised emissions are M_{22} (with an efficiency loss shown by the heavily shaded area in Figure 8.8b).

If the tax rate had been set at t_2, efficient emissions result if the true value of MC lies in the neighbourhood of MC_2, but it imposes a massively deficient emissions outcome (here zero) if MC_1 is the actual value. Overall we see that the non-linearity in damages implies that a price-based policy has attractive properties where errors are not too large. However, when the estimation error goes just beyond some critical size, the efficiency loss can switch to a very large magnitude.

We leave the reader to explore the use of quantity controls. You should find that if the EPA set a control at the quantity M_1 or M_2 (depending on which MC function it deems to be relevant), the likelihood of extremely large efficiency losses is reduced, but at the expense of losing some efficiency for relatively small errors in estimation.

Hartwick and Olewiler conjecture that a best policy in the case analysed in this section is one that combines a tax (price) control and an emissions (quantity) control. They propose a tax equal to the lower value of the MD function, and an emissions limit equal to the threshold level. The tax bites – and generates efficient emissions – if marginal abatement cost lies in the neighbourhood of MC_1. Where MC is sufficiently large to intersect MD in its upper segment, the quantity constraint bites. Such a composite policy does not eliminate efficiency losses, but it prevents such losses being excessively large. Finally, the authors argue that such a combined policy is also prudent where uncertainty surrounds the position of the MD function. We leave analysis of this case as an exercise for the reader.

8.3.3.4 General conclusions

Collecting the relevant results together, we can summarise as follows. Consider first the case where functions are linear, and uncertainty relates to the marginal abatement cost (MC) function. Then an EPA should prefer a quantity policy (licences) to an emissions tax if MC is flatter than MD, and an emissions tax to a licence system if the reverse is true, if it wishes to minimise the efficiency losses arising from incorrect information. However, where uncertainty pertains to the MD function, knowledge of relevant slopes does not contain information that is useful in this way.

Once the existence of non-linearity and/or threshold effects is admitted, general results become much harder to find. In some circumstances at least, combined tax–quantity-control programmes may have attractive properties.

It is clear that the presence of uncertainty substantially weakens the general presumption in favour of incentive-based instruments over quantitative regulations that we developed in the previous chapter. They may be better in some circumstances

---

6 This result arises from the fact that the MD curve is horizontal in this neighbourhood. If it were not, this efficiency property would not hold exactly.

but not in all. Finally, we note that experience with using taxes/subsidies or quantity controls will tend to reveal information through time that may help to reduce uncertainty. The logic behind this claim will be explained in the next section.

8.3.4   Information requirements: asymmetric information and incentive compatibility

The analysis so far in this chapter has shown that imperfect information puts restrictions on the ability of the EPA to devise 'good' targets and to attain them at least cost. It also considerably complicates its choice of instrument because comparative advantages depend on the prevailing circumstances. Moreover, limited information and uncertainty may prevent the EPA from knowing which circumstance actually pertains.

Faced with all this, there are strong incentives on the EPA to become better informed. One would expect that it would invest in systems that deliver greater information. There are three ways that the EPA might do this:

- undertake its own research to gather data;
- build long-term institutional relationships with regulated businesses;
- create reward structures that give firms incentives to reveal information truthfully to the regulator.

There are limits to how far the first two of these can be taken. Section 6.14 gave some insight into the kind of research that could be undertaken to yield estimates of abatement cost functions. Elsewhere in the book (in Chapters 10, 12 and 13) we give an indication of how research might reveal information about the benefits of pollution abatement. It is clear that undertaking (or commissioning another body to undertake) research is a costly exercise. Moreover, it is possible that, well before complete knowledge has been attained, the incremental costs of additional research activity will exceed its benefits.

The second method – building institutional relationships with polluting businesses – has much to offer, particularly in terms of the prospect of access to private company-level information. But the approach also has drawbacks. Most importantly perhaps is the possibility of 'regulatory capture', in which the relationships threaten to undermine the independence of the regulator from the regulated parties. (See Section 8.2.)

Environmental economists have focused increasingly on the third of these options, looking for 'incentive-compatible instruments'. An instrument is *incentive-compatible* if the incentives faced by those to whom the instrument applies generate behaviour compatible with the objectives of the regulator. In general, none of the instruments we have discussed so far has this property. Where polluters think that the numbers they report can influence the severity of regulation, they have an incentive to lie about the costs of complying with abatement targets. This is true whether the instrument being used is command and control, emissions tax, abatement subsidy or a marketable permit scheme.

In the following section, we illustrate two examples of such incentive effects. If firms expect tax schemes to be used they have an incentive to understate abatement costs. If they expect a marketable permit scheme, the incentive is to overstate these costs. We also outline one possible instrument – a mixture of abatement subsidy and marketable permits – that is incentive-compatible.

8.3.4.1 The incentives to be untruthful under tax and marketable permit regimes

Case 1: Firms expect a permit system to be in operation

Suppose that firms expect the EPA to use a marketable permit system. Moreover, they believe that the total number of permits issued will be equal to what the EPA estimates to be the economically efficient level of emissions. Finally, firms realise that the EPA will make its choice of permit quantity only

---

[7]   The functions shown are aggregate (industry-wide) curves, not those for a single polluter.

[8] M^* is the target if an efficiency criterion is used by the EPA. But the arguments used in this section do not depend on targets being

chosen in that way. Any upward-sloping function (replacing the marginal damage function) would generate the same results about incentives to lie.

(a)

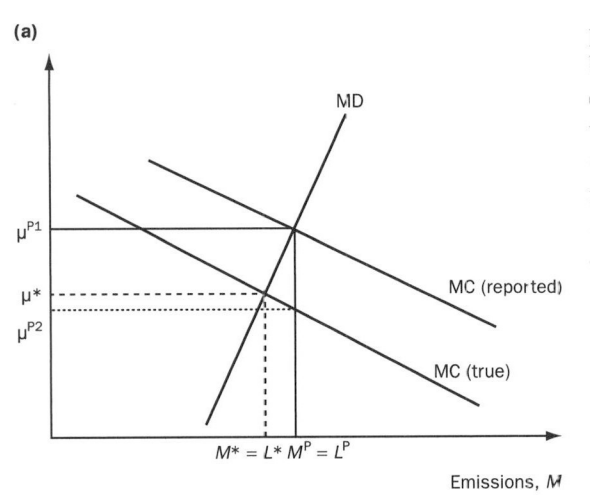

(b)

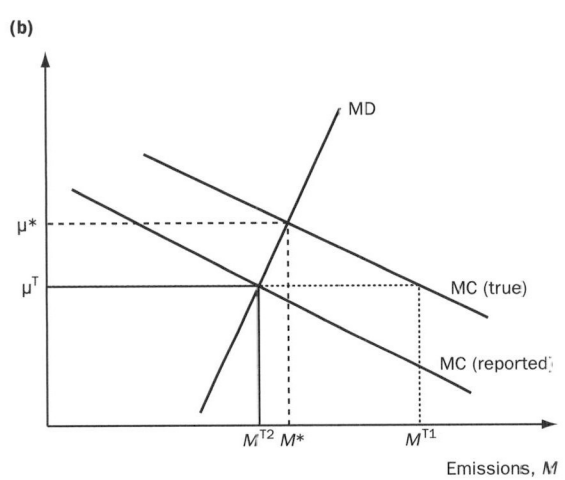

Figure 8.9 (a) Incentive effects with permit systems;
(b) Incentive effects with an emissions tax

after firms have provided the EPA with information about their emissions abatement costs.

Using Figure 8.9(a), we will show that it is in the interest of firms to exaggerate their marginal abatement costs (MC).[7] If firms honestly report their actual abatement costs, L^* permits are issued, allowing an efficient emissions level M^*.[8] In a competitive

permits market the equilibrium permit price would be μ^*. If firms lie, and overstate their abatement costs, the EPA incorrectly believes that the efficient target is M^P, and so issues that number of permits (L^P). Exaggerating abatement costs is better for firms than being truthful as more permits are issued, and so they incur lower real emission abatement costs.[9]

Note in passing a point that we will return to later, and which was alluded to earlier in remarking that the use of instruments will reveal useful information. The EPA expects the permit price to be μ^{P1}, although the actual price will turn out to be μ^{P2} (because the true marginal abatement cost function is the demand curve for permits).

Case 2: Firms expect an emissions tax to be in operation

Now we suppose that firms expect the EPA to use an emissions tax system. Equivalently to Case 1, firms expect that the EPA will set what it believes to be the efficient tax rate only after firms have informed the EPA of their abatement costs.

Figure 8.9(b) shows that firms have an incentive to understate their abatement costs. If abatement costs are reported truthfully, a tax rate of μ^* is set, leading to emissions of M^* (the efficient level). However, if firms understate their abatement costs the EPA incorrectly believes that the efficient tax rate is μ^T, and sets that rate. This results in a quantity of emissions M^{T1}. Firms benefit because they emit more than if they told the truth (and so incur lower real abatement costs). Also, the tax rate is lower than it would be otherwise.[10]

Note also that the EPA expects the quantity of emissions to be M^{T2} whereas in this scenario it will turn out to be M^{T1}. Once again, this information will prove useful to the regulator. Indeed, whether a tax or a permit system is used, untruthful behaviour is revealed after the event to the EPA. The EPA observes a difference between what it expects the permit price to be and what it actually is (or between

---

9   The size of the actual financial gain also depends on whether or not permits are initially allocated without charge. If they are, the only change to firms' financial position is the reduction in abatement costs. If the permits are purchased via auction, then there is an additional factor to take into account: the permit price is lower,

but more permits are bought. Nevertheless, firms must still gain overall.
10   The total tax bill might rise because more emissions take place; but firms must still gain overall, as one option they have available is to emit no more but pay the lower tax on those emissions.

the actual and expected levels of emissions). Moreover, it will be able to deduce in which direction abatement costs have been misreported. So one possibility open to the EPA is to adopt an iterative process, changing the number of permits it issues (or tax rate) until there is no difference between actual and expected outcomes. But this may not be politically feasible, or it may involve large costs in making successive adjustments.

8.3.4.2 An incentive-compatible instrument

Can an instrument be found which will encourage truthful behaviour *and* allow the EPA to achieve its objective? More specifically, what we are looking for here is an instrument that creates an incentive to report abatement costs truthfully and which allows the EPA to achieve whatever target it wants in a cost-effective way. Several schemes with such properties have been identified. We examine one of them, proposed by Kwerel (1977).

The scheme involves a combination of marketable permits and subsidies on 'excess' emissions reduction. Some intuition can help to understand why this will work. The costs that firms report have two effects: they influence the number of permits issued, and they also influence the subsidy received for excess emissions reduction. The scheme balances these two influences so as to reward truthful reporting.

Kwerel's scheme works in the following way. Firms are told that:

1. permits will be allocated through auction;
2. they will receive a subsidy for any emissions reduction over and above the number of permits they hold;
3. the subsidy rate will be set at the intersection of the marginal damage curve and the reported marginal abatement cost curve.

Given this information, firms are then asked to report their abatement costs, the subsidy is set accordingly, and the permit auction takes place.

The total cost of the scheme to all firms in the industry is equal to actual emission abatement cost plus the cost of acquiring permits less the subsidy payments received on any emissions reduction over and above the permitted amount of emissions. We use the following notation: L = number of permits made available to industry; P = price of permits; s = subsidy per unit of emissions reduction. Then we can write an expression for pollution abatement costs (PCC) for the whole industry.

$$\text{PCC} = \frac{\text{Abatement costs}}{\text{(area under MC curve)}} + \frac{\text{Permit costs}}{P \times L}$$
$$- \frac{\text{Emissions reduction subsidy}}{s \times (L - M)}$$

To demonstrate that this instrument is incentive-compatible, we compare the benefits to firms of being truthful with the benefits of (a) understating costs and (b) exaggerating costs.

Case 1: Firms understate abatement costs
(see Figure 8.10(a))

Understating causes permits to be scarce ($\check{L}$ rather than L^*). The permit price is driven up to $\check{P}$, the level determined by true abatement costs. Hence total costs rise because (a) fewer emissions licences means it must do more abatement (shaded area) and it has to pay a higher permit price (hatched area). The combined area of these is larger the greater is the permit price. Note that the firms' total costs are increasing in the permit price. It follows from this that firms' costs are minimised when the costs reported are actual costs, which drives the permit price down to its lowest level.

Case 2: Firms exaggerate abatement costs
(see Figure 8.10 (b))

At first sight, exaggeration of abatement costs seems to be advantageous to firms: it increases allowed emissions (to $\bar{L}$) and it increases the subsidy rate (to $\bar{s}$). But there is another factor that dominates these considerations. The existence of the subsidy, $\bar{s}$, puts a floor (a minimum level) on the permit price. That price cannot fall below $\bar{s}$. For if it began to do so, firms would buy permits in order to receive the (higher-valued) subsidy payment from holding more permits. But if the permit price is equal to $\bar{s}$, then the amount of permits actually bought will be $\bar{M}$ (even though a larger quantity $\bar{L}$ is available for purchase).

Figure 8.10(b) shows the losses that firms make as a result of exaggerating abatement costs. The shaded area is the additional abatement costs, the hatched

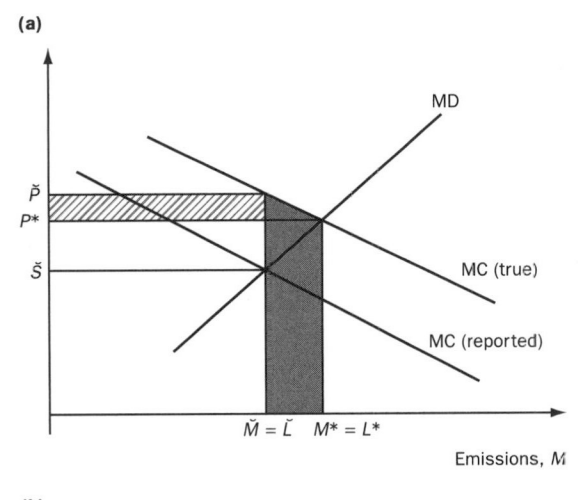

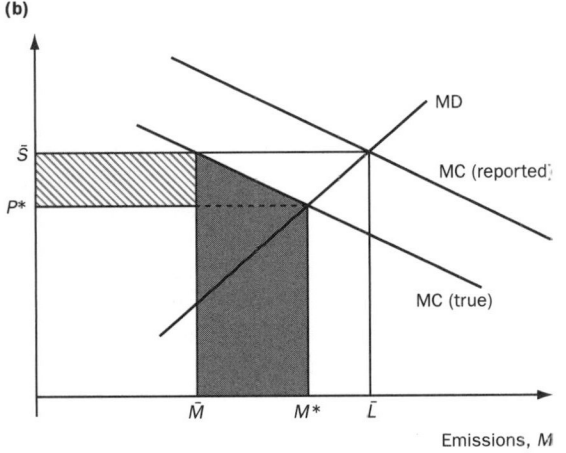

Figure 8.10 (a) An incentive-compatible instrument and under-reporting costs; (b) An incentive-compatible instrument and over-reporting costs

area is the additional price paid for permits. It can be seen that as MC (reported) goes towards MC (true), these losses disappear. The best that the firm can do is to be truthful!

8.4 Transactions costs and environmental regulation

In carrying out its responsibilities, an environmental protection agency necessarily incurs transaction costs. This is a generic term for a variety of costs that include:

- acquiring relevant information;
- creating, monitoring and enforcing contracts (of which one category is the EPA's regulations);
- establishing, implementing and revising the instruments it employs;
- monitoring performance, and ensuring compliance.

It is important to be clear about what should and should not be included in the term 'transactions costs'. They *do include* the costs of the personnel and the structures an organisation puts in place that allow it to carry out its activities, and any equivalent costs imposed on other parties, including the regulated firms or individuals. They *do not include* what are sometimes called the real resource costs of the controls – that is, the costs of pollution control equipment, higher fuel bills for cleaner fuel, more expensive exhaust systems and so on. They also *do not include* any induced indirect costs that might occur such as loss of national competitiveness or increased unemployment. Summing up all those costs gives the total compliance costs of environmental regulation. Clearly, transactions costs are just one part – albeit a not insignificant part – of that overall total.

To clarify these ideas, it is helpful to look at Figure 8.11. We assume that the marginal gross benefits of pollution abatement (the damages avoided) are correctly represented by the curve labelled as D in the picture. Curve A represents the marginal real resource costs of pollution abatement. If there were no other costs, an efficient outcome would require Z_A units of abatement. There may also be induced, indirect costs, including impacts on unemployment and trade competitiveness. Adding these to the resource abatement costs, the composite cost curve B is obtained, with a correspondingly lower efficient abatement level, Z_B. Note that Figure 8.11 assumes that these induced indirect impacts are adverse to the economy in question. It is possible, though, that they may be beneficial. Double dividend effects could be interpreted as beneficial induced effects; moreover, there are reasons for believing that tighter environmental standards – particularly minimum technological requirements – might increase the dynamic growth potential of the economy. If the induced effects were beneficial rather than adverse overall,

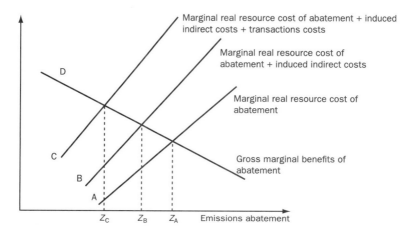

Figure 8.11 The net benefits of regulation

curve B would lie to the right (rather than to the left) of curve A.

Finally, curve C adds in transactions costs to the previous two categories of costs. The efficient abatement level, taking all relevant items of information into consideration, is Z_c. Figure 8.11 is intended only to illustrate and organise our thinking. Nevertheless, it does provide a useful way of thinking about instrument selection. Suppose that a choice of abatement target had already been made. That would then fix a particular point along the abatement axis that we are committed to reach. If we were comparing the relative merits of two instruments, we might construct two versions of Figure 8.11, one for each instrument. The preferred instrument would be the one that has the lower total cost of achieving that particular target. Even if one instrument is superior in terms of real resource cost of abatement, it need not be superior when induced effects and transactions costs are also considered.

Deviating for a moment from the main thrust of the argument, note that there is another interesting inference to be drawn from Figure 8.11. The notion that an EPA could devise an efficient target first, without consideration of instrument to be used, and then choose an instrument to best attain that target, may not be sensible. To see why, return to the idea that we might choose between instruments by constructing alternative versions of Figure 8.11, one for each instrument. It is evident that if the cost functions differ, so might the efficient abatement level.

The independence of targets from instruments does not seem to go through. This should be intuitively clear after a little reflection, or by a slight change in our argument. Suppose that under existing technology instrument I is least-cost for achieving a target Z_I. Now suppose that an innovation creates a new instrument II, that is lower cost than I. It should be selected. But if it were selected, efficient abatement would now be higher, as some units of emission that could only be abated at a marginal cost exceeding the marginal benefit would now yield positive net benefit.

Let us now return to the issue of transactions costs. These arise, principally, because of uncertainty. The greater is that uncertainty, the larger will be these costs. In practice, these costs sometimes constitute a substantial proportion of the total costs of pollution control. One estimate of the size of transaction costs, for water quality control programmes in the USA, can be deduced from the information given in Box 8.1. It is evident that transaction costs are very large in that case. Moreover, it matters greatly how well the instrument referred to there compares with other control techniques that are available. Unfortunately, the source of information for Box 8.1 did not supply such information.

At this point there is little more that can be said *a priori* about optimal instrument choice. We have seen that total control costs might differ according to which kinds of instruments are used and also what kind of pollution problem is being considered.

Box 8.1 US EPA estimates of the costs of the Clean Water TMDL programme

A recent draft report released by the US Environmental Protection Agency, in conjunction with a National Academy of Sciences study, estimated costs of the total maximum daily load (TMDL) programme, one tool used under the Clean Water Act for cleaning up United States rivers, lakes and streams. TMDLs are pollution limits set for a waterway, depending on its use. The limits are used to allocate any needed controls among all the pollutant sources, both point sources (industrial and municipal dischargers) and non-point sources (agriculture and urban runoff).

The programme could cost between $900 million and $4.3 billion dollars annually. These figures relate to programme abatement costs (that is, the costs of installing measures to reduce pollution) which would be borne primarily by dischargers, but do not include monitoring and compliance costs. These cost estimates include about 90 per cent of the waters currently on state lists for which the EPA currently has sufficient data to estimate clean-up costs. The EPA notes

that the worst-case (but highly unlikely) scenario estimate of more than $4 billion to fully implement the clean-up is a fraction of current US expenditures for clean water.

In addition to these abatement costs, the EPA estimates the costs to states of additional data gathering to support the TMDL programme at $17 million per year. Once good data have been collected, states will need to spend up to $69 million annually over the next 15 years to develop plans to clean up some 20 000 impaired waters currently on state lists. State costs to develop a clean-up plan for each of these 20 000 waters are projected to average about $52 000 per plan. The costs quoted in this paragraph comprise some (but not all) of the programme's monitoring, compliance enforcement, and other transactions costs. Clearly, such costs are not negligible relative to the abatement costs.

Source information:
US EPA Press Release 3 August 2001
A copy of the report and additional information
available online at: www.epa.gov/owow/tmdl

However, the magnitudes of transactions costs depend on prevailing circumstances, and probably have to be examined on a case-by-case basis. We have seen that economists sometimes have a presumption in favour of the use of incentive-based systems, as these can, under special circumstances, generate least-cost attainment of targets without knowledge of the cost structures of individual firms. However, arguments in this and the previous chapter have shown circumstances in which this line of reasoning may not be valid. For example, while the ambient permit system described in Chapter 7 is capable of being cost-efficient, it is likely to be very difficult or costly to design and implement where information is imperfect. Moreover, once established, it would not easily admit piecemeal changes that could be done using command and control. It is perhaps for these reasons that we rarely, if ever, find pure cases of ambient tradable permit schemes in practice.

When transactions costs are added in to relative cost comparisons, the cost-efficiency rankings of instruments may change, and it is far more difficult to reach general conclusions about the relative

merits of different instruments. For example, required minimum technology standards are quick and simple to introduce, are relatively easy to monitor, and can be implemented in flexible ways. In other words, they generate low transactions costs. Standard arguments point to the likely cost-inefficiency of technology controls, which force firms to adopt a particular method of emissions reduction irrespective of whether it is the cheapest way in which that reduction could be achieved. The cost-inefficiency referred to here concerns the real resource costs of abating pollution. However, transaction cost advantages may outweigh that real resource cost disadvantage, and make technology controls a superior option to market-based instruments.

8.4.1 Regulatory failure

In this chapter and in Chapter 7, we have discussed the properties and relative advantages of various instruments that may be used to attain environmental policy targets. Much of our discussion has been premised on the assumption that efficiency losses can be minimised, or sometimes avoided entirely, by appropriate regulatory intervention.

Yet we have also noted that regulatory intervention is not costless. Regulation incurs a variety of transactions costs. These costs have to be set against the net benefits of regulation (the gross benefits of regulation minus the real resource costs of pollution abatement and minus any induced, indirect costs). In general, the presence of transactions costs will reduce the amount of pollution abatement that is warranted (see again Figure 8.11). In extreme cases, transactions costs may be sufficiently large to completely negate the expected net gains from regulation. Put another way, regulation costs exceed the attained benefits, and so regulation would lower – rather than increase – social net benefits. This situation could be described as one of regulatory failure to signify the fact that, as with market failure,

social net benefit-maximising outcomes are not delivered.

But there are other causes of regulatory failure, two of which we finish our discussions with. First, regulatory action may also fail because of inadequate foresight or because of unintended consequences. Some interesting examples in the context of the United States Clean Air Act Amendments are outlined in Box 8.2.

Second, regulatory failure may occur because of regulatory capture. This idea is outlined in Box 8.3. Finally, the reader may have noticed that our discussion has taken place under the implicit assumption that some authority has the ability to implement and administer a coordinated control programme. But many pollution problems spill over national boundaries, and cannot be properly dealt with by any single EPA. We discuss international coordination of environmental policy in Chapter 10.

Box 8.2 Regulatory failure in the case of the United States Clean Air Act Amendments of 1970 and 1977

Some interesting examples of regulatory failure arising from inadequate foresight and unintended consequences are provided by Joskow and Schmalensee (2000) in their discussion of the control of SO_2 emissions from large electricity utility sources. The 1970 Clean Air Act Amendments (CAAA) established a system of national maximum ambient air quality standards, and gave states the principal responsibility to ensure compliance with those standards. To meet local standards, some states imposed minimum stack height requirements. While contributing to local clean-up, this did not reduce total emissions. Indeed, it almost certainly led to increased acid rain deposition (over a much wider area), as SO_2 at higher levels of the atmosphere persists longer and is a more effective precursor of acid rain formation. A second feature of the 1970 CAAA was the 'new source performance standards' (NSPS) for newly commissioned generating sources. NSPS set maximum emissions *rates*, in terms of mass of SO_2 per mass of fuel burned. These regulations created a substantial gap in allowable emissions rates between old and new plant, and so provided a powerful incentive to prolong the life of old (and dirtier) plant.

The 1977 CAAA extended the scope of emissions control and required that coal-fired plant built after 1978 meet both the 1970 emission rate requirement and either

(a) to remove 90% or more of potential SO_2 emissions, or
(b) to remove 70% or more of potential SO_2 emissions and to operate with an emissions rate no more than half of the 1970 requirement.

This was widely interpreted as a major tightening of emissions control, and was welcomed by environmentalists. However, the 'percentage reduction' component of the legislation required all generators to use flue gas desulphurisation equipment (scrubbers) *even if* they already used low-sulphur coal. This had the consequence of largely removing the cost advantage of low-sulphur coal as means of compliance. However, drawing on some observations made by Ackerman and Hassler (1981), the authors note that in spite of there now being stricter emissions limits on new sources, the 1977 CAAA probably led to greater overall air pollution by encouraging utilities to burn high-sulphur coal and by prolonging the life of old generating plant.

Box 8.3 Regulatory capture

The notion of regulatory capture is one aspect of principal–agent theory. It refers to the idea that a regulator, entrusted with the task of shaping the behaviour of economic agents so as to achieve various stated public-policy objectives, may find itself 'captured' by those whom it is supposed to regulate, and effectively becomes a means by which the latter regulate themselves in a self-serving manner.

At one level, regulatory capture is an assertion about what actually exists, or has existed at various times and places. It can also be thought of as a hypothesis about what is possible under various structures of incentives and relationships, and as a guide to how a regulatory regime might be designed to minimise the chances of those outcomes occurring.

The theoretical foundation for regulatory capture can be found in the so-called 'new political economy'. Here the policy maker is seen as making rational (optimising) choices subject to patterns of incentives and networks of pressures (Arrow, 1951; Olson, 1965). Several schools of thought have emerged within this framework, including public choice theory, in which political behaviour reflects maximisation of the probability of electoral success (Buchanan and Tullock, 1962) and the political economy of regulation (Stigler, 1971; Peltzman, 1976). A key component of the latter is the capture theory of regulation.

The major principles underlying regulatory capture can be summarised as follows. Actual or potential regulated parties (firms, let's say) may be adversely affected by regulation. Where they do stand to lose from regulatory action, firms have incentives to avert those adverse consequences. To do so, firms may be able to bring to bear on policy makers or policy administrators a variety of pressures and influences (to be outlined below). Of course, regulation in principle offers the prospect of benefiting the general public. Therefore one might expect countervailing pressure to be brought to bear by the public through electoral and other political processes.

However, the relatively small numbers of firms means that their cost of organising to bring about pressure are small relative to those of the general public. Moreover, each individual regulated party will usually have much more to lose than an individual citizen, and so has a stronger incentive to incur costs to head off that regulation.

By what means can potentially regulated firms exert pressure to manipulate policy or its implementation in their favour? There are several, including:

- Lobbying pressure in the policy-making and legislative processes.
- Funds for supporting candidates in elections or in their search for administrative office: financial contributions may buy support for future influence.
- Long-term relationships between regulators and regulated. In many command and control regimes, regulation is highly decentralised, and is reliant on flows of information that derive from continuous working relationships. In these circumstances, regulators will tend to become increasingly imbued with the corporate ethos and culture of the regulated parties.
- Revolving-door career profiles. In some cases, those in mid-career as agents of regulatory agencies secure senior positions in firms within the regulated sector, acting as directors, advisers or lobbyists. Where these career patterns become common and expected by both sides, the independence of regulators may be compromised. Sanjour (1992), safeguarded in employment in the US EPA by whistle-blower protection, provides an insider account of revolving-door career profiles and other reciprocal influence relationship positions between the EPA and the hazardous waste industry.

In the final analysis, the extent to which regulatory capture actually takes place is an empirical question. However, it is clear from these brief comments that, to the extent it does take place, regulatory capture partly involves influence at the policy- or law-making stage, and partly in the processes by which by which laws are implemented and administered. Downing (1981) provides an illuminating model of the implementation of pollution control legislation. Three groups – polluters, victims of pollution, and the regulator – participate in this regulatory game. The environmental protection agency seeks to maximise some function of three underlying objectives: environmental improvement, increased agency budget, and its discretionary power. Each of these objectives gives opportunities for networks of influence to be established.

Box 8.3 *continued*

Firms will not necessarily act in a unified way, of course. In general, each sector, region or firm is out to get as much as it can from the implementation process, and so to some degree a zero-sum game is being played out. Nor does regulatory capture necessarily reduce the extent of regulation. Milliman and Prince (1989) discuss the incentives of firms to innovate, and show that those firms that succeed in developing low-cost control innovations may lobby for greater regulation in order to gain competitive advantage. Maxwell *et al.* (1996) demonstrate that polluters may sometimes have incentive to undertake limited voluntary clean-up to head off the likelihood of pollution victims organising to press for stricter regulatory control.

Joskow and Schmalensee (2000) provide a detailed case study of the political economy of US SO$_2$ control and acid rain legislation. They argue that the 1970 and 1977 Clean Air Act legislation was

an excellent example of interest group politics mediated through legislative and regulatory processes. . . . Concentrated and well-organized interests in a few states that produced and burned high-sulfur coal were able to shape the Clean Air Act Amendments *(CAAA)* of 1970 and, particularly, 1977 to protect high-sulfur coal and impose unnecessary costs on large portions of the rest of the country.

Even with the 1990 CAAA, those states with powerfully organised Congressional presence were able to secure substantial benefits in their allocations of emissions allowances for Phase I units (the class of old and dirty electricity generators). However, the authors note that allocations for Phase II units were not consistent with simple interest-group models.

If anything, the resulting allocation of Phase II allowances appears more to be a majoritarian equilibrium than one heavily weighted towards a narrowly defined set of economic or geographical interests.

(pp. 642–643)

Summary

- Whatever criterion is used, or objective sought, setting pollution targets and choosing among pollution control instruments is made difficult by uncertainty.
- In many circumstances, the EPA will not only be unaware of the abatement costs of individual firms but it will not even know the aggregate emissions abatement cost function. It will be difficult or impossible to determine efficient targets in those circumstances.
- In a world of certainty, where the EPA knows all relevant information, no instrument has an advantage over any other in cost-efficiency terms, provided that transactions costs do not differ among instruments.
- If transactions costs do exist, and they differ from one type of instrument to another, this can be important in selection of an appropriate pollution control instrument.
- Under uncertainty, instruments differ in cost-efficiency properties.
- For uniformly mixing pollutants, economic incentive instruments have the important advantage over command and control that the EPA needs to know less in order to attain targets cost-effectively. Specifically, it does not require knowledge of individual firms' abatement costs. In contrast, an emissions tax, abatement subsidy or marketable permit scheme can be used to achieve a predetermined emissions target at least total cost with the EPA knowing only the aggregate abatement cost schedule.
- Even if the EPA did not know the aggregate abatement cost schedule, use of any of these economic-incentive instruments would achieve some target at least cost.

- Where the pollutant is not uniformly mixing, two of the three incentive-based instruments – emissions taxes and abatement subsidies – lose their relative advantage over command and control licences. Only marketable permits (in the form of an ambient permit system described in Section 7.5) allow the EPA to reach pollution targets at least cost in the absence of perfect knowledge about firms' costs.

- For linear functions, when the EPA has uncertainty about the marginal abatement cost function, it should prefer a quantity policy (licences) to an emissions tax if MC is flatter than MD, and an emissions tax to a licence system if the reverse is true, if it wishes to minimise the efficiency losses arising from incorrect information.

- While economists attach great importance to efficiency and optimality as criteria in setting policy targets, operationalising these criteria is often very difficult because of limited information and uncertainty.

- In the presence of uncertainty, it may be appropriate for pollution policy to take some account of the precautionary principle. This is likely to be particularly appropriate where uncertainty is acute, damage effects are thought to be catastrophic, and non-linearities may be present in pollution–damage relationships.

Further reading

Baumol and Oates (1988) is a classic source in the area of environmental regulation. The whole book is relevant but it is quite difficult and formal. Hartwick and Olewiler (1998) is less difficult, and contains some good expositions of policy making with imperfect information.

Two seminal works on the new political economy are Arrow (1951) and Olson (1965). The classic work in public choice theory (in which political behaviour reflects maximisation of probability of electoral success) is Buchanan and Tullock (1962). Important original works in the political economy of regulation are Stigler (1971) and Peltzman (1976). Sanjour (1992) gives an insider's account of EPA regulatory failure in relation to the US EPA and the hazardous waste industry. Downing (1981) develops a political economy model of the implementation of pollution control legislation. Milliman and Prince (1989), Salop et al. (1984) and Hackett (1995) analyse the incentives to innovate in abatement technology. Maxwell et al. (1996) argue that polluters have incentive to undertake limited voluntary clean-up to head off victims organising to press for stricter regulatory control. Joskow and Schmalensee (2000) provide a detailed analysis of the political economy of regulation for the case of the US acid rain programme. The EPA web site (at May 2002) contains an interesting set of documents relating to whether or not environmental regulation is effective and beneficial. Goodstein (1999) provides some interesting evidence regarding the 'revolving-door' effect. Government failure is the central theme of Weimer and Vining (1992).

Discussion of the idea of a safe minimum standard of conservation can be found in Bishop (1978) and Randall and Farmer (1995). Stebbing (1992) discusses the notion of a precautionary principle applied to pollution policy. A number of texts provide collections of papers, several of which are relevant to pollution control policy under imperfect information; these include Bromley (1995) and, at a more rigorous level, the three 'Handbooks' edited by Kneese and Sweeney (1985a, b, 1993).

Discussion question

1. Asymmetric information typically involves the regulator having less relevant information than the regulated parties. Find out what is meant by 'adverse selection' and show why it can lead to asymmetric information. Why does adverse selection make it difficult to regulate pollution efficiently?

Problems

1. If the control authority does not know the marginal damage function, it will not be able to identify the economically efficient level of pollution abatement, nor the efficient tax or subsidy level. Demonstrate that
   (a) knowledge of the pollution abatement cost schedule alone means that it can calculate the required rate of tax to achieve any target level it wishes;
   (b) if the regulator knew neither the marginal damage nor the marginal abatement cost schedules, then it could arbitrarily set a tax rate, confident in the knowledge that whatever level of abatement this would generate would be attained at minimum feasible cost.

2. We examined in this chapter a particular form of asymmetric information where a firm knows its emissions abatement costs but the regulator does not. The regulator must ask firms to reveal abatement costs in order to select an efficient emission reduction target. We demonstrated that where a firm expects the EPA to use a marketable permit system, it may be in the interest of firms to exaggerate their marginal abatement costs (MC). In contrast, where a firm expects the EPA to use an emissions tax, firms have an incentive to understate their abatement costs.

   Suppose that the regulator committed itself to randomly selecting either a fee or a marketable permit system (each with a probability of one-half), but only after it received cost information from firms. Would this system generate truthful reporting by firms?

3. A regulator requires a company to reduce its emissions to a level below its (pre-regulation) profit-maximising level of emissions. The requirement will be implemented by the issue of a non-transferable licence. However, imperfect monitoring means that if the firm does not adhere to the regulation, the probability of this being discovered is p, which will in general be significantly less than one. If the company is discovered to have not adhered to the licence, however, it will face a financial penalty of £x per unit emitted in excess of its allowed (licensed) amount.

   Show how the amount which it is optimal for your company to emit (i.e. the amount which will maximise your expected profits) depends on the values of p and x. Would the company's decision be different if the penalty were a fixed fine, irrespective of the magnitude of its transgression?

4. You are given the following information:
   (a) A programme of air pollution control would reduce deaths from cancer from 1 in 8000 to 1 in 10 000 of the population.
   (b) The cost of the programme is expected to lie in the interval £2 billion (£2000 million) to £3 billion annually.
   (c) The size of the relevant population is 50 million persons.
   (d) The 'statistical value' of a human life is agreed to lie in the interval £300 000 to £5 million.

   If the only benefit from the programme is the reduced risk of death from cancer, can the adoption of the programme be justified using an economic efficiency criterion?

CHAPTER 9

Economy-wide modelling

A model is simply an ordered set of assumptions about a complex system. . . . The model we have constructed is, like every other model imperfect, oversimplified, and unfinished.

Meadows *et al.* (1972) p. 20

Learning objectives

In this chapter you will
- learn about the basic input–output model of an economy and its solution
- find out how the basic input–output model can be extended to incorporate economy–environment interactions
- encounter some examples of environmental input–output models and their application
- learn how the input–output models, specified in terms of physical or constant-value flows, can be reformulated to analyse the cost and price implications of environmental policies, such as pollution taxes, and how these results can be used to investigate the distributional implications of such policies
- study the nature of computable general equilibrium (CGE) models and their application to environmental problems

Introduction

Appropriate environmental policy measures require a detailed understanding of the environmental impact of particular economic activities, and hence there is the need to model the relationships between the economy and the environment. For instance, which economic activities result in the emission of carbon dioxide, and by how much would particular economic activity levels have to be reduced to bring about a reduction of, say, 20% in CO_2 emissions? What level of 'carbon tax' would be necessary to bring about such a reduction? What would be the effects of such a tax on different types of household? For many policy purposes it is not enough to know simply the nature and direction of the changes that would be brought about by a particular measure (or by the failure to implement a measure) – a quantitative estimate of the effects of the policy (or of its absence) is needed. It is for this purpose that models of interaction between the economy and the environment are constructed.

By using models to assess and compare the simulated quantitative effects of a range of feasible policy options, governments can hope to identify the 'best' (or least bad) policy or policy mix, avoid policy combinations that are inconsistent or that work in opposite directions, and achieve some kind of optimal trade-off between different, and potentially conflicting, economic and environmental objectives[1]. Moreover, such simulation exercises underpin the formulation and implementation of proactive environmental policies, which attempt to anticipate or avoid undesirable outcomes by appropriate preventive measures. Although formal simulation

---

[1] Of course, what is optimal to a government may not seem optimal to some interest groups, such as environmentalists, or the unemployed, or the political opposition, each of whom may, and most probably will, have different social welfare functions (or different perceptions of *the* social welfare function), and will attach different weights to particular economic and environmental outcomes.

modelling is not a precondition for proactive environmental policies, it can powerfully influence public attitudes and policy making, a recent example being predictions and simulations of the effects of greenhouse gases on global warming. In the absence of quantitative models of economy–environment interaction, policy is more likely to be reactive than proactive, and may be too late if environmental damage is irreversible (for example, species extinction).

A variety of model types have been used to examine economy–environment interactions: input–output models, computable general equilibrium models, and linear and non-linear programming (optimisation) models. This chapter is largely devoted to a discussion of environmental input–output (I/O) models and their application; these have been used quite extensively in environmental economics, particularly in studies related to energy and pollution. They are the basis for computable general equilibrium (CGE) models, which will also be discussed. It must be stressed that the availability and quality of data, both economic and environmental, are serious impediments to the development of all kinds of models of links between the economy and the environment.

The following section presents and explains the basic input–output model and its solution, while the next section shows how the basic model can be extended to incorporate economy–environment interactions, and includes examples of environmental input–output models and their application. These applications are concerned with the 'real' side of the economy, that is, with physical or constant-value flows. We then show in Section 9.3 how the equations of the model can be reformulated to analyse the cost and price implications of environmental policies, such as pollution taxes, and how these results can be used to investigate the distributional implications of such policies. The last section of the chapter reviews the nature of CGE models and their application to environmental problems. The first appendix makes extensive use of matrix algebra to present a very general framework for environmental input–output analysis, while the second works through the algebra of the simple two-sector CGE model used in the final section of the chapter.

9.1 Input–output analysis

I/O models incorporate a number of simplifying assumptions which require a degree of caution in interpreting their results, but they are mathematically tractable and less demanding of data than many other multisectoral models. The basis for input–output modelling is the availability of suitable economic data, and we begin with a discussion of the accounting conventions according to which such data are made available.

9.1.1 Input–output accounting

The basis of the input–output system is the transactions table, which is essentially an extended version of the national accounts in which interindustry transactions – that is, flows of goods and services between industries – are explicitly included and indeed form the centrepiece of the system of accounts. This contrasts with the conventional national accounts in which inter-industry transactions

Table 9.1 Input–output transactions table, $ million

Sales to:		Intermediate sectors			Final demand		
	Purchases from	Agriculture	Manufacturing	Services	Households	Exports	Total output
Intermediate sectors	Agriculture	0	400	0	500	100	1000
	Manufacturing	350	0	150	800	700	2000
	Services	100	200	0	300	0	600
Primary inputs	Imports	250	600	50			
	Wages	200	500	300			
	Other value added	100	300	100			
	Total input	1000	2000	600			

are 'netted out', and the accounts record only the value added by each industry, and the value of sales to final buyers.

Table 9.1 is a hypothetical example of a transactions table, in which all production activities in the economy have been allocated to one of three sectors. Looking across any row of the table shows what the sector on the left sold to each sector at the top, for example:

$$\frac{\text{Agriculture sales}}{\text{(to)}} = \frac{0}{\text{(Agriculture)}}$$

$$+ \frac{400}{\text{(Manufacturing)}} + \frac{0}{\text{(Services)}} + \frac{500}{\text{(Households)}}$$

$$+ \frac{100}{\text{(Exports)}} = \frac{1000}{\text{(Total output)}}$$

Notice that sales are divided between those to intermediate sectors (agriculture, manufacturing and services) and to final demand (households and exports).[2]

The sum of intermediate and final sales for each sector is gross, or total, output. Again, for simplicity, we assume no government or investment expenditure, which normally would be included as additional components of final demand. Looking down any column of the table shows what the sector listed at the top purchased from each sector on the left, for example:

$$\frac{\text{Manufacturing}}{\text{purchases}} = \frac{400}{\text{(Agriculture)}} + \frac{0}{\text{(Manufacturing)}}$$

$$+ \frac{200}{\text{(Services)}} + \frac{600}{\text{(Imports)}} + \frac{500}{\text{(Wages)}} + \frac{300}{\text{(OVA)}}$$

$$= \frac{2000}{\text{(Total input)}}$$

Notice that purchases are divided between those from intermediate sectors (agriculture, manufacturing and services), and so-called 'primary input' purchases (imports, wages and other value added).

Like the national accounts, transactions tables are normally compiled on an annual basis. They are also typically expressed in value terms, in order to provide a standard unit of account across sectors, though in principle it would be possible to use sector-specific units of account (tonnes, metres, numbers, therms), or a combination of physical and monetary units.

A real transactions table will normally be larger than Table 9.1 because more sectors will be separately identified but the interpretation of it will be the same. A recently compiled input–output table for the UK, for example, contains 123 intermediate sectors, and the most recent table for the United States has 480 intermediate sectors. Tables of this size provide a highly detailed snapshot of the structure of an economy in a particular year, and show the pervasive interdependence of sectors and agents.

Because of the accounting conventions adopted in the construction of an I/O transactions table, the following will always be true:

1. For each industry: Total output ≡ Total input, that is, the sum of the elements in any row is equal to the sum of the elements in the corresponding column.
2. For the table as a whole: Total intermediate sales ≡ Total intermediate purchases, and Total final demand ≡ Total primary input

Note the use here of the identity sign, ≡, reflecting the fact that these are accounting identities, which always hold in an I/O transactions table.

The standard national income accounts can be readily derived from the input–output accounts. For example, GDP can be derived from Table 9.1

1. On the Income side as:

Wages	$1000m
+ OVA	$500m
= GDP	$1500m

or

2. On the Expenditure side as:

Household expenditure	$1600m
+ Exports	$800m
− Imports	$900m
= GDP	$1500m

---

[2]   As a further simplification, transactions between undertakings within the same sector (intra-industry transactions) have been netted out, so that the main diagonal of Table 9.1 has zeros everywhere.

Reading across rows the necessary equality of total output with the sum of its uses for each industry or sector can be written as a set of 'balance equations':

$$X_i \equiv \sum_j X_{ij} + Y_i, \quad i = 1, \ldots, n \qquad (9.1)$$

where X_i = total output of industry i
$\quad\quad X_{ij}$ = sales of commodity i to industry j
$\quad\quad Y_i$ = sales of commodity i to final demand
$\quad\quad n$ = the number of industries (3 in Table 9.1)

9.1.2 Input–output modelling

To go from accounting to analysis, the basic input–output modelling assumption is that

$$X_{ij} = a_{ij} X_j \qquad (9.2)$$

where a_{ij} is a constant. That is, it is assumed that intermediate inputs are constant proportions of the output of the purchasing industry. So for example if X_j represents the output of the steel industry (tonnes valued at constant prices) and X_{ij} records purchases of iron ore (tonnes valued at constant prices) by the steel industry, we are assuming that iron ore purchases are a constant fraction of the value of steel output (expressed in constant prices); if the output of steel doubles, inputs (purchases) of iron ore will double.

Substituting equation 9.2 into 9.1 gives

$$X_i = \sum_j a_{ij} X_j + Y_i, \quad i = 1, \ldots, n \qquad (9.3)$$

as a system of n linear equations in $2n$ variables, the X_i and Y_i, and n^2 coefficients, the a_{ij}. If the Y_i – the final demand levels – are specified, there are n unknown X_i – the gross output levels – which can be solved for using the n equations. Given that the equations are linear, the solution can readily be accomplished using matrix algebra.[3] In matrix notation, equations 9.3 become

$$\mathbf{X} = \mathbf{AX} + \mathbf{Y}$$

which on rearrangement is

$$\mathbf{X} - \mathbf{AX} = \mathbf{Y} \qquad (9.4)$$

where $\mathbf{X}$ is an $n \times 1$ vector of gross outputs, X_i, $\mathbf{A}$ is an $n \times n$ matrix of intermediate input coefficients, a_{ij}, and $\mathbf{Y}$ is an $n \times 1$ vector of final demands, Y_i.

With $\mathbf{I}$ as an $n \times n$ identity matrix, equation 9.4 can be written as

$$(\mathbf{I} - \mathbf{A})\mathbf{X} = \mathbf{Y}$$

which has the solution

$$\mathbf{X} = (\mathbf{I} - \mathbf{A})^{-1}\mathbf{Y} \qquad (9.5)$$

where $(\mathbf{I} - \mathbf{A})^{-1}$ is the 'inverse' of $(\mathbf{I} - \mathbf{A})$. This solution can be written as

$$\mathbf{X} = \mathbf{LY} \qquad (9.6)$$

where $\mathbf{L} = (\mathbf{I} - \mathbf{A})^{-1}$, and the notation $\mathbf{L}$ used as this inverse is often referred to as the 'Leontief inverse' in recognition of the progenitor of input–output analysis, Wassily Leontief.

This is the basic input–output model. Its use involves a number of assumptions – notably equation 9.2 and the constancy of the a_{ij} – which are clearly approximations to reality, but used judiciously input–output modelling can be a cost-effective and powerful tool in a number of applications. In the next section it is shown how the basic model can be extended to incorporate economy–environment interactions. Before doing that, it will be useful to consider further what it is that the basic model does, and to work through a numerical illustration of its application based on Table 9.1. For the reader who wishes to verify the calculations, or who wishes to see how Excel can be used to do the kinds of matrix algebra calculations used in input–output analysis, the numerical example is reproduced in its entirety in an Excel file in the *Additional Materials* for Chapter 9, *IO.xls*.

For a three-sector economy, the matrix equation 9.6 can be written in ordinary algebra as the three equations

$$X_1 = l_{11}Y_1 + l_{12}Y_2 + l_{13}Y_3$$
$$X_2 = l_{21}Y_1 + l_{22}Y_2 + l_{23}Y_3 \qquad (9.7)$$
$$X_3 = l_{31}Y_1 + l_{32}Y_2 + l_{33}Y_3$$

where the l_{ij} are the elements of the Leontief inverse, $\mathbf{L}$. Each equation here gives the gross output of an industry as depending on the levels of final demand for each of the three commodities. The l_{ij} give the level of output in the ith industry to meet the direct

---

[3]   Readers who are unfamiliar with matrix algebra will find the essentials in Appendix 6.1 in Chapter 6.

and indirect requirements for a unit of final demand for commodity j. Thus, for example, the delivery of one unit of commodity 2 to final demand requires an output level l_{22} in industry 2. This level will meet both the direct requirement and the indirect requirement arising from the fact that commodity 2 is used in the production of commodities 1 and 3, which are used in the production of commodity 2. The actual gross output requirement for commodity 2, X_2, depends, in the same way, on the levels of delivery of all three commodities to final demand, as given by l_{21}, l_{22} and l_{23}, and similarly for X_1 and X_3.

From the data in Table 9.1, and using equation 9.2, the elements of the matrix **A** are calculated as follows:

$$a_{11} = 0, \ a_{12} = 400/2000 = 0.2000, \ a_{13} = 0$$

$$a_{21} = 350/1000 = 0.3500, \ a_{22} = 0, \ a_{23} = 150/600$$
$$= 0.2500$$

$$a_{31} = 100/1000 = 0.1000, \ a_{32} = 200/2000$$
$$= 0.1000, \ a_{33} = 0$$

Hence,

$$\mathbf{A} = \begin{bmatrix} 0.0000 & 0.2000 & 0.0000 \\ 0.3500 & 0.0000 & 0.2500 \\ 0.1000 & 0.1000 & 0.0000 \end{bmatrix}$$

and

$$\mathbf{I} - \mathbf{A} = \begin{bmatrix} 1.0000 & -0.2000 & 0.0000 \\ -0.3500 & 1.0000 & -0.2500 \\ -0.1000 & -0.1000 & 1.0000 \end{bmatrix}$$

so that[4]

$$\mathbf{L} = (\mathbf{I} - \mathbf{A})^{-1} = \begin{bmatrix} 1.0833 & 0.2222 & 0.0556 \\ 0.4167 & 1.1111 & 0.2778 \\ 0.1500 & 0.1333 & 1.0333 \end{bmatrix}$$

Substituting into equation 9.6 gives

$$\mathbf{X} = \begin{bmatrix} 1.0833 & 0.2222 & 0.0556 \\ 0.4167 & 1.1111 & 0.2778 \\ 0.1500 & 0.1333 & 1.0333 \end{bmatrix} \begin{bmatrix} Y_1 \\ Y_2 \\ Y_3 \end{bmatrix}$$

which is the same as:

$$X_1 = 1.0833Y_1 + 0.2222Y_2 + 0.0556Y_3$$

$$X_2 = 0.4167Y_1 + 1.1111Y_2 + 0.2778Y_3$$

$$X_3 = 0.1500Y_1 + 0.1333Y_2 + 1.0333Y_3$$

If the Y_i here are replaced by the total final demand levels from Table 9.1 ($Y_1 = 600$ for agriculture, $Y_2 = 1500$ for manufacturing, $Y_3 = 300$ for services) this gives the gross output levels

Agriculture $X_1 = 999.96$
Manufacturing $X_2 = 2000.01$
Services $X_3 = 599.94$

which are the same, allowing for inevitable small errors on account of rounding, as the total output levels shown in Table 9.1.[5] This must be the case, given that the final demand levels are the same.

Now suppose that it is known that there will be an increase in the export demand for all commodities. What are the implications for gross output levels? Suppose that the new export demand levels are

Agriculture 200
Manufacturing 1000
Services 100

so that the new final demand levels are:

$$Y_1 = 700$$
$$Y_2 = 1800$$
$$Y_3 = 400$$

Using these with the elements of the Leontief inverse, as above, gives as the new gross output levels:

$$X_1 = (1.0833 \times 700) + (0.2222 \times 1800)$$
$$+ (0.0556 \times 400) = 1180.51$$

$$X_2 = (0.4167 \times 700) + (1.1111 \times 1800)$$
$$+ (0.2778 \times 400) = 2402.79$$

$$X_3 = (0.1500 \times 700) + (0.1333 \times 1800)$$
$$+ (0.0333 \times 400) = 758.26$$

Note that for every industry the increase in gross output exceeds the increase in the final demand for

---

[4] While the inverse for a small matrix can be found using a calculating machine, using a method described in, for example, Chiang (1984), the calculation is tedious and prone to error. Even for small matrices, it is better to use the routine included in most spreadsheet packages for PCs. One such routine is explained in the Word document *Matrix.doc* and illustrated in the Excel file

Matrix.xls. These are both available from the *Additional Materials* for Chapter 6.
[5] This calculation, and others in this chapter, were done with a pocket calculator. If an Excel spreadsheet is used, as in the file *Matrix.xls* in the *Additional Materials* to Chapter 6, a higher degree of accuracy will be obtained.

the commodity that it produces. This is because commodities are used in the production of commodities. Input–output analysis is the investigation of the quantitative implications of such inter-industry relations.

9.2 Environmental input–output analysis

Proposals to extend input–output tables and models to include aspects of economy–environment links were first mooted in the late 1960s. The next 10–15 years saw a rapid development of environmental input–output models. Although there are some important differences between the models developed by different authors – so that for particular applications the choice of model is important – they all share a common basis of input–output methodology, including constant returns to scale production functions which permit no substitution between inputs (Leontief production functions), as described in the preceding section. A general input–output framework for economy–environment linkages is presented, using matrix algebra, in Appendix 9.1. Here we consider some particular, but useful and widely used, approaches to accounting and modelling.

Suppose that in addition to the data of Table 9.1 we also know that the use of oil by the three industries was

Agriculture	Manufacturing	Services
50	400	60

where the units are petajoules, PJs. A joule is a unit of measurement used in recording the use of energy in the economy (one joule is the energy conveyed by one watt of power for one second) and the prefix 'peta' stands for 10^{15}. With O_i for oil use by the ith industry, paralleling equation 9.2, assume

$$O_i = r_i X_i \qquad (9.8)$$

so that

$r_1 = 0.05$ for agriculture
$r_2 = 0.2$ for manufacturing
$r_3 = 0.1$ for services

These coefficients can be used to figure the implications for total oil use of changes in deliveries to final

demand by applying them to the changes in the X_i associated with the change in final demand. Thus, for example, in the previous section the following changes to final demand deliveries

$$\Delta Y_1 = 100 \quad \Delta Y_2 = 300 \quad \Delta Y_3 = 100$$

were found to imply

$$\Delta X_1 = 180.51 \quad \Delta X_2 = 402.79 \quad \Delta X_3 = 158.26$$

so that the oil use changes are

$$\Delta O_1 = 9.03 \quad \Delta O_2 = 80.56 \quad \Delta O_3 = 15.83$$

with an increase in total oil use from 510 to 615.41 PJ.

A similar approach can be used in regard to waste emissions. If the emissions levels of a particular kind, E_i, are known, then, paralleling equation 9.8, assume

$$E_i = w_i X_i \qquad (9.9)$$

and the implications of final demand changes for these emissions can be figured as just described for oil. Clearly, the same procedure can be followed for any number of particular kinds of emissions (or resource inputs), if the data are available.

In a recent study McNicoll and Blackmore (1993) calculated emissions coefficients for 12 pollutants for a (preliminary) 29-sector version of the 1989 input–output tables for Scotland. Coefficients were expressed in tonnes per £ million output, except radioactivity, which is measured in thousand becquerels. Applications of the model included a number of simulation studies, two of which involved assessing the impact on pollution emissions of (i) partial substitution by consumers of coal for gas, and (ii) partial substitution for road and air transport by rail transport. For SIM1 (coal for gas), final demand for coal was reduced by £30m, while that for gas was increased by £30m. For SIM2 (greater use of rail), final demand for road transport was reduced by £50m, and air transport by £20m, while final demand for rail transport was raised by £70m. In both cases aggregate final demand was kept unchanged in order to show the effects of different patterns of expenditure. Although the figures used are purely illustrative, the approach and discussion are suggestive of how environmental input–output models can be used to quantify and evaluate the

Table 9.2 SIM1 and SIM2 impacts on outputs and emissions

Sector	Δ Gross output[a]		Emission	Δ Emissions[b]	
	SIM1	SIM2		SIM1	SIM2
1	−0.04	+0.64	CO_2	−404.7	−287.7
2	−0.001	−0.04	CO_2(weight)	−110.4	−78.5
3	−0.02	+0.22	SO_2	−3.0	+0.11
4	−30.21	+0.08	Black smoke	−0.35	−0.06
5	−0.02	−0.02	NO_x	−0.88	−3.84
6	−0.73	−1.06	VOC	−0.14	−3.25
7	−0.27	+2.25	CO	−0.35	−21.16
8	+30.98	+0.60	Methane	−11.46	+0.09
9	−0.01	+0.17	Waste	−655.2	+24.26
10	−0.11	+0.07	Lead	−0.000005	−0.01
11	+0.03	+1.02	RA air	−0.001	+0.009
12	+0.004	+0.27	RA water	−0.00006	+0.0005
13	−0.09	+0.21	RA solid	0.0143	+0.121
14	−0.15	+0.14			
15	−0.009	+1.20			
16	−0.19	+2.13			
17	+0.02	+0.83			
18	+0.05	+0.97			
19	−0.08	+0.48			
20	+0.01	+1.65			
21	−0.42	+15.25			
22	+0.02	+70.29			
23	−0.04	−49.2			
24	+0.01	+0.21			
25	+0.09	−20.49			
26	+0.61	+2.80			
27	+2.64	+5.47			
28	−0.24	+2.89			
House	−5.84	+71.47			

Notes: [a] Units are £ × 10⁶

[b] Units are tonnes × 10³, except for RA

Source: Adapted from McNicoll and Blackmore (1993)

effects of policies which influence the pattern, as well as the level, of economic activity. Especially in SIM2, for example, it is interesting that although rail travel is usually considered more environmentally friendly than road or air transport, the substitution suggests an increase in the output of certain pollutants.

Results of the simulations are summarised in Table 9.2. The left-hand columns record the estimated effects of the substitutions on sector outputs, compared with actual 1989 outputs. The right-hand columns show the estimated changes in emissions which would result from the substitutions. For SIM1, the switch from coal to gas results in a fall in the output of all pollutants except solid radioactive waste. For SIM2, the switch from road/air to rail, the results are less clear-cut; emissions of six pollutants decline, but six increase.

As well as permitting this kind of analysis, input–output methods can be used to account for resource use and/or pollution generation in terms of deliveries to final demand. Consider the case of use of the oil resource first. For the three-industry case, using equation 9.8 with equation 9.7 gives

$$O_1 = r_1 X_1 = r_1 l_{11} Y_1 + r_1 l_{12} Y_2 + r_1 l_{13} Y_3$$
$$O_2 = r_2 X_2 = r_2 l_{21} Y_1 + r_2 l_{22} Y_2 + r_2 l_{23} Y_3$$
$$O_3 = r_3 X_3 = r_3 l_{31} Y_1 + r_3 l_{32} Y_2 + r_3 l_{33} Y_3$$

and adding vertically gives

$$O_1 + O_2 + O_3 = (r_1 l_{11} + r_2 l_{21} + r_3 l_{31}) Y_1$$
$$+ (r_1 l_{12} + r_2 l_{22} + r_3 l_{32}) Y_2$$
$$+ (r_1 l_{13} + r_2 l_{23} + r_3 l_{33}) Y_3$$

which can be written as

$$O_1 + O_2 + O_3 = i_1 Y_1 + i_2 Y_2 + i_3 Y_3 \tag{9.10}$$

where $i_1 = r_1l_{11} + r_2l_{21} + r_3l_{31}$ etc. The left-hand side of equation 9.10 is total oil use. The right-hand side allocates that total as between final demand deliveries via the coefficients i. These coefficients give the oil intensities of final demand deliveries, oil use per unit, taking account of direct and indirect use. The coefficient i_1, for example, is the amount of oil use attributable to the delivery to final demand of one unit of agricultural output, when account is taken both of the direct use of oil in agriculture and of its indirect use via the use of inputs of manufacturing and services, the production of which uses oil inputs.

For the data on oil use given above with the data of Table 9.1, the oil intensities are

Agriculture	Manufacturing	Services
0.1525	0.2467	0.1617

which with final demand deliveries of

Agriculture	Manufacturing	Services
600	1500	300

gives total oil use, 510 PJ, allocated across final demand deliveries as

Agriculture	Manufacturing	Services
91.50	370.05	48.51

Note that as compared with the industry uses of oil from which the r_i were calculated, these numbers have more oil use attributed to agriculture and less to manufacturing and services. This reflects the fact that producing agricultural output uses oil indirectly when it uses inputs from manufacturing and services.

In matrix algebra, which would be the basis for doing the calculations where the number of sectors is realistically large, n, the foregoing is

$$O = \mathbf{RX} = \mathbf{RLY} = \mathbf{iY} \tag{9.11}$$

to define the intensities, where

O is total resource use (a scalar)
$\mathbf{R}$ is a $1 \times n$ vector of industry resource input coefficients
$\mathbf{i}$ is a $1 \times n$ vector of resource intensities for final demand deliveries

and $\mathbf{X}$, $\mathbf{L}$ and $\mathbf{Y}$ are as previously defined. The resource uses attributable to final demand deliveries can be calculated as

$$\mathbf{O} = \mathbf{R}^* \mathbf{Y} \tag{9.11$'$}$$

where

$\mathbf{O}$ is an $n \times 1$ vector of resource use levels
$\mathbf{R}^*$ is an $n \times n$ matrix with the elements of $\mathbf{R}$ along the diagonal and 0s elsewhere.

With suitable changes of notation, all of this applies equally to calculation concerning waste emissions. Where there are several, m, resources, or types of emissions, being considered, the vector $\mathbf{R}$ in 9.11 becomes an $m \times n$ matrix, and with suitable dimensional adjustments elsewhere, the above carries through, and all the intensities for final demand deliveries can be calculated in one operation.

In the case of CO_2 emissions arising in fossil fuel combustion, it is not necessary to know the emissions levels for each industry, as these can be calculated using data on the fossil fuel inputs to each industry and a standard set of coefficients which give the amount of CO_2 released per unit of a particular fossil fuel burned:[6]

	Tonnes CO_2 per PJ
Natural gas	54 900
Oil	73 200
Black coal	104 100
Brown coal	112 700

In this case, fossil fuel intensities can be converted to CO_2 intensities by using these coefficients and aggregating across the fuels. Table 9.3 gives results so obtained (Common and Salma, 1992a) for Australia for 1986/7 for CO_2 intensities and levels for deliveries to final demand: the figures in parentheses are rankings. A CO_2 intensity is the quantity of CO_2 emitted per unit delivery to final demand. In the first column of Table 9.3 CO_2 units are thousands of tonnes, and final demand delivery units are millions of Australian dollars. The first point to note here is that deliveries of the output of the agriculture, forestry and fishing sector to final demand are

---

[6] Actually slightly different coefficient sets can be found in different sources: for an examination of the sensitivity of results to such variations, see Common and Salma (1992a).

Table 9.3 CO_2 intensities and levels for final demand deliveries, Australia 1986/7

Sector	CO_2[a]	CO_2[b]	Percentage of total
Agriculture, forestry, fishing, hunting	1.8007 (6)	13.836(8)	4.74
Mining	0.9854(11)	9.953(12)	3.41
Meat and milk products	1.0368(10)	8.515(13)	2.92
Food products	1.5325(8)	11.540(10)	4.00
Beverages and tobacco	0.9213(12)	3.399(20)	1.17
Textiles, clothing and footwear	0.5561(24)	3.062(21)	1.05
Wood, wood products, furniture	0.8771(14)	2.034(23)	0.70
Paper, products, printing, publishing	0.8707(15)	1.390(24)	0.48
Chemicals	1.2335(9)	2.579(22)	0.88
Petroleum and coal products	10.7272(2)	37.788(2)	12.95
Non-metallic mineral products	2.1930(5)	0.357(26)	0.12
Basic metals, products	4.4977(4)	20.25(4)	6.94
Fabricated metal products	1.7055(7)	3.484(19)	1.19
Transport equipment	0.7406(20)	4.706(17)	1.61
Machinery and equipment	0.8834(13)	5.296(16)	1.82
Miscellaneous manufacturing	0.7727(18)	1.012(25)	0.35
Electricity	15.2449(1)	43.747(1)	14.99
Gas	9.9663(3)	4.675(18)	1.60
Water	0.6630(22)	0.205(27)	0.07
Construction	0.7567(19)	28.111(3)	9.64
Wholesale and retail, repairs	0.4978(25)	18.225(5)	6.25
Transport, storage, communication	0.8157(17)	13.386(9)	4.58
Finance, property, business services	0.6242(23)	5.719(14)	1.96
Residential property	0.1992(27)	5.504(15)	1.89
Public administration, defence	0.8409(16)	14.352(7)	4.92
Community services	0.4437(26)	17.802(6)	6.10
Recreational, personal services	0.7205(21)	10.830(11)	3.71
Total		291.756	100.00

[a] tonnes $\times 10^3/(\$A \times 10^6)$
[b] tonnes $\times 10^6$
Source: Adapted from Common and Salma (1992a)

relatively CO_2- and fossil-fuel-intensive, ranking sixth, and ahead of several manufacturing sectors. This counter-intuitive result arises because the sector is a large indirect user of fossil fuels, with, particularly, large inputs of fertiliser, the production of which is fossil-fuel-intensive. It means that expansion of Australia's agricultural industry would, per unit, increase Australian CO_2 emissions by more than expansion of several manufacturing outputs. A second point worthy of noting explicitly is that while service sectors – such as wholesale and retail, repairs, or public administration, defence – rank low by intensity, they climb well up the ranking according to emissions levels, on account of their large size. The third point to be made here concerns electricity. It is frequently stated that for Australia – and the case is much the same in most other industrialised economies – electricity generation accounts for approximately 45% of CO_2 emissions associated with fossil fuel combustion. In Table 9.3, electricity

accounts for only some 15% of total emissions. It is true that 45% of emissions are through the stacks of power stations. However, much of the electricity so generated is used as input to other productive activities, rather than consumed by households. The accounting in Table 9.3 attributes the emissions associated with electricity as an intermediate commodity to the sectors that use electricity in that way, and the CO_2 total for electricity relates solely to its use by final consumers. For many purposes, accounting for emissions in terms of final demand deliveries is more useful than accounting in terms of the location of fossil fuel combustion. It aligns, as the next section will show, with the impact of carbon taxation on relative prices.

The work from which Table 9.3 is taken also conducted some simulation experiments which illustrate the usefulness of input–output analysis in exploring the potential for alternative routes to the abatement of CO_2 emissions. Some examples are as follows.

Cutting the final demand for electricity by 10% would reduce total emissions by 1.5%. Cutting the final demand for the output of the construction industry by 10% would reduce total emissions by 1.0%. This surprising result arises because, when indirect use is taken account of, construction is a relatively CO_2-intensive sector, and it is a large sector. If in the matrix of inter-industry coefficients, $\mathbf{A}$, those for electricity inputs are all cut by 10%, then for the original set of final demands, total CO_2 emissions reduce by 4.4%. If, instead, the coefficients for basic metal inputs to all industries are cut by 10%, there is a 1.4% reduction in total emissions. Given that the basic metal industry is relatively energy- and CO_2-intensive, conserving on inputs of its commodity is energy-conserving and CO_2-abating. Materials conserving technical change is energy-conserving, and CO_2-abating, because the extraction and processing of materials uses energy, which is currently predominantly based on fossil fuel use.

9.3   Costs and prices

In the preceding sections inputs and outputs were expressed in constant-value terms for economic flows and in physical units for environmental extractions (resource inputs) and insertions (waste emissions). The accounting and analysis were concerned with the 'real' side of the economy, and with questions such as 'if final demand changes, what will happen to emissions?' However, many of the most interesting and controversial issues in environmental economics involve questions of costs and prices. For instance, how would a 'carbon tax' affect the prices facing households, and hence the cost of living?

These questions can be explored using the dual of the input–output model system outlined above. Analogous to equation 9.1 based on the rows of the transactions table, we can write for the columns of that table

$$X_j \equiv \sum_i X_{ij} + M_j + W_j + OVA_j \quad j = 1, \ldots, n \tag{9.12}$$

that is, the value of output of sector j covers the cost of purchases from other sectors $\sum_i X_{ij}$, plus the cost of imports used in the production of product M_j, plus

labour costs, W_j, plus other value added, OVA_j, which includes profit and is essentially the balancing item in the accounting identity. To simplify the exposition, we aggregate imports, labour costs and other value added, so that

$$X_j \equiv \sum_i X_{ij} + V_j, \quad j = 1, \ldots, n \tag{9.13}$$

where V_j is primary input cost. We now assume as before that intermediate inputs are a fixed proportion of industry output, as in equation 9.2. Substituting in equation 9.13 this gives

$$X_j = \sum_i a_{ij} X_j + V_j, \quad j = 1, \ldots, n \tag{9.14}$$

Now, the inter-industry flows in the transactions table are expenditure flows, that is price times quantity. When we use the data to consider questions about the 'real' side of the economy, we are dealing with commodities where quantities are measured in units which are 'millions of dollars worth'. Such quantities have, in the accounts, prices which are unity. With P_j for the price of the jth commodity, equation 9.14 can then be written

$$P_j X_j = \sum_i a_{ij} P_j X_j + V_j, j = 1, \ldots, n$$

and dividing by X_j gives

$$P_j = \sum_i a_{ij} P_j + V_j / X_j, j = 1, \ldots, n$$

or

$$P_j = \sum_i a_{ij} P_j, + v_j, j = 1, \ldots, n \tag{9.15}$$

where v_j is primary input cost per unit output.

In matrix algebra equation 9.15 is

$$\mathbf{P} = \mathbf{A}'\mathbf{P} + \mathbf{v} \tag{9.16}$$

where $\mathbf{P}$ is an $n \times 1$ vector of prices, $\mathbf{A}'$ is the transpose of the $n \times n$ matrix of input–output coefficients, $\mathbf{A}$, and $\mathbf{v}$ is an $n \times 1$ vector of primary input cost coefficients.

From Equation 9.16

$$\mathbf{P} - \mathbf{A}'\mathbf{P} = \mathbf{v}$$

and with $\mathbf{I}$ as the identity matrix

$$(\mathbf{I} - \mathbf{A}')\mathbf{P} = \mathbf{v}$$

so that

$$\mathbf{P} = (\mathbf{I} - \mathbf{A}')^{-1}\mathbf{v}$$

This last result can be written more usefully as

$$\mathbf{P}' = \mathbf{v}'(\mathbf{I} - \mathbf{A})^{-1} = \mathbf{v}'\mathbf{L} \tag{9.17}$$

where $\mathbf{P'}$ is a $1 \times n$ vector of prices (the transpose of $\mathbf{P}$), $\mathbf{v'}$ is a $1 \times n$ vector of primary input cost coefficients (the transpose of $\mathbf{v}$) and $\mathbf{L}$ is the $n \times n$ Leontief inverse matrix.

According to equation 9.17, commodity prices can be calculated using the Leontief inverse and the primary input cost coefficients. This can be illustrated using data from the transactions table given in Table 9.1. The primary input cost coefficients are:

Agriculture	Manufacturing	Services
0.55	0.70	0.75

Using these in equation 9.17 with the Leontief inverse

$$\mathbf{L} = \begin{bmatrix} 1.0833 & 0.222 & 0.0556 \\ 0.4167 & 1.1111 & 0.2778 \\ 0.1500 & 0.1333 & 1.0333 \end{bmatrix}$$

gives $P_1 = 1.00$, $P_2 = 1.00$ and $P_3 = 1.00$. For $n = 3$, equation 9.14 is

$$X_1 = X_{11} + X_{21} + X_{31} + V_1$$
$$X_2 = X_{12} + X_{22} + X_{32} + V_2$$
$$X_3 = X_{13} + X_{23} + X_{33} + V_3$$

and following the steps above leads to equations 9.15 as

$$P_1 = a_{11}P_1 + a_{21}P_1 + a_{31}P_1 + v_1$$
$$P_2 = a_{12}P_2 + a_{22}P_2 + a_{32}P_2 + v_2$$
$$P_3 = a_{13}P_3 + a_{23}P_3 + a_{33}P_3 + v_3$$

where on substituting for the a and v coefficients, it can readily be confirmed that $P_1 = P_2 = P_3 = 1$ is the solution.

Given that we already knew that all prices are unity in an input–output transactions table, equation 9.17 does not appear very useful. In looking at the 'real' side of things, using the Leontief inverse calculated from the transactions table with the final demand given in the transactions table in equation 9.6 would simply give the gross outputs reported in the transactions table. The usefulness of computing the Leontief inverse from the transactions table was in considering the implications for gross outputs, and flows to and from the environment, of different levels and patterns of final demand. Here, the point is that equation 9.17 can be used to consider the commodity price implications of v coefficients other than those derived from the transactions table.

Suppose that for the hypothetical economy to which Table 9.1 refers, carbon taxation were under consideration. In the preceding section we gave data on the use of oil by each of the three sectors, and noted that the use of 1 PJ of oil meant the emission of 73.2×10^3 tonnes of CO_2. This means that the CO_2 emissions arising in each sector are, in kilotonnes $= 10^3$ tonnes:

Agriculture	Manufacturing	Services
3660	29280	4392

Suppose that the rate of carbon taxation under consideration is $20 per tonne. From equation 9.17 the change in prices for a change in the v coefficients is

$$\Delta\mathbf{P'} = \Delta\mathbf{v'L} \qquad (9.18)$$

where $\Delta\mathbf{v'}$ is the transposed vector of changes in the primary input cost coefficients and $\Delta\mathbf{P'}$ is the transposed vector of consequent price changes. For the postulated rate of carbon taxation, using the figures above for emissions and the data from Table 9.1 gives

$$\Delta v_1 = 0.0682, \quad \Delta v_2 = 0.2265, \quad \Delta v_3 = 0.1277$$

for which equation 9.18, with $\mathbf{L}$ as given above, yields

$$\Delta P_1 = 0.1874, \quad \Delta P_2 = 0.2838, \quad \Delta P_3 = 0.1987$$

Given that prior to the imposition of the carbon tax all the prices were unity, these are proportionate price increases; that is, the price of the commodity which is the output of the agricultural sector would increase by 18.74%. Note, for example, that whereas the manufacturing sector uses four times as much oil per unit gross output, and hence emits four times as much CO_2, as the agriculture sector, the ratio of price increases in manufacturing relative to agriculture, 1.5, is smaller than four. Using input–output analysis picks up the implications for pricing of the fact that the agriculture sector uses oil, so that delivering its output to final demand is responsible for CO_2 emissions, indirectly as well as directly.

It should also be noted that this analysis involves the assumption that the input–output coefficients, the a_{ij}, and the coefficients for oil inputs do not change in response to the imposition of a carbon tax. It involves the assumption, that is, that making oil inputs more expensive does not induce any

Table 9.4 Price increases due to a carbon tax of A$20 per tonne

Sector	Percentage price increase	
Agriculture, forestry, fishing, hunting	1.77	(9)
Mining	1.69	(12)
Meat and milk products	1.77	(9)
Food products	1.46	(16)
Beverages and tobacco	0.84	(24)
Textiles, clothing and footwear	0.95	(21)
Wood, wood products, furniture	1.31	(15)
Paper, products, printing, publishing	1.12	(20)
Chemicals	1.56	(16)
Petroleum and coal products	9.97	(4)
Non-metallic mineral products	1.89	(8)
Basic metals, products	9.00	(5)
Fabricated metal products	2.76	(6)
Transport equipment	0.82	(23)
Machinery and equipment	0.71	(26)
Miscellaneous manufacturing	0.89	(23)
Electricity	31.33	(1)
Gas	21.41	(2)
Water	1.34	(18)
Construction	1.60	(13)
Wholesale and retail, repairs	10.14	(3)
Transport, storage, communication	2.28	(7)
Finance, property, business services	1.21	(19)
Residential property	0.42	(27)
Public administration, defence	1.73	(11)
Community services	0.93	(21)
Recreational, personal services	1.62	(13)

Source: Adapted from Common and Salma (1992b)

Table 9.5 CPI impacts of carbon taxation

Decile	Accounting for direct and indirect impacts %	Accounting for only direct impacts %
1	2.89	1.53
2	3.00 H	1.66 H
3	2.97	1.60
4	2.85	1.44
5	2.88	1.45
6	2.77	1.35
7	2.80	1.31
8	2.77	1.28
9	2.67	1.16
10	2.62 L	1.10 L
All households	2.79	1.31
H/L ratio	1.15	1.51

Source: Adapted from Common and Salma (1992b)

substitution responses on the part of producers. In so far as any such responses would involve using less oil per unit output, and less of relatively oil-intensive commodities as intermediate inputs, they would reduce the price increases consequent on the introduction of the carbon tax. The input–output results can, that is, be regarded as setting upper bounds to the price increases that would actually occur. In so far as substitution responses take time to implement, it would be expected that those upper bounds would approximate the short-run impacts, rather than the long-run impacts.

Table 9.4 gives the results of calculations essentially the same as those described above using the same input–output data for Australia as were used for the results given in Table 9.3. The calculations differ in so far as there are several fuels, rather than

just oil, used, and in so far as the Australian input–output data involve a distinction between the prices received by sellers and those paid by buyers, which reflects indirect taxation and the way in which the accounts treat distribution margins. It is because of the latter that the rankings in Table 9.4, shown in parentheses, do not exactly match those shown in Table 9.3 for the CO_2 intensities of deliveries to final demand.

It is widely believed that carbon taxation would be regressive in its impact, would hurt the poor more than the rich. Input–output analysis of the impact on commodity prices can provide one input to a quantitative analysis of this question. The other necessary input is data on the expenditure patterns of households at different positions in the income distribution which is, or can be made, compatible with the input–output data in terms of its commodity classification. Where such data are available, the change in the cost of living for a household is given by

$$\Delta CPI_h = \sum_j \beta_{hj} \Delta P_j, \quad h = 1, \dots, m \quad (9.19)$$

where CPI stands for consumer price index, h indexes households, and β_{hj} is the budget share of commodity j for the hth household. Table 9.5 gives results for Australia, using the price changes from Table 9.4 here with data on Australian household expenditure patterns by expenditure decile.[7] In

---

[7] The household expenditure data is for 1984, which was at the time that the study was done the most recent such data available by decile. For results using more recent household expenditure data, by quintile, see Common and Salma (1992b), which also gives a more detailed account of data and methods.

Table 9.5 H identifies the highest CPI effect, L the lowest. The presumption that carbon taxation would be regressive in its impact comes from the observation, generally valid for industrial economies, that lower-income groups spend a larger proportion of their income on fuel than upper-income groups. The third column in Table 9.5 shows the CPI impacts when j in equation 9.19 indexes only the fuel commodities: electricity, gas, and petroleum and coal products. The second column shows the CPI impact when j indexes all 27 commodities, picking up the indirect as well as the direct price effects of carbon taxation. There is by the H/L ratio a regressive impact in both columns, but it is smaller in the second column. Just looking at direct fuel purchases overstates the regressive impact of carbon taxation (and, equivalently, of higher fuel prices). Carbon dioxide taxation affects all commodity prices, roughly, in proportion to their carbon dioxide intensity. Thus, while the poor spend proportionately more on direct fuels purchases, the rich spend more on things, such as overseas travel, in which fuels are, directly and indirectly, used as inputs, and this reduces regressivity.

Two points need to be kept in mind when considering results such as those shown in Table 9.5. The first is that using equation 9.19 involves the assumption that household expenditure patterns do not change in response to the changed relative prices induced by carbon taxation. The assumption of fixed budget shares for households is directly analogous to the assumption of fixed input–output coefficients in production, and has similar implications for the results of the analysis. Given changed relative prices following the introduction of carbon taxation, households would be expected to substitute commodities for which price had risen less for those for which it had risen more. Such behaviour would reduce the CPI impact of carbon taxation: results based on equation 9.19 would, for each decile, represent an upper limit. The second point is that the impacts on households arising from carbon taxation would not be confined to the expenditure side. There would also be income effects. As noted above, producers would also be expected to make substitution responses, which would have implications for employment opportunities and incomes. Also, carbon taxation would give rise to government revenue

which could be used in a variety of ways, including increased welfare payments and/or lower income taxation for low-income households, for example. If substitution responses, and discretion in the use of the tax receipts, are to be allowed for, analysing the full implications of the introduction of carbon taxation, and other environmental policies, is beyond the scope of input–output analysis. Such issues can, in principle, be investigated using the methods to be discussed in the next section.

9.4 Computable general equilibrium models

Environmental input–output models are undoubtedly useful for applied work in policy simulation, forecasting and structural analysis. They are transparent and computationally straightforward. However, they are seen by many economists as suffering from several serious deficiencies. Utility- and profit-maximising behaviour play no role in input–output models: there are no demand and supply equations and no capacity constraints. Concern with the rather limited behavioural basis of input–output models has led to a growing interest in applied, or computable, general equilibrium models. We will use the term 'computable general equilibrium' (CGE) models.

CGE models are essentially empirical versions of the Walrasian general equilibrium system and employ the theoretical (neoclassical) assumptions of that system, which, as remarked above, are absent from the input–output system. In general, CGE models cannot be solved algebraically, but thanks to recent increases in computing power, and the development of solution algorithms, they can be solved computationally. These developments have stimulated a rapid growth in applied CGE modelling, particularly on issues related to taxation, trade, structural adjustment and the environment.

9.4.1 An illustrative two-sector model

Here we will use constructed data for an imaginary economy and a simple CGE model of that economy

Table 9.6 Transactions table for the two-sector economy

	Agriculture	Manufacturing	Consumption	Total output
Agriculture	0	1.3490	3.1615	4.5105
Manufacturing	1.1562	0	3.1615	4.3177
Wages	2.5157	1.4844		
Other value added	0.8386	1.4843		
Total input	4.5105	4.3177		

Table 9.7 Physical data for the two-sector economy

	Agriculture	Manufacturing	Consumption	Total output
Agriculture	0	0.5508	1.2909	1.8417
Manufacturing	0.3687	0	1.0083	1.3770
Labour	2.5157	1.4844		
Oil	0.7217	1.2774		
Emissions	52.8484	93.5057		

to illustrate the essentials of CGE modelling in relation to environmental problems.[8] Table 9.6 is the transactions table for a two-sector economy. This economy uses labour and oil as inputs to production, and in Table 9.6 'Other value added' refers to payments to the owners of oil deposits. The units of measurement are $\$ \times 10^6$ everywhere. The only component of final demand is consumption by the households which supply labour and own oil deposits – there is no foreign trade. The implication that households sell costlessly extracted oil to the producing sectors of the economy keeps what follows as simple as possible, while not affecting the essentials.

The prices of both produced commodities and of both primary inputs are known for the year to which Table 9.6 relates. Since, as we shall see, it is for present purposes only relative prices that matter, we set the price of labour at unity and express all other prices in terms of the 'wage rate' as numeraire. Then, the known prices are:

Agriculture	$P_1 = 2.4490$
Manufacturing	$P_2 = 3.1355$
Labour	$W = 1$
Oil	$P = 1.1620$

With these prices we can convert the transactions table into an input–output table expressed in physical units (Table 9.7). Take it that the units in

Table 9.7 are: tonnes $\times 10^6$ for agriculture and manufacturing; person-years for labour and PJs for oil. Table 9.7 has an additional row labelled 'Emissions'. Each PJ of oil used gives rise to 73.2×10^3 tonnes of CO_2, and in Table 9.7 emissions are reported in units of kilotonnes.

Suppose now that we want to consider policy in regard to CO_2 emissions. If we restrict ourselves to the assumptions of input–output modelling, we can, as discussed in the second section of this chapter, consider the implications of alternative final demand scenarios, and/or the implications of changes to the economy's technology, as reflected in the matrix **A**. We could also, as described in Section 9.3, consider the implications for commodity prices of the imposition of a carbon tax at various rates. Note that in the latter case, imposing a tax on emissions would not affect emissions levels.

The argument for CGE modelling is that by using the assumptions of general equilibrium theory, we can do more useful policy analysis, where agents respond to the policy intervention. Essentially, CGE modelling employs four sorts of assumption:

(1) market clearing – all markets are in equilibrium;
(2) Walras's law – all markets are connected;
(3) utility maximisation by households;
(4) profit maximisation by firms.

---

[8]   For a good summary of work on CGE modelling and applications see Greenaway *et al.* (1993).

Using assumptions (1) and (2) is a relatively straightforward matter of model specification. Using assumptions (3) and (4) requires additional assumptions and/or data.

In regard to (1), consider for example the commodity markets. The market clearing assumption there is that for each commodity, the amount produced is taken off the market by the sum of all the demands. Here, given intermediate uses of produced commodities, that is

$$X_1 = X_{11} + X_{12} + C_1$$

$$X_2 = X_{21} + X_{22} + C_2$$

In regard to the use of intermediate goods in production, we will make the standard input–output modelling assumption, equation 9.2. In that case, we have

$$X_1 = a_{11}X_1 + a_{12}X_2 + C_1$$
$$X_2 = a_{21}X_1 + a_{22}X_2 + C_2$$
(9.20)

In regard to (2), we know, for example, that for this simple economy

$$Y = W(L_1 + L_2) + P(R_1 + R_2)$$
(9.21)

where Y is total household income, W is the wage rate, L_i is labour used in the ith sector, P is the price of oil and R_i is oil used in the ith sector.

Together with demand equations for primary inputs and demand and supply equations for produced commodities, equation 9.21 ties together various markets in the economy.

The derivation of numerical demand and supply equations from the assumptions of utility and profit maximisation is less straightforward. Consider utility maximisation and household commodity demands. We will assume, as is typical in CGE modelling, that there is just one household. The general form of the commodity demand equations is then:

$$C_1 = C_1(Y, P_1, P_2)$$
$$C_2 = C_2(Y, P_1, P_2)$$
(9.22)

If it were the case that we had adequate time series data on this economy for C_1, C_2, Y, P_1 and P_2 we could use it to test alternative functional forms for these demand equations, and to estimate the parameters for the preferred functional form. In fact, this 'econometric' approach is generally not adopted in actual CGE modelling exercises, as there are not adequate time series data. The alternative, and widely used, approach is known as 'calibration'. This involves assuming some plausible functional form and setting its parameters so that the resulting equations are numerically consistent with the available data. Very often this 'benchmark' data is for a single year, as is the case with Table 9.6, the associated price data, and Table 9.7.

Let us assume, then, that the utility function for the household in this economy is

$$U = C_1^\alpha C_2^\beta$$
(9.23)

Maximising equation 9.23 subject to the budget constraint

$$Y = P_1C_1 + P_2C_2$$

leads, as shown in Appendix 9.2, to the demand functions:

$$C_1 = [\alpha/(\alpha + \beta)P_1]Y$$
$$C_2 = [\beta/(\alpha + \beta)P_2]Y$$
(9.24)

Using the data for Y, P_1, P_2, C_1 and C_2, these can be written as

$$\alpha/(\alpha + \beta) = 0.5$$
$$\beta/(\alpha + \beta) = 0.5$$
(9.25)

which are two equations in two unknowns. Unfortunately, and not untypically, equations 9.25 do not have a unique solution for the values of α and β. The solution to equations 9.25 is $\alpha = \beta$. We need some more information. A typical approach in practice would be to 'import' a value for one of these parameters as estimated with some other data for a different economy. We shall simply impose the plausible value $\alpha = 0.5$.

As regards the other sources of demand for produced commodities, numerical parameterisation is straightforward, given that we are making the standard input–output assumptions about intermediate demands. From Table 9.7 we derive the matrix of, physical, input–output coefficients as:

$$\mathbf{A} = \begin{bmatrix} 0 & 0.4 \\ 0.2 & 0 \end{bmatrix}$$

Now consider the production side of the model. We assume, as is typical in CGE practice, that each sector comprises a single firm, which behaves as a price-taker in its output market and the factor markets. We assume constant returns to scale and Cobb–Douglas production functions, with labour and oil as arguments. While the Cobb–Douglas assumption is adopted here mainly for simplicity, the first is generally used in actual CGE modelling, and has important consequences for model structure. As shown in Appendix 9.2, with constant returns to scale, profits are zero at all output levels and so there is no supply function. It is then necessary to construct the model such that firms produce to meet demand. As shown in Appendix 9.2, given the output level, the assumption of cost minimisation means that equations for factor demands per unit output can be derived. There remains the problem of fixing numerical values for the parameters of the production functions, and hence, the factor demand equations. The situation in regard to the production and factor demand side of the economy is as discussed above for household demand equations. While econometric estimation is possible in principle, it is generally, though not always, precluded by the non-availability of the necessary data. Most usually, numerical parameter values are determined by importing some of them from other sources – or on grounds of 'plausibility' – and determining the remainder by calibration against the benchmark data set, here Table 9.7.

We shall not go into this any further here beyond saying that Box 9.1 lists the equations of our CGE model with numerical parameter values which pass the calibration test – running the model listed there does, as shown in the lower part of the box, reproduce the data of Tables 9.6 and 9.7, and give the relative prices that go with that data. Equations (1) and (2) in the box are the household commodity demands, derived as discussed above. Equations (3) and (4) are the commodity balance equations using the values from the matrix **A** given above. Then we have a pair of simultaneous equations in P_1 and P_2. Given that U_{L1} and U_{R1}, for example, are respectively the use of labour and oil per unit output in sector 1, equations (5) and (6) are the same as the

pricing equations used in input–output analysis – see equation 9.15 from the previous section – and go with zero profit in each line of production.

There follow eight equations relating to factor demands. Equations (7), (9), (11) and (13) give the quantity of factor input per unit output, and equations (8), (10), (12) and (14) convert the results to factor demand levels using the corresponding output levels. The form of these equations is derived from cost minimisation, as described in Appendix 9.2. The numerical values appearing in equations (7), (9), (11) and (13) in Box 9.1 go with the following numerical specifications for the production functions:

$$X_1 = L_1^{0.75} R_1^{0.25}$$
$$X_2 = L_2^{0.5} R_2^{0.5}$$
$$(9.26)$$

Equation (15) gives the total of emissions as the sum of the emissions of CO_2 associated with oil combustion in each sector. Equation (16) is equation 9.21, giving total household income as arising from the sales of labour services and oil to both producing sectors. Finally, equations (17) and (18) say that there is a fixed total amount of each factor, L^* and R^*, available to the economy, and that there is full employment of the available amount, taking the two sectors together. These factor endowments are exogenous variables in this model. There are 18 endogenous variables: W, P, Y, E; and for $i = 1, 2$ U_{Li}, U_{Ri}, C_i, P_i, X_i, L_i and R_i.

The solution algorithm is based on the economic idea of price moving to clear excess demand/supply, exploits the fact that we are concerned only with relative prices, and is simplified by using the Walras law.[9] It first takes in the numerical values for the parameters and the given total factor endowments L^* and R^*. In the light of the concern for relative prices, labour is selected as numeraire, and W is set at some fixed value, which, given the discussion of the data above, is 1. Given an assumed, temporary, value for P the next step is to use equations (7), (9), (11) and (13) from Box 9.1 to calculate the unit factor demands. These are used with the solution to the commodity pricing equations, equations (5) and (6)

Box 9.1 The illustrative CGE model specification and simulation results

Computable general equilibrium model specification

(1) $C_1 = Y/2P_1$
(2) $C_2 = Y/2P_2$
(3) $X_1 = 0.4X_2 + C_1$
(4) $X_2 = 0.2X_1 + C_2$
(5) $P_1 = 0.2P_2 + WU_{L1} + PU_{R1}$
(6) $P_2 = 0.4P_1 + WU_{L2} + PU_{R2}$
(7) $U_{L1} = [3(P/W)]^{0.25}$
(8) $L_1 = U_{L1}X_1$
(9) $U_{L2} = [P/W]^{0.5}$

(10) $L_2 = U_{L2}X_2$
(11) $U_{R1} = [0.33(W/P)]^{0.75}$
(12) $R_1 = U_{R1}X_1$
(13) $U_{R2} = [W/P]^{0.5}$
(14) $R_2 = U_{R2}X_2$
(15) $E = E_1 + E_2 = e_1R_1 + e_2R_2$
(16) $Y = W(L_1 + L_2) + P(R_1 + R_2)$
(17) $L_1 + L_2 = L^*$
(18) $R_1 + R_2 = R^*$

Table 9.8 Computable general equilibrium model results

	Base case A	Base case B	50% emissions reduction	Reduction case as proportion of base case
W	1	5	1	1
P	1.1620	5.7751	2.3990	2.0645
P_1	2.4490	12.2410	3.0472	1.2443
P_2	3.1355	15.6702	4.3166	1.3767
X_1	1.8416	1.8421	1.4640	0.7950
X_2	1.3770	1.3770	1.0341	0.7510
L_1	2.5157	2.5164	2.3983	0.9533
L_2	1.4844	1.4836	1.6017	1.0790
R_1	0.7216	0.7226	0.3332	0.4618
R_2	1.2774	1.2780	0.6677	0.5227
R	2	2	1	0.5000
E_1	52.8484	52.8484	24.3902	0.4618
E_2	93.5057	93.5057	48.8756	0.5227
E	146.3541	146.3541	73.2658	0.5000
Y	6.324	31.615	6.3990	1.0119
C_1	1.2909	1.2912	1.0503	0.8136
C_2	1.0083	1.0087	0.7415	0.7354
U	1.1409	1.1412	0.8825	0.7735

(the nature of which solution was discussed in the previous section of the chapter), to derive commodity prices, and with an assumed, temporary, value for X_1 to find L_1 according to equation (8) and R_1 according to equation (12). L_2 is then calculated as $L^* - L_1$. We can then find X_2 from L_2 and the unit factor demand for labour in manufacturing, and given this value for X_2 the manufacturing demand for oil can be found using equation (14). Given values for L_1, L_2, R_1 and R_2, Y can be calculated according to equation (16), and hence household commodity demands from equations (1) and (2).

At this point, the value of $R_1 + R_2$ is compared with that for R^*. If $R_1 + R_2$ is greater than R^*, the value of P is increased by a small amount, to reduce

the excess demand for oil, and the calculation described in the previous paragraph repeated. If $R_1 + R_2$ is less than R^*, the value of P is reduced, to reduce the excess supply of oil, and the calculation described in the previous paragraph repeated. These iterations are repeated until a value for P is found for which, to some close approximation, $R_1 + R_2 = R^*$. At this point, the iteration process ceases. We know by virtue of the calculations as described that the oil market, the X_1 market, and the labour market are in equilibrium. And, by virtue of Walras's law, we then know that the remaining market, for X_2, must also be in equilibrium. The computer program which implements the algorithm reports the values of all of the endogenous variables, and stops.

The results for base cases A and B are those that the model produces when L^* is set at 4 and R^* is set at 2, the total labour and oil use in Table 9.7, and when $e_i = 73.2$, as indicated by the data there. The input to the two base case runs of the model differs only in the value given to W, 1 in A and 5 in B. The point of reporting results from these two runs is to illustrate the point that in a CGE model it is only relative prices that matter. Comparing the columns, we see, first, that for B the entries for W, P, P_1 and P_2 are all five times those for A, and, second, that all of the remaining entries, for the 'real' variables, are the same (leaving aside inevitable small differences due to the impact of the rule for stopping iterations in the algorithm). We also see that base case A reproduces the data on prices and quantities that we started with, the model calibrates.

The results in the third column arise when the model is run with base case A input, except that R^* is set at 1, 50% of the total amount of oil used in the original data set. Because emissions are linked to oil use by fixed coefficients, cutting total oil use by 50% will cut emissions by 50%. The results in the fourth column show those in the third as a proportion of those in the first. Looking at the results for the 50% emissions cut in comparison with base case A, we see first that P, the price of oil, increases by more than 100%. The prices of commodities 1 and 2 increase, with P_1 increasing less than P_2. Consistent with this, X_1, the total output of 1, falls by less than X_2. It is not the case that all factor inputs fall. Labour use in the production of commodity 1 goes down, but labour use in 2 goes up – recall that the model is structured so that there is always full employment of the labour available, so that in a two-sector model a reduction in labour input in one sector must be balanced by an increase in the other.

As a result of the reduced availability and hence higher price of oil, both producing sectors use less oil, and produce smaller amounts of emissions. Note, however, that it is not the case that R_1 and R_2, and E_1 and E_2, are reduced by equal amounts, of 50%. Oil use and emissions fall by more than 50% in the production of commodity 1, by less than 50% in the production of commodity 2. This is the efficient loading of total abatement across sources discussed in Chapters 6 and 7, arising because the model mimics competitive firms responding to their relative cost structures.

Household consumption of both commodities falls, with that of the commodity, 1, the price of which rose least, falling least. National income, here the simple sum of household incomes, which is equal to $P_1C_1 + P_2C_2$, increases because the rise in the price of oil more than compensates for the reduced quantity used, and the additional income is more than absorbed by the higher prices for C_1 and C_2. National income as reported in Box 9.1 is not corrected for the change in the general price level, and so misrepresents the welfare change, to the extent in this case of getting the sign for the direction of movement wrong. However, utility as a function of quantities consumed falls. In regard to this, it is important to note that the model has utility dependent only on commodity consumption levels. Emissions are not an argument in the utility function. This is typical of CGE models used for the analysis of the effects of programmes to reduce emissions or improve the environment. To the extent that people do derive benefit from reduced pollution, considering the utility change computed in a CGE model which does not allow for that benefit, means that the reported utility change will be an underestimate. Again, the extent of this may be such that the direction of change is misrepresented – the unrecognised utility gain from reduced emissions could be larger than the utility loss due to reduced commodity consumption.

In this model the reduction in total oil use and emissions has to be simply imposed as action by a *deus ex machina*, and the impact is transmitted through a higher price for oil, which is received directly by the owners of oil deposits, who are the household sector. An actual study of the implications of prospective action on carbon dioxide emissions would be looking not at action by a *deus ex machina* but at some kind of change of policy by government. While it could be argued that a model without a government sector, like that considered above, gives some kind of first-cut feel for the implications of reducing emissions, it is clear that an interesting analysis of government policy requires that the government sector be explicitly represented in the model. Without a government sector, we would have to treat, for example, tradable emissions (or oil use) permits as equivalent to emissions (or oil) taxation, whereas the interesting questions are about how they compare. About the only interesting policy question that the above model could address is a comparison of an efficient policy – permits or tax – with an inefficient policy – making all sources cut in equal proportional amounts. Clearly, it is also the case that to be useful for policy analysis for a trading economy a CGE model would also need a trade sector. Extending the model in these ways makes it complex, and requires more data, or more assumptions about parameter values.

Rather than develop the illustrative model further in these directions, we now look briefly at results from two substantive exercises which serve to illustrate the sort of analysis that can be done when trade and government are explicitly represented in a CGE model.[10] Both exercises deal with aspects of greenhouse gas abatement. As discussed in Chapter 10, CGE models have been extensively used to analyse policy for the abatement of greenhouse gas emissions, focusing particularly on carbon dioxide emissions. A good recent survey is in the report of IPCC Working Group III published as Bruce *et al.* (1996).

9.4.2 The international distribution of abatement costs

Here we consider the modelling work of Whalley and Wigle (1991). In this model the world is divided into six regional economies, as shown in Table 9.9. Two types of energy source are distinguished, the fossil-fuel and other, non-carbon, sources such as nuclear power. These are substitutable for one another in production, and energy and other inputs

are also substitutes in production. International trade involves fossil-fuel energy but not non-fossil energy, and commodities produced using both energy sources. The entries in Table 9.9 are percentage changes in GDP. There is a cost where there is a minus sign, and a gain where there is a plus sign. Given that all fossil fuels are aggregated to a single composite 'fossil fuel', carbon taxation is actually achieved by taxing the fossil-fuel commodity, it being assumed that the only way to reduce emissions is to reduce fuel use.

The results shown in Table 9.9 refer to three alternative routes to the achievement in the model of a global 50% reduction in emissions on what would otherwise have been the case. In options 1 and 2 each economy acts to cut its emissions by 50%. In 1 this is done by the imposition of the required rate of tax on the production of fossil fuels. In 2 it is the consumption of fossil fuels that is taxed. It should be noted that in terms of the discussion of alternative instruments for pollution abatement in Chapter 7, both of these are, at the global level, quantity control, or command and control, type instruments. Each economy is required to cut by 50%, so we are dealing, from the global perspective, with uniform emissions reductions across all sources. Each 'source' in this case is a regional economy, which uses taxation to achieve the emissions cutback required of it. Hence, at the global level standard theory would suggest that neither of these is an efficient way to achieve an overall 50% cut in emissions. This is shown in Table 9.9, where world costs are higher with both 1 and 2 than with option 3, which is the use of fossil fuel taxation at the same rate across all sources. In the model, the uniform global tax is levied and collected by an international agency. In this case it does not make any difference whether the tax is levied on production or consumption.

The results for the individual economies show how the distribution of costs varies with instrument choice. In options 1 and 2, tax revenues accrue to the individual economies, and are spent there. Option 1 then benefits carbon-energy, i.e. fossil-fuel, exporters at the expense of importers, especially the 'rest of world'. Under option 1 GDP increases in the 'oil

Table 9.9 Costs associated with alternative instruments for global emissions reductions

Region	Option 1	Option 2	Option 3
EC	−4.0	−1.0	−3.8
N. America	−4.3	−3.6	−9.8
Japan	−3.7	+0.5	−0.9
Other OECD	−2.3	−2.1	−4.4
Oil exporters	+4.5	−18.7	−13.0
Rest of world	−7.1	−6.8	1.8
World	−4.4	−4.4	−4.2

Source: Adapted from Whalley and Wigle (1991)

---

[10] Dinwiddy and Teale (1988) develop, in terms of the algebra and solution algorithms, an illustrative two-industry model to include government expenditure and taxation and foreign trade.

exporters' economy. The 'rest of world' economy includes the developing nations and the formerly centrally planned economies. It does slightly less badly where the 50% reductions in each economy are achieved by a fossil fuel consumption tax. In this case, the oil exporters suffer heavily, and Japan actually gains. With the tax levied on consumption, the costs to fossil fuel importers are reduced because the pre-tax world price of fossil fuel tax falls, due to reduced demand, and the tax revenues are recycled within the importing economies.

Under option 3 a uniform global tax is levied and collected by an international agency which disposes of the revenues by grants to each economy based on their population size. The per capita grant is the same throughout the world. In this case, not only do we have minimised cost to the global economy, but we also have a distributional impact that works to reduce inequity, by, generally, transferring funds to the 'rest of world' economy, which comprises mainly developing economies. This economy actually gains under option 3 when the joint effect of the tax and revenue distribution is considered. As is clear from the discussion in Chapter 10, equity is important here not only for itself, but also for the incentives for participation that arise. The large developing economies, such as India and China, would gain substantially under option 3. Note that a tradable permits regime could have effects similar to those shown for option 3, if the initial allocation of the permits was arranged so as to favour developing countries. This could be done by doing the initial allocation on the basis of equal per capita shares in the global total of emissions, which was the target, or equivalently in total global fossil fuel use. Each country would get an initial allocation equal to one per capita share times its population size.

9.4.3 Alternative uses of national carbon tax revenue

We now consider some CGE modelling results to illustrate the effects of different assumptions about the way in which any environmental tax revenue is used. Table 9.10 reports results for Australia obtained using a model called ORANI which includes a government sector and Australia's overseas trade. The columns refer to two different simulations of

Table 9.10 Effects of carbon taxation according to use of revenue

	S1	S2
Real Gross Domestic Product	0.07	−0.09
Consumer Price Index	−0.18	0.42
Budget Balance*	−0.02	0.31
Employment	0.21	−0.04
CO_2 Emissions	−3.9	−4.7

* As percentage of GDP
Source: Adapted from Common and Hamilton (1996)

the ORANI model where Australia unilaterally introduces carbon taxation:

> S1: Carbon taxation is levied so as to raise revenue of A$2 billion, which is used to reduce payroll taxation by the same amount. The tax rate involved is A$7.40 per tonne of carbon dioxide.

> S2: Carbon taxation is levied so as to raise revenue of A$2 billion, which is used to reduce the government deficit by that amount.

The results shown for these two simulations in Table 9.10 are in terms of the percentage differences from the base case without carbon taxation.

In each of these simulations the model standard CGE modelling practice is not followed in that the model is configured with money wage rates fixed, and the market clearing assumption in the labour market is dropped. This allows the model to examine the employment effects of alternative policies. It is regarded as a way of modelling the short-run effects of policy changes. ORANI modellers wishing to examine long-run effects, where 'long run' means enough time for complete adjustment, would set the model with flexible wage rates which would ensure market clearing in the labour market. This illustrates the point that CGE modelling results have to be understood in the light of the assumptions and intentions of the modellers. The same model can produce different results according to the way it is configured for a particular simulation.

The introduction of carbon taxation has an output and a substitution effect in the labour market. There is a reduction in the demand for labour on account of the contraction of economic activity due to fixed money wages and the trade effects of acting unilaterally. There is an increase in the demand for labour on account of the higher price of fossil fuel inputs relative to labour inputs. Where the carbon tax revenue is used to reduce payroll taxation, the non-wage costs to employers of using labour are reduced, thus reinforcing the substitution effect of the carbon tax itself.

This is seen in the comparison of the results for S1 and S2. Employment actually increases where payroll tax is cut in S1. Given the relative shares of labour and fossil fuel in expenditures on inputs, the switch from a tax on labour input to a tax on fossil fuel input leads to a reduction in the consumer price index. The overall impact gives an increase in real GDP. Where, in S2, the carbon tax revenue is used to reduce the budget deficit, employment falls, as does GDP, and the consumer price index increases.

9.4.4 Benefits and costs of CGE modelling

As compared with I/O models, CGE models have the benefit that they incorporate behavioural responses to the price changes induced by policy actions on the part of producers and consumers. This entails costs. The structure of the behavioural sub-models reflects the assumptions of economic theory. To economists this is the natural and obvious way to proceed. However, many non-economists would argue that producers and consumers do not actually behave according to those assumptions, and there is quite a lot of evidence that can be cited in support of this view. Economists tend to respond to this line of argument, and the evidence, to the effect that the evidence is flawed and/or that the critics are missing the point, which is that the standard assumptions, and CGE models, are not really about predicting short-run and ephemeral movements but about underlying long-run tendencies. Many non-economists, and some economists, are prone to overlook such caveats and regard CGE models as forecasting models. This appears to be less the case with I/O models, perhaps because their limitations are more readily apparent.

Going from I/O to CGE not only involves more assumptions, but also more data so that those assumptions, or their implications, can be quantified for incorporation into the model. As we have seen, the required data are frequently unavailable, so that the behavioural sub-models often use assumed parameter values that are plausible and consistent with a single benchmark data set for the variables included in the model. CGE model results are sensitive to changes in the parameter values used. Again, this is less of a problem to the extent that such models are seen as vehicles for gaining broad quantitative, or even purely qualitative, insights into policy questions, rather than forecasting models.

The use of CGE, and other economic models, in policy debate is often less fruitful than it might be due to a lack of awareness of the inherent limitations of the models themselves combining with a lack of awareness of the limits to the accuracy with which the variables that they track can actually be measured. National income can be measured in three ways, and the same result should arise whichever way it is done. In fact published official national income accounts always include as the 'residual error' the difference between the results of measurement according to two of the conventions. This residual error as a percentage of the measure regarded as most accurate varies over time, but typically is of the order of 0.5%, and goes as high as 1%. CGE model results for the national income cost of environmental policies should be looked at with this in mind. In Table 9.9, for example, we noted that the results for the world GDP costs of alternative instruments for a 50% reduction in global emissions did show, as theory predicts, that uniform taxation is the least-cost instrument. Note, however, that the difference between the least cost and the cost with the other instruments is just 0.2%. One might say, then, that while the model confirms the theory, it also suggests that the gain to going for the least-cost approach, rather than the alternatives considered, is quite small. It should be noted also that the model result is not anyway independent confirmation of the least-cost property of uniform taxation – the model incorporates the same assumptions as the standard theory, and could not produce a different result.

Similar considerations apply to the results in Table 9.10, and to those reported in Chapter 10. As regards the exercise reported on in Table 9.10, the real point is the demonstration that a standard economic model says that, in the short run at least, unilateral carbon taxation need not imply an increase in unemployment and a reduction in national income if the revenue is used to reduce a distortionary tax. This is not a point that I/O modelling could make.

Summary

Economy-wide models take a comprehensive view of the economy as a whole and the interactions between various sectors in the economy. These models can be used to simulate the consequences, direct, indirect and induced of shocks or policy changes on the overall economy and its individual sectors.

Input–output models often have a high level of sectoral disaggregation, permitting the analyst to model changes in a richly detailed way. When augmented with an environmental sector, or environmental activities, I/O models may be used to investigate economy–environment relationships. In this way, they can form the basis for an investigation of environmental policy options, or for the analysis of the impacts of a variety of 'exogenous' changes.

However, the maintained assumptions that underpin input–output modelling, both in its standard and in its environmentally augmented forms, are very strong, and impose highly restrictive assumptions about the extent of substitution possibilities in consumption and production.

Computable general equilibrium (CGE) models generalise the I/O framework, in particular by allowing for substitution effects to take place in response to changes in relative prices. In recent years CGE models have been employed with increasing frequency as a way of simulating different ways of achieving environmental policy objectives. However, while these models are capable of having a very rich specification, and a theoretically consistent foundation, their usefulness in practice is often limited by difficulty in obtaining appropriate data.

Further reading

Our treatment of input–output analysis and its application to questions concerning natural resources and environmental pollution in the text is simplified though essentially valid. For a comprehensive guide to input–output analysis, including environmental and energy input–output models, see Miller and Blair (1985). Vaze (1998c) presents environmental input–output accounts for the United Kingdom for 1993, and reports the results of simulations based upon them. Proops *et al.* (1993) is an extended account of the use of input–output methods to analyse CO_2 emissions and options for their abatement.

Xie (1996) is a good introduction to the use of CGE modeling to study environmental policy issues, and reports results for a Chinese application. Most CGE models are, like the illustrative model discussed in the text, comparative static models. This is a limitation, particularly in the context of a problem like that of thinking about policies for abating CO_2 emissions. The OECD has developed for this problem a dynamic CGE model, which is described and used in Nicoletti and Oliveira-Martins (1993) and Burniaux *et al.* (1994).

Discussion questions

1 Examine critically the basic assumptions of input–output models, in particular those related to the input–output (Leontief) production function and to factor supplies, and discuss the importance of these assumptions in affecting the validity and accuracy of environmental input–output applications.

2 In discussing the results in Table 9.9 it was asserted that with uniform global taxation, the result would be the same using either fossil fuel production or consumption as tax base. Why is this?

Problems

1. (a) Calculate import, wage and other value-added coefficients from Table 9.1 analogous to the intermediate input coefficients a_{ij}. Check that for each industry, the sum of the intermediate and primary input coefficients is unity.

   (b) In the text we used coefficients derived from the data of Table 9.1 to find the gross output levels implied by new higher levels of export demand. Use those new gross output levels to derive a new transactions table, assuming constant input coefficients for both intermediate and primary inputs. Calculate the new level of GDP.

2. Suppose now we can add the following information about tonnes of waste emissions to the dataset of Table 9.1:

   Industry of origin:

Agriculture	Manufacturing	Services	Total
4000	2500	150	6650

   Calculate the change in the industry and total emissions levels that would be associated with an across-the-board increase of 20% in household expenditure.

3. The transactions table for a closed economy is:

	Agriculture	Manufacturing	Final demand
Agriculture	10	20	50
Manufacturing	20	50	80
Primary inputs	50	80	

The agriculture industry purchased 10 units of energy, the manufacturing sector 40 units.

   (a) Calculate the energy intensities for deliveries to final demand by the agriculture and manufacturing industries.

   (b) If the use of 1 unit of energy releases 3.5 units of CO_2, calculate total CO_2 emissions and allocate them to deliveries to final demand by the agriculture and manufacturing industries.

   (c) Calculate what total CO_2 emissions would be for deliveries to final demand of 100 from agriculture and 240 from manufacturing.

4. Using the data of Table 9.1, and noting that $(I - A')^{-1} = [(I - A)^{-1}]'$, calculate the effect on prices of a 50% increase in the import costs in the agriculture sector, due to the imposition of a tax on fuel imports. Why is your calculation likely to overestimate the effects of this cost increase?

5. (a) Calculate the real income change that goes with the results given in Box 9.1 for a 50% reduction in emissions.

   (b) If the utility function is assumed to have the form $C_1^{0.5} C_2^{0.5} E^\delta$, find the value of δ for which it would be true that utility did not fall with the 50% reduction in emissions.

Appendix 9.1 A general framework for environmental input–output analysis

Figure 9.1 sets out schematically a general input–output system for analysing the interconnections between economic activity and the natural environment. The basis is the recognition that there are three types of linkage between the economy and the environment, which should properly be treated jointly. First, economic agents extract or exploit natural resources, including obvious forms of exploitation such as extraction of ores and minerals, fish har-

vesting and so on, but also in less obvious ways such as the 'consumption' of fresh air and landscape.

Second, the processing and consumption of these environmental resources yields residuals which are returned to the environment, and which may have undesirable economic, social or health effects, such as air pollution, soil degradation and loss of habitat. Attempts to eliminate, mitigate or compensate for these effects lead to the third type of

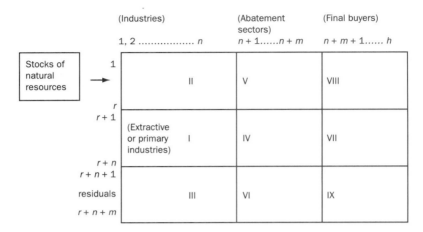

Figure 9.1 An extended input–output system

economy–environment link, namely activities devoted to abatement or environmental renewal.

In Figure 9.1, the submatrices I and VII correspond to the conventional input–output table: I recording flows of goods and services between the *n* intermediate sectors of the economy, and VII recording deliveries to final buyers or users (private and government consumption, investment, exports). For simplicity, we assume here, as we did in the chapter itself, that each 'industry' produces a unique homogeneous 'commodity', thus avoiding the need for a more complex system of accounts which links industries and commodities.

Submatrix II records the extraction or direct use of natural resources by industries, involving a reduction in the vector of stocks of natural resources. The cell *ij* of submatrix II records the amount or volume of resource *i*, measured in physical units, used or consumed by industry *j* during a particular time period, say one year. Thus if resource *i* is water and industry *j* is water supply, the entry in cell *ij* records the volume of water collected and processed by the water supply sector: subsequent sales or deliveries of water to industry and households would appear in row $r + j$ of submatrices I and VII.

Following conventional input–output modelling practice, if we assume a constant proportional relation between inputs of resources and outputs of industries, we can derive a submatrix of resource input coefficients in which the typical coefficient r_{ij} indicates the amount of resource *i* (in physical units)

required per unit of output (typically measured in value units) of industry *j*. Pursuing the example above, r_{ij} would record the number of gallons of water required per million dollars output of the water supply industry.

Many of the cells in submatrix II will be zero, since only a limited number of industries are engaged in the direct extraction or harvesting of natural resources. Processed natural resources will be classified as industrial products and distributed along the rows of submatrices I, IV and VII.

Submatrix III records residual wastes generated by each industry, there being a separate row for each type of residual: thus an entry in cell *gk* in III records the amount of residual *g* generated by industry *k* in the accounting period concerned. Again following standard input–output practice, if we assume a constant proportional relationship between industry output and residuals generation, we can derive a submatrix of waste coefficients in which the typical element w_{gk} indicates the amount of waste element *g* produced per million dollars output of industry *k*. Note that although the elements of submatrix III are outputs rather than inputs, they are treated here in an identical way to the input flows in submatrices II and I. Obvious examples of this type of waste production are pollutants generated by industrial production and distribution, an example of which will be considered later in this appendix.

Columns $n + 1$ to $n + m$ (submatrices IV, V and VI) represent residuals abatement or treatment activities.

Note that although abatement activities are here accorded the status of separate industries, in practice such activities may be undertaken by and within the industries which are responsible for generating the residual concerned. For instance a firm which generates waste water may undertake water purification 'on site' before discharging the water back into the environment. In the accounting system here, the mainstream production and purification activities would be recorded separately. Note also that in this schema, certain abatement/treatment activities may operate at zero levels.

Like other industries, abatement industries purchase goods and services from other industries (submatrix IV), and may also absorb natural resources directly (submatrix V, though this submatrix could well be empty). Moreover, like other industries the abatement sectors may themselves generate residual wastes (submatrix VI).

The output of the abatement industries may be expressed in value terms, as are typically the other industries in the table, or in physical units, as the amount of residual treated or eliminated. In the latter case the input coefficients (submatrix IV) would measure (constant) dollar inputs per ton of residual treated or eliminated. Again, for these industries we assume the Leontief technology of fixed proportional input coefficients.

The final columns of the table record sales or deliveries to final buyers, typically household (private) consumption, government consumption, investment, changes in stocks, exports and (a negative column of) imports, but each of these categories may be further disaggregated. One possibility is to disaggregate the investment column to separately identify capital expenditures directed towards the renewal of natural resources, such as reforestation, soil regeneration, fish stocks renewal, and so on. These activities then provide a link to the vector of stocks of natural resources at the beginning of the environment–economy–environment sequence in Figure 9.1, and are a step towards closure of the model system.

Submatrix VIII allows for the possibility of direct extraction or use of natural resources by final buyers (for example, fresh air, untreated water, fish caught

for personal consumption, and so on), while submatrix IX includes residual wastes generated by households and other final buyers (CO_2, solid wastes, scrap, and so on).

More complex versions can be constructed, and alternative systems of accounting can be utilised, but the above schema captures the essential features of the environmental input–output system, from which a model can be constructed. Like the basic input–output model described in the chapter, the version presented below is an open, comparative-static model in which final demands are exogenous (determined outside the model). There are no explicit capacity constraints on outputs, or limits to the supply of factors of production, which is equivalent to treating factor supplies as completely elastic at prevailing factor prices.[11]

To simplify the algebra, we assume in what follows that submatrices V and VIII are empty. For the n 'conventional' input–output sectors the balance equations are

$$X_i - \sum_{j=1}^{n} a_{ij}X_j - \sum_{q=n+1}^{n+m} a_{iq}Z_q = F_i \quad (9.27)$$

or

$$\mathbf{X} - \mathbf{A_1X} - \mathbf{A_2Z} = \mathbf{F} \quad (9.28)$$

where $\mathbf{X}$ is the output vector for the conventional industries, $\mathbf{Z}$ is the output vector for the abatement industries (to be discussed below) and $\mathbf{F}$ is a vector of deliveries to final buyers. (For convenience we assume here that $\mathbf{F}$ is a vector.) The coefficients $a_{ij} \in \mathbf{A_1}$ and $a_{iq} \in \mathbf{A_2}$ are derived from the system of accounts in Figure 9.1 as

$$a_{ij} = X_{ij}/X_j \quad (9.29)$$

where X_{ij} is purchases of commodity i to produce output X_j, and

$$a_{iq} = X_{iq}/Z_q \quad (9.30)$$

where Z_q is the output of abatement sector q (or volume of residual q eliminated).

These assumptions of constant proportional input coefficients mirror those of the basic input–output

[11] Other than natural resources, inputs of factors of production (labour and capital) are not shown in Figure 9.1, but the system could readily be extended to include them, in a manner similar to that used for natural resource flows.

model of the chapter text, and reflect the properties of the Leontief production function, notably constant returns to scale and zero substitution between inputs, in contrast to the more usual neoclassical function used elsewhere in this book.

For the residuals submatrices (III, VI and IX), the production or generation of residuals can be written as

$$P_g = \sum_{j=1}^{n} w_{gj}X_j + \sum_{q=n+1}^{n+m} w_{gq}Z_q + w_{gF} \qquad (9.31)$$

where P_g is the amount of residual g generated by production, by abatement activities and by final demand.

In matrix form

$$\mathbf{P} = \mathbf{W_1X} + \mathbf{W_2Z} + \mathbf{W_F} \qquad (9.32)$$

Equation 9.32 measures gross production of residuals. The net production is gross production less the volume treated or eliminated, which is the measured output of the abatement sector. How is this determined? For residual g, the net production (the volume of the residual returned to the environment) can be written

$$D_g = Z_g - P_g = Z_g - \sum w_{gj}X_j - \sum w_{gq}Z_q - w_{gF} \qquad (9.33)$$

where Z_g is the volume of residual g eliminated (the output of abatement sector g) and D_g is the net production of g (the volume not eliminated). Unless there is complete elimination, D_g will typically be negative, but its level may be amenable to control, and in ideal circumstances may be taken as a measure of the permitted level of net emission, waste or damage, where marginal damage and abatement costs are equal. By specifying this level as a negative final demand for the residual concerned, we have an equilibrium condition which enables us to determine the output of the abatement activity for that residual.

In matrix form,

$$\mathbf{Z} - \mathbf{W_1X} - \mathbf{W_2Z} = \mathbf{D} + \mathbf{W_F} \qquad (9.34)$$

We now write the complete model in the following partitioned form:

$$\begin{bmatrix} \mathbf{X} \\ \mathbf{Z} \end{bmatrix} - \begin{bmatrix} \mathbf{A_1} & \mathbf{A_2} \\ \mathbf{W_1} & \mathbf{W_2} \end{bmatrix} \begin{bmatrix} \mathbf{X} \\ \mathbf{Z} \end{bmatrix} = \begin{bmatrix} \mathbf{F} \\ \mathbf{D} + \mathbf{W_F} \end{bmatrix} \qquad (9.35)$$

$\mathbf{F}$ and $\mathbf{D}$ are the vectors of independent variables: $\mathbf{F}$ is final demand for the standard commodities, and $\mathbf{D}$ is tolerated or permitted emission, waste or damage levels. Once $\mathbf{F}$ and $\mathbf{D}$ are specified, we can solve for $\mathbf{X}$ (industry output levels) and $\mathbf{Z}$ (abatement levels):

$$\begin{bmatrix} \mathbf{X} \\ \mathbf{Z} \end{bmatrix} = \begin{bmatrix} \mathbf{I} - \mathbf{A_1} & -\mathbf{A_2} \\ -\mathbf{W_1} & \mathbf{I} - \mathbf{W_2} \end{bmatrix}^{-1} \begin{bmatrix} \mathbf{F} \\ \mathbf{D} + \mathbf{W_F} \end{bmatrix} \qquad (9.36)$$

Given the solution vector [$\mathbf{X}$ $\mathbf{Z}$], the level of natural resource consumption can be calculated as

$$\mathbf{N} = \mathbf{R}[\mathbf{X}\ \mathbf{Z}] \qquad (9.37)$$

where $\mathbf{R}$ is a matrix of natural resource input coefficients.

Although there have been numerous applications of environmental input–output models, none has attained the degree of detail and comprehensiveness of the model structure outlined above. Data problems have been severe, particularly in relation to the cost and production structures of abatement activities, but also in the definition and measurement of certain types of environmental degradation.

For this extended environmental input–output system, cost–price calculations can be introduced in a manner similar to that outlined in the third section of the chapter. In practice a range of approaches have been adopted, governed partly by data availability and partly by the particular form of model. For instance, cost–price equations for the abatement sectors (submatrices IV, V and VI of Figure 9.1) could be formulated so that the price of a unit of abatement is determined by its cost of production. In practice, abatement or elimination activity may be undertaken by and within the industry or industries which generate the pollution, and it may be difficult to identify the costs of the abatement activity.

If adequate data on abatement costs are available or can be collected, price equations can be formulated for the abatement sectors as

$$P_g = \sum a_{ij}P_i + v_g \qquad (9.38)$$

where P_g is the price or cost of eliminating one unit of pollutant g. How these equations are used in the extended model depends on the mechanism adopted for paying for abatement or elimination. If legislation obliges the polluter to pay, then polluting industries will buy abatement services from the abatement sectors, and the cost of these services will be included in the polluting industries' prices. The output price for industry j now becomes

$$P_j = \Sigma a_{ij} P_i + \Sigma a_{gj} P_g + v_j \tag{9.39}$$

where a_{gj} is the quantity of abatement service g per unit of output which industry j is required to purchase, and P_g is the unit cost of abatement service g. The general solution to the extended price model then becomes

$$\mathbf{P} = (\mathbf{I} - \mathbf{A'})^{-1} \mathbf{v} \tag{9.40}$$

where $\mathbf{P}$, $\mathbf{v}$ and $\mathbf{A}$ now include the abatement sectors. Alternatively, abatement/treatment may be financed through general taxation. In this case, polluting industry prices are unaffected (at least directly). Abatment services are provided by or purchased by government (central or local) and delivered to consumers as a public service (for example, river purification, household waste collection, nuclear waste disposal).

Appendix 9.2 The algebra of the two-sector CGE model

The utility maximisation problem for the household is

$$\text{Max } C_1^\alpha C_2^\beta \text{ subject to } Y = P_1 C_1 + P_2 C_2$$

for which the Lagrangian is

$$\Psi = C_1^\alpha C_2^\beta + \lambda [Y - P_1 C_1 - P_2 C_2]$$

giving the first-order conditions:

$$\partial \Psi / \partial C_1 = \alpha C_1^{\alpha-1} C_2^\beta - \lambda P_1 = 0 \tag{9.41}$$

$$\partial \Psi / \partial C_2 = \beta C_1^\alpha C_2^{\beta-1} - \lambda P_2 = 0 \tag{9.42}$$

$$\partial \Psi / \partial \lambda = Y - P_1 C_1 - P_2 C_2 = 0 \tag{9.43}$$

Moving the terms in λ to the right-hand side in equations 9.41 and 9.42 and then dividing the first equation by the second gives

$$(\alpha C_1^{\alpha-1} C_2^\beta)/(\beta C_1^\alpha C_2^{\beta-1}) = P_1/P_2$$

which can be solved for C_2 as

$$C_2 = (\beta P_1/\alpha P_2) C_1$$

which on substitution for C_2 in equation 9.43 solves for

$$C_1 = [\alpha/(\alpha + \beta) P_1] Y \tag{9.44}$$

Using equation 9.44 to eliminate C_1 from the budget constraint and solving for C_2 yields

$$C_2 = [\beta/(\alpha + \beta) P_2] Y \tag{9.45}$$

Equations 9.44 and 9.45 are equations 9.25 in the text of the chapter.

Now consider the derivation of factor demands and the supply function for a profit-maximising firm,

where the production function is Cobb–Douglas in labour, L, and oil, R:

$$X = L^a R^b \tag{9.46}$$

With W and P for the prices of labour and oil respectively, total cost is given by:

$$TC = WL + PR \tag{9.47}$$

For cost minimisation, the Lagrangian is

$$\Psi = WL + PR + \lambda [X - L^a R^b]$$

and the necessary conditions are

$$\partial \Psi / \partial L = W - \lambda a L^{a-1} R^b = 0 \tag{9.48}$$

$$\partial \Psi / \partial R = P - \lambda b L^a R^{b-1} = 0 \tag{9.49}$$

$$\partial \Psi / \partial \lambda = X - L^a R^b = 0 \tag{9.50}$$

Moving the terms in λ to the right-hand side in equations 9.48 and 9.49 and dividing the first of the resulting equations by the second so as to eliminate λ, we get

$$W/P = (a/b) L^{-1} R$$

or

$$L/R = (a/b) P W^{-1} = (a/b)(P/W) \tag{9.51}$$

which gives the ratio of factor use levels for cost minimisation as depending on the factor price ratio, and the parameters of the production function.

From equation 9.50 we can write

$$L = (X/R^b)^{1/a}$$

and using this in equation 9.51 to eliminate L yields, after rearrangement,

$$R = [(b/a)(W/P)]^{a/(a+b)} X^{1/(a+b)} \qquad (9.52)$$

for the firm's demand for oil as depending on factor prices and the level of output. Using equation 9.50 again gives

$$R = (X/L^a)^{1/b}$$

which, used in equation 9.51 to eliminate R, leads to

$$L = [(a/b)(P/W)]^{b/(a+b)} X^{1/(a+b)} \qquad (9.53)$$

for the firm's demand for labour.

Equations 9.52 and 9.53 are known as 'conditional factor demands', since they give demands conditional on the output level. To get, unconditional, factor demand equations we need to determine the profit-maximising output level. With P_X for the price of output, profits are

$$\pi = P_X X - WL - PR$$

and substituting from the conditional factor demand equations, this is

$$\pi = P_X X - W[(a/b)(P/W)]^{b/(a+b)} X^{1/(a+b)} \\ + P[(b/a)(W/P)]^{a/(a+b)} X^{1/(a+b)}$$

or

$$\pi = P_X X - ZX^{1/(a+b)} \qquad (9.54)$$

where

$$Z = W[(a/b)(P/W)]^{b/(a+b)} + P[(b/a)(W/P)]^{a/(a+b)} \qquad (9.55)$$

Taking the derivative of equation 9.54 with respect to X and setting it equal to zero gives

$$P_X - [1/(a+b)]ZX^{1-\{1/(a+b)\}} = 0 \qquad (9.56)$$

as necessary for profit maximisation. Solving equation 9.56 for X gives the profit-maximising output level as:

$$X = [\{(a+b)P_X\}/Z]^{\{(a+b)/(a+b-1)\}} \qquad (9.57)$$

Equation 9.57 is a supply function giving profit-maximising output as depending on the output price, P_X, and factor prices, P and W.

As in the chapter here, CGE models frequently employ the assumption of constant returns to scale in production. In this case, there is no supply func-

tion. For the Cobb–Douglas production function, constant returns to scale means $a + b = 1$, which means that the exponent of X in equation 9.56 is zero. This means that the equation does not involve X and cannot be solved for it to give a supply function. For $a + b = 1$, equation 9.56 becomes

$$P_X = Z$$

which, using equation 9.55 with $a + b = 1$, is:

$$P_X = W[(a/b)(P/W)]^{(1-a)} + P[(b/a)(W/P)]^a \qquad (9.58)$$

Now, using $a + b = 1$ in equations 9.52 and 9.53 gives

$$R = [(\{1-a\}/a)(W/P)]^a X$$

and

$$L = [(a/\{1-a\})(P/W)]^{(1-a)} X$$

so that, dividing by X,

$$U_R = R/X = [(\{1-a\}/a)(W/P)]^a \qquad (9.59)$$

and

$$U_L = L/X = [(a/\{1-a\})(P/W)]^{(1-a)} \qquad (9.60)$$

These two equations give the use of each factor per unit output as functions of the relative prices of the factors. If we knew the level of output X, we could use them to derive factor demands, by multiplying U_R and U_L by the output level.

On rearrangement, equation 9.58 with $a + b = 1$ is

$$P_X = W^a P^{(1-a)}(a/\{1-a\})^{(1-a)} \\ + P^{(1-a)} W^a (\{1-a\}/a)^a$$

so that it and equations 9.59 and 9.60 mean that

$$P_X = W U_L + P U_R \qquad (9.61)$$

which is the unit cost equation. It has the implication, well known from basic microeconomics, that for constant returns to scale in production, profits are zero at all levels of output. To see this, note that

$$W U_L + P U_R = W(L/X) + P(R/X) = (WL + PR)/X$$

which is average cost, so that equation 9.61 says that price equals average cost. Although demonstrated here for a Cobb–Douglas production function, this result holds for any constant-returns-to-scale production function. With constant returns to scale, the firm produces to satisfy demand, using the factor input mix that follows from cost minimisation, and makes zero profit.

CHAPTER 10

International environmental problems

The nation-state is here to stay for the near horizon. Thus, practical solutions for today's global challenges must adjust for this reality.

Sandler (1997), p. 212

Learning objectives

During the course of this chapter we address a set of important questions that relate to international environmental problems. After studying this chapter, the reader should understand the implications of these questions, be able to answer them in general terms, and have the ability to apply those general answers to specific international environmental problems.

The questions we deal with are as follows:

- In which ways do international environmental problems differ from purely national (or sub-national) problems?
- What additional issues are brought into contention by virtue of an environmental problem being 'international'?
- What insights does the body of knowledge known as game theory bring to our understanding of international environmental policy?
- What determines the degree to which cooperation takes place between countries and policy is coordinated? Put another way, which conditions favour (or discourage) the likelihood and extent of cooperation between countries?
- Why is cooperation typically a gradual, dynamic process, with agreements often being embodied in treaties or conventions that are general frameworks of agreed principles, but in which subsequent negotiation processes determine the extent to which cooperation is taken?
- Is it possible to use such conditions to explain how far efficient cooperation has gone concerning acid rain, lower-atmosphere ozone, and greenhouse-gas pollution?

Introduction

Previous chapters have shown that markets are likely to generate inefficient outcomes in the presence of externalities and public goods. The interdependencies that they create are not, and cannot be, adequately addressed through unregulated market mechanisms. However, when all generators and victims of an externality – or all individuals affected by a public good – reside within a single country, mechanisms exist by which government may be able to induce or enforce an efficient resource allocation where markets fail to do so.[1] These mechanisms can operate because the primacy given to the nation state in political affairs provides the legitimacy and authority needed to support them.

However, many important environmental problems concern public goods or external effects where affected individuals live (or are yet to live) in many or all nation states. These *international and global environmental problems* are the subject of this chapter. Important examples include global warming, ozone-layer depletion, acid rain, biodiversity loss, and the control of infectious diseases. One property common to these problems is that the level of an

---

[1] There are two important caveats here. First, where there is widespread dispute about the appropriate boundaries of a nation state, government may not possess the legitimacy required to secure compliance with its regulations. Second, even where it is legitimate, government may have insufficient information or means to achieve efficient outcomes.

environmental cost borne, or benefit received, by citizens of one country does not depend only on that country's actions but also depends on the actions of other countries. Reflect for a moment on these examples. It is evident that in each case the relevant costs and benefits depend on the behaviour of many nations. This adds an important dimension to environmental analysis. Where environmental impacts spill over national boundaries, there is typically no international organisation with the power to induce or enforce a collectively efficient outcome. Will countries behave selfishly in these circumstances? If so, what will be the consequences of that behaviour? Does mutually beneficial cooperation take place between independent nation states? If it does, how large are the gains from that cooperation? And what can be done to increase the chances of cooperative behaviour? These are the kinds of questions we try to answer in this chapter.

We begin our consideration of international environmental problems by discussing international environmental agreements. Box 10.1 lists some characteristics of such agreements. The items in this list are 'stylised facts' – assertions that are widely accepted as being valid statements about the phenomena being studied. Subsequent sections of this chapter will illustrate these stylised facts with several examples, and will use economic theory to explain and support them.

The main tool used to explain these assertions is game (or games) theory. Game theory analysis of international environmental problems has been one of the major developments in the recent environmental economics literature. We begin by looking at a simple two-country, two-strategy game played just once. This simple model is then generalised to take account of many countries, continuous rather than discrete choices (for example, *how much* pollution abatement rather than *whether or not* to abate pollution), and games played repeatedly rather than just a single time.

Game theory is applied here in the context of decisions about the provision of an international public good. This focus is taken because many – if not most – international and global problems concern the provision (or maintenance) of public goods, and because the theory of public goods has underpinned much of the recent literature about international and global environmental problems. However, much of the content of this chapter could also be interpreted in terms of externalities that spill over national boundaries.

In addition to the examples discussed as we go along, the chapter also examines in greater depth the problems of global climate change, acid rain and depletion of the ozone layer. As you read through these cases, you will see the power of insight that game theory brings to bear on these problems. The chapter concludes by looking at the trade–environment relationship. The notion that free trade can improve economic welfare is a central tenet of economic theory. It goes some way to explain the attachment that many economists have to measures that liberalise international trade. However, free trade may not be welfare-enhancing once environmental impacts are brought into the picture. We explore the conditions under which trade liberalisation is likely to have beneficial – and deleterious – environmental consequences.

Questions at the end of the chapter – and the *Additional Materials* for Chapter 10 – invite you to apply the ideas developed in this chapter to other important examples: tropical deforestation, wilderness conversion and the loss of biological diversity.

10.1 International environmental cooperation

More than 170 international environmental treaties have been adopted to date, covering a wide range of actual or potential environmental problems.[2] Many of the early treaties concerned regulation of behaviour at sea: marine fishing (see Chapter 17), transportation in international waters, dumping and disposal of wastes, and exploitation of the sea beds. Another set related to regional pollution spillover problems. In recent years, great attention has been paid to attempts to develop agreements about the use

---

[2] Further details of these international treaties can be found in *Treaties.doc* in *Additional Materials*, Chapter 10. A hyperlink from there points you to various summary listings of these treaties available on various web sites, and to a variety of sources of further information about international environmental agreements.

of two global public goods: composition of the atmosphere and the stock of biological diversity.

The main vehicle that has been used in attempts to reach cooperative solutions to regional and global environmental problems is that of the intergovernmental conference. The proactive role played by the United Nations (UN) system of international institutions has been one of the successes of international diplomacy in the post-Cold War period. The adoption of a treaty through such a framework does not of itself imply that objectives and targets will be met. However, the moral, financial and political pressures that such treaties can bring to bear may be large. Also noteworthy is the way in which the UN environmental strategy has attempted to link issues of environmental protection, environmental sustainability and economic development (the latter particularly in the poorer nations).

Initiatives through the United Nations are not the only, or even the most important, framework within which international environmental cooperation has taken place. Much of what is important has been dealt with at regional or bilateral levels, and takes place in relatively loose, informal ways. Why is there a need for international treaties at all? The answer to this question has already been sketched out in the Introduction. Political sovereignty resides principally in nation states. And as the epigraph to this chapter suggests, that state of affairs is likely to remain so for the foreseeable future. There is one important exception to this statement. Countries of the European Union have moved some way towards creating a supranational political institution. However, it is not yet evident that member states have relinquished substantial sovereign power to the European Union.

The environmental impacts of economic activity do not respect national boundaries, however. As the scale and pervasiveness of these activities increases, so the proportion of activity that has international (rather than intra-national) consequences rises, or at least becomes more evident to us. In the absence of a formal supranational political apparatus with decision-making sovereignty, the coordination of behaviour across countries seeking environmental improvements must take place through other forms of international cooperation. Formal international treaties represent the most visible outcome of that cooperation.

How effective has international cooperation been? Does it merely reflect what countries would have done anyway, and so offers little real improvement over the status quo? Or have there been significant environmental (and efficiency) gains arising from cooperation? Three often-repeated assertions about effectiveness warrant particular attention:

- Treaties tend to codify actions that nations were already taking.
- When the number of affected countries is very large, treaties can achieve very little, no matter how many signatories there are.
- Cooperation can be hardest to obtain when it is needed most.

We shall examine the validity of these, and a series of related, assertions in this chapter. To set the scene – and to provide an agenda of issues for analysis in later sections – we present, in Box 10.1, a set of 'stylised facts' about international environmental cooperation. There is now a huge literature on the economics and politics of international environmental agreements. The stylised facts listed in the box have been extracted from conclusions that have been found with some regularity in that literature. Nevertheless, you should treat these as hypotheses rather than facts, and examine them in the light of the evidence given – and the theoretical explanations offered – in the chapter.

10.2 Game theory analysis[3,4]

A powerful technique for analysing behaviour where actions of individuals or firms are interdependent is game theory. We shall make extensive use of game theory to investigate behaviour in the presence of global or regional public goods. The arguments

---

[3] This section, and others in the chapter, draw heavily on the works of two writers: Todd Sandler and Scott Barrett. Sandler's book *Global Challenges* (1997) is a superb non-technical account of game theory applied to international environmental problems. The sequencing and much of the content of our game theory arguments owe much to the pieces by Barrett listed in the Further Reading to this chapter.

[4] The games we shall consider here are played by two or more countries. Another variant of game theory is known as games against nature, which is concerned with choices by just one player under conditions of uncertainty.

Box 10.1 Conditions that are conducive to effective cooperation between nations in dealing with international environmental problems

Game theory suggests that some conditions are conducive to effective international cooperation. These conditions include the following (each of which will be illustrated at some point in this chapter):

- The existence of an international political institution with the authority and power to construct, administer and enforce a collective agreement.
- The output of the international agreement would yield private rather than public goods.
- A large proportion of nation-specific or localised benefits relative to transnational benefits coming from the actions of participating countries.
- A small number of cooperating countries.
- Relatively high cultural similarity among the affected or negotiating parties.
- A substantial concentration of interests among the adversely affected parties.
- The adoption of a leadership role by one 'important' nation.
- A small degree of uncertainty about the costs and benefits associated with resolving the problem.
- The agreement is self-enforcing.
- There is a continuous relationship between the parties.
- The existence of linked benefits.
- The short-run cost of implementation is low, and so current sacrifice is small.
- The time profile of benefits is such that a high proportion of the available benefits are obtained currently and in the near future.
- The costs of bargaining are small relative to the gains expected from cooperation.

also apply to externalities that spill over national boundaries.

Game theory is used to analyse choices where the outcome of a decision by one player depends on the decisions of the other players, and where decisions of others are not known in advance. This interdependence is evident in environmental problems. Where pollution spills over national boundaries, expenditures by any one country on pollution abatement will give benefits not only to the abating country but to others as well. Similarly, if a country chooses to spend nothing on pollution control, it can obtain benefits if others do so. So in general the pay-off to doing pollution control (or not doing it) depends not only on one's own choice, but also on the choices of others.

10.2.1 Two-player binary-choice games

We investigate first a two-player game. Each player has a simple binary choice to make: selecting either Strategy 1 or Strategy 2. The game is played just once. The two players are identical. The elements of this game can be represented in the generic form shown in Figure 10.1:

Y's strategy / X's strategy	*Strategy 1*	*Strategy 2*
Strategy 1	a, a	b, c
Strategy 2	c, b	d, d

Figure 10.1 Two-player binary-choice games

The pair of letters in each cell of the matrix denotes the net benefit (or pay-off) that each country receives for a particular choice of strategy by X and by Y. The first letter denotes the pay-off to X, the second the pay-off to Y. When the letters in Figure 10.1 are replaced by numerical values, a particular form of game is generated, and we can explore its outcome. As there are many alternative structures of pay-off matrix, there is a large number of possible game forms. We begin with a game that has been widely used to analyse international environmental problems: the *Prisoner's Dilemma.*

10.2.1.1 A 'Prisoner's Dilemma' game

This was first introduced in Chapter 5. Let the players in this game be two countries, X and Y. Each country must choose whether or not to abate pollution. Pollution abatement is assumed to be a public good so that abatement by either country benefits both. Each unit of pollution abatement comes at a cost of 7 to the abater, but confers benefits of 5 to both countries. If both abate both experience benefits of 10. The pay-offs from the four possible outcomes are indicated in Figure 10.2.

Y's strategy / X's strategy	Pollute	Abate
Pollute	**0, 0**	5, –2
Abate	–2, 5	3, 3

Figure 10.2 A two-player pollution abatement game

Pollute is taken to be the status quo strategy. If neither country abates, there are no costs or benefits (relative to the status quo) to either country, and so the net benefit to each is 0. Other pay-offs can be deduced from the information given above. For example, if X chooses *Abate* and Y *Pollute* the pay-offs are –2 to X (a benefit of 5 minus a cost of 7) and 5 to Y (a benefit of 5 at no cost).

10.2.1.1.1 The non-cooperative solution

To predict the outcome of this game, it is necessary to consider how the countries handle their strategic interdependence. Let us investigate the consequences of two different ways in which that interdependence may be handled. The first approach is to assume that each country maximises its own net benefit, conditional on some expectation about how the other will act, and without collaboration taking place between the countries. We describe this kind of behaviour as 'non-cooperative'. If this leads to an equilibrium outcome, that outcome is called a non-cooperative solution to the game. Alternatively, 'cooperative behaviour' takes place when countries collaborate and make agreements about their strategic choices. If an equilibrium outcome exists, it is called a cooperative solution to that game.

We begin by looking at non-cooperative behaviour. One important concept that is widely used in looking for solutions to non-cooperative games is the idea of dominant strategy. A player has a dominant strategy when it has one strategy that offers a higher pay-off than any other irrespective of the choice made by the other player. A widely accepted tenet of non-cooperative game theory is that dominant strategies are selected where they exist.

Let us examine the pay-off matrix to see whether either country has a dominant strategy. First, look at the game from Y's point of view. If X chooses

Pollute, Y's preferred choice is *Pollute*, as the pay-off of 0 from not abating exceeds the pay-off of –2 from abating. Conversely, if X chooses *Abate*, Y's preferred strategy is *Pollute*. We see that whatever X chooses, *Pollute* is best for Y, and so is Y's dominant strategy. You should confirm that the dominant strategy for X is also *Pollute*. Non-cooperative game theory analysis leads us to the conclusion that the equilibrium solution to this game consists of both countries not abating pollution.

It is worth remarking on three characteristics of this solution. First, the fact that neither country chooses to abate pollution implies that the state of the environment will be worse than it could be. Second, the solution is a *Nash equilibrium*. A set of strategic choices is a Nash equilibrium if each player is doing the best possible given what the other is doing. Put another way, neither country would benefit by deviating unilaterally from the outcome, and so would not unilaterally alter its strategy given the opportunity to do so. Third, the outcome is inefficient. Both countries could do better if they had chosen to abate (in which case the pay-off to each would be three rather than zero).

Why has this state of affairs come about? There are two facets to the answer. The first is that the game has been played non-cooperatively. We shall examine shortly how things might be different with cooperative behaviour. The second concerns the pay-offs used in Figure 10.2. These pay-offs determine the structure of incentives facing the countries. They reflect the assumptions we made earlier about the costs and benefits of pollution abatement. In this case, the incentives are not conducive to the choice of abatement.

Not surprisingly, the structure of incentives can be crucial to the outcome of a game. The pay-off matrix in Figure 10.2 is an example of a so-called *Prisoner's Dilemma* game. The Prisoner's Dilemma is the name given to all games in which the pay-offs, when put in ordinal form, are as shown in Figure 10.3. The ordinal form of the pay-off matrix *ranks* pay-offs rather than showing them in nominal values. Thus in Figure 10.3, the number 1 denotes the least preferred pay-off and 4 the most preferred pay-off. Take a moment to confirm to yourself that the rankings in Figure 10.3 do correspond to the nominal pay-offs in Figure 10.2.

X's strategy / Y's strategy	Defect (Pollute)	Cooperate (Abate)
Defect (Pollute)	**2, 2**	4, 1
Cooperate (Abate)	1, 4	3, 3

Figure 10.3 The two-player pollution abatement Prisoner's Dilemma game: ordinal form

In *all* Prisoner's Dilemma games, there is a single Nash equilibrium (the outcome highlighted in bold in Figures 10.2 and 10.3). This Nash equilibrium is also the dominant strategy for each player. Moreover, the pay-offs to both countries in the dominant strategy Nash equilibrium are less good than those which would result from choosing their alternative (dominated) strategy. As we shall see in a moment, not all games have this structure of pay-offs. However, so many environmental problems appear to be examples of Prisoner's Dilemma games that environmental problems are routinely described as Prisoner's Dilemmas.

10.2.1.1.2 *Cooperative solution*

Suppose that countries were to cooperate, perhaps by negotiating an agreement. Would this alter the outcome of the game? Intuition would probably leads us to answer yes. If both countries agreed to abate – and did what they agreed to do – pay-offs to each would be 3 rather than 0. So in a Prisoner's Dilemma cooperation offers the prospect of greater rewards for both countries, and superior environmental quality.

But there is a problem here. Can these greater rewards be sustained? If self-interest governs behaviour, they probably cannot. To see why, note that the {*Abate, Abate*} outcome is not a Nash equilibrium. Each country has an incentive to defect from the agreement – to unilaterally alter its strategy once the agreement has been reached. Imagine that the two countries are at the cooperative solution, and then look at the incentives facing Y. Given that X has chosen to abate, Y can obtain an advantage by defecting from the agreement ('free-riding'), leaving

X to abate but not abating itself. In this way, country Y could obtain a net benefit of 5 units. Exactly the same argument applies to X, of course. There is a strong incentive operating on each player to attempt to obtain the benefits of free-riding on the other's pollution abatement. These incentives to defect from the agreement mean that the cooperative solution is, at best, an unstable solution.

10.2.1.1.2.1 A binding agreement? Is it possible to transform this game in some way so that the {*Abate, Abate*} strategy pair becomes a stable cooperative solution? There are ways in which this might be done, several of which we shall examine later in the chapter. One possibility would be to negotiate an agreement with built-in penalty clauses for defection. For example, the agreement might specify that if either party defects (pollutes) it must pay a fine of $3\frac{1}{2}$ to the other. If you construct the pay-off matrix that would correspond to this agreement, it will be seen that the game structure has been transformed so that it is no longer a Prisoner's Dilemma game. Moreover, both countries would choose to abate.

But we should be hesitant about accepting this conclusion. Countries might make such promises but, given the incentive to defect, would they keep them or could they be made to keep them? As we have seen there is an incentive to renege on promises here. Cheating (or reneging or free-riding) on agreements might confer large gains on individual cheaters, particularly if the cheating is not detectable. And countries could only be forced to keep their promises (or pay their fines) if there were a third party who could enforce the agreement. So to secure the collectively best outcome, and to make the agreement binding in a game-theory rather than legal sense, it would seem that an enforcer is required. But in a world of sovereign states, no such enforcer exists. So agreements between nations must be *self-enforcing* if they are to be sustained.[5] The only self-enforcing equilibrium here seems to be the non-cooperation outcome.

All of this suggests that cooperation cannot be relied upon to prevail over individual countries acting non-cooperatively in ways which they perceive to be in their own interests. Non-cooperative outcomes

---

[5] Later in this chapter we shall give a precise explanation of what is meant by a self-enforcing agreement.

can and do happen, even where it would be in the interest of all to behave cooperatively. It is for this reason that the game we have been discussing was called a dilemma. Players acting in an individually rational way end up in a bad state. If they attempt to collaborate, incentives on the other to cheat on the deal expose each to the risk of finishing up in the worst of all possible states. Mutual defection seems to be inevitable.

Fortunately, not all games have the structure of the Prisoner's Dilemma. And, despite what has been said above, we shall see there *may* be ways in which a Prisoner's Dilemma game could be successfully transformed to a type that is conducive to cooperation. Box 10.2 briefly describes two other forms of game – the Assurance Game and the Chicken Game – that are useful in exploring international environmental problems.

Box 10.2 Other forms of game

Not all games have the form of the Prisoner's Dilemma. Indeed, Sandler (1997) states that there are 78 possible ordinal forms of the 2-player, 2-strategy game, found from all the permutations of the rankings 1 through to 4. Two other structures of pay-off matrix appear to be highly relevant to environmental problems. These structures generate the Chicken game and the Assurance game.

X's strategy \ Y's strategy	Pollute	Abate
Pollute	–4, –4	**5, –2**
Abate	**–2, 5**	3, 3

Figure 10.4 A two-player Chicken game

Chicken game

Let us revisit the previous game in which each of two countries must choose whether or not to abate pollution. We suppose, as before, that each unit of pollution abatement comes at a cost of 7 to the abater and, being a public good, confers benefits of 5 to both countries. However, in this example, doing nothing exposes both countries to serious pollution damage, at a cost of 4 to both countries. The pay-off matrix for this 'Chicken game' is presented in Figure 10.4.[6] The only difference between this set of payoffs and that in Figure 10.2 is the negative (as opposed to zero) pay-offs in the cell corresponding to both countries selecting *Pollute*.

This difference fundamentally changes the nature of the game.[7] Consider, first, non-cooperative behaviour. Neither player has a dominant strategy. Moreover, there are two Nash equilibria (the cells in bold).

Game theory predicts that in the absence of a dominant strategy equilibrium, a Nash equilibrium will be played (if one exists). Here there are two Nash equilibria (bottom left and top right cells), so there is some indeterminacy in this game. How can this indeterminacy be removed? One possibility arises from commitment or reputation. Suppose that X commits herself to pollute, and that Y regards this commitment as credible. Then the bottom row of the matrix becomes irrelevant, and Y, faced with pay-offs of either –2 or –4, will choose to abate. (We may recognise this form of behaviour in relationships between bullies and bullied.) Another possibility arises if the game is played *sequentially* rather than simultaneously. Suppose that some circumstance exists so that country X chooses first.[8] Y then observes X's choice and decides on its own action. In these circumstances, the *extensive form* of the game is

---

[6] The description 'Chicken game' comes from the fact that this form of pay-off matrix is often used to describe a game of daring in which two motorists drive at speed towards each other. The one who loses nerve and swerves is called Chicken. Relabelling the strategy *Pollute* as *Maintain Course* and *Abate* as *Swerve* generates a plausible pay-off matrix for that game.

[7] If you transform the Chicken game pay-off matrix into its ordinal form, you will see that the difference in ordinal forms of the Prisoner's Dilemma and the Chicken game lies in the reversal of the positions in the matrices of the 1 and 2 rankings.

[8] A commitment or a reputation might be interpreted in this way. That is, the other player (in this case Y) regards X as already having made their choice of strategy.

Box 10.2 *continued*

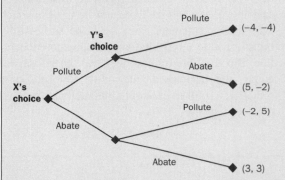

Figure 10.5 Extensive form of the Chicken game

relevant for analysis of choices. This is illustrated in Figure 10.5. The solution to this game can be found by the method of backward induction. If X chooses *Pollute*, Y's best response is *Abate*. The pay-off to X is then 5. If X chooses *Abate*, Y's best response is *Pollute*. The pay-off to X is then −2. Given knowledge about Y's best response, X will choose *Pollute* as her pay-off is 5 (rather than −2 if she had selected *Abate*). This is one example of a more general result: in games where moves are made sequentially, it is *sometimes* advantageous to play first – there is a 'first-mover advantage'. First-mover advantages exist in Chicken games, for example.[9]

Now consider another possibility. Suppose there is asymmetry in the top left cell so that the penalty to X of not abating is −1 rather than −4, but all else remains unchanged. (This is no longer a Chicken game, however, as can be seen by inspecting the ordinal structure of pay-offs.) The outcome of this game is determinate, and the strategy combination corresponding to the top right cell will be chosen. Backward induction shows that X has a dominant strategy of *Pollute*. Given that Y expects X to play her dominant strategy, Y plays *Abate*.[10]

This is reminiscent of decisions relating to ozone-layer depletion. For a while, at least, some countries expected the USA to reduce

ozone-depleting emissions, and were content to free-ride on this. Indeed, the USA did play a major role in leading the way towards reducing their usage of ozone-depleting substances. Two reasons seemed to lie behind this. First, US EPA studies published in 1987 had shown that health costs from ozone depletion were dramatically higher than control costs. (Specifically, a 50% cut in CFC emissions was estimated to create long-term benefits in the form of avoided cancer damage valued at $6.4 trillion, while long-run abatement costs would be in the range $20–40 billion.[11]) Second, chemical businesses in the USA were confident of being able to achieve competitive advantage in the production of substitute products to CFC substances. The USA would be in a very strong position were a CFC ban to be introduced. Overall, the USA perceived that the benefits to her of abatement were high relative to the benefits of not abating. This was not true for all countries, however, and it is this that creates an asymmetry in the pay-off matrix. Those countries which were, initially at least, free-riders had less relative advantage in abating.

Cooperative behaviour

A strategy in which both countries abate pollution could be described as a cooperative solution to the Chicken game as specified in Figure 10.4. The mutually abate strategy is collectively best for the two countries. But that solution is not stable, because it is not a Nash equilibrium. Given the position in which both countries abate, each has an incentive to defect (provided the other does not). A self-enforcing agreement in which the structure of incentives leads countries to negotiate an agreement in which they will all abate *and* in which all will wish to stay in that position once it is reached does not exist here. However, where the structure of pay-offs has the form of a Chicken game, we expect that *some* protective action will take place. Who will do it, and who will free-ride, depends on particular circumstances.

---

[9] However, some other structures of pay-off matrix lead to the opposite result, in which it is better to let the other player move first and then take advantage of that other player.

[10] Dixit and Nalebuff (1991) give a more complete account of the reasoning that lies behind strategic choices in these kinds of games.

[11] Some later (1989) US EPA estimates are presented in Table 10.5 below. While the estimates are rather different, the huge surplus of benefits over costs remains in the later figures.

Box 10.2 *continued*

Assurance game

The other game-form to which some attention will be given in this chapter is the Assurance game. We consider this in terms of an example in which each of two countries must decide whether or not to contribute to a global public good. The cost to each country of contributing is 8. Benefits of 12 accrue to each country only if both countries contribute to the public good. If one or neither country contributes there is no benefit to either country. What we have here is a form of threshold effect: only when the total provision of the public good reaches a certain level (here 2 units) does any benefit flow from the public good. Situations in which such thresholds exist may include the control of infectious disease, conservation of biodiversity, and the reintroduction of species variety into common-property resource systems. The pay-off matrix which derives from the cost and benefit values described above is given in Figure 10.6.

Inspection of the pay-off matrix reveals the following. Looking first at non-cooperative behaviour, neither country has a dominant strategy. There are two Nash equilibria (shown in bold in the matrix). Which is the more likely to

A's strategy	B's strategy *Do not contribute*	*Contribute*
Do not contribute	**0, 0**	0, −8
Contribute	−8, 0	**4, 4**

Figure 10.6 A two-player Assurance game

occur? Perhaps surprisingly, game theory cannot be of much help in answering that question for a single-shot game. However (as we show later), if the game were to be played repeatedly there is a strong presumption that both would contribute. Moreover, the greater is the difference between the payoffs in the two Nash equilibria, the more likely is it that the 'both countries contribute' outcome will result.

The cooperative solution is that in which both contribute. This solution is stable because it is self-enforcing. If one player cooperates, it is in the interest of the other to do so too. Once here, neither would wish to renege or renegotiate. The incentive structure here is supportive of cooperation.

10.2.2 Games with multiple players

The analysis so far has been restrictive, as it has involved only two-country games. But most international environmental problems involve several countries, and global problems a large number. However, much of what we have found so far generalises readily to problems involving more than two countries. Let N be the number of countries affected by some environmental problem, where $N \geq 2$.

We begin by revisiting the Prisoner's Dilemma example, discussed first in Section 10.2.1.1. As before, each unit of pollution abatement comes at a cost of 7 to the abating country; it confers benefits of 5 to the abating country and to all other countries. For the case where $N = 10$, the pay-off matrix can be described in the form of Table 10.1.

Here we look at things from the point of view of one country, the ith country let us say. Table 10.1 lists the pay-off to country i from polluting and from abating for all possible numbers of countries **other**

than i that choose to abate. It is evident that irrespective of how many other countries decide to abate, it is individually rational for country i to not abate. Given that all countries are symmetrical, the non-cooperative solution is *Not Abate* by all 10 countries. The basic properties of the two-country Prisoner's Dilemma are again evident. Nations following their self-interest each finish up with worse outcomes (0 each) than if all were to cooperate and abate pollution (43 each). But the cooperative solution remains unstable. Given an agreement to

Table 10.1 The Prisoner's Dilemma example with 10 countries

	Number of abating nations other than i									
	0	1	2	3	4	5	6	7	8	9
Nation i pollutes	0	5	10	15	20	25	30	35	40	45
Nation i abates	−2	3	8	13	18	23	28	33	38	43

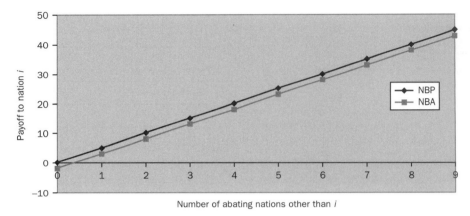

Figure 10.7 The pay-offs to one country from abating and from not abating as the number of other countries abating varies

Abate, any individual country does better by reneging on the agreement and polluting.

As before, the structure of pay-offs is critical in determining whether cooperation can be sustained. To explore this idea further, let us think about the pay-offs to choices in a more general way than we have so far. Following Barrett (1997), we denote NB_A as the net benefit to a country if it abates and NB_P as the net benefit to a country if it pollutes (does not abate). Let there be N identical countries, of which K choose to abate. We define the following pay-off generating functions:

$$NB_P = a + bK; \ NB_A = c + dK$$

where a, b, c and d are parameters. By altering these parameter values, we generate different pay-off matrices. For example, for the problem in Figure 10.2 and in Table 10.1 we have $a = 0$, $b = 5$, $c = -7$ and $d = 5$. You should verify that these two expressions do indeed generate the numbers shown in the examples. Note that for 'Nation i pollutes' row in Table 10.2 K is equal to the 'Number of abating nations other than i', whereas for the 'Nation i abates' row K is equal to the 'Number of abating nations other than i' plus 1.

It will be convenient to portray the information shown in Table 10.1 in another way – in the form of Figure 10.7. You should now examine Figure 10.7, and verify that this also represents the information correctly. (If you wish to see the calculations that lie behind this chart, look at the Excel file *games.xls*.) It is again clear from this chart that the net benefit of

Table 10.2 The Prisoner's Dilemma example with alternative parameter values

	Number of abating nations other than i									
	0	1	2	3	4	5	6	7	8	9
Nation i pollutes	12	15	18	21	24	27	30	33	36	39
Nation i abates	0	7	14	21	28	35	42	49	56	63

pollution is always larger than the net benefit of abating, irrespective of how many other countries abate. The only stable outcome is that in which no countries abate.

But this conclusion is *not* true for all pay-off structures. For example, suppose that the parameters of the pay-off functions take the following values: $a = 12$, $b = 3$, $c = -7$ and $d = 7$. Then if we generate the counterparts to Table 10.1 and Figure 10.7, we obtain Table 10.2 and Figure 10.8.

It is evident from either of these two descriptions that if less than three countries agree to cooperate (abate), none will cooperate (i.e. all will pollute). However, if three or more cooperate, all will cooperate. Here we have an outcome in which two stable equilibria are possible: either all will abate, or none will. To see that they are both stable equilibria, reason as follows. First, suppose that no country abates. Then, can any country individually improve its pay-off by abating rather than polluting? The answer is no. Next, suppose that every country abates. Can any country individually improve its pay-off by

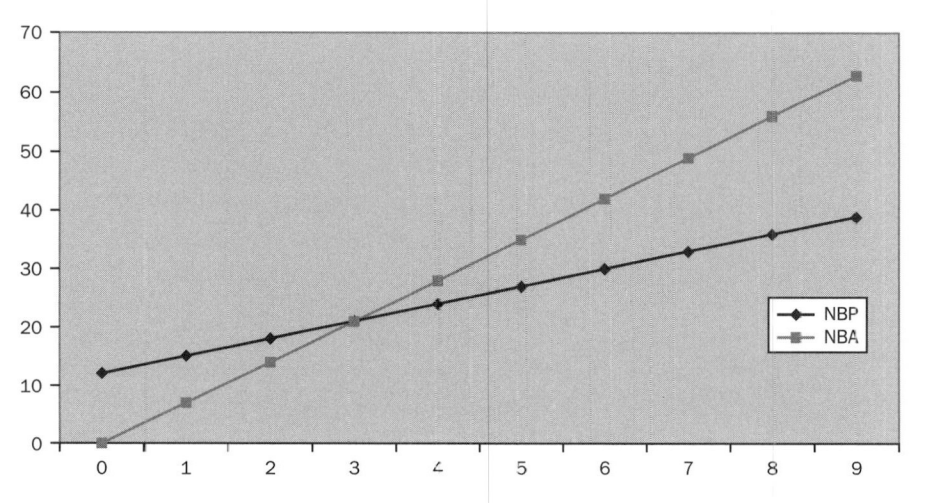

Figure 10.8 The pay-offs to one country from abating and from not abating as the number of other countries abating varies: alternative set of parameter values

Table 10.3 The Prisoner's Dilemma example with third set of parameter values ($a = 0$, $b = 5$, $c = 3$ and $d = 3$)

	Number of abating nations other than i									
	0	1	2	3	4	5	6	7	8	9
Nation i pollutes	0	5	10	15	20	25	30	35	40	45
Nation i abates	6	9	12	15	18	21	24	27	30	33

polluting rather than abating? The answer is again no. However, no other combination of polluting and abating countries is stable. For example, suppose that you are polluting and two other countries are abating (and so the remaining seven also pollute). You get 18 and they get 14 each. But each of the two abaters has an incentive to defect (i.e. pollute). For if one were to do so, its pay-off would rise from 14 to 15. Verify that this is so.

As a third example, now consider the parameter set $a = 0$, $b = 5$, $c = 3$ and $d = 3$. This is represented in Table 10.3 and Figure 10.9. This structure of pay-offs generates an incomplete self-enforcing agreement with 3 signatories and 7 non-signatories. Notice that the pay-off to each cooperating (abating) country is lower than that to each non-cooperating country. In this respect the game is similar to a Chicken game. The collective pay-off to all countries is greater than where no cooperation takes place, but is less than from complete cooperation. In this respect,

the game is reminiscent of a Prisoner's Dilemma that has been partly solved. The lesson of this story is that if a Prisoner's Dilemma pay-off matrix can be transformed by altering the structure of pay-offs (so that, for example, it resembles one of the two later examples) stable cooperation becomes possible. But cooperation may still be less than complete. We will return to this theme in a short while. Before we do so, one further generalisation is necessary.

10.2.3 Continuous choices about the extent of abatement

Our discussion so far has been rather limiting as we have assumed that nations face a simple binary choice decision: participate in an environmental agreement and abate pollution, or do not participate in the agreement and do not abate. But in practice, the relevant decision is not an all-or-nothing choice. Even if one chooses to participate in an agreement, there is a further choice to make: by how much should that country agree to abate the pollutant. Let us now generalise the discussion by allowing countries to choose – or rather negotiate – abatement levels.

This can be done with some simple algebra. Our previous analysis has shown that in terms of the participation choice, three kinds of outcome are possible: none abate, all abate, and some abate but others

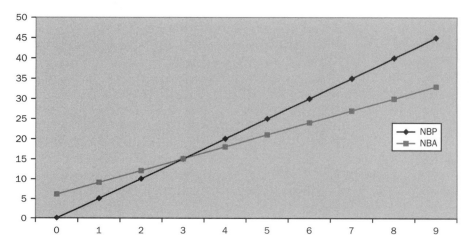

Figure 10.9 The pay-offs to one country from abating and from not abating as the number of other countries abating varies: third set of parameter values ($a = 0$, $b = 5$, $c = 3$ and $d = 3$)

do not. For simplicity, we deal first with just the first two of these alternatives. Let us assume that there are N identical countries, indexed by $i = 1, \ldots, N$. We first look at each country's pay-off function.

The pay-off functions

Each country is taken to maximise some net benefit (or pay-off) function, Π_i. Let z_i denote pollution abatement by country i, and $Z = \sum_{i=1}^{N} z_i$ be the total abatement of the pollution. Once again, pollution abatement is taken to be a public good. Then the pay-off (or net benefit) of abatement to country i is the benefits (B) of abatement (which depends on the total amount of abatement by all countries) minus costs (C) to country i of abatement (which depends on its own level of abatement). Thus we have

$$\Pi_i = B(Z) - C(z_i), \text{ for } i = 1, \ldots, N \qquad (10.1)$$

10.2.3.1 Non-cooperative behaviour

Non-cooperative (or unilateral) behaviour involves each country choosing its level of abatement to maximise its pay-off, independently of – and without regard to the consequences for – other countries. That is, each country chooses z to maximise equation 10.1 conditional on z being fixed in all other countries.

Country i's abatement choice is the solution to the first-order condition

$$\frac{dB(Z)}{dZ} \frac{dZ}{dz_i} = \frac{dC(z_i)}{dz_i} \qquad (10.2)$$

Noting that $dZ/dz_i = 1$, and that, given our assumption of symmetry, all countries' efficient abatement will be identical, the solution can be written as

$$\frac{dB(Z^U)}{dZ} = \frac{dC(z^U)}{dz} \text{ where } Z^U = \sum_{i=1}^{N} z^U \qquad (10.3)$$

and the superscript U denotes the unilateral (non-cooperative) solution. Intuitively, each country abates up to the point where its own marginal benefit of abatement is equal to its marginal cost of abatement.

10.2.3.2 Full cooperative behaviour

Full cooperative behaviour consists of the N countries *jointly* choosing levels of abatement to maximise their collective pay-off. This is equivalent to what would happen if the N countries were unified as a single country that behaved rationally.[12] The solution requires that abatement in each country be chosen jointly to maximise the collective pay-off

$$\Pi = NB(Z) - \sum_{i=1}^{N} C(z_i)$$

---

[12] The joint decision process may also involve negotiations about how the additional benefits from cooperation are to be distributed between the parties but we shall leave this matter for consideration later.

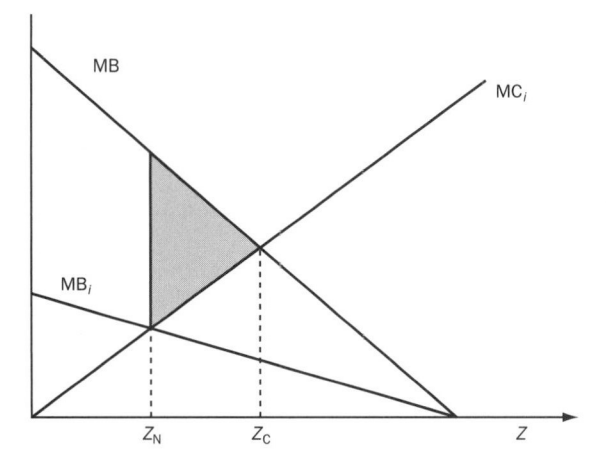

Figure 10.10 A comparison of the non-cooperative and full cooperative solutions to an environmental public good problem

The necessary conditions for a maximum are

$$N\frac{dB(Z)}{dZ}\frac{dZ}{dz_i} = \frac{dC(z_i)}{dz_i} \quad \text{for all } i.$$

Once again (for the same reasons as given earlier) these can be written as

$$N\frac{dB(Z^C)}{dZ} = \frac{dC(z^C)}{dz} \quad \text{where } Z^C = \sum_{i=1}^{N} z^C$$

where the superscript C denotes the full cooperative solution. This is the usual condition for efficient provision of a public good. That is, in each country, the marginal abatement cost should be equal to the sum of marginal benefits over all recipients of the public good.

The full cooperative solution can be described as collectively rational: it is welfare-maximising for all N countries treated as a single entity. Indeed, if some supranational governmental body existed, acting to maximise total net benefits, and had sufficient authority to impose its decision, then the outcome would be the full cooperative solution described here.

The non-cooperative and cooperative solutions can be visualised graphically, and are represented in Figure 10.10. The diagram is adapted from Barrett (1994a). Z denotes pollution abatement. In the absence of cooperation, equilibrium abatement is Z_N. Here, each country equates its own marginal benefit of abatement (MB_i) and marginal cost of abatement (MC_i). In contrast, the full cooperation abatement level Z_C has each country equating the sum of the marginal benefit of abatement across all countries (MB) with its own and marginal cost of abatement. This picture is useful because it shows us what determines the size of two magnitudes of interest:

- the amount by which full cooperation abatement exceeds non-cooperative abatement (i.e. $Z_C - Z_N$);
- the magnitude of the efficiency gain from full cooperation (the shaded triangular area in the diagram).

It is evident that these depend on two things:

1. the relative slopes of the MB_i and MC_i curves;
2. the number of competing countries, N (as this determines the relative slopes of the MB_i and MB curves.

Problem 10.2 invites you to examine these matters further, and to draw inferences about the conditions under which international cooperation is likely to deliver large decreases in emissions.

10.2.3.3 Partial cooperation and incomplete environmental agreements

As in our earlier analysis of binary-choice decisions, the outcome of a negotiation about an international environmental problem is not restricted to only one of full cooperation or no cooperation at all. A third possibility is partial cooperation: some countries agree to abate pollution (by negotiated amounts), while others act independently, doing the best they can given what the cooperators have agreed. This could be described as an incomplete environmental agreement. In this section, we briefly explore how such incomplete cooperation may be an equilibrium outcome. To do this, we use a concept that has been touched on before, but without being defined: a self-enforcing international agreement.

An agreement is self-enforcing if its terms create incentives on all parties – cooperators and non-cooperators – to adhere to the agreement once it has come into effect. For this to be the case, the agreement must satisfy the following conditions for each country, $i = 1, \ldots, N$:

- There is no incentive to renegotiate the agreement.
- Pay-offs must be such that cheating is deterred.

- Penalties to countries other than i should not be a disincentive to country i.
- Penalties to country i should not encourage country i to renegotiate.

Let us think about the kinds of choices that have to be made in arriving at such an agreement. First, each country that participates in negotiation of the treaty must decide whether or not to participate. Secondly, the terms of the agreement must be decided upon. These terms concern how much abatement a signatory will undertake. More precisely, this requires a schedule of abatement levels, one for each possible number of other countries acceding to the agreement. Therefore, implicitly or explicitly, the terms include penalties and rewards that reflect what signatories will do if a country were to accede to, or to leave, the group of cooperating countries. This last point is at the heart of how self-enforcing treaties work. Essentially, what happens is that there will be some mechanism whereby if a country accedes the signatories increase their abatement (thus rewarding accession), or reduce their abatement if a country leaves (thus punishing defection).

We can describe this a little more formally as follows. A self-enforcing international environmental agreement (IEA) is an equilibrium outcome to a negotiated environmental problem that has the following properties:

- There are N countries in total, of which K choose to cooperate and so $N - K$ do not cooperate (defect).
- Each cooperating country selects an abatement level that maximises the aggregate pay-off of all countries that cooperate.
- Each defecting country pursues its individually rational unilateral policy.

Choices by each country must also satisfy the two conditions:

- no signatory can gain by unilaterally withdrawing from the agreement;
- no non-signatory can gain by unilaterally acceding to the agreement;

which can be represented by the inequalities $\Pi_s(k^*) \geq \Pi_n(k^* - 1)$ and $\Pi_n(k^*) \geq \Pi_s(k^* + 1)$.

10.2.3.4 Key results

The derivation of a solution to this problem is outlined in Appendix 10.1. Several writers have examined what kind of self-enforcing IEA we would expect to see – if any – under a variety of different circumstances. Here we just note some of the main results of that research.

- Non-signatories and signatories would both do better if all cooperate. (In this respect, self-enforcing IEAs resemble a Prisoner's Dilemma game.)
- Non-signatories do better than signatories. (In this respect, the game is like Chicken.)
- Full cooperation is not usually stable (it is not self-enforcing and so renegotiation-proof).
- An IEA may enjoy a high degree of cooperation but only if the difference between global net benefits under the full cooperative and non-cooperative solutions is small; when this difference is large, a self-enforcing IEA cannot support a large number of countries.
- When N is very large, treaties can achieve very little, no matter how many signatories there are.

Barrett (1994a, 1995) was the first to state these results, and provides the following reasoning and intuition. The larger are the potential gains to cooperation, the greater are the benefits of free-riding and so the larger are the incentives to defect. But the larger are the incentives to defect, the smaller will be the number of signatories. The reason here is that when N is large, defection or accession by any country has only a negligible effect on the abatement of the other cooperators. This bodes badly for attempts to control greenhouse gas emissions. There the gains from cooperation are very large, and so defection is very likely. Given this, it will be difficult to secure agreement among a large number of countries.

If the test of effectiveness of agreements is by comparison of the Nash and cooperative outcomes, the literature on self-enforcing IEAs suggests that they are very limited in their effectiveness. It suggests that treaties tend to codify actions that nations were already doing. It suggests that a treaty with large numbers of signatories – such as the Biodiversity Convention which has been ratified by more than 140 countries – is limited in its capacity to deliver social benefits. Compare this case with the Antarctic Treaty which has been ratified by fewer than 25 countries. (See Barrett, 1994a, b and 1995.) A qualification is in order, however. These results have been derived only for some functional specifications and some possible sets of assumptions (including identical countries, marginal benefits of abatement are constant, and many others). It is not clear how generally robust they are.

10.3 Factors contributing to enhancing probability of international agreements or achieving a higher degree of cooperation

The notion of self-enforcing agreements has proved itself to be a very useful way of thinking about international environmental cooperation. However, as we have seen, it does tend to generate rather pessimistic conclusions about the effectiveness of agreements. Agreements do not have to be self-enforcing, however; there are other mechanisms by which cooperation could deliver large benefits. We discuss several of these in this section.

10.3.1 Role of commitment

Cooperating countries may voluntarily make commitments to do things irrespective of what others do. By giving up the right to change abatement levels in response to changes in K, any agreement that is obtained will not in general be self-enforcing. However, if the commitments are regarded as credible, then – depending on what kinds of commitments are made – it can be possible to achieve and sustain a full (complete) IEA. The difficulty here, of course, is that as commitments typically lead to self-sacrifice in some circumstances, it may be hard to make them credible.

10.3.2 Transfers and side-payments

Suppose that a self-enforcing IEA is only capable of supporting a small number of signatories, K. Now imagine that the signatories offer side-payments to induce non-signatories to enter. If these side-payments are larger than the inducements in the original IEA, others will join in cooperation. In some circumstances, such side-payments can bring about a complete IEA, and so maximise collective benefits. However, as the resulting agreement will, by construction, not be self-enforcing, we have the same difficulty as mentioned in the previous paragraph. Such IEAs may not be credible. It seems that side-payment systems will require that signatories find a way to make a credible commitment to the system (and in effect suspend the self-enforcing constraints).

10.3.3 Linkage benefits and costs and reciprocity

It may be possible to secure greater cooperation than the analysis to date has indicated if other benefits are brought into consideration jointly. Doing this in effect alters the pay-off matrix to the game. To see what might be involved here, we note that countries typically cooperate (or at least try to do so) over many things: international trade restrictions, anti-terrorism measures, health and safety standards, and so on. There may be economies of scope available by linking these various goals. Moreover, reputations for willingness to act in the common interest in any one of these dimensions may secure benefits in negotiations about another. What policy makers might try and obtain is linkages over two or more policy objectives so that the set of agreements about these objectives creates overall positive net benefits for the entire set of participants, and net gains which are distributed so that every participant perceives a net linkage gain. In these cases, there can be very substantial gains from international cooperation.

Of course, it must also be recognised that there may be 'additional' costs of cooperation too. These include transaction and enforcement costs, and perceived costs of interdependency itself (such as feelings about loss of sovereignty). The larger are these costs, the smaller are the possible net gains from cooperation.

10.3.4 Repeated games

Another mechanism that may enhance the extent of cooperation is repeated interaction between nations.

A's strategy \ B's strategy	Defect	Cooperate
Defect	P, P	T, S
Cooperate	S, T	R, R

Figure 10.11 A one-shot Prisoner's Dilemma game

A's strategy \ B's strategy	Defect	Cooperate
Defect	2P, 2P	T+P, S+P
Cooperate	S+P, T+P	R+P, R+P

Figure 10.12 The two-shot Prisoner's Dilemma game

Thus far in this chapter we have implicitly been assuming that choices are being made just once. But most environmental problems are long-lasting and require that decisions be made repeatedly. To examine how this may alter outcomes, let us look first at Figure 10.11 which represents the pay-offs in a one-shot game. Here we suppose that the pay-offs have the ranking $T > R > P > S$ and that $S + T < 2R$. The dominant strategy for each player in this game is P.

Now imagine this game being played twice (in two consecutive periods, let us say). The pay-off matrix for this two-shot Prisoner's Dilemma game, viewed from the first of the two periods, is shown in Figure 10.12. Once again, the dominant strategy is P. In fact, this result is true for any fixed, known number of repetitions. However, observation of actual cooperation and experimental games both suggest that cooperation occurs more commonly than theory predicts. What seems to lie behind this? First, cooperation seems to be more likely when communication is allowed. Most importantly, the likelihood of cooperation increases greatly if interaction is never-ending, or its end point is unknown.

A large literature exists that analyses games played repeatedly. We cannot survey that literature here. Suffice it to say that among the many strategies that are possible, some variety of tit-for-tat strategy seems to be sensible. Tit-for-tat strategies tend to encourage cooperation. However, some results reminiscent of those we have found earlier also emerge. In particular, as N becomes large, cooperation tends to be more difficult to sustain. Indeed Barrett (1994a)

shows that even in infinitely repeated games his previous conclusions remain true: an IEA will only be able to support a large number of signatories when gains to cooperation are small; and when the gains are large a self-enforcing IEA can sustain only a smaller number of signatories. Once again, some form of commitment seems to be required if large gains are to be obtained.

10.4 International treaties: conclusions

Many important examples of environmental problem affect only small numbers of countries. Where this is the case, cooperative bargaining agreements are relatively easy to obtain. These can often be embodied in ad hoc agreements and loose structures. Where the number of countries affected by an environmental problem is large, successful cooperation is harder to achieve. These difficulties are lessened if there are large nation-specific gains, and if influential nations are willing to act in the role of leaders. The configuration of pay-offs can be made more conducive to cooperation by linkages between various policy goals (such as debt-for-nature swaps).

10.5 Acid rain pollution

Acid rain originates from the emissions of a variety of pollutants that are subsequently chemically converted into acid form, particularly sulphuric and nitric acids. Its international dimension arises from the property that some proportion of the pollutant emissions in question – the precursors of acid rain – are transported over national boundaries by natural processes. Examples include oxides of nitrogen and sulphur, which can be moved over distances of several hundred miles. Unlike greenhouse gases, these substances are not uniformly mixing, and so impacts are regional or international rather than global. Figure 10.13 shows the incremental sulphur dioxide concentrations attributable to a single oil combined cycle power station located near Stuttgart in Germany. Significant SO_2 depositions are felt over distances of up to 1000 miles and over most European states.

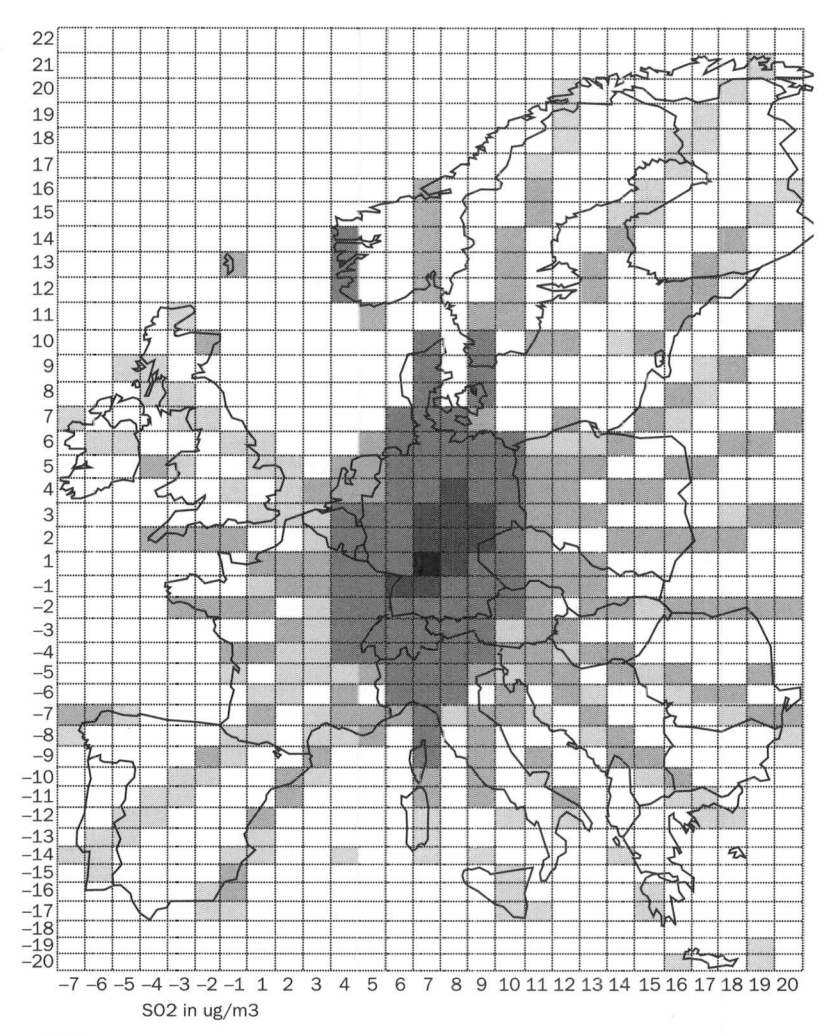

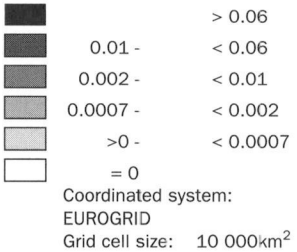

> 0.06

0.01 -   < 0.06

0.002 -   < 0.01

0.0007 -   < 0.002

>0 -   < 0.0007

= 0

Coordinated system:
EUROGRID
Grid cell size: 10 000km^2

Figure 10.13 Incremental SO_2 concentrations from an oil combined cycle power station located in Lauffen, Germany
Source: ExternE (1995), p. 61

In the following parts of this section, we present a relatively brief account of acid rain. More extensive detail on each of the aspects discussed here is available in the file *Acid Rain.doc* in the *Additional Materials*, Chapter 10.

10.5.1 Causes of acid rain pollution

The physical processes underlying acid rain are well understood. Atmospheric stocks of sulphur dioxide and nitrous oxide accumulate primarily from stationary sources such as fossil-fuel-burning power generation, ore smelters and industrial boilers. Of secondary importance are emissions of unburned hydrocarbons and oxides of nitrogen (NO_x) from mobile sources, principally vehicle exhaust emissions. Stocks of potentially acidic material are transported in the higher levels of the atmosphere for distances of up to 600 miles.[13]

Acid rain occurs through two principal processes. In dry deposition, deposited particulate matter is chemically transformed into acid through contact with surface water. Dry deposition is the principal mechanism of acidification in the south-western United States. By contrast, wet deposition is characterised by the formation of acidic substances, particularly sulphuric and nitric acids, in the atmosphere, which are subsequently deposited through rain or the movement of moist air.

Acid rain deposition is principally associated with the heavily industrialised regions of Europe, China, the former Soviet Union and North America. Acid rain is often regarded as a reciprocal externality or spillover problem. However, meteorological patterns imply that many depositions are predominantly one-way, and so it is often better to view acid rain as a unidirectional spillover.

10.5.2 Consequences of acid rain pollution

Major studies of the consequences of acid rain pollution in Europe have been conducted by the Commission of the European Communities (CEC, 1983) and the World Conservation Union (WCU, 1990). The National Acid Rain Precipitation Program began an important long-term study in the USA in 1980. These research programmes have identified the following consequences (see French, 1990).

1. increased acidity of lakes;
2. increased acidity of soils which reduces the number of plants that may be grown;
3. forest destruction;

4. human health effects via acidification of domestic water supplies and sulphate pollution in general;
5. building and infrastructure erosion;
6. loss of visibility, caused by fine sulphate particles produced by airborne sulphuric acid.

10.5.3 Pollution control techniques and instruments

10.5.3.1 National control

Reductions in the level of acid rain deposition require reductions in those substances that are precursors of acid rain. There are several ways in which this can be achieved. These include changes in the fuel mix used in power generation (for example, changes from high-sulphur to low-sulphur coal, substitution of coal by natural gas, and greater use of non-fossil-fuel sources), and the introduction of technologies that reduce the emissions to energy output ratios (such as more efficient combustion techniques, sulphur scrubbing equipment, and other forms of clean-up technology).

To enforce or induce uptake of these control techniques, the full set of policy instruments discussed in Chapter 7 is available to national environmental protection agencies. These include command and control instruments (such as quantity-of-emissions regulation, requirements to install emission control technologies, prohibitions on use of particular fuels), and economic-incentive-based instruments (in particular, emissions taxes and tradable permit schemes).

In the United States, the first substantial control programmes were launched after the passage of the 1970 Clean Air Act. This established a system of local ambient air quality standards, and conferred powers on states to enforce emission quantity regulations. The system proved to be rather disappointing. For example, the legislation led to taller emission stacks, which succeeded in attaining local ambient standards, but at the cost of largely passing on the problem to neighbouring areas.

---

[13] It is interesting to note that tall chimneys were introduced partly to reduce the ambient levels of pollution in the vicinity of the pollution sources. But a chimney does not eradicate a pollutant – it relocates it. Tall chimneys have been significant in disseminating pollutants over long distances.

Subsequent amendments to the legislation, resulting in the 1990 Clean Air Act, will have far stronger abatement effects. The Act requires nitrogen oxide emissions to be reduced by 2.5 million tonnes and sulphur dioxide to be reduced by over 50% to 10 million tonnes (relative to 1980 emission levels). Attainment of the 1990 Clean Air Act targets will be effected through a system of marketable permits in emissions of the precursors of acid rain. The programme's introduction is in two phases: in the first stage (in 1995) permits were issued for 110 large coal-burning utilities, followed later by permit issues for 2400 smaller generators. Permits, issued at no charge to generators, allow emissions of between 30% and 50% of 1985 pollution levels. Portney (1989) estimated the annual benefits to the USA to lie in the interval $2–9 billion while control costs are predicted to be $4 billion. The UK approach to sulphur emissions control has centred on mandatory abatement investments, including flue-gas desulphurisation technology.

10.5.3.2 International control

The existence of a federal governmental system in the USA facilitates the introduction of pollution control programmes that have effect over much (but not all) of the areas affected by its acid rain pollutants. How easy has it been to abate the precursors of acid rain in Europe where no such unified sovereign governmental structure exists?

The abatement record in Europe has turned out to be quite impressive, and the cooperative process that has taken place between European countries is often regarded as a model for international environmental cooperation. That cooperation has been most visibly manifested in one convention and a set of associated protocols. These are:

- the Long Range Transboundary Air Pollution Convention, 1979 (ratified 1983);
- the Geneva Protocol, 1984 (finance of EMEP[14]) (in force 1988, 30 ratifiers by November 1995);
- the Helsinki Protocol, 1985 (in force 1987: sulphur);

- the Sofia Protocol, 1988 (in force 1991: NOx);
- Large Combustion Plant Directive, 1988 (in force 1993 after ratification);
- Oslo Protocol, 1994 (sulphur);
- Geneva Protocol, 1995 (VOC).

The 1985 Helsinki Protocol bound 21 European states to a 30% reduction in sulphur dioxide emissions (in terms of 1980 base levels) by 1993. In June 1988, EC Environment Ministers agreed to national reductions in emissions from large combustion plants. These and other agreements have met with some success, with SO_2 emissions falling by more than 20% between 1980 and 1989. At national levels, emission reductions have largely been implemented through command and control regulations, although some countries (including France and Sweden) have introduced emission taxes. In the long term, larger-scale reductions in acid rain precursors in Europe will necessitate the use of either uniform emission taxes or tradable permit schemes. As yet, no Europe-wide example of either exists.

European cooperation about acid rain illustrates a number of themes commented upon earlier in the chapter. First, securing agreement was facilitated by the existence of an international political institution (the European Commission, later to be the European Union). Second, cooperation is helped when there is a relatively high degree of cultural similarity between the cooperating countries. Third, regional problems that affect relatively few countries are likely to be addressed successfully through supranational cooperation. This appears to be exemplified by the case of sulphur control in Europe, where agreement involved a relatively small numbers of parties.

That international treaties are often incomplete (at least initially) is attested to in this case by 13 countries in the geographically relevant area not being signatories to the Helsinki Protocol. Also note-worthy here is the fact that agreement is most likely when participants have strong local incentives to act (even without international cooperation). One European country – the United Kingdom – had very weak incentives to enter into voluntary regulation,

[14] EMEP is the European Monitoring and Evaluation Programme. This is a model of acid rain transport over Europe, used in the design of sulphur emission controls.

with approximately 70% of its sulphur emissions being transported outside UK boundaries by the prevailing westerly winds, and with the UK receiving little acid rain deposition from other countries. However, membership of the European Union has required the UK to reduce sulphur and nitrogen oxide emissions, even though the UK had earlier refused to accede to the Helsinki Protocol.

Until the collapse of communism in Eastern Europe, a particularly intractable problem had been reciprocal transfers of acid rain pollutants between the countries of Eastern and Western Europe. The scope for internationally negotiated reductions in sulphur and nitrogen emissions has increased with the demise of COMECON, and the prospects for membership of the European Union by a number of central European states will further enhance the likelihood that mutually beneficial reductions in those pollutants occur. Even though a full solution to acid rain problems in Europe involves many countries, it has been beneficial to start with a relatively small set of crucial participants.

Agreements to reduce emissions of the precursors of acid rain have also benefited from technological change (which has reduced abatement costs), high and well-understood pollution damages, and a reasonably high degree of similarity in the burdens that the agreements have imposed upon participating states (all of which correspond to lessons we mentioned above).

Considerably more progress has been made in reducing sulphur rather than nitrogen emissions.

Why should this be so? Sandler (1997) offers two explanations. First, there is usually a greater degree of self-pollution from sulphur, and so the incentives to clean up sulphur emissions are high even in the absence of international cooperation. In contrast, NOx emissions are much less characterised by local benefits. Second, sulphur emission problems are more concentrated than those associated with nitrogen, largely because they are much less dependent on car and other mobile pollution sources. This implies that sulphur abatement tends to be easier to implement and more cost-effective.

We argued earlier that a test of the effectiveness of international cooperation should be based on comparison of the Nash (non-cooperative) and cooperative outcomes. Given that a high proportion of national sulphur depositions are accounted for by national emissions, the Nash equilibrium would be likely to involve significant reductions in national emissions, and one would not expect to find a large divergence between Nash and cooperative outcomes. Indeed, Sandler has argued that the reductions in SO_2 emissions agreed by parties to the Long Range Transboundary Air Pollution Convention are no greater than they would have been in the absence of a formal agreement. So using this effectiveness criterion, cooperation to reduce acid rain has been much less effective than is often thought. Acid rain control agreements have tended to codify actions that nations were already doing. Not all would accept this conclusion, however. One example of a different assessment is given in Box 10.3.

Box 10.3 Acid rain games in Europe

In a paper entitled 'Acid rain games in Europe', George Halkos and John Hutton (1993) concluded that acid rain causes greater environmental damage than would occur if countries act cooperatively. Using estimates of sulphur dioxide damage and abatement costs, Halkos and Hutton calculated the potential gains to some West European countries from cooperative SO_2 emissions control.

Halkos and Hutton commence by determining cost-efficient abatement cost functions for each

country, which measure the cost of eliminating SO_2 emissions from the process of power generation. Abatement costs differ between countries as a result of country-specific factors such as the fuel mix used, the sulphur content of fuels, capacity utilisation and the scale for installations. Figure 10.14 illustrates total abatement costs for one country, the United Kingdom. The 'staircase' shape of the abatement cost curve results from marginal cost increases as abatement rises; at higher abatement, polluters

Box 10.3 *continued*

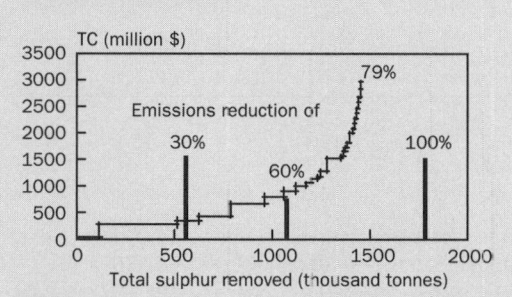

Figure 10.14 United Kingdom year 2000 total abatement cost curve
Source: Adapted from Halkos and Hutton, 1993, p. 5

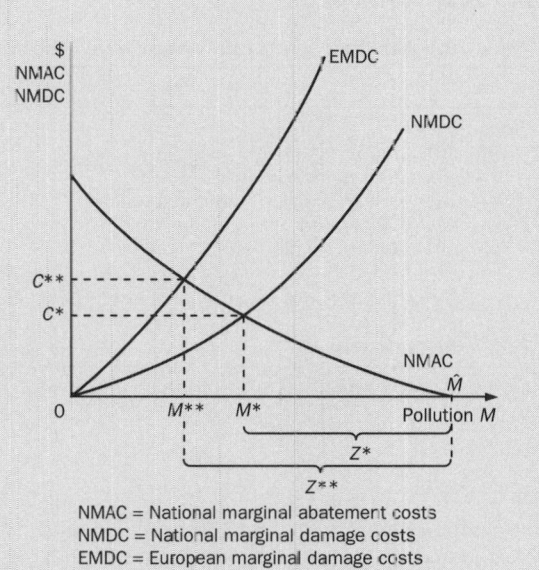

NMAC = National marginal abatement costs
NMDC = National marginal damage costs
EMDC = European marginal damage costs

Figure 10.15 Cooperative and non-cooperative pollution outcomes in the presence of international pollution spillovers

are forced to use more expensive control technologies. Note that the total abatement cost function provides information about the maximum level of pollution abatement that can be obtained for any given size of control budget. The second step in the exercise uses studies conducted by the Norwegian Meteorological Institute to construct a matrix of transfer coefficients, indicating what proportion of the total emissions from any particular country is eventually deposited in each of the 27 countries being studied.

Halkos and Hutton then proceed to estimate total SO_2 damage functions. First they assume, on the basis of recent evidence, that the damage function is convex, rather than linear (see Chapter 6 for an explanation of convexity). It is not possible to estimate directly the parameters of the damage function, given the almost complete absence of relevant data. However, Halkos and Hutton assume that, for each country, national marginal abatement costs are equated with national marginal damage costs. To understand this, look at Figure 10.15. Halkos and Hutton assume that, when acting uncooperatively, each country considers the costs of pollution control (represented by NMAC) and the damages which it will avoid in its own country by doing that abatement (represented by the function labelled NMDC). A country will reduce pollution from the uncontrolled level, to the privately efficient level, M^*. The cooperative solution is obtained when each country equates its national marginal abatement costs with the European (and not national) marginal damage function. By doing so,

the outcome is identical to that which would be economically efficient if all Europe were a single country, and the European environmental protection agency equates European marginal costs and damages. This would yield M^{**} as the fully efficient pollution level or Z^{**} as the abatement. Notice that the cooperation result is a higher abatement level, Z^{**}, than the non-cooperative solution, Z^*.

Returning to the main thread of our argument, it can be seen from Figure 10.15 that Halkos and Hutton are assuming that each country undertakes Z^* pollution abatement. The unobserved marginal damage can be calculated by noting that it is equal to the observable level of marginal abatement costs, C^*, given that assumption. Using this information for each of the 27 countries studied, the parameters of a damage function can then be calibrated. Once this is done, the matrix of transfer coefficients can be used to calculate the total damage each country will experience for any level of SO_2 emissions by each of the 27 countries.

The final step in the analysis involves estimating the magnitudes of the gains that would be obtained from cooperative behaviour

Box 10.3 *continued*

Table 10.4 Acid rain: gains from cooperative behaviour

	Austria	Italy	FRG	UK	FRG	GDR
Percentages						
1992 Abatement	18.35	8.40	45.1	11.2	45.1	0.72
Privately efficient abatement (Z^*)	29.49	29.2	62.77	16.7	66.17	1.90
Socially efficient (Europe-wide) abatement (Z^{**})	35.4	35.5	62.41	24.81	63.46	25.24
Total costs of abatement and damage ($m 1985):						
Privately efficient abatement (Z^{**})	233.9	720.68	1813.46	479.63	1991.00	84.15
		(954.58)		(2293.09)		(2075.15)
Socially efficient (Europe-wide) abatement (Z^{**})	215.51	729.27	1780.15	496.21	1843.50	156.20
		(944.78)		(2276.36)		(1999.70)
Total efficiency gain		[9.80]		[16.73]		[75.45]

Source: Adapted from Halkos and Hutton (1993)

as compared with non-cooperative behaviour. Halkos and Hutton's results are presented in Table 10.4, for three pairs of countries. To understand the information given, let us read across the rows.

The first three rows of numbers refer to levels of abatement in percentages. In the '1992 Abatement' row we find percentage levels of abatements that the countries actually undertook in 1992; these show very marked variations. For example, in the GDR (the former East Germany), less than 1% of potential SO_2 emissions were actually abated in 1992; in the FRG (the former West Germany) the much greater priority given to environmental conservation led to over 45% abatement relative to the theoretical unconstrained level. Figures in the second row give the privately efficient abatement percentages (corresponding to Z^* in Figure 10.15). In all cases, these exceed the 1992 abatement levels, implying that none of the five countries abated sulphur dioxide even to the level that would pay positive returns in terms of the own-country pollution reductions that would arise from abatement. The third row presents the socially efficient abatement levels, assuming that each of the pairs of countries shown in the table act in a cooperative manner. Socially efficient pollution abatement occurs when, for the two countries indicated, the sum of total abatement costs and total pollution costs for that pair of countries is minimised. In the case of the FRG and the GDR, cooperative efficiency actually required the FRG to do a little less abatement than would be privately optimal, while the GDR would have to do much more.

The lower part of the table shows the sum of total abatement and total damage costs for each country and for each pair of countries (in parentheses). Continuing to look at the case of the FRG and the GDR, note that the sum of costs is lower by 75.45 in the socially efficient case (Z^{**}) (costs = 1999.7) as compared with the privately efficient case (Z^*) (costs = 2075.15).

A scrutiny of the costs for individual countries brings out another aspect of this example. For West Germany, total abatement and damage costs fall by $147 million in moving to the cooperative solution, whereas for East Germany total costs rise by $72 million. For a cooperative solution to be possible it would be necessary for the FRG to give a side-payment to the GDR of at least $72 million (but less than $147 million), otherwise both parties would not benefit from the cooperation.

By way of contrast, the figures demonstrate that for the FRG/UK pair of countries, total costs would rise for the UK in the cooperation case. To induce the UK to undertake cooperation, side-payments of at least £16.58 million annually by the FRG to the UK would be required. It must be stressed that the 'total efficiency gains' referred to in the table are obtained by comparison of costs at Z^* and Z^{**}. However, the actual levels of current abatement are less in all cases than Z^*, and so the total net benefits in moving from 1992 abatement levels to the socially efficient levels would be greater (and probably substantially greater) than those indicated here.

Source: Adapted from Halkos and Hutton (1993)

10.6 Stratospheric ozone depletion

10.6.1 Summary of problem

Ozone is produced in the upper layers of the atmosphere by the action of ultraviolet light on oxygen molecules. The processes determining the concentrations of upper-atmospheric ozone are complex and incompletely understood. It is known that ozone concentration is in a constant state of flux, resulting from the interaction of decay and creation processes. Several naturally occurring catalysts act to speed up natural rates of decay; these catalysts include oxides of chlorine, nitrogen and hydrogen. There are large, naturally caused variations in these concentrations by time, spatial location and altitude. For example, normal dynamic fluctuations in ozone concentrations are as large as 30% from day to night, and 10% from day to day (Kemp, 1990).

During the early 1970s, scientific claims that ozone was being depleted in the stratosphere were first made. These original claims were not satisfactorily verified, but in the mid-1980s the discovery of the so-called hole in the ozone layer over Antarctica led the scientific community to conclude that serious reductions in ozone concentrations were taking place in certain parts of the atmosphere. The downward trend in ozone concentrations was attributed to inadvertent human interference with the chemistry of the atmosphere, related to the prevailing pattern of air pollution. Over the continent of Antarctica, the fall in concentration (relative to its 1975 level) was estimated to be in the interval 60–95%, depending upon the place of measurement (Everest, 1988).

Although much progress has been made towards understanding the chemistry of ozone depletion, we are still uncertain even as to the recent historical rates of depletion. Estimates of the actual rates of depletion experienced have been considerably lowered since the initial studies were published, and forecast depletion rates are now much less than early predictions. Current models forecast depletion to be no more than 5% on average over the next 50 years, as compared with initial predictions of depletions of up to 20%.

There are several ways in which human impacts on the ozone layer take place. Two of these – nuclear radiation and aircraft emissions – appear to have relatively little effect at present, but are potentially important. Evidence also implicates a number of other chemicals as ozone depleters, in particular nitrous oxide (associated with traffic and agricultural activity), carbon tetrachloride and chloroform. The dominant anthropogenic cause of ozone depletion appears to be the emission of chlorofluorocarbon (CFC) gases into the atmosphere. These substances act as catalysts to the decay of ozone, adding to the effects of the natural catalysts we mentioned earlier. Many forms of CFC exist and are being produced currently, two of them – CFC-11 and CFC-12 – being the dominant forms. The most important sources of CFC emissions by quantity are the production, use and disposal of aerosol propellants, cushioning foams, cleaning materials and refrigerative materials. In some cases, such as in aerosol uses, the release of the gas occurs at the time of manufacture or within a relatively short lapse of time after manufacture. In other cases, the release can occur at much later dates as items of hardware such as refrigerators and air-conditioning units are scrapped. Estimates by Quinn (1986) suggest that CFCs have very high income elasticities of demand. Hence, if CFC gases were not subject to control, their use would rise very rapidly as world incomes increase.

What would be the effects of a continuing depletion of the atmospheric ozone layer? The consequences follow from the fact that ozone plays a natural, equilibrium-maintaining role in the stratosphere through

(a) absorption of ultraviolet (UV) radiation, and

(b) absorption of infrared (IR) radiation.

The absorption of IR radiation implies that CFC substances are greenhouse gases, contributing to global climate change. This aspect of ozone depletion is discussed in the following section. Here we focus on the role played by halons and CFCs in depleting the concentration of ozone in the upper atmosphere and leading to increased UV radiative flows. The ozone layer protects living organisms from receiving harmful UV radiation. It is now virtually certain that ozone depletion has increased the incidence of skin cancer among humans. Connor (1993) estimates that a 1% depletion in ozone concentration would

Table 10.5 Costs and benefits of CFC control in the United States

Level of control	Discounted benefits ($ billion)	Discounted costs ($ billion)
80% cut	3533	22
50% cut	3488	13
20% cut	3396	12
Freeze	3314	7

Source: Adapted from EPA (1989)

increase non-malignant skin cancers by more than 3%, but by rather less for malignant melanomas. The United States Environmental Protection Agency (EPA) has estimated that human-induced changes in the ozone layer will cause an additional 39 million contractions of skin cancer during the next century, leading to 800 000 additional deaths (Kemp, 1990).

Effects which may occur, but about which much doubt remains, include effects on human immune systems (including activation of the AIDS virus), radiation blindness and cataract formation, genetic damage to plants and animals, and losses to crops and other plant or animal damage. Of particular concern is the apparent damage to marine plankton growth – the importance of plankton in many food chains suggests that this may become a critical issue during the next century. Increased UV radiative flows are also likely to accelerate the degradation of polymer plastic materials.

Some indication of the likely magnitudes of the costs and benefits of control is given in a United States EPA 1989 study, the results of which are reported in Table 10.5. It is sometimes thought that rapidly rising marginal costs of abatement mean that very large proportionate reductions in pollutant emissions would be prohibitively expensive. If these estimates are trustworthy that is not true in this case. It is clear from Table 10.5 that the costs of CFC reduction do rise as the magnitude of abatement is increased, but not in a sharply increasing manner. Moreover, the benefits rise substantially as abatement is increased. Given these numbers, almost complete elimination of the pollutant emissions is economically warranted.

The North is currently far more important than the South in terms of the quantities of emissions of ozone-depleting substances (WR, 1994). However,

this seems set to change in the future as economies of the South undergo rapid economic growth, while those in the North attempt to adhere to political commitments.

10.6.2 Action to date on abating emissions of ozone-depleting substances

The first steps towards international control measures were taken at the Vienna Convention in 1985, at which agreements were made for international co-operation in research, monitoring and the exchange of information. By 1989, 27 countries had ratified the Vienna Convention. It is now generally agreed that preliminary agreements of this form are of great importance. The acquisition of information about the costs and benefits of an environmental control programme reduces uncertainty and improves the chances of an effective response. For global problems, such as ozone-layer depletion, the accumulation of scientific evidence seems to be required before nations perceive the need to act. The discovery of the hole in the ozone layer in 1985, and publications in 1987 and 1989 of research by the US EPA were also pivotal in generating international support for control of ozone-depleting substances.

The Montreal Protocol was agreed in 1987, and came into effect in 1989. By 1995, at which time amendments were made to the treaty, 149 countries had ratified the Protocol. In September 1988, signatories to the Montreal Protocol (at that time 24 mainly industrialised countries) agreed to phased reductions in domestic consumption and production of ozone-depleting substances, and in particular to cease the production of chlorofluorocarbons (CFCs) by 1996. Developing countries could increase CFC production until 1999, after which it must be progressively reduced until it ends in 2010. The London Protocol, signed in July 1990 by 59 nations, agreed to a complete phasing out of halons and CFCs by the year 2000. In addition, controls were agreed on two other substances implicated in the depletion of ozone, carbon tetrachloride (to be eliminated by 2000) and methyl chloroform (by 2005). Financial support was made available to assist in the funding of projects to substitute from ozone-depleting substances in poorer counties.

International action to control the production and use of CFCs is widely regarded as the outstanding success of international environmental diplomacy. The agreements led to a rapid decline in global CFC emissions, although most of this was achieved in the developed countries (with the United States adopting a tradable permit scheme for domestic CFC usage).

Two factors mentioned in Table 10.1 have been important contributors in ozone depletion control. First, there has been a high concentration of interests among adversely affected parties. For example, in 1986 just three countries – the Soviet Union, the USA and Japan – accounted for 46% of global CFC emissions. A high concentration of interests implies that there are relatively few parties to the problem. This implies, in turn, that those countries attempting to negotiate an agreement need have little concern about free-riding among treaty non-participants, and so are more willing to become signatories.

Second, we see here the importance of one influential nation being willing to adopt a leadership role, particularly where that country has a large beneficial stake in the outcome of negotiations. The USA was a major driving force in discussions that led to the Montreal and subsequent protocols. As we shall see later, the absence of any major country willing to act in this way constitutes a serious obstacle to progress on control of global warming.

More pessimistically, a continuing decline will depend upon the developing countries substituting away from CFCs as industrial output rises; at present CFC production is increasing very rapidly in these economies. In China, for example, government forecasts expect CFC emissions to increase from 48 000 metric tonnes in 1991 to 177 000 in 1999 in the absence of control, and to rise rapidly thereafter. China has indicated a willingness to gradually phase out the use of CFCs, but this is conditional upon similar action being taken elsewhere, and upon technological transfers and financial assistance. As yet there is no sign that the rapid rate of growth of CFC and halon use in China is being halted. Even if target reductions are met on time, the ozone layer will not return to its normal state until the second half of the 21st century, before which ultraviolet levels are expected to rise by a further 10–15%, with a comparable increase in the incidence of skin cancers.

10.7 The greenhouse effect

10.7.1 Greenhouse gas emissions

Our discussion of the greenhouse effect focuses on policy aspects. However, we begin with a very brief summary of some of the underlying processes. The reader who wishes to learn more about the underlying science can find good accounts in the references given at the end of this chapter.

Economic activity gives rise to flows of greenhouse gas (GHG) emissions. Greenhouse gases are uniformly mixing pollutants; the geographical location of the pollution impacts is independent of the location of the emission source. Since all nations are emitters and each is affected by the emissions of all others, greenhouse gas emissions can be thought of both as a reciprocal spillover problem and as a global public 'bad'.

The principal GHG – carbon dioxide – derives mainly from fossil-fuel use, but an important contribution is also made by deforestation. Agricultural activity and the decomposition and disposal of waste are important emitters of methane, another GHG. Chlorofluorocarbon (CFC) emissions also act as potential global-warming substances. Climate change is driven by the atmospheric *concentration* of greenhouse gases, and by the rate of change of those concentrations through time. At any point in time, GHG concentrations depend on the levels of emissions at all previous points in time, and on the extent to which sinks have sequestered atmospheric GHGs, or the amounts that have decayed into harmless forms, at all previous points in time. How much global climate change will occur over the next century and beyond is partly predetermined (because of its dependence on previous net emissions) but also depends on future GHG emissions and actions that affect the size of various carbon sinks.

Forecasts about emissions over long-term horizons are very sensitive to the assumptions made, particularly about population and economic growth rates, changes in fuel mix, rates of technological progress and energy efficiency improvement, and, of course, policy choices. As a result, the range of predictions is large, even for relatively short forecast horizons. This creates problems in building up a consistent research picture about climate change. In the early days of climate change research, modelling teams tended to work to independent agenda, making the task of comparison of research output rather difficult. More recently, formal and informal coordination of research efforts has led to some 'standardisation' of agenda. In particular, the Intergovernmental Panel on Climate Change (IPCC) – in the activities leading to its Third Assessment Report (TAR) – developed a set of emissions scenarios. These are described in Box 10.4. In commissioning research from a number of independent research teams, the IPCC asked for those scenarios to be used in the teams' simulations.

A scenario can be thought of as a possible development path. Each one assumes a particular, plausible path for the way in which GHG emissions will evolve over time. The scenarios are richly specified, encompassing not just narrowly economic and technological dimensions, but also broader socio-economic policies and trends, such as those relating to development, sustainability and equity.

The scenarios do *not* include additional climate control initiatives. Each generates a 'reference' or baseline projection, conditional on a set of socio-economic and technological assumptions. The consequences of alternative climate-change control strategies can be analysed under each scenario. IPCC analyses show that climate change policy will both be affected by, and have impacts on, these broader dimensions of change, and that alternative development paths can lead to very different GHG emissions and concentrations levels, even for identical mitigation policies. Several of the 'lower' emissions scenarios being studied by IPCC are only attainable under substantially different patterns of energy resource development from those being pursued now.

Box 10.4 IPCC Special Report on Emission Scenarios (SRES)

This box describes the emissions scenarios developed by the IPCC Special Report on Emission Scenarios, and some of the uses of scenario analysis by the IPCC. None of the scenarios incorporates additional climate-change mitigation strategies and so, for example, do not assume implementation of the Kyoto Protocol.

The scenarios

A1 Future of very rapid economic growth, global population peaks in the middle of the 21st century and declines thereafter, and rapid introduction of new and more efficient technologies. Underlying themes are regional convergence, capacity-building, increased social and cultural interactions, substantial reduction in regional differences in per capita income. Three sub-groups:

- **A1FI** fossil-intensive
- **A1T** non-fossil technology emphasis
- **A1B** balanced fossil/non-fossil emphasis

A2 Heterogeneous world of self-reliance and preservation of local identities. Fertility patterns converge only slowly, so global population continues to increase. Per capita economic growth and technological progress more fragmented and slower than in other scenarios.

B1 Future of very rapid economic growth, global population peaks in the middle of the 21st century and declines thereafter. Rapid changes in economic structures towards a service- and information-oriented economy. Reductions in material intensity and introduction of cleaner, resource-efficient technologies. Underlying themes are global solutions to sustainability problems, improved equity, but without additional climate initiatives.

B2 World in which emphasis is on local solutions to sustainability problems. Continuously increasing population (but at a rate slower than in A2). Intermediate levels of economic development, less rapid and more diverse technological change than in A1 and B1. Environmental protection and social equity focused on at local and regional levels.

A summary of the qualitative assumptions being used is shown in Figure 10.16. This portrays the directions and strengths of change of several indicators under each of the six SRES scenarios.

IPCC uses of scenarios for projection of CO_2 emissions and concentrations

The IPCC has employed several modelling teams to undertake simulation analysis. Among other

Box 10.4 *continued*

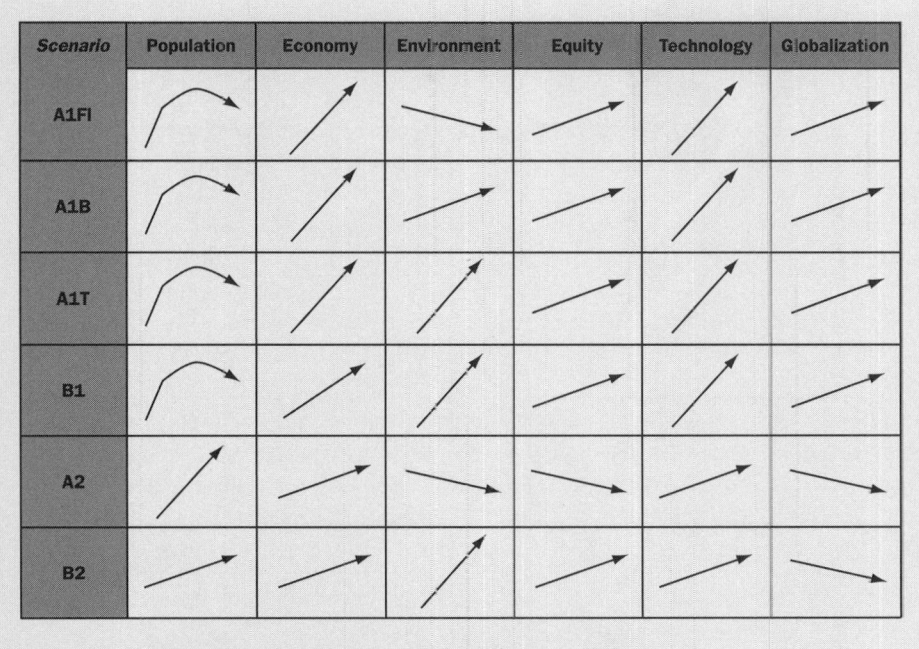

Figure 10.16 Qualitative directions of SRES scenarios for different indicators
Source: IPCC(3), Figure TS.1, p. 24

things, each team was given the following brief. For each scenario, estimate the path of CO_2 emissions until 2100 under the assumption that no additional emissions reduction policies are adopted.[15] This yields a variety of 'Reference case' emission projections. These will differ from one modelling group to another because of variations in (a) model structures and parameterisations and (b) auxiliary assumptions employed by each group.

Each of the six panels of Figure 10.17 illustrates, for one SRES scenario, the range over modelling teams in which total CO_2 anthropogenic emissions (in gigatonnes of carbon) from all sources are projected to lie over the period up to 2100 in the scenario reference case. This information is shown in the grey shaded bands.

Figure 10.17 also contains information about what it calls 'mitigation strategies'. How was this information generated? First, the panel has chosen to focus on several alternative stabilised

CO_2 concentration rates: these are 450, 550, 650 and 750 ppmv. (The value of 550 ppmv has proved to be of particular interest. It corresponds to an approximate doubling of CO_2 concentrations since pre-industrial times, and many research teams have chosen to study such an objective.) Second, a set of mitigation strategies has been assessed by IPCC Working Group III. Using this information, the following can be done. For each scenario, and for each mitigation strategy, identify the time path of emissions that would be consistent with attaining each particular stabilised concentration by 2100. Clearly, different model groups would arrive at different answers to this question (for the reasons given above). Figure 10.17 summarises the results of this exercise. The bands in the diagram show the emissions ranges (over all mitigation strategies investigated) required to stabilise CO_2 concentrations at the levels indicated on the right-hand-side axis.

[15] The IPCC TAR, somewhat confusingly, calls any programme to reduce GHG emissions rates or concentration levels a 'mitigation strategy'.

Box 10.4 *continued*

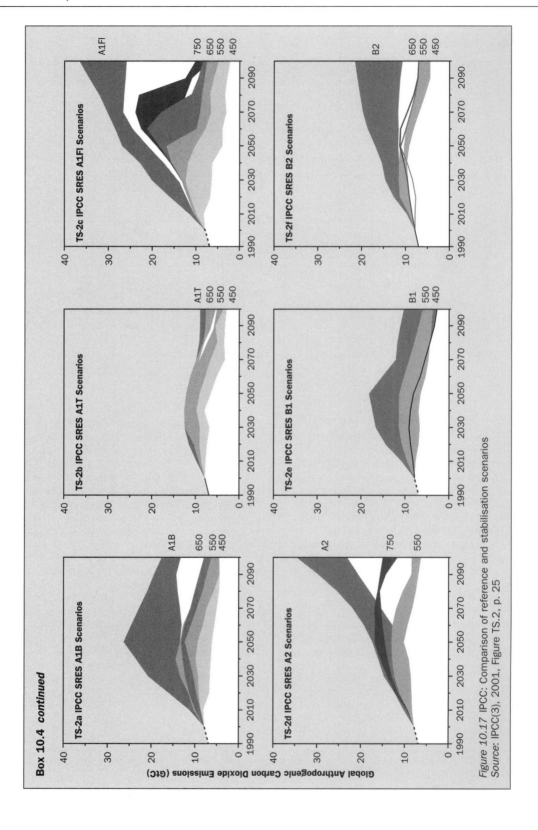

Figure 10.17 IPCC: Comparison of reference and stabilisation scenarios
Source: IPCC(3), 2001, Figure TS.2, p. 25

10.7.2 Stocks and flows: the relationship between emissions and concentrations

Although much of the debate about the greenhouse effect is couched in terms of emissions, it is important to appreciate that what ultimately determines global mean temperature is the concentration rate of greenhouse gases in the atmosphere. So any analysis of the greenhouse effect requires that the predicted path through time of GHG emissions be mapped into the implied atmospheric GHG concentrations.

The way in which emissions affect concentrations is apparently simple: emissions add to the stock and decay reduces the stock. The relationship between pollution flows and stocks will be analysed in some depth in Chapter 16. Boxes 16.1 and 16.2 in that chapter show how one research team – Nordhaus and his colleagues with the RICE-99 model – have modelled this stock–flow relationship for GHGs. Two matters that we discuss in Chapter 16 apply *a fortiori* to GHG concentrations. First, the rate of decay of the GHG stock depends on the 'active' residence time of GHG molecules in the atmosphere. The expected lives of GHG molecules range from a few weeks for tropospheric ozone to 100 years or more for CFCs. It follows that as the composition of different gases in the overall stock of GHGs alters, so the average lifetime of the composite GHG stock will alter. The second complication arises from the operations of various 'sinks' that sequester carbon dioxide and other greenhouse gases. It is known, for example, that the oceans absorb some carbon dioxide. But we have imperfect knowledge about how the capacity of oceans to absorb CO_2 will change as mean temperatures change or as GHG concentrations change.

Conditional on the best estimates that can be made of emissions–concentration relationships for greenhouse gases, analysis can proceed in three ways:

1. Forecasts of emission paths through time are made, and then mapped into their implied paths for GHG concentration rates.

2. Target paths for concentration rates are selected, from which are calculated the implied GHG emission paths.
3. Target paths for emissions rates are selected, from which are calculated the implied GHG concentration paths.

These three approaches really process the same information in different ways. The first approach is typically followed when researchers are simulating what might happen under a 'business as usual' (otherwise known as reference or baseline) policy regime in which no additional climate-change control policy is introduced. For example, we stated earlier that the IPCC, in its TAR, used six scenarios as the basis for its analysis of possible future climate change. On the basis of emissions projections under each of the six illustrative SRES scenarios (see Box 10.4), the IPCC central estimates imply that by 2100 CO_2 concentrations would be in the range 540 to 970 ppm. These values are 90% to 250% above the pre-industrial (1750) concentration level of 280 ppm. However, modelling uncertainties imply that the outcomes (with 95% confidence) may vary within each scenario by between −10% and +30% of the central estimates. Hence the total range of 'reasonably possible' concentrations is 490 ppm to 1260 ppm (75% to 350% above the 1750 level).[16]

For policy analysis the second approach may be useful. Here one can imagine that policy makers are presented with a choice between alternative GHG concentrations (with their associated long-term climate-change outcomes). Once a choice of concentration target has been made, the analyst can reason backwards to find out what emission path (or paths) are consistent with that target. Policy instruments can then be set accordingly. Much of what one reads in the IPCC TAR can be seen in this light.

Setting emission targets is less appealing intellectually, as emission rates are intermediate targets, and rather far removed from final objectives. Put another way, emissions flows are not of any intrinsic interest, as they do not directly relate to the goals we are trying to achieve. It is noteworthy, therefore, that current policy targets – embodied in the Kyoto

---

[16] The IPCC report (IPCC(1), 2001) also notes that there is much more variability in projections of the concentration of non-CO_2 greenhouse gases than for CO_2 itself.

Protocol – are cast in terms of emissions (rather than concentrations or global mean temperatures).

10.7.3 Climate change models

Climatic change models are designed to simulate the climate consequences of particular paths of GHG concentrations over time. Researchers are interested not only in global mean temperature changes, but also in their variation across space. This is typically done through the use of global circulation models (also called carbon cycle models), which simulate atmospheric and oceanic dynamic processes. Global circulation model simulations generate information about what the global mean temperature – and its spatial variation – would be at various points in time if GHG concentrations were to increase along particular paths and stabilise at particular levels.

What kinds of conclusions emerge from such global circulation model simulation runs? For this we turn to the IPCC Third Assessment Report (TAR) which is widely recognised as providing authoritative answers. The salient features are summarised in Box 10.5, first in terms of what we know has happened in the recent past due to anthropogenic GHG emissions, and then for what is likely to happen in the future.

Since publication of the IPCC Second Assessment Report (1995), confidence in the ability of models to project future climate has increased. This is largely due to a better understanding of the roles played by water vapour, sea-ice dynamics and ocean heat transport. Large uncertainties persist in several aspects of the models, however, particularly with regard to the feedback effects of changing cloud cover and their interaction with radiation and aerosols. For policy purposes, the main limitation of our scientific understanding of the greenhouse effect relates to spatial disaggregation. The estimates reported in Box 10.5 concern global land-surface averages. Although the confidence with which regional predictions can be made has sharply increased in the last five years, we still know relatively little about climate change at regional and national levels. But it is exactly this kind of information we require in order to make well-founded estimates about the impacts of climate change.

10.7.4 The impacts of climate change and the monetary value of potential damages

As can be seen in Table 10.6, the variety of possible future physical, biological and ecological impacts of climate change is immense. Some of these impacts are likely to be beneficial for humans, but most are expected to be adverse. For many – particularly the ecological impacts – uncertainty is pronounced. The 2001 IPCC TAR projects that the global average sea-level will rise by an amount in the interval 0.1 to 0.9 metre between 1990 and 2100 (over the full range of SRES scenarios – see Box 10.4) in the absence of large-scale policy change. This alone could have catastrophic consequences for some parts of the world. As we have seen, global average temperature is projected to rise under all SRES scenarios, and several inner continental areas would experience higher probabilities of severe drought and soil degradation.

Natural systems can be very sensitive to climate change because of limited adaptive capacity. Many of these impacts are irreversible. Those systems most at risk are listed in Table 10.6. It is likely that biodiversity decline will take place in these systems, at a rate which will depend on extent and rate of climate change. The table also lists several of the more sensitive human systems. Potential impacts which have been intensively studied include changes in crop yields (expected to be adverse overall), water availability (expected to worsen where water is already scarce), risks to human health and disease, and exposure to extreme events such as flooding. Finally, there will be further induced impacts on the economic system, particularly in the energy and industry sectors, and in financial services.

Of most concern are impacts which may arise from threshold effects in climate change (such as discontinuous changes in ocean circulation patterns, large reduction in Greenland and West Antarctic ice sheets, and accelerated global warming due to feedback effects such as release of carbon from permafrost). While the probability of such changes is low, their consequences would be catastrophic and largely irreversible.

A recurrent theme in climate-change impact studies is that those who are already relatively

---

Box 10.5 Climate change consequences of anthropogenic greenhouse-gas emissions

Recent historical changes in climate

- Global average surface temperature has increased over the 20th century by 0.6 ± 0.2 °C (95% confidence range).
- Regional variations in warming can, and have, departed appreciably from the global average.
- The diurnal temperature range (maximum minus minimum daily) has decreased widely, although not everywhere.
- Snow cover and ice cover have decreased.
- Northern hemisphere sea-ice amounts are decreasing, but no significant trends are apparent in Antarctic sea-ice.
- Global average sea level has risen (between 0.1 and 0.2 metre during the 20th century).
- Global ocean heat content has increased since the late 1950s.
- Other important aspects of climate have changed: precipitation amounts have increased in middle-to-high latitudes of the Northern hemisphere (except East Asia). Changes have taken place in the frequency of heavy precipitation. There has been increased cloud cover.
- Concentrations of atmospheric GHGs and their radiative forcing have continued to increase as a result of human activities.
- Natural factors have made small contributions to radiative forcing over the past century.
- In recent years there has been new, and stronger, evidence that most of the warming observed over the last 50 years is attributable to human activities.

Looking ahead

- Human influences will continue to change atmospheric concentration throughout the 21st century.
- By 2100, CO_2 concentrations projected to be in range 540 to 970 ppm for illustrative SRES scenarios (90% to 250% above 1750 value of 280 ppm). Uncertainties cause -10 to $+30\%$ variation around each scenario. Total range of concentrations is 490 to 1260 ppm (75 to 350% above 1750 level).
- There is much more variability in concentration projections of non-CO_2 gases than for CO_2 itself.
- Stabilisation of CO_2 concentrations at 450, (650 or 1000) ppm would require global anthropogenic CO_2 emissions to fall below 1990 levels within a few decades (a century, or about two centuries), *and* decrease thereafter. Eventually, CO_2 emissions would have to be a very small fraction of current emissions.
- Global average temperature and sea level are projected to rise under all IPCC SRES scenarios.
- Globally averaged surface temperature is projected to rise by 1.4 °C to 5.8 °C over period 1990 to 2100. (Results over the full range of SRES scenarios.) These projections are higher than those in the Second Assessment Report (IPCC, 1995), primarily due to lower projected sulphur emissions in newer SRES scenarios. (The Second Assessment Report gave an interval of 1.0 °C to 3.5 °C.)
- Global average sea level is projected to rise by 0.1 to 0.9 metre between 1990 and 2100, for the full range of SRES scenarios.
- Anthropogenic climate change will persist for many centuries. Global mean surface temperature increases and rising sea level are projected to rise for hundreds of years after stabilisation of GHG concentrations (even at present levels) owing to the long timescales on which the deep ocean adjusts to climate change. Ice sheets will continue to react for thousands of years.
- The possibility for large and irreversible changes in the climate system exists, but there is large uncertainty about the mechanisms involved and so about the likelihood or timescales of such transitions.

---

disadvantaged are likely to suffer the largest adverse impacts. This arises partly because adaptation to climate change is a necessary part of any climate change policy – it is simply not feasible to prevent climate change from occurring. However, communities with low income and wealth will have the lowest ability to adapt. It also follows from the spatial distribution of climate change impacts. For example, the most serious impacts on farming are projected to occur in areas already experiencing high population growth and/or decreasing soil fertility.

Table 10.6 Recent historical and potential future impacts of climate change

Potential Impacts	Comments
Physical:	
Shrinkage of glaciers, thawing of permafrost	Changes in mountain and high-latitude ecosystems
Later freezing and earlier break-up of river and lake ice	
Sea-level rise	Major implication for coastal settlement patterns. Flood damage. Permanent inundation of some river delta areas
Higher incidence of floods and of droughts in some regions	It is unclear to what extent already observed changes in flood and drought frequencies are attributable to climate change or to other socio-economic factors
Biological:	
Lengthening of mid-to-high-latitude growing seasons	
Poleward and altitudinal shifts of plant and animal ranges	
Declines of some plant and animal populations	
Early tree flowering, emergence of insects and birds' egg laying	
Damage to natural systems which are very sensitive to climate change because of limited adaptive capacity	Systems at risk include glaciers, coral reefs, mangroves, boreal and tropical forests, polar and alpine ecosystems, prairie wetlands and remnant native grasslands
Many of these impacts are irreversible	Biodiversity declines highly likely in these cases, and will depend on extent and rate of climate change
Human-system impacts:	
Systems at risk include water resources, agriculture and forestry, coastal zones and marine systems	General reductions in crop yields in most tropical, sub-tropical and mid-latitude regions (But increased crop yield potential at mid-latitudes for small temperature rises)
Decreased water availability in regions where water already scarce	
Human health and risk of disease	Increase in number of people exposed to vector-borne (e.g. malaria) and water-borne (e.g. cholera) diseases Increase in heat stress in some regions, but reduced winter mortality in others
Changes in climate extremes	Widespread increase in risk of flooding (higher precipitation and sea-level rise) Effects of changes in extremes expected to fall disproportionately on the poor
Energy demand changes	Via impacts on air-conditioning and space heating

Source: Compiled from IPCC(2), 2001

10.7.4.1 Damage valuation

Suppose that policy makers wished to identify an efficient (or optimal) level of GHG control. Conventional economic approaches would require that money values be put on the costs and benefits of climate change, or equivalently on the costs and benefits of control measures to reduce climate change. Either way, this would require some economic measure of the damages of climate change. Such a measure is usually expressed in monetary units.

There are many ways in which this could be done. We shall explore these methods at some length in Chapters 12 and 13. The general technique is straightforward in principle. Once impacts have been estimated in their original 'physical' units, one assigns monetary values to those impacts using some technique which tries to proxy for what individuals are willing to pay to secure a benefit or willing to accept in compensation to avoid an impact that would otherwise occur.

It is generally accepted that this can be a legitimate exercise when done for small changes that take place within a single national economy. Even then, the caveat 'can be' is important, as we shall see in our discussions about valuation in Chapters 12 and

13. But it is an altogether more problematic exercise when attempted for large-scale changes, and/or for changes that occur in several countries simultaneously. There are two problems here. The first is that conventional *operational* welfare measures are constructed on the assumption that changes are small, and do not move an economy far from its original resource allocation. Marginal valuations may be inappropriate for large changes. The second problem is often described as one relating to aggregation difficulties. However, it also involves a wider aspect of economic methodology, concerning how international comparisons can be made legitimately when the global distribution of income and wealth is far from what could be regarded as optimal. We shall explain these problems at some length in discussing cost–benefit analysis in Chapter 11. It is noteworthy that the Report of Working Group III of the IPCC Second Assessment Group (IPCC, 1995c) did come up with numerical damage estimates. These estimates, though, generated considerable controversy; this may explain why the Third Assessment Group Report (IPCC(3), 2001) avoided giving any additional monetary evaluations of damages.

If these methodological problems have substance – as we shall argue that they do – then they will have significant implications for international policy towards climate change. Impacts may well be very large, will bear down unequally between countries, and impact on a world in which the wealth distribution is extremely skewed. The size of possible impacts can be gauged from the fact that, for doubling of CO_2 concentration scenarios, studies typically place damages in the range 1% to 1.5% of GDP per year for developed countries, and 2% to 9% for developing countries. However, there is no reason to believe that concentrations will only rise to that extent, and it is quite possible that average temperatures will eventually increase by more than 10 °C. Damages would then be considerably greater than those just indicated.

As far as the regional distribution of damages arising from climate change is concerned, the current consensus view is that there will be few, if any, 'big winners' but there will almost certainly be some very large losers. (See Nordhaus, 1990a; Hansen, 1990, Nordhaus and Boyer, 1999. Numerical estimates from the last mentioned of those references are given in Box 10.6.) On average, damage is expected to be inversely related to per capita income. Furthermore, those economies with the greatest incentive to cut emissions (or otherwise limit climate change) tend to have the poorest resource base to implement policies that adapt to climate change and minimise the most serious forms of damage.

10.7.5 Routes towards stabilisation of greenhouse-gas atmospheric concentrations

There are two ways in which we could move towards a goal of reducing the rate of growth of atmospheric greenhouse-gas concentrations in the atmosphere:

1. increase the capacity of 'pools' that sequester carbon dioxide and other greenhouse gases from the atmosphere;
2. decrease the rate of emissions of greenhouse gases (thereby reducing GHG inflows into the atmosphere).

An ultimate objective of stabilising GHG atmospheric concentrations could be achieved by the second of these alone, or by some combination of the two methods. Let us briefly explore the first route: increasing the capacity of what we shall, loosely speaking, call 'carbon pools'.[17] Research suggests that forests, agricultural lands and other terrestrial ecosystems offer significant carbon reduction potential. This potential operates through several channels. First, increased planting rates and volumes would increase the amount of biomass that accumulates through natural growth; it is this biomass which sequesters carbon. Secondly, some changes in the species or varieties mix of crops and biological material mass can enhance the amount of biomass that is stored. Thirdly, changes in agricultural practice and land use patterns can conserve existing stocks of carbon more effectively (preventing its discharge into the atmosphere).

---

[17] We use the term 'pool' here to denote a stock; the flow of carbon into this pool can be called a sink. As the pool reaches its full capacity, the sink reduces.

Box 10.6 Estimates of greenhouse gas damages given in Nordhaus and Boyer (1999)

Table 10.7 list estimates made by Nordhaus and Boyer (1999, Table 4-10) of the impacts – measured in percentage gains or losses in net output – of a rise in global mean temperature of 2.5 °C by the year 2100. These estimates incorporate what the authors regard as potential catastrophic impacts. It should be noted that catastrophic impacts are expected by Nordhaus and Boyer 'to become far larger for higher temperature changes, and begin to dwarf the estimates shown . . . at 5 °C increases or above'.

Table 10.7 Estimated GDP gains or losses arising from a rise in global mean temperature of 2.5 °C by the year 2100

Country/Region	Net output gain/loss	Comments
Russia	+0.65	Significant agricultural benefits Gains from non-market time use
Eastern Europe	−0.71	
USA	−0.45	Temperate climate Low dependence on agriculture Advanced health system Positive amenity of warmer climate
China	−0.22	
Japan	−0.50	
Middle-income	−2.44	
High-income OPEC	−1.95	
Lower-middle-income	−1.81	
OECD Europe	−2.83	Potential of catastrophic climate change due to shifts in ocean currents Significant coastal and agricultural impacts
Other high-income	+0.39	Canada: Significant agricultural benefits Gains from non-market time use
Africa	−3.91	Potential for adverse health impacts
India	−4.93	Extreme vulnerability to climate change due to importance of monsoons on agriculture Disamenity of higher temperatures on non-market time Potential for adverse health impacts
Other low-income	−2.64	
Global average	−1.50 (output-weighted) −1.88 (population-weighted)	

Source: Adapted from Nordhaus and Boyer (1999)

The IPCC estimates that the potential here is large but nevertheless limited. There are two kinds of limit. The first concerns the feasible size of the pools. IPCC sees a total cumulative sequestration potential of 100 GtC by 2050, equivalent to between 10% and 20% of potential fossil-fuel emissions during that period. The second limit concerns duration through time. A once-for-all forestation project would store carbon for the lifetime of the timber, but once that timber decays or burns, its carbon is returned to other pools, including the atmosphere. Put another way, larger biomass stocks today imply greater flows to the atmosphere in the future. Taking a longer view, this approach may merely reschedule the temporal pattern of carbon flows to and from the atmosphere, and pose a risk of substantially greater CO_2 emissions in the future. A permanent reduction of atmospheric carbon stocks would require, loosely speaking, a permanent increase in the stock of the biomass in question.

Even if this option is feasible, it may not be economically sensible. That depends on the costs of sequestering carbon in this way compared, for example, to the costs of reducing equivalent amounts of carbon emissions. Those cost comparisons need also to take into consideration opportunity costs of the land on which biomass is accumulated. Doing this may incur opportunity costs in the form of lost alternative uses of that land. A sensible approach might be to look for sequestration projects that generate synergies, by being complementary to other activities or land uses, such as wildlife or biodiversity reserves, or recreational activities. The IPCC argues that the best long-term goal is to substitute wood for other materials to generate some permanency of carbon pools.

Preliminary IPCC estimates suggest that the (undiscounted) marginal costs of these schemes are in the region of \$0.1/tC to \$20/tC in several tropical countries; and from \$20/tC to \$100/tC in non-tropical countries. However, these costs underestimate full long-run marginal costs, as they do not include opportunity costs of land, infrastructure and some other associated 'indirect costs'. Moreover, marginal costs will rise as the best carbon pool projects are taken up.

As a practical proposition, it is clear that increased carbon pools can only partially offset expected fossil-fuel emissions. Given the limited scope for larger terrestrial sinks, a large component of any programme must involve GHG emissions reductions. How large these would have to be is discussed next. To think about how they might be achieved, it is worth looking at the following accounting identity (which assumes that carbon emissions arise entirely in energy use)

$$M = \frac{m}{e} \cdot \frac{e}{q} \cdot \frac{q}{v} \cdot v \cdot N$$

where M is total emissions, N is total population, $m = M/N$ is emissions per person, e is the energy used per person (in producing material output), q is material output per person, and v is the value of output per person. The first three components on the right-hand side are expressed as ratios of per capita terms, and reflect various kinds of 'intensities'. The fourth and fifth components, v and N, measure the scale of the economy in different ways. What does this identity tell us? Total emissions will fall if any term on the right-hand side falls, other things being equal. Hence we can arrive at the following conclusions (assuming that other things stay constant in each case):

1. Emissions will fall if m/e – which reflects the emissions intensity of energy production – can be reduced. This could be achieved by changes in fuel mix (from fossil to renewable energy, for example).
2. Emissions will fall if e/q – the energy intensity of material output – falls. This could be achieved by changes in material output mix, or by producing output in more energy-conserving ways.
3. Emissions will fall if q/v falls. This concept is subtle, but possibly of some significance. As we have seen, q is an index of (per capita) material output. It is best thought of in volume terms. In contrast, v is a (per capita) measure of the value of output, where value reflects the contribution to well-being of an individual. It is possible for output value to rise even if output volume remains constant (or falls). For example, computers are now immensely more valuable to users now than they were twenty years ago, even though the volume of computer output – measured in material terms – has fallen sharply. But, more importantly, as economies become more service-oriented – and as the relative importance of recreational services and environmental amenities rise – we might expect to see q/v falling.
4. Emissions will fall if N falls. There is no prospect of this for many decades. Indeed, for some time rising global population will be a contributory factor to growing emissions. But as Chapter 2 showed, global population might fall by the end of the 21st century, and certainly cannot grow without limit indefinitely.

One must be wary of trying to extract too much from accounting identities of this kind. However, they can provide some insight into how policy to reduce GHG emissions might operate. It would be a useful exercise to take an energy or carbon tax and

Table 10.8 Estimates of potential global GHG-emission reductions by sector, arising from available technological options (1998 prices, US dollars)

Sector	1990 emissions (MtC$_{eq}$/yr)	Potential emissions reduction in 2010 (MtC$_{eq}$/yr)	Potential emissions reduction in 2020 (MtC$_{eq}$/yr)	Net direct costs per ton of C avoided
Buildings	1650	700–750	1000–1100	Most at negative cost
Transport	1080	100–300	300–700	Less than $25/tC Two studies suggest > $50/tC
Industry – energy and material efficiency	2470	600–800	1300–1500	More than half of energy efficiency at negative cost. Costs uncertain for material efficiency
Agriculture	1460–3010	150–300	350–700	Most between zero and $100/tC. Limited opportunities for negative cost
Waste	240	200	200	75% at negative cost 25% at $20/tC
Montreal Protocol replacements	0	100	na	Less than $200/tC
Energy supply and conversion	1620	50–150	350–700	Limited negative cost opportunities Most at < $100/tC
TOTAL	6900–8400	1900–2600	3600–5050	Half at negative cost Half at < $100/tC

Source: IPCC(3) 2001. Table 3.37, p. 264
Notes:
Estimates here acquired by aggregation of large number of sector- and geographically specific studies. Should be regarded as indicative only. Discount rates used in their calculation were in range 5% to 12% per annum.
Negative cost means here that direct benefits (energy saved) exceed direct cost (net capital, operating and maintenance).
Additional costs mean that total costs exceed those shown above. These include set-up and development costs.
Attaining these reductions would require technology transfer, the overcoming of a number of barriers, additional R&D, and possibly a variety of support policies.

see how it might alter the components we have been discussing. We leave this as an exercise for the reader.

Returning now to IPCC deliberations, the IPCC has estimated the extent of feasible emissions reductions, achievable at 'reasonable' cost, that can be obtained from individual sectors of the economy. Table 10.8 illustrates its findings. These estimates seem to be based on bottom-up, engineering approaches and may not be reliable. If they prove to be soundly based, however, total reductions in annual emissions of around 60% of 1990 levels are possible. Moreover, a substantial proportion of those reductions are claimed to be available at negative real cost: the projects involve a double dividend. It is also clear, however, that realising these gains makes very strong assumptions about future technological improvements and international technology transfer.

10.7.6 The costs of greenhouse gas reductions

In the period since 1990, there has been something close to an industry developing within the economics profession researching the likely costs of greenhouse gas abatement. It would be impossible to adequately survey this literature in the space we have available. We shall restrict ourselves to reporting some general results that have emerged from this literature, and then describe the findings of one recent reference source, the report entitled '*Climate Change 2001: Mitigation*' of the Third Working Group of the IPCC (IPCC(3), 2001). This provides a comprehensive statement of what is currently known. The general conclusions that have emerged are as follows:

- Estimates of costs (and benefits) of greenhouse gas abatement vary considerably among modelling teams. In particular, they seem to be rather sensitive to (i) what measure of welfare changes is used; (ii) the scope and structure of model employed; (iii) choices of parameter values; (iv) underlying assumptions, particularly about baseline emissions scenarios.

- The cost of stabilising CO_2 concentrations increases as the concentration stabilisation target declines.
- Emissions constraints in Annex 1 countries are unlikely to be independent of emissions outcomes in non-Annex 1 countries. There are a variety of possible externality or spillover effects that may operate. One important form of negative spillover is 'carbon leakage'; tighter constraints on, or costs of, carbon emissions in some locations may result in geographical relocations of some industries. Estimates of the extent of carbon leakage vary widely, but are often thought to be in the order of 5% to 20% of Annex 1 constraints.
- Climate-change decision-making is essentially a sequential process under uncertainty. The value of new information is likely to be very high, and so there are important quasi-option values that should be considered.
- Significant technical progress relevant to GHG emissions reduction has been made since the second IPCC assessments in 1995; that progress has been faster than was anticipated.
- There is some scope for GHG emissions to be reduced at zero or negative net social cost. The magnitude of this scope is uncertain. It depends primarily on the size of three forms of 'no-regrets' opportunities and the extent to which they can be exploited:

1. overcoming market imperfections (and so reducing avoidable inefficiencies);
2. ancillary or joint benefits of GHG abatement (such as reductions in traffic congestion);
3. double dividend effects (see Box 6.3 on pp. 175–6).

10.7.6.1 IPCC estimates of the costs of attaining Kyoto emissions targets

Many estimates have been made of the costs of complying with the Kyoto protocol. Weyant and Hill (1999) point out that several of those studies have put the cost of abatement as envisaged under Kyoto at around $1 trillion in present value. Evidently, then, these costs are not trivial, particularly given that they would have to be incurred in the near-term future. Nordhaus and Boyer put this in an interesting way:

> It is no hyperbole to say that the issue of greenhouse warming invokes the highest form of global citizenship – where nations are being called upon to sacrifice hundreds of billions of dollars of present consumption in an effort which will largely benefit people in other countries, where the benefits will not come until well into the next century and beyond, and where the threat is highly uncertain and based on modelling rather than direct observation.
>
> *(Nordhaus and Boyer, 1999: electronic manuscript version page 1–3)*

Some relevant numerical information has already been provided in Chapter 6. Table 6.5 listed estimates made by 15 modelling teams of the marginal abatement costs for attainment of the Kyoto targets by the year 2010. This information is summarised in Table 10.9. These costs are calculated for three GHG emissions permit trading scenarios. In the first case, no international trading of GHG permits is allowed, and so each country (or here, bloc of countries) must obtain its Kyoto target by domestic abatement alone. Marginal abatement costs will, therefore, vary from country to country. Table 10.9 shows several measures of cost: the range over the whole set of 4 blocs and 15 models; the median value of marginal abatement cost over all countries and all models; and the median value for each country bloc over the 15 models. What is most evident from this data is the large variation across different models. But it is also noteworthy that there are large variations in the median value of abatement costs between different country blocs (ranging from $US168 to $US304 per tonne). It is evident that in the absence of trading, overall targets are not being met at least-cost.

The second and third scenarios allow limited trading (among Annex 1 countries only) and unrestricted, global trading. Summary statistics are provided for these cases in the lower two rows. The marginal costs of attaining Kyoto targets with emissions trading are far lower than without trading;

Table 10.9 Costs of attaining Kyoto targets under various permit trading regimes

Trading conditions permitted	Marginal cost per tonne of carbon abated (US $)	Reduction in 2010 projected GDP (%)
Absence of international emissions trading	Range over all countries and models: 20 to 665 Median over all countries and models: 201 Country-group medians: US: 168; OECD-Europe: 204 Japan: 304; CANZ: 179	Country-group medians: US: 1.06 OECD-Europe: 0.81 Japan: 0.72 CANZ: 1.83
Emissions trading among Annex 1 countries only	Range over all models: 14 to 135 Median over all models: 65	Country-group medians: US: 0.51 OECD-Europe: 0.28 Japan: 0.19 CANZ: 0.63
Global emissions trading	Range over all models: 5 to 86 Median over all models: 23	Country-group medians: US: 0.20 OECD-Europe: 0.09 Japan: 0.02 CANZ: 0.32

moreover, full global trading leads to significantly lower marginal costs than under Annex 1 trading only.

10.7.7 International cooperation in climate change policy

10.7.7.1 Towards Kyoto

Attempts to secure internationally coordinated reductions in greenhouse gas emissions have taken place largely through a series of international conventions organised under the auspices of the United Nations. First steps were taken at the 1988 Toronto Conference, at which the principle of carbon dioxide targets was first set. The conference recommended that CO_2 emissions should be reduced by 20% from 1988 levels by 2005. It is noteworthy that the idea that GHG control should be specified in terms of quantitative emissions targets – rather than in terms of price incentives such as carbon tax rates – has stuck since then. The year 1988 also saw the establishment of the IPCC which was charged with finding out what was known about the process of climate change, its potential impacts, and policy options for controlling climate change. IPCC Assessment Reports have been produced each fifth year from 1990.

At the so-called Earth Summit in Rio de Janeiro, Brazil, in 1992, the Framework Convention on Climate Change (FCCC) required signatories to conduct national inventories of GHG emissions and to submit action plans for controlling emissions. That 150 countries were signatories to the FCCC appears to be impressive; but the large number prepared to sign reflects the situation that FCCC required no country to commit itself to a particular emissions reduction nor a timetable for any such reduction.

The parties to the Rio agreement were still unable to agree strict emissions limits at the Berlin summit in 1995, agreeing only on a procedure for negotiating such limits (to be concluded by 1997) and accepting in principle the need for industrialised countries to reduce emissions below 1990 levels. Progress in securing agreement at Berlin was primarily hampered by the existence of marked differences of interest between various sub-groups within the nations present.

10.7.7.2 The Kyoto Protocol and its provisions

The Kyoto Protocol (1997) constitutes the first substantial agreement to set GHG emissions limits and a timetable for their attainment. To come into force and be binding on all signatories, it must be ratified by at least 55 countries, responsible for at least 55% of 1990 CO_2 emissions of Annex 1 (as defined in the FCCC) countries. The conference focused on five principal GHGs, and set the objective of cutting combined emissions of GHGs from developed countries by 5% from 1990 levels by the years

Table 10.10 National GHG emission targets set at Kyoto, 1997

Country	Kyoto target 2008–12 (percent change from 1990 emissions)	Projected emissions 2000 (percentage change from 1990 emissions)
Australia	+8	+15
Bulgaria	−8	−28
Canada	−6	+10
Croatia	−5	na
Estonia	−8	−46
European Union	−8	+3
Hungary	−6	−18
Iceland	+10	+5
Japan	−6	+4
Latvia	−8	−26
Liechtenstein	−8	+18
Lithuania	−8	na
Monaco	−8	na
New Zealand	0	+16
Norway	+1	+11
Poland	−6	−17
Romania	−8	na
Russian Federation	0	−17
Slovakia	−8	−16
Slovenia	−8	na
Switzerland	−8	−3
Ukraine	0	na
United States	−7	+4

2008–2012. Moreover, it specifies the amount each industrialised nation must contribute towards the overall target. These country-specific targets are listed in Table 10.10. The Protocol did not set any binding commitments on developing countries.

10.7.7.2.1 The Kyoto Protocol's flexible mechanisms

The Kyoto Protocol is notable for its advocacy of several so-called flexible mechanisms. These are particularly interesting to economists. By generating incentives for control to take place in those countries that have the lowest abatement costs, they create the potential for greatly reducing the total cost of attaining overall policy targets.

(1) Emissions Trading The Protocol endorsed the principle of emissions trading among Annex 1 countries, whereby countries in which emissions fall short of their allowed targets may sell 'credits' to other nations, which can add these to their allowed targets. First steps towards formulating details of

the operations of the emissions trading system were taken at the 1998 negotiating session in Buenos Aires, but still remain undecided.

A point of contention concerns what has become known as 'hot-air' trading. The economic collapse or restructuring through which many of the transition economies of Russia and central Europe have passed means that their GHG emissions will be well below 1990 (or other) baseline levels, even by 2010. Emissions trading will allow these economies to sell large quantities of pollution credits to other Annex 1 countries. Many environmentalists have criticised this provision as allowing some countries – particularly the more affluent ones such as the USA with the means to purchase credits – to buy their way out of abatement, without there being any corresponding increase in abatement elsewhere. In retrospect, it seems that unduly generous emissions limits were set for the transition economies. However, when growth in the transition economies has eliminated their emissions shortfalls, trading provisions will serve the objective of attaining overall (global) targets cost effectively, and so are economically attractive.

(2) Banking Emissions targets do not have to be met every year, only on average over the period 2008–2012. Moreover, emissions reductions above Kyoto targets attained in the years 2008–2012 can be banked for credit in the following control period. This provision will allow economies flexibility in the timing of their abatement programmes (thereby reducing overall abatement costs), while giving countries incentives to act early.

(3) Joint Implementation (JI) Joint Implementation allows for bilateral bargains among Annex 1 countries, whereby one country can obtain 'Emissions Reduction Units' for undertaking in another country projects that reduce net emissions, provided that the reduction is additional to what would have taken place anyway. Clearly, if the cost of reducing net emissions is lower abroad than at home, this provision will contribute to cost-efficiency. However, it is likely that the transaction costs of arranging these bargains will be high, offsetting some proportion of such efficiency gains. Moreover, there remains the problem of identifying which projects genuinely are additional ones.

(4) Clean Development Mechanism (CDM) The Clean Development Mechanism creates the potential for further efficiency gains in policy implementation. These arise where projects that reduce emissions in developing countries are less costly than equal-sized reductions in Annex 1 nations. By funding such projects, Annex 1 countries can gain emissions credits to offset against their abatement obligations. Effectively, the CDM generalises the JI provision to a global basis. However, at the time of writing, it is unclear whether the CDM will apply to sequestration schemes (such as forestry programmes) as well as emissions reductions. There is also concern that many trades under CDM could be spurious in that the project would have taken place anyway (and so should not create offsets elsewhere). As with JI, the difficult task remains of establishing criteria for assessing whether a project really is additional.

10.7.8 An appraisal of the provisions of the Kyoto Protocol

The Kyoto Protocol constitutes the most well-known outcomes of a more-or-less continuous series of international negotiating meetings under the auspices of the FCCC. Since then there have been several other meetings of the negotiating parties, with several further scheduled. As of May 2002, the two most recent meetings of the negotiating parties took place in Bonn (COP 6 [Conference of the Parties], July 2001) and Marrakesh (COP 7, November 2001). At these meetings two major developments took place.

First, agreements were made for financial and technological transfers from developed to developing nations to support implementation of the Kyoto Protocol. Second, the institutional structures and mechanisms required to implement the protocol were put in place. This includes agreements about various 'rules of the game', such as how emissions and reductions are to be measured, the extent to which CO_2 absorbed by sinks will be counted towards Kyoto targets, and compliance mechanisms. The administrative structures for some of the flex-

ible mechanisms – specifically JIP, CDM and emissions trading were agreed.

By May 2002, 40 countries had ratified the Protocol. As yet only one industrialised country (Romania) has ratified the treaty. For the Protocol to become operational, 55 countries must sign, including industrialised countries that account for at least 55% of GHG emissions. The continuing unwillingness of the USA to support the Protocol remains a cause for concern.

10.7.8.1 The extent and depth of international cooperation

The game-theoretic literature that we discussed earlier in this chapter does not point to a high likelihood of efficient outcomes when it comes to attempts to control climate change. Many commentators (for example Barrett and Sandler) characterise the greenhouse effect as a classic Prisoner's Dilemma in which inactivity is a dominant strategy. International cooperation is made difficult by several conditions, including the fact that negotiation concerns benefits that are largely public (rather than private) good in nature, the large number of countries affected, and nation-specific or localised benefits being small relative to transnational benefits.

Under these conditions, game theory suggests that agreements are difficult to secure and implement. This is true above all for attempts to reduce emissions of greenhouse gases. It is not surprising, therefore, that many countries have been reluctant to undertake substantial amounts of GHG reduction; the costs to many individual countries would be very high, the benefits are highly uncertain and very unevenly distributed, and the number of relevant parties is very large.[18]

Many commentators have argued that the only practicable way forward is to secure agreement to very modest emissions reductions in the near term (or more precisely, reductions relative to forecast future trajectories) with some form of commitment to a programme of gradually tightening targets in the future. Given the widespread disparities in levels of economic development, it also seems to be

---

[18] While several of these features are also true for control of CFC emissions, it is noteworthy that control costs are very much lower and benefits more evenly spread in that case. These factors possibly explain the relatively successful efforts on that front.

inevitable that the major share of the abatement cost burden will have to be borne by the more affluent, industrialised economies.

It is too early to say whether or not the outcome will be more than modest reductions. The industrialised countries have agreed in principle to a 5% reduction in GHG emissions by 2010 relative to 1990 levels; if realised that would constitute a significant real cutback. The second of these observations, though, appears to be borne out in practice already. The Kyoto Protocol has adopted the principle that only the richer, industrialised nations should be committed to GHG emissions reductions for the medium-term future. But it is the manner in which the overall burden should be shared that has constituted the most difficult obstacle to significant emissions reductions, and explains the unwillingness of the USA to adopt the treaty.

10.7.8.2 Are Kyoto targets economically defensible?

Are the Kyoto targets economically defensible? Not surprisingly, views differ on this. Some economists are of the opinion that the Kyoto targets are probably not substantially different from *optimal* targets (where optimality is measured in terms of the solutions of optimal-growth stock pollution models of the kind we examine in depth later in Chapter 16). Barrett (1998) uses some rule-of-thumb calculations to support the conclusion that the Kyoto targets are close to being efficient *if* implemented in full, *and* achieved cost-effectively. He quotes Clinton Administration (1998) estimates of the marginal cost of meeting Kyoto targets to be in the range $14–23/ton and claims, on the basis of 1996 IPCC results, that most estimates of the marginal damage of GHG emissions are of a similar magnitude. Others, though, argue that Kyoto targets are excessively stringent. For one such view, see Box 16.2 in Chapter 16. There Nordhaus argues that a path which limits GHG emissions to a doubling of CO_2 atmospheric concentrations is close to being 'optimal' and that present (Kyoto-consistent) policies are highly inefficient with abatement costs being ten times larger benefits than avoided damages.

One could of course argue that given the presence and pervasiveness of fundamental uncertainty regarding many aspects of climate change processes, a control programme that is stricter than one suggested by a conventional cost–benefit approach is warranted. This is what the precautionary principle or a Safe Minimum Standard of Conservation argument would suggest. Some take the opposite view, arguing that there is little point in taking radical cooperative action until these uncertainties are much closer to being resolved. However, there are good reasons for action to be taken – and that in the first instance it should be targeted at reducing that uncertainty. Moreover, coordinating action through simple international institutions has the important advantage that, in the event of substantial abatement being required, it will have been facilitated by those previous ad hoc cooperative efforts.

10.7.8.3 The magnitude of gains from flexibility

You will have noticed Barrett's qualification that Kyoto will only be efficient if it is implemented at least cost. As we saw earlier, the various flexible mechanisms provided for in the Protocol are critical to whether this possibility will be realised. Box 10.7 gives some indication about the magnitude of such flexibility gains.

10.7.8.4 Other aspects of the Kyoto Protocol

Although some commentators write about Kyoto as being a binding agreement (on its signatories), the agreement is not binding in the sense that economists would like to use. It is not a self-enforcing agreement; nor does it contain any compliance enforcement mechanisms or any formal free-rider deterrence provisions. This raises two possibilities.

First, the agreement itself – assuming that the required minimum number of countries ratify – may not be sustainable. Second, agreement may well be substantially less than full. If it is less than full, the cost-effectiveness of the Kyoto scheme will suffer badly, and trade leakages will almost certainly diminish the achieved emissions reductions. We explain this point further in Section 10.8, on international trade.

Some writers have criticised the Kyoto approach to greenhouse gas policy for posing choices in terms of emissions limits rather than GHG concentration targets. The issue here is that concentration levels

---

Box 10.7 How large might the efficiency gains from Kyoto's flexible mechanism be?

We can obtain some insight into the size of efficiency gains from flexibility by comparing marginal abatement costs with and without flexibility. This was essentially what we were doing in Section 10.7.6.1.

Without flexibility

In Table 10.9 we saw that the median estimate of marginal abatement costs in developed economies was $201 per tonne of carbon. (This figure sits more-or-less centrally between the corresponding figures from two often quoted models: $125 in the Nordhaus and Boyer (1999) model and $240 in Manne and Richels (1990).). As Barrett (1998) argues, with emissions uncontrolled in the non-Annex 1 countries, marginal abatement costs are effectively zero. Hence costs savings from the Clean Development Mechanism could be at least $200 per tonne at the margin.

With flexibility

With complete flexibility (global permits trading and all other flexibility mechanisms working perfectly), Table 10.9 suggests that optimised marginal abatement costs are $23 per tonne of carbon. Again these figures correspond reasonably closely to some others: $14–23 per tonne (Clinton Administration, 1998), $11 per tonne in 2010 (Nordhaus and Boyer, 1999),

and $70 per ton in 2010 (Manne and Richels, 1990).

Cost differences

Barrett (1998) calculates – on the basis of these numbers and the emissions reductions implied by the Kyoto Protocol – how large the total costs might be for one country, the USA. Using Clinton Administration estimates, he concludes that the total costs to the USA could be $7–12 billion per year with full efficiency, but ten times as large without any flexibility. Using Manne and Richels estimates, the corresponding figures are $20 billion per year in 2010 – equal to 0.25 per cent of GDP – with full efficiency – but four times as large without any flexibility.

On the basis of similar reasoning, Nordhaus and Boyer (1999) estimate cost reduction to be by a factor of seven (comparing with and without trading). Manne and Richels themselves note that with full intertemporal flexibility, marginal abatement costs could fall by a factor of 10 (the same value we obtained earlier in Section 10.7.6.1).

It should be noted that all these estimates compare extremes, and assume that all emissions in any individual country are achieved with full cost-efficiency, a rather implausible assumption. To the extent that this is not achieved, the flexibility gains referred to in this box will be reduced.

---

are closer to what it is that we are ultimately trying to attain, and that framing policy in terms of emissions is at best an indirect way of thinking about goals; and at worst it is arbitrary. During the 1980s and early 1990s, much of the debate about greenhouse effect policy was couched in terms of concentration rates. In particular, many scientists conjectured what levels of GHG concentration would be 'acceptable' in terms of their expected impacts. This way of framing analysis remains important today in much of the work being undertaken by the IPCC working groups, at least in so far as much of its research about mitigation is done for a variety of concentration rate scenarios.

However, ultimate goals are not set in terms of emissions or concentrations. They refer, in the final

analysis, to temperature and other climate changes, or perhaps, to some indicator of welfare. Thus neither emissions nor concentrations have any real advantage over one another as objectives; they are both intermediate targets.

Finally, we note a rarely-commented-upon aspect of the Kyoto framework. It has largely focused policy analysis in terms of quantities rather than prices. This is an interesting feature of the agreement. Under different configurations of events, it might have turned out to be the case that policy was couched in terms of prices, considering, for example, what rates of carbon tax should be applied worldwide.

This has important implications for the consequences of policy under conditions of uncertainty, as our discussions in Chapter 8 have shown. Working in terms of quantities leads to uncertain price (or tax) outcomes. Working in terms of prices (or taxes) creates uncertain quantity outcomes. Moreover, as we remarked earlier, the relative efficiency losses (using price- as opposed to quantity-based controls) from setting 'wrong' targets depends on the relative slopes of the marginal benefit and marginal cost functions. This warrants more attention than it has been given thus far.

10.8 International trade and the environment

Our earlier discussions have suggested that the prospects for international environmental cooperation are increased by the presence of linkages between countries. International trade is, arguably, the strongest of such linkages. One might expect environmentalists, therefore, to be enthusiastic supporters of trade liberalisation and, in the final analysis, free trade internationally. However, environmentalists are typically guarded in their attitude towards the liberalisation of international trade. Indeed, in recent years, it appears at times to have been the case that environmentalists have taken a strong line against free trade, at least in the form discussed in current WTO meetings. Why should this be so?

The answer has, at least partially, to do with the belief that trade liberalisation can be environmentally damaging. In this section, we briefly summarise why this might be so, and review some of the evidence. The issue can be approached in two ways. First, one can ask whether an individual country's environmental quality will improve or deteriorate as a result of its becoming more heavily involved in international trade. Secondly, one can ask whether, looking at all countries together, in the aggregate the environment gains or loses from trade liberalisation.

It is not easy to obtain unambiguous results in either approach; it is particularly difficult to do so when looking at countries collectively. Not surprisingly, therefore, economic theory does not deliver clear-cut results, nor does empirical evidence point overwhelmingly in one direction or the other. At the moment, we must conclude that the jury is out, although as trade–environment relationships are now among the most actively researched topics in environmental economics, uncertainties might be reduced in the near future.

We begin by considering individual country effects. The proposition that free trade can improve economic welfare in each of the participating countries is one of the oldest, and most widely accepted, principles of economics. It has played a part in shaping much of the international political, economic and institutional framework that has been built up since 1945 (for example, single-market areas such as the European Union, and GATT, now known as the World Trade Organization). Is the validity of this proposition affected by the existence of environmental pollution?

To examine this we investigate a simple world of two countries, X and Y, each of which produces two goods, A and B.[19] Each country acts as a price-taker, regarding the world price of a good as fixed and beyond its control. It is generally thought that free trade will bring positive net benefits to both countries compared with a situation where no trade is allowed. To see why, we can examine the changes in consumers' surplus and producers' surplus that arise from the introduction of trade.[20] Figure 10.18 portrays the demand and supply curves for good A in each of the two countries. In the absence of international trade, country X produces and consumes the quantity A_X at price P_X, country Y produces and consumes A_Y at price P_Y.

The opening of free trade establishes a common world price, P_W. As the world price is below its pre-trade domestic price, X becomes an importer of good A; Y becomes an exporter of good A. Let us identify the changes that take place in consumer and producer surpluses with respect to good A in the two countries. For country X, in Figure 10.18(a), the opening of trade causes domestic production to fall to A_{SX} while domestic consumption increases to A_{DX}.

---

[19] The argument could be generalised to many countries and many goods but for simplicity we shall not do so.

[20] The concepts of consumers' and producers' surplus were explained in Chapter 5.

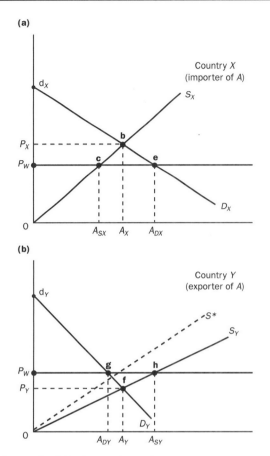

(a)

(b)

Figure 10.18 Trade and the environment

Imports make up the shortfall of domestic production relative to domestic consumption. Consumer surplus – the area below the demand function but above the price paid by consumers – increases from the area $P_X b d_X$ to the area $P_W e d_X$. Producer surplus – the area above the supply function but below the price received by sellers – falls from $0 b P_X$ to $0 c P_W$. The gain in consumer surplus is greater than the loss of producer surplus by an amount equal to the area *ceb*, and so the importing country has a net gain in welfare from trade in good A.

By inspection of Figure 10.18(b), it can be seen that the exporting country also experiences a net welfare gain from the opening of trade. With trade,

domestic production of good A is A_{SY} while domestic consumption is A_{DY}. The surplus production is exported to country X. Consumer surplus associated with good A falls from the area $P_Y f d_Y$ to the area $P_W g d_Y$. Producer surplus increases from $0 f P_Y$ to $0 h P_W$. The gain in producer surplus is greater than the loss of consumer surplus by an amount equal to the area *fhg*, and so the exporter has a net gain in welfare from trade in good A.[21]

This is just one version of the familiar argument for free trade. However, it should be noted that the argument as it stands is only strictly valid if there are no 'distortions' present anywhere in the economies in question (that is, if all the conditions set out in Chapter 5 are satisfied). But does this argument for free trade carry over to a situation where production generates adverse environmental externalities? Suppose that producing good A generates an adverse externality that affects only the citizens of the producing country (that is, there is no international pollution spillover). For the importing country, we have already seen that the opening of trade reduces its domestic production of the good, and so the magnitude of the environmental externality will also fall there. Bringing external effects into the picture reinforces the argument for trade for this country.

But matters are not clear-cut for the country that becomes an exporter. Its increased volume of production raises external costs, which reduces the net gains from the opening of trade. The rise in pollution externalities may be larger than the previously explained net surplus gain, in which case the country will experience a net welfare loss. Further information is needed to derive an unambiguous conclusion about whether trade will benefit the exporting country (or indeed the two countries collectively). However, it is clear that the presence of production externalities undermines the case for free trade.

Next suppose that the opening of an economy to international trade is accompanied by the introduction of some pollution control programme. Is it possible to be any more precise about the consequences of such a package? If, for example, a uniform tax rate were imposed on units of emission in the

---

[21] Although it is not shown in Figure 10.18, equivalent conclusions must follow from examination of changes in welfare associated with trade in the other good (although the direction of trade flows would be reversed). So it does no harm to our analysis to focus on just one good.

exporting country, the supply function would rotate anticlockwise to a position such as that shown by the function $0S^*$ in Figure 10.18(b). As compared with the trade-but-no-pollution-control situation, emissions will fall and so external costs will be reduced. However, producer surplus will also be smaller, as is evident from inspection of the figure. In general it is not possible to know whether the reduction in pollution externalities will be more or less than the fall in producer surplus, once again leaving the overall welfare effect ambiguous.

There is, however, one case where the outcome is not ambiguous. If the pollution control programme – whether it uses taxes, permits or other controls – is economically efficient then, as we demonstrated in Chapter 6, the gain in avoided pollution costs must exceed the fall in producer surplus – see particularly Figures 6.4 and 6.5 and the accompanying discussion. In this particular circumstance, therefore, we do have a clear result. Opening economies to international trade will result in net welfare gains provided that this is accompanied by the introduction of an economically efficient pollution control programme to internalise any pollution externality (provided that was the only distortion present).

As a matter of practice, however, one should note that the world is one in which distortions are pervasive, environmental pollution problems are rarely if ever fully internalised, and it is almost impossible to design fully efficient pollution control programmes. Whether free trade is welfare-maximising – or whether trade liberalisation leads to net welfare gains – is, therefore, a moot point. Now let us consider some other routes through which international trade may impact upon the environment.

Two hypotheses dominate theoretical discussions about trade–environment linkages:

- The factor endowment hypothesis: in this classical view of trade (sometimes known as the Heckscher–Ohlin–Samuelson model) relative factor abundance determines comparative advantage, and so the directions of trade flows. Under this hypothesis, on the assumption that capital-intensive industry is more pollution-intensive than labour-intensive industry, heavily polluting capital-intensive processes will migrate to capital-abundant affluent economies with trade.

- The pollution haven hypothesis: in this view, income differences between countries generate differences in the tightness of environmental regulations; higher-income countries have stricter regulation than lower-income countries. Then, on the assumption that production costs rise with the level of regulation, relatively low-income countries will become more pollution-intensive as a result of international trade.

Notice that both of these hypotheses agree that trade will have environmental consequences; they disagree about how those consequences are distributed. However, neither hypothesis tells us anything about what will happen to the environment in aggregate – whether measured in terms of quantity or quality.

It is not necessary to choose between these hypotheses, as they are not mutually exclusive. Both could be – and probably are – true. However, we note in passing that recent empirical work casts considerable doubt on the economic importance of the pollution haven hypothesis. A series of empirical studies (including Tobey, 1990, Grossman and Krueger, 1995, Jaffe *et al.*, 1995) find that trade seems to reflect factor endowments, not differing emissions abatement costs (as proxied by the strictness of environmental regulation).

An important recent work by Antweiller *et al.* (2001) helps us to gain further insight into trade–environment linkages. The authors build a theoretical model to address these issues. The impacts of greater openness arising from trade liberalisation are decomposed into three effects:

1. *Scale effects*: Trade liberalisation promotes economic growth. Scale effects of trade liberalisation refer to changes in pollution that arise if the economy were to be simply scaled up, other things being equal.
2. *Production technique effects*: These concern emission intensities, which vary across techniques of production. As real incomes increase, producers are expected to switch to cleaner techniques with lower emissions intensity.
3. *Composition effects*: These relate to the industrial structure of an economy. An economy that devotes more of its resources to producing polluting goods will pollute more.

The model of Antweiller *et al.* is constructed to provide an account, firmly grounded in economic theory, that can generate a consistent explanation of the expected signs and magnitudes of these three types of trade effect. The model nests as special cases the two hypotheses mentioned above. The authors find that trade liberalisation will generate increased scale that increases pollution, but the magnitude of this effect is outweighed by the environmentally beneficial production technique effects. (Their empirical work suggests that the net effect of scale and technique effects is such that if trade liberalisation were to raise GDP per person by 1%, then pollution concentrations would fall by about 1%.) With respect to composition effects, they find that openness *per se* should not be related in any systematic way to emissions. Moreover, composition effects are predicted to be relatively small in magnitude.

Using sulphur dioxide emissions as an example, Antweiller *et al.* find strong support for their theoretical conclusions. The scale effect increases emissions, but is outweighed by a beneficial technique effect. As predicted, the composition (and so pollution-intensity) effect is found to be relatively small. Overall, the authors conclude that free trade has a beneficial effect (at the aggregate level) on the environment.

Despite our earlier comments that the 'pollution haven' hypothesis has found little empirical support so far, it would be unwise to conclude on that basis alone that it has had no effect and that it will not have one in the future. As environmental regulations tighten generally, so the scope for gaining competitive advantage by free-riding with lower standards increases. Some countries may deliberately choose to trade off more environmental pollution for a better competitive position in terms of output and employment gained by lower environmental standards (see Esty, 1994). Perhaps of more concern is the effect that this perception may have on the development of international environmental control. The fear of losing international competitiveness by acting ahead of, or to a greater degree than, others in terms of environmental regulation may slow the adoption of stricter environmental controls.

These arguments suggest another role that can usefully be played by international cooperation –

constructing a framework by which pollution policy is coordinated so that the degree of regulation is similar everywhere, and so preventing the development of 'pollution havens'. In a similar vein, the question is raised as to whether it is appropriate for international institutions to seek unconditionally the objective of completely free, unregulated trade. There are parallels here with the issue of exploitation of child or slave labour to gain trade advantages through low private costs of production. Many would argue that the usual presumption in favour of free trade should be suspended in those circumstances.

What is really at issue here is, once again, policy integration. GATT (the General Agreement on Tariffs and Trade) and its successor the WTO (World Trade Organization) have been the principal international institutions responsible for liberalising world trade and policing trading arrangements. While GATT has always admitted some restrictions on free trade (such as giving a country the right to impose tariffs against a country 'dumping' its exports), these exceptions were intended to foster a climate in which trade restrictions would be penalised (and so free trade more effectively promoted). Meanwhile, alternative institutional arrangements have been introduced to seek international cooperation in achieving international environmental targets, such as the conservation of biodiversity or greenhouse gas reduction. There are clearly gains to be made by integrating policy objectives and so ensuring that gains on one policy dimension are not partially or wholly offset by adverse side effects on others. Much of the recent debate about the operation of the WTO has been concerned with how the pursuit of environmental goals can be made consistent with its fundamental commitment to the liberalisation of trade.

Learning outcomes

Near the start of this chapter, it was stated that our objective was to provide the reader with the means to answer several fundamental questions, and to apply those answers to specific problems. We here repeat those questions, and provide (very briefly) some preliminary answers implied by the analysis of this chapter.

- In which ways do international environmental problems differ from purely national (or sub-national) problems? The main point here is that these problems involve people living (or yet to be born) in more than one country. There are spillovers or externalities that cross national boundaries. This poses difficulties because political sovereignty is typically given to the nation state.

- What additional issues are brought into contention by virtue of an environmental problem being 'international'? Given the previous comments, it is evident that outcomes are likely to be inefficient or sub-optimal unless nations cooperate and policy is coordinated.

- What insights does the body of knowledge known as game theory bring to our understanding of international environmental policy? Game theory provides a framework for analysing behaviour where the payoffs to choices are strategically interdependent (that is, where the payoff to one player from a decision depends upon the choices of all other players in the 'game').

- What determines the degree to which cooperation takes place between countries and policy is coordinated? What conditions favour (or discourage) the likelihood and extent of cooperation between countries? We have brought together, in Box 10.1, a statement of these

conditions. You should re-read that now. Of particular importance seem to be reciprocity and repetition. If parties interact continuously – either having to repeatedly make a particular choice, or negotiate with each other repeatedly but about different things, the chances of effective cooperation are greatly enhanced.

- Why is cooperation typically a gradual, dynamic process, with agreements often being embodied in treaties or conventions that are general frameworks of agreed principles, but in which subsequent negotiation processes determine the extent to which cooperation is taken? It is often best to enter a cooperative process by making small commitments; cooperation may then be stepped up gradually as parties are observed to stick to agreed principles, and as new knowledge arrives.

- Is it possible to use such conditions to explain how far efficient cooperation has gone concerning about acid rain, lower-atmosphere ozone and greenhouse gas pollution? The answer seems to be that the appropriate theory can be, and has been, used with considerable success.

- Most importantly, these insights will help in the design of future cooperative processes and ventures. Well-designed bargaining mechanisms can, in some circumstances, generate substantial mutual net benefits to participants (relative to non-cooperative outcomes).

Further reading

Trade

Anderson (1992a) provides a careful analysis of the benefits of free trade and associated conditions. Anderson (1992b) examines through a case study the environmental implications of increased world trade in agricultural products. Esty (1994) considers the argument that differing regulatory standards will lead to pollution havens. Runge (1995) gives an excellent general account of trade–environment relationships. Cairncross (1992) and Porter (1990) suggest that environmental regulation may enhance rather than detract from national competitiveness by

operating as a technology promoter. Mäler (1990) provides a very readable account of policy coordination issues using game theory.

Game theory

A good discussion of game theory, at an elementary level, is to be found in Varian (1987), chapters 27, 31 and 32. See also Mäler (1990). Barrett (1990, 1994a) explores cooperative and non-cooperative outcomes for a range of types of spillover, and develops the concept of self-enforcing international agreements. Hoel (1989) demonstrates the worrying result that 'unselfish' unilateral action can result in outcomes that lead to greater levels of emission than in its absence. Dasgupta (1990) shows that cooperation need not require an outside agency to enforce agreements and that such cooperation could be sustained over time by means of norms of conduct. Victor *et al.* (1998) discuss the effectiveness of international commitments. A good general text on game theory (but not explicitly linked to issues of environmental policy) is Rasmusen (2001). Evolutionary games are discussed in Axelrod (1984), a beautiful and easy-to-read classic, and the more difficult text by Gintis (2000).

International coordination of policy and the use of tradable permits

Grubb (1989a) provides an excellent critical survey of the various initial allocation options for marketable permit systems to achieve internationally agreed pollution control targets. Other analyses are found in Hahn and Hester (1989b), Bertram *et al.* (1989) and Tietenberg (1984, 1990). These sources also discuss the distributional consequences of various alternative methods of allocating permits between countries. See also WR (1996), chapter 14.

Acid rain

The scientific basis is well described in Kemp (1990) and a definitive study is to be found in NAPAP (1990). A good analysis of the acid rain issue is to be found in Adams and Page (1985). *World Resources*, published every two years, provides regular updates of the scientific evidence and economic assessments of the damages caused. Good economic analyses may be found in Feldman and Raufer (1982) and Tietenberg (1989). Two articles in the summer 1998 issue of the *Journal of Economic Perspectives* – Schmalensee *et al.* (1998) and Stavins (1998) – give authoritative appraisals of the United States SO$_2$ emissions trading programme.

Ozone depletion

Kemp (1990), WMO (1991) and French (1990) describe the scientific basis of ozone depletion. *World Resources* provides regular updates. An excellent economic analysis is in Bailey (1982). See also Office of Air and Radiation *et al.* (1995).

The greenhouse effect and global climate change

The most comprehensive and up-to-date surveys of climate change science, economics and policy is found in the three most recent reports of the IPCC (IPCC(1), IPCC(2) and IPCC(3), all published in 2001). A *Summary for Policy Makers* and a *Technical Summary* for each of these three volumes – together with a variety of background papers – can be downloaded from the IPCC web site at www.ipcc.ch. A series of papers that together constitute a comprehensive general survey is found in Toman (2001). Other general surveys include Rao (2000) and DeCanio *et al.* (2000), which has a web site at www.pewclimate.org/projects/directions.cfm. Hall and Howarth (2001) examine the long-term economics of climate change.

A presentation of the 'scientific basis' for the greenhouse effect, written from the perspective of an economist, is given in Cline (1991). For information on the warming contribution of different GHGs, the reader should study Grubb (1989b), Nordhaus (1991a) and Lashof and Ahuja (1990). The most complete account is provided in the text by Houghton *et al.* (1990). Emissions forecasts and/or scenarios are covered in Reilly *et al.* (1987), IPCC (1992, 1994), IPCC(1, 2 and 3) (2001), IEA (1995), World Energy Council (1993) and in report DOE/EIA-0484 (95) from the Energy Information Administration (1995). Further information on impacts and damages is given in Schneider (1989), Cline (1989, 1991), Nordhaus (1990a, b), EPA (1988, 1989), IPCC (1995a), Hansen *et al.* (1988), IPCC(2) (2001), and Mendelsohn (2001). Common (1989), Hansen (1990) and Nordhaus (1991a) discuss the uncertainties involved in damage estimation.

Early studies concerning the costs of CO$_2$ (and other GHG) abatement can be found in Department of Energy (1989) for the UK, Manne and Richels (1989), IPCC (1995b), Nordhaus (1990a, b, 1991a, b), Barker (1990), Jorgensen and Wilcoxen (1990a, b, c), Anderson and Bird (1990a, b), Cline (1991), Edmonds and Barns (1990a, b), Edmonds and Reilly (1985) and Mintzer (1987). Early CGE-based simulations can be found in Whalley and Wigle (1989, 1990, 1991) and Burniaux *et al.* (1991a, b, 1992). More recent studies of GHG abatement costs are to be found in White *et al.* (2001) and Hall and Howarth (2001). Green (2000) considers scale-related problems in estimating the costs of CO_2 mitigation policies. Good examples of attempts to use economic analysis to develop policy options and/or GHG policy targets are Nordhaus (2001) and Goulder and Mathai (2000), which examines optimal abatement in the presence of induced technological change.

Policy instruments and global warming are discussed in Opschoor and Vos (1989) and Pearce (1991b). For appropriate responses under uncertainty, see Barbier and Pearce (1990) and Hansen (1990). More recent analyses can be found in Chichilnisky and Heal (2000), Weyant (2000), with web site at www.pewclimate.org/projects/econ*w*introduction.cfm, Hohmeyer and Rennings (1999), Fankhauser *et al.* (1999) and Petsonk *et al.* (1999), with web site at www.pewclimate.org/projects/pol*w*market.html. Tietenberg (1984, 1990) discusses tradable emissions

permits; Grubb (1989a) argues that internationally tradable permits represent the best approach for international action towards the greenhouse effect. Edmonds *et al.* (1999) examine the effects of international emissions trading on abatement costs (with web site at www.pewclimate.org/projects/econ*w*emissions.cfm). Adger *et al.* (1997) consider climate change mitigation and European land use policies. Barrett (1998) provides an interesting discussion of the 'political economy' of the Kyoto Protocol. Interesting information about the evolving markets for emissions trading may be obtained at the UK Emissions Trading Group web site at www.uketg.com. Optimal policy towards greenhouse effect given uncertainty and learning is analysed in Kolstad (1996).

Biodiversity

Montgomery *et al.* (1999) discuss the pricing of biodiversity.

Discussion questions

1. Discuss the proposition that marketable emissions permits are more appropriate than emissions taxes for controlling regional and global pollutants because of the much lower transfer costs associated with the former instrument.

2. Consider the following extracts from an article in the *Independent* newspaper (28 March 1995) by the economist Frances Cairncross:

   Work by William Cline, a scrupulous and scientifically literate American economist, suggests that the benefits of taking action do not overtake the costs until about 2150. And Mr Cline sees global warming largely in terms of costs. Yet it is inconceivable that a change of such complexity will not bring gains ... as well as losses.

   Given the difficulties of doing something about climate change, should we try? Some measures are certainly worth taking because they make sense in their own right. ... Removing such [energy] subsidies would make the economy work more efficiently and benefit the environment, too.

   Indeed, wise governments should go further, and deliberately shift the tax burden away from earning and saving ... towards energy consumption.

   Beyond that, governments should do little. The most rational course is to adapt to climate change, when it happens. ... Adaptation is especially appropriate for poor countries once they have taken all the low-cost and no-cost measures they can find. Given the scarcity of capital, it makes good sense for them to delay investing in expensive ways to curb carbon dioxide output. Future economic growth is likely to make them rich enough to offset those effects of climate change that cannot be prevented.

   Provide a critical assessment of these arguments.

3. Compare and contrast the cost-effectiveness of
   (a) a sulphur dioxide emission tax;
   (b) a sulphur dioxide emission tax levied at the same rate as in (a), together with an arrangement by which emissions tax revenues are used to subsidise capital

equipment designed to 'scrub' sulphur from industrial and power-generation emissions.

4. The text mentioned that forests, agricultural lands and other terrestrial ecosystems offer significant carbon-reduction potential. Choose one country, and consider the ways in which this potential might be realised. What are the limits to the extent to which these methods could be used?

Problems

1. The world consists of two countries, X which is poor and Y which is rich. The total benefits (B) and total costs (C) of emissions abatement (A) are given by the functions

$$B_X = 8(A_X + A_Y), \quad B_Y = 5(A_X + A_Y),$$
$$C_X = 10 + 2A_X + 0.5A_X^2 \quad \text{and}$$
$$C_Y = 10 + 2A_Y + 0.5A_Y^2$$

where the subscripts are used in the same way as in Box 10.2.

(a) Obtain the non-cooperative equilibrium levels of abatement for X and Y.
(b) Obtain the cooperative equilibrium levels of abatement for X and Y.
(c) Calculate the utility levels enjoyed by X and by Y in the non-cooperative and cooperative solutions. Does the cooperative solution deliver Pareto improvements for each country, or would one have to give a side-payment to the other to obtain Pareto improvements for each with cooperation?
(d) Obtain the privately optimising level of abatement for X, given that Y decides to emit at the level of emissions that Y would emit in the cooperative equilibrium.

(You should find that the answer to (d) above is that X does the same amount of abatement that she would have done in the non-cooperative case. What property or properties of the cost and benefit function used in this example cause this particular result?)

(e) Suppose that Y acts as a 'swing abater', doing whatever (non-negative) amount of abatement is required to make the combined world abatement equal to the combined total under a full cooperative solution. How much abatement is undertaken in the two countries?

2. Refer to Figure 10.10. Show how the relative slopes of the MB and MC functions, and the number of countries, N, determine

(a) the magnitude of the efficiency gain from full cooperation, and
(b) the amount by which the cooperative level of abatement exceeds the non-cooperative (Nash) abatement level.

What conclusions can be drawn from your results?

Appendix 10.1 Some algebra of international treaties

Let signatories be indexed by s and non-signatories by n.

Non-signatories

Non-signatories choose z_n to solve

$$\frac{dB(Z)}{dZ}\frac{dZ}{dz_n} = \frac{dC(z_n)}{dz_n}$$

Noting that $dZ/dz_n = 1$, and that – given our assumption of symmetry – all countries' efficient abatement will be identical, the solution can be written as

$$\frac{dB(Z)}{dZ} = \frac{dC(z_n)}{dz} \tag{10.4}$$

where $Z = Z_n + Z_s$, $Z_n = (N - k)z_n$ and $Z_s = kz_s$.

Signatories

Choose abatement levels that maximise aggregate payoffs of all signatories:

$$\text{Max } \Pi_s = kB(Z) - \sum_{j=1}^{k} C(z_j)$$

The solution requires

$$k\frac{dB(Z)}{dZ}\left[\frac{\partial Z}{\partial Z_s} \cdot \frac{\partial Z_s}{\partial Z_j} + \frac{\partial Z}{\partial Z_n} \cdot \frac{\partial Z_n}{\partial Z_s} \cdot \frac{\partial Z_s}{\partial Z_j}\right] = \frac{dC(z_j)}{dz_j}$$

for all $j = 1, \ldots, k$ (10.5)

$$k\frac{dB(Z)}{dZ}\left[1 \cdot \frac{\partial Z_s}{\partial Z_j} + 1 \cdot \frac{\partial Z_n}{\partial Z_s} \cdot \frac{\partial Z_s}{\partial Z_j}\right] = \frac{dC(z_j)}{dz_j}$$

for all $j = 1, \ldots, k$

What determines $\partial Z_n/\partial Z_s$? It is chosen so that signatories would not wish to revise their choices after the choices of non-signatories. Those non-signatory choices are determined by 10.4 above.

Totally differentiating 10.4 and noting that $dZ = dZ_s + dZ_n$ and $dz_n = dZ_n/(N-k)$ we obtain

$$\frac{\partial Z_n}{\partial Z_s} = \frac{\dfrac{d^2 B(Z)}{dZ^2} \cdot (N-k)}{\dfrac{d^2 C(z)}{dz^2} - \dfrac{d^2 B(Z)}{dZ^2} \cdot (N-k)}$$ (10.6)

Then substitute equation (10.6) into (10.5), and add (10.4). This gives two equations which we shall not reproduce here, but will just label as equations (10.7) and (10.8). A self-enforcing agreement also requires that

- no signatory can gain by unilaterally withdrawing from the agreement;
- no non-signatory can gain by unilaterally acceding to the agreement;

which together imply that

$$\Pi_s(k^*) \geq \Pi_n(k^* - 1) \text{ and } \Pi_n(k^*) \geq \Pi_s(k^* + 1)$$ (10.9)

Equations 10.7, 10.8 and 10.9 give us three equations in 3 unknowns from which we can solve for z_n^*, z_s^* and k^*.

PART III

Project appraisal

CHAPTER 11

Cost–benefit analysis

Almost all economists are intellectually committed to the idea that the things people want can be valued in dollars and cents. If this is true, and things such as clean air, stable sea levels, tropical forests and species diversity can be valued that way, then environmental issues submit – or so it is argued – quite readily to the disciplines of economic analysis . . . most environmentalists not only disagree with this idea, they find it morally deplorable.

The Economist, 31 January 2002

Learning objectives

In this chapter you will
- learn about the conditions necessary for intertemporal efficiency
- revisit the analysis of optimal growth introduced in Chapter 3
- find out how to do project appraisal
- learn about cost–benefit analysis and its application to the environment
- be introduced to some alternatives to cost–benefit analysis

Introduction

By 'cost–benefit analysis' we mean the social appraisal of investment projects. Here, 'social' signifies that the appraisal is being conducted according to criteria derived from welfare economics, rather than according to commercial criteria. Cost–benefit analysis, that is, attempts to appraise investment projects in ways that correct for market failure. If there were no market failure, social and commercial criteria would coincide. An 'investment project' is something that involves a current commitment with

consequences stretching over future time. It need not, that is, be an 'investment' in the sense of the accumulation of capital, though, of course, it may be and frequently is. As generally used, the term 'cost–benefit analysis' would also embrace, for example, the appraisal of the adoption now of a government policy intended to have future effects.

Cost–benefit analysis relates to the environment in two main ways. First, many projects intended to yield benefits in the form of the provision of goods and services have environmental impacts – consider damming a river in a wilderness area to generate electricity. To the extent that such impacts are externalities (see Chapter 5) there is market failure and they do not show up in private, commercial, appraisals. The costs of such projects are understated in ordinary financial appraisals. Second, there are projects the main purpose of which is to have beneficial environmental impacts – consider the construction of a sewage treatment plant. Here also the impacts typically involve external effects, and so would not appear in an ordinary financial appraisal. Projects where environmental market failure relates to incidental damage arise in both the private and public sectors – in the dam case there is saleable output and it could be privately or publicly financed. Projects intended to provide environmental benefits typically come up as public-sector projects – they provide outputs which are (again see Chapter 5) public goods. There are, of course, projects which have both desirable and undesirable impacts on the environment – waste incinerators are intended to reduce the need for landfill disposal but they generate atmospheric emissions.

In all cases, the basic strategy of cost–benefit analysis is the same. It is to attach monetary values to the environmental impacts, desired and undesired, so that they are considered along with, and in the same way as, the ordinary inputs (labour, capital, raw materials) to and outputs (goods and/or services) from the project. In this chapter we are primarily concerned with the rationale for, and the methods of, cost–benefit analysis in relation to the environment. The methods which economists have developed to value the environment so that it can be accounted for in cost–benefit analysis are dealt with principally in the next chapter, Chapter 12, but also come up in Chapter 13.

This chapter is organised as follows. As noted above, cost–benefit analysis is based on welfare economics. Also as noted above, it is essentially about dealing with situations where the consequences of a decision are spread out over time. Our previous treatment of welfare economics, in Chapter 5, ignored the temporal dimension. Hence, the first thing to be done here is to review the basics of intertemporal welfare economics. The second section of the chapter builds on that review to discuss the economics of project appraisal, starting with the private and moving from there to social appraisal, i.e. cost–benefit analysis. The third section then looks specifically at cost–benefit analysis and the environment, and considers some of the objections that have been raised about the basic idea of dealing with environmental impacts in the same way as 'ordinary' commodities. It also looks briefly at some alternative models for social decision-making where environmental impacts are important.

Finally here a word about terminology. What we call 'cost–benefit analysis' some writers refer to as 'benefit–cost analysis' – CBA, as we shall henceforward refer to it, is the same thing as BCA. Cost-effectiveness analysis is not the same thing as CBA, and we will discuss it briefly toward the end of this chapter.

11.1 Intertemporal welfare economics

Chapter 5 introduced the basic ideas in welfare economics in a timeless context. Those basic ideas, such as efficiency and optimality, carry over into the analysis of situations where time is an essential feature of the problem. In Chapter 5, we saw that efficiency and optimality at a point in time require equality conditions as between various rates of substitution and transformation. Once the passage of time is introduced into the picture, the number and range of such conditions increases, but the intuition as to the need for them remains the same. In going from intratemporal, or static, to intertemporal, or dynamic, welfare economics we introduce some new constructions and some new terminology, but no fundamentally new ideas.

The primary motivation for this discussion here of intertemporal welfare economics is to provide the foundations for an appreciation of CBA. It should be noted, however, that intertemporal welfare economics is also the background to much of the analysis of natural resource exploitation economics to be considered in Part IV of this book. We also drew upon some of the material to be presented here in our discussion of some aspects of the ethical basis for the economic approach to environmental problems in Chapter 3. Appendices 11.1 and 11.2 work through the material to be discussed in this section using the Lagrangian multipliers method in the same way as was done in the appendices to Chapter 5. The reader might find it helpful at this point to quickly revisit Chapter 5 on efficiency and optimality, and the way in which, given ideal circumstances, a system of markets could produce an efficient allocation.

11.1.1 Intertemporal efficiency conditions

In Chapter 5 we considered a model economy in which two individuals each consumed two commodities, with each commodity being produced by two firms using two scarce inputs. Appendices 11.1 and 11.2 consider that model generalised so that it deals with two periods of time. Also considered there are some specialisations of that model, which bring out the essentials of intertemporal allocation issues while minimising the number of variables and notation to keep track of. In the text here we will just look at a special model so as to deal with the essentials in the simplest possible way. Readers are, however, advised to work through the more general treatment in the appendices so as to appreciate the ways in which what follows is special.

We consider two individuals and two time periods, which can be thought of as 'now' and 'the future' and are identified as periods 0 and 1. Each individual has a utility function, the arguments of which are the levels of consumption in each period:

$$U^A = U^A(C_0^A, C_1^A)$$
$$U^B = U^B(C_0^B, C_1^B) \tag{11.1}$$

As in Chapter 5, an allocation is efficient if it is impossible to make one individual better off without thereby making the other individual worse off. Here, the allocation question is about how total consumption is divided between the two individuals in each period, and about the total consumption levels in each period, which are connected via capital accumulation. In order to focus on the essentially intertemporal dimensions of the problem, we are assuming that there is a single 'commodity' produced using inputs of labour and capital. The output of this commodity in a given period can either be consumed or added to the stock of capital to be used in production in the future. We shall assume that the commodity is produced by a large number of firms.

Given this, efficiency requires the satisfaction of three conditions:

1. equality of individuals' consumption discount rates;
2. equality of rates of return to investment across firms;
3. equality of the common consumption discount rate with the common rate of return.

We will now work through the intuition of each of these conditions. Formal derivations of the conditions are provided in Appendix 11.1.

11.1.1.1 Discount rate equality

This condition concerns preferences over consumption at different points in time. Figure 11.1 shows intertemporal consumption indifference curves for A and B. The curve shown in panel a, for example, shows those combinations of C_0^A and C_1^A that produce a constant level of utility for A. The curve in panel b does the same thing for individual B. In Chapter 5 we worked with marginal rates of utility substitution which are the slopes of indifference curves, multiplied by -1 to make them positive numbers. We can do that here, defining $MRUS_{C0,C1}^A$ in terms of the slope of a panel a indifference curve and $MRUS_{C0,C1}^B$ in terms of the slope of a panel b indifference curve. Given that, we can say that for an allocation to be intertemporally efficient it is necessary that

$$MRUS_{C0,C1}^A = MRUS_{C0,C1}^B$$

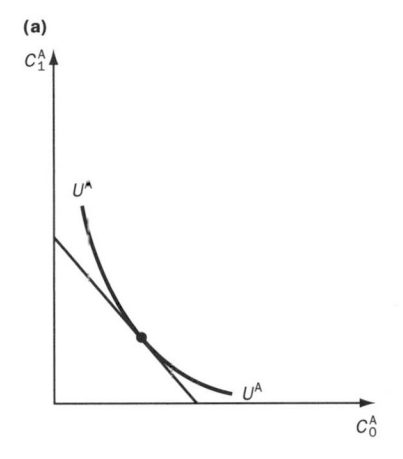
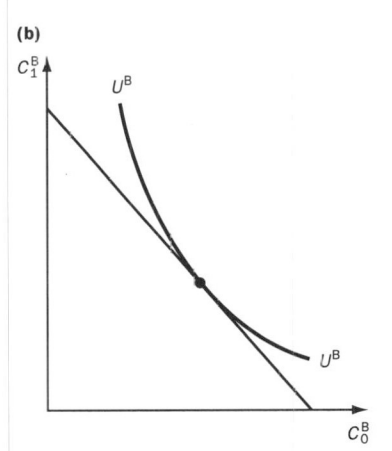

Figure 11.1 Equality of consumption discount rates

where the intuition is the same as in the static case – if the marginal rates of utility substitution differ, then there exists a rearrangement that would make one individual better off without making the other worse off. In fact, Figure 5.1 applies here if we just treat X there as period 0 consumption and Y there as period 1 consumption.

Following the practice in the literature, we state this condition using the terminology of consumption discount rates. For example, A's consumption discount rate is defined as

$$r^A_{C0,C1} \equiv \text{MRUS}^A_{C0,C1} - 1$$

i.e. the consumption indifference curve slope (times −1) minus 1. In that terminology, and dropping the subscripts, the intertemporal consumption efficiency condition is:

$$r^A = r^B = r \qquad (11.2)$$

Note that although consumption discount rates are often written like this, they are not constants – as Figure 11.1 makes clear, for a given utility function, the consumption discount rate will vary with the levels of consumption in each period.

11.1.1.2 Rate of return equality

This condition concerns the opportunities for shifting consumption over time. Consider the production of the consumption commodity in periods 0 and 1 by one firm. At the start of period 0 it has a given amount of capital, and we assume that it efficiently uses it together with other inputs to produce some level of output, denoted Q_0. That output can be used for consumption in period 0 or saved and invested so as to increase the size of the capital stock at the start of period 1. In Figure 11.2 $\bar{C}_0$ is period 0 consumption output from this firm when it does no investment. In that case, the capital stock at the start of period 1 is the same as at the start of period 0, and $\bar{C}_1$ is the maximum amount of consumption output possible by this firm in period 1. Suppose that all of period 0 output were invested. In that case the larger capital stock at the start of period 1 would mean that the maximum amount of consumption output possible by this firm in period 1 was C_1^{max}. The solid line $C_1^{max}A$ shows the possible combinations of consumption output in each period available as the level of

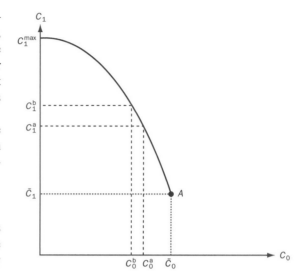

Figure 11.2 Shifting consumption over time

investment varies. It is the consumption transformation frontier.

Figure 11.2 shows two intermediate – between zero and all output – levels of investment, corresponding to C_0^a and C_0^b. The levels of investment are, respectively, given by the distances $C_0^a\bar{C}_0$ and $C_0^b\bar{C}_0$. Corresponding to these investment levels are the period 1 consumption output levels C_1^a and C_1^b. The sacrifice of an amount of consumption $C_0^bC_0^a$ in period 0 makes available an amount of consumption $C_1^aC_1^b$ in period 1. The rate of return to, or on, investment is a proportional measure of the period 1 consumption payoff to a marginal increase in period 0 investment. It is defined as

$$\delta \equiv \frac{\Delta C_1 - \Delta I_0}{\Delta I_0}$$

where ΔC_1 is the small period 1 increase in consumption – $C_1^aC_1^b$ for example – resulting from the small period 0 increase ΔI_0 in investment which corresponds to $C_0^bC_0^a$. The increase in investment ΔI_0 entails a change in period 0 consumption of equal size and opposite sign, i.e. a decrease in C_0. With ΔI equal to $-\Delta C_0$, the definition of the rate of return can be written as

$$\delta = \frac{\Delta C_1 - (-\Delta C_0)}{-\Delta C_0} = \frac{\Delta C_1 + \Delta C_0}{-\Delta C_0} = -\frac{\Delta C_1}{\Delta C_0} - 1$$

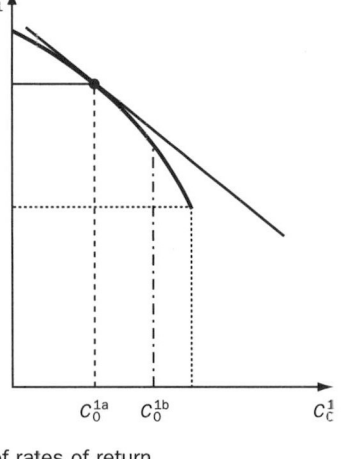
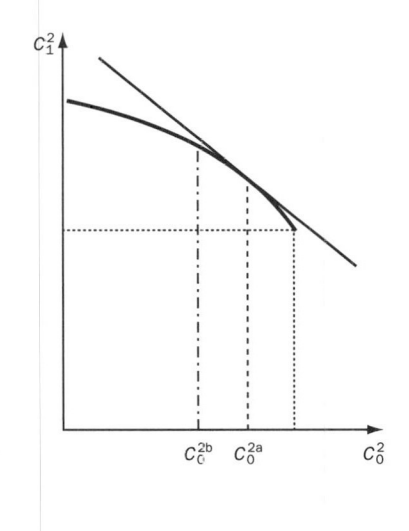

Figure 11.3 Equality of rates of return

which is the negative of the slope of the consumption transformation frontier minus 1. This can be written

$$1 + \delta = -s$$

where s is the slope of $C_1^{max}A$. The curvature of the line $C_1^{max}A$ in Figure 11.2 reflects the standard assumption that the rate of return declines as the level of investment increases.

Now, there are many firms producing the consumption commodity. Figure 11.3 refers to just two of them, identified arbitrarily as 1 and 2 with superscripts, and shows why the second condition for intertemporal efficiency is that rates of return to investment must be equal, as they are for C_0^{1a} and C_0^{2a}. Suppose that they were not, with each firm investing as indicated by C_0^{1b} and C_0^{2b}. In such a situation, period 1 consumption could be increased without any loss of period 0 consumption by having firm 1, where the rate of return is higher, do a little more investment, and firm 2, where the rate of return is lower, do an equal amount less. Clearly, so long as the two rates of return differ, there will be scope for this kind of costless increase in C_1. Equally clearly, if such a possibility exists, the allocation cannot be efficient as, say, A's period 1 consumption could be increased without any reduction in her period 0 consumption or in B's consumption in either period. Hence, generalising to $i = 1, \ldots, N$ firms, we have

$$\delta_i = \delta, \, i = 1, \ldots, N \tag{11.3}$$

as the second intertemporal efficiency condition.

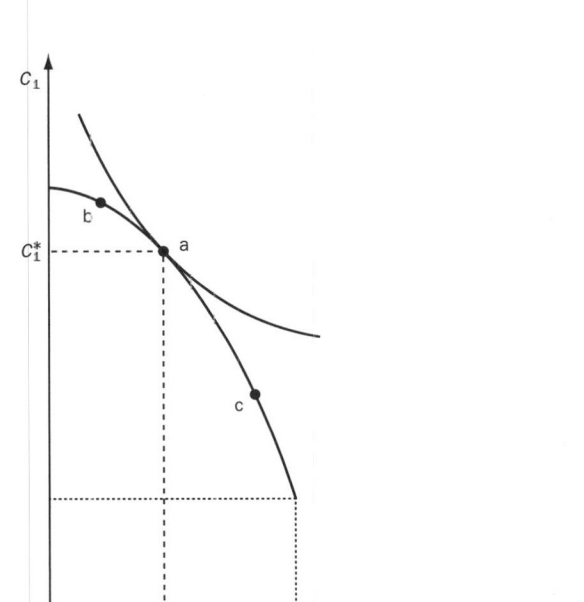

Figure 11.4 Equality of rate of return and discount rate

11.1.1.3 Equality of discount rate with rate of return

If we take it that the conditions which are equations 11.2 and 11.3 are satisfied, we can discuss the third condition in terms of one representative individual and one representative line of production. Figure 11.4 shows the situation for these representatives. Clearly, the point a corresponds to intertemporal efficiency, whereas points b and c do not. From either b or c it is possible to reallocate consumption as between periods 0 and 1 so as to move onto a higher consumption indifference curve. It is impossible to do this only where, as at a, there is a point of tangency between a consumption indifference curve and the consumption transformation frontier.

At a the slopes of the consumption indifference curve and the consumption transformation frontier are equal. We have already noted that r is the slope of the former minus 1. The slope of the latter is $\Delta C_1/\Delta C_0$, so that from the definition of δ it is equal to that slope minus 1. It follows that slope equality can also be expressed as the equality of the rate of return and the discount rate:

$$\delta = r \tag{11.4}$$

11.1.2 Intertemporal optimality

In our discussion of the static, intratemporal, allocation problem in Chapter 5 we noted that efficiency requirements do not fix a unique allocation. To do that we need a social welfare function with individuals' utility levels as arguments. The situation is exactly the same when we look at intertemporal allocations. The conditions for static efficiency plus the conditions stated above as equations 11.2, 11.3 and 11.4 do not fix a unique allocation. For any given data for the economic problem – resource endowments, production functions, preferences and the like – there are many intertemporally efficient allocations. Choosing among the set of intertemporally efficient allocations requires a social welfare function of some kind.

In general terms there is nothing more to be said here beyond what was said in the discussion of the static case in Chapter 5. We shall come back to the relationship between intertemporal efficiency and optimality shortly when we make some observations on intertemporal modelling. Before that we discuss the role of markets in the realisation of intertemporal efficiency. This way of proceeding makes sense given that there is another important carry-over from the static to the dynamic analysis – while in both cases it can be claimed that market forces alone might, given ideal circumstances, realise efficiency in allocation, in neither case can it be claimed, under any circumstances, that market forces alone will necessarily bring about welfare-maximising outcomes.

11.1.3 Markets and intertemporal efficiency

Economists have considered two sorts of market institution by means of which the conditions required for intertemporal efficiency might be realised, and we will briefly look at both here. In doing that we will take it that in regard to intratemporal allocation the ideal circumstances discussed in Chapter 5 are operative so that the static efficiency conditions are satisfied. This assumption is not made as an approximation to reality – we have already seen that static market failure is quite pervasive. It is made in order to simplify the analysis, to enable us, as we did above, to focus on those things that are the essential features of the intertemporal allocation problem.

11.1.3.1 Futures markets

One way of looking at the problem of allocative efficiency where time is involved, considered in Appendix 11.1, is simply to stretch the static problem over successive periods of time. Thus, for example, we could take the economy considered in Chapter 5 – with two individuals, two commodities, and two firms producing each commodity, each using two inputs – and look at it for two periods of time. This approach could be, and in the literature has been, extended to many individuals, many commodities, many firms, many inputs, and many time periods. In following it, one thinks of the same physical thing at different times as different things. Thus, for example, the commodity X at time t is defined as a different commodity from X at time $t + 1$. This approach leads to more general versions of the intertemporal conditions stated in the previous section.

In terms of markets, the parallel analytical device is to imagine that date-differentiated things have date-differentiated markets. Thus, for example, there is market for commodity X at time t and a separate market for commodity X at time $t + 1$. It is assumed that at the beginning of time binding contracts are made for all future exchanges – the markets in which such contracts are made are 'futures markets'. Now, by this device, time has essentially been removed from the analysis. Instead of thinking about N

commodities and M periods of time, one is thinking about $M \times N$ different commodities. Trade in all of these commodities takes place at one point in time. Clearly, the effect of this device is, formally, to make the intertemporal allocation problem just like the static problem, and everything said about the latter applies to the former. This includes what can be said about markets. If all of the ideal circumstances set out in Chapter 5 apply to all futures markets, then it can be formally shown that the conditions for intertemporal efficiency will be satisfied.

This is an interesting analytical construct. It will be immediately apparent that the connection between a complete set of futures markets characterised by the ideal circumstances and 'the real world' is remote in the extreme. Recall, for example, that in the static case we saw in Chapter 5 that for a pure market system to produce an efficient allocation it was necessary that all agents had complete information. In the context of the futures market construct, this involves agents now having complete information about circumstances operative in the distant future.

While futures markets do exist for some commodities – mainly standardised raw material inputs to production and financial instruments – there is very far from the complete set of them that would be required for there to be even a minimal case for seriously considering them as a means for the attainment of intertemporal efficiency. In actual market systems the principal way in which allocation over time is decided is via markets for loanable funds, to which we now turn.

11.1.3.2 Loanable funds market

We will assume, in order to bring out the essentials as simply as possible, that there is just one market for loanable funds – the bond market. A bond is a financial instrument by means of which borrowing and lending are effected. In our two-period context we will assume that trade in bonds takes place at the beginning of period 0. All bond certificates say that on day 1 of period 1 the owner will be paid an amount of money x by the bond issuer. There are many sellers and buyers of such bonds. If the market price of such bonds is established as P_B, which will be less than x, then the interest rate is:

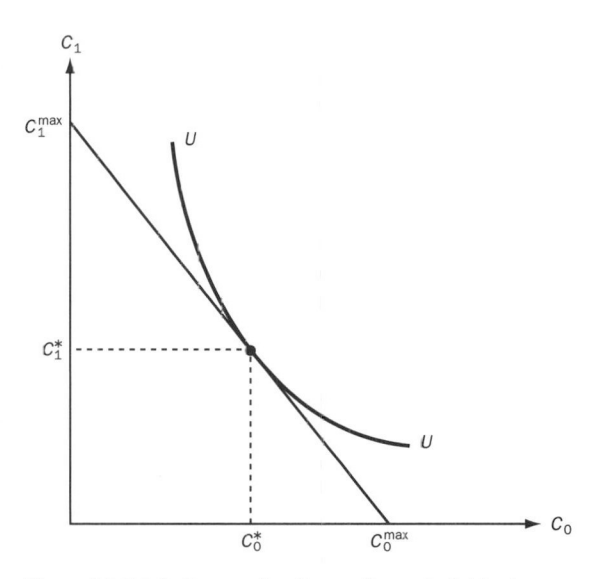

Figure 11.5 Intertemporal optimum for an individual

$$i = \frac{x - P_B}{P_B}$$

A seller of a bond is borrowing to finance period 0 consumption: repayment is made on the first day of period 1, and will reduce period 1 consumption below what it would otherwise be. A buyer is lending during period 0, and as a result will be able to consume more in period 1 by virtue of the interest earned.

Now consider an individual at the start of period 0, with given receipts M_0 and M_1 at the beginning of each period, and with preferences over consumption in each period given by $U = U(C_0, C_1)$. The individual maximises utility subject to the budget constraint given by M_0 and M_1 and the market rate of interest, at which she can borrow/lend by trading in the market for bonds. Note that the individual takes the market rate of interest as given – in this context i is a constant. The individual's maximisation is illustrated in Figure 11.5. UU is a consumption indifference curve, with slope $-(1 + r)$, where r is the consumption discount rate. The budget constraint is $C_1^{max} C_0^{max}$ which has the slope $-(1 + i)$, because by means of bond market transactions $(1 + i)$ is the rate at which the individual can shift consumption between the two periods. The individual's optimum consumption levels are C_0^* and C_1^* given by the tangency of the budget constraint to the consumption

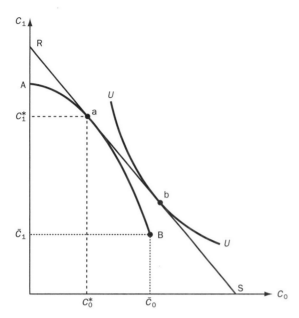

Figure 11.6 Present value maximisation

indifference curve. It follows that the optimum is characterised by the equality of r and i. But this will be true for all individuals, so with a single bond market clearing interest rate of i, consumption discount rates, r, will be equalised across individuals, thus satisfying the first condition for an intertemporally efficient allocation, equation 11.2. Individuals for whom C_0^* is less than M_0 will be lenders, and hence buyers in the bond market; individuals for whom C_0^* is greater than M_0 will be borrowers, and hence sellers in the bond market.

Now consider the period 0 investment decisions made by firms. The owners of firms can shift their consumption over time in two ways. First, by investing in their firm, and second by borrowing/lending via the bond market. The terms on which they can do the latter have just been discussed. What they want to do is to invest in their firm up to the point that puts them in the best position in relation to the opportunities offered by the bond market. In Figure 11.6 the curve AB shows the combinations of C_0 and C_1 available to the firm's owners as they vary their period 0 investment in the firm from zero, at B, to the maximum possible, at A with zero period 0 consumption. The straight line RS has the slope $-(1+i)$

and it gives the terms on which consumption can be shifted between periods via bond market transactions. The optimum level of investment in the firm in period 0 is shown as $C_0^*\bar{C}_0$, such that AB is tangential to RS. The line AB has the slope $-(1+\delta)$, where δ is the rate of return on investment for this firm. So, AB tangential to RS means that i is equal to δ. The firm invests up to the level where the rate of return is equal to the rate of interest.

Why is this the optimum? First note that if the owners invest so as to get to a, they can then borrow/lend via the bond market so as to end up with the consumption levels given by point b where RS is tangential to the consumption indifference curve UU. Now consider an investment decision that leads to a point to the right or the left of a along AB. Such a point will lie on a line parallel to but inside, beneath, RS. Moving along such a line so as to maximise utility, it will not be possible to get to as high a level of utility as that corresponding to UU.

The point here is that given the existence of the bond market, utility maximisation for the owners of firms involves two distinct steps. First, choose the level of investment in the firm so as to maximise its present value. Second, then use the bond market to borrow and lend so as to maximise utility. The present value of the firm is the maximum that its owners could borrow now and repay, with interest, from future receipts. In this two-period case, the firm's present value is $M_0 + [1/(1+i)]M_1$, where M_0 and M_1 are receipts in periods 0 and 1, and $[1/(1+i)]M_1$ is the 'discounted value' of M_1. Discounted values in a multiperiod context will be discussed below.

Now, this two-stage maximisation process applies to the owners of all firms. In each firm investment is undertaken up to the level where the rate of return is equal to the rate of interest. It follows that rates of return are equalised across firms, as is required by the second condition for efficiency in intertemporal allocation, equation 11.3.

We have seen that with a market for loanable funds, all consumption discount rates will be equal to the market rate of interest, and that all rates of return will equal the market rate of interest. It follows that the common consumption discount rate is equal to the common rate of return, as is required by the third condition, equation 11.4, for an intertemporally efficient allocation.

So, the conditions for intertemporal efficiency could be satisfied by an ideal system of markets that includes a market for loanable funds. In order for the conditions to be satisfied, that market – the bond market as the story was told here – is itself required to satisfy certain conditions. It must, for example, be a competitive market in the sense that all participants act as price-takers. As we emphasised in Chapter 5, the purpose of this kind of analysis is not to propagate the idea that actual market systems do bring about efficient outcomes. It is to define the conditions under which market systems would do that, and hence to support policy analysis.

11.1.4 Intertemporal modelling

The main purpose of this section is to relate the foregoing analysis to some standard models and issues. In this section we will be revisiting some of the topics and models, and using some of the notation, introduced in Section 3.5 – you may find it helpful to read that material again before proceeding here.

11.1.4.1 Optimal growth models

In much of the literature, including this book, the model used for looking at intertemporal allocation problems frequently involves just one individual at each point in time. For the two-period case, instead of the two utility functions $U^A = U^A(C_0^A, C_1^A)$ and $U^B = U^B(C_0^B, C_1^B)$, such models have the single function $W = W\{U(C_0), U(C_1)\}$. In such models, as well as aggregating over commodities and looking just at 'consumption', we are also aggregating over individuals and looking at a single 'representative' individual. The preference system represented by $W\{.\}$ has two components. $U(C_0)$ and $U(C_1)$ are contemporaneous utility functions which map consumption at a point in time into utility at a point in time.[1] It is assumed that $U(.)$ is invariant over time, and that it exhibits decreasing marginal utility. The function $W\{.\}$ maps a sequence of contemporaneous utility levels into a single measure for the whole sequence. In the literature, $W\{.\}$ is frequently given the particular form

$$W = U(C_0) + \left(\frac{1}{1+\rho}\right)U(C)$$

where ρ is the utility discount rate, a parameter, introduced in Chapter 3.

The function $W\{.\}$ can be, and is in the literature, interpreted in two ways. It can be treated as a particular functional form for the intertemporal utility function of a representative individual alive in both periods, one which is additively separable in discounted contemporaneous utilities. Alternatively, it can be treated as an intertemporal social welfare function where there are distinct, non-overlapping, generations alive in each period, each generation being represented by a single individual. It is this second interpretation that fits best with the notation used here – W for welfare and U for the contemporaneous utility of the representative of each generation over which welfare is defined. We looked at this kind of intertemporal social welfare function in our consideration of utilitarian ethics and discounting in Chapter 3.

The way in which the function $W\{.\}$ is widely used in the literature is in 'optimal growth' models. In such models it is assumed that the conditions for efficiency in allocation are satisfied. Clearly, with just one commodity and one individual explicitly modelled there is little to be said about either intratemporal or intertemporal efficiency. Note that where there are many individuals and commodities, efficiency requires equality across individuals' commodity consumption discount rates and across investment rates of return in the production of commodities. If it is assumed that these conditions are satisfied, working with a single commodity and a representative individual follows naturally. It is, then, the matter of the intertemporal distribution of utility, via saving and investment, that is investigated in such models. For our two-period case this investigation uses the problem of maximising

$$W = U(C_0) + \left(\frac{1}{1+\rho}\right)U(C_1) \tag{11.5a}$$

subject to the constraints

$$Q_0(K_0) - (K_1 - K_0) = C_0 \qquad (11.5b)$$

$$Q_1(K_1) - (K_2 - K_1) = C_1 \qquad (11.5c)$$

where Q_t is the output of the commodity during period t, and K_t is the capital stock at the beginning of period t. Assuming that capital is the only input to production further serves to simplify and sharpen the focus on the central issue, without the loss of anything essential. Note that the efficiency problem here is trivial. From 11.5b and 11.5c it is clear that no further conditions are required to ensure that consumption, and hence utility, in one period can only be increased at the cost of a reduction in consumption, and hence utility, in the other period.

Appendix 11.1 works through such an exercise and shows that

$$\frac{U_{C1}}{U_{C0}} = \frac{1 + \rho}{1 + \delta} \qquad (11.6)$$

is a necessary condition for intertemporal welfare maximisation. For ρ less than δ, U_{C1} is less than U_{C0}, which for decreasing marginal utility means that C_1 is larger than C_0 – consumption is increasing over time. This makes sense, given that ρ measures the rate at which future utility is discounted, while δ measures the pay-off to deferring consumption and utility by investing. For ρ equal to δ equation 11.6 says that consumption would be the same in both periods.

Without the restriction to two periods, this kind of intertemporal welfare function becomes:

$$W = U(C_0) + \left(\frac{1}{1 + \rho}\right) U(C_1) + \left(\frac{1}{1 + \rho}\right)^2 U(C_2)$$

$$+ \ldots + \left(\frac{1}{1 + \rho}\right)^T U(C_T) = \sum_{t=0}^{T} \left(\frac{1}{1 + \rho}\right)^t U(C_t)$$

Most analysis of intertemporal distribution issues uses continuous time,

$$W = \int_{t=0}^{t=T} U(C_t) e^{-\rho t} dt$$

and frequently the time horizon is indefinitely far into the future so that

$$W = \int_{t=0}^{t=\infty} U(C_t) e^{-\rho t} dt \qquad (11.7a)$$

The corresponding formulation of the constraint reflecting the possibilities for shifting consumption over time, equations 11.5b and 11.5c for the two-period model above, is

$$\dot{K} = Q(K_t) - C_t \qquad (11.7b)$$

where $\dot{K}$ is the time derivative of K, i.e. the rate of investment. The maximisation of equation 11.7a subject to equation 11.7b is the basic standard optimal growth model. The mathematics of the solution to this maximisation problem are set out in Appendix 14.1. Corresponding to equation 11.6 above for the two-period case, for this continuous-time infinite-horizon version of the problem a necessary condition is:

$$\frac{\dot{U}_C}{U_C} = \rho - \delta \qquad (11.8)$$

The left-hand side here is the proportional rate of change of marginal (instantaneous) utility, and along the optimal consumption path this is equal to the difference between the utility discount rate and the rate of return to investment. The former is a parameter, while the rate of return varies and is generally assumed to fall as the size of the capital stock increases. Given the assumption of diminishing marginal utility, $\delta < \rho$ implies that the left-hand side of equation 11.8 is negative which implies that consumption is growing along the optimal path. For $\delta = \rho$, growth is zero. Given the standard assumptions about the instantaneous utility and production functions, optimal growth for an intertemporal welfare function which adds discounted utilities takes the general form shown in Figure 11.7, which was previously seen as panel a of Figure 3.6 in Chapter 3.

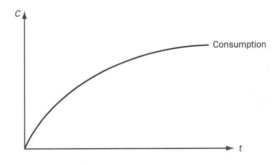

Figure 11.7 Optimal growth

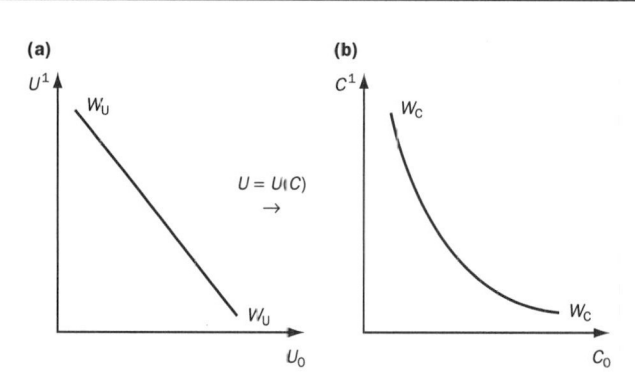

Figure 11.8 Indifference curves in utility and consumption space

In Part IV of this book we focus on models where natural resources are used, with capital and labour, in production. In the terminology introduced in Chapter 2, the natural resources that we shall be concerned with there are 'stock' resources, and are potentially exhaustible. In analysing the use of such resources, attention focuses mainly on the patterns of use over time. An example of the sort of problem that you will be looking at in Part IV, and have already looked briefly at in Chapters 3 and 4, is the maximisation of

$$W = \int_{t=0}^{t=\infty} U(C_t)e^{-\rho t}dt \tag{11.9a}$$

subject to the constraints

$$\dot{K} = Q(K_t, R_t) - C_t \tag{11.9b}$$

$$\dot{S} = -R_t \tag{11.9c}$$

The first of the constraints says, as before, that output, Q, can either be used for consumption, C, or investment, $\dot{K}$. It differs from equation 11.7b in that the production of output now involves two inputs, capital, K, and some natural resource, R. In equation 11.9c, S stands for stock, and this constraint says that the natural resource being used is non-renewable.

This problem will be considered in some detail in Chapter 14, and variants of it – such as for the case of a renewable resource – will take up most of Part IV. The point that we want to make here is that whereas in the maximisation problem defined by equations 11.7 intertemporal efficiency is trivially guaranteed, in the case of equations 11.9 it is an essentially important feature of the problem. Notwithstanding that just one commodity is produced in the model of equations 11.9, there are two forms that investment can take. As before, current consumption can be forgone and output instead added to the capital stock. Additionally, there is now the possibility of reducing the current rate of use of the resource so as to leave more of it for future use. In terms of the analysis of the preceding sections there is now a role for an intertemporal efficiency condition. Intertemporal efficiency requires the equalisation of the rates of return to capital accumulation and resource conservation.

11.1.4.2 Utility and consumption discount rates

Panel a of Figure 11.8 shows, as $W_U W_U$, a welfare indifference curve drawn in utility space for the intertemporal welfare function:

$$W = U(C_0) + \left(\frac{1}{1+\rho}\right)U(C_1)$$

Points along $W_U W_U$ are combinations of U in period 0 and U in period 1 that yield equal levels of W. $W_U W_U$ is a straight line with slope $-(1 + \rho)$. Given that in each period U depends solely on that period's consumption, we can map $W_U W_U$ into $W_C W_C$, shown in panel b of Figure 11.8, the corresponding welfare indifference curve in consumption space.

In regard to Figure 11.1, we defined, for each individual, the consumption discount rate as the slope of the indifference curve in consumption space, multiplied by -1, minus 1. It is shown in Appendix 11.1 that the slope of $W_C W_C$ in panel b of Figure 11.8 is

$$-\frac{U_{C0}}{[1/(1 + \rho)]U_{C1}}$$

so that

$$r = \frac{U_{C0}}{[1/(1 + \rho)]U_{C1}} - 1 = \frac{(1 + \rho)U_{C0}}{U_{C1}} - 1 \quad (11.10)$$

gives the relationship between the consumption rate of interest and utility discount rate for an intertemporal welfare function which is the sum of discounted contemporaneous utilities. Although derived here for the two-period case, this result holds generally. Also as shown in Appendix 11.1, working in continuous time, it can be established that

$$r = \rho + \eta g \quad (11.11)$$

where η is the elasticity of marginal utility for the instantaneous utility function, and g is the growth rate for consumption. Equation 11.11 was introduced and used in Chapter 3 in the discussion of discounting in relation to ethics.

From either 11.10 or 11.11, it can be seen that constant consumption implies that the consumption and utility discount rates would be equal. For consumption growing, the consumption discount rate is greater than the utility discount rate. In fact, unless η is zero, growing consumption would imply a positive consumption discount rate if the utility discount rate were zero. Discounting future consumption does not, that is, necessarily entail discounting future utility.

11.2 Project appraisal

In the preceding section of the chapter we set out some of the basic ideas of intertemporal welfare economics. In this section we are going to consider how those ideas are applied using CBA. While it is in the next section of the chapter that we will look specifically at CBA and the environment, Box 11.1 appears here so as to 'set the scene' for the material to be covered in this section – the analysis that it reports distinguishes between the commercial and the social appraisal of afforestation projects.

We begin this section by looking at project appraisal as it would be conducted by a private-sector agent according to commercial criteria. This provides a useful way into CBA in terms of the principles and practice involved.

Box 11.1 A CBA of temperate-zone forestry

Is there an economic case for government support for afforestation programmes in temperate zones such as the UK? What are the benefits and costs of such programmes? David Pearce argues that afforestation programmes are multiple-output activities. The outputs he identifies are listed below.

T Timber values
R Recreational amenities
D Biological diversity
L Landscape values
W Water-related effects: watershed protection, affecting soil erosion and water run-off, fixation of airborne pollutants, typically increasing pollutant concentrations locally but reducing them elsewhere
M Microclimate effects
G Carbon stores
S Economic security
I Community integration

Each of these outputs can be beneficial, relative to alternative uses of the land. However, in some cases the benefits may be negative. For example, if single-species spruce afforestation displaces the provision of wilderness areas, biological diversity is likely to diminish. On the other hand, the creation of urban forests in areas of industrial dereliction would, in most cases, increase diversity.

What are the costs of afforestation? These costs comprise land acquisition, planting, maintenance, thinning and felling. Denoting the present values for total benefits by B and total costs by C afforestation is economically justified if

$B - C > 0$

Pearce notes that only one of the joint products – the produced timber – is actually traded through market exchanges. All other products are beneficial (or sometimes adverse) external effects, not captured in market valuations. On the other

Box 11.1 *continued*

hand, the costs of afforestation are internalised in market transactions. The consequence of this is that afforestation programmes in temperate regions such as the UK are rarely commercially profitable. By way of example, Pearce quotes results from an earlier study. He introduces time into his analysis, discounts consumption-equivalent benefits and costs at a discount rate of 6%, and then estimates the net present value of various types of forestry plantations (on various types of land) under a variety of assumptions about the costs of land.

Pearce investigates eight types of forestry scheme. For each scheme, the commercial NPV is calculated under high and low (and sometimes zero) assumed costs of land. Of the 17 cases this generates, all but one result in negative NPVs. The sole exception is mixed fir/spruce and broadleaf plantations in lowlands, assuming the true value of land is zero (that is, the land has no alternative use)!

Having evaluated the commercial returns to afforestation, Pearce then investigates each of the non-marketed benefits, so as to investigate the social returns. He estimates the net benefits for each of the outputs R, D, L, W, G, S and I. For two of these (R and G) the benefits are quantified in money terms; for others (D, W, S and I) Pearce identifies and describes the benefits but does not attempt any monetary quantification. Unquantified benefits will have to be judgementally taken into account when project decisions are made.

Recreational benefits for various forms of afforestation are taken from Benson and Willis (1991). The gross values for recreational benefits in the UK range from £3 per hectare on low-amenity woodlands in the uplands to £424 per hectare on very high-amenity lowland woodlands (in 1989 prices). Pearce suggests these values are likely to grow in real terms by at least 1% per annum. Wildlife conservation and biodiversity benefits (W) and landscape amenity values (L) are two outputs that Pearce does not quantify and monetise. He argues that these benefits will vary widely depending upon woodland form and location, but that they are likely to be positive in the UK, where land for afforestation tends to be drawn from low-wildlife-value agricultural land. However, if afforestation takes the form of non-native conifer species, and is at the expense of previously semi-natural land use, these effects on both landscape amenities and biological diversity could be strongly negative. The picture is thus a very

Table 11.1 The values of alternative classes of woodlands

Forest type	Assumptions giving positive NPV at $r = 6\%$
FT5 Community forests	Very high recreational values
FT4 Spruce in uplands	Moderate recreational values and land values at 0.5 × market price
FT8 Fir, spruce, broadleaf trees in lowlands	High recreational values and land values at 0.8 × market price
FT7 Pine in lowlands	Moderate recreational values and land values at 0.5 × market price

Source: Adapted from Pearce (1994)

mixed one, with the magnitude (and direction) of the effects varying greatly from one case to another.

Water-related ecological outputs (W) discussed by Pearce include the effects of afforestation on water supply, water quality, the deposition of air pollution, soil erosion, and the impacts of fertiliser and pesticide use and harvesting practices. Qualitative estimates only are presented for these impacts.

Greenhouse-warming-related effects are quantified in monetary terms by Pearce. His estimates of the present value of benefits from carbon fixing, in pounds per hectare at a 6% discount rate, range from £142 on upland semi-natural pinelands to £254 on lowland mixed woodlands.

Pearce's conclusions

In terms of the commercial costs and benefits, together with the two benefit categories that he was able to quantify (recreation and carbon-fixing), Pearce concludes that only four of the eight general classes of woodlands he investigates have a clear justification for increased afforestation at a discount rate of 6%. His summary conclusions are presented in Table 11.1.

As explained above, these conclusions are drawn without looking at non-monetised benefits (or costs). In those cases where the NPV of an afforestation project is negative, however, the decision maker may regard the project as socially desirable if he or she forms a judgement that the non-monetised benefits are sufficiently large to offset the negative (monetised) NPV.

Source: Adapted from Pearce (1994)

11.2.1 Private appraisal

The commercial viability of a project can be assessed in two equivalent ways – the net present value test and the internal rate of return test. Since the rationale is clearer in the former, we begin by looking at that.

11.2.1.1 The net present value test

At the interest rate i, £1 lent for one year grows to £$(1 + i)$. If at the end of the year, the principal and the interest earned are re-lent – left to accumulate in a savings account say – then after 2 years the amount due will be £$\{(1 + i)(1 + i)\} = $ £$(1 + i)^2$. After being lent for 3 years, the amount due will be £$\{(1 + i)(1 + i)(1 + i)\} = $ £$(1 + i)^3$. And so on and so on. This is the process of compounding.[2] Generally, a principal lent at the rate i, with annual compounding, will be worth V_t after t years where

$$V_t = PV(1 + i)^t \qquad (11.12)$$

where PV stands for the principal, the sum initially lent, or 'invested'.

What would a, completely reliable, promise to pay £$(1 + i)$ a year hence be worth now? In the previous section we called such a promise a 'bond'. Then, the question is: what is the value today of a bond with value £$(1 + i)$ a year from now? Given that £1 invested today at i will be worth £$(1 + i)$ a year from now, the answer to this question is clearly £1. This process of converting future amounts to current equivalents is discounting, which is compounding in reverse. Just as compounding can be extended over many years, so can discounting. What would be the value of a bond that promised to pay £V t years from now? The answer is the amount of money that would have to be invested now at the ruling interest rate to realise £V t years from now. By equation 11.12 that is

$$PV = V_t/(1 + i)^t \qquad (11.13)$$

where PV stands for 'present value' in the terminology used when looking at things this way round,

Table 11.2 Example net cash flow 1

Year	Expenditure	Receipts	Net cash flow
0	100	0	−100
1	10	50	40
2	10	50	40
3	10	45.005	35.005
4	0	0	0

and $1/(1 + i)^t$ is the discount factor for t years at interest rate i.

The present value of a sum of money in the future is its current equivalent, where equivalence is in the sense that, given the existence of facilities for lending and borrowing, an individual or firm would currently be indifferent between the certain promise of the future sum and the offer of the present value now.

Project appraisal is the consideration of whether it makes sense to make some expenditure commitment now given the expectation of future receipts as a result. Consider a simple example. Suppose that a firm can buy a machine for £100 now. If it does this, it can use the machine for some time, and its use will give rise to additional receipts of £50 for each of the two following years, and then of £45.005 the year after that. Then, the machine will be useless, and its scrap value 0. Using the machine will add £10 each year to costs. The impact of acquiring the machine on the firm over time is given by Table 11.2.

Should the firm buy the machine? Summing the net cash flow over time gives a positive number £15.005. However, as is typical with investment projects, there is a negative cash flow now and the positive cash flow is in the future. Just looking at the total over the life of the project ignores this time profile. The net present value approach to project appraisal is a technique for assessing projects which takes account of the futurity of the positive elements in the net cash flow. It can be thought of as a way of normalising the cash flows associated with projects so that alternatives can be properly compared. To see the need for such normalisation, suppose that the firm considering the project described above

---

[2] Compounding proceeds according to exponential growth. An interesting question is how long it takes for something growing exponentially, like an untouched savings account, to double in size.

From equation 11.12, $V_t/PV = (1 + i)^t$ so to find the doubling time solve $2 = (1 + i)^t$ or $\ln 2 = t \cdot \ln(1 + i)$ for t. For $i = 0.015$, for example, the doubling time is 47 years, and for $i = 0.03$ it is just 24 years.

Table 11.3 Example net cash flow 2

Year	Expenditure	Receipts	Net cash flow
0	100	0	−100
1	0	0	0
2	0	0	0
......	......	......	......
......	......	......	......
49	0	0	0
50	0	115.005	115.005
51	0	0	0

could alternatively now invest £100 in a project which would give rise to the net cash flow shown in Table 11.3.

For both of these projects, the total net cash flow over their lifetimes is £15.005. On this basis the firm would be indifferent between the two projects, which clearly does not make sense.

The net present value, NPV, of a project is the present value of the net cash flow associated with it. If an investment has a non-negative NPV, then it should be undertaken, otherwise not. The decision rule is, that is, go ahead with the project only if NPV ≥ 0. The rationale for this rule is that following it will lead to going ahead only with projects that leave unchanged or increase net worth. A firm wishing to maximise its net worth should rank available projects by NPV, and undertake those for which NPV ≥ 0.

Denote expenditure in year t as E_t, and receipts as R_t so that $N_t = R_t - E_t$ is the net cash flow in year t, and denote the project lifetime by T. Then the present value of expenditures is

$$PV_E = E_0 + \frac{E_1}{1+i} + \frac{E_2}{(1+i)^2} + \ldots + \frac{E_T}{(1+i)^T}$$

$$= \sum_0^T \frac{E_t}{(1+i)^t} \qquad (11.14)$$

the present value of receipts is

$$PV_R = R_0 + \frac{R_1}{1+i} + \frac{R_2}{(1+i)^2} + \ldots + \frac{R_T}{(1+i)^T}$$

$$= \sum_0^T \frac{R_t}{(1+i)^t} \qquad (11.15)$$

and the net present value of the project is

$$NPV = PV_R - PV_E = \sum_0^T \frac{R_t}{(1+i)^t} - \sum_0^T \frac{E_t}{(1+i)^t}$$

$$(11.16)$$

which can also be written

$$NPV = N_0 + \frac{N_1}{1+i} + \frac{N_2}{(1+i)^2} + \ldots + \frac{N_T}{(1+i)^T}$$

$$= \sum_0^T \frac{N_t}{(1+i)^t} \qquad (11.17)$$

Applying 11.16 or 11.17 to the data of Table 11.2 gives

(i)   for $i = 0.05$, NPV = £4.6151
(ii) for $i = 0.075$, NPV = £0
(iii) for $i = 0.10$, NPV = −£4.27874

so that while the project fails the NPV test at 10%, it passes at 7.5% and 5%, and has a higher NPV for an interest rate of 5% than it would for an interest rate of 7.5%. A close examination of how these results arise demonstrates the logic and meaning of the NPV test. This is made clearer if it is assumed that the firm finances the project by issuing one-year bonds.

Take the 5% case first. In order to acquire the machine, the firm must on day one of year 0 sell its bonds to the value of £100. Given $i = 0.05$, it thus incurs the liability to redeem the bonds for £105 on day one of year 1. At that time, it will have net receipts from using the machine of £40, a shortfall of £65. It covers this shortfall by issuing new bonds in amount £65, which generates a liability of £68.25 (65 × 1.05) for day one of year 2. At that time its receipts in respect of using the machine are £40, so there is a shortfall of £28.25 as between net receipts and expenditure on bond redemption. This can be covered by issuing further one-year bonds to the value of £28.25, incurring a liability of £29.6625 (28.25 × 1.05) for day one of year 3. On that day, net receipts will be 35.005, so that there will be a current surplus of 35.005 − 29.6625 = £5.3425 at the end of the project lifetime. What is the present value of this surplus when considered at the time, day one of year 0, that a decision has to made on the project? It is 5.3425 × 1/(1 + i)³ = 5.3425/1.1576 = £4.6151, which is the answer given by the NPV formula for this project with an interest rate of 5%, see (i) above.

The NPV of a project is the amount by which it increases net worth in present value terms.

Working through the 7.5% case in the same way –

t

0 sell £100 of bonds

1 redeem bonds for £107.5, sell £67.5 of new bonds (107.5 – 40)

2 redeem bonds for £72.5625, sell £32.5625 of new bonds (72.5625 – 40)

3 redeem bonds for £35.005, surplus of £0

and 11.16 or 11.17 produces the answer NPV = 0. For the 10% case

t

0 sell £100 of bonds

1 redeem bonds for £110, sell £70 of new bonds (110 – 40)

2 redeem bonds for £77, sell £37 of new bonds (77 – 40)

3 redeem bonds for £40.7, surplus of –£5.695 (35.005 – 40.7)

and the formula produces the answer NPV = –£4.27874. This is the present value at 10% of –£5.695 three years hence. £4.27874 is what would have to be initially invested at 10% to yield enough to meet the £5.695 liability that would arise after three years if the firm went ahead with this project.

Projects with positive NPV increase net worth, while those with negative NPV reduce it. If the NPV is 0, the project would leave net worth unchanged.

In this example, for a given project net cash flow, a higher interest rate means a lower NPV. It is sometimes assumed that this is always true. It is not. It is true where the time profile is one with negative net receipts early followed by positive net receipts. But, and this can be important where projects have long-term environmental impacts, when proper account is taken of all costs and benefits the time profile may not be like this.

Table 11.3 provided the data for an alternative project, which involved £100 expenditure now for a one-off net receipt of £115.005 in year 50. For this project with 5% interest rate

NPV = { 115.005/1.05^{50} } – 100

   = { 115.005/11.4 } – 100

   = 10.0289 – 100

   = –£89.9711

The logic of the NPV test for project appraisal has been developed here for a situation where the firm is going to borrow the funds to finance the project, as this makes clearer what is going on. However, the test is equally appropriate where the firm can fund the project from its own cash reserves. This is because the firm could, instead of using its own cash to finance the project, lend the money at the market rate of interest. If the NPV for the project is negative, the firm would do better for the present value of its net worth by lending the money rather than committing to the project. If the NPV is 0, it is a matter of indifference. If the project has a positive NPV, then the money would do more for the present value of net worth by being put into the project than being lent at interest.

Where the project lifetime is more than a few years, finding the NPV from data on the projected net cash flow is straightforward but tedious. Most spreadsheet software includes a routine that calculates NPV, and the internal rate of return which we now discuss.

11.2.1.2 The internal rate of return test

An alternative test for project appraisal is the internal rate of return, IRR, test, according to which a project should be undertaken if its internal rate of return is greater than the rate of interest. The internal rate of return for a project is the rate at which its net cash flow must be discounted to produce an NPV equal to 0.

Recall that NPV is given by:

$$\text{NPV} = N_0 + \frac{N_1}{1+i} + \frac{N_2}{(1+i)^2} + \ldots + \frac{N_T}{(1+i)^T}$$

$$= \sum_0^T \frac{N_t}{(1+i)^t}$$

A project's IRR is found by setting the left-hand side here equal to zero, and then solving the equation for the interest rate, which solution is the IRR. The IRR is, that is, the solution for x in

$$0 = N_0 + \frac{N_1}{1+x} + \frac{N_2}{(1+x)^2} + \ldots + \frac{N_T}{(1+x)^T}$$

$$= \sum_0^T \frac{N_t}{(1+x)^t} \tag{11.18}$$

The IRR test will, for the same input data, give the same result as the NPV test. The reason for this, and the underlying logic of the IRR test, is apparent from the discussion of the NPV test. In some cases, because of the time profile of the net cash flow, the solution to 11.18 involves multiple solutions for x. This problem does not arise with the NPV test, and it is the recommended test.

Table 11.4 One project, two possible cash flows

Year	Net cash flow 1 Probability 0.6	Net cash flow 2 Probability 0.4
0	−100	−100
1	40	35
2	40	35
3	35.005	25
4	0	0

11.2.1.3 Dealing with risk

Thus far it has been assumed that at the time of appraising a project, the firm knows what the net cash flow that it would give rise to is. This, of course, is generally not the case. The net cash flow figures that are input to NPV or IRR calculations are derived from projections, or estimates, of future receipts and expenditures, and an important question is: how do we incorporate into project appraisal the fact that it is dealing with imperfect knowledge of the future?

If the firm is prepared to assign probabilities to possible alternatives regarding the determination of the net cash flow, a simple modification of the NPV criterion can be used. Instead of requiring that the NPV be positive, it is required that the expected NPV be positive. The expected value, or expectation, of a decision is the probability weighted sum of the values of the mutually exclusive outcomes. Suppose that for the project considered above, instead of the single known net cash flow considered thus far, the firm considers that there are two possible outcomes with the probabilities shown in Table 11.4.

Table 11.5 shows the calculations to calculate the expected NPV. In this case it is negative and the project should not be undertaken.

Basing the decision rule on the expected NPV assumes that the decision maker is 'risk-neutral',

which means that she regards an expected value of £x as the same as the certainty of £x. Thus, a risk-neutral decision maker would regard the offer of £4 if a tossed coin comes up heads, where the expected value of the offer is $(0.5 \times 4) + (0.5 \times 0) = £2$, as equivalent to the offer of £2 cash in hand. Decision makers are in fact frequently observed to be 'risk-averse' rather than risk-neutral, e.g. would prefer £2 cash in hand to £4 if heads comes up. There are a variety of ways to modify the basic NPV decision rule to deal with decision makers who are risk-averse. References to the literature are provided in the Further Reading section at the end of the chapter. We will revisit the question of imperfect knowledge of project consequences, in the context of social appraisal, i.e. CBA, in Chapter 13. Our discussion of CBA in this chapter will, in the main, assume that project consequences are known.

A flexible way of informally considering the impact of risk would be to compute the NPV for different assumptions about future expenditures and receipts, to examine the sensitivity of the decision to assumptions built into the net cash flow projections. This kind of sensitivity analysis does not produce a unique decision, but it can illuminate key areas of the underlying project analysis.

Table 11.5 Calculation of expected NPV

Year	Expected net cash flow	Present value of expected cash flow
0	$-(0.6 \times 100) + \{-(0.4 \times 100)\} = -100$	−100
1	$(0.6 \times 40) + (0.4 \times 35) = 38$	$38/1.075 = 35.35$
2	$(0.6 \times 40) + (0.4 \times 35) = 38$	$38/1.075^2 = 32.88$
3	$(0.6 \times 35.005) + (0.4 \times 25) = 31.003$	$31.003/1.075^3 = 24.96$
4	$(0.6 \times 0) + (0.4 \times 0) = 0$	
Expected NPV		−6.81

11.2.2 Social appraisal

CBA is used in circumstances where it is felt that some of the consequences of going ahead with a project would not be adequately represented using market prices. Where there are consequences that are not traded in markets, as is the case with, but not only with, many environmental impacts, reliance on market prices would mean completely ignoring those consequences. In such circumstances, a non-market evaluation procedure is required to assess the project properly from a social, as opposed to private, commercial, perspective.

11.2.2.1 Utility-based appraisal

The key principle that underpins CBA ideally is very simple. The impact of the project on the utility of each and every affected person at each point in time is identified. The typical project will involve some winners and some losers. Some kind of social welfare function is then used to aggregate across affected individuals. The project is approved if its net impact on social welfare is positive.

For simplicity, imagine that three individuals (A, B and C) are affected in each of four consecutive intervals of time, labelled 0, 1, 2 and 3, where we take period 0 to be the present period. Table 11.6 presents the impacts on each person's utility at each time. Thus $\Delta U_{B,2}$ denotes the change in utility during time period 2 that would be experienced by individual B on account of the project if it went ahead.

If there existed a generally agreed social welfare function with dated individual utilities as arguments, the analyst could compute

$$\Delta W = W(\Delta U_{A,0}, \ldots, \Delta U_{C,3})$$

and consider its sign. If positive the project should go ahead. Alternatively, we could imagine that there

existed an intratemporal social welfare function which mapped individual utilities into a social aggregate, ΔU_t, in each period, and an intertemporal social welfare function for aggregating over time. The analyst would then compute

$$\Delta W = W(\Delta U_0, \Delta U_1, \Delta U_2, \Delta U_3)$$

and the decision would be based on the sign here. A widely entertained particular form for the intertemporal social welfare function, considered in the previous section, is

$$\Delta W = \Delta U_0 + \frac{\Delta U_1}{1 + \rho} + \frac{\Delta U_2}{(1 + \rho)^2} + \frac{\Delta U_3}{(1 + \rho)^3}$$

where aggregation over time involves exponential discounting – so called because the aggregation weights decrease exponentially with time. Note that here these weights are given by the utility discount rate.

There are several problems with all of this. First, there is no generally agreed social welfare function of any of the above forms. It is not even generally agreed that interpersonal utility comparisons are admissible. Finally, utilities are not observable.

11.2.2.2 Consumption-based appraisal

For these reasons, what is actually recommended as the ideal CBA procedure involves consumption, rather than utility, changes. Under this procedure, the analyst would trace all of the consequences of the project through to their final impact on consumption by individuals. Thus, stated in monetary units, the impacts can be referred to as net benefits, being positive for consumption increases, benefits, and negative for decreases, costs. Table 11.7 corresponds to Table 11.6.

Appraisal involves, first, adding net benefits across individuals at a point in time to get contemporaneous

Table 11.6 Changes in utility (ΔU) consequent on an illustrative project

Individual	Time period				
	0	1	2	3	Overall
A	$\Delta U_{A,0}$	$\Delta U_{A,1}$	$\Delta U_{A,2}$	$\Delta U_{A,3}$	ΔU_A
B	$\Delta U_{B,0}$	$\Delta U_{B,1}$	$\Delta U_{B,2}$	$\Delta U_{B,3}$	ΔU_B
C	$\Delta U_{C,0}$	$\Delta U_{C,1}$	$\Delta U_{C,2}$	$\Delta U_{C,3}$	ΔU_C
Society	ΔU_0	ΔU_1	ΔU_2	ΔU_3	

Table 11.7 Net benefit (NB) impacts consequent upon an illustrative project

Individual	Time period				
	0	1	2	3	Overall
A	$NB_{A,0}$	$NB_{A,1}$	$NB_{A,2}$	$NB_{A,3}$	NB_A
B	$NB_{B,0}$	$NB_{B,1}$	$NB_{B,2}$	$NB_{B,3}$	NB_B
C	$NB_{C,0}$	$NB_{C,1}$	$NB_{C,2}$	$NB_{C,3}$	NB_C
Society	NB_0	NB_1	NB_2	NB_3	

net benefits $NB_0, \ldots, NB_3$, where $NB_t = NB_{A,t} + NB_{B,t} + NB_{C,t}$. The NPV of this project is then the discounted, using the consumption discount rate, sum of net benefits:

$$NPV = NB_0 + \frac{NB_1}{1 + r} + \frac{NB_2}{(1 + r)^2} + \frac{NB_3}{(1 + r)^3}$$

Generally, for T periods:

$$NPV = \sum_{t=0}^{t=T} \frac{NB_t}{(1 + r)^t}$$

The decision rule is to go ahead with the project if its NPV is positive. The rationale for this decision rule can be put in several, equivalent, ways.

Following from the discussion above of private-sector appraisal, a positive NPV indicates that, with due allowance for the dating of costs and benefits, the project delivers a surplus of benefit over cost. The consumption gains involved are, that is, greater than the consumption losses, taking account of the timing of gains and losses. The existence of a surplus means that those who gain from the project could compensate those who lose and still be better off. Note that the NPV test is a potential compensation test. It does not require that compensation is actually paid. All the discussion of potential, as opposed to actual, compensation tests in Chapter 5 applies to the NPV test.

Identifying the NPV test as a potential compensation test indicates that CBA is concerned with allocative efficiency, is intended to select projects that move the economy toward an efficient allocation of its resources. Another way to appreciate this is as follows. There are two steps. First, as compared with a private appraisal, CBA takes account of *all* impacts on consumption, irrespective of whether or not they show up in, or are properly valued in, market transactions. Think of this as correcting market failure in a static sense. Second, as we saw in the previous section, supposing that there is a single market for loanable funds from which market failure is absent, the equilibrium rate of interest, i, in that market will be equal to the consumption discount rate, r, and the marginal rate of return to investment, δ.

It follows that if scarce resources were not used in the project under consideration they could be invested elsewhere at a rate of return r per period.

The NPV of a project will only exceed zero if its internal rate of return exceeds r. Therefore scarce funds will only be allocated to the project by the NPV test if its rate of return is at least as good as the best alternative return available. But this is precisely what efficient investment appraisal requires – allocating scarce funds to their highest valued use. It is clear from this that CBA is a technique whose object is to ensure the attainment of economic efficiency in the allocation of resources.

While some economists are content to treat CBA as a means for achieving efficiency objectives, leaving distributional objectives to be pursued by other means, others argue that CBA should be conducted so that projects that pass its test are welfare-enhancing. To do this, it is suggested that, in terms of Table 11.7, contemporaneous total net benefit should be defined as the weighted sum of individual net benefits, with marginal utilities of consumption as weights, rather than as the simple sum. That is, using

$$NB_t = U_C^A NB_{A,t} + U_C^B NB_{B,t} + U_C^C NB_{C,t}$$

where U_C^i is the ith individual's marginal utility of consumption, instead of

$$NB_t = NB_{A,t} + NB_{B,t} + NB_{C,t}$$

This suggestion is rarely followed in practice. It requires identifying the individuals, or groups of individuals, affected by the project, and then ascertaining the marginal utilities for those individuals or groups.

11.2.3 Choice of discount rate

There are a number of technical aspects of the application of CBA that warrant extended discussion. One of these is the means by which the correct, i.e. market-failure-correcting, contemporary valuations are assigned to project impacts. We devote the whole of the next chapter, and some of the one after that, to this topic, albeit exclusively in regard to environmental impacts. Space precludes dealing with the other issues properly: see the Further Reading suggestions at the end of the chapter. However, we will briefly discuss here the question of the discount rate to be used in CBA, because it is important, and because the discussion should provide further insight into the nature of CBA.

Table 11.8 Present values at various discount rates

Discount rate %	Time horizon Years			
	25	50	100	200
2	60.95	37.15	13.80	1.91
4	37.51	14.07	1.98	0.04
6	23.30	5.43	0.29	0.0009
8	14.60	2.13	0.05	0.00002

There is disagreement among economists about the principles according to which the discount rate to be used in CBA should be determined, as well as about the actual number to use at any particular time in any particular economy. This is important because the decision reached on a project using the NPV test can be very sensitive to the number used for the discount rate. This is particularly the case where, as with many projects involving environmental impacts, the time horizon for the NPV test is many years into the future. In this connection it is important to note that the proper time horizon for the appraisal of a project is the date at which its impacts cease, not the date at which it ceases to serve the purpose for which it was intended. Thus, for example, for a nuclear fission plant the time horizon is not the 40 years to the time when it ceases to generate electricity but the time over which it is necessary to devote resources to storing the plant's waste products – hundreds of years.

Table 11.8 gives the present value of £100 arising from 25 to 200 years ahead at discount rates from 2% to 8%. This range of discount rates is not arbitrary – rates across this range have been proposed for use in CBA by economists. Clearly, the choice of discount rate matters. Even for 25 years out, the present value at 2% is four times that at 8%.

In an important article on the choice of discount rate for CBA, Joseph Stiglitz states that:

> The question of the appropriate rate of discount to use for public projects has been a subject of extensive controversy. The reason for this controversy is that the number of projects for which there is an acceptable benefit–cost ratio is critically dependent on the value of this rate.[3]
>
> *(p. 154)*

The benefit–cost ratio is an alternative way of doing the NPV test – the project should go ahead if the ratio of the present value of benefit to the present value of cost is greater than one. Stiglitz finds that there is no simple resolution of the controversy. The discount rate to be used

> depends on a number of factors, and indeed I have argued that it might vary from project to project depending, for instance, on the distributional consequences of the project. These results may be frustrating for those who seek simple answers, but such are not to be found. The decision on the appropriate rate of discount thus will inevitably entail judgements.
>
> *(p. 155)*

The need for judgements arises because of what Stiglitz calls 'constraints'. By this terminology he means that the world in which we want to do CBA is not the ideal world where there is no market failure. Many of the departures from ideal circumstances are not amenable to corrective action – if public goods are to be supplied, they must be financed by government, which given the infeasibility of lump-sum taxation necessarily introduces 'distortions'. A distortion that cannot be corrected is a constraint. A full discussion of the implications of distortions for the conduct of CBA is well beyond the scope of this text, and the interested reader should consult the Further Reading section at the end of the chapter. We can, however, sketch the nature of some of the basic issues in relation to the CBA of a project to supply a public good.

If we lived in a world that, from the economic viewpoint, was entirely free of distortions and constraints, the choice of discount rate problem would not arise. As discussed above, in such a market-failure-free world we would have the market rate of interest equal to the consumption discount rate equal to the marginal rate of return to investment. In such a world, the question of the choice of discount rate for CBA would not arise as there would be just one rate. Actually, in such a world we would not need to do CBA. In the world in which we do live we cannot directly observe the consumption discount rate. We do observe a variety of market interest

---

[3]   The article is reprinted as Stiglitz (1994).

Box 11.2 Discount rate choices in practice

What values have been used 'officially' for CBA discount rates in the USA and the UK?

In 1969, a United States Congressional hearing found that agencies were using discount rates from zero to 20%, with no clear logic dictating the level in any particular instance. Very often, rates are set reflecting political pressures and goals. For example, in the years of the Nixon administration, the federal government chose to use rates near the top of the then prevailing 3–12% band in order to reduce the level of public expenditure. From time to time, single target rates have been set by the federal authorities. In 1970, the Office of Management and Budget required all federal agencies to use a 10% discount rate, although some project areas were treated differently. In particular, discount rates for water resource projects were set annually by the US Treasury Department, and have typically been around 2.5%. In 1986, the US Congressional Budget Office required the general use of a 2% discount rate, roughly equal to the real cost of borrowing on world markets. A detailed analysis of US discounting practices can be found in the March 1990 Special Issue of the *Journal of Environmental Economics and Management* (Vol. 18, no 2, Part 2).

Little more consistency seems to characterise choices of social discount rates in the UK. Some recent choices have been:

1988: UK Treasury 'Test' Discount Rate of 5%
1990: UK Treasury: 6% rate on most public sector investments, but 8% for public transport
1994: UK Treasury 'Target' Discount Rate for public-sector investment, 8%. Forestry projects to be discounted at 6% if non-market benefits included

One particularly awkward matter has been the use of different discount rates where project areas are deemed to carry positive external benefits. In the USA, this has been true for water-resource project appraisal, while in the UK, forestry projects have often been discounted at unusually low rates. This practice is not desirable; the appropriate way of proceeding is to measure externalities in a project appraisal, rather than to assume they exist and set *ex ante* an adjusted discount rate to reflect this assumption.

---

rates, and of rates of return to investments actually undertaken.

In regard to the former, the standard assumption is that they reflect consumption discount rates where there are many such rates according to the degree of risk associated with various instruments for effecting borrowing and lending. We discuss CBA and risk in Chapter 13. The basic idea is that it should be conducted in terms of the expected values of costs and benefits, that an explicit allowance be made for the cost of bearing risk, and that the relevant consumption discount rate is then the risk-free market interest rate. This is taken to be the interest rate on government bonds. This varies over time, but is generally of the order of 2% to 5%. If we are going to do NPV tests using r, then, we are looking at a discount rate of, say, 4%.

In regard to rates of return to investment in the private sector, what we actually observe are average rather than marginal rates of return. If firms ranked investment projects by rate of return and undertook

those with higher rates before those with lower rates, the average rate of return would exceed the marginal rate. Average rates of return vary over time, and across countries, but we are looking in general terms at something of the order of 6% to 10%. Certainly economists take it that in the world that we actually live in, we should assume that the marginal rate of return to private-sector investment, δ, is considerably higher – of the order of twice as high – than the consumption discount rate, r. One of the reasons advanced as explaining the failure of markets to bring δ and r closer together is taxation, and particularly the taxation of profits. It is the pre-tax profit that is relevant for δ. Box 11.2 provides some information on actual practice in setting discount rates for the CBA of public-sector projects.

It should be noted that there is universal agreement among economists on one thing in this area. That is that it is 'real' rates that should be used in CBA, not 'nominal' rates. Nominal rates are those stated, while real rates are nominal rates adjusted for inflation. If the stated rate of interest on a savings account, for example, is 7% per annum and inflation is 4% per annum, then the real rate of interest on offer is $7 - 4 = 3\%$ per annum. The rates cited above, and in Box 11.2, are real rates.

Now, let us revert to our simple two-period analysis to consider the choice between δ and r, given that the former is larger. Suppose that the government is considering a project to supply a public good costing ΔI_0. CBA_1 uses the consumption discount rate and says go ahead if

$$\frac{\Delta C_1}{1 + r} > \Delta I_0 \tag{11.19}$$

whereas CBA_2 uses the rate of return as discount rate and says go ahead if

$$\frac{\Delta C_1}{1 + \delta} > \Delta I_0 \tag{11.20}$$

For $\delta > r$, the ΔC_1 required to pass 11.20 will be larger than that required to pass 11.19 – a project could pass 11.19 but fail 11.20.

Suppose that the public-sector project would be at the expense of, would 'crowd out', the marginal private-sector project. In that case, with $\delta > r$, there is an argument for using 11.20 rather than 11.19, as follows. If 11.19 is satisfied and the project goes ahead, we know that consumers are, over the two periods, better off. However, they would have been even better off if ΔI_0 had been committed to the marginal private-sector project. Therefore we should evaluate public-sector projects using the rate of return as discount rate.

Suppose, on the other hand, that the decision on the public-sector project makes absolutely no difference to what happens in the private sector – there is no crowding out of private- by public-sector investment. In that case, the argument of the previous paragraph does not apply. The rate of return to private-sector investment is irrelevant to public-sector decision making, which should use the consumption discount rate.

The former situation here corresponds to one where there is a distortion in that the total amount of investment is fixed, rather than being determined by rates of return as in the latter situation. Basically, an argument for not using the consumption discount rate rests on the claim that there is some kind of

distortion that must be taken as a given for the purposes of the CBA.

In making this point here, we have not actually conducted the CBA according to ideal standards. The problem is that we have not converted everything into consumption-equivalent terms. In setting out 11.19 and 11.20 we have used the cost of the public-sector project in terms of the money spent on it, ΔI_0. This is not a proper measure of the consumption cost of this public-sector project if it is being assumed that it crowds out the marginal private-sector project. It is a proper measure of the consumption cost under the assumption that going ahead with it would have no effect on private-sector investment. In the case of complete crowding out, a private-sector project that would have delivered consumption in amount $(1 + \delta)\Delta I_0$ in period 1 does not take place. The present value, in period 0 when the decision is taken, of that loss is

$$\frac{1 + \delta}{1 + r}\Delta I_0$$

and using this in 11.19 gives that test as

$$\frac{\Delta C_1}{1 + r} > \frac{1 + \delta}{1 + r}\Delta I_0$$

which, multiplying both sides by $1 + r$, is

$$\Delta C_1 > (1 + \delta)\Delta I_0$$

which is

$$\frac{\Delta C_1}{1 + \delta} > \Delta I_0$$

which is 11.20.

The point here is that in this case doing things in terms of the money cost of the investment, ΔI_0, and using the rate of return as discount rate would give the same result as doing things in terms of consumption-equivalent flows and using the consumption discount rate. Many economists would argue that the latter is the proper way to proceed, and that doing things the other way happens to come out right in this case because two cancelling mistakes are made – not converting to consumption-equivalent flows, and using the rate of return rather than the consumption discount rate. These economists would argue that the proper way to proceed, always, in

CBA is to convert everything to consumption-equivalent flows and discount using the consumption discount rate.

However, as our quotation from Stiglitz indicates, not everyone agrees. The foregoing is a counsel of perfection. Converting everything to consumption equivalents can be very difficult and involves a number of somewhat arbitrary assumptions. In the crowding-out case considered here it was straightforward because the nature of the distortion was extreme and therefore clear. In practice, crowding out is neither 100% nor 0%, but depends on such factors as the marginal propensity to save, and whether or not there are unemployed resources in the economy. In the practice of CBA there is the need for judgement and scope for legitimate disagreement. For this reason, it is important that any exercise in CBA should include sensitivity analysis – examining the effect on the decision of variations around the central estimates/assumptions employed in the analysis.

11.3 Cost–benefit analysis and the environment

We now wish to discuss CBA in relation to the environment. This is a wide field with an extensive literature. In order to fix ideas we will consider a wilderness forest area, in which some development – a mine, a hydroelectric plant, timber harvesting or perhaps a theme park and tourist resort – is proposed. Currently, the area is relatively inaccessible and is used only for low-intensity recreation, such as backpacking for example. It also provides habitat for numerous species of flora and fauna, and thus plays a role in biodiversity conservation. If the development goes ahead, the area's value to wilderness recreationalists will be reduced, as will its effectiveness in biodiversity conservation. The question at issue is whether the development project should be allowed to go ahead.

For economists, this question is to be answered by CBA. The development project should be appraised by the methods discussed in the previous section of this chapter, taking due account of any losses suffered by individuals on account of the reduction in its wilderness recreation and conservation services. These services do not pass through markets, so they cannot be taken into account in CBA using market prices. Economists have developed a variety of techniques for 'non-market valuation' so that services such as wilderness recreation and biodiversity conservation can be included in CBA. We consider these techniques in some detail in the next chapter. For now, we shall simply say that the essential point of these techniques is that the intention is to ascertain what the affected individuals collectively would be willing to pay if there were markets for these services. This is what the logic of bringing them within the ambit of applied welfare economics requires.

To emphasise that, in circumstances where a project involves environmental impacts that are not valued in markets, a proper CBA should take account of such impacts, let us call it environmental cost–benefit analysis, ECBA. The scope of ECBA is much wider than the appraisal of development projects in wilderness areas, but looking at it in that context does bring out the most important issues.

11.3.1 Environmental cost–benefit analysis

We know that to do a cost–benefit analysis we calculate

$$NPV = \sum_{t=0}^{t=T} \frac{NB_t}{(1 + r)^t}$$

and that the project should go ahead if $NPV > 0$. Net benefits are the excess of benefits over costs in each period and we can write

$$NPV = \sum_{t=0}^{t=T} \frac{B_t - C_t}{(1 + r)^t}$$

with B for benefits and C for costs. In ECBA benefits and costs are to include, respectively, the value of environmental improvement and of environmental deterioration consequent upon going ahead with the project. In fact, in discussing ECBA it is convenient for expositional purposes to keep ordinary benefits and costs separate from environmental benefits and costs. By 'ordinary' benefits and costs we mean the value of standard, non-environmental, outputs from and inputs to the project – such as, in the case of a mine, the extracted ore on the benefit side, and on the cost side inputs of labour, capital equipment, fuel and so on. As noted in the previous section, ideally all these inputs and outputs would be expressed in consumption-equivalent terms.

Let B_d be the discounted value of the ordinary benefit stream over the project lifetime, and let C_d represent the discounted value of the ordinary cost stream over the project lifetime, so that ignoring environmental impacts we can write

$$NPV = \sum_{t=0}^{t=T} \frac{B_t - C_t}{(1 + r)^t} = \sum_0^T \frac{B_t}{(1 + r)^t} + \sum_0^T \frac{C_t}{(1 + r)^t}$$

$$= B_d - C_d$$

To denote an NPV that ignores environmental impacts, use NPV′ for it. Then, taking account of environmental impacts, the 'proper' NPV is given by

$$NPV = B_d - C_d - EC = NPV' - EC \qquad (11.21)$$

where EC is the present value of the stream of the net value of the project's environmental impacts over the project's lifetime. Note that in principle EC could be negative, with the value of environmental benefits exceeding the value of environmental costs, so that NPV > NPV′. The net value of the environmental consequences of the project, could, that is, be such as to strengthen, rather than weaken, the case for the project. However, we shall assume that EC is positive. In fact, it will be convenient to make the stronger assumption that there are no desirable environmental consequences of going ahead with the project, that it causes only environmental damage. This assumption appears to sit well with development in a wilderness area, and is what is typically assumed about such development in the literature. Given this, EC stands for 'environmental cost'. It could also be taken to stand for 'external cost' as the unpriced environmental damages are externalities associated with the project.

Using equation 11.21 the ECBA decision rule is that the project should go ahead if

$$NPV' = B_d - C_d > EC \qquad (11.22)$$

The application of this criterion requires the identification and measurement of the impacts on the wilderness area, and then their valuation and aggrega-

tion to arrive at EC, which is a monetary measure of the environmental benefits of not going ahead with the project.

Assuming that the environmental impacts on individuals can be identified and measured, the basic strategy for valuation is to treat them as arguments in utility functions, to treat them, that is, in the same way as ordinary produced goods and services. Then, as discussed in the next chapter, demand theory can be used to establish the existence and nature of monetary measures of the impacts. The implementation of this ECBA approach to social decision making then requires the estimation of the sizes of the appropriate monetary measures for affected individuals and their aggregation to obtain an estimate for EC.

Now clearly, if NPV′ < 0 then the project should not go ahead, independent of any consideration of the environmental damage that it might entail. A development of this observation, where NPV′ has been assessed as some positive number, is to ask: how large would EC have to be in order, according to ECBA, for the project not to go ahead? The answer is obvious. The project should not go ahead if

$$EC \geq NPV' = B_d - C_d$$

so that

$$EC^* = NPV' = B_d - C_d \qquad (11.23)$$

defines a threshold value for EC. For EC ≥ EC* the project should not go ahead.

This suggests that what we can call an 'inverse ECBA' might usefully precede or accompany an ECBA. ECBA itself requires the identification, measurement and valuation of the project's environmental impacts on affected households. Such an exercise involves non-trivial expenditures, and may, nevertheless, produce results that do not command universal assent, as discussed in the next chapter. Inverse ECBA simply means properly figuring NPV′, and then asking what average valuation of the environmental impacts would have to be to produce a negative verdict on the project. It involves, that is, calculating the threshold for total environmental cost, EC*, and dividing it by N, the size of the relevant population of individuals. In some cases the result of this calculation will be such a small amount that it could be generally agreed, or at least widely agreed, that the project obviously should not go ahead.

Even where this is not the case, and a serious attempt to estimate EC/N is undertaken, the value for EC^*/N will provide a useful benchmark against which to consider the result for EC/N produced by the application of the techniques to be considered in the next chapter. Given the problems that will be seen to attend the results from the various environmental valuation techniques, estimating EC/N as, say, 10 times EC^*/N produces a very different decision situation from estimating EC/N as, say, 1.5 times EC^*/N. In the former case one might be reasonably confident that the project should not go ahead; in the latter case much less so.

Thinking about wilderness development projects in inverse ECBA terms directs attention to the question of the size of N, the number of individuals that would be affected if the project went ahead. In regard to recreational use of the undeveloped area, this would be the number of visitors, which would be of the order of tens of thousands perhaps. In regard to biodiversity conservation, it is not necessary for an individual to actually, or even potentially, be a visitor to the area for them to be affected by a reduction in its conservation value. There is evidence from a variety of sources that many individuals are willing to pay to promote wildlife conservation in areas that they will never visit. In regard to conservation, the whole population of the nation in which the threatened wilderness area is located is generally seen as the relevant population, in which case we are looking at a value for N of the order of millions. Indeed, for wilderness areas that are internationally famous for their wildlife it could plausibly be argued that it is a proportion (the relatively affluent inhabitants of the developed world) of the global population that is the relevant population, making N of the order of tens or hundreds of millions. In that case, the per capita valuation of the conservation cost of development required to give a value for EC greater than the project's NPV' may be

very small. Box 12.4 in the next chapter illustrates these points about inverse ECBA for an Australian experience with ECBA.

11.3.2 The Krutilla–Fisher model

NPV is the result of discounting and summing over the project's lifetime an annual net benefit stream which is

$$NB_t = B_{d,t} - C_{d,t} - EC_t \qquad (11.24)$$

where $B_{d,t}$, $C_{d,t}$ and EC_t are the annual, undiscounted, amounts for $t = 1, 2, \ldots, T$, and where T is the project lifetime, corresponding to the present values B_d, C_d and EC. The environmental costs of going ahead with the project, the EC_t, are at the same time the environmental benefits of not proceeding with it. Instead of EC_t we could write $B(P)_t$ for the stream of environmental benefits of preservation.[4] If we also use $B(D)_t$ and $C(D)_t$ for the benefit and cost streams associated with development when environmental impacts are ignored, so that $B(D)_t - C(D)_t$ is what gets discounted to give NPV', then equation 11.24 can also be written as:

$$NB_t = B(D)_t - C(D)_t - B(P)_t \qquad (11.25)$$

It will now be convenient to treat time as continuous, so that instead of

$$NPV = \sum_0^T \{B(D)_t - C(D)_t - B(P)_t\}/(1 + r)^t$$

we use

$$NPV = \int_0^T \{B(D)_t - C(D)_t - B(P)_t\}e^{-rt}dt$$

which can be written:

$$NPV = \int_0^T \{B(D)_t - C(D)_t\}e^{-rt}dt - \int_0^T B(P)_t e^{-rt}dt$$

$$(11.26)$$

---

[4] In some of the literature on wilderness development there would also be distinguished $C(P)$ for the costs of preservation, where such costs are those associated with, for example, managing the national park set up to realise preservation. Here we do not explicitly introduce such costs as this simplifies without any essential loss. Our $B(P)$ can be interpreted as preservation benefits net of any such costs. Clearly, such an interpretation does not substantially affect the plausibility of the assumptions about relative price movements to be introduced shortly.

Krutilla and Fisher (1975) introduced important and persuasive arguments as to why it should be assumed that the value of wilderness amenity services will, relative to the prices of the inputs to and outputs from development, be increasing over time. The arguments concern substitution possibilities, technical progress and the income elasticity of demand for wilderness services.

In the Krutilla–Fisher model the development option is seen as producing extracted intermediate outputs. It is typically the case that these intermediate outputs have relatively close substitutes. Moreover, the degree of substitutability tends to increase over time as technical knowledge develops. If we consider hydroelectric power, for example, it is clear that this form of power has many close substitutes, such as power from fossil fuel and nuclear sources. Technological advances have increased these substitution possibilities in recent decades, and will almost certainly continue to do so in the foreseeable future. If fusion power were to become technically and commercially viable, very long-term substitution possibilities will have been opened up. Finally, one would expect that rising demand for the extractive outputs of the development use can be met at decreasing real costs over time, as energy production and conversion benefits from technological innovation.

This contrasts strongly with the case of wilderness preservation benefits. The substitution possibilities here are often effectively zero, and there is no reason to suppose that they will become greater due to technical progress. Second, it is plausible and consistent with the evidence that environmental amenity services, and especially those of wilderness areas, have a high income elasticity of demand. But, third, technological progress itself cannot augment the supply of such services.

With economic growth and technological change it is reasonable to assume a tendency for the relative value of amenity services from undeveloped environmental assets to increase. A simple way to introduce this into equation 11.26 is to assume that preservation benefits grow at the rate a, while development benefits and costs are constant, so that

$$\text{NPV} = \int_0^T \{B - C\}\,e^{-rt}dt - \int_0^T \{Pe^{at}\}e^{-rt}dt \quad (11.27)$$

where B and C are the constant development benefit and cost flows, while Pe^{at} is the growing flow of preservation benefits. This can be written as

$$\text{NPV} = \text{NPV}' - \int_0^T Pe^{-(r-a)t}dt \quad (11.28)$$

Note here, first, that for $a > 0$, NPV will be less than for $a = 0$, for given NPV'. This means that for a given NPV', a development project is less likely to pass the intertemporal allocative efficiency test if the Krutilla–Fisher arguments are accepted and incorporated into ECBA. The second point to note is that if $a = r$ then, in effect, preservation benefits are not discounted. If it were to be assumed that $a > r$, then those benefits would effectively get discounted at a negative rate, and the discounted stream for P_t would itself be growing over time.

Now, let us suppose that $T \to \infty$. There are two reasons for making this assumption. First, it means that we can use a standard mathematical result which greatly simplifies the analysis.[5] The result is that

$$\int_0^\infty xe^{-rt} = x\int_0^\infty e^{-rt} = \frac{x}{r}$$

where x is some constant. The present value of a constant sum x for ever is x divided by the relevant interest rate r. This result is actually quite a good approximation where T is of the order of 100. For $r = 0.05$, the present value of

x for 50 years is $0.9128(x/r)$
x for 75 years is $0.9742(x/r)$
x for 100 years is $0.9924(x/r)$
x for 125 years is $0.9978(x/r)$

and for T fixed, the approximation gets closer as r increases.

The second reason for having $T \to \infty$ is that in practice for wilderness development projects, T is

---

Table 11.9 $P/(r - a)$ for $P = 1$

a	For $r = 0.05$	For $r = 0.075$
0	20	13.33
0.01	25	15.37
0.02	33.33	18.18
0.03	50	22.22
0.04	100	28.57
0.05	∞	40
0.06		66.67
0.075		∞

appropriately taken to be a very large number. T is the project lifetime, which is defined not by the date at which the project ceases to serve the function for which it was undertaken, but the date at which the longest-lived consequence of the project ceases. Thus, for example, if the project is a mine with an extraction life of 50 years, but where vegetation will take 200 years to recover after the closure of the mine, then T is 250.

Applying the result above in equation 11.28, it becomes:

$$NPV = NPV' - P/(r - a)$$ (11.29)

Note that as a increases, so $P/(r - a)$ increases, so that for NPV′ given, NPV decreases. This is illustrated in Table 11.9, which shows how the second term in equation 11.29 varies with the value of a for $r = 0.05$ and $r = 0.075$, where $P = 1$. Note that the long-term rate of economic growth is generally taken to be around 2.5%, that is, 0.025, and that it can be argued that this provides a plausible lower bound for the value that should be assumed for a. Note also that for $a > r$ the standard result used to go from equation 11.28 to equation 11.29 does not hold, because, as noted above, the discounted P_t are growing over time. For P at some value other than 1, the entries in Table 11.9 are the factors by which P, the current value of preservation benefits, would be multiplied to give the value of their loss for ever.

11.3.3 Discount rate adjustment?

Conservationists sometimes argue that when doing an ECBA of a project giving rise to long-lasting environmental damage, a lower discount rate should be used as this will give more weight to environ-

mental costs far into the future, thus making it less likely that the project will get the go-ahead. This argument is not generally valid. We can consider what is involved by first writing equation 11.27 as

$$NPV = \{B - C\}\int_0^T e^{-rt}dt - P\int_0^T e^{-(r-a)t}dt$$

or, using D for net development benefits,

$$NPV = D\int_0^T e^{-rt}dt - P\int_0^T e^{-(r-a)t}dt$$

Using the standard result from above as an approximation for very large T, this is:

$$NPV = \frac{D}{r} - \frac{P}{r - a}$$ (11.30)

Now, thus far in treating $D = (B - C)$ as constant over all t we have overlooked one feature of development projects, which is that they typically involve a short initial period with capital expenditure but no sales revenue – digging the mine or building the dam for the hydroelectric facility – followed by a long period with running costs and sales revenues. The stylised facts here can be captured by rewriting equation 11.30 as

$$NPV = -X + \frac{D}{r} - \frac{P}{r - a}$$ (11.31)

where X is the initial start-up cost, which does not get discounted.

Suppose that X is 1000, D is 75 and P is 12.5 in monetary units, say millions of pounds. Consider first a case where it is assumed that $a = 0$. Then

$$NPV = -X + \frac{D - P}{r}$$ (11.32)

and for $r = 0.055$ NPV is 136.37, while for $r = 0.045$ NPV is 388.89. For these numbers, lowering the discount rate has increased the NPV. This is because reducing the discount rate affects both development net benefits and environmental costs in the same way. From Equation 11.32 it is clear that, for $(D - P)$ positive, reducing r will increase NPV. Of course, to the extent that both D and P are not everlasting, we are dealing here with an approximation. But for time horizons of 100 years or more, it will be a close approximation.

Now suppose that it is assumed that a in equation 11.31 is 0.025. In this case, for $r = 0.055$ the NPV is -53.03, while for $r = 0.045$ the NPV is 41.67. Reducing the discount rate shifts the ECBA decision from rejection of the project to going ahead with it. Lowering r increases D/r by more than it increases $P/(r - a)$. The point here is not that reducing the interest rate for this kind of project will increase the NPV for any values for D and P and any initial r. From equation 11.31 it is clear that this would not be the case. The point is to provide an illustration of a counter-example to the proposition that reducing r will always work against projects with damaging and long-lasting environmental effects. That proposition is not generally true. While reducing r gives more weight to environmental damage very far into the future, it also gives more weight to net development benefits moderately far into the future, and far into the future if they continue that long.[6]

11.3.4 Objections to environmental cost–benefit analysis

In order to do ECBA it is necessary to figure out what EC is. The non-market valuation methods by which economists seek to measure EC are considered in the next chapter. As we shall see there, there is some dispute about the accuracy of the methods. Some argue that the methods do not produce reliable information for inclusion in ECBA. Some, mainly economists, who take this position consider that the existing methods can be improved so as to provide reliable information, and/or that new methods can be developed that will produce reliable information. Others take the view that there are inherent limitations to the accuracy of non-market valuation, and hence to that of ECBA. As we shall see in the next chapter, the environmental valuation methods require that environmental impacts are arguments in well-behaved utility functions. Some, economists and others, argue, and provide evidence to support the argument, that this assumption is not satisfied, in

that people do not, in fact, relate to the environment in this way. If this is true, then non-market valuation methods cannot do what ECBA requires them to.

These arguments will be reviewed in the next chapter, after we have worked through the methods to which they relate. Here we are concerned with a different sort of objection to ECBA. Many people, who are mainly but not exclusively non-economists, take the view that it is simply the wrong way, on ethical grounds, to inform social decision making where there are serious environmental impacts at issue.

ECBA is applied welfare economics. We discussed the ethical basis for welfare economics in Chapter 3. Here we can summarise by saying that welfare economics is based on a particular form of utilitarianism, which is 'consequentialist' and 'subjectivist' in nature. It is consequentialist in that actions are to be judged in terms of their consequences for human individuals. It is only human individuals that are of interest – only humans have 'moral standing'. It is subjectivist in that the measure of what is good for a human individual is that human individual's own assessment. The individual's assessment is to be ascertained from his or her preferences as revealed in behaviour. All of this is roughly encapsulated in the idea of 'consumer sovereignty'. There are two classes of ethical objection to this way of proceeding.

The first accepts that only human individuals have moral standing but rejects consumer sovereignty, arguing that individual preferences are a poor guide to individual human interests. Following Penz (1986), four particular arguments can be distinguished:

1. Individuals may be inadequately informed as to the consequences for themselves of the alternatives they face.
2. Individuals may be insufficiently deliberative in assessing the consequences of alternative choices.
3. Individuals may lack self-knowledge in the sense that they cannot properly relate the consequences of alternative choices to their preferences.

---

[6] The analysis here is based on Porter (1982), where there is a more rigorous and extended discussion. See also chapter 8 of Common (1995) for a detailed numerical illustration of these points.

4. Individuals' preferences may not reflect their true interests due to 'preference shaping' arising from socialisation processes and advertising.

These arguments are not restricted to the environmental context, but have been argued to have special force there: see, for example, Vatn and Bromley (1995) and Norton (1994). The philosopher Mark Sagoff (1988, 1994, 1998) particularly has argued against social choice on the basis of 'preference satisfaction', and for social choice by 'deliberative citizens' rather than 'consumers' in the environmental context. His point is that where serious environmental issues are involved, it is simply wrong to appeal to the self-interested preferences that might be acceptable as the criterion for deciding how much whisky as opposed to beer to produce. Sagoff argues that the correct way to make decisions with serious environmental implications is as the result of the deliberations of citizens – individuals whose views reflect their assessment of what is good for society.[7]

A second class of argument is that the scope of ethical concern should not be restricted to humans, that animals and plants (and in some versions non-living entities) should have 'moral standing': see, for examples, Naess (1972), Goodpaster (1978), Regan (1981) and Singer (1979, 1993). Booth (1994) argues that 'cost–benefit analysis cannot be legitimately applied where, as they should be, non-human natural entities are viewed as morally considerable' (p. 241), and that the ethically correct principle for social decision making is that 'Destruction of the natural environment shall not be undertaken unless absolutely necessary to maintain the real incomes of all human individuals at a level required for the living of a decent human life' (p. 251). This has affinities with the safe minimum standard idea, mentioned in Chapter 6 and to be discussed further in Chapter 13. That idea is based upon a consequentialist theory restricted to human interests, but recognises the uncertainties that attend predicting the future costs of current environmental damage.

11.3.4.1 Sustainable development and environmental valuation

We considered sustainability and sustainable development in Chapters 2, 3 and 4, where we argued that a commitment to sustainable development involves an appreciation of the facts of economy–environment interdependence and an ethical position. We saw that such a commitment could take the form of adopting a different objective function from the one routinely used in welfare economics, or of retaining the standard objective function and maximising it subject to sustainability constraints.

Common and Perrings (1992) show that observing sustainability constraints may involve overriding the outcomes that are consistent with consumer sovereignty. Individuals' preferences may be consistent with the requirements for sustainable development, but there is no guarantee that they will be, even if it is assumed that individuals are well informed. It follows that market failure correction, which is what ECBA and environmental valuation seek to deliver, is not sufficient for sustainability.

Suppose that we could ascertain accurately the aggregate monetary measure of the loss that consumers would suffer as the result of a decline in some environmental indicator. It does not follow that an ECBA on the project involved would produce an outcome consistent with sustainability requirements. It may be, for example, that the project would lead to the extinction of some species of termite that plays a key role in ecosystem function, and hence loss of resilience, but that EC would be, nonetheless, insufficient to stop the project. There is a reason for the choice of this example. Ecologists understand that termites do, in fact, play key roles in ecosystem function. There are good reasons – introspection and evidence from non-market valuation exercises – to suppose that the monetary measure of the loss

---

[7] It should be noted that self-interest as assumed in economics does not exclude the possibility of altruism – other individuals' consumption could well be arguments in my utility function with positive derivatives (negative derivatives would imply envy). Sen (1977) distinguishes between this kind of altruism, which he calls 'sympathy' and altruism as 'commitment' which is where my concern for others is based on ethical principles and could involve my acting in their interests even though it reduces my own utility. Commitment would be a characteristic of Sagoff's 'citizens' but not of his 'consumers'.

suffered on account of the extinction of a termite species would be small.

In Chapter 4 we noted that 'weak' and 'strong' sustainability are different views about substitution possibilities rather than different views about what sustainability is. Strong sustainability proponents argue for the maintenance of natural capital on the grounds that human-made capital cannot substitute for it so as to permit constant consumption. Weak sustainability proponents, a group that includes most economists, argue for keeping the total stock of capital, human-made and natural, intact, and consumption constant, by substituting human-made for natural capital as the latter is depleted. This is not an ethical difference. Weak and strong sustainabilists have the same concern for intergenerational justice. They differ about the facts, the circumstances in which what that concern means in terms of action must be worked out.

Some of those who object to ECBA do so on the grounds that it implicitly involves the same assumptions about substitution possibilities as the weak sustainability position does, which assumptions are, in fact, incorrect. As noted above, there is no reason why a properly conducted ECBA would not allow a project known to entail species extinction to go ahead. The critics argue that this means that it is effectively being assumed that the services that the species provides can be substituted for by some other species and/or human-made capital, and that this assumption is wrong. They would argue that the domain of ECBA should be limited to cases where it is known that the project in question will not have impacts that entail the loss of environmental services for which there is no susbstitute. Given that these critics generally assume that possibilities for substituting for environmental services are very limited, this argument would greatly limit the range of applicability of ECBA.

11.3.5 Alternatives to environmental cost–benefit analysis

In order to briefly review the nature of some of the alternatives to ECBA that have been advocated, it will be convenient to consider a simple constructed example of a decision-making problem.[8]

Suppose that there are two towns linked by a four-lane highway built before both grew rapidly in population. The highway is frequently affected by severe traffic jams, and the government is considering three options for dealing with this problem. Option A is simply to build another four-lane highway between the two towns. Option B is to do that but to reserve one lane in each direction for specially built buses, with a view to reducing the emissions of CO_2 per person-mile travelled on this route. The third option considered is to build a new railway link rather than a new highway. It is thought that this could further reduce emissions and have less impact on wildlife and visual amenity.

However the decision is eventually to be taken, the first step is to assemble the basic information about each option in terms of costs, impact on the perceived problem, and environmental impact. This involves having engineers produce designs and hence costings for each option. Given the designs, the engineers can estimate the impact of each option on traffic flows on the existing highway and the new facilities, and hence the impact on the congestion problem. Traffic flow data will also permit of estimates of the CO_2 emissions associated with each option. Given the designs and routes, environmental scientists can be asked to assess the impacts on wildlife and landscape amenity values.

This whole exercise would often be referred to as an environmental impact assessment, or an environmental and social impact assessment, or an impact assessment. The point is that at this stage what is at issue is just what would happen under each option – the objective here is not to evaluate the options, but simply to determine what they each involve. The complete separation of impact assessment from evaluation is possible conceptually, and helps to make clear what is involved in the various approaches to the evaluation and decision-making stages. In practice the separation is not clear-cut. Some commentators use the term 'environmental impact assessment' to include processes which are actually about evaluation rather than impact description. Many accounts

---

[8] The example used is based on one provided in Janssen and Munda (1999) who go into more detail on multi-criteria analysis.

Table 11.10 Options for reducing traffic delays

	A. Highway	B. Highway and Buses	C. Railway
Cost 10^6£	250	300	500
Time Saving 10^6 hours per year	10 000	8000	6000
CO_2 Emissions 10^3 tonnes per year	1 000	800	200
Wildlife and Amenity Qualitative	Bad	Bad	Moderate

of cost–benefit analysis focus exclusively on the evaluation of impacts, which can suggest that assessing the impacts is less of a problem than their evaluation. In fact, for many projects impact assessment is itself a large and difficult task.

It also needs to be noted that it would really be more descriptive of what is involved at this stage to refer to impact estimation rather than assessment. What will happen in the future under each option cannot be known with certainty in any of the dimensions of impact. Even cost data are estimates, which in the case of large engineering projects almost always turn out in the event to be significant underestimates. In what follows here we largely ignore imperfect knowledge of project impacts; Chapter 13 is mainly about the implications of risk and uncertainty for the ECBA approach to decision making.

One way of thinking about the distinction between impact assessment and evaluation is in terms of the role of expertise. Impact assessment is that part of the overall decision-making process where most people would regard it as appropriate to rely primarily on expert opinion. If we want an estimate of the effects on CO_2 emissions of alternative transport projects, for example, it would generally be agreed that it is better to ask trained traffic engineers and economists than to conduct a poll of a random sample of the population. If, on the other hand, it is a matter of choosing between two projects with given impacts, it could be argued that the choice should not be left to experts, but should reflect the preferences of the affected population as between the two sets of impacts. Impact assessment is that part of project appraisal that it would be generally agreed should be left to the relevant experts.

For our illustrative transport problem, assume that the impact assessment has been done and produces the data shown in Table 11.10. The impacts of the three options on the problem that is the origin of the various options, traffic jams and extended journey times, are measured in terms of (estimated) millions of hours saved per year. In terms of time savings, the more costly the option the less effective it is. CO_2 emissions effects are measured as tonnes arising per year under each option, and incurring more cost does more to reduce emissions. Whereas cost, time savings and emissions estimates can all be expressed quantitatively, we are assuming that the expert assessment of the wildlife and amenity impacts can only be expressed qualitatively. This is what is actually the case for many types of impact considered in actual environmental impact assessment exercises.

Before looking at some of the alternatives to it, let us briefly consider how ECBA would be used to appraise these projects and make a decision as between them. In our earlier account of project appraisal and cost–benefit analysis, we assumed that a decision had to be made as to whether or not to go ahead with a single project. Whether looked at from the commercial or the social perspective, the rule is to go ahead with the project if it has positive net present value – what differs as between commercial and social appraisals is that the latter takes account of costs and benefits that do not have market prices attached to them. It will be clear from our account of the logic of the net present value criterion, and from the earlier discussion of intertemporal efficiency, that where a choice has to be made between two projects, the one with the higher NPV should be undertaken. Equivalently, the one with the higher rate of return should be undertaken. Where there are several competing projects they should be ranked by NPV/rate of return.

In the case now being considered, the ECBA decision rule is to adopt the option which has the highest NPV, provided that that is positive, or equivalently to adopt the option with the highest rate of return, provided that it is higher than the test rate. Implementing this rule means setting out the time profile of each option in terms of arising flows of costs and non-monetary impacts, assigning monetary values to those impacts, and then using the agreed discount rate to arrive at an NPV figure for each option. The means by which monetary values would be assigned are discussed in detail in the next chapter. Broadly, time savings could be valued based on observed data about earnings per unit time, whereas there are no observed data that could be used to put a money value on either CO_2 emissions or wildlife and amenity impacts – people would have to be asked about their willingness to pay to secure improvements or avoid deteriorations here.

The important point is that it is the preferences of those affected that are to be used to evaluate the options. As already noted, objections take two basic forms. One argues that those preferences cannot be ascertained accurately. The other is that preferences are the wrong way to evaluate the options.

We now consider some alternatives to ECBA in the context of this simple constructed example.

11.3.5.1 Cost-effectiveness analysis

The basic idea of cost-effectiveness analysis is to select the option which achieves some specified objective at the least cost. Suppose, for example, that it had been decided that the minimum acceptable time saving was 8000 million hours per year. In that case the impact assessment rules out Option C, the railway. If just the monetary costs of construction are considered, Option A would be selected as it (over)achieves the target and costs less than the other option that meets the objective. However, there is no reason in principle why the monetary valuation methods that would be used to conduct an ECBA could not be used to bring emissions and wildlife and amenity impact into the ambit of the costs considered. In that case, people's preferences could be such that the poorer performance of A in emissions terms would lead to B being the selected option. Using preferences in this way would, of course, expose cost-effectiveness analysis to the same criticism as ECBA. In any case, cost-effectiveness involves, as ECBA does not, giving absolute priority to one aspect of performance.

11.3.5.2 Multi-criteria analysis

Multi-criteria analysis, MCA, is usually described as analysis which uses the preferences of decision

makers to resolve situations where, as in our constructed example, the options get ranked differently on the various criteria that are considered relevant. We will come back to the matter of using the preferences of the decision makers after explaining how MCA uses preferences. There are actually many MCA methods, differentiated by the way in which the option evaluations on different criteria are combined to produce a single choice of option. Here we will use the simplest method, weighted summation, to illustrate what MCA basically involves: more detailed accounts of MCA and the methods that it can utilise are provided in the references given in the Further Reading section at the end of the chapter.

Some of the methods that have been proposed for MCA can work with qualitative data, but the weighted sums method cannot, so the first step is to convert the qualitative data in Table 11.10 to quantitative data. This is done by simply identifying each qualitative rating with a number as in

Bad	Moderate	Slight
3	2	1

in which case the evaluations of the three options on the four criteria are:

	A. Highway	B. Highway and Buses	C. Railway
Cost 10^6£	250	300	500
Time Saving 10^6 hours per year	10 000	8000	6000
CO_2 Emissions 10^3 tonnes per year	1 000	800	200
Wildlife and Amenity Qualitative	3	3	2

The numbers for the Wildlife and Amenity assessments could, of course, have been assigned the other way round, with a higher number going with a smaller impact. One of the Problems at the end of the chapter invites you to see the effect that that would have on what follows here.

The next step is to convert the data to dimensionless form, so as to permit aggregation. This is done by expressing the criterion outcome for each option as a ratio to the best outcome for the criterion which is set equal to 1. Consider Time Saving. On this criterion Option A is the best, so it gets set at 1, B at 8000/10 000 = 0.8, and C at 6000/10 000 = 0.6. For Cost, best is smallest, which is Option A at 250. Then B/A = 300/250 = 1.2 for which the reciprocal is 0.8333, and C/A = 500/250 = 2 with reciprocal 0.5. Proceeding in the same way for Emissions and Wildlife and Amenity, we get the dimensionless evaluation table:

	Highway	Highway and Buses	Railway
Cost	1.0000	0.8333	0.5000
Time Saving	1.0000	0.8000	0.6000
CO_2 Emissions	0.2000	0.2500	1.0000
Wildlife and Amenity	0.6667	0.6667	1.0000

The final step to is aggregate for each option across its criteria evaluations using weights that reflect the preferences of the decision makers, in terms of the relative importance attached to the various criteria. Suppose that the weights are agreed by the decision makers involved to be

Costs	0.3
Time Saving	0.3
CO_2 Emissions	0.2
Wildlife and Amenity	0.2

Then multiplying the entries in the dimensionless evaluation table by the weights and summing down columns gives

	Highway	Highway and Buses	Railway
Cost	0.3000	0.2500	0.1500
Time Saving	0.3000	0.2400	0.1800
CO_2 Emissions	0.0400	0.0500	0.2000
Wildlife and Amenity	0.1333	0.1333	0.2000
Sum	0.7733	0.6733	0.7300

so that the options are ranked: Highway, Railway, Highway and Buses.

For the weights

Costs	0.2
Time Saving	0.2
CO_2 Emissions	0.4
Wildlife and Amenity	0.2

we get

	Highway	Highway and Buses	Railway
Cost	0.2000	0.1667	0.1000
Time Saving	0.2000	0.1600	0.1200
CO_2 Emissions	0.0800	0.1000	0.4000
Wildlife and Amenity	0.1333	0.1333	0.2000
Sum	0.6133	0.5600	0.8200

and the ranking is: Railway, Highway, Highway and Buses.

As noted above, in discussing MCA it is usually taken that the weights used for summation reflect the preferences of the decision makers. However, it is clear that there is nothing inherent in MCA that would prevent those decision makers basing the weightings used on assessments of the preferences of the affected population, or at least taking account of those preferences in forming their own. The government could, for example, commission an opinion poll on the weights. We noted above that one of the objections that is raised against the use of the population's preferences in ECBA is that those preferences might well be based on inadequate information. Clearly, exactly the same objection could be raised in the present context. We also noted that Sagoff (1988, 1994) argues that the correct way to make decisions with serious environmental implications is through the *deliberations* of citizens. The point here is that Sagoff, and many others, think that individuals interacting and debating with one another will produce more informed preferences. We now note two ways that decision makers could use to get information on informed preferences.

11.3.5.3 Deliberative polling

Deliberative polling involves running an opinion poll then asking respondents to attend a meeting at which they will collectively consider the issues, by hearing and questioning expert witnesses and debating among themselves. At the end of this process, the participants are asked to again respond to the original survey instrument. As reported in Fishkin (1997) the results, in regard to the movement of opinion as between the first poll and that conducted after deliberation, are often striking. As an example, consider the results from three such exercises conducted in Texas. In Texas regulated public utilities are required to consult the public as part of their Integrated Resource Planning, and three chose to use deliberative polling to do this in regard to electricity supply planning. Respondents were asked to specify their first choice for the provision of additional power from four alternatives: renewable sources, fossil fuel sources, energy conservation, buying in electricity. As between the two polls respondents attended meetings at which they were provided with, *inter alia*, cost data on these four alternatives. In each case there was the same pattern of response variation as between the before and after polls. As first choice, renewable sources fell from 67% to 16%, 71% to 35%, and 67% to 28%, while conservation rose from 11% to 46%, 7% to 31%, and 16% to 50%. The cost data showed conservation to be less expensive than renewable sources.

An obvious problem with deliberative polling is that it is very costly. The idea is to poll a random sample of sufficient size to produce results up to the standard usual in opinion polling. This may mean hundreds of people, which makes the information provision and deliberative parts of the exercise expensive, especially where the population of interest covers a large geographical area. As practised to date, deliberative polling has usually involved opinions on somewhat broadbrush issues of interest to large media organisations. However, as exemplified by the example from Texas, the general strategy could, given funding, be applied to more narrowly defined decision problems, with respondents being required to consider resource constraints and their implications.

11.3.5.4 Citizens' juries

A citizens' jury exercise is less expensive than deliberative polling. In a report on experience with citizens' juries in the UK, Coote and Lenaghan (1997, p. ii) describe what is involved as follows:

> Citizens' juries involve the public in their capacity as ordinary citizens with no special axe to grind. They are usually commissioned by an organisation which has power to act on their recommendations. Between 12 and 16 jurors are recruited, using a combination of random and stratified sampling, to be broadly representative of their community. Their task is to address an important question about policy or planning. They are brought together for four days, with a team of two moderators. They are fully briefed about the background to the question, through written information and evidence from witnesses. Jurors scrutinise the information, cross-examine the witnesses and discuss different aspects of the question in small groups and plenary sessions. Their conclusions are compiled in a report that is returned to the jurors for their approval before being submitted to the commissioning authority. The jury's verdict need not be unanimous, nor is it binding. However, the commissioning authority is required to publicise the jury and its findings, to respond within a set time and either to follow its recommendations or to explain publicly why not.

Obviously the particulars described here are not immutable, and there could be considerable variation consistent with the underlying rationale.

In regard to underlying rationale, Coote and Lenaghan (p. ii, italics in original) put it as follows:

> Compared with other models, citizens' juries offer a unique combination of *information, time, scrutiny, deliberation and independence.*

Coote and Lenaghan report positively on the citizens' jury process. Of particular interest here, they judge that 'Jurors readily adopt a community perspective', that most 'accept that resources are finite and were willing to participate in decisions about priority setting', and that 'a substantial minority of jurors said they had changed their minds in the course of the session'. It should also be noted that a number of the participating jurors expressed 'strong doubts about the jury's capacity to influence the commissioning authority'. Experience in using citizens' juries in relation to decisions concerning the natural environment is limited; some references will be found under Further Reading.

11.3.5.5 Overview

In practice, decisions with serious environmental implications are generally taken by the management of private firms, or by politicians (or their delegated officers). The hope is that where private commercial decisions have serious environmental implications, those decisions will require in some way to be approved by government (or its delegated agency) taking the social welfare view of the options involved. We say 'the hope is' because in order for this to be the case law must be drafted so as to define the circumstances in which private decisions need governmental approval. It is in the nature of the case – imperfect knowledge of the future consequences of current action – that there can be no guarantee that all private decisions that will turn out to have serious environmental consequences will be subject to governmental, or other social, review. Equally, there will be circumstances in which public-sector projects which turn out to have serious environmental consequences do not get properly scrutinised.

Focusing on those cases where scrutiny is exercised, we have seen that the appraisal method preferred by economists has many critics, and that there are alternative methods. Basically all involve two stages. First, expert knowledge is used to estimate project impacts, then, preferences are used to reach a decision on the basis of the information about impacts. One argument often used in favour of ECBA is that the preferences that it uses are those of the affected general public rather than those of the experts. However, as we have seen, this 'democratisation' at the preference stage is not unique, or at least need not be unique, to ECBA. We have also, in this chapter and earlier chapters, seen that the efficiency criterion of ECBA does not necessarily imply that any particular concept of equity will be honoured in decision making, and does not guarantee sustainability. It is equally the case that MCA, for example, may, depending on the preferences used, produce decisions that are inefficient, inequitable, and inconsistent with sustainability. Advocates of deliberative processes have yet to demonstrate that these necessarily produce, for example, decisions consistent with sustainability requirements.

Finally, we can note that those charged with reaching a decision on a project thought to involve serious environmental consequences do not have to regard ECBA, MCA and deliberative processes as mutually exclusive means for the provision of advice. In each case a necessary first step is the attempt to document all of the consequences of the project, or of each of the options under consideration. This is itself an important discipline on the decision-making process. There is then no reason why the impact assessment data should not be input to an ECBA, an MCA and, say, a citizens' jury. Unless these all produce the same result, a decision still has to be made by politicians or their appointed agents. All project appraisal methods should be regarded, as a practical matter, as providing information to decision makers rather than as providing them with the answer.

Summary

Cost–benefit analysis is an application of welfare economics which is intended to select projects according to efficiency criteria. The chapter began with a review of the welfare economics from which the intertemporal efficiency conditions derive, and with a statement of those conditions. We then looked at the net present value test for project appraisal, first as conducted by private agents, and second as conducted on behalf of society. In the latter context we discussed the important, and somewhat controversial, matter of the choice of discount rate. The third part of the chapter looked at the application of cost–benefit analysis to environmental issues, such as wilderness preservation. Finally, we looked at some objections to cost–benefit analysis as the basis on which social choices concerning the environment should be made, and briefly considered some alternative methodologies and techniques.

The treatment of the derivation of the conditions for intertemporal efficiency in introductory and intermediate microeconomics texts usually leaves much to be desired. An exception is Varian (1987). Chapter 4 of Dasgupta and Heal (1979), which is an environmental and resource economics text, covers the basic issues. Dasgupta (1994) covers the basic optimal growth model with and without the use of a non-renewable resource as input to production. Many microeconomics texts do cover well the analytics of intertemporal behaviour by firms and individuals: see, for example, Gravelle and Rees (1981) and Hirshliefer (1980). Common (1995) uses numerical examples to work through the basic ideas in intertemporal efficiency, behaviour in the market for loanable funds, and optimal growth.

Most intermediate microeconomics texts discuss project appraisal according to both commercial and social criteria: see, for examples, Gravelle and Rees (1981), Layard and Walters (1978) and Varian (1987). Cost–benefit analysis as such is the subject matter of Pearce and Nash (1981) and Hanley and Spash (1993) – the latter is especially about environmental application. The introduction to Layard and Glaister (1994) is a good overview of all of the main issues in cost–benefit analysis – subsequent chapters in the book deal with particular issues in more detail, or review applications in particular areas.

Applications of cost–benefit analysis to environmental issues will be found in journals such as the *Journal of Environmental Economics and Management, Environmental and Resource Economics* and *Environment and Development Economics*. Government departments and agencies frequently carry out or commission cost–benefit analyses and publish the results, often making them available via the internet. The Innovative Strategies and Economics Group of the US Environmental Protection Agency makes many papers and reports available at the Economics and Cost Analysis web site, www.epa.gov/ttn/ecas. See also the web site of the National Center for Environmental Economics which can be reached via the links from the EPA site, or directly at www.yosemite.epa.gov/ee/epa/eed.nsf/pages/homepage?Opendocument. A useful way into

UK government publications is to go to the web site for the Department of Environment Food and Rural Affairs, www.defra.gov.uk, and search on cost–benefit analysis.

There is an extensive literature on the principles and practice of the choice of discount rate for cost–benefit analysis. Arrow *et al.* (1996) provides an excellent point of entry to this literature, and is the source of the distinction between the prescriptive and descriptive approaches that was discussed in Chapter 3 here. Stiglitz (1994) is an excellent account of the main issues; see also Harberger (1971), Heal (1981), Marglin (1963), Broome (1992) and Common (1995). Lind (1982) investigates discounting and risk in energy policy. Mikesell (1977) looks in detail at the practical choice of discount rates, and the implications of that choice. Price (1993) is a critique of the conventional wisdom on all aspects of discounting.

The 1970s saw the publication of a number of books and papers concerning wilderness development. Many of these originated with the Washington DC organisation Resources for the Future, and involved the names Krutilla and Fisher. Particularly worth reading still are Krutilla and Fisher (1975) and Krutilla (1967). Porter (1982) provides an overview and synthesis of much of this literature. Resources for the Future publications span the whole range of resource and environmental economics, and can now be accessed at www.rff.org.

Foster (1997) is a collection of papers which cover most of the range of the ethical objections to environmental cost–benefit analysis, and discuss some alternative ways in which social decisions about the use of the environment might be made. The journal *Environmental Values* frequently includes papers about the ethical foundations of social choice in regard to the natural environment: Vol. 9, no 4 (November 2000) was, for example, a special issue on 'The accommodation of value in environmental decision-making'. *Ecological Economics* also frequently includes papers on these issues: see, for example, the special issue on 'Social processes of environmental valuation', Vol. 34, no 2, published in August 2000.

Glasson *et al.* (1994) is a very good introduction to the principles and practice of environmental impact assessment. Lee and Kirkpatrick (2000) is a collection of papers focusing mainly on the application of environmental impact assessment in developing countries. Janssen and Munda (1999) is a very useful brief survey of the principles and methods of multi-criteria analysis, on which see also Janssen (1992) for a fuller treatment. The UK Department for Transport, Local Government and the Regions produced (DTLR, 2001) a manual on multi-criteria analysis and its applications, which can be accessed at www.dtlr.gov.uk/about/multicrteria. Munda *et al.* (1994) is about qualitative assessment and Van Pelt (1993) relates multi-criteria analysis to sustainable development. Stirling (1997) makes a case for multi-criteria mapping as a means for informing decision making, rather than as a decision-making tool.

The August 2000 issue of *Ecological Economics* includes papers on multi-criteria analysis and citizens' juries.

Jacobs (1997) reviews the arguments for citizen deliberation as the basis for environmental decision-making, discusses the role of citizens' juries and related procedures, and provides useful references. The Jefferson Center, in the USA, is a non-profit organisation interested in 'providing tools for decision makers to more fully understand what citizens want to do about key issues'. Information about its experiences with citizens' juries can be found at www.jefferson-center.org. Information on experience in Australia with citizens' juries on environmental issues can be found at http://cjp.anu.edu.au. In 2001, Vol. 19, no 4 of *Environment and Planning C* was a special issue on participation and deliberation in environmental valuation and decision making.

Discussion questions

1. Should decisions about environmental policy be made on the basis of cost–benefit analysis?

2. In the context of a proposed hydroelectric development in a wilderness area, has the Krutilla–Fisher argument about the relative price movements that should be assumed in ECBA been affected by recent concerns about the implications for climate change of carbon dioxide emissions in fossil-fuel combustion and about nuclear power stations?

Problems

1. Derive the optimality conditions for the model specified in Appendix 11.1.

2. Consider the two social welfare functions

   $W_U = U(1) + U(2)$ (utilitarian)

   $W_R = \min\{U(1), U(2)\}$ (Rawlsian)

   where $U_i = \ln(X_i)$ is the utility enjoyed by the *i*th generation from the consumption X_i, $i = 1, 2$. Consider two projects:
   Project A: Generation 1 reduces consumption by 10 units. The investment yields 20 additional units of consumption for Generation 2.
   Project B: Generation 1 reduces consumption by 15 units. The investment yields 15 additional units of consumption for Generation 2.

   Let the pre-project level of consumption in Generation 1 be 100 units. Now consider three scenarios:

Scenario	Pre-project level of X_2
(i) No technology change	100
(ii) Technology improvement	120
(iii) Technology worsening (or loss of inputs)	80

   Use a tick to denote *Do project* or a cross to denote *Do not do project* in each cell of the following table to show whether the project (A or B) should be undertaken under each of the three scenarios, for the two cases of a utilitarian SWF (U) and a Rawlsian SWF (R).

		Scenario					
		(i)		(ii)		(iii)	
		U	R	U	R	U	R
Project	A						
	B						

3. The Safe Water Drinking Act required the United States Environmental Protection Agency to establish action standards for lead in drinking water. The EPA evaluated three options (labelled A, B and C below) using cost–benefit techniques. A selection of the results of this analysis is presented in the following table.

	Option		
	A	B	C
Total benefits	$68 957	$63 757	$24 325
Total costs	$6 272	$4 156	$3 655
Benefit to cost ratio	11.0	15.3	6.7
Marginal benefit (MB)	$5 192	$39 440	$24 325
Marginal cost (MC)	$2 117	$500	$3 665
MB to MC ratio	2.5	78.8	6.67

Monetary values in the table are 1988 $ million, based on a 20-year life, discounted to present value at 3%. Option A involves the strictest standard, Option C the least strict, with B intermediate. The marginal cost and benefit figures refer to incremental costs/benefits incurred in moving from no control to Option C, from Option C to Option B, and from Option B to A respectively. *Source*: EPA (1991). The EPA decision is discussed at length in Goodstein (1995), pp. 133–140.

The US Environmental Protection Agency selected Option B. Is Option B the economically efficient choice?

4. Solve equation 11.31 for a with NPV set at 0 to get an expression for a^*, the value of a that makes the project marginal, in terms of r, X, P and D. Treat X, P and D as parameters and find $\partial a^*/\partial r$. What can be said about its sign? What is its sign for the values used in the chapter when discussing discount rate adjustment, $X = 1000$, $D = 75$ and $P = 12.5$? Confirm the answer by evaluating a^* for $r = 0.055$ and $r = 0.045$, and explain it.

5. Rework the MCA example considered in the chapter:
   a. With the following scoring of the qualitative assessment of the wildlife and amenity impacts

Bad	Moderate	Slight
1	2	3

   b. With the following scoring of the qualitative assessment of the wildlife and amenity impacts

Bad	Moderate	Slight
10	20	30

Is it possible to find an order-preserving scoring that affects the result of the weighted summation MCA?

Appendix 11.1 Conditions for intertemporal efficiency and optimality

Appendix 5.1 considered the conditions for efficiency and optimality in a timeless economy. To do that it explicitly analysed an economy in which two individuals each consumed two commodities, each of which was produced by two firms, each using two kinds of input, capital and labour. We noted that having just two of everything simplified the analysis without any loss in regard to the essentials. In the same spirit, here we consider just two periods of time, which we label 0 and 1. Considering the Appendix 5.1 economy for just two periods would still produce a model with lots of variables and symbols. To keep things as simple as possible, while not overlooking anything essential, we will have each commodity produced by just one firm, and we will assume that the only input to production is capital. As will be seen, the result is still a fairly complicated, or at least cluttered, model, and in much of the literature intertemporal analysis works with models that involve aggregations of various kinds. We will look at some of the widely employed specialisations of the basic model at the end of this appendix. It is worth looking at the general model, as doing so makes clear the implicit assumptions in the aggregated models.

You may find it useful to take a look again at the appendices to Chapter 5 before working through this appendix and the next, so as to refresh your memory in regard to notation etc.

A11.1.1 Intertemporal rates of substitution and transformation

There are two individuals A and B, each of whom consumes two commodities X and Y, in each of two periods 0 and 1. Their utility functions are

$$U^A = U^A(X_0^A, X_1^A, Y_0^A, Y_1^A) \text{ and}$$
$$U^B = U^B(X_0^B, X_1^B, Y_0^B, Y_1^B)$$

where a superscript identifies an individual and a subscript a period. For derivatives, the notation to be used here is an extension of that used in Appendix 5.1 so as to indicate period. Thus, for example, we write U_{X0}^A for $\partial U^A/\partial X_0^A$, A's marginal utility with respect to the consumption of X in period 0.

We can now define intratemporal – within period – and intertemporal – across period – marginal rates of utility substitution. Thus, for examples, A's intratemporal MRUS with respect to X and Y in period 0 is

$$MRUS_{X0,Y0}^A \equiv -\frac{dY_0^A}{dX_0^A}$$

for $dX_1^A = dY_1^A = 0$, while A's intertemporal MRUS with respect to X in period 0 and X in period 1 is

$$MRUS_{X0,X1}^A \equiv -\frac{dX_1^A}{dX_0^A}$$

for $dY_0^A = dY_1^A = 0$. These MRUSs have the same interpretation as previously. Thus, for example, $MRUS_{X0,X1}^A$ is the slope of an indifference curve in

X_1^A/X_0^A space, multiplied by -1 so that MRUS is a positive number. Considering

$$dU^A = U_{X0}^A dX_0^A + U_{X1}^A dX_1^A = 0$$

for example, leads to

$$MRUS_{X0,X1}^A \equiv -\frac{dX_1^A}{dX_0^A} = \frac{U_{X0}^A}{U_{X1}^A}$$

The full set of marginal rates of utility substitution for individual A is:

$$MRUS_{X0,Y0}^A = \frac{U_{X0}^A}{U_{Y0}^A}, \quad MRUS_{X1,Y1}^A = \frac{U_{X1}^A}{U_{Y1}^A},$$

$$MRUS_{X0,X1}^A = \frac{U_{X0}^A}{U_{X1}^A}, \quad MRUS_{X0,Y1}^A = \frac{U_{X0}^A}{U_{Y1}^A},$$

$$MRUS_{Y0,Y1}^A = \frac{U_{Y0}^A}{U_{Y1}^A}, \quad MRUS_{Y0,X1}^A = \frac{U_{Y0}^A}{U_{X1}^A} \quad (11.33)$$

An exactly equivalent set can be written for individual B.

Consider the production of commodity X. The production function for period 0 is

$$X_0 = X_0(K_0^X)$$

where K_0^X is the amount of capital existing at the beginning of period 0, and hence the amount employed in the production of X during period 0. We make the assumption that the commodity X is such that it can either be consumed or added to the capital stock for the production of X. This greatly simplifies the analysis. Actually, of course, what happens is that the producers of X use some of the proceeds from sales of X to buy capital equipment. Our assumption short-circuits this and avoids the need to introduce further notation for capital goods and the price thereof. The output of X is, then, either sold for consumption, X^C, or invested, $X^I = K_1^X - K_0^X$, where K_1^X is the capital stock at the beginning of period 1. Thus, we have

$$X_0^C = X_0(K_0^X) - X_0^I = X_0(K_0^X) - (K_1^X - K_0^X)$$
$$= X_0(K_0^X) - K_1^X + K_0^X \quad (11.34a)$$

for period 0, and proceeding in the same way for period 1 gives

$$X_1^C = X_1(K_1^X) - X_1^I = X_1(K_1^X) - (K_2^X - K_1^X)$$
$$= X_1(K_1^X) - K_2^X + K_1^X \quad (11.34.b)$$

We are interested in the marginal shifting of the consumption of X as between periods 0 and 1 by a marginal change in the level of investment in period 0. We define the, intertemporal, marginal rate of transformation for X_0^C and X_1^C as

$$\text{MRT}_{0,1}^X \equiv -\frac{dX_1^C}{dX_0^C}$$

From equations 11.34

$$dX_0^C = X_{K0}dK_0^X - dK_1^X + dK_0^X$$

and

$$dX_1^C = X_{K1}dK_1^X - dK_2^X + dK_1^X$$

where $X_{K0} = \partial X_0/\partial K_0^X$ is the marginal product of capital in period 0, and similarly for X_{K1}. With $dK_0^X = dK_2^X = 0$

$$\frac{dX_1^C}{dX_0^C} = \frac{X_{K1}dK_1^X + dK_1^X}{-dK_1^X}$$

so that

$$\text{MRT}_{0,1}^X \equiv -\frac{dX_1^C}{dX_0^C} = 1 + X_{K1} \qquad (11.35a)$$

and similarly

$$\text{MRT}_{0,1}^Y \equiv -\frac{dY_1^C}{dY_0^C} = 1 + Y_{K1} \qquad (11.35b)$$

A11.1.2 Efficiency conditions

The problem to be considered to derive the intertemporal efficiency conditions is

Max $U^A = U^A(X_0^A, X_1^A, Y_0^A, Y_1^A)$

subject to

$$U^B(X_0^B, X_1^B, Y_0^B, Y_1^B) = Z$$

$$X_0(K_0^X) - (K_1^X - K_0^X) = X_0^A + X_0^B$$

$$X_1(K_1^X) - (K_2^X - K_1^X) = X_1^A + X_1^B$$

$$Y_0(K_0^Y) - (K_1^Y - K_0^Y) = Y_0^A + Y_0^B$$

$$Y_1(K_1^Y) - (K_2^Y - K_1^Y) = Y_1^A + Y_1^B$$

Here, Z is some arbitrary fixed level for B's utility, and the opening and closing stocks of capital in each line of production are taken as given. The allocation problem concerns the commodity consumptions of A and B in each period, and the amount of investment in each line of production.

The Lagrangian is

$$
\begin{aligned}
L = U^A = {}& U^A(X_0^A, X_1^A, Y_0^A, Y_1^A) \\
& + \lambda_1[U^B(X_0^B, X_1^B, Y_0^B, Y_1^B) - Z] \\
& + \lambda_2[X_0(K_0^X) - K_1^X + K_0^X - X_0^A - X_0^B] \\
& + \lambda_3[X_1(K_1^X) - K_2^X + K_1^X - X_1^A - X_1^B] \\
& + \lambda_4[Y_0(K_0^Y) - K_1^Y + K_0^Y - Y_0^A - Y_0^B] \\
& + \lambda_5[Y_1(K_1^Y) - K_2^Y + K_1^Y - Y_1^A - Y_1^B]
\end{aligned}
$$

giving the first-order conditions

$$\frac{\partial L}{\partial X_0^A} = U_{X0}^A - \lambda_2 = 0 \qquad (11.36a)$$

$$\frac{\partial L}{\partial X_1^A} = U_{X1}^A - \lambda_3 = 0 \qquad (11.36b)$$

$$\frac{\partial L}{\partial Y_0^A} = U_{Y0}^A - \lambda_4 = 0 \qquad (11.36c)$$

$$\frac{\partial L}{\partial Y_1^A} = U_{Y1}^A - \lambda_5 = 0 \qquad (11.36d)$$

$$\frac{\partial L}{\partial X_0^B} = \lambda_1 U_{X0}^B - \lambda_2 = 0 \qquad (11.36e)$$

$$\frac{\partial L}{\partial X_1^B} = \lambda_1 U_{X1}^B - \lambda_3 = 0 \qquad (11.36f)$$

$$\frac{\partial L}{\partial Y_0^B} = \lambda_1 U_{Y0}^B - \lambda_4 = 0 \qquad (11.36g)$$

$$\frac{\partial L}{\partial Y_1^B} = \lambda_1 U_{Y1}^B - \lambda_5 = 0 \qquad (11.36h)$$

$$\frac{\partial L}{\partial K_1^X} = -\lambda_2 + \lambda_3 X_{K1} + \lambda_3 = 0 \qquad (11.36i)$$

$$\frac{\partial L}{\partial K_1^Y} = -\lambda_4 + \lambda_5 Y_{K1} + \lambda_5 = 0 \qquad (11.36j)$$

From the eight conditions on consumption, 11.36a to 11.36h, using the MRUS definitions from Section A11.1.1, we have:

$$\text{MRUS}_{X0,Y0}^A = \text{MRUS}_{X0,Y0}^B = \lambda_2/\lambda_4 \qquad (11.37a)$$

$$\text{MRUS}_{X1,Y1}^A = \text{MRUS}_{X1,Y1}^B = \lambda_3/\lambda_5 \qquad (11.37b)$$

$$\text{MRUS}_{X0,X1}^A = \text{MRUS}_{X0,X1}^B = \lambda_2/\lambda_3 \qquad (11.37c)$$

$$\text{MRUS}_{X0,Y1}^A = \text{MRUS}_{X0,Y1}^B = \lambda_2/\lambda_5 \qquad (11.37d)$$

$$MRUS^A_{Y0,Y1} = MRUS^B_{Y0,Y1} = \lambda_4/\lambda_5 \qquad (11.37e)$$

$$MRUS^A_{Y0,X1} = MRUS^B_{Y0,X1} = \lambda_4/\lambda_3 \qquad (11.37f)$$

Note that these are an extended version of the consumption efficiency conditions for the intratemporal allocation problem – the two individuals must have the same MRUS for all possible pairs of commodities. In saying this we are treating the same physical commodity at two different dates as two different commodities – we are, for example, treating X in period 0 as a different commodity from X in period 1.

If we had explicitly shown a labour input to production, we would have obtained intratemporal production efficiency conditions, the same as those in Chapter 5, for each line of production in each period.

The necessary conditions relating to investment, 11.36i and 11.36j, can be written

$$1 + X_{K1} = \lambda_2/\lambda_3 \qquad (11.38a)$$

and

$$1 + Y_{K1} = \lambda_4/\lambda_5 \qquad (11.38.b)$$

and comparing these with 11.37c and 11.37e, using the definitions for the marginal rates of transformation provided in Section A.11.1.1 above, gives

$$MRUS^A_{X0,X1} = MRUS^B_{X0,X1} = MRT^X_{0,1} \qquad (11.39a)$$

$$MRUS^A_{Y0,Y1} = MRUS^B_{Y0,Y1} = MRT^Y_{0,1} \qquad (11.39b)$$

For each commodity, the intertemporal MRUS has to equal the MRT.

In the chapter, the conditions for intertemporal efficiency were stated, following the practice in much of the literature, in terms of rates of return to investment in different lines of production and the consumption discount rate. To demonstrate the equivalence of the conditions derived here with that statement of the conditions requires some definitions and an assumption.

Taking the assumption first. Assume that for both individuals

$$MRUS_{X0,Y0} = MRUS_{X1,Y1} \qquad (11.40)$$

which by 11.37a and 11.37b implies

$$\frac{\lambda_2}{\lambda_4} = \frac{\lambda_3}{\lambda_5}$$

or

$$\frac{\lambda_2}{\lambda_3} = \frac{\lambda_4}{\lambda_5}$$

which by 11.38a and 11.38b gives:

$$X_{K1} = Y_{K1} \qquad (11.41)$$

Efficiency requires the equalisation of the marginal product of capital in each of the lines of production.

This is equivalent to requiring equality of rates of return to investment, as in equation 11.3 in the chapter. The rate of return to investment is defined as difference between the increase in the next period consumption pay-off and the associated increase in current investment, expressed as a proportion of the increase in investment. In terms of X, the definition is

$$\delta_X \equiv \frac{dX^C_1 - dX^I_0}{dX^I_0}$$

where the increase in investment dX^I_0 entails an equal decrease consumption dX^C_0. Substituting $-dX^C_0$ for dX^I_0 in the definition

$$\delta_X = \frac{dX^C_1 - (-dX^C_0)}{-dX^C_0} = \frac{dX^C_1 + dX^C_0}{-dX^C_0} = -\frac{dX^C_1}{dX^C_0} - 1$$

which, using 11.35a, gives:

$$\delta_X = X_{K1}$$

Marginal products and rates of return are the same things. Hence, 11.41 can be written, as in the chapter, in terms of rates of return as:

$$\delta_X = \delta_Y \qquad (11.42)$$

Consider A's intertemporal marginal utility rate of substitution for commodity X and define as A's consumption discount rate for commodity X:

$$r^A_{X0,X1} \equiv MRUS^A_{X0,X1} - 1 \qquad (11.43a)$$

We can also define

$$r^A_{Y0,Y1} \equiv MRUS^A_{Y0,Y1} - 1 \qquad (11.43b)$$

for A, and

$$r^B_{X0,X1} \equiv MRUS^B_{X0,X1} - 1 \qquad (11.43c)$$

and

$$r^B_{Y0,Y1} \equiv MRUS^B_{Y0,Y1} - 1 \qquad (11.43d)$$

for B. With these definitions we can restate the intertemporal MRUS conditions from 11.37 in terms of commodity consumption discount rates as

$$r^{A}_{X0,X1} = r^{B}_{X0,X1} \tag{11.43e}$$

$$r^{A}_{Y0,Y1} = r^{B}_{Y0,Y1} \tag{11.43f}$$

in the same manner as equation 11.2 in the body of the chapter.

Using the definitions for commodity consumption discount rates, from 11.37c and 11.38a, replacing marginal product by rate of return gives

$$1 + r^{A}_{X0,X1} = 1 + r^{B}_{X0,X1} = 1 + X_{K1} = 1 + \delta_X$$

and similarly from 11.37e and 11.38b

$$1 + r^{A}_{Y0,Y1} = 1 + r^{B}_{Y0,Y1} = 1 + Y_{K1} = 1 + \delta_Y$$

from which

$$r^{A}_{X0,X1} = r^{B}_{X0,X1} = \delta_X$$

and

$$r^{A}_{Y0,Y1} = r^{B}_{Y0,Y1} = \delta_Y$$

which by the equality of rates of return, 11.42, is

$$r = \delta \tag{11.44}$$

where sub- and superscripts can be dropped as consumption discount rates, across commodities and individuals, are required to be equalised along with rates of return, across commodities. Equation 11.44 here is the same as equation 11.4 in the body of the chapter.

It is important to be clear that although consumption discount rates and rates of return are often written without subscripts in the literature, as in equations 11.4 and 11.44 here and elsewhere in this text, they are *not* parameters. It is partly because getting to them via marginal rates of transformation and substitution may help to make this clear that we have done things that way.

The assumption 11.40 is that for each commodity pair, individuals indifferently exchange at the margin at a rate which is time-invariant. In terms of individuals facing given prices, this is, as will be made explicit in Appendix 11.2 below, the assumption that the relative prices of commodities are constant over time.

Note that there is another assumption that does the same job as 11.40. We could assume that for both consumers within both periods the two commodities are perfect substitutes for each other. In that case the intratemporal marginal rates of utility substitution are unity, i.e.

$$\text{MRUS}^{A}_{X0,Y0} = \text{MRUS}^{B}_{X0,Y0} = 1$$

and

$$\text{MRUS}^{A}_{X1,Y1} = \text{MRUS}^{B}_{X1,Y1} = 1$$

which by 11.37a and 11.37b gives

$$\frac{\lambda_2}{\lambda_4} = \frac{\lambda_3}{\lambda_5} = 1$$

so that

$$\frac{\lambda_2}{\lambda_3} = \frac{\lambda_4}{\lambda_5}$$

which gives equal marginal products, $X_{K1} = Y_{K1}$, by 11.38a and 11.38b. This is the assumption effectively adopted in the chapter, and in much of the literature, to simplify the exposition. See also Section A11.1.4.1, on aggregation over commodities, below.

A11.1.3 Optimality conditions

The relationship between the optimality problem and the efficiency problem, and between the necessary conditions arising in each case, is the same as in the static case examined in Appendix 5.1. Confirming this is left as an exercise for the reader – see Problem 1.

A11.1.4 Some specialisations

A11.1.4.1 Aggregation over commodities

In order to focus more on the intertemporal dimensions of the efficiency and optimality problems, we can specify them in terms of a single commodity, Q say, which can be either consumed or invested. Then the efficiency problem is

$$\text{Max } U^{A}(C^{A}_0, C^{A}_1)$$

subject to

$$U^{B}(C^{B}_0, C^{B}_1) = Z$$

$$Q_0(K_0) - (K_1 - K_0) = C^{A}_0 + C^{B}_0$$

$$Q_1(K_1) - (K_2 - K_1) = C^{A}_1 + C^{B}_1$$

For

$$L = U^A(C_0^A, C_1^A) + \lambda_1[U^B(C_0^B, C_1^B) - Z]$$
$$+ \lambda_2[Q_0(K_0) - K_1 + K_0 - C_0^A - C_0^B]$$
$$+ \lambda_3[Q_1(K_1) - K_2 + K_1 - C_1^A - C_1^B]$$

necessary conditions are

$$U_{C0}^A - \lambda_2 = 0$$

$$U_{C1}^A - \lambda_3 = 0$$

$$\lambda_1 U_{C0}^B - \lambda_2 = 0$$

$$\lambda_1 U_{C1}^B - \lambda_3 = 0$$

$$-\lambda_2 + \lambda_3 Q_{K1} + \lambda_3 = 0$$

from which it is now straightforward to derive the intertemporal efficiency condition as

$$\text{MRUS}_{C0,C1}^A = \text{MRUS}_{C0,C1}^B = \text{MRT}_{0,1}^C$$

which can also be stated as

$$r^A = r^B = \delta \qquad (11.45)$$

i.e. the equality of the (common) consumption discount rate with the rate of return to investment.

Given this aggregation, the optimality problem is

$$\text{Max } W\{U^A(C_0^A, C_1^A), U^B(C_0^B, C_1^B)\}$$

subject to

$$Q_0(K_0) - (K_1 - K_0) = C_0^A + C_0^B$$

$$Q_1(K_1) - (K_2 - K_1) = C_1^A + C_1^B$$

It is left to the reader to confirm that the necessary conditions for a welfare optimum here are 11.45 plus

$$\frac{W_A}{W_B} = \frac{U_{C0}^B}{U_{C0}^A} = \frac{U_{C1}^B}{U_{C1}^A} \qquad (11.46)$$

where $W_A = \partial W/\partial U^A$ and $W_B = \partial W/\partial U^B$.

With this specification of the problem there is no condition requiring the equality of rates of return to investment. This condition can be recovered by modifying the specification so that there is a single commodity produced by many firms across which production functions differ. The outputs of the various firms are, that is, perfect substitutes in consumption. In this case, with $i = 1, \ldots, N$ firms, the efficiency problem is

$$\text{Max } U^A(C_0^A, C_1^A)$$

subject to

$$U^B(C_0^B, C_1^B) = Z$$

$$\sum_1^N \{Q_0^i(K_0^i) - (K_1^i - K_0^i)\} = C_0^A + C_0^B$$

$$\sum_1^N \{Q_1^i(K_1^i) - (K_2^i - K_1^i)\} = C_1^A + C_1^B$$

for which the necessary conditions are

$$U_{C0}^A - \lambda_2 = 0$$

$$U_{C1}^A - \lambda_3 = 0$$

$$\lambda_1 U_{C0}^B - \lambda_2 = 0$$

$$\lambda_1 U_{C1}^B - \lambda_3 = 0$$

$$-\lambda_2 + \lambda_3 Q_{K1}^i + \lambda_3 = 0, \, i = 1, 2, \ldots, N$$

from which

$$r^A = r^B = \delta_i$$

for all i.

A11.1.4.2 Aggregation over individuals

In order to focus solely on matters intertemporal, we could further specialise the problem specification by explicitly considering just one 'representative' individual. In that case we consider

$$\text{Max } U(C_0, C_1)$$

subject to

$$Q_0(K_0) - (K_1 - K_0) = C_0$$

$$Q_1(K_1) - (K_2 - K_1) = C_1$$

with Lagrangian

$$L = U(C_0, C_1) + \lambda_2[Q_0(K_0) - K_1 + K_0 - C_0]$$
$$+ \lambda_3[Q_1(K_1) - K_2 + K_1 - C_1]$$

for necessary conditions

$$U_{C0} - \lambda_2 = 0$$

$$U_{C1} - \lambda_3 = 0$$

$$-\lambda_2 + \lambda_3 Q_{K1} + \lambda_3 = 0$$

from which we get

$$\text{MRUS} = \text{MRT}$$

or

$$r = \delta \qquad (11.47)$$

A widely used variant of $U(C_0, C_1)$ is

$$W\{U(C_0), U(C_1)\} = U(C_0) + \left(\frac{1}{1+\rho}\right)U(C_1)$$

which has overall utility as the sum of current utility and discounted future utility; the parameter ρ is the utility discount rate. Some observations on terminology and notation here appear in the text of the chapter.

With this form of maximand, the two-period optimisation problem becomes

$$\text{Max } W = U(C_0) + \left(\frac{1}{1+\rho}\right)U(C_1)$$

subject to

$$Q_0(K_0) - (K_1 - K_0) = C_0$$

$$Q_1(K_1) - (K_2 - K_1) = C_1$$

with Lagrangian

$$L = U(C_0) + \left(\frac{1}{1+\rho}\right)U(C_1)$$

$$+ \lambda_2[Q_0(K_0) - K_1 + K_0 - C_0]$$
$$+ \lambda_3[Q_1(K_1) - K_2 + K_1 - C_1]$$

for necessary conditions

$$U_{C0} - \lambda_2 = 0$$

$$\left(\frac{1}{1+\rho}\right)U_{C1} - \lambda_3 = 0$$

$$-\lambda_2 + \lambda_3 Q_{K1} + \lambda_3 = 0$$

from which we get

$$\frac{U_{C0}}{[1/(1+\rho)]U_{C1}} = 1 + Q_{K1}$$

or

$$\frac{U_{C1}}{U_{C0}} = \frac{1+\rho}{1+Q_{K1}} \qquad (11.48)$$

Note that 11.48 implies, given decreasing marginal utility, $U_{CC} < 0$, that:

For $\rho > Q_{K1}$, $C_1 < C_0$

For $\rho = Q_{K1}$, $C_1 = C_0$

For $\rho < Q_{K1}$, $C_1 > C_0$

The model just considered is the simple optimal growth model considered in the chapter here, and in Chapter 3. For given utility and production functions, a given utility discount rate and given initial and terminal stocks of capital, it determines period 0 saving/investment, and hence consumption levels in the two periods. Such a model takes it as given that the intratemporal and intertemporal efficiency conditions are satisfied, and aggregates over commodities and individuals.

A11.1.4.3 Consumption and utility discount rates

Given that in

$$W\{U(C_0), U(C_1)\} = U(C_0) + \left(\frac{1}{1+\rho}\right)U(C_1)$$

contemporaneous utility is a function only of current consumption, $W\{.\}$ can be expressed with consumption levels as arguments. Utility discounting then implies consumption discounting. The consumption discount rate is defined as

$$r \equiv -\frac{dC_1}{dC_0} - 1$$

For

$$W = U(C_0) + \left(\frac{1}{1+\rho}\right)U(C_1)$$

we have

$$dW = U_{C0}dC_0 + \left(\frac{1}{1+\rho}\right)U_{C1}dC_1$$

so that with $dW = 0$, the MRUS is

$$-\frac{dC_1}{dC_0} = \frac{U_{C0}}{[1/(1+\rho)]U_{C1}}$$

and

$$r = \frac{U_{C0}}{[1/(1+\rho)]U_{C1}} - 1 = \frac{(1+\rho)U_{C0}}{U_{C1}} - 1 \qquad (11.49)$$

This shows that the consumption discount rate depends on the utility discount rate, and on the levels of marginal utility, and hence, given the utility function, on the consumption levels, in each period. In fact, with diminishing marginal utility, we can see that for given consumption levels r increases as ρ

increases, and that for given ρ r increases as the ratio of C_1 to C_0 increases. Working in continuous time it is possible to derive the expression for r in terms of ρ and the growth of C that was used in Chapter 3 in the discussion of the ethics of discounting. First write equation 11.49 in terms of any two adjacent periods t and $t + 1$ as

$$r = \frac{U_{C,t} - [1/(1 + \rho)]U_{C,t+1}}{[1/(1 + \rho)]U_{C,t+1}}$$

which in continuous time is

$$r = \frac{\frac{d}{dt}[e^{-\rho t}U'(C_t)]}{e^{-\rho t}U'(C_t)}$$

which gives

$$r = \rho - \frac{U''(C_t)\dot{C}_t}{U'(C_t)} \tag{11.50}$$

Define as the elasticity of marginal utility

$$\eta \equiv -\frac{U''(C_t)C_t}{U'(C_t)} \tag{11.51}$$

and 11.50 can be written as

$$r = \rho + \eta g \tag{11.52}$$

where g is the growth rate for consumption, $\dot{C}_t/C_t$.

Appendix 11.2 Markets and intertemporal allocation

Given the ideal circumstances discussed in the chapter, the literature looks at two sorts of market system as potential institutional means for the support of an efficient intertemporal allocation.

A11.2.1 Futures markets

Here it is imagined that contracts are made for all future exchanges at the beginning of period 0. Contracts referring to future periods are futures contracts, and the markets in which they are traded are futures markets. Letting M represent the total value of all future commodity expenditure that an individual can legitimately commit to, the individual's problem is

Max $U(X_0, X_1, Y_0, Y_1)$

subject to

$M = P_{X0}X_0 + P_{Y0}Y_0 + P_{X1}X_1 + P_{Y1}$

M could be thought of as the total sum of money paid to the individual in respect of the amounts of labour that they contract to supply in all future periods. The Lagrangian here is

$L = U(X_0, X_1, Y_0, Y_1)$
$\quad + \lambda[M - P_{X0}X_0 - P_{Y0}Y_0 - P_{X1}X_1 - P_{Y1}Y_1]$

with first-order conditions:

$U_{X0} - \lambda P_{X0} = 0$

$U_{Y0} - \lambda P_{Y0} = 0$

$U_{X1} - \lambda P_{X1} = 0$

$U_{Y1} - \lambda P_{Y1} = 0$

From these we derive for two individuals A and B both facing the same prices:

$$\text{MRUS}^A_{X0,Y0} = \text{MRUS}^B_{X0,Y0} = \frac{P_{X0}}{P_{Y0}} \tag{11.53a}$$

$$\text{MRUS}^A_{X1,Y1} = \text{MRUS}^B_{X1,Y1} = \frac{P_{X1}}{P_{Y1}} \tag{11.53b}$$

$$\text{MRUS}^A_{X0,X1} = \text{MRUS}^B_{X0,X1} = \frac{P_{X0}}{P_{X1}} \tag{11.53c}$$

$$\text{MRUS}^A_{X0,Y1} = \text{MRUS}^B_{X0,Y1} = \frac{P_{X0}}{P_{Y1}} \tag{11.53d}$$

$$\text{MRUS}^A_{Y0,Y1} = \text{MRUS}^B_{Y0,Y1} = \frac{P_{Y0}}{P_{Y1}} \tag{11.53e}$$

$$\text{MRUS}^A_{Y0,X1} = \text{MRUS}^B_{Y0,X1} = \frac{P_{Y0}}{P_{X1}} \tag{11.53f}$$

Comparing these with equations 11.37 shows that the extended consumption efficiency conditions are satisfied.

Consider production first in terms of the firm producing commodity X. Its objective is the maximisation of its net receipts at the beginning of period 0, which relate to contracts to supply X to individuals in that and all future periods. The way we have set production conditions up means that the firm has no monetary outgoings – we have not explicitly represented any inputs other than capital, and we have had capital accumulation as a process internal to the firm. The firm's net receipts are then its receipts from its sales to consumers. Its decision is how much to sell, and hence to invest, in period 0. That is to

$$\text{Max } \pi = P_{X0}[X_0(K_0^X) - (K_1^X - K_0^X)]$$
$$+ P_{X1}[X_1(K_1^X) - (K_2^X - K_1^X)]$$

by choice of K_1. The first-order necessary condition is

$$\partial\pi/\partial K_1^X = -P_{X0} + P_{X1}X_{K1} + P_{X1} = 0$$

from which

$$1 + X_{K1} = \frac{P_{X0}}{P_{X1}} \tag{11.54}$$

Comparing this with 11.53c and using the MRT definition we have

$$\text{MRT}_{0,1}^X = \text{MRUS}_{X0,X1}^A = \text{MRUS}_{X0,X1}^B \tag{11.55a}$$

and proceeding in the same way for commodity Y leads to

$$\text{MRT}_{0,1}^Y = \text{MRUS}_{Y0,Y1}^A = \text{MRUS}_{Y0,Y1}^B \tag{11.55b}$$

Equations 11.55 say that for each commodity we have, intertemporally, that MRT equals MRUS, as required for efficiency – see 11.39. When considering 11.39 we showed that, given an assumption, the statement of the required condition in terms of MRUSs and MRTs was equivalent to a statement in terms of consumption discount rates and rates of return. Clearly, the same applies here to the satisfaction of the condition in this system of markets – the overall efficiency condition of a common consumption discount rate equal to a common rate of return will be satisfied.

Regarding the assumption

$$\text{MRUS}_{X0,Y0} = \text{MRUS}_{X1,Y1}$$

note that by 11.53a and 11.53b, this will hold if

$$\frac{P_{X0}}{P_{Y0}} = \frac{P_{X1}}{P_{Y1}}$$

that is if relative prices are the same in both periods.

A11.2.2 Loanable funds market

Suppose that there exists a market in which funds can be borrowed or lent at the interest rate i. All contracts, other than those involving borrowing or lending, refer only to the one period of time at the beginning of which they are made.

The individual's problem is

$$\text{Max } U(X_0, X_1, Y_0, Y_1)$$

subject to

$$M_0 + [1/(1 + i)]M_1 = \{p_{X0}X_0 + p_{Y0}Y_0\}$$
$$+ [1/(1 + i)]\{p_{X1}X_1 + p_{Y1}Y_1\}$$

The left-hand side here is the present value of the sum of the individual's receipts at start of each period. The individual pays for each period's consumption at the start of each period, and the right-hand side is the present value of expenditures. The constraint simply says that the present value of receipts equals the present value of expenditures. Note the different notation here for prices as compared with that used in Section A11.2.1. In the case of futures markets everything is determined at the beginning of period 0, and prices such as P_{X0} refer to money sums then payable. With loanable funds markets, commodity trades take place at the start of each period, and prices such as p_{X0} refer to money sums then payable.

The Lagrangian for this problem is

$$L = U(X_0, X_1, Y_0, Y_1) + \lambda[M_0 + [1/(1 + i)]M_1$$
$$- \{p_{X0}X_0 + p_{Y0}Y_0\} - [1/(1 + i)]\{p_{X1}X_1 + p_{Y1}Y_1\}$$

where the first-order conditions are:

$$U_{X0} - \lambda p_{X0} = 0$$

$$U_{Y0} - \lambda p_{Y0} = 0$$

$$U_{X1} - \lambda[1/(1 + i)]p_{X1} = 0$$

$$U_{Y1} - \lambda[1/(1 + i)]p_{Y1} = 0$$

From these we derive for two individuals A and B both facing the same prices:

$$\text{MRUS}^A_{X0,Y0} = \text{MRUS}^B_{X0,Y0} = \frac{p_{X0}}{p_{Y0}} \qquad (11.56\text{a})$$

$$\text{MRUS}^A_{X1,Y1} = \text{MRUS}^B_{X1,Y1} = \frac{p_{X1}}{p_{Y1}} \qquad (11.56\text{b})$$

$$\text{MRUS}^A_{X0,X1} = \text{MRUS}^B_{X0,X1} = \frac{p_{X0}}{[1/(1+i)]p_{X1}} \qquad (11.56\text{c})$$

$$\text{MRUS}^A_{X0,Y1} = \text{MRUS}^B_{X0,Y1} = \frac{p_{X0}}{[1/(1+i)]p_{Y1}} \qquad (11.56\text{d})$$

$$\text{MRUS}^A_{Y0,Y1} = \text{MRUS}^B_{Y0,Y1} = \frac{p_{Y0}}{[1/(1+i)]p_{Y1}} \qquad (11.56\text{e})$$

$$\text{MRUS}^A_{Y0,X1} = \text{MRUS}^B_{Y0,X1} = \frac{p_{Y0}}{[1/(1+i)]p_{X1}} \qquad (11.56\text{f})$$

Comparing equations 11.56 with equations 11.37 we see that the consumption conditions for efficiency are satisfied.

In the context of a loanable funds market the problem for the firm producing X, for example, is to maximise the present value of net receipts by choice of investment level in period 0. That is to

$$\text{Max } \pi = p_{X0}[X_0(K_0^X) - (K_1^X - K_0^X)] \\ + [1/(1+i)]p_{X1}[X_1(K_1^X) - (K_2^X - K_1^X)]$$

by choice of K_1. The first-order necessary condition is

$$\partial\pi/\partial K_1^X = -p_{X0} + [1/(1+i)]\{p_{X1}X_{K1} + p_{X1}\} = 0$$

from which

$$1 + X_{K1} = \frac{p_{X0}}{[1/(1+i)]p_{X1}} \qquad (11.57)$$

Comparing this with 11.56c and using the MRT definition we have

$$\text{MRT}^X_{0,1} = \text{MRUS}^A_{X0,X1} = \text{MRUS}^B_{X0,X1} \qquad (11.58\text{a})$$

and proceeding in the same way for commodity Y leads to

$$\text{MRT}^Y_{0,1} = \text{MRUS}^A_{Y0,Y1} = \text{MRUS}^B_{Y0,Y1} \qquad (11.58\text{b})$$

The intertemporal efficiency conditions are satisfied.

Assuming that $p_{X0} = p_{X1}$, 11.57 becomes

$$1 + X_{K1} = 1 + i$$

which is

$$1 + \delta_X = 1 + i$$

or

$$\delta_X = i \qquad (11.59\text{a})$$

and in the same way for $p_{Y0} = p_{Y1}$

$$\delta_Y = i \qquad (11.59\text{b})$$

which establishes that equality of rates of return with the market rate of interest condition is satisfied. Given the same assumptions about relative prices over time, equations 11.56c to 11.56e have all the commodity consumption discount rates equal to the rate of interest determined in the market for loanable funds.

The discussion in the text of the chapter was conducted in terms of aggregate consumption. Suppose that there are $j = 1, 2, \ldots, J$ individuals, each determining period 0 and 1 consumption levels, given receipts M_0 and M_1, according to

$$\text{Max } U^j(C_0^j, C_1^j)$$

subject to

$$M_0^j + \left(\frac{1}{1+i}\right)M_1^j = C_0^j + \left(\frac{1}{1+i}\right)C_1^j$$

Then, as you can readily confirm, for each individual

$$r_j = i \qquad (11.60)$$

i.e. the consumption discount rate is equal to the market rate of interest.

Now suppose that each of these individuals is the owner of a firm producing the consumption/capital good. In that role, each individual's problem is to invest so as to maximise the present value of their firm. From

$$\text{Max } [Q_0^j(K_0^j) - (K_1^j - K_0^j)] \\ + [1/(1+i)][Q_1^j(K_1^j) - (K_2^j - K_1^j)]$$

we get

$$1 + Q_{K1}^j = 1 + i$$

which is the same as

$$\delta^j = i \qquad (11.61)$$

which says that rates of return will be equalised and equal to the market interest rate, as efficiency requires.

In their roles as owners of firms, individuals choose a level of investment such that the rate of return equals the interest rate, and thus fix receipts in each period, M_0^j and M_1^j. Given these, each individual determines, given their preferences and the market rate of interest, C_0^j and C_1^j as set out above. Those for whom $C_0^j > M_0^j$ become period 0 borrowers, and those for whom $C_0^j < M_0^j$ become period 0 lenders.

CHAPTER 12

Valuing the environment

If the environment is one of the world's bloodiest political battlefields, economics provides many of the weapons. Environmental lawsuits and regulatory debates would be starved of ammunition if economists did not lob their damage estimates into the fray. The trouble with these number wars is that the estimate's accuracy is often more akin to that of second-world-war bombers than precision-guided missiles.

The Economist, 3 December 1994, p. 106

Learning objectives

In this chapter you will
- learn about the categories of economic value assigned to the natural environment, and the distinction between use and non-use values
- work through the utility theory on which environmental valuation techniques are based
- find out how the Travel Cost Method uses data on actual behaviour to infer use value
- learn about the ways in which the Contingent Valuation Method generates and uses data which are individuals' responses to hypothetical questions to infer non-use value
- be introduced to some of the controversies about the Contingent Valuation Method
- find out about Choice Modelling as an alternative to Contingent Valuation
- learn about Hedonic Pricing for valuing pollution
- be introduced to valuation methods that are based on production function analysis

---

Introduction

This chapter is about the ways in which economists attach values to the unpriced services provided by the natural environment. 'Environmental valuation' is a very active and rapidly expanding field. It is also somewhat controversial. Many non-economists regard putting prices on environmental services as totally misconceived, if not wicked. While most economists accept the desirability of environmental valuation, there is disagreement over the prospects for actually doing it in a satisfactory way.

The original, and still the principal, motivation for environmental valuation was to enable environmental impacts to be included in cost–benefit analysis. Impacts can be favourable or unfavourable. Taking the latter first, suppose that there is proposed some development – a mine or a tourist resort – in a wilderness area. The argument for valuing the services provided by the wilderness area, which would be reduced, and perhaps totally lost, if the development goes ahead, is that only then can they be compared with the standard costs and benefits of the project so that a proper decision on it can be made. Introducing pollution control standards will have favourable impacts on the environment, but will involve abatement costs. As discussed in Chapter 6, efficiency in allocation requires that a standard be set such that marginal costs and benefits are equal. For this to be done, it is necessary to have a monetary measure of the variation of pollution reduction benefits with the level of reduction.

Environmental valuation for cost–benefit analysis has a history of some 30 years. In the past few years there have emerged two further sources of demand for environmental valuations. The first is the perceived need to take account of environmental damage in measuring economic performance, to be discussed in Chapter 19. Second, in the USA, since the late 1980s, economists' valuations of environmental damage are now admissible evidence in fixing the compensation to be paid by those the courts hold responsible for the damage.

The basic strategy for environmental valuation is the 'commodification' of the services that the natural environment provides. The services are used by households and firms, and are treated as arguments in utility and production functions, respectively. The standard theories for consumer and producer behaviour can then be used to derive methods for assigning values to environmental services. Most of the environmental valuation literature is about services which flow to households rather than firms, and we shall follow that emphasis in this chapter. We shall also focus mainly on a context which is the appraisal of a project with the potential to reduce the flow of environmental services from a wilderness area to households. The principles, and lessons from practice, that emerge in this context are of general applicability. By a 'household' here we mean an entity that takes and acts upon decisions about consumption. As in much of the economics literature, we shall also refer to such an entity as an 'individual' or as a 'consumer', depending on the context.

The chapter is organised as follows. The first section considers the way economists treat environmental services, and the classes of economic value that they ascribe to them. The second section deals with the utility theory that underpins standard environmental valuation techniques relating to services

to households. We then give extended accounts of two of those valuation techniques – the travel cost method which infers recreational valuations from observed behaviour, and the contingent valuation method which involves asking people about their valuations and is mainly used where observed behaviour cannot provide the required information. The chapter ends with brief overviews of some of the other techniques that are used.

12.1 Dimensions of value

In Chapter 2 (see Figure 2.1 especially) we distinguished four categories of service that the natural environment provides for humans and their economic activities:

- resource inputs to production by firms, here to be referred to as I;
- sinks for the assimilation of wastes generated in production and consumption, W;
- amenity services to households, A;
- life-support services for firms and households, L.

In order to introduce some of the basic ideas concerning environmental valuation we will first consider an old-growth forest. In Table 12.1 we list, in the first column, 11 potential 'outputs' from the forest area, and, in the second column, we assign each output to one or more of the above categories. The first point to be made is that this particular listing of outputs is somewhat arbitrary. The enumeration of forest outputs could be different. Some economists might choose, for example, to take flora and fauna together as 'biodiversity', as was the case in Box 11.1

Table 12.1 Forest outputs

Output	Service	Users	Rivalry	Excludability	Marketed
Harvested timber	I	F	R	E	M
Standing timber	A	H	NR	NE	NM
Minerals	I	F	R	E	M
Flora	I, A, L	F, H	R, NR	E, NE	M, NM
Fauna	I, A, L	F, H	R, NR	E, NE	M, NM
Flood protection	L	F, H	NR	NE	NM
Water quality	W, A, I	F, H	R, NR	E, NE	NM
Soil protection	L, I	F	NR	NE	NM
Local climate	L	F, H	NR	NE	NM
Carbon fixation	W, L	F, H	NR	NE	NM

in the previous chapter. A biologist would, no doubt, write the list in a quite different way. It is not a matter of right or wrong, but of fitness for purpose. The purpose in Table 12.1 is to provide a basis for discussing the way economists approach environmental valuation.

The identification in Table 12.1 of an output with a service category is clearly somewhat arbitrary in some cases, and some outputs obviously entail more than one class of service. Harvested timber is unambiguously and uniquely an input to production, undertaken by firms, as indicated by the F for User in the third column. Table 12.1 has standing timber as, at least potentially, a source of amenity services via opportunities for recreation and aesthetic appreciation, provided to households as indicated by H in the third column. One might wish to argue that standing trees also provide life-support services by virtue of their role in ecosystem function. In Table 12.1 we have implicitly got standing timber in again as a subset of the output 'flora', and it is there that its life support services are accounted for. If minerals were extracted within the forest area, they would clearly be resource inputs. Flora and fauna get classified as I because they may be inputs to production, as, for example, in the cases of grazing and wild honey collection, which may both be commercial activities conducted by firms. In the old-growth forest context, flora and fauna would more usually be thought of as contributing to recreational and aesthetic opportunities, A, and to ecosystem function and hence life-support, L.

We leave it to the reader to consider the remaining output categories and their service classifications in Table 12.1. The fourth and fifth columns in Table 12.1 relate to the characteristics of rivalry and excludability introduced in Chapter 5 in the discussion of the differences between private and public goods (and bads), using R to indicate rivalry and NR for non-rivalry, and similarly for E and NE. The final column shows whether the output is marketed, M, or not, NM, and the entries follow from those in columns four and five. Again, in some cases here, there is some ambiguity given the broad 'output' classifications used. As noted in Chapter 5 rivalry and excludability may be assessed in terms of current institutional arrangements or in terms of underlying physical characteristics. Harvested timber is clearly

a private good, sold through markets. Given that we have classified standing timber as providing amenity services to households, we have marked it as non-rival and non-excludable. However, there is no physical reason why a private, or public for that matter, forest owner should not construct a fence and so introduce excludability in regard to access for the enjoyment of the amenity services. Classification as non-rival implies that there is no congestion. Clearly, if the level of recreational use is such that an additional recreationalist would reduce the amenity service level provided for existing recreationalists, then there is rivalry.

12.1.1 Environmental cost–benefit analysis

Now, suppose that the forest is undeveloped wilderness. There is no timber harvesting, no mineral extraction, no harvesting of any of the flora and fauna. The forest wilderness is used for recreational purposes, and provides the other non-extractive outputs and associated services listed in Table 12.1. Next suppose that there is a proposal for some development project to occur in the area – a mine, a hydroelectric plant or timber harvesting, say. The question is whether the project should go ahead, in which case the environmental services that it supplies, as wilderness, to households will be reduced. As economists, we know, as discussed in Chapter 11, that the question of whether a project should go ahead or not is to be decided by environmental cost–benefit analysis, ECBA, with market failure corrected for – all of the impacts arising from going ahead with the project should be taken account of, irrespective of whether or not they have market prices attached to them.

As set out in the previous chapter, the project should go ahead only if NPV > 0, where

$$NPV = B_d - C_d - EC \tag{12.1}$$

with B_d as the present value of the stream of development benefits, C_d as the present value of the stream of development costs, and EC for the present value of the environmental, or external, costs of the project. An alternative way of stating this criterion is that the project should go ahead only if

$$B_d - C_d > EC \tag{12.2}$$

In either form, use of this criterion requires the identification and measurement of the impacts of the project on the wilderness area, and then their valuation and aggregation to arrive at EC, which is a monetary measure of the environmental benefits of not going ahead with the project.

Assuming that the impacts involved are limited to those affecting households, and that these can be identified and measured, the basic strategy for valuation is to treat the environmental services impacted as arguments in household utility functions, as commodities. Then, as discussed in the next section, demand theory can be used to establish the existence and nature of monetary measures of the impacts on utility. The implementation of this ECBA approach to social decision making then requires the estimation of the sizes of the appropriate monetary measures for affected households and their aggregation to obtain an estimate for EC. Techniques for doing this are discussed in subsequent sections of this chapter. Here we can note that there are two basic approaches to the estimation of the monetary measures of impact for individuals: the indirect and the direct. Both derive from the fact that markets do not exist for the environmental services impacted by the project, due to non-excludability and/or non-rivalry. The indirect approach involves recovering estimates from the observed behaviour of individuals in regard to marketed commodities; the direct approach involves asking individuals questions relating to the affected environmental services.

12.1.2 Categories of environmental benefit

EC is the environmental cost of going ahead with the development project in the forest area. Equally, it can be seen as the environmental benefits arising from not going ahead with the project. We can divide EC into four classes of benefit potentially accruing to individuals:

- use value (UV) arises from the actual and/or planned use of the service by an individual, for recreation for example;
- existence value (EV) arises from knowledge that the service exists and will continue to exist, independently of any actual or prospective use by the individual;

- option value (OV) relates to willingness to pay to guarantee the availability of the service for future use by the individual;
- quasi-option value (QOV) relates to willingness to pay to avoid an irreversible commitment to development now, given the expectation of future growth in knowledge relevant to the implications of development.

EC is the sum of these four sorts of value across all of the affected individuals:

$$EC = UV + EV + OV + QOV$$

Of course, for any particular project, and for some individuals, some, or all, of UV, EV, OV and QOV may be zero.

OV and QOV arise only where there is incomplete knowledge of future conditions, whereas UV and EV can exist where there is complete certainty about future conditions. Incomplete knowledge is, of course, the operative case. However, we shall in this chapter assume complete knowledge and consider just UV and EV, leaving discussion of OV and QOV to the next chapter, which deals explicitly with risk and uncertainty.

There is not in the literature a single standard categorisation, nor is terminology uniform. What we have called EC is sometimes known as total value, TV, and it is stated that

$$TV = UV + NUV$$

or that

$$TV = UV + PUV$$

where NUV stands for non-use value and PUV for passive use value. Two categories of use value are sometimes distinguished – direct (DUV) and indirect (IUV). In this categorisation DUV is essentially UV as defined above, while IUV refers to the life-support services role of the natural environment, which are 'indirectly used' by individuals (and by firms). In the first categorisation, the value attached to life-support services is covered by EV.

The existence for an individual of EV is often taken to imply some kind of altruism, and in the literature EV is itself sometimes subdivided on the basis of the object of the altruism. A 'philanthropic' motive relating to the provision of amenity services to human contemporaries is, for example, sometimes distinguished from a 'bequest' motive relating to amenity and life-support services for future human generations. Again, a concern for the well-being of non-human entities is sometimes distinguished from a concern for the well-being of other humans, with the former referred to as 'intrinsic' value. However, in practice these distinctions are typically overlooked and the objective is simply to estimate total EV. It is also the case that most applications of the techniques developed to date seek to estimate total non-use value, rather than trying to estimate separately EV, OV and QOV. The point is that while there is a large literature distinguishing between the components of NUV, in practice the operative distinction is between UV, as direct use, and NUV. It is generally understood that whereas techniques based on indirect approaches can only be used to estimate use value, techniques based on direct approaches can be used to estimate both use and non-use values. The basis for this understanding is discussed in the next section, which deals with the extension of the theory of consumer behaviour to deal with 'commodities' that are environmental services.

12.2   The theory of environmental valuation

In this section we deal with the theoretical foundations for the techniques that economists have developed for environmental valuation in relation to services to households. The first step in that development is the assumption that environmental services, or indicators relating to environmental services, can be treated as arguments in well-behaved utility functions. This is an important first step as the conditions under which preferences can be represented by well-behaved utility functions are non-trivial, and, as we shall discuss later in the chapter, some commentators argue that preferences over both 'ordinary commodities' and 'environmental commodities' are unlikely, in many cases, to satisfy those conditions. For an account of the axiomatic basis for well-behaved utility functions the reader should consult a microeconomics text such as Kreps (1990), or Deaton and Muellbauer (1980) on the theory of consumer behaviour.

In this section we set out the standard theory of environmental valuation, simply assuming the existence of the required utility functions. Given that, we discuss the proper monetary measures of utility change, and the extent to which such measures are, in principle, observable, or can be approximated by measures which are observable. Finally here we discuss the conditions for the use of the indirect methods, and which define existence value. Appendix 12.1 covers much the same ground in a more general and formal way.

12.2.1 Price changes: equivalent and compensating variation

For the purpose of doing ECBA we require an estimate of EC. Given the assumption that the relevant environmental damages affect only consumers, what we require is a monetary measure of the utility changes experienced on account of the environmental damage done by the project. In Chapter 5 we discussed, in relation to the practice of partial equilibrium analysis, consumers' surplus, the area under the demand function minus actual expenditure (see Figure 5.11 and its discussion especially). Given an individual's demand function, we could define individual consumer surplus in an exactly analogous way, and the consumers' surplus discussed in Chapter 5 would be the sum of the individual consumer surpluses. For an individual, the change in consumer surplus can be treated as a monetary measure of the individual's utility change when, for example, the price of some commodity falls. However, this is a valid measure of the utility change only under some restrictive assumptions. It would be required, for example, that the marginal utility of income be constant. Hicks (1941) developed a set of money measures of utility change which do not require such restrictive assumptions, and these are what we use, ideally, to estimate EC. As we shall see, in practice we frequently have to use consumer surplus, and one of the major concerns in the literature is the closeness of it to the proper, Hicksian, measures. We shall use MCS to refer to consumer surplus, where the M is for Marshall, the 19th-century economist who popularised the use of consumers' surplus, the CS part, for welfare analysis.

To begin, we leave aside matters environmental. We wish to obtain a monetary measure of an individual's welfare change arising from a reduction in the price of some good C_1 from P'_1 to P''_1. Define a second good, C_2, as the composite good which is all goods other than C_1, let the price of C_2 be unity, and suppose that the individual has a fixed money income, Y_0. The consumer's budget constraint, prior to the price fall, can then be written as:

$$P'_1 C_1 + C_2 = Y_0 \qquad (12.3)$$

A utility-maximising consumer will choose C_1 and C_2 so as to maximise $U = U(C_1, C_2)$ subject to this budget constraint. The solution is two consumption quantities, C'_1 and C'_2, and a maximised level of utility U_0, and is illustrated in Figure 12.1. We may interpret the vertical axis as being in units of money income. To see this, note from the budget constraint that if no expenditure took place on good 1 (so $C_1 = 0$), then C_2 is equal to the money income level Y_0.

Now consider the consequence of the price fall of good C_1 from P'_1 to P''_1. The budget constraint rotates anticlockwise about the point Y_0 on the vertical axis to the new constraint

$$P''_1 C_1 + C_2 = Y_0 \qquad (12.4)$$

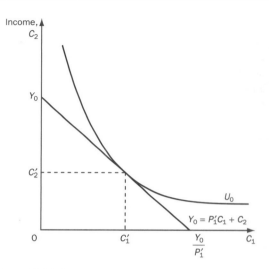

Figure 12.1 Utility maximisation subject to a budget constraint

as shown in Figure 12.2. Utility maximisation now implies consumption levels of C''_1 and C''_2, and a higher utility level, U_1. The increase in the consumption of C_1 from C'_1 to C''_1 can be decomposed into a substitution effect, C'_1 to C^*_1, and an income effect, C^*_1 to C''_1.

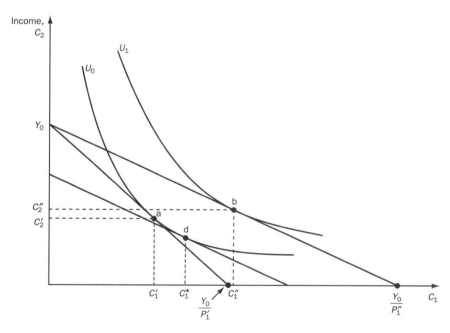

Figure 12.2 The income and substitution effects of a price reduction

There are two 'Hicksian' monetary measures of the utility change associated with a price change:

- The compensating variation (CV) is the change in income that would 'compensate' for the price change.
- The equivalent variation (EV) is the change in income that would be 'equivalent' to the proposed price change.

We will first examine CV and EV for a price fall for good C_1. The CV is the quantity of money income which, when taken from the individual together with the price fall, leaves the individual at his or her initial level of utility. It is, therefore, the maximum amount that the individual would pay to have the price fall occur. The EV is the quantity of money income which, if given to the individual without the price fall, would give the same level of utility as he or she would have attained if the price fall had occurred. It is, therefore, the minimum compensation that the individual would accept in lieu of the price fall.

In Figure 12.3(a) the points labelled a and b denote the utility-maximising consumption choices before and after the price fall. Begin at point b, at which the slope of the budget constraint is given by the final price, after the price fall. Keeping relative prices constant, reduce money income until the individual is constrained to have only the original level of utility, U_0, at the point marked d. The required income reduction is the amount $Y_0 - Y_1$, which is the compensating variation of the price fall. The CV measures, in units of money income, the utility change from U_0 to U_1, given that prices are fixed at their final level. The EV is given by amount $Y_2 - Y_0$ in Figure 12.3(a), leaving the individual at point f, and it measures, in units of money income, the utility change from U_0 to U_1, given that prices are fixed at their initial level. The two variations each measure the utility change from U_0 to U_1 in money-income units. They differ from one another because these changes are valued at different sets of prices and use different reference points.

An alternative geometrical interpretation for CV and EV is given in Figure 12.3(b), where two types of demand function are shown. We know that a price change will, in general, have both substitution and income effects. The Marshallian and Hicksian demand functions shown in Figure 12.3(b) differ in the way in which they deal with these two effects. The Marshallian demand function shows how the quantity of C_1 demanded varies with P_1, when the consumer's income and all other prices are held constant. It is the standard demand function from introductory microeconomics texts. A Hicksian demand function is the relationship between the quantity demanded of a particular good and the price of that good, holding all other prices and utility constant. It is constructed in such a way that compensation is made which eliminates the income effect of a price change. Movements along a Hicksian demand curve thus represent the pure substitution effect of a price change. Hicksian demand functions are sometimes referred to as 'compensated demand functions', and Marshallian as 'uncompensated'.

To derive the compensated demand function for our example, look again at the exercise we undertook in identifying the CV of a price fall, which we showed to be $Y_0 - Y_1$. Now consider the two points a and d in Figure 12.3(a). The move from a to d is the consequence of a fall in the price of the good, holding all other prices constant (in this case just the price of C_2) and holding utility constant (at U_0), and therefore represents the substitution effect of the fall in price of C_1. Points a and d constitute two points on the Hicksian demand curve for $U = U_0$, as shown in Figure 12.3(b). Note that a second Hicksian demand function can be obtained for the utility level $U = U_1$. The two combinations b and f constitute points on this Hicksian demand function.

We are now in a position to provide an alternative geometrical interpretation of CV and EV for a price fall. To do this, the Marshallian uncompensated demand curve and the two Hicksian compensated demands have been redrawn in Figure 12.4. CV is the area to the left of $H(U_0)$ and between the prices P_0 and P_1. EV is the area to the left of $H(U_1)$ and between the prices P_0 and P_1. Note that the area to the left of the Marshallian demand – the Marshallian consumer surplus, MCS, for the price change – is not exactly equal to either of the two Hicksian measures of utility change.

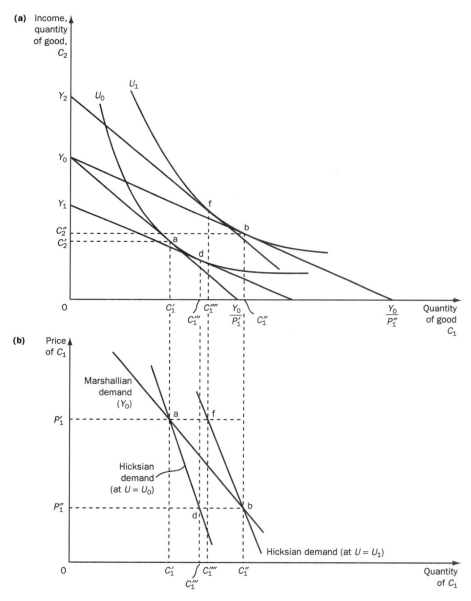

Figure 12.3 (*a*) The compensating variation of a price fall; (*b*) Hicksian and Marshallian demands

For a fall in the price of C_1:

$$CV = \int_{P_1''}^{P_1'} H(U_0)\,dP = \text{shaded area}$$

$$EV = \int_{P_1''}^{P_1'} H(U_1)\,dP = \text{shaded area} + \text{hatched area}$$

Repeating the arguments that we have gone through for a price fall for a price increase leads to CV for a price increase as the minimum compensation that would leave an individual's utility unchanged, and EV as the maximum that the individual would be willing to pay to have the price increase not take place. Using WTP for willingness to pay and WTA for willingness to accept, Table 12.2 summarises the relationships between WTP/WTA and CV/EV.

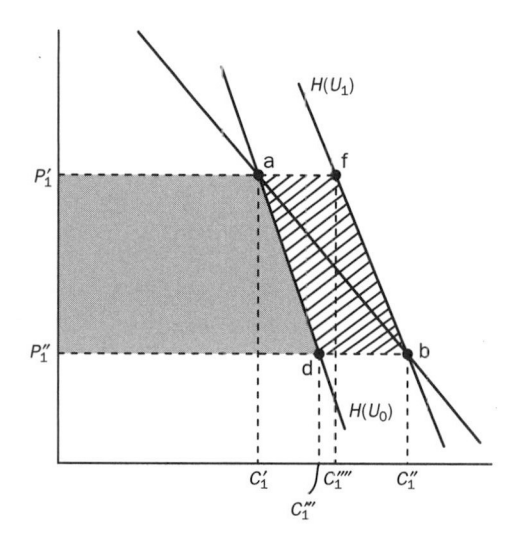

For a fall in the price of C_1:

$$CV = \int_{P_1''}^{P_1'} H(U_0)\, dP = \text{shaded area}$$

$$EV = \int_{P_1''}^{P_1'} H(U_1)\, dP = \text{shaded area} + \text{hatched area}$$

Figure 12.4 Compensating variation and equivalent variation

Table 12.2 Monetary measures for price change effects

	CV	EV
Price fall	WTP for the change occurring	WTA compensation for the change not occurring
Price rise	WTA compensation for the change occurring	WTP for the change not to occur

From Figure 12.4 it is clear that for a price fall we have

$$CV < MCS < EV$$

which is the same as

$$WTP < MCS < WTA$$

For a price increase we get

$$CV > MCS > EV$$

or

$$WTA > MCS > WTP$$

What this means is that, for the 'normal' sort of commodity for which Figures 12.3 and 12.4 are drawn, we have

$$WTP < MCS < WTA \qquad (12.5)$$

So, in principle, we can get at proper monetary measures of the utility effects of price changes for an individual if we can ascertain his or her WTP or WTA. If we cannot do that, but we know the individual's ordinary uncompensated (Marshallian) demand function, we can measure MCS, which we know is not a correct measure for either increases or decreases in price, though we also know that it lies between the two correct measures. Two questions arise. First, which of CV and EV should be used in any particular case? Second, if only MCS is feasible, how wrong will it be in relation to the correct measure?

Taking the second question first, the answer is 'not very much'. From the foregoing it should be apparent that the size of the error involved in using MCS will depend on the size of the income effect associated with a price change for the commodity of concern, as Hicksian demand functions correct for the income effect whereas Marshallian demand functions do not. It is generally understood, based on Willig (1976), that for most cases of practical concern the error involved in using MCS, with respect to either CV or EV, will be 5% or less. A special case is worth noting. When the income elasticity of demand for the good in question is zero, then the Hicksian demands become identical to the Marshallian demand function, and so EV = CV = MCS. The reason for this is that the income effect of the price change is zero.

The answer to the first question is that it depends on the circumstances and purposes of the analysis. If we think about it in terms of using WTP or WTA, it is really a question of whether we want to treat the status quo as a reference point to which the individual has some kind of entitlement, or not. We shall return to this question in the context of a discussion of monetary measures of changes in the consumption levels of environmental services, which is the subject of the next subsection. It will also come up again in our discussion of contingent valuation, a technique which seeks to directly ascertain WTP or WTA by asking individuals about them.

12.2.2 Quality changes: equivalent and compensating surplus

We now want to consider monetary measures for the utility change implications of changes in the quality or quantity of environmental services. To follow the preceding analysis, let us take C_1 as the environmental commodity, and change the notation from C_1 to E. We are assuming, then, that the individual has a well-behaved utility function $U = U(E, C_2)$. Changes in the level of E can refer to quantity changes or quality changes, depending on the particular environmental service involved. Both usages are encountered in the literature. It is important to be clear that analytically both usages refer to the same thing, changes in the level of E. Where there is reference to 'environmental quality', there is generally some quantitative measure involved, as with, for example, water quality. The measure may be ordinal rather than cardinal, and may be based on subjective evaluations.

Typically, as quality or quantity, E would be non-exclusive and non-divisible, so that the individual cannot adjust his or her consumption level. For present purposes, we shall assume that E is a public good, something like water quality in a lake, say. There are two monetary measures of the utility change associated with a change in the level of E, compensating surplus (CS) and equivalent surplus (ES). They are shown, for the case of an improvement, or increase, from E' to E'' in Figure 12.5(a) and (b) respectively, where the mode of analysis is essentially the same as in the previous subsection.

In Figure 12.5(a), the individual is initially at a utility U_0. As a result of some policy change, E increases from E' to E'' and the individual's utility increases. Increasing E with nothing else changing is equivalent to a reduction in the price of E. The slope of the budget line Y_0d gives the price ratio implicit in the quantity increase, tangential to an indifference curve for a higher level of utility, U_1, at b. Now, draw Y_Ne parallel to Y_0d and cutting the indifference curve for U_0 at f where the level of E is E''. This is not a point of tangency, reflecting the fact that the individual is constrained to experience E''. Now CS is bf $= Y_0 - Y_N$, the amount of money that, if forgone by the individual with the policy change, would result in their experiencing the pre-change level of

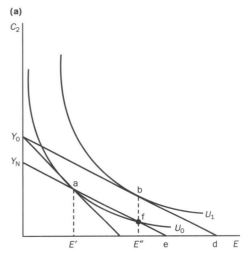

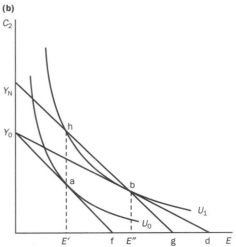

Figure 12.5 Equivalent and compensating surplus

utility. Put another way, it is the maximum willingness to pay for the environmental improvement – if the individual experienced E going from E' to E'' and paid an amount $Y_0 - Y_N$, he or she would remain at a constant level of utility U_0.

Now look at Figure 12.5(b). Again, the increase in E means a move to b with the implicit new price ratio given by the slope of Y_0d. Now draw Y_Ng parallel to the original budget line Y_0f and passing through b. It cuts the indifference curve for U_1 at h. ES is $Y_N - Y_0 = ha$. It is the amount of money that, at the original prices, would, if paid to the individual, move him or her to the same utility level as the environmental improvement would have done, given

Table 12.3 Monetary measures for environmental quality changes

	CS	ES
Improvement	WTP for the change occurring	WTA compensation for the change not occurring
Deterioration	WTA compensation for the change occurring	WTP for the change not to occur

that the improvement does not, in fact, take place. Put another way, ha is the individual's minimum willingness to accept compensation for the prospective environmental improvement not happening.

If we consider a deterioration in the environment, a reduction in E, and examine CS and ES for that case, we find that CS is willingness to accept compensation for the lower E while ES is willingness to pay to avoid it. Table 12.3 summarises the situation in regard to monetary measures of the utility changes associated with changes in the quality/quantity of an environmental service, paralleling Table 12.2 for changes in the price of some commodity (which could be an environmental service that is not a public good).

In the case of Table 12.2 we made statements about the relative sizes of CV, EV and MCS. Until recently it was thought that similar statements could be made about CS, ES and MCS for a change in environmental quality. Since the publication of Bockstael and McConnell's paper (1993) it is realised that this is not the case – the results for CV, EV and MCS do not carry over to CS, ES and MCS. This means that for environmental quality changes it is not possible to use MCS as an approximation for the proper monetary measure of utility change.

Given that environmental quality is generally an unpriced public good, so that ordinary Marshallian demand functions cannot be estimated, the inability to say anything about MCS as an approximation to a proper measure would appear to be a non-problem. If MCS itself cannot be estimated, it might appear that it does not really matter that we do not know how it relates to CS and ES, so that the Bockstael and McConnell results are of little interest. However, their results are seen as important in relation to the indirect methods for environmental valuation, the theoretical basis for which we discuss next.

12.2.3 Weak complementarity

The basic idea behind the indirect methods of environmental valuation is to infer the monetary value of a change in the level of the environmental service of interest from observed market data on some ordinary commodity. If, for example, we observed an increase in the demand for fishing permits following an improvement in water quality, we could try to use the observed increase in demand for the permits to put a value on the water quality change.

In order to explain how this might work, we need first to revisit the difference between the variation and surplus measures of utility change. We associated CV and EV with price changes, and CS and ES with changes in quality or quantity. Reviewing the discussion, it will be seen that in the price change case the individual can adjust his or her consumption level for the commodity the price of which changes, whereas in the quality/quantity change case the consumption level for the environmental service is beyond the individual's control. In the latter case the change in the level of E is exogenously imposed on the individual.

Consider an individual consuming N ordinary commodities, let C_1 be the quantity of daily fishing permits purchased, and let E be the level of water quality in the lake to which the permits relate. Then, we can write the compensated demand function for fishing days as:

$$C_1 = H_1(P_1, \ldots, P_N, E, U_0) \qquad (12.6)$$

A change in the level of E will shift this demand function for a given set of $P_1, \ldots, P_N$, so that E is a parameter of the function, as illustrated in Figure 12.6. An improvement in water quality, an increase in E from E^o to E^n, shifts the demand for fishing days so that at the constant permit price P_1^F, the individual's consumption increases from C_1' to C_1''. The price $P_1^C(E^o)$ is the price which would drive demand to zero – the 'choke price' – with E equal to E^o, and $P_1^C(E^n)$ is the price which would drive demand to zero for E equal to E^n.

Now, it follows from the analysis of Figure 12.4 that in Figure 12.6 the shaded area $aP_1^C(E^o)P_1^C(E^n)b$, call it A, gives the CV change associated with the increased consumption of C_1 due to the parametric shift of the Hicksian demand function for C_1. For

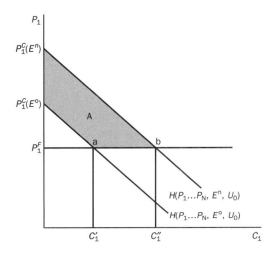

Figure 12.6 Environmental quality as a commodity demand function parameter

the purposes of environmental valuation, what is actually wanted is the CS associated with the environmental improvement that is the cause of the parametric shift in the compensated demand function for C_1. It has been established that the area A is exactly equal to the required CS if two conditions hold. The conditions are that C_1 is non-essential and that C_1 and E are weak complements:

> For an individual, C_1 is non-essential if it is possible to compensate him or her for the complete loss of C_1. In terms of the fishing example, suppose that an individual who has been using the lake is prohibited from doing so. Then C_1, days spent fishing at this lake, is a non-essential commodity for this individual if there is some income level that would enable his or her original level of utility to be regained after the prohibition.
>
> The complementarity between E and C_1 is weak if it is the case that for $C_1 = 0$, utility is not affected by variations in the level of E. In the example here, fishing and water quality are weak complements for an individual if it is the case that given that the individual does not go fishing, perhaps because the price of a permit is above his or her choke price, then he or she does not care about variations in water quality in the lake.[1]

Now, given that all this is in terms of the un-observable Hicksian demand for C_1, the fact that, if non-essentialness and weak complementarity hold, the area A is exactly equal to the willingness to pay for the environmental improvement is not in itself of much use as A is inherently unknown. However, one could hope to determine a Marshallian, uncompensated, demand function for C_1 and thus derive the MCS associated with a change in E. We saw above that, for price changes, Willig (1976) established that MCS is close to CV. If this were also true for quantity changes, MCS could be used to give a close approximation to the CV associated with the change in the consumption of C_1, and hence to the CS monetary measure of the utility change arising from the improvement in environmental quality. Unfortunately, as we noted above, Bockstael and McConnell (1993) showed that the Willig results for variational measures do not, as was once thought, carry over to the surplus measures. Using an environmental-quality-induced change in MCS as an estimate of either CS or ES involves errors for which little is known about the potential size, or indeed the sign. Notwithstanding this, environmental economists continue to use indirect methods based on Marshallian demand functions, in the hope that the errors involved, with respect to the true surplus measures, are not too great.

We noted above that the contingent valuation method involves asking people about their willingness to pay (or accept), so that for some environmental improvement it could be used to directly get at CS, avoiding the problem outlined above. This direct method has not supplanted indirect methods because it too has problems, as we will see below. There is one circumstance, however, where a direct method such as contingent valuation has to be used. In terms of the lake water-quality example, suppose that the weak complementarity condition is violated such that for $C_1 = 0$ it is the case that the individual's utility is affected by variations in E. In this case, there is, as discussed above, existence value, which cannot be estimated by indirect methods since it leaves no behavioural traces in observed behaviour in relation to marketed commodities. Simply using

---

[1] These conditions are stated more formally in Appendix 12.1.

some indirect method, such as travel cost, across many individuals to value a water-quality improvement in the lake would result in a downward-biased result to the extent that there were individuals for whom there was existence value. Note that since actual use of the lake by an individual for fishing, or anything else, is not necessary for that individual to have existence value in regard to it, the relevant population for estimating total value is not just those who actually use the lake. It may be very much larger.

12.3 Environmental valuation techniques

The literature on environmental valuation techniques and their application is now very extensive, and we shall not be able to cover it all here. What we will do is to give a reasonably comprehensive account of the main features of two of the most widely used techniques, and to provide a brief introduction to the essential features of several other techniques. The first technique considered in some depth is the travel cost method (TCM), which is an example of the indirect approach. The second is the contingent valuation method (CVM), which is an example of the direct approach. The techniques to be covered more briefly are choice modelling, hedonic pricing, and those based on production functions. We will consider some of the problems attending these techniques that have engaged economists. More fundamental questions about the appropriateness of the economic approach to environmental decision making, and hence the role of these valuation techniques, were considered in the previous chapter.

12.4 The travel cost method

This appears to have first been proposed in outline in a letter from Hotelling (known for the Hotelling rule, on which see Chapter 15 below) to the US Park Service in 1947. It was developed principally in papers by Clawson (1959) and Clawson and Knetsch (1966). That work preceded the theoretical work on weak complementarity considered above,

and was based on the simple idea that it ought to be possible to infer the values placed by visitors on environmental amenity services from the costs that they incurred in order to experience the services. However, it can be seen now that the TCM is an application of the weak complementarity idea. The original TCM proposals related to national parks where entry was unpriced. In terms of Figure 12.6, in that context E is the amenity service that is enjoyed by a park visitor and C_1 is travel to the park. Then E and C_1 are complementary. The non-essentialness assumption is that there is some income level that would compensate for the closure of the park. The weak complementarity assumption is that if the individual does not visit the park, he or she does not care about the services that it provides.

We will fix ideas here by considering a situation where some project threatens the amenity services currently provided by a protected area, a national park say, for which there is no access fee. Those responsible for deciding whether the project should go ahead are going to use ECBA, and wish to know the environmental cost to compare with the net development benefit. For the purposes of exposition, we shall assume that if the project goes ahead the value of the recreational amenity services from the area in question will go to zero.

In practical terms the first basic assumption for the TCM is that visits to the park are determined by a trip- or visit-generating function

$$V_i = f(C_i, X_{1i}, X_{2i}, \ldots, X_{Ni}) \qquad (12.7)$$

where V_i is visits from the ith origin or by the ith individual, C_i is the cost of a visit from origin i or by individual i, and the Xs are other relevant variables. The second basic assumption is that the cost of a visit comprises both travel costs T_i, varying with i, and admission price, P, constant across i, and that visitors treat travel costs and the price of admission as equivalent elements of the total cost of a visit. Visitors respond, that is, in exactly the same way to increases/decreases in total cost whether they are due to increases/decreases in travel cost or admission price, with $\partial V_i / \partial C_i < 0$. If we assume that the function $f(\cdot)$ is linear in costs, and suppress the role of other variables, this means that the trip generating equation to be estimated is

$$V_i = \alpha + \beta C_i + \varepsilon_i = \alpha + \beta(T_i + P) - \varepsilon_i \qquad (12.8)$$

where ε_i is the stochastic component, or error term, assumed to be normally and independently distributed, with zero expectation. Travel and the recreational amenity services of the park are being assumed to be weak complements and it is assumed that travel and access costs are behaviourally equivalent. Note that the way that we have written equation 12.8 means that β is assumed to be negative.

In the data for the case we are considering, P is zero.[2] However, given the second assumption here, α and β can be estimated from data on V_i and T_i and used to figure the effects on visits of hypothetical changes in P. Note that this could be useful for figuring the effects on visits of the introduction of access charging, as well as for figuring a monetary measure of the utility of the recreational amenity with free access. Note also that equation 12.8 is a Marshallian, uncompensated, demand function for visits. Given the assumption of zero expectation for the error term in equation 12.8, the relationship between expected visits from origin i or by individual i and the price of access to the park is

$$E[V_i] = \alpha + \beta P + \beta T_i \qquad (12.9)$$

where E[ ] is the expectation operator. Equation 12.9 is shown diagrammatically in Figure 12.7 as the downward-sloping straight line. There $E[V_i^*]$ is visits when the access price is zero, and P_i^* is the choke price that drives $E[V_i]$ to zero. Setting $E[V_i]$ equal to zero in equation 12.9 and solving for P gives

$$P_i^* = -(\alpha/\beta) - T_i \qquad (12.10)$$

and for P equal to zero:

$$E[V_i^*] = \alpha + \beta T_i \qquad (12.11)$$

Marshallian consumer surplus for origin/individual i at $P = 0$ is given by the area of the triangle $OE[V_i^*]P_i^*$ in Figure 12.7. The area of a triangle is half base times height, which in this case is 0.5 times $OE[V_i^*]$ times OP_i^*. Using equations 12.10 and 12.11 that is

$$0.5\{\alpha + \beta T_i\}\{-(\alpha/\beta) - T_i\}$$

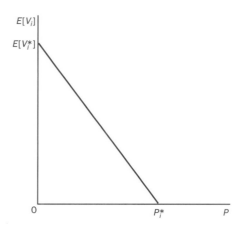

Figure 12.7 The linear trip-generating function

or

$$\{-0.5/\beta\}\{\alpha + \beta T_i\}\{\alpha + \beta T_i\}$$

so that using equation 12.11 again we have

$$MCS_i = \frac{-(E[V_i^*])^2}{2\beta} \qquad (12.12)$$

Summing over i, total consumer surplus when $P = 0$ is

$$MCS = \frac{-\sum_i (E[V_i^*])^2}{2\beta} \qquad (12.13)$$

In some applications of the TCM, surplus for $P = 0$ is calculated across i using the actual observed visits for each origin/individual, as in:

$$MCS = \frac{-\sum_i V_i^2}{2\beta} \qquad (12.14)$$

In either case, the crucial nature of the assumption that visits respond in the same way to changes in P as to variations in travel cost is apparent. Given this assumption, the operational problem is to estimate α and β from data on V_i and T_i. These data are most usually obtained by surveying visitors to the site, in this case the park, though sometimes data are

2   Having P fixed, and the same for all i, at some non-zero value, say P', would not materially affect the account of the TCM that follows here. One would still estimate α and β from data on travel costs and visits and use the results as discussed in connection

with Figure 12.7. The only difference would be that in computing MCS_i one would subtract actual expenditure on access fees, the area under a horizontal line at height OP'.

gathered on visitors and non-visitors by means of a, usually postal, survey of a sample of the population considered to be relevant as potential visitors. Survey respondents could be asked about their travel costs, but this is rare and typically travel costs are assigned to respondents by the analyst on the basis of distance travelled, which itself is usually estimated by the analyst by assigning respondents, on the basis of information supplied by them such as a postal or zip code, to a number of zones and measuring distance from the centre of each zone using a map. The regression is then, usually, of the number of visits per unit population from zone i on travel cost from zone i. For some sites and some surveys it is possible to have i index individuals, when the dependent variable is the number of visits in a period of time by individual i and the explanatory variable is travel costs per visit for individual i. Where the data are such that either approach could be followed, there is some dispute as to whether it is better to use the individual data or to average costs over individuals in given zones and regress total zonal visits per unit population on average zonal travel costs. Most TCM applications employ the zonal average approach, often simply because of data limitations.

The MCS figure that is produced by the TCM as described here is the total MCS for the sample of visitors included in the survey. Unless the survey has been such that the sample is the population,

there remains the question of how to go from this figure to the MCS figure to be used in ECBA. This can be quite complicated and the answer depends on the nature and timing of the survey in relation to the characteristics of the site concerned. One fairly standard procedure is to divide the MCS figure produced as described here by the total number of visits covered by the survey to get a figure for MCS per visit, which is then multiplied by the (usually estimated) number of visits per year to get a figure for MCS per year for use in the ECBA. In Willis and Garrod (1991a) MCS per visit is estimated using both individual data on visits per year and zonal data on visits per unit population as dependent variable, with explanatory variables defined appropriately in each case. Across six forest sites in the UK MCS per visit ranged from £1.43 to £2.60 (average £2.03) using the zonal averaging approach, and from £0.06 to £0.96 (average £0.48) using individual data. The two methods did not even rank the sites in the same order. Clearly, given annual total visitor numbers of the order of one million, one could draw quite different conclusions as to the use value of one of these sites according to which of these approaches was used.

Box 12.1 works through an illustrative, zonal average, TCM application where the numbers have been constructed so as to make the calculations simple and bring out the basic ideas as clearly as possible.

Box 12.1 An illustrative zonal average TCM example

The basic data for a national park with no admission charge are:

Zone	Visits	Population (thousands)	Distance (miles)
1	15 000	2 000	10
2	48 000	8 000	15
3	11 250	2 500	20
4	45 000	15 000	25
5	34 000	22 660	30

where distance is measured from the centre of the zone, and we are assuming, in the interest of keeping the story simple, that we know the total number of visits in the year from each zone. We will also assume that we know the travel cost per

mile to be £1. The first step is to estimate the parameters of the trip generating function

$$v_i = \alpha + \beta(T_i + P) + \varepsilon_i$$

where v_i is visits per thousand population from the ith zone, T_i is travel cost from the ith zone, P is the admission price which is zero, and ε_i is the error term. We get ordinary least squares estimates for α and β using:

$$\hat{\beta} = \frac{\sum_i (v_i - \bar{v})(T_i - \bar{T})}{\sum_i (T_i - \bar{T})^2}$$

and

$$\hat{\alpha} = \bar{v} - \hat{\beta}\bar{T}$$

Box 12.1 *continued*

From

	v_i	T_i	$v_i - \bar{v}$	$T_i - \bar{T}$	$(v_i - \bar{v})^2$	$(T_i - \bar{T})^2$	$(v_i - \bar{v})(T_i - \bar{T})$
	7.5	10	3	−10	9	100	−30
	6	15	1.5	−5	2.25	25	−7.5
	4.5	20	0	0	0	0	0
	3	25	−1.5	5	2.25	25	−7.5
	1.5	30	−3	10	9	100	−30
Sum	22.5	100				250	−75
Mean	4.5	20					

we get the estimated trip generating equation as

$$\hat{v}_i = 10.5 - 0.3(T_i + P)$$

The second step is to use this estimate to derive the relationship between visits and the price of admission, which is often referred to in the literature as the surrogate demand function. We will consider P varying in steps of £5. For $P = £5$ predicted visits from each zone, $\hat{V}_i$, and total predicted visits are calculated using the estimated trip generating function as follows:

Zone	$C_i = T_i + P$	$\hat{v}_i = 10.5 - 0.3C_i$	$\hat{V}_i$
1	10	6	12 000
2	15	4.5	36 000
3	20	3	7 500
4	25	1.5	22 500
5	30	0	0
Total			78 000

Proceeding in the same way for $P = £10$ and so on, we get the following simulated price/visits data for the surrogate demand function:

P	V
0	153 250
5	78 000
10	36 750
15	18 000
20	3 000
25	0

Figure 12.8 shows the surrogate demand function. The third step is to get from this the estimate of consumers' surplus for the year. Given that in fact $P = 0$, total consumers' surplus is the total area under this demand function, which is

$[(153\ 250 - 78\ 000) \times 5 \times 0.5] + [78\ 000 \times 5]$

plus

$[(78\ 000 - 36\ 750) \times 5 \times 0.5] + [36\ 750 \times 5]$

plus

$[(36\ 750 - 18\ 000) \times 5 \times 0.5] + [18\ 000 \times 5]$

plus

$[(18\ 000 - 3000) \times 5 \times 0.5] + [3000 \times 5]$

plus

$[3000 \times 5 \times 0.5]$

which is £1 061 875.

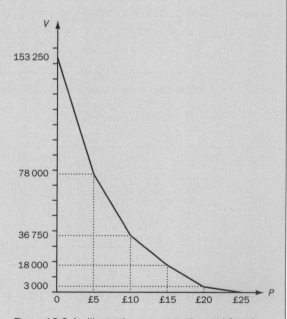

Figure 12.8 An illustrative surrogate demand function

12.4.1 Some TCM problems

There are a number of other problems that can arise in the implementation of the TCM. Here we briefly discuss four of them. It should be noted that while we discuss each problem in isolation, they can, and do, occur simultaneously in particular TCM applications. References to fuller discussions of these problems, and of others, will be found in the Further Reading section at the end of the chapter.

12.4.1.1 Functional form

In going from equation 12.7 to equation 12.8 we imposed linearity. There was no particular reason, apart from convenience, for doing this. The economic theory of constrained optimisation with weak complementarity does not imply any particular functional form for the trip generating equation. On *a priori* grounds, the trip generating equation could as well have been written as linear in logarithms:

$$\log(V_i) = \alpha + \beta\log(C_i) + \varepsilon_i \qquad (12.15)$$

Given no *a priori* guidance, it is tempting to let the data decide, and, for example, to choose between the linear and linear-in-logarithms specifications according to which fits the data better. The functional form chosen can have non-trivial implications for the result obtained. Hanley (1989a) reports the results for MCS per visit for four different specifications of the trip generating equation fitted to travel cost and visit data, using the zonal averaging approach, for a forest site. The range is from £0.32 to £15.13. Many of the TCM applications reported in the literature do not provide this kind of sensitivity analysis, simply reporting an MCS result for the chosen functional form.

12.4.1.2 Estimation

In many of the early applications of the TCM the trip generating equation parameters are estimated by the method of ordinary least squares, but latterly it has been realised that there are a number of reasons why this may give rise to biased estimates of the parameters. The development of improved estimation techniques to deal with particular problems arising in different sorts of TCM application is now a very active area of research. If, for example, the data are collected from a survey of actual visitors to the site of interest, rather than from a sample of the population of potential visitors, then the dependent variable in the trip generating equation is constrained to be equal to or greater than one, where i indexes individuals and the dependent variable is visits per period. In this case, a form of maximum likelihood estimation which takes account of the nature of the data generating system is superior to ordinary least squares. It needs to be noted that this is true so long as there are no other problems with the data and the analysis. If the 'wrong' functional form for the trip generating function is used, estimation using a method appropriate for censored and truncated data may produce more biased parameter estimates than estimation by ordinary least squares. Note carefully that we say 'may', not 'will', here. There is relatively little numerical guidance on these matters – we do not, that is, have much idea about how wrong parameter estimates will be under various circumstances.

12.4.1.3 Substitute sites

In going from equation 12.7 to equation 12.8 we suppressed the role of other variables in the trip generating function so as to focus on the key assumption of the equivalence of travel and access costs in the TCM. Clearly, one would not expect either visits by an individual or visits from a geographical area or zone to depend only on travel and access costs. Income, for example, could be expected to vary across i and to affect visitation rates. To the extent that relevant variables, such as income, are omitted from the trip generating equation that is estimated, the result will be biased estimation of α and β, and hence of MCS_i and MCS.[3] TCM researchers do now

---

[3] A 'relevant' variable is one that does have a systematic effect on the dependent variable. Strictly, the statement in the text is true only if the omitted variable is not orthogonal to the variables included in the regression; that is, where the omitted relevant variable is totally uncorrelated with the included variables there is not a problem of biased estimation. However, such a situation would be unusual for a relevant variable, and is in any case hard to properly test for, so the standard working assumption is that omitted variables give rise to biased estimation. For further discussion see an econometrics text such as, for example, Greene (1993).

routinely collect in their surveys data on such matters as respondent income and include such variables in the estimated trip generating equation. A particular case of the general class of omitted variables problem here that has attracted a lot of attention in the TCM literature is the question of sites that are substitutes for the site of interest. In principle, the problem could be dealt with by estimating

$$V_{1i} = \alpha + \beta_1 C_{1i} + \sum_{j=2}^{j=J} \beta_j C_{ji} + \varepsilon_i \qquad (12.16)$$

where j indexes sites, and site 1 is the site of interest. However, implementing this solution requires identifying substitute sites and collecting the relevant data for all so identified, and TCM applications generally do not deal adequately with the substitute sites issue.

12.4.1.4 Travel cost measurement

One might think that the question of measuring the travel costs on which the TCM relies so heavily would have received a lot of attention in the literature. With the exception of the time costs of travel, this has not, in fact, been the case.

The matter of including the time costs of travel in C_i in equation 12.7 has been considered in the literature since the earliest interest in the TCM. The basic idea is that time spent travelling involves an opportunity cost, and should therefore be included in C_i at a unit price that reflects that opportunity cost. This idea has been formalised in the 'household production function' (HPF) formulation of the basis for the TCM. The HPF approach treats the recreational experience that is an argument in the utility function as a commodity produced by the household using inputs of other commodities – such as motor vehicles and fuel – and time. As in the standard approach, observed consumption levels are interpreted as the result of utility maximisation, but the HPF approach explicitly recognises two constraints, the standard income constraint together with a time constraint. Further, the two constraints are linked in so far as time spent producing recreational experience is not available for work to produce income. This leads naturally to the idea that time spent travelling should be valued using the cost of not working.

There are a number of problems with this simple idea. Simply measuring time spent travelling is not always straightforward. The obvious thing to do, ask survey respondents about it, can lead to strange results, as can be seen in Table 12.4 in Box 12.2. If it is accepted that the cost of not working is the proper way to value time, the problem arises that this cost is going to vary widely over individuals and households. Again, experience suggests that survey responses on such things as wage rates can be unreliable unless great care is taken in survey design and administration. More fundamentally, a non-trivial proportion of visitors will not be in the labour force, and for those who are there is frequently no leisure/work choice to be made as weekly hours and annual holidays are fixed. Again, for some sites and some visitors it is intuitively plausible that time spent travelling would have positive utility as part of the total recreational experience, and should be assigned a negative cost. This has been confirmed empirically in some studies. Despite these difficulties, a number of TCM applications have included some measure of the value of time spent travelling in the definition of T_i, or included it as an additional variable to the money cost of travel. Results for MCS are sensitive to the valuation of time in either of these cases. Some TCM practitioners take the view that the whole matter is so fraught with difficulties of principle and practice that the best way to proceed is to ignore time cost and to treat the MCS based on solely monetary travel costs as a lower bound to some true but unknown MCS.

However, there a number of problems that attend the measurement of those monetary costs themselves, which have not received much attention, nor been satisfactorily resolved, in the literature. Some examples follow. First, consider the matter of a visitor to a site who travels to it from a location where he or she is spending a vacation. Should site travel cost be assessed as just the expenditure incurred in getting to the site from the vacation location, or should some proportion of the expenses of getting to the vacation location from the normal place of residence be included? If the latter, how should the proportion be decided? Second, consider those who visit several sites during the course of a day trip from home. How should the total travel costs for the day be allocated over the sites visited?

Third, there is the matter of discretionary expenses, such as meals consumed while travelling. For lengthy trips, eating along the way will be necessary, and it will generally involve greater expense than eating at home. In such cases, even if the nature of the addition to more straightforward travel costs, such as motor vehicle expenses, could be agreed, there could remain considerable difficulties in getting accurate information from survey respondents.

These examples should suffice to indicate that the measurement of travel costs involving actual monetary expenditure is something which involves judgement on the part of the TCM analyst. Different TCM analysts use different judgements and follow different conventions in measuring monetary travel costs. In Randall (1994) it is argued that for TCM the theoretically correct way to measure travel costs is according to the perceptions of those doing the travelling. This is rarely done. Most TCM applications involve, as described above, the TCM analyst calculating respondents' travel cost using some convention together with information from the survey. Randall calls the results 'researcher-assigned visitation cost estimates' and argues that when they are used: 'The resulting travel costs and welfare estimates remain artefacts of the travel cost accounting and specification conventions selected for imposition' (1994, p. 93). As a result, Randall claims that 'the *best* that we can expect [from TCM applications that use researcher-assigned visitation cost estimates] is ordinally measurable welfare estimates' (1994, p. 95, emphasis added).

Since the purpose of a TCM exercise is generally understood to be the production of cardinal monetary welfare measures, this is a fundamental criticism of TCM as usually practised to date, which would apply even if all TCM analysts used the same conventions for measuring travel costs, which they do not. Not all economists would agree that travel costs should, in principle, be assessed using survey respondent perceptions. However, if the argument for perceived costs is rejected, the question remains as to what convention should be followed in computing 'researcher-assigned visitation cost estimates'. In Box 12.2 we report some results which give some sense of the potential magnitudes of error associated with different conventions.

The implications of adopting different conventions for measuring travel costs for the purpose of estimating consumers' surplus for ECBA can be investigated using the computer-based technique of Monte Carlo analysis. This involves generating data in the computer according to known parameter values, and then using some procedure to estimate the parameters from the data so generated and stored in the computer. Comparison of the known values with the estimated values shows the errors involved.

In this case, data were generated using

$$V_i = 4 - 0.001T_i + \varepsilon_i: \varepsilon_i \sim N(0, \sigma_\varepsilon^2) \quad (12.17)$$

where

$$T_i = (20 + \mu_i)D_i: \mu_i \sim N(0, \sigma_\mu^2) \quad (12.18)$$

for $D_i = i$ for $i = 1, 2, \ldots, 80$, where T_i is the perceived cost of a visit from location i, D_i is distance to the site from location i, and ε_i and μ_i are normally distributed random variables, each with an expected value of zero, and with variances σ_ε^2 and σ_μ^2 respectively. The Tidbinbilla study (Box 12.2) used 80 origins for visits. The parameter value of -0.001 for β is used in equation 12.17 as it is an approximation to the value reported in Table 12.4 when using perceived travel costs, ECPK, and 4 for α comes about in the same way. The figure 20 for the expectation of perceived unit travel cost in equation 12.18 comes from the entry for the mean of ECPK in Table 12.4, being adjusted so that when used in equation 12.17 no negative values for V_i are generated. This use of, approximate, parameter values from previous empirical work in Monte Carlo experiments is sometimes known as 'bootstrapping'. It puts the results from the Monte Carlo analysis in a meaningful context.

The data on V_i generated in this way were used to estimate α and β by ordinary least squares together with travel cost data generated according to two rules:

$$C_i = 10D_i \quad (12.19)$$

$$C_i = 50D_i \quad (12.20)$$

The first of these mimics the situation where the TCM analyst computes travel costs using only the fuel costs of vehicle use – 10 is approximately the mean for FCPK in Table 12.4. The second mimics the use of the full costs of vehicle use – the mean for CPK in Table 12.4 is 49.02.

Box 12.2 The implications of alternative travel cost measurement conventions

A visitor survey was conducted at the Tidbinbilla nature reserve in 1994. The reserve is in the Australian Capital Territory (ACT), and the majority of visitors are residents of ACT and the nearby city of Queanbeyan in New South Wales. For these visitors there are no alternative sites that could be considered close substitutes for Tidbinbilla. The reserve is managed by the ACT Parks and Conservation Service. In 1994 there was no entry charge at Tidbinbilla and opportunities for on-site expenditure were restricted to a small information centre at the entrance selling a limited range of postcards and posters. A survey was completed by 800 visitors during two parts of the year, corresponding to peak and off-peak visitation periods, as determined from visitor number records kept by the ACT Parks and Conservation Service. Respondents were asked (among other things) to provide information on:

- their point of departure for the visit;
- their place of residence;
- their travel mode (there is no bus or rail route which serves Tidbinbilla; some respondents were cyclists);
- the make and model of their motor vehicle, if that mode was used;
- whether their trip from their point of departure involved visiting any other destinations;
- their number of visits to Tidbinbilla in the previous year;
- their perception of the one-way transport cost of this visit – respondents were asked Question 11: How much do you think the journey *to* Tidbinbilla has cost (i.e. one-way expenses incurred in getting here such as petrol and 'wear and tear' on the car)?
- their perception of the time taken for the one-way trip – respondents were asked Question 19: How long did the trip *here* take?

In order to avoid the problem of apportioning travel costs, responses where the trip involved destinations other than Tidbinbilla were removed from the data set. In order to minimise problems about discretionary travel-related expenditures, and to make for accurate distance measurement, responses where the place of residence was other than the ACT or Queanbeyan were also removed, as were the small number of responses from cyclists. Some respondents did not provide sufficient information to accurately identify the make and model of their motor vehicle, and these responses were not used. For the remaining 410 observations, distance was measured from a large-scale map as the distance from the centre of the respondent's ACT suburb, or Queanbeyan, to the entrance to the nature reserve. ACT suburbs are unambiguously identified and known to residents, and are small in area and population size (average 4000 residents). Hence, the measurement of distance travelled was less problematic than in many TCM applications.

An Australian motoring organisation, the NRMA, produces estimates of the costs per kilometre of using different makes and models of motor vehicle. For each vehicle type, the NRMA produces a figure for fuel cost per kilometre, here referred to as FCPK, and for total cost per kilometre, where the latter includes depreciation, maintenance and so on and is referred to here as CPK. For each respondent, the perceived unit price of travel, ECPK, was calculated as the perceived one-way cost, the answer to Question 11, divided by the one-way distance. Also, for each respondent, average travel speed, SPEED, was calculated by dividing one-way distance by one-way time.

The first three columns of Table 12.4 report some descriptive statistics for this data set. Costs are in Australian cents per kilometre: speed is kilometres per hour. Mean perceived cost, ECPK, lies between mean fuel cost and mean total vehicle cost per unit distance, but its range is greater than that for both FCPK and CPK. In regard to SPEED, note that from any origin considered in this data set the trip includes both urban and rural segments, and that the urban speed limit is, at most, 80 kph, while the rural is 100 kph.

The last column in Table 12.4 gives the estimated value for β, the coefficient on travel cost in the trip generating equation, obtained using each of these three measures of unit distance cost applied to distance travelled. The important point here is that the estimated coefficient on travel costs varies in orders of magnitude according to the way that variable is measured. Going from researcher-assigned full costs, CPK, to researcher-assigned fuel cost, FCPK, increases the absolute size of the estimated coefficient by a factor of 7. The ratio of the estimated coefficient using fuel costs, FCPK, to that using respondents' perceived costs, ECPK, is 9.

Table 12.4 Tidbinbilla survey results

	Mean	Minimum	Maximum	Estimated β
FCPK	8.84	5.00	14.00	−0.0072
CPK	49.02	21.00	92.00	−0.0011
ECPK	31.34	0.00	177.78	−0.0008
SPEED	63.92	10.33	168.00	

FCPK – Fuel cost per kilometre
CPK – Full cost per kilometre
ECPK – Perceived price per kilometre
Source: Common *et al.* (1999)

One Monte Carlo experiment involves 50 repetitions of the following steps:

(a) using equations 12.17 and 12.18 to generate data on T_i and V_i, for given values for the variances of the random variables ε and μ, and to calculate total MCS;
(b) using the V_i data with C_i data from either equation 12.19 or equation 12.20 to estimate, by ordinary least squares, the intercept and slope coefficients of the trip generating equation which follow from using either the fuel- or the full-cost convention (note that given the way the data are generated in this experiment, ordinary least squares is an appropriate estimation method);
(c) using the results at (b) to calculate an estimate of MCS;
(d) averaging the results at (a), (b) and (c) across the 50 repetitions, and reporting the averages arising.

A number of such experiments were run for different values of the variances of the random variables ε and μ. However, one of the interesting results was that estimated coefficients of the trip generating equation and MCS were not very sensitive to the values for these variances. Hence here we report, in Table 12.5, only the results for the case where both variances were set at zero.

These results suggest that the TCM analyst's choice of convention for measuring travel costs may well have serious implications for the social decision making that the TCM as input to ECBA is supposed to inform. Consider the following. Suppose that the recreational site to which the results in Table 12.5 apply is the site for a project for which the net present value, leaving aside the impact on recreational value, is $B_d - C_d$, that going ahead with the project would mean that recreational benefits went to zero, and that non-use value was always zero. Let X represent the present value of the lost recreational benefits evaluated on the basis of perceived travel cost. Then, from the Table 12.5 results, evaluation using the full-cost convention would give $2.5X$, while using the fuel-cost convention would give $0.5X$, in round numbers. If, then, the proper basis for social decision making is recreationalists' perceived cost, four cases can be distinguished:

(a) $B_d - C_d < 0.5X$: the project should not go ahead, and this will be the decision whichever cost convention is used;
(b) $0.5X < B_d - C_c < X$: the project should not go ahead, but the decision will be to go ahead if the fuel-cost convention is used, otherwise the decision will be correct;
(c) $X < B_d - C_d < 2.5X$: the project should go ahead, but the decision will go against the project if the full-cost convention is used, otherwise the decision will be correct;
(d) $B_d - C_d > 2.5X$: the project should go ahead, and this will be the decision whichever cost convention is used.

If it is taken that full cost is the proper basis for social decision making, then the cases are:

(e) $B_d - C_d < 0.5X$: the project should not go ahead, and this will be the decision whichever convention is used;
(f) $0.5X < B_d - C_d < X$: the project should not go ahead, but the decision will be to go ahead if the fuel-cost convention is used, otherwise the decision will be correct;
(g) $X < B_d - C_d < 2.5X$: the project should not go ahead, which will be the decision only if the full-cost convention is used;
(h) $B_d - C_d > 2.5X$: the project should go ahead, which will be the decision whichever convention is used.

The $ value of the band widths here depend on the value of X, which depends on the per-trip consumers' surplus as estimated, the annual number of trips in the population, the length of time for which it is assumed that recreation benefit is lost, and the discount rate. Clearly, in some applications the bands could be wide, and, depending on the size of $B_d - C_d$, use of the incorrect cost convention could lead to large social losses.

Given the several problems attending the implementation of the TCM, one might wonder whether it is worth devoting scarce intellectual resources to

Table 12.5 Some Monte Carlo results

	Slope coefficient	MCS
FCPK	−0.002	$208 000
ECPK	−0.001	$416 000
CPK	−0.0004	$1 040 000

it as currently practised, and what are the prospects for improving matters. Smith and Kaoru (1990) attempted an implied answer to the first question by looking directly at the question: are the MCS numbers produced in different TCM applications just random noise? To answer this question they conducted a meta-analysis which involved regressing MCS per visit from a large number of TCM studies on some of the characteristics of the studies, such as the type of recreation activity, whether the price of a substitute was included as an explanatory variable in the trip generating function, the functional form for that equation, and the estimation method used. They found that 43% of the variation in MCS across the TCM applications could be explained in terms of the different characteristics of the studies, and concluded that the MCS results are not just random noise. This may be somewhat reassuring, but clearly means that there is a lot of variation, 57%, in the results that cannot be explained by the characteristics considered. It is of some interest that the convention adopted for measuring travel costs is not one of the characteristics considered by Smith and Kaoru.

If Randall's argument for perceived costs is accepted, then progress requires that all TCM surveys collect data on respondents' perceived travel costs. The range of data for ECPK and SPEED in Table 12.4 in Box 12.2 might be taken as suggesting, consistently with other studies, that eliciting respondents' perceptions requires great care, and hence considerable expense, if it is to produce useful results. If the argument for perceived costs is not accepted, then comparability across TCM applications requires that all analysts adopt the same conventions for travel cost measurement. This seems unlikely to happen, and anyway leaves other problems noted above to be addressed. A more realistic hope might be that all TCM application results will include sensitivity analysis in respect of such matters as travel cost measurement conventions, functional forms for the trip generating equation, and estimation method.

It should be recalled, finally, that we have here been discussing the problems attending the use of the TCM for the estimation of MCS, whereas we know from the preceding section that this is not the correct welfare measure, and that, for quantity/quality changes, we do not know how it relates to the correct welfare measure.

12.5 Contingent valuation

The contingent valuation method (CVM) is a direct method in that it involves asking a sample of the relevant population questions about their WTP or WTA. It is sometimes referred to as a stated preference method. It is called 'contingent valuation' because the valuation is contingent on the hypothetical scenario put to respondents. Its main use is to provide inputs to analyses of changes in the level of provision of public goods/bads, and especially of environmental 'commodities' which have the characteristics of non-excludability and non-divisibility. As compared with indirect methods it is seen by many economists as suffering from the problem that it asks hypothetical questions, whereas indirect methods exploit data on observed, actual, behaviour. On the other hand, the CVM has two advantages over indirect methods. First, it can deal with both use and non-use values, whereas the indirect methods cover only the former, and involve weak-complementarity assumptions. Second, in principle, and unlike the indirect methods, CVM answers to WTP or WTA questions go directly to the theoretically correct monetary measures of utility changes.

While the CVM can be used for both use and non-use values, its actual use has mainly been in regard to the latter. Particularly, most CVM applications have concerned existence, or passive-use, values. Given this, and the fact that indirect methods cannot address existence values, we shall discuss the CVM in the context of trying to ascertain existence values. This reflects the balance of the literature, and is where most of the debates and controversy are located.

We discussed the theoretically correct monetary measures of utility changes in Section 12.2. Here we will confine our attention to changes in environmental quality indicators, in which case it is the surplus measures that are relevant, and Table 12.6 is a rearranged Table 12.3. If we can elicit the correct answer to an appropriate WTP/WTA question from an individual, the answer is the correct monetary measure sought for that individual. For either an improvement or a deterioration, the individual can be asked about WTP or WTA. Which is the correct question? From what they measure, CS or ES, and our previous discussion it is clear that the answer to

Table 12.6 WTP and WTA for environmental quality changes

	WTP	WTA compensation
Improvement	For the change to occur is CS	For the change not occurring is ES
Deterioration	For the change not to occur is ES	For the change occurring is CS

this question is really a statement about the entitlements assumed. CS measures relate to the initial utility level and imply entitlements to the status quo. Thus, asking about WTP for an environmental improvement implies that the individual is entitled to the existing level, as does asking about WTA compensation for a deterioration. ES measures relate to the new level of utility. Asking about WTA compensation for a possible environmental improvement not actually occurring implies an entitlement to the higher level, while asking about WTP to avoid an environmental deterioration implies only an entitlement to the lower level.

12.5.1 CVM steps

The steps involved in applying the CVM can be stated as follows:

1. Creating a survey instrument for the elicitation of individuals' WTP/WTA. This can be broken down into three distinct, but related, components:
   (a) designing the hypothetical scenario,
   (b) deciding whether to ask about WTP or WTA,
   (c) creating a scenario about the means of payment or compensation.
2. Using the survey instrument with a sample of the population of interest.
3. Analysing the responses to the survey.
   This can be seen as having two components:
   (a) using the sample data on WTP/WTA to estimate average WTP/WTA for the population,
   (b) assessing the survey results so as to judge the accuracy of this estimate.
4. Computing total WTP/WTA for the population of interest for use in an ECBA.
5. Conducting sensitivity analysis.

An exhaustive discussion of each of these steps is well beyond the scope of this text. Here we simply comment on some of the more important aspects of CVM practice, and its evolution over time. Box 12.3 summarises a state-of-the-art application in the USA according to the steps enumerated above. References to fuller discussions of the details of CVM practice will be found in the Further Reading section at the end of the chapter.

Box 12.3 Using the CVM to estimate damages from the *Exxon Valdez* oil spill

In 1989 the *Exxon Valdez* ran into submerged rocks shortly after leaving the port of Valdez loaded with crude oil, and 11 million gallons of its cargo flowed from ruptured tanks into the waters of Prince William Sound on the coast of Alaska. This was the largest oil spill in US waters, and was widely regarded as a major environmental disaster, occurring as it did in a wilderness area of outstanding natural beauty. In anticipation of legal action against the ship's owners, the government of Alaska commissioned a team of economists to conduct a CVM study to estimate the damages from the oil spill as the lost existence, or passive use, value that the spill caused. In terms of the five steps in doing CVM work identified and discussed in the text, what the research team did can be summarised as follows.

(1) In designing the scenario and selecting a payment vehicle, the team's primary goal was to develop a survey instrument that would produce a valid and theoretically correct measure of the lost passive use values due to the natural resource injuries caused by the spill. This was seen as entailing:
(a) a scenario which fully described the spill's impacts and was intelligible to all potential respondents;
(b) a plausible payment vehicle;
(c) a scenario that would be seen by respondents as neutral as between the interests of the government, the oil company and environmentalists;
(d) a conservative approach to scenario construction, erring on the side of understating the environmental effects of the oil spill.

Box 12.3 *continued*

Requirement (a) was taken to imply the extensive use of maps, colour photographs and other visual aids, and extensive testing of alternative versions of the scenario and payment vehicle prior to the conduct of the survey itself. It also pointed to conducting the survey by means of face-to-face interviews of respondents. Given previous experience suggesting that respondents have difficulty with WTA questions, requirement (b) was taken to imply that the question asked should be a WTP question. Plausibility was also taken, in part on the basis of the testing of alternatives in focus groups and the like, to require that the payment vehicle should be a one-off tax payment. The focus group work also assisted in designing an instrument that would be seen as neutral. In regard to (d), where scenario construction necessitated choices between options for which neither theory nor survey research practice gave a strong ranking, the option was chosen which would, it was thought, if it had any effect, produce a lower WTP. Thus, for example, respondents were not shown pictures of oiled birds.

The development of the survey instrument used took place over a period of 18 months, and involved initially focus groups, followed by trial interviews and pilot surveys. The form that it finally took was as follows. After being asked about their views on various kinds of public goods and knowledge of the *Exxon Valdez* incident, respondents were presented with information about Prince William Sound, the port of Valdez, the spill and its environmental effects, and a programme to prevent damage from another spill. The programme would involve two coastguard vessels escorting each loaded tanker on its passage through Prince William Sound. These vessels would have two functions: first, reducing the likelihood of a grounding or collision, and second, should an accident occur, keeping the spill from spreading beyond the tanker. The interviewer then stated that the programme would be funded by a one-off tax on oil companies using the port of Valdez and that all households would also pay a one-off tax levy. Before asking about willingness to pay this tax, the interviewer presented material about the reasons why a respondent might not want to pay such a tax,

Table 12.7 Monetary values used in WTP questionnaire for various treatments and various questions

Treatment	A-15	A-16	A-17
A	10	30	5
B	30	60	10
C	60	120	30
D	120	250	60

so as to make it clear that a 'no' vote was socially acceptable.

The WTP question was whether the respondent would vote for the programme, given that the one-off household tax would be an amount x. The survey involved four different treatments in which the amount x varied as shown in Table 12.7 in the column headed A-15, which was the first WTP question number in the survey instrument. Depending on the answer to that question, a second WTP question was put to the interviewee. If the A-15 answer was 'yes', the respondent was asked whether he or she would vote for the programme if the tax cost were to be the higher amount shown in the column headed A-16. If the answer at A-15 was 'no', the interviewee was asked about voting given a tax cost at the lower amount shown in the column headed A-17.

After the WTP questions, the interviewer asked a number of debriefing type questions about the motives for the responses given, about attitudes and beliefs relevant to the scenario, and about the respondent's demographic and socio-economic characteristics.

(2) The survey was conducted using a stratified random sample of dwelling units in the USA. Approximately 1600 units were selected. Given the cost that producing and using foreign-language versions of the survey instrument would have involved, non-English-speaking households were dropped from the sample. Within the remaining households, one respondent was randomly selected. Respondents were randomly assigned to one of the four WTP treatments. The response rate, based on sample size after dropping non-English-speaking households, was 75.2%.

(3) The second column of Table 12.8 gives the proportion of 'yes' responses to the first WTP question, A-15, across the four treatments.

Box 12.3 *continued*

Table 12.8 Response proportions

Treatment	Yes	Yes–Yes	Yes–No	No–Yes	No–No
A ($10, 30, 5)	67.42	45.08	22.35	3.03	29.55
B ($30, 60, 10)	51.69	26.04	26.04	11.32	36.60
C ($60, 120, 30)	50.59	21.26	29.13	9.84	39.76
D ($120, 250, 60)	34.24	13.62	20.62	11.67	54.09

The next four columns give the proportions for response patterns over the two WTP questions that all respondents were asked. Thus, for example, in the third column 45.08% of respondents asked initially about $10 said 'yes' to it and to the $30 that they were subsequently asked about, while in the fifth column 11.67% of the respondents initially asked about $120 said 'no' to it but 'yes' to the $60 that they were subsequently asked about. For the 'yes' answer to the first WTP question, and for the 'yes–yes' and 'no–no' patterns over the two questions, the entries in Table 12.8 look consistent with the basic idea that the probability of a 'yes' vote falls with the price tag attached. Note that the group answering 'no–no' may, as well as including respondents whose WTP lies between zero and the second $x put to them, include respondents who do not think that the escort ship plan would work or think that, as a matter of principle, the oil shippers should bear the whole cost.

(3a) To use the response data to estimate a measure of average WTP, it is necessary to adopt some statistical model assumed to be generating the responses. In this study it was assumed that the underlying distribution of WTP is a Weibull distribution. Estimating the parameters of this distribution using maximum likelihood estimators and the response data gave an estimate of $30.30 (95% confidence interval $26.18 – $35.08) for the median WTP and of $97.18 (95% confidence interval $85.82 – $108.54) for mean WTP. In using the response data here, 'not sure' responses to either WTP question were treated as 'no' responses, consistent with the goal of producing a conservative estimate of average WTP.

(3b) A valuation function, using data on respondents' beliefs, attitudes and characteristics to construct explanatory variables for a regression with WTP as dependent variable, was estimated and the result was taken as demonstrating construct validity. It was found, for example, that a belief that in the absence of the escort ship programme the damage occurring in the future would be greater than in the *Exxon Valdez* case was positively associated with WTP, other things being equal, while a belief that the damage would be less was negatively associated with WTP. Again, it was found that a respondent's self-identification as an environmentalist was positively associated with WTP, other things being equal, as was an expectation of a future visit to Alaska. WTP was found to be positively associated with income level.

(4) Taking the estimated median WTP of $30.30 as the relevant average and multiplying it by the number of English-speaking households in the USA gives a total WTP for the escort ship programme of $2.75 billion. This was interpreted as representing an estimate of the lower bound on the correct, WTA-based, valuation of the passive use value lost as a result of the *Exxon Valdez* oil spill.

(5) Sensitivity analysis was conducted using the estimated valuation function. Thus, for example, the dummy variables representing beliefs about what the impact of a future spill would be in the absence of the escort vessels were all set to zero and the estimated function was then used to generate respondents' WTP. The intention here was to produce estimates of the WTP responses that would have arisen if all respondents had had the same belief in the efficacy of the escort vessel programme. The median of the individual WTP estimates so produced was $27, to be compared with $30.30 based on the actual responses. On the basis of several such experiments using the valuation function it was concluded that the result used at step (4) was reasonably robust.

Another type of sensitivity test involved re-running the survey. The survey described here was conducted in 1991. Two years later the same survey instrument was used again with a national sample, and 'almost identical' results were obtained.

Source: Carson *et al.* (1995a)

12.5.1.1 The survey

There appears now to be a fairly wide consensus about the form that the survey instrument should take, briefly summarised as follows. In regard to point (1)(a), it should posit some programme or policy intended to have clearly stated environmental impacts, either by way of improving matters (better air quality, say) or by way of preventing some deterioration (protecting biodiversity, say). Individuals should then, (1)(b), be asked about their WTP for such a programme or policy by means of, (1)(c), some kind of tax payment. The WTP question should take the form of specifying a sum of money and asking the respondent whether he or she would be willing to pay that sum. This type of WTP question requiring a yes/no answer is referred to as a 'dichotomous choice format' question. Note, especially given that it relates to a tax payment, that it is rather like being asked to cast a vote. The form of survey instrument described here is sometimes referred to as the 'referendum model' for CVM scenario structure. In some applications the respondent is asked to vote twice, with the amount offered at the second pass dependent on the first response, as in Box 12.3.

A number of potential 'biases' have been identified in the CVM literature, and survey design is seen as an exercise in eliminating and reducing bias as much as possible. Two classes of problem are subsumed by the term 'bias' as used in the literature. The first concerns getting respondents to answer the question that would, if they answered honestly, elicit respondents' true WTP in regard to the policy issue that the exercise is intended to inform. The second concerns getting respondents to answer honestly. The basic problems in regard to the revelation of preferences for public goods were discussed in Chapter 5.

An example of 'bias' of the first class is where the environmental 'commodity' perceived as being of concern by the respondent differs from that intended by the CVM analyst. This is known as amenity misspecification bias. Dealing with this class of biases is mainly a matter of the design of the scenario presented, especially in terms of the background information to be given to respondents.

An example of 'bias' of the second class is where the respondent perceives what the analyst intends, but provides a response which is not his or her true WTP but is intended to influence the provision of the environmental 'commodity' and/or his or her level of payment for it. This is called strategic bias. Suppose, for example, that the scenario concerns a programme to protect biodiversity by taking wilderness land into public ownership as a national park, and that respondents are asked what they would be willing to pay toward the cost of acquisition. A respondent who regards the cost collection part of the exercise as purely hypothetical and is desirous of having greater biodiversity protection might overstate his or her true WTP so as to increase the probability of the park coming into being, at no personal cost. On the other hand, a respondent, desiring the park, who thinks that he or she would have to pay the price that he or she stated as their WTP might understate their true WTP in the hope of free-riding on other respondents who honestly report higher WTP. Simply asking respondents to state what they would be willing to pay, as here, is known as 'open-ended bid elicitation' and was fairly common in early CVM applications. One of the reasons why CVM practice has evolved from using the open-ended bid format to the dichotomous choice model, with taxation as the payment vehicle, described above, has been the belief that the latter is less subject to strategic bias. Many CVM practitioners argue that with good survey instrument design strategic bias is not a major problem nowadays.

Good survey instrument design is now seen as involving extensive pre-testing, and the use of focus groups. These are small groups of individuals, up to a dozen or so, who are led by a facilitator through a loosely structured discussion of the issues raised by the scenario and payment vehicle. The purpose of this exercise is to avoid bias of the first kind noted above in regard to the scenario itself, and of the second kind in regard to the payment vehicle and related matters.

12.5.1.2 Getting responses

Given a survey instrument, there are three broad options for obtaining responses from the sample respondents. Conducting face-to-face interviews offers several potential advantages, notably a high response rate and effective information provision, but it is very expensive. Mail surveys are much cheaper, but get lower response rates and tend to restrict the amount of information that can be provided and the number of questions that can be asked. Telephone interviewing is cheap, but restricts the information that can be provided – graphics cannot be used, for example. Clearly, which of these methods is to be used will influence the details of survey instrument design. While the sample should be randomly selected from the population, possibly with some stratification, precisely how it is selected will clearly vary with how the survey is to be administered.

12.5.1.3 Averaging responses

In regard to reporting the average WTP across respondents, the options are the mean and the median. The median is less affected by outliers, which are a few very high WTP responses, and is generally found to be lower than the mean. Most CVM applications report both the mean and the median, but use the median for calculating total WTP. Where the survey follows the single-pass referendum model, responses are analysed using logit analysis and logistic regression methods, and the median WTP is calculated as the sum of money which when used with the estimated regression parameters gives the probability of a 'yes' response as 0.5. For any given sum of money put to them in such a survey, some respondents will say 'no' because they object to the question, rather than because the sum is greater than their WTP. It is now seen as important that the survey takes a form which enables such 'protest' responses to be distinguished from 'no' responses which do reflect the fact that the sum offered is greater than WTP. Where this is done, protest responses are usually ignored in calculating average WTP. Clearly, the treatment of outliers and protest responses can have significant implications for estimated median and, especially, mean WTP.

12.5.1.4 Evaluating responses

A standard procedure for assessing the results of a survey is to use the responses to estimate a valuation or bid function. Typically the survey would ask respondents about their demographic and socio-economic status, and about some of their attitudes,

as well as simply asking them about WTP. The estimation of the valuation function takes the WTP response as the dependent variable in a regression with demographic, socio-economic and attitudinal indicators as explanatory variables. If the estimated parameters are consistent with economic theory and previous experience, this is taken as evidence that some confidence may be placed in all of the survey results, including estimated average WTP. If this is not the case, then the inference would be that the survey had not worked well. Thus, for example, theory and experience have respondents with higher incomes having, other things being equal, higher WTP, so that if the valuation function for a survey involved a regression coefficient on income which was negative and statistically significant, one would have little confidence in its average WTP result.

12.5.1.5 Total WTP

Given average WTP, total WTP is just that average times the size of the relevant population. A question which arises is: what is the relevant population? At one level the question is answered by the conduct of the CVM exercise in regard to sample selection. Thus, if the sample is randomly selected from the electoral rolls for a nation, then the population size is the nation's population. At another level, the question may be open and unresolved. If it is the existence value associated with a world-famous wilderness area known for its biodiversity – the Amazon rainforest, say – that is at issue, it is not obvious that individuals with positive WTP will all be located within the boundaries of the nation where the area is located. But, for practical reasons, global surveys for environmental valuation are not undertaken. Another issue which can be numerically important is the question of on whose behalf respondents state WTP. Should respondents be understood to be stating what is strictly their own WTP, or WTP on behalf of the households that they belong to? Supposing that by good survey design the analyst can be sure that responses are of the first kind, there then remains the question of whether the arising average WTP should be multiplied by the population or by the number of adults in the population? Clearly, for any given average WTP, the answer to this question can make a large difference to calculated total WTP.

12.5.1.6 Sensitivity analysis

Sensitivity analysis can take several forms. The estimated valuation function can be used to figure how the average WTP is affected by variations in the demographic, socio-economic and attitudinal composition of respondents included in the sample used for calculating it. Average WTP can be recalculated following different procedures in relation to outliers and possible or actual protest responses. The survey can be repeated using a different sample, and possibly with minor variations to the scenario. The problem with the last approach to sensitivity analysis is that it is expensive. It will generally be useful to compare the total WTP estimated with the money sum to which the decision that the CVM is supposed to inform would be sensitive, as illustrated in Box 12.4.

12.5.2 Experience with the CVM

A bibliography of CVM 'studies and papers' (Carson *et al.*, 1995b) published at the beginning of 1995 contained 2131 entries. Even supposing that only 50% of the entries are reports of CVM applications, as opposed to theoretical exercises, and bearing in mind the growth in activity since 1995, this suggests a range of experience impossible to properly report here. What follows is, then, selective. The Further Reading section at the end of the chapter includes survey articles which provide many references to the literature: see especially Kriström (1999) and Smith (2000). We have chosen here to discuss four aspects of experience which have been seen as 'problems' for CVM.

Box 12.4 Mining at Coronation Hill?

In 1990 there emerged a proposal to develop a mine at Coronation Hill in the Kakadu national park, which is listed as a World Heritage Area. The Australian federal government referred the matter to a recently established advisory body, the Resource Assessment Commission, which undertook a very thorough exercise in environmental valuation using the CVM, implemented via a survey of a sample of the whole Australian population. This exercise produced a range of estimates for the median individual WTP to preserve Coronation Hill from the proposed development, the smallest of which was $53 per year, which implies a very large figure for total Australian WTP. If it is assumed, conservatively, that the $53 figure is WTP per household, and this annual WTP is converted to a present-value capital sum in the same way as the commercial NPV for the mine was calculated, the EC to be compared with the mine NPV is, in round numbers, $1500 million.

 The publication of this result gave rise to much comment, mainly critical, and some hilarity. It was pointed out that given the small size of the actual area directly affected, the implied per-hectare value of Coronation Hill greatly exceeded real-estate prices in Manhattan, whereas it was 'clapped-out

buffalo country' of little recreational or biological value. In fact, leaving aside environmental considerations and proceeding on a purely commercial basis gave the NPV for the mine as $80 million, so that the threshold per Australian household WTP required to reject the mining project was $5 per year, one-tenth of the low end of the range of estimated individual WTP on the part of Australians. Given that Kakadu is internationally famous for its geological formations, biodiversity and indigenous culture, a case could be made for extending the existence value relevant population, at least, to North America and Europe. On that basis, the size of WTP per Australian household required to block the project would be much smaller than $5.

 In the event, the Australian federal government did not allow the mining project to go ahead. It is not clear that the CVM application actually played any part in that decision. What is clear is that even if the CVM result overestimated true Australian WTP by a factor of 10, it would still be the case that ECBA would reject the mining project even if the Australian population were taken to be the entire relevant population.

Source: Resource Assessment Commission (1991)

12.5.2.1 The size of total WTP

The first problem is the contention that the CVM produces results for total WTP which are implausibly large. Box 12.4 illustrates this with an Australian experience. As illustrated by the 'back of the envelope' calculations in the box, where existence values are involved so that the population is large even a small average WTP will give a very large total WTP. As to the implausibility of the $53 per year for the average, it can be noted that this is approximately equivalent to one small glass of beer per week at Australian prices. It is not obviously implausible that an average individual would say, if asked, that he or she was prepared to make that kind of sacrifice to preserve part of the national heritage.

12.5.2.2 Price and scope sensitivity

The second and third problems – lack of price sensitivity and lack of sensitivity to the extent of the environmental 'commodity' – can be illustrated jointly in the context of another CVM application in Australia by the Resource Assessment Commission, the main features of which are reported in Box 12.5. The term 'preservation values' used there has the same meaning as our 'non-use values'; a TCM exercise was jointly conducted to assess 'use values'. As noted above, where, as here, the single-pass dichotomous choice model is used to elicit WTP, the results can be analysed using the logit model and logistic regression. The respondent is asked whether he or she is willing to pay $X, and answers 'yes' or 'no'. For analysis, the response is treated as a binary variable taking the value 1 or 0. In this application a 'no' is given the value 1 and a 'yes' the value 0. In that case for the logit model

$$\text{Pr(no)} = e^{-z}/(1 + e^{-z}) \qquad (12.21)$$

so that with Pr(yes) equal to one minus Pr(no)

$$\text{Pr(yes)} = 1/(1 + e^{-z}) \qquad (12.22)$$

where $z = f(x)$ is some linear function of the variables determining a yes or no response. If we define the 'odds' as

$$\text{Odds} = \text{Pr(yes)}/\text{Pr(no)}$$

from equations 12.21 and 12.22 we get

$$\text{Odds} = e^z$$

so that

$$\ln(\text{Odds}) = z = f(x) \qquad (12.23)$$

A logistic regression package estimates the parameters of $f(x)$ from the data on individual respondents' yes/no answers and the values taken by the variables specified as arguments in $f(x)$ for individuals. In the case considered in Box 12.5 the arguments of $f(x)$ considered are the cost put to a respondent, X, income, Y, and age, A. With this notation we have

$$\ln(\text{Odds}) = \alpha + \beta_1 X + \beta_2 Y + \beta_3 A \qquad (12.24)$$

where theory says that β_1 is negative and β_2 positive, so that the relative probability of a 'yes' decreases with increases in the 'price' asked of a respondent and increases with income. The results in Table 12.9 in Box 12.5 show the right signs.

However, and this is the second of the problems being illustrated, if we look at the estimated coefficients on $X we see that for one preservation scenario the result is not significant at 5%, and that in all three cases the coefficients appear small. To see this consider the scenario where price sensitivity is the greatest, the 50% preservation scenario. There a coefficient of -0.0029 means that a $100 increase in $X would reduce ln(Odds) by 0.29, that is, would reduce the relative probability of 'yes' by 1.3364, whereas a $1 increase in income would increase ln(Odds) by 0.1325, that is, increase the relative probability of a 'yes' by 1.1416. This lack of price sensitivity was one of the reasons why the Resource Assessment Commission lacked confidence in the results of this CVM application.

Another reason for this lack of confidence is the illustration of the third problem that we are considering, which we described as a lack of sensitivity to the extent of the environmental 'commodity', and which has also been called 'scope insensitivity'. In one of the original papers calling attention to this problem it took the form that WTP for cleaning up the lakes in one region of the Canadian province of Ontario was 'strikingly similar' to that for cleaning up all the lakes in that province. In another CVM application it was found that WTP to prevent bird deaths did not differ significantly across scenarios in which the programme prevented 2000, 20 000 and 200 000 deaths. In the case of Box 12.5, the problem

Box 12.5 The Resource Assessment Commission South-East Forest CV study

Management of the forests of the Australian states of New South Wales and Victoria has been the focus of considerable debate over many years, and in 1990 the Resource Assessment Commission was requested to conduct an Inquiry into forest management. One of several research projects undertaken as part of the 'Forest and Timber Inquiry' was a CV study directed at estimating 'preservation values' for the 'South-East forests'. While the major aim of the study was to collect information relevant to the preservation value of all the forest areas in south-eastern Australia that are on the Register of the National Estate, preservation values were estimated under three different scenarios: setting 100 per cent of the National Estate forests aside for preservation, setting 50 per cent aside, and setting 10 per cent aside. The total sample of respondents comprised three sub-samples, each of which received a different scenario in terms of the area to be set aside for preservation.

Within each of these sub-samples, a further 11 sub-samples were employed to provide variation in the stated costs (X) of preservation put to respondents, which ranged from $2 per year to $400 per year. A mail survey was employed which was administered by a consultancy firm. Reminder cards were sent out ten days after initial dispatch, and a further copy of the questionnaire was sent out ten days after this. The final valid response rate was slightly over 50 per cent.

The questionnaire was pre-tested with focus groups. The final questionnaire, which began with a map of the region in question, was also designed to provide data for a travel cost study of recreation values. In addition to the CV relevant questions and general attitudinal and socio-economic questions, information was collected on recreation statistics such as expenses, activities undertaken, time spent at location, and so forth.

The CV section of the questionnaire began by asking respondents to look at the map again. This was followed with:

We are now going to ask you some questions about what you would like to see happen to the forests in the striped areas shown on the map.

The Resource Assessment Commission is considering two options (A and B) for the future use of the forests in the striped areas of the map: we would like to know which of these options you prefer.

Respondents were then presented with concise summaries, in bullet point form, of both of the options. Option A, referred to as 'Wood Production', was described as involving the setting aside of half of the area in question to grow trees for wood and each year a different 2% of the wood-producing area would be logged, and then allowed to regrow until the next logging. The wood-producing areas were described as having younger trees on average; they would cause habitat disturbance to some rare and endangered species; current job opportunities in the local region would be maintained as a result. Option B, referred to as 'Conservation Reserves', would set an area aside from wood production and consequently would have caused some job losses.

The remainder of the CV question was as follows:

If you choose option B it could cost you $X each year.
This is because:
– with less wood being available the prices of timber products you buy, such as house frames and paper, could rise; and government charges you pay could be increased to pay for the conservation of the areas.
When you make your choice between Options A and B, keep in mind that there may also be other forests in Australia that you may wish to pay further money to have conserved. Which option do you prefer?

Response data was analysed using the logit model. The logistic regression results for $z = f(x)$ for each preservation scenario are given in Table 12.9.

Table 12.9 Logistic regression results for three preservation scenarios

	10% preservation	50% preservation	100% preservation
Constant	−1.5227	0.1533	−1.1976
	(1.18)	(0.12)	(0.94)
$X	−0.0006	−0.0029*	−0.0017*
	(0.75)	(3.47)	(1.98)
Income (logarithm)	0.2942*	0.1325	0.2556*
	(2.47)	(1.01)	(2.13)
Age (years)	−0.0293*	−0.0234*	−0.0296*
	(4.15)	(3.40)	(4.22)
Median WTP	$200.00	$140.00	$43.50

* Indicates statistical significance at 5%, two-tailed test
Source: Adapted from Blamey *et al.* (1995)

is even worse. Median WTP actually decreases as the area to be set aside for preservation increases.

The results in Box 12.5 are an illustration of two insensitivity problems that have appeared in a number of CVM applications. It is not the case that all CVM applications have produced results demonstrating these insensitivities. Carson (1995) reports results from over 30 CVM applications where the hypothesis of scope insensitivity can be tested and is rejected. He argues that where there is scope insensitivity it is a consequence of 'poor' survey design and administration. Others take the view that, at least in some cases, these insensitivities reflect problems with the behavioural assumptions underlying the CVM. These positions are not necessarily mutually exclusive. It may be that while survey respondents have an inclination not to act as economists require, they can be induced to overcome that inclination by avoiding 'poor' survey design and administration. This raises questions which we return to later in this section.

12.5.2.3 WTP or WTA?

The fourth problem to be briefly considered here concerns WTP and WTA results obtained in CVM applications. As noted in the section on the theory of environmental valuation (12.2), the CVM has an advantage over indirect methods in that it goes, in principle, directly to the correct monetary measures of utility change, rather than producing results for MCS. Given that where it is quality change that is at issue, the typical case in the environmental context, the approximation involved in using MCS is of unknown size, this is seen by many economists as an important advantage. However, the question remains as to whether to ask about WTP or WTA. Suppose that we are concerned with an ECBA of a proposed development in a wilderness area, so that the quality change at issue is a deterioration. Then, from Table 12.6 we see that we could try to elicit ES via a WTP question or CS via a WTA question. Which should we use?

In the early days of CVM application it was widely supposed that for a given scenario the result should not materially depend on which question was used. This belief persisted after it was recognised that the Willig (1976) result did not transfer from

the CV/EV context (price changes) to the CS/ES context (quality changes). Randall and Stoll (1980) established that although the contexts differed, CS and ES would be close together for commodities for which expenditure was small in relation to income, so that WTP and WTA questions should produce similar results. However, in CVM applications where both questions were asked, it was routinely found that WTA was much greater than WTP. In the first study to estimate both, for example, Hammack and Brown (1974) reported WTA four times larger than WTP for the same change. The apparent persistent mismatch between the predictions of utility theory and CVM results troubled economists working in the field. Acceptance of the theory implied that CVM practice was in some way deficient. However, similar results were emerging from experimental economics.

In 1986 a paper by Hanemann showed that it was the understanding of the predictions of the theory that was incorrect (now available as Hanemann, 1991). He showed that utility theory actually predicts that for commodities where there are limited possibilities for substitution, WTA could be much larger than WTP. While this resolves the apparent contradiction between theory and evidence, it leads to another problem for using CVM as input to ECBA. If the theory says that WTA and WTP answers can be very different in circumstances likely to be typical in ECBA, then it matters which one is asked about. Given the observed size differences as between WTA and WTP results, which of them is used in an ECBA could make the difference between approving and rejecting a wilderness-threatening project. As noted earlier, the choice between CS and ES is really a decision about property rights. To ask about WTA and use CS is to take it that the status quo is the relevant reference point, so that individuals have an implicit property right in a public good which is an undisturbed wilderness, whereas to ask about WTP and use ES takes the situation with a damaged wilderness as the relevant reference point, and implies no such property rights. The policy implications arising are discussed in Knetsch (1990).

The general view appears to be that ECBA should in this kind of context proceed on the former basis, and properly use WTA questions. This is where the problem arises, as experience with CVM indicates that many individuals have difficulty with WTA questions. Where the WTA format has been used, there is a consistently high level of protest responses, with many individuals either refusing to accept any amount of compensation or accepting only indefinitely large amounts. In some cases the WTA format has produced protest response rates as high as 50% (Mitchell and Carson, 1989). This suggests that whatever the theoretical arguments for the WTA format, its use in practice is undesirable. Hence, there appears to be an emerging consensus that good CVM practice involves using the WTP format, and treating it as providing a lower bound for the more appropriate WTA result.

12.5.3 Respondent behaviour

Experience with the use of CVM to determine existence values has revealed several problems:

- high incidence of protest responses;
- high estimates of average WTP;
- low sensitivity of yes/no responses to price variation (in dichotomous choice formats);
- low scope-sensitivity;
- large differences between WTP and WTA.

We now briefly review some contributions to the literature which argue that these problems arise from the fact that at least some of those who are subjects of CVM surveys are not behaving according to the theoretical model set out earlier in this chapter, where a consumer maximises a single well-behaved utility function defined over commodities and environmental services.

12.5.3.1 Citizen responses

In our discussion of ethical objections to ECBA in the previous chapter, we noted that Sagoff has argued that social choices involving important environmental impacts should be made by reference to citizens' deliberations rather than consumers' preferences. Sagoff has also advanced the behavioural hypothesis that many individuals will, in fact, be unable, or unwilling, to make trade-offs between ordinary commodities and important environmental services and attributes. The claim here is that, where

existence values are at issue, responses are not typically on the basis of a single utility function with arguments that are both ordinary commodities and environmental services. Sagoff argues that there is a consumer self which deals with trade-offs between commodities, and a citizen self which deals with important environmental (and other) matters.

If some CVM responses do reflect citizen behaviour, then one could expect to find a lack of price sensitivity in them, where the dichotomous choice format is used, with respondents behaving as voters largely disregarding the price information contained in the question. For the CVM application reported in Box 12.5, Blamey et al. (1995) report results that support the Sagoff hypothesis; see also Blamey (1996). Blamey and Common (1994) report results from some classroom experiments where the majority of subjects offered the choice, before being presented with any price information, between a political and a market-based approach to social decision making about preservation, opted for the former; see also Common et al. (1997). These subjects were, after committing to one or the other institutional setting, presented with a cost, which varied across subjects, and asked if they would be willing to meet it. Subjects opting for the political institutional framework were asked dichotomous-choice questions regarding reallocations of government expenditure. The proportion answering 'yes' declined as the amount to be taken away from other government programmes increased. This suggests that individuals as citizens may be 'price'-sensitive when they are asked questions that conform to their understanding of the proper context for dealing with the issues.

12.5.3.2 Lexicographic preferences

Cognitive psychologists have observed the use by individuals of non-compensatory strategies for choice. One form of non-compensatory decision rule is the lexicographic preference ordering, in which alternatives are compared on the most important dimension only, unless equal scores are obtained, in which case scores on the second most important dimension are considered, and so on until a decision is reached. If individuals have lexicographic preferences, well-behaved utility functions do not exist in the sense that indifference curves cannot be drawn.[4]

Edwards (1986) suggested that individuals' ethical attitudes could give rise to lexicographic preference orderings of ordinary commodities and environmental attributes, based on a moral commitment in favour of environmental protection. Edwards (1992) considered bounded lexicographic preferences where, for example, species preservation is always preferred to more income, so long as income is above some threshold level. Lexicographic preferences would imply a lack of price sensitivity, and could give rise to high estimates of average WTP for preservation. Spash and Hanley (1995) identified lexicographic preferences in a CVM study using open-ended questioning about WTP where respondents stated a zero WTP for the reason that biodiversity should be protected by law, and where respondents stated that animals/ecosystems/plants should be protected irrespective of the costs and refused to give a WTP amount. Common *et al.* (1997) conducted some experiments to investigate the possibility of lexicographic preferences with respect to environmental goods and obtained results consistent with lexicographic preferences for approximately a quarter of respondents.

Ethical commitments are not the only possible source of lexicographic preference orderings. It appears consistent with work in psychology that they may alternatively reflect a rule of thumb strategy adopted to deal with information processing difficulties, or with uncertainty as to the consequences of choice. In the study reported in Common *et al.* (1997), an additional quarter of subjects reported preferences that were incomplete or intransitive. Faced with a dichotomous-choice CVM question in a postal survey, individuals do not have the option of reporting such difficulties. They must answer 'yes' or 'no', or not respond at all.

12.5.3.3 Responsibility considerations

Individuals are likely to think that treatment of problems is the responsibility of those who caused them in the first place, and/or those who most stand to benefit from their solution. Since most CVM questions imply that the respondent has some responsibility to help protect the environment, thereby justifying some sort of payment, the extent to which this aligns with the individual's own perception of responsibilities regarding the issue in question has an important influence on the likelihood of a 'yes' response to a WTP question, and on the likelihood of protest where the format allows it. Harris and Brown (1992) stress the important influence responsibility ascriptions may have on CV responses. Peterson *et al.* (1996) investigated the effects of different levels of moral responsibility on CV responses and concluded (p. 156) that:

> when in a role of agency for the public interest, people tend to use a different utility function than when in the role of individual consumer. When compared with shared responsibility, sole responsibility for choices among public circumstances tends to increase the relative value of public goods and services, with the effect being greatest for environmental goods.

An important question that arises is whether 'no' responses to the question 'would you be willing to pay $x?' that are motivated by denial of responsibility can be considered legitimate from a CBA standpoint. Denial of responsibility is likely to result in protest responses and outliers, which are not generally considered legitimate CVM responses for CBA. In fact, CVM surveys frequently have not investigated the basis for 'no' or 'yes' responses. If a proportion of 'no' responses are motivated by responsibility denial protest, and if it is accepted that such responses are not valid for CBA, then including such responses in the estimation of average WTP will produce results that are biased with respect to the desired outcome. Stevens *et al.* (1991) found that the majority of respondents would not pay any money for the existence of bald eagles or wild turkeys in New England, or for salmon restoration. In this study response motivations were investigated. In the case of bird preservation, 40% of zero WTP responses protested the payment vehicle used in the CVM question on responsibility grounds, stating

---

[4]   In technical terms the continuity condition for the existence of well-behaved utility functions is violated when preferences are lexicographic – see Deaton and Muellbauer (1980).

that 'these species should be preserved but that the money should come from taxes or license fees'. Stevens *et al.* also report that: 'Twenty-five percent protested for ethical reasons, claiming that wildlife values should not be measured in dollar terms' (p. 397).

12.5.3.4 The purchase of moral satisfaction

A controversial paper by Kahneman and Knetsch (1992a) sought to explain scope insensitivity in CVM studies in terms of respondents using their participation in a CVM to get a 'warm inner glow' from the (hypothetical) purchase of moral satisfaction by saying 'yes' to a WTP question about the 'good cause' of environmental protection. According to Kahneman and Knetsch an important feature of the warm inner glow hypothesis is that the 'warm glow of moral satisfaction . . . increases with the size of the contribution: for this unusual good, the expenditure is an essential aspect of consumption' (p. 64). The hypothesis is claimed to explain scope insensitivity in that the 'moral satisfaction associated with contributions to an inclusive cause, extends with little loss to any subset of that cause'. This claim is disputed in a number of papers: see, for example, Smith (1992) and Harrison (1992). Kahneman and Knetsch (1992b) is a response to some of the criticism that their work attracted. Subsequent contributions to this debate are Diamond *et al.* (1993), Plott (1993) and Kemp and Maxwell (1993). One of the issues raised in the debate is that the warm glow hypothesis proper has moral satisfaction attaching to actual donations to good causes, whereas responses to CVM questions do not entail actual expenditure.

Schkade and Payne (1993, 1994) used verbal protocol analysis to investigate the thought processes driving CVM responses, and found that 23% of respondents 'suggested a desire to signal concern for larger or more inclusive issues [than those covered in the CVM question] such as preserving the environment or leaving the planet for their progeny'. They interpret this as support for the Kahneman and Knetsch hypothesis. Given our remarks above, it is not clear that it is, though it clearly is consistent with an influence from ethical attitudes to CVM responses for some individuals.

12.5.3.5 Expressive benefits and decisiveness discounting

We consider next a behavioural hypothesis for CVM respondents which has affinities with the Kahneman and Knetsch hypothesis, but is not subject to the difficulty that whereas the warm inner glow hypothesis proper relates to actual expenditure, CVM responses concern hypothetical expenditure. Public choice theory seeks to explain voting behaviour in terms of the instrumental pursuit of self-interest – individuals vote for the candidate who promises to deliver what they want. However, in purely instrumental terms, it is difficult to see why any individual should incur the costs of voting, given the low probability that his or her vote will be decisive. Brennan and Lomasky (1993) offer an explanation of voting in terms of, on the one hand, the benefits that individuals derive from the act of expressing what we have called ethical attitudes, and on the other the fact that whereas the instrumental benefits of voting are discounted by the low probability of being decisive, these expressive benefits are not so discounted.

Blamey (1998) argues that the Brennan and Lomasky argument applies to CVM responses, which are more like casting a vote than buying a commodity in relation to the likely salience of ethical attitudes and the decisiveness discounting of any instrumental personal benefits. This hypothesis can explain both a lack of price-responsiveness- and scope-insensitivity-type phenomena in CVM studies. Blamey also argues that this hypothesis about CVM responses can explain seemingly lexicographic preference revelation there.

12.5.3.6 An ethical explanation of WTP and WTA divergences

We have noted that it is now understood that the standard theory can accommodate the observed large discrepancies between WTP and WTA. Here we note that there may be an alternative explanation in terms of ethical attitudes. Recall Sagoff's behavioural distinction between the citizen self and the consumer self, and consider such a dualistic individual confronted with a CVM questionnaire. Requested to pay for environmental preservation as a consumer, the citizen will find the question inappropriate, but not wildly so. Asked to accept individual compensation for allowing damage to a collective asset such as the natural environment, and to say how much, the citizen will find the question wildly inappropriate. Consider an analogy. An individual might believe that poverty relief is properly a matter for the state, yet have few qualms about making a contribution, when asked, to a charity engaged in helping the poor. Now consider such an individual asked the question: how much would you need to be paid to compensate you for the abolition of all state-financed poverty relief? For many, but not all, such individuals, there is likely to be a very large, but non-infinite, answer to such a question – some price at which the prospective consumer gain will compensate for the mental costs of acting against an ethical attitude.

12.5.4 Assessing the CVM

Particularly where non-use values are at issue, the use of the CVM is controversial. It is useful to distinguish two areas of debate. The first, although often focusing on CVM for non-use values, is actually about ECBA and the use there of monetary valuations. We covered this area of debate, mainly between economists and non-economists, in the previous chapter. In the second area of debate, which is mainly the subject matter of exchanges within the economics profession, the role of ECBA and the arising need for environmental valuation are taken as given, and the question is whether CVM can provide accurate valuations.

Within economics, it is accepted that decisions should be made according to efficiency criteria, and that for this to happen information about individuals' preferences, as captured in such measures as CS and ES, is needed. Economists are generally much more comfortable with preference information revealed through actual behaviour than through answers to hypothetical questions. Given that, suspicion about CVM results for existence values persists because there is no way that they can be compared with what is known to be the truth to assess CVM performance. Assessing the validity and usefulness of CVM results is a matter of judgement based on evidence of various kinds from various sources. Drawing on work in psychology, where attempts are made to measure concepts like intelligence, it has been suggested that in coming to a judgement about the CVM it is useful to distinguish and consider three kinds of validity.

- Content validity concerns the extent to which all of the aspects of the concept are adequately covered. Assessing a particular CVM application for its content validity is a matter of forming a view about whether the scenario in all of its dimensions is likely to be conducive to the revelation of true WTP or WTA for the 'commodity' intended. Experience, in terms of protest responses and with focus groups, has led to content validity being considered more likely with a WTP format than with a WTA format.
- Construct validity concerns the degree to which the estimated CVM measure agrees with other measures as predicted by theory. Two particular forms have been distinguished in the literature. Convergent validity concerns agreement of the CVM result with a result for the same 'commodity' obtained by another method, such as the TCM, for example. Of course, such convergence does not definitively establish that the CVM result is correct: problems with the TCM were discussed above. Also, it should be noted that this assessment of convergent validity is only possible where it is use values that are at issue. Theoretical validity is assessed by considering the relationship between the CVM result and other variables that theory suggests are related to it in some particular way. An example of generating evidence on theoretical validity would be the use of the estimated valuation or bid function described in Box 12.3, in which case the results were taken as establishing theoretical construct validity. Another would be looking at scope sensitivity, as described in discussing Box 12.5, in which case the results were against theoretical construct validity.
- Criterion validity is assessed by comparing a CVM result with something, the criterion, that is definitely closer to what it is intended that the CVM measure than the CVM result itself. Clearly, the ideal criterion would be market price data, but, equally clearly, such are not currently available – if they were nobody would be doing

a CVM application. In the case of existence values, actual market price data could never be available. In the case of use values, it may be possible to create a market where one did not previously exist, and thus to test a CVM result. Simulated markets have been used to consider criterion validity, and involve setting up experimental situations where individuals actually pay or get compensation.

We have discussed environmental valuation generally and CVM particularly in the context of ECBA. In the USA the courts have decided that CVM-based evidence on non-use values may be admissible in determining the compensation payments to be made where actual damage has occurred. The sums of real money involved can be large – billions of dollars. This has sharpened the controversy. The US government agency responsible for setting the rules for the assessment of damages from oil spills, the National Oceanic and Atmospheric Administration (NOAA) of the US Department of Commerce, convened a panel of experts, co-chaired by two Nobel laureates in economics (Kenneth Arrow and Robert Solow), to advise on the reliability of CVM for the role allowed it by the courts. The panel's report (US Department of Commerce, 1993) gave CVM for what it referred to as passive-use values a qualified endorsement. It states that

> The Panel starts from the premise that passive-use loss – interim or permanent – is a meaningful component of the total damage resulting from environmental accidents.

and comments that

> It has been argued in the literature and in comments addressed to the Panel that the results of CV studies are variable, sensitive to the details of the survey instrument used, and vulnerable to upward bias. These arguments are plausible. However, some antagonists of the CV approach go so far as to suggest that there can be no useful information content to CV results. The Panel is unpersuaded by these extreme arguments.

The Panel identified 'a number of stringent guidelines for the conduct of CV studies', concluding that

> under those conditions . . . CV studies convey useful information. We think it is fair to describe such information as reliable by the standards that seem to

be implicit in similar contexts, like market analysis for new and innovative products and the assessment of other damages normally allowed in court proceedings

and that

> CV studies can produce estimates reliable enough to be the starting of a judicial process of damage assessment, including lost passive-use values.

The Panel's guidelines covered all aspects of the design and conduct of a CVM application. The *Exxon Valdez* exercise reported in Box 12.3 can be considered as exemplifying compliance with the guidelines. Particularly, the Panel recommended face-to-face interviewing, the use of the WTP question, and the 'use of a dichotomous question that asks respondents to vote for or against a particular level of taxation'. Discussing the problem of eliciting reliable 'CV estimates', the Panel stated that:

> The simplest way to approach the problem is to consider the CV survey as essentially a self-contained referendum in which respondents vote on whether to tax themselves or not for a particular purpose.

Other economists are less optimistic about the prospects for CVM providing useful information on non-use values, whether for damage assessment in litigation or for use in ECBA. There is a widespread view that it is necessarily the case that 'if you ask hypothetical questions you get hypothetical answers'. Peterson (1992) expressed the assessment, which he thought shared by many, that

> CV works where it is not needed (for example, to measure the value of private goods), but is flawed and useless for measuring those values for which it may be the only hope (for example, such extreme public goods as existence value or subsistence use of natural resources).

Such a judgement depends, as does that of the NOAA Panel, on what is meant by 'works'. Recall that the purpose of the CVM as originally envisaged was the accurate estimation of the correct monetary measures of utility changes associated with environmental quality change as required for input to ECBA. This is Peterson's criterion. The NOAA Panel uses a different criterion. By 'works' it means the provision of 'useful information' about the taxes that people are willing to pay in connection with programmes intended to protect the environment, as in the *Exxon Valdez* case. For the Panel, a CV exercise is 'essentially a self-contained referendum in which respondents vote on whether to tax themselves or not for a particular purpose'. A 'particular purpose' cannot be an environmental service as such, and is clearly envisaged by the Panel in setting out its guidelines for good practice as being some governmental programme – recall that in the *Exxon Valdez* case, Box 12.3, respondents were asked about their WTP for a programme to prevent damage from any future spill.

The point is that if we follow the NOAA Panel's recommendations, a CVM exercise is no longer about valuing the environment according to consumers' preferences. It is about obtaining useful information on voters' willingness to pay taxes for environmental programmes. This is an important shift in perspective on CVM exercises. The NOAA Panel's position is not that far from that of some of the critics of ECBA considered in the previous chapter. Those critics were objecting, mainly, to the use of consumers' preferences over states of the environment and ordinary commodities as the criterion for decision making. They were not objecting to asking a sample of voters about how they would respond to different levels of tax increase intended to finance environmental protection programmes. In so far as the NOAA Panel's position is representative of economists, there is some convergence in the area of environmental decision-making methods between economists and their critics.

In a recent paper Sagoff (1998), for example, effectively moves toward the Panel's operational position. In it he argues not for the abandonment of CVM but for its modification. His argument is that CVM can only take into account, as it should, individuals' 'principled views of the public interest, not private preferences about their own consumption' if it 'moves toward a deliberative, discursive, jury-like research method emphasizing informed discussion leading toward a consensus'. Among Sagoff's arguments for the appropriateness of deliberation is that 'individuals do not come to CV surveys with predetermined preferences but must construct them'. This is effectively agreed in much of the CVM design literature, and, as Sagoff notes, 'social learning' is also involved in the construction of preferences

over ordinary, marketed, commodities. The practical problems of involving citizens in deliberation about environmental decisions are, as noted in the previous chapter, being investigated by researchers from a range of disciplines.

12.6 Other techniques

For completeness, we now briefly review some other techniques for environmental valuation developed in recent decades. We do not go into any detail, merely sketching the basic nature of the techniques. In every case there are problems and issues similar in nature to those discussed above for the TCM and CVM, which have been more or less extensively canvassed and addressed in the literature. More information on the theoretical basis for and applications of these techniques can be found in the references provided in the Further Reading section at the end of the chapter.

12.6.1 Hedonic pricing

This is an indirect method, first proposed and used in the early 1970s, based on weak complementarity assumptions. As such, it is subject to the problems about the relationship between what can be estimated, an MCS monetary measure, and that which is required by the theory, a CS or ES monetary measure, that were discussed in the section on the theory of environmental valuation. There are also a number of problems attending the estimation of MCS itself. The basic approach can be indicated in the context of atmospheric pollution, where the hedonic pricing technique has been widely used. While clean air is not a traded good, it is an attribute which seems to influence residential property prices. Evidence from revealed preferences suggests that, other things being equal, a positive relationship exists between the prices that people are willing to pay for housing and the quality of ambient air standards. Examination of property prices might, therefore, enable one to impute the value of clean air.

Assume that data can be collected on housing rents (or house prices, from which rents can be imputed), air quality and a set of attributes which influence housing rents, such as house size, amenities, proximity to employment and neighbourhood characteristics. A representative sample of properties should be drawn, in such a way that properties in the sample are chosen from a variety of localities with differing levels of ambient air quality. Multiple regression analysis can then be used to estimate the relationship between rents and all of the attributes relevant to rents. That estimated relationship can then be used to figure the relationship between rent and air pollution, holding all the other determinants of rent constant. The estimated equation for the determination of rents is known as a 'hedonic price equation'; the derived relationship between rent and pollution is often referred to as a 'rent-pollution function' or a 'rent gradient'. Box 12.6 presents one application for the purpose of estimating the value of air quality improvements in Los Angeles.

The hedonic travel cost method is a variant of the travel cost method which seeks to use data on the attributes of recreational sites together with data on visitation rates and travel costs to value site attributes. The basic idea can be illustrated by considering just two sites which are the same in all respects save that one has some attribute that the other does not. The valuation of that attribute would then be inferred from the difference in the relationship between visitation and travel costs at the two sites.

12.6.2 Choice modelling

Choice modelling, CM, is a recent innovation in stated preference methods which has the same point of departure as hedonic pricing – the idea, originally formalised in Lancaster (1966), that a 'commodity' is most usefully treated as the embodiment of a bundle of attributes or characteristics, which are the things of real interest to consumers. We will present the basic nature of choice modelling by considering a simple constructed example.[5] We will not go into any details, which can be followed up in the references provided in the Further Reading section at the end of the chapter.

Suppose that it is proposed that a forested area currently subject to timber harvesting in parts, and with uncontrolled recreational access in the remainder, becomes a conservation area with no logging and restricted recreational access. Going ahead with the proposal would involve the government paying compensation to the logging firms, so an ECBA is to be undertaken to see whether it should go ahead. Basically, the question is whether the present value of total WTP is equal to or greater than the compensation costs of conservation.

This question could be addressed by means of CVM study. After providing information on the area in question, the central question in such a study would be:

Box 12.6 Valuing improvements in air quality in Los Angeles

Brookshire *et al.* (1982) took a sample of 634 sales of single-family homes which occurred between January 1977 and March 1978 in the Los Angeles metropolitan area. Data on two air pollution variables – nitrogen dioxide (NO_2) and total suspended particulates (TSP) – that are collected regularly at air monitoring stations in the area were used in the study. The objective of the study was to estimate rent differentials associated with air quality improvements for various localities within Los Angeles.

Housing sale prices were assumed to be a function of four sets of variables, H, N, A, and Q, where

H = housing structure variables (living area, number of bathrooms, etc.)
N = neighbourhood variables (crime rate, school quality, population density, etc.)
A = accessibility variables (distances to centres of employment, beaches, etc.)
Q = air quality variables (total suspended particulate matter and NO_2)

Two hedonic price equations were estimated, one for each measure of pollution. Brookshire *et al.* searched through a variety of alternative functional forms for the hedonic equations, and those reported here are the ones that had the best

---

[5] The example and discussion here are based on Bennett and Adamowicz (2001).

Box 12.6 *continued*

statistical fit. In these two equations, note that the dependent variable is the natural logarithm of the home-sale price (in 1978 US$1000). Thus a change of one unit in any one of the explanatory variables results in a proportionate change of the dollar house-sale price, where the magnitude of that proportionate change is given by the estimated coefficient attached to the variable in question. However, in the cases where an explanatory variable also enters in log form, the associated coefficient gives the proportionate change in house-sale price that results from a unit proportionate change in the explanatory variable; it is an elasticity.

So, for example, if distance to the beach is increased by one unit (one unit is probably one mile, although the paper does not define units), then the home-sale price will fall by 0.011 586 in proportionate terms (by 1.1586 per cent), if all other variables are held constant. A unit proportionate increase in NO_2 concentration (a 100 per cent increase, or a doubling) results, *ceteris paribus*, in a proportionate decrease in house prices of 0.224 07 (that is 22.407 per cent).

In regard to the results in Table 12.10, note that

(a) Approximately 90 per cent of the variation in the home-sale price is accounted for by variation in the explanatory variables of the models (see the R^2 statistics).
(b) All coefficients have the expected sign and, except for those on crime, all are statistically significant at the one per cent level. Particularly, the pollution variables have their expected negative influence on sale price and are highly significant.
(c) With the exception only of ethnic composition, the estimated coefficients on variables are very similar across the two reported equations.

Brookshire *et al.* use this information to calculate the rent premium that would be implied if air quality were to improve, for identical homes in given localities. These rent premia differ from one locality to another, but the results indicate rent differentials from $15.44 to $45.92 per month (in 1978 prices) for an improvement from 'poor' to 'fair' air quality, and from $33.17 to $128.46 (in 1978 prices) for an improvement from 'fair' to 'good' air quality. In each case, the higher figures are associated with higher-income communities.

Table 12.10 Estimated hedonic rent gradient equations
Dependent variable = log (home-sale price, in $1000)

Independent variable	NO_2 equation		TSP equation	
Housing structure variables:				
Sale date	0.018591	(9.7577)	0.018654	(9.7727)
Age	−0.018171	(2.3385)	−0.021411	(2.8147)
Living area	0.00017568	(12.126)	0.00017507	(12.069)
Bathrooms	0.15602	(9.609)	0.15703	(9.6636)
Pool	0.058063	(4.6301)	0.058397	(4.6518)
Fireplaces	0.099577	(7.1705)	0.099927	(7.1866)
Neighbourhood variables:				
Log (Crime)	−0.08381	(1.5766)	−0.10401	(1.9974)
School quality	0.0019826	(3.9450)	0.001771	(3.5769)
Ethnic composition (per cent White)	0.027031	(4.3915)	0.043472	(6.2583)
Housing density	−0.000066926	(9.1277)	−0.000067613	(9.2359)
Public safety expenditures	0.00026192	(4.7602)	0.00026143	(4.7418)
Accessibility variables:				
Distance to beach	−0.011586	(7.8321)	−0.011612	(7.7822)
Distance to employment	−0.28514	(14.786)	−0.26232	(14.148)
Air pollution variables:				
log (TSP)			−0.22183	(3.8324)
log (NO_2)	−0.22407	(4.0324)		
Constant	2.2325	(2.9296)	1.0527	(1.4537)
R^2	0.89		0.89	

(Figures in brackets are *t*-statistic for the null hypothesis that the coefficient is zero.)
Source: Adapted from Brookshire *et al.* (1982).

The government is proposing to designate area Y as a conservation area. If it did, the number of rare bird species present would increase from 5 to 10, and the extent of the old-growth forest would increase from 1500 to 1800 hectares. It would be necessary to restrict the number of visitors to 2000 per year. In order to finance the compensation of the logging firms for their lost rights, the government would have to raise additional tax revenue in the form of a one-off levy of £X on all income tax payers. Would you vote for this proposal? Please tick 'yes' or 'no' below.

The size of X would vary across sub-samples. Responses to this question, and others put to respondents at the same time, would be analysed as outlined in the previous section.

Now consider the CM approach to the same issue. First, the various dimensions of the decision are treated as attributes which can take a small number of specified levels. In this case, the attributes and their possible levels are:

Species, number	5	10	15
Old-growth forest, hectares	1500	1800	2000
Visitors per year	4000	3000	2000
Cost per taxpayer, £s	0	10	20

A set of levels for each attribute is known in the CM terminology as an alternative. Each respondent in a CM survey is presented with several choice sets, each of which requires the respondent to select their preferred alternative from among the three or four offered in a single choice set. Each respondent gets the same number of choice sets, but the composition of the set of choice sets presented varies across respondents. Each choice set must include the status quo as one alternative. Thus, in the hypothetical case being considered, one choice set as presented to a respondent could be as follows:

Please consider carefully each of the following options. Given that only these options are available, which one would you choose?			
Attribute	Alternative 1 Status quo	Alternative 2	Alternative 3
Bird species	5	15	10
Hectares of old-growth	1500	1800	1500
Annual visitors	2000	1000	2000
Cost to you	0	20	10
Please circle your preferred option. I would choose the status quo at no cost to me.............. 1 I would choose alternative 1 at a cost to me of £20.......... 2 I would choose alternative 2 at a cost to me of £10.......... 3			

Figure 12.9 One choice set for the hypothetical CM survey example

The data that the CM survey generates is analysed on the assumption that respondents have chosen between alternatives on the basis of selecting the one from among those available which confers the highest utility. The precise form that the statistical analysis of responses takes is determined by what is assumed about the form of the random, or stochastic, element necessarily involved. Most often, the choices that individuals make are analysed using a multinomial logit model. Three main sorts of information can then be extracted from the response data:

- the trade-offs between attributes – how much access they would give up for more bird species, for example;
- given that one of the attributes is a money cost, such trade-offs can be expressed in willingness to pay terms – an implicit price can be estimated for each non-monetary attribute;

- it is then possible to estimate willingness to pay for movement from the status quo to an alternative comprising any bundle of attribute levels, and the result is the compensating surplus measure that is required for use in an ECBA for that alternative.

Whereas the CVM gets the required answer for just one alternative to the status quo, the CM can generate answers about a range of alternatives.

This is seen by many of its proponents as the key advantage of CM over CVM. It is also claimed that it enables the analyst to better control the frame that respondents will use to form their preferences, thus, for example, greatly reducing the CVM scope insensitivity problem. It is also argued that strategic behaviour is less likely with CM responses. The main widely recognised problem with CM as compared with CVM is that it places greater strain on respondents' cognitive capacities. There is the danger that respondents adopt rules of thumb to choose between the alternatives presented.

While there is quite a lot of experience with choice modelling in market research, where Lancaster's work has had considerable impact, there is relatively little experience with it in the environmental valuation context. It is clear, however, that environmental choice modelling faces similar problems to the CVM in regard to survey design and administration. It also shares with CVM the problem that respondents may not be behaving as the utility theory requires, in which case the numbers that it generates are not what are required as inputs to ECBA. As with the CVM, an unresolved problem is the extent to which good survey design can induce respondents to behave as the utility theory requires.

12.6.3 Production-function-based techniques

In our discussion of environmental valuation we have thus far considered environmental services or indicators only as arguments in utility functions. As Table 12.1 makes clear, environmental conditions are of relevance to production, and this is not just a matter of resource inputs to production as usually

understood. In Table 12.1 we have 'harvested timber' as a resource input service used exclusively by firms, but we also have, for example, 'local climate' as a life-support service used by firms and households. We now consider several environmental valuation techniques based on environmental services or indicators as arguments in production functions.

We can represent the basis for these techniques as the production function

$$Q = f(L, K, E) \tag{12.25}$$

where L and K have the usual meanings, and where E is some environmental indicator, and we have

$$\partial Q/\partial L > 0, \; \partial Q/\partial K > 0, \; \partial Q/\partial E > 0 \tag{12.26}$$

To fix ideas, consider an example such as a river fishery where E is water quality.[6] Suppose that some policy to improve water quality is under consideration. If we knew the algebraic form of the production function and the parameter values, we could use that information to map some change in water quality, ΔE, into a change in harvest, ΔQ, for constant levels of L and K. If we could then convert ΔQ into a monetary measure we would have valued the environmental quality change as it affects production. Of course, if E were also an argument in utility functions, this would not be the end of the story – we would have to estimate the value of ΔE in consumption, as well as production, by one of the techniques already discussed.

As regards the effect on production, this is an outline description of what is often called the 'dose–response' valuation technique. It is tempting to think that to convert ΔQ to a monetary measure it is necessary only to multiply it by the unit price of Q, in this case caught fish, to get the change in revenue. This is, in fact, what many applications of the dose–response method do. It is, however, for ECBA purposes strictly incorrect. This is because it takes no account of changes in the opportunity cost of producing Q, and no account of the elasticity of the demand function. Ellis and Fisher (1987) show how this should, in general terms, be done using measures of changes in the sum of producer and

---

[6]   Given our previous discussions of production function specification, see Chapter 2 especially, equations 12.25 and 12.26 are

clearly gross oversimplifications, but they serve to make the point here.

consumer surplus, and give illustrative calculations for a case where E is wetland acreage and Q is the harvest of blue crabs.

Two closely related techniques that have been used for environmental valuation in relation to production are 'avoided cost' and 'averting expenditure'. Write the production function as

$$Q = f(L, K, E, A) \qquad (12.27)$$

where

$$\partial Q/\partial L > 0,\ \partial Q/\partial K > 0,\ \partial Q/\partial E < 0,\ \partial Q/\partial A > 0 \qquad (12.28)$$

In this case increases in the environmental indicator E reduce output for given levels of input of L, Q and A, which is some 'averting' input. We are now considering, say, a factory for the production of computer components where clean air is important. E is ambient air quality where the factory is located, and A is inputs of air-filtration services. According to the averting expenditure approach, air quality deteriorations would be valued in terms of increases in expenditure on A. According to the avoided cost approach, air quality improvements would be valued in terms of reduced expenditure on A.

The use of production functions for valuation is not confined to firms. The 'household production function' approach has households using purchased commodities with their own time and effort to produce some of the arguments that appear in its utility function. We have already noted that the TCM can be understood in this way.

The averting expenditure and avoided cost approaches to valuations for households can also be derived from a household production function formulation.

Summary

The use of environmental cost–benefit analysis requires the availability of monetary measures of the utility changes that would follow from the decision under consideration. In considering how changes in the level of provision of environmental services impact on individuals' utilities it is conventional to distinguish between use and non-use values. In the former case valuation can use indirect methods, which exploit data on observed behaviour in related contexts. The Travel Cost Method and Hedonic Pricing are the main techniques of this class. In regard to non-use values there is no observed behaviour that contains relevant information, so that stated preference, or direct, methods have to be used. These involve asking individuals about their willingness to pay, or to accept, in regard to hypothetical changes in the level of provision. While stated preference methods are mainly used in respect of non-use values, they can also be used to elicit information on use values. The most widely used technique from the stated preference class is Contingent Valuation, which has proved somewhat controversial. A more recently introduced stated preference technique is Choice Modelling.

Further reading

Surveys of environmental valuation, with a practical orientation, are to be found in Winpenny (1991), Turner and Bateman (1990), Pearce and Markandya (1989), Johansson (1987) and Kneese (1984). Randall (1986) discusses categories of value attaching to environmental services. Environmental valuation has generated a very large literature in the past three decades, and provided a substantial proportion of the articles in the most prestigious environmental economics journal, the *Journal of Environmental Economics and Management*. Smith (2000) looks at the role of this journal in development of environmental valuation over the quarter-century that the journal has existed. *Land Economics,*

Environmental and Resource Economics and *Ecological Economics* are other journals where papers on environmental valuation regularly appear. Bishop and Woodward (1995) provide an excellent account of the utility theory for environmental valuation, and Appendix 12.1 here is based on their approach.

The travel cost method is examined and applied, for example, in Freeman (1979), Hanley (1989a), Bockstael *et al.* (1987a, b) and Smith *et al.* (1983). A survey that concentrates mainly on theoretical developments is Bockstael (1995); see also the Kling and Crooker (1999) survey article.

Useful expositions and/or applications of contingent valuation are Randall *et al.* (1974), Hanley (1988), Bishop and Heberlein (1979), Schulze *et al.* (1981b), Bishop and Welsh (1992), Cummings *et al.* (1986) and Mitchell and Carson (1984). Mitchell and Carson (1989) is perhaps now the standard

contingent valuation text, and includes an extensive review of applications. Useful review articles are Bishop *et al.* (1995) and Kriström (1999). Hausman (1993) is a collection of critiques of various aspects of the CVM. Blamey and Common (1999) review the literature on the relevance of ethical attitudes for responses to contingent valuation questions.

Discussions of the application of hedonic pricing are Freeman (1979), Hufschmidt *et al.* (1983) and Kneese (1984). The technique is surveyed in Nelson (1982), Freeman (1995), and most recently Palmquist (1999). Interesting applications may also be found in Marin and Psacharopoulos (1982) and Willis and Garrod (1991a).

Bennett and Blamey (2001) is a collection of papers on the theory and application of choice modelling, with a very comprehensive bibliography: see also Boxall *et al.* (1996) and Adamowicz *et al.* (1994).

Discussion questions

1. Discuss the contention that contingent valuation is, in general, superior to all other techniques for valuing non-marketed goods or services as it is the only technique capable of incorporating non-use values as well as use values.

2. Discuss the contention that, where use values are at issue, contingent valuation is superior to indirect methods as it goes directly to the appropriate theoretical construct for welfare analysis.

3. Should decisions about environmental policy be made on the basis of cost–benefit analysis?

Problems

1. Suppose an individual has the following utility function, where U denotes total utility and Q the quantity of a good or service consumed in a given period of time:

$$U(Q) = \alpha Q + \frac{\beta Q^2}{2}$$

    (a) Obtain the individual's marginal utility function.
    Assume $\alpha = 10$ and $\beta = -1/2$, and that the individual's consumption rises from Q_1 to Q_2, where $Q_1 = 2$ and $Q_2 = 4$.

    (b) What is the individual's marginal utility at Q_1 and Q_2?
    (c) Show that total utility can be interpreted as an area under an appropriate marginal utility function, and use this result to obtain the increase in total utility when consumption rises from Q_1 to Q_2.

2. Suppose that an individual has the utility function

$$U = E^{0.25} + Y^{0.75}$$

where E is some index of environmental quality and Y is income. From an initial situation where

$E = 1$ and $Y = 100$, calculate CS and ES for an increase in E to the level 2, and for a decrease in E to the level 0.5. (It may be useful to refer back to Table 12.3.)

3. With E as some index of environmental quality and C_1 and C_2 as two 'ordinary' commodities, consider the following utility functions in regard to whether C_1 is non-essential and whether C_1 and E are weak complements:

(a) $U = E^\alpha + C_1^\beta + C_2^\delta$
(b) $U = E^\alpha C_1^\beta C_2^\delta$
(c) $U = E^\alpha C_1^\beta + C_2^\delta$

4. This problem illustrates the problem with the TCM in regard to the dependence of estimated consumers surplus on estimated travel costs per unit distance. Re-work the steps in Box 12.1 assuming that the per-mile travel cost is £1.2 rather than the £1 assumed there.

Appendix 12.1 Demand theory and environmental evaluation

We first state some standard results from consumer demand theory (see Deaton and Muellbauer, 1980, or Kreps, 1990) extended by the inclusion of environmental services as parametric arguments in the utility function, using the following notation:[7]

$c = [C_1, \ldots, C_N]$ is a vector of consumption levels for ordinary commodities

$p = [P_1, \ldots, P_N]$ is the corresponding vector of prices

$e = [E_1, \ldots, E_M]$ is a vector of levels of environmental quality indicators

Y is income

The Marshallian demand functions

$$C_i = C_i(p, Y, e) \tag{12.29}$$

are obtained from the problem

$$\text{Max } U(c, e) \text{ subject to } pc = Y \tag{12.30}$$

while the Hicksian demand functions

$$C_i = H_i(p, U, e) \tag{12.31}$$

can be obtained either from the cost minimisation dual to equation 12.30

$$\text{Min } pc \text{ subject to } U(c, e) = U \tag{12.32}$$

or by differentiation of the cost function

$$M = M(p, U, e) \tag{12.33}$$

which gives the minimum expenditure required to achieve some U level. The cost function is sometimes referred to as the expenditure function. The indirect utility function

$$U = V(p, Y, e) \tag{12.34}$$

gives the maximum utility attainable, and is the inverse of the cost function.

Now, let

superscript o refer to the original situation prior to some policy intervention
superscript n refer to the new situation resulting from the policy intervention
superscript * to a vector symbol refer to that vector with one element missing

so that

$$U^o = V(P_i^o, p^*, Y, e) \tag{12.35}$$

and

$$U^n = V(P_i^n, p^*, Y, e) \tag{12.36}$$

respectively refer to maximum attainable utility in the original and new situations where the intervention takes the form of a change in the price of the commodity i.

Then, considering a change in the price of the ith commodity we have

---

[7]   Please note that we have not used bold notation for vectors in this appendix.

$$CV = M(P_i^o, p^*, U^c, e) - M(P_i^n, p^*, U^o, e)$$

$$= -\int_{P_i^o}^{P_i^n} H_i(P_i, p^*, U^o, e)\mathrm{d}P_i \qquad (12.37)$$

and

$$EV = M(P_i^n, p^*, U^n, e) - M(P_i^o, p^*, U^n, e)$$

$$= \int_{P_i^o}^{P_i^n} H_i(P_i, p^*, U^n, e)\mathrm{d}P_i \qquad (12.38)$$

while

$$MCS = \int_{P_i^o}^{P_i^n} C_i(P_i, p^*, Y, e)\mathrm{d}P_i \qquad (12.39)$$

Considering a change in the level of the jth environmental quality indicator, the surplus measures are:

$$CS = M(p, U^o, E_j^o, e^*) - M(p, U^o, E_j^n, e^*) \qquad (12.40)$$

and

$$ES = M(p, U^n, E_j^n, e^*) - M(p, U^n, E_j^o, e^*) \qquad (12.41)$$

Expressing the variation and surplus measures in terms of cost functions makes apparent their relationship to willingness to pay and to accept, and hence the way that, in principle, a well-designed contingent valuation exercise would directly elicit these measures for individuals. The basis for the indirect approach can also be set out in these terms. Recall Figure 12.6 and the accompanying discussion of the example where an improvement in water quality increased the consumption of fishing days and the purchase of fishing permits, at a constant price. There we used C_1 for the commodity, which is fishing days, and we will do that here. We will let the water quality indicator be E_1, and consider a policy intervention which improves E_1 from E_1^o to E_1^n. The shaded area A in Figure 12.6 is the change in CV associated with the increased consumption of C_1 which results from the shift in the demand function for C_1 caused by the improvement in water quality.

The change in the CV is given by:

$$\Delta CV = \int_{P_1^F}^{P_1^C(E_1^n)} H_1(P_1, p^*, U^o, E_1^n, e^*)\mathrm{d}P_1$$

$$- \int_{P_1^F}^{P_1^C(E_1^o)} H_1(P_1, p^*, U^o, E_1^o, e^*)\mathrm{d}P_1 \qquad (12.42)$$

Using equation 12.37 and noting the minus sign on the right-hand side, we can substitute cost function differences for the integrals in equation 12.42 so that

$$\Delta CV = M(P_1^C(E_1^n), p^*, U^o, E_1^n, e^*)$$
$$- M(P_1^F, p^*, U^o, E_1^n, e^*)$$
$$+ M(P_1^F, p^*, U^o, E_1^o, e^*)$$
$$- M(P_1^C(E_1^o), p^*, U^o, E_1^o, e^*)$$

$$= \{M(P_1^F, p^*, U^o, E_1^o, e^*)$$
$$- M(P_1^F, p^*, U^o, E_1^n, e^*)\}$$
$$+ \{M(P_1^C(E_1^n), p^*, U^o, E_1^n, e^*)$$
$$- M(P_1^C(E_1^o), p^*, U^o, E_1^o, e^*)\} \qquad (12.43)$$

From equation 12.40, the first term in braces in equation 12.43 is just the CS associated with the environmental quality change from E_1^o to E_1^n, so that equation 12.43 can be written

$$\Delta CV = CS + \{M(P_1^C(E_1^n), p^*, U^o, E_1^n, e^*)$$
$$- M(P_1^C(E_1^o), p^*, U^o, E_1^o, e^*)\}$$

and given two conditions to be discussed, the second right-hand-side term here can be shown to be zero, so that

$$\Delta CV = CS \qquad (12.44)$$

The two conditions are those stated in the text of the chapter when discussing Figure 12.6. The non-essentialness condition can now be stated as the existence of some consumption bundle c_b^* with C_{1b} equal to zero such that:

$$U(C_{1a}, c_a^*, e) = U(0, c_b^*, e) \qquad (12.45)$$

where C_{1a} is any non-zero level for C_1. The weak complementarity condition is

$$\partial U(0, c^*, E_1, e^*)/\partial E_1 = 0 \qquad (12.46)$$

The proof that these conditions give equation 12.44 was originally due to Mäler (1974); see also Bockstael and McConnell (1993).

CHAPTER 13

Irreversibility, risk and uncertainty

To know one's ignorance is the best part of knowledge.

Lao Tzu, *The Tao*, no. 71

Learning objectives

In this chapter you will

- learn about the difference between risk and uncertainty
- find out how risk affects environmental decision making and have the concepts of option value and option price explained
- see how irreversibility affects environmental decision making and learn about quasi-option value
- consider decision making in the face of uncertainty
- be introduced to the safe minimum standard and the precautionary principle
- learn how environmental performance bonds could work

Introduction

Much of our analysis has assumed that the consequences of decisions are known with certainty and are reversible. However, many of our discussions have implied that these assumptions are not factually correct. Resource decisions concern the future as well as the present, and we cannot know the future with certainty. Many such decisions have consequences that are irreversible. The ecological consequences of economic behaviour especially are frequently a matter of considerable ignorance, beyond the presumption of irreversible change. The assumption of certainty and reversibility in much of

the literature is a simplifying device: it is convenient to assume away some real-world complexities in order to develop analytical insights. But simplifying things in this way is only appropriate when the thing being ignored does not have major consequences for the results of the analysis. It is important, therefore, to see what difference it makes to the analysis if it is assumed that the future is not known with certainty and may involve irreversible change.

The central objective of this chapter, then, is to consider how recognition of imperfect knowledge about the future and irreversibility affects resource and environmental economics. To orient our analysis, we shall consider the use of environmental cost–benefit analysis (ECBA) and particularly we shall make extensive use of the context used to fix ideas in the previous two chapters – the decision about whether to conserve a wilderness area or to allow it to be developed with the consequent loss of wilderness values. The insights developed in this context apply generally where there is incomplete knowledge and irreversibility.

The chapter is organised as follows. In the first section of the chapter we distinguish two kinds of imperfect knowledge, risk and uncertainty, and discuss individual behaviour in a risky world, leaving decision making in the face of uncertainty for later consideration. We then consider, in the second and third sections, option value and quasi-option value, which were mentioned, but not explained, as components of total environmental value in the previous chapter. These arise when individual and social decisions have to be made in the face of risk. The fourth section draws on that discussion to consider ECBA which recognises risk. The penultimate section of the chapter discusses decision making in the face of uncertainty, and in the final section this analysis is used to consider the idea that, in the face of uncertainty combined with irreversibility, environmental policy should be cautious and adopt the safe minimum standard approach.

13.1 Individual decision making in the face of risk

In considering the implications of imperfect knowledge of the future, it is useful to distinguish between risk and uncertainty. Situations involving risk are those where the possible consequences of a decision can be completely enumerated, and probabilities assigned to each possibility. The possibilities are often referred to in the literature as 'states of the world' or 'states of nature', or just 'states'. Where the assignment of probabilities to all states is not possible, we are dealing with uncertainty. Two sorts of uncertainty can be distinguished. We mean by 'uncertainty' the situation where the possible consequences of a decision can be fully enumerated, but where the decision maker cannot assign probabilities. A more profound kind of uncertainty exists where the decision maker cannot enumerate all of the possible consequences of a decision – we call this radical uncertainty.

The distinction that we make between risk and uncertainty, originally due to Knight (1921), is not followed universally in the economics literature. Much modern usage conflates risk and uncertainty in Knight's sense under the general heading of uncertainty. So, for example, Freeman's definitive text on environmental valuation (Freeman, 1993, p. 220) uses the term 'individual uncertainty' to refer to 'situations in which an individual is uncertain as to which of two or more alternative states of nature will be realized'. However, in the context of environmental and resource economics, where some decisions must be made in the face of what can only be properly described as ignorance, we feel that it is useful to continue with Knight's distinction.

The classic risk situations are gambling and insurance. In the former case, unless cheating is involved, probabilities can be assigned to outcomes on the basis of the known properties of the gamble – as with betting on the toss of a coin or the spin of a roulette wheel. In insurance, probabilities are assigned on the basis of lots of past experience – as with life expectancies of individuals at different ages and in different circumstances, or with the incidence of accidents for motor vehicle drivers of different ages. In some gambling situations, such as horse racing, probabilities are also assigned on the basis of past 'form', albeit differently by different observers. Where there is no past 'form' and/or the underlying properties of the situation to be affected by the decision are not well understood, probabilities cannot be assigned by these means. This sort of situation is exemplified by the so-called greenhouse effect in relation to prospective climate change, discussed in Chapter 10.

In many environmental decision contexts probabilities are derived from models of the processes of interest. In the case of urban air pollution, for example, for given levels of emissions from a given set of sources, ambient pollution levels at locations will vary with meteorological conditions. Physical models of the airshed can be used to simulate probabilities of different ambient levels at locations of interest: see the discussion of ambient pollution levels in Chapters 6 and 8. Again, models of nuclear reactors have been used to calculate the probabilities of various kinds of accident, there being little 'form' to go on, and experimentation to establish actual empirical knowledge being out of the question.

Where probabilities are assigned on the basis of form or knowledge, they are sometimes referred to as 'objective' probabilities. Some economists deal with situations where the assignment of objective probabilities is seen as impossible by treating the decision-making problem as being dealt with by the assignment of 'subjective' probabilities. The idea is that the decision maker proceeds by assigning, on the basis of judgement, to each of the possible outcomes that he or she has identified a set of weights that satisfy the requirements for probabilities – basically they comprise positive numbers that sum to unity. However, this assumes that the decision maker feels able to do this, and, more fundamentally, feels able to enumerate all possible outcomes. In our view, it is more appropriate to admit that there are environmental decision-making problems, as exemplified by the greenhouse effect, which are not well characterised by these assumptions, and to consider uncertainty as distinct from risk. We defer discussion of decision making in the face of uncertainty until the final two sections of the chapter. Until then we proceed on the assumption that probabilities can somehow – possibly subjectively – be assigned to a complete enumeration of the outcomes considered possible.

13.1.1 The St Petersburg paradox

Consider the following potential gamble. A fair coin will be tossed. If it falls head up at the first toss, the gambler gets £1. If it falls head up at the second toss, the gambler gets £2, at the third toss £4, at the fourth £8, and so on. Tossing continues until the coin falls head down. How much would somebody be willing to pay for such a gamble? The answer might appear to be 'an infinite amount' because the expected monetary value of the gamble is infinite. The expected value is the sum of the probability-weighted possible outcomes, which in this case is the infinite series

$$(0.5 \times 1) + (0.5^2 \times 2) + (0.5^3 \times 4) + (0.5^4 \times 8)$$
$$+ \ldots = 0.5 + 0.5 + 0.5 + 0.5 + \ldots$$

which has an infinite sum. That anybody would be prepared to pay a very large amount of money for such a gamble violates everyday experience, and the example is known as the Bernoulli, or St Petersburg, paradox.[1]

The paradox can be resolved by assuming that individuals assess gambles in terms of expected utility, rather than expected monetary value, and that the utility function exhibits diminishing marginal utility. The relevant outcome is then the infinite series

$$0.5U(1) + 0.5^2U(2) + 0.5^3U(4) + 0.5^4U(8) + \ldots$$

which has a finite sum, so long as there is some upper limit to U, which is what diminishing marginal utility implies. Diminishing marginal utility is

a very natural assumption for economists. In economics, the basic approach to the analysis of individual behaviour in any kind of risky situation is to assume the maximisation of expected utility and diminishing marginal utility.

13.1.2 Basic concepts for risk analysis

The basic concepts used by economists here are expected value, expected utility, risk neutrality/ aversion/preference, certainty equivalence and the cost of risk bearing. To develop these, consider an individual facing a gamble – though it could be any risky choice – where there are just two possible outcomes expressed in terms of the individual's income, Y_1 and Y_2. The probabilities associated with Y_1 and Y_2 are p_1 and p_2, where, by virtue of the fact that one of the outcomes must occur, $p_2 = (1 - p_1)$. Then, the expected value of the income outcome of the gamble is

$$E[Y] = p_1Y_1 + (1 - p_1)Y_2 \tag{13.1}$$

where E[.] is the expected value operator. It says that we are referring to the expected value of whatever appears inside the square brackets. The term 'expectation' is sometimes used for 'expected value', so that equation 13.1 would be said to give the expectation of the gamble. The expected utility of the gamble is:

$$E[U] = p_1U(Y_1) + (1 - p_1)U(Y_2) \tag{13.2}$$

If the utility function is given the algebraic form $U = Y^a$ where a is a positive fraction so that $\partial U/\partial Y > 0$ and $\partial^2 U/\partial Y^2 < 0$, this is

$$E[U] = p_1Y_1^a + (1 - p_1)Y_2^a \tag{13.3}$$

The certainty equivalent to this gamble is the Y corresponding to its expected utility; that is, the result of solving

$$U(Y) = E[U]$$

for Y. For our case with $U(Y) = Y^a$ this is

$$Y^a = p_1Y_1^a + (1 - p_1)Y_2^a \tag{13.4}$$

to be solved for Y, given p_1, Y_1, Y_2 and a.

---

[1] This paradox was posed by Bernoulli in the 18th century, and is sometimes known by his name. The origin of the name for the paradox used in the text lies in the Bernoulli family's long association with St Petersburg.

Now consider Figure 13.1 for this gamble. Y^{**} is the expected value of the gamble. The straight line ACB is the locus of expected value/expected utility combinations for a gamble with just two outcomes Y_1 and Y_2 as p_1 varies. If $p_1 = 1$, so that $p_2 = 0$ and Y_1 is certain, using equations 13.1 and 13.2 we get point A with Y_1 and $U(Y_1)$. If $p_1 = 0$, we get B with Y_2 and $U(Y_2)$. If $p_1 = 0.5$, we get Y^{**} halfway between Y_1 and Y_2, $E[U]$ equal to the vertical distance $Y^{**}C$. To the left of C along CA $p_1 > 0.5$, to the right along CB $p_1 < 0.5$.

The utility function maps certain income into utility. If $Y^{**} = E[Y]$ were certain income, rather than the expected value of a gamble, the utility level corresponding would be that at point E on the $U(Y)$ curve, with $U(E[Y])$ corresponding. The horizontal line C to $E[U]$ cuts the $U(Y)$ curve at D, which corresponds to an income of Y^*. This is the certainty equivalent for this gamble, the solution for Y in equation 13.4, as it is the certain level of income that yields the same utility as the expected utility of the gamble.

Y^* is, in Figure 13.1 and generally for $U = Y^a$ with $0 < a < 1$, less than Y^{**}. The certainty equivalent is less than the expected value of the gamble. Put another way, the utility of the certain payment of Y^{**} is greater than the utility of a gamble with expected value Y^{**}. If this individual were offered the sum of money Y^{**} or a free ticket to the gamble described here, he or she would not be indifferent but would prefer the sum of money over the actuarially equal gamble. We say that such an individual is risk-averse. If in $U = Y^a$, a took the value 1 then the graph for $U(Y)$ in Figure 13.1 would be a straight line with ADEB coinciding with ACB, and the individual would be indifferent between the money sum and the free ticket; in other words, risk-neutral. If an individual had a utility function such that $\partial U/\partial Y > 0$ and $\partial^2 U/\partial Y^2 > 0$, instead of $\partial U/\partial Y > 0$ and $\partial^2 U/\partial Y^2 < 0$, then in a diagram like Figure 13.1 the arc ADEB would lie below the straight line ACB and the ticket to gamble would be preferred to the sum of money. Such an individual would be said to exhibit risk-preference.

Reflecting everyday experience, in economics it is assumed that the typical individual is risk-averse, as

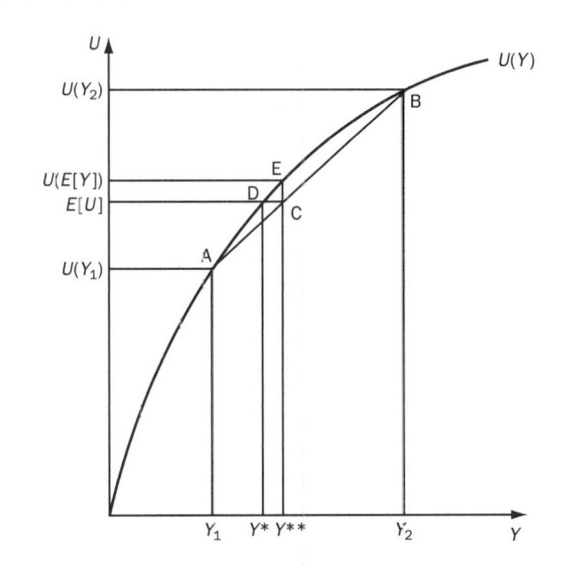

Figure 13.1 Risk aversion and the cost of risk bearing

depicted in Figure 13.1. For such individuals, taking a risk is costly in utility terms, which cost can be expressed in a monetary measure using the concepts developed here. The cost of risk bearing, CORB, is defined as the difference between the expected value of the gamble and its certainty equivalent:

$$\text{CORB} = Y^{**} - Y^* \tag{13.5}$$

CORB is analogous to the measures of surplus and variation developed in the previous chapter, in that it is a monetary measure of a utility difference, which in this case would arise, for a risk-averse individual, from being in a risky as opposed to an actuarially equivalent certain situation.

While we have here developed these concepts for the case of a gamble with just two equiprobable outcomes, they are not restricted to such a context, which was adopted solely for expositional convenience. The number of possible outcomes does not have to be just two, nor do all possible outcomes have to have equal probabilities attached to them. The situation underlying the outcomes does not have to be a gamble as generally understood – it could, for example, be a choice about whether to insure or not, or climatic conditions affecting agricultural output.[2]

---

2   Our treatment here of the economic analysis of individual behaviour in the face of risk has been neither rigorous ror comprehensive. For fuller accounts see, for example, Kreps (1990).

Or, as discussed in the next section, the basic ideas can be used to consider the situation of individuals who do not know for sure what they will demand in the future, or what its availability will be.

13.2   Option price and option value

We now return to the context of a wilderness area for which some development is proposed and under consideration. The basic idea of option value was introduced by Weisbrod (1964) in considering a national park and the prospect of its closure. Park closure is equivalent, from the point of view of use value, to development driving the value of the wilderness area's amenity services to zero. We will adopt the particular Weisbrod context here. Weisbrod saw that as well as a loss to current visitors, closure would entail a loss to potential future visitors. He argued that the benefit of keeping the park open would be understated by just measuring current consumer surplus for visitors, and that there should be added to that a measure of the benefit of future availability. He called this additional component of preservation benefit 'option value'.

Weisbrod's definition of option value, and the claim that it was a preservation benefit additional to consumer surplus, led to some controversy. Eventually, Cicchetti and Freeman (1971) established a set of definitions that proved generally acceptable, and appeared to support the basic thrust of Weisbrod's position, at least in so far as individuals are risk-averse. We now set out a simplified version of their analysis, using the concepts developed in the previous section.

13.2.1 Risky availability

Consider an individual and a national park wilderness area. In Figure 13.2, $U(A)$ is the level of utility that the individual attains for some given level of income, Y_A, if he or she wants to visit and the park is open. 'A' is for available. Using N for not available, $U(N)$ is the utility experienced if the individual wants to visit and the park has been closed. Given non-availability, how much would the individual be

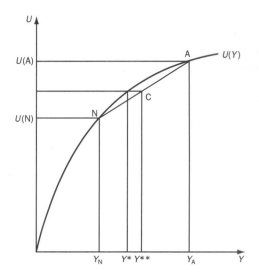

Figure 13.2 Risk aversion, option price and option value

willing to pay for availability? The answer is the sum of money $Y_A - Y_N$, which would restore utility to the level $Y(A)$.

Now, that question and the answer imply that the individual is either in a situation where access to the park is available, or in a situation where it is not. The idea of option value relates rather to a situation in which the individual does not know for sure whether future access will be available or not. Figure 13.2 deals with this situation along the lines set out for Figure 13.1 in relation to a gamble. Assign a probability of p_1 to the N situation and $1 - p_1$ to the A situation. Then the straight line NCA in Figure 13.2 is the locus of U/Y combinations as p_1 varies – at N p_1 is 1, at A it is zero. As before, Y^{**} is the expected value of the outcome for some given p_1, and Y^* is the certainty equivalent.

The sum of money $Y_A - Y^{**}$ is the expected value of the individual's compensating surplus, E[CS]. For p_1 at 1, Y^{**} would coincide with Y_N, and willingness to pay for availability would be $Y_A - Y_N$. For $p_1 = 0$, Y^{**} would coincide with Y_A and CS would be zero. For situations where $0 < p_1 < 1$, the expected value of compensating surplus as willingness to pay is determined by the value for p_1. As Figure 13.2 is drawn, $p_1 = 0.5$ and Y^{**} is halfway between Y_N and Y_A.

The sum of money $Y_A - Y^*$, where Y^* is the certainty equivalent for this 'gamble' on availability, is what is known as 'option price', OP, the maximum amount that the individual would be willing to pay for an option which would guarantee access to an open park. As Figure 13.2 is drawn, $Y^{**} > Y^*$, so that OP is greater than E[CS]. Cicchetti and Freeman called the difference between OP and E[CS] 'option value', OV, with

$$OP = E[CS] + OV \qquad (13.6)$$

with OV positive. From the previous section of this chapter we know that the way Figure 13.2 is drawn reflects the assumption of risk aversion. For a risk-neutral individual the straight line NCA would coincide with the arc NA, so that Y^* and Y^{**} would coincide, and OV would be zero with OP = E[CS]. As Cicchetti and Freeman put it, 'Option value is a risk aversion premium' (1971, p. 536). Weisbrod's idea was, in this framework, that E[CS] would understate the preservation benefits of keeping the park open, because risk-averse individuals are willing to pay a premium to avoid risk.

13.2.2 *Ex ante* and *ex post* measurement

Our report of the Cicchetti and Freeman analysis, in the interest of getting at the basic idea, was not entirely accurate. In particular, we treated risk as attaching to availability where the individual knows that he or she will want to visit in the future, whereas in the original formulation it (also) attaches to the individual's future preferences in an analysis of the policy decision as to whether to allow development to close the park or keep it open. We now explore option value further in that context, distinguishing between *ex ante* and *ex post* perspectives.[3] The *ex ante* view is prior to outcomes being revealed; the *ex post* is after the event, when the outcomes are known.

We need now to introduce some additional notation. We will use s_k to denote one of S possible and mutually exclusive states of nature, $k = 1, 2, \ldots, S$, and p_k for the corresponding probabilities. We will use δ_j for $j = 0, 1$ to denote one of the two possible environmental policy settings between which a decision is being made. Individuals are assumed to be able to rank, *ex post*, realised outcomes according to

a utility function of the form $U(Y, \delta_j \mid s_k)$ where Y denotes the individual's income as before, and where the | means 'given that' so that $U(Y, \delta_j \mid s_k)$ is the utility for some Y and δ_j given that some particular s_k obtains. The | symbol can also be read as 'conditional on', so that $U(Y, \delta_j \mid s_k)$ is the utility associated with the Y and δ_j conditional on the state s_k.

Let δ_0 represent one policy setting and δ_1 represent the alternative. Then

$$U(Y, \delta_1 \mid s_k) > U(Y, \delta_0 \mid s_k) \qquad (13.7)$$

describes an *ex post* winner if δ_1 is adopted rather than δ_0, while

$$U(Y, \delta_1 \mid s_k) < U(Y, \delta_0 \mid s_k) \qquad (13.8)$$

represents a loser. In either case *ex post* compensating surplus is defined by:

$$U(Y - CS_k, \delta_1 \mid s_k) = U(Y, \delta_0 \mid s_k) \qquad (13.9)$$

Note that there is a k subscript on CS here – equation 13.9 defines compensating surplus given the kth state of nature. For a winner, CS_k is willingness to pay for the change of policy setting; for a loser, CS_k is willingness to accept compensation. Of course, the fact that an individual is a winner under a policy setting in one state of nature does not mean that he or she will be a winner under that policy in other states of nature. The expected value of compensating surplus, or expected compensating surplus, denoted E[CS] is the expectation of the compensated surpluses under each of the s possible states of nature:

$$E[CS] = \sum_{k=1}^{s} p_k CS_k \qquad (13.10)$$

We can illustrate this in the Weisbrod park closure context. There are just two possible states of nature – s_1 where the individual wants to visit the park, and s_2 where he or she does not. The respective probabilities are p_1 and $1 - p_1$. Let δ_1 be the policy setting where the park is open (wilderness preserved) and δ_0 be the park closed (development allowed to go ahead). Then the individual is an *ex post* winner if the park is open and

$$U(Y, \delta_1 \mid s_1) > U(Y, \delta_0 \mid s_1)$$

---

[3] The discussion here largely follows that of Ready (1995).

with

$$U(Y - \text{CS}_1, \delta_1 \mid s_1) = U(Y, \delta_0 \mid s_1)$$

defining CS_1, which would be WTP to have the park open. In this case CS_2 is zero because in the event that he or she does not want to visit the park, the individual will require no compensation for its closure. The individual is not a winner under δ_1, but neither is he or she a loser. Note that we are here assuming that the individual attaches no existence value to the park being open, to the wilderness remaining in an undeveloped state. In this case then,

$$\begin{aligned}
\text{E[CS]} &= p_1 \cdot \text{CS}_1 + (1 - p_1) \cdot \text{CS}_2 \\
&= p_1 \cdot \text{CS}_1 + (1 - p_1) \cdot 0 = p_1 \cdot \text{CS}_1
\end{aligned}$$

Imagine the policy decision being taken repeatedly over time. Given that p_1 is the probability that the individual will suffer from a decision for closure, expected compensating surplus can be regarded as the average over many repetitions of his or her willingness to pay to avoid it.

Now consider matters *ex ante*, before the outcome is known, first in the general case. *Ex ante*, an individual's utility depends on the potential outcomes and their probabilities as assessed by that individual. If we use the ordinary utility function notation for *ex ante* utility,

$$U(Y, \delta_1) > U(Y, \delta_0) \tag{13.11}$$

simply means that before the outcome is known the individual prefers δ_1 to δ_0, so that if policy setting δ_1 were to eventuate he or she would, *ex post*, be a winner. On the other hand,

$$U(Y, \delta_1) < U(Y, \delta_0) \tag{13.12}$$

says that *ex ante* the individual prefers δ_0 to δ_1, so that if policy setting δ_1 were to eventuate he or she would, *ex post*, be a loser. Given this,

$$U(Y - \text{OP}, \delta_1) = U(Y, \delta_0) \tag{13.13}$$

defines OP as the option price for δ_1. For the equation 13.11 case OP would be WTP, *ex ante*, for δ_1 rather than δ_0, while for the equation 13.12 case OP would be WTA compensation to accept δ_1 rather than δ_0.

Ex ante, the individual's utility is a function of the potential outcomes and their associated probabilities, that is,

$$U(Y, \delta) = \sum_{k=1}^{s} p_k U(Y, \delta \mid s_k) \tag{13.14}$$

This says that *ex ante* the utility associated with a Y/δ pair is the expected value of the *ex post* utilities that would go with that pair under different states of nature. Substituting from equation 13.14 into equation 13.13 we get

$$\sum_{k=1}^{s} p_k U(Y - \text{OP}, \delta_1 \mid s_k) = \sum_{k=1}^{s} p_k U(Y, \delta_0 \mid s_k) \tag{13.15}$$

as defining OP for δ_1.

Consider the Weisbrod park policy decision again. We can define OP for the park staying open according to

$$U(Y - \text{OP}, \delta_1) = U(Y, \delta_0) \tag{13.16}$$

or

$$p_1 U(Y - \text{OP}, \delta_1 \mid s_1) = p_1 U(Y, \delta_0 \mid s_1) \tag{13.17}$$

Note that we do not find s_2 appearing in equation 13.17 for the reason discussed above. Note also that instead of the δ notation, we could use here the A/N notation that we used when first considering the question of option value using Figure 13.2. Equations 13.16 and 13.17 could, that is, be written as

$$U(Y - \text{OP}, \text{A}) = U(Y, \text{N}) \tag{13.18}$$

and

$$p_1 U(Y - \text{OP}, \text{A} \mid s_1) = p_1 U(Y, \text{N} \mid s_1) \tag{13.19}$$

To make this more concrete, let us consider a simple numerical example. Suppose that what determines whether the individual wants to visit the park or not on a weekend is the weather. In fine weather the individual will definitely want to go, while in bad weather he or she will definitely not want to go. Suppose that the park is open for free and that the individual's WTP for entry on a fine weekend is £10, and that the probability of fine weather is 0.5. Then, their E[CS] is £5. Now suppose that he or she is told that the park might be closed next weekend, then offered a ticket guaranteeing them access. On an actuarial basis, with no risk aversion, the value of the ticket is £5 = (0.5 × £10) + (0.5 × £0), E[CS]. If in order to avoid the risk of wanting to go to the park (fine weather) but not being able to (it is closed), the individual is WTP £6 for such a ticket, then OP = £6 and OV = £1.

According to this analysis, OV is not so much a separate category of preservation benefit as the difference between an *ex ante* measure, OP, and the expected value of an *ex post* measure, E[CS]. The question which arises is: which is the correct measure to use in ECBA? The consensus view emerging in the literature is that an *ex ante* measure is the right one. Essentially the basis for this is the acceptance of consumer sovereignty. In actually taking decisions concerning 'ordinary commodities', consumers proceed on an *ex ante* basis, and the argument is that the best measure of an individual's own preferences and attitude to risk for policy analysis is his or her own *ex ante* utility function that informs decisions about 'ordinary commodities'.[4]

Unfortunately, OP cannot be estimated from data on observable behaviour. However, E[CS] in some circumstances can be estimated from observable behaviour. In the Weisbrod park context, for example, and leaving aside the problems discussed in the previous chapter, one could use the TCM. If it were known that OV were positive, then from equation 13.6 it would follow that OP was greater than E[CS] and an estimate of E[CS] based on observable behaviour could be treated as a lower bound for OP. However, while Figure 13.2 suggests that risk aversion necessarily implies a positive OV, recent analysis shows that even for a risk-averse individual OV could in some circumstances be negative. Given this, E[CS] would not necessarily represent a lower bound for OP.

In principle, this need not be a major problem, as instead of trying to get at OP via observed behaviour, one could use the CVM with an appropriate *ex ante* scenario to directly elicit OP as WTP/WTA. In practice, the design of 'an appropriate *ex ante* scenario' – that is, one that effectively puts respondents in the intended hypothetical market and risk situation – is extremely difficult. We discussed in the previous chapter some of the problems with the CVM where respondents are put in situations where outcomes are to be treated as certain. These problems tend to be made worse when an effort to introduce risk into the scenario is undertaken, and there have been only a few CVM applications that have tried to elicit OP.

13.3 Risk and irreversibility

In the previous section we saw that, usually, for a risk-averse individual option price is greater than expected compensating surplus by an amount which is option value. To the extent that social decision making adopts the principle of consumer sovereignty, and given that most individuals are risk-averse, this leads to the conclusion that option price, rather than expected compensating surplus, should be used in ECBA. With respect to, for example, wilderness development, this suggests that the level that net development benefits have to attain to justify development is greater than would be the case in a world in which the future was certain. This conclusion is dependent on adopting a risk-averse position. In this section we consider arguments that work in the same direction, but do not require risk aversion. Since we are not assuming risk aversion, we can, and do, work with expected values, sums of money, rather than expected utilities.

The arguments which lead to an increase in the net development benefits required to justify development depend on the future being imperfectly known and on development being irreversible. Economic analysis usually assumes that allocation decisions are reversible. However, there is an implicit assumption in the foregoing discussions of wilderness development that once development occurs, it is irreversible. If this were not so, when the project ceased to do what it was intended for – when the mine was exhausted or the dam at the end of its safe life – then it would be possible, at some cost, to restore the wilderness, and this should be reflected in an ECBA. At least on a timescale relevant to human decision making, the assumption that once lost, the benefits of wilderness preservation are lost for ever, appears to be a reasonable approximation to the relevant stylised facts of wilderness development. A

---

[4] Ready (1995) argues for the use of *ex ante* OP from consideration of the properties of *ex ante* and *ex post* versions of compensation tests.

decision in favour of preservation, on the other hand, is clearly reversible.

While the argument that we are interested in involves both irreversibility and risk, it will make things clearer to begin by considering just irreversibility alone.

13.3.1 Irreversibility with the future known

To introduce some of the implications of irreversibility, then, we begin with the, unrealistic, assumption that the future is known with certainty. We will consider a wilderness area yielding flows of amenity services, to be denoted A. We will assume that A is a function of the proportion of the wilderness area preserved from, say, logging. As the size of the area where logging is permitted increases, A falls. We consider benefits and costs as a function of A. The benefits are the preservation benefits, in terms of use and non-use values as discussed in the previous chapter, and we assume that marginal benefits decline as A increases. Consistently with our previous treatment, we assume that the costs of preservation as such are zero. However, we assume that preservation does entail forgone development benefits, which we treat here as costs of preservation. We assume that marginal costs increase with the area set aside from logging, and hence increase with A.

These assumptions are shown in Figure 13.3(a), where there is also shown as A^* the level of amenity service flow that goes with allocative efficiency. Figure 13.3(b) shows the corresponding behaviour for benefits minus costs, that is, net benefit, NB. Net benefits attain a maximum at A^*. Figure 13.3(c) shows the corresponding behaviour for the derivative of net benefit, which is marginal net benefit, MNB, which is zero at the level of A for which NB attains a maximum, A^*. MNB(A) = 0 is an alternative way of stating the necessary condition for maximum NB. In what follows here it will be convenient to work with MNB. The downward-sloping MNB function that we work with is a fairly generally appropriate assumption. The assumed linearity makes it possible, in Appendix 13.1, to do some simple algebra which supports the discussion in the text here.

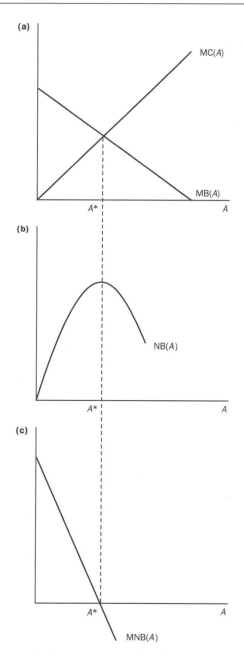

Figure 13.3 Alternative ways of identifying maximum net benefit

We divide time into two periods, now and 'the future'. Now consider Figure 13.4, which, in (a) shows MNB_1 for period 1, now, and in (b) shows MNB_2 for period 2, 'the future'. Future net benefits are expressed in terms of their present value. As

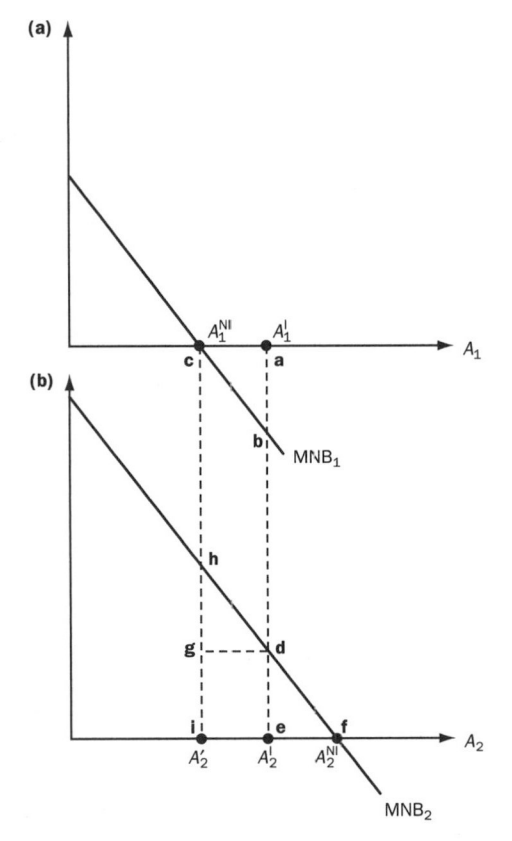

Figure 13.4 Irreversibility and development with the future known

Figure 13.4 is drawn, even after discounting, period 2 MNB is greater than period 1 MNB for a given level of the service flow. Generally, this reflects the considerations advanced in Chapter 11 in connection with the Krutilla–Fisher model concerning the relative prices of environmental amenity services and produced commodities. Particularly, in Figure 13.4 MNB_2 has the same slope as MNB_1 but a larger intercept.

Consider now the level of amenity service flow in each period that goes with current and intertemporal allocative efficiency if there is no irreversibility. Given that we are dealing with period 2 in terms of appropriately discounted net benefit, in the absence of irreversibility, an efficient outcome would involve choosing a consumption level for environmental amenity services in each period for which MNB_1 and MNB_2 are equal to zero, A_1^{NI} and A_2^{NI}. Note that $A_2^{NI} > A_1^{NI}$.

Now assume that development is irreversible. How does this affect things? It constrains the choices in the two periods such that A_2 cannot be greater than A_1. If at the outset a level of period 1 development A_1^{NI} were chosen, myopically ignoring irreversibility, then period 2 A could be at most A_2'. If the decision on the period 1 level of development were taken in the light of the irreversibility constraint, the outcome would be A_1^I and A_2^I. As compared with the myopic decision-making outcome, taking account of irreversibility means a higher level of A (less development) in period 1 and period 2.

Taking irreversibility into account means, as compared with the situation where irreversibility is ignored, incurring costs in period 1 so as to secure benefits in period 2. The period 1 costs arise from selecting a level of A_1 above that where MNB_1 is equal to 0. The period 2 benefits resulting are due to a level of A_2 for which MNB_2 is nearer to 0 than at A_2'. For efficiency, costs and benefits must be equal at the margin. This is the case in Figure 13.4, where **ab**, MNB_1 at A_1^I, is equal to **de**, MNB_2 at A_2^I. Taking the irreversibility constraint into account leads to an outcome where MNB_1 and MNB_2 are equal but of opposite sign. Recall that MNB_2 refers to period 2 net benefits considered in present-value terms in period 1.

As compared with a situation where development is reversible, irreversibility entails costs. In Figure 13.4 these costs are given by comparing A_1^{NI} with A_1^I and A_2^{NI} with A_2^I. In period 1 the cost is given by the area of the triangle **abc**, and in period 2 by the area of triangle **def**. If there is irreversibility, ignoring it entails costs. Given irreversibility, the efficient outcome is A_1^I/A_2^I, but if irreversibility is ignored the actual outcome will be A_1^{NI}/A_2^I. Ignoring irreversibility leads to a gain in period 1 given by the area of triangle **abc**, but to a loss in period 2 given by the area **edhi**. The loss is greater than the gain, so that there is a net cost to ignoring irreversibility.

We have been assuming here that the future is known with certainty. In reality, when considering such matters as wilderness development, irreversibility is combined with imperfect future knowledge. We next use this simple framework for considering the implications of irreversibility taking account of imperfect knowledge of the future.

In order to do that we use the analysis of decision making given imperfect knowledge of the future introduced in the first section of this chapter.

13.3.2 Irreversibility in a risky world

Figure 13.5(a) is the same as Figure 13.4(a), apart from the appearance of A_1^{IR}, to be explained. Figure 13.5(b) shows the same MNB function as Figure 13.4(b), but here it is labelled MNB_2^2 instead of just MNB_2. The superscript 2 now appears

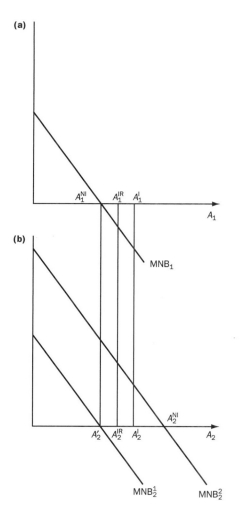

Figure 13.5 Irreversibility and development with imperfect future knowledge

because we also have MNB_2^1, which has the same intercept and slope as MNB_1 in Figure 13.5(a). We are now considering a situation where MNB as a function of A is known for period 1, but where the decision maker does not know for period 2 which of two MNB functions will eventuate, MNB_2^1 which is the same as MNB_1, or MNB_2^2, which has the same slope as MNB_1 but a larger intercept. While it is not known, when deciding on the level of period 1 development and hence the level of A_1, which of MNB_2^1 or MNB_2^2 will obtain in period 2, the decision maker can assign probabilities p to MNB_2^1 and $q = (1 - p)$ to MNB_2^2.

In Figure 13.5 A_1^{NI} is the same level of A_1 as A_1^{NI} in Figure 13.4 and both refer to the outcome of decision making which ignores irreversibility. Given irreversibility, A_2 must equal (strictly be no greater than) A_1, so A_1^{NI} the same in both figures implies A_2' the same in both. A_1^I and A_2^I in Figure 13.5 are also the same as in Figure 13.4, and refer to the outcome where there is irreversibility but no risk and it is known that the period 2 MNB function will be MNB_2^2 which is the same as MNB_2 in Figure 13.4. A_1^{IR} and A_2^{IR} are the outcomes for a decision-making process that takes on board both irreversibility and risk, and adopts risk neutrality. In this case, adding imperfect future knowledge about MNB to irreversibility leads to lower levels of amenity – higher levels of development – than irreversibility alone, but which are higher – lower levels of development – than would have resulted if irreversibility were ignored.

This is established in Appendix 13.2. The results are reasonably intuitive. If irreversibility is ignored, then in the first period the level of A_1 can be chosen by setting MNB_1 equal to zero, and the fact that which of MNB_2^1 or MNB_2^2 will eventuate is unknown is irrelevant. Given that irreversibility is a fact, though ignored, the choice of the period 1 level of A immediately gives its period 2 level, and we get A_1^{NI} and A_2'. If the decision-making process recognises irreversibility and assumes MNB_2^2, the situation is as discussed for Figure 13.4 and we get A_1^I and A_2^I. Where it also recognises that period 2 might involve MNB_2^1 or MNB_2^2, it uses the weighted average of these two alternatives, with weights that are the assigned probabilities, and ends up in an intermediate situation, A_1^{IR} and A_2^{IR}.

13.3.3 Quasi-option value

We now consider the implications of irreversibility in a world where there is imperfect knowledge of the future, but where more knowledge will become available after a decision has been made. We again look at the matter of wilderness development. This is the context in which Arrow and Fisher (1974) introduced the concept of quasi-option value, and our treatment follows that of Arrow and Fisher quite closely. To simplify, we now consider a situation where development is 'all or nothing' in the sense that either development occurs and drives wilderness amenity benefits to zero, or development does not occur. This is like the decision considered by Weisbrod – either the national park is permanently closed (to allow development), or it remains open.

The essential point that this special formulation makes clear is that where there is the prospect of improved information 'the expected benefits of an irreversible decision should be adjusted to reflect the loss of options it entails' (Arrow and Fisher, 1974, p. 319). The adjustment is required even if the decision maker is risk-neutral. The size of the adjustment is quasi-option value. While we discuss quasi-option value in an all-or-nothing development context, the basic idea carries over to situations where the wilderness area can be partially developed – indeed, it carries over to any situation where one course of action is irreversible and where there will in the future be improved information about the future situation.

As before, time is divided into two periods, 1 being 'now' and 2 'the future'. The decision maker has complete knowledge of all relevant period 1 conditions. At the start of period 1, period 2 outcomes can be listed and probabilities attached to them. A decision involving irreversible consequences must be taken at the start of period 1. At the end of period 1, complete knowledge about period 2 will become available to the decision maker.

The decision to be taken at the start of period 1 is whether to permit development of a wilderness area. The options are shown in Table 13.1. As before, D is for development, P is for preservation, and period 2 costs and benefits are to be understood as discounted present values. R^i is the return associated with the ith option, B_{pt} is preservation benefits, B_{dt}

Table 13.1 Two-period development/preservation options

Option	Period 1	Period 2	Return
1	D	D	$R^1 = (B_{d1} - C_{d1}) + B_{d2}$
2	P	D	$R^2 = B_{p1} + (B_{d2} - C_{d2})$
3	P	P	$R^3 = B_{p1} + B_{p2}$
4	D	P	Is infeasible

is development benefits, C_{dt} is development costs, which are treated as arising only in the period in which the development project is undertaken, and as before we do not explicitly distinguish preservation costs. Option 1 involves initiating development at the start of period 1, and given irreversibility development in period 1 implies development in period 2. Hence, option 4, having the area developed in 1 but preserved in 2, is shown in Table 13.1 as infeasible. The operative alternatives to having the area in a developed state in both periods are option 2 – preservation followed by development at the start of period 2 – and option 3 – never develop.

Let us label the return to the decision taken at the start of period 1 to proceed immediately with development R^d, so that:

$$R^d = R^1 = (B_{d1} - C_{d1}) + B_{d2} \quad (13.20)$$

The return to the decision taken at the start of period 1 to preserve is either R^2 or R^3, depending on whether or not development is initiated at the start of period 2 given the information then available. If B_{p2} then is known to be bigger than $B_{d2} - C_{d2}$, the area will be preserved in period 2, giving R^3. If $B_{d2} - C_{d2}$ is then known to be bigger than B_{p2}, development will be undertaken at the start of period 2, giving R^2. We can express this as

$$R^p = B_{p1} + \max\{B_{p2}, (B_{d2} - C_{d2})\} \quad (13.21)$$

where R^p is the return to the period 1 decision for preservation, and the right-hand side is to be read as B_{p1} plus whichever is the greater of B_{p2} and $(B_{d2} - C_{d2})$ – 'max' is short for 'the largest of the terms appearing inside the braces'. Note that B_{p1} is common to both R^2 and R^3.

Now, suppose for the moment that the decision maker does have complete knowledge of the relevant future circumstances, that at the start of period 1 he or she knows all the B_{pt}, B_{dt} and C_{dt}. Then the decision maker also knows R^d and R^p, and the decision will be to go ahead with development immediately if $R^d > R^p$, which is if $R^d - R^p > 0$, which on substituting from equations 13.20 and 13.21 is

$$(B_{d1} - C_{d1}) + B_{d2} - B_{p1} - \max\{B_{p2}, (B_{d2} - C_{d2})\} > 0 \tag{13.22}$$

which can be written

$$N_1 + B_{d2} - \max\{B_{p2}, (B_{d2} - C_{d2})\} > 0 \tag{13.23}$$

where $N_1 = (B_{d1} - C_{d1}) - B_{p1}$. In other words, N_1 is that which would actually be known to the decision maker at the start of period 1.

The other terms in the expression 13.23 could not, in fact, be known to the decision maker at the start of period 1, so 13.23 is not an operational decision rule. We are, however, assuming that the possible outcomes for B_{d2}, B_{p2} and $(B_{d2} - C_{d2})$ are known to the decision maker and that he or she can attach probabilities to the mutually exclusive outcomes. In that case, it is tempting to simply replace known outcomes in the expression 13.23 by the corresponding expectations, or expected values, and to write an operational decision rule as: go ahead with development at the start of period 1 if

$$N_1 + E[B_{d2}] - \max\{E[B_{p2}], E[(B_{d2} - C_{d2})]\} > 0 \tag{13.24}$$

However, using this rule ignores the fact that more information will be available at the start of period 2. If the area is developed at the start of period 1 this information cannot be used, since the area will necessarily be in a developed state in period 2. If the area is not developed at the start of period 1, the new information could be used at the start of period 2 to decide between development and preservation then.

The proper decision rule is one that takes this on board, as the expression 13.24 does not. Now, of course, a decision has to be taken at the start of period 1, and the decision maker does not then have the information that will become available at the start of period 2. But, by assumption, the decision maker does at the start of period 1 know what the informational possibilities are and the probabilities to attach to outcomes in that respect. So, he or she could use the decision rule: go ahead with development at the start of period 1 if

$$N_1 + E[B_{d2}] - E[\max\{B_{p2}, (B_{d2} - C_{d2})\}] > 0 \tag{13.25}$$

Whereas in expression 13.24 the decision maker uses the maximum of the expected values of period 2 preservation benefits and net development benefits, in 13.25 he or she uses the expectation of the maximum of period 2 preservation benefits and net development benefits. The left-hand side of expression 13.25 will be larger than the left-hand side of 13.24, so that the former decision rule is a harder test for development to pass at the start of period 1. The difference between the left-hand sides of expressions 13.25 and 13.24 is quasi-option value. It is the amount by which a net development benefit assessment which simply replaces outcomes by their expectations should be reduced, given irreversibility, to reflect the pay-off to keeping options open, by not developing, until more information about future conditions is available.

This analysis can be illustrated with a simple numerical example. Suppose that there are just two possible period 2 situations, A and B, differentiated only by what the preservation benefits for 'the future' will be learned to be. B_{d2} and C_{d2} are the same for A and B, and for both $(B_{d2} - C_{d2}) = 6$. For A, B_{p2} is 10; for B, B_{p2} is 5. At the beginning of period 1, A and B are seen as equiprobable so that $p^A = p^B = 0.5$. In this case, for 13.24 we have for the third term to the left of the > sign

$$\max\{E[B_{p2}], E[(B_{d2} - C_{d2})]\} = \max\{[(0.5 \times 10) + (0.5 \times 5)], [(0.5 \times 6) + (0.5 \times 6)]\}$$
$$= \max\{7.5, 6\} = 7.5$$

so the development will get the go-ahead if

$$N_1 + E[B_{d2}] - 7.5 > 0 \tag{13.26}$$

Now consider 13.25. We have two possible outcomes:

A where $B_{p2} > (B_{d2} - C_{d2})$, $B_{p2} = 10$, $p^A = 0.5$

B where $B_{p2} < (B_{d2} - C_{d2})$, $(B_{d2} - C_{d2}) = 6$, $p^B = 0.5$

Hence,

$$E[\max\{B_{p2}, (B_{d2} - C_{d2})\}] = (0.5 \times 10) + (0.5 \times 6)$$
$$= 8$$

and following this decision rule, development will get the go-ahead if

$$N_1 + E[B_{d2}] - 8 > 0 \tag{13.27}$$

Suppose $N_1 + E[B_{d2}] = 7.75$. Then, using 13.24/13.26 development would be decided on at the start of period 1, while using 13.25/13.27 the decision would be to preserve in period 1. The test based on 13.25 is harder to pass than the 13.24-based test. As compared with 13.24, 13.25 adds a premium to the value for $N_1 + E[B_{d2}]$ required to justify a decision for development at the start of period 1. That premium is quasi-option value, which in this example is $0.5 = 8 - 7.5$.

Positive quasi-option value is a general result. This is straightforward, and instructive, to establish where $E[B_{p2}] > E[(B_{d2} - C_{d2})]$, as in this numerical example.[5] Consider first 13.24 under that assumption, in which case it becomes

$$N_1 + E[B_{d2}] - E[B_{p2}] > 0 \qquad (13.28)$$

Now consider $\max\{B_{p2}, (B_{d2} - C_{d2})\}$ from 13.25. This is either B_{p2} or a number larger than B_{p2}. So long as the possibility that $(B_{d2} - C_{d2}) > B_{p2}$ is entertained by the decision maker, $E[\max\{B_{p2}, (B_{d2} - C_{d2})\}]$ will be greater than $E[B_{p2}]$, and 13.25 which is

$$N_1 + E[B_{d2}] - E[\max\{B_{p2}, (B_{d2} - C_{d2})\}] > 0$$

will be a harder test to pass than 13.28, with

$$E[\max\{B_{p2}, (B_{d2} - C_{d2})\}] - E[B_{p2}] = QOV$$

where QOV is for quasi-option value.

The basic point about the existence of quasi-option value is that, where more knowledge about future conditions will become available after an irreversible decision has been made, even with risk neutrality, simply replacing random variables with their expectations and then optimising will lead to the wrong decision. Recall that in Figure 13.5 (and see also Appendix 13.2) we found that adding imperfect future knowledge to irreversibility led to a higher current level of development. We did not there incorporate any quasi-option value into the, risk-neutral, decision-making procedure, because we did not assume that more information would become available at the end of period 1. In general the assumption of increased information in the future would be more appropriate than the contrary assumption, and social decision making should include quasi-option value. However, it is clear from the discussion here that in order to estimate quasi-option value it would be necessary to know, or to assume, a lot about possible outcomes, their current probabilities and the prospects for additional information in the future. In practice ECBA exercises rarely take any account of quasi-option value in any formal quantitative way.

13.4 Environmental cost–benefit analysis revisited

Let us briefly bring together some of the foregoing ideas in the following context. An area of completely undeveloped wilderness land is currently privately owned. A large mineral deposit has been discovered and the owner plans to open a mine. The government is considering purchasing the land and making it a national park so as to preserve the amenity and life-support services that the area provides in its undeveloped state. If the mine went ahead there would be start-up costs with a present value of £20 million, to open the mine and construct the necessary infrastructure. Once operational the mine would yield net revenues of £6 million for 100 years, after which the ore body would be exhausted. Using the standard result for the present value of £x per annum for ever as an approximation, at an interest rate of 5%, £6 million for 100 years has a present value of £120 million. Hence, we have NPV' for the mine equal to £100 million. This is the capitalised value of the area used for mining, the opportunity cost of the creation of a national park.

Consider first inverse ECBA. What is the minimum value of the environmental services yielded by the land in its undeveloped state that would justify stopping the mine and creating the park? We will assume that the only cost involved in the park option is the cost of acquiring the land. In that case, the answer is £100 million, in present-value terms. If the relevant population were collectively willing to pay £100 million now, or more, the government would on standard allocative efficiency grounds be justified

---

in buying the land to create a national park. The per capita test for going ahead with the park would be: is the average member of the population willing to pay a once-off sum now of £(100/N), where N is the population size in millions? For a population of 20 million, roughly the number of adults in the UK, this is a lump sum of £5. This can be converted to an equivalent annual payment for a given number of years.

Actually, if the arguments of Krutilla and Fisher about the relative prices of wilderness services and 'ordinary' commodities, considered in Chapter 11, are accepted, this way of calculating the threshold value for the value of environmental services lost if the mine goes ahead is biased in favour of the mine. Equation 11.29 can be read as saying that for the mine

$$\text{NPV} = 0 \text{ if NPV}' = P/(r - a)$$

where for the present example NPV' is £100 million and $r = 0.05$. Suppose that P, the initial value for preservation benefits, is taken to be just £1 million per annum. What would a, the growth rate for the value of environmental services relative to ordinary commodities, then have to be to justify creating the park? Solving

$$100 = 1/(0.05 - a)$$

gives $a = 0.04$.

So, if it were known that the mine's NPV' were £100 million, that current population willingness to pay for the services of the area undeveloped was £1 million, that development would be irreversible in its impact on those services, and that their relative value would grow by 4% per annum or more, then the government would be justified in acquiring the land and creating the park. Of course, in fact, things are not known in this way, and the question that arises is: how should ECBA take account of risk? It is tempting to answer that it is simply a matter of replacing known outcomes by their expected values. In that case, using continuous time notation for convenience, instead of calculating NPV according to equation 11.26,

$$\text{NPV} = \int_0^T \{B(\text{D})_t - C(\text{D})_t\} e^{-rt} dt - \int_0^T \{B(\text{P})_t\} e^{-rt} dt$$

we would use the probabilities for the various possibilities in regard to B(D), C(D) and B(P) to calculate

$$\text{E}[\text{NPV}] = \int_0^T \{\text{E}[B(\text{D})]_t - \text{E}[C(\text{D})]_t\} e^{-rt} dt$$

$$- \int_0^T \{\text{E}[B(\text{P})]_t\} e^{-rt} dt \tag{13.29}$$

However, if individuals are risk-averse and this is to be reflected in ECBA, this is incorrect. Some allowance for risk aversion must be made. Then the proper test for the mining project, and for the creation of the park, is

$$\text{NPV*} = \int_0^T \{\text{E}[B(\text{D})]_t - \text{E}[C(\text{D})]_t\} e^{-rt} dt$$

$$- \int_0^T \{\text{E}[B(\text{P})]_t\} e^{-rt} dt - \int_0^T \text{CORB}_t e^{-rt} dt \tag{13.30}$$

where CORB_t is the cost of risk bearing at time t. It is sometimes suggested that risk can be dealt with by using expected values and an increased rate of discount, as in

$$\text{NPV**} = \int_0^T \{\text{E}[B(\text{D})]_t - \text{E}[C(\text{D})]_t\} e^{-(r+b)t} dt$$

$$- \int_0^T \{\text{E}[B(\text{P})]_t\} e^{-(r+b)t} dt \tag{13.31}$$

where b is the 'risk premium' to be added to the standard discount rate. Apart from the problem of deciding on a proper value for b, this implies that the cost of risk bearing is decreasing exponentially over time. This can be seen by writing equation 13.31 as

$$\text{NPV**} = \int_0^T \{\text{E}[B(\text{D})]_t - \text{E}[C(\text{D})]_t\} \{\text{CORBe}^{-bt}\} e^{-rt} dt$$

$$- \int_0^T \{\text{E}[B(\text{P})]_t\} \{\text{CORBe}^{-bt}\} e^{-rt} dt$$

where CORB is some initial value for the cost of risk bearing, which thereafter declines at the rate b. While the assumption of an exponentially decreasing cost of risk may be appropriate in some cases, it clearly is not generally valid. The correct way to proceed is to estimate $CORB_t$ over the life of the project and incorporate those estimates as in equation 13.30.

It has been argued (see Arrow and Lind, 1970) that when a project is undertaken by government on behalf of society as a whole, no allowances for risk need be made. The reasoning here is that when government undertakes risky projects, the risks are spread (or pooled or diversified) over many individuals. In aggregate, therefore, there is no risk attached to collectively undertaken investments, and no need to include estimates of $CORB_t$. This argument is not now accepted as being applicable in the context of projects that have environmental impacts. The reason for this is that environmental services are typically public goods – they are non-rival and non-excludable, so that the assumption of risk spreading does not hold.

The problem then remains of estimating $CORB_t$. As we have seen, this is now looked at under the 'option-value' rubric – in the ECBA context option-value is the cost of risk bearing. What this means is that, leaving aside existence values for the moment, an ECBA which does not simply ignore risk should use either 13.30 with $E[B(P)]_t$ replaced by $E[CS]_t$ and $CORB_t$ replaced by OV_t, or, more directly, replace both $E[B(P)]_t$ and $CORB_t$ with OP_t, where CS is compensating surplus and OP is option price. It should use, that is, either

$$NPV^* = \int_0^T \{E[B(\mathrm{D})]_t - E[C(\mathrm{D})]_t\}e^{-rt}dt$$

$$- \int_0^T \{E[CS]_t\}e^{-rt}dt - \int_0^T OV_t e^{-rt}dt \quad (13.32)$$

or

$$NPV^* = \int_0^T \{E[B(\mathrm{D})]_t - E[C(\mathrm{D})]_t\}e^{-rt}dt$$

$$- \int_0^T OP_t e^{-rt}dt \quad (13.33)$$

In principle, as previously noted, OP could be obtained directly from suitable application of the CVM. In practice this is difficult. It is understood that in most cases OV will be positive, so that if equation 13.32 is used with OV set at zero, NPV* will be overestimated. Of course, as discussed in the previous chapter, what actually gets estimated by, for example, the TCM, is Marshallian consumer surplus, MCS, rather than the theoretically correct Hicksian measure. The relationship between MCS and CS where it is quantity/quality change, rather than price change, that is at issue is, as discussed in the previous chapter, complex and they may diverge widely in unknown ways.

What all this means is that while at a theoretical level the proper way to do ECBA accounting for risk aversion is clear enough, the practical implementation of the procedures is difficult. In practice, an ECBA exercise of the kind we are considering here would use

$$NPV = \int_0^T \{B(\mathrm{D})_t - C(\mathrm{D})_t\}e^{-rt}dt - \int_0^T \{B(\mathrm{P})_t\}e^{-rt}dt$$

where $B(P)$ would include estimated use and existence value for the relevant population, and then subject the central-case result to sensitivity analysis. ECBA practitioners are aware of the importance of option value and quasi-option value, but find it hard to put numbers to these concepts. It is rather a matter of considering whether plausible variations to the central-case numbers can produce a negative NPV, when some judgemental allowance is made for option and quasi-option value.

13.5 Decision theory: choices under uncertainty

In the first section of this chapter we made the distinction between risk and uncertainty. Thus far we have been considering individual and social decision making in circumstances of risk, that is where the decision maker proceeds on the assumption that he or she can enumerate all possible future states and assign probabilities to them. We now consider decision making in the face of uncertainty, where the

Table 13.2 A pay-off matrix

	C	D	E
A Conserve the wilderness area as a national park	120	50	10
B Allow the mine to be developed	5	30	140

decision maker enumerates all possible states relevant to the decision but cannot attach probabilities to those states. The approach that we adopt is called 'decision theory' and is a branch of the theory of games.

We focus on social decision making and treat what we shall call 'society' as one of the players of a game. The other 'player' is by convention called 'nature' and the games that we shall be considering are often called 'games against nature'. Society must select a move (or strategy) in ignorance about which state of nature will occur, and is unable to attach probabilities to states of nature. However, it is assumed that society can estimate its 'pay-off matrix'. The pay-off matrix is a statement of the alternative strategies open to society, the possible states of nature, and the pay-offs associated with each combination of strategy and state of nature. Table 13.2 is an example of a pay-off matrix constructed for the context that we considered in the previous section of the chapter – the decision as to whether to stop development in a wilderness area by making it a national park.

There are two strategies, A and B, and three possible states of nature C, D and E. The entries in Table 13.2 are millions of £s of NPV associated with the corresponding strategy–state-of-nature combination. If state C eventuates and the park exists, a large number of individuals choose to visit the park and enjoy its wilderness amenities, while if the mine is allowed to go ahead it turns out that it is a commercial failure. State E is the converse of this: if the park exists few individuals choose to visit it and the value attached to its existence by non-visitors is low, while the mine turns out to be very successful commercially. The state of nature D is intermediate between C and E: the mine is moderately successful if it goes ahead, as is the park if it does.

If C eventuates, society is richly rewarded *ex post* for adopting strategy A, receiving a pay-off of 120. In contrast, its returns to strategy B are very poor,

obtaining a pay-off of just 5. The remaining four cells in the matrix show society's pay-offs from A or B when the state of nature is either D or E. Note that the best of all possible outcomes is that given by the lower right cell, where society allows the mine to go ahead and it is commercially successful.

Which strategy, A or B, should the government acting on behalf of society select? Should it allow the mine to proceed or create a national park? Let us examine four of the decision rules that have been proposed for games against nature.

1) Maximin rule

Government sets out the pay-off matrix and selects the strategy with the least-bad worst outcome. The label 'maximin' signifies that the strategy that maximises the minimum possible outcome is selected. Inspection of the pay-off matrix in Table 13.2 reveals A to be the maximin strategy. If B is selected, the worst possible outcome is 5, while if A is selected the worst outcome is 10.

While avoiding worst possible outcomes has some attraction, the maximin rule can easily lead to choices which seem to contradict common sense. This arises because the maximin rule ignores most of the information in the pay-off matrix. In particular, the pay-offs in best possible cases are ignored. Moreover, the maximin decision rule means that decisions are made entirely on the basis of the most adverse possibilities. If one strategy was only marginally better than a second in terms of its worst outcome, the first would be preferred no matter how much more preferable the second may be under all other states of nature.

2) Maximax rule

In contrast to what may be regarded as the very cautious maximin strategy, the 'maximax' decision rule is very adventurous. Each available strategy is examined to identify its best outcome. The one selected is that with the best of the best outcomes. This rule implies that government should adopt strategy B, as its best outcome is 140, in state E, whereas the best outcome from adopting A is 120, in state C.

Table 13.3 A regret matrix

	C	D	E
A	0	0	130
B	115	20	0

The maximax rule suffers from a similar weakness to the maximin rule, as it ignores most of the information in the pay-off matrix. In this case, all pay-offs other than the best possible ones are ignored. Once again, the choices implied by this rule can fly in the face of common sense.

3) Minimax regret rule

The essence of the 'minimax regret' rule is the avoidance of costly mistakes. To implement this rule, a regret matrix is derived from the pay-off matrix. This is done by identifying for each state of nature the strategy with the largest pay-off and then expressing all the other pay-offs for that state of nature as deviations from the largest. The entries in the regret matrix are the difference between the actual pay-off for the strategy–state-of-nature combination and what the pay-off would have been if the best strategy for the state of nature had been chosen. The regret matrix for our illustrative example is shown in Table 13.3.

Once the regret matrix has been calculated, government plays a minimax game using these regrets. Each row of the regret matrix is examined to identify the largest possible regret. The strategy with the lowest of the largest regrets is then chosen. The minimax regret rule leads to selection of B in this example, as its most costly mistake is 115 in state C, whereas for A the most costly mistake is 130 in state E.

4) Assignment of subjective probabilities

According to 'the principle of insufficient reason', in the absence of any better information the decision maker should assign equal probabilities to the mutually exclusive outcomes, and adopt the strategy that then has the pay-off with the greatest expected value. For our example, this leads to selection of strategy A, which has an expected value of 60 whereas the expected value for B is 58.33.

The equal probabilities are just subjective probabilities. In some situations there may be information available which enables the assignation of unequal subjective probabilities. Unlike the previous decision rules, selecting the strategy with the largest expected value on the basis of subjective probabilities does consider all alternatives in the pay-off matrix.

It is clear from this brief exposition of decision theory that while it can provide insights into how decision makers might behave in the face of uncertainty, it cannot tell us which is the best way to make choices in an uncertain world. Indeed, the concept of rational behaviour is problematic in the face of uncertainty – there is no way of making decisions that can be unambiguously identified as doing the best for the decision maker in the relevant circumstances. It may be that this is why many economists are uncomfortable with uncertainty, and prefer to deal with situations where the assignment of 'objective' probabilities is impossible by treating decision makers as assigning 'subjective' probabilities.

13.6 A safe minimum standard of conservation

In the first section of this chapter we defined radical uncertainty as a situation in which the decision maker is not able to list all of the possible outcomes. This is the context in which the idea of the 'safe minimum standard' was originally formulated. To see what is involved, let us modify the illustrative example just considered. Let us confine the possibilities to state E, but suppose that it is known that the construction of the proposed mine will mean that a population of some plant will be destroyed, and that this population is thought to be the only one in existence. The mine proponents have undertaken to attempt the re-establishment of the plant in another location, and the cost of so doing is included in their project appraisal. It is unknown whether the attempt will be successful.

To consider the park/mine decision now, we can specify just two states of nature, F and U: F stands for 'favourable' and is where the relocation is

Table 13.4 A regret matrix for the possibility of species extinction

	F	U
A	130	0
B	0	z

successful, while U is for 'unfavourable', in which state of nature the relocation is unsuccessful. What pay-off should be assigned to having the mine go ahead if the state U eventuates? The problem is that not only is it impossible to assign probabilities to success and failure – it has never been tried before – but that it is also unknown whether any other populations of the plant species exist. In this case the state of nature U may imply extinction of the species. In this case, the regret matrix is then as shown in Table 13.4, where z is an unknown number. For state F the regrets in Table 13.4 are the same as in Table 13.3. For state U, the park option A would avoid the species extinction, whereas B could entail that extinction, which carries a large, but unknown, regret, z.

In fact, as Table 13.4 is constructed, it is implicit, by virtue of the 0 entry for A/U, that although we have said that z is an unknown number, it is supposed large enough that A, stop the mine, is the correct strategy in state U. But this presumption does not, following minimax regret, indicate which strategy to adopt. One way to proceed would be to assume that although the cost of species extinction is unknown, it can be presumed large enough to make A the right strategy. It is exactly this presumption that underlies the idea of the safe minimum standard as originally put forward. As made by Bishop (1978) the argument for this presumption is as follows. Species extinction involves an irreversible reduction in the stock of potentially useful resources which is the existing portfolio of species. In a state of radical uncertainty there is no way of knowing how large the value to humans of any of the existing species might turn out to be in the future. Two kinds of ignorance are involved here. First, there is social ignorance about future preferences, needs and technologies. Second, there is scientific ignorance about the characteristics of existing species as they relate to future social possibilities and needs. The extinction of any species is, there-

fore, to be presumed to involve future costs that may be very large, even when discounted into present-value terms. The argument here is essentially that the species that may become extinct may turn out to be one for which there is no substitute.

Applying the safe minimum standard for conservation (SMS) criterion as stated to projects which could entail species extinction would mean rejecting all such projects. All that is required for rejection is the possibility that going ahead with the project could involve species extinction. SMS is a very conservative rule. It means forgoing current gains, however large, in order to avoid future losses of unknown, but presumed very large, size. A modified SMS has been proposed according to which the strategy that ensures the survival of the species should be adopted, unless it entails unacceptably large costs. This is less conservative, but leaves it to be determined whether any given cost is 'unacceptably large'.

The SMS criterion can also be applied to target setting for pollution policy, where it would imply that targets should be set so that threats to the survival of valuable resource systems from pollution flows are eliminated, provided that this does not entail excessive cost. Alternatively, one may view the SMS criterion here in terms of constraints – pollution policy should in general be determined using an efficiency criterion, as discussed in Chapter 6, but subject to the overriding constraint that an SMS is satisfied. This formulation of pollution policy recognises the importance of economic efficiency but accords it a lower priority than conservation when the two conflict, provided that the opportunity costs of conservation are not excessive. This compromise between efficiency and conservation criteria implies that 'correct' levels of pollution cannot be worked out analytically. Instead, judgements will need to be made about what constitutes excessive costs, and which resources are deemed sufficiently valuable for application of the SMS criterion.

As will be seen in Chapter 17, the standard economic approach to the question of the proper rate at which renewable resources should be harvested is based on intertemporal efficiency criteria. Basically, the harvest rate should be such that the rate of return on the stock of such a resource is equal to the rate of return on other forms of investment. However, this approach ignores unpredictable exogenous shocks that could, given harvesting, threaten the sustainability of the resource. In Chapter 17, we shall examine a proposal that the proper rate of renewable resource harvesting should be determined on a modified SMS basis, so as to avoid this threat.

13.6.1 Environmental performance bonds

The precautionary principle is closely related to the modified safe minimum standard and is gaining widespread acceptance, at the governmental and intergovernmental levels, as a concept that should inform environmental policy. Statements of the precautionary principle have been made by a number of governments, by individuals, and as part of international agreements. Thus, for example, Principle 15 of the June 1992 Rio Declaration is that:

> In order to protect the environment, the precautionary approach shall be widely applied by States according to their capabilities. Where there are threats of serious or irreversible damage, lack of full scientific certainty shall not be used as a reason for postponing cost-effective measures to prevent environmental degradation.[6]

Like the SMS, the precautionary principle can be taken as saying that there is a presumption against going ahead with projects that have serious irreversible environmental consequences, unless it can be shown that not to go ahead would involve unacceptable costs. The question which arises is whether there are any policy instruments that are consistent with this approach to irreversibility and uncertainty, which could constitute a feasible means for its implementation in such a way as to avoid an outcome that simply prohibits such projects.

Environmental performance bonds have recently been suggested as a response to the problem of devising a means of project appraisal which takes on board the ideas behind the SMS and the precautionary principle. The basic ideas involved can be discussed by considering some firm which wishes to undertake a project involving major technological innovation, so that there is no past experience according to which probabilities can be assigned to all possible outcomes. Indeed, in so far as genuine novelty is involved, there is radical uncertainty in that not all of the possible outcomes can be anticipated. An example of such a project would have been the construction of the first nuclear power plant.

We assume that there is in existence an environmental protection agency (EPA) without permission from which the firm cannot go ahead with the project. The EPA takes independent expert advice on the project, and comes to a view about the worst conceivable environmental outcome of the project's going ahead. Approval of the project is then conditional on the firm depositing with the EPA ('posting') a bond of x, where this is the estimate of the social cost of the worst conceivable outcome. The bond is fully or partially returned to the firm at the end of the project's lifetime (defined by the longest-lasting conceived consequence of the project, not by the date at which it ceases to produce output) according to the damage actually occurring over the lifetime. Thus, if there is no damage the firm gets back x, plus some proportion of the interest. The withheld proportion of the interest is to cover EPA administration costs and to finance EPA research. If the damage actually occurring is y, the firm gets back $x - y$, with appropriate interest adjustment. For x equal to y, the firm gets nothing back, forfeiting the full value of the bond. It is, of course, possible that y will turn out to be greater than x, in which case also the firm gets back $0.

The advantages claimed for such an instrument are in terms of the incentives it creates for the firm to undertake research to investigate environmental impact and means to reduce it, as well as in terms of stopping projects. Taking the latter point first, suppose that the EPA decides on x as the size of the bond, and that the firm assesses lifetime project net returns to it as $(x - 1)$, and accepts that x is the appropriate estimate of actual damage to arise. Then it will not wish to go ahead with the project. If, however, the firm took the view that actual damage would be $(x - 2)$ or less, it would wish to

---

go ahead with the project. The firm has, then, an incentive to itself assess the damage that the project could cause, and to research means to reduce that damage. Further, if it does undertake the project it has an ongoing incentive to seek damage-minimising methods of operation, so as to increase the eventual size of the sum returned to it, $x - $y. This incentive effect could be enhanced by having the size of the bond posted periodically adjustable. Thus, if the firm could at any point in time in the life of the project, on the basis of its research, convince the EPA that the worst conceivable lifetime damage was less than $x, the original bond could be returned and a new one for an amount less than $x be posted.

At the end of the project's lifetime, the burden of proof as to the magnitude of actual damage would rest with the firm, not the EPA. The presumption would be, that is, that the bond was not returnable. It would be up to the firm to convince the EPA that actual damage was less than $x if it wished to get any of its money back. This would generate incentives for the firm to monitor damage in convincing ways, as well as to research means to minimise damage. In the event that damage up to the amount of the bond, $x, occurred, society, as represented by the EPA, would have received compensation. If damage in excess of $x had occurred, society would not receive full compensation. Recall that $x is to be set at the largest amount of damage seen as conceivable by the EPA at the outset, on the basis of expert advice. A socially responsible EPA would have an incentive to take a cautious view of the available evidence, implying a high figure for $x, so that society would not find itself uncompensated. This, it is argued, would coincide with the selfish motivations of EPA staff, since a higher $x would mean more funding available for EPA administration and research.

Environmental performance bonds are clearly an interesting idea for an addition to the range of instruments for environmental protection, given the pervasiveness of uncertainty and the need for research addressed to reducing it. In the form discussed here, they do not appear to be in use anywhere. Their usefulness would appear, as with other environmental policy instruments, to vary with particular circumstances, and clearly further consideration of the details of their possible implementation is warranted.

Summary

In this chapter our objective was to study the ways in which irreversibility and the fact that the future environmental consequences of current decisions are imperfectly known affect decision making about projects with environmental impacts. In regard to imperfect future knowledge, we distinguished between risk and uncertainty. In a risky world, cost–benefit analysis works with expected values together with a risk premium which reflects risk aversion. Where a project has irreversible environmental impacts, it should go ahead only if net present value using expected values less quasi-option value is positive, even if risk neutrality is assumed. In a risky world, possible project impacts are known and probabilities can be assigned to them. Many people take the view that in many cases the possible environmental impacts of a project cannot be fully anticipated, or that where they can be probabilities cannot meaningfully be assigned. In such an uncertain world, decision makers cannot work with expected values, and we discussed some alternative procedures. The safe minimum standard and the precautionary principle have been advocated as cautious approaches to environmental standard setting in an uncertain world.

Further reading

The economic analysis of individual decision making in the face of risk is covered in standard intermediate and advanced microeconomics texts such as Deaton and Muellbauer (1980) or Kreps (1990).

Our treatment of option price and option value draws heavily on Ready (1995), which provides lots of references to the original literature, where important papers include Weisbrod (1964), Cicchetti and Freeman (1971), Bishop (1982), Freeman (1985), Plummer and Hartman (1986), Desvousges *et al.* (1987) and Boyle and Bishop (1987).

Arrow and Fisher (1974) introduced quasi-option value in the wilderness development context, on which see also Krutilla and Fisher (1975) and Fisher and Krutilla (1974). Henry (1974) independently published essentially the same arguments. Fisher and Hanemann (1986) discuss quasi-option value in the context of pollution with irreversible consequences, and illustrate its estimation. Graham-Tomasi (1995) provides a generalisation of the setting and arguments originally proposed by Arrow and Fisher.

Dixit and Pindyck (1994) consider project appraisal and show that an irreversible investment opportunity that need not be implemented immediately should only be undertaken now if its expected net present value exceeds the opportunity cost of keeping the investment option alive. The value of these options can be estimated using standard techniques for the valuation of call options developed in the financial markets literature. Coggins and Ramezani (1998) use those techniques to show explicitly that the value of the right to delay a decision equals Arrow and Fisher's quasi-option value.

Funtowicz and Ravetz (1991) consider uncertainty, as we define it, in the context of scientific knowledge about environmental problems, and argue that quality assurance requires the 'democratisation' of science. Faucheux and Froger (1995) consider decision making in the face of uncertainty in the context of policies for sustainable development. Dixit and

Nalebuff (1991) is an excellent, and very easy-to-read, account of using game theory to make strategic choices in the context of uncertainty.

Young (2001) develops a critique of the use of expected utility for environmental decision making and argues that G.L.S. Shackle's model of decision making in the face of uncertainty, originally developed for analysing business behaviour, provides a superior explanation of how decision makers actually proceed, and is a better prescriptive model. The arguments are supported with a case study of the appraisal of a highway project in a developing country.

The safe minimum standard for conservation idea was originally proposed by Ciriacy-Wantrup (1968), and further developed by Bishop (1978). Barbier *et al.* (1994) review some contributions to the safe minimum standard and the precautionary principle in the context of biodiversity preservation; see also Chapters 11, 12 and 13 in Heywood (1995). Perrings (1991) considers the theoretical content of the precautionary principle in relation to problems of uncertain environmental impact of large spatial and temporal dimension. Cameron and Abolucher (1991) give another useful discussion of the precautionary principle. As described in the text here, environmental performance bonds appear to have first been proposed by Perrings (1989), and are discussed further in Costanza and Perrings (1990); see Shogren *et al.* (1993) for a critique of the Costanza and Perrings proposals.

A substantial literature now exists about pollution targets and instruments in a risky or uncertain world. References to some useful reading in this area were given in Part II of this book. The greenhouse effect, considered in Chapter 10, is an example *par excellence* of a pollution problem where all dimensions are subject to uncertainty. Risk and uncertainty also have a bearing, of course, on efficient and optimal resource depletion and harvesting, to be dealt with in Part IV of this book, where references to the literature will be provided.

1. Is the loss of a species of plant or animal necessarily of economic concern? Is this true for every species that currently exists? Do we now suffer as a consequence of earlier extinctions?

2. How could the value of an environmental performance bond be set?

3. Should the safe minimum standard approach be applied to setting standards for environmental pollution? If so, how could it be done?

1. Consider an individual for whom Y is initially £100 and $U(Y) = Y^a$, offered a bet on the toss of a fair coin at a price of £5. For each of the pay-outs A and B, calculate the expected value of the Y outcome, the individual's expected utility, certainty equivalent and cost of risk bearing, for a taking the values 0.9, 0.95, 0.99. 0.999 and 1.0. In situation A, the individual gets £15 if he or she calls the way the coin falls correctly, and nothing if he or she gets it wrong. In B, the pay-out on a correct call is £10. Note that A is actuarially a very good bet, while B is actuarially fair, and identify the circumstances in which the individual would take the bet. Note also that from equation 13.4 the certainty equivalent is expected utility raised to the power $1/a$.

2. In Figure 13.4 with $MNB_1 = 10 - (A_1/2)$ and $MNB_2 = 20 - (A_2/2)$ known with certainty, find the levels of A_1 and A_2, (a) if there is no irreversibility, (b) if irreversibility applies but is ignored in decision making, and (c) if irreversibility is taken into account. Hence calculate the cost of ignoring irreversibility. Suppose now that there is imperfect knowledge of the future, and a risk-neutral decision-maker aware of and taking into account irreversibility assigns equal probabilities to the mutually exclusive future states where $MNB_2 = 10 - (A_1/2)$ and

$MNB_2 = 20 - (A_2/2)$. What will be the selected levels for A_1 and A_2?

3. The construction of a hydroelectric plant in a wilderness valley is under consideration. It is known that the valley contains an insect species found nowhere else, and the project includes relocating the insects. It is not known whether they can be successfully located. The pay-off matrix is

		State of nature	
		F	**A**
	P	+70	−20
Decision			
	A	+20	+20

where F and A stand for favourable and unfavourable, P is the decision to go ahead with the hydroelectric plant, A is the decision to proceed instead with a coal-fired plant, and the cell entries are NPV millions of £s. Favourable is the state of nature where species relocation is successful, unfavourable is where it is not. Ascertain the decisions following from adopting: (a) the principle of insufficient reason, (b) the maximin rule and (c) the maximax rule. Derive the regret matrix and ascertain the implications of the minimax regret rule, and compare the outcome with that arising from the safe minimum standard approach.

Appendix 13.1 Irreversibility and development: future known

In the absence of irreversibility, the efficient levels of development would be chosen, so as to

Max $F_1(A_1) + F_2(A_2)$

where $F_1(A_1)$ and $F_2(A_2)$ are the net benefit functions. The necessary conditions are:

$$\partial F_1/\partial A_1 = 0 \quad (13.34a)$$

$$\partial F_2/\partial A_2 = 0 \quad (13.34b)$$

With the linear MNB functions shown in Figure 13.4, these conditions are

$$\alpha - \beta A_1 = 0 \quad (13.35a)$$

$$k\alpha - \beta A_2 = 0 \quad (13.35b)$$

where $k > 1$. Using the notation of Figure 13.4, solving equations 13.35 gives:

$$A_1^{NI} = \alpha/\beta \quad (13.36a)$$

$$A_2^{NI} = k(\alpha/\beta) = kA_1^{NI} \quad (13.36b)$$

If there is irreversibility but it is not taken account of in decision making, the result will be:

$$A_1' = A_1^{NI} = \alpha/\beta \quad (13.37a)$$

$$A_2' = A_1' = \alpha/\beta \quad (13.37b)$$

With irreversibility taken into account in decision making, the problem is to

Max $F_1(A_1) + F_2(A_2)$

subject to

$$A_1 = A_2$$

for which the Lagrangian

$$L = F_1(A_1) + F_2(A_2) + \lambda[A_1 - A_2]$$

gives the necessary conditions:

$$\partial F_1/\partial A_1 + \lambda = 0 \quad (13.38a)$$

$$\partial F_2/\partial A_2 - \lambda = 0 \quad (13.38b)$$

$$A_1 - A_2 = 0 \quad (13.38c)$$

Substituting $\alpha - \beta A_1$ for $\partial F_1/\partial A_1$ and $k\alpha - \beta A_2$ for $\partial F_2/\partial A_2$ in equations 13.38a and 13.38b and solving leads to:

$$A_1^I = A_2^I = (\alpha/\beta)\{(1 + k)/2\} \quad (13.39)$$

Comparing equation 13.39 with equations 13.36 and 13.37, for $k > 1$ it is seen that

$$A_1^I > A_1^{NI} = A_1' \quad (13.40)$$

and

$$A_2' < A_2^I < A_2^{NI} \quad (13.41)$$

as shown in Figure 13.4.

Now consider the cost of irreversibility, when it is taken into account in decision making. As discussed in the chapter, this cost is the sum of the triangles **abc** and **def** in Figure 13.4. The area of **abc** is given by $0.5 \times$ **ac** $\times$ **ab** where

$$\mathbf{ac} = A_1^I - A_1^{NI} = (\alpha/\beta)\{(1 + k)/2\} - (\alpha/\beta)$$
$$= (\alpha/\beta)\{(k - 1)/2\} \quad (13.42)$$

and

$$\mathbf{ab} = \alpha - \beta A_1^I = \alpha - \beta(\alpha/\beta)\{(1 + k)/2\}$$
$$= \{\alpha(1 - k)/2\} \quad (13.43)$$

so that

$$\mathbf{abc} = \{\alpha^2(k - 1)(1 - k)\}/8\beta \quad (13.44)$$

Proceeding in the same way, we get

$$\mathbf{ef} = A_2^{NI} - A_2^I = k(\alpha/\beta) - \{(1 + k)/2\}(\alpha/\beta)$$
$$= (\alpha/\beta)\{(k - 1)/2\} \quad (13.45)$$

and

$$\mathbf{de} = k\alpha - \beta A_2^I = k\alpha - \beta(\alpha/\beta)\{(1 + k)/2\}$$
$$= \alpha\{(k - 1)/2\} \quad (13.46)$$

so that

$$\mathbf{def} = \{\alpha^2(k - 1)(k - 1)\}/8\beta \quad (13.47)$$

Comparing equations 13.43 and 13.46 we see that **ab** and **de** are equal, as stated in the text discussion of Figure 13.4, but of opposite sign. Equation 13.44 shows **abc** as negative, so to get the cost of irreversibility we use the absolute value for **abc** (the right-hand side of 13.44 multiplied by −1) plus **def**. This gives

$$|\mathbf{abc}| + \mathbf{def} = 2 \times \{\alpha^2(k - 1)^2\}/8\beta$$
$$= \{\alpha^2(k - 1)^2\}/4\beta \quad (13.48)$$

for the cost of irreversibility.

Now consider the cost of ignoring irreversibility in decision making. This leads to A_1^{NI} instead of A_1^1, and to A_2' instead of A_2^1. As shown in Figure 13.4, in the first period there is a gain equal to the area of triangle **abc**, and in the second a loss equal to the area **edhi**. If **edhi** > **abc**, there is a net loss. Since **abc** and **def** have the same areas, this condition is **edhi** > **def**. Clearly, **edhi** is greater than **def** if **ie** = **ef**, which it does as **ie** = **ac** and by equations 13.42 and 13.45 **ac** and **ef** are equal.

So there is a cost to ignoring irreversibility when it exists. For the linear MNB functions used in Figure 13.4, we can show that the cost of ignoring irreversibility is greater than the cost of irreversibility. The cost of ignoring irreversibility is area **edhi**,

which is area **hgd** plus area **gdei**. Consider the latter first. We have

$$\mathbf{gdei} = \mathbf{de} \times \mathbf{ie} = \alpha\{(k-1)/2\} \times \mathbf{ie}$$

using equation 13.46 for **de**. The distance **ie** is $A_2^1 - A_2'$, so that, using equations 13.39 and 13.37,

$$\mathbf{gdei} = \alpha\{(k-1)/2\} \times [(\alpha/\beta)\{(1+k)/2\} - (\alpha/\beta)]$$

which, on simplifying, is

$$\mathbf{gdei} = \{\alpha^2(k-1)^2\}/4\beta \qquad (13.49)$$

Comparing equations 13.48 and 13.49 gives **gdei** equal to the cost of irreversibility. But the cost of ignoring irreversibility is **gdei** plus **hdg**, so the cost of ignoring irreversibility is greater than the cost of irreversibility.

Appendix 13.2 Irreversibility, development and risk

Consider first the case of a risk-neutral decision-maker where there is no irreversibility. With the two possible period 2 benefit functions as $F_2^1(A_2)$ and $F_2^2(A_2)$, where the respective probabilities are p and q with $q = 1 - p$, the decision maker's problem is to

$$\text{Max } F_1(A_1) + E[F_2(A_2)]$$
$$= F_1(A_1) + pF_2^1(A_2) + qF_2^2(A_2)$$

for which the necessary conditions are:

$$\partial F_1/\partial A_1 = 0 \qquad (13.50a)$$

$$p(\partial F_2^1/\partial A_2) + q(\partial F_2^2/\partial A_2) = 0 \qquad (13.50b)$$

For the linear MNB functions of Figure 13.5, we have

$$\partial F_1/\partial A_1 = \alpha - \beta A_1 \qquad (13.51a)$$

$$\partial F_2^1/\partial A_2 = \alpha - \beta A_2 \qquad (13.51b)$$

$$\partial F_2^2/\partial A_2 = k\alpha - \beta A_2 \qquad (13.51c)$$

and substituting these into equations 13.50 gives the necessary conditions as:

$$\alpha - \beta A_1 = 0 \qquad (13.52a)$$

$$p(\alpha - \beta A_2) + q(k\alpha - \beta A_2) = 0 \qquad (13.52b)$$

From equation 13.52a

$$A_1^{RNI} = \alpha/\beta \qquad (13.53)$$

and from equation 13.52b

$$A_2^{RNI} = (\alpha/\beta)(p + qk) \qquad (13.54)$$

give the period 1 and 2 levels of A, where the superscript RNI is for 'risk, no irreversibility'. The effect of the introduction of risk alone can be seen by comparing equations 13.53 and 13.54 with equations 13.36 from Appendix 13.1. There is no effect on the period 1 level of A. The size of the effect on the second-period level depends on the sizes of p and q, but except for $p = 0$ it is the case that $A_2^{RNI} < A_2^{NI}$. This is because equation 13.54 can be rewritten, using $q = 1 - p$, as

$$A_2^{NRI} = k(\alpha/\beta) + p(\alpha/\beta)(1 - k)$$

where the second term is negative.

With irreversibility incorporated into the decision problem it becomes

$$\text{Max } F_1(A_1) + E[F_2(A_2)] \text{ subject to } A_1 = A_2$$

for which the Lagrangian is

$$L = F_1(A_1) + pF_2^1(A_2) + qF_2^2(A_2) + \lambda[A_1 - A_2]$$

giving as necessary conditions

$$\partial F_1/\partial A_1 + \lambda = 0 \qquad (13.55a)$$

$$p(\partial F_2^1/\partial A_2) + q(\partial F_2^2/\partial A_2) - \lambda = 0 \qquad (13.55b)$$

$$A_1 = A_2 \qquad (13.55c)$$

Substituting for the derivatives in equations 13.55 from 13.51 and solving leads to

$$A_1^{IR} = A_2^{IR} = \{\alpha(1 + p + qk)\}/2\beta \qquad (13.56)$$

where the superscript IR stands for 'irreversibility, risk'. In Appendix 13.1 the result for the case where there is irreversibility but perfect future knowledge was established as

$$A_1^I = A_2^I = (\alpha/\beta)\{(1 + k)/2\} \qquad (13.57)$$

Consider the first-period levels. A_1^{IR} is less than A_1^I if

$$\alpha(1 + p + qk)/2\beta < (\alpha/\beta)\{(1 + k)/2\} \qquad (13.58)$$

which, using $q = 1 - p$, reduces to

$$p < pk$$

which follows from $k > 1$, for any $p > 0$. So, A_1^{IR} is less than A_1^I, as shown in Figure 13.5. The condition for $A_2^{IR} < A_2^I$, as shown in Figure 13.5, is also the expression 13.58, so that is also established for $k > 1, p > 0$.

Figure 13.5 also shows $A_1^{IR} > A_1^{NI}$ and $A_2^{IR} > A_2'$. From 13.46 in Appendix 13.1 and 13.56 the condition for $A_1^{IR} > A_1^{NI}$ is

$$\{\alpha(1 + p + qk)\}/2\beta > \alpha/\beta \qquad (13.59)$$

which, using $q = 1 - p$, reduces to

$$k > p(k - 1)$$

which is true for $k > 1$ and $0 < p < 1$. The condition for $A_2^{IR} > A_2'$ is also expression 13.59.

PART IV

Natural resource exploitation

CHAPTER 14

The efficient and optimal use of natural resources

The Golden Rule is that there are no golden rules.

George Bernard Shaw, Maxims for Revolutionists, in *Man and Superman*

Learning objectives

Having read this chapter, the reader should be able to
- understand the ideas of 'efficient' and 'optimal' allocations of environmental resources
- recognise the relationship between – but also the difference between – the concepts of efficency and optimality
- understand how questions relating to efficient and optimal use of environmental resources over time can be analysed using a class of models known as 'optimal growth models'
- appreciate the ways in which resource use patterns are linked with sustainability

Introduction

In this chapter, we construct a framework to analyse the use of natural resources over time. This will provide the basis for our investigations of non-renewable resource depletion and the harvesting of renewable resources that follow in Chapters 15 to18. Our objectives in the present chapter are:

- to develop a simple economic model, built around a production function in which natural resources are inputs into the production process;
- to identify the conditions that must be satisfied by an economically efficient pattern of natural resource use over time;
- to establish the characteristics of a socially optimal pattern of resource use over time in the special case of a utilitarian social welfare function.

We shall be constructing a stylised model of the economy in order to address questions about the use of resources. Although the economics of our model are straightforward, some mathematics is required to analyse the model. To keep technical difficulties to a minimum, the main body of text avoids the use of mathematical derivations. It shows the logic behind, and the economic interpretations of, important results. Derivations of results are presented separately in appendices at the end of the chapter. It is not vital to read these appendices to follow the arguments in the chapter, but we strongly recommend that you do read them. The derivations are explained thoroughly. Appendix 14.1 is of particular importance as it takes the reader through a key mathematical technique, dynamic optimisation using the maximum principle. You are also urged to read Appendices 14.2 and 14.3 to see how the results discussed in the text are obtained.

PART I A SIMPLE OPTIMAL RESOURCE DEPLETION MODEL

14.1 The economy and its production function

We begin by specifying the model used in this chapter. The economy produces a single good, Q, which can be either consumed or invested. Consumption increases current well-being, while investment increases the capital stock, permitting greater consumption in the future. Output is generated through a production function using a single 'composite' non-renewable resource input, R. Beginning in this way, with just one type of natural resource, abstracts from any substitution effects that might take place between different kinds of natural resource. In Chapter 15, we shall see how our conclusions alter when more than one type of natural resource enters the production function.

In addition to the non-renewable resource, a second input – manufactured capital, K – enters the production function, which is written as

$$Q = Q(K, R) \qquad (14.1)$$

This states that output has some functional relationship to the quantities of the two inputs that are used, but it does not tell us anything about the particular form of this relationship.[1] One possible type of production technology is the Cobb–Douglas (CD) form, consisting of the class of functions

$$Q = AK^{\alpha}R^{\beta} \qquad (14.2)$$

where A, α and $\beta > 0$. An alternative form, widely used in empirical analysis, is the constant elasticity of substitution (CES) type, which comprises the family of functional forms

$$Q = A(\alpha K^{-\theta} + \beta R^{-\theta})^{-\varepsilon/\theta} \qquad (14.3)$$

where A, ε, α, $\beta > 0$, $(\alpha + \beta) = 1$, and $-1 < \theta \neq 0$.[2]

The CD and CES forms of production function do not exhaust all possibilities. In this chapter, we shall

not be making any assumption as to which type of production function best represents the production technology of an economy, but rather work with a general form that might be CD, might be CES, or might be some other. Which functional form is the 'correct' one is an empirical question, and cannot be answered by theoretical argument alone.

14.2 Is the natural resource essential?

The characteristics of an optimal resource depletion path through time will be influenced by whether the natural resource is 'essential'. Essentialness of a resource could mean several things. First, a resource might be essential as a waste disposal and reprocessing agent. Given the ubiquitous nature of waste and the magnitude of the damages that waste can cause, resources do appear to be necessary as waste-processing agents. A resource might also be essential for human psychic satisfaction. Humans appear to need solitude and the aesthetic enjoyment derived from observing or being in natural environments. Thirdly, some resource might be ecologically essential in the sense that some or all of a relevant ecosystem cannot survive in its absence.

In this chapter, we are concerned with a fourth meaning: whether a resource is directly essential for production. Some resources are undoubtedly essential for specific products – for example, crude oil is an essential raw material for the production of petrol and paraffin. But here we are conceptualising resources at a high degree of aggregation, dealing with general classes such as non-renewable and renewable resources. A productive input is defined to be essential if output is zero whenever the quantity of that input is zero, irrespective of the amounts of other inputs used. That is, R is essential if $Q = Q(K, R = 0) = 0$ for any positive value of K.

In the case of the CD production function, R and K are both essential, as setting any input to zero in

---

[1] Each output level Q satisfying the production function is the maximum attainable output for given quantities of the inputs, and implies that inputs are used in a technically efficient way. The production function does not contain labour as a productive input; we have omitted labour to keep the algebra as simple as possible.

One could choose to interpret K and R as being in per capita units, so that labour does implicitly enter as a productive input.
[2] It can be shown that the CD function is a special case of the CES functional form as θ goes to zero in the limit.

equation 14.2 results in $Q = 0$. Matters are not so straightforward with the CES function. We state (but without giving a proof) that if $\theta < 0$ then no input is essential, and if $\theta > 0$ then all inputs are essential.

What is the relevance of this to our study of resource use over time? If we wish to answer questions about the long-run properties of economic systems, the essentialness of non-renewable resources will matter. Since, by definition, non-renewable resources exist in finite quantities it is not possible to use constant and positive amounts of them over infinite horizons. However, if a resource is essential, then we know that production can only be undertaken if some positive amount of the input is used. This seems to suggest that production and consumption cannot be sustained indefinitely if a non-renewable resource is a necessary input to production.

However, if the rate at which the resource is used were to decline asymptotically to zero, and so never actually become zero in finite time, then production could be sustained indefinitely even if the resource were essential. Whether output could rise, or at least stay constant over time, or whether it would have to decline towards zero will depend upon the extent to which other resources can be substituted for non-renewable resources and upon the behaviour of output as this substitution takes place.

14.3 What is the elasticity of substitution between K and R?

The extent of substitution possibilities is likely to have an important bearing on the feasibility of continuing economic growth over the very long run, given the constraints which are imposed by the natural environment. Let us examine substitution between the non-renewable resource and capital. The elasticity of substitution, σ, between capital and the non-renewable natural resource (from now on just called the resource) is defined as the proportionate change in the ratio of capital to the resource in response to a proportionate change in the ratio of the marginal products of capital and the resource, conditional on total output Q remaining constant (see Chiang, 1984). That is,

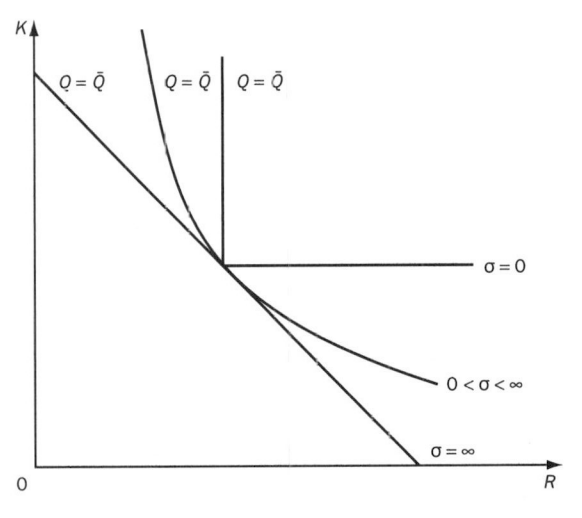

Figure 14.1 Substitution possibilities and the shapes of production function isoquants

$$\sigma = \frac{d(K/R)}{K/R} \bigg/ \frac{d(Q_K/Q_R)}{Q_K/Q_R} \,|\, Q = \text{constant}. \quad (14.4)$$

where the partial derivative $Q_R = \partial Q/\partial R$ denotes the marginal product of the resource and $Q_K = \partial Q/\partial K$ denotes the marginal product of capital.[3] The elasticity of substitution lies between zero and infinity. Substitution possibilities can be represented diagrammatically. Figure 14.1 shows what are known as production function isoquants. For a given production function, an isoquant is the locus of all combinations of inputs which, when used efficiently, yield a constant level of output. The three isoquants shown in Figure 14.1 each correspond to the level of output, $\bar{Q}$, but derive from different production functions. The differing substitution possibilities are reflected in the curvatures of the isoquants.

---

[3] It can also be shown (see Chiang, 1984, for example) that if resources are allocated efficiently in a competitive market economy, the elasticity of substitution between capital and a non-renewable resource is equal to

$$\sigma = \frac{d(K/R)}{K/R} \bigg/ \frac{d(P_R/P_K)}{P_R/P_K}$$

where P_R and P_K denote the unit prices of the non-renewable resource and capital, respectively. That is, the elasticity of substitution measures the proportionate change in the ratio of capital to non-renewable resource used in response to a change in the relative price of the resource to capital.

In the case where no input substitution is possible (that is, σ = 0), inputs must be combined in fixed proportions and the isoquants will be L-shaped. Production functions of this type, admitting no substitution possibilities, are sometimes known as Leontief functions. They are commonly used in input–output models of the economy. At the other extreme, if substitution is perfect (σ = ∞), isoquants will be straight lines. In general, a production function will exhibit an elasticity of substitution somewhere between those two extremes (although not all production functions will have a constant σ for all input combinations). In these cases, isoquants will often be convex to the origin, exhibiting a greater degree of curvature the lower the elasticity of substitution, σ. Some evidence on empirically observed values of the elasticity of substitution between different production inputs is presented later in Box 14.1.

For a CES production function, we can also relate the elasticity of substitution to the concept of essentialness. It can be shown (see, for example, Chiang, 1984, p. 428) that σ = 1/(1 + θ). We argued in the previous section that no input is essential where θ < 0, and all inputs are essential where θ > 0. Given the relationship between σ and θ, it can be seen that no input is essential where σ > 1, and all inputs are essential where σ < 1. Where σ = 1 (that is, θ = 0), the CES production function collapses to the CD form, where all inputs are essential.

14.4 Resource substitutability and the consequences of increasing resource scarcity

As production continues throughout time, stocks of non-renewable resources must decline. Continuing depletion of the resource stock will lead to the non-renewable resource price rising relative to the price of capital. The results obtained in Chapter 11 imply that as the relative price of the non-renewable resource rises the resource to capital ratio will fall, thereby raising the marginal product of the resource and reducing the marginal product of capital. However, the magnitude of this substitution effect will depend on the size of the elasticity of substitution. Where the elasticity of substitution is high, only small changes in relative input prices will be necessary to induce a large proportionate change in the quantities of inputs used. 'Resource scarcity' will be of little consequence as the economy is able to replace the scarce resource by the reproducible substitute. Put another way, the constraints imposed by the finiteness of the non-renewable resource stock will bite rather weakly in such a case.

On the other hand, low substitution possibilities mean that as resource depletion pushes up the relative price of the resource, the magnitude of the induced substitution effect will be small. 'Resource scarcity' will have more serious adverse effects, as the scope for replacement of the scarce resource by the reproducible substitute is more limited. Where the elasticity of substitution is zero, then no scope exists for such replacement.

14.4.1 The feasibility of sustainable development

In Chapter 4, we considered what sustainability might mean, how economists have attempted to incorporate a concern with sustainability into their work, and why one might wish to incorporate sustainability into the set of objectives that society pursues. What we did not discuss there was whether sustainable development is actually possible.

To address this question, two things are necessary. First, a criterion of sustainability is required; unless we know what sustainability is it is not possible to judge whether it is feasible. Second, we need to describe the material transformation conditions available to society, now and in the future. These conditions – the economy's production possibilities – determine what can be obtained from the endowments of natural and human-made capital over the relevant time horizon.

To make some headway in addressing this question a conventional sustainability criterion will be adopted: non-declining per capita consumption maintained over indefinite time (see Chapter 4). Turning attention to the transformation conditions, it is clear that a large number of factors enter the picture. What is happening to the size of the human population? What kinds of resources are available and in what quantities, and what properties do they possess? What will happen to the state of technology in the future? How will ecosystems be affected by the continuing waste loads being placed upon the environment, and how will ecosystem changes feed back upon productive potential? To make progress, economists typically simplify and narrow down the scope of the problem, and represent the transformation possibilities by making an assumption about the form of an economy's production function. A series of results have become established for several special cases, deriving mainly from papers by Dasgupta and Heal (1974), Solow (1974a) and Stiglitz (1974). For the CD and CES functions we have the following.

Case A: Output is produced under fully competitive conditions through a CD production function with constant returns to scale and two inputs, a non-renewable resource, R, and manufactured capital, K, as in the following special case of equation 14.2:

$$Q = K^{\alpha}R^{\beta} \quad \text{with } (\alpha + \beta) = 1$$

Then, in the absence of technical progress and with constant population, it is feasible to have constant consumption across generations if the share of total output going to capital is greater than the share going to the natural resource (that is, if $\alpha > \beta$).

Case B: Output is produced under fully competitive conditions through a CES production function with constant returns to scale and two inputs, a non-renewable resource, R, and manufactured capital, K, as in equation 14.3:

$$Q = A(\alpha K^{-\theta} + \beta R^{-\theta})^{-\varepsilon/\theta} \quad \text{with } (\alpha + \beta) = 1$$

Then, in the absence of technical progress and with constant population, it is feasible to have constant consumption across generations if the elasticity of substitution $\sigma = 1/(1 + \theta)$ is greater than or equal to one.

Case C: Output is produced under conditions in which a backstop technology is permanently available. In this case, the non-renewable natural resource is not essential. Sustainability is feasible, although there may be limits to the size of the constant consumption level that can be obtained.

It is relatively easy to gain some intuitive understanding of these results. For the CD case, although the natural resource is always essential in the sense we described above, if $\alpha > \beta$ then capital is sufficiently substitutable for the natural resource so that output can be maintained by increasing capital as the depletable resource input diminishes. However, it should be noted that there is an upper bound on the amount of output that can be indefinitely sustained in this case; whether that level is high enough to satisfy 'survivability' (see Chapter 4) is another matter. For the CES case, if $\sigma > 1$, then the resource is not essential. Output can be produced even in the absence of the natural resource. The fact that the natural resource is finite does not prevent indefinite production (and consumption) of a constant, positive output. Where $\sigma = 1$, the CES production function collapses to the special case of CD, and so Case A applies. Where a backstop exists (such as a renewable energy source like wind or solar power, or perhaps nuclear-fusion-based power) then it is always possible to switch to that source if the limited natural resource becomes depleted. We explore this process further in the next chapter.

These results assumed that the rate of technical progress and the rate of population growth were both zero. Not surprisingly, results change if one or both of these rates is non-zero. The presence of permanent technical progress increases the range of circumstances in which indefinitely long-lived constant per capita consumption is feasible whereas constant population growth has the opposite effect. However, there are circumstances in which constant per capita consumption can be maintained even where population is growing provided the rate of technical progress is sufficiently large and the share of output going to the resource is sufficiently low. Details of this result are given in Stiglitz (1974). Similarly, for a CES production function, sustained consumption is possible even where $\sigma < 1$ provided that technology growth is sufficiently high relative to population growth.

The general conclusion from this analysis is that sustainability requires either a relatively high degree of substitutability between capital and the resource, or a sufficiently large continuing rate of technical progress or the presence of a permanent backstop technology. Whether such conditions will prevail is a moot point.

14.4.2 Sustainability and the Hartwick rule

In our discussion of sustainability in Chapter 4, mention was made of the so-called Hartwick savings rule. Interpreting sustainability in terms of non-declining consumption through time, John Hartwick (1977, 1978) sought to identify conditions for sustainability. He identified two sets of conditions which were sufficient to achieve constant (or, more accurately, non-declining) consumption through time:

- a particular savings rule, known as the Hartwick rule, which states that the rents derived from an efficient extraction programme for the non-renewable resource are invested entirely in reproducible (that is, physical and human) capital;
- conditions pertaining to the economy's production technology. These conditions are essentially those we described in the previous section, which we shall not repeat here.

We shall discuss the implications of the Hartwick rule further in Chapter 19. But three comments about it are worth making at this point. First, the Hartwick rule is essentially an *ex post* description of a sustainable path. Hence if an economy were not *already* on a sustainable path, then adopting the Hartwick rule is not sufficient for sustainability from that point forwards. This severely reduces the practical usefulness of the 'rule'. (See Asheim, 1986, and Pezzey, 1996, and Appendix 19.1 in the present book.) Second, even were the economy already on a sustainable path, the Hartwick rule requires that the rents be generated from an *efficient* resource extraction programme in a competitive economy. Third, even if the Hartwick rule is pursued subject to this qualification, the savings rule itself does not guarentee sustainability. Technology conditions may rule out the existence of a feasible path. As we noted in the previous section, feasibility depends very much upon the extent of substitution possibilities open to an economy. Let us now explore this a little further.

14.4.3 How large are resource substitution possibilities?

Clearly, the magnitude of the elasticity of substitution between non-renewable resources and other inputs is a matter of considerable importance. But how large it is cannot be deduced by *a priori* theoretical reasoning – this magnitude has to be inferred empirically. Whereas many economists believe that evidence points to reasonably high substitution possibilities (although there is by no means a consensus on this), natural scientists and ecologists stress the limited substitution possibilities between resources and reproducible capital. Indeed some ecologists have argued that, in the long term, these substitution possibilities are zero.

These disagreements reflect, in large part, differences in conceptions about the scope of services that natural resources provide. For example, whereas it appears to be quite easy to economise on the use of fossil energy inputs in many production processes, reproducible capital cannot substitute for natural capital in the provision of the amenities offered by wilderness areas, or in the regulation of the earth's climate. The reprocessing of harmful wastes is less clear-cut; certainly reproducible capital and labour can substitute for the waste disposal functions of the environment to some extent (perhaps through increased use of recycling processes) but there appear to be limits to how far this substitution can proceed.

Finally, it is clear that even if we were to establish that substitutability had been high in the past, this does not imply that it will continue to be so in the future. It may be that as development pushes the economy to points where natural constraints begin to bite, substitution possibilities reduce significantly. Recent literature from natural science seems to suggest this possibility. On the other hand, a more optimistic view is suggested by the effect of technological progress, which appears in many cases to have contributed towards enhanced opportunities for substitution. You should now read the material on resource substitutability presented in Box 14.1.

Up to this point in our presentation, natural resources have been treated in a very special way. We have assumed that there is a single, non-renewable resource, R, of fixed, known size, and (implicitly) of uniform quality. Substitution possibilities have been limited to those between this resource and other, non-natural, resources. In practice, there are a large number of different natural resources, with substitution possibilities between members of this set. Of equal importance is the non-uniform quality of resource stocks. Resource stocks do not usually

---

Box 14.1 Resource substitutability: one item of evidence

A huge amount of empirical research has been devoted to attempts to measure the elasticity of substitution between particular pairs of inputs. Results of these exercises are often difficult to apply to general models of the type we use in this chapter, because the estimates tend to be specific to the particular contexts being studied, and because many studies work at a much more disaggregated level than is done here. We restrict comments to just one estimate, which has been used in a much-respected model of energy–environment interactions in the United States economy.

Alan Manne, in developing the ETA Macro model, considers a production function in which gross output (Q) depends upon four inputs: K, L, E and N (respectively capital, labour, electric and non-electric energy). Manne's production function incorporates the following assumptions:

(a) There are constant returns to scale in terms of all four inputs.
(b) There is a unit elasticity of substitution between capital and labour.
(c) There is a unit elasticity of substitution between electric and non-electric energy.
(d) There is a constant elasticity of substitution between the two pairs of inputs, capital and labour on the one hand and electric and non-electric energy on the other. Denoting this constant elasticity of substitution by the symbol σ, the production function used in the ETA Macro model that embraces these assumptions is

$$Q = [a(K^{\alpha}L^{1-\alpha})^{-\theta} + b(E^{\beta}N^{1-\beta})^{-\theta}]^{-1/\theta}$$

where, as noted in the text,

$$\sigma = \frac{1}{1 + \theta}$$

Manne selects the value 0.25, a relatively low figure, for the elasticity of substitution σ between the pair of energy inputs and the other input pair. How is this figure arrived at? First, Manne argues that the elasticity of substitution is approximately equal to the absolute value of the price elasticity of demand for primary energy (see Hogan and Manne, 1979). Then, Manne collects time-series data on the prices of primary energy, incomes and quantities of primary energy consumed. This permits a statistically derived estimate of the long-run price elasticity of demand for primary energy to be obtained, thereby giving an approximation to the elasticity of substitution between energy and other production inputs. Manne's elasticity estimate of 0.25 falls near the median of recent econometric estimates of this elasticity of substitution.

Being positive, this figure suggests that energy demand will rise relative to other input demand if the relative price of other inputs to energy rises, and so the composite energy resource is a substitute for other productive inputs (a negative sign would imply the pair were complements). However, as the absolute value of the elasticity is much less than one, the degree of substitutability is very low, implying that relative input demands will not change greatly as relative input prices change.

Source: Manne (1979)

---

exist in a fixed amount of uniform quality, but rather in deposits of varying grade and quality. As high-grade reserves become exhausted, extraction will turn to lower-grade deposits, provided the resource price is sufficiently high to cover the higher extraction costs of the lower-grade mineral. Furthermore, while there will be some upper limit to the physical occurrence of the resource in the earth's crust, the location and extent of these deposits will not be known with certainty. As known reserves become depleted, exploration can, therefore, increase the size of available reserves. Finally, renewable resources can act as backstops for non-renewable: wind and wave power are substitutes for fossil fuels, and

wood products are substitutes for metals for some construction purposes, for example.

Dasgupta (1993) examines these various substitution possibilities. He argues that they can be classified into nine innovative mechanisms:

1. an innovation allowing a given resource to be used for a given purpose. An example is the use of coal in refining pig-iron;
2. the development of new materials, such as synthetic fibres;
3. technological developments which increase the productivity of extraction processes. For example, the use of large-scale earthmoving

equipment facilitating economically viable strip-mining of low-grade mineral deposits;

4. scientific and technical discovery which makes exploration activities cheaper. Examples include developments in aerial photography and seismology;

5. technological developments that increase efficiency in the use of resources. Dasgupta illustrates this for the case of electricity generation: between 1900 and the 1970s, the weight of coal required to produce one kilowatt-hour of electricity fell from 7 lb to less than 1 lb;

6. development of techniques which enable one to exploit low-grade but abundantly available deposits. For example, the use of froth-flotation, allowing low-grade sulphide ores to be concentrated in an economical manner;

7. constant developments in recycling techniques which lower costs and so raise effective resource stocks;

8. substitution of low-grade resource reserves for vanishing high-grade deposits;

9. substitution of fixed manufacturing capital for vanishing resources.

In his assessment of substitution possibilities, Dasgupta (p. 1126) argues that only one of these nine mechanisms is of limited scope, the substitution of fixed manufacturing capital for natural resources:

> Such possibilities are limited. Beyond a point fixed capital in production is complementary to resources, most especially energy resources. Asymptotically, the elasticity of substitution is less than one.

There is a constant tension between forces which raise extraction and refining costs – the depletion of high-grade deposits – and those which lower such costs – discoveries of newer technological processes and materials. What implications does this carry for resource scarcity? Dasgupta argues that as the existing resource base is depleted, profit opportunities arise from expanding that resource base; the expansion is achieved by one or more of the nine mechanisms just described. Finally, in a survey of the current stocks of mineral resources, Dasgupta notes that after taking account of these substitution mechanisms, and assuming unchanged resource stock to demand ratios:

> the only cause for worry are the phosphates (a mere 1300 years of supply), fossil fuels (some 2500 years), and manganese (about 130 000 years). The rest are available for more than a million years, which is pretty much like being inexhanstible.

However, adjusting for population and income growth,

> the supply of hydrocarbons . . . will only last a few hundred years . . . So then, this is the fly in the ointment, the bottleneck, the binding constraint.

Dasgupta's optimism is not yet finished. He conjectures that profit potentials will induce technological advances (perhaps based on nuclear energy, perhaps on renewables) that will overcome this binding constraint. Not all commentators share this sanguine view, as we have seen previously, and we shall have more to say about resource scarcity in the next chapter. In the meantime, we return to our simple model of the economy, in which the heterogeneity of resources is abstracted from, and in which we conceive of there being one single, uniform, natural resource stock.

14.5 The social welfare function and an optimal allocation of natural resources

Chapters 5 and 11 established the meaning of the concepts of efficiency and optimality for the allocation of productive resources in general. We shall now apply these concepts to the particular case of natural resources. Our objective is to establish what conditions must be satisfied for natural resource allocation to be optimal, in the sense that the allocation maximises a social welfare function. The presentation in this chapter focuses upon non-renewable resources, although we also indicate how the ideas can be applied to renewable resources.

The first thing we require is a social welfare function. You already know that a general way of writing the social welfare function (SWF) is:

$$W = W(U_0, U_1, U_2, \ldots, U_T) \qquad (14.5)$$

where U_t, $t = 0, \ldots, T$, is the aggregate utility in period t.[4] We now assume that the SWF is utilitarian in form. A utilitarian SWF defines social welfare as a weighted sum of the utilities of the relevant individuals. As we are concerned here with intertemporal welfare, we can interpret an 'individual' to mean an aggregate of persons living at a certain point in time, and so refer to the utility in period 0, in period 1, and so on. Then a utilitarian intertemporal SWF will be of the form

$$W = \alpha_0 U_0 + \alpha_1 U_1 + \alpha_2 U_2 + \ldots + \alpha_T U_T \quad (14.6)$$

Now let us assume that utility in each period is a concave function of the level of consumption in that period, so that $U_t = U(C_t)$ for all t, with $U_C > 0$ and $U_{CC} < 0$. Notice that the utility function itself is not dependent upon time, so that the relationship between consumption and utility is the same in all periods. By interpreting the weights in equation 14.6 as discount factors, related to a social utility discount rate ρ that we take to be fixed over time, the social welfare function can be rewritten as

$$W = U_0 + \frac{U_1}{1 + \rho} + \frac{U_2}{(1 + \rho)^2} + \cdots + \frac{U_T}{(1 + \rho)^T} \quad (14.7)$$

For reasons of mathematical convenience, we switch from discrete-time to continuous-time notation, and assume that the relevant time horizon is infinite. This leads to the following special case of the utilitarian SWF:

$$W = \int_{t=0}^{t=\infty} U(C_t) e^{-\rho t} dt \quad (14.8)$$

There are two constraints that must be satisfied by any optimal solution. First, all of the resource stock is to be extracted and used by the end of the time horizon (as, after this, any remaining stock has no effect on social well-being). Given this, together with the fact that we are considering a non-renewable

resource for which there is a fixed and finite initial stock, the total use of the resource over time is constrained to be equal to the fixed initial stock. Denoting the initial stock (at $t = 0$) as S_0 and the rate of extraction and use of the resource at time t as R_t, we can write this constraint as

$$S_t = S_0 - \int_{\tau=0}^{\tau=t} R_\tau d\tau \quad (14.9)$$

Notice that in equation 14.9, as we are integrating over a time interval from period 0 to any later point in time t, it is necessary to use another symbol (here τ, the Greek letter tau) to denote any point in time in the range over which the function is being integrated. Equation 14.9 states that the stock remaining at time t (S_t) is equal to the magnitude of the initial stock (S_0) less the amount of the resource extracted over the time interval from zero to t (given by the integral term on the right-hand side of the equation). An equivalent way of writing this resource stock constraint is obtained by differentiating equation 14.9 with respect to time, giving

$$\dot{S}_t = -R_t \quad (14.10)$$

where the dot over a variable indicates a time derivative, so that $\dot{S}_t = dS/dt$. Equation 14.10 has a straightforward interpretation: the rate of depletion of the stock, $-\dot{S}_t$, is equal to the rate of resource stock extraction, R_t.

A second constraint on welfare optimisation derives from the accounting identity relating consumption, output and the change in the economy's stock of capital. Output is shared between consumption goods and capital goods, and so that part of the economy's output which is not consumed results in a capital stock change. Writing this identity in continuous-time form we have[5]

$$\dot{K}_t = Q_t - C_t \quad (14.11)$$

---

[4] Writing the SWF in this form assumes that it is meaningful to refer to an aggregate level of utility for all individuals in each period. Then social welfare is a function of these aggregates, but not of the distribution of utilities between individuals within each time period. That is a very strong assumption, and by no means the only one we might wish to make. We might justify this by assuming that, for each time period, utility is distributed in an optimal way between individuals.

[5] Notice that by integration of equation 14.11 we obtain

$$K_t = K_0 + \int_{\tau=0}^{\tau=t} (Q_\tau - C_\tau) d\tau$$

in which K_0 is the initial capital stock (at time zero). This expression is equivalent in form to equation 14.9 in the text.

It is now necessary to specify how output, Q, is determined. Output is produced through a production function involving two inputs, capital and a non-renewable resource:

$$Q_t = Q(K_t, R_t) \tag{14.12}$$

Substituting for Q_t in equation 14.11 from the production function 14.12, the accounting identity can be written as

$$\dot{K}_t = Q(K_t, R_t) - C_t \tag{14.13}$$

We are now ready to find the solution for the socially optimal intertemporal allocation of the non-renewable resource. To do so, we need to solve a constrained optimisation problem. The objective is to maximise the economy's social welfare function subject to the non-renewable resource stock–flow constraint and the national income identity. Writing this mathematically, therefore, we have the following problem:

Select values for the choice variables C_t and R_t for $t = 0, \ldots, \infty$ so as to maximise

$$W = \int_{t=0}^{t=\infty} U(C_t)e^{-\rho t}dt$$

subject to the constraints

$$\dot{S}_t = -R_t$$

and

$$\dot{K}_t = Q(K_t, R_t) - C_t$$

The full solution to this constrained optimisation problem, and its derivation, are presented in Appendix 14.2. This solution is obtained using the maximum principle of optimal control. That technique is explained in Appendix 14.1, which you are recommended to read now. Having done that, then read Appendix 14.2, where we show how the maximum principle is used to solve the problem that has been posed in the text. If you find this appendix material difficult, note that the text of this chapter has been written so that it can be followed without having read the appendices. In the following sections, we

outline the nature of the solution, and provide economic interpretations of the results.

14.5.1 The nature of the solution

Four equations characterise the optimal solution:

$$U_{C,t} = \omega_t \tag{14.14a}$$
$$P_t = \omega_t Q_{R,t} \tag{14.14b}$$
$$\dot{P}_t = \rho P_t \tag{14.14c}$$
$$\dot{\omega}_t = \rho\omega_t - Q_{K,t}\omega_t \tag{14.14d}$$

Before we discuss the economic interpretations of these equations, it is necessary to explain several things about the notation used and the nature of the solution:

- The terms $Q_K (= \partial Q/\partial K)$ and $Q_R (= \partial Q/\partial R)$ are the partial derivatives of output with respect to capital and the non-renewable resource. In economic terms, they are the marginal products of capital and the resource, respectively. Time subscripts are attached to these marginal products to make explicit the fact that their values will vary over time in the optimal solution.

- The terms P_t and ω_t are the shadow prices of the two productive inputs, the natural resource and capital. These two variables carry time subscripts because the shadow prices will vary over time. The solution values of P_t and ω_t, for $t = 0, 1, \ldots, \infty$, define optimal time paths for the prices of the natural resource and capital.[6]

- The quantity being maximised in equation 14.8 is a sum of (discounted) units of utility. Hence the shadow prices are measured in utility, not consumption (or money income), units. You should now turn to Box 14.2 where an explanation of the relationship between prices in utils and prices in consumption (or income) units is given.

Now we are in a position to interpret the four conditions 14.14. First recall from the discussions in

---

[6]   A shadow price is a price that emerges as a solution to an optimisation problem; put another way, it is an implicit or 'planning' price that a good (or in this case, a productive input) will take if resources are allocated optimally over time. If an economic planner

were using the price mechanism to allocate resources over time, then $\{P_t\}$ and $\{\omega_t\}$, $t = 0, 1, \ldots, \infty$, would be the prices he or she should establish in order to achieve an efficient and optimal resource allocation.

Box 14.2 Prices in units of utility: what does this mean?

The notion of prices being measured in units of utility appears at first sight a little strange. After all, we are used to thinking of prices in units of money: a Cadillac costs $40 000, a Mars bar 30 pence, and so on. Money is a claim over goods and services: the more money someone has, the more goods he or she can consume. So it is evident that we could just as well describe prices in terms of consumption units as in terms of money units. For example, if the price of a pair of Levi 501 jeans were $40, and we agree to use that brand of jeans as our 'standard commodity', then a Cadillac will have a consumption units price of 1000.

We could be even more direct about this. Money can itself be thought of as a good and, by convention, one unit of this money good has a price of one unit. The money good serves as a numeraire in terms of which the relative prices of all other goods are expressed. So one pair of Levi's has a consumption units price of 40, or a money price of $40.

What is the conclusion of all this? Essentially, it is that prices can be thought of equally well in terms of consumption units or money units. They are alternative but equivalent ways of measuring some quantity. Throughout this book, the terms 'benefits' and 'costs' are usually measured in units of money or its consumption equivalent. But we sometimes refer to prices in

utils – units of utility – rather than in money/consumption units. It is here that matters may be a little baffling. But this turns out to be a very simple notion. Economists make extensive use of the utility function:

$$U = U(C)$$

where U is units of utility and C is units of consumption. Now suppose that the utility function were of the simple linear form $U = kC$ where k is some constant, positive number. Then units of utility are simply a multiple of units of consumption. So if $k = 2$, three units of consumption are equivalent to six units of utility, and so on.

But the utility function may be non-linear. Indeed, it is often assumed that utility rises with consumption but at a decreasing rate. One form of utility function that satisfies this assumption is $U = \log(C + 1)$, with log denoting the common logarithmic operator, and in which the argument of the function includes the additive constant 1 to keep utility non-negative. The chart in Figure 14.2 shows the relationship between utility and consumption for this particular utility function.

It is equally valid to refer to prices in utility units as in any other units. From Figure 14.2 it is clear that a utility price of 2 corresponds to a 'consumption' (or money) price of approximately

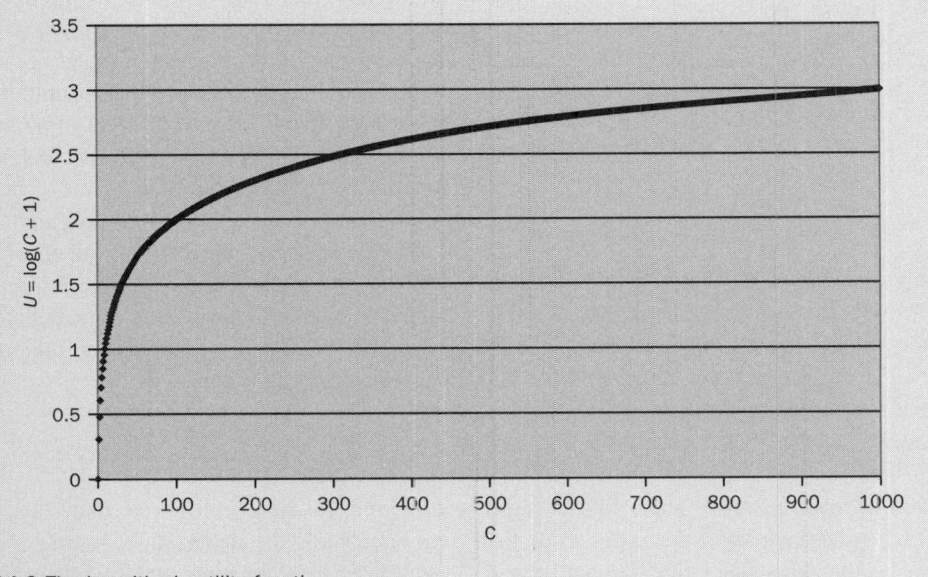

Figure 14.2 The logarithmic utility function

Box 14.2 continued

100 (in fact, 99 exactly). Also, a consumption price of 999 corresponds to a utility price of 3. What is the consumption units price equivalent to a price of 2.5 units of utility? (Use a calculator to find the answer, or read it off approximately from the diagram.)

Which units prices are measured in will depend on how the problem has been set up. In the chapters on resource depletion, what is being maximised is social welfare; given that the SWF is specified as a sum of utilities (of different people or generations), it seems natural to denominate it in utility units as well, although our discussion makes it clear that we could

convert units from utility into money/ consumption terms if we wished to do so. In other parts of the book, what is being maximised is net benefit. That measure is typically constructed in consumption (or money income) units, and so it is natural to use money prices when dealing with problems set up in this way.

In conclusion, it is up to us to choose which units are most convenient. And provided we know what the utility function is (or are willing to make an assumption about what it is) then we can always move from one to the other as the occasion demands.

Chapters 5 and 11 that for any resource to be allocated efficiently, two kinds of conditions must be satisfied: static and dynamic efficiency. The first two of these conditions – 14.14a and 14.14b – are the static efficiency conditions that arise in this problem; the latter two are the dynamic efficiency conditions which must be satisfied. These are examined in a moment. The first two conditions – 14.14a and 14.14b – also implicitly define an optimal solution to this problem. We shall explain what this means shortly.

14.5.2 The static and dynamic efficiency conditions

You will recall from our discussions in Chapters 5 and 11 that the efficient allocation of any resource consists of two aspects.

14.5.2.1 The static efficiency conditions

As with any asset, static efficiency requires that, in each use to which a resource is put, the marginal value of the services from it should be equal to the marginal value of that resource stock *in situ*. This ensures that the marginal net benefit (or marginal value) to society of the resource should be the same in all its possible uses.

Inspection of equations 14.14a and 14.14b shows that this is what these equations do imply. Look first at equation 14.14a. This states that, in each period, the marginal utility of consumption $U_{C,t}$ must be

equal to the shadow price of capital ω_t (remembering that prices are measured in units of utility here). A marginal unit of output can be used for consumption now (yielding $U_{C,t}$ units of utility) or added to the capital stock (yielding an amount of capital value ω_t in utility units). An efficient outcome will be one in which the marginal net benefit of using one unit of output for consumption is equal to its marginal net benefit when it is added to the capital stock.

Equation 14.14b states that the value of the marginal product of the natural resource must be equal to the marginal value (or shadow price) of the natural resource stock. This shadow price is, of course, P_t. The value of the marginal product of the resource is the marginal product in units of output (i.e. $Q_{R,t}$) multiplied by the value of one unit of output, ω_t. But we have defined ω_t as the price of a unit of capital; so why is this the value of one unit of output? The reason is simple. In this economy, units of output and units of capital are in effect identical (along an optimal path). Any output that is not consumed is added to capital. So we can call ω_t either the value of a marginal unit of capital or the value of a marginal unit of output.

14.5.2.2 The dynamic efficiency conditions

Dynamic efficiency requires that each asset or resource earns the same rate of return, and that this rate of return is the same at all points in time, being equal to the social rate of discount. Equations 14.14c and 14.14d ensure that dynamic efficiency is satisfied. Consider first equation 14.14c. Dividing each side by P we obtain $\dot{P}_t/P_t = \rho$ which states that the growth rate of the shadow price of the natural resource (that is, its own rate of return) should equal the social utility discount rate. Finally, dividing both sides of 14.14d by ω, we obtain

$$\frac{\dot{\omega}_t}{\omega_t} + Q_{K,t} = \rho$$

which states that the return to physical capital (its capital appreciation plus its marginal productivity) must equal the social discount rate.

14.5.3 Hotelling's rule: two interpretations

Equation 14.14c is known as Hotelling's rule for the extraction of non-renewable resources. It is often expressed in the form

$$\frac{\dot{P}_t}{P_t} = \rho \tag{14.15}$$

The Hotelling rule is an intertemporal efficiency condition which must be satisfied by any efficient process of resource extraction. In one form or another, we shall return to the Hotelling rule during this and the following three chapters. One interpretation of this condition was offered above. A second can be given in the following way. First rewrite equation 14.15 in the form used earlier, that is

$$\dot{P}_t = \rho P_t \tag{14.16}$$

By integration of equation 14.16 we obtain

$$P_t = P_0 e^{\rho t} \tag{14.17}$$

P_t is the undiscounted price of the natural resource. The discounted price is obtained by discounting P_t at the social utility discount rate ρ. Denoting the discounted resource price by P^*, we have

$$P_t^* = P_t e^{-\rho t} = P_0 \tag{14.18}$$

Equation 14.18 states that the discounted price of the natural resource is constant along an efficient resource extraction path. In other words, Hotelling's rule states that the discounted value of the resource should be the same at all dates. But this is merely a special case of a general asset–efficiency condition; the discounted (or present value) price of any effici-

ently managed asset will remain constant over time. This way of interpreting Hotelling's rule shows that there is nothing special about natural resources *per se* when it comes to thinking about efficiency. A natural resource is an asset. All efficiently managed assets will satisfy the condition that their discounted prices should be equal at all points in time. If we had wished to do so, the Hotelling rule could have been obtained directly from this general condition.

Before moving on, note the effect of changes in the social discount rate on the optimal path of resource price. The higher is ρ, the faster should be the rate of growth of the natural resource price. This result is eminently reasonable given the two interpretations we have offered of the Hotelling rule. Its implications will be explored in the following chapter.

14.5.4 The growth rate of consumption

We show in Appendix 14.2 that equations 14.14a and 14.14d can be combined to give

$$\frac{\dot{C}}{C} = \frac{Q_K - \rho}{\eta}$$

The term η, the elasticity of marginal utility with respect to consumption, is necessarily positive under the assumptions we have made about the utility function. It therefore follows that

$$\frac{\dot{C}}{C} > 0 \Leftrightarrow Q_K > \rho$$

$$\frac{\dot{C}}{C} = 0 \Leftrightarrow Q_K = \rho$$

$$\frac{\dot{C}}{C} < 0 \Leftrightarrow Q_K < \rho$$

Some intuition may help to understand these relations. The social discount rate, ρ, reflects impatience for future consumtion; Q_K (the marginal product of capital) is the pay-off to delayed consumption. The relations imply that along an optimal path:

(a) consumption is increasing when 'pay-off' is greater than 'impatience';
(b) consumption is constant when 'pay-off' is equal to 'impatience';
(c) consumption is decreasing when 'pay-off' is less than 'impatience'.

Therefore, consumption is growing over time along an optimal path if the marginal product of capital (Q_K) exceeds the social discount rate (ρ); consumption is constant if $Q_K = \rho$; and consumption growth is negative if the marginal product of capital is less than the social discount rate.

This makes sense, given that:

(a) when 'pay-off' is greater than 'impatience', the economy will be accumulating K and hence growing;

(b) when 'pay-off' and 'impatience' are equal, K will be constant;

(c) when 'pay-off' is less than 'impatience', the economy will be running down K.

14.5.5 Optimality in resource extraction

The astute reader will have noticed that we have described the Hotelling rule (and the other conditions described above) as an efficiency condition. But a rule that requires the growth rate of the price of a resource to be equal to the social discount rate does not give rise to a unique price path. This should be evident by inspection of Figure 14.3, in which two different initial prices, say 1 util and 2 utils, grow over time at the same discount rate, say 5%. If ρ were equal to 5%, each of these paths – and indeed an infinite quantity of other such price paths – satisfies Hotelling's rule, and so they are all efficient paths. But only one of these price paths can be optimal, and so the Hotelling rule is a necessary but not a sufficient condition for optimality.

How do we find out which of all the possible efficient price paths is the optimal one? An optimal solution requires that all of the conditions listed in equations 14.14a–d, together with initial conditions relating to the stocks of capital and resources and terminal conditions (how much stocks, if any, should be left at the terminal time), are satisfied simultaneously. So Hotelling's rule – one of these conditions – is a necessary but not sufficient condition for an optimal allocation of natural resources over time.

Let us think a little more about the initial and final conditions for the natural resource that must be satisfied. There will be some initial resource stock; similarly, we know that the resource stock must converge to zero as elapsed time passes and the economy approaches the end of its planning horizon. If the initial price were 'too low', then this would lead to 'too large' amounts of resource use in each period, and all the resource stock would become depleted in finite time (that is, before the end of the planning horizon). Conversely, if the initial price were 'too high', then this would lead to 'too small' amounts of resource use in each period, and some of the resource stock would (wastefully) remain undepleted at the end of the planning horizon. This suggests that there is one optimal initial price that would bring about a path of demands that is consistent with the resource stock just becoming fully depleted at the end of the planning period.

In conclusion, we can say that while equations 14.14 are each efficiency conditions, taken jointly as a set (together with initial values for K and S) they implicitly define an optimal solution to the optimisation problem, by yielding unique time paths for K_t and R_t and their associated prices that maximise the social welfare function.

PART II EXTENDING THE MODEL TO INCORPORATE EXTRACTION COSTS AND RENEWABLE RESOURCES

In our analysis of the depletion of resources up to this point, we have ignored extraction costs. Usually the extraction of a natural resource will be costly. So it is desirable to generalise our analysis to allow for the presence of these costs.

It seems likely that total extraction costs will rise as more of the material is extracted. So, denoting

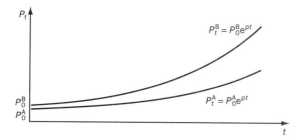

Figure 14.3 Two price paths, each satisfying Hotelling's rule

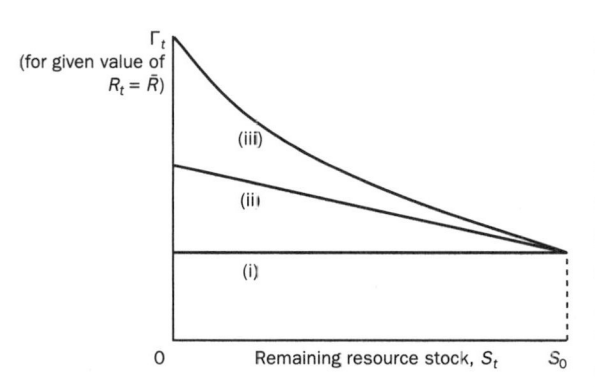

Figure 14.4 Three possible examples of the relationship between extraction costs and remaining stock for a fixed level of resource extraction, R

$\Gamma_t = \Gamma(S_t, R_t)$

Case (i) $\Gamma_t = \Gamma_1(R_t) \rightarrow \partial\Gamma_t/\partial S_t = 0$

Case (ii) $\Gamma_t = \Gamma_2(S_t, R_t) = \beta_1 R_t + \beta_2 S_t$ $\quad(\beta_1 > 0, \beta_2 < 0)$

$\qquad \rightarrow \partial\Gamma_t/\partial S_t = \beta_2 < 0$

Case (iii) $\Gamma_t = \Gamma_3(S_t, R_t) = \beta_1 R_t + \beta_2 S_t^{0.5}$ $\quad(\beta_1 > 0, \beta_2 < 0)$

$\qquad \rightarrow \partial\Gamma_t/\partial S_t = \frac{1}{2}\beta_2 S_t^{-0.5} < 0$

total extraction costs as Γ and the amount of the resource being extracted as R, we would expect that Γ will be a function of R. A second influence may also affect extraction costs. In many circumstances, costs will depend on the size of the remaining stock of the resource, typically rising as the stock becomes more depleted. Letting S_t denote the size of the resource stock at time t (the amount remaining after all previous extraction) we can write extraction costs as

$$\Gamma_t = \Gamma(R_t, S_t) \qquad (14.19)$$

To help understand what the presence of the stock term in equation 14.19 implies about extraction costs look at Figure 14.4. This shows three possible relationships between total extraction costs and the remaining resource stock size for a constant level of resource extraction. The relationship denoted (i) corresponds to the case where the total extraction cost is independent of the stock size. In this case, the extraction cost function collapses to the simpler form $\Gamma_t = \Gamma_1(R_t)$ in which extraction costs depend only on the quantity extracted per period of time. In case (ii), the costs of extracting a given quantity of the resource increase linearly as the stock becomes increasingly depleted. $\Gamma_S = \partial\Gamma/\partial S$ is then a constant negative number. Finally, case (iii) shows the costs of extracting a given quantity of the resource

increasing at an increasing rate as S falls towards zero; Γ_S is negative but not constant, becoming larger in absolute value as the resource stock size falls. This third case is the most likely one for typical non-renewable resources. Consider, for example, the cost of extracting oil. As the available stock more closely approaches zero, capital equipment is directed to exploiting smaller fields, often located in geographically difficult land or marine areas. The quality of resource stocks may also fall in this process, with the best fields having been exploited first. These and other similar reasons imply that the cost of extracting an additional barrel of oil will tend to rise as the remaining stock gets closer to exhaustion.

14.6 The optimal solution to the resource depletion model incorporating extraction costs

The problem we now wish to solve can be expressed as follows:

Select values for the choice variables C_t and R_t for $t = 0, \ldots, \infty$ so as to maximise

$$W = \int_{t=0}^{t=\infty} U(C_t)e^{-\rho t}dt$$

subject to the constraints

$$\dot{S}_t = -R_t$$

and

$$\dot{K}_t = Q(K_t, R_t) - C_t - \Gamma(R_t, S_t)$$

Comparing this with the description of the optimisation problem for the simple model, one difference can be found. The differential equation for $\dot{K}$ now includes extraction costs as an additional term. Output produced through the production function $Q(K, R)$ should now be thought of as gross output. Extraction costs make a claim on this gross output, and net-of-extraction cost output is gross output minus extraction costs (that is, $Q - \Gamma$).

The solution to this problem is once again obtained using the maximum principle of optimal control. If you wish to go through the derivations, you should follow the steps in Appendix 14.2, but this time ensuring that you take account of the extraction cost term which will now appear in the differential equation for $\dot{K}$, and so also in the Hamiltonian. From this point onwards, we shall omit time subscripts for simplicity of notation unless their use is necessary in a particular context. The necessary conditions for a social welfare optimum now become:

$$U_C = \omega \tag{14.20a}$$

$$P = \omega Q_R - \omega \Gamma_R \tag{14.20b}$$

$$\dot{P} = \rho P + \omega \Gamma_S \tag{14.20c}$$

$$\dot{\omega} = \rho \omega - Q_K \omega \tag{14.20d}$$

Note that two of these four equations – 14.20a and 14.20d – are identical to their counterparts in the solution to the simple model we obtained earlier, and the interpretations offered then need not be repeated. However, the equations for the resource net price and for the rate of change of net price differ. Some additional comment is warranted on these two equations.

First, it is necessary to distinguish between two kinds of price: gross price and net price. This distinction follows from that we have just made between gross and net output. These two measures of the resource price are related by net price being equal to gross price less marginal cost. Equation 14.20b can be seen in this light:

$$P_t \quad = \quad \omega_t Q_R \quad \text{less} \quad \omega_t \Gamma_R$$
Net price $=$ Gross price less Marginal cost

The term $\omega_t \Gamma_R$ is the value of the marginal extraction cost, being the product of the impact on output of a marginal change in resource extraction and the price of capital (which, as we saw earlier, is also the value of one unit of output). Equation 14.20b can be interpreted in a similar way to that given for equation 14.14b. That is, the value of the marginal net product of the natural resource ($\omega Q_R - \omega \Gamma_R$, the marginal gross product less the marginal extraction cost) must be equal to the marginal value (or shadow net price) of a unit of the natural resource stock, P.

If profit-maximising firms in a competitive economy were extracting resources, these marginal costs would be internal to the firm and the market price would be identical to the gross price. Note that the level of the net (and the gross) price is only affected by the effect of the extraction rate, R, on costs. The stock effect does not enter equation 14.20b.

The stock effect on costs does, however, enter equation 14.20c for the rate of change of the net price of the resource. This expression is the Hotelling rule, but now generalised to take account of extraction costs. The modified Hotelling rule (equation 14.20c) is:

$$\dot{P} = \rho P + \Gamma_S \omega$$

Given that $\Gamma_S = \partial \Gamma / \partial S$ is negative (resource extraction is more costly the smaller is the remaining stock), efficient extraction over time implies that the rate of increase of the resource net price should be lower where extraction costs depend upon the resource stock size. A little reflection shows that this is eminently reasonable. Once again, we work with an interpretation given earlier. Dividing equation 14.20c by the resource net price we obtain

$$\rho = \frac{\dot{P}}{P} - \frac{\Gamma_S \omega}{P}$$

which says that, along an efficient price path, the social rate of discount should equal the rate of return from holding the resource (which is given by its rate of capital appreciation, plus the present value of the extraction cost increase that is avoided by not extracting an additional unit of the stock, $-\Gamma_S \omega / P$.)

There is yet another possible interpretation of equation 14.20c. To obtain this, first rearrange the equation to the form:

$$\rho P = \dot{P} - \Gamma_S \omega \tag{14.20*}$$

The left-hand side of 14.20* is the marginal cost of not extracting an additional unit of the resource; the right-hand side is the marginal benefit from not extracting an additional unit of the resource. At an efficient (and at an optimal) rate of resource use, the marginal costs and benefits of resource use are balanced at each point in time. How is this interpretation obtained? Look first at the left-hand side. The net price of the resource, P, is the value that would be obtained by the resource owner were he or she to extract and sell the resource in the current period. With ρ being the social utility discount rate, ρP is the utility return forgone by not currently extracting one unit of the resource, but deferring that extraction for one period. This is sometimes known as the holding cost of the resource stock. The right-hand side contains two components. $\dot{P}$ is the capital appreciation of one unit of the unextracted resource;

the second component, $-\Gamma_S \omega$, is a return in the form of a postponement of a cost increase that would have occurred if the additional unit of the resource had been extracted.

Finally, note that whereas the static efficiency condition 14.20b is only affected by the current extraction rate, R, the dynamic efficiency condition (Hotelling's rule, 14.20c) is only affected by the stock effect on costs.

In conclusion, the presence of costs related to the level of resource extraction raises the gross price of the resource above its net price but has no effect on the growth rate of the resource net price. Note that net price is what we referred to as rent in Chapter 4: it is also sometimes referred to as royalty. In contrast, a resource stock size effect on extraction costs will slow down the rate of growth of the resource net price. In most circumstances, this implies that the resource net price has to be higher initially (but lower ultimately) than it would have been in the absence of this stock effect. As a result of higher initial prices, the rate of extraction will be slowed down in the early part of the time horizon, and a greater quantity of the resource stock will be conserved (to be extracted later).

14.7 Generalisation to renewable resources

We reserve a lengthy analysis of the allocation of renewable resources until Chapters 17 and 18, but it will be useful at this point to suggest the way in which the analysis can be undertaken. To do so, first note that we have been using S to represent a fixed and finite stock of a non-renewable resource. The total use of the resource over time was constrained to be equal to the fixed initial stock. This relationship arises because the natural growth of non-renewable resources is zero except over geological periods of time. Thus we wrote

$$S_t = S_0 - \int_{\tau=0}^{\tau=t} R_\tau d\tau \Rightarrow \dot{S}_t = -R_t$$

However, the natural growth of renewable resources is, in general, non-zero. A simple way of modelling this growth is to assume that the amount of growth of the resource, G_t, is some function of the current stock level, so that $G_t = G(S_t)$. Given this we can write the relationship between the change in the resource stock and the rate of extraction (or harvesting) of the resource as

$$\dot{S}_t = G(S_t) - R_t \tag{14.21}$$

Not surprisingly, the efficiency conditions required by an optimal allocation of resources are now different from the case of non-renewable resources. However, a modified version of the Hotelling rule for rate of change of the net price of the resource still applies, given by

$$\dot{P} = \rho P - P G_S \tag{14.22}$$

where $G_S = dG/dS$, and in which we have assumed, for simplicity, that harvesting does not incur costs, nor that any natural damage results from the harvesting and use of the resource. Inspection of the modified Hotelling rule for renewable resources (equation 14.22) demonstrates that the rate at which the net price should change over time depends upon G_S, the rate of change of resource growth with respect to changes in the stock of the resource. We will not attempt to interpret equation 14.22 here as that is best left until we examine renewable resources in detail later. However, it is worth saying a few words about steady-state resource harvesting.

A steady-state harvesting of a renewable resource exists when all stocks and flows are constant over time. In particular, a steady-state harvest will be one in which the harvest level is fixed over time and is equal to the natural amount of growth of the resource stock. Additions to and subtractions from the resource stock are thus equal, and the stock remains at a constant level over time. Now if the demand for the resource is constant over time, the resource net price will remain constant in a steady state, as the quantity harvested each period is constant. Therefore, in a steady state, $\dot{P} = \rho P - P G_S = 0$. So in a steady state, the Hotelling rule simplifies to

$$\rho P = P G_S \tag{14.23}$$

and so

$$\rho = G_S \tag{14.24}$$

It is common to assume that the relationship between the resource stock size, S, and the growth of

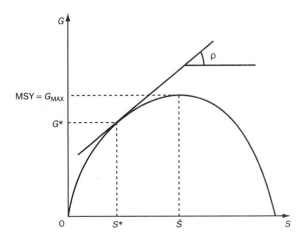

Figure 14.5 The relationship between the resource stock size, *S*, and the growth of the resource stock, *G*

the resource, *G*, is as indicated in Figure 14.5. This relationship is explained more fully in Chapter 17. As the stock size increases from zero, the amount of growth of the resource rises, reaches a maximum, known as the maximum sustainable yield (MSY), and then falls. Note that $G_S = dG/dS$ is the slope at any point of the growth–stock function in Figure 14.5.

We can deduce that if the social utility discount rate ρ were equal to zero, then the efficiency condition of equation 14.24 could only be satisfied if the steady-state stock level is $\hat{S}$, and the harvest is the MSY harvest level. On the other hand, if the social discount rate was positive (as will usually be the case), then the efficiency condition requires that the steady-state stock level be less than $\hat{S}$. At the stock level S^*, for example, G_S is positive, and would be an efficient stock level, yielding a sustainable yield of G^*, if the discount rate were equal to this value of G_S. Full details of the derivation of this and other results relating to the Hotelling rule are given in Appendix 14.3.

14.8 Complications

The model with which we began in this chapter was one in which there was a single, known, finite stock of a non-renewable resource. Furthermore, the whole stock was assumed to have been homogeneous in quality. In practice, both of these assumptions are

often false. Rather than there existing a single non-renewable resource, there are many different classes or varieties of non-renewable resource, some of which may be relatively close substitutes for others (such as oil and natural gas, and iron and aluminium). While it may be correct to assume that there exists a given finite stock of each of these resource stocks in a physical sense, the following situations are likely:

1. The total stock is not known with certainty.
2. New discoveries increase the known stock of the resource.
3. A distinction needs to be drawn between the physical quantity of the stock and the economically viable stock size.
4. Research and development, and technical progress, take place, which can change extraction costs, the size of the known resource stock, the magnitude of economically viable resource deposits, and estimates of the damages arising from natural resource use.

Furthermore, even when we focus on a particular kind of non-renewable resource, the stock is likely to be heterogeneous. Different parts of the total stock are likely to be uneven in quality, or to be located in such a way that extraction costs differ for different portions of the stock.

By treating all non-renewable resources as one composite good, our analysis in this chapter had no need to consider substitutes for the resource in question (except, of course, substitutes in the form of capital and labour). But once our analysis enters the more complex world in which there are a variety of different non-renewable resources which are substitutable for one another to some degree, analysis inevitably becomes more complicated. One particular issue of great potential importance is the presence of backstop technologies (see Chapter 15). Suppose that we are currently using some non-renewable resource for a particular purpose – perhaps for energy production. It may well be the case that another resource exists that can substitute entirely for the resource we are considering, but may not be used at present because its cost is relatively high. Such a resource is known as a backstop technology. For example, renewable power sources such as wind energy are backstop alternatives to fossil-fuel-based energy.

The existence of a backstop technology will set an upper limit on the level to which the price of a resource can go. If the cost of the 'original' resource were to exceed the backstop cost, users would switch to the backstop. So even though renewable power is probably not currently economically viable, at least not on a large scale, it would become so at some fossil-fuel cost, and so the existence of a backstop will lead to a price ceiling for the original resource.

Each of the issues we have raised in this section, and which we have collectively called 'complications', need to be taken account of in any comprehensive account of resource use. We shall do so in the next four chapters.

14.9 A numerical application: oil extraction and global optimal consumption

In this section we present a simple, hypothetical numerical application of the theory developed above. You may find the mathematics of the solution given in Box 14.3 a little tedious; if you wish to avoid the maths, just skip the box and proceed to Table 14.1 and Figures 14.6–14.8 at the end of the section where the results are laid out. (The derivation actually uses the technique of dynamic optimisation explained in Appendix 14.1, but applied in this case to a discrete-time model.)

Suppose that the welfare function to be maximised is

Box 14.3 Solution of the dynamic optimisation problem using the maximum principle

The current value of the Hamiltonian is

$$H_t = U(C_t) + P_{t+1}(-R_t) + q_{t+1}(Q(K_t, R_t) - C_t)$$

$$(t = 0, 1, \ldots, T-1)$$

where P_t is the shadow price of oil (at time t), and q_t is the shadow price of capital. The four necessary conditions for an optimum are:

1. $P_{t+1} - P_t = pP_t - \dfrac{\partial H_t}{\partial S_t} = pP_t$

which implies Hotelling's efficiency rule

$$P_{t+1} = (1 + \rho)P_t \quad (t = 1, \ldots, T)$$

2. $q_{t+1} - q_t = pq_t - \dfrac{\partial H_t}{\partial K_t} = pq_t - q_{t+1}Q_{Kt}$

which implies

$$q_{t+1} = \frac{1 + \rho}{1 + Q_{Kt}} q_t \quad (t = 1, \ldots, T)$$

where $Q_{Kt} = Q_{Kt}(K_t, R_t) = \dfrac{\partial Q(K_t, R_t)}{\partial K_t}$

3. $\dfrac{\partial H_t}{\partial R_t} = 0 = -P_{t+1} + q_{t+1}Q_{Rt}$

$$(t = 0, 1, \ldots, T-1)$$

where $Q_{Rt} = Q_{Rt}(K_t, R_t) = \dfrac{\partial Q(K_t, R_t)}{\partial R_t}$

4. $\dfrac{\partial H_t}{\partial C_t} = 0 = U'(C_t) - q_{t+1}$

$$(t = 0, 1, \ldots, T-1)$$

where $U'(C_t) = \dfrac{dU(C_t)}{dC_t}$

Since we know $S_T = K_T = 0$, there are $6T$ unknowns in this problem as given below. The unknowns are:

Number	$T+1$	$T+1$	$T+1$	$T-1$	$T-1$
Unknowns	$\{P_t\}_1^{T+1}$	$\{q_t\}_1^{T+1}$	$\{K_t\}_1^{T+1}$	$\{S_t\}_1^{T-1}$	$\{C_t\}_0^{T-1} \quad \{R_t\}_0^{T-1}$

$$= 6T$$

We have $6T$ equations to solve for these $6T$ unknowns. The equations are:

$$U'(C_t) = q_{t+1} \quad (t = 0, 1, \ldots, T-1) \qquad [T \text{ equations}]$$

$$P_{t+1} = q_{t+1}Q_{Rt} \quad (t = 0, 1, \ldots, T-1) \qquad [T \text{ equations}]$$

$$S_{t+1} = S_t - R_t \quad (t = 0, 1, \ldots, T-1) \qquad [T \text{ equations}]$$

$$P_{t+1} = (1 + \rho)P_t \quad (t = 1, \ldots, T) \qquad [T \text{ equations}]$$

$$q_{t+1} = \frac{1 + \rho}{1 + Q_{Kt}} q_t \quad (t = 1, \ldots, T) \qquad [T \text{ equations}]$$

$$K_{t+1} = K_t + Q(K_t, R_t) - C_t \quad (t = 0, 1, \ldots, T-1) \qquad [T \text{ equations}]$$

$$W = \sum_{t=0}^{t=T-1} \frac{U(C_t)}{(1 + \rho)^t}$$

where C_t is the global consumption of goods and services at time t; U is the utility function, with $U(C_t) = \log C_t$; ρ is the utility discount rate; and T is the terminal point of the optimisation period. The relevant constraints are

$$S_{t+1} = S_t - R_t$$

$$K_{t+1} = K_t + Q(K_t, R_t) - C_t$$

$$S_T = K_T = 0$$

S_0 and K_0 are given.

S_t denotes the stock of oil; R_t is the rate of oil extraction; K_t is the capital stock; and $Q(K_t, R_t) = AK_t^{0.9}R_t^{0.1}$ is a Cobb–Douglas production function, with A being a fixed 'efficiency' parameter. In this application, we assume that oil extraction costs are zero, and that there is no depreciation of the capital stock. Note that we assume that there are fixed initial stocks of the state variables (non-renewable resource and the capital stock), and that we specify that the state variables are equal to zero at the end of the optimisation period.

We also assume that a backstop technology exists that will replace oil as a productive input at the end (terminal point) of the optimisation period, $t = T$. This explains why we set $S_T = 0$, as there is no point having any stocks of oil remaining once the backstop technology has replaced oil in production. We assume that the capital stock, K_t, associated with the oil input, will be useless for the backstop technology, and therefore will be consumed completely by the end of the optimisation period, so $K_T = 0$.

Implicitly in this simulation, we assume that a new capital stock, appropriate for the backstop technology, will be accumulated out of the resources available for consumption. So C_t in this model should be interpreted as consumption plus new additions to the (backstop) capital stock. The question of how much should be saved to accumulate this new capital stock is beyond the scope of our simple model.

As the notation will have made clear, this is a discrete-time model. We choose each period to be 10 years, and consider a 10-period ($t = 0, 1, \ldots, 9$) time horizon of 100 years beginning in 1990 ($t = 0$). The following data are used in the simulation:

Estimated world oil reserve
= 11.5 (units of 100 billion barrels)

World capital stock
= 4.913 (units of 10 trillion \$US)

Efficiency parameter $A = 3.968$

Utility discount rate = 5%

The value of the efficiency parameter is estimated under the assumption that world aggregate output over the 1980s was \$US179.3 trillion, and aggregate oil extraction was 212.7 billion barrels.

We cannot obtain an analytical solution for this problem. But it is possible to solve the problem numerically on a computer. Table 14.1 and Figures 14.6–14.8 show the numerical solution. Figure 14.6 shows that consumption rises exponentially through the whole of the optimisation period (the figure only shows the first part of that period, from 1990 up to 2080); output (F_t) also rises continuously, but its growth rate slows down towards the end of the period shown in the figure; this arises because at the terminal point (not shown in these figures), the capital stock has to fall to zero for the reason indicated above.

In Figure 14.7 we observe the shadow price growing over time at the rate ρ, and so satisfying Hotelling's rule; the shadow price of capital falls continuously through time. In Figure 14.8, we see that the oil stock falls gradually from its initial level towards zero; note that as the shadow price of oil rises over time, so the rate of extraction falls towards zero. Not surprisingly, the optimal solution will require that the rate of extraction goes to zero at exactly the same point in time, t_f, that the stock is completely exhausted. Note that within 100 years, the oil stock has fallen to a level not significantly different from zero; it is optimal to deplete the stock of oil fairly rapidly in this model. What happens after the year 2090? You should now try to deduce the answer to this question.

Table 14.1 Numerical solution to the oil extraction and optimal consumption problem

Welfare (p.v.) = 46.67668

time	C_t	$Q(K_t, R_t)$	K_t	R_t	S_t	$q(t+1)$	$P(t+1)$	$\partial Q/\partial K(t)$
1990s	3.7342	18.0518	4.9130	2.2770	11.5000	0.2678	0.2123	3.3069
2000s	13.6819	60.8347	19.2306	1.9947	9.2230	0.0731	0.2229	2.8471
2010s	45.3301	182.8353	66.3834	1.7232	7.2283	0.0221	0.2341	2.4788
2020s	137.2777	493.8224	203.8886	1.4637	5.5051	0.0073	0.2458	2.1798
2030s	383.6060	1 204.3708	560.4334	1.2167	4.0413	0.0026	0.2581	1.9341
2040s	997.3350	2 654.7992	1 381.1982	0.9824	2.8247	0.0010	0.2710	1.7299
2050s	2 430.1080	5 261.7198	3 038.6624	0.7611	1.8423	0.0004	0.2845	1.5584
2060s	5 584.8970	9 217.1125	5 870.2742	0.5525	1.0812	0.0002	0.2987	1.4131
2070s	12 174.5621	13 608.6578	9 502.4897	0.3564	0.5287	0.0001	0.3137	1.2889
2080s	25 298.4825	14 361.8971	10 936.5854	0.1724	0.1724	0.0000	0.3293	1.1819
2090s			0.0	0.0000	0.0000	0.0000	0.3548	

$$\underbrace{\hspace{10cm}}_{\times\ 10\ \text{trillion US\$}}\qquad \underbrace{\hspace{5cm}}_{\times\ 100\ \text{billion barrels}}$$

% Growth rates:

2000	266.3899	237.0006	291.4222	−12.4012	−19.8004	−74.0064	5.0000	
2010	231.3150	200.5443	245.1973	−13.6071	−21.6271	−71.2545	5.0000	
2020	202.8399	170.0914	207.1378	−15.0607	−23.8402	−68.5517	5.0000	
2030	179.4380	143.8874	174.8723	−16.8783	−26.5885	−65.9180	5.0000	
2040	159.9894	120.4304	146.4518	−19.2530	−30.1053	−63.3685	5.0000	
2050	143.6602	98.1965	120.0019	−22.5320	−34.7797	−60.9136	5.0000	
2060	129.8209	75.1730	93.1861	−27.4081	−41.3110	−58.5599	5.0000	
2070	117.9908	47.6456	61.8747	−35.4951	−51.0972	−56.3110	5.0000	
2080	107.7979	5.5350	15.0918	−51.3311	−67.3996	−54.1679	5.0000	

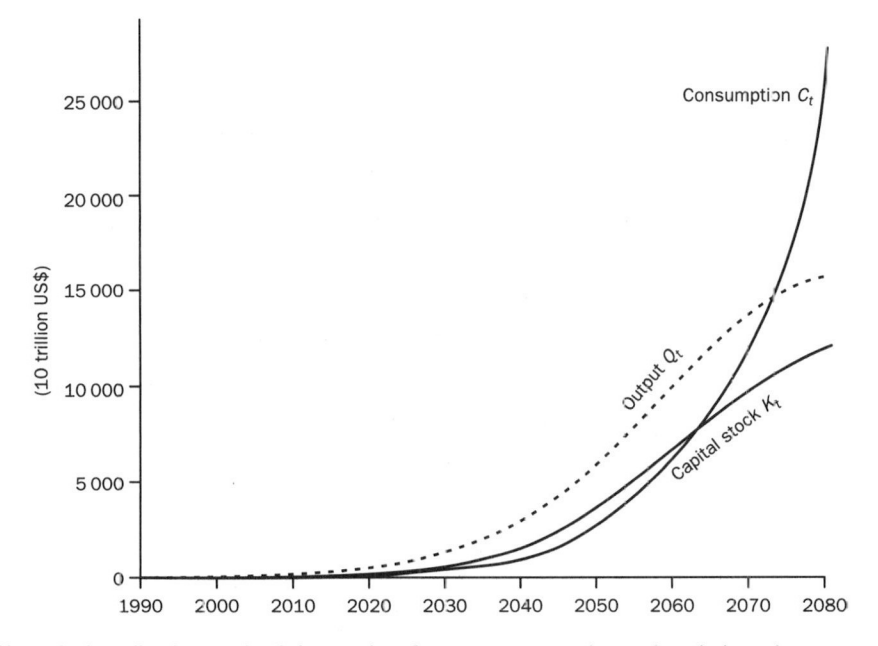

Figure 14.6 Numerical application: optimal time paths of output, consumption and capital stock

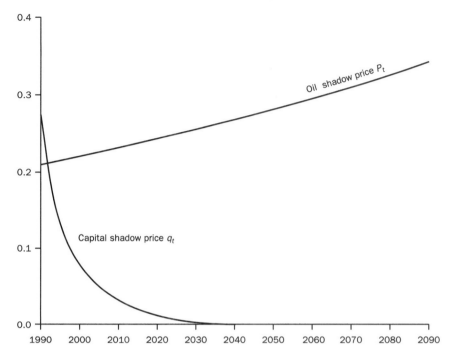

Figure 14.7 Numerical application: optimal time paths of the oil and capital shadow prices

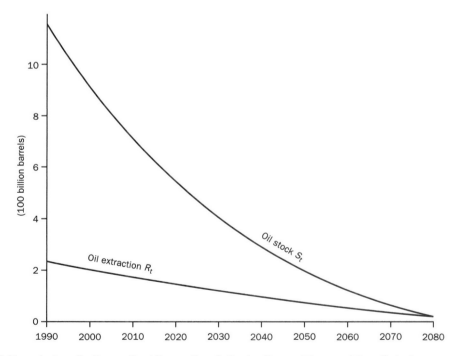

Figure 14.8 Numerical application: optimal time paths of oil extraction and the remaining oil stock

Summary

- In this chapter, we have constructed a simple economic model of optimal resource depletion, and studied several of its variants. The framework we use is a version of the so-called optimal growth models, built around a production function in which natural resources are inputs into the production process.
- The solution to an optimal resource depletion model should be one in which a set of static and intertemporal efficiency conditions – as discussed in Chapters 5 and 11 – are satisfied. In addition, optimality requires that, of the many possible efficient depletion paths that may be available, the one chosen is that which maximises the relevant objective function (in this case the intertemporal social welfare function).
- The characteristics of a socially optimal pattern of natural resource use over time will depend on the particular nature of the social welfare function that is deemed to be appropriate. In this chapter – as generally throughout the text – the special case chosen is that of the utilitarian social welfare function, in which future utility is discounted at the positive rate ρ.
- Given that the objective function used here is specified in terms of units of utility, all prices and values referred to in this chapter are also specified in units of utility. This poses a practical problem in that utility is an unobservable variable. However, given the form of the utility function $U = U(C)$, all results could be stated equivalently in terms of units of consumption (or income).
- One efficiency property to which resource economists pay considerable attention is the so-called Hotelling rule. This intertemporal efficiency condition requires that the real rate of return to a resource owner should equal the social discount rate.
- For a non-renewable resource available in known, fixed quantity, the Hotelling rule implies that the net price of the resource, specified in utility units, should grow at the proportionate rate ρ.
- The Hotelling rule has general applicability and does not apply only to non-renewable resources. We briefly state how the rule applies to renewable resources. This will be examined at length in Chapter 17. Although we did not discuss it in this chapter, the rule also applies where resource extraction or use generates adverse external effects. This case is examined at length in Chapter 16.

Further reading

The mathematics underlying our analyses is presented simply and clearly in Chiang (1984, 1992). Kamien and Schwartz (1981) is also an excellent reference for optimal control theory. Excellent advanced-level presentations of the theory of efficient and optimal resource depletion can be found in Baumol and Oates (1988), Dasgupta and Heal (1979), and Heal (1981). Kolstad and Krautkraemer (1993) is particularly insightful and relatively straightforward. Dasgupta and Heal (1974) is also a comprehensive study, and is contained along with several other useful (but difficult) papers in the May 1974 special issue of the *Review of Economic Studies*.

Less difficult presentations are given in Hartwick and Olewiler (1998), Anderson (1985, 1991), and the Fisher and Peterson survey article in the March 1976 edition of the *Journal of Economic Literature*. For an application of this theory to the greenhouse effect, see Barbier (1989b) or Nordhaus (1982, 1991a). Barbier (1989a) provides a critique of the conventional theory of resource depletion, and other critical discussions are found in Common (1995) and Common and Perrings (1992).

1. Are non-renewable resources becoming more or less substitutable by other productive inputs with the passage of time? What are the possible implications for efficient resource use of the elasticity of substitution between non-renewable resources and other inputs becoming
   (a) higher, and
   (b) lower
   with the passage of time?

2. Discuss the possible effects of technical progress on resource substitutability.

3. Recycling of non-renewable resources can relax the constraints imposed by finiteness of non-renewable resources. What determines the efficient amount of recycling for any particular economy?

1. Using the relationship

$$r = \rho + \eta \frac{\dot{C}}{C}$$

demonstrate that if the utility function is of the special form $U(C) = C$, the consumption rate of discount (r) and the utility rate of discount are identical.

2. Using equation 14.15 in the text (that is, the Hotelling efficiency condition), demonstrate the consequences for the efficient extraction of a non-renewable resource of an increase in the social discount rate, ρ.

3. The simplest model of optimal resource depletion is the so-called 'cake-eating' problem in which welfare is a discounted integral of utility, utility is a function of consumption, and consumption is equal to the amount of the (non-renewable) resource extracted. That is:

$$W = \int_{t=0}^{t=\infty} U(C_t) e^{-\rho t} dt$$

$$C_t = R_t \quad \text{and}$$

$$\dot{S}_t = -R_t$$

   (a) Obtain the Hamiltonian, and the necessary first-order conditions for a welfare maximum.
   (b) Interpret the first-order conditions.
   (c) What happens to consumption along the optimal path?
   (d) What is the effect of an increase in the discount rate?

Appendix 14.1 The optimal control problem and its solution using the maximum principle

Optimal control theory, using the maximum principle, is a technique for solving constrained dynamic optimisation problems. In this appendix we aim to

- explain what is meant by a constrained dynamic optimisation problem;
- show one technique – the maximum principle – by which such a problem can be solved.

We will not give any proofs of the conditions used in the maximum principle. Our emphasis is on explaining the technique and showing how to use it. For the reader who wishes to go through these proofs, some recommendations for further reading are given above. After you have finished reading this appendix, it will be useful to go through Appendices 14.2 and 14.3. Appendix 14.2 shows how the maximum principle is used to derive the optimal solution to the simple non-renewable resource depletion problem discussed in Part 1 of this chapter. Appendix 14.3 considers the optimal allocation

Table 14.2 The optimal control problem and its solution[7]

Objective function (see note 1)	$J(\mathbf{u}) = \max \displaystyle\int_{t_0}^{t_T} L(\mathbf{x}, \mathbf{u}, t)\mathrm{d}t + F(\mathbf{x}(t_T))$			
System	$\dot{\mathbf{x}} = \mathbf{f}(\mathbf{x}, \mathbf{u}, t)$ $\mathbf{x}(t_0) = \mathbf{x}_0$			
Terminal state	$\mathbf{x}(t_T) = \mathbf{x}_T$		$\mathbf{x}(t_T)$ free	
Terminal point	t_T fixed	t_T free	t_T fixed	t_T free
Hamiltonian	$H = H(\mathbf{x}, \mathbf{u}, t, \lambda)$ $= L(\mathbf{x}, \mathbf{u}, t) + \lambda \mathbf{f}(\mathbf{x}, \mathbf{u}, t)$			
Equations of motion	$\dot{\mathbf{x}} = \mathbf{f}(\mathbf{x}, \mathbf{u}, t)$ $\dot{\lambda} = -\dfrac{\partial H}{\partial \mathbf{x}}$			
Max H (see note 2)	$\dfrac{\partial H}{\partial \mathbf{u}} = 0$			
Transversality condition	$\mathbf{x}(t_T) = \mathbf{x}_T$		$\lambda(t_T) = 0$ if $t_T = \infty$ or $F(\cdot) = 0$ otherwise $\lambda(t_T) = F'(\cdot)$	
		$H(t_T) = 0$		$H(t_T) = 0$

Notes to Table 14.2
1. The term $F(\mathbf{x}(t_T))$ may not be present in the objective function, and cannot be if $t_T = \infty$.
2. The Max H condition given in the table is for the special case of an interior solution (u is an interior point). A more general statement of this condition (the 'maximum principle') is: $\mathbf{u}(t)$ maximises H over $\mathbf{u}(t) \in U$, for $0 \leq t \leq t_T$.

[7] Notation:
x(t)   is the vector of state variables
u(t)   is the vector of control variables
J(**u**)   is the objective function to be maximised, which may be augmented by a final function F(·)
λ(t)   is the vector of co-state variables
f(**x**, **u**, t)   are the state equation functions, describing the relevant physical–economic system
t_0 is the initial point in time
t_T is the terminal point in time
H   is the Hamiltonian function
F(**x**(t_T))   is a 'final function', which defines some endpoint condition that has to be satisfied

Table 14.3 The optimal control problem with a discounting factor and its solution[8]

Objective function (see note 1)	$J(\mathbf{u}) = \max \displaystyle\int_{t_0}^{t_T} L(\mathbf{x}, \mathbf{u}, t)\mathrm{e}^{-\rho t}\mathrm{d}t + F(\mathbf{x}(t_T))\mathrm{e}^{-\rho T}$			
System	$\dot{\mathbf{x}} = \mathbf{f}(\mathbf{x}, \mathbf{u}, t)$ $\mathbf{x}(t_0) = \mathbf{x}_0$			
Terminal state	$\mathbf{x}(t_T) = \mathbf{x}_T$		$\mathbf{x}(t_T)$ free	
Terminal point	t_T fixed	t_T free	t_T fixed	t_T free
Present-value Hamiltonian	$H = H(\mathbf{x}, \mathbf{u}, t, \lambda)$ $= L(\mathbf{x}, \mathbf{u}, t) + \lambda \mathbf{f}(\mathbf{x}, \mathbf{u}, t)$			
Current-value Hamiltonian	$H_C = H\mathrm{e}^{\rho t} = L(\mathbf{x}, \mathbf{u}, t)$ $+ \mu \mathbf{f}(\mathbf{x}, \mathbf{u}, t), (\mu = \lambda \mathrm{e}^{\rho t})$			
Equations of motion	$\dot{\mathbf{x}} = \mathbf{f}(\mathbf{x}, \mathbf{u}, t)$ $\dot{\mu} = \rho\mu - \dfrac{\partial H_C}{\partial \mathbf{x}}$			
Max H_C (see note 2)	$\dfrac{\partial H}{\partial \mathbf{u}} = 0$			
Transversality condition	$\mathbf{x}(t_T) = \mathbf{x}_T$		$\mu(t_T) = 0$ if $t_T = \infty$ or if $F(\cdot) = 0$ otherwise $\mu(t_T) = F'(\cdot)$	
		$H_C(t_T) +$ $\partial F/\partial T = 0$		$H_C(t_T) +$ $\partial F/\partial T = 0$

Notes to Table 14.3
Note 1: The term $F(\mathbf{x}(t_T))\mathrm{e}^{-\rho T}$ may not be present in the objective function, and cannot be if $t_T = \infty$.
Note 2: two versions of the Hamiltonian function are given. The first is known as the 'present-value' Hamiltonian, as the presence of the term $\mathrm{e}^{-\rho t}$ in the objective function (which converts magnitudes into present-value terms) carries over into the Hamiltonian, H_P. The second is known as the current-value Hamiltonian (see Chiang, 1992, p. 210). Premultiplying H_P by $\mathrm{e}^{\rho t}$ removes the discounting factor from the expression, and hence H_C is expressed in current-value terms. For mathematical convenience, it is usually better to work with the Hamiltonian in current-value terms.
Note 3: The Max H_C condition given in the table is for the special case of an interior solution (**u** is an interior set). A more general statement of this condition (the 'maximum principle') is: $\mathbf{u}(t)$ maximises H_C over $\mathbf{u}(t) \in U$, for $0 \leq t \leq t_T$.
Note 4: The term $\partial F/\partial T$ does not enter the transversality condition in the final line of the table if $F(\cdot) = 0$.

[8] Notation is as defined in Table 14.2. The term ρ denotes the utility social discount rate.

of a renewable or non-renewable resource in the case where extraction of the resource involves costs – the model discussed in Part 2 of this chapter.

Let us begin by laying out the various elements of a constrained dynamic optimisation problem. In doing this, you will find it useful to refer to Tables 14.2 and 14.3, where we have summarised the key elements of the optimal control problem and its solution.

1. The function to be maximised is known as the objective function, denoted $J(\mathbf{u})$. This takes the form of an integral over a time period from an initial time t_0 to the terminal time t_T. Two points should be borne in mind about the terminal point in time, t_T:

- In some optimisation problems t_T is fixed; in others it is free (and so becomes an endogenous variable, the value of which is solved for as part of the optimisation exercise).
- In some optimisation problems the terminal point is a finite quantity (it is a finite number of time periods later than the initial time); in others, the terminal point is infinite ($t_T = \infty$). When a problem has an infinite terminal point in time, t_T should be regarded as free.

2. The objective function will, in general, contain as its arguments three types of variable:
   - $\mathbf{x}(t)$, a *vector* of n state variables at time t;
   - $\mathbf{u}(t)$, a *vector* of m control (or instrument) variables at time t;
   - t, time itself.

   Although the objective function may contain each of these three types of variables, it is not necessary that all be present in the objective function (as you will see from the examples worked through in Appendices 14.2 and 14.3).

3. The objective function may (but will often not) be augmented with the addition of a 'final function', denoted by the function $F(\cdot)$ in Tables 14.2 and 14.3. Its role (where it appears) will be explained below. (The applications in Chapter 14 did not involve the use of a final function.)

4. The solution to a dynamic optimal control problem will contain, among other things, the values of the state and control variables at each point in time over the period from t_0 to t_T. It is this that makes the exercise a dynamic optimisation exercise.

5. Underlying the optimal control problem will be some economic, biological or physical system (which we shall call simply 'the economic system'), describing the initial values of a set of state variables of interest, and how they evolve over time. The evolution of the state variables over time will, in general, be described by a set of differential equations (known as state equations) of the form:

$$\dot{\mathbf{x}} = \mathbf{f}(\mathbf{x}, \mathbf{u}, t)$$

where $\dot{\mathbf{x}} = d\mathbf{x}/dt$ is the time derivative of $\mathbf{x}$ (the rate of change of $\mathbf{x}$ with respect to time). Note that as $\mathbf{x}$ is a vector of n state variables, there will in general be n state equations. Any solution to the optimal control problem must satisfy these state equations. This is one reason why we use the phrase 'constrained' dynamic optimisation problems.

6. A second way in which constraints may enter the problem is through the terminal conditions of the problem. There are two aspects here: one concerns the value of the state variables at the terminal point in time, the other concerns the terminal point in time itself.
   - First, in some problems the values that the state variables take at the terminal point in time are fixed; in others these values are free (and so are endogenously determined in the optimisation exercise).
   - Secondly, either the particular problem that we are dealing with will fix the terminal point in time, or that point will be free (and so, again, be determined endogenously in the optimisation exercise).

7. The optimisation exercise must satisfy a so-called transversality condition. The particular transversality condition that must be satisfied in any particular problem will depend upon which of the four possibilities outlined in (6) applies. (Four possibilities exist because for each of the two possibilities for the terminal values of the state variables there are two possibilities for the terminal point in time.) It follows from this that when we read Tables 14.2 and 14.3, then (ignoring the column of labels) there are four columns referring to these four possibilities. Where cells are merged and so cover more than one column, the condition shown refers to all the possibilities it covers. We shall come back to the transversality condition in a moment.

8. The control variables (or instruments) are variables whose value can be chosen by the decision maker in order to steer the evolution of the state variables over time in a desired manner.

9. In addition to the three kinds of variables we have discussed so far – time, state and control variables – a fourth type of variable enters optimal control problems. This is the vector of co-state variables λ (or μ in the case where the objective function contains a discount factor). Co-state variables are similar to the Lagrange multiplier variables one finds in static constrained optimisation exercises. But in the present context, where we are dealing with a dynamic optimisation problem over some sequence of time periods, the value taken by each co-state variable will in general vary over time, and so it is appropriate to denote $\lambda(t)$ as the vector of co-state variables at time t.

10. The analogy of co-state variables with Lagrange multipliers carries over to their economic interpretation: the co-state variables can be interpreted as shadow prices, which denote the decision maker's marginal valuation of the state variable at each point in time (along the optimal time path of the state and control variables).

11. Finally, let us return to the transversality condition. Looking at the final rows in Tables 14.2 and 14.3 you will see four possible configurations of transversality condition. All relate to something that must be satisfied by the solution at the terminal point in time. Where the terminal value of the state variables is fixed, this will always be reflected in the transversality condition. On the other hand, where the terminal value of the state variables

is free, the transversality condition will usually[9] require that the shadow price of the state variables be zero. Intuitively, this means that if we do not put any constraints on how large the stocks of the state variables must be at the terminal point in time, then they must have a zero value at that time. For if they had any positive value, it would have been optimal to deplete them further prior to the end of the planning horizon. Note also that whenever the terminal point in time is free (whether or not the state variables are fixed at the terminal point), an additional part of the transversality condition requires that the Hamiltonian have a zero value at the endogenously determined terminal point in time.[10] If it did not, then the terminal point could not have been an optimal one!

The general case referred to in Tables 14.2 and 14.3, and special cases

In the description we have given above of the optimal control problem, we have been considering a general case. For example, we allow there to be n state variables and m control variables. In some special cases, m and n may each be one, so there is only one state and one control variable. Also, we have written the state equation for the economic system of interest as being a function of three types of variables: time, state and control. In many particular problems, not all three types of variables will be present as arguments in the state equation. For example, in many problems, time does not enter explicitly in the state equation. A similar comment applies to the objective function: while in general it is a function of three types of variables, not all three will enter in some problems. Finally, often the objective function will not be augmented by the presence of a 'final function'.

---

[9] Strictly speaking, the shadow price will be zero where the time horizon is of infinite length or if there is no final function in the objective function. However, where the objective function contains a final function, the shadow price must equal the first derivative of that final function with respect to the state variable. This is shown in Tables 14.2 and 14.3.

[10] Or, as shown in Table 14.3, the additional part of the transversality condition requires that the Hamiltonian plus the derivative of F with respect to T have a zero value at the endogenously determined terminal point in time.

Limitations to the optimal control technique outlined in this appendix

The statement of the optimal control problem and its solution given in this appendix is not as general as it might be. For example, the terminal condition might require that a control variable must be greater than some particular quantity (but is otherwise unconstrained). As neither this (nor any other) complication arises in the examples discussed in this book, we do not go through them here. Details can be found in Chiang (1992).

The presence of a discount factor in the objective function

For some dynamic optimisation problems, the objective function to be maximised, $J(\mathbf{u})$, will be an integral over time of some function of time, state variables and control variables. That is:

$$J(\mathbf{u}) = \int_{t_0}^{t_T} L(\mathbf{x}, \mathbf{u}, t)\,dt$$

However, in many dynamic optimisation problems that are of interest to economists, the objective function will be a discounted (or present-value) integral of the form:

$$J(\mathbf{u}) = \int_{t_0}^{t_T} L(\mathbf{x}, \mathbf{u}, t)\,e^{-\rho t}\,dt$$

For example, equation 14.8 in the text of this chapter is of this form. There, L is actually a utility function $U(\cdot)$ (which is a function of only one control variable, C). Indeed, throughout this book, the objective functions with which we deal are almost always discounted or present-value integral functions.

The solution of the optimal control problem

The nature of the solution to the optimal control problem will differ depending on whether or not the objective function contains a discounting factor. Table 14.2 states formally the optimal control problem and its solution using general notation, for the

case where the objective function does not include a discount factor. Table 14.3 presents the same information for the case where the objective function is a discounted (or present-value) integral. Some (brief) explanation and discussion of how the conditions listed in Tables 14.2 and 14.3 may be used to obtain the required solution is provided below those tables. However, we strongly urge you also to read Appendices 14.2 and 14.3, so that you can get a feel for how the general results we have described here can be used in practice (and how we have used them in this chapter).

Interpreting the two tables

It will help to focus on one case: we will look at an optimal control problem with a discounting factor, an infinite time horizon (so that t_T is deemed to be free), and no restriction being placed on the values of the state variable in the terminal time period (so that $x(t_T)$ is free. The relevant statement of the optimal control problem and its solution is, therefore, that given in the final column to the right in Table 14.3.

We can express the problem as

$$J(\mathbf{u}) = \max \int_{t_0}^{t_T} L(\mathbf{x}, \mathbf{u}, t)\,e^{-\rho t}\,dt$$

subject to

$$\dot{\mathbf{x}} = \mathbf{f}(\mathbf{x}, \mathbf{u}, t) \text{ and } \mathbf{x}(t_0) = \mathbf{x}_0, \mathbf{x}(0) \text{ given, } \mathbf{x}(t_T) \text{ free.}$$

To obtain the solution we first construct the current-value Hamiltonian:

$$H_C = L(\mathbf{x}, \mathbf{u}, t) + \mu\mathbf{f}(\mathbf{x}, \mathbf{u}, t)$$

The current-value Hamiltonian consists of two components:

- The first $L(\mathbf{x}, \mathbf{u}, t)$ is the function which, after being multiplied by the discounting factor and then being integrated over the relevant time horizon, enters the objective function. Note carefully by examining Table 14.3 that in the Hamiltonian the L function itself enters, not its integral. Furthermore, although the discounting factor enters the objective function, it does not enter in the current-value Hamiltonian.

- The second component that enters the Hamiltonian is the right-hand side of the state variable equations of motion, $\mathbf{f}(\mathbf{x}, \mathbf{u}, t)$, after having been premultiplied by the co-state variable vector in current-value form. Remember that in the general case there are n state variables, and so n co-state variables, one for each state equation. In order for this multiplication to be conformable, it is actually the transpose of the co-state vector $\boldsymbol{\mu}$ that premultiplies the vector of functions from the state equations.

Our next task is to find the values of the control variables $\mathbf{u}$ which maximise the current-value Hamiltonian at each point in time; it is this which gives this approach its name of 'the maximum principle'. If the Hamiltonian function H_C is non-linear and differentiable in the control variables $\mathbf{u}$, then the problem will have an interior solution, which can be found easily. This is done by differentiating H_C with respect to $\mathbf{u}$ and setting the derivatives equal to zero. Hence in this case one of the necessary conditions for the solution will be

$\partial H_C/\partial \mathbf{u} = 0$ (a set of m equations, one for each of the m control variables).

More generally, there may be a corner solution. Obtaining this solution may be a difficult task in some circumstances, as it involves searching for the values of $\mathbf{u}(t)$ which maximises $H_C(t)$ (at all points in time) in some other way.

Bringing together all the necessary conditions for the complete solution of the optimisation problem we have:

- The maximum principle conditions (assuming an interior solution and no final function present):

$$\frac{\partial H_C}{\partial \mathbf{u}} = 0 \text{ (a set of } m \text{ equations, one for each}$$

of the m control variables).

- Those given in the row labelled 'Equations of motion' in Table 14.3, that is

$\dot{\mathbf{x}} = \mathbf{f}(\mathbf{x}, \mathbf{u}, t)$ (a set of n equations)

$$\dot{\boldsymbol{\mu}} = \rho\boldsymbol{\mu} - \frac{\partial H_C}{\partial \mathbf{x}} \text{ (a set of } n \text{ equations)}$$

- The initial condition $\mathbf{x}(t_0) = \mathbf{x}_0$

- The transversality condition $H_C(t_T) = 0$

Solving these necessary conditions simultaneously, we can obtain the optimal time path for each of the m control variables over the (infinite) time horizon. Corresponding to this time path of the control variables are the optimised time paths of the n state variables and their associated current-value shadow prices (values of the co-state variables) along the optimal path.

It should be clear that obtaining this complete solution could be a daunting task in problems with many control and state variables. However, where the number of variables is small and the relevant functions are easy to handle, the solution can often be obtained quite simply. We demonstrate this assertion in the following two appendices.

One final point warrants mention. Tables 14.2 and 14.3 give necessary but not sufficient conditions for a maximum. In principle, to confirm that our solution is indeed a maximum, second-order conditions should be checked as well. However, in most problems of interest to economists (and in all problems investigated in this book), assumptions are made about the shapes of functions which guarantee that second-order conditions for a maximum will be satisfied, thereby obviating the need for checking second-order conditions.

Let us try to provide some intuitive content to the foregoing by considering a problem where there is just one state variable, x, and one control variable, u, where t does not enter either the objective function or the equation describing the system, no final function is present, and where $t_0 = 0$ and we have an infinite terminal point ($t_T = \infty$). Then the problem is to maximise[11]

$$\int_0^\infty L(x_t, u_t)e^{-\rho t}dt$$

subject to

---

[11] As x and u are now single variables, not vectors, we now drop the bold (vector) notation.

$\dot{x} = f(x_t, u_t)$ and $x(t_0) = x_0$

for which the current-value Hamiltonian is

$$H_{C_t} = L(x_t, u_t) + \mu_t f(x_t, u_t) = L(x_t, u_t) + \mu_t \dot{x}_t$$

In the original problem, we are looking to maximise the integral of the discounted value of $L(x_t, u_t)$. The first term in the Hamiltonian is just $L(x_t, u_t)$, the instantaneous value of that we seek the maximum of. Recalling that co-state variables are like Lagrangian multipliers and that those are shadow prices (see Appendix 4.1), the second term in the Hamiltonian is the increase in the state variable, some stock, valued by the appropriate shadow price. So, H_{C_t} can be regarded as the value of interest at t plus the increase in the value of the stock at t. In that case, the maximum principle condition $\partial H_{C_t}/\partial u_t = 0$ makes a good deal of sense. It says, at every point in time, set the control variable so that it maximises H_C, which is value plus an increase in value. It is intuitive that such maximisation at every point in time is required for maximisation of the integral. The equation of motion condition $\dot{x} = f(x_t, u_t)$ ensures that the optimal path is one that is feasible for the system. Aside from transversality, the remaining condition is $\dot{\mu} = \rho\mu_t - \partial H_C/\partial x_t$ which governs how the shadow, or imputed, price of the state variable must evolve over time.

This condition can be given some intuitive content by considering a model which is, mathematically, further specialised, and which has some economic content. Consider the simplest possible optimal growth model in which the only argument in the production function is capital. Then, the optimal paths for consumption and capital accumulation are given by maximising

$$\int_0^{\infty} U(C_t)e^{-\rho t}dt$$

subject to

$$\dot{K} = Q(K_t) - C_t$$

giving the current-value Hamiltonian

$$H_{C_t} = U(C_t) + \mu_t(Q(K_t) - C_t) = U(C_t) - \mu_t\dot{K}$$

Here the Hamiltonian is current utility plus the increase in the capital stock valued using the shadow

price of capital. In Appendices 19.1 and 19.2 we shall explore this kind of Hamiltonian in relation to the question of the proper measurement of national income.

The maximum principle condition here is $\partial H_{C_t}/\partial C_t = \partial U_t/\partial C_t - \mu_t = 0$ which gives the shadow price of capital as equal to the marginal utility of consumption. Given that a marginal addition to the capital stock is at the cost of a marginal reduction in consumption, this makes sense. Here the condition governing the behaviour of the shadow price over time is

$$\dot{\mu} = \rho\mu_t - \partial H_{C_t}/\partial K_t = \rho\mu_t - \mu_t\partial Q_t/\partial K_t$$

where $\partial Q_t/\partial K_t$ is the marginal product of capital. This condition can be written with the proportionate rate of change of the shadow price on the left-hand side, as

$$\dot{\mu}/\mu_t = \rho - (\partial Q_t/\partial K_t)$$

where the right-hand side is the difference between the utility discount rate and the marginal product of capital adjusted for the marginal utility of consumption. The first term on the right-hand side reflects impatience for future consumption and the second term the pay-off to delayed consumption. According to this expression for the proportional rate of change of the shadow price of capital:

(a) μ is increasing when 'impatience' is greater than 'pay-off';
(b) μ is constant when 'impatience' is equal to 'pay-off';
(c) μ is decreasing when 'impatience' is less than 'pay-off'.

This makes sense, given that:

(a) when 'impatience' is greater than 'pay-off', the economy will be running down K;
(b) when 'impatience' and 'pay-off' are equal, K will be constant;
(c) when 'impatience' is less than 'pay-off', the economy will be accumulating K.

These remarks should be compared with the results in Table 14.1 where it will be seen that the calculated shadow price of capital decreases over time, while the shadow price of oil, which is becoming scarcer, increases over time.

Appendix 14.2 The optimal solution to the simple exhaustible resource depletion problem

In this appendix, we derive the optimal solution to the simple exhaustible resource depletion problem discussed in Part 1 of this chapter. In doing this, we will make extensive reference to the solution method outlined in Appendix 14.1.

The objective function to be maximised is:

$$W = \int_{t=0}^{t=\infty} U(C_t)e^{-\rho t}dt$$

Comparing this with the form and notation used for an objective function in Tables 14.2 and 14.3 it is evident that:

- we are here using W (rather than J) to label the objective function;
- the initial time period (t_0) is here written as $t = 0$;
- the terminal time (t_T) is infinity: therefore we describe the terminal point as free;
- there is a discounting factor present in the objective function: Table 14.3 is therefore appropriate;
- the integral function which in general takes the form $L(\mathbf{x}, \mathbf{u}, t)$ (ignoring the discounting term) here has the form $U(C_t)$. It is a function of one variable only, consumption, which is a control variable (u). Note that we have written this variable as C_t rather than C to make it explicit that the value of the control variable changes over time. No state variable enters the objective function in this problem, nor does time, t, enter the integral function directly (it enters only through the discounting factor).

Be careful not to confuse U and u. The term U in Appendix 14.2 denotes utility; it is what is being maximised in the objective function; $\mathbf{u}$ in Tables 14.2 and 14.3 is the notation used for control variables.

There are two state variables (the $\mathbf{x}$ variables in Table 14.3) in this problem: S_t and K_t, the resource stock at time t and the capital stock at time t, respectively. Corresponding to these two state variables are two state equations of motion (the equations $\dot{\mathbf{x}} = \mathbf{f}(\mathbf{x}, \mathbf{u}, t)$ in Table 14.3). These are

$$\dot{S}_t = -R_t$$

and

$$\dot{K}_t = Q_t - C_t$$

There are two control variables in this problem: C_t and R_t (the rate of resource extraction). These are the two variables whose values are chosen by the decision maker to form a time path that will maximise the objective function. Note that in neither of the state equations of motion does a state variable ($\mathbf{x}$) or time (t) appear as an argument of the function.

The economic system consists of:

- the two state equations;
- initial values for the state variables: the initial resource stock (S_0, see equation 14.9) and the initial capital stock (K_0, see footnote 5 in the main text);
- a production function, linking output Q (which is neither a state nor a control variable) to the capital stock and rate of resource extraction at each point in time:

$$Q_t = Q(K_t, R_t)$$

One final thing remains to be specified: the terminal state conditions. We do not state these explicitly in the text. However, by implication, the problem is one in which both the capital stock and the resource stock become zero at the end of the (infinite) planning horizon, so we have $K_{t=\infty} = 0$ and $S_{t=\infty} = 0$ (i.e. $\mathbf{x}(t_T) = \mathbf{x}_T = 0$, in the notation of Table 14.3). As a result of $\mathbf{x}(t_T) = 0$ and t_T free (with an infinite horizon), it is the third column from the right in Table 14.3 which is relevant for obtaining the solution to this problem.

The current-value Hamiltonian for this problem is

$$H_{C_t} = U(C_t) + P_t(-R_t) + \omega_t(Q_t - C_t)$$

in which P_t and ω_t are the co-state variables (shadow prices) expressed in units of current-value utility associated with the resource stock and the capital stock at time t respectively. After substituting for Q_t from the production function, the Hamiltonian is

$$H_{C_t} = U(C_t) + P_t(-R_t) + \omega_t(Q\{K_t, R_t\} - C_t)$$

The necessary conditions for a maximum include:

$$\frac{\partial H_{C_t}}{\partial C_t} = U_{C,t} - \omega_t = 0 \tag{14.25a}$$

$$\frac{\partial H_{C_t}}{\partial R_t} = -P_t + \omega_t Q_{R,t} = 0 \tag{14.25b}$$

$$\dot{P}_t = -\frac{\partial H_{C_t}}{\partial S_t} + \rho P_t \Leftrightarrow \dot{P}_t = \rho P_t \tag{14.25c}$$

$$\dot{\omega}_t = -\frac{\partial H_{C_t}}{\partial K_t} + \rho \omega_t \Leftrightarrow \dot{\omega}_t = \rho \omega_t - Q_{K,t} \omega_t \tag{14.25d}$$

The pair of equations 14.25a and 14.25b correspond to the 'Max H' condition $\partial H_C/\partial \mathbf{u} = 0$ in Table 14.3, for the two control ($\mathbf{u}$) variables R and C. The second pair, 14.25c and 14.25d, are the equations of motion for the two co-state variables [$\dot{\boldsymbol{\mu}} = \rho\boldsymbol{\mu} - \partial H_C/\partial \mathbf{x}$] that are associated with the two state variables S and K. Note that in 14.25c the term $-\partial H_C/\partial S = 0$ as S does not enter the Hamiltonian function. The four equations 14.14a to 14.14d given in the main text of this chapter are identical to equations 14.25a to 14.25d above (except that the equations in the text, rather loosely, use H rather than H_C).

Obtaining an expression for the growth rate of consumption

An expression for the growth rate of consumption along the optimal time path can be obtained by combining equations 14.25a and 14.25d as follows (dropping the time subscripts for simplicity). First, differentiate equation 14.25a with respect to time, yielding:

$$\dot{\omega} = U''(C)\dot{C} \tag{14.26}$$

Next, combine equations 14.26 and 14.25d to obtain:

$$U''(C)\dot{C} = \rho\omega - Q_K\omega$$

Hence

$$\dot{C}U''(C) = \omega(\rho - Q_K)$$

But since from equation 14.25a we know that $U'(C_t) = \omega_t$ the previous equation can be re-expressed as

$$\dot{C}U''(C) = U'(C)(\rho - Q_K)$$

Therefore

$$\frac{\dot{C}U''(C)}{C} = \frac{U'(C)(\rho - Q_K)}{C}$$

and so

$$\frac{\dot{C}}{C} = \frac{1}{\left[\dfrac{U''(C)C}{U'(C)}\right]}(\rho - Q_K) \tag{14.27}$$

Now by definition the elasticity of marginal utility with respect to consumption, η, is

$$\eta = -\frac{\partial MU/MU}{\partial C/C}$$

Noting that $MU = U'(C)$, then the expression for η can be rearranged to give

$$\eta = -\frac{U''(C)C}{U'(C)}$$

Then 14.27 can be rewritten as

$$\frac{\dot{C}}{C} = -\frac{1}{\eta}(\rho - Q_K) = \frac{Q_K - \rho}{\eta}$$

which is the expression we gave for the growth rate of consumption in the text.

Appendix 14.3 Optimal and efficient extraction or harvesting of a renewable or non-renewable resource in the presence of resource extraction costs

In this appendix, we derive the optimal solution to the exhaustible resource depletion problem discussed in Part 2 of this chapter. We allow for the resource to be either renewable or non-renewable, and its extraction or harvesting to be costly. Once

again, we use the solution method outlined in Appendix 14.1.

Utility is a function of the level of consumption:

$$U_t = U(C_t)$$

The objective function to be maximised is:

$$W = \int_{t=0}^{t=\infty} U(C_t)\mathrm{e}^{-\rho t}\mathrm{d}t$$

There are two state variables in this problem: S_t, the resource stock at time t, and K_t, the capital stock at time t. Associated with each state variable is a shadow price, P (for the resource stock) and ω (for the capital stock). The two state equations of motion are

$$\dot{S}_t = G(S_t) - R_t \tag{14.28}$$

$$\dot{K}_t = Q(K_t, R_t) - C_t - \Gamma(R_t, S_t) \tag{14.29}$$

There are several things to note about these equations of motion:

- If the environmental resource being used is a non-renewable resource, $G(S) = 0$ and so equation 14.28 collapses to the special case $\dot{S}_t = -R_t$.
- Equation 14.29 incorporates resource extraction costs, which are modelled as reducing the amount of output available for either consumption or addition to the stock of capital.
- Equation 14.29 incorporates a production function of the same form as in Appendix 14.2.

There are two control variables in this problem: C_t (consumption) and R_t (the rate of resource extraction). Initial and terminal state conditions are identical to those in Appendix 14.2. The current-value Hamiltonian is

$$H_C = U(C_t) + P_t(G(S_t) - R_t) + \omega_t(Q\{K_t, R_t\} - C_t - \Gamma(R_t, S_t))$$

Ignoring time subscripts and the subscript $_C$ on the expression for the current-value Hamiltonian, the necessary conditions for a maximum are:

$$\frac{\partial H_C}{\partial C} = U_C - \omega = 0 \tag{14.30a}$$

$$\frac{\partial H_C}{\partial R} = -P + \omega Q_R - \omega \Gamma_R = 0 \tag{14.30b}$$

$$\dot{P} = -\frac{\partial H}{\partial S} + \rho P \Leftrightarrow \dot{P} = \rho P - P G_S + \omega \Gamma_S \tag{14.30c}$$

$$\dot{\omega} = -\frac{\partial H}{\partial K} + \rho \omega \Leftrightarrow \dot{\omega} = \rho \omega - Q_K \omega \tag{14.30d}$$

Special cases of these conditions

Let us first concentrate on the simplifications which take place in the Hotelling efficiency condition for the shadow price of the environmental resource (equation 14.30c) when some special cases are considered.

(a) Non-renewable resources. For non-renewables, as noted above, $G(S) = 0$. The Hamiltonian does not, therefore, contain the term G_S. This implies that condition 14.30c simplifies to

$$\dot{P} = \rho P + \Gamma_S \omega$$

which is identical to the Hotelling rule given in the text for optimal depletion of a non-renewable resource that incurs extraction costs (equation 14.20c).

(b) Extraction costs do not depend on the size of the resource stock. Next suppose that we are considering a non-renewable resource for which extraction costs are zero or, more generally, are positive but do not depend on the size of the remaining resource stock. In this case, we have either $\Gamma = 0$ or $\Gamma = \Gamma(R)$. In both cases, $\Gamma_S = 0$. Therefore, the final term in equation 14.30c is zero and so (for non-renewable resources) the Hotelling rule collapses to equation 14.14c, the one we used in Part 1 of the chapter. That is, $\dot{P} = \rho P$.

CHAPTER 15

The theory of optimal resource extraction: non-renewable resources

Behold, I have played the fool, and have erred exceedingly.

1 Samuel 26:21

Learning objectives

After the end of this chapter the reader should be able to

- understand the concept of non-renewable resources
- appreciate the distinctions between alternative measures of resource stock, such as base resource, resource potential and resource reserves
- understand the role of resource substitution possibilities and the ideas of a backstop technology and a resource choke price
- construct and solve simple discrete time and continuous time models of optimal resource depletion
- understand the meaning of a socially optimal depletion programme, and why this may differ from privately optimal programmes
- carry out simple comparative dynamic analysis in the context of resource depletion models, and thereby determine the consequences of changes in interest rates, known stock size, demand, price of backstop technology, and resource extraction costs
- compare resource depletion outcomes in competitive and monopolistic markets
- identify the consequences of taxes and subsidies on resource net prices and resource revenues
- understand the concept of natural resource scarcity, and be aware of a variety of possible measures of scarcity

Introduction

Non-renewable resources include fossil-fuel energy supplies – oil, gas and coal – and minerals – copper and nickel, for example. They are formed by geological processes over millions of years and so, in effect, exist as fixed stocks which, once extracted, cannot be renewed. One question is of central importance: what is the optimal extraction path over time for any particular non-renewable resource stock?

We began to answer this question in Chapter 14. There the optimal extraction problem was solved for a special case in which there was one homogeneous (uniform-quality) non-renewable resource. By assuming a single homogeneous stock, the possibility that substitute non-renewable resources exist is ruled out. The only substitution possibilities considered in Chapter 14 were between the non-renewable resource and other production inputs (labour and capital).

But in practice, non-renewable resources are heterogeneous. They comprise a set of resources varying in chemical and physical type (such as oil, gas, uranium, coal, and the various categories of each of these) and in terms of costs of extraction (as a result of differences in location, accessibility, quality and so on). This chapter investigates the efficient and optimal extraction of one component of this set of non-renewable resources where substitution possibilities exist. Substitution will take place if the price of the resource rises to such an extent that it makes alternatives economically more attractive. Consider, for example, the case of a country that has been exploiting its coal reserves, but in which coal extraction costs rise as lower-quality seams are mined. Meanwhile, gas costs fall as a result of the application of superior extraction and distribution technology. A point may be reached where electricity producers will substitute gas for coal in power generation. It is this kind of process that we wish to be able to model in this chapter.

Although the analysis that follows will employ a different (and in general, simpler) framework from that used in Chapter 14, one very important result carries over to the present case. The Hotelling rule is a necessary efficiency condition that must be satisfied by *any* optimal extraction programme. The chapter begins by laying out the conditions for the extraction path of a non-renewable resource stock to be socially optimal. It then considers how a resource is likely to be depleted in a market economy. As you would expect from the analysis in Chapters 5 and 11, the extraction path in competitive market economies will, under certain circumstances, be socially optimal. It is usually argued that one of these circumstances is that resource markets are competitive. We investigate this matter by comparing extraction paths under competitive and monopoly market structures against the benchmark of a 'first-best' social optimum.

The model used in most of this chapter is simple, and abstracts considerably from specific detail. The assumptions are gradually relaxed to deal with increasingly complex situations. To help understanding, it is convenient to begin with a model in which only two periods of time are considered. Even from such a simple starting point, very powerful results can be obtained, which can be generalised to analyses involving many periods. If you have a clear understanding of Hotelling's rule from Chapter 14, you might wish to skip the two-period model in the next section. Then, having analysed optimal depletion in a two-period model, a more general model is examined in which depletion takes place over T periods, where T may be a very large number.

There are two principal simplifications used in the chapter. First, we assume that utility comes directly from consuming the extracted resource. This is a considerably simpler, yet more specialised, case than that investigated in Chapter 14 where utility derived from consumption goods, obtained through a production function with a natural resource, physical capital (and, implicitly, labour) as inputs. Although doing this pushes the production function into the background, more attention is given to another kind of substitution possibility. As we remarked above, other non-renewable resources also exist. If one or more of these serve as substitutes for the resource being considered, this is likely to have important implications for economically efficient resource depletion paths.

Second, we do not take any account of adverse external effects arising from the extraction or consumption of the resource. The reader may find this rather surprising given that the production and consumption of non-renewable fossil-energy fuels are the primary cause of many of the world's most serious environmental problems. In particular, the combustion of these fuels accounts for between 55% and 88% of carbon dioxide emissions, 90% of sulphur dioxide, and 85% of nitrogen oxide emissions (IEA, 1990). In addition, fossil fuel use accounts for significant proportions of trace-metal emissions.

However, the relationship between non-renewable resource extraction over time and environmental degradation is so important that it warrants separate attention. This will be given in Chapter 16. Not surprisingly, we will show that the optimal extraction path will be different if adverse externalities are present causing environmental damage. The depletion model developed in this chapter will be used in Chapter 16 to derive some important results about efficient pollution targets and instruments.

Finally, a word about presentation. A lot of tedious – although not particularly difficult – mathematics is required to derive our results. The main text of this chapter lays emphasis on key results and the intuition which lies behind them; derivations, where they are lengthy, are placed in appendices. You may find it helpful to omit these on a first reading.

For much of the discussion in this chapter, it is assumed that there exists a known, finite stock of each kind of non-renewable resource. This assumption is not always appropriate. New discoveries are made, increasing the magnitude of known stocks, and technological change alters the proportion of mineral resources that are economically recoverable.

Later sections indicate how the model may be extended to deal with some of these complications. Box 15.1 – which you should read now – considers several measures of resource stock, and throws some light on the issue of whether it can be reasonable to assume that there are fixed quantities of non-renewable resources.

Box 15.1 Are stocks of non-renewable resources fixed?

Non-renewable resources include a large variety of mineral deposits – in solid, liquid and gaseous forms – from which, often after some process of refining, metals, fossil fuels and other processed minerals are obtained. The crude forms of these resources are produced over very long periods of time by chemical, biological or physical processes. Their rate of formation is sufficiently slow in timescales relevant to humans that it is sensible to label such resources non-renewable. At any point in time, there exists some fixed, finite quantities of these resources in the earth's crust and environmental systems, albeit very large quantities in some cases.

So, in a physical sense, it is appropriate to describe non-renewable resources as existing in fixed quantities. However, that description may not be appropriate in an economic sense. To see why not, consider the information shown in Table 15.1. The final column – *Base resource* – indicates the mass of each resource that is thought to exist in the earth's crust. This is the measure closest to that we had in mind in the previous paragraph. However, most of this base resource consists of the mineral in very dispersed form, or at great depths below the surface. Base resource figures such as these are the broadest sense in which one might use the term 'resource stocks'. In each case, the measure is purely physical, having little or no relationship to economic measures of stocks. Notice that each of these quantities is extremely large relative to any other of the indicated stock measures.

The column labelled *Resource potential* is of more relevance to our discussions, comprising estimates of the upper limits on resource extraction possibilities given current and expected technologies. Whereas the resource base is a pure physical measure, the resource potential is a measure incorporating physical and technological information. But this illustrates the difficulty of classifying and measuring resources; as time passes, technology will almost certainly change, in ways that cannot be predicted today. As a result, estimates of the resource potential will change (usually rising) over time. To some writers, the possibility that resource constraints on economic activity will bite depends primarily on whether or not technological improvement in extracting usable materials from the huge stocks of base resources (thereby augmenting resource potential) will continue more-or-less indefinitely.

However, an economist is interested not in what is technically feasible but in what would become available under certain conditions. In other words, he or she is interested in resource supplies, or potential supplies. These will, of course, be shaped by physical and technological factors. But they will also depend upon resource market prices and the costs of extraction via their influence on exploration and research effort and on expected profitability. Data in the column labelled *World reserve base* consist of estimates of the upper bounds of resource stocks (including reserves that have not yet been discovered) that are economically recoverable under 'reasonable expectations' of future price, cost and technology possibilities. Those labelled *Reserves* consist of quantities that are economically recoverable under present configurations of costs and prices.

In economic modelling, the existence of fixed mineral resource stocks is often used as a simplifying assumption. But our observations suggest that we should be wary of this. In the longer term, economically relevant stocks are not fixed, and will vary with changing economic and technological circumstances.

Box 15.1 continued

Table 15.1 Production, consumption and reserves of some important resources: 1991 (figures in millions of metric tons)

	Production	Reserves		World reserve base		Consumption	Resource potential	
		Quantity	Reserve life (yrs)	Reserve base	Base life (yrs)			Base resource (crustal mass)
Aluminium	112.22	23 000	222	28 000	270	19.46	3 519 000	1 990 000 000 000
Iron ore	929.75	150 000	161	230 000	247	959.6	2 035 000	1 392 000 000 000
Potassium	na	20 000	800	na	>800	na	na	408 000 000 000
Manganese	25	800	32	5 000	200	22	42 000	31 200 000 000
Phosphorus	na	110	na	na	270	25	51 000	28 800 000 000
Fluorine	na	2.5	na	na	12	na	20 000	10 800 000 000
Sulphur	56.87	na	na	na	na	57.5	na	9 600 000 000
Chromium	13	419	32	1 950	150	13	3 260	2 600 000 000
Zinc	7.137	140	20	330	46	6.993	3 400	2 250 000 000
Nickel	0.922	47	51	111	119	0.882	2 590	2 130 000 000
Copper	9.29	310	33	590	64	10.714	2 120	1 510 000 000
Lead	3.424	63	18	130	38	5.342	550	290 000 000
Tin	0.179	8	45	10	56	0.218	68	10 000 000 000
Tungsten	0.0413	3.5	80	>3.5	>80	0.044	51	26 400 000
Mercury	0.003	0.130	43	0.240	80	0.005	3.4	2 100 000
Silver	0.014	0.28	20	na	na	0.02	2.8	1 800 000
Platinum	0.0003	0.37	124	na	na	0.00029	1.2	1 100 000

Source: Figures compiled from a variety of sources

15.1   A non-renewable resource two-period model

Consider a planning horizon that consists of two periods, period 0 and period 1. There is a fixed stock of known size of one type of a non-renewable resource. The initial stock of the resource (at the start of period 0) is denoted $\bar{S}$. Let R_t be the quantity extracted in period t and assume that an inverse demand function exists for this resource at each time, given by

$$P_t = a - bR_t$$

where P_t is the price in period t, with a and b being positive constant numbers. So, the demand functions for the two periods will be:

$$P_0 = a - bR_0$$

$$P_1 = a - bR_1$$

These demands are illustrated in Figure 15.1.

A linear and negatively sloped demand function such as this one has the property that demand goes to zero at some price, in this case the price a. Hence, either this resource is non-essential or it possesses a substitute which at the price a becomes economically more attractive. The assumption of linearity of demand is arbitrary and so you should bear in mind that the particular results derived below are conditional upon the assumption that the demand curve is of this form.

The shaded area in Figure 15.1 (algebraically, the integral of P with respect to R over the interval $R = 0$ to $R = R_t$) shows the total benefit consumers obtain from consuming the quantity R_t in period t. From a social point of view, this area represents the gross social benefit, B, derived from the extraction and consumption of quantity R_t of the resource.[1] We can express this quantity as

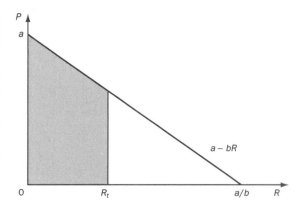

Figure 15.1 The non-renewable resource demand function for the two-period model

$$B(R_t) = \int_0^{R_t} (a - bR)\,dR$$

$$= aR_t - \frac{b}{2}R_t^2$$

where the notation $B(R_t)$ is used to make explicit the fact that the gross benefit at time t (B_t) is dependent on the quantity of the resource extracted and consumed (R_t).

However, the gross benefit obtained by consumers is not identical to the net social benefit of the resource, as resource extraction involves costs. In this chapter, we assume that these costs are fully borne by the resource-extracting firms, and so private and social costs are identical.[2] This assumption will be dropped in the following chapter. Let us define c to be the constant marginal cost of extracting the resource $(c \geq 0)$.[3] Then total extraction costs, C_t, for the extracted quantity R_t units will be

$$C_t = cR_t$$

The total net social benefit from extracting the quantity R_t is

---

[1] A demand curve is sometimes taken as providing information about the marginal willingness to pay (or marginal benefit) for successive units of the good in question. The area under a demand curve up to some given quantity is, then, the sum of a set of marginal benefits, and is equal to the total benefit derived from consuming that quantity.

[2] We also assume that benefits represented in the resource demand function are the *only* benefits to society, so there are no beneficial externalities.

[3] Constancy of marginal costs of extraction is a very strong assumption. In the previous chapter, we investigated a more general case in which marginal extraction costs are not necessarily constant. We do not consider this any further here. Later in this chapter, however, we do analyse the consequences for extraction of a once-and-for-all rise in extraction costs.

$$NSB_t = B_t - C_t$$

where NSB denotes the total net social benefit and B is the gross social benefit of resource extraction and use.[4] Hence

$$NSB(R_t) = \int_0^{R_t} (a - bR)dR - cR_t = aR_t - \frac{b}{2}R_t^2 - cR_t$$

$$(15.1)$$

15.1.1 A socially optimal extraction policy

Our objective in this subsection is to identify a socially optimal extraction programme. This will serve as a benchmark in terms of which any particular extraction programme can be assessed. In order to find the socially optimal extraction programme, two things are required. The first is a social welfare function that embodies society's objectives; the second is a statement of the technical possibilities and constraints available at any point in time. Let us deal first with the social welfare function, relating this as far as possible to our discussion of social welfare functions in Chapters 3 and 5.

As in Chapter 3, the social welfare function that we shall use is discounted utilitarian in form. So the general two-period social welfare function

$$W = W(U_0, U_1)$$

takes the particular form

$$W = U_0 + \frac{U_1}{1 + \rho}$$

where ρ is the social utility discount rate, reflecting society's time preference. Now regard the utility in each period as being equal to the net social benefit in each period.[5] Given this, the social welfare function may be written as

$$W = NSB_0 + \frac{NSB_1}{1 + \rho}$$

Only one relevant technical constraint exists in this case: there is a fixed initial stock of the non-renewable resource, $\bar{S}$. We assume that society wishes to have none of this resource stock left at the end of the second period. Then the quantities extracted in the two periods, R_0 and R_1, must satisfy the constraint:[6]

$$R_0 + R_1 = \bar{S}$$

The optimisation problem can now be stated. Resource extraction levels R_0 and R_1 should be chosen to maximise social welfare, W, subject to the constraint that total extraction of the resources over the two periods equals $\bar{S}$. Mathematically, this can be written as

$$\operatorname*{Max}_{R_0,\ R_1} W = NSB_0 + \frac{NSB_1}{1 + \rho}$$

subject to

$$R_0 + R_1 = \bar{S}$$

There are several ways of obtaining solutions to constrained optimisation problems of this form. We use the Lagrange multiplier method, a technique that was explained in Appendix 3.1. The first step is to form the Lagrangian function, L:

$$L = W - \lambda(\bar{S} - R_0 - R_1) = (NSB_0) + \left(\frac{NSB_1}{1 + \rho}\right)$$

$$- \lambda(\bar{S} - R_0 - R_1) = \left(aR_0 - \frac{b}{2}R_0^2 - cR_0\right)$$

$$+ \left(\frac{aR_1 - \frac{b}{2}R_1^2 - cR_1}{1 + \rho}\right) - \lambda(\bar{S} - R_0 - R_1) \quad (15.2)$$

---

[4] Strictly speaking, social benefits derive from consumption (use) of the resource, not extraction *per se*. However, we assume throughout this chapter that all resource stocks extracted in a period are consumed in that period, and so this distinction becomes irrelevant.

[5] In order to make such an interpretation valid, we shall assume that the demand function is 'quasi-linear' (see Varian, 1987). Suppose there are two goods, X, the good whose demand we are interested in, and Y, money to be spent on all other goods. Quasi-

linearity requires that the utility function for good X be of the form $U = V(X) + Y$. This implies that income effects are absent in the sense that changes in income do not affect the demand for good X. In this case, we can legitimately interpret the area under the demand curve for good X as a measure of utility.

[6] The problem could easily be changed so that a predetermined quantity S^* ($S^* \geq 0$) must be left at the end of period 1 by rewriting the constraint as $R_0 + R_1 + S^* = \bar{S}$. This would not alter the essence of the conclusion we shall reach.

in which λ is a 'Lagrange multiplier'. Remembering that R_0 and R_1 are choice variables – variables whose value must be selected to maximise welfare – the necessary conditions include:

$$\frac{\partial L}{\partial R_0} = a - bR_0 - c + \lambda = 0 \tag{15.3}$$

$$\frac{\partial L}{\partial R_1} = \frac{a - bR_1 - c}{1 + \rho} + \lambda = 0 \tag{15.4}$$

Since the right-hand side terms of equations 15.3 and 15.4 are both equal to zero, this implies that

$$a - bR_0 - c = \frac{a - bR_1 - c}{1 + \rho}$$

Using the demand function $P_t = a - bR_t$, the last equation can be written as

$$P_0 - c = \frac{P_1 - c}{1 + \rho}$$

where P_0 and P_1 are gross prices and $P_0 - c$ and $P_1 - c$ are net prices. A resource's net price is also known as the resource rent or resource royalty. Rearranging this expression, we obtain

$$\rho = \frac{(P_1 - c) - (P_0 - c)}{(P_0 - c)}$$

If we change the notation used for time periods so that $P_0 = P_{t-1}$, $P_1 = P_t$ and $c = c_t = c_{t-1}$, we then obtain

$$\rho = \frac{(P_t - c_t) - (P_{t-1} - c_{t-1})}{(P_{t-1} - c_{t-1})} \tag{15.5}$$

which is equivalent to a result we obtained previously in Chapter 14, equation 14.15, commonly known as Hotelling's rule. Note that in equation 15.5, P is a gross price whereas in equation 14.15, P refers to a net price, resource rent or royalty. However, since $P - c$ in equation 15.5 is the resource net price or royalty, these two equations are identical (except for the fact that one is in discrete-time notation and the other in continuous-time notation).

What does this result tell us? The left-hand side of equation 15.5, ρ, is the social utility discount rate, which embodies some view about how future utility

should be valued in terms of present utility. The right-hand side is the proportionate rate of growth of the resource's net price. So if, for example, society chooses a discount rate of 0.1 (or 10%), Hotelling's rule states that an efficient extraction programme requires the net price of the resource to grow at a proportionate rate of 0.1 (or 10%) over time.

Now we know how much higher the net price should be in period 1 compared with period 0, if welfare is to be maximised; but what should be the level of the net price in period 0? This is easily answered. Recall that the economy has some fixed stock of the resource that is to be entirely extracted and consumed in the two periods. Also, we have assumed that the demand function for the resource is known. An optimal extraction programme requires two gross prices, P_0 and P_1, such that the following conditions are satisfied:

$$P_0 = a - bR_0$$

$$P_1 = a - bR_1$$

$$R_0 + R_1 = \bar{S}$$

$$P_1 - c = (1 + \rho)(P_0 - c)$$

This will uniquely define the two prices (and so the two quantities of resources to be extracted) that are required for welfare maximisation. Problem 1, at the end of this chapter, provides a numerical example to illustrate this kind of two-period optimal depletion problem. You are recommended to work through this problem before moving on to the next section.

15.2   A non-renewable resource multi-period model

Having investigated resource depletion in the simple two-period model, the analysis is now generalised to many periods. It will be convenient to change from a discrete-time framework (in which there is a number of successive intervals of time, denoted period 0, period 1, etc.) to a continuous-time framework which deals with rates of extraction and use at particular points in time over some continuous-time horizon.[7]

---

[7]   The material in this section, in particular the worked example investigated later, owes much to Heijman (1990).

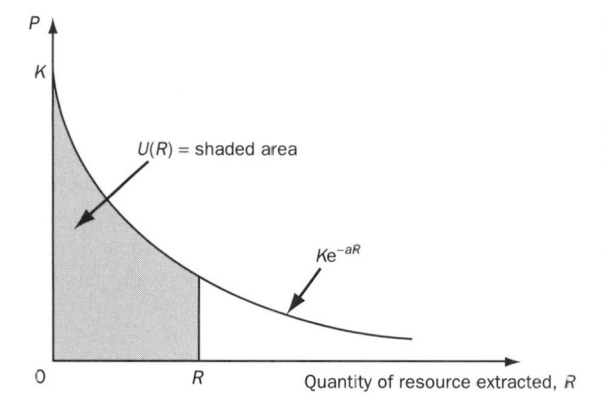

Figure 15.2 A resource demand curve, and the total utility from consuming a particular quantity of the resource

To keep the maths as simple as possible, we will push extraction costs somewhat into the background. To do this, P is now defined to be the net price of the non-renewable resource, that is, the price after deduction of the cost of extraction. Let $P(R)$ denote the inverse demand function for the resource, indicating that the resource net price is a function of the quantity extracted, R. The social utility from consuming a quantity R of the resource may be defined as

$$U(R) = \int_0^R P(R)\,dR \qquad (15.6a)$$

which is illustrated by the shaded area in Figure 15.2. You will notice that the demand curve used in Figure 15.2 is non-linear. We shall have more to say about this particular form of the demand function shortly.

By differentiating total utility with respect to R, the rate of resource extraction and use, we obtain

$$\frac{\partial U}{\partial R} = P(R) \qquad (15.6b)$$

which states that the marginal social utility of resource use equals the net price of the resource.

Assume, as for the two-period model, that the intertemporal social welfare function is utilitarian. Future utility is discounted at the instantaneous social utility discount rate ρ. Then the value of social welfare over an interval of time from period 0 to period T can be expressed as[8]

$$W = \int_0^T U(R_t)e^{-\rho t}\,dt$$

Our problem is to make social-welfare-maximising choices of

(a) R_t, for $t = 0$ to $t = T$ (that is, we wish to choose a quantity of resource to be extracted in each period), and
(b) the optimal value for T (the point in time at which depletion of the resource stock ceases), subject to the constraint that

$$\int_0^T R_t\,dt = \bar{S}$$

where $\bar{S}$ is the total initial stock of the non-renewable resource. That is, the total extraction of the resource is equal to the size of the initial resource stock. Note that in this problem, the time horizon to exhaustion is being treated as an endogenous variable to be chosen by the decision maker.

We define the remaining stock of the natural resource at time t, S_t, as

$$S_t = \bar{S} - \int_0^t R_t\,dt$$

then by differentiation with respect to time, we obtain

---

[8] It may be helpful to relate this form of social welfare function to the discrete-time versions we have been using previously. We have stated that a T-period discrete-time discounted welfare function can be written as

$$W = U_0 + \frac{U_1}{1 + \rho} + \frac{U_2}{(1 + \rho)^2} + \dots + \frac{U_T}{(1 + \rho)^T}$$

We could write this equivalently as

$$W = \sum_{t=0}^{t=T} \frac{U_t}{(1 + \rho)^T}$$

A continuous-time analogue of this welfare function is then

$$W = \int_{t=0}^{t=T} U_t e^{-\rho t}\,dt$$

$$\dot{S}_t = -R_t$$

where $\dot{S} = \mathrm{d}S/\mathrm{d}t$, the rate of change of the remaining resource stock with respect to time.

So the dynamic optimisation problem involves the choice of a path of resource extraction R_t over the interval $t = 0$ to $t = T$ that satisfies the resource stock constraint and which maximises social welfare, W. Mathematically, we have:

$$\mathrm{Max}\, W = \int_0^T U(R_t)\mathrm{e}^{-\rho t}\mathrm{d}t$$

subject to $\dot{S}_t = -R_t$

It would be a useful exercise at this point for you to use the optimisation technique explained in Appendix 14.1 to derive the solution to this problem. Your derivation can be checked against the answer given in Appendix 15.1.

Thinking point

Before moving on to interpret the main components of this solution, it will be useful to pause for a moment to reflect on the nature of this model. It is similar in general form to the model we investigated in Chapter 14, and laid out in full in Appendix 14.2. However, the model is simpler in one important way from that of the previous chapter as utility is derived directly from the consumption of the natural resource, rather than indirectly from the consumption goods generated through a production function. There is a fixed, total stock available of the natural resource, and this model is sometimes called the 'cake-eating' model of resource depletion.

It would also be reasonable to interpret this model as one in which a production function exists implicitly. However, this production function has just one argument – the non-renewable natural resource input – as compared with the two arguments – the natural resource and human-made capital – in the model of Chapter 14.

It is clear that this model can at most be regarded as a partial account of economic activity. One possible interpretation of this partial status is that the economy also produces, or could produce, goods and services through other production functions, using capital, labour and perhaps renewable resource inputs. In this interpretation the non-renewable resource is like a once-and-for-all gift of nature. Using this non-renewable resource provides something over and above the welfare possible from production in its absence. It is this *additional welfare* that is being measured by our term W.

An alternative interpretation is more commonly found in the literature. Here, non-renewable resources consist of a diverse set of different resources. Each element of this set is a particular resource that is fixed and homogeneous. Substitution possibilities exist between at least some elements of this set of resources. For historical, technical or economic reasons, production might currently rely particularly heavily on one kind of resource. Changing technological or economic conditions might lead to this stock being replaced by another. With the passage of time, a sequence of resource stocks are brought into play, with each one eventually being replaced by another. In this story, what our resource depletion model investigates is one stage in this sequence of depletion processes. This interpretation will be used later in the chapter when the concepts of a backstop technology and a choke price are introduced.

These comments raise a general issue about choices that need to be made in doing resource modelling. It is often too difficult to explain everything of interest in one framework. Sometimes, one needs to pick 'horses for courses'. In the previous chapter, we were concerned with substitution between natural resources and physical capital; that required that we explicitly specify a conventional type of production function. In this chapter, that is not of central concern, and so the production function can be allowed to slip somewhat into the background. However, we do wish here to place emphasis on substitution processes between natural resources. That can be done in a simple way, by paying greater attention to the nature of resource demand functions, and to the idea of a choke price for a resource.

Whether or not you have succeeded in obtaining a formal solution to this optimisation problem, intuition should suggest one condition that must be satisfied if W is to be maximised. R_t must be chosen so that the *discounted* marginal utility is equal at each point in time, that is,

$$\frac{\partial U}{\partial R}e^{-\rho t} = \text{constant}$$

To understand this, let us use the method of contradiction. If the discounted marginal utilities from resource extraction were not equal in every period, then total welfare W could be increased by shifting some extraction from a period with a relatively low discounted marginal utility to a period with a relatively high discounted marginal utility. Rearranging the path of extraction in this way would raise welfare. It must, therefore, be the case that welfare can only be maximised when discounted marginal utilities are equal. What follows from this result? First note equation 15.6b again:

$$\frac{\partial U_t}{\partial R_t} = P_t$$

So, the requirement that the discounted marginal utility be constant is equivalent to the requirement that the discounted net price is constant as well – a result noted previously in Chapter 14. That is,

$$\frac{\partial U_t}{\partial R_t}e^{-\rho t} = P_t e^{-\rho t} = \text{constant} = P_0$$

Rearranging this condition, we obtain

$$P_t = P_0 e^{\rho t} \tag{15.7a}$$

By differentiation[9] this can be rewritten as

$$\frac{\dot{P}_t}{P_t} = \rho \tag{15.7b}$$

This is, once again, the Hotelling efficiency rule. It now appears in a different guise, because of our switch to a continuous-time framework. The rule states that the net price or royalty P_t of a non-renewable resource should rise at a rate equal to the social utility discount rate, ρ, if the social value of the resource is to be maximised.

We now know the rate at which the resource net price or royalty must rise. However, this does not fully characterise the solution to our optimising problem. There are several other things we need to know too. First, we need to know the optimal initial value of the resource net price. Secondly, we need to know over how long a period of time the resource should be extracted – in other words, what is the optimal value of T? Thirdly, what is the optimal rate of resource extraction at each point in time? Finally, what should be the values of P and R at the end of the extraction horizon?

It is not possible to obtain answers to these questions without one additional piece of information: the particular form of the resource demand function. So let us suppose that the resource demand function is

$$P(R) = Ke^{-aR} \tag{15.8}$$

which is illustrated in Figure 15.2.[10] Unlike the demand function used in the two-period analysis, this function exhibits a non-linear relationship between P and R, and is probably more representative of the form that resource demands are likely to take than the linear function used in the section on the two-period model. However, it is similar to the previous demand function in so far as it exhibits zero demand at some finite price level.

To see this, just note that $P(R = 0) = K$. K is the so-called *choke price* for this resource, meaning that

---

[9] Differentiation of equation 15.7a with respect to time gives

$$dP_t/dt \equiv \dot{P}_t = P_0\rho e^{\rho t}$$

By substitution of equation 15.7a into this expression, we obtain

$$\dot{P}_t = \rho P_t$$

and dividing through by P_t we obtain

$$\dot{P}_t/P_t = \rho$$

as required.

[10] For the demand function given in equation 15.8, we can obtain the particular form of the social welfare function as follows. The social utility function corresponding to equation 15.6a will be:

$$U(R) = \int_0^R P(R)dR = \int_0^R Ke^{-aR}dR = \frac{k}{a}(1 - e^{-aR})$$

The social welfare function, therefore, is

$$W = \int_0^T U(R_t)e^{-\rho t}dt = \int_0^T \frac{K}{a}(1 - e^{-aR_t})e^{-\rho t}dt$$

the demand for the resource is driven to zero or is 'choked off' at this price. At the choke price people using the services of this resource would switch demand to some alternative, substitute, non-renewable resource, or to an alternative final product not using that resource as an input.

As we shall demonstrate shortly, given knowledge of

- a particular resource demand function,
- Hotelling's efficiency condition,
- an initial value for the resource stock, and
- a final value for the resource stock,

it is possible to obtain expressions for the optimal initial, interim and final resource net price (royalty) and resource extraction rates. What about the final stock level? This is straightforward. An optimal solution must have the property that the stock goes to zero at exactly the same point in time that demand and extraction go to zero.[11] If that were not the case, some resource will have been needlessly wasted. So we know that the solution must include $S_T = 0$ and $R_T = 0$, with resource stocks being positive, and positive extraction taking place over all time up to T. As you will see below, that will give us sufficient information to fully tie down the solution.

Before we proceed to obtain all the details of the solution, one important matter must be reiterated. The solution to a problem of this type will depend upon the demand function chosen. Hence the particular solutions derived below are conditional upon the demand function chosen, and will not be valid in all circumstances. Our model in this chapter assumes that the resource has a choke price, implying that a substitute for the resource becomes economically more attractive at that price. If you wish to examine the case in which there is no choke price – indeed, where there is no finite upper limit on the resource price – you may find it useful to work through some of the exercises provided in the *Additional Materials* for this chapter, which deal with this case among others.

As the mathematics required to obtain the full solution are rather tedious (but not particularly diffi-

Table 15.2 Optimality conditions for the multi-period model

	Initial ($t = 0$)	Interim ($t = t$)	Final ($t = T$)
Royalty, P	$P_0 = Ke^{-\sqrt{2\rho \bar{S}a}}$	$P_t = Ke^{\rho(t-T)}$	$P_T = K$
Extraction, R	$R_0 = \sqrt{\dfrac{2\rho\bar{S}}{a}}$	$R_t = \dfrac{\rho}{a}(T-t)$	$R_T = 0$
Depletion time			$T = \sqrt{\dfrac{2\bar{S}a}{\rho}}$

cult), the derivations are presented in Appendix 15.1. You are strongly recommended to read this now, but if you prefer to omit these derivations, the results are presented in Table 15.2. There it can be seen that all the expressions for the initial, interim and final resource royalty (or net prices) and rate of resource extraction are functions of the parameters of the model (K, ρ and a) and T, the optimal depletion time. As the final expression indicates, T is itself a function of those parameters. Given the functional forms we have been using in this section, if the values of the parameters K, ρ and a were known, it would be possible to solve the model to obtain numerical values for all the variables of interest over the whole period for which the resource will be extracted.

Figure 15.3 portrays the solution to our optimal depletion model. The diagram shows the optimal resource extraction and net price paths over time corresponding to social welfare maximisation. As we show subsequently, it also represents the profit-maximising extraction and price paths in perfectly competitive markets. In the upper right quadrant, the net price is shown rising exponentially at the social utility discount rate, ρ, thereby satisfying the Hotelling rule. The upper left quadrant shows the resource demand curve with a choke price K. The lower left quadrant gives the optimal extraction path of the non-renewable resource, which is, in this case, a linear declining function of time.

The net price is initially at P_0, and then grows until it reaches the choke price K at time T. At this point, demand for the resource goes to zero, and the accumulated extraction of the resource (the shaded

---

[11] In terms of optimisation theory, this constitutes a so-called terminal condition for the problem.

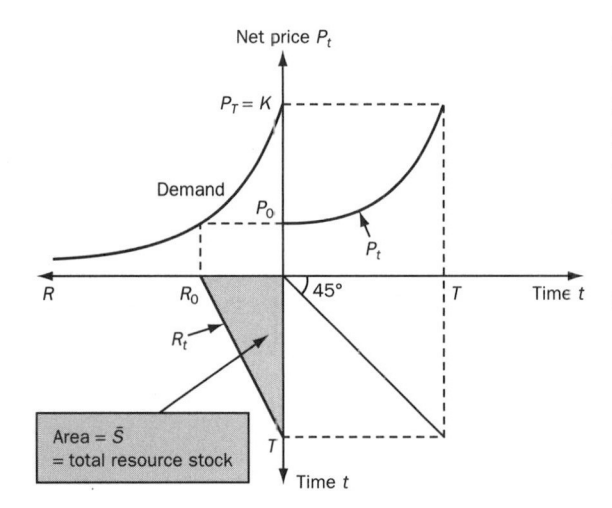

Figure 15.3 Graphical representation of solutions to the optimal resource depletion model

area beneath the extraction path) is exactly equal to the total initial resource stock, $\bar{S}$. The lower right quadrant maps the time axes by a 45° line. A worked numerical example illustrating optimal extraction is presented in Appendix 15.3.

15.3 Non-renewable resource extraction in perfectly competitive markets

Until this point, we have said nothing about the kind of market structure in which decisions are made. It is as if we have been imagining that a rational social planner were asked to make decisions that maximise social welfare, given the constraints facing the economy. The optimality conditions listed in Table 15.2, plus the Hotelling efficiency condition, are the outcome of the social planner's calculations.

How will matters turn out if decisions are instead the outcome of profit-maximising decisions in a perfectly competitive market economy? This section demonstrates that, *ceteris paribus*, the outcomes will be identical. Hotelling's rule and the optimality conditions of Table 15.2 are also obtained under a perfect competition assumption.

Suppose there are *m* competitive firms in the market. Use the subscript *j* to denote any one of these

m firms. Assume, for simplicity, that all firms have equal and constant marginal costs of extracting the resource. Now as all firms in a competitive market face the same fixed selling price at any point in time, the market royalty will be identical over firms. Given the market royalty P_t, each firm chooses an amount to extract and sell, $R_{j,t}$, to maximise its profits.

Mathematically, the *j*th firm's objective is to maximise

$$\int_0^T \Pi_{j,t} e^{-it} dt$$

subject to

$$\int_0^T \left(\sum_{j=1}^m R_{j,t} \right) dt = \bar{S}$$

where $\Pi_j = P \cdot R_j$ is firm *j*'s profit and *i* is the market interest rate. Note that the same stock constraint operates on all firms collectively; the industry as a whole cannot extract more than the fixed initial stock over the whole time horizon. The profit-maximising extraction path is obtained when each firm selects an extraction $R_{j,t}$ at each time, $t = 0$ to $t = T$, so that its discounted marginal profit will be the same at any point in time *t*, that is,

$$M\Pi_{j,t} e^{-it} = \frac{\partial \Pi_{j,t}}{\partial R_{j,t}} e^{-it} = \frac{\partial PR_{j,t}}{\partial R_{j,t}} e^{-it} = P_t e^{-it}$$

$$= \text{constant, for } t = 0 \text{ to } t = T$$

where $M\Pi_j$ is firm *j*'s marginal profit function. If discounted marginal profits were *not* the same over time, total profits could be increased by switching extraction between time periods so that more was extracted when discounted profits were high and less when they were low. The result that the discounted marginal profit is the same at any point in time implies that

$$P_t e^{-it} = P_0 \text{ or } P_t = P_0 e^{it}$$

Not surprisingly, Hotelling's efficiency rule continues to be a required condition for profit maximisation, so that the market net price of the resource must grow over time at the rate *i*. The interest rate in this profit maximisation condition is the market rate of interest. Our analysis in Chapter 11 showed that, in perfectly competitive capital markets and in the absence of transactions costs, the market interest rate will be equal to r, the consumption rate of interest, and also to δ, the rate of return on capital.

We appear now to have two different efficiency conditions,

$$\frac{\dot{P}}{P} = \rho \text{ and } \frac{\dot{P}}{P} = i$$

the former emerging from maximising social welfare, the latter from private profit maximisation. But these are in fact identical conditions under the assumptions we have made in this chapter; by assuming that we can interpret areas under demand curves (that is, gross benefits) as quantities of utility, we in effect impose the condition that $\rho = r$. Given this result, it is not difficult to show, by cranking through the appropriate maths in a similar manner to that done in Appendix 15.1, that all the results of Table 15.2 would once again be produced under perfect competition, provided the private market interest rate equals the social consumption discount rate. We leave this as an exercise for the reader.

Finally, note that the appearance of a positive net price or royalty, $P_t > 0$, for non-renewable resources reflects the fixed stock assumption. If the resource existed in unlimited quantities (that is, the resource were not scarce) net prices would be zero in perfect competition, as the price of the product will equal the marginal cost (c), a result which you may recall from standard theory of long-run equilibrium in competitive markets. In other words, scarcity rent would be zero as there would be no scarcity.

15.4 Resource extraction in a monopolistic market

It is usual to assume that the objective of a monopoly is to maximise its discounted profit over time. Thus, it selects the net price P_t (or royalty) and chooses the output R_t so as to maximise

$$\int_0^T \Pi_t e^{-it} dt$$

subject to

$$\int_0^T R_t dt = \bar{S}$$

where $\Pi_t = P(R_t)R_t$.

For the same reason as in the case of perfect competition, the profit-maximising solution is obtained by choosing a path for R so that the discounted marginal profit will be the same at any time. So we have

$$M\Pi_t e^{-it} = \frac{\partial \Pi_t}{\partial R_t} e^{-it} = \text{constant} = M\Pi_0$$

that is,

$$M\Pi_t = M\Pi_0 e^{it} \tag{15.9}$$

Looking carefully at equation 15.9, and comparing this with the equation for marginal profits in the previous section, it is clear why the profit-maximising solutions in monopolistic and competitive markets will differ. Under perfect competition, the market price is exogenous to (fixed for) each firm. Thus we are able to obtain the result that in competitive markets, marginal revenue equals price. However, in a monopolistic market, price is not fixed, but will depend upon the firm's output choice. Marginal revenue will be less than price in this case.

The necessary condition for profit maximisation in a monopolistic market states that the marginal profit (and not the net price or royalty) should increase at the rate of interest i in order to maximise the discounted profits over time. The solution to the monopolist's optimising problem is derived in Appendix 15.2. If you wish to omit this, you will find the results in Table 15.3.

15.5 A comparison of competitive and monopolistic extraction programmes

Table 15.3 summarises the results concerning optimal resource extraction in perfectly competitive and monopolistic markets. The analytical results presented are derived in Appendices 15.1 and 15.2. For convenience, we list below the notation used in Table 15.3.

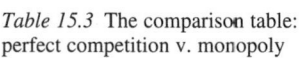

Table 15.3 The comparison table: perfect competition v. monopoly

	Perfect competition	Monopoly
Objective	$\max \int_0^T P_t R_t^j e^{-it} dt$	$\max \int_0^T P_t R_t e^{-it} dt$
Constraint	$\int_0^T \left(\sum_j R_t^j \right) dt = \bar{S}$	$\int_0^T R_t dt = \bar{S}$
Demand curve	$P_t = K e^{-aR_t}$	$P_t = K e^{-aR_t}$
	Optimal Solution	
Exhaustion time	$T = \sqrt{\dfrac{2\bar{S}a}{i}}$	$T = \sqrt{\dfrac{2\bar{S}ah}{i}}$
Initial royalty	$P_0 = K e^{-\sqrt{2i\bar{S}a}}$	$P_0 = K e^{-\sqrt{\frac{2i\bar{S}a}{h}}}$
Royalty path	$P_t = P_0 e^{it}$	$P_t = P_0 e^{(it/h)}$
Extraction path	$R_t = \dfrac{i}{a}(T - t)$	$R_t = \dfrac{i}{ha}(T - t)$
	where $R_t = \sum_j R_t^j$	where $R_t = \sum_j R_t^j$
	$R_0 = \sqrt{\dfrac{2i\bar{S}}{a}}$	$R_0 = \sqrt{\dfrac{2i\bar{S}}{ha}}$

P_t is the net price (royalty) of non-renewable resource with fixed stock $\bar{S}$
R_t is the total extraction of the resource at time t
R_t^j is the extraction of individual firm j at time t
i is the interest rate
T is the exhaustion time of the natural resource
K and a are fixed parameters
$h = (1.6)^2$

Two key results emerge from Tables 15.2 and 15.3. First, under certain conditions, there is equivalence between the perfect competition market outcome and the social welfare optimum. If all markets are perfectly competitive, and the market interest rate is equal to the social consumption discount rate, the profit-maximising resource depletion programme will be identical to the one that is socially optimal.

Secondly, there is non-equivalence of perfect competition and monopoly markets: profit-maximising

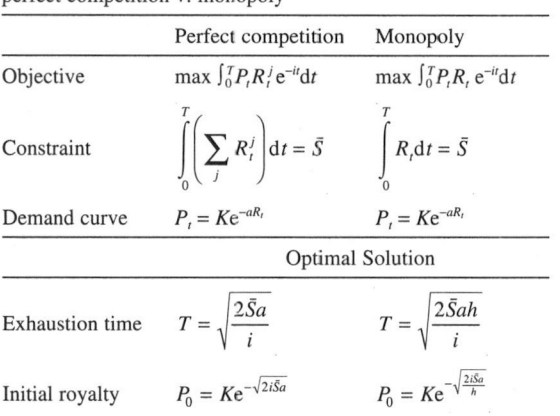

Figure 15.4 A comparison of resource depletion in competitive and monopolistic markets

extraction programmes will be different in perfectly competitive and monopolistic resource markets. Given the result stated in the previous paragraph, this implies that monopoly must be sub-optimal in a social-welfare-maximising sense.

For the functional forms we have used in this section, a monopolistic firm will take $\sqrt{h} = 1.6$ times longer to fully deplete the non-renewable resource than a perfectly competitive market in our model. As Figure 15.4 demonstrates, the initial net price will be higher in monopolistic markets, and the rate of price increase will be slower. Extraction of the resource will be slower at first in monopolistic markets, but faster towards the end of the depletion horizon. Monopoly, in this case at least, turns out to be an ally of the conservationist, in so far as the time until complete exhaustion is deferred further into the future.[12] As the comparison in Figure 15.4 illustrates, a monopolist will restrict output and raise prices initially, relative to the case of perfect competition. The rate of price increase, however, will be slower than under perfect competition. Eventually, an effect of monopolistic markets is to increase the time horizon over which the resource is extracted. We illustrate these results numerically in the Excel file *polcos.xls*, the contents of which are explained in

---

[12] Note that this conclusion is not *necessarily* the case. The longer depletion period we have found is a consequence of the particular assumptions made here. Although in most cases one would expect this to be true, it is possible to make a set of assumptions such that a monopolist would extract the stock in a shorter period of time.

the Word file *polcos.doc*. These can both be found in the *Additional Materials* for Chapter 15.

15.6   Extensions of the multi-period model of non-renewable resource depletion

To this point, a number of simplifying assumptions in developing and analysing our model of resource depletion have been made. In particular, it has been assumed that

- the utility discount rate and the market interest rate are constant over time;
- there is a fixed stock, of known size, of the non-renewable natural resource;
- the demand curve is identical at each point in time;
- no taxation or subsidy is applied to the extraction or use of the resource;
- marginal extraction costs are constant;
- there is a fixed 'choke price' (hence implying the existence of a backstop technology);
- no technological change occurs;
- no externalities are generated in the extraction or use of the resource.

We shall now undertake some comparative dynamic analysis. This consists of finding how the optimal paths of the variables of interest change over time in response to changes in the levels of one or more of the parameters in the model, or of finding how the optimal paths alter as our assumptions are changed. We adopt the device of investigating changes to one parameter, holding all others unchanged, comparing the new optimal paths with those derived above for our simple multi-period model. (We shall only discuss these generalisations for the case of perfect competition; analysis of the monopoly case is left to the reader as an exercise.)

The reader interested in doing comparative dynamics analysis by Excel simulation may wish to explore the file *hmodel.xls* (together with its explanatory document, *hmodel.doc*) in the *Additional Materials* to Chapter 15. The consequences of each of the changes described in the following subsections can be verified using that Excel workbook.

15.6.1 An increase in the interest rate

Let us make clear the problem we wish to answer here. Suppose that the interest rate we had assumed in drawing Figure 15.3 was 6% per year. Now suppose that the interest rate was not 6% but rather 10%; how would Figure 15.3 have been different if the interest rate had been higher in this way? This is the kind of question we are trying to answer in doing comparative dynamics.

The answer is shown in Figure 15.5. The thick, heavily drawn line represents the original optimal price path, with the price rising from an initial level of P_0 to its choke price, K, at time T. Now suppose that the interest rate rises. Since the resource's net price must grow at the market interest rate, an increase in i will raise the growth rate of the resource royalty, P_t; hence the new price path must have a steeper slope than the original one. The new price path will be the one labelled C in Figure 15.5. It will have an initial price lower than the one on the original price path, will grow more quickly, and will reach its final (choke) price earlier in time (before $t = T$). This result can be explained by the following observations. First, the choke price itself, K, is not altered by the interest rate change. Second, as we have already observed, the new price path must rise more steeply with a higher interest rate. Third, we can deduce that it must begin from a lower initial price level from using the resource exhaustion constraint. The change in interest rate does not alter the

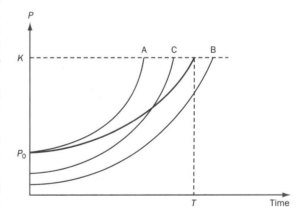

Figure 15.5 The effect of an increase in the interest rate on the optimal price of the non-renewable resource

quantity that is to be extracted; the same total stock is extracted whatever the interest rate might be. If the price path began from the same initial value (P_0) then it would follow a path such as that shown by the curve labelled A and would reach its choke price before $t = T$. But then the price would always be higher than along the original price path, but for a shorter period of time. Hence the resource stock will not be fully extracted along path A and that path could not be optimal.

A path such as B is not feasible. Here the price is always lower (and so the quantity extracted is higher) than on the original optimal path, and for a longer time. But that would imply that more resources are extracted over the life of the resource than were initially available. This is not feasible. The only feasible and optimal path is one such as C. Here the price is lower than on the original optimal path for some time (and so the quantity extracted is greater); then the new price path crosses over the original one and the price is higher thereafter (and so the quantity extracted is lower).

Note that because the new path must intersect the original path from below, the optimal depletion time will be shorter for a higher interest rate. This is intuitively reasonable. Higher interest rate means greater impatience. More is extracted early on, less later, and total time to full exhaustion is quicker. The implications for all the variables of interest are summarised in Figure 15.6.

15.6.2 An increase in the size of the known resource stock

In practice, estimates of the size of reserves of non-renewable resources such as coal and oil are under constant revision. *Proven reserves* are those unextracted stocks known to exist and can be recovered at current prices and costs. *Probable reserves* are stocks that are known, with near certainty, to exist but which have not yet been fully explored or researched. They represent the best guess of additional amounts that could be recovered at current price and cost levels. *Possible reserves* are stocks in geological structures near to proven fields. As prices rise, what were previously uneconomic stocks become economically recoverable.

Consider the case of a single new discovery of a fossil fuel stock. Other things being unchanged, if the royalty path were such that its initial level remained unchanged at P_0, then given the fact that the rate of royalty increase is unchanged, some proportion of the reserve would remain unutilised by the time the choke price, K, is reached. This is clearly neither efficient nor optimal. It follows that the initial royalty must be lower and the time to exhaustion is extended. At the time the choke price is reached, T', the new enlarged resource stock will have just reached complete exhaustion, as shown in Figure 15.7.

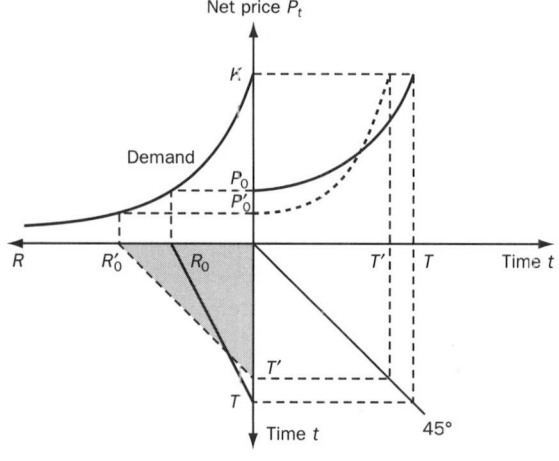

Figure 15.6 An increase in interest rates in a perfectly competitive market

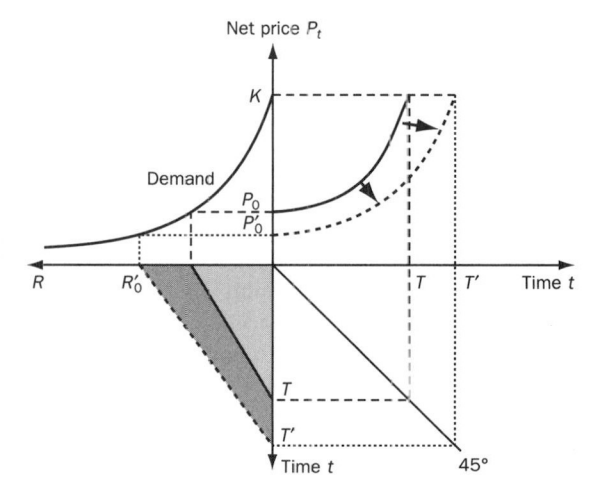

Figure 15.7 An increase in the resource stock

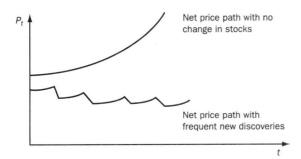

Figure 15.8 The effect of frequent new discoveries on the resource net price or royalty

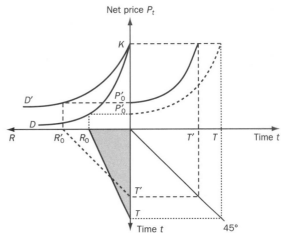

Figure 15.9 The effect of an increase in demand for the resource

Now suppose that there is a sequence of new discoveries taking place over time, so that the size of known reserves increases in a series of discrete steps. Generalising the previous argument, we would expect the behaviour of the net price or royalty over time to follow a path similar to that illustrated in Figure 15.8. This hypothetical price path is one that is consistent with the actual behaviour of oil prices.

15.6.3 Changing demand

Suppose that there is an increase in demand for the resource, possibly as a result of population growth or rising real incomes. The demand curve thus shifts outwards. Given this change, the old royalty or net price path would result in higher extraction levels, which will exhaust the resource before the net price has reached K, the choke price. Hence the net price must increase to dampen down quantities demanded; as Figure 15.9 shows, the time until the resource stock is fully exhausted will also be shortened.

15.6.4 A fall in the price of backstop technology

In the model developed in this chapter, we have assumed there is a choke price, K. If the net price were to rise above K, the economy will cease consumption of the non-renewable resource and switch to an alternative source – the backstop source. Suppose that technological progress occurs, increasing the efficiency of a backstop technology. This

will tend to reduce the price of the backstop source, to P_B ($P_B < K$). Hence the choke price will fall to P_B. Given the fall in the choke price to P_B, the initial value of the resource net price on the original optimal price path, P_0, cannot now be optimal. In fact, it is too high since the net price would reach the new choke price before T, leaving some of the economically useful resource unexploited. So the initial price of the non-renewable resource, P_0, must fall to a lower level, P_0', to encourage an increase in demand so that a shorter time horizon is required until complete exhaustion of the non-renewable resource reserve. This process is illustrated in Figure 15.10. Note that when the resource price reaches the new, reduced choke price, demand for the non-renewable resource falls to zero.

15.6.5 A change in resource extraction costs

Consider the case of an increase in extraction costs, possibly because labour charges rise in the extraction industry. To analyse the effects of an increase in extraction costs, it is important to distinguish carefully between the net price and the gross price of the resource. Let us define:

$$p_t = P_t - c$$

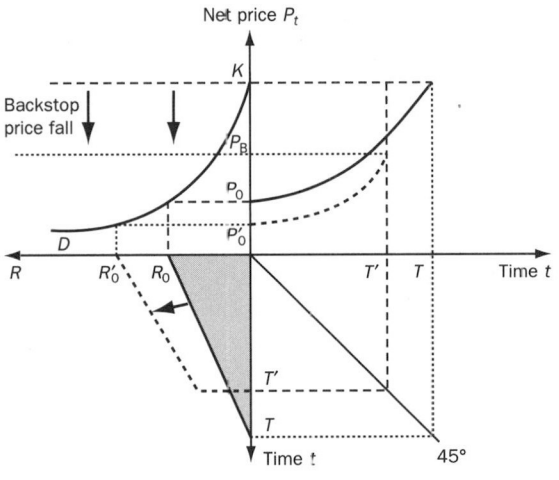

Figure 15.10 A fall in the price of a backstop technology

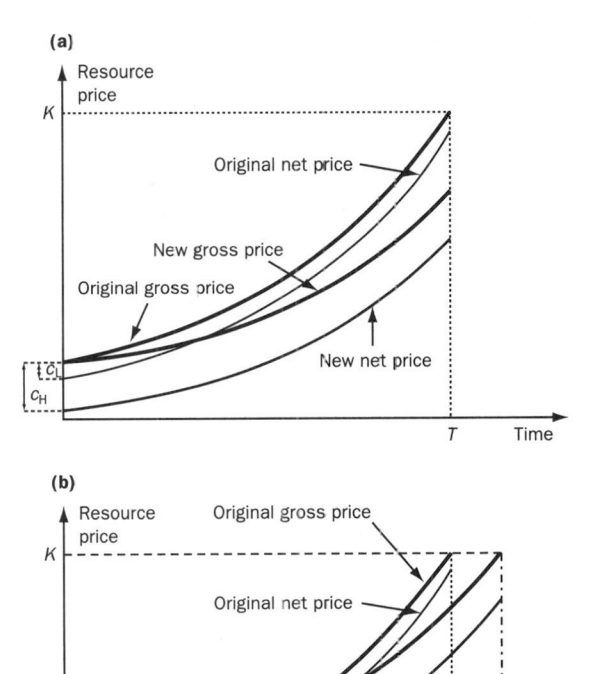

Figure 15.11 (a) An increase in extraction costs: deducing the effects on gross and net prices; (b) An increase in extraction costs: actual effects on gross and net prices

where p_t is the resource net price, P_t is the gross price of the non-renewable resource, and c is the marginal extraction cost, assumed to be constant. Hotelling's rule requires that the resource *net price* grows at a constant rate, equal to the discount rate (which we take here to be constant at the rate i). Therefore, efficient extraction requires that

$$p_t = p_0 e^{it}$$

Now look at Figure 15.11(a). Suppose that the marginal cost of extraction is at some constant level, c_L, and that the curve labelled *Original net price* describes the optimal path of the net price over time (i.e. it plots $p_t = p_0 e^{it}$); also suppose that the corresponding optimal gross price path is given by the curve labelled *Original gross price* (i.e. it plots $P_t = p_t + c_L = p_0 e^{it} + c_L$).

Next, suppose that the cost of extraction, while still constant, now becomes somewhat higher than was previously the case. Its new level is denoted c_H. We suppose that this change takes place at the initial time period, period 0. Consider first what would happen if the gross price remained unchanged at its initial level, as shown in Figure 15.11(a). The increase in unit extraction costs from c_L to c_H would then result in the net price being lower than its original initial level. However, with no change having occurred in the interest rate, the net price must *grow*

at the same rate as before. Although the net price grows at the same rate as before, it does so from a lower starting value, and so it follows that the new net price p_t would be lower at all points in time than the original net price, and it will also have a flatter profile (as close inspection of the diagram makes clear). This implies that the new gross price will be lower than the old gross price at all points in time except in the original period.

However, the positions of the curves for the new gross and net prices in Figure 15.11(a) cannot be optimal. If the gross (market) price is lower at all points in time except period 0, more extraction would take place in every period. This would cause the reserve to become completely exhausted before

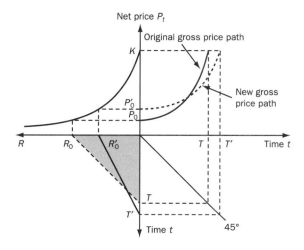

Figure 15.12 A rise in extraction costs

the choke price (K) is reached. This cannot be optimal, as any optimal extraction path must ensure that demand goes to zero at the same point in time as the remaining resource stock goes to zero.

Therefore, optimal extraction requires that the new level of the gross price in period 0, P'_0, must be greater than it was originally (P_0). It will remain above the original gross price level for a while but will, at some time before the resource stock is fully depleted, fall below the old gross price path. This is the final outcome that we illustrate in Figure 15.11(b). As the new gross price eventually becomes lower than its original level, it must take longer before the choke price is reached. Hence the time taken before complete resource exhaustion occurs is lengthened.

All the elements of this reasoning are assembled together in the four-quadrant diagram shown in Figure 15.12. A rise in extraction costs will raise the initial gross price, slow down the rate at which the gross price increases (even though the net price or royalty increases at the same rate as before), and lengthen the time to complete exhaustion of the stock.

What about a fall in extraction costs? This may be the consequence of technological progress decreasing the costs of extracting the resource from its reserves. By following similar reasoning to that we used above, it can be deduced that a fall in extraction costs will have the opposite effects to those just

described. It will lower the initial gross price, increase the rate at which the gross price increases (even though the net price increases at the same rate as before), and shorten the time to complete exhaustion of the stock.

If the changes in extraction cost were very large, then our conclusions may need to be amended. For example, if a cost increase were very large, then it is possible that the new gross price in period 0, P'_0, will be above the choke price. It is then not economically viable to deplete the remaining reserve – an example of an economic exhaustion of a resource, even though, in physical terms, the resource stock has not become completely exhausted.

One remaining point needs to be considered. Until now it has been assumed that the resource stock consists of reserves of uniform, homogeneous quality, and the marginal cost of extraction was constant for the whole stock. We have been investigating the consequences of increases or decreases in that marginal cost schedule from one fixed level to another. But what if the stock were not homogeneous, but rather consisted of reserves of varying quality or varying accessibility? It is not possible here to take the reader through the various possibilities that this opens up. It is clear that in this situation marginal extraction costs can no longer be constant, but will vary as different segments of the stock are extracted. There are many meanings that could be attributed to the notion of a change in marginal extraction costs. A fall in extraction costs may occur as the consequence of new, high-quality reserves being discovered. An increase in costs may occur as a consequence of a high-quality mine becoming exhausted, and extraction switching to another mine in which the quality of the resource reserve is somewhat lower. Technical progress may result in the whole profile of extraction costs being shifted downwards, although not necessarily at the same rate for all components.

We do not analyse these cases in this text. The suggestions for further reading point the reader to where analysis of these cases can be found. But it should be evident that elaborating a resource depletion model in any of these ways requires dropping the assumption that there is a known, fixed quantity of the resource. Instead, the amount of the resource that is 'economically' available becomes an endogenous variable, the value of which depends upon resource demand and extraction cost schedules. This also implies that we could analyse a reduction in extraction costs as if it were a form of technological progress; this can increase the stock of the reserve that can be extracted in an economically viable manner. Hence, changes in resource extraction costs and changes in resource stocks become interrelated – rather than independent – phenomena.

15.7 The introduction of taxation/subsidies

15.7.1 A royalty tax or subsidy

A royalty tax or subsidy will have no effect on a resource owner's extraction decision for a reserve that is currently being extracted. The tax or subsidy will alter the present value of the resource being extracted, but there can be no change in the rate of extraction over time that can offset that decline or increase in present value. The government will simply collect some of the mineral rent (or pay some subsidies), and resource extraction and production will proceed in the same manner as before the tax/subsidy was introduced.

This result follows from the Hotelling rule of efficient resource depletion. To see this, define α to be a royalty tax rate (which could be negative – that is, a subsidy), and denote the royalty or net price at time t by p_t. Then the post-tax royalty becomes $(1 - \alpha)p_t$. But Hotelling's rule implies that the post-tax royalty must rise at the discount rate, i, if the resource is to be exploited efficiently. That is:

$$(1 - \alpha)p_t = (1 - \alpha)p_0 e^{it}$$

or

$$p_t = p_0 e^{it}$$

Hotelling's rule continues to operate unchanged in the presence of a royalty tax, and no change occurs to the optimal depletion path. This is also true for a royalty subsidy scheme. In this case, denoting the royalty subsidy rate by β, we have the efficiency condition

$$(1 + \beta)p_t = (1 + \beta)p_0 e^{it} \Rightarrow p_t = p_0 e^{it}$$

We can conclude that a royalty tax or subsidy is neutral in its effect on the optimal extraction path. However, a tax may discourage (or a subsidy encourage) the exploration effort for new mineral deposits by reducing (increasing) the expected payoff from discovering the new deposits.

15.7.2 Revenue tax/subsidy

The previous subsection analysed the effect of a tax or subsidy on resource royalties. We now turn our attention to the impact of a revenue tax (or subsidy). In the absence of a revenue tax, the Hotelling efficiency condition is, in terms of net prices and gross prices,

$$p_t = p_0 e^{it}$$
$$\Rightarrow (P_t - c) = (P_0 - c) e^{it}$$

Under a revenue tax scheme, with a tax of α per unit of the resource sold, the post-tax royalty or net price is

$$p_t = (1 - \alpha)P_t - c$$

So Hotelling's rule becomes:

$$[(1 - \alpha)P_t - c] = [(1 - \alpha)P_0 - c] e^{it} \quad (0 < \alpha < 1)$$

$$\Rightarrow \left(P_t - \frac{c}{1 - \alpha} \right) = \left(P_0 - \frac{c}{1 - \alpha} \right) e^{it}$$

Since $c/(1 - \alpha) > c$, an imposition of a revenue tax is equivalent to an increase in the resource extraction cost. Similarly, for a revenue subsidy scheme, we have

$$\left(P_t - \frac{c}{1 + \beta} \right) = \left(P_0 - \frac{c}{1 + \beta} \right) e^{it} \quad (0 < \beta < 1)$$

A revenue subsidy is equivalent to a decrease in extraction cost. We have already discussed the effects of a change in extraction costs, and you may recall the results we obtained: a decrease in extraction costs will lower the initial gross price, increase the rate at which the gross price increases (even though the net price or royalty increases at the same rate as before) and shorten the time to complete exhaustion of the stock.

15.8   The resource depletion model: some extensions and further issues

15.8.1 Discount rate

We showed above that resource extraction under a system of perfectly competitive markets might produce the socially optimal outcome. But this equivalence rests upon several assumptions, one of which is that firms choose a private discount rate identical to the social discount rate that would be used by a rational planner. If private and social discount rates differ, however, then market extraction paths may be biased toward excessive use or conservation relative to what is socially optimal.

15.8.2 Forward markets and expectations

The Hotelling model is an abstract analytical tool; its operation in actual market economies is dependent upon the existence of a set of particular institutional circumstances. In many real situations these institutional arrangements do not exist and so the rule lies at a considerable distance from the operation of actual market mechanisms. In addition to the discount rate equivalence mentioned in the previous section, two assumptions are required to ensure a social optimal extraction in the case of perfect competition, First, the resource must be owned by the competitive agents. Secondly, each agent must know at each point in time all current and future prices. One might just assume that agents have perfect foresight, but this hardly seems tenable for the case we are investigating. In the absence of perfect foresight, knowledge of these prices requires the existence of both spot markets and a complete set of forward markets for the resource in question. But no resource does possess a complete set of forward markets, and in these circumstances there is no guarantee that agents can or will make rational supply decisions.

15.8.3 Optimal extraction under uncertainty

Uncertainty is prevalent in decision making regarding non-renewable resource extraction and use. There is uncertainty, for example, about stock sizes, extraction costs, how successful research and development will be in the discovery of substitutes for non-renewable resources (thereby affecting the cost and expected date of arrival of a backstop technology), pay-offs from exploration for new stock, and the action of rivals. It is very important to study how the presence of uncertainty affects appropriate courses of action. For example, what do optimal extraction programmes look like when there is uncertainty, and how do they compare with programmes developed under conditions of certainty?

Let us assume an owner of a natural resource (such as a mine) wishes to maximise the net present value of utility over two periods:[13]

$$\text{Max}\left(U_0 + \frac{U_1}{1 + \rho}\right)$$

If there is a probability (π) of a disaster (for example, the market might be lost) associated with the second period of the extraction programme, then the owner will try to maximise the *expected* net present value of the utility (if he or she is risk-neutral):

$$\text{Max}\left(U_0 + \pi \cdot 0 + (1 - \pi)\frac{U_1}{1 + \rho}\right)$$

$$= \text{Max}\left(U_0 + (1 - \pi)\frac{U_1}{1 + \rho}\right) = \text{Max}\left(U_0 + \frac{U_1}{1 + \rho^*}\right)$$

where

$$\frac{1}{1 + \rho^*} = \frac{1 - \pi}{1 + \rho}$$

Note that

$$(1 + \rho^*)(1 - \pi) = 1 + \rho$$

$$\Rightarrow \rho^* - \rho = \pi(1 + \rho^*) > 0 \qquad \text{(if } 1 \geq \pi > 0)$$

$$\Rightarrow \rho^* > \rho$$

---

[13] This argument follows very closely a presentation in Fisher (1981).

Therefore, in this example, the existence of risk is equivalent to an increase in the discount rate for the owner, which implies, as we have shown before, that the price of the resource must rise more rapidly and the depletion is accelerated.

15.9   Do resource prices actually follow the Hotelling rule?

The Hotelling rule is an economic theory. It is a statement of how resource prices should behave under a specified (and very restrictive) set of conditions. Economic theory begins with a set of axioms (which are regarded as not needing verification) and/or a set of assumptions (which are treated as being provisionally correct). These axioms or assumptions typically include goals or objectives of the relevant actors and various rules of how those actors behave. Then logical reasoning is used to deduce outcomes that should follow, given those assumptions.

But a theory is not necessarily correct. Among the reasons it may be wrong are inappropriateness of one or more of its assumptions, and flawed deduction. A theory may also fail to 'fit the facts' because it refers to an idealised model of reality that does not take into account some elements of real-world complexity. However, failing to fit the facts does not make the theory *false*; the theory only applies to the idealised world for which it was constructed.

But it would be interesting to know whether the Hotelling principle is sufficiently powerful to fit the facts of the real world. Indeed, many economists take the view that a theory is useless unless it has predictive power: we should be able to use the theory to make predictions that have a better chance of being correct than chance alone would imply. A theory is unlikely to have predictive power if it cannot describe or explain current and previous behaviour. Of course, even if it could do that, this does not necessarily mean it will have good *ex ante* predictive power.

In an attempt to validate the Hotelling rule (and other associated parts of resource depletion theory), much research effort has been directed to empirical testing of that theory. What conclusions have emerged from this exercise? Unfortunately, no consensus of opinion has come from empirical analysis. As Berck (1995) writes in one recent survey of results 'the results from such testing are mixed'.

A simple version of the Hotelling rule for some marketed non-renewable resource was given by equation 15.7b; namely

$$\frac{\dot{p}_t}{p_t} = \rho$$

In this version, all prices are denominated in units of utility, and ρ is a utility discount rate. These magnitudes are, of course, unobservable, so equation 15.7b is not directly testable. But we can rewrite the Hotelling rule in terms of money-income (or consumption) units that can be measured:

$$\frac{\dot{p}_t^*}{p_t^*} = \delta \tag{15.10}$$

Here, p^* denotes a price in money units, and δ is a consumption discount rate. Empirical testing normally uses discrete time-series data, and so the discrete-time version of Hotelling's rule is employed:

$$\frac{\Delta p_t^*}{p_t^*} = \delta \tag{15.11}$$

or, expressed in an alternative way,

$$p_{t+1}^* = p_t^*(1 + \delta) \tag{15.12}$$

Notice right away that equations 15.11 and 15.12 are assuming that there is a constant discount rate over time. If this is not correct (and there is no reason why it has to be) then δ should enter those two equations with a time subscript, and the Hotelling principle no longer implies that a resource price will rise at a fixed rate. But this is a complication we ignore in the rest of this section.

One way of testing Hotelling's rule seems to be clear: collect time-series data on the price of a resource, and see if the proportionate growth rate of the price is equal to δ. This was one thing that Barnett and Morse (1963) did in a famous study. They found that resource prices – including iron, copper, silver and timber – fell over time, which was a most disconcerting result for proponents of the standard theory. Subsequent researchers, looking at different resources or different time periods, have come up with a bewildering variety of results. There is no clear picture of whether resource prices typically rise or fall over time. We can no more be confident that the theory is true than that it is not true – a most unsatisfactory state of affairs.

But we now know that the problem is far more difficult than this to settle, and that a direct examination of resource prices is not a reasonable way to proceed. Note first that the variable p^* in Hotelling's rule is the *net* price (or rent, or royalty) of the resource, not its *market* price. Roughly speaking, these are related as follows:

$$P^* = p^* + \text{MC} \tag{15.13}$$

where P^* is the gross (or market) price of the extracted resource, p^* is the net price of the resource *in situ* (i.e. unextracted), and MC is the marginal extraction cost. It is clear from equation 15.13 that if the marginal cost of extraction is falling, P^* might be falling even though p^* is rising. We noted this earlier in doing comparative statics to examine the effect of a fall in extraction costs. So evidence of falling market prices cannot, in itself, be regarded as invalidating the Hotelling principle.

This suggests that the right data to use is the resource net price. But that is an unobservable variable, for which data do not therefore exist. And this is not the only unobservable variable: δ is also unobserved, as we shall see shortly. In the absence of data on net price, one might try to construct a proxy for it. The obvious way to proceed is to subtract marginal costs from the gross, market price to arrive at net price. This is also not as easy as it seems: costs are observable, but the costs recorded are usually averages, not marginals. We shall not discuss how this (rather serious) difficulty has been dealt with. However, many studies have pursued this approach. Slade (1982) made one of the earliest studies of this type; she concluded that some resources have U-shaped quadratic price paths, having fallen in the past but latterly rising. Other studies of this type are Stollery (1983), which generally supported the Hotelling hypothesis, and Halvorsen and Smith (1991), which was unable to support it.

Any attempt to construct a proxy measure for net price comes up against an additional problem. The measure that is obtained is a proxy, and it will contain estimation errors. If this variable is simply treated as if it were the unobserved net price itself, a statistical problem – known to econometricians as an errors-in-variables problem – will occur, and estimates of parameters will in general be biased (and so misleading) no matter how large is the sample of data available to the researcher. This casts doubt on all studies using proxies for the net price which have not taken account of this difficulty. Appropriate statistical techniques in the presence of errors-in-variables are discussed in most intermediate econometrics texts, such as Greene (1993). Harvey (1989) is a classic text on the Kalman filter, which is one way of resolving this problem.

Other approaches have also been used to test the Hotelling rule, and we shall mention only two of them very briefly. Fuller details can be found in the survey paper by Berck (1995). Miller and Upton (1985) use the valuation principle. This states that the stock market value of a property with unextracted resources is equal to the present value of its resource extraction plan; if the Hotelling rule is valid this will be constant over time, and so the property's stock market value will be constant. Evidence from this approach gives reasonably strong support for the Hotelling principle. Farrow (1985) adopts an approach that interprets the Hotelling rule as an asset-efficiency condition, and tests for efficiency in resource prices, in much the same way that finance theorists conduct tests of market efficiency. These tests generally reject efficiency, and by implication are taken to not support the Hotelling rule. However, it has to be said that evidence in favour of efficient asset markets is rarely found, but that does not stop economists assuming (for much of the time) that asset markets are efficient.

Let us now return to a comment we made earlier. The right-hand side of the Hotelling rule equation consists of the consumption discount rate δ. But this is also a theoretical construct, not directly observable. What we do observe are market rates of interest, which will include components reflecting transaction costs, various degrees of risk premia, and other market imperfections. Even if we could filter these out, the market rate of interest measures realised or *ex post* returns; but the Hotelling theory is based around an *ex ante* measure of the discount rate, reflecting expectations about the future. This raises a whole host of problems concerning how expectations might be proxied that are beyond the scope of this text.

Finally, even if we did find convincing evidence that the net price of a resource does not rise at the rate δ (or even that it falls), should we regard this as evidence that invalidates the Hotelling rule? The answer is that we should not draw this conclusion. There are several circumstances where resource prices may fall over time even where a Hotelling rule is being followed. For example, in Figure 15.8 we showed that a sequence of new mineral discoveries could lead to a downward-sloping path of the resource's net price. Pindyck (1978) first demonstrated this in a seminal paper. If resource extraction takes place in non-competitive markets, the net price will also rise less quickly than the discount rate (see Figure 15.4). And in the presence of technical progress continually reducing extraction costs, the market price may well fall over time, thereby apparently contradicting a simple Hotelling rule.

The history of attempts to test the Hotelling principle is an excellent example of the problems faced by economists in all branches of that discipline. Many of the variables used in our theories are unobservable or latent variables. Shadow prices are one class of such latent variables. The best we can do is to find proxy variables for them. But if the theory does not work, is that because the theory is poor or because our proxy was not good? More generally, a theory pertains to a particular model. So unless it contains a logical error, a theory can never be wrong. What can be, and often is, incorrect, is a presumption that a theory that is correct in the context of one particular model will generate conclusions that are valid in a wide variety of 'real' situations.

15.10 Natural resource scarcity

Concern with the supposed increasing scarcity of natural resources, and the possibility of running out of strategically important raw materials or energy sources, is by no means new. Worries about resource scarcity can be traced back to medieval times in Britain, and have surfaced periodically ever since. The scarcity of land was central to the theories of Malthus and the other classical economists. In the 20th century, fears about timber shortages in several countries led to the establishment of national forestry authorities, charged with rebuilding timber stocks. As we have seen earlier, pessimistic views about impending resource scarcity have been most forcibly expressed in the *Limits to Growth* literature (see Chapter 2 of this text for examples); during the 1970s, the so-called oil crises further focused attention on mineral scarcities.

What do we mean by resource scarcity? One use of the term – what might be called absolute scarcity – holds that all resources are scarce, as the availability of resources is fixed and finite at any point in time, while the wants which resource use can satisfy are not limited. Where a market exists for a resource, the existence of any positive price is viewed as evidence of absolute scarcity; where markets do not exist, the existence of a positive shadow price – the implicit price that would be necessary if the resource were to be used efficiently – similarly is an indicator of absolute scarcity for that resource.

But this is not the usual meaning of the term in general discussions about natural resource scarcity. In these cases, scarcity tends to be used to indicate that the natural resource is becoming harder to obtain, and requires more of other resources to obtain it. The relevant costs to include in measures of scarcity are both private and external costs; it is important to recognise that if private extraction costs are not rising over time, social costs may rise if negative externalities such as environmental degradation or depletion of common property resources are increasing as a consequence of extraction of the natural resource. Thus, a rising opportunity cost of obtaining the resource is an indicator of scarcity – let us call this use of the term *relative scarcity*. In the rest of this section, our comments will be restricted to this second form.

Before we take this matter any further, it is necessary to say something about the degree of aggregation used in examining resource scarcity. To keep things as simple as possible, first consider only non-renewable natural resources. There is not one single resource but a large number, each distinct from the others in some physical sense. However, physically distinct resources may be economically similar, through being substitutes for one another. Non-renewable resources are best viewed, then, as a structure of assets, components of which are substitutable to varying degrees. In Chapter 14, when we discussed the efficient extraction of a single non-renewable resource, what we had in mind was some aggregate set of resources in this particular sense. Moreover, when the class of resources is extended to incorporate renewable resources, so the structure is enlarged, as are the substitution possibilities.

Except for resources for which no substitution possibilities exist – if indeed such resources exist – it is of limited usefulness to enquire whether any individual resource is scarce or not. If one particular resource, such as crude oil, were to become excessively costly to obtain for any reason, one would expect resource use to substitute to another resource, such as natural gas or coal. A well-functioning price mechanism should ensure that this occurs. Because of this, it is more useful to consider whether natural resources in general are becoming scarcer: is there any evidence of increasing generalised resource scarcity?

What indicators might one use to assess the degree of scarcity of particular natural resources, and natural resources in general? There are several candidates for this task, including physical indicators (such as reserve quantities or reserve-to-consumption ratios), marginal resource extraction cost, marginal exploration and discovery costs, market prices, and resource rents. We shall now briefly examine each of these. In doing so, you will see that the question of whether resources are becoming scarce is closely related to the question of whether the Hotelling rule is empirically validated.

15.10.1 Physical indicators

A variety of physical indicators have been used as proxies for scarcity, including various measures of reserve quantities, and reserve-to-consumption ratios. Several such measures were discussed earlier in this chapter and appropriate statistics listed (see Box 15.1 and Table 15.1). Inferences drawn about impending resource scarcity in the *Limits to Growth* literature were drawn on the basis of such physical indicators. Unfortunately, they are severely limited in their usefulness as proxy measures of scarcity for the reasons discussed in Box 15.1. Most import-

antly, most natural resources are not homogeneous in quality, and the location and quantities available are not known with certainty; extra amounts of the resource can be obtained as additional exploration, discovery and extraction effort is applied. A rising resource net price will, in general, stimulate such effort. It is the absence of this information in physical data that limits its usefulness.

15.10.2 Real marginal resource extraction cost

We argued earlier that scarcity is concerned with the real opportunity cost of acquiring additional quantities of the resource. This suggests that the marginal extraction cost of obtaining the resource from existing reserves would be an appropriate indicator of scarcity. The classic study by Barnett and Morse (1963) used an index of real unit costs, c, defined as

$$c = \frac{(\alpha L + \beta K)}{Q}$$

where L is labour, K is capital and Q is output of the extractive industry, and α and β are weights to aggregate inputs. Rising resource scarcity is proxied by rising real unit costs. Note that ideally marginal costs should be used, although this is rarely possible in practice because of data limitations. An important advantage of an extraction costs indicator is that it incorporates technological change. If technological progress relaxes resource constraints by making a given quantity of resources more productive, then this reduction in scarcity will be reflected in a tendency for costs to fall. However, the measure does have problems. First, the measurement of capital is always difficult, largely because of the aggregation that is required to obtain a single measure of the capital stock. Similarly, there are difficulties in obtaining valid aggregates of all inputs used. Secondly, the indicator is backward-looking, whereas an ideal indicator should serve as a signal for future potential scarcity. Finally, it may well be the case that quantities and/or qualities of the resource are declining seriously, while technical progress that is sufficiently rapid results in price falling. In extreme cases, sudden exhaustion may occur after a period of prolonged price falls. Ultimately, no clear inference about scarcity can be drawn from extraction cost data alone.

Barnett and Morse (1963) and Barnett (1979) found no evidence of increasing scarcity, except for forestry. As we mentioned previously, they concluded that agricultural and mineral products, over the period 1870 to 1970, were becoming more abundant rather than scarcer, and explained this in terms of the substitution of more plentiful lower-grade deposits as higher grades were depleted, the discovery of new deposits, and technical change in exploration, extraction and processing. References for other, subsequent studies are given at the end of the chapter.

15.10.3 Marginal exploration and discovery costs

An alternative measure of resource scarcity is the opportunity cost of acquiring additional quantities of the resource by locating as-yet-unknown reserves. Higher discovery costs are interpreted as indicators of increased resource scarcity. This measure is not often used, largely because it is difficult to obtain long runs of reliable data. Moreover, the same kinds of limitations possessed by extraction cost data apply in this case too.

15.10.4 Real market price indicators and net price indicators

The most commonly used scarcity indicator is time-series data on real (that is, inflation-adjusted) market prices. It is here that the affinity between tests of scarcity and tests of the Hotelling principle is most apparent. Market price data are readily available, easy to use and, like all asset prices, are forward-looking, to some extent at least. Use of price data has three main problems. First, prices are often distorted as a consequence of taxes, subsidies, exchange controls and other governmental interventions; reliable measures need to be corrected for such distortions. Secondly, the real price index tends to be very sensitive to the choice of deflator. Should nominal prices be deflated by a retail or wholesale price index (and for which basket of goods), by the GDP deflator, or by some input price index such as manufacturing wages? There is no unambiguously correct answer to this question, which is unfortunate as very different

conclusions can be arrived at about resource scarcity with different choices of deflator. Some evidence on this is given in the chapter on resource scarcity in Hartwick and Olewiler (1986); these authors cite an analysis by Brown and Field (1978) which compares two studies of resource prices using alternative deflators. For eleven commodities, Nordhaus (1973) used capital goods prices as a deflator and concluded that all eleven minerals were becoming less scarce. However, Jorgensen and Griliches (1967) used a manufacturing wages deflator and concluded that three of the minerals – coal, lead and zinc – were becoming scarcer over the same period.

The third major problem with resource price data is one we came across earlier. Market prices do not in general measuring the right thing; an ideal price measure would reflect the net price of the resource. Hotelling's rule shows that it is this that rises through time as the resource becomes progressively scarcer. But we have seen that net resource prices are not directly observed variables, and so it is rather difficult to use them as a basis for empirical analysis.

Despite the limitations of market price data, the early studies show a broad agreement between this measure and the others discussed in this section. One illustration is given in Figure 15.13, taken from

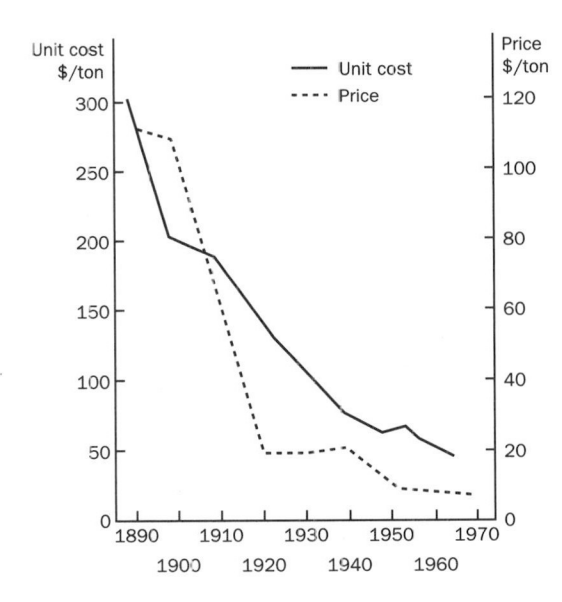

Figure 15.13 Price and unit costs for all metals, 1890–1970
Source: Brown and Field (1979). Copyright, Resources for the Future, Inc.

Brown and Field (1979), which suggests that, for an aggregate index of all metals, scarcity was decreasing over the period 1890 to 1970. More recent studies present a much less clear picture, however – as we noted above.

Can any general conclusions about resource scarcity be obtained from the literature? The majority of economic analyses conducted up to the early 1980s concluded that few, if any, non-renewable natural resources were becoming scarcer. In the last 20 years, concern about increasing scarcity of non-renewable resources has increased, and an increasing proportion of studies seems to lend support to an increasing scarcity hypothesis.

Paradoxically, these studies also suggested it was in the area of *renewable* resources that problems of increasing scarcity were to be found, particularly in cases of open access. The reasons why scarcity may be particularly serious for some renewable resources will be examined in Chapter 17.

Summary

- Non-renewable resources consist of energy and material stocks that are generated very slowly through natural processes; these stocks – measured in terms of base resource – can be thought of as existing in fixed, finite quantities. Once extracted, they cannot regenerate in timescales that are relevant to humans.

- Resource stocks can be measured in several ways, including base resource, resource potential, and resource reserves. It is important to distinguish between purely physical measures of stock size, and 'economic' measures of resource stocks.

- Non-renewable resources consist of a large number of particular types and forms of resource, among which there may be substitution possibilities.

- The demand for a resource may exhibit a 'choke price'; at such a price demand would become zero, and would switch to an alternative resource or to a 'backstop' technology.

- The chapter has shown – for two-period discrete time and for continuous time – how models of optimal resource depletion can be constructed and solved.

- One element of the solution of such models is that an efficient price path for the non-renewable resource must follow the Hotelling rule.

- In some circumstances, a socially optimal depletion programme will be identical to a privately optimal (profit-maximising) depletion programme. However, this is not always true. In particular, the equivalence will not hold if social and private discount rates diverge.

- Using comparative dynamic analysis, we have been able to determine the consequences of changes in interest rates, known stock size, demand, price of backstop technology, and resource extraction costs.

- Frequent new discoveries of the resource are likely to generate a price path which does not resemble constant exponential growth.

- Resource depletion outcomes differ between competitive and monopolistic markets. The time to depletion will be longer in a monopoly market, the resource net price will be higher in early years, and the net price will be lower in later years.

- Taxes or subsidies on royalties (or resource rents or net prices) will not affect the optimal depletion path, although they will affect the present value of after-tax royalties. However, revenue-based taxes or subsidies will affect depletion paths, being equivalent to changes in extraction costs.

- We explained the concept of natural resource scarcity. There are many measures that have been proposed, or are used, as measures of scarcity. The more theoretically attractive measures typically are unobtainable as they depend upon unobservable quantities.

Further reading

The references for further reading given at the end of Chapter 14 are all relevant for further reading on the material covered in this chapter. In particular, very good (but rather advanced-level) presentations of the theory of efficient and optimal resource depletion can be found in Baumol and Oates (1988), Dasgupta and Heal (1979), Heal (1981) and the collection of papers in the May 1974 special issue on resource depletion of the *Review of Economic Studies*. As stated previously, less difficult presentations are given in Hartwick and Olewiler (1986), Anderson (1991) and Fisher (1981). Pindyck (1978) is the classic reference on resource exploration.

Good general discussions of resource scarcity can be found in Hartwick and Olewiler (1986, chapter 5), which provides an extensive discussion of the evidence, Barbier (1989a), Fisher (1979, 1981) and Harris (1993). Important works in the field of resource scarcity include Barnett (1979), Barnett and Morse (1963), Brown and Field (1979), Deverajan and Fisher (1980, 1982), Hall and Hall (1984), Jorgensen and Griliches (1967), Leontief *et al.* (1977), Nordhaus (1973), Norgaard (1975), Slade (1982), Smith (1979) and Smith and Krutilla (1979). Examinations of the extent to which the Hotelling rule are satisfied in practice are extensively referenced in the text, but the best place to go next is probably Berck (1995).

An excellent discussion on natural resource substitutability can be found in Dasgupta (1993). Adelman (1990, 1995) covers the economics of oil depletion. Prell (1996) deals with backstop technology.

Discussion questions

1. Discuss the merits of a proposal that the government should impose a tax or subsidy where an non-renewable resource is supplied monopolistically in order to increase the social net benefit.

2. 'An examination of natural resource matters ought to recognise technical/scientific, economic, and socio-political considerations.' Explain.

3. 'The exploitation of resources is not necessarily destructive . . . need not imply the impoverishment of posterity . . . It is the diversion of national income from its usual channels to an increased preservation of natural wealth that will harm posterity' (Anthony Scott). Explain and discuss.

4. The notion of sustainability is used differently in economics than in the natural sciences. Explain the meaning of sustainability in these two frameworks, and discuss the attempts that have been made by economists to make the concept operational.

Problems

1. Consider two consecutive years, labelled 0 and 1. You are currently at the start of year 0. The following information is available. There is a single fixed stock of a non-renewable resource; the magnitude of this stock at the start of year 0 is 224 (million tonnes). The inverse resource demand functions for this resource in each of the years are

$$P_0 = a - bR_0 \quad \text{and} \quad P_1 = a - bR_1$$

in which $a = 107$ and $b = 1$. The constant marginal cost of resource extraction is 5. All (non-physical) units are in European units of utility. The social welfare function is discounted utilitarian in form, with a social utility discount rate of 0.1. Given that the objective is to maximise social welfare over periods 0 and 1,

calculate the amounts of resource that should be extracted in each period, subject to the restriction that at least 104 units of the resource should be left (unextracted) for the future at the end of period 1. What is the resource price in each period
(a) in utility units;
(b) in euros, given that $U = \log(C)$, where U is utility units, log is the natural logarithm operator, and C is consumption (or income), measured in euros?

2. The version of Hotelling's rule given in equation 15.5 requires the net price to grow proportionately at the rate ρ. Under what circumstances would this imply that the gross price also should grow at the rate ρ?

3. In equation 15.5, if $\rho = 0$, what are the implications for

(a) P_0 and P_1?
(b) R_0 and R_1?
(Problems 4, 5 and 6 are based on Table 15.3.)

4. Explain, with diagrams, why a monopolistic non-renewable resource market is biased towards conservation and therefore will increase the 'life' of the resource.

5. In the case of perfect competition, if the private discount rate is higher than the correct social discount rate, explain, with diagrams, why the market will exhaust the resource too quickly.

6. Discuss, with diagrams, the consequences of the discovery of North Sea oil for
(a) the price and output levels for the oil market;
(b) the date of exhaustion of oil reserves.
What will be the probable path over time of oil prices if there are frequent discoveries of oil?

Appendix 15.1 Solution of the multi-period resource depletion model

We wish to maximise

$$W = \int_{t=0}^{t=T} U(R_t)e^{-\rho t}dt$$

subject to

$$\dot{S} = -R_t$$

The current-valued Hamiltonian for this problem is

$$H = U(R_t) + P_t(-R_t)$$

The necessary conditions for maximum social welfare are

$$\dot{P}_t = \rho P_t \tag{15.14}$$

$$\frac{\partial H}{\partial R} = -P_t + \frac{dU}{dR} = 0 \tag{15.15}$$

Rearranging equation 15.15 we obtain

$$P_t = \frac{dU}{dR}$$

so that the resource shadow price, P_t, is equal to the marginal utility of the non-renewable resource, an equality used in the main text. Equation 15.14 is, of

course, the Hotelling efficiency condition, given as equation 15.7b in the chapter.

As we noted in the chapter, an optimal solution must have the property that the stock goes to zero at exactly the point that demand goes to zero. In order for demand to be zero at time T (which we determine in a moment) the net price must reach the choke price at time T. That is,

$$P_T = K$$

This, together with equation 15.7a in the main text, implies

$$K = P_0 e^{\rho T} \tag{15.16}$$

To solve for R_t, it can be seen from equations 15.7a and 15.8 that

$$P_0 e^{\rho t} = K e^{-aR}$$

Substituting for K from equation 15.16 we obtain

$$P_0 e^{\rho T} = P_0 e^{-(aR - \rho T)}$$

$$\Rightarrow \rho t = -aR + \rho T$$

$$\Rightarrow R_t = \frac{\rho}{a}(T - t) \tag{15.17}$$

This gives an expression for the rate at which the resource should be extracted along the optimal path. To find the optimal time period, T, over which extraction should take place, recall that the fixed stock constraint is:

$$\int_0^T R_t dt = \bar{S}$$

and so by substitution for R_t from equation 15.17 we obtain

$$\int_0^T \left[\frac{\rho}{a}(T - t) \right] dt = \bar{S}$$

Therefore

$$\frac{\rho}{a} \left[Tt - \frac{t^2}{2} \right]_0^T = \bar{S}$$

$$\frac{1}{2}\frac{\rho}{a}T^2 = \bar{S}$$

or

$$T = \sqrt{\frac{2\bar{S}a}{\rho}}$$

Next we solve, using equation 15.16, for the initial royalty level, P_0:

$$P_0 = Ke^{-\rho T} = Ke^{-\sqrt{2\rho \bar{S}a}}$$

To obtain an expression for the resource royalty at time t, we substitute equation 15.7a into the expression just derived for the initial royalty level to obtain the required condition:

$$P_t = Ke^{\rho(t-T)}$$

The optimal initial extraction level is, from equation 15.17,

$$R_0 = \frac{\rho}{a}(T - 0) = \frac{\rho T}{a} = \sqrt{\frac{2\rho \bar{S}}{a}}$$

Appendix 15.2 The monopolist's profit-maximising extraction programme

To solve for the monopolist's profit-maximising extraction programme, we need to do some additional calculation. First, let us derive an expression for the firm's marginal profit function, $M\Pi$:

$$M\Pi_t = \frac{\partial \Pi_t}{\partial R_t} = \frac{\partial (P(R)R_t)}{\partial R_t} = \frac{\partial P_t}{\partial R_t}R_t + P(R)$$

$$(15.18)$$

Now, substituting for $P(R)$ from the resource demand function (equation 15.8) we can express this equation as

$$M\Pi_t = -aR_t Ke^{-aR_t} + Ke^{-aR_t}$$
$$= K(-aR_t + 1)e^{-aR_t} \approx Ke^{-ahR_t} \quad (15.19)$$

where $h = 2.5$. Notice the approximation here. We use this because otherwise it is not possible to obtain an analytical solution, given the double appearance of R_t.

Since resource extraction at the end of the planning horizon must be zero ($R_T = 0$) we have

$$M\Pi_t = Ke^{-ahR(T)} = K \quad (15.20)$$

To obtain $M\Pi_0$, using equation 15.9 we obtain

$$M\Pi_0 = M\Pi_T e^{-iT} = Ke^{-iT} \quad (15.21)$$

To obtain an expression for $M\Pi_t$, using equations 15.9 and 15.21, we have

$$M\Pi_t = M\Pi_0 e^{it} = Ke^{i(t-T)} \quad (15.22)$$

Now we may obtain a solution equation for R_t, using equations 15.9 and 15.22:

$$Ke^{-ahR_t} = Ke^{i(t-T)}$$

$$\Rightarrow i(t - T) = -ahR_t$$

$$\Rightarrow R_t = \frac{i}{ha}(T - t) \quad (15.23)$$

In order to obtain the optimal depletion time period T we use the fixed-stock constraint together with equation 15.23, the result we have just obtained:

$$\int_0^T R_t dt = \bar{S}$$

$$\Rightarrow \int_0^T \frac{i}{ha}(T - t)\,dt = \bar{S}$$

$$\Rightarrow \frac{i}{ha}\left[Tt - \frac{t^2}{2}\right]_0^T = \bar{S}$$

$$\frac{1}{2}\frac{i}{ha}T^2 = \bar{S}$$

Therefore $T = \sqrt{\dfrac{2\bar{S}ha}{i}}$

To solve the initial extraction R_0, from equation 15.22:

$$R_0 = \frac{i}{ha}(T - 0) = \frac{iT}{ha} = \sqrt{\frac{2i\bar{S}}{ha}}$$

Finally, to solve the initial net price P_0, from equation 15.8, (the demand curve)

$$P_0 = Ke^{-aR_0} = K\exp\left(-\sqrt{\frac{2i\bar{S}a}{h}}\right)$$

Appendix 15.3 A worked numerical example

Let us take 1990 as the 'initial year' of the study. In 1990, the oil price was $P_0 = \$20$ per barrel, and oil output was $R_0 = 21.7$ billion barrels. From our demand function (equation 15.8)

$$P_0 = Ke^{-aR_0}$$

we obtain

$$R_0 = \frac{\ln K}{a} - \frac{1}{a}\ln P_0$$

The price elasticity of the initial year is, therefore,

$$\varepsilon_0 = \frac{dR_0}{dP_0}\frac{P_0}{R_0} = \left[-\frac{1}{aP_0}\right]\frac{P_0}{R_0} = -\frac{1}{aR_0}$$

Assume that $\varepsilon = -0.5$; then we can estimate a:

$$a = -\frac{1}{\varepsilon R_0} = \frac{1}{0.5 \times 21.7} \approx 0.1$$

We can also estimate the parameter K as follows:

$$K = P_0 \exp(aR_0) = 20 \exp(0.1 \times 21.7) \approx 175$$

The global oil reserve stock is $S = 1150$ billion barrels. The optimal oil extraction programme under the assumptions of a discount rate $\rho = 3\%$ and perfect competition are given by the following.

The optimal exhaustion time is:

$$T^* = \sqrt{\frac{2Sa}{\rho}} = \sqrt{\frac{2 \times 1150 \times 0.1}{0.03}} = 87.5 \text{ years}$$

The optimal initial oil output is

$$R_0^* = \sqrt{\frac{2\rho S}{a}} = \sqrt{\frac{2 \times 0.03 \times 1150}{0.1}}$$
$$= 26.26 \text{ billion barrels}$$

The corresponding optimal initial oil price is

$$P_0^* = K\exp(-aR_0^*) = 175\exp(-0.1 \times 26.26)$$
$$= \$12.7/\text{barrel}$$

The optimal oil output is obviously higher than the actual output in 1990, and the optimal price is lower than the actual one. So there is apparent evidence of distortion (inefficiency) in the world oil market.

CHAPTER 16

Stock pollution problems

Look before you leap.

Proverb, source unknown; most likely source is Aesop's fables

Learning objectives

In this chapter you will

- investigate two models of optimal emissions which are suitable for the analysis of persistent (long-lasting) pollutants. Each of these models is a variant of the optimal growth model framework that we have addressed before at several places in the text
- investigate a simple 'aggregate stock pollution model'. This model is appropriate for dealing with pollution problems where the researcher considers it appropriate to link emissions flows to the processes of resource extraction and use
- use the aggregate stock pollution model to identify how optimal pollution targets can be obtained from generalised versions of the resource depletion models we investigated in Chapters 14 and 15
- follow the development of a second resource use and depletion model. This model – which we call a 'model of waste accumulation and disposal' – provides a framework that is suitable for analysing stock pollution problems of a local, or less pervasive, type, such as the accumulation of lead in water systems or contamination of water systems by effluent discharges
- investigate in some depth the dynamics of pollution generation and pollution regulation processes, using phase plane analysis

Introduction

Our analysis of pollution targets in Chapter 6 recognised that some residuals are durable. Their emissions accumulate, impose loads upon environmental systems which persist through time, and can result in harmful impacts. Processes of this form were called stock pollution problems. In this chapter, we revisit our previous analysis of pollution targets (in Chapter 6). Two modelling frameworks will be examined. We refer to these as an 'aggregate stock pollution model' and a 'model of waste accumulation and disposal'.[1] The first is appropriate for dealing with pollution problems at a highly aggregated level, and where it is necessary to place pollution problems explicitly in the context of the material basis of the economy, by linking residual flows to the processes of resource extraction and use. In doing so, it will be possible to generate pollution targets from the resource depletion models we investigated in Chapters 14 and 15.

This approach is appropriate for dealing with economy-wide or global stock pollution problems arising from the use of fossil fuels. Climate change modelling falls into this category, and several of the illustrations we use in the chapter refer to that example. Most climate change models are highly aggregated using, for example, an aggregate 'fossil

---

[1] The term 'model of waste accumulation and disposal' is borrowed from the title of Plourde's (1972) seminal paper.

fuels' resource as an input into production. And they require that the material basis of the pollution in question – in this case, finite stocks of fossil fuels – is properly built into the modelling framework.

The second framework – the waste accumulation and disposal model – is appropriate for analysing stock pollution problems of a local, or less pervasive, type. Examples of such problems include the accumulation of lead, mercury and other heavy metals in water systems, the accumulation of particulates in air, the build-up of chemicals from pesticides and fertilisers in soils, and contamination of inland and coastal water systems by effluent discharges. In these cases, resource use is of a sufficiently small scale (in the problem being considered) that limits on resource stocks do not become binding constraints. Hence, the researcher can focus on the dynamics of the pollution problem but need not explicitly build into the model a component which links pollutant emissions to the resources from which they are derived.

For both modelling frameworks, though, we shall take the analysis of previous chapters further by giving a more complete account of the dynamics of the pollution processes, the properties of their steady states (if they exist), and the implications for pollution control targets and instruments.

16.1 An aggregate dynamic model of pollution

Pollution problems come in many forms. Yet many have one thing in common: they are associated with the use of fossil fuels. In this section, we present a simple and highly aggregated stock pollution model. To fix ideas, it will be useful to think of this as a global climate change model, although that is by no means the only context in which the model could be used.

16.1.1 Basic structure of the model

The model developed in this section is a simple, aggregate stock pollution model. It can be thought of as an optimal growth model – of the type covered in Chapter 14 – but including some additional components, one of which models the way in which pollution flows are related to the extraction and use of a composite non-renewable resource. We employ here equivalent notation to that used in Chapter 14 and, wherever appropriate, adopt equivalent functional forms. Being an optimal growth model, we look for its 'solution' by using dynamic optimisation techniques. Specifically, we are trying to find the characteristics of an emissions path for the pollutant that will maximise a suitably defined objective function.

We suppose that the production process utilises two inputs: capital and a non-renewable environmental resource. Obtaining that non-renewable resource involves extraction and processing costs. There is a fixed (and known) total stock of the non-renewable resource. From now on we shall refer to this resource as 'fossil fuels'. Use of fossil fuels involves two kinds of trade-offs. First, there is an intertemporal trade-off: given that the total stock is fixed, using fossil fuels today means that less will be available tomorrow. So different paths of fossil-fuel extraction can affect the welfare of different generations. Second, using fossil fuels leads to more production (which is welfare-enhancing) but also generates more pollution (which is welfare-detracting). The principal concern of Chapters 14 and 15 was with the intertemporal trade-off. Here we are interested in both of these trade-offs.

The pollution model used is an extension of that developed in Chapter 14. Its structure – elements and key relationships – is illustrated in Figure 16.1. We retain the assumption that extracting the resource is costly, but simplify the earlier analysis by having those costs dependent on the rate of extraction but not on the size of the remaining stock. Pollution is generated from the use of the fossil-fuel resource.

16.1.2 Pollution damages

There are various ways in which pollution damages can be incorporated into a resource depletion model. Two of these are commonly used in environmental economics:

- damages operating through the utility function;
- damages operating through the production function.

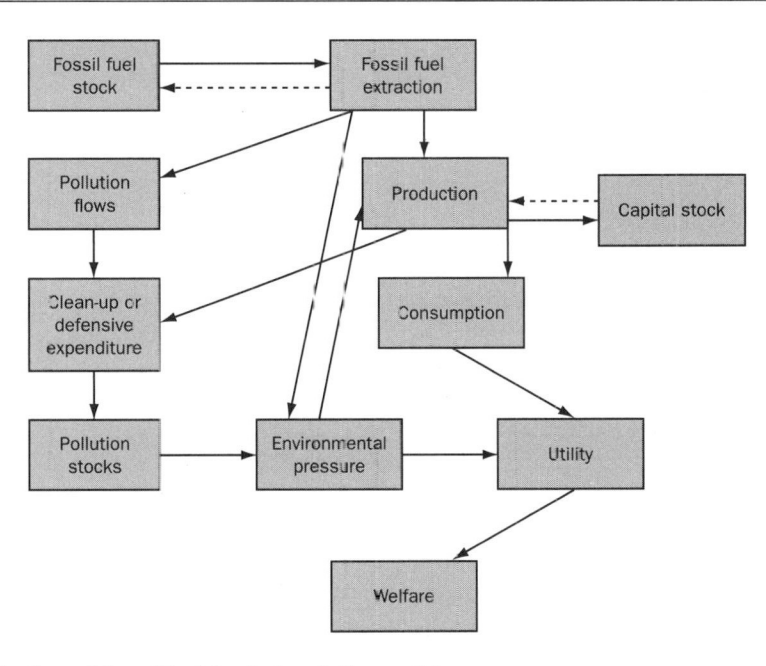

Figure 16.1 The structure of the aggregate stock pollution model

In order to handle these kinds of effects in a fairly general way, we use the symbol E to denote an index of environmental pressures. These environmental pressures have a negative effect upon utility. To capture these effects, we write the utility function as

$$U = U(C, E) \tag{16.1}$$

in which, by assumption, $U_C > 0$ and $U_E < 0$. The index of environmental pressures E depends on the rate of fossil-fuel use (R) and on the accumulated stock of pollutant in the relevant environmental medium (A). So we have

$$E = E(R, A) \tag{16.2}$$

Higher rates of fossil-fuel use and higher ambient pollution levels each increase environmental pressures, so that $E_R > 0$ and $E_A > 0$. Substituting equation 16.2 into equation 16.1 we obtain

$$U = U(C, E(R, A)) \tag{16.3}$$

This deals with the case where damages operate through the utility function. But many forms of damage operate through production functions. For example, greenhouse-gas-induced climate change might reduce crop yields, or tree growth may be damaged by sulphur dioxide emissions. A production function that incorporates damages of this kind is

$$Q = Q(R, K, E(R, A)) \tag{16.4}$$

Obtaining the non-renewable resource involves extraction and processing costs, Γ, which depend on the quantity of the resource used; hence we have

$$\Gamma = \Gamma(R)$$

16.1.3 The resource stock–flow relationship

The utility and production functions both depend on A, the ambient level of pollution. The way in which A changes over time is modelled in the same way as in Chapter 6. That is:

$$\dot{A} = M(R) - \alpha A \tag{16.5}$$

which assumes that a constant proportion α of the ambient pollutant stock decays at each point in time. Note that equation 16.5 specifies that emissions depend upon the amount of resource use, R. By integration of equation 16.5 we obtain

$$A_t = \int_0^t (M(R_\tau) - \alpha A_\tau)\,\mathrm{d}\tau$$

So for a pollutant which is not infinitely long-lived $(\alpha > 0)$ the pollution stock at time t will be the sum of all previous pollution emissions less the sum of all previous pollution decay, while for a perfectly persistent pollutant ($\alpha = 0$) A grows without bounds as long as M is positive.

16.1.4 Defensive or clean-up expenditure

We now introduce an additional control variable (or instrument) – expenditure on cleaning-up pollution. Expenditure on V is an alternative use of output to investment expenditure, consumption, or resource extraction and processing costs, and so must satisfy the identity

$$Q \equiv \dot{K} + C + \Gamma + V$$

In the model clean-up activity operates as additional to natural decay of the pollution stock. For example, rivers may be treated to reduce biological oxygen demand or air may be filtered to remove particles. The level of such activity will be measured by expenditure on it, V. We shall refer to V as 'defensive expenditure'. This is a term which is widely used in the literature but in an ambiguous way. Sometimes it refers to expenditure on coping with, or ameliorating the effects of, an existing level of pollution. Thus, for example, in some contexts the term would be used to cover expenditure by individuals on personal air filters, 'gas masks', for wear while walking the streets of a city with an air pollution problem. As we use the term here, it would in that context refer to expenditure on an activity intended to reduce the level of air pollution in the city.

The consequences of defensive expenditure on the pollutant stock is described by the equation:

$$F = F(V) \tag{16.6}$$

in which $F_V > 0$. The term F, therefore, describes the reduction in the pollution stock brought about by some level of defensive expenditure V. Incorporating this in the differential equation for the pollutant stock gives

$$\dot{A} = M(R) - \alpha A - F(V) \tag{16.7}$$

which says that the pollution stock is increased by emissions arising from resource use and is decreased by natural decay and by defensive expenditure.

16.1.5 The optimisation problem

The dynamic optimisation problem can now be stated as:

Select values for the control variables C_t, R_t and V_t for $t = 0, \ldots, \infty$ so as to maximise

$$W = \int_{t=0}^{t=\infty} U(C_t, E(R_t, A_t)) e^{-\rho t} dt$$

subject to the constraints

$$\dot{S}_t = -R_t$$

$$\dot{A}_t = M(R_t) - \alpha A_t - F(V_t)$$

$$\dot{K}_t = Q(K_t, R_t, E(R_t, A_t)) - C_t - \Gamma(R_t) - V_t$$

As shown in Table 16.1, there are three state variables in this problem: S_t, the resource stock at time t; A_t, the level of ambient pollution stock at time t; and K_t, the capital stock at time t. Associated with each state variable is a shadow price, P (for the resource stock), ω (for the capital stock) and λ (for the ambient pollution stock). Be careful to note that, because we are maximising a utility-based social welfare function, the discount rate being used here is a utility discount rate (not a consumption discount rate) and the shadow prices are denominated in units of utility (not in units of consumption). This should be taken into account when comparing the shadow price of the ambient pollution stock in this chapter (λ) with the shadow price μ used in Chapter 6 (which was measured in consumption units).

In the production function specified by equation 16.4 we assume that $Q_E < 0$ (and also, as before,

Table 16.1 Key variables and prices in the model

Variables ($t = 0, \ldots, \infty$)	
Instrument (control) variables:	
C_t	
R_t	
V_t	
State variables:	Co-state variables (shadow prices) ($t = 0, \ldots, \infty$)
S_t	P_t
K_t	ω_t
A_t	λ_t

$E_R > 0$ and $E_A > 0$). The rate of extraction of environmental resources thus has a direct and an indirect effect upon production. The direct effect is that using more resources increases Q. The indirect effect is that using more resources increases environmental pressures, and so reduces production. The overall effect of R on Q is, therefore, ambiguous and cannot be determined *a priori*.

16.1.6 The optimal solution to the model

The current-valued Hamiltonian is

$$H = U(C_t, E(R_t, A_t)) + P_t(-R_t)$$
$$+ \omega_t(Q[K_t, R_t, E(R_t, A_t)] - C_t - \Gamma(R_t) - V_t)$$
$$+ \lambda_t(M(R_t) - \alpha A_t - F(V_t))$$

Ignoring time subscripts, the necessary conditions for a social welfare maximum are:[2]

$$\frac{\partial H}{\partial C} = U_C - \omega = 0$$

$$\frac{\partial H}{\partial R} = U_E E_R - P + \omega Q_R + \omega Q_E E_R - \omega \Gamma_R + \lambda M_R$$

$$= 0$$

$$\frac{\partial H}{\partial V} = -\omega - \lambda F_V = 0$$

$$\dot{P} = -\frac{\partial H}{\partial S} + \rho P \Leftrightarrow \dot{P} = \rho P$$

$$\dot{\omega} = -\frac{\partial H}{\partial K} + \rho \omega \Leftrightarrow \dot{\omega} = \rho \omega - Q_K \omega$$

$$\dot{\lambda} = -\frac{\partial H}{\partial A} + \rho \lambda$$
$$\Leftrightarrow \dot{\lambda} = \rho \lambda + \alpha \lambda - U_E E_A - \omega Q_E E_A$$

These can be rewritten as:

$$U_C = \omega \tag{16.8a}$$

$$P = U_E E_R + \omega Q_R + \omega Q_E E_R - \omega \Gamma_R + \lambda M_R \tag{16.8b}$$

$$\omega = -\lambda F_V \tag{16.8c}$$

$$\dot{P} = \rho P \tag{16.8d}$$

$$\dot{\omega} = \rho \omega - Q_K \omega \tag{16.8e}$$

$$\dot{\lambda} = \rho \lambda + \alpha \lambda - U_E E_A - \omega Q_E E_A \tag{16.8f}$$

16.1.7 Interpreting the solution

Three of these first-order conditions for an optimal solution – Equations 16.8a, 16.8d and 16.8e – have interpretations essentially the same as those we offered in Chapter 14. No further discussion of them is warranted here, except to note that equation 16.8d is a Hotelling dynamic efficiency condition for the resource net price, which can be written as:

$$\frac{\dot{P}}{P} = \rho$$

Provided that the utility discount rate is positive, this implies that the resource net price must always grow at a positive rate. Note that the ambient pollution level does not affect the growth rate of the resource net price.

Three conditions appear that we have not seen before, equations 16.8b, 16.8c and 16.8f. The last of these is a dynamic efficiency condition which describes how the shadow price of pollution, λ, must move along an efficient path. As this condition is not central to our analysis, and because obtaining an intuitive understanding of it is difficult, we shall consider it no further. However, some important interpretations can be drawn from equations 16.8b and 16.8c. We now turn to these.

16.1.7.1 The static efficiency condition for the resource net price

Equation 16.8b gives the shadow net price of the environmental resource. It shows that the net price of the environmental resource equals the value of the marginal net product of the environmental resource (that is, ωQ_R, the value of the marginal product less $\omega \Gamma_R$, the value of the extraction costs) minus three kinds of damage cost:

---

[2] We will leave you to verify that these first-order conditions are correct, using the method of the maximum principle explained in Appendix 14.1.

- $U_E E_R$, the loss of utility arising from the impact of a marginal unit of resource use on environmental pressures;
- $\omega Q_E E_R$, the loss of production arising from the impact of a marginal unit of resource use on environmental pressures;
- λM_R the value of the damage arising indirectly from resource extraction and use. This corresponds to what we have called previously stock-damage pollution damage. This 'indirect' damage cost arises because a marginal increase in resource extraction and use results in pollution emissions and then an increase in the ambient pollution level, A. To convert this into value terms, we need to multiply this by a price per unit of ambient pollution.

Note that we have stated that these three forms of damage cost must be *subtracted* from the marginal net product of the environmental resource, even though they are each preceded by an addition symbol in equation 16.8b. This can be verified by noting that U_E and Q_E are each negative, as is the shadow price λ_t, given that ambient pollution is a 'bad' rather than a 'good' and so will have a negative price.

In a competitive market economy, none of these pollution damage costs will be internalised – they are not paid by whoever it is that generates them. This has implications for efficient and optimal pollution policy. A pollution control agency could set a tax rate per unit of resource extracted equal to the value of marginal pollution damages, $U_E E_R + \omega Q_E E_R + \lambda M_R$.

The nature of the required tax is shown more clearly in Figures 16.2 and 16.3. To interpret these diagrams, it will be convenient to rearrange equation 16.8b to:

$$\omega Q_R = P + \omega \Gamma_R - U_E E_R - \omega Q_E E_R - \lambda M_R$$

We can read this as saying that:

Gross price = net price + extraction cost + value of flow damage operating on utility + value of flow damage operating on production + value of stock damage

Figure 16.2 can be interpreted in the following way. In a perfectly functioning market economy

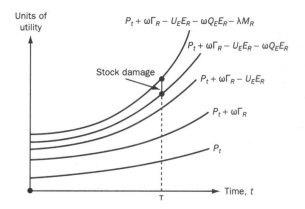

Figure 16.2 Optimal time paths for the variables of the pollution model

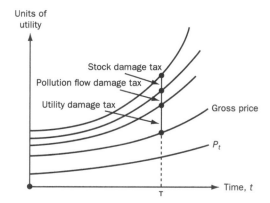

Figure 16.3 Optimal 'three-part' pollution taxes

with no market failure, in which all costs and benefits are fully and correctly incorporated in market prices, the gross (or market) price of the resource would follow a path through time indicated by the uppermost curve in the diagram. We can distinguish several different cost components of this *socially optimal* gross price:

1. the net price of the resource (the rent that must be paid to the resource owner to persuade him or her to extract the resource);
2. the marginal cost of extracting the resource;
3. the marginal pollution damage cost. This consists of three different types of damage:
   - pollution flow damage operating through the utility function;
   - pollution flow damage operating through the production function;

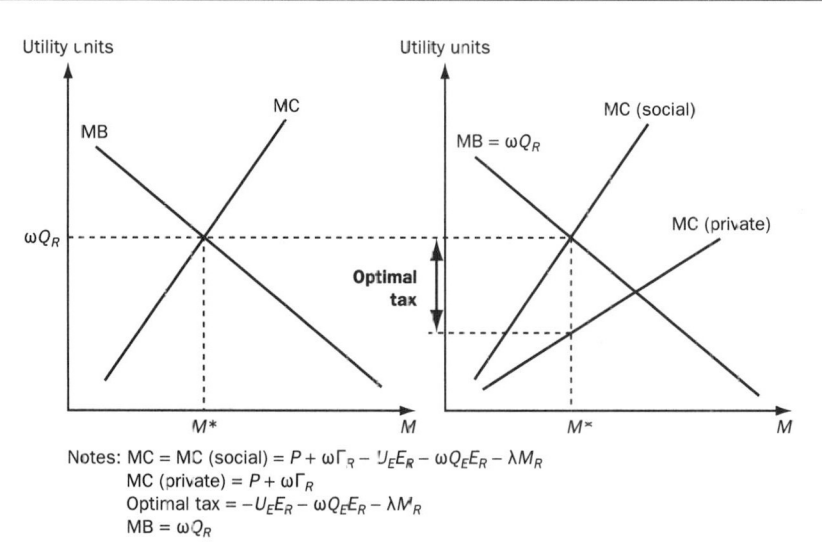

Notes: MC = MC (social) = $P + \omega\Gamma_R - U_E E_R - \omega Q_E E_R - \lambda M_R$
MC (private) = $P + \omega\Gamma_R$
Optimal tax = $-U_E E_R - \omega Q_E E_R - \lambda M_R$
MB = ωQ_R

Figure 16.4 Optimal taxes and the wedge between private and social costs

- pollution stock damage (which in our model can work through both production and utility functions).

However, in a competitive market economy where damage costs are not internalised and so do not enter firms' cost calculations, the market price will not include the pollution damage components, and so would not be equal to the gross price just described. The market price would only include two components: the net price (or resource royalty) and the marginal extraction cost. It would then be given by the curve drawn second from the bottom in Figure 16.2.

But now suppose that government were to introduce a socially optimal tax in order to bring market prices into line with the socially optimal gross price. It is now easy to see what such a tax would consist of. The tax should be set at a rate equal in value (per unit of resource) to the sum of the three forms of damage cost, thereby internalising the damages arising from resource use. We could regard this tax as a single pollution tax, or we might think of it as a three-part tax (one on utility flow damages, one on production flow damages and one on stock damages). Such an interpretation is shown in Figure 16.3. The three-part tax has the advantage that it shows clearly what the government has to calculate in order to arrive at a socially optimal tax rate.

Figure 16.4 shows this interpretation of the optimal tax rate in terms of a 'wedge' between the private and the social marginal costs. As you can see from the notes that accompany the diagram, the private marginal cost is given by $P + \omega\Gamma_R$. The optimal tax is set equal to the marginal value of the three damage costs. When imposed on firms, the wedge between private and social marginal costs is closed. Be careful to note, however, that Figure 16.4 can only be true at one point in time. We know that all the components of costs change over time, and so the functions shown in the diagram will be shifting as well.

16.1.7.2 Efficiency in defensive expenditure

The necessary conditions for a solution of our pollution problem include one equation, equation 16.8c, that concerns defensive expenditure, $\omega = -\lambda F_V$. To understand this condition, let us recall the meanings of its terms. First, the variable ω is the shadow price of capital; it is the amount of utility lost when one unit of output is diverted from consumption (or investment in capital) to be used for defensive expenditure. Be careful to note that these values are being measured at the optimal solution. That is, it is the amount of utility lost when output is diverted to pollution clean-up when consumption and clean-up are already at their socially optimal levels.[3] You can imagine that finding out what these values are going to be is a very difficult task indeed; this is a matter we shall return to shortly.

Second, λ is the optimal value of one unit of ambient pollution; remember that this is a negative quantity, as pollution is harmful. Third, F_V is the amount of pollution stock clean-up from an additional unit of defensive expenditure.

Putting these pieces together, we can deduce the meaning of equation 16.8c. The right-hand side, $-\lambda F_V$, is the utility value gained from pollution clean-up when one unit of output is used for defensive expenditure. This must be set equal to the value of utility lost by reducing consumption (or investment) by one unit. Put in another way, the optimal amount of pollution clean-up expenditure will be the level at which the marginal costs and the marginal benefits of clean-up are equal.

16.2   A complication: variable decay of the pollution stock

Throughout this chapter, we have assumed that the proportionate rate of natural decay of the pollution stock, α, is constant. Although a larger amount of decay will take place the greater is the size of the pollution stock, the proportion that naturally decays is unaffected by the pollution stock size (or by anything else). This assumption is very commonly employed in environmental economics analysis.

However, this assumption is usually made for convenience and analytical simplicity. Whether it is reasonable or not depends on the problem under study. Often it will not be reasonable, because the rate of decay changes over time, or depends on the size of the pollution stock. Of particular importance are the existence of threshold effects, irreversibilities, and time lags in flows between various environmental media (as with greenhouse gases). For an example of threshold effects and irreversibilities, consider river pollution. At some threshold level of biological oxygen demand (BOD) on a river, the

decay rate of a pollutant may collapse to zero. An irreversibility exists if the decay rate of the pollutant in the environmental medium remains below its previous levels even when the pollutant stock falls below the threshold level. An irreversibility implies some hysteresis in the environmental system: the history of pollutant flows matters, and reversing pollution pressures does not bring one back to the *status quo ex ante*.

Another way of thinking about this issue is in terms of carrying capacities (or assimilative capacities, as they are sometimes called) of environmental media. In the case of water pollution, for example, we can think of a water system as having some pollution-assimilative capacity. This enables the system to carry and to continuously transform some proportion of these pollutants into harmless forms through physical or biological process. Our model has in effect assumed unlimited carrying capacities: no matter how large the load on the system, more can always be transformed at a constant proportionate rate.

Whether this assumption is plausible is, in the last resort, an empirical question. However, there are good reasons to believe that it is not plausible for many types of pollution. Where the assumption is grossly invalid, it will be necessary to respecify the pollutant stock–flow relationship in an appropriate way. Box 16.1 illustrates how one important climate change model – the RICE-99 model of Nordhaus and Boyer (1999) – deals with variable decay rates of atmospheric greenhouse gases. Suggestions for further reading at the end of this chapter point you to some literature that explores models with variable pollution-decay rates.

16.3   Steady-state outcomes

In some of the previous chapters, we have examined steady-state outcomes – equilibria in which the levels of variables of interest are unchanging through time. Is the notion of a steady state useful, or even meaningful, in the context of the modelling

---

[3] The reason why we can use the value lost by diverting expenditure from either consumption or investment follows from this point: at the social optimum, the value of an incremental unit of consumption will be identical to the value of an incremental unit of investment. They will not be equal away from such an optimum.

Box 16.1 Decay rates for greenhouse gases in the RICE-99 model

In early versions of Nordhaus's climate change models, the GHG emissions–concentrations relationship adopted an extended form of equation 16.7, although without the $F(V)$ term being present. Estimates of the decay rate parameters were obtained from historical data on M and A. Notice that in equation 16.7 (and other similar expressions) a clear distinction is drawn between stocks and flows: A is a stock of accumulated pollutants, measured in units of mass at some point in time; M is a flow of pollutant emissions, measured in units of mass per period of time.

A problem with this approach when it comes to climate change modelling is that a constant decay rate parameter implies that the deep oceans are an infinite sink for carbon, which does not appear to be consistent with either theory or evidence.

RICE-99 (see Box 16.2) uses a structural approach to the model GHG decay rates, based on current thinking about the carbon cycle. There are three reservoirs for carbon in the model: (i) the atmosphere; (ii) the upper oceans and biosphere; and (iii) the deep oceans. Carbon emissions, labelled ET in the equations below, enter the atmosphere reservoir. There are exchanges of carbon mass (the various M terms on the right-hand sides of the equations below) between the three reservoirs. Some carbon flows from the atmosphere to the upper oceans/ biosphere, and some flows in the opposite direction. These flows need not be equal (and indeed would only be equal in a steady-state equilibrium of the system). A two-way flow relationship also exists between the upper oceans/biosphere and the deep oceans. Two-way mixing also takes place between the upper oceans/biosphere and the deep oceans but is

very slow. There is, though, no direct interchange of carbon mass between the atmosphere and the deep oceans, although the structure of the model implies that some carbon emissions are indirectly taken up by deep oceans. The model equations also have the property that the deep oceans provide a finite – rather than an infinite – sink for carbon in the long term. This has important implications for climate change modelling.

Carbon flows within and between the sinks are given by the following three equations, in which M denotes carbon mass (*not* emissions, which are notated as ET), and the subscripts AT, UP and LO denote the atmosphere, upper oceans/ biosphere, and lower (deep) oceans respectively.[4] Note that in this three-box carbon cycle model, not only are all the terms denoted by the letter M stocks (being measured in mass units) *but so too are 'emissions'*. The term 'emissions' is, therefore, being used by Nordhaus and Boyer here in a different way than in the rest of this chapter, where they are treated as a flow variable.

$$M_{AT}(t) = 10 \times ET(t) + \phi_{11}M_{AT}(t-1) - \phi_{12}M_{AT}(t-1) + \phi_{21}M_{UP}(t-1)$$

$$M_{UP}(t) = \phi_{22}M_{UP}(t-1) + \phi_{12}M_{AT}(t-1) - \phi_{21}M_{UP}(t-1) + \phi_{32}M_{LO}(t-1) - \phi_{23}M_{UP}(t-1)$$

$$M_{LO}(t) = \phi_{33}M_{LO}(t-1) - \phi_{32}M_{LO}(t-1) + \phi_{23}M_{UP}(t-1)$$

It is evident by inspection of this system of dynamic equations that it does not specify a constant decay rate of *atmospheric* GHGs (whether that is measured in proportionate or absolute terms).[5] Chapter 3 of Nordhaus and Boyer (1999) explains how these equations are parameterised from existing carbon cycle models.

---

[4]   See equations 2.13a–2.13c in Nordhaus and Boyer (1999), p. 2–24, electronic manuscript version.
[5]   To verify this, just consider the role played by the final term in the first of the three equations.

framework we have been examining? In the rest of this section, we show that it is *not* a meaningful concept if the optimising model used above is used to think about policy over indefinitely long spans of time. In that case, some attention must be paid to renewable resources too, and a steady state can only make sense where those resources are brought into consideration.

However, one may object in principle to the use of optimal growth models for policy analysis when major pollution problems are the object of concern, perhaps arguing that policy should be constrained by some form of precautionary principle (see Chapter 6). For example, in thinking about the greenhouse effect, using the precautionary principle suggests that the policy maker should try and identify what kinds of

Box 16.2 Nordhaus: DICE and RICE models of global warming

During the last fifteen years, Nordhaus – with various collaborators – has been developing a suite of integrated economic–scientific models of global warming. The most recent version, the RICE-99 model, is described in Nordhaus and Boyer (1999). This model is publicly accessible; Nordhaus's personal web site (at www.econ.yale.edu/~nordhaus/homepage/homepage.htm) contains links to the full electronic version of the book, together with versions of the model programmed in GAMS and in Excel. The latter is relatively easy to use.

RICE (Regional Integrated model of Climate and the Economy) employs an optimal growth modelling framework, augmented by the addition of an environmental sector. As in all optimal growth models, choices essentially concern a trade-off between consumption today and in the future. GHG emissions control reduces current consumption but increases future consumption. Optimisation is used to manage this trade-off to maximise social welfare. In this respect, RICE is broadly similar in structure to the optimal growth model we developed in Section 16.1. Table 16.2 shows the similarity between RICE and the model you examined earlier, and notes several of the particular characteristics of the RICE model.

Not only is RICE an operational, empirically parameterised model, but also it is far more richly developed than the simple, stylised model we developed earlier. As its name implies RICE is regionally disaggregated. The world is composed of 13 large sovereign countries or groups of countries. Each 'country' selects values of the control variables – consumption, investment in tangible capital, and climate investment (GHG reduction) to maximise a utilitarian intertemporal social welfare function subject to relevant economic and technological constraints. Utility is discounted at a positive pure rate of time preference, which is assumed to decline over time (due to decreasing impatience) from 3% per year in 1995 to 1.8% in 2200. Global social welfare is a population-weighted sum of individual country per capita social welfares.

Table 16.2 A comparison between the RICE model and the dynamic pollution model of Section 16.1

Component	Model in Section 16.1	RICE-99
Objective function	$$W = \int_{t=0}^{t=\infty} U(C_t, E(R_t, A_t))e^{-\rho t}dt$$	RICE has a similar objective function. Differences and specifics: Discrete time model; no environmental degradation index term (E) enters utility function; RICE has a global objective function which aggregates over regions. Specifically, objective function is a discounted sum of population-weighted sum of utility of per capita consumption. Logarithmic form of utility function embodies assumption of diminishing valuation of consumption as consumption rises. Utility discount rate falls over time.
Control (instrument) variables	C_t, R_t and V_t for $t = 0, \ldots, \infty$	RICE does not deal with defensive expenditure as such.
Resource stock constraint	$\dot{S}_t = -R_t$	RICE recognises the finiteness of fossil-fuel stocks. A carbon supply curve describes the availability of carbon fuels at rising marginal costs. As stocks are increasingly depleted, price rises along a Hotelling-type path over time.
Pollution stock–flow relationship	$\dot{A}_t = M(R_t) - \alpha A_t - F(V_t)$	RICE does not deal with defensive expenditure as such, nor does it assume a constant decay parameter (see Box 16.1).
Production function	$Q_t = Q(K_t, R_t, E(R_t, A_t))$	RICE does not include E in function, but labour (= population) is specified as an input. Production function is constant returns to scale, Cobb–Douglas form. Population growth is exogenous. Exogenous technological change has two forms, economy-wide and energy-saving.
Capital accumulation	$\dot{K}_t = Q_t - C_t - \Gamma(R_t) - V_t$	

Box 16.2 *continued*

RICE consists of two main sectors: a (relatively conventional) economic sector, and a geophysical sector (which embodies climate change modelling). In RICE's economic sector, each country is endowed with initial stocks of capital, labour and region-specific technology. Capital and labour, together with a composite 'carbon energy' resource, are inputs in each economy's production function. The carbon energy resource is in finite supply, and becomes available at a rising marginal cost. Using the carbon energy resource generates CO_2 emissions as a joint product. The production function is calibrated against data on energy use, energy prices and energy-use elasticities. This generates an empirically based CO_2 marginal abatement cost function.

The geophysical component of RICE consists of simplified versions of current best-practice climate science. It contains a three-box carbon cycle (see Box 16.1); a radiative forcing equation; climate change equations; and climate damage relationships. The global impact is derived by aggregation of regional impact estimates. The latter include market, non-market and potential catastrophic impacts.

Policy analysis

To undertake policy analysis, RICE can be used to simulate the effects of policy makers imposing a carbon tax or issuing tradable emissions permits, under a variety of assumptions about whether tax rates are equal, and whether emissions trading is allowed, between alternative configurations of blocs of countries. A country-specific carbon-tax rate can also be interpreted as the price of a carbon emission permit in that country. A uniform rate of carbon tax over all countries is equivalent to a system of marketable permits in which trading is allowed between all countries. RICE also allows permit trading to take place within blocs, so that the carbon tax (permit price) is equalised within a bloc. Setting the carbon tax at zero yields the Reference or Baseline case. With these various configurations of policy instruments, RICE can be used to analyse the relative costs and benefits of a wide

variety of possible global warming policies. In particular, a Pareto optimal policy (inducing the economically efficient level of emissions) can be achieved *either* (a) by setting a uniform carbon tax in every country equal to the global environmental shadow price of carbon – that being the present value of all future consumption reductions in all regions of one unit of carbon emissions today, *or* (b) by distributing to each country permits equal to the quantity of emissions they would produce if the Pareto optimal tax were imposed.

Major results

1. The Reference case is used to simulate the consequences of climate change where no action is taken by policy makers to reduce global warming. Nordhaus finds that impacts differ sharply between regions. Russia and some high-income countries (principally Canada) will benefit slightly from a modest global warming. Low-income countries – particularly African and India – appear to be quite vulnerable to climate change. For example, regional impacts of a 2.5 degrees C global warming ranges from a net benefit of 0.7% of output for Russia to damage of 5% of output for India.

2. RICE can be used to compare the relative efficiency of different approaches to climate change policy. A path that limits CO_2 concentrations to no more than a doubling of pre-industrial levels is close to the 'optimal' or efficient policy. Current approaches – such as that in the Kyoto Protocol – are highly inefficient, with abatement costs approximately ten times their benefits in avoided damages.

3. Investigating the role of carbon taxes (as a measure of the stringency of global warming policy) gives the optimal carbon price in the range $5 to $10 per ton of carbon. Kyoto policy targets yield carbon taxes close to $100 per ton. These fail a cost–benefit test because they impose excessive near-term abatement.

See also Table 10.9 in Chapter 10.

---

states are acceptable in terms of avoiding risks of catastrophic climate change. Such states might be defined in terms of maximum allowable global mean temperature levels, or perhaps (less directly) in terms of maximum allowable GHG concentration rates. Much

of the current discussion about the greenhouse effect is couched in this kind of framework – particularly about what GHG concentration rates are acceptable.

Article 2 of the United Nations Framework Convention on Climate Change (UNFCCC) states that

'The ultimate objective of this convention . . . is to achieve . . . stabilization of GHG concentrations in the atmosphere at a level that would prevent dangerous anthropogenic interference with the climate system'.[6] There is no consensus as to what this level is, nor perhaps could there be, given the judgement that inevitably must surround the word 'dangerous'. When global warming first began to attract the attention of policy analysts, many scientists implicitly took stabilisation of atmospheric concentrations at the then current levels as the appropriate target, and posed the question of what level of GHG emissions reduction would be required to achieve this. Not surprisingly, the answer given to this question typically suggested massive reductions in emissions. It soon became clear that stabilisation at current concentration rates was politically infeasible, and probably economically indefensible. A widely held opinion among natural and physical scientists today is that the target should be set at twice the pre-industrial concentration (i.e. at 560 ppm of CO_2 or 1190 GtC in the atmosphere). Many climate-change research teams have employed this value for one of the scenarios they have investigated. As we mentioned in Box 16.2, Nordhaus's RICE model simulations suggest that this is close to an optimal target.

16.3.1 Is a steady state meaningful in our current model?

For the pollution model we have just been studying, however, the notion of a steady state is logically inconsistent and so not meaningful. No constant positive quantity of a non-renewable resource can be extracted indefinitely, given the limited stock size. The only constant amount that could be used indefinitely is zero. That case is of no interest in our model as it stands. For if R were zero, production would be using produced capital as the sole input. That is at odds with the laws of thermodynamics: unless the capital itself were consumed in the process of production, it implies that physical output could be produced without using any physical inputs, which is clearly impossible.

It is evident that production cannot rely forever only on the use of non-renewable resources. At some point in time it will be necessary to make use of renewable resources as productive inputs. This points us to a way in which the model investigated above should be extended if it is to be useful for very long-term analysis. And as we shall see, it also leads to the notion of a steady state being a meaningful and relevant concept.

To fix ideas, let us return to the example of using fossil fuels as a non-renewable resource input. Fossil fuels cannot be used for ever. Eventually one of three things must happen. Stocks will become completely exhausted; or the price of fossil fuels will rise so high as to make them uneconomic (in which case the economically relevant stock becomes zero); or the pollution consequences of using fossil fuels will become intolerable, and we will be forced to cease using them. In each of these cases, production will switch from the non-renewable to a renewable resource input. If a steady state is ever attained, it would be one in which the renewable resource is used at a constant rate through time.

That suggests that we should generalise the model specified above so that the production function is of the form $Q = Q(R_1, R_2, K, E)$ where R_1 and R_2 denote non-renewable and renewable natural resources respectively. The index of environmental pressures, E, may depend on R_2 as well as on R_1. We leave it to you as an exercise to investigate how the model we have been examining could be generalised in this way, and what its steady state would be. A possible answer is provided in the file *Enlarged model.doc* in the *Additional Materials* for Chapter 16.

16.4   A model of waste accumulation and disposal

In this section, we investigate efficient emissions targets for stock pollutants where it is not necessary to take account of resource constraints in the way we did in Section 16.2. Ignoring such constraints may be appropriate where pollution derives from

---

[6]   The full wording of the Convention can be found at http://unfccc.int.

the extraction and use of some resource on a scale sufficiently small that resource stock constraints are not binding. We might call these 'local' models of stock pollution. They are typically much less highly aggregated than those previously studied. Examples include models of pollution associated with the use of nitrates in agricultural chemicals, with discharges of toxic substances and radioactive substances, and with various forms of groundwater and marine water contamination.

The models we are looking at here are best thought of as examples of partial equilibrium cost–benefit analysis, albeit in a dynamic modelling framework. Because variables are now being measured in monetary (or consumption unit) terms, rather than in utility units, the appropriate rate of discount is now r rather than ρ. We shall pay particular attention to the economically efficient steady-state model outcome. Box 16.3 lays out the problem we shall be considering and the first-order conditions for its solution.

16.4.1 The steady state

In a steady state, all variables are constant over time and so $d\mu/dt$ is zero. Time subscripts are no longer necessary. The two first-order conditions become

$$\frac{dB}{dM} = -\mu \tag{16.13}$$

$$\frac{dD}{dA} = -(r + \alpha)\mu \tag{16.14}$$

Also, in a steady state the pollution-stock differential equation

$$\frac{dA_t}{dt} = M_t - \alpha A_t$$

collapses to

$$M = \alpha A \tag{16.15}$$

Equation 16.14 can also be written as

$$-\mu = \frac{\dfrac{dD}{dA}}{r + \alpha} \tag{16.16}$$

The variable μ is the shadow price of one unit of pollutant emissions. It is equal to the marginal social

---

Box 16.3 The local stock pollution model

The problem

The objective is to choose a sequence of pollutant emission flows, M_t, $t = 0$ to $t = \infty$, to maximise

$$\int_{t=0}^{t=\infty} (B(M_t) - D(A_t))e^{-rt}dt$$

subject to

$$\frac{dA_t}{dt} = M_t - \alpha A_t \tag{16.9}$$

$A_0 = A(0)$, a non-negative constant

$M_t \geq 0$

Optimisation conditions

The current-valued Hamiltonian for this problem is

$$H_t = B(M_t) - D(A_t) + \mu_t(M_t - \alpha A_t) \tag{16.10}$$

The necessary first-order conditions for a maximum (assuming an interior solution) include:

$$\frac{\partial H_t}{\partial M_t} = 0 \Rightarrow \frac{dB_t}{dM_t} + \mu_t = 0 \tag{16.11}$$

$$\frac{d\mu}{dt} = r\mu_t - \frac{\partial H_t}{\partial A_t} = r\mu_t + \frac{dD}{dA_t} + \alpha\mu_t \tag{16.12}$$

---

value of a unit of emissions at a social net benefits maximum. As pollution is a bad, not a good, the shadow price, μ, will be negative (and so $-\mu$ will be positive).

The conditions 16.13 and 16.16 say that two things have to be equal to $-\mu$ at a net benefit maximum. Therefore those two things must be equal to one another. Combining those conditions we obtain:

$$\frac{dB}{dM} = \frac{\dfrac{dD}{dA}}{r + \alpha} \tag{16.17}$$

Equation 16.17 is one example of a familiar marginal condition for efficiency: in this case, an efficient solution requires that the present value of net benefit of a marginal unit of pollution equals the present value of the loss in future net benefit that arises from the marginal unit of pollution. However, it is quite tricky to get this interpretation from equation 16.17, so we shall take you through it in steps.

The term on the left-hand side of equation 16.17 is the increase in *current* net benefit that arises when the rate of emissions is allowed to rise by one unit. This marginal benefit takes place in the current period only. In contrast, the right-hand side of equation 16.17 is the present value of the loss in future net benefit that arises when the output of the pollutant is allowed to rise by one unit. Note that dD/dA itself lasts for ever; it is a form of perpetual annuity (although an annuity with a negative effect on utility). To obtain the present value of an annuity, we divide its annual flow, dD/dA, by the relevant discount rate, which in this case is r. The reason why we *also* divide the annuity by α is because of the ongoing decay process of the pollutant. If the pollutant stock were allowed to rise, then the amount of decay in steady state will also rise by a proportion α of that increment in the stock size. This reduces the magnitude of the damage. Note that α acts in an equivalent way to the discount rate. The greater is the rate of decay, the larger is the 'effective' discount rate applied to the annuity and so the smaller is its present value.

For the purpose of looking at some special cases of equation 16.17, it will be convenient to rearrange that expression as follows:

$$\frac{dD}{dA} = \frac{dB}{dM}\alpha + \frac{dB}{dM}r \tag{16.18}$$

and so

$$\frac{dD}{dA}\frac{1}{\alpha} = \frac{dB}{dM} + \frac{dB}{dM}\frac{r}{\alpha} \tag{16.19}$$

Given that in steady state $A = (1/\alpha)M$, then from the damage function $D = D(A)$, and using the chain rule of differentiation, we can write

$$\frac{dD}{dM} = \frac{dD}{dA}\cdot\frac{dA}{dM} = \frac{dD}{dA}\frac{1}{\alpha}$$

This allows us to write equation 16.19 as

$$\frac{dD}{dM} = \frac{dB}{dM} + \frac{dB}{dM}\frac{r}{\alpha}$$

or

$$\frac{dD}{dM} = \frac{dB}{dM}\left(1 + \frac{r}{\alpha}\right) \tag{16.20}$$

If we knew the values of the parameters α and r, and the functions dB/dA and dD/dM (or dD/dA, from which dD/dM could be derived for any given value of α), equation 16.20 could be solved for the numerical steady-state solution value of M, M^*. Then from the relationship $A = (1/\alpha)M$ the steady-state solution for A is obtained, A^*.

Four special cases of equation 16.20 can be obtained, depending on whether $r = 0$ or $r > 0$, and on whether $\alpha = 0$ or $\alpha > 0$. These were laid out in Table 6.4 in Chapter 6. We briefly summarise here our earlier conclusions.

Case A: $r = 0$, $\alpha > 0$

Given that $\alpha > 0$, the pollutant is imperfectly persistent and eventually decays to a harmless form. With $r = 0$, no discounting of costs and benefits is being undertaken. Equation 16.20 collapses to:[7]

$$\frac{dD}{dM} = \frac{dB}{dM} \tag{16.21}$$

An efficient steady-state rate of emissions for a stock pollutant requires that the contribution to benefits from a marginal unit of pollution flow be equal to the contribution to damage from a marginal unit of pollution flow. We can also write this expression as

$$\frac{dD}{dA}\frac{1}{\alpha} = \frac{dB}{dM} \tag{16.22}$$

which says that the contribution to damage of a marginal unit of emissions flow should be set equal to the damage caused by an additional unit of ambient pollutant stock divided by α.

---

[7] We can arrive at this result another way. Recall that $NB(M) = B(M) - D(A)$. Maximisation of net benefits requires that the following first-order condition is satisfied: $dNB/dM = dB/dM - dD/dM = 0$. Differentiating (using the chain rule in the damage function) and then rearranging, we obtain $dB/dM = (1/\alpha)(dD/dA) = dD/dM$.

Case C: $r > 0$, $\alpha > 0$

Equation 16.20 remains unchanged here:

$$\frac{dD}{dM} = \frac{dB}{dM}\left(1 + \frac{r}{\alpha}\right)$$

The marginal equality we noted in Case A remains true but in an amended form (to reflect the presence of discounting at a positive rate). Discounting, therefore, increases the steady-state level of emissions. Intuitively, the reason it does so is because a larger value of r reduces the present value of the future damages that are associated with the pollutant stock. In effect, higher weighting is given to present benefits relative to future costs the larger is r. However, the shadow price of one unit of the pollutant emissions becomes larger as r increases.

Cases B ($r > 0$, $\alpha = 0$) and D ($r = 0$, $\alpha = 0$)

Given that $\alpha = 0$, cases B and D are each one in which the pollutant is perfectly persistent – the pollutant does not decay to a harmless form. No positive and finite steady-state level of emissions can be efficient. The only possible steady-state level of emissions is zero. If emissions were positive, the stock would increase without bound, and so stock-pollution damage would rise to infinity. The steady-state equilibrium solution for any value of r when $\alpha = 0$, therefore, gives zero pollution. The pollution stock level in that steady state will be whatever level A had risen to by the time the steady state was first achieved, say time T. Pollution damage continues indefinitely, but no additional damage is being caused in any period.

This is a very strong result – any activity generating perfectly persistent pollutants that lead to any positive level of damage cannot be carried on indefinitely. At some finite time in the future, a technology switch is required so that the pollutant is not emitted. If that is not possible, the activity itself must cease. Note that even though a perfectly persistent pollutant has a zero natural decay rate, policy makers may be able to find some technique by which the pollutant may be artificially reduced. This is known as clean-up expenditure. We examined this possibility in Section 16.1.4.

16.4.2 Dynamics

The previous subsection outlined the nature of the steady-state solution to the local stock pollution model. However, without some form of policy intervention, it is very unlikely that variables will actually be at their optimal steady-state levels. How could the policy maker 'control' the economy to move it from some arbitrary initial position to its optimal steady state?

To answer this question, we need to carry out some analysis of the dynamics of the model solution. Our interest is with the dynamics of the state variable (A_t) and the instrument or control variable (M_t) in our problem. Specifically, we are looking for two differential equations of the form:

$$\frac{dA}{dt} = f(A, M)$$

$$\frac{dM}{dt} = g(A, M)$$

We already have the first of these – it is given by equation 16.9, the pollution stock–flow relationship. To obtain the second of this pair of differential equations we proceed as follows. First, take the time derivative of equation 16.11, yielding:

$$\frac{d\mu}{dt} = -\left(\frac{d^2 B}{dM^2}\right)\frac{dM}{dt} \tag{16.23}$$

Then substituting equation 16.23 into equation 16.12 we have:

$$(r + \alpha)\mu + \frac{dD}{dA} = -\left(\frac{d^2 B}{dM^2}\right)\frac{dM}{dt} \tag{16.24}$$

Finally, substituting equation 16.11 into equation 16.24 yields the second differential equation we require:[8]

$$\frac{dM}{dt} = \frac{(r + \alpha)\left(\dfrac{dB}{dM}\right) - \dfrac{dD}{dA}}{\dfrac{d^2 B}{dM^2}} \tag{16.25}$$

The differential equations 16.25 and 16.9 will provide the necessary information from which the

---

8 Notice that D and B are functions of M or A.

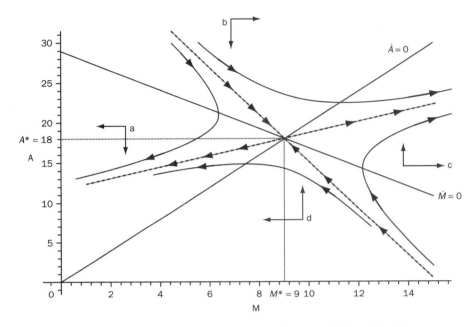

Figure 16.5 Steady-state solution and dynamics of the waste accumulation and disposal model

efficient time paths of $\{M_t, A_t\}$ can be obtained. In the absence of particular functions, the solutions can only be qualitative. However, if we select particular functions and parameter values, then a quantitative solution can be obtained. In the example which follows, we choose the functions and parameter values used earlier in the text, in Box 6.7 of Chapter 6. There we had $\alpha = 0.5$, $r = 0.1$, $D = A^2$ and $B = 96M - 2M^2$, and so $dB/dM = 96 - 4M$, $dD/dA = 2A$ and $dD/dM = 8M$ (in steady state).

It will be convenient to obtain the steady-state solution before finding the dynamic adjustment path. Inserting the function and parameter values given in the previous paragraph into the differential equations 16.9 and 16.25 gives

$$\frac{dA}{dt} = M - 0.5A \qquad (16.9')$$

$$\frac{dM}{dt} = \frac{(0.6)(96 - 4M) - 2A}{-4} = 0.6M + 0.5A - 14.4 \qquad (16.25')$$

In steady state, variables are unchanging through time, so $dA/dt \equiv \dot{A} = 0$ and $dM/dt \equiv \dot{M} = 0$. Imposing these values, and solving the two resulting equations yields $M^* = 9$ and $A^* = 18$ (as we found previously).

This steady-state solution is shown in the 'phase plane' diagram, Figure 16.5. The intersection of the two lines labelled $\dot{A} = 0$ and $\dot{M} = 0$ (which are here $A = 2M$ and $A = (-0.6/0.5)M + 28.8$ from 16.9' and 16.25') gives $M^* = 9$ and $A^* = 18$.

Next, we establish in which direction A and M will move over time from any pair of initial values $\{A_0, M_0\}$. The two lines $\dot{A} = 0$ and $\dot{M} = 0$ (known as isoclines) divide the space into four quadrants. Above the line $\dot{A} = 0$, $A > 2M$, decay exceeds emissions flows, and so A is falling. Conversely, below the line $\dot{A} = 0$, $A < 2M$, decay is less than emissions flows, and so A is rising. These movements are shown by the downward-facing directional arrows in the two quadrants labelled **a** and **b**, and by upward-facing directional arrows in the two quadrants labelled **c** and **d**.

Above the line $\dot{M} = 0$, $0.6M > 14.4 - 0.5A$, and so from equation 16.25' we see that M is rising. Below the line $\dot{M} = 0$, $0.6M < 14.4 - 0.5A$, and so M is falling. These movements are shown by the leftward-facing directional arrows in the two quadrants labelled **a** and **d**, and by rightward-facing directional arrows in the two quadrants labelled **b** and **c**.

Taking these results together we obtain the pairs of direction indicators for movements in A and M for each of the four quadrants when the system is not in steady state. The curved and arrowed lines illustrate four paths that the variables would take from particular initial values. Thus, for example, if the initial values in quadrant **d** with $M = 15$ and $A = 2$, the differential equations which determine A and M would at first cause M to fall and A to rise over time. As this trajectory crosses the $\dot{M} = 0$ isocline into quadrant c, A will continue to rise but now M will also rise too. Left alone, the system would not reach the steady-state optimal solution, diverging ever further from it as time passes.

Inspection of the other three trajectories shows that these also fail to attain the steady-state optimum, and eventually diverge ever further from it. Indeed, there are only two paths which do lead to that optimum. These are shown by the dotted lines whose arrows point towards what is known as the bliss point, together known as the stable arm of the problem. For any dynamic process with a saddle-point equilibrium such as this, the only way of reaching the optimum is for the policy maker to control M so as to reach the stable arm, and then to adjust M accordingly along the stable arm until the bliss point is reached.

From all of this we have the following conclusion. If the initial level of pollution stock lies to the left of the stable arm, emissions should be increased until they reach the level indicated by the stable arm (for that level of pollution stock). The pollution stock will then rise (fall) if A_0 were less (more) than A^*, and the policy maker would need to increase

(decrease) emissions to stay on the stable path until the bliss point was reached.

There are several instruments by means of which the environmental protection agency could control emissions in this way. For example, it could issue quantity regulations (by issue of licences); it could use a marketable permit system; or it could use an emissions tax or abatement subsidy. Note that the regulator will need to keep in mind both the steady-state solution which it wishes to be ultimately achieved, and the transition path to it. For the latter purpose, regulation will typically change in severity over time if an optimal approach to the equilibrium is to be achieved.

In the steady state, the terminal condition (transversality condition) will be satisfied. $A_{t=T} = A^*$ and $M_{t=T} = M^*$. Here $M_t = M_T = \alpha A_T$ so that $dA/dt = 0$, and the pollution stock remains at the steady-state level. The terminal conditions for pollution emissions are $M_T = \alpha A_T$ from equation 16.9 and, from equation 16.17,

$$(r + \alpha) \frac{dB(M_T)}{dM_T} - \frac{dD(A_T)}{dA_T} = 0$$

If the reader would like to see in more detail how these properties can be discovered using a computer software package, we suggest you examine the Maple file *Stock pollution 1.mws*. This file is set up to generate the picture reproduced here as Figure 16.5. For a much more extensive account of the techniques of dynamic analysis using phase-plane diagrams, see the file *Phase.doc*. Both of these are available in the *Additional Materials* for Chapter 16.

Summary

In this chapter we have developed and studied two further models of optimal emissions. Each of these is a variant of the optimal growth modelling framework used before at several places in the text. The two models developed here are appropriate for the specific circumstance in which emissions result in the accumulation of persistent (long-lasting) pollutants. They have the attractive property that choices about resource use and choices about pollution control are brought together in one integrated modelling exercise.

The first of the two models discussed in this chapter has been called an aggregate stock pollution model. This model is particularly useful for dealing with national, international or global pollution problems arising from the extraction or use of fossil fuels, and where the pollutant is long-lasting and accumulates over time. In effect, what we have done within this modelling framework is to show how optimal pollution targets can, at least in principle, be obtained from generalised versions of the resource depletion models we investigated in Chapters 14 and 15. There are, of course, severe practical problems in implementing such models, particularly given the conditions of limited information and uncertainty in which researchers and policy makers must operate.

The second model investigated here – what we termed 'the model of waste accumulation and disposal' – showed how one might think about the setting of emissions targets for various stock pollution problems that are more local, or less pervasive, than those we addressed with the previous model. Examples of these types of problems would include the accumulation of lead in water systems, contamination of water supplies by agricultural pesticide use, and contamination of water systems by effluent discharges.

In all modelling exercises of the kind developed in this chapter, the time dimension is of the essence. Optimal (or merely efficient) pollution targets are not necessarily constant over time, even where flows are unchanging over time. Rather, targets should be specified in terms of paths of emissions (or emissions controls) over some relevant time horizon.

All of this means that dynamics matter. The chapter has shown how dynamic analysis – particularly the use of phase plane diagrams – can provide valuable insights into the analysis of pollution policy.

Further reading

Baumol and Oates (1988) is a classic source in this area, although the analysis is formal and quite difficult. Other useful treatments which complement the discussion in this chapter are Dasgupta (1982, chapter 8) and Smith (1972) which gives a very interesting mathematical presentation of the theory. Several excellent articles can be found in the volume edited by Bromley (1995).

The original references for stock pollution are Plourde (1972) and Forster (1975). Conrad and Olson (1992) apply this body of theory to one case, Aldicarb on Long Island. One of the first studies about the difficulties in designing optimal taxes (and still an excellent read) is Rose-Ackerman (1973). Pezzey (1996) surveys the economic literature on assimilative capacity, and an application can be found in Tahvonen (1995). Forster (1975) analyses a model of stock pollution in which the decay rate is variable.

Some journals provide regular applications of the economic theory of pollution. Of particular interest are the *Journal of Environmental Economics and Management*, *Ambio*, *Environmental and Resource Economics*, *Land Economics*, *Ecological Modelling*, *Marine Pollution Bulletin*, *Ecological Economics* and *Natural Resources Journal*.

Discussion question

1. In what principal ways do stock pollution models differ from models of flow pollutants?

Problem

1. Using equation 11.18, deduce the effect of an increase in α for a given value of r, all other things being equal, on:

(a) M^* (b) A^*

CHAPTER 17

Renewable resources

It will appear, I hope, that most of the problems associated with the words 'conservation' or 'depletion' or 'overexploitation' in the fishery are, in reality, manifestations of the fact that the natural resources of the sea yield no economic rent. Fishery resources are unusual in the fact of their common-property nature; but they are not unique, and similar problems are encountered in other cases of common-property resource industries, such as petroleum production, hunting and trapping, etc.

Gordon (1954)

Learning objectives

After studying this chapter, the reader should be able to
- understand the biological growth function of a renewable resource, and the notions of compensation and depensation in growth processes
- interpret the simple logistic growth model, and some of its variants, including models with critical depensation
- understand the idea of a sustainable yield and the maximum sustainable yield
- distinguish between steady-state outcomes and dynamic adjustment processes that may (or may not) lead to a steady-state outcome
- specify, and solve for its bioeconomic equilibrium outcome, an open-access fishery, a static private-property fishery, and a present value (PV)-maximising fishery
- undertake comparative statics analysis and simple dynamic analysis for open-access and private-property models
- explain under what conditions the stock, effort and harvesting outcomes of private fisheries will not be socially efficient
- describe conditions which increase the likelihood of severe resource depletion or species extinction
- understand the workings, and relative advantages, of a variety of policy instruments that are designed to conserve renewable resource stocks and/or promote socially efficient harvesting

---

Introduction

Environmental resources are described as renewable when they have a capacity for reproduction and growth. The class of renewable resources is diverse. It includes populations of biological organisms such as fisheries and forests which have a natural capa- city for growth, and water and atmospheric systems which are reproduced by physical or chemical processes. While the latter do not possess *biological* growth capacity, they do have some ability to assimilate pollution inputs (thereby maintaining their quality) and, at least in the case of water resources, can self-replenish as stocks are run down (thereby maintaining their quantity).

It is also conventional to classify arable and grazing lands as renewable resources. In these cases reproduction and growth take place by a combination of biological processes (such as the recycling of organic nutrients) and physical processes (irrigation, exposure to wind, etc.). Fertility levels can regenerate naturally so long as the demands made on the soil are not excessive. We may also consider more broadly defined environmental systems (such as wilderness areas or tropical moist forests) as being sets of interrelated renewable resources.

The categories just described are renewable stock resources. A broad concept of renewables would also include flow resources such as solar, wave, wind and geothermal energy. These share with biological stock resources the property that current harnessing of the flow does not mean that the total magnitude of the future flow will necessarily be smaller. Indeed, many forms of energy-flow resources are, for all practical purposes, non-depletable.

Given this diversity of resource types, it will be necessary to restrict what will, and will not, be discussed here. Most of the literature on the economics of renewable resources is about two things: the harvesting of animal species ('hunting and fishing') and the economics of forestry. This chapter is largely concerned with the former; forestry economics is the subject of the following chapter. Agriculture could also be thought of as a branch of renewable resource harvesting. But agriculture – particularly in its more developed forms – differs fundamentally from other forms of renewable resource exploitation in that the environmental medium in which it takes place is designed and controlled. The growing medium is manipulated through the use of inputs such as fertilisers, pesticides, herbicides; temperatures may be controlled by the use of greenhouses and the like; and plant stocks are selected or even genetically modified. In that sense, there is little to differentiate a study of (developed) agricultural economics from the economics of manufacturing. For this reason, we do not survey the huge literature that is 'agricultural economics' in this text, although some of the environmental consequences of agricultural activity are discussed in *Agriculture.doc* in the *Additional Materials*. For reasons of space, we also do not cover the economics of renewable flow resources. Again, a brief outline of some of the main issues is given in *Renewables.doc* in the *Additional Materials*.

It is important to distinguish between stocks and flows of the renewable resource. The stock is a measure of the quantity of the resource existing at a point in time, measured either as the aggregate mass of the biological material (the biomass) in question (such as the total weight of fish of particular age classes or the cubic metres of standing timber), or in terms of population numbers. The flow is the change in the stock over an interval of time, where the change results either from biological factors, such as 'recruitment' of new fish into the population through birth or 'exit' due to natural death, or from harvesting activity.

One similarity between renewable and non-renewable resources is that both are capable of being fully exhausted (that is, the stock being driven to zero) if excessive and prolonged harvesting or extraction activity is carried out. In the case of non-renewable resources, exhaustibility is a consequence of the finiteness of the stock. For renewable resources, although the stock can grow, it can also be driven to zero if conditions interfere with the reproductive capability of the renewable resource, or if rates of harvesting continually exceed net natural growth.

It is evident that enforceable private property rights do not exist for many forms of renewable resource. In the absence of regulation or collective control over harvesting behaviour, the resource stocks are subject to open access. We will demonstrate that open-access resources tend to be overexploited in both a biological and an economic sense, and that the likelihood of the resource being harvested to the point of exhaustion is higher than where private property rights are established and access to harvesting can be restricted.

As we have said, this chapter is principally about the harvesting of animal resources. Our exposition focuses on marine fishing. With some modifications, the fishery economics modelling framework can be used to analyse most forms of renewable resource exploitation. We begin by setting out a simple model of the biological growth of a fish population. Then the properties of commercial fisheries are examined under two sets of institutional arrangements: an open-access fishery and a profit-maximising fishery in which enforceable private property rights exist.

For the case of the private-property fishery, the analysis proceeds in two steps. First we examine what is usually known as the static private-property fishery. The analysis is kept simple by abstracting from the need to deal explicitly with the passage of time. We do this by focusing attention on steady-state (or equilibrium) outcomes in which variables are taken to be unchanging over time. Some unspecified interval of time is chosen to be representative of all periods in that steady state. The equilibrium is found by solving the model for its profit-maximising solution. By construction that equilibrium would apply to every time period, provided that economic and biological conditions remain unchanged.

The second step involves a generalisation in which the passage of time is modelled explicitly. In this case we investigate a private-property fishery that is managed so as to maximise its present value over an infinite lifetime. All nominal-value flows are discounted at some positive rate to convert to present-value equivalents. Describing the second variant as a generalisation of the first is appropriate because – as we shall show – the static private fishery turns out to be a special case of the present-value-maximising fishery in which owners adopt a zero discount rate. Where discounting takes place at some positive rate, the outcomes of the two models differ.

In common with the practice throughout this text, we also examine the outcomes of the various commercial fishery regimes against the benchmark of a *socially efficient* fishery. We demonstrate that under some conditions the harvesting programme of a competitive fishery where private property rights to the resource stocks are established and enforceable will be socially efficient. However, actual resource harvesting regimes are typically not socially efficient, even where attempts have been made to introduce private property rights. Among the reasons why they are not is the existence of various kinds of externalities. Open-access regimes will almost certainly generate inefficient outcomes. The chapter concludes by examining a set of policy instruments

that could be introduced in an attempt to move harvesting behaviour closer to that which is socially efficient.

17.1 Biological growth processes

In order to investigate the economics of a renewable resource, it is first necessary to describe the pattern of biological (or other) growth of the resource. To fix ideas, we consider the growth function for a population of some species of fish. This is conventionally called a fishery. We suppose that this fishery has an intrinsic (or potential) growth rate denoted by g. This is the proportional rate at which the fish stock would grow when its size is small relative to the carrying capacity of the fishery, and so the fish face no significant environmental constraints on their reproduction and survival. The intrinsic growth rate g may be thought of as the difference between the population's birth and natural mortality rate (again, where the population size is small relative to carrying capacity). Suppose that the population stock is S and it grows at a fixed rate g. Then in the absence of human predation the rate of change of the population over time is given by[1]

$$\frac{dS}{dt} \equiv \dot{S} = gS \qquad (17.1)$$

By integrating this equation, we obtain an expression for the stock level at any point in time:

$$S_t = S_0 e^{gt}$$

in which S_0 is the initial stock level. In other words, for a positive value of g, the population grows exponentially over time at the rate g and without bounds. This is only plausible over a short span of time. Any population of fish exists in a particular environmental milieu, with a finite carrying capacity, which sets bounds on the population's growth possibilities.

A simple way of representing this effect is by making the actual (as opposed to the potential)

---

[1] Be careful not to confuse a rate of change with a rate of growth. A rate of change refers to how much extra is produced in some interval of time. A rate of growth is that rate of change divided by its current size (to measure the change in proportionate terms).

Note that we shall sometimes refer to an 'amount of growth' (as opposed to a growth rate); this should be read as the population size change over some interval of time.

growth rate depend on the stock size. Then we have what is called density-dependent growth. Using the symbol χ to denote the actual growth rate, the growth function can then be written as

$$\dot{S} = \chi(S)S$$

where $\chi(S)$ states that χ is a function of S, and shows the dependence of the actual growth rate on the stock size. If this function has the property that the proportionate growth rate of the stock ($\dot{S}/S$) declines as the stock size rises then the function is said to have the property of compensation.

Now let us suppose that under a given set of environmental conditions there is a finite upper bound on the size to which the population can grow (its carrying capacity). We will denote this as S_{MAX}. A commonly used functional form for $\chi(S)$ which has the properties of compensation and a maximum stock size is the simple logistic function:

$$\chi(S) = g\left(1 - \frac{S}{S_{MAX}}\right)$$

in which the constant parameter $g > 0$ is what we have called the intrinsic or potential growth rate of the population. Where the logistic function determines the actual population growth rate, we may therefore write the biological growth function as

$$\dot{S} \equiv \frac{dS}{dt} = g\left(1 - \frac{S}{S_{MAX}}\right)S \qquad (17.2)$$

The changes taking place in the fish population that we have been referring to so far are 'natural' changes. But as we want to use the notation $\dot{S}$ and dS/dt in the rest of this chapter to refer to the *net* effect of natural changes and human predation, we shall use the alternative symbol G to refer to stock changes due only to natural causes. (More completely, we shall use the notation $G(S)$ to make it clear that G depends on S.) With this change the logistic biological growth function is

$$G(S) = g\left(1 - \frac{S}{S_{MAX}}\right)S \qquad (17.3)$$

The logistic form is a good approximation to the natural growth processes of many fish, animal and bird populations (and indeed to some physical systems such as the quantity of fresh water in an underground reservoir). Some additional information on the simple logistic growth model, and alternative forms of logistic growth, is given in Box 17.1. Problem 1 at the end of the chapter also explores the logistic model a little further, and invites you to explore another commonly used equation for biological growth, the Gompertz function.

Box 17.1 The logistic form of the biological growth function

Logistic growth is one example of density-dependent growth: processes where the growth rate of a population depends on the population size. It was first applied to fisheries by Schaefer (1957). The equation for logistic growth of a renewable resource population was given by equation 17.3.

Simple logistic growth is illustrated in Figure 17.1(a), which represents the relationship between the stock size and the associated rate of change of the population due to biological growth. Three properties should be noted by inspection of that diagram.

(a) S_{MAX} is the maximum stock size that can be supported in the environmental milieu. This value is, of course, conditional on the particular environment circumstances that

happen to prevail, and would change if any of those circumstances (such as ocean temperature or stocks of nutrients) change.

(b) By multiplication through of the terms on the right-hand side of equation 17.3, it is clear that the amount of growth, G, is a quadratic function of the resource stock size, S. For the simple logistic function, the maximum amount of growth (S_{MSY}) will occur when the stock size is equal to half of S_{MAX}.

(c) The amount of biological growth G is zero only at a stock size of zero and a stock size of S_{MAX}. For all intermediate values, growth is positive.

This last property may appear to be obviously true, but it turns out to be seriously in error in many cases. It implies that for any population

Box 17.1 *continued*

(a)

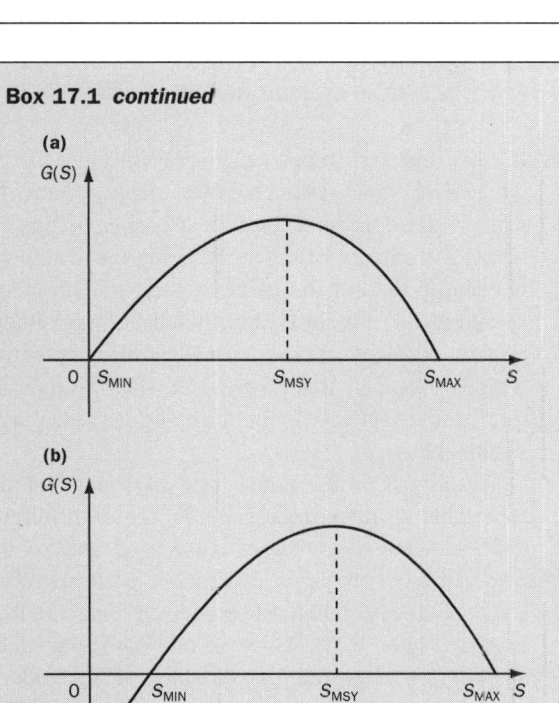

(b)

(c)

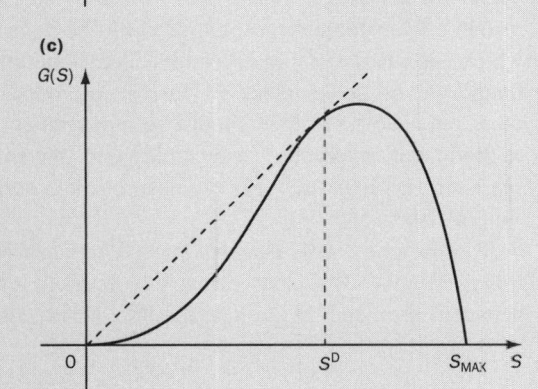

(d)

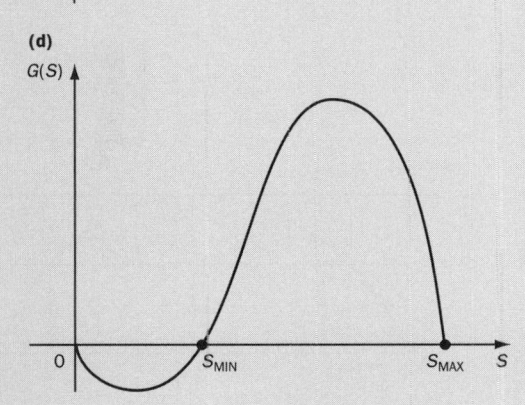

size greater than zero natural growth will lead to a population increase if the system is left undisturbed. In other words, the population does not possess any positive lower threshold level.

However, suppose there is some positive population threshold level, S_{MIN}, such that the population would inevitably and permanently decline to zero if the actual population were ever to fall below that threshold. A simple generalisation of the logistic growth function that has this property is:

$$G(S) = g(S - S_{MIN})\left(1 - \frac{S}{S_{MAX}}\right) \qquad (17.4)$$

Note that if $S_{MIN} = 0$, equation 17.4 collapses to the special case of equation 17.3. The generalisation given by equation 17.4 is illustrated in Figure 17.1(b). Several other generalisations of the logistic growth model exist. For example, the modified logistic model:

$$G(S) = gS^{\alpha}\left(1 - \frac{S}{S_{MAX}}\right)$$

has the property that for $\alpha > 1$ there is, at low stock levels, *depensation*, which is a situation where the proportionate growth rate $(G(S)/S)$ is an increasing function of the stock size, as opposed to being a decreasing function (compensation) in the simple logistic case where $\alpha = 1$. A biological growth function exhibiting depensation at stock levels below S^D (and compensation thereafter) is shown in Figure 17.1(c).

Finally, the generalised logistic function

$$G(S) = g\left(\frac{S}{S_{MIN}} - 1\right)\left(1 - \frac{S}{S_{MAX}}\right)S$$

exhibits what is known as *critical depensation*. As with equation 17.4, the stock falls irreversibly to zero if the stock ever falls below S_{MIN}. This function is represented in Figure 17.1(d). It should be evident that if a growth process does exhibit critical depensation, then the probability of the stock being harvested to complete depletion is increased, and increased considerably if S_{MIN} is a large proportion of S_{MAX}.

Figure 17.1 (a) Simple logistic growth; *(b)* Logistic growth with a minimum population threshold; *(c)* Logistic growth with depensation; *(d)* Logistic growth with critical depensation

17.1.1 The status and role of logistic growth models

The logistic growth model is a stylised representation of the population dynamics of renewable resources. The model is most suited to non-migratory species at particular locations. Among fish species, demersal or bottom-feeding populations of fish such as cod and haddock are well characterised by this model. The populations of pelagic or surface-feeding fish, such as mackerel, are less well explained by the logistic function, as these species exhibit significant migratory behaviour. Logistic growth does not only fit biological growth processes. Brown and McGuire (1967) argue that the logistic growth model can also be used to represent the behaviour of a freshwater stock in an underground reservoir.

However, a number of factors which influence actual growth patterns are ignored in this model, including the age structure of the resource (which is particularly important when considering stocks of long-lived species such as trees or whales) and random or chance influences. At best, therefore, it can only be a good approximation to the true population dynamics.

Judging the logistic model on whether it is the best available at representing any particular renewable resource would be inappropriate for our present purposes. One would not expect to find that biological or ecological modellers would use simple logistic growth functions. They will use more complex growth models designed specifically for particular species in particular contexts. But the needs of the environmental economist differ from those of ecological modellers. The former is willing to trade off some realism to gain simple, tractable models that are reasonably good approximations. It is for this reason that much economic analysis makes use of some version of the logistic growth function

Of more concern, perhaps, is the issue of whether it is appropriate to describe a biological growth process by any purely deterministic equation such those given in Box 17.1. Ecological models typically specify growth as being stochastic, and linked in complex ways to various other processes taking place in more broadly defined ecosystems and subsystems. We shall briefly explore these matters later in the chapter.

17.2 Steady-state harvests

In this chapter, much of our attention will be devoted to steady-state harvests. Here we briefly explain the concept. Consider a period of time in which the amount of the stock being harvested (H) is equal to the amount of net natural growth of the resource (G). Suppose also that these magnitudes remain constant over a sequence of consecutive periods. We call this *steady-state* harvesting, and refer to the (constant) amount being harvested as a *sustainable yield*.

Defining $\dot{S}$ as the actual rate of change of the renewable resource stock, with $\dot{S} = G - H$, it follows that in steady-state harvesting $\dot{S} = 0$ and so the resource stock remains constant over time. What kinds of steady states are feasible? To answer this, look at Figure 17.2. There is one particular stock size (S_{MSY}) at which the quantity of net natural growth is at a maximum (G_{MSY}). If at a stock of S_{MSY} harvest is set at the constant rate H_{MSY}, we obtain a *maximum sustainable yield* (MSY) steady state. A resource management programme could be devised which takes this MSY in perpetuity. It is sometimes thought to be self-evident that a fishery, forest or other renewable resource should be managed so as to produce its maximum sustainable yield. We shall see later that economic theory does not, in general, support this proposition.

H_{MSY} is not the only possible steady-state harvest. Indeed, Figure 17.2 shows that any harvest level between zero and H_{MSY} is a feasible steady-state

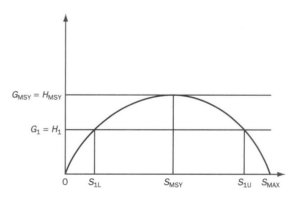

Figure 17.2 Steady-state harvests

harvest, and that any stock between zero and S_{MAX} can support steady-state harvesting. For example, H_1 is a feasible steady-state harvest if the stock size is maintained at either S_{1L} or S_{1U}. Which of these two stock sizes would be more appropriate for attaining a harvest level of H_1 is also a matter we shall investigate later.

Before moving on, it is important to understand that the concept of a steady state is a heuristic device: useful as a way of organising ideas and structuring analysis. But, like all heuristic devices, a steady state is a mental construct and using it uncritically can be inappropriate or misleading. Fisheries and other resource stocks are rarely, if ever, in steady states. Conditions are constantly changing, and the 'real world' is likely to be characterised by a more-or-less permanent state of disequilibrium. For some problems of renewable resource exploitation the analysis of transition processes is more important or insightful than information about steady states. We shall examine some of these 'dynamic' matters later in the chapter. Nevertheless, we will proceed on the assumption that looking at steady states *is* useful, and next investigate their properties under various institutional circumstances.

17.3 An open-access fishery

Our first model of renewable resource exploitation is an open-access fishery model. In conformity with the rest of this book, we study this using continuous-time notation. However, the equations which constitute the discrete-time equivalent of this continuous-time model (and others examined later in the chapter) are listed in full in Appendix 17.1. These will be used at various places in the chapter to give numerical illustrations of the arguments. The numerical values shown in our illustrative examples are computed using an Excel spreadsheet. Should the reader wish to verify that the values shown are correct, or to see how they would change under

alternative assumptions, we have made the two spreadsheets used in our computations available to the reader in the *Additional Materials: Comparative statics.xls* and *Fishery dynamics.xls*. While we hope that some readers (or instructors) will find them useful, they are *not* necessary for an understanding of the contents of this chapter.

It is important to be clear about what an open-access fishery is taken to mean in the environmental economics literature. The open-access fishery model shares two of the characteristics of the standard perfect competition model. First, if the fishery is commercially exploited, it is assumed that this is done by a large number of independent fishing 'firms'. Therefore, each firm takes the market price of landed fish as given. Second, there are no impediments to entry into and exit from the fishery. But the free entry assumption has an additional implication in the open-access fishery, one which is *not* present in the standard perfect competition model.

In a conventional perfect competition model, each firm has enforceable property rights to its resources and to the fruits of its production and investment choices. However, in an open-access fishery, while owners have individual property rights to their fishing capital and to any fish that they have actually caught, they have no enforceable property rights to the *in situ* fishery resources, including the fish in the water.[2] On the contrary, any vessel is entitled or is able (or both) to fish wherever its owner likes. Moreover, if any boat operator chooses to leave some fish in the water in order that future stocks will grow, that owner has no enforceable rights to the fruits of that investment. It is as if a generalised 'what one finds one can keep' rule applies to fishery resources. We shall see in a moment what this state of affairs leads to. First, though, we need to set up the open-access fishery model algebraically.

The open-access model has two components:

1. a biological sub-model, describing the natural growth process of the fishery;
2. an economic sub-model, describing the economic behaviour of the fishing boat owners.

---

[2] This lack of *de facto* enforceability may derive from the fact that the fish are spatially mobile, or from the fact that boats are spatially mobile (or both).

Table 17.1 The open-access fishery model

		General specification	Specific forms assumed
BIOLOGICAL SUB-MODEL:			
Biological growth	(17.5, 17.3)	$dS/dt = G(S)$	$G(S) = g\left(1 - \dfrac{S}{S_{MAX}}\right)S$
ECONOMIC SUB-MODEL:			
Fishery production function	(17.6, 17.7)	$H = H(E, S)$	$H = eES$
Net growth of fish stock	(17.8)	$dS/dt = G(S) - H$	$dS/dt = g\left(1 - \dfrac{S}{S_{MAX}}\right)S - H$
Fishery costs	(17.9, 17.10)	$C = C(E)$	$C = wE$
Fishery revenue	(17.11)	$B = PH$, P constant	$B = PH$, P constant
Fishery profit	(17.12)	$NB = B - C$	$NB = B - C = PeES - wE$
Fishing effort dynamics: open-access entry rule	(17.13)	$dE/dt = \delta \cdot NB$	$dE/dt = \delta(PeES - wE)$
BIOECONOMIC EQUILIBRIUM CONDITIONS:			
Biological equilibrium	(17.14)	$G = H$	$G = H$
Economic equilibrium	(17.15)	$E = E^*$ at which $NB = 0$	$E = E^*$ at which $NB = 0$

Note: Numbers in parentheses refer to the appropriate equation number in the text.

The model is laid out in full in Table 17.1. Subsequent parts of this section will take you through each of the elements described there. We shall be looking for two kinds of 'solutions' to the open-access model. The first is its equilibrium (or steady-state) solution. This consists of a set of circumstances in which the resource stock size is unchanging over time (a biological equilibrium) *and* the fishing fleet is constant with no net inflow or outflow of vessels (an economic equilibrium). Because the steady-state equilibrium is a joint biological–economic equilibrium, it is often referred to as *bioeconomic* equilibrium.

The second kind of solution we shall be looking for is the adjustment path towards the equilibrium, or from one equilibrium to another as conditions change. In other words, our interest also lies in the dynamics of renewable resource harvesting. This turns out to have important implications for whether a fish population may be driven to exhaustion, and indeed whether the resource itself could become extinct. The properties of such adjustment paths are examined in Section 17.4.

17.3.1 The model described

17.3.1.1 Biological sub-model

In the absence of harvesting and other human interference, the rate of change of the stock depends on the prevailing stock size

$$dS/dt = G(S) \qquad (17.5)$$

For our worked numerical example, we assume that the particular form taken by this growth function is the simple logistic growth model given by equation 17.3.

17.3.1.2 Economic sub-model

17.3.1.2.1 *The harvest function (or fishery production function)*

Many factors determine the size of the harvest, H, in any given period. Our model considers two of these. First, the harvest will depend on the amount of resources devoted to fishing. In the case of marine fishing, these include the number of boats deployed and their efficiency, the number of days when fishing is undertaken and so on. For simplicity, assume that all the different dimensions of harvesting activity can be aggregated into one magnitude called *effort*, E.

Second, except for schooling fisheries, it is probable that the harvest will depend on the size of the resource stock.[3] Other things being equal, the larger the stock the greater the harvest for any given level of effort. Hence, abstracting from other determinants of harvest size, including random influences, we may take harvest to depend upon the effort applied and the stock size. That is

$$H = H(E, S) \tag{17.6}$$

This relationship can take a variety of particular forms. One very simple form appears to be a good approximation to actual relationships (see Schaefer, 1954 and Munro, 1981, 1982), and is given by

$$H = eES \tag{17.7}$$

where e is a constant number, often called the catch coefficient.[4] Dividing each side by E, we have

$$\frac{H}{E} = eS$$

which says that the quantity harvested per unit effort is equal to some multiple (e) of the stock size. We have already defined the fish-stock growth function with human predation as the biological growth function less the quantity harvested. That is,

$$\dot{S} = G(S) - H \tag{17.8}$$

17.3.1.2.2 The costs, benefits and profits of fishing

The total cost of harvesting, C, depends on the amount of effort being expended

$$C = C(E) \tag{17.9}$$

For simplicity, harvesting costs are taken to be a linear function of effort,

$$C = wE \tag{17.10}$$

where w is the cost per unit of harvesting effort, taken to be a constant.[5]

Let B denote the gross benefit from harvesting some quantity of fish. The gross benefit will depend on the quantity harvested, so we have

$$B = B(H)$$

In a commercial fishery, the appropriate measure of gross benefits is the total revenue that accrues to firms. Assuming that fish are sold in a competitive market, each firm takes the market price P as given and so the revenue obtained from a harvest H is given by[6]

$$B = PH \tag{17.11}$$

Fishing profit is given by

$$NB = B - C \tag{17.12}$$

17.3.1.2.3 Entry into and exit from the fishery

To complete our description of the economic submodel, it is necessary to describe how fishing effort is determined under conditions of open access. A crucial role is played here by the level of economic profit prevailing in the fishery. Economic profit is

---

[3] See Discussion Question 4 for more on this matter and the notion of schooling and non-schooling fisheries.

[4] The use of a constant catch coefficient parameter is a simplification that may be unreasonable, and is often dropped in more richly specified models. Note also that equation 17.7 can be regarded as a special case of the more general form $H = eE^{\alpha}S^{\beta}$ in which the exponents need not be equal to unity. In empirical modelling exercises, this more general form may be more appropriate. Another form of the harvest equation sometimes used is the exponential model $H = S(1 - \exp(-eE))$.

[5] The equation $C = wE$ imposes the assumption that harvesting costs are linearly related to fishing effort. However, Clark et al. (1979) explain that this assumption will be incorrect if capital costs

are sunk (unrecoverable); moreover, they show that even in a private-property fishery (to be discussed later in the chapter), it can then be privately optimal to have severely depleted fish stocks as the fishery approaches its steady-state equilibrium (although the steady-state equilibrium itself is not affected by whether or not costs are sunk). We return to this matter later.

[6] We could justify this assumption either by saying that the harvesting industry being examined is a small part of a larger overall market, or by arguing that the resource market is competitive, in which case each firm acts as if the market price is fixed (even though price will actually depend *ex post* on the realised total market supply).

the difference between the total revenue from the sale of harvested resources and the total cost incurred in resource harvesting. Given that there is no method of excluding incomers into the industry, nor is there any way in which existing firms can be prevented from changing their level of harvesting effort, effort applied will continue to increase as long as it is possible to earn positive economic profit.[7] Conversely, individuals or firms will leave the fishery if revenues are insufficient to cover the costs of fishing. A simple way of representing this algebraically is by means of the equation

$$dE/dt = \delta \cdot NB \tag{17.13}$$

where δ is a positive parameter indicating the responsiveness of industry size to industry profitability. When economic profit (NB) is positive, firms will enter the industry; and when it is negative they will leave. The magnitude of that response, for any given level of profit or loss, will be determined by δ. Although the true nature of the relationship is unlikely to be of the simple, linear form in equation 17.13, this suffices to capture what is essential.

17.3.1.2.4 Bioeconomic equilibrium

We close our model with two equilibrium conditions that must be satisfied jointly. Biological equilibrium occurs where the resource stock is constant through time (that is, it is in a steady state). This requires that the amount being harvested equals the amount of net natural growth:

$$G = H \tag{17.14}$$

Economic equilibrium requires that the amount of fishing effort be constant through time. Such an equilibrium is only possible in open-access fisheries when rents have been driven to zero, so that there is no longer an incentive for entry into or exit from the industry, nor for the fishing effort on the part of existing fishermen to change. We express this by the equation

$$NB = B - C = 0 \tag{17.15}$$

which implies (under our assumptions) that $PH = wE$. Notice that when this condition is satisfied, $dE/dt = 0$ and so effort is constant at its equilibrium (or steady-state) level $E = E^*$.

17.3.2 Open-access steady-state equilibrium

We can envisage an open-access fishery steady-state equilibrium by means of what is known as the fishery's yield–effort relationship. To obtain this, first note that in a biological equilibrium $H = G$. Then, by substituting the assumed functions for H and G from equations 17.7 and 17.3 respectively we obtain:

$$gS\left(1 - \frac{S}{S_{MAX}}\right) = eES \tag{17.16}$$

which can be rearranged to give

$$S = S_{MAX}\left(1 - \frac{e}{g}E\right) \tag{17.17}$$

Equation 17.17 is one equation in two endogenous variables, E and S (with parameters g, e and S_{MAX}). It implies a unique equilibrium stock at each level of effort.[8] Next substitute equation 17.17 into equation 17.7 ($H = eES$), giving

$$H = eES_{MAX}\left(1 - \frac{e}{g}E\right) \tag{17.18}$$

In an open-access economic equilibrium, profit is zero, so

$$PH = wE \tag{17.19}$$

Equations 17.18 and 17.19 constitute two equations in two unknowns (H and E); these can be solved for the equilibrium values of the two unknowns as functions of the parameters alone. The steady-state stock solution can then be obtained by substituting the expressions for H and E into equation 17.7. We list these steady-state solutions in Box 17.2, together with the numerical values of E, H and S under the

---

[7] The terms rent, economic rent, royalties and net price are used as alternatives to economic profit. They all refer to a surplus of revenue over total costs, where costs include a proper allowance for the opportunity of capital tied up in the fishing fleet.

[8] This uniqueness follows from the assumption that $G(S)$ is a simple logistic function; it may not be true for other biological growth models.

Box 17.2 Analytical expressions for the open-access steady-state equilibrium and numerical solutions under baseline parameter assumption

The analytical expressions for E^*, S^* and H^* (where an asterisk denotes the equilibrium value of the variable in question) as functions of the model parameters alone are:

$$E^* = \frac{g}{e}\left(1 - \frac{w}{PeS_{MAX}}\right) \qquad (17.20)$$

$$S^* = \frac{w}{Pe} \qquad (17.21)$$

$$H^* = \frac{gw}{Pe}\left(1 - \frac{w}{PeS_{MAX}}\right) \qquad (17.22)$$

Derivations of expressions 17.20–17.22 are given in full in Appendix 17.2. Throughout this chapter, we shall be illustrating our arguments with results drawn from fishery models using the parameter values shown in Table 17.2. At various points in the chapter we shall refer to these as the 'baseline' parameter values. It can be easily verified that for this set of parameter values, the steady-state solution is given by $E^* = 8.0$, $S^* = 0.2$ and $H^* = 0.024$.

Table 17.2 Parameter value assumptions for the illustrative numerical example

Parameter	Assumed numerical value
g	0.15
S_{MAX}	1
e	0.015
δ	0.4
P	200
w	0.6

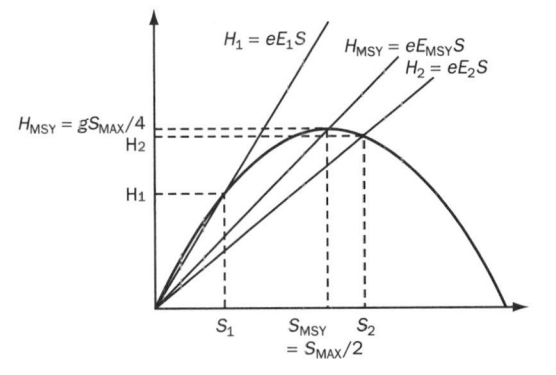

Figure 17.3 Steady-state equilibrium fish harvests and stocks at various effort levels

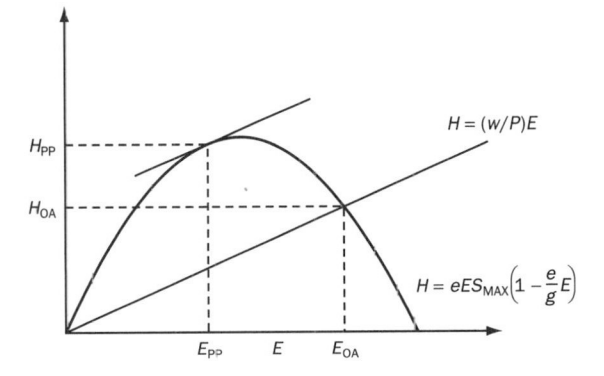

Figure 17.4 Steady-state equilibrium yield–effort relationship

function determines a steady-state harvest level H_1 at stock S_1. The lower effort level E_2 determines a second steady-state equilibrium (the pair $\{H_2, S_2\}$). We leave the reader to deduce why the label E_{MSY} has been attached to the third harvest–stock relationship. The various points of intersection satisfy equation 17.17, being equilibrium values of S for particular levels of E. Clearly there is an infinite quantity of possible equilibria, depending on what constant level of fishing effort is being applied.

The points of intersection in Figure 17.3 not only satisfy equation 17.17 but they also satisfy equation 17.18. Put another way, the equilibrium $\{E, S\}$ combinations also map into equilibrium $\{E, H\}$ combinations. The result of this mapping from $\{E, S\}$ space into $\{E, H\}$ space is shown in Figure 17.4. The inverted U-shape curve here portrays the steady-state harvests that correspond to each possible effort

particular set of assumptions about numerical values of the parameters given in Table 17.2.

This solution method can also be represented graphically, as shown in Figures 17.3 and 17.4. Figure 17.3 shows equilibrium relationships in stock–harvest space. The inverted U-shape curve is the logistic growth function for the resource. Three rays emanating from the origin portray the harvest–stock relationships (from the function $H = eES$) for three different levels of effort. If effort were at the constant level E_1, then the unique intersection of the harvest–stock relationship and biological growth level. It describes what is often called the fishery's yield–effort relationship. Mathematically, it is a plot of equation 17.18.

The particular point on this yield–effort curve that corresponds to an open-access equilibrium will be the one that generates zero economic profit. How do we find this? The zero economic profit equilibrium condition $PH = wE$ can be written as $H = (w/P)E$. For given values of P and w, this plots as a ray from the origin with slope w/P in Figure 17.4. The intersection of this ray with the yield–effort curve locates the unique open-access equilibrium outcome.

Alternatively, multiplying both functions in Figure 17.4 by the market price of fish, P, we find that the intersection point corresponds to $PH = wE$. This is, of course, the zero profit condition, and confirms that $\{E_{OA}, H_{OA}\}$ is the open-access effort–yield equilibrium.

17.4   The dynamics of renewable resource harvesting

Our discussion so far has been exclusively on steady states: equilibrium outcomes which, once achieved, would remain unchanged provided that relevant economic or biological conditions remain constant. However, we may also be interested in the *dynamics* of resource harvesting. This would consider questions such as how a system would get to a steady state if it were not already in one, or whether getting to a steady state is even possible. In other words, dynamics is about transition or adjustment paths. Dynamic analysis might also give us information about how a fishery would respond, through time, to various kinds of shocks and disturbances.

A complete description of fishery dynamics is beyond the scope of this book. But some important insights can be obtained relatively simply. In this section, we undertake some dynamics analysis for the open-access model of Section 17.3. Suppose a mature fishery exists that has not previously been commercially exploited. The stock size is, therefore, at its carrying capacity. The fishery now becomes available for unregulated, open-access commercial exploitation. If the market price of fish, P, is reasonably high and fishing cost (per unit of effort), w, is

reasonably low, the fact that stocks are high (and so easy to catch) implies that the fishery will be, at least initially, profitable for those who enter it. Have in mind equations 17.7, 17.10, 17.11 and 17.12 when thinking this through.

If a typical fishing boat can make positive economic profit then further entry will take place. How quickly new capacity is built up depends on the magnitude of the parameter δ in equation 17.13. In this early phase, effort is rising over time as new boats are attracted in, and stocks are falling. Stocks fall because harvesting is taking place while new recruitment to stocks is low: the logistic growth function has the property that biological growth is near zero when the stock is near its maximum carrying capacity (equation 17.3). This process of increasing E and decreasing S will persist for some time, but it cannot last indefinitely. As stocks become lower, fish become harder to catch and so the cost per fish caught rises. Profits are squeezed from two directions: harvesting cost per fish rises, and fewer fish are caught.

Eventually, this profit squeeze will mean that a typical boat makes a loss rather than a profit, and so the process we have just described goes into reverse, with stocks rising and effort falling. In fact, for the model we are examining, the processes we are describing here are a little more subtle than this. The changes do not occur as discrete switches but instead are continuous and gradual. We also find that stocks and effort (and also harvest levels) have oscillatory cycles with the stock cycles slightly leading the effort cycles. In some circumstances, these oscillations dampen down as time passes, and the system eventually settles to a steady-state outcome such as that described in the previous section. We illustrate such a transition process in Figure 17.5, where parameter values are given by those shown in Table 17.2. Note that the oscillations shown in this diagram are particularly acute and have massive amplitude; for other combinations of parameter values, the cycles may be far less pronounced. In this case, you should be able to discern that, given enough time, the levels of S and E will settle down to the steady-state values $S^* = 0.2$ and $E^* = 8.0$.

The oscillations exhibited by the dynamic adjustment path in Figure 17.5 – with the variables repeatedly over- and under-shooting equilibrium

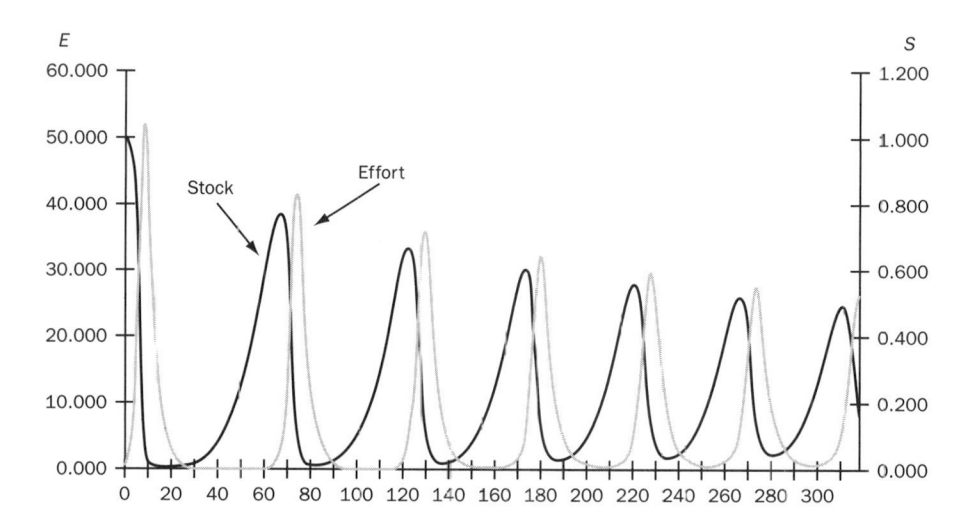

Figure 17.5 Stock and effort dynamic paths for the illustrative model

outcomes – is a characteristic feature of open-access fisheries. In this case, the steady-state outcome obtained by solving equations 17.20–22 is eventually achieved (albeit very slowly). But that is not necessarily true. It is evident that if the oscillations were even larger, the population may be driven down to a level from which it cannot recover, and the fishery is driven out of existence, irrespective of whether or not the equilibrium equations imply that a steady state exists with positive stock and effort. For example, if price had been £270 rather than £200, the steady-state solution gives, to two decimal places, $S = 0.15$ and $E = 8.52$. Verify this by substituting the new parameter values in equations 17.21 and 17.20. However, successive iterations of the discrete-time equations from initial values of $S = 1$ and $E = 1$ show that the stock collapses to zero after only 7 periods. (It does so because effort explodes so rapidly to such a huge level that the stock is completely harvested in a short finite span of time.)

Other things being equal, the probability that effort oscillations might cause a population to collapse before it can attain a steady-state solution is increased when

(a) the growth function has $S_{MIN} > 0$, and
(b) the growth function or environmental conditions are stochastic.

The first of these should be self-evident. A positive minimum population size – found when the growth

function exhibits critical depensation, for example – implies that low populations that would otherwise recover through natural growth may collapse irretrievably to zero. The second is also relatively straightforward. If in practice there is a stochastic component to growth then the *achieved* growth in any period may be smaller or larger than its underlying mean value as determined by the growth equation 17.3. In some cases, the stochastic component may be such that growth is actually negative. If the population were at a very low level already, then a random change inducing lower than normal or negative net growth could push the resource stock below the point from which biological recovery is possible.

Another way of describing this is in terms of a so-called phase-plane diagram. This is shown in Figure 17.6. The diagram defines a space consisting of pairs of values for S and E. The steady-state equilibrium ($S^* = 0.2$ and $E^* = 8.0$) lies at the intersection of two straight lines the meaning of which will be explained in a moment. The adjustment path through time is shown by the curved line which converges through a series of diminishing cycles on the steady-state equilibrium. In the story we have just told, the stock is initially at 1 and effort begins at a small value (just larger than zero). Hence we begin at the top left point of the curved adjustment path. As time passes, stock falls and effort rises – the adjustment path heads 'south-eastwards'. After some time, the

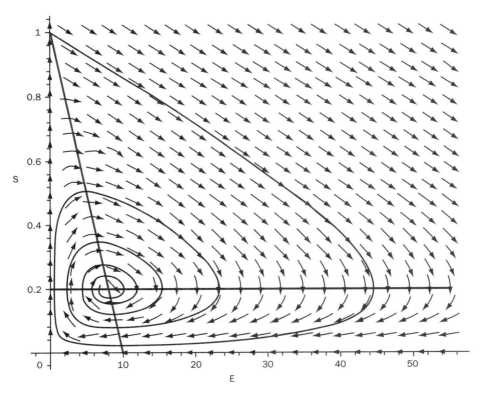

Figure 17.6 Phase-plane analysis of stock and effort dynamic paths for the illustrative model

stock continues to fall but so too does effort – the adjustment path follows a 'south-west' direction. Comparing Figures 17.5 and 17.6, you will see that the latter presents the same information as the former but in a different way.

But the phase-plane diagram also presents some additional information not shown in Figure 17.5. First, the arrows denote the directions of adjustment of S and E whenever the system is not in steady state from any arbitrary starting point. It is evident that the open-access model we are examining here *in conjunction with* the particular baselines parameter values being assumed has strong stability properties: irrespective of where stock and effort happen to be the adjustment paths will lead to the unique steady-state equilibrium, albeit through a damped, oscillatory adjustment process.

Second, the phase-plane diagram explicitly shows the steady-state solution. As noted above this lies at the intersection of the two straight lines. The

horizontal line is a locus of all economic equilibrium points at which profit per boat is zero, and so effort is unchanging ($dE/dt = 0$). The downward sloping line is a locus of all biological equilibrium points at which $G = H$, and so stock is unchanging ($dS/dt = 0$). Clearly, a bioeconomic equilibrium occurs at their intersection.

Although the calculations required to carry out the kind of dynamic analyses described in this section could be done by hand, this would be extremely tedious to do. It would be far easier to use some mathematical package (such as Maple or Mathematica) or a spreadsheet program (such as Excel). For the reader interested in seeing how a spreadsheet package can be used for dynamic simulation (and also to calculate numerical values for steady-state stock, harvest and effort) we have provided an annotated Excel workbook *Fishery dynamics.xls* in the *Additional Materials*. In essence, dynamic simulations are done in Excel in the following way. First choose initial values for E and S. Then using the discrete-time versions of our model equations (listed in Appendix 17.1) calculate the values of H, E and S the next time period. Next use the **Fill Down** function in Excel to copy the formulae which embody these model equations down the spreadsheet. In this way, Excel will recursively calculate levels of the variables over any chosen span of successive time periods. The steady-state solution can be found by plotting successive values of H, E and S and observing at which numerical values the variables eventually settle down.

The Excel file implements the calculations used to obtain Figure 17.5, carries out some additional dynamic simulations, and also illustrates other fishery models examined in this chapter. The workbook is set up so that the reader can easily carry out other simulations, and contains instructions for using the spreadsheet and an explanation of the simulation technique.

Trying to generate a phase-plane diagram by pen-and-paper calculations would be immensely time-consuming. Diagram 17.6 was obtained by setting up the open-access model within the Maple package. We provide, in the *Additional Materials*, file *Phase.doc*, a more complete account of phase-plane analysis and an explanation of how Maple – an easy-to-use and very powerful package – can generate the graphical output of the form in Figure 17.6. The Maple file used to generate the picture is included as *Chapter 17.mws*.

In our analysis to date, we have presumed that environmental conditions remain unchanged over time. However, in practice these conditions do change, usually unpredictably, and sometimes very rapidly. When open access to a resource is accompanied by worsening environmental conditions, and when these changes are either rapid or unforeseen or both, harvesting outcomes can be catastrophic. The recent history of the Peruvian anchovy fishery, described in Box 17.3, illustrates such an outcome. Another facet of open access is also shown in Box 17.3. Overfishing does not usually happen because of ignorance; it tends to result from the forces of competition in conditions where access is poorly regulated. The New England fisheries demonstrate that self-regulation on the part of fishermen may do little to overcome the consequences of open access.

17.5   Some more reflections on open-access fisheries

The absence of enforceable private property rights does not *necessarily* imply that renewable resources will fail to be harvested in a rational or conservationist manner. In this respect it is important to distinguish between 'common property' and 'open access' resources. In the former private property rights are not vested in individuals but rather in communities. Here, relationships of trust and social norms may be sufficiently well developed and entrenched to create patterns of resource exploitation that are both sustainable and rational for the group as a whole (see for example Bromley, 1999). In contrast, open access is usually taken to mean the absence of any such binding norms with a tendency for exploitation to take place under conditions of 'free-for-all' individualistic competition.

It is possible that any resource stock could be harvested to exhaustion, or a species driven to extinction, under open access. Indeed, we show later that this is true under almost any regime, including those with enforceable private property rights. Nevertheless, it remains true that open-access conditions increase the probabilities of those outcomes occurring. Why is this? The main reason is that in these circumstances there is no collectively rational management of harvesting taking place. Even where what should be done is evident, an institutional mechanism to bring this about is missing. When you compare open-access outcomes with those of private-property regimes in the sections that follow, you will see that harvest rates are typically higher under conditions of open access; other things being equal, the greater are harvesting rates, the higher is the likelihood of extinction.

Another way of thinking about this is in terms of stock externality effects and economic inefficiency. Open-access harvesting programmes are inefficient because the resource harvesters are unable to appropriate the benefits of investment in the resource. If a single fisher were to defer the harvesting of some fish until a later period, all fishers would benefit from this activity. It would be in the interests of all if a bargain were made to reduce fishing effort by the industry. However, the conditions under which such

Box 17.3 A story of two fish populations

One species of fish – the Peruvian anchovy – and one group of commercial fish – New England groundfish – provide us with case studies of the mismanagement and economic inefficiency which often characterise the world's commercial fisheries. In this box, we summarise reviews of the recent historical experiences of these two fisheries; the reviews are to be found in WR (1994), chapter 10.

Peruvian anchovy are to be found in the Humboldt Upswelling off the west coast of South America. Upswellings of cold, nutrient-rich water create conditions for rich commercial fish catches. During the 1960s and 1970s, this fishery provided nearly 20% of the world's fish landings. Until 1950, Peruvian anchovy were harvested on a small scale, predominantly for local human consumption, but in the following two decades the fishery increased in scale dramatically as the market for fishmeal grew. The maximum sustainable yield (MSY) was estimated as 9.5 million tonnes per year, but that figure was being exceeded by 1970, with harvests beyond 12 million tonnes. In 1972, the catch plummeted. This fall was partially accounted for by a cyclical natural phenomenon, the arrival of the El Niño current. However, it is now recognised that the primary cause of the fishery collapse (with the catch down to just over 1 million tonnes in the 1980s) was the conjunction of overharvesting with the natural change associated with El Niño. Harvesting at rates above the MSY can lead to dramatic stock collapses that can persist for decades, and may be irreversible (although, in this case, anchovy populations do now show signs of recovery).

The seas off the New England coast have been among the most productive, the most intensively studied and the most heavily overfished in the world since 1960. The most important species in commercial terms have been floor-living species including Atlantic cod, haddock, redfish, hake, pollock and flounder. Populations of each are now near record low levels. Although overfishing is not the only contributory factor, it has almost certainly been the principal cause of stock collapses. The New England fisheries are not unusual in this; what is most interesting about this case is the way in which regulatory schemes have failed to achieve their stated goals. In effect, self-regulation has been practised in these fisheries and, not surprisingly perhaps, regulations have turned out to avoid burdening current harvesters. This is a classic example of what is sometimes called 'institutional capture': institutions which were intended to regulate the behaviour of firms within an industry, to conform with some yardstick of 'the common good', have in effect been taken over by those who were intended to be regulated, who then design administrative arrangements in their own interest. The regulations have, in the final analysis, been abysmal failures when measured against the criterion of reducing the effective quantity of fishing effort applied to the New England ground fisheries.

Long-term solutions to overfishing will require strict quantity controls over fishing effort, either by direct controls over the effort or techniques of individual boats, or through systems of transferable, marketable quotas. We investigated some of these instruments in Chapter 7 and do so further later in this chapter.

a bargain could be made and not reneged upon are very unlikely to exist. Each potential bargainer has an incentive to free-ride once a bargain has been struck, by increasing his or her harvest while others reduce theirs. Moreover, even if all existing parties were to agree among themselves, the open-access conditions imply that others could enter the market as soon as rents became positive. Open-access resources thus have one of the properties of a public good – non-excludability – and this alone is sufficient to make it likely that markets will fail to reach efficient outcomes.

17.6 The private-property fishery

In an open-access fishery, firms exploit available stocks as long as positive profit is available. While this condition persists, each fishing vessel has an incentive to maximise its catch. But there is a dilemma here, both for the individual fishermen and for society as a whole. From the perspective of the fishermen, the fishery is perceived as being overfished. Despite each boat owner pursuing maximum profit, the collective efforts of all drive profits down to zero. From a social perspective, the fishery will be economically 'overfished' and the stock level may (but will not necessarily) be driven down to biologically dangerous levels.

What is the underlying cause of this state of affairs? Although reducing the total catch today may be in the collective interest of all (by allowing fish stocks to recover and grow), it is not rational for any fisherman to individually restrict fishing effort. There can be no guarantee that he or she will receive any of the rewards that this may generate in terms of higher catches later. Indeed, there may not be any stock available in the future. In such circumstances, each firm will exploit the fishery today to its maximum potential, subject only to the constraint that its revenues must at least cover its costs.

We shall now discuss a particular set of institutional arrangements that could overcome some of these dilemmas. These arrangements could be described as the private-property fishery. This kind of fishery – and several variants of it – have been explored in depth in the fishery economics literature. However, discussions of the private-property fishery rarely make explicit the institutional assumptions that lie behind it. It is important to do that, however, and so we shall now describe what the private-property fishery is usually taken to mean (and the sense in which we shall be using the term).

The private-property fishery has the following three characteristics:

1. There is a large number of fishing firms, each behaving as a price-taker and so regarding price as being equal to marginal revenue. It is for this reason that the industry is often described as being competitive.
2. Each firm is profit- (or wealth-) maximising.
3. There is a particular structure of well-defined and enforceable property rights to the fishery, such that owners can control access to the fishery and appropriate any rents that it is capable of delivering.

What exactly is this particular structure of property rights? Within the literature there are several (sometimes implicit) answers to this question. We shall outline two of them. One view regards 'the fishery' as an aggregate of a large number of smaller individual fisheries. Each of these sub-fisheries is privately owned by one firm that has property rights to the fish which are there currently and at all points in time in the future.[9] All harvested fish, however, sell in one aggregate market at a single market price. A second view regards the fishery as being managed by a single entity which controls access to the fishery and coordinates the activity of individual operators to maximise total fishery profits (or wealth). Nevertheless, harvesting and pricing behaviour are competitive rather than monopolistic.

Neither of these accounts is satisfactory as a statement of what actually does exist, nor what might realistically exist. The first faces problems in deciding how to specify ownership rights to migratory fish. Moreover, it could only be descriptively accurate if the fishery in question is a huge, highly spatially aggregated, fishery. The researcher does not want to study at this level of aggregation. The second concept – the coordinated fishery – seems problematic in that we rarely, if ever, find examples of such *internally* coordinated fisheries (except in the case of fish farming and the like). And even if one were to find examples, it is difficult to imagine that they would operate as competitive fisheries rather than as monopolies or cartels.[10]

But to label one or both of these views as descriptively unrealistic is to miss the point somewhat. They should be thought of in 'as if' terms. That is, we want a specification such that the industry behaves *as if* each firm has its own 'patch' of fishery that others are not permitted to exploit or *as if* it were coordinated in the way mentioned above. Given either of these *as if* assumptions, the researcher can then reasonably assume that owners undertake economically rational management decisions, and are in a position to make investment decisions confident

---

[9] The owners of any fishing firm may, of course, lease or sell their property rights to another set of individuals.

[10] In fact, two other variants of the private-property fishery sometimes discussed in the literature are actually these: the monopoly fishery and the cartel fishery. However, given the fact that they are so uncommon in practice, we do not deal with those models in this text, except for a brief reference to monopoly fishery in Appendix 17.3.

in the belief that the returns on any investment made can be individually appropriated. This is what distinguishes a private-property fishery fundamentally from an open-access fishery.

An important benefit from thinking about property rights carefully in this way is the help it gives in developing public policy towards fishery regulation and management. If we are confident that a particular property rights structure would bring about socially efficient (or otherwise desirable) outcomes, then policy instruments can be designed to mimic that structure. We will argue below that an individual transferable quota (ITQ) fishing permit system can be thought of in this way.

17.6.1 The static profit-maximising private-property fishery model

As we explained in the Introduction, our analysis of the private-property fishery proceeds in two steps. The first, covered in this section, develops a simple static model of a private-property fishery in which the passage of time is not explicitly dealt with. In effect, the analysis supposes that biological and economic conditions remain constant over some span of time. It then investigates what aggregate level of effort, stock and harvest would result if each individual owner (with enforceable property rights) managed affairs so as to maximise profits in any arbitrarily chosen period of time. This way of dealing with time – in effect, abstracting from it, and looking at decisions in only one time period (but which are replicated over successive periods) – leads to its description as a *static* fishery model. We shall demonstrate later that this analytical approach only generates wealth-maximising outcomes if fishermen do not discount future cash flows. More specifically, the static private-property fishery turns out to be a special case of a multi-period fishery model: the special case in which owners use a zero discount rate.

The biological and economic equations of the static private-property fishery model are identical to those of the open-access fishery in all respects but one: the open-access entry rule ($dE/dt = \delta \cdot NB$), which in turn implies a zero-profit economic equilibrium, no longer applies. Instead, owners choose effort to maximise economic profit from the fishery.

Table 17.3 Steady-state solutions under baseline parameter value assumptions

	Open access	Static private property
Stock	0.200	0.600
Effort	8.000	4.000
Harvest	0.024	0.036

This can be visualised with the help of Figure 17.4. As we did earlier, multiply both functions by the market price of fish. The inverted U-shape yield–effort equation then becomes a revenue–effort equation. And the ray emerging from the origin now becomes $PH = wE$, with the right-hand side thereby denoting fishing costs. Profit is maximised at the effort level which maximises the surplus of revenue over costs. Diagrammatically, this occurs where the slopes of the total cost and total revenue curves are equal. This in indicated in Figure 17.4 by the tangent to the yield–effort function at E_{PP} being parallel to the slope of the $H = (w/P)E$ line.

An algebraic derivation of the steady-state solution to this problem – showing stock, effort and harvest as functions of the parameters – is given in Box 17.4. It is easy to verify from the solution equations given there that the steady-state values of E, S and H are given by $E_{PP}^* = 4.0$, $S_{PP}^* = 0.60$ and $H_{PP}^* = 0.0360$. To facilitate comparison, the numerical values of the steady-state equilibrium stock, harvest and effort under our baseline parameter assumptions, for both open-access and static private-property fishery, are reproduced in Table 17.3. Under the assumptions we have made about functional forms, the static private-property equilibrium will always lead to a higher resource stock level and a lower effort level than that which prevails under open access. This is confirmed for our particular parameter assumptions, with the private-property stock being three times higher and effort only half as large as in open access.

The steady-state harvest may be higher, lower or identical. This is evident from inspection of Figure 17.4. For the particular set of parameter values used in our illustrative example, private-property harvest is *larger* than open-access harvest, as shown in the diagram. But it will not always be true that private-property harvests exceed those under open access. For example, if P were 80 (rather than 200) and all

The derivation initially follows exactly that given in Section 17.3.2, with equations 17.16 to 17.18 remaining valid here. However, the zero profit condition (equation 17.19) is no longer valid, being replaced by the profit-maximisation condition:

$$\text{Maximise NB} = PH - wE \qquad (17.23)$$

Remembering that $H = eES$, and treating E as the instrument variable, this yields the necessary first-order condition,

$$\partial(PeES)/\partial E = \partial(wE)/\partial E \qquad (17.24)$$

Substituting equation 17.17 into 17.24 we have

$$\partial\left(PeES_{MAX}\left(1 - \frac{\epsilon}{g}E\right)\right)/\partial E = \partial(wE)/\partial E$$

from which we obtain after differentiation

$$PeS_{MAX} - 2PES_{MAX}\left(\frac{e^2}{g}\right) = w \qquad (17.25)$$

That is, the marginal revenue of effort is equal to the marginal cost of effort. This can be solved for E_{PP}^* (the subscript denoting 'private property') to give

$$E_{PP}^* = \frac{1}{2}\frac{g}{e}\left(1 - \frac{w}{PeS_{MAX}}\right) \qquad (17.26)$$

Substitution of E_{PP}^* into 17.17 gives

$$S_{PP}^* = \frac{1}{2}\frac{PeS_{MAX} + w}{Pe} \qquad (17.27)$$

and then using $H = eES$ we obtain[11]

$$H_{PP}^* = \frac{1}{4}g\left(S_{MAX} - \frac{w^2}{P^2e^2S_{MAX}}\right) \qquad (17.28)$$

---

[11] In the Excel spreadsheets, an alternative (but exactly equivalent) version of this expression has been used to generate the Excel formulas, namely

$$H_{PP}^* = \frac{1}{4}\frac{g(PeS_{MAX} - w)(PeS_{MAX} + w)}{P^2e^2S_{MAX}}$$

other parameter values were those specified in the baseline set (listed in Table 17.2) then an open-access fishery would produce $H = 0.0375$, the maximum sustainable yield of the fishery! In contrast, a private-property fishery would in those circumstances yield only $H = 0.0281$.

The source of this indeterminacy follows from the inverted U shape of the yield–effort relationship. Although stocks will be higher under private property than open access, the quadratic form of the stock–harvest relationship implies that harvests will not necessarily be higher with higher stocks.

17.6.2 Comparative statics

For convenience, we list in Table 17.4 the expressions obtained in earlier sections for the steady-state equilibria of E, H and S. We can use these expressions to make qualitative predictions about the effects of changing a particular parameter on the equilibrium levels of S^*, E^* and H^*. Doing this is known as comparative statics. For example, how will S^* change as w rises or as P increases? Inspection of the formula in the top left cell shows that open-access S^* will increase if w increases and will decrease if P increases. This is also true in the case of the static private-property steady state, as can be seen by inspection of the top right-hand-side cell.

Where the sign of a relationship cannot easily be found by inspection, we may be able to obtain it from the appropriate partial derivative. For example, although it is easy in this case to confirm by inspection that a rise in w will increase open-access S^*, this inference is corroborated by the fact that the partial derivative of S^* with respect to w is $1/Pe$. As P and e are both positive numbers, the partial derivative

Table 17.4 Steady-state open-access and static private-property equilibria compared

	Open access	Static private property
Stock	$S^* = \dfrac{w}{Pe}$	$S_{PP}^* = \dfrac{1}{2}\dfrac{PeS_{MAX} + w}{Pe}$
Effort	$E^* = \dfrac{g}{e}\left(1 - \dfrac{w}{PeS_{MAX}}\right)$	$E_{PP}^* = \dfrac{1}{2}\dfrac{g}{e}\left(1 - \dfrac{w}{PeS_{MAX}}\right)$
Harvest	$H^* = \dfrac{gw}{Pe}\left(1 - \dfrac{w}{PeS_{MAX}}\right)$	$H_{PP}^* = \dfrac{1}{4}g\left(S_{MAX} - \dfrac{w^2}{P^2e^2S_{MAX}}\right)$

Table 17.5 Comparative static results

	P	w	E	g	δ
Open access					
S^*	–	+	–	0	0
E^*	+	–	?	+	0
H^*	?	?	?	+	0
Static private property					
S^*_{PP}	–	+	–	0	0
E^*_{PP}	+	–	?	+	0
H^*_{PP}	+	–	+	+	0

$1/Pe$ is also positive. Sometimes, of course, the direction of an effect cannot be signed unambiguously; this should usually be evident by inspection of the partial derivative.

Table 17.5 lists the signs of these effects from the appropriate partial derivatives. A plus sign means that the derivative is positive, a minus sign means that the derivative is negative, 0 means that the derivative is zero, and ? means that no sign can be unambiguously assigned to the derivative (and so we cannot say what the direction of the effect will be without knowing the actual values of the parameters that enter the partial derivative in question). Note that variations in δ have no effect on any steady-state outcome (although they do affect how fast, if indeed at all, such an outcome may be achieved).

17.6.3 The present-value-maximising fishery model

The present-value-maximising fishery model generalises the model of the static private-property fishery. In doing so it formulates a model that has a more sound theoretical basis and generates a richer set of results. The essence of this model is that a rational private-property fishery will organise its harvesting activity so as to maximise the value of the fishery. We shall refer to this value as the present value (PV) of the fishery. In this section, we outline how a model of a present-value-maximising fishery can be set up, state the main results, and provide interpretations of them. Full derivations have been placed in Appendix 17.3. The individual components of our model are very similar to those of the static private fishery model. However, we now bring time explicitly into the analysis by using an intertemporal optimisation framework. Initially we shall develop results using general functional forms. Later in this section, solutions are obtained for the specific functions and baseline parameter values assumed earlier in this chapter.

As in previous sections of the chapter, we assume that the market price of fish is a constant, exogenously given, number. Moreover, as before, the market is taken to be competitive. However, Appendix 17.3 will also go through the more general case in which the market price of fish varies with the size of total industry catch, and will briefly examine a monopolistic fishery.

It will be convenient to regard harvest levels as the instrument (control) variable. To facilitate this, we specify fishing costs as a function of the quantity harvested and the size of the fish stock. Moreover, it is assumed that costs depend positively on the amount harvested and negatively on the size of the stock.[12,13] That is,

$$C_t = C(H_t, S_t) \quad C_H > 0, C_S < 0$$

The initial population of fish is S_0, the natural growth of which is determined by the function $G(S)$. The fishery owners select a harvest rate for each period over the relevant time horizon (here taken to be

---

[12] The reader may be confused about our formulation of the harvest cost function. In an earlier section, we wrote $C = C(E)$, equation 17.9. But note that we have also assumed that $H = H(E, S)$, equation 17.6. If 17.6 is written as E in terms of H and S, and that expression is then substituted into 17.9, we obtain $C = C(H, S)$. It is largely a matter of convenience whether we express costs in terms of effort or in terms of harvest and stock. In our discussion of open-access equilibrium, we chose to regard fishing effort as a variable of interest and did not make that substitution. In this section, our interest lies more in the variable H and so it is convenient to make the substitution. But the results of either approach can be found from the other.

[13] There is another issue here that we should mention. The costs of fishing should include a proper allowance for all the opportunity costs involved. For land-based resources, the land itself is likely to have alternative uses, and so its use in any one activity will have a land opportunity cost. For fisheries, however, there is rarely an alternative *commercial* use of the oceans, and so this kind of opportunity cost is not relevant. However, from a social point of view there may be important alternative uses of the oceans (for example, as conserved sources of biodiversity). Hence a difference can exist between costs as seen from a social and a private point of view.

infinity) to maximise the present value (or wealth) of the fishery, given an interest rate i. Algebraically, we express this as

$$\text{Max} \int_0^\infty \{PH_t - C(H_t, S_t)\} e^{-it} dt$$

subject to

$$\frac{dS}{dt} = G(S_t) - H_t$$

and initial stock level $S(0) = S_0$. The necessary conditions for maximum wealth include

$$p_t = P - \frac{\partial C(H, S)}{\partial H_t} \tag{17.29}$$

$$\frac{dp_t}{dt} = ip_t - p_t \frac{dG(S)}{dS_t} + \frac{\partial C(H, S)}{\partial S_t} \tag{17.30}$$

It is very important to distinguish between upper-case P and lower-case p in equation 17.29, and in many of the equations that follow. P is the market, or landed, price of fish; it is, therefore, an observable quantity. As the market price is being treated here as an exogenously given fixed number, no time subscript is required on P. In contrast, lower-case p_t is a shadow price, which measures the contribution to wealth made by an additional unit of fish stock at the wealth-maximising optimum. We call it the net price of fish. Two properties of this net price deserve mention. First, it is typically an unobservable quantity. Second, like all shadow prices, it will vary over time (unless the fishery is in a steady-state equilibrium). In general, therefore, it is necessary to attach a time label to this net price.

Equation 17.29 defines the net price of the resource (p_t) as the difference between the market price and marginal cost of an incremental unit of harvested fish. Equation 17.30 governs the behaviour over time of the net price, and implicitly determines the harvest rate in each period. This equation is interpreted in the discussions below.

17.6.3.1 Steady-state equilibrium in the present-value-maximising fishery

Let us investigate the properties of a PV-maximising fishery steady-state equilibrium. An explanation of how such a state may be achieved is left to Appendix 17.3. In a steady state all variables are unchanging with respect to time, so $dp/dt = 0$. We have $G(S) = H$ and the optimising conditions 17.29 and 17.30 collapse to the simpler forms

$$p = P - \frac{\partial C(H, S)}{\partial H} \tag{17.31}$$

$$ip = p \frac{dG(S)}{dS} - \frac{\partial C(H, S)}{\partial S} \tag{17.32}$$

17.6.3.2 Interpretation of equation 17.32

How is the present value of profits maximised? The key to understanding profit-maximising behaviour when access to the resource can be regulated lies in capital theory. A renewable resource is a capital asset. To fix ideas, think about a fishery with a single owner who can control access to the resource and appropriate all returns from it. We wish to consider the owner's decision about whether to marginally change the amount of fish harvesting currently being undertaken.

Choosing not to harvest some fish is equivalent to a capital investment. The uncaught fish will be there next period; moreover, biological growth will mean that there is an additional increment to the stock next period (over and above the quantity of fish left unharvested). This amounts to saying that the asset – in this case the fishery – is productive. A decision about whether to defer some harvesting until the next period is made by comparing the marginal costs and benefits of adding additional units to the resource stock. By choosing not to harvest an incremental unit, the fisher incurs an opportunity cost in holding a stock of unharvested fish. Holding these units sacrifices an available return. The marginal cost of the investment is ip. How is this obtained? Sale of the harvested fish would have led to revenue which can be invested at the prevailing rate of return on capital, i. The forgone revenue is equal to the net price of the resource, p. Note that this is actually a net revenue as $p = P - C_H$, where P is the market price and $C_H = \partial C / \partial H$ is the marginal cost of one unit of the harvested resource. However, since we are considering a decision to defer this revenue by one period, the present value of this sacrificed return is ip.

The owner compares this marginal cost with the marginal benefit obtained by the resource investment (not harvesting the incremental unit). There are two categories of benefit:

1. As a consequence of an additional unit of stock being added, *total* harvesting costs will be reduced by the quantity $C_S = \partial C/\partial S$ (note that $\partial C/\partial S < 0$).
2. The additional unit of stock will grow by the amount dG/dS. The value of this additional growth is the amount of growth valued at the net price of the resource.

A present-value-maximising owner will add units of resource to the stock provided the marginal cost of doing so is less than the marginal benefit. That is:

$$ip < \frac{dG}{dS}p - \frac{\partial C}{\partial S}$$

This states that a unit will be added to stock provided its 'holding cost' (ip) is less than the sum of its harvesting cost reduction and value-of-growth benefits. Conversely, a present-value-maximising owner will harvest additional units of the stock if marginal costs exceed marginal benefits:

$$ip > \frac{dG}{dS}p - \frac{\partial C}{\partial S}$$

These imply the asset equilibrium condition, equation 17.32. When this is satisfied, the rate of return the resource owner obtains from the fishery is equal to i, the rate of return that could be obtained by investment elsewhere in the economy. This is one of the intertemporal efficiency conditions we identified in Chapter 11. To confirm that this equality exists, divide both sides of equation 17.32 by the net price p to give

$$i = \frac{dG}{dS} - \frac{\left(\frac{\partial C}{\partial S}\right)}{p} \tag{17.33}$$

Equation 17.33 is one (steady-state) version of what is sometimes called the 'fundamental equation' of renewable resources. The left-hand side is the rate of return that can be obtained by investing in assets

elsewhere in the economy. The right-hand side is the rate of return that is obtained from the renewable resource. This is made up of two elements:

- the natural rate of growth in the stock from a marginal change in the stock size;
- the value of the reduction in harvesting costs that arises from a marginal increase in the resource stock.

Equation 17.33 is an implicit equation for the unknown PV-maximising equilibrium value of S. Solving 17.33 for S gives an analytical solution for the equilibrium stock. (This solution is given in Appendix 17.3.) Given that, expressions for the PV optimal solutions for H and E can be obtained using the biological growth function and the fishery production function, equation 17.6.

We have used the spreadsheet *Comparative statics.xls* to calculate the equilibrium values of S, E and H for interest rates between zero and 100 per cent (and two higher values), conditional on our assumed functional forms and other baseline parameter values. These equilibria are listed in Table 17.6. For purposes of comparison we also show the equilibrium values for a static private-property fishery and an open-access fishery. Note that for these last two models, equilibrium values do not vary with the interest rate.

Three important results are evident from an inspection of the data in Table 17.6:

1. In the special case where the interest rate is zero, the steady-state equilibria of a static private-property fishery and a PV-maximising fishery are identical. For all other interest rates they differ.
2. For non-zero interest rates, the steady-state fish stock (fishing effort) in the PV profit-maximising fishery is lower (higher) than that in the static private fishery, and becomes increasingly lower (higher) the higher is the interest rate.
3. As the interest rate becomes arbitrarily large, the PV-maximising outcome converges to that of an open-access fishery.

At the moment we just note these results. We shall explain them later.

Table 17.6 Steady-state equilibrium outcomes from the illustrative spreadsheet model for baseline parameter values in (a) a static private-property fishery, (b) open-access fishery and (c) a PV-maximising fishery with various interest rates

	Static private fishery*			PV-maximising fishery			Open-access fishery*		
i	S	E	H	S	E	H	S	E	H
0.0	0.6	4.0	0.036	0.6000	4.0000	0.0360	0.20	8.0	0.024
0.1	0.6	4.0	0.036	0.4239	5.7607	0.0366	0.20	8.0	0.024
0.2	0.6	4.0	0.036	0.3333	6.6667	0.0333	0.20	8.0	0.024
0.3	0.6	4.0	0.036	0.2899	7.1010	0.0309	0.20	8.0	0.024
0.4	0.6	4.0	0.036	0.2677	7.3333	0.0293	0.20	8.0	0.024
0.5	0.6	4.0	0.036	0.2527	7.4734	0.0283	0.20	8.0	0.024
0.6	0.6	4.0	0.036	0.2434	7.5660	0.0276	0.20	8.0	0.024
0.7	0.6	4.0	0.036	0.2369	7.6314	0.0271	0.20	8.0	0.024
0.8	0.6	4.0	0.036	0.2320	7.6798	0.0267	0.20	8.0	0.024
0.9	0.6	4.0	0.036	0.2283	7.7171	0.0264	0.20	8.0	0.024
1.0	0.6	4.0	0.036	0.2253	7.7467	0.0260	0.20	8.0	0.024
10.0	0.6	4.0	0.036	0.2024	7.9759	0.0242	0.20	8.0	0.024
100.0	0.6	4.0	0.036	0.2002	7.9976	0.0240	0.20	8.0	0.024

* Static private fishery and open-access fishery steady-state equilibrium values do not vary with the interest rate. These equilibrium values have been copied into every row for purposes of comparison.
Source of data: The Excel file *Comparative statics.xls*, to be found in the *Additional Materials* for Chapter 17

17.6.4 The consequence of a dependence of harvest costs on the stock size

The specific functions used in this chapter for harvest quantity and harvest costs are $H = eES$ and $C = wE$ respectively. Substituting the former into the latter and rearranging yields $C = wE/eS$. It is evident from this that, under our assumptions, harvest costs depend on both effort and stock. However, suppose that the harvest equation were of the simpler form $H = eE$. In that case we obtain $C = wE/e$ and so costs are independent of stock. But in such cases (which are rather unlikely in general), when harvesting costs do *not* depend on the stock size, $\partial C/\partial S = 0$ and so the steady-state PV-maximising condition (17.32) simplifies to $i = dG/dS$.

This is an interesting result. It tells us that a private PV-maximising steady-state equilibrium, where access can be controlled and costs do not depend upon the stock size, will be one in which the resource stock is maintained at a level where the rate of biological growth (dG/dS) equals the market rate of return on investment (i) – exactly what standard capital theory suggests should happen. This is illustrated in Figure 17.7. At the present-value-maximising resource stock size (which we denote by S_{PV}), $i = dG/dS$. It is clear from this diagram that as the interest rate rises, the profit-maximising stock size will fall.

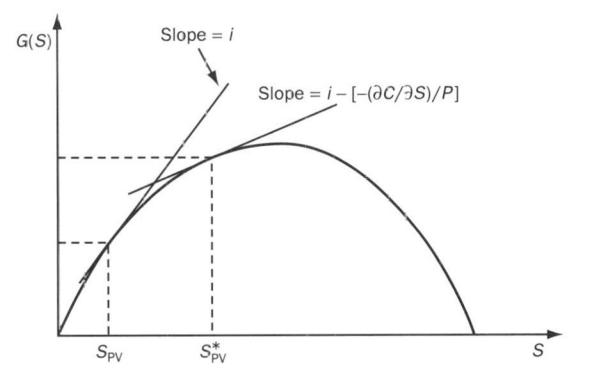

Figure 17.7 Present-value-maximising fish stocks with and without the dependence of costs on stock size, and for zero and positive interest rates

Furthermore, it is also clear from inspection of Figure 17.7 that if $i > 0$ and $\partial C/\partial S = 0$, then S_{PV} is less than the maximum sustainable yield stock, S_{MSY}. With positive discounting and no stock effect on costs, the stock is drawn down below the maximum sustainable yield as future losses in income from higher harvests are discounted and there is no penalty from harvest cost increases.

A further deduction can be made from equation 17.32, and is also illustrated with the help of Figure 17.7. If harvesting costs do not depend on the stock size, *and* decision makers use a zero discount rate, then the stock rate of growth (dG/dS) should be zero, and so the present-value-maximising steady-state stock level would be the one which leads to the maximum sustainable yield, S_{MSY}. (In Figure 17.7, the straight line is horizontal and is tangent to the growth function at S_{MSY}.) It makes sense to pick the stock level that gives the highest yield in perpetuity if costs are unaffected by stock size and the discount rate is zero. This result is of little practical relevance in commercial fishing, however, as it is not conceivable that owners would select a zero discount rate.

However, for many marine fisheries, it is likely to be the case in practice that harvesting costs will rise as the stock size falls. This property is built into the equations used in the illustrative example in this chapter. We have found that when costs depend negatively on the stock size, the present-value-maximising stock is higher than it would be otherwise. This follows from the result that the discount rate i must be equated with $dG/dS - \{\partial C/\partial S\}/p$), rather than with dG/dS alone. Given that $\{\partial C/\partial S\}/p$ is a negative quantity, this implies that dG/dS must be lower for any given interest rate, and so the equilibrium stock size must be greater than where there is no stock effect on costs. The intuition behind this is that benefits can be gained by allowing the stock size to rise (which causes harvesting costs to fall). This is also illustrated in Figure 17.7, which compares the present-value optimal stock levels with (S^*_{PV}) and without (S_{PV}) the dependence of costs on the stock size.

Note from equation 17.32 that as i rises, it will be necessary for dG/dS to fall to maintain the equality. That requires a smaller stock size. Hence we find that i and S will be negatively related for a PV-maximising fishery, whether or not costs depend on the stock size. This is consistent with our findings in Table 17.6.

Finally, note that in the general case where a positive discount rate is used and $\partial C/\partial S$ is non-zero, the steady-state present-value-maximising stock level may be less than, equal to, or greater than the maximum sustainable yield stock. Which one applies depends on the relative magnitudes of i and $(\partial C/\partial S)P$. Indeed inspection of Figure 17.7 shows the following:

$$i = -(\partial C/\partial S)P \Leftrightarrow S^*_{PV} = S_{MSY}$$

$$i > -(\partial C/\partial S)P \Leftrightarrow S^*_{PV} < S_{MSY}$$

$$i < -(\partial C/\partial S)P \Leftrightarrow S^*_{PV} > S_{MSY}$$

This confirms an observation made earlier in this chapter: a maximum sustainable yield (or a stock level S_{MSY}) is not in general economically efficient, and will only be so in special circumstances. For our illustrative numerical example, using baseline parameter values, it turns out that this special case is that in which $i = 0.05$; only at that interest rate does the PV-maximising model yield the MSY outcome.[14]

17.7 Dynamics in the PV-maximising fishery

Our analysis of the open-access fishery showed complex patterns of dynamic behaviour. Out of equilibrium, the processes of adjustment over time were (under baseline assumptions) characterised by oscillatory paths for stock, effort and harvest, with levels of these variables repeatedly over-shooting and under-shooting their steady-state values. In the case investigated, the dynamic adjustment processes were dynamically stable, eventually converging to equilibrium levels. For other sets of parameter values, other patterns of dynamic behaviour can be found, including fishery collapse and chaotic behaviour. (See Clark, 1990, and Conrad and Clark, 1987 for further details.)

These various dynamic processes reflect the unplanned, uncoordinated and myopic behaviour of fishing effort in an open-access fishery. Given the assumptions that have been made in this chapter about the PV-maximising fishery (and about the static private-property fishery) we would not expect to find those dynamic processes there. It is assumed that either owners in private fisheries coordinate their behaviour in a rational maximising way, or that the individual private property assumption rules out the intertemporal stock externality effect (whereby each boat's harvest reduces the future

---

[14] You can verify this yourself using the spreadsheet *Comparative Statics.xls*. Note also that if P were chosen differently, then another value of i would be required to bring about an MSY solution.

stock available for others) that exists in an open-access fishery.

A brief description of adjustment dynamics in PV-maximising private-property fisheries is given in Appendix 17.3. We suggest there that the efficient (wealth-maximising) paths to steady-state equilibrium outcomes will typically not be oscillatory. In fact, for the model examined in this section where the market price of fish is exogenously fixed, adjustment takes a particularly simple form, known as the most rapid approach path (MRAP). This is characterised by a simple rule

$$H_t = \begin{cases} 0 & \text{when } S_t < S_{PV}^* \\ H_{MAX} & \text{when } S_t > S_{PV}^* \end{cases}$$

That is, do no harvesting when stocks are less than the equilibrium value, and harvest at the maximum possible rate when stocks exceed the PV equilibrium.[15] Matters are more complicated where the price is endogenous, depending on the harvest rate. Relevant results, obtained using phase-plane analysis, are presented below in Appendix 17.3.

17.8 Bringing things together: the open-access fishery, static private-property fishery and PV-maximising fishery models compared

17.8.1 Steady-state characteristics

For pedagogical reasons, we have used a variety of methods of deriving results for the three fishery models investigated in this chapter. In addition, a variety of graphical techniques have been employed. It turns out that all of these can be related to one another and so what might appear to be three fundamentally different sets of models and results can all be reconciled with one another and encompassed within a single framework.

Let us look first at the difference between the two private-property fishery models. Earlier remarks have – without proof – stated that the static private-

property fishery is nothing more than a special case of the PV fishery – the special case being that the interest rate is zero. Put another way, the steady-state PV-maximising fishery results collapse to those of the simple private fishery model when the interest (discount) rate is zero. One way of verifying this assertion would be to substitute the value $i = 0$ into the expressions for PV-maximising stock, effort and harvest levels (shown in Appendix 17.3). It will be found that they collapse to the simpler expressions for static private-property equilibria in Table 17.4.

To understand intuitively why this happens, return to the dynamic asset-equilibrium condition given by equation 17.32:

$$ip = p\frac{dG}{dS} - \frac{\partial C}{\partial S}$$

When $i = 0$, this collapses to

$$\frac{dG}{dS}p = \frac{\partial C}{\partial S}$$

The left-hand side of this expression is the marginal revenue (with respect to stock changes) and the right-hand side is the marginal cost (with respect to stock changes). Profit-maximising equilibrium (in the static private-property fishery model without discounting) requires that these be equal. This is, of course, the standard result for any static profit-maximising model. Indeed, if the reader obtains the derivatives dG/dS and $\partial C/\partial S$ for our particular model equations, substitutes these into the expression above, and then solves for the equilibrium level of stock, they will find that the result is identical to that derived in Section 17.4 (and listed in the column labelled 'Static private property' in Table 17.4). We recommend that you try this exercise; it can be checked against our solution, given in Appendix 17.2.

Finally, is there any way in which we can bring the open-access fishery model into this encompassing framework? We can do so, by observing that an open-access fishery can be thought of as one in which the absence of enforceable property rights means that fishing boat owners have an infinitely

---

[15] Our Excel workbook does not exhibit this MRAP form of adjustment for a private (nor for a PV-maximising) fishery. Instead, the workbook uses a gradual adjustment rule in which effort increases (decreases) when marginal profit of effort is positive (negative). This rule generates a correct steady-state outcome, but the adjustment to it is slower than optimal.

high discount rate. Hence it is appropriate to modify a statement made earlier. The interest rate of boat owners in an open-access fishery is, in effect, infinity, irrespective of what level the prevailing interest rate in the rest of the economy happens to be. We have already demonstrated that as increasingly large values of i are plugged into the PV-maximising solution expression, outcomes converge to those derived from the open-access model.

17.9 Socially efficient resource harvesting

As with all resource allocation decisions, there can be no guarantee that privately maximising decisions will be socially efficient (let alone socially optimal). In this section, we review some of the reasons why divergences may take place. First of all, though, we establish the conditions that must be satisfied for socially efficient harvesting.

Let r be the *social* consumption discount rate. Socially efficient harvesting emerges as the solution to the maximisation problem

$$\text{Max} \int_0^\infty \{BS(H_t) - CS(S_t, H_t)\} e^{-rt} dt$$

subject to

$$\frac{dS}{dt} = G(S_t) - H_t$$

and initial stock level $S(0) = S_0$. In this expression $BS(H)$ denotes the social benefits as a function of quantity of fish landed, and $CS(S, H)$ denotes the social costs as a function of stock size and harvest rate. The current-value Hamiltonian, L, for this problem is

$$L(H, S)_t = BS(H_t) - CS(S_t, H_t) + \lambda_t(G(S_t) - H_t)$$

where λ_t is the (social) shadow net price of a unit of the stock of the renewable resource. The necessary conditions for a maximum include

(i) $\quad \dfrac{\partial L_t}{\partial H_t} = 0 = \dfrac{dBS}{dH_t} - \dfrac{\partial CS}{\partial H_t} - \lambda_t \qquad (17.34)$

(ii) $\quad \dfrac{d\lambda_t}{dt} = r\lambda_t - \lambda_t \dfrac{dG}{dS_t} + \dfrac{\partial CS}{\partial S_t} \qquad (17.35)$

and the resource net growth equation

(iii) $\quad \dfrac{dS}{dt} = G(S_t) - R_t$

We continue to assume that the market price of fish is exogenously fixed at P. Now consider also the following additional conditions:

(i) The market price, P, correctly reflects all social benefits (which then, together with the assumption of exogenously given prices, implies $dBS/dH = P$).

(ii) There are no fishing externalities on the cost side so that $CS(S, H) = C(S, H)$.

(iii) The private and social consumption discount rates are identical, $i = r$.

If these additional conditions are satisfied, and are imposed on equations 17.34 and 17.35, the first-order conditions for social efficiency are identical to those for the PV-maximising fishery (equations 17.29 and 17.30) except for the fact that the shadow price is denoted as λ in the former and p in the latter. But since shadow prices are themselves solutions to optimising problems, and the problems are in this case identical, it follows that p and λ must also be identical. Hence the PV-maximising fishery is socially efficient under the set of conditions we have just described. But, of course, it also follows that if one or more of those conditions is *not* satisfied, private fishing will not be socially efficient. We investigate next some reasons why such a divergence might arise.

17.9.1 Externalities in the benefits function

The first case is that in which social benefits depend not only on the size of the resource harvest but also on the level of the resource stock. For many biological species that are harvested, intentionally or unintentionally (as by-catch), it is evident that society does place a value on the existence of these species and is concerned about the number of them that do exist. This is clearly true for many large animals such as big cats, whales and apes, and surely extends much more widely than that. In this case, the social-welfare-maximising problem should be generalised to

$$\text{Max} \int_0^\infty \{\text{BS}(H_t, S_t) - \text{CS}(H_t, S_t)\} e^{-rt} dt$$

subject to

$$\frac{dS}{dt} = G(S_t) - H_t$$

Note that S now enters the benefits function (in which it had not appeared previously). Intuition suggests that the optimal solution to this model will be different from that obtained from the model where benefits only depend on the harvest rate, H. This intuition is correct. Assuming that utility is an increasing function of S, the solution will in general be one in which the optimal stock level is higher, reflecting the positive utility that the resource stock generates. We invite the reader to work through the maths to obtain this result. To check your analysis, we have placed such a derivation in a separate document in the *Additional Materials, Stock Dependent Utility.doc*.

More generally, society is likely to have multiple objectives which are not well represented by the private harvester's own objective function (which will tend to be dominated by catch quantity considerations). This is very important for many terrestrial resources, particularly woodlands and forests as we shall see in the next chapter. But it also applies to marine resources. For example, society may have an interest in the maintenance of population diversity or genetic diversity; it may be willing to pay a larger risk premium to ensure high resistance to disease among marine organisms; or it may prefer to maintain stock levels much higher than would private harvesters – at a safe minimum standard – in response to uncertainty and the threats of catastrophic change. All these could be thought of as additional arguments that would appear in the social objective function (but which would not usually enter private profit functions).

Alternatively, we might choose to model some or all of the externalities in terms of costs. That is, private owners are likely to fail to make adequate provision for the full social opportunity costs of their activities, and so externalities are not being intern-

alised. This leads us to the next category of sources of inefficiency.

17.9.2 Externalities in the fishery production function

A second source of social inefficiency arises from externalities operating through the fishery production function. There are two important types of harvesting externality. First, it often happens that resource harvesting inadvertently destroys other species. Beam trawling, for example, (in which a net is weighed down to the sea bed by heavy beams and is trawled along the sea bed to catch bottom-feeding fish such as cod), causes immense damage to other sea-bed creatures, and can cause those populations to collapse. This is a classic externality problem and it is clear that outcomes are most unlikely to be efficient in such cases. Some form of regulation of fishing practices seems to be appropriate here. We return to this matter later.

A second kind of externality is often known as a 'crowding' diseconomy. Suppose that each boat's harvest depends on its effort and on the effort of others. Then each boat's catch imposes a contemporaneous external cost on every other boat. In effect, boats are getting in each other's way. When any boat is fishing, the costs of harvesting a given quantity of fish become higher for all other boats. This externality drives the average costs of fishing for the fleet as a whole above the marginal costs of an individual fisher.

If a crowding effect of this kind exists, the function $C(H, S)$ from the point of view of an individual boat operator may differ from the function $CS(H, S)$ from the social point of view. Whether it does or not depends on what institutional conditions apply. If the private (or PV-maximising) fishery is one in which effort is somehow or other coordinated in the common interest, then it would be sensible to assume that the size of the fishing fleet as a whole (and the spatial patterns of fishing) would be optimally chosen. The optimal size of fleet would balance the additional benefits of extra boats against the additional external costs of extra boats. The crowding diseconomies become internalised in this way, leading to efficient outcomes. Alternatively, if the fishery were in private-property ownership but were carefully and effectively *regulated*, then it is conceivable that such regulation might also internalise the externality.

Under conditions of open access, there is virtually no possibility that crowding effects would be internalised by the actions of fishermen alone. The kind of coordination we referred to above cannot happen in the competitive struggle to grab fish. Almost certainly, the unregulated industry would consist of more harvesters and more harvesting capital than is economically efficient. However, it is still possible that some form of regulation might achieve the required coordination. We discuss this further below.

It is important to note that the crowding diseconomy we have just referred to is entirely different from the 'stock externality' effect which arises in open access. Crowding externalities are contemporaneous; stock externalities are intertemporal. The latter exist when the taking of fish today imposes additional costs in the future by virtue of the reduced future stock size. We have already remarked that this kind of externality fundamentally distinguishes the open-access and private (and PV-maximising) fishery cases. Realistically or not, modellers typically assume that the stock externality will not be internalised in open-access conditions but will be in a private fishery. The first part of this assumption is surely true. Indeed, there is ample evidence that fishing effort is massively excessive and inefficient in many open-access fisheries throughout the world.

It is of interest to note that the Schaefer (1957) form of fishery production function we have used in this chapter ($H = eES$) rules out the existence of crowding externalities. For a given stock size, H will change in proportion to changes in E. In other words, the marginal product of effort is constant, precluding crowding effects.

17.9.3 Difference between private and social discount rates

Maximised social and private net benefits also diverge when social and private discount rates differ.

We have already remarked that this is one way of explaining the excessive harvesting that takes place in open-access fisheries, but it should be clear that the problem is more wide-reaching than that case alone.

17.9.4 Monopolistic fisheries

The existence of monopoly ownership of a fishery may also generate inefficient outcomes. A resource market is monopolistic if there is one single price-making harvester. It is known from standard microeconomic theory that marginal revenue exceeds marginal cost at a monopolistic market equilibrium.[16] A monopoly owner would tend to harvest less each period, and sell the resource at a higher market price, than is socially efficient. Therefore, if a renewable resource were harvested under monopolistic rather than competitive conditions, an economically inefficient harvesting level may result. The qualifier 'may' in the previous sentence arises from second-best considerations. In a world where there are other market failures pushing harvest rates to excessive levels, monopoly harvests may be closer to the second-best efficient allocation than those from 'competitive' PV-maximising fisheries.

17.10 A safe minimum standard of conservation

Our discussion of the 'best' level of renewable-resource harvesting has focused almost exclusively on the criterion of economic efficiency. However, if harvesting rates pose threats to the sustainability of some renewable resource (such as North Atlantic fisheries or primary forests) or jeopardise an environmental system itself (such as a wildlife reserve containing extensive biodiversity) then the criterion of efficiency may be insufficient or inappropriate. We observed earlier that even in a deterministic world – in which population growth rates are known with certainty – the pursuit of an efficiency criterion is not sufficient to guarantee the survival of a

---

[16] Similar conclusions also apply to imperfectly competitive markets in which a small number of harvesters dominate the industry.

renewable resource stock or an environmental system in perpetuity, particularly when resource prices are high, harvesting costs are low, or discount rates are high. Where biological systems are stochastic, or where uncertainty is pervasive, threats to sustainability are even more pronounced.

Many writers – some economists, but particularly non-economists – argue that correcting market failure and eliminating efficiency losses should be given secondary importance to the pursuit of sustainability. This would suggest that policy be targeted to the prevention of species extinction or the loss of biological diversity whenever that is reasonably practical. Efficiency objectives can be pursued within this general constraint.

Such considerations brings us back to the principle that policy be oriented around the criterion of a safe minimum standard of conservation (SMS), an idea examined earlier in Chapter 13. How does this idea apply to renewable resource policy? A strict version of SMS would involve imposing constraints on resource harvesting and use so that all risks to the survival of a renewable resource are eliminated. This is unlikely to be of much practical relevance. Virtually all human behaviour entails some risks to species survival, and so a strict SMS would prohibit virtually all economic activity. In order to make the concept usable, it is necessary to impose weaker constraints, so that the adoption of an SMS approach will entail that, under *reasonable* allowances for uncertainty, threats to survival of valuable resource systems are eliminated, provided that this does not entail excessive cost. For decisions to be made that are consistent with that weaker criterion, judgements will be necessary particularly about what constitutes 'reasonable uncertainty' and 'excessive cost', and which resources are deemed 'sufficiently valuable' for application of the SMS criterion.

Let us explore the concept of an SMS in this context by following the exposition in a recent paper by Randall and Farmer (1995). Suppose there is some renewable resource the expected growth of which over time is illustrated by the curve labelled 'Regeneration function' in Figure 17.8. The function

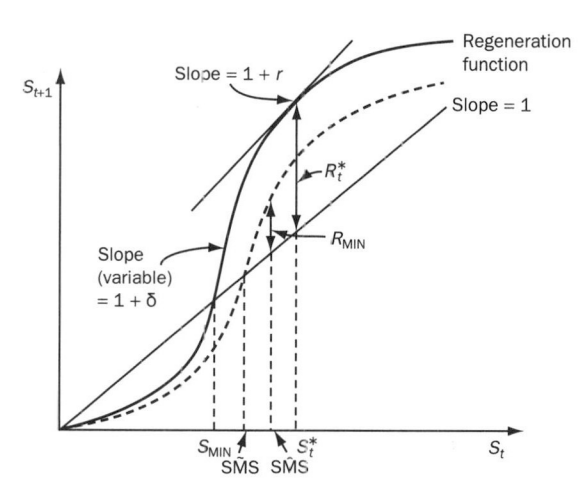

Figure 17.8 A safe minimum standard of conservation
Source: Adapted from Randall and Farmer (1995)

shows the resource stock level that will be available in period $t + 1$ (S_{t+1}) for any level of stock that is conserved in period t (S_t). Notice that the greater is the level of stock conservation in period t, the higher will be the stock level available in the following period.[17]

Randall and Farmer restrict their attention to sustainable resource use, interpreting sustainability to mean a sequence of states in which the resource stock does not decline over time. Therefore, only those levels of stock in period t corresponding to segments of the regeneration function that lie on or above the 45° line (labelled 'slope = 1') constitute sustainable stocks. The minimum *sustainable* level of stock conservation is labelled S_{MIN}.

The efficient level of stock conservation is S_t^*. To see this, construct a tangent to the regeneration function with a slope of $1 + r$, where r is a (consumption) social discount rate, and let δ denote the rate of growth of the renewable resource.[18] At any point on the regeneration function, a tangent to the function will have a slope of $1 + \delta$. For the particular stock level S_t^* we have

$$1 + r = 1 + \delta \quad \text{or} \quad r = \delta$$

and so the rate of growth of the renewable resource, δ, is equal to the social discount rate, r. This is a

---

[17] The non-linear relationship shown here is plausible for many types of biological resource, but will not be a good representation for all such resources.

[18] Strictly speaking, δ is the derivative of the amount of resource growth with respect to the stock size; it is what we have earlier written as dG/dS.

condition for *economically efficient* steady-state renewable resource harvesting that we have met earlier in Section 17.7.1. That is, it is the form that equation 17.32 takes in steady-state equilibrium where harvest costs are independent of stock size. Note also that at the efficient stock level, the amount of harvest that can be taken in perpetuity is R_t^*. By harvesting at this rate, the post-harvest stock in period $t + 1$ is equal to that in period t, thus satisfying the sustainability requirement.

Now suppose that the regeneration function is subject to random variation. For simplicity, assume that the worst possible outcome is indicated by the dotted regeneration function in Figure 17.8. At any current stock, the worst that can happen is that the available future stock falls short of the expected quantity by an amount equal to the vertical distance between the solid and dotted functions. Now even in the worst outcome, if SM̃S is conserved in each period, the condition for perpetual sustainability of the stock will be maintained. We might regard SM̃S as a stock level that incorporates the safe minimum standard of conservation, reflecting the uncertainty due to random variability in the regeneration function. Put another way, whereas S_{MIN} is an appropriate minimum stock in the absence of uncertainty, SM̃S takes account of uncertainty in a particular way.

In fact, SM̃S is not what Randall and Farmer propose as a safe minimum standard of conservation. They argue that any sustainable path over time must involve some positive, non-declining level of resource harvesting and consumption in every period. Suppose that R_{MIN} is judged to be that minimum required level of resource consumption. Then Randall and Farmer's safe minimum standard of conservation is SM̂S. If the stock in period t is kept from falling below this level then, even in the worst possible case, R_{MIN} can be harvested without interference with sustainability.

The SMS principle implies maintaining a renewable resource stock at or above some safe minimum level such as SM̂S. In Figure 17.8, there is no conflict between the conservation and efficiency criteria. The safe minimum standard of conservation actually implies a lower target for the resource stock than that implied by economic efficiency. This will not always be true, however, and one can easily imagine circumstances where an SMS criterion implies more cautious behaviour than the economically efficient outcome.

Finally, what can be said about the qualification that the SMS should be pursued only where it does not entail excessive cost? Not surprisingly, it is difficult to make much headway here, as it is not clear how one might decide what constitutes excessive cost. Randall and Farmer suggest that no society can reasonably be expected to decimate itself. Therefore, if the SMS conflicted with the survival of human society, that would certainly entail excessive cost. But most people are likely to regard costs far less than this – such as extreme deprivation – as being excessive. Ultimately, the political process must generate views as to what constitutes excessive costs.

17.11 Resource harvesting, population collapses and the extinction of species

It will be useful to draw together some of the results obtained in this chapter that relate to the possibilities of major population declines or the extinction of species. Human activity can have adverse effects on biological resources in a variety of ways. Two general classes of effects can be distinguished. One operates on particular species (or local populations of a species) that are the direct targets of harvesting activity. In this category we shall also include effects on related species or populations that are strongly dependent on or interrelated with the targets. The second class concerns more widely diffused, indirect impacts on systems of biological resources, induced in the main by disruptions of ecosystems. Much of this generalised impact on biological resources is brought together under the rubric of decline of biological diversity. We consider the causes of biodiversity decline in a separate document in the *Additional Materials*.

As we have seen, property rights have important consequences for patterns of resource exploitation. In general, harvesting effort will be higher and stock sizes lower where a renewable resource is open-access than when enforceable property rights exist. But stronger claims are often made. In particular, it is sometimes argued that populations of renewable resources will inevitably be degraded, suffer serious collapse, or even be driven to zero under open-access conditions. The *inevitability* of these events finds no support in the models we have examined so far. Indeed, in examining the steady-state equilibrium of an open-access fishery, our numerical example generated a maximum-sustainable-yield stock size. And for higher values of harvesting costs or lower prices the stock would be even higher, possibly as large as S_{MAX}, the environmental carrying capacity of the resource.

To confirm this, look again at Figures 17.3 and 17.4. Consider, for example, the consequence of an increase in w. The ray which plots $H = (w/P)E$ in Figure 17.4 shifts anticlockwise, and so leads to lower effort. Lower effort rotates the *eES* curve in Figure 17.3 clockwise, leading to a higher steady-state stock. For a sufficiently high value of w, no positive steady-state fishing effort will be profitable, and the population will rise to its environmental carrying capacity. Clearly, there is nothing inevitable about population collapses in open-access conditions. Much depends on economic factors that may be favourable or unfavourable to large population sizes. Nevertheless, the possibility that a population may be driven to zero is greater

- when the resource is harvested under conditions of open access than where enforceable property rights prevail;
- the higher is the market price of the harvested resource;
- the lower is the cost of harvesting a given quantity of the resource;
- when prices are endogenous, the more that market price rises as catch costs rise or as harvest quantities fall;
- the lower the natural growth rate of the stock;
- the lower the extent to which marginal extraction costs rise as the stock size diminishes;
- the higher is the discount rate.

Even under private property conditions an optimal harvesting programme may drive a fish stock to zero. This is most likely where the prey is simple to catch even when the stock approaches a critical minimum threshold level, and where the harvested resource is very valuable. In this case, the optimal harvest level could exceed biological growth rates at all levels of stock.

As the analyses in this chapter have been derived from a simple logistic biological growth model one should be wary about claiming too much generality for our results. Clearly, other biological growth functions could have generated different results. Three matters are noteworthy here:

- The biological growth function may have a positive (and possibly quite large) minimum sustainable population size, as in Figures 17.1(b) and (c). If for any reason the stock falls below this level, the population cannot survive. Many large mammal species appear to be cases in point.
- The growth process may be stochastic (have a random component); stochastic shocks or disturbances might lead to population collapses.
- Populations are often interdependent in ecosystems. Changes in other populations may lead to the collapse of some population in which we are interested. The word file *Models of Biological Interaction* in the *Additional Materials* for Chapter 17 examines this matter at some length.

But there is another set of reasons why we should be cautious. Our comments so far in this section have been largely about steady-state or equilibrium outcomes. But systems are not always (or perhaps not even very often) in such a state. Indeed, our Excel spreadsheet simulations of an open-access fishery show that the fishery may be in disequilibrium over very long periods of time even where parameters and environmental conditions are unchanging. Where those factors are frequently changing – as we would expect to find in practice – disequilibrium states will prevail more-or-less indefinitely, and it is very difficult to predict outcomes. It is clearly possible that harvest rates may be persistently above natural population growth rates. Also, ignorance, uncertainty or institutional failure could lead to a population falling below its minimum threshold size even where that event is (*ex post*) irrational.

Notice in particular that the existence of a steady-state equilibrium is no guarantee that such a state may be attained. Even if we restrict attention to the adjustment paths along which effort and stock levels travel in the open-access model of Section

17.3, the Excel simulations described in *Fishery dynamics.xls* demonstrate that the population might collapse to its minimum threshold size (and never recover) even though a positive steady-state equilibrium stock level exists. Non-targeted species may be casualties in this process too. Many forms of resource harvesting, particularly marine fishing, directly or indirectly reduce stocks of other plants or animals that happen to be in the neighbourhood, or which have some biologically complementary relationship with the target resource.

Extinction of species is more likely, other things being equal, where the critical minimum threshold population size is relatively large. In this case, a greater proportion of possible harvesting programmes will lead to harvest rates that cannot be maintained over time. The existence of uncertainty also plays a very important role. Uncertainty may relate to the size of the minimum threshold population, to the actual stock size, or to the current and forecast harvesting rates. If errors are made in estimating any of these magnitudes, then it is clear that the likelihood of stock extinction is increased.

Another influence is the role of chance or random factors. Our presentation has assumed that all functions are deterministic – for given values of explanatory variables, there is a unique value of the explained variable. But many biological and economic processes are stochastic, with chance factors playing a role in shaping outcomes. In these circumstances, there will be a distribution of possible outcomes rather than one single outcome for given values of explanatory variables. We discussed some consequences of risk and uncertainty in Chapter 13.

Elementary theories of commercial resource harvesting tend to ignore these possibilities, as we did in much of the exposition given to this point in this chapter. Steady-state fishing involves a balance between regeneration and harvesting rates, and so precludes population collapses. Even sophisticated dynamic models of commercial resource harvesting suggest that species extinction, while being possible in principle, is likely only under very special circumstances. For example, Clark (1990) shows that a privately optimal harvesting programme (where access to the resource is controlled) may be one in which it is 'optimal' to harvest a resource to extinction, but also demonstrates that this is highly improbable.

But even a casual inspection of the evidence suggests that much resource harvesting does not fit comfortably with the theoretical models we have outlined, nor does it appear to have the consequences that those models predict. Reading the sections on the state of renewable resources in recent issues of *World Resources* makes it clear that the world is experiencing extensive losses of many renewable resource-population stocks, and unprecedented rates of species extinction. Some examples of these phenomena, looking particularly at cases where harvesting rates of target animal populations have been high relative to natural rates of regeneration, are presented in the file *Population Collapses* in the *Additional Materials*.

17.12 Renewable resources policy

What goals might one reasonably expect of governmental policy towards the use of renewable resources? Several seem relevant, including efficiency, biological and ecological sustainability, and regional employment and cultural support.

Efficiency goals have been the main focus of this chapter. When the use of resources is economically inefficient, there are potential welfare benefits to the community from policy which leads to efficiency gains. This suggests that policy may be directed towards removing externalities, improving information, developing property rights, removing monopolist industrial structures, and using direct controls or fiscal incentives to alter rates of harvesting whenever there is reason to believe that harvesting programmes are inefficient. Efficiency gains, in the form of improved intertemporal resource extraction programmes, may also be obtained if government assists in the establishment of forward or futures markets. As we saw in Chapter 5, efficient outcomes are not possible in general unless all relevant markets exist. The absence of forward markets for most natural resources suggests that it is most unlikely that extraction and harvesting programmes will be intertemporally efficient. Chapter 7 examined the policy instruments available to attain environmental pollution targets, and much of what was written there is relevant for our present discussion. We will examine two particular instances of incentive-based policy instruments later in this section.

The provision of information matters not only to the pursuit of efficiency but also to biological and ecological sustainability. Given that uncertainty is so great in matters relating to natural resources, the government's role in the provision of information is likely to be crucial. In the case of commercial fisheries, for example, individual fishermen will not be in a position to know, in quantitative terms, how previous and current behaviour has affected and is likely to affect the population levels of relevant species. The consequences of cyclical natural phenomenon, such as the El Niño current mentioned in Box 17.3, will similarly be largely unpredictable by individual agents. Obtaining this kind of information requires a significant monitoring and research effort which is unlikely to be undertaken by the industry itself. Even if it were obtained privately, the dissemination of such information would probably be sub-optimal, as those who devote resources to collecting the information may well seek to limit its availability to others.

17.12.1 Command and control regulations

Throughout the world most fisheries have been, and remain, in essence open-access fisheries. By far the most common way of regulating fisheries is some form of command and control approach. The large set of restrictions and regulations that fall under this heading can be loosely classified in the following way:

1. regulations aimed at reducing fishing effort. Examples include restrictions on the boat size or other capital equipment used by fishermen, closed fishery seasons, limits on days of fishing permitted per boat;
2. restrictions on fishing gear and mesh or net size, aimed at controlling the qualitatitive nature of the catch. Particular targets have included protection of juvenile fish, reduction of by-catch and catch discards, and reducing environmental damage associated with harvesting;
3. spatial restrictions on harvesting activity, aimed at reducing conflict among fishing operators;
4. fleet size reductions;

5. quantity restrictions on catches. This is the centrepiece of fishing regulation in the European Union, for example, in the Total Allowable Catch system.

A difficulty with the first three of these command and control approaches is that objectives are reached at the cost of decreased harvesting efficiency (in effect, a reduction in the catch coefficient, e, in equation 17.7) and/or large financial costs to fishing operators. These controls deliberately impose economic inefficiency on the industry, in an effort to reduce harvest sizes, and so cannot be cost-efficient methods of attaining harvest reduction targets.

The fourth approach – fleet size reduction – may avoid cost-inefficiencies if the fishing industry capital stock is reduced to its optimal (cost-minimising) level. Governments have tried to attain this by incentives for firms to leave the industry. But there are two serious limitations at work here. First, capital reductions in some fisheries (particularly in those of the industrialised economies) result in older vessels being sold cheaply to fisheries elsewhere; the effective capacity is not actually cut. Second, such controls are useless in a state of generalised overcapacity when reduced effort by one set of operators is just matched by increased effort from other firms.

The fifth approach, quantity of catch restrictions, may be attractive if enforceable, but its record of achievement is extremely poor. Box 17.5 shows that even one of the few examples of quota schemes that was thought to be successful turned out not to be so on closer examination. The widespread failure of catch quota instruments is partly the consequence of the mobile and geographically dispersed nature of the industry and its prey. That is being overcome by modern electronic-based methods of monitoring, control and surveillance. However, in the final analysis, this instrument – like others in the list – is flawed by its focus on proximate causes. It fails to tackle the fundamental causes of the excess fishing-capacity problem. This has its roots, as we have seen, in the absence of well-defined and enforceable property rights, such that many fisheries are *de facto* open-access resources. Where property rights do not exist, perverse incentive structures result. Individual fishing firms have incentives to buy larger boats, or more boats, or install more sophisticated harvesting

---

Box 17.5 Quota restrictions in the Pacific halibut fishery

Gordon (1954) provides an interesting account of the use of quota restrictions in the Pacific halibut fishery. During the 1930s, Canada and the USA agreed to fixed catch limits. For many years, the scheme was hailed as an outstanding success; with catch per unit effort quantities rising over two decades, it was one of the few quota schemes to have achieved this goal.

However, Gordon shows that the improvements were not the result of quotas, but of a natural cyclical improvement in Pacific halibut stocks. Catches rose rather than fell during the period when quotas were introduced. Even then, the total catch taken was only a small fraction of the estimated population *reduction* prior to the introduction of regulation.

Furthermore, the efficiency loss of the regulations was enormous. The actual duration of the fishing season (the time span until quotas were met) fell from six months in 1933 to between one and two months in 1952. Despite their widespread use, these quantitative restrictions on either effort or catch have very little justification in either economic or biological terms.

---

technology in order to win a larger share of the fixed quota for themselves. These things happen at the same time as government is trying to buy boats out of fishing. The failure to effectively limit capacity (and attain quota targets) then results in regulators imposing shorter fishing seasons.[19] As a result of processes like this, the larger capital stock either lies idle for even longer periods, or boats turn to exploit other, less tightly regulated, fisheries, thereby imposing stock depletion problems elsewhere.

17.12.2 Incentive-based instruments: a landing tax

Compliance with regulations is often so poor, and illegal, unregulated and unreported (IUU) fishing so widespread, that command and control techniques may simply fail to reach their objectives at all. Not surprisingly, this has led to a search for alternative policy instruments. We have seen in several earlier parts of this book that a tax instrument can sometimes internalise an externality so as to bring about an efficient solution. The 'problems' associated with open-access fisheries can also be interpreted as externality problems. In this section we show how – at least in principle – an open-access fishing industry might be induced to harvest in a socially efficient manner through the use of a tax instrument.

Specifically, the tax being looked at here is a fish landings tax. It is levied at a fixed rate per unit of the fish resource landed. How should the level of such a tax be set? Consider the steady-state present-value-maximising condition 17.32:

$$ip = p\frac{dG}{dS} - \frac{\partial C}{\partial S} \qquad (17.36)$$

Remember that p in this equation is the net price of a unit of the fish resource. Rewrite this equation in the form

$$p = \frac{\frac{dG}{dS}p}{i} - \frac{\frac{\partial C}{\partial S}}{i} \qquad (17.37)$$

How can we interpret this equation? Consider a decision to *not* harvest an additional unit of the resource. The left-hand side of this expression is the net price of the fish; it is, therefore, the rent forgone by not harvesting that unit. As that rent would be obtained immediately if the fish were harvested, the left-hand side is already in present-value terms. The right-hand side of 17.37 consists of the present value of the benefits obtained by not harvesting that unit of fish. This benefit has two components:

- $[(dG/dS)p]/i$ is the present value of the extra biological growth that would result from leaving the fish unharvested (including any new growth of fish that could be attributed to it);
- $-[(\partial C/\partial S)/i$ is the present value of the reduced fishing costs that would result from leaving the fish unharvested (noting that the costs per unit harvest will generally be smaller the larger is the fish stock level).

---

[19] For example, the season for eastern Pacific yellowfin tuna fell from nine months prior to catch quotas being introduced to just three months after a quota restriction was imposed.

How do we know that these two terms are in present values? It follows from the expression for the present value of an infinite-duration annuity. The present value of an infinite annuity of A at an interest rate i is A/i. As we are considering steady states only here, the numerator term in each of the two components is an infinitely repeated benefit or cost. Dividing one repetition of either by the interest rate gives us its present value, therefore.

The right-hand side of equation 17.37 is often known as the *user cost* of fishing. We note that the user cost of fishing is taken into account in optimal (present-value-maximising) harvesting choices. However, in an open-access fishery, even though each fisherman may well be aware of these two components of costs, the user cost of fishing will *not* be taken into account in choices about effort or harvesting. Why not? The open-access property gives the fisherman no incentive to leave fish in the sea (to encourage more growth in the future). Others would simply harvest any fish left by one fisherman. The fisherman would be unable to appropriate the fruits of his investment in the future. Each fisherman in effect sees the present value of these future benefits as zero (even though collectively they would not be zero if all abstained together).

Recall that in open-access conditions, fishing effort expands until a point is reached at which the net price (or rent) from an additional unit of effort is zero. That is, in equilibrium $p = P - \partial C/\partial H = 0$ where p is the *net* price of the fish resource. However, the condition that must be satisfied by optimal (present-value-maximising) fishing is, using equation 17.37:

$$p - \left(\frac{\frac{dG}{dS}p}{i} - \frac{\frac{\partial C}{\partial S}}{i} \right) = 0$$

and so

$$(P - C_H) - \left(\frac{\frac{dG}{dS}p}{i} - \frac{\frac{\partial C}{\partial S}}{i} \right) = 0 \qquad (17.38)$$

where $C_H = \partial C/\partial H$ is the marginal cost of each fish harvested for an additional unit of effort. But now suppose that the open-access fisherman is required to pay a tax (t) on each unit of fish landed equal to the user cost of fishing

$$\frac{\frac{dG}{dS}p}{i} - \frac{\frac{\partial C}{\partial S}}{i}.$$

Then, the post-tax open-access equilibrium condition would be amended so that post-tax net price is zero. That is,

$$P - t - C_H = P - \left(\frac{\frac{dG}{dS}p}{i} - \frac{\frac{\partial C}{\partial S}}{i} \right) - c = 0$$

which is identical to the present-value-maximising fishing rule. A tax on landed fish equal in value to the user cost of fishing would therefore bring about an efficient outcome.

In fact, there may be an additional tax adjustment required to bring about a socially efficient outcome. In the models discussed in this chapter, we have adopted simplified functions which impose equality of average and marginal fishing costs, and rule out the existence of crowding diseconomies. Where crowding diseconomies do exist, these warrant a second component to the optimal tax; that component would be set at a value that internalises crowding externalities. Overall, therefore, an optimal landing tax will have two components: one part corrects for the fact that fishermen in open access take no account of the future benefits to be obtained by refraining from harvesting; the second part internalises crowding diseconomies. Despite their theoretical attractiveness, tax systems of this kind are very uncommon (or perhaps non-existent).

17.12.3 Incentive-based instruments: property rights and transferable harvesting quotas

A central theme of this chapter has been the key role played by property rights – or their absence – in renewable resource exploitation. Where enforceable property rights do not exist, the resource is said to be subject to open access. An obvious way of trying to achieve efficient resource harvesting is to define and allocate exclusive property rights to it. Where resources are exclusively owned, and where that ownership generates for its owner or owners the full income flow attributable to that resource, owners have incentives to maximise its present value and so to take whatever investment or conservation decisions are consistent with that goal.

Many nations have extended the limits of their national jurisdictions over marine resources to 200 miles from their coasts. Is this sufficient to meet the conditions we have just described for exclusive and enforceable property rights? The answer is, in most cases, that by itself it is not sufficient. Even if a government were willing and able to prevent all access to its fisheries by foreign nationals, there may still be *de facto* open access to fishing boats of the nation in question. The problem is not resolved, and clearly something additional is required.

One way of thinking what additional instrument is required is to follow up on a device we used when introducing the notion of a 'private-property fishery'. There we presented two 'scenarios'. The first envisaged a fishery consisting of a large number of sub-fisheries, each exclusively owned by one operator. The second envisaged a fishery in which enforceable property rights are collectively vested in a particular large set of fishing firms *and* in which the behaviour of those individual owners was somehow or other coordinated to be collectively rational. We did not specify, though, what either of these mechanisms might be in practice.

There is a large number of ways in which one or other of these scenarios could be achieved or, rather, mimicked. We shall investigate just one in this section. It involves the state or regulator acting as co-ordinator, and allocating exclusive property rights to particular quantities of harvested fish to a particular set of fishing operators. Note that this will involve more than merely allocating quotas or allowable catches to the fleet as a whole: the allocations are to individuals (or possibly to some small collective units that can be relied upon to internally coordinate their actions).

Moreover, if these exclusive property rights are to have their full worth to those to whom they are allocated, they must – like all property rights – be transferable or marketable. Bearing in mind results we obtained in Chapter 7, the reader will notice that this marketability characteristic will be consistent with the objective of achieving whatever target is sought at least cost. This corresponds with the requirement we are looking for that the system in some way mimics a coordinated present-value-maximising fishery.

One scheme that has these properties is the 'individual transferable quota' (ITQ) system. This operates (approximately) in the following way for some particular stock of a controlled species. Scientists assess current and potential stock levels, and determine a maximum total allowable catch (TAC). The TAC is then divided among fishers. Each fisher can catch and land up to the amount of the quota they hold. Alternatively, some or all of the ITQs that an operator holds can be sold to others. No entitlement exists to harvest fish in the absence of holding ITQs.

To see how the ITQ system can result in the harvest of a given target quantity of fish in a cost-efficient manner, consider the following hypothetical example in which, for arithmetical simplicity only, the industry consists of just two fishing firms. The two firms differ in terms of harvesting costs, one being low-cost ($2 per tonne) and the other high-cost ($4 per tonne). A tonne of fish can be sold for $10. Each firm has historically caught and sold 100 tonnes of fish each period. Now consider what will happen if the government imposes an industry TAC of 100 tonnes. Suppose that a non-transferable quota of 50 tonnes is imposed on each firm. The total catch will be 100 tonnes, at a total cost of $300 (that is, $50 \times 4 + 50 \times 2$). Next, suppose that a transferable quota of 50 tonnes is allocated to each fisher; what will happen in this case? Given that the low-cost fisher makes a profit (net price) of $8 per tonne, while the high-cost fisher makes a profit of $6 per tonne, a mutually advantageous trade opportunity arises. Suppose, for example, that an ITQ price is agreed at $7 per tonne of landed fish. The high-cost producer will sell quotas at this price, obtaining a higher value per sold quota ($7) than the profit forgone on fish it could otherwise catch ($6). The low-cost producer will purchase ITQs at $7, as this is lower than the marginal profit ($8) it can make from the additional catch that is permitted by possession of an ITQ. A Pareto gain takes place, relative to the case where the quotas are non-transferable. This gain is a gain for the economy as a whole as can be seen by noting the total costs after ITQ trading. In this case, all 50 ITQs will be transferred, and so 100 tonnes will be harvested by the low-cost fisher, at a total cost of $200.

This example is, of course, unrealistically simple. We really want our story to apply to large numbers, not just two. And the idea that the industry consists of two sets of fishers, each with a constant (but different) set of harvesting costs, will not hold in practice. Nevertheless, the underlying principle is correct and applies generally to marketable permit or quota systems in a wide set of circumstances. Transferability ensures that a market will develop in the quotas. In this market, high-cost producers will sell entitlements to harvest, and low-cost producers will purchase rights to harvest. The market price will be set at some level intermediate between the net prices or profits of the different producers. (We demonstrated in Chapter 7 that this efficiency property is also shared by a tax system; indeed, a tax rate of $7 per tonne of harvested fish would bring about an identical outcome to that described above. Why is this so?)

The transferable quota system has been used successfully in several fisheries, including some in Canada and New Zealand. Some aspects of its practical experience are examined in Box 17.6.

In this section we have focused on one specific form of property rights – exclusive individual private-property rights – and one particular form of policy instrument – individual transferable quotas. However, we do not wish to imply that these are the only ways of achieving efficient outcomes. In principle, many forms of property rights regime, and many forms of policy instrument, can deliver efficient outcomes. The suggestions for further reading at the end of this chapter point you to, and elaborate on, some other possibilities.

Box 17.6 The individual transferable quota system in New Zealand fisheries

In 1986, New Zealand introduced an individual transferable quota (ITQ) system for its major fisheries. The ITQ management system operates in the way we described earlier. Government scientists annually assess fish stock levels, and determine maximum total allowable catches (TAC) for controlled species. New Zealand legislation requires that the TAC levels are consistent with the stock levels that can deliver maximum sustainable yields. The TAC is then divided among fishers, with the shares being allocated on the basis of individual catches in recent years. Each fisher can catch fish up to the amount of the quota it holds, or the quotas can be sold or otherwise traded.

The ITQ system has a number of desirable properties. First, fishermen know at the start of each season the quantity of fish they are entitled to catch; this allows effort to be directed in a cost-minimising efficient manner, avoiding the mad dash for catches that characterises free-access fishery. Secondly, as a market exists in ITQs, resources should be allocated in such a way that firms with low harvesting costs undertake fishing. The reasoning behind this assertion is explained in the main text.

The ITQ system operates in conjunction with strictly enforced exclusion from the fishery of those not in possession of quotas. This access restriction generates appropriate dynamic incentives to conserve fish stocks for the future whenever the net returns of such 'investments' are sufficiently high.

The evidence of the ITQ system in operation suggests that, in comparison with alternative management regimes that might have been implemented, it has been successful both as a conservation tool and in terms of reducing the size of the uneconomically large fleets. The ITQ system has not eliminated all problems, however. The fishing industry creates continuous pressure to push TAC levels upwards, and great uncertainty remains as to the levels at which the TAC can be set without jeopardising population numbers. The ITQ system has failed to find a clear solution to the problems of by-catch – the netting of unwanted, untargeted species – and highgrading – the discarding of less valuable species or smaller-sized fish, in order to maximise the value of quotas set in terms of fish quantities.

The ITQ system now operates, to varying extents, in the fisheries of Australia, Canada, Iceland and the United States.

Source: WR (1994), chapter 10

Summary

- Simple models, such as the logistic growth equation, can be used to describe the biological growth properties of renewable resources. However, for some species – those which exhibit critical depensation – there will be some positive level of population size below which the stock cannot be sustained (and so will eventually collapse to zero).

- The notion of a sustainable yield is a useful heuristic device for analysing resource harvesting. Resource owners are sometimes recommended to manage stocks so as to extract a maximum sustainable yield. This is only economically efficient under special circumstances.

- Open-access fisheries are characterised by conditions of individualistic competition combined with an inability of each boat owner to appropriate the gains of their investment in fish stocks. An open-access fishery is likely to be characterised by an economically excessive amount of fishing effort.

- It is important – particularly when conditions of open access prevail – to distinguish between steady-state equilibrium outcomes and dynamic adjustment paths for a renewable resource stock. In some cases equilibrium outcomes are unobtainable (and so irrelevant) because stocks are pushed beyond critical threshold points during adjustment processes.

- Open-access conditions do not *necessarily* imply stock collapses. But economic (and biological) over-harvesting is more likely to occur where the stock is exploited under conditions of open access than where access can be regulated and enforceable property rights exist.

- Comparative statics analysis (for both open-access and private-property models) suggests that steady-state stocks will be higher (fishing effort will be lower) when resource prices fall and when harvesting costs rise. Increases in the efficiency of fishing effort will reduce stocks. The effects of parameter changes on harvest quantities cannot be unambiguously signed, as harvest quantities depend on the particular configuration of stock and effort changes (which may be in opposite directions).

- Where resource owners have a positive discount rate, and aim to maximise the resource net present value (PV), resource stocks will typically be kept at smaller levels than where no discounting of cash flows is undertaken. As the discount rate becomes arbitrarily large, a PV-maximising fishery model converges in its outcomes to that of an open-access fishery.

- There are several reasons why privately rational resource exploitation decisions are not socially efficient or optimal. These include poorly defined or unenforceable property rights, a failure to internalise the value of the resource stock size (and various other kinds of harvesting external effects) in the objective function, and a divergence between private and social discount rates.

- Resource harvesting may, under certain circumstances, lead to the biological exhaustion of stocks or even extinction of species. Sometimes the stocks in question are target species; but they may also be incidental (untargeted) sufferers of harvesting behaviour.

- Outcomes in which fishery stocks are economically depleted are common in practice, as are outcomes in which stocks are being harvested beyond safe biological limits. Occasionally these processes have led to species extinction.

- Fisheries regulatory instruments have typically taken the form of some kind of total-allowable-catch licence system, combined with controls over effort, such as fishing seasons, closure of fisheries, and boat or gear restrictions. Controls have also been targeted at controlling catch 'quality' or composition (such as minimum mesh sizes). It is difficult to find any evidence that such instruments are effective in achieving their stated goals.

- Market-based instruments, particularly transferable fishing licences, are theoretically more attractive and have shown much promise where used to date. However, they are not a panacea for attaining fishery objectives.

■ As with all environmental assets, renewable resources typically provide a multiplicity of valuable services. Their value for supply of food or materials – which drives private harvesting behaviour – is only a partial reflection of total resource values. It is not surprising, therefore, that socially optimal resource exploitation will need to use several instruments, and/or be subject to a variety of constraints.

Further reading

General reviews

Excellent reviews of the state of various renewable resources in the world economy, and experiences with various management regimes are contained in the biannual editions of *World Resources*. See, in particular, the sections in *World Resources 1994–95* on biodiversity (chapter 8) and marine fishing (chapter 10). Various editions of the *United Nations Environment Programme, Environmental Data Report* also provide good empirical accounts.

Renewable resources

Clark (1990), Conrad and Clark (1987) and Dasgupta (1982) provide graduate-level accounts, in quite mathematical form, of the theory of renewable resource depletion, as do Wilen (1985), Conrad (1995) and Rettig (1995). Good undergraduate accounts are to be found in Fisher (1981, chapter 3), the survey paper by Peterson and Fisher (1977), Neher (1990), Hartwick and Olewiler (1998) and Tietenberg (2000). Gordon (1954) is a classic paper developing the idea of open-access resources. Bromley (1999) examines common property resource regimes, and argues that many fisheries have transformed to open access with population growth. Ostrom *et al.* (2002) provides a multi-disciplinary reappraisal of the role of the notion of the commons as an explanation of human activity. Other references on open access are Ostrom (1998) and Baland and Platteau (1996), the latter of which includes a game-theoretic approach.

Fisheries

A Word document describing the current state of global fisheries is available in the *Additional* Materials as *The current state of marine fisheries.doc*. Comprehensive accounts of the world's fisheries can be found from the UN FAO at www.fao.org. In particular, see the FAO's publication *State of World Fisheries and Aquaculture*, updated every few years and available online. FAO (2002) gives a good account of recent thinking about sustainability, property rights, and the precautionary principle in fisheries management. Works which focus specifically on fisheries include the early classics by Munro (1981, 1982); Hannesson (1993); and Cunningham, Dunn and Whitmarsh (1985). Van Kooten and Bulte (2000) contains an excellent survey of the economics of fishing, covering with great care harvesting under various forms of uncertainty. Iudicello *et al.* (1999) examines the economics of overfishing. Anderson (1986) deals with fisheries management. More advanced discussions of fisheries management can be found in Conrad and Clark (1987), Harris (1998) which discusses 'high grading', Neher (1990), Graves *et al.* (1994), Salvanes and Squires (1995), Sutinen and Anderson (1985), Ludwig *et al.* (1993), Tahvonen and Kuuluvainen (1995), and L.G. Anderson (1977, 1981, 1995), the last of which examines gear restrictions and the ITQ system. F.J. Anderson (1985, chapter 7) gives a very thorough and readable analysis of policy instruments that seek to attain efficient harvesting of fish stocks, using evidence from Canadian experience. That book also provides a good account of models of fluctuating fish populations, an issue of immense practical importance. Rettig (1995) considers the problem of management with migratory and transboundary populations.

There are now several very useful Web-based sources of information on fishery problems and fishery management. One such source is the web site of the International Institute of Fisheries Economics and Trade (IIFET) at http://osu.orst.edu/Dept/IIFET (search via 'Resources') which contains conference proceedings and contributions on ITQ management and many other fisheries- and resource-related topics.

Empirical models include Wilen (1976) on North Pacific fur seal; Amundsen *et al.* (1995) on North Atlantic minke whale; Bjorndal and Conrad (1987) on North Sea herring; Henderson and Tugwell (1979) on a lobster fishery; and Huppert (1990) on Alaskan groundfish.

Ecological considerations

Ecologists have a fundamentally different notion of population viability to that held by many environmental economists. In particular, they typically reject the largely deterministic bioeconomic models examined in this chapter, and would argue that ecological complexities cannot be properly dealt with by a fixed number for S_{MIN}, nor by the simple inclusion of a stochastic factor in an otherwise deterministic growth function. It is, therefore, sensible to read some expositions of issues relating to resource exploitation and conservation, and the nature of stochasticity in biological systems written from an ecological perspective. Krebs (1972, 1985) contain good expositions of ecology. MacArthur and Wilson (1967) consider spatial aspects of biological population dynamics (island biogeography; metapopulations); Lande *et al.* (1994) discuss extinction risk in fluctuating populations. The following three references all give accounts written from an ecological perspective on issues discussed in this chapter and elsewhere throughout the text.

May (1994) provides an excellent short account of the economics of extinction;
Ludwig *et al.* (1993) provide a historical perspective to resource scarcity and resource conservation; and Hilborn *et al.* (1995) investigate sustainable resource management.

Sethi and Somanathan (1996) discuss the use of evolutionary game theory to examine ecological systems.

Species extinction and biodiversity decline

Several references to the meaning, measurement of, and estimates regarding the extent of biodiversity decline were given at the end of Chapter 6. The various causes of biodiversity loss are surveyed in a separate document in the *Additional Materials*, *What is causing the loss of biodiversity.doc*. A simple, non-technical account of species loss arising from harvesting and human predation is given in Conrad (1995). For a more rigorous and complete account, see Clark (1990). Barbier *et al.* (1990b) examine elephants and the ivory trade from an economics perspective. In addition to those, important ecological accounts of the issue are Lovelock (1989, developing the Gaia principle), Ehrenfeld (1988) and Ehrlich and Ehrlich (1981, 1992). The classic book in this field is Wilson (1988). More recent evidence is found in Groombridge (1992), Hawksworth (1995), Jeffries (1997) and UNEP (1995).

Perrings (1995), Jansson *et al.* (1994) and Perrings *et al.* (1995) examine biodiversity loss from an integrated ecology–economy perspective. Several other ecological accounts, together with more conventional economic analyses of the causes, are found in Swanson (1995a, b) and OECD (1996c). Repetto and Gillis (1988) examine biodiversity in connection with forest resource use. The economics of biodiversity is covered at an introductory level in Pearce and Moran (1994), McNeely (1988) and Barbier *et al.* (1994).

Other economics-oriented discussions are in Simon and Wildavsky (1993). There is also a journal devoted to this topic, *Biodiversity and Conservation*. Articles concerning biodiversity are regularly published in the journal *Ecological Economics*. Policy options for conserving biodiversity are covered in OECD (1996c). Common and Norton (1992) study conservation in Australia.

Conservation

A large literature now exists examining the economics of wilderness conservation, including Porter (1982), Krutilla (1967) and Krutilla and Fisher (1975).

Excellent accounts of the notion of a safe minimum standard of conservation are to be found in Randall and Farmer (1995) and Bishop (1978). Other good references in this area include Ciriacy-Wantrup (1968), Norgaard (1984, 1988), Ehrenfeld (1988) and Common (1995).

Water

Water may, of course, be regarded as a renewable resource. Good discussions of the valuation of water quality improvements are found in Desvousges *et al.* (1987) and Mitchell and Carson (1984) (which both emphasise valuation issues), Ecstein (1958) and Maass *et al.* (1962), both of which focus on CBA. Water quality management is considered by Johnson and Brown (1976), Kneese (1984) and Kneese and Bower (1968). The US EPA web site contains much useful information about groundwater (and drinking water) resources (web links include www.epa.gov/safewater/protect/sources.html and www.epa.gov/OGWDW). It may also be helpful to check out the site of the Groundwater Foundation (a non-profit organisation) at www.groundwater.org/GWBasics/gwbasics.htm and the US Geological Survey (USGS) groundwater information web sites (http://ga.water.usgs.gov).

Dams

Large dam construction and operations can have dramatic effects on human and biological populations. A large literature on this topic has been spawned by the World Bank Operations Evaluation Department and the IUCN–The World Conservation Union. Follow their respective web sites. See also the World Commission on Dams (2000) with web site at www.damsreport.org.

Land use policy

El-Swaify and Yakowitz (1998) is a general survey.

Discussion questions

1. Would the extension of territorial limits for fishing beyond 200 miles from coastlines offer the prospect of significant improvements in the efficiency of commercial fishing?

2. Discuss the implications for the harvest rate and possible exhaustion of a renewable resource under circumstances where access to the resource is open, and property rights are not well defined.

3. To what extent do environmental 'problems' arise from the absence (or unclearly defined assignation) of property rights?

4. Fish species are sometimes classified as 'schooling' (such as herring, anchovies and tuna) or 'searching' (non-schooling) classes, with the former being defined by the tendency to 'school' in large numbers. In the text we specified fishery harvest by the equation $H = H(E, S)$. For some species, the level of stocks has a much less important effect on harvest, and so (as an approximation) we may write $H = H(E)$. Is this more plausible for schooling or searching species, and why?

Problems

Problems marked with an asterisk * require that the reader either construct his or her own spreadsheet program, or adapt the file *exploit5.xls*.

1. (a) The simple logistic growth model given as equation 17.3 in the text

$$G(S) = g\left(1 - \frac{S}{S_{MAX}}\right)S$$

gives the amount of biological growth, G, as a function of the resource stock size, S. This equation can be easily solved for $S = S(t)$, that is, the resource stock as a function of time, t. The solution may be written in the form

$$S(t) = \frac{S_{MAX}}{1 + ke^{-gt}}$$

where $k = (S_{MAX} - S_0)/S_0$ and S_0 is the initial stock size (see Clark, 1990, p. 11 for details of the solution). Sketch the relationship between $S(t)$ and t for:

(i) $S_0 > S_{MAX}$
(ii) $S_0 < S_{MAX}$

*(b) An alternative form of biological growth function is the Gompertz function

$$G(S) = gS\ln\left(\frac{S_{MAX}}{S}\right)$$

Use a spreadsheet program to compare – for given parameters g and S_{MAX} – the growth behaviour of a population under the logistic and Gompertz growth models.

2. A simple model of bioeconomic (that is, biological and economic) equilibrium in an open-access fishery in which resource growth is logistic is given by

$$G(S) = g\left(1 - \frac{S}{S_{MAX}}\right)S - eES$$

and

$$B - C = PeES - wE = 0$$

with all variables and parameters defined as in the text of the chapter.

(i) Demonstrate that the equilibrium fishing effort and equilibrium stock can be written as

$$E = \frac{g}{e}\left(1 - \frac{w}{PeS_{MAX}}\right) \text{ and } S = \frac{w}{Pe}$$

(ii) Using these expressions, show what happens to fishing effort and the stock size as the 'cost-price ratio' w/P changes. In particular, what happens to effort as this ratio becomes very large? Explain your results intuitively.

3. In what circumstances would it be plausible to assume that, as a first approximation, harvest costs do *not* depend on stock size?

4. (i) The results of this chapter have shown that the outcomes (for S, E and H) are identical in what has been called the PV-maximising model and the static private-fishery profit-maximising model when the discount rate is zero. Explain why this is so. Also explain why the stock level is higher under zero discounting than under positive discounting.

(ii) It has also been shown in this chapter that as the interest rate becomes arbitrarily large, the PV-maximising outcome converges to that found under open access. Why should this be the case? (If you are using the *exploit5.xls* spreadsheet, this result can be quickly verified. In the worksheet 'Steady states (2)', note that at $i = 1000$, the present-value outcome is more or less identical to that which emerges under open access.)

5. Calculate the 'growth rate', dG/dS, at which the fish population is growing in the open-access equilibrium, the static private-property equilibrium, and the present-value-maximising equilibrium with costs dependent on stock size and $i = 0.1$, for the baseline assumptions given in Table 17.3. At what stock size is $dG/dS = 0$ (the maximum sustainable yield harvest level)? Explain and comment on your findings.

6. Demonstrate that open access is not cost-minimising.

Appendix 17.1 The discrete-time analogue of the continuous-time fishery models examined in Chapter 17

The analysis in the chapter text uses *continuous-time* notation. However, when a spreadsheet is used for dynamic simulation (as in *exploit5.xls*) we necessarily adopt *discrete-time*, as spreadsheets are set up to do calculation recursively in discrete time intervals. Tables 17.7 and 17.8 present discrete-time analogues of the continuous-time equations (with the latter reproduced from Table 17.1 for convenience).

Table 17.7 The fishery models: general function specification

	Continuous-time model	Discrete-time model
Biological growth	$dS/dt = G(S)$	$S_{t+1} - S_t = G(S_t)$
Fishery production function	$H = H(E, S)$	$H_t = H(E_t, S_t)$
Net growth of fish stock	$dS/dt = G(S) - H$	$S_{t+1} - S_t = G(S_t) - H_t$
Fishery costs	$C = C(E)$	$C_t = C(E_t)$
Fishery revenue	$B = PH$, P constant	$B_t = PH_t$, P constant
Fishery profit	$NB = B - C$	$NB_t = B_t - C_t$
FISHING EFFORT DYNAMICS		
Open-access entry rule	$dE/dt = \delta NB$	$E_{t+1} - E_t = \delta NB_t$
Private-property entry rule	$dE/dt = \delta(dNB/dE) \times E$	$E_{t+1} - E_t = \delta(dNB_t/dE_t) \times E$
STEADY-STATE CONDITIONS		
Biological equilibrium	$G = H$	$G_t = H_t$
Economic equilibrium	$E(t) = E^*$	$E_{t+1} = E_t = E^*$

Table 17.8 The fishery models: with assumed functional forms

	Continuous-time model	Discrete-time model
Pure biological growth	$G(S) = g\left(1 - \dfrac{S}{S_{MAX}}\right)S$	$S_{t+1} - S_t = g\left(1 - \dfrac{S_t}{S_{MAX}}\right)S_t$
Fishery production function	$H = eES$	$H_t = eE_tS_t$
Net growth of fish stock	$G(S) = g\left(1 - \dfrac{S}{S_{MAX}}\right)S - H$	$S_{t+1} - S_t = g\left(1 - \dfrac{S_t}{S_{MAX}}\right)S_t - H_t$
Fishery costs	$C = wE$	$C_t = wE_t$
Fishery revenue	$B = PH$, P constant	$B_t = PH_t$, P constant
Fishery profit	$NB = B - C = PeES - wE$	$NB_t = B_t - C_t = PeE_tS_t - wE_t$
FISHING EFFORT DYNAMICS		
Open-access entry rule	$dE/dt = \delta(PeES - wE)$	$E_{t+1} - E_t = \delta(PeE_tS_t - wE_t)$
Private-property entry rule	$dE/dt = \delta(dNB/dE) \times E$	$E_{t+1} - E_t = \delta(dNB_t/dE_t) \times E_t$

Appendices 17.2 and 17.3 are available on the *Additional Materials* web pages of the accompanying websites for this text.

CHAPTER 18

Forest resources

This was the most unkindest cut of all.

William Shakespeare, *Julius Caesar* III.ii (188)

Learning objectives

Having completed this chapter, the reader should be able to

- understand the various functions provided by forest and other woodland resources
- describe recent historical and current trends in forestation and deforestation
- recognise that plantation forests are renewable resources but natural – particularly primary – forests are perhaps best thought of as non-renewable resources in which development entails irreversible consequences
- explain the key differences between plantation forests and other categories of renewable resource
- understand the concepts of *site value* of land and *land rent*
- use a numerically parameterised timber growth model, in conjunction with a spreadsheet package, to calculate appropriate physical measures of timber growth and yield; and given various economic parameters, to calculate appropriate measures of cost and revenue
- obtain and interpret an expression for the present value of a single-rotation stand of timber
- using the expression for present value of a single rotation, obtain the first-order condition for maximisation of present value, and recognise that this can be interpreted as a modified Hotelling rule
- undertake comparative static analysis to show how the optimal stand age will vary with changes in relevant economic parameters such as timber prices, harvesting costs and interest (or discount) rate
- specify an expression for the present value of an infinite sequence of identical forest rotations, obtain an analytic first-order expression for maximisation of that present value with respect to the rotation age, and carry out comparative static analysis to ascertain how this varies with changes in economic parameters

---

Introduction

This chapter is concerned with forests and other wooded land. In the first section, the present state of global forest resources is briefly described. We then consider several salient characteristics of forest resources. This draws your attention to some of the particular characteristics of forest resources that differentiate its study from that of fisheries, the principal focus of Chapter 17.

Roughly speaking, forest resources can be divided into three categories: natural forests, semi-natural (disturbed or partly developed) forests, and plantation forests.[1] As we shall see, these are very different in terms of the services that they provide. Our attention

---

[1] Except where it is necessary to distinguish between the two, we shall use the word 'forest' to refer to both forested land and (the less densely stocked) woodland.

in this chapter is largely given to the two 'extreme' cases of natural and plantation forests. Semi-natural forests are a hybrid form, and will share characteristics of the two other cases depending on the extent to which they have been disturbed or managed.

Section 18.3 considers plantation forests. The analysis of plantation forestry is well developed, and it has been the object of an important sub-discipline within economics for well over a century. A plantation forest is a renewable resource, and the techniques we outlined in the previous chapter can be applied to the analysis of it. However, the long span of time taken by trees to reach maturity means that the age at which a stand of trees is cut – the rotation period – is of central (but not exclusive) importance, and is the dimension on which our analysis focuses.

Initially, our emphasis is on the timber yielded by managed forest land. However, all forests – even pure plantation forests – provide a wide variety of other, non-timber, benefits. Forestry policy in many countries is giving increasing weight to non-timber values in forest management choices. Section 18.4 investigates the question of how forests should be managed when they are used, or generate values, in multiple ways.

Not surprisingly, natural (undisturbed) forests are biologically the most diverse and perform a much broader range of ecological, amenity and recreational and other economic services than do plantation forests. We devote the latter part of this chapter, therefore, to looking at deforestation of natural woodland. Particular attention is paid to tropical deforestation, an issue that has become the subject of extensive study within environmental economics in recent decades.

Plantation forests are renewable resources. Does the same hold for undisturbed natural forests? The fact that trees can grow and reproduce suggests that this is so. But a little reflection suggests that matters are not quite so straightforward. If we think about natural forests as ecosystems providing multiple services, and recognise that the ways in which such forests are typically 'developed' or disturbed generate irreversible changes, it becomes clear that they share some of the characteristics of non-renewable resources. Hence it may be preferable, under present conditions at least, to regard natural forests as existing in more-or-less fixed quantities and once

'mined' as being irreversibly lost as natural forests. Although trees may subsequently grow in areas once occupied by natural forest, the gestalt of what constitutes a natural forest cannot be replaced (except over extremely long spans of time). We examine these issues in Section 18.6.

Sections 18.2 and 18.3 make extensive use of economic models of forestry. Several illustrative examples are used in those parts of the chapter. To allow the reader to replicate our results, and to explore the properties of these models a little further, all calculations in this chapter – and all associated diagrams – are performed using Excel workbooks. *Chapter18.xls* contains the calculations and charts used in the main body of the chapter. *Palc18.xls* contains computations used in Appendix 18.2 and some of the problems at the end of this chapter. Details of other associated Excel files are given below at appropriate places. These files can be found on the *Additional Materials* web page.

18.1 The current state of world forest resources

The latest available comprehensive assessment of the state of the world's forest resources is contained in the Global Forest Resources Assessment 2000 (known as 'FRA 2000'), undertaken by the Food and Agriculture Organisation of the United Nations (FAO, 2001). The complete report is available online by searching from the forestry section of the FAO web site at www.fao.org/forestry/index.jsp. Material in this section is largely drawn from that report.

The information found in that report can be usefully summarised by means of two tables. Table 18.1 shows forested and wooded area disaggregated by continents and sub-continental regions; Table 18.2, at a higher but different level of aggregation, shows changes in forested area by forest type for tropical and non-tropical areas. It is evident by inspection of these tables that forested area is in a state of flux, with areas being both won and lost to forest and other woodland. The overall effect, however, is one of falling total forest area, with 9.4 million hectares being lost in net terms in the decade to 2000.

Table 18.1 Global forest resource

Country/Area	Total forest area 1990 000 ha	Total forest area 2000 000 ha	2000 forest area as percentage of land area %	Forest cover annual rate of change 1990–2000 %	Forest land area Closed 000 ha	Open 000 ha	Plantation 000 ha	Other wooded land Shrubs/Trees 000 ha	Forest fallow 000 ha	Total plantation area, 2000 000 ha	Annual planting rate, 2000 000 ha
TOTAL WORLD	**3 963 429**	**3 869 455**	**29.7**	**-0.2**	**3 334 790**	**444 585**	**112 844**	**1 302 768**	**126 823**	**186 733**	**4458**
Total Africa	**702 502**	**649 866**	**21.8**	**-0.7**	**352 700**	**288 906**	**4 571**	**377 996**	**52 083**	**8 036**	**194**
North Africa	5 930	6 262	1.0	0.6	2 481	2 236	1 207	4 560	0	1 693	60
West Sahelian Africa	46 818	43 570	8.2	-0.7	12 191	34 587	80	45 750	4 284	543	27
East Sahelian Africa	109 271	96 612	19.3	-1.2	27 984	81 362	183	110 897	0	1 156	39
West Africa	51 803	41 594	20.3	-2.0	16 755	33 458	385	26 609	3 963	1 252	33
Central Africa	235 861	227 637	57.1	-0.3	196 648	36 802	30	29 917	10 319	301	6
Tropical Southern Africa	230 306	212 884	38.2	-0.8	79 890	97 707	612	93 931	33 517	989	10
Temperate Southern Africa	9 475	9 453	7.5	0.0	5 084	2 754	1 739	64 812	0	1 729	14
Insular Africa	13 038	11 854	20.1	-0.9	11 667	0	335	1 520	0	374	6
Total Asia	**551 448**	**547 793**	**17.8**	**-0.1**	**416 207**	**58 321**	**53 791**	**122 308**	**20 031**	**115 847**	**3500**
Temperate and Middle East Asia	227 356	248 569	12.0	0.9	172 730	9 645	53 120	86 819	7 234	61 222	1242
South Asia	88 889	87 310	15.3	-0.2	58 219	28 951	405	13 303	120	34 652	1571
Continental South East Asia	87 761	80 896	42.5	-0.8	59 609	19 450	173	18 882	12 018	7 596	351
Insular South East Asia	147 442	131 018	53.3	-1.1	125 649	275	93	3 304	659	12 376	336
Total Oceania	**201 271**	**197 623**	**23.3**	**-0.2**	**196 345**	**1 145**	**2 691**	**423 519**	**451**	**2 848**	**15**
Total Europe	**1 030 475**	**1 039 251**	**46.0**	**0.1**	**1 002 979**		**32 036**	**29 484**		**32 015**	**5**
Total North and Central America	**569 115**	**563 417**	**26.6**	**-0.1**	**508 298**	**27 367**	**16 681**	**308 585**	**26 055**	**17 533**	**234**
Temperate North America	466 684	470 564	25.6	0.1	453 162	0	16 238	250 477	0	16 238	121
Central America and Mexico	84 765	75 680	29.5	-1.1	52 225	27 243	421	58 083	25 295	1 241	112
Caribbean Subregion	17 666	17 173	71.7	-0.3	17 011	124	22	25	760	67	1
Total South America	**908 618**	**871 505**	**50.1**	**-0.4**	**858 261**	**68 846**	**3 074**	**40 876**	**28 203**	**10 455**	**509**
Non-tropical South America	54 029	51 476	14.1	-0.5	21 965	28 733	2 323	14 670	0	3 565	261
Tropical South America	854 589	820 029	59.7	-0.4	822 196	40 113	751	26 206	28 203	6 877	248

Source: Adapted from information drawn from Forest Resource Assessments 2000 (FAO, 2001)

Table 18.2 Forest area changes 1990–2000 in tropical and non-tropical areas (million ha/year)

Domain	Natural forest					Forest plantations			Total forest
	Losses			Gains	Net change	Gains		Net change	Net change
	Deforestation (to other land use)	Conversion (to forest plantations)	Total loss			Conversion from natural forest (reforestation)	Afforestation		
Tropical	−14.2	−1	−15.2	+1	−14.2	+1	+0.9	+1.9	−12.3
Non-tropical	−0.4	−0.5	−0.9	+2.6	+1.7	+0.5	+0.7	+1.2	+2.9
Global	−14.6	−1.5	−16.1	+3.6	−12.5	+1.5	+1.6	+3.1	−9.4

Source: FRA 2000. Table 49–1, p. 334

As Table 18.1 shows, in the year 2000 forests – defined to be areas with at least 10% canopy cover – covered nearly 3.9 billion hectares, of which 95% was natural forest and 5% forest plantations. The former is typically not managed at all (and where it is managed, is not done so primarily for timber production), whereas plantations are commercially operated resources, managed predominantly for timber revenues. While the proportion of plantation forests in total forest land is relatively small, it is growing quickly, at an average of 3.1 million hectares per year during the 1990s. Of this, 1.5 million hectares was converted from natural forest and 1.6 million was on land previously under non-forestry use.

Although the area of plantation forests is relatively small (5% of all forest area), their importance in timber supply is substantially greater (35% of all roundwood – all wood in the rough, for both domestic and industrial purposes – is derived from plantations). Moreover the expansion of plantations has important effects on fuelwood availability, reducing the pressures on natural forests to provide this resource.

Of total forest area, 47% is found in the tropical zone, 9% in the sub-tropics, 11% in the temperate zone and 33% in the boreal zone. Natural forests continue to be lost or converted to other uses at high rates. Between 1990 and 2000, 4.2% of the world's total natural forest area (16.1 million hectares) was lost, with most of this occurring in the tropics (15.2 million hectares). Overall, the picture portrayed in Tables 18.1 and 18.2 shows

- a net loss of world forest area during the 1990s of 2.4%;
- a large loss in tropical forest cover with a much smaller gain in non-tropical forest area;

- a large loss in natural forest area with a much smaller gain in forest plantation area;
- for the broad aggregates considered here, a loss in total forest area in all regions except Europe and temperate North America.

The loss of natural (or primary) forests is a major cause for concern, and one we investigate at length later in the chapter. However, it does appear (see FAO, 2001, p. 343 in web manuscript version) that the net loss of forest land was slower in the 1990s than in the 1980s. This seems to be due to the more rapid expansion of secondary natural forests in the later period, with forest returning to land in which agriculture has been discontinued. Whether the services currently being lost from disappearing primary forests are replaced by the services of maturing secondary natural forests is a moot, but highly important, point.

18.2 Characteristics of forest resources

Let us begin by summarising some of the key characteristics of forest resources, noting several similarities and differences between forest and fish resources.

1. While fisheries typically provide a single service, forests are multi-functional. They directly provide timber, fuelwood, food, water for drinking and irrigation, stocks of genetic resources, and other forest products. Moreover, as ecosystems, forests also provide a wide variety of services, including removal of air pollution, regulation of atmospheric quality, nutrient cycling, soil creation, habitats for

humans and wildlife, watershed maintenance, recreational facilities and aesthetic and other amenities. Because of the wide variety of functions that forests perform, timber managed for any single purpose generates a large number of important external effects. We would expect that the management of woodland resources is often economically inefficient because of the presence of these external effects.

2. Woodlands are capital assets that are intrinsically productive. In this, they are no different from fisheries, and so the techniques we developed earlier for analysing efficient and optimal exploitation should also be applicable (albeit with amendments) to the case of forest resources.

3. Trees typically exhibit very long lags between the date at which they are planted and the date at which they attain biological maturity. A tree may take more than a century to reach its maximum size. The length of time between planting and harvesting is usually at least 25 years, and can be as large as 100 years. This is considerably longer than for most species of fish, but not greatly different from some large animals.

4. Unlike fisheries, tree harvesting does not involve a regular cut of the incremental growth. Forests, or parts of forests, are usually felled in their entirety. It is possible, however, to practise a form of forestry in which individual trees are selectively cut. Indeed, this practice was once common, and is now again becoming increasingly common, particularly where public pressure to manage forests in a multiple-use way is strong. This form of felling is similar to the 'ideal' form of commercial fishing in which adult fish are taken, leaving smaller, immature fish unharvested for a later catch.

5. Plantation forestry is intrinsically more controllable than commercial marine fishing.

Tree populations do not migrate spatially, and population growth dynamics are simpler, with less interdependence among species and less dependence on relatively subtle changes in environmental conditions.

6. Trees occupy potentially valuable land. The land taken up in forestry often has an opportunity cost. This distinguishes woodlands from both ocean fisheries (where the ocean space inhabited by fish stocks usually has no value other than as a source of fish) and mineral deposits (where the space occupied by deposits has little or no economic value).

7. The growth in volume or mass of a single stand of timber, planted at one point in time, resembles that illustrated for fish populations in the previous chapter.

To illustrate the assertion made in point 7, we make use of some data reported in Clawson (1977). This refers to the volume of timber in a stand of US Northwest Pacific region Douglas firs. Let S denote the volume, in cubic feet, of standing timber and t the age in years of the stand since planting. (For simplicity, we shall use a year to denote a unit of time.) The age–volume relationship estimated by Clawson for a typical single stand is

$$S = 40t + 3.1t^2 - 0.016t^3$$

Figure 18.1(a) plots the volume of timber over a period up to 145 years after planting. The volume data is listed in the second column in Table 18.3. It is evident from the diagram that an early phase of slow growth in volume is followed by a period of rapid volume growth, after which a third phase of slow growth takes place as the stand moves towards maturity. The stand becomes biologically mature (reaches maximum volume with zero net growth) at approximately 135 years.[2]

How does the amount of annual growth vary with the volume of timber, S? The amount of growth is listed in the third column of Table 18.3, and the growth–volume relationship is plotted in Figure 18.1(b).[3] Although the biological growth function is

---

[2] Inspection of Clawson's estimated timber growth equation shows that growth becomes negative after (approximately) 135 years. The equation should be regarded as being a valid repres-entation of the growth process only over the domain $t = 0$ to $t = 135$.

[3] Table 18.3 (in a more complete form) and Figures 18.1 (a) and (b) are all generated in the Excel workbook *Chapter18.xls*.

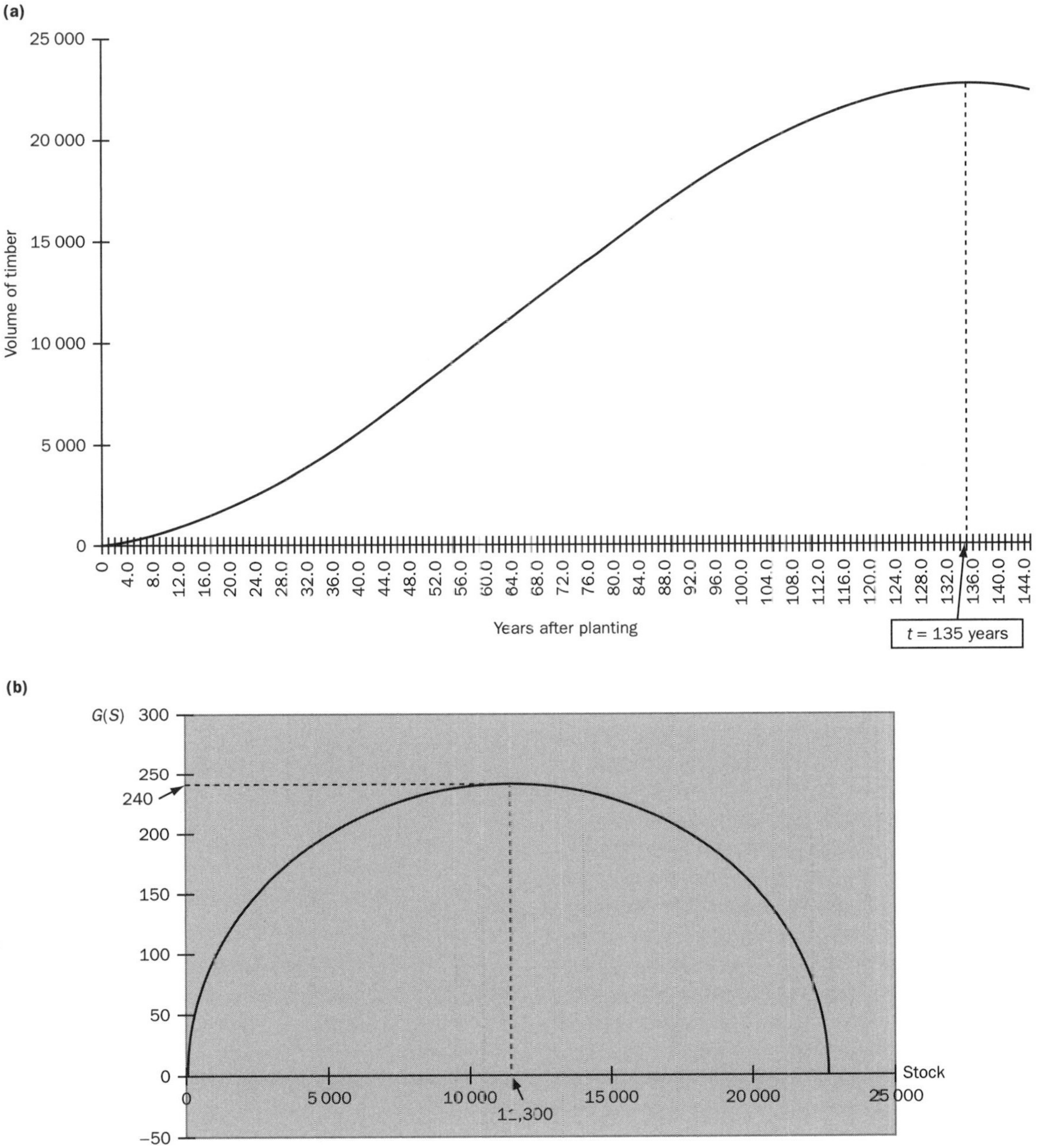

(a)

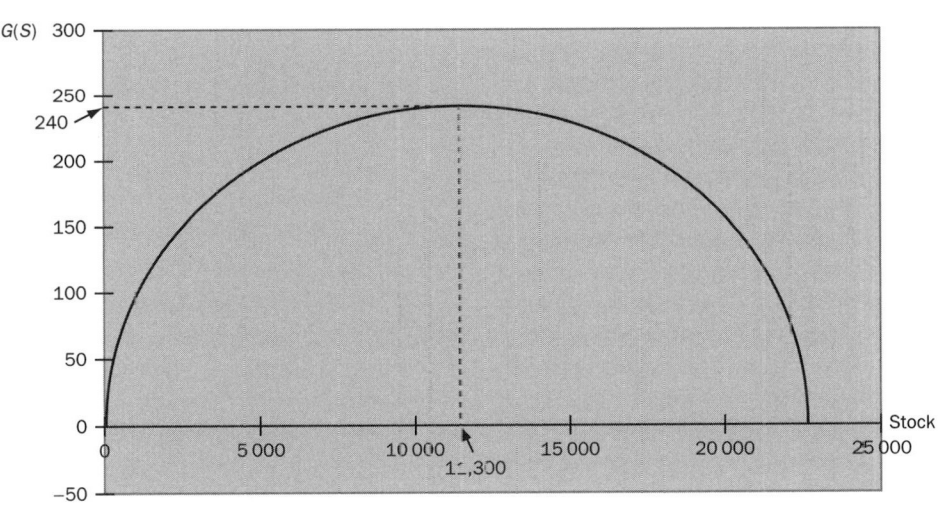

Volume of timber

Years after planting

$t = 135$ years

(b)

$G(S)$

Stock

Figure 18.1 (a) The volume of timber in a single stand over time; (b) Biological growth of a single stand of timber

not logistic in this case, it is very similar in form to simple logistic growth, being a quadratic function (with an inverted U-shaped profile).

Inspection of Figure 18.1(b) or Table 18.3 shows that the biological growth function for one stand

reaches a peak annual increment of 240 cubic feet 65 years after planting at a total standing-timber volume of approximately 11 300 cubic feet. When discussing a fishery, we labelled the periodic increment at which the growth function is maximised the

Table 18.3 Present values of revenues, costs and net benefits undiscounted and discounted at 3%

Age of stand t years	Volume of timber S (cu. ft.)	Annual growth $S_t - S_{t-1}$	Interest rate i = 0.00			Interest rate i = 0.03		
			Revenue R1	Cost C1	Net benefit NB1	Revenue R2	Cost C2	Net benefit NB2
1	43.1	43.1	430.8	5 086.2	−4 655.3	418.1	5083.6	−4665.5
5	275.5	66.9	2 755.0	5 551.0	−2 796.0	2 371.3	5474.3	−3103.0
10	694.0	94.6	6 940.0	6 388.0	552.0	5 141.3	6028.3	−887.0
15	1 243.5	119.8	12 435.0	7 487.0	4 948.0	7 928.9	6585.8	1343.1
20	1 912.0	142.6	19 120.0	8 824.0	10 296.0	10 493.3	7098.7	3394.6
24	2 524.4	159.2	25 244.2	10 048.8	15 195.3	12 287.6	7457.5	4830.1
25	2 687.5	163.1	26 875.0	10 375.0	16 500.0	12 694.8	7539.0	5155.9
27	3 025.0	170.6	30 249.7	11 050.0	19 199.8	13 456.8	7691.4	5765.5
30	3 558.0	181.1	35 580.0	12 116.0	23 464.0	14 465.8	7893.2	6572.6
32	3 930.1	187.7	39 301.1	12 860.2	26 441.0	15 048.1	8009.6	7038.5
35	4 511.5	196.8	45 115.0	14 023.0	31 092.0	15 787.4	8157.5	7630.0
39	5 326.0	207.5	53 260.0	15 652.0	37 608.0	16 530.1	8306.0	8224.1
40	5 536.0	210.0	55 360.0	16 072.0	39 288.0	16 674.1	8334.8	8339.3
50	7 750.0	229.3	77 500.0	20 500.0	57 000.0	17 292.6	8458.5	8834.1
60	10 104.0	239.0	101 040.0	25 208.0	75 832.0	16 701.8	8340.4	8361.4
65	11 303.5	240.2	113 035.0	27 607.0	85 428.0	16 082.0	8216.4	7865.6
70	12 502.0	239.0	125 020.0	30 004.0	95 016.0	15 309.5	8061.9	7247.6
80	14 848.0	229.5	148 480.0	34 996.0	113 784.0	13 469.8	7694.0	5775.8
90	17 046.0	210.4	170 460.0	39 092.0	131 368.0	11 455.9	7291.2	4164.7
100	19 000.0	181.7	190 000.0	43 000.0	147 000.0	9 459.5	6891.9	2567.6
110	20 614.0	143.4	206 140.0	46 228.0	159 912.0	7 603.1	6520.7	1082.5
120	21 792.0	95.4	217 920.0	48 584.0	169 336.0	5 954.4	6190.9	−236.5
130	22 438.0	37.9	224 380.0	49 876.0	174 504.0	4 541.9	5908.4	−1366.5
135	22 531.5	5.6	225 315.0	50 063.0	175 252.0	3 925.5	5785.1	−1859.6
140	22 456.0	−29.2	224 560.0	49 912.0	174 648.0	3 367.4	5673.5	−2305.1
145	22 199.5	−66.4	221 995.0	49 399.0	172 596.0	2 865.2	5573.1	−2707.8

'maximum sustainable yield'. But for a stand of trees all planted at one point in time, the concept of a sustainable yield of timber is not meaningful (except for specialised activities such as coppicing). While one can conceive of harvesting mature fish while leaving younger fish to grow to maturity, this cannot happen on a continuous basis in a single-aged forest stand. However, when there are many stands of trees of different ages, it is meaningful to talk about sustainable yields. This is something we shall discuss later.

18.3 Commercial plantation forestry

There is a huge literature dealing with efficient timber extraction. We attempt to do no more than present a flavour of some basic results, and refer the reader to specialist sources of further reading at the end of the chapter. An economist derives the criterion for an efficient forest management and felling programme by trying to answer the following question:

> What harvest programme is required in order that the present value of the profits from the stand of timber is maximised?

The particular aspect of this question that has most preoccupied forestry economists is the appropriate time after planting at which the forest should be felled. As always in economic analysis, the answer one gets to any question depends on what model is being used. We begin with one of the most simple forest models, the single-rotation commercial forest model. Despite its lack of realism, this model offers useful insights into the economics of timber harvesting. However, as we shall see later in the chapter, that which is privately optimal may not be socially efficient. In particular, where private costs and benefits fail to match their social counterparts, a wedge may be driven between privately and socially efficient behaviour. For the moment, we put these considerations to one side.

18.3.1 A single-rotation forest model

Suppose there is a stand of timber of uniform type and age. All trees in the stand were planted at the same time, and are to be cut at one point in time. Once felled, the forest will not be replanted. So only one cycle or rotation – plant, grow, cut – is envisaged. For simplicity, we also assume that

- the land has no alternative uses so its opportunity cost is zero;
- planting costs (k), marginal harvesting costs (c) and the gross price of felled timber (P) are constant in real terms over time;
- the forest generates value only through the timber it produces, and its existence (or felling) has no external effects.

Looked at from the point of view of the forest owner (which, for simplicity, we take to be the same as the landowner), what is the optimum time at which to fell the trees? The answer is obtained by choosing the age at which the present value of profits from the stand of timber is maximised. Profits from felling the stand at a particular age of trees are given by the value of felled timber less the planting and harvesting costs. Notice that because we are assuming the land has no other uses, the opportunity cost of the land is zero and so does not enter this calculation. If the forest is clear-cut at age T, then the present value of profit is

$$(P - c)S_T e^{-iT} - k = pS_T e^{-iT} - k \qquad (18.1)$$

where S_T denotes the volume of timber available for harvest at time T, p (in lower-case, note) is the net price of the harvested timber, and i is the private consumption discount rate (which we suppose is equal to the opportunity cost of capital to the forestry firm).

The present value of profits is maximised at that value of T which gives the highest value for $pS_T e^{-iT} - k$. To maximise this quantity, we differentiate equation 18.1 with respect to T, using the product rule, set the derivative equal to zero and solve for T:[4]

---

[4] Note from the first of these steps that k does not enter the first derivative, and so immediately we find that in a single rotation model, planting costs have no effect on the efficient rotation length

(provided that k is not so large as to make the maximised present value negative).

$$\frac{d}{dT}(pS_T e^{-iT} - k) = \frac{d}{dT}(pS_T e^{-iT})$$

$$= pe^{-iT}\frac{dS}{dT} + pS_T\frac{de^{-iT}}{dT}$$

which, setting equal to zero, implies that

$$pe^{-iT}\frac{dS}{dT} - ipS_T e^{-iT} = 0$$

and so

$$p\frac{dS}{dT} = ipS_T$$

or

$$i = \frac{p\frac{dS}{dT}}{pS_T} \qquad (18.2)$$

Equation 18.2 states that the present value of profits is maximised when the rate of growth of the (undiscounted) net value of the resource stock is equal to the private discount rate. Note that with the timber price and harvesting cost constant, this can also be expressed as an equality between the proportionate rate of growth of the volume of timber and the discount rate. That is,

$$i = \frac{\frac{dS}{dT}}{S_T} \qquad (18.2')$$

We can calculate the optimal, present-value-maximising age of the stand for the illustrative data in Table 18.3. These calculations, together with the construction of the associated graphs are reproduced in the Excel workbook *Chapter18.xls* which can be downloaded from the *Additional Materials* web page. In these calculations, we assume that the market price per cubic foot of felled timber is £10, total planting costs are £5000, incurred immediately the stand is established, and harvesting costs are £2 per cubic foot, incurred at whatever time the forest is felled. The columns labelled R1, C1 and NB1 list the present values of revenues and costs and profits (labelled Net benefit in the table) for a discount rate of zero. Note that when $i = 0$, present values are identical to undiscounted values. The level of the present value of profits (NB1) over time is shown in Figure 18.2. Net benefits are maximised at 135 years, the point at which the biological growth of the stand (dS/dt) becomes zero. With no discounting and fixed timber prices, the profile of net value growth of the timber is identical to the profile of net volume growth of the timber, as can be seen by comparing Figures 18.1(a) and 18.2.

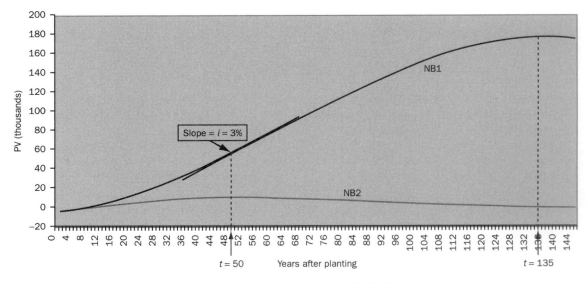

Figure 18.2 Present values of net benefits at $i = 0.00$ (NB1) and $i = 0.03$ (NB2)

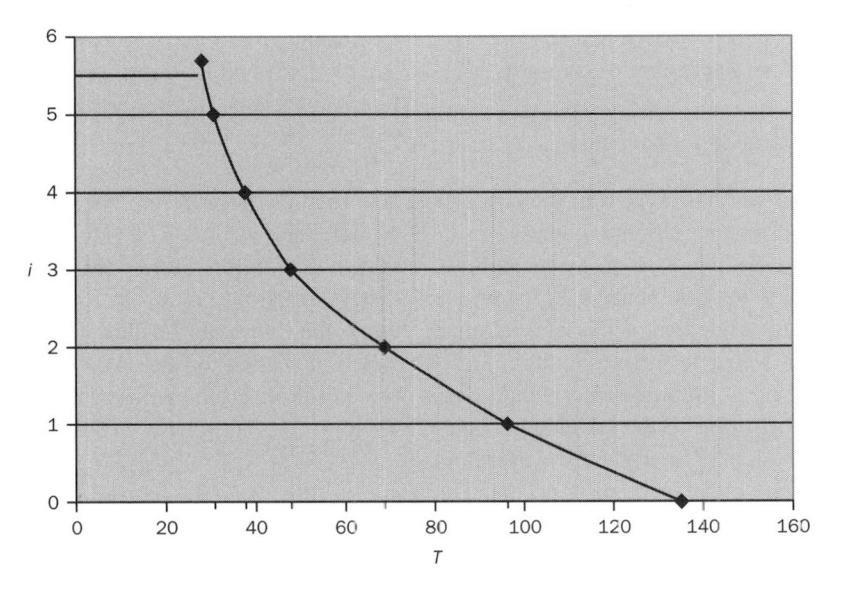

Figure 18.3 The variation of the optimal felling age with the interest rate, for a single-rotation forest

It is also useful to look at this problem in another way. The interest rate to a forest owner is the opportunity cost of the capital tied up in the growing timber stand. When the interest rate is zero, that opportunity cost is zero. It will, therefore, be in the interests of the owner to not harvest the stand as long as the volume (and value) growth is positive, which it is up to an age of 135 years. Indeed, inspection of equation 18.2′ confirms this; given that S is positive, when $i = 0$ dS/dt must be zero to satisfy the first-order maximising condition.

Now consider the case where the discount rate is 3%. The columns labelled R2, C2 and NB2 in Table 18.3 refer to the present values of revenues, costs and profits when the interest rate is 3%. The present value of profits at a discount rate of 3% is also plotted in Figure 18.2, under the legend NB2. With a 3% discount rate, the present value of the forest is maximised at a stand age of 50 years.

Expressed in a way that conforms to equation 8.2, the growth of *undiscounted* profits,

$$\frac{p\dfrac{\mathrm{d}S}{\mathrm{d}T}}{pS_T}$$

equals i (at 3%) in year 50, having been larger than 3% before year 50 and less than 3% thereafter. This is shown by the '$i = 3\%$' line which has an identical slope to that of the NB1 curve at $t = 50$ in Figure 18.2. At that point, the growth rate of undiscounted timber value equals the interest rate. A wealth-maximising owner should harvest the timber when the stand is of age 50 years – up to that point, the return from the forest is above the interest rate, and beyond that point the return to the forest is less than the interest rate.

The single-rotation model we have used shows that the optimal time for felling will depend upon the discount rate used. It can be seen from our calculations that this effect can be huge. A rise in the discount rate from zero to 3% not only dramatically lowers the profitability of the forest but also significantly changes the shape of the present-value profile, reducing the age at which the forest should be felled (in our illustrative example) from 135 to 50 years.

More generally, it is clear from our previous arguments that as the interest rate rises the age at which the stand is felled will have to be lowered in order to bring about equality between the rate of change of undiscounted net benefits and the discount rate. In Figure 18.3, we illustrate how the optimal felling age varies with the interest rate for our illustrative data. While the exact relationship shown is only valid under the assumptions used here, it does suggest that small changes in interest rates might dramatically alter privately optimal harvesting programmes.

18.3.2 Infinite-rotation forestry models

The forestry model we investigated in the previous section is unsatisfactory in a number of ways. In particular, it is hard to see how it would be meaningful to have only a single rotation under the assumption that there is no alternative use of the land. If price and cost conditions warranted one cycle then surely, after felling the stand, a rational owner would consider further planting cycles if the land had no other uses? So the next step is to move to a model in which more than one cycle or rotation occurs. The conventional practice in forestry economics is to analyse harvesting behaviour in an infinite time horizon model (in which there will be an indefinite quantity of rotations). A central question investigated here is what will be the optimal length of each rotation (that is, the time between one planting and the next).

When the harvesting of one stand of timber is to be followed by the establishment of another, an additional element enters into the calculations. In choosing an optimal rotation period, a decision to defer harvesting incurs an additional cost over that in the previous model. We have already taken account of the fact that a delay in harvesting has an opportunity cost in the form of interest forgone on the (delayed) revenues from harvesting. But a second kind of opportunity cost now enters into the calculus. This arises from the delay in establishing the next and all subsequent planting cycles. Timber that would have been growing in subsequent cycles will be planted later. So an optimal harvesting and replanting programme must equate the benefits of deferring harvesting – the rate of growth of the undiscounted net benefit of the present timber stand – with the costs of deferring that planting – the interest that could have been earned from timber revenues and the return lost from the delay in establishing subsequent plantings.

Our first task is to construct the present-value-of-profits function to be maximised for the infinite-rotation model. We continue to make several simplifying assumptions that were used in the single-rotation model: namely, the total planting cost, k, the gross price of timber, P, and the harvesting cost of a unit of timber, c, are constant through time. Given this, the net price of timber $p = P - c$ will also be constant.

Turning now to the rotations, we assume that the first rotation begins with the planting of a forest on bare land at time t_0. Next, we define an infinite sequence of points in time that are ends of the successive rotations, $t_1, t_2, t_3, \ldots$. At each of these times, the forest will be clear-felled and then immediately replanted for the next cycle. The net present value of profit from the first rotation is

$$pS_{(t_1-t_0)}e^{-i(t_1-t_0)} - k$$

that is, the volume of timber growth between the start and end of the cycle multiplied by the discounted net price of a unit of timber, less the forest planting cost. Notice that because the planting cost is incurred at the start of the rotation, no discounting is required to bring it into present-value terms. But as the timber is felled at the end of the rotation (t_1), the timber revenue has to be discounted back to its present (t_0) value equivalent.

The net present value of profits over this infinite sequence is given by

$$\Pi = [pS_{(t_1-t_0)}e^{-i(t_1-t_0)} - k]$$
$$+ e^{-i(t_1-t_0)}[pS_{(t_2-t_1)}e^{-i(t_2-t_1)} - k]$$
$$+ e^{-i(t_2-t_0)}[pS_{(t_3-t_2)}e^{-i(t_3-t_2)} - k] \quad (18.3)$$
$$+ e^{-i(t_3-t_0)}[pS_{(t_4-t_3)}e^{-i(t_4-t_3)} - k]$$
$$+ \ldots$$

Reading this, we see that the present value of profits from the infinite sequence of rotations is equal to the sum of the present values of the profit from each of the individual rotations.

Provided conditions remain constant through time, the optimal length of any rotation will be the same as the optimal length of any other. Call the interval of time in this optimal rotation T. Then we can rewrite the present-value function as

$$\Pi = [pS_T e^{-iT} - k]$$
$$+ e^{-iT}[pS_T e^{-iT} - k]$$
$$+ e^{-2iT}[pS_T e^{-iT} - k] \quad (18.4)$$
$$+ e^{-3iT}[pS_T e^{-iT} - k]$$
$$+ \ldots$$

Next, factorise out e^{-iT} from the second term on the right-hand side of equation 18.4 onwards to give

$$\Pi = [pS_T e^{-iT} - k] + e^{-iT}\{[pS_T e^{-iT} - k] + e^{-iT}[pS_T e^{-iT} - k] + e^{-2iT}[pS_T e^{-iT} - k] + \dots\}$$ (18.5)

Now look at the term in braces on the right-hand side of equation 18.5. This is identical to Π in equation 18.4. Therefore, we can rewrite equation 18.5 as

$$\Pi = [pS_T e^{-iT} - k] + e^{-iT}\Pi$$ (18.6)

which on solving for Π gives[5]

$$\Pi = \frac{pS_T e^{-iT} - k}{1 - e^{-iT}}$$ (18.7)

Equation 18.7 gives the present value of profits for any rotation length, T, given values of p, k, i and the timber growth function $S = S(t)$. The wealth-maximising forest owner selects that value of T which maximises the present value of profits. For the illustrative data in Table 18.3, we have used a spreadsheet program to numerically calculate the present-value-maximising rotation intervals for different values of the discount rate. (The spreadsheet is available in *Additional Materials*, Chapter 18, as *Chapter18.xls*, Sheet 2.) Present values were obtained by substituting the assumed values of p, k and i into equation 18.7, and using the spreadsheet to calculate the value of Π for each possible rotation length, using Clawson's timber growth equation. The results of this exercise are presented in Table 18.4 (along with the optimal rotation lengths for a single rotation forest, for comparison). Discount rates of 6% or higher result in negative present values at any rotation, and the asterisked rotation periods shown are those which minimise present-value losses; commercial forestry would be abandoned at those rates. With our illustrative data, at any discount rate which yields a positive net present value for the forest the optimal rotation interval in an

Table 18.4 Optimal rotation intervals for various discount rates

i	Optimal T (years) in infinite-rotation model	Optimal T (years) in single-rotation model
0	99	135
1	71	98
2	51	68
3	40	50
4	33	38
5	29	31
6	26*	26*
7	24*	22*
8	22*	19*
9	21*	17*
10	20*	15*

Notes to table:
1. Data simulated by Excel, using workbook *Chapter18.xls*
2. * For both single- and infinite-rotation models, at interest rates of 6% and above (for the price, cost and growth data used here) the PV is negative even at optimal T, so the land would not be used for commercial forestry. The value of T shown in these cases is that which minimises the PV loss.
3. To simulate the solution for $i = 0$, we used a value of i sufficiently close to (although not exactly equal to) zero so that the optimal rotation, in units of years, was unaffected by a further reduction in the value of i.

infinite-rotation forest is lower than the age at which a forest would be felled in a single rotation model. For example, with a 3% discount rate, the optimal rotation interval in an infinite sequence of rotations is 40 years, substantially less than the 50-year harvest age in a single rotation. We will explain why this is so shortly.

It is also useful to think about the optimal rotation interval analytically, as this will enable us to obtain some important comparative statics results. Let us proceed as was done in the section on single-rotation forestry. The optimal value of T will be that which maximises the present value of the forest over an infinite sequence of planting cycles. To find the optimal value of T, we obtain the first derivative of Π with respect to T, set this derivative equal to zero, and solve the resulting equation for the optimal rotation length.

---

[5] A more elegant method of obtaining equation 18.7 from 18.4 is as follows. Equation 18.4 may be rewritten as

$$\Pi = (pS_T e^{-iT} - k)(1 + e^{-iT} + (e^{-iT})^2 + (e^{-iT})^3 + \dots)$$

The final term in parentheses is the sum of an infinite geometric progression. Given the values that i and T may take, this is a con-

vergent sum. Then, using the result for such a sum, that term can be written as $1/(1 - e^{-iT})$, and so

$$\Pi = \frac{(pS_T e^{-iT} - k)}{1 - e^{-iT}}$$

The algebra here is simple but tedious, and so we have placed it in Appendix 18.1. Two forms of the resulting first-order condition are particularly useful, each being a version of the Faustmann rule (derived by the German capital theorist Martin Faustmann in 1849; see Faustmann (1968)). The first is given by

$$\frac{p\dfrac{dS_T}{dT}}{pS_T - k} = \frac{i}{1 - e^{-iT}} \tag{18.8a}$$

and the second, after some rearrangement of 18.8a, is given by

$$p\frac{dS_T}{dT} = ipS_T + i\Pi \tag{18.8b}$$

Either version of equation 18.8 is an efficiency condition for present-value-maximising forestry, and implicitly determines the optimal rotation length for an infinite rotation model in which prices and costs are constant.[6] Given knowledge of the function $S = S(t)$, and values of p, i and k, one could deduce which value of T satisfies equation 18.8 (assuming the solution is unique, which it usually will be). The term Π in equation 18.8b is called the site value of the land – the capital value of the land on which the forest is located. This site value is equal to the maximised present value of an endless number of stands of timber that could be grown on that land.

The two versions of the Faustmann rule offer different advantages in helping us to make sense of optimal forest choices. Equation 18.8b gives some intuition for the choice of rotation period. The left-hand side is the increase in the net value of the timber left growing for an additional period. The right-hand side is the value of the opportunity cost of this choice, which consists of the interest forgone on the capital tied up in the growing timber (the first term on the right-hand side) and the interest forgone by not selling the land at its current site value (the second term on the right-hand side). An efficient choice equates the values of these marginal costs and benefits. More precisely, equation 18.8b is a form of Hotelling *dynamic* efficiency condition for the harvesting of timber. This is seen more clearly by rewriting the equation in the form:

$$\frac{p\left(\dfrac{dS}{dT}\right)}{pS_T} = i + \frac{i\Pi}{pS_T} \tag{18.9}$$

Equation 18.9 states that, with an optimal rotation interval, the proportionate rate of return on the growing timber (the term on the left-hand side) is equal to the rate of interest that could be earned on the capital tied up in the growing timber (the first term on the right-hand side) plus the interest that could be earned on the capital tied up in the site value of the land ($i\Pi$) expressed as a proportion of the value of the growing timber (pS_T).

We can use the other version of the Faustmann rule – equation 18.8a – to illustrate graphically how the optimal rotation length is determined. This is shown in Figure 18.4. The curves labelled 0%, 1%, 2% and 3% plot the right-hand side of equation 18.8a for these rates of interest. The other, more steeply sloped, curve plots the left-hand side of the equation. At any given interest rate, the intersection of the functions gives the optimum T. The calculations required to generate Figure 18.4 are implemented in *Sheet 3* of the Excel file *Chapter18.xls*, together with the chart itself.

The lines plotting the right-hand side of equation 18.8a are generated assuming particular values for P, c, k and i, and also a particular natural growth function describing how timber volume S changes over time. The reader is invited to copy this worksheet, and to study the way in which optimised T varies as p (that is, $P - c$), or k changes, *ceteris paribus*.

18.3.2.1 Comparative static analysis

The results of the previous section have shown that in the infinite-rotation model the optimum rotation depends on:

- the biological growth process of the tree species in the relevant environmental conditions;
- the interest (or discount) rate (i);
- the cost of initial planting or replanting (k);
- the net price of the timber (p), and so its gross price (P) and marginal harvesting cost (c).

---

[6]   Unlike in the case of a single-rotation model, planting costs k do enter the first derivative. So in an infinite-rotation model, planting costs do affect the efficient rotation length.

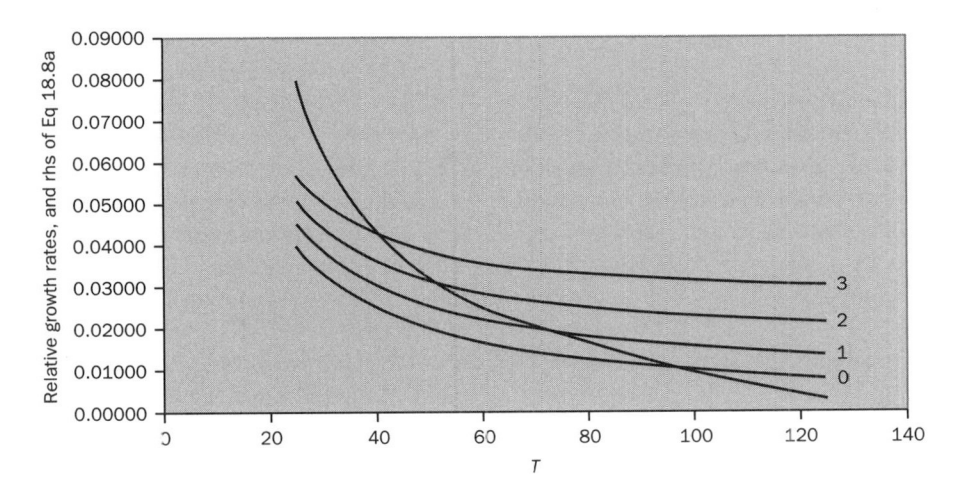

Figure 18.4 Optimal rotation lengths, *T*, as determined by equation 18.8a

Table 18.5 The infinite-rotation model: comparative static results

Change in:	i	k	$p = P - c$
Effect on optimal rotation length	$dT/di < 0$	$dT/dk > 0$	$dT/dp < 0$

Comparative static analysis can be used to make qualitative predictions about how the optimal rotation changes as any of these factors vary. We do this algebraically using equation 18.8b. Derivations of the results are given in Appendix 18.2. Here we just state the results (for convenience, they are tabulated in Table 18.5) and provide some intuition for each of them.

Changes in the interest rate

The result that $dT/di < 0$ means that the interest rate and the optimal rotation period are negatively related. An increase (decrease) in *i* causes a decrease (increase) in *T*. Why does this happen? Once planted, there are costs and benefits in leaving a stand unfelled for a little longer. The marginal benefit derives from the marginal revenue product of the additional timber growth. The marginal costs are of two kinds: first, the interest earnings forgone in having capital (the growing timber) tied up a little longer; and second, the interest earnings forgone from not clearing and then selling the bare land at its capital (site) value. If the interest rate increases, the terms of this trade-off change, because the opportunity costs of deferring felling become larger.[7] Foresters respond to this by shortening their forest rotation period.

Changes in planting costs

The result that $dT/dk > 0$ means that a change in planting costs changes the optimal rotation in the same direction. A fall in *k*, for example, increases the site value of the land, Π. With planting costs lower, the profitability of all future rotations will rise, and so the opportunity costs of *delaying* replanting will rise. The next replanting should take place sooner. The optimal stand age at cutting will fall.

Changes in the net price of timber

The result that $dT/dp < 0$ means that the net price of timber (*p*) and the optimal rotation length are negatively related. Therefore, an increase in timber prices (*P*) will decrease the rotation period, and an increase in harvest costs will increase the rotation period. We leave you to deduce the intuition behind this for

---

[7] There is a trap to watch out for here. An increase in discount rates will increase the opportunity cost of each unit of tied-up capital; but at the same time, it will reduce the magnitude of Π, which you will recall is measured in present-value terms. However, inspection of equation 18.8.4 in Appendix 18.2 confirms that the effect of a change in *i* on *T* must be negative.

yourself, in the light of what we have suggested for the two previous cases.

An Excel spreadsheet model (*palc18.xls*) can be used to explore these changes *quantitatively*, for an assumed growth process and particular values of the relevant economic parameters. We recommend that you work through that Excel file, and then experiment further with it. The workbook allows you to reproduce the numbers given in the textbook, to answer the Problems at the end of the chapter, and to see how the comparative static results work out quantitatively.

18.3.2.2 Comparing single and infinite rotations: how does a positive site value affect the length of a rotation?

To see the effect of land site values on the optimal rotation interval, compare equation 18.9 (the Hotelling rule taking into consideration positive site values) with equation 18.10, which is the Hotelling rule when site values are zero (and is obtained by setting $\Pi = 0$ in equation 18.9):

$$\frac{p\dfrac{dS}{dT}}{pS_T} = i \qquad (18.10)$$

In this case, an optimal rotation interval is one in which the rate of growth of the value of the growing timber is equal to the interest rate on capital alone.

But it is clear from inspection of equation 18.9 that for any given value of i, a positive site value will mean that $(dS/dt)/S$ will have to be larger than when the site value is zero if the equality is to be satisfied. This requires a shorter rotation length, in order that the rate of timber growth is larger at the time of felling. Intuitively, the opportunity cost of the land on which the timber is growing requires a compensating increase in the return being earned by the growing timber. With fixed timber prices, this return can only be achieved by harvesting at a point in time at which its biological growth is higher, which in turn requires that trees be felled at a younger age. Moreover, the larger is the site value, the shorter will be the optimal rotation.

It is this which explains why the optimal rotation intervals (for forests that are commercially viable) shown in Table 18.3 are shorter for infinite rotations than for a single rotation. In an infinite-rotation model, land is valuable (because the timber that can be grown on it in the future can yield profits), and the final term in equation 18.9 comes into play.

The reader should note that the way in which bare land is valued by the Faustmann rule – the present value of profits from an infinite sequence of optimal timber rotations – is not the only basis on which one might choose to arrive at land values. Another method would be to value the land at its true opportunity cost basis – that is, the value of the land in its most valuable use other than forestry. In many ways, this is a more satisfactory basis for valuation. This approach can give some insights into forestry location. In remote areas with few alternative land uses, low land prices may permit commercial forest growth even at high altitude where the intrinsic rate of growth of trees is low. In urban areas, by contrast, the high demand for land is likely to make site costs high. Timber production is only profitable if the rate of growth is sufficiently high to offset interest costs on tied-up land capital costs. There may be no species of tree that has a fast enough growth potential to cover such costs. In the same way, timber production may be squeezed out by agriculture where timber growth is slow relative to crop potential (especially where timber prices are low). All of this suggests that one is not likely to find commercial plantations of slow-growing hardwood near urban centres unless there are some additional values that should be brought into the calculus. It is to this matter that we now turn.

18.4 Multiple-use forestry

In addition to the timber values that we have been discussing so far, forests are capable of producing a wide variety of non-timber benefits. These include soil and water control, habitat support for a biologically diverse system of animal and plant populations, recreational and aesthetic amenities, wilderness existence values, and climate control. Where forests do provide one or more of these benefits to a significant extent, they are called multiple-use forests.

Efficiency considerations imply that the choices of how a forest should be managed and how frequently it should be felled (if at all) should take account of the multiplicity of forest uses. If the forest owner is able to appropriate compensation for these non-timber benefits, those benefits would be factored into his or her choices and the forest should be managed in a socially efficient way. If these benefits cannot be appropriated by the landowner then, in the absence of government regulation, we would not expect them to brought into the owner's optimising decisions. Decisions would be privately optimal but socially inefficient.

For the moment we will assume that the owner can appropriate the value generated by all the benefits of the forest: both timber and non-timber benefits. Our first task is to work out how the inclusion of these additional benefits into the calculations alters the optimal rotation age of a forest. Once again we imagine beginning at time zero with some bare land. Let NT_t denote the *undiscounted* value of the flow of non-timber benefits t years after the forest is established. The present value of these non-timber value flows over the whole of the first rotation of duration T is

$$\int_{t=0}^{t=T} NT_t e^{-it} dt$$

Now for simplicity denote this integral as N_T, so that we regard the present value of the stream of non-timber values (N) during one rotation as being a function of the rotation interval (T). Adding the present value of the non-timber benefits to the present value of timber benefits, the present value of all forest benefits for the first rotation is

$$PV_1 = (pS_T - k)e^{-iT} - k + N_T$$

For a single rotation, the optimal age at which the stand should be felled is that value of T which maximises PV_1. Is the rotation age lengthened or shortened? In this special case (a single rotation only) the answer is unambiguous. Provided that non-timber values are positive, the optimal felling age will be increased. This is true irrespective of whether the non-timber values are constant, rising or falling through time. To see why, note that if these values

are always positive, the NPV of non-timber benefits will increase the longer is the rotation. This must increase the age at which it is optimal to fell the forest. Problem 5 at the end of this chapter invites you to use an Excel file, *Non timber.xls*, to explore this matter and verify these conclusions.

Matters are more complicated in the case of an infinite succession of rotations of equal duration. Then the present value of the whole infinite sequence is given by

$$\begin{aligned} \Pi* = &[pS_T e^{-iT} - k + N_T] \\ &+ e^{-iT}[pS_T e^{-iT} - k + N_T] \\ &+ e^{-2iT}[pS_T e^{-iT} - k + N_T] \\ &+ e^{-3iT}[pS_T e^{-iT} - k + N_T] \\ &+ \dots \end{aligned}$$
(18.11)

which is just a generalisation of equation 18.4 including non-timber benefits. Alternatively, we could interpret equation 18.11 as saying that the present value of all benefits from the rotation ($\Pi*$) is equal to the sum of the present value of timber-only benefits from the rotation (Π) and the present value of non-timber-only benefits from the infinite sequence of rotations.

A forest owner who wishes to maximise the net present value of timber and non-timber benefits will choose a rotation length that maximises this expression. Without going through the derivation (which follows the same steps as before), wealth maximisation requires that the following first-order condition is satisfied:

$$p\frac{dS}{dT*} + N_{T*} = ipS_{T*} + i\Pi*$$
(18.12)

in which asterisks have been included to emphasise the point that the optimal rotation interval when all benefits are considered ($T*$) will in general differ from the interval which is optimal when only timber benefits are included in the function being maximised (T). For the same reason, the optimised present value (and so the land site value) will in general be different from their earlier counterparts, and we will denote these as $\Pi*$.

What effect does the inclusion of non-timber uses of forests have on the optimal rotation length? Inspection of equation 18.12 shows that non-timber benefits affect the optimal rotation in two ways:

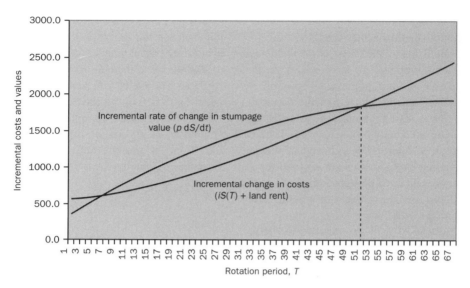

Figure 18.5 Incremental change in value and costs with rotation stand age

■ the present value of the flows of non-timber benefits over any one rotation (N_T^*) enter equation 18.12 directly; other things being equal, a positive value for N_T^* implies a reduced value of dS/dT, which means that the rotation interval is lengthened;

■ positive non-timber benefits increase the value of land (from Π to Π^*) and so increase the opportunity cost of maintaining timber on the land; this will tend to reduce the rotation interval.

Which of these two opposing effects dominates depends on the nature of the functions $S(t)$ and $N(t)$. Therefore, for infinite-rotation forests it is not possible to say *a priori* whether the inclusion of non-timber benefits shortens or lengthens rotations. However, some qualitative results can be obtained from equation 18.8(b), which for convenience is given again here:

$$p\frac{\mathrm{d}S}{\mathrm{d}T} = ipS_T + i\Pi$$

Recall that Π is called the site value of the land, and is equal to the maximised present value of an endless number of stands of timber that could be grown on the land. The second term on the right-hand side – often called land rent – is thus the interest forgone

by not selling the land at its current site value. The first term on the right-hand side constitutes the interest forgone on the value of the growing timber. Adding these two costs together, we arrive at the full opportunity cost of this choice, the marginal cost of deferring harvesting. The left-hand side is the increase in the net value of the timber left growing for an additional period, and so is the marginal benefit of deferring harvesting. An efficient choice equates the values of these marginal costs and benefits.

This equality is represented graphically in Figure 18.5. The inclusion of non-timber values potentially changes the left-hand side of equation 18.8b. If non-timber values are greater in old than in young forests (are rising with stand age) then non-timber values have a positive annual increment; adding these to the timber values will increase the magnitude of the change in overall (timber + non-timber) benefits, shifting the incremental benefits curve upwards. Its intersection with the incremental costs curve will shift to the right, generating a longer optimal rotation. An equivalent, but opposite, argument shows that falling non-timber benefits will shorten the optimal rotation.

Only if the flow of non-timber benefits is constant over the forest cycle will the optimal rotation interval be unaffected. Hence it is variation over the cycle in non-timber benefits, rather than their existence as such, that causes the rotation age to change.

It is often assumed that NT (the annual magnitude of undiscounted non-timber benefits) increases with the age of the forest. While this may happen, it need not always be the case. Studies by Calish *et al.* (1978) and Bowes and Krutilla (1989) suggest that some kinds of non-timber values rise strongly with forest age (for example, the aesthetic benefits of forests), others decline (including water values) and yet others have no simple relationship with forest age. There is also reason to believe that total forest benefits are maximised when forests are heterogeneous (with individual forests being specialised for specific purposes) rather than being managed in a uniform way (see Swallow and Wear, 1993; Vincent and Blinkley, 1993). All that can be said in general is that it is most unlikely that total non-timber benefits will be independent of the age of forests, and so the inclusion of these benefits into rotation calculations will make some difference.

Note also that in extreme cases the magnitude and timing of non-timber benefits may be so significant as to result in no felling being justified. Where this occurs, we have an example of what is called 'dominant-use' forestry. It suggests that the woodland in question should be put aside from any further commercial forest use, perhaps being maintained as a national park or the like.

18.5 Socially and privately optimal multiple-use plantation forestry

Our discussions of multiple-use forestry have assumed that the forest owner either directly receives all the forest benefits or is able to appropriate the values of these benefits (presumably through market prices). In that case, what is privately optimal will also be what is socially optimal (provided, of course, that there is no divergence between social and private consumption discount rates). But it is most implausible that forest owners can appropriate all forest benefits. Many of these are public goods; even if exclusion could be enforced and markets brought into existence, market prices would undervalue the marginal social benefits of those public

goods. In many circumstances, exclusion will not be possible and open-access conditions will prevail.

Where there is a divergence between private and social benefits, the analysis of multiple-use forestry we have just been through is best viewed as providing information about the socially optimal rotation length. In the absence of efficient bargaining (see Chapter 5), to achieve such outcomes would involve public intervention. This might consist of public ownership and management, regulation of private behaviour, or the use of fiscal incentives to bring social and private objectives into line. The fact that forestland often satisfies multiple uses suggests that there are likely to be efficiency gains available where government integrates environmental policy objectives with forestry objectives.

18.6 Natural forests and deforestation

A series of recent studies, including FAO (1995), FAO (2001), and various editions of *World Resources* (by the World Resources Institute), paint a vivid picture of the pattern and extent of natural forest loss and conversion (deforestation). The extent of human impact on the natural environment can be gauged by noting that by 1990 almost 40% of the earth's land area had been converted to cropland and permanent pasture. Most of this has been at the expense of forest and grassland.

Until the second half of the 20th century, deforestation largely affected temperate regions. In several of these, the conversion of temperate forests has been effectively completed. North Africa and the Middle East now have less than 1% of land area covered by natural forest. It is estimated that only 40% of Europe's original forestland remains, and most of what currently exists is managed secondary forest or plantations. The two remaining huge tracts of primary temperate forest – in Canada and Russia – are now being actively harvested, although rates of conversion are relatively slow. Russia's boreal (coniferous) forests are now more endangered by degradation of quality than by quantitative change, and the same is true for all forms of temperate woodland throughout Europe, which appear to be experiencing severe pollution damage, with about a quarter of trees suffering moderate to severe defoliation. The picture is not entirely bleak, however. China has recently undertaken a huge reforestation programme, and the total Russian forest area is currently increasing. And in developed countries, management practices in secondary and plantation forests are becoming more environmentally benign, partly as a result of changing public opinion and political pressure.

Not surprisingly, the extent of deforestation tends to be highest in those parts of the world which have the greatest forest coverage. With the exceptions of temperate forests in China, Russia and North America, it is tropical forests that are the most extensive. And it is tropical deforestation that is now perceived as the most acute problem facing forest resources. In the thirty years from 1960 to 1990 one-fifth of all natural tropical forest cover was lost, and the rate of deforestation increased steadily during that period. FAO (2001) tentatively suggests, though, that this rate may have slightly slowed in the final decade of the 20th century. Box 18.1 contains a

---

Box 18.1 Tropical deforestation

Tropical deforestation has many adverse consequences. As far as the countries in which the forests are are concerned, valuable timber assets are irretrievably lost, and the loss of tree cover (particularly when it is followed by intensive agriculture or farming) can precipitate severe losses of soil fertility. Indigenous people may lose their homelands (and their distinctive cultures), water systems may be disrupted, resulting in increased likelihood of extreme hydrological conditions (more droughts and more floods, for example), and local climates may be subtly altered. Perhaps most pernicious are the losses in potential future incomes which deforestation may lead to. Tropical forests are immense stores of biological diversity and genetic material, and quasi-option values (see Chapters 12 and 13) are forfeited as this diversity is reduced. With the loss of animal and plant species and the gestalt of a primary tropical forest will go recreational amenities and future tourism potential.

All of this is reinforcing a point made earlier: tropical forests are multiple-service resources *par excellence*. Many of these forest services benefit the world as a whole of course, rather than just local inhabitants. Of particular importance here are the losses of stores of diverse genetic material, the climate control mechanisms that are part of tropical forest systems, and the emission of greenhouse gases when forests are cleared (see Chapter 10 for further details).

Given these adverse consequences, why are tropical forests being lost? There appears to be no single, predominant cause. As with earlier discussions of biodiversity loss, it is convenient to distinguish between proximate (or immediate) causes and fundamental causes. Economists tend to focus on the latter. And important in this latter category – especially for tropical forests – is the absence of clearly defined and enforceable property rights. The lack of access restrictions must at least partially explain the fact that less than 0.1% of tropical logging is currently being done on a sustainable yield basis (WR, 1996).

Many commentators give a large role to population pressure, especially when significant numbers of people in burgeoning populations have no land entitlement or are living close to the margin of poverty. However, it is now being realised that too much weight has been attributed to this cause, and that emphasis has been given to it in part at least because most models of deforestation have been constructed to be population-driven (see FAO, 2001). This reflects a point well worth remembering about economic modelling: what you get out (here the conclusions) depends very much on what you put in (here, modelling structures and assumptions).

Nevertheless, it is not difficult to understand why many governments, faced with growing populations, mounting debt and growing problems in funding public expenditure, will tend to regard tropical forests as capital assets that can be quickly turned into revenues. Moreover, cleared forestland can also provide large additional sources of land for agriculture and ranching, each of which may offer far greater financial returns than are obtainable from natural forests.

This suggests that the conversion of forestland to other uses (principally agriculture) may well be optimal from the point of view of those who make land-use choices in tropical countries.

Box 18.1 *continued*

Of course, it may be the case that the incentive structures are perverse, as a result of widespread market failure. Tropical deforestation is *not* simply the result of ignorance, short-sightedness, or commercial pressure from organised business (although any of these may have some bearing on the matter). It is the result of the patterns of incentives that exist. This way of thinking is important because it suggests ways of changing behaviour, based on altering those incentive structures.

Several writers have developed models of tropical forest conversion arising from optimising rational behaviour. Hartwick (1992) suggests that the use of any single piece of land will be determined by the relative magnitudes of B^F, the net benefits of the land in forestry (which includes both timber and non-timber values) and B^A, the net benefits of the land in agriculture. At the level of the whole economy, there will be many individual natural forest stands, and we can envisage deforestation as a gradual process by which an increasing proportion of these stands is converted to agriculture over time. The socially efficient rate of conversion at any point in time is that at which these benefits are equalised at the margin. That is $MB^F = MB^A$. One might expect MB^F to rise as the remaining area of tropical forest becomes ever smaller. This would tend to slow down forest conversion. However, this effect may be offset by a rise in MB^A which could arise because of population increases or higher incomes. It is not inconceivable that the outcome of this process would be one in which all forestland is converted. That likelihood is increased if MB^F only includes timber benefits, but excludes the non-timber, or environmental, benefits. For the reasons we gave in the text, there are good reasons to believe that the non-timber benefits will be excluded from the optimising exercise.

Barbier and Burgess (1997) develop Hartwick's ideas a little further. Their optimising model specifies a demand-and-supply function for forestland conversion to agriculture. At any point in time, the supply and demand for forestland conversion, taking account of both timber and non-timber benefits, can be represented by the functions labelled S_t^* and D_t^* in Figure 18.6. The price shown on the vertical axis is the opportunity cost of land converted to agriculture: that is, forgone timber and non-timber benefits. The demand function is of the form:

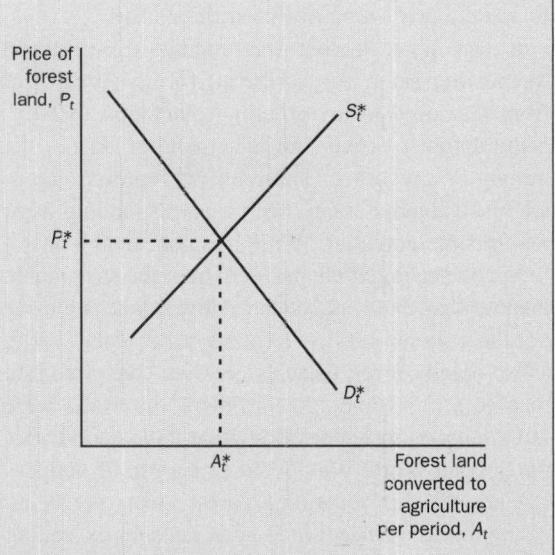

Figure 18.6 The optimal rate of conversion of forested land at time *t*

$$D = D(P, Y, \text{POP}, Q)$$

where Y is income, POP is the level of population and Q is an index of agricultural yields. Barbier and Burgess expect that $dD/d\text{POP}$ is positive, and so population increases will shift the demand curve rightwards, thus increasing deforestation.

If, however, forest owners are unable to appropriate non-timber benefits, the supply curve will shift to the right relative to that shown in the diagram (which supposes that both timber and non-timber benefits are appropriable by forest owners). Clearly this would also increase the rate of deforestation (by depressing the price of forestland).

We mentioned in the text that the non-timber benefits of tropical forests are received by people throughout the world, not just in the forest vicinities. The benefits are global environmental goods. An interesting attempt to estimate the size of these benefits has recently been made. Kramer and Mercer (1997) used a contingent valuation approach (see Chapter 12) to estimate the size of the one-off monetary payment that US residents would be willing to pay to conserve 5% of tropical forests. Kramer and Mercer's survey responses gave an average value per household of between $21 and $31. Aggregated over the US population, this is equivalent to a total single payment of between $1.9 billion and $2.8 billion.

summary of the consequences of tropical deforestation and a discussion of its various causes.

It was noted earlier that natural (or primary) forests warrant a very different form of treatment from that used in investigating plantation forestry. Natural forest conversion is something akin to the mining of a resource. These forests represent massive and valuable assets, with a corresponding huge real income potential. While it is conceivable that a forest owner might choose to extract the sustainable income that these assets can deliver, that is clearly not the only possibility. In many parts of the world, as we noted earlier, these assets were converted into income a long time ago. In others, the assets were left almost entirely unexploited until the period after the Second World War. What appears to be happening now is that remaining forest assets are being converted into current income at rates far exceeding sustainable levels.

Where a natural forest is held under private property, and the owner can exclude others from using (or extracting) the forest resources, the management of the resource can be analysed using a similar approach to that covered in Chapter 15 (on non-renewable resources). The basic point is that the owner will devise an extraction programme that maximises the present value of the forest. Whether this results in the forest being felled or maintained in its natural form depends on the composition of the benefits or services the forest yields, and from which of these services the owner can appropriate profits. This explanation is developed further in Box 18.1.

Where private ownership exists, the value of the forest as a source of timber is likely to predominate in the owner's management plans even where the forest provides a multiplicity of socially valuable services. This is because the market mechanism does not provide an incentive structure which reflects the relative benefits of the various uses of the forest. Timber revenues are easily appropriated, but most of the other social benefits of forestry are external to the owner. The signals given to owners by the relative returns to the various forest services lead to a socially inefficient allocation of resources, as we explained in Chapter 5 in discussing the consequences of externalities and public goods. These

mechanisms go a long way to explain why the rate of conversion of natural forests is so high, why forestland is often inefficiently converted to other land uses, and why the incentives to replant after clearing are sometimes too low to generate reforestation or to ensure its success.

Our arguments have been premised on the assumption that forestland is privately owned and its use correspondingly controlled. But this analysis is of little relevance in circumstances where forests are not privately owned or where access cannot be controlled. There are two main issues here: the first is the consequence of open-access conditions, and the second is the temptation to 'mine' forests for quick returns.

Many areas of natural forest are *de facto* open-access resources. There is no need to repeat the analysis in Chapter 17 of the consequences of open access for renewable resource exploitation. However, in some ways, the consequences will be more serious in this instance. We argued that open-access fisheries have a built-in defence against stocks being driven to zero: as fish numbers decline to low levels, marginal harvesting costs rise sharply. It usually becomes uneconomic to harvest fish to the point where stock levels have reached critical minimum levels. This does not apply in the case of woodland, however. Trees are not mobile and harvesting costs tend to be affected very little by the stock size. So as long as timber values are high (or the return from other uses of the land is sufficiently attractive), there is no in-built mechanism stopping stock declining to zero. Open access also implies that few individuals are willing to incur the large capital costs in restocking felled timber, particularly when returns are so far into the future.

The second issue we raised above was the temptation of governments and individuals granted tenure of land to convert natural timber assets into current income, or to switch land from forestry to another use which offers quicker and more easily appropriated returns. There is, of course, nothing new about this. It has been happening throughout history, and goes a long way to explaining the loss of natural forest cover in Europe, North Africa and the Middle East. The process is now most acute in tropical forests.

18.7   Government and forest resources

Given the likelihood of forest resources being inefficiently allocated and unsustainably exploited, there are strong reasons why government might choose to intervene in this area. For purely single-use plantation forestry, there is little role for government to play other than guaranteeing property rights so that incentives to manage timber over long time horizons are protected.

Where forestry serves multiple uses, government might use fiscal measures to induce managers to change rotation intervals. It is straightforward to see how this can be done. Well-designed taxes or subsidies can be thought of as changing the net price of timber (by changing either the gross price, P, or the marginal harvest cost, c). We will leave you to deduce what kind of taxes and subsidies would have this effect. In principle, any desired rotation length can be obtained by an appropriate manipulation of the after-tax net price.

Where non-timber values are large and their incidence is greatest in mature forests, no felling may be justified. Government might seek such an outcome through fiscal incentives, but is more likely to do so through public ownership. The most important role for government, though, concerns its policy towards natural forestland. It is by no means clear that public ownership *per se* has any real advantages over private ownership in this case. What matters here is how the assets are managed, and what incentive structures exist.

Finally, we need to give some attention to international issues here. Many of the non-timber values of forest resources are derived by people living not only outside the forest area but also in other countries. Many of the externalities associated with tropical deforestation, for example, cross national boundaries. This implies limits to how much individual national governments can do to promote efficient or sustainable forest use. Internationally concerted action is a prerequisite of efficient or sustainable outcomes. We discussed these issues – including internationally organised tax or subsidy instruments, debt-for-nature swap arrangements and international conservation funds – in Chapter 10.

Summary

- If all markets exist, all the conditions described in Chapter 5 for the efficient allocation of resources are satisfied throughout the economy, and if the interest rate used by private foresters is identical to the social consumption discount rate, privately optimal choices in forestry will be socially efficient, and, given appropriate distributions of initial endowments of property rights, could be socially optimal too.
- These conditions are not likely to be satisfied. Apart from the fact that the 'rest of the economy' is unlikely to satisfy all the necessary efficiency conditions, there are particular aspects of forestry that imply a high likelihood of private decisions not being socially efficient. What are these aspects?

  1. Where forests are privately owned, externalities tend to drive a wedge between privately and socially efficient incentive structures whenever forests serve multiple uses. Forests are multi-functional, providing a wide variety of economic and other benefits. Private foresters are unlikely to incorporate all these benefits into their private net benefit calculations, as they often have very weak or no financial incentives to do so. Non-timber benefits may be very substantial. Where plantation forests are being managed, the presence of these benefits is likely to cause the length of socially optimal rotations to diverge from what is privately optimal.

2. In the case of natural forests, it will also be difficult for whoever has responsibility for land-use decisions to extract appropriate monetary values for these non-timber benefits, particularly when the benefits are received by citizens of other countries. These problems are particularly acute in the case of tropical forests and other open-access woodlands.

■ Governments might attempt to internalise externalities by fiscal measures or by the regulation of land use. Alternatively, public ownership of forestland may be used as a vehicle for promoting socially efficient forest management.

■ The record of public ownership does not, however, give much cause for confidence that forest policy will be pursued prudently.

Further reading

Excellent reviews of the state of forest resources in the world economy, and experiences with various management regimes, are contained in *World Resources*, published every two years. See, in particular, the sections in WR (1994) and WR (1996). This source also contains an excellent survey concerning trends in biodiversity. Various editions of the *United Nations Environment Programme, Environmental Data Report* also provide good empirical accounts. Extensive references on biodiversity were given in Chapter 17.

A more extensive account of forestry economics (at about the same level as this text), examining the effects of various tax and subsidy schemes, is to be found in Hartwick and Olewiler (1998), chapter 10. Other excellent surveys of the economics of forestry can be found in Anderson (1991), Pearse (1990), Berck (1979) and Johansson and Löfgren (1985). Montgomery and Adams (1995) contains a good account of optimal management, but at a relatively advanced level.

Bowes and Krutilla (1985, 1989) are standard references for multiple-use forestry. Hartman (1976) is an early work in the area, which is also examined in Calish *et al.* (1978), Swallow *et al.* (1990), Swallow and Wear (1993), Pearce (1994) and Vincent and Blinkley (1993).

The value of forests for recreation is analysed by Clawson and Knetsch (1966), Benson and Willis (1991) and Cobbing and Slee (1993), although you should note that these references are primarily concerned with the techniques of valuation of non-marketed goods that we discuss in Chapter 14. Browder (1988) examines the conversion of forestland in Latin America. The state of tropical and other natural-forest resources, with an emphasis on sustainability and policy, is discussed in Sandler (1993), Barbier and Burgess (1997), Vincent (1992) and Repetto and Gillis (1988). For the effects of acid rain on forests, see CEC (1983) and Office of Technology Assessment (1984).

Tahvonen and Salo (1999) present a synthesis of the Fisher two-period consumption-saving model with the Faustmann model, thereby allowing owner preferences to shape forest management choices.

Discussion questions

1. Is it reasonable for individuals living in Western Europe today to advise others to conserve tropical forests given that the countries in which they live effectively completed the felling of their natural forests centuries ago?

2. Discuss the implications for the harvest rate and possible exhaustion of a renewable resource under circumstances where access to the resource is open, and property rights are not well defined.

3. Discuss the contention that it is more appropriate to regard natural forests as non-renewable than as renewable resources.

4. In what circumstances, and on what criterion, can the conversion of tropical forestry into agricultural land be justified?

5. How will the optimal rotation interval be affected by extensive tree damage arising from atmospheric pollution?

Problems

1. Using a spreadsheet program, calculate the volume of timber each year after planting for a period of up to 130 years for a single unfelled stand of timber for which the age–volume relationship is given by $S = 50t + 2t^2 - 0.02t^3$ (where S and t are defined as in the text of this chapter). Is it meaningful to use this equation to generate stock figures up to this stand age?

   Also calculate:
   (a) The year after planting at which the amount of biological growth, $G(S)$, is maximised.
   (b) The present-value-maximising age for clear felling (assuming the stand is not to be replanted) for the costs and prices used in Table 18.3 and a discount rate of 5%.
   (We suggest that you attempt to construct your own spreadsheet program to answer this question. If you find that this is not possible, you can obtain the answers by adapting *Sheet 4* in *Chapter18.xls*.)

2. Demonstrate that a tax imposed on each unit of timber felled will increase the optimal period of any rotation (that is, the age of trees at harvesting) in an infinite-rotation model of forestry. What effect would there be on the optimal rotation length if the expected demand for timber were to rise?

3. How would the optimal rotation interval be changed as a result of
   (a) an increase in planting costs;
   (b) an increase in harvesting costs;
   (c) an increase in the gross price of timber;
   (d) an increase in the discount rate;
   (e) an increase in the productivity of agricultural land?

4. The following three exercises require that you use the Excel file *palc18.xls*.
   (a) Calculate the optimal rotation lengths for a single-rotation forest for the interest rates 1, 2, 4, 5 and 6%. These should match those shown in Table 18.4.
   (b) Calculate the interest rate above which the PV of the forest becomes negative for *any* rotation length in a single rotation forest. Do the same for an infinite-rotation forest.
   (c) Identify what happens to the gap between the optimal rotation lengths in single- and infinite-rotation models as the interest rate becomes increasingly large (beginning from 0%). Explain the convergence that you should observe. What happens to the PV of the forest at this convergence?

5. The Excel workbook *Non Timber.xls* (see *Additional Materials*) models the consequences of including non-timber values in a single-rotation forest model. The first sheet – *Parameter values* – defines various parameter values, and gives three alternative sets of non-timber present values. Results of the computations are shown in *Sheet 1*. Examine how the inclusion of non-timber benefits alters the optimal stand age at which felling takes place. Does the change vary from one set of non-timber values to another? Do your conclusions differ between the cases where the discount rate is 2% and 4%?

Appendix 18.1 Mathematical derivations

(1) The present-value-maximising first-order condition derived from equation 18.7

$$\Pi = \frac{pS_T e^{-iT} - k}{1 - e^{-iT}} \qquad (18.7)$$

$$\Pi = \frac{pS_T - ke^{iT}}{e^{iT} - 1}$$

$$\Pi = \frac{pS_T - k}{e^{iT} - 1} - k \qquad (18.7b)$$

Differentiating 18.7b with respect to T and setting the result equal to zero gives

$$\frac{d\Pi}{dT} = -1(pS_T - k)(e^{iT} - 1)^{-2} ie^{iT} + (e^{iT} - 1)^{-1} p\frac{dS_T}{dT} = 0$$

$$\frac{d\Pi}{dT} = -\frac{(pS_T - k)ie^{iT}}{(e^{iT} - 1)^2} + \frac{p\dfrac{dS_T}{dT}}{(e^{iT} - 1)} = 0$$

$$\frac{(pS_T - k)ie^{iT}}{(e^{iT} - 1)^2} = \frac{p\dfrac{dS_T}{dT}}{(e^{iT} - 1)}$$

$$\frac{(pS_T - k)ie^{iT}}{(e^{iT} - 1)} = p\frac{dS_T}{dT}$$

$$\frac{p\dfrac{dS_T}{dT}}{(pS_T - k)} = \frac{ie^{iT}}{(e^{iT} - 1)} = \frac{i}{1 - e^{-iT}}$$

equation 18.8a, as required

(2) Obtaining the alternative version of the first-order condition

$$\frac{p\dfrac{dS_T}{dT}}{(pS_T - k)} = \frac{i}{1 - e^{-iT}} \qquad (18.8a)$$

$$p\frac{dS_T}{dT} = \frac{i(pS_T - k)}{1 - e^{-iT}}$$

$$p\frac{dS_T}{dT} = \frac{ipS_T - ik}{1 - e^{-iT}}$$

$$p\frac{dS_T}{dT} = \frac{ipS_T - ipS_T e^{-iT} + ipS_T e^{-iT} - ik}{1 - e^{-iT}}$$

$$p\frac{dS_T}{dT} = \frac{ipS_T(1 - e^{-iT}) + ipS_T e^{-iT} - ik}{1 - e^{-iT}}$$

$$p\frac{dS_T}{dT} = ipS_T + i\left(\frac{pS_T e^{-iT} - k}{1 - e^{-iT}}\right)$$

$$p\frac{dS_T}{dT} = ipS_T + i\Pi \qquad (18.8b)$$

(3) The optimal rotation at $i = 0$

$$\frac{p\dfrac{dS_T}{dT}}{(pS_T - k)} = \frac{i}{1 - e^{-iT}} \qquad (18.8a)$$

By l'Hopital's rule:

$$\lim_{i \to 0} \frac{i}{1 - e^{-iT}} = \frac{1}{T}$$

L'Hopital's rule:

Suppose $f(a) = g(a) = 0$, $f'(a)$ and $g'(a)$ exist, and $g'(a) \neq 0$, then

$$\lim_{x \to a} \frac{f(x)}{g(x)} = \frac{f'(a)}{g'(a)}$$

Hence, as i goes to zero in the limit we have

$$\frac{p\dfrac{dS_T}{dT}}{(pS_T - k)} = \frac{1}{T} \quad \text{or}$$

$$p\frac{dS_T}{dT} = \frac{(pS_T - k)}{T}$$

This implies that cutting will be done at an age T which maximises the average economic yield, $(pS_T - k)/T$. This point is illustrated in Figure 18.7 (using a diagram that is an adaptation of one used in Clark, 1990, p. 273). At the tangency point vertically above $T = 99$, the average economic yield (given by the slope of the ray from the origin) is at its maximum.

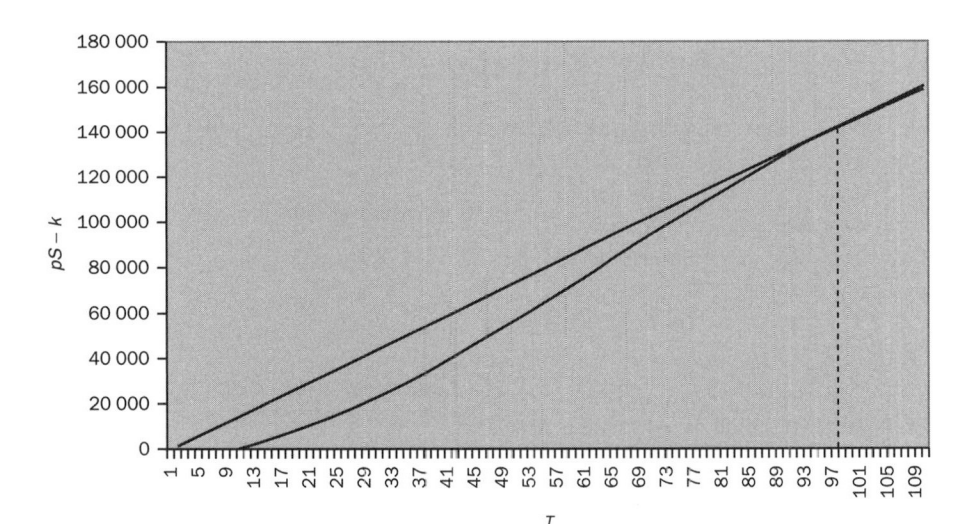

Figure 18.7 The optimising rotation at $i = 0$: maximising average economic yield

Appendix 18.2 The length of a forest rotation in the infinite-rotation model: some comparative statics

In this appendix, we deal with the same infinite-rotation model (and all the associated assumptions) as given in Section 18.3.

The optimum rotation length, T

Our analysis has found that the optimal rotation length, T^*, is the value of T which maximises Π (the present value of an infinite cycle of rotations) in the equation

$$\Pi = [pS_T e^{-iT} - k] + e^{-iT}\Pi \qquad (18.6)$$

or equivalently, in

$$\Pi = \frac{pS_T e^{-iT} - k}{1 - e^{-iT}} \qquad (18.7)$$

It is clear from inspection of either equation that the present value of profits for any rotation length, and implicitly T^*, will depend on the values of the parameters p, k and i, and on the timber growth function $S(t)$.

We know from standard optimisation theory that maximisation of Π requires that T be chosen so that the first derivative of Π with respect to T is equal to zero. Using this first-order condition, we obtained, after some rearrangement, the equation:

$$p\frac{dS_T}{dT} = ipS_T + i\Pi \qquad (18.8b)$$

It will be useful for what follows to put this into the alternative form

$$p\frac{dS}{dT} - ipS_T - i\Pi = 0 \qquad (18.8^*)$$

Comparative statics

We are now ready to do the comparative statics. First, it will be useful to give some general perspective on how this is to be done. As you will see, the key thing we shall need to use is the total differential of a function.

Looking again at equation 18.7, you see will that the value function being maximised is of the general form

$$\Pi = \Pi(i, p, S, T, k)$$

Optimisation requires that the first derivative of Π with respect to T is zero at $T = T^*$. That is,

$$\frac{\partial \Pi(i, p, S, T, k)}{\partial T*} = f(i, p, S, T, k) = 0$$

Now imagine asking what must happen to the *optimal* rotation period, $T*$, if one of the other determinants of Π changes.[8] Suppose, for example, that the other determinant is the discount rate, i. To get the answer, we obtain the *total differential* of the first-order condition:

$$\frac{\partial f}{\partial T} dT + \frac{\partial f}{\partial i} di$$

Note that this total differential is examining how the function changes as the variables in which we are interested change. There are two variables we are allowing to change here: the interest rate, i, and the forest rotation period, T. So our total differential contains two 'change' terms, di and dT.

However, the value of the function will *not* change here. Although Π itself will probably change, the *slope of Π with respect to T* (which is the function we are examining here) must remain at zero at any optimising value of T. So the value of this differential must be zero, given that T and i are being chosen simultaneously to maximise present value. Therefore

$$\frac{\partial f}{\partial T} dT + \frac{\partial f}{\partial i} di = 0$$

or

$$\frac{\partial f}{\partial T} dT = -\frac{\partial f}{\partial i} di$$

Inspection of this shows that if the terms $\partial f/\partial T$ and $-\partial f/\partial i$ are each positive (or are each negative), then dT/di must then be positive. *Be careful to take account of the negative sign here.* Similarly, if the terms $\partial f/\partial T$ and $-\partial f/\partial i$ are of opposite sign, then dT/di must then be negative. This gives us a method for establishing our comparative static results, as we show below. And if we want to find the effect of changes in other variables (such as planting costs) on the optimal rotation, it is simply a matter of having the appropriate variables in the total differential.

Before obtaining our results, it will be convenient to write equation 10.8* in yet one more form:

$$\frac{dS_T}{dT} - iS_T = \frac{i}{p}\Pi \tag{18.8.1}$$

remembering that

$$\Pi = \frac{pS_T e^{-iT} - k}{1 - e^{-iT}} \qquad \text{from equation 18.7}$$

A change in the discount rate, i

Totally differentiate equation 18.8.1 with respect to T and i, to obtain the total differential

$$\frac{\partial\left[\dfrac{dS_T}{dT} - iS_T\right]}{\partial T} dT - S_T di = \frac{\Pi}{p} di + \frac{i}{p}\left[\frac{\partial \Pi}{\partial i}\right] di \tag{18.8.2}$$

Noting that

$$\frac{\partial \Pi}{\partial i} = -\frac{pSTe^{-iT}}{1 - e^{-iT}} - \frac{(pSe^{-iT} - k)Te^{-iT}}{(1 - e^{-iT})^2} \tag{18.8.3}$$

we can substitute 18.8.3 into 18.8.2 and simplify to give

$$\frac{\partial\left[\dfrac{dS_T}{dT} - iS_T\right]}{\partial T} dT = \left(\frac{\Pi}{p} + S_T\right)\left[1 - \frac{iT}{e^{iT} - 1}\right] di \tag{18.8.4}$$

Hint

Doing differentiation by hand can be difficult. Try learning and using Maple or Mathematica to do calculus for you. See the Maple file *Timber.mws* to see how easy this is. One way of learning these packages is to read Ron Shone's *Economic Dynamics* (1997). The web site associated with that book is full of Maple and Mathematica example files to take you through the package. The book is also a superb account of economic dynamics.

---

[8]   In the rest of this note, as in the text of the book itself, for notational simplicity we omit the * symbol being used on any variable to denote its optimal value. Whether the optimal value or any other value is being referred to should be clear from the context.

Under reasonable assumptions about the form of the timber biological growth function, the coefficient associated with dT is negative. (You could check this in the Excel spreadsheet.) It should also be clear that the coefficient associated with the term di is positive. It follows from the reasoning given above that dT/di must be negative.

A change in planting costs, k

As we are now investigating the effect of a change in k on the optimal value of T, the total differential required now contains terms in dT and dk. Totally differentiating equation 18.8.1, we obtain:

$$\frac{\partial\left[\frac{dS_T}{dT} - iS_T\right]}{\partial T}dT = \frac{i}{p}\frac{\partial\Pi}{\partial k}dk = \frac{i}{p}\left[\frac{-e^{iT}}{e^{iT} - 1}\right]dk$$

(18.8.5)

Inspection of equation 18.8.5 shows that the coefficients associated with dT and dk are negative, and therefore dT/dk is positive. A *fall* in planting/replanting costs would then result in a shortening of the optimal rotation length.

A change in timber net price, $p = P - c$

Totally differentiate equation 18.8.1 with respect to T and p:

$$\frac{\partial\left[\frac{dS_T}{dT} - iS_T\right]}{\partial T}dT = \frac{-i\Pi}{p^2}dp + \frac{i}{p}\left[\frac{\partial\Pi}{\partial p}\right]dp$$

(18.8.6)

and so

$$\frac{\partial\left[\frac{dS_T}{dT} - iS_T\right]}{\partial T}dT = \frac{i}{p}\left[\frac{-pS_T + e^{iT}k}{(e^{iT} - 1)p} + \frac{S_T}{e^{iT} - 1}\right]dp$$

which simplifies to

$$\frac{\partial\left[\frac{dS_T}{dT} - iS_T\right]}{\partial T}dT = \frac{ik}{p^2}\left(\frac{e^{iT}}{e^{iT} - 1}\right)dp$$

(18.8.7)

As the coefficient on dT is negative and the coefficient with dp is positive, it follows that dT/dp is negative. This implies that dT/d$P < 0$ and dT/d$c > 0$.

CHAPTER 19 Accounting for the environment

There is a dangerous asymmetry today in the way we measure, and hence, the way we think about, the value of natural resources. Man-made assets – buildings and equipment, for example – are valued as productive capital and are written off against the value of production as they depreciate. This practice recognizes that a consumption level maintained by drawing down the stock of capital exceeds the sustainable level of income. Natural resource assets are not so valued, and their loss entails no debit charge against current income that would account for the decrease in potential future production. A country could exhaust its mineral resources, cut down its forests, erode its soils, pollute its aquifers, and hunt its wildlife to extinction, but measured income would not be affected as these assets disappeared.

Repetto *et al.* (1989), p. 4

Statisticians are trying to adjust measures of national wealth for pollution and depleted resources. This turns out to be all but impossible.

***The Economist*, 18 April 1998**

Learning objectives

In this chapter you will

- find out about the steps that many countries are taking to use environmental indicators to report the state of the environment
- learn about what economic theory says about defining national income so that what gets measured is sustainable income
- have explained proposals made by national income statisticians with the aim of having the published national income accounts report on resource depletion and environmental degradation
- consider the idea of genuine saving as saving net of resource depletion so that non-negative genuine saving is necessary to prevent total wealth declining
- encounter the difficulties that arise when trying to measure genuine saving
- learn about some suggested alternatives to national income as a measure of economic welfare
- be introduced to ecological footprinting as an indicator of environmental impact

Introduction

There is now a wide measure of agreement that the conventional system of national accounts, in most countries based upon the System of National Accounts (SNA) designed by the United Nations Statistical Division, is not adequate as a means of measuring or monitoring the impact of environmental changes on income or welfare. This is not surprising, as the development of national accounting (mainly in the 1940s and 1950s) took place in a period in which there was less concern about the impact of economic development on the environment. The conceptual basis and scope of the national accounts were governed by definitions of income and wealth which did not make any allowance for the depletion of natural resources or the costs of environmental damage such as pollution.

It is now widely appreciated that production and consumption activities have environmental effects which impose considerable costs, some of which will be borne by future generations. There is a perceived requirement for information that will permit economic activity to be so managed that it is sustainable. This chapter is about emerging responses to that perception. The response that has most engaged economists is directed at modifications to national income accounting conventions such that what would get measured is sustainable income, which, as indicated in the quotation which heads this chapter, is not what currently gets measured. This is one area where there is a high level of agreement between environmental economists and environmental activists, most of whom also want to see changes to the national income accounting conventions. Many economists and environmentalists argue that such changes are essential for the pursuit of sustainability.

Criticism of current accounting conventions centres on three main issues: the absence of any allowance for the depletion of natural resources, the absence of any adjustment for degradation of environmental amenity, and the fact that activity to offset environmental damage is counted as part of income. The work done by economists on 'environmental accounting' – also sometimes referred to as 'natural resource accounting' or 'green accounting' – falls into two distinct, but related, parts. First, as

discussed in the second part of this chapter, theoretical economists have used abstract models to consider how income should properly be measured, given the interdependence of the economy and the environment. Second, as discussed in the third part of this chapter, national income statisticians have developed proposals for the modification of the existing accounting conventions.

Not everybody who sees the need for information about environmental conditions is explicitly concerned about sustainability. There is a demand for biophysical data concerning the state of the environment which is independent of any interest in sustainable income. In any case, such data are a logical prerequisite to monetary data which can be used in economic accounts. Hence, in the next section we precede consideration of environmental accounting with a discussion of environmental indicators.

It will be seen that actually measuring sustainable income is extremely difficult. Indeed, some of the economists, and others, who have considered the problem in its practical as well as theoretical dimensions have come to the conclusion that it is impossible. Abandoning the goal of measuring sustainable income does not mean taking the view that it is impossible to provide information that could assist in the pursuit of sustainability. In the fourth section of this chapter we discuss 'sustainability indicators' of two kinds. First, there are economic indicators that are intended to signal whether some conditions for sustainability as conceived by economists are being met. Second, we review some proposals for using biophysical, and mixed socio-economic and biophysical, indicators to monitor performance in relation to broader sustainability criteria.

The chapter ends with some concluding remarks on environmental accounting and sustainability.

19.1 Environmental indicators

Simply listing all of the features of the natural environment that are of direct concern to humans would take a long time, and providing information about such features and their behaviour over time would be expensive. But human interest in the natural environment extends beyond those things of direct

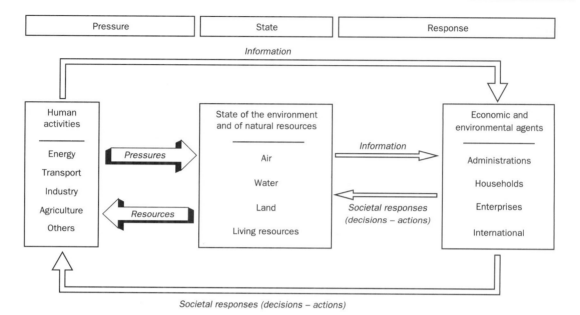

Figure 19.1 The OECD pressure state response model
Source: OECD (1994a)

concern. While there is much that is not known about the functioning of natural systems, we do know that the state of things of direct concern – soil quality, for example – depends on many things not of direct concern – soil microfauna, for example. Indeed, one of the reasons for generating and reporting data on the natural environment is to improve understanding of how the environment 'works' in relation to human interests, so that it can be better managed for human interests. So, a major problem in providing biophysical information is deciding what to report on. The term 'environmental indicators' is usually taken to refer to the provision of information by some public agency for the general public, rather than the generation of data for scientific research. This still leaves a very long list of potential indicators.

Agencies responsible for compiling and publishing data on environmental indicators have, therefore, to select from among potential indicators those that they will report. A long list runs the risk of information overload so that the public misses the overall picture and its important features, while a short list runs the risk that something important will be left out. Another selection criterion is the availability of data – indicators for which there are no

data cannot be reported. Of course, it is always possible to decide to collect data where this was not previously done, but this entails spending money, so that decisions have to be made about costs and benefits across a range of potential, but currently unrecorded, indicators. Biophysical data on natural resources and the environment were first systematically collected and published in Norway in the mid-1970s. Since then, many other, mainly developed, countries have followed suit, and now publish environmental indicator data. Table 19.1 shows the key indicators selected by the Canadian environment ministry.

Even where the list of indicators is relatively short, as in Table 19.1, comprehending the information provided can be difficult. One response to this is to use some framework, or model, to classify and organise the indicator data. The statistical office of the OECD has played a major role in the development of thinking about environmental indicators, and in OECD (1994a) it proposed a 'core' indicator list (40–50 items), and the 'pressure state response' model, shown in Figure 19.1, for their organisation. The idea is to report over time on indicators that signal the pressures that human activities are generating, on indicators that measure how the state of

Table 19.1 Canada's preliminary environmental indicators, 1991

Category	Issue	Indicator
Atmosphere	Climate change	Canadian energy-related emissions of carbon dioxide (CO_2) Atmospheric concentrations of CO_2 Global air temperature
	Stratospheric ozone depletion	Canadian production and importation of ozone-depleting chemicals Stratospheric ozone levels
	Radiation exposure	Levels of radioactivity in the air
	Acid rain	Sulphur dioxide (SO_2) and nitrogen oxides (NO_x) emissions
	Outdoor urban air quality	Common air pollutants: nitrogen dioxide (NO_2) and carbon monoxide (CO) levels in urban air and emissions Common air pollutants: SO_2 and total suspended particulates (TSP) levels in urban air and emissions Ground-level ozone concentrations Air toxics: lead concentrations in urban air
Water	Freshwater quality	Population served by treated water supply Municipal discharges to fresh water: BOD (biochemical oxygen demand), TSS (total suspended solids) and phosphorus Pulp and paper mill discharges to fresh water: TSS and BOD Discharges of regulated substances by petroleum refineries to water Concentration of phosphorus and nitrogen in water Maximum observed concentrations of pesticides in water: 2,4-D, atrizine and lindane
	Toxic contaminants in the freshwater system	Contaminant levels in herring gull eggs in the Great Lakes Basin: PCBs (polychlorinated biphenyls) and system DDE (dichlorodiphenyldichloroethylene) Contaminant levels in Lake Trout, a sport fish from the Great Lakes Basin: PCBs and DDT (dichlorodiphyenyltrichloroethane)
	Marine environmental quality	Municipal discharges to coastal waters: TSS and BOD Pulp and paper mill discharges to coastal waters: TSS and BOD Volume of significant marine spills Area closed to shellfish harvesting Contaminant levels in seabird eggs: PCBs Contaminant levels in seabird eggs: dioxins and furans
Biota (living organisms)	Biological diversity at risk	Wildlife species at risk
	State of wildlife	Levels of migratory gamebird populations
Land	Protected areas	Land under protected status
	Urbanisation	Rural to urban land conversion
	Solid waste management	Municipal solid waste disposal trends
Natural economic resources	Forestry	Regeneration success versus total forest area harvested
	Agriculture	Changes in agricultural land use Amount of chemical fertiliser used and its associated nutrient content Agricultural pesticide application on cultivated land
	Fisheries	Total commercial fish catches in Canadian waters off the Atlantic coast Commercial fish harvest in the Great Lakes
	Water use	Total water withdrawal compared with growth in Gross Domestic Product (GDP) Rates of water withdrawal and consumption by key economic sectors Rates of water recirculation by key industrial sectors Daily household water use per capita
	Energy	Total per capita primary energy use Emissions of CO_2 per unit of energy consumed Fossil fuel intensity of primary energy demand

Source: Environment Canada (1991), published in MacGillivray (1994)

Table 19.2 Suggested environmental indicators for the UK

Theme	Potential indicator idea	PSR[a]	Data[b]	Meaningful[c]	Resonant[d]
Biodiversity	1 Extinct species	S	x	✔	?
	2 SSSI damage	S/P	x	✔	?
	3 Farmland species index	S	✔a	✔	✔
	4 Declining species	S	x	✔	✔
	5 Habitat status	S	x	✔	✔
	6 Land under active conservation management	R	?	✔	✔
	7 Species Action Plans	R	x	?	x
Quality of life	8 Sustainable Economic Welfare	S	✔p	✔	✔
	9 Asthma cases reported by GPs	S	✔a	?✔	✔
Footprints abroad	10 Timber imports from sustainable sources	P	✔a	✔	✔
	11 Cotton imports from sustainable sources	P	?a	✔	✔
Atmosphere	12 CO_2 emissions	P	✔a	✔	✔
	13 NO_x emissions (from transport)	P	✔a	✔	✔
	14 SO_2 emissions	P	✔a	✔	✔
	15 Areas of SSSI at risk from acid rain	S	x	?	?
	16 HCFC production	P	x	x	?
	17 Critical load exceedance	P/S	x	✔	?
	18 Population exposed to poor air quality	S	?a	x	✔
	19 Other air quality measures	S	?	?	?
Land	20 Hedgerow loss	S/P	✔p	✔	✔
	21 Land use	S	?	?	?
	22 Tree health survey	S	✔a	?	✔
	23 Rates and types of new tree planting	S/R	?a	x	✔
	24 Soil condition	S	x	x	?
Water	25 Nitrate in groundwater	S	✔a	✔	?
	26 Water consumption	P	✔a	✔	?
	27 Water pollution incidents	P	✔a	x	✔
	28 Water quality measures	S	✔a	✔?	✔
Marine	29 Bathing beach standards	S	✔a	?	✔
	30 Coast watch litter	S/P	✔?a	?	✔
	31 Oiled seabirds	S	✔p	?	✔
	32 Fish stocks and catches	S/P	✔a	✔	✔
	33 Oil spill incidents	P	✔a	?	✔
	34 Eutrophication	P	✔a	✔	x
Agriculture	35 Decline in farmland bird species	S	✔a	✔	✔
	36 Expenditure on agri-environment	P/R	✔a	?	✔
	37 Applications of fertiliser/pesticide per farmed hectare	P	✔a	x	?
Energy	38 Energy consumption by fuel type	P	✔a	✔	x
	39 Energy intensity of the economy	S?	✔a	x?	x
Industry	40 Special waste intensity	P	✔a	x	x
	41 Toxic releases	P	x	x	✔
	42 Contaminated land	S	x	x	✔?
Transport	43 Transport km by mode	P	✔a	✔	?
	44 Length of motorways/trunk road lanes	P	✔a	✔	?
	45 Journey length/time	P	✔p	✔	?
Waste	46 Toxic waste trade	P	✔a	✔?	✔

Source: MacGillivray (1994)

[a] P = environmental pressures, S = state of the environment, or R = societal response to the situation.

[b] Is data available and reliable? a, annual; p, periodic.

[c] Represents an important phenomenon.

[d] Likely to strike a chord with a public audience.

the environment is being affected by those pressures, and on indicators signalling how human activities are responding to changes in the state of the environment.

This model has found favour with a number of national environmental and statistical agencies in OECD member countries. Table 19.2 lists 46 indicators proposed for the UK in a recent report, where the indicators are characterised according to the OECD model. The selection of indicators was governed by the following criteria:

- a time series of the indicator should be available, including recent observations;
- the indicators should be sensitive to action by the UK authorities, and should allow the setting of meaningful targets for the monitoring of actions;
- the data should be uncontentious (as far as this is ever possible) and be from official or otherwise accessible sources;
- they should require little or no additional collection or processing;
- the indicator should have resonance with the intended audience; that is, be readily understood and be considered appropriate by that audience.

Comparing Tables 19.1 and 19.2 it is apparent that while the coverage of the 'Issue' and 'Theme' lists is similar, the indicator lists show greater differences.

The exercises reported on in Tables 19.1 and 19.2 are examples of what is called 'state of the environment reporting'. In such exercises, as illustrated in these examples, there is an emphasis on issues relating to environmental quality, as opposed to issues relating to natural resource use and availability. State of the environment reports are typically intended for an audience which is the concerned general public, as indicated by the final criterion used in selecting the UK list of indicators. They report, again as illustrated in these two examples, mainly in biophysical units. While this approach avoids the problem of assigning monetary values to physical or qualitative flows which are not exchanged through a market, it makes it difficult, and some would argue impossible, to aggregate the effects of a number of environmental changes since there is no standard unit of measurement or agreed system of weights. In the next two sections we discuss, under the rubric of 'environmental accounting', work, mainly by economists, which is directed at using monetary valuation to capture in a smaller set of numbers the implications for human welfare of changes in the state of the natural environment. To date, this work has focused mainly on issues concerning the use of natural resources in production and the measurement of sustainable income, but many working in the area envisage that

environmental quality issues can be handled in similar ways.

19.2 Environmental accounting: theory

In a lecture delivered at the Washington DC 'think tank' Resources for the Future in 1992 (Solow, 1992, 1993), the Nobel laureate economist Robert Solow suggested that 'an innovation in social accounting practice could contribute to more rational debate and perhaps more rational action in the economics of non-renewable resources and the approach to a sustainable economy'. We use the title of his lecture as the heading to the next subsection. In it he outlined the basis in economic theory for his view that proper national income accounting would promote sustainability. As we have noted, many environmentalists share this view, as do many economists. For the economists, the theory outlined by Solow is the basis for their views on this matter. In this section we shall consider that theory, and the modifications to current national income accounting conventions that it is taken to imply. We shall also make the important point that there appears to be some misunderstanding of the theory and its implications for the ability of revised national income accounting conventions to promote sustainability. In the text here we shall try to tell the story in fairly intuitive terms. Appendices 19.1 and 19.2 tell the same story in mathematical terms. The theory to be considered here builds on the theory of natural resource use covered thus far in this Part of the book – Chapters 14, 15, 17 especially.

19.2.1 An almost practical step toward sustainability

We consider an economy that uses a non-renewable resource and human-made, reproducible, capital to produce output, which can be either consumed or added to the stock of capital. There is no technical progress. A sustainable path is one that involves constant utility for ever. Given that there is just one commodity produced and consumed, and that utility depends only on consumption, constant utility is the same as constant consumption. We are going to consider the question: what kind of economic behaviour is necessary for sustainability in this sense? There is, of course, a prior question, which is: can such an economy be sustainable? Given that the stock of the resource is finite, it is obvious that the answer to this question depends, as discussed in Chapters 4 and 14, on the possibilities for substitution in production as between the resource and reproducible capital. If those possibilities are such that sustainability is infeasible – as they would be if the production function was $Q = K^\alpha R^\beta$, $\alpha + \beta = 1$ and $\beta < \alpha$ – then following the rules for economic behaviour that are the answer to the first question could not deliver sustainability. Those rules are necessary but not sufficient conditions for sustainability. We return to the question of feasibility at the end of this section.

As set out by Solow, the theory involves two 'key propositions'. The first is that 'properly defined net national product'

> measures the maximum current level of consumer satisfaction that can be sustained forever

and is therefore

> a measure of sustainable income given the state of the economy

The second proposition is that

> Properly defined and properly calculated, this year's net national product can always be regarded as this year's interest on society's total stock of capital

where the total stock of capital includes both reproducible capital and the resource stock. When these two propositions are put together, we get the rule for economic behaviour that gives sustainability. It is to maintain society's total stock of capital intact, by consuming only the interest on that capital. This implies adding to the stock of reproducible capital an amount equal to the depreciation of the resource stock – which is Hartwick's rule, discussed in Chapters 4 and 14 – where the depreciation of the resource stock is measured by the Hotelling rent arising in its extraction.

In his lecture, Solow was careful to state, several times, a caveat that attends these propositions as guides to policy in an actual economy. This is that the 'right prices' are used to value the capital stock and the resource stock. Note that without prices we could not add together the stocks of reproducible capital and the resource to get a figure for 'society's total wealth'. In order to be 'right', the prices must be, as Solow puts it, such that they 'make full allowance even for the distant future, and will even take account of how each future generation will take account of its future'. The theory ensures that the prices do this by working with a model in which there is a single representative agent with perfect future knowledge, who works out and follows a plan for consumption, investment and resource depletion on the basis of maximising the discounted sum of future utilities subject to the constraints imposed by the availability of the resource and the need to forgo consumption in order to invest in reproducible capital. Such a model is set out in Appendix 19.1, and was previously considered in Chapters 3, 4, 14 and 15.

The justification for using such a model to think about these questions is that, given some very strong assumptions about agents' foresight and institutions, competitive markets would produce the same price behaviour. The model shows, for example, that the resource price is required to evolve according to Hotelling's rule, and, given strong assumptions, it can be shown that resource prices determined in competitive markets will follow the same rule. Solow is absolutely explicit about the relationship between actual market prices and the 'right prices' for guiding the economic behaviour that is necessary for sustainability:

> This story makes it obvious that everyday market prices can make no claim to embody that kind of foreknowledge. Least of all could the prices of natural resource products, which are famous for their volatility, have this property; but one could entertain legitimate doubts about other prices, too. The hope has to be that a careful attempt to average out speculative movements and to correct for the other imperfections I listed earlier would yield adjusted prices that might serve as a rough approximation to the theoretically correct ones. We act as if that were true in other contexts. The important hedge is not to claim too much.

Unfortunately, in their enthusiasm to use economic theory to promote sustainability, some economists do not explicitly qualify their contributions to policy analysis with 'the important hedge'.

There is, as set out in Appendix 19.1 and discussed below, a further 'hedge' of some importance, not made explicit in Solow's lecture, and which tends to be glossed over in much of the literature. This is the fact that, even within the context of the representative agent model itself, the prices may not be 'right'. The 'right' prices are those which go with a constant consumption path. However, the representative agent will not necessarily choose a constant consumption path, unless constrained to do so. Hence, the prices ruling along the optimal path in such a model will not be the correct prices to use for the implementation of Hartwick's rule in pursuit of sustainability, unless it so happens that the representative agent's optimal path is one with constant consumption.

What has all this got to with environmental accounting? What is Solow's 'almost practical step'? It is the idea that if at a point in time we knew what sustainable income for the economy was we would know whether or not we were behaving in the interests of the future. Consumption in excess of sustainable income would indicate that we were not, while consumption equal to or less than sustainable income would indicate that we were. The step is 'almost practical' because of the need to use not currently observable market prices, but the 'right' prices.

19.2.2 A resource owner in a competitive economy

The idea that to behave sustainably involves keeping wealth intact by consuming just the interest income on that wealth has considerable intuitive appeal. We can make that appeal explicit by considering the situation of a resource owner in a competitive economy. Doing this will also serve to provide some insight into how the Hartwick rule works when it does, and some basis for a further discussion of the caveats noted above.

Consider, then, an individual who owns an oil deposit and sells extraction permits to a company in the oil production business. The individual pays the proceeds from permit sales into his or her bank account, from which is paid his or her expenditure on consumption. Let us use here the following notation:

B is the size of the bank account, units £s
C is consumption expenditure, units £s

W is total wealth, units £s
R is the total of permit sales, units tonnes
X is the size of the remaining stock of mineral, units tonnes
h is the price of a permit, £s per tonne
V is the value of the mine, units £s
r is the interest rate, assumed constant over time

Let us also use $t - 1$ to denote the first day of the relevant period of time, say a year, and t to denote the last day of the period. At $t - 1$ the mine owner sells permits and banks the revenue. At t he or she writes a cheque on the bank account to pay for his or her consumption during the period. While this construction is somewhat special it serves to make what is going on clear. In this context, considering, as we shall, an infinite time horizon and the question of constant consumption by an individual for ever is obviously rather strange. Individuals do not live for ever. However, pretending that they do, or at least that they behave as if they do by treating their heirs as simple extensions of themselves, is not uncommon in economics, and does serve to generate some useful insights.

The behaviour over time of B is given by

$$B_t = (1 + r)B_{t-1} + (1 + r)h_{t-1}R_{t-1} - C_t \qquad (19.1)$$

because B_{t-1} is the principal at the start of the year, to which is added, to earn interest over the year, the proceeds from permit sales at the start of the year. Equation 19.1 can be written as

$$B_t - B_{t-1} = rB_{t-1} + (1 + r)h_{t-1}R_{t-1} - C_t \qquad (19.2)$$

At t the value of the mine is given by the permit price at t multiplied by the amount of oil remaining, which is the amount remaining at the start of the period less the amount for which permits were sold at the start of the period. That is:

$$V_t = h_t(X_{t-1} - R_{t-1}) \qquad (19.3)$$

The price of an extraction permit in a competitive economy will be the difference between the marginal cost of extraction and the price for which extracted oil sells; that is, the Hotelling rent. That is why we have used 'h' here as the symbol for the price of an extraction permit. Again given a competitive economy, we know from Chapter 15 that Hotelling's rule governs the behaviour of rent, and hence the price of extraction permits, over time so that

$$h_t = (1 + r)h_{t-1}$$

and substituting in equation 19.3 gives

$$V_t = (1 + r)h_{t-1}(X_{t-1} - R_{t-1})$$
$$= (1 + r)(h_{t-1}X_{t-1} - h_{t-1}R_{t-1})$$

or

$$V_t = (1 + r)(V_{t-1} - h_{t-1}R_{t-1}) \qquad (19.4)$$

from which we get

$$V_t - V_{t-1} = rV_{t-1} - (1 + r)h_{t-1}R_{t-1} \qquad (19.5)$$

The individual's wealth is just the sum of the bank deposit and the value of the mine:

$$W_t = B_t + V_t$$

so that the change in wealth over a period is:

$$W_t - W_{t-1} = (B_t - B_{t-1}) + (V_t - V_{t-1}) \qquad (19.6)$$

Substituting in equation 19.6 from equations 19.2 and 19.5 gives

$$W_t - W_{t-1} = rB_{t-1} + (1 + r)h_{t-1}R_{t-1} - C_t + rV_{t-1}$$
$$- (1 + r)h_{t-1}R_{t-1}$$

or

$$W_t - W_{t-1} = rB_{t-1} + rV_{t-1} - C_t \qquad (19.7)$$

which is

$$W_t - W_{t-1} = rW_{t-1} - C_t \qquad (19.8)$$

Now, for constant wealth, $W_t - W_{t-1} = 0$, we get from equation 19.8

$$C_t = rW_{t-1} \qquad (19.9)$$

so that if a period's consumption is equal to the interest earned on total wealth at the start of the period, wealth will be the same at the end of the period as at the start. Further, equation 19.9 holds for all t and $t - 1$, for all periods, so that if we use the subscript 0 for the start of some initial period

$$C_t = rW_0 \qquad (19.10)$$

will clearly be the maximum constant consumption level for all subsequent periods. Readers who are unconvinced that rW_0 is the largest possible constant consumption stream can convince themselves

that this is the case by some numerical experiments. A numerical example on which such experiments could be based is given in chapter 9 of Common (1996).

Given the result that the present value of x for ever is x/r (see Chapter 13) the present value of the consumption stream rW_0 for ever is

$$W_0^* = W_0 \qquad (19.11)$$

so that wealth as the current value of total assets and wealth as the present value of the largest future constant consumption level that is indefinitely sustainable are the same.

For this individual a period's income, Y, is given by the interest payment on the bank deposit plus the revenue from permit sales and the interest earned thereon:

$$Y_t = rB_{t-1} + (1 + r)h_{t-1}R_{t-1} \qquad (19.12)$$

Equation 19.7 for $W_t - W_{t-1} = 0$ gives

$$C_t = rB_{t-1} + rV_{t-1}$$

and if we define investment, I, as the difference between income and consumption we have

$$I_t = Y_t - C_t = rB_{t-1} + (1 + r)h_{t-1}R_{t-1} - rB_{t-1} - rV_{t-1}$$
$$= (1 + r)h_{t-1}R_{t-1} - rV_{t-1} \qquad (19.13)$$

From equation 19.5, this can be written as

$$I_t = -(V_t - V_{t-1}) \qquad (19.14)$$

which says that the individual is investing an amount equal to the depreciation of the mine. This is Hartwick's rule applied to this individual – investing in his or her reproducible capital, the bank account, in every period an amount equal to the depreciation of his or her resource stock, the oil deposit. The depreciation of the oil deposit is simply the reduction in its value over the period on account of the reduced size of the resource stock. Note that equation 19.14 can also be read as saying that net investment – that is, investment less depreciation – is zero when wealth is maintained intact.

A widely used definition of 'sustainable income' is that it is the amount that can be consumed during a period without reducing wealth. Here it follows immediately from the preceding discussion that with $Y_{sus,t}$ for the individual's sustainable income for the period starting on $t - 1$ and ending on t, it is:

$$Y_{\text{sus},t} = rW_{t-1} \tag{19.15}$$

Recall that Solow stated that properly measured net national product, or income, is both the interest on wealth and the level of consumption that can be maintained for ever. Equation 19.15 gives sustainable income for the individual as the interest on wealth. We have already established in this context (equation 19.9) that this is a level of consumption that can be maintained for ever.

All of this is the basic result set out by Solow as discussed in the previous subsection – for sustainable consumption, maintain wealth intact by consuming just the interest on the constant wealth – but here it is shown to work for a non-renewable-resource-stock-owning individual in a competitive economy with a constant interest rate rather than for an economy as a whole.[1] We look at the transferability of the result to an economy in the next subsection, but before doing that there are some further points to be made about the situation of an individual.

The first is to note the key role of the efficiency condition that the proportional rate of increase in rent is equal to the single ruling interest rate. If we have $h_t = (1 + b)h_{t-1}$ rather than $h_t = (1 + r)h_{t-1}$, then we cannot derive equation 19.7.

We have shown that by consuming just the interest on wealth an individual resource-stock owner achieves the highest sustainable level of consumption. We have not shown that such an individual would choose such a consumption pattern. In fact an individual would do so only in special circumstances, as we now show. There is a substantial and technically sophisticated literature on the choice of intertemporal consumption plans by individuals, but for our purposes a very simple formulation of the problem will suffice. We assume that the problem of choosing a consumption plan can be represented as

$$\text{Max} \int_0^\infty U(C_t)e^{-\rho t}dt$$

subject to $dW/dt = rW_t - C_t$

where the notation is as before, but we have introduced the symbol ρ for the rate (assumed constant)

at which the individual discounts future utility. For this problem, we get from the current-value Hamiltonian necessary conditions which include

$$\partial H_t/\partial C_t = U_{Ct} - \lambda_t = 0$$

and

$$d\lambda/dt - \rho\lambda_t = -\partial H_t/\partial W_t = -\lambda_t r$$

where from the second condition we can write

$$d\lambda/dt = (\rho - r)\lambda_t$$

and we have, on standard assumptions about diminishing marginal utility,

$$\rho = r \rightarrow d\lambda/dt = 0 \rightarrow U_{Ct} \text{ constant}, C_t \text{ constant}$$

$$\rho > r \rightarrow d\lambda/dt > 0 \rightarrow U_{Ct} \text{ increasing}, C_t \text{ decreasing}$$

$$\rho < r \rightarrow d\lambda/dt < 0 \rightarrow U_{Ct} \text{ decreasing}, C_t \text{ increasing}$$

Thus, we see that the individual will choose constant consumption as his or her optimal plan only if their intertemporal utility discount rate is equal to the interest rate.

Suppose that our individual started out with C_t increasing and then decided for some reason at the start of period $T - 1$ to T decided to switch to C_t constant. Given the foregoing it should be clear that the individual would thereafter be acting to consume the interest on the wealth at $T - 1$ and maintaining that wealth intact and sustaining constant consumption for ever, but that the wealth maintained intact would be less than the individual's initial wealth and the constant indefinitely sustainable consumption level would be lower than if such behaviour had been adopted at the outset. Again, the reader who wishes to confirm these points can do so by simple numerical experimentation.

There is another point here that can also be confirmed in that way. We have not yet mentioned the eventual exhaustion of the oil deposit, and what happens when that occurs. In fact, in regard to consumption and wealth, nothing happens. By the time the oil is exhausted, given the behaviour from the outset that keeps wealth constant, the entire initial

---

[1] Note that if the interest rate r is not constant, sustainable consumption would not maintain wealth intact. Wealth would have to move in the opposite direction to any change in the interest rate, so that the product rW remains constant.

value of the oil stock will have been transferred to the bank deposit, and our individual can continue to have constant consumption for ever as the interest on the bank deposit at the same level as initially.

Finally, we should note that, in order to establish a reference point for talking about economies as opposed to individuals, we have thus far ignored one area of opportunity open to an individual. We have assumed that the individual's consumption opportunities over time are given solely by the way he or she manages the asset portfolio, which comprises the bank account and the mine. In fact, an individual can borrow to alter his or her consumption path from that given by the asset portfolio, incurring debts for later repayment from the income stream that it generates. We considered behaviour in loanable funds markets in Chapter 11. It was shown there that, given standard assumptions, the individual would manage assets so as to maximise wealth, and then choose a consumption path reflecting his or her intertemporal preferences and the opportunities available by borrowing and repaying. There is, that is, a 'separation theorem' which shows that the problems of asset portfolio management and consumption planning can be treated sequentially – first maximise wealth ignoring intertemporal preferences, then arrange consumption over time subject to the constraint arising from maximised wealth. We make this point to emphasise that our discussion here has been intended only as a means of providing some sense of economists' basic way of thinking about sustainability, rather than as a proper account of intertemporal consumption planning by an individual.[2]

19.2.3 Consumption, income and wealth for an economy

We now consider an economy which uses reproducible capital and a non-renewable resource to produce output, which can be either consumed or saved and added to the capital stock. The first point to be made is that there is an important distinction between an open economy, which trades with other economies, and a closed economy where there is no foreign trade. If we assume that an open economy is 'small', so that it takes world prices for traded goods as given, that there is complete freedom of international capital movements (with respect to which the economy is also 'small') and that all markets are competitive, then the situation for an open economy is essentially as set out above for an individual. We will return to this point in discussing two essential differences between a resource-owning individual and a resource-exploiting economy in relation to sustainability as constant consumption for ever. Note that the global economy is a closed economy, and that the sustainability problem is really a global problem.

The first essential difference primarily concerns the feasibility of constant consumption for ever. Equation 19.12 is the production function for the individual's income. It is linear, implying that the bank account and the oil deposit are perfect substitutes in the production of income, and that the oil deposit is not essential in the production of income. As we noted above, for the individual mine owner exhaustion of the mine does not, if behaviour has previously been such as to maintain wealth intact, imply any reduction in wealth or sustainable consumption. In the economics literature on sustainability, it is not generally regarded as appropriate to assume for an economy that the resource is inessential in production. Note, however, that most of the literature is concerned with a closed economy. For a small open economy which can export the resource and invest in overseas assets the situation is essentially as for an individual and an income production function like equation 19.12 would be appropriate. For a closed economy, it can be shown that even where the resource is essential, sustainability as constant consumption may be feasible. This is, as already noted, the case where the production function is

$$Q_t = K_t^\alpha R_t^\beta : \alpha + \beta = 1 \text{ and } \beta < \alpha \qquad (19.16)$$

where K_t is the stock of reproducible capital and R_t is the resource use at time t.

---

[2] Most standard intermediate and advanced microeconomics texts provide an analysis of the individual intertemporal utility maximisation: see, for examples, Hirshleifer (1980) and Deaton and Muellbauer (1980). Chapter 16 in Hirshleifer (1980) discusses the separation theorem, on which see also chapter 6 of Common (1996).

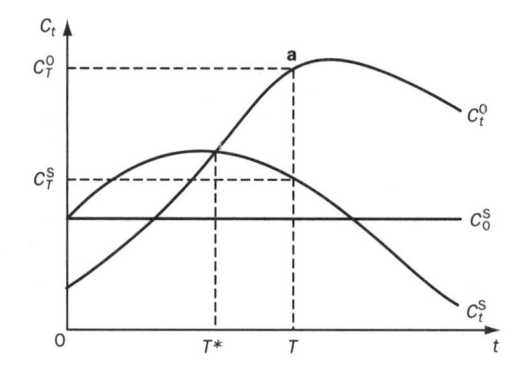

Figure 19.2 Optimal and sustainable consumption paths

The second essential difference concerns the behavioural rule that will give sustainability, if it is feasible. The point here is that whereas for an individual in a competitive economy, or for a small open economy in a competitive world economy, prices are exogenous and unaffected by the behaviour of the individual, or of a small open economy, for a closed economy prices are endogenous and depend upon the economy's behaviour. Also, for the individual analysed in the previous subsection, the marginal product of the bank account in producing income is constant, and equal to r, the single interest rate ruling throughout the economy. For a closed economy with equation 19.16 as its production function, on the other hand, the behaviour of the marginal product of capital over time depends upon the time paths chosen for K_t and R_t, as does the marginal product of resource use. Analysing properly the full implications of the endogeneity of prices and rates of return on assets is difficult, and we will not attempt it here. Some analysis is provided in Appendix 19.1. We can, however, use Figure 19.2 to show some of the results.

In Figure 19.2 C_t^O is the optimal path for consumption from a representative agent model of a closed economy, where the integral of the discounted utility of consumption is maximised, subject to the constraints involving resource use and the allocation of output as between consumption and capital accumulation.[3] This is essentially the model considered in Chapters 3, 4 and 14; see also Appendix 19.1.

C_0^S is the constant consumption level that could be maintained for ever if at the outset the agent went for the highest feasible level of constant consumption, rather than the optimal path C_t^O; and C_t^S gives the time path under the optimal plan for the maximum level of consumption that would be indefinitely sustainable at each date. At T, for example, C_T^O is optimal consumption and C_T^S is the maximum constant level of consumption sustainable after T, given that the optimal plan is followed until T.

Now, the theory appealed to by Solow as discussed above has been interpreted as having the implication that if an economy had been following the optimal path and were at the point a on C_t^O the ruling prices and interest rate could be used with the stock of capital and of the resource to compute wealth and sustainable income for which the corresponding future constant consumption level would be C_T^O. In fact, as Figure 19.2 shows, C_T^O would not be sustainable at T, given that C_t^O had been followed to that time. The maximum constant consumption level that could be indefinitely sustained forward from T, given that C_t^O had been followed until T, is C_T^S. Note that it is not being asserted that using prices and quantities from the optimal path will always overstate wealth, sustainable income and future constant consumption. To the left of T^* C_t^S is greater than C_t^O. The point is that, in general, using the prices and quantities that go with the optimal path will give incorrect signals regarding the level of sustainable income and constant future consumption as interest on wealth. To get the right signals at time T it would be necessary to use the prices and quantities that would hold at T on the path C_t^S. Note that both the efficiency condition (rent increasing proportionately at the rate of interest) and the Hartwick rule (zero total net investment) hold along C_0^S, given that the prices that go with that time path for consumption are used in stating them.

As we have already noted, in the case of an individual it is also true that the optimal consumption plan will, generally, not involve maximum constant consumption. And, to the extent that it does not, an individual who follows it initially will subsequently have stocks of assets that are different from those

---

[3] Figure 19.2 is based on Figure 4 in Pezzey (1997).

that would exist if the maximum constant consumption path had been followed. However, the prices and interest rate facing the individual, being independent of his or her behaviour, will not be affected. He or she could, should at some point he or she wish to follow a constant-consumption path, use the ruling prices and interest rate to work out the maximum constant level of consumption possible, given the actual asset portfolio.

In discussing the case of the closed economy here we have been looking at a model economy tracking the optimal path, which is usually taken to being equivalent to thinking about the path that a fully competitive perfect-foresight economy would track. Of course, as emphasised by Solow, actual economies do not involve perfect foresight and competition. The model economy considered is special in a number of other ways also – it exploits just one non-renewable resource, there is no population growth and no technical progress. Models without such restrictions have been examined in the literature, and references are provided in the Further Reading section at the end of the chapter. We have focused here on this very simple model in order to highlight in it a point that applies generally – measuring sustainable income, and hence future constant consumption possibilities, requires using the prices that go with sustainability to measure total wealth. These are not, generally, the prices that obtain along the path that a competitive perfect-foresight economy would track, and are not the prices that we observe in actual economies. These 'important hedges' are often overlooked, with the result that the prospects for actually measuring sustainable income for an actual economy are frequently oversold.

In saying this, it is implied that there is a sustainable income to be measured, that constant consumption for ever is feasible. As we have noted, this is not assured. There is an extensive literature on feasibility conditions in the simple model considered here, and on extensions to encompass multiple resource inputs (renewable and non-renewable), population growth and technical progress. Again, we refer the reader to the Further Reading section, and move to considering the adjustments to standard measures of national income that this sort of economic theory, which we shall refer to as 'capital theory' in what follows, suggests are required.

19.2.4 Measuring national income

The simplest capital theory model used to address the question of the proper measurement of national income, or product, is a representative agent model of a closed economy where a single commodity is produced using just (non-depreciating) reproducible capital, which is accumulated by abstaining from consumption of the produced commodity. As shown in Appendix 19.2, the basic result derived is that the proper measure of national income is

$$\text{NDP}_t = C_t + I_t \tag{19.17}$$

where NDP stands for Net Domestic Product, C for consumption and I for investment in reproducible capital. This 'proper measure of national income' is taken to be a measure of sustainable income, as that term was used in the previous subsections.

Theoretical arguments about how sustainable income should be measured are developed in terms of modifications to equation 19.17 based on consideration of models that all have the same structure and nature except in regard to what is assumed about the way the economy relates to the environment in terms of arguments in the production and utility functions. A number of such models are presented in Appendix 19.2. Here we shall briefly review some of the results reported there.

For the model that is the basis for Figure 19.2, where production requires inputs of a single non-renewable resource as well as reproducible capital, and using EDP (environmentally adjusted domestic product) for sustainable income, the result is that

$$\text{EDP}_t = \text{NDP}_t - Q_{Rt}R_t = \text{NDP}_t - h_t R_t \tag{19.18}$$

where Q_{Rt} is the marginal product of the resource in production, R_t is the amount used, and h_t is, as previously in this section, the Hotelling rent. In this model, resource extraction is costless, so that Hotelling rent is equal to marginal product. The second term on the right-hand side of equation 19.18 is the depreciation of the resource stock. Two points need to be made here.

First, if we substitute equation 19.17 into equation 19.18 we get

$$\text{EDP}_t = C_t + I_t - h_t R_t$$

so that if total net investment is zero – investment in reproducible capital equals resource depreciation, the Hartwick rule – we have consumption equal to sustainable income and, given the caveats of the previous subsection, constant wealth.

The second point concerns the interpretation of Hotelling rent times resource use as depreciation of the resource stock. Earlier, at equation 19.5, we gave depreciation in the value of the mine as:

$$V_t - V_{t-1} = rV_{t-1} - (1 + r)h_{t-1}R_{t-1}$$

Rearranging 19.5 we get depreciation as the change in the value of the mine as

$$V_t/(1 + r) - V_{t-1} = h_{t-1}R_{t-1} \qquad (19.19)$$

where the right-hand side refers to the start of a period, so that the value of the mine at the end of the period, V_t, has to be discounted by $(1 + r)$ on the left-hand side for comparability. In both discrete and continuous time, depreciation of the resource stock/mine is equal to Hotelling rent times the amount extracted.

In the model which is the basis for Figure 19.2 and for which equation 19.18 is derived resource extraction is costless, and there is no exploration activity that can increase the size of the known resource stock. In a model economy where resource extraction involves cost, and new known reserves can be established at some cost, we find that

$$\begin{aligned} EDP_t &= NDP_t - (Q_{Rt} - G_{Rt})(R_t - N_t) \\ &= NDP_t - h_t(R_t - N_t) \end{aligned} \qquad (19.20)$$

where Q_{Rt} is the marginal product of the resource, G_{Rt} is marginal extraction cost, and N_t is additions to the known stock as the result of exploration. Note that where extraction is costly, Hotelling rent is the difference between the marginal product of the resource and its marginal cost of extraction.

Suppose that a renewable resource rather than a non-renewable resource is used in production. Then we find that

$$\begin{aligned} EDP_t &= NDP_t - (Q_{Rt} - G_{Rt})(R_t - F\{S_t\}) \\ &= NDP_t - h_t(R_t - F\{S_t\}) \end{aligned} \qquad (19.21)$$

where G_{Rt} is the marginal cost of harvesting, and $F\{S_t\}$ is the growth function for the resource stock, where S_t is the stock size. Note that equation 19.21 has exactly the same structure as equation 19.20, with $F\{S_t\}$ playing the role in 19.21 that N_t plays in 19.20. Note also that for sustainable yield exploita-

tion of the renewable resource, $R_t = F\{S_t\}$, there is no depreciation to account for, and $EDP_t = NDP_t$.

While some renewable resources are solely of economic interest as an input to production, some are also of direct interest to consumers. An example would be some tree species which is harvested and used in the production of commodities such as paper, and which as standing timber is a source of recreational services. In such a case we find that

$$EDP_t = NDP_t - (U_{St}/U_{Ct})S_t - h_t(R_t - F\{S_t\}) \qquad (19.22)$$

where U_{St} is the marginal utility of standing trees and U_{Ct} is the marginal utility of produced commodity consumption. As compared with equation 19.21 we now have an additional adjustment to make to net national income as conventionally measured. We have written this adjustment for the amenity value of standing timber valuing it using a ratio of marginal utilities because, typically, there will be no market price that we can observe for the amenity services of standing timber. If we want to measure sustainable income taking account of such amenity services, then we cannot rely on market prices. We could, in principle, think in terms of getting some kind of price to use with S_t from the methods discussed in Chapter 12, where we also discussed the problems that attend such methods.

More fundamentally, there is the question of whether there should be such an adjustment to NDP_t for any particular tree species. In the model which leads to equation 19.22 it is assumed that standing timber yields services to consumers. In the model which leads to equation 19.21 this assumption is not made. The different prescriptions about adjustments to NDP_t arise from different models about how the economy relates to the environment. For any particular tree species we could, in principle, decide which is the appropriate model by using the methods of Chapter 12 to test for $U_S = 0$. While this is true, given many renewable resources which *a priori* could have direct utility it does imply a large research agenda for actually doing environmental accounting. In the absence of such empirical resolution, the prescriptions from capital theory for adjusting conventional income measurement to account for the environment are dependent on the assumptions embodied in the model.

As shown in Appendix 19.2, the point here also applies when we start to consider adjustments on account of the environmental deterioration due to emissions arising in production. What capital theory tells us about how to do environmental accounting and measure sustainable income depends on the model of economy–environment interdependence that is used. Given the current state of knowledge, there is no unique and generally agreed model. Given the uncertainty, as ignorance, that is central to the sustainability problem, it is unlikely that there will ever be such a model. It would, in any case, be a very complicated model, and unlikely to generate simple prescriptions for national income accounting purposes. While capital theory can provide some general insights, it cannot provide generally agreed definitive rules for practising national income accountants to follow. Further, the pricing caveats discussed in the context of the simplest model with production using a costlessly extracted non-renewable resource carry through to all the more complex models. And, as we shall see in the next section, even where the theory offers clear and unambiguous prescriptions over a limited area of the total problem, as with non-renewable resource depletion, implementation remains problematic.

19.3 Environmental accounting: practice[4]

In this section we consider environmental accounting from a perspective which is that of a national income statistician rather than an economic theorist. We begin with some observations on current national income accounting conventions, and their deficiencies in relation to matters environmental as argued by many commentators. We then look at proposals emanating from the United Nations for addressing such concerns. The second subsection of this section looks at the different ways in which non-renewable resource depreciation can be, and has been, measured in practice. The section finishes by looking at some unofficial attempts to produce a measure which better reflects a nation's economic progress, or the lack of it, when due account is taken of its environmental impacts.

Current national income accounting conventions actually produce a variety of measures relating to national income. The most widely used are Gross National Product (GNP) and Gross Domestic Product (GDP). The difference between GNP and GDP is not great for most economies, and its origins are not very relevant to our central concerns here. We shall conduct our discussion by referring to GDP.[5] The conventions now used for GDP measurement have their origin in the information requirements for management of the macroeconomy. For this purpose, what is needed is a measure of the total demand for the outputs of produced commodities. Given that GDP measures total demand, it also measures the output produced to meet that demand, and GDP has come to be seen as a measure of economic performance, or welfare. Indeed, for many commentators it has effectively become *the* performance/welfare indicator, notwithstanding that economists have long been aware of many ways in which it is a very poor performance/welfare indicator, even leaving aside environmental considerations.

GDP can be measured in three ways. First, GDP is the total output sold by firms measured by value added. In measuring national income, purchases of intermediate goods are netted out, as discussed in Chapter 9. Second, GDP is the sum of the incomes earned by persons in the economy. This is the most obvious rationale for calling GDP 'national income'. The sum of incomes is equal to the value of total

---

[4] Our discussion here is at the national level. National-level accounts are compiled from data obtained from, among other sources, the accounts and records of corporations. Ultimately, successful national-level environmental accounting will require changes to accounting practices at the level of companies. Gray (1994) provides a good critical account of research and debate on environmental accounting at that level.

[5] The national income accounting conventions are discussed in most macroeconomics texts. Beckerman (1980) provides a fuller

discussion of the conventions than most such texts, and looks at the principles underlying them. Usher (1980) gives a very thorough discussion of the use of national income accounting data to measure economic growth, and contains an early discussion of adjustments for resource depletion and environmental deterioration. National statistical agencies publish detailed guides to the practices followed in their own accounts and publications; see also the United Nations publications cited in the Further Reading section at the end of this chapter.

output produced by firms by virtue of the convention that output is measured in terms of value added. Third, GDP is total expenditure by individuals on consumption plus expenditure by firms on items of capital equipment; that is, investment.

Given these conventions, each way of measuring GDP should produce the same numerical result. The value-added measure of firms' total output equals the incomes generated in firms equals total expenditure on non-intermediate goods. In practice, the three ways of measuring GDP do not produce the same numbers due to errors arising in the collection of data from the very large number of firms and individuals in an actual economy. To preserve the principle of the conventions, published national income accounts introduce a residual error term, and write the final output, expenditure and income numbers as the same after adding in that term. The expenditure measure of GDP is generally regarded as the most reliable. The size of the residual error term varies from year to year, but is often in excess of 0.5% of GDP. National income accounting is not an exact science.

It is universally agreed that, leaving aside environmental considerations, the proper measure of national income for purposes of monitoring national economic performance and welfare is Net Domestic Product (NDP). This is GDP less that part of it required to make good the depreciation of reproducible capital as it is used in production. In principle, depreciation for a period is measured as the reduction in the value of the economy's existing stock of capital equipment over that period, on account of its use in production. In fact, GDP is much more widely used than NDP. The reason for this is that it is very difficult to measure the depreciation of capital equipment accurately. National income statisticians prefer a number which is an accurate measure of an admittedly unsatisfactory concept to an inaccurate measure of a more satisfactory concept. This needs to be kept in mind when considering proposals for modifying national income measurement so as to account for the depreciation of environmental assets.

As noted in the introduction to this chapter, environmentally driven criticism of current accounting conventions focuses on three areas: depletion of natural resources, environmental degradation and defensive expenditure.

As regards natural-resource depletion, the widely agreed principle is that stocks of natural resources such as oil and gas reserves, stocks of fish, and so on should be treated in the same way as stocks of human-made capital, so that a deduction should be made to allow for the depletion or consumption of these natural resources as they are used in production – that is, their depreciation. In this regard, there is a distinction between resources that yield monetised flows (such as commercial forests, exploited oils and minerals, and so on) and those that yield non-monetised benefits (such as fresh air, lakes and oceans, and similar natural resources to which there are no exclusive property rights). In principle, the depreciation of the former ought to be observable in market data, while this will not be true of the latter. Where renewable resources are not traded in markets, or where they are exploited on an open-access basis, it is clearly going to be difficult to get firm data relating to depreciation. As well as the problem of valuation, there are often problems of physical measurement, given that there are no incentives for private measurement activity, as there are in the case of traded resources where exclusive property rights exist.

Degradation occurs when there is a decline in the quality of the natural environment, in particular of air, water and land quality. As with renewable and non-renewable resources, land, air and water can be viewed as assets, the degradation of which should be treated as depreciation and accounted for in the same way as depletion of reproducible capital. At the level of theory, there is no difference between this case and that of the depletion of natural resources. However, as a practical matter it is not always obvious how degradation should be defined and, even if satisfactorily defined, how it should be valued. An approach that has been suggested is to establish certain desirable quality standards, and then to measure degradation as the deviation from these quality levels. The value of the degradation can then be calculated as the cost of making good the degradation that has occurred or the cost of achieving the targeted quality standards. However, there is clearly the possibility of an arbitrary element in this since quality standards may be set which are higher than would occur in the 'natural' environment. It is unlikely that the quality standards established would be those which correspond to the efficient level of abatement – that is, where the marginal social cost of the pollution equals the marginal abatement cost. If the use of the costs of achieving standards is considered inappropriate, alternative methods of valuing degradation must be sought. Willingness to pay (WTP) to avoid the degradation, or to make it good, has been proposed. The assessment of WTP in relation to the natural environment was considered in Chapter 12. Leaving aside the problems discussed there, from a national accounting standpoint there is the difficulty that WTP includes consumers' surplus whereas the standard components of the national accounts are valued using market prices.

Expenditures that are expressly designed to prevent degradation or to counteract the effects of degradation that has already taken place – so-called defensive expenditures – will be included in GDP as currently measured. Expenditure incurred by producers – for example, waste treatment by enterprises – will be reflected in product prices but not be separately identifiable in the national accounts. Expenditure by households, government or non-profit-making institutions, or capital expenditure by enterprises, will be included on the expenditure side of GDP and should in principle be separately identifiable in the accounts currently produced. As noted, some commentators argue that such defensive expenditures should be deducted from GDP as now measured to arrive at a proper measure of national income. As a practical matter, quite apart from the difficulty of measuring defensive expenditure, it can be argued that there is no reason why defensive environmental expenditure should be treated differently from other forms of defensive expenditure, such as expenditure on armed forces, preventive medicine, policing and so on. A consistent approach to defensive expenditure would require major changes in the measurement of national income, beyond those required on environmental grounds. Some commentators argue that given the difficulties that such an approach would face, the construction of a measure of sustainable economic welfare should, rather than involve adjustments to national income, start somewhere else. We discuss some efforts of this nature in the final part of this section of the chapter.

19.3.1 The UNSTAT proposals: satellite accounting

The practical possibilities for environmental modifications to national income accounting conventions have been under active consideration by many individuals and institutions for a number of years. In the wake of the emergence of, and interest in, the idea of sustainable development, the United Nations Statistical Division (UNSTAT) has proposed draft guidelines for new national income accounting conventions, the System of integrated Environmental and Economic Accounting (SEEA). Here we provide an informal outline of the essentials of the guidelines; a more formal account is given in Appendix 19.3.

The essential idea is to measure the 'environmental cost' of economic activity in a period. Environmental cost (EC) is defined as the difference between the opening and closing value of the stock of environmental assets

$$EC_t \equiv \sum a_{it}v_{it} - \sum a_{it-1}v_{it-1} \qquad (19.23)$$

where the summation is over $i = 1, 2, \ldots, n$ assets, a_i represents the physical measure of the ith environmental asset, v_i the unit value assigned to the ith asset, and where $t - 1$ refers to the start of the period and t to the end of the period. For the ith asset, $a_{it}v_{it} - a_{it-1}v_{it-1}$ is its depreciation over the period. EC_t is the change in the balance sheet value of all n environmental assets over the period, the depreciation of what is sometimes called 'natural capital'. In line with the discussion of the previous section, environmentally adjusted net domestic product could then be defined as

$$EDP_t \equiv NDP_t - EC_t \equiv (GDP_t - D_{Mt}) - D_{Nt} \qquad (19.24)$$

where NDP stands for Net Domestic Product, D_M for the depreciation of human-made reproducible capital, and $D_N \equiv EC$ for the depreciation of natural capital.

The UNSTAT proposals do not envisage replacing the publication of the standard GDP/NDP accounts with the publication of EDP accounts. They do envisage complementing the standard accounts with balance sheets for natural capital, from which users of the accounts could work out EDP. This would leave intact the current conventions for the measurement of GDP and NDP, so that adoption of the proposal would mean that figures on these constructs would continue to be available on a consistent basis with past data. The balance sheets for environmental assets are, therefore, referred to as 'satellite accounts'. The potential, discussed below, for large year-on-year changes in estimates of the depreciation of non-renewable resources is another reason why most of those concerned with the production of national income accounts favour the satellite accounting approach, rather than producing only figures for environmentally adjusted national income. The idea is to publish each year conventional national income accounts accompanied by opening and closing balance sheet accounts for environmental assets.

In principle, the satellite accounts could cover all environmental assets relevant to production and consumption. This would require physical data and valuations for all relevant assets, and this is not now available even in those countries where the official statistical agencies have invested heavily in generating, collating and publishing environmental data. The problems are seen as especially acute with respect to valuation data for those assets not subject to market transactions. We shall see shortly, however, that even for mineral deposits subject to private property rights, there are quite serious problems about both physical data and valuation for depreciation. The UNSTAT proposals envisage that the range of assets used for the calculation of environmental cost be extended over time, starting with non-renewable resources and renewable resources involving market transactions.

As well as resource depletion and environmental degradation, we have noted that some commentators argue for the deduction of defensive environmental expenditures from the measure of NDP. The UNSTAT proposals do not involve treating defensive expenditures as an element of environmental cost for the adjustment of NDP to EDP, for two main reasons. First, as a practical matter, it is very difficult to definitively identify and measure such expenditures. Second, and more fundamentally, such subtraction might open the door to questioning the whole basis of measured national income as a welfare indicator. Leaving the natural environment aside, much of the expenditure counted in national income could be regarded as defensive – we eat and incur medical expenses to stay alive, we buy clothes to defend against the weather and social disapproval, and so on. The UNSTAT proposals do, however, involve identifying and separately reporting defensive environmental expenditures in the accounting system.

It must be emphasised that we have been discussing proposals and guidelines. No nation's official statistical office currently produces comprehensive satellite environmental accounts along with its standard national income accounts. Some have produced estimates of balance sheets for some natural resources, as exemplified by the data for Australia and the UK discussed in the next subsection, but these appear as special one-off publications, or are classified as 'preliminary estimates', rather than as routine elements of the national income accounting system. Some independent analysts have made attempts to produce measures of EDP. Two such efforts, for Indonesia and Australia, are discussed below.

19.3.2 Measuring the depreciation of non-renewable resources

A somewhat extended treatment of this particular of the practice of environmental accounting is justified because, given that non-renewable resources are generally subject to private property rights and traded in markets, they are, from the general class of environmental assets, the case where it is most straightforward to come up with numbers for depreciation. In fact, as we shall see, even in this case, obtaining a single 'correct' number for the depreciation of a particular resource is problematic, notwithstanding the availability of market data.

As we have seen, the theoretically correct measure of the depreciation of an economy's stock of a non-renewable resource is the total Hotelling rent (THR) arising in its extraction. With P for the price of the extracted resource, c for the marginal cost of extraction, R for the amount extracted, N for new discoveries, and D for the depreciation of the resource stock:

$$D = \text{THR} = (P - c)(R - N) \qquad (19.25)$$

Given standard assumptions for a fully competitive economy, we would have

THR = CIV

where CIV is the change in the value of the economy's stock of the non-renewable resource in question. In principle, and given the standard assumptions, D could be measured as either THR given by equation 19.25 or as CIV, with the same result.

In practice, neither of these measures of D appears to have been used, nor are they proposed for use in the literature concerning how environmental accounts might actually be constructed. The most obvious problem with equation 19.25 is that c, the marginal cost of extraction, is not observable in published, or readily available, data. As we shall see, there are other problems with using equation 19.25 to measure D. If there existed competitive firms that were solely in the business of selling the rights to extract from the resource stock, which they owned, then stock market valuations of such firms could be used to measure CIV. Generally such firms do not exist, resource ownership and extraction being vertically integrated in mining firms. Stock market valuations of mining firms are available, but these data confound the changes in other asset values with those of the mineral deposits owned, and reflect changes in overall stock market 'sentiment'. In any case, the minerals sector of an economy is rarely such that it can properly be characterised as 'competitive'.

There are three main methods that appear in the literature concerned with the practical implementation of environmental accounting.

19.3.2.1 Net price

This uses average cost, C, instead of marginal cost to compute rent, which is taken as the measure of depreciation, so that:

$$D = (P - C)(R - N) \tag{19.26}$$

Note that for $c > C$, $(P - C) > (P - c)$ so that on this account there would arise an overestimation of THR using equation 19.26. In many applications of the net price method, N is ignored. In what follows we shall refer to the net price method with new

discoveries ignored as 'Net price I', and to the use of equation 19.26 with the N adjustment as 'Net price II'. Given that actual accounts refer to periods of time, rather than to instants of time as in the theoretical literature, applications of equation 19.26, with or without N, also vary as to the treatment of P and C in terms of dating. Clearly, each could be measured at the start or the end of the period, or as some average over the period. These three measures will only coincide if P and C are unchanging throughout the period, which in the case of P is uncommon.

19.3.2.2 Change in net present value

With 0 indicating the start of the accounting period and 1 its close, this method uses

$$D = \sum_{t=0}^{T_0} [(P_t - C_t)R_t/(1 + r)^t] - \sum_{t=1}^{T_1} [(P_t - C_t)R_t/(1 + r)^t] \tag{19.27}$$

where T_0 and T_1 are deposit lifetimes, and r is the interest rate. Apart from the use of C rather than c, this method can be seen as an alternative (to stock market valuations) method of measuring CIV. As actually used this method requires some specialising assumptions, as discussed below.

19.3.2.3 El Serafy's (user cost) rule

El Serafy was the economist who proposed this method, which is intended to measure depreciation as 'user cost'. The rationale for and derivation of the rule is discussed in Appendix 19.4. According to the rule

$$D = R(P - C)/(1 + r)^T \tag{19.28}$$

where r is the interest rate, and T is the deposit lifetime assuming a constant rate of extraction.

19.3.2.4 Measurements of non-renewable resource depreciation for Australia and the United Kingdom

It is generally understood that the net price method is liable to produce large year-on-year fluctuations in estimated D, and this method is not recommended in the UNSTAT guidelines for environmental accounting. Those guidelines recommend the change in net present value method. The net price method is, however, quite widely used by analysts seeking a figure for D in respect of non-renewable resource stocks. It avoids the need for information/assumptions about mine lifetimes and interest rates, which arises with both of the other methods.

We now consider some results based on officially published data, measured by different methods for two countries. In the case of Australia the results for a wide range of non-renewable resources were added to estimate total depreciation for all mineral resources. In the case of the United Kingdom, attention was restricted to oil and natural gas.

The Australian Bureau of Statistics has produced preliminary balance sheet estimates for a range of assets including 'Subsoil assets', that is, non-renewable mineral resources (ABS, 1995).[6] Table 3.3 of ABS (1995) gives for each of 33 minerals:

1. the size of 'Economic Demonstrated Resources' (EDR) at 30 June 1989, 1990, 1991 and 1992;
2. the price of the extracted mineral at 30 June 1989, 1990, 1991 and 1992;
3. the average cost of extraction at 30 June 1989, 1990, 1991 and 1992;
4. production of the mineral in the years ending 30 June 1989, 1990, 1991 and 1992.

From these data there is calculated for each of the 33 minerals, for each of four years, the NPV of the resource stock according to

$$PV_s = \sum_{t=1}^{T_s} [(P_t - C_t)R_t/(1 + r)^t]$$

where s refers to the balance sheet date (30 June 1989, 1990, 1991 and 1992) and T_S is the estimated stock lifetime at that date. Several specialising assumptions are made. First, R_t is set equal to R for all t where

$$R = 0.25(R_{88/9} + R_{89/90} + R_{90/1} + R_{91/2})$$

At each s the resource lifetime, T, is calculated as:

$$T_s = EDR_s/R$$

Table 19.3 Alternative estimates of minerals depreciation for Australia 1988/9 to 1991/2, AUS$ $\times 10^6$

Year	El Serafy rule	Net price I	Net price II	ABS NPV change
1988/89	952	8 511		
1989/90	1 228	9 872	−19 321	−6 500
1990/91	1 922	12 023	−147 035	−19 900
1991/92	2 328	13 624	299 075	−9 700

It is assumed that for all t, $(P_t - C_t) = (P_s - C_s)$. Using an interest rate of 7.5% the PV_s results are summed across minerals to give balance sheet valuations of Australia's 'subsoil assets' at 30 June 1989, 1990, 1991 and 1992.

The figures shown in Table 19.3 under 'ABS NPV change' are the differences between the closing and opening valuations for all Australian non-renewable resources, and are the results for the change in NPV method as described above.[7] The figures shown in Table 19.3 under 'El Serafy rule' are calculated according to equation 19.28 using the same P, C and T data from ABS (1995), and the same 7.5% interest rate. The 'Net price II' figures use the net price method, taking account of new discoveries, calculating rent as $(P_s - C_s)(R_s - N_s)$ where P_s, C_s and R_s are taken direct from the ABS data, and N_s is inferred from $(EDR_s - EDR_{s-1})$ and R_s in those data. ABS (1995) notes a number of problems regarding the EDR data. Of particular concern are changes due to variation in P, technological change, and revisions of resource classification. The figures for 'Net price I' in Table 19.3 are the least affected by specialising assumptions and the problems attending the EDR data, being calculated as $(P_s - C_s)R_s$ – in other words, ignoring new discoveries.

From a comparison of equation 19.26, with N equal to zero, and equation 19.28, it is clear that, for the same data, the 'Net price I' figure must always be larger than the 'El Serafy rule' figure. From equation 19.26, assuming that N must be non-negative means that 'Net price II' must always be smaller than 'Net price I'. In Table 19.3, for 1989/90 and 1990/1 across all minerals new discoveries are positive and

---

[6] For further information on the ABS data and details of the calculations for Table 19.3 here, see Common and Sanyal (1998).

[7] The ABS also did the calculations for interest rates of 5% and 10%. Their results illustrate the sensitivity of depreciation as measured by the change in NPV method to the interest rate used.

large enough to produce a negative figure for depreciation. However, for 1991/2 'Net price II' depreciation is much larger than 'Net price I' depreciation. This is primarily because of a reduction in the EDR figure for bauxite for 30 June 1992 by an amount which exceeds the previous year's production, 0.04 gigatonnes, by 3.96 gigatonnes, implying negative new discoveries. The pattern in the 'ABS NPV change' figures follows that for 'Net price II' with dampened swings, as would be expected given the method of calculation described above.

Which of these is the 'correct' way to measure depreciation? The capital-theoretic approach could be taken to suggest 'Net price II', were it not for the fact that it uses average, rather than marginal, costs. Given marginal costs greater than average costs, one could argue, this measure should be taken as an upper bound on depreciation. However, given the problems about measuring 'new discoveries', the implications of this argument in practice can, as shown in Table 19.3, lead to negative figures for non-renewable-resource depletion. The change in NPV method, as implemented by ABS, also gives rise to negative depreciation for minerals, as shown in the final column of Table 19.3. A negative figure for depreciation means that the effect of accounting for the depletion of non-renewable resources would be, other things equal, to make sustainable national income larger than conventionally measured national income. Notice also that the 'Net price II' and 'ABS NPV change' results in Table 19.3 are more volatile than those for 'El Serafy rule' and 'Net price I'. Using either of the former to adjust conventionally measured national income would make the time series resulting highly volatile.

The point of reporting these results is not to criticise the work of the Australian Bureau of Statistics. It is, on the contrary, to demonstrate that even thorough work by a highly respected national statistical agency does not result in unambiguous measurement of the depreciation of non-renewable natural resources.

The results in Table 19.4 make the same point with data for the UK taken from a 1992 publication from the national statistical agency. In a subsequent publication, Vaze (1998a), the same agency reports three sets of oil and gas depreciation estimates through to 1994. In addition to estimates according

Table 19.4 Alternative estimates of depletion of the UK oil and natural gas reserves (£m)

Year	User cost method 1	Depreciation method[a] 2	Ratio 2/1
1980	2600	6 600	2.54
1981	4200	9 400	2.24
1982	5300	10 700	2.02
1983	5200	12 400	2.39
1984	7700	15 400	2.00
1985	2900	14 200	4.90
1986	2800	4 500	1.61
1987	3400	5 100	1.50
1988	2000	2 000	1.00
1989	1700	1 800	1.06
1990	1600	2 200	1.38

[a] Based on the method proposed by Repetto *et al.* (1989), i.e. Net price II
Source: Adapted from Central Statistical Office estimates from Bryant and Cook (1992)

to the depreciation method (described as the net price method in the second publication) and the user cost method, estimates according to the present value method are reported. The estimates vary across methods to a similar extent to that shown in Table 19.4. It is stated that the agency's 'preferred approach is to use the net present value methodology' in an environmental satellite account.

19.3.3 Environmentally adjusted national income for Indonesia and Australia

The quotation from Repetto *et al.* (1989) which heads this chapter is from the introduction to a report in which a World Resources Institute team adjusted official national income measures for Indonesia by their estimates of the depreciation of three environmental assets – oil deposits, timber and soil. They proceeded by first constructing physical accounts, then applying unit values. In the case of oil opening stocks were valued at the current market price of the extracted oil less estimated average extraction cost. Closing stocks were computed by subtracting extraction during the year and adding new discoveries, and valued in the same way as the opening stocks using the price ruling at the end of the period. This is an application of the Net price II method. The procedure followed with timber is the same except that it allows for estimated natural growth over the year. The physical data here are recognised as being

Table 19.5 GDP and an EDP estimate for Indonesia 1971–1984

Year	GDP	EDP	EDP/GDP
1971	1	1	1.20
1972	1.09	0.90	0.99
1973	1.22	0.97	0.96
1974	1.32	1.48	1.36
1975	1.38	0.98	0.85
1976	1.47	1.12	0.92
1977	1.60	1.08	0.81
1978	1.73	1.19	0.78
1979	1.83	1.19	0.78
1980	2.01	1.28	0.76
1981	2.17	1.48	0.82
1982	2.22	1.58	0.86
1983	2.32	1.49	0.78
1984	2.44	1.68	0.83

Source: Based on Repetto *et al.* (1989)

Table 19.6 GDP and EDP estimates for Australia 1980–88

Year	GDP	EDP$_1$	EDP$_2$	GDP/Pop	EDP$_2$/Pop
1980	1	1	1	1	1
1981	1.03	1.03	1.16	1.01	1.13
1982	1.07	1.07	1.14	1.03	1.10
1983	1.04	1.03	1.15	0.98	1.09
1984	1.09	1.09	1.04	1.00	0.96
1985	1.17	1.17	1.34	1.06	1.22
1986	1.22	1.22	1.62	1.08	1.44
1987	1.25	1.26	1.09	1.09	0.95
1988	1.31	1.32	1.52	1.12	1.30
Growth rate	3.4%	3.5%	5.4%	1.4%	3.3%

Source: Based on Young (1990)

less firmly based than in the case of oil. For soil erosion, estimated physical losses over the year were valued using estimates of the loss of agricultural output entailed.

Table 19.5 reports the results obtained by Repetto *et al.* in index number form, where EDP is GDP minus the depreciation of the three environmental assets considered. The average per annum growth rates are 7.1% for GDP and 4.1% for EDP. EDP grows more slowly than GDP over the period 1971–1984, and behaves more erratically. The fourth column shows the ratio of the EDP estimate to GDP. The erratic behaviour of the EDP series is principally due to the effect of changes in the price of extracted oil, and of new discoveries of oil. The EDP figures for 1973 and 1974 show the effects of the increase in the world price of oil. If EDP is understood as sustainable income, these figures show sustainable income increasing by 51% in one year, 1973 to 1974.

Young (1990) undertook a similar exercise for Australia, with the results shown in Table 19.6. Young treated all mineral resources in the way that Repetto *et al.* treated just oil, and also followed them in considering from among the renewable resources only timber. However, Young's valuation of the depreciation of this asset is based only on an estimate of its implications for wildlife habitat loss. As regards soil degradation, Young uses estimates of the value of agricultural productivity losses. Unlike Repetto *et al.*, Young incorporates an estimate of the

degradation of environmental assets by pollution. This is done by subtracting from GDP an estimate of expenditure by households and government to offset the effects of pollution. The problems associated with this way of measuring environmental degradation were noted above.

Young describes his calculations as 'back of the envelope', and claims to have been 'environmentally generous' in producing his figures. In Table 19.6, Young's results are reported in index number form for GDP, EDP$_1$ and EDP$_2$, where

$$EDP_1 = GDP - \text{Depreciation on account of land} \\ \text{degradation} \\ - \text{Depreciation on account of} \\ \text{timber production} \\ - \text{Defensive expenditures}$$

and

$$EDP_2 = EDP_1 - \text{Depreciation on account of} \\ \text{mineral depletion}$$

'Pop' stands for population, and the last two columns give the index numbers for GDP per capita and EDP$_2$ per capita. Shown at the bottom of each column is the average annual growth rate implied by the index numbers above.

Several points are worth noting. First, the behaviour of GDP and EDP$_1$ is quite similar. Second, as with the Repetto *et al.* figures, EDP$_2$ is quite erratic over time. This is, again, due to the effects of price changes and new discoveries. Third, the average growth rate for EDP$_2$ is actually substantially greater than that for GDP. In 1980 the EDP$_2$ to GDP ratio was 0.84; in 1988 the ratio was 0.97. The fourth point concerns the adjustment for population growth. Clearly, if we wish to give national income a welfare interpretation, it needs to be measured per capita. Official national statistical publications do not generally report on a per capita basis, and commentary is frequently based on those unadjusted figures. The Repetto *et al.* results in Table 19.5 are for Indonesia's total national income, not per capita national income. For Australia, Table 19.6 shows that adjusting for population growth reduces GDP growth by 2% per annum, whereas adjusting GDP for environmental depreciation actually increases national income growth. Fifth, on these figures, per capita sustainable income after allowing for environmental depreciation, is growing at 3.3% per annum.

It should be noted that Young, and Repetto *et al.*, do not subtract from GDP the depreciation of human-made capital. If this were done, it would reduce their EDP figures in terms of levels, but it is unlikely that it would much affect the growth rate results.

19.3.4 Measuring sustainable economic welfare

In recent years a number of economists interested in sustainability and welfare have taken the view that NDP is not the place from which to start the search for a satisfactory measurement.[8] Rather, they have constructed indices which start with personal consumption expenditure as recorded in the national income accounts and then make a series of adjustments to it which are intended to produce a better account of welfare which is sustainable. The result is usually called an 'index of sustainable economic welfare' (ISEW) or a 'genuine progress indicator' (GPI). Figure 19.3 shows the results obtained, in comparison with the movement of GNP, for the UK by Jackson and Marks (1994). In common with many ISEW/GPI results for industrialised economies, the main feature is that whereas national income grew more or less continually over recent decades, 'properly' measured sustainable welfare grew much more slowly overall, and actually went into decline starting around the mid-1970s; see, for example, Daly and Cobb (1989) for the USA, Stockhammer *et al.* (1997) for Austria, and Hamilton (1997) for Australia.

The original ISEW was calculated for the USA by Daly and Cobb (1989), and we now briefly discuss their method and results. The definition that they use is

$$ISEW \equiv \{(C/D) + (E + F + G + H)$$
$$- (I + J + K + L + M + N + O + P + Q$$
$$+ R + S + T + U) + (V + W)\}/Pop \qquad (19.29)$$

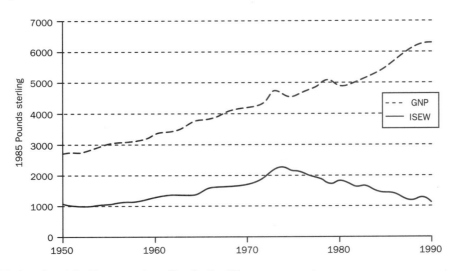

Figure 19.3 Index of sustainable economic welfare for the UK
Source: Jackson and Marks (1994).

---

[8]   For references to some of the precursors of the work discussed here see Daly and Cobb (1989).

where

C is personal consumption expenditure

D is an index of distributional inequality

E is an imputed value for extra-market labour services

F is an estimate of the flow of services from consumer durables

G is an estimate of the value of streets and highway services

H is an estimate of the value of publicly provided health and education services

I is expenditure on consumer durables

J is an estimate of private defensive spending on health and education

K is expenditure on advertising at the national level

L is an estimate of commuting cost

M is an estimate of the costs of urbanisation

N is an estimate of the costs of automobile accidents

O is an estimate of water pollution costs

P is an estimate of air pollution costs

Q is an estimate of noise pollution costs

R is an estimate of the costs of wetlands loss

S is an estimate of the costs of farmland loss

T is an estimate of the cost of non-renewable-resource depletion

U is an estimate of the cost of long-term environmental damage

V is an estimate of net additions to the stock of reproducible capital

W is the change in net overseas indebtedness

Daly and Cobb (1989) report, in an appendix, the sources used and the estimation methods employed, and admit to the somewhat arbitrary assumptions that it was necessary to make in many cases. In effect, equation 19.29 is a welfare function, which reflects the authors' judgements about the determinants of welfare, and what sustains them. Others may have different views about these matters. It should be noted, for example, that according to equation 19.29, sustainable economic welfare increases when, other things constant, unpaid household labour increases. It should also be noted, on the other hand, that the value of leisure time does not appear as an argument in the welfare function. Many people would, one imagines, feel that their welfare

Table 19.7 GDP and ISEW average annual growth rates for the USA

	1950–1986	1951–1986
GDP	3.34	2.55
GDP per capita	2.02	1.52
ISEW	0.87	1.00
ISEW1	1.09	0.76
ISEW2 = ISEW1 − E	3.14	2.01
ISEW2 = ISEW1 + T	1.13	0.80
ISEW3 = ISEW1 + L + M + N	1.12	0.78

had improved if they did less work around the house and worked shorter hours in paid employment. That said, it should also be noted that per capita national income takes no account of time spent in paid work, nor of unpaid work.

Table 19.7 gives the results from calculations using the data provided in the appendix to Daly and Cobb (1989), which illustrate the sensitivity of the ISEW to the removal of some of its components. The two columns of numbers show the effect of changing, by one year, the base year from which the average annual growth rates for GDP, ISEW and ISEW variants are measured. Note that the difference between the growth of per capita GDP and ISEW is reduced from 1.15% to 0.52%. ISEW1 is ISEW without the adjustment for the distribution of income; that is, it is the result if the term *D* in equation 19.29 is fixed at 1. The results for ISEW2, which is ISEW1 without the adjustment for unpaid extra market labour, shows that this adjustment has a major impact on the behaviour of ISEW. Without this adjustment, ISEW2 grows faster than GDP per capita whichever base year is used, and for the 1950 base ISEW2 grows by more than 1% faster. On the other hand, adding back in the adjustment for non-renewable-resource depletion, to get ISEW3, makes little difference to the growth rate obtained for ISEW1. As the last row shows, the non-renewable-resource depletion adjustment has an effect of essentially the same size as the adjustment for the costs of commuting, urbanisation and automobile accidents.

Other ISEW/GPI constructions make adjustments to personal consumption which, while generally similar in nature to those of Daly and Cobb, differ in detail on account of the judgements of the constructors and/or the availability of data. However, as noted above, they generally show similar patterns in relation to the behaviour of GDP per capita. What most ISEW/GPI constructions appear to have in common is an adjustment for unpaid labour, and we have noted for the case of the Daly and Cobb (1989) ISEW the large leverage that this exerts on the final result.

19.4 Sustainability indicators

From the preceding sections it is clear that it is difficult both in principle and in practice to measure sustainable income, or some alternative such as sustainable economic welfare. This has led to an interest in 'sustainability indicators' – measurements which, while not intended to capture the whole picture in a single number, are supposed to provide information useful to the pursuit of sustainability.

19.4.1 The Pearce–Atkinson indicator: measuring genuine saving

In the second section of this chapter we discussed the capital-theoretic approach to sustainability and environmental accounting. The essential ideas from there suggest a necessary, but not sufficient, condition for sustainability with considerable intuitive appeal – that an economy's saving be sufficient to make good the depreciation of both its human-made and natural capital. Making good depreciation is an appealing guide to prudent asset management. This has led to an interest in an indicator which is intended to record whether an economy is satisfying this necessary condition for sustainability. As the indicator appears to have first been suggested in Pearce and Atkinson (1993) we shall refer to this as the Pearce–Atkinson indicator; see also Atkinson and Pearce (1993) and Pearce and Atkinson (1995). We will work through the basis for the Pearce–Atkinson indicator, and then present some results for Australia.

With W for wealth, we can write

$$W_t - W_{t-1} = Y_t - C_t - D_t \qquad (19.30)$$

where Y is income, C is consumption and D is the depreciation of the asset portfolio. If we impose the condition that wealth is constant, this becomes

$$0 = Y_t - C_{\max,t} - D_t \qquad (19.31)$$

where $C_{\max,t}$ is the maximum level of consumption consistent with constant wealth. Rearranging equation 19.31 we can write

$$C_{\max,t} = Y_t - D_t$$

and, defining sustainable income as the maximum that can be consumed without reducing wealth, this gives

$$Y_{\text{sus},t} = Y_t - D_t \qquad (19.32)$$

where $Y_{\text{sus},t}$ stands for sustainable income. With $Y_t = C_t + S_t$, equation 19.32 can be written as

$$Y_{\text{sus},t} - C_t = S_t - D_t$$

so that we have

$$C_t > Y_{\text{sus},t} \leftrightarrow S_t - D_t < 0 \leftrightarrow W_t - W_{t-1} < 0$$

$$C_t = Y_{\text{sus},t} \leftrightarrow S_t - D_t = 0 \leftrightarrow W_t - W_{t-1} = 0 \quad (19.33)$$

$$C_t < Y_{\text{sus},t} \leftrightarrow S_t - D_t > 0 \leftrightarrow W_t - W_{t-1} > 0$$

If W_t comprises both human-made capital and natural capital, and we use D_{Mt} for the depreciation of the former and D_{Nt} for the depreciation of the latter, then

$$S_t \geq D_{Mt} + D_{Nt} \qquad (19.34a)$$

is necessary for sustainability. An alternative way of stating this condition is as

$$GS_t = S_t - D_{Mt} - D_{Nt} \geq 0 \qquad (19.34b)$$

where GS stands for 'genuine saving'. Pearce and Atkinson actually look at genuine saving as a proportion of national income, but clearly if GS as defined by 19.34b is positive then so will be GS divided by income.

As we have seen, even where attention is restricted to the non-renewable resource component of natural capital, the measurement of D_N is problematic. As is well documented in the national income accounting literature, the measurement of D_M is also problematic. However, Pearce and Atkinson argue that looking at genuine saving is a useful, practical sustainability indicator in so far as it will, at relatively low cost, generate information about the attainment, or otherwise, of a minimal necessary condition for sustainability. If we find that genuine saving is positive, we certainly should not conclude

Table 19.8 Saving and depreciation in Australia 1979/80 to 1994/5

Year	S A\$ $\times 10^6$	D_M A\$ $\times 10^6$	D_N A\$ $\times 10^6$	$S - D_M - D_N$ A\$ $\times 10^6$	D_N/D_M
1979/80	28 846	18 137	1845	8 684	0.102
1980/1	35 192	21 105	1665	12 422	0.079
1981/2	41 456	24 188	1743	15 525	0.072
1982/3	41 105	27 801	2099	11 205	0.076
1983/4	44 325	29 940	2937	11 448	0.098
1984/5	51 016	32 539	3064	15 413	0.094
1985/6	59 303	37 478	3417	18 408	0.091
1986/7	64 475	42 590	2726	19 159	0.064
1987/8	72 354	46 737	2658	22 959	0.057
1988/9	85 146	51 372	1332	32 442	0.026
1989/90	89 479	55 996	3010	30 473	0.054
1990/1	81 336	58 303	4956	18 077	0.085
1991/2	77 347	59 836	4311	13 200	0.072
1992/3	81 767	62 789	3893	15 085	0.062
1993/4	87 007	65 121	2743	19 143	0.042
1994/5	96 732	66 658	2057	28 017	0.031

Source: Adapted from Common and Sanyal (1998)

that sustainability is assured, but if we find that it is negative then there are grounds for doubting that current behaviour is consistent with sustainability.

Table 19.8 gives some results for Australia, where only non-renewable resources are considered. As previously discussed, economists take the view that the proper measure of depreciation of natural resources is the rent arising in a competitive economy. In the context of the Pearce–Atkinson indicator, a natural way to estimate the total rents actually arising in minerals extraction is via the national income accounts, as follows. For countries with well-developed national statistical services the published national income accounts give data for the Net Capital Stock (of reproducible, human-made, capital equipment), K, and Gross Operating Surplus, GOS, reported by industrial sectors. With N indicating the mining sector, the return on capital in sectors other than mining can be calculated as

$$g = GOS_{non-N}/K_{non-N}$$

which can be used to estimate a normal GOS in mining as

$$EGOS_N = gK_N$$

Mining rent is then given by the difference between the normal and actual GOS in the mining sector, and identifying rent with depreciation, we have:

$$D_N = GOS_N - EGOS_N$$

The results arising are shown in Table 19.8, together with data for S and D_M. There are several points of interest. The first is that GS = $S - D_M - D_N$ is always positive, so that according to this indicator, we cannot say that Australia was behaving unsustainably over 1979/80 to 1994/5. Over this period, GS as measured in Table 19.8 varied between 3.4% and 9.8% of GDP. The second point to note is that D_M is very much larger than D_N, although Australia is, among developed countries, a country where minerals extraction is relatively high as a proportion of GDP. The size of D_N relative to D_M is falling over time in Table 19.8. In Table 19.3 we reported four different D_N estimates for Australia for some of the years shown in Table 19.8. The third point is then that we have here a fifth estimate for D_N, which is different from the other four. Comparing the two tables, it will be seen that the Table 19.8 estimate falls between the El Serafy rule and net price estimates from Table 19.3, and, like them, is much less volatile than the Net price II and NPV change estimates.

Pearce and Atkinson (1995) report results for their indicator for 18 countries, for 8 of which GS is negative. All of these 8 are developing countries. The exact coverage of, and method of calculation for, D_N by country is not reported. It appears that both vary across countries, and that for some 'natural capital' is broader than just mineral resources, which is the definition of 'natural capital' for the Australian results reported in Table 19.8. The World Bank has produced estimates for GS in which 'natural capital' includes renewable resources as well as minerals, and where D_N includes an estimate for damage arising on account of a country's emissions of greenhouse gases. In World Bank (1995) the depreciation of both mineral stocks and renewable resources is calculated as the quantity extracted/harvested multiplied by 50% of the price of the extracted/harvested resource. On this basis, GS for Australia averaged over 1989–91 is reported as between −1% and 1% of GNP. Australia, according to these results (see also World Bank, 1996), has a GS performance which is borderline in terms of satisfying the Pearce–Atkinson indicator condition for sustainability, among the worst of the developed countries, and worse than that of a number of developing countries. Again, we see that one can get substantially different results according to the conventions followed and estimates used.

19.4.2 The Proops–Atkinson indicator: accounting for international trade

Given international trade, one nation's inhabitants can depreciate natural capital in another nation. Thus, for example, Japan is frequently cited as a country which has high domestic saving and investment in human-made capital, and low natural-capital depreciation domestically, but which is responsible for much natural-capital depreciation overseas when it imports raw materials. The obverse case would be somewhere like Saudi Arabia, where natural-capital depreciation is high on account of exported natural-resource extraction. The Pearce–Atkinson indicator does not allow for such effects. Proops and Atkinson (1996) have proposed a method which modifies the indicator so as to allow for trade effects. The essential idea is to treat each economy as a sector in the global economy, and to use the techniques of input–output modelling discussed in Chapter 9.

Consider two trading economies, 1 and 2. Let x_{12} be exports from 1 to 2, and x_{21} be exports from 2 to 1. Let y represent total output, and f represent final demand, comprising c for consumption and s for saving/investment. We can then write:

$$y_1 = x_{12} + c_1 + s_1 = x_{12} + f_1$$
$$y_2 = x_{21} + c_2 + s_2 = x_{21} + f_2$$
(19.35)

If we define coefficients $q_{12} = x_{12}/y_2$ and $q_{21} = x_{21}/y_1$, equations 19.35 can be written as

$$y_1 = 0 + q_{12}y_2 + f_1$$
$$y_2 = q_{21}y_1 + 0 + f_2$$

which in matrix notation, using upper-case letters for matrices and lower-case for column vectors, is

$$\mathbf{y} = \mathbf{Qy} + \mathbf{f}$$

with the solution

$$\mathbf{y} = (\mathbf{I} - \mathbf{Q})^{-1}\mathbf{f} = \mathbf{Lf}$$
(19.36)

where $\mathbf{I}$ is the identity matrix.

Now, let

$$D_1 = D_{M1} + D_{N1} = d_{m1}y_1 + d_{n1}y_1 = z_1y_1$$
$$D_2 = D_{M2} + D_{N2} = d_{m2}y_2 + d_{n2}y_2 = z_2y_2$$

so that we can write for total global depreciation

$$D = z_1y_1 + z_2y_2$$

or, in matrix notation,

$$D = \mathbf{z'y}$$
(19.37)

where $\mathbf{z'}$ is $[z_1 \ z_2]$. Substituting for $\mathbf{y}$ in equation 19.37 from equation 19.36 gives

$$D = \mathbf{z'Lf}$$

or

$$\mathbf{T} = \mathbf{ZLF}$$
(19.38)

where $\mathbf{Z}$ and $\mathbf{F}$ are matrices with the elements of $\mathbf{z}$ and $\mathbf{f}$ along the diagonals, and zeros elsewhere. For the two-country case, equation 19.38 is:

$$\begin{bmatrix} t_{11} & t_{12} \\ t_{21} & t_{22} \end{bmatrix} = \begin{bmatrix} z_1l_{11}f_1 & z_1l_{12}f_2 \\ z_2l_{21}f_1 & z_2l_{22}f_2 \end{bmatrix}$$

In the matrix $\mathbf{T}$ the row elements give depreciation in a country arising by virtue of final demand in that and other countries, while column elements give depreciation in all countries by virtue of final demand in one country. So, row sums, D_i^{IN}, give depreciation in i, and column sums, D_i^{ATT}, give depreciation attributable to i. Thus, in the two-country case

Table 19.9 D^{IN} and D^{ATT} for Australia, US\$ $\times 10^6$

Year	D^{IN}	D^{ATT}
1984	23 110	24 214
1986	31 989	33 319
1988	39 069	40 647

Source: Adapted from Common and Sanyal (1998)

here $t_{11} + t_{12}$ is the depreciation of total capital actually taking place in country 1, while $t_{11} + t_{21}$ is the depreciation of capital in the global economy that is on account of, attributable to, final demand in country 1.

Table 19.9 gives the results arising for the world economy treated as two economies – Australia and the rest of the world (ROW). For Australia, the depreciation of natural capital is calculated as described above for the results shown in Table 19.8. For ROW the data are those used in Proops and Atkinson (1996): for D_N they mainly derive their data from national income accounting data as described above for Table 19.8.[9] According to these results, the depreciation of human-made capital and non-renewable resources for which Australian residents are responsible is slightly greater than the depreciation which occurs in Australia. Given that Australia is a major exporter of minerals, and that such exports account for a large proportion of its total exports, these results might seem surprising. However, as shown in Table 19.8, when estimated from national income accounts sources D_N is small in relation to D_M in Australia, and Australian imports involve both D_M and D_N overseas, where it is also generally the case that D_M is much larger than D_N.

However, the main point to be made here is that the differences between D^{IN} and D^{ATT} shown in Table 19.9 are small in relation to the differences between the differently based estimates of D_N in Tables 19.3 and 19.8. In Table 19.9 D^{ATT} exceeds D^{IN} by less than 5%, whereas in Table 19.3, for one example, 'Net price I' exceeds 'national accounts' by at least 140%.

A slight extension of the method of Proops and Atkinson allows for consideration of these issues on a per capita basis. Let **P** be the matrix with the

reciprocals of population sizes along the diagonal and zeros elsewhere. Then, for the two-country case,

$$\mathbf{A} = \mathbf{TP} = \mathbf{ZLFP} \qquad (19.39)$$

is

$$\begin{bmatrix} a_{11} & a_{12} \\ a_{21} & a_{22} \end{bmatrix} = \begin{bmatrix} z_1 l_{11}(f_1/p_1) & z_1 l_{12}(f_2/p_2) \\ z_2 l_{21}(f_1/p_1) & z_2 l_{22}(f_2/p_2) \end{bmatrix}$$

so that column sums from **A**, d_i^{ATT}, give depreciation in all countries attributable to per capita final demand in country i. And,

$$\mathbf{B} = \mathbf{PT} = \mathbf{PZLF} \qquad (19.40)$$

is

$$\begin{bmatrix} b_{11} & b_{12} \\ b_{21} & b_{22} \end{bmatrix} = \begin{bmatrix} (z_1/p_1)l_{11}f_1 & (z_1/p_1)l_{12}f_2 \\ (z_2/p_2)l_{21}f_1 & (z_2/p_2)l_{22}f_2 \end{bmatrix}$$

so that row sums from **B**, d_i^{IN}, give per capita depreciation in country i on account of global final demand. These depreciation measures can be compared with s_i, per capita saving in i.

The following interesting question can now be addressed: taking account of international trade, how does the average citizen of economy A compare with one of B in regard to contributions to the global difference between saving and the depreciation of total, human-made and natural, capital? This is an interesting question because, given trade, the sustainability question is really a global question – exhausting domestic natural resources is not a problem for a trading economy, provided that it has acquired other assets as it runs down its domestic resource stock, the income from which can replace its earnings from resource exportation. The problem really bites at the global level – the global economy is a closed economy which cannot import anything from anywhere. It is for this reason that most of the capital theory literature on sustainability, and the derived literature on accounting, deals with a closed economy.

To answer the question, we can calculate the elements of **A** and **B** above, and for each country use them to calculate the difference between its saving and its depreciation measured on the 'in' and

---

9   We are very grateful to John Proops for supplying these data on which Table 19.10 here is also based.

Table 19.10 Excesses of per capita saving over depreciation – difference from global excess

	$(s_i - d_i^{IN}) - (s - d)$ US$				
	1980	1982	1984	1986	1988
E. Europe	−79	−58	70	78	35
USSR	55	−76	289	278	285
W. Europe	570	341	344	522	764
Canada	838	808	760	525	953
USA	153	−200	38	−429	−401
Japan	1278	1377	1557	2603	4066
Oceania	349	11	62	−109	113
Africa	−102	−68	−113	−140	−238
Latin America	124	79	5	−66	−42
Other America	−142	−68	−363	−311	−206
Middle East	−578	853	−1024	−1135	−978
Other Asia	−132	−38	−67	−70	−163
s − d	**173**	**76**	**106**	**109**	**220**

	$(s_i - d_i^{ATT}) - (s - d)$ US$				
	1980	1982	1984	1986	1988
E. Europe	−53	−35	97	84	57
USSR	47	−100	276	266	286
W. Europe	440	249	306	528	754
Canada	984	1002	1020	774	1186
USA	48	−271	−141	−613	579
Japan	1123	1265	1512	2673	4110
Oceania	318	−45	62	−114	172
Africa	−102	−79	−119	−146	−246
Latin America	103	70	16	−66	−35
Other America	−158	−76	−236	−252	−236
Middle East	238	−273	−708	−950	−779
Other Asia	−139	−44	−70	−72	−161

'attributable' basis. Some results are given in Table 19.10, where the entries are for the difference between $s_i - d_i$ for country i and $s - d$ for the global economy, where s is per capita saving and d is per capita depreciation. The upper part of the table refers to d_i calculated on the 'in' basis, the lower part to it calculated on the 'attributable' basis. Clearly, for the global economy it makes no difference which way d is measured, and so there is just one row for $s - d$ in the middle of the table.

The results in Table 19.10 use exactly the same data as Proops and Atkinson (1996) and therefore follow their categorisation of the global economy into 12 national and regional economies. There are several interesting points about these results that are worth calling attention to. Note first that for the world as a whole, in each of the years distinguished, saving exceeded depreciation – genuine saving was positive. In noting this, we must also note that these

data only cover the non-renewable resource component of natural capital. Overall, the picture in the upper part of the table is much the same as in the lower part – our appreciation of per capita national and regional contributions to the excess of global saving over depreciation is little affected by looking at things on an 'attributable' basis. Japan's per capita contribution is always greater than the global average, while that of Africa is always smaller. The situation for the USA is mixed, and in two years it does make a difference which way depreciation is measured. Note also that for the USA in every year except 1988, going from the 'in' to the 'attributable' basis for measuring depreciation reduces a positive entry or makes a negative one bigger.

Given our earlier discussion of the problems of measuring the depreciation of non-renewable resources, and our noting of the fact that measuring the depreciation of reproducible capital is itself difficult, these results should not be invested with too much significance at the level of detail. The point is rather that the methodology developed by Proops and Atkinson provides an interesting perspective on the global sustainability problem. It can be seen as complementary to looking at the way consumption levels, and patterns, vary between countries, and the arising implications for resources use, as reported, for example, in UNDP (1998). In that context, it should be noted that the results as presented in Table 19.10 take no account of ability to save – Japan and the USA, for examples, have much higher per capita income levels than, for examples, Africa and Other Asia.

19.4.3 Biophysical and composite indicators

Pearce and Atkinson (1995) describe the inequality we state as 19.34 above as a 'weak sustainability rule'. This refers to the distinction made in some of the literature between 'weak' and 'strong' sustainability, which we discussed in Chapter 4. As explained there, what is involved is not two views of what sustainability is, but two views about the substitution possibilities as between human-made and natural capital. Proponents of weak sustainability take the view that substitutability is such that sustainability as constant consumption is feasible, given sufficient human-made capital accumulation. Strong sustainability refers to the view that substitution possibilities are limited so that constant consumption requires that the natural capital stock is maintained constant in size. Based on this view that substitution possibilities are limited, many commentators argue that all we need to know to promote the pursuit of sustainability is not, and cannot be, captured solely in economic data and indicators. There is now a large literature on biophysical sustainability indicators, and here we can do no more than suggest something of its nature with some examples. We also give some examples of proposals for combining biophysical indicators with socio-economic indicators.

We have at various points throughout this book referred to the problem of biodiversity loss, which many see as a major threat to the sustainability of the global system. In terms of the weak/strong sustainability distinction, the argument is that biodiversity is part of the life-support services that the natural environment supplies (see the discussion accompanying Figure 2.1 in Chapter 2), and that reproducible capital can substitute for those services to a very limited extent. Several proximate causes of species extinction and biodiversity loss can be distinguished, but one way of looking at the matter is in terms of the appropriation of solar radiation. Ultimately, this is the basis for all life, and one effect of increasing human numbers and per capita consumption has been that the human species is appropriating to itself a larger share of the fixed solar budget. In Box 2.2 in Chapter 2, we reported estimates by Vitousek et al. (1986) of the human appropriation of net primary production. They provided low, intermediate and high estimates of the global percentage appropriated by humans as 3, 19 and 25. The basis of the different estimates is in conventions about what is counted as 'human appropriation'. In relation to their high estimate, they comment that

> An equivalent concentration of resources into one species and its satellites has probably not occurred since land plants first diversified

and they argue that even the lower estimate implies a threat to the sustainability of the global system.

Rojstaczer et al. (2001) report the results of a similar study using a wider range of more recent data,

confining their attention to terrestrial net primary production and looking only at the intermediate basis for estimation. As well as reporting the mean estimate for human appropriation, Rojstaczer et al. used Monte Carlo methods to assess the range of uncertainty implied by the available data. Their mean estimate of the proportion of terrestrial net primary production appropriated by humans is 32%, which is almost exactly the same as that of Vitousek et al., 31% in Table 2.2 here, for intermediate terrestrial appropriation. The 95% confidence limits reported by Rojstaczer et al. are 32% ± 22%, i.e. a lower bound of 10% and an upper bound of 54%. They comment:

> Although there is a large degree of uncertainty, it is clear that human impact on TNPP [terrestrial net primary production] is significant. The lower bound on our estimate . . . indicates that humans have had more impact on biological resources than any single species of megafauna known over the history of the earth.

Estimating the human appropriation of the products of photosynthesis is one way of quantifying the extent to which our species dominates the global ecosystem. A related indicator is the ecological footprint, an ideal definition of which (Wackernagel and Rees, 1997) is:

> the aggregate area of land and water in various ecological categories that is claimed by participants in the economy to produce all the resources they consume, and to absorb all the wastes they generate on a continuing basis, using prevailing technology.

We describe this as an 'ideal' definition because to date estimates of the size of ecological footprints have been based on just subsets of consumed resources and generated wastes, and are in that sense conservative estimates. It should also be noted that the footprint size will vary with technology as well as with levels and patterns of production and consumption. Wackernagel et al. (2002) report estimates of the size of the footprint for each of the years from 1961 to 1999, for the whole global economy. Considering the demands for land and water on account of

- growing crops
- grazing domesticated animals
- harvesting timber

- fishing
- space for locating human artefacts such as houses, factories, roads, etc.
- sequestering the CO_2 released in fossil-fuel combustion

in relation to the available amounts in the biosphere, they find that the ratio of the former demand to the latter supply increased from approximately 0.7 in 1961 to approximately 1.2 in 1999, and conclude that as presently constituted the global economy is not sustainable in that it would 'require 1.2 earths, or one earth for 1.2 years, to regenerate what humanity used in 1999'. On a per capita basis the global average demand for biologically productive space is 2.3 hectares, whereas other studies have estimated per capita footprints of 9.7 hectares for the USA, 5.4 for the UK and 4.7 for Germany. The implication is that if the developing world were to attain the consumption levels of the developed world, the total footprint for the world would be the size of several earths.

In Chapter 4 we noted the set of biophysical indicators proposed by Schaeffer *et al.* (1988):

- changes in the number of native species;
- changes in the standing crop of biomass;
- changes in mineral micronutrient stocks;
- changes in the mechanisms of and capacity for damping oscillations.

Azar *et al.* (1996) and Rennings and Wiggering (1997) are examples of arguments for the need for consideration in pursuit of sustainability of a set of indicators which includes both biophysical indicators of the type suggested by Schaeffer *et al.*, and socio-economic indicators. Both of these papers provide further references to the literature in this area, and make the point that there is a need for more basic biophysical information on the state of the environment. Ekins and Simon (1998) argue for the identification of 'sustainability gaps' as the difference between some biophysical indicator's current level and the level taken to be consistent with sustainability requirements. They also argue for a monetary value being placed on such a gap, but specifically argue against the use of such a valuation being used to adjust the measure of national income to produce a measure of sustainable income.

As a global problem, the sustainability problem includes the problem of poverty in the developing world. UNDP publishes an annual report which since 1990 has included the results for the calculation of a Human Development Index (HDI) for each of some 170 countries; see UNDP (2001) for the latest set of results. The HDI has undergone some changes in the details of its construction over the years but has retained its essential features intact. The HDI itself is defined over three sub-indices which relate to per capita national income, longevity and education, and the definition is such that the value for a country's HDI score must lie between 0 and 1. While the HDI is open to criticism (see, for example, Sagar and Najam, 1998), it is a readily accessible source of data across a wide range of countries, on a reasonably consistent basis over a period of years, and should continue to be available in the future. Also, the annual publication gives the data from which the HDI and its sub-indices are calculated. Common (1995) reports results from the use of data for two of these sub-indices with a biophysical indicator to produce what is argued to be a low-cost indicator of relevance to monitoring sustainable development. The indicator is longevity multiplied by annual per capita income, divided by greenhouse gas emissions per capita. It is argued that a country that improved its performance on this indicator could be said, as a first approximation, to be improving its performance against sustainable development criteria. The numerator is average lifetime income, and the denominator is the per capita contribution to a major global environmental problem. An increase in this ratio would indicate that more lifetime income was being generated per unit greenhouse gas emission.

19.5 Concluding remarks

Here we offer some remarks on where we think that we have got to, not just in this chapter but also in the course of the book as a whole. These remarks necessarily involve the authors' values and judgements, as well as technical economic considerations. The reader may come to different conclusions. Our purpose here is to offer our assessments for consideration, rather than to make pronouncements.

It will be clear that we do not see measuring sustainable national income as a practical step, or even an almost practical step, toward sustainability. Even if the capital-theoretic characterisation of the sustainability problem is accepted, and leaving aside the question of feasibility, it is our judgement that the practical problems involved are unlikely ever to be satisfactorily resolved. As well as the difficulty of ascertaining the 'right prices' for aggregation across quantities of reproducible and natural capital assets, there is the difficulty of measuring the quantities themselves.

It is not even clear that measuring sustainable national income is a particularly desirable thing to do in pursuit of sustainability. The problem involved is multi-faceted and complex and involves uncertainty. Dealing with it requires that these characteristics are recognised. Attempts to capture in a single number the answer to the question 'Are we behaving sustainably?' tend to obscure the essential characteristics of the problem. And, one of those essential characteristics is that it is, at bottom, a global rather than a national problem.

It is clear that economic analysis can contribute much to the discussion of other, in our view, more practical steps than trying to measure sustainable income. We noted that the 'right prices' problem for that endeavour is something of a chicken and egg problem. If we are behaving as capital theory says we should for sustainability the right prices would be readily observable. If we are not, the prices that we do observe tell us little about how we should be behaving. However, while we may not know the 'right prices', so that computations of sustainable income are rather meaningless, we do in many cases have a good idea in which direction from current prices the right prices lie. In many contexts it is clear that using economic instruments – taxes, tradable permits and the like – would move actual prices paid by the users of environmental resources in the right direction. Making, for example, the use of fossil fuels more expensive would, we can be reasonably sure, do much for the amelioration of several of the environmental dimensions of the sustainability problem. In and of itself it could increase poverty, but

that is a problem that can be addressed in other ways which economists are well equipped to advise on.

Of course, while economists can advise on dealing with the regressive impact of higher energy prices, this does not ensure that the appropriate measures will be put in place. That requires political action, as would the adoption of the fossil-fuel price-increasing measures in the first place. However good the analysis and the information, action will only occur if there is the political will for it. The hope is that good analysis and information will increase the political will to do 'the right thing'. It appears that for many, economist and non-economist, advocates of environmental accounting as the measurement of sustainable national income or some related concept, the real rationale for the activity is that it will produce results that affect the political climate. On this view, it does not really matter that the number produced is wrong or meaningless, so long as it moves perceptions in the 'right' direction. However, it is not clear that announcing in this way that economic performance is worse than had previously been thought, if that is the way the numbers do turn out, could be relied upon to have this effect.

On the other hand, we can be reasonably sure, on the basis of historical evidence, that actually changing prices does influence behaviour. It appears to us that, if the objective is to promote the cause of sustainability, it is much more important to move actual prices in the right direction than to get the right shadow prices for the computation of a number for sustainable income. To do this does require that decision makers and those who vote for them are well informed about the issues and the alternatives. Economists have an important role in providing some of this information, but there is an important role for other kinds of information, assessment and advice. Economists need to be honest about the quality of the information that they can provide, and the ethical basis for the advice that they offer. In saying this, we are not implying that economists are peculiar in this respect. All 'experts' contributing to public debate and deliberation on the many issues involved in the sustainability problem need to be circumspect about the limits of, and basis for, their expertise. It is simply that this book is addressed to students doing an economics course.

Further reading

The capital-theoretic literature which is relevant to environmental accounting is extensive and growing rapidly. We shall here just note some of the major original contributions, and some recent papers that themselves provide fuller references to the literature. Dasgupta and Heal (1974) was perhaps the first rigorous consideration of the optimal path for consumption in a representative-agent single-commodity model, where the agent maximises the sum of discounted utility and production uses inputs of capital and a non-renewable resource. Solow (1974a) rigorously examined the feasibility of constant consumption for ever in such a model, given various assumptions about substitutability in production, population growth and technical progress. Weitzman (1976) established the interpretation of net national product as sustainable income as the return on wealth, but did not explicitly consider natural resources. Hartwick (1977) showed that for an economy with a constant returns to scale Cobb–Douglas production function with capital and a non-renewable resource as arguments, zero net investment – investment in reproducible capital equal to resource depreciation – would give constant consumption. Hartwick's rule was generalised, in terms of the production conditions in which it held, in a number of subsequent papers by himself and others: see for examples Hartwick (1978) and Dasgupta and Mitra (1983). Solow (1986) brought together the contributions of Weitzman and Hartwick, and set out the basic theory drawn upon in Solow (1992, 1993).

The literature on neoclassical growth theory, what we referred to as capital theory, in relation to sustainability was reviewed in Toman *et al.* (1995); see also Pezzey and Toman (2002), a Resources for the Future discussion paper available at www.rff.org/disc*w*papers/PDF*w*files/0203.pdf. Sustainability in small open economies is discussed in Asheim (1986) and Brekke (1997). Papers drawing on capital theory to derive propositions about the proper measurement of net national income as sustainable income, given the dependence of production and consumption on environmental inputs, include: Hartwick (1990), Mäler (1991), Dasgupta (1995), Hamilton (1994) and Cairns (2002). Volume 5, Parts 1 and 2, the February and May 2000 issue of *Environment and Development Economics*, is a special issue on 'Advances in green accounting' which includes papers on theory and practice. Faucheux *et al.* (1997) consider sustainability in the context of an overlapping generations model and argue that standard capital theory does not provide a satisfactory basis for environmental accounting. Weitzman (1997) looks at technical progress in relation to sustainability, and argues that on account of technical progress properly measured net national income will understate sustainable income. Dasgupta (2001) is a book on measuring the quality of life given the role of the natural environment in economic activity.

The UNSTAT proposals for satellite accounting are set out in UN (1992, 1993b). Work on the UNSTAT proposals included the preparation of illustrative accounts for a hypothetical country, and of preliminary accounts for Mexico and Papua New Guinea, reported in chapters in Lutz (1993); see also Bartelmus (1994). Up-to-date information on progress with the proposals can be obtained by visiting the UNSTAT web site at http://unstats.un.org. An 'operational manual', UN (2000), can be accessed electronically at http://unstats.un.org/unsd/sna1993/doc/F78e.pdf.

The difficulties involved in actually measuring sustainable income are considered in Neumayer (1999), see especially chapter 5. Hamilton (2000) reviews the theory of genuine savings measurement and reports 1997 results for some 150 countries. This World Bank publication can be accessed at www.worldbank.org.

Vitousek *et al.* (1997) review a range of indicators for the extent to which the human species now dominates most ecosystems; see also Field (2001). Wackernagel and Rees (1996) is a simple introduction to ecological footprints which describes methods of calculation and reports a variety of results. The organisation Redefining Progress is active in promoting the idea of ecological footprinting, and further information is available at www.redefiningprogress.org, where there can also be found work on Genuine Progress Indicators. In March 2000, *Ecological Economics*, Vol. 32, no 3, included a forum comprising 12 short papers on the ecological footprint. Several of these papers set out the limitations of the concept as a guide to policy.

Discussion questions

1. Five European countries have access to the water resources of the River Rhine, which are intensively used for commercial and industrial purposes. Discuss (a) methods of valuation of Rhine water-quality degradation caused by human use, and (b) the allocation of these costs between the countries affected.

2. Discuss the arguments for and against the exclusion, or deduction, of defensive or preventive environmental expenditure from GDP. Identify other components of GDP which, it could be argued, should be excluded for identical or similar reasons.

3. Discuss the distinction between 'economic' and 'non-economic' environmental assets. Compile a short list of three or four specific non-economic environmental assets, and identify the costs and benefits associated with those assets, and how these might be valued for national accounts purposes.

4. There is lot more coal remaining than there is natural gas, in the world as a whole. The combustion of coal releases more CO_2, and other pollutants, per unit energy released, than is the case with natural gas. Which should have the higher shadow price for the purposes of environmental accounting?

5. Devise a checklist for the qualitative and quantitative information which a university should be asked to furnish as a basis for an environmental audit of its functional activities.

6. Given the valuation problems inherent in assessing many forms of environmental damage or degradation, is it better to concentrate efforts on developing a comprehensive system of physical environmental accounts, rather than attempt to incorporate environmental costs and benefits into the conventional system of national accounts?

Problems

1. A mineral resource is extracted and sold, yielding £20m annual gross revenue to the owners. Purchases of goods and services used for extraction are £4m, labour costs are £2m and capital equipment is valued at £30m. The average rate of return on capital in the mineral extraction sector is 4.5%. At current extraction rates, reserves will be economically exhausted in 5 years. Assume a constant rate of extraction, a fixed extraction technology, and constant relative prices. Calculate a depletion rate for this mineral resource and hence the contribution of this extraction activity to gross and net national product, stating any necessary additional assumptions.

2. At the start of 1998 oil reserves in country X were 504×10^9 barrels. During 1998 country X produced 8×10^9 barrels, and there were no new discoveries of oil there. The world price of oil was constant at £3.125 per barrel throughout 1998, and the interest rate in X was also constant, at 5%. Total oil production costs in X,

including a normal return on capital employed, were $£20 \times 10^6$.

(a) Calculate the depreciation of country X's oil stock using
   - the net present value method,
   - El Serafy's user cost rule.

(b) Repeat (a) using an interest rate of 10%.

(c) Repeat the calculation for a 5% interest rate, but with the world price of oil being £3.00 at the start of the year and £5.00 at the end of the year.

(d) Comment on your results.

3. In this chapter we showed that the owner of an oil deposit in a fully competitive economy would keep his or her wealth constant and achieve the highest consistent level of constant consumption by following the Hartwick rule. Show that this would also be the case for the sole owner of a fishery, given sustainable yield harvesting. Show that it would also be the case for someone owning an oil deposit and a fishery.

Appendix 19.1 National income, the return on wealth, Hartwick's rule and sustainable income

Jack Pezzey, Environment Department, University of York

In this appendix and the next we use the dot notation for derivatives with respect to time so as to reduce clutter in the exposition. For the same reason we omit the t subscript when referring to derivatives such as marginal utilities and marginal products, writing, for example, U_C rather than U_{C_t} for $\partial U_t/\partial C_t$.

National income and the return on wealth

We begin here with the simplest optimal growth model where there is a single produced good which may be consumed or added to the stock of reproducible capital, which does not depreciate, and where the environment affects neither utility nor production. The problem to be considered is

$$\text{Max} \int_0^\infty U(C_t)\,e^{-\rho t}\mathrm{d}t \ \text{ subject to } \dot{K}_t = Q(K_t) - C_t$$

$$(19.41a)$$

for which the current-value Hamiltonian is

$$H_t = U(C_t) + w_t(Q\{K_t\} - C_t)$$

where the necessary conditions are

$$\partial H_t/\partial C_t = U_C - w_t = 0 \qquad (19.41b)$$

$$\dot{w}_t - \rho w_t = -\partial H_t/\partial K_t = -w_t Q_K \qquad (19.41c)$$

Replacing $Q(K_t) - C_t$ by $\dot{K}_t$, we can write the maximised value of the Hamiltonian as

$$H_t^* = U(C_t) + w_t \dot{K}_t$$

which by equation 19.41b can also be written as

$$H_t^* = U(C_t) + U_C \dot{K}_t \qquad (19.41d)$$

where C_t and $\dot{K}_t$ are the *optimal* values for the maximisation problem 19.41a. We can interpret H_t^*

as instantaneous national income measured in units which are utils. Observe that the right-hand side of 19.41d is the current flow of utility plus the value of the change in the capital stock measured in units which reflect its contribution to future, maximised, utility.

This interpretation of H_t^* can be further supported by noting that if we linearise the utility function so that $U(C_t) = U_C C_t$, we can write equation 19.41d as

$$H_t^* = U_C C_t + U_C \dot{K}_t$$

so that

$$H_t^*/U_C = C_t + I_t$$

where I_t for investment is $\dot{K}_t$.[12] Given the assumption that K does not depreciate, the right-hand side here is just the usual expression for net national income and if we use NDP for this, we have

$$\text{NDP}_t = H_t^*/U_C = C_t + I_t \qquad (19.41e)$$

Now introduce the use of a non-renewable natural resource into production, as in the simple exhaustible resource depletion problem considered in Chapter 14, and see Appendix 14.2 there. We saw there that for

$$\text{Max} \int_0^\infty U(C_t)\,e^{-\rho t}\mathrm{d}t \ \text{ subject to } \dot{S}_t = -R_t$$

$$\text{and } \dot{K}_t = Q(K_t R_t) - C_t$$

the current-value Hamiltonian is

$$H_t = U(C_t) + P_t(-R_t) + w_t(Q\{K_t R_t\} - C_t)$$

so that the necessary conditions are

$$\partial H_t/\partial C_t = U_C - w_t = 0 \qquad (19.42a)$$

$$\partial H_t/\partial R_t = -P_t + w_t Q_R = 0 \qquad (19.42b)$$

---

[12] Strictly speaking, linearising the utility function makes the Hamiltonian linear in consumption, and so gives rise to what are known as 'corner' or 'non-interior' solutions to the optimal control problem, for which equations like 19.41a and 19.41b do not hold. However, in common with much of the relevant literature, we will overlook this technicality.

$$\dot{w}_t - \rho w_t = -\partial H_t / \partial K_t = -w_t Q_K \qquad (19.42c)$$

$$\dot{P}_t - \rho P_t = -\partial H_t / \partial S_t = 0 \qquad (19.42d)$$

These can respectively be written as

$$w_t = U_C \qquad (19.42e)$$

$$\dot{P}_t / P_t = \dot{w}_t / w_t + \dot{Q}_R / Q_R \qquad (19.42f)$$

$$Q_K = \rho - \dot{w}_t / w_t \qquad (19.42g)$$

$$\dot{P}_t / P_t = \rho \qquad (19.42h)$$

Note that equation 19.42f comes from differentiating equation 19.42b with respect to time, dividing both sides by P, and then substituting for P on the right-hand side from equation 19.42b. For constant consumption, equations 19.42g and 19.42a then give, since U_C constant means $\dot{U}_C = 0$,

$$Q_K = \rho - \dot{U}_C / U_C = \rho \qquad (19.42i)$$

Finally, equations 19.42g, 19.42f and 19.42h together give

$$\dot{Q}_R / Q_R = Q_K \qquad (19.42j)$$

as an alternative statement of the Hotelling rule which is used later.

However, our main interest here is in the Hamiltonian itself. Using the equations of motion, the maximised Hamiltonian can be written

$$H_t^* = U(C_t) + w_t \dot{K}_t + P_t \dot{S}_t \qquad (19.42k)$$

and proceeding to linearise the utility function as for the simple model above, this becomes

$$H_t^* / U_C = C_t + I_t + (P_t / w_t) \dot{S}_t$$

which by equation 19.42b, and substituting for $\dot{S}_t$ from the equation of motion, can be written

$$H_t^* / U_C = C_t + I_t - Q_R R_t = \text{NDP}_t - Q_R R_t = \text{EDP}_t \qquad (19.42l)$$

where we still use NDP$_t$ for national income as conventionally measured, and now introduce EDP$_t$ to refer to national income as properly measured given the use of the natural resource in production. According to equation 19.42l, EDP$_t$ is NDP$_t$ minus the rent $Q_R R_t$ arising in the extraction of the resource, where that rent is the measure of the depreciation of the asset which is the resource stock. Depreciation is the amount extracted valued at the

marginal product of the resource, which in this model with costless extraction is the unit rent.

We could write equation 19.42l as

$$\text{EDP}_t = C_t + I_t - (P_t / w_t) R_t \qquad (19.42m)$$

where P_t / w_t is the relative (to the price of the numeraire commodity which is the consumption/capital good) price of the extracted resource, which in a model with costless extraction is the same as the price of the resource *in situ*. As we saw in Chapter 14, in a fully competitive economy the relative price of the resource would move over time as required by the necessary conditions for the maximisation of discounted utility. This is the basis for taking equation 19.42m as a guide to how the conventional measure of national income should be adjusted to account for non-renewable-resource depletion in an actual economy. The assumption is, that is, that actual economies should be treated as if they were fully competitive economies. Recall from Chapter 14 that the conditions characterising a fully competitive economy are strong.

Now, note that we have $H_t^* = H_t^*(K, S, w, P)$ and consider the differentiation of H_t^* with respect to time. We have

$$\dot{H}_t^* = (\partial H^* / \partial K)\dot{K}_t + (\partial H^* / \partial S)\dot{S}_t + (\partial H^* / \partial w)\dot{w}_t + (\partial H^* / \partial P)\dot{P}_t$$

Using equation 19.42c for $(\partial H^* / \partial K)$, equation 19.42d for $(\partial H^* / \partial S)$, and $\partial H^* / \partial w = \dot{K}_t$ and $\partial H^* / \partial P = \dot{S}_t$ from equation 19.42k, we get

$$\dot{H}_t^* = \rho w_t \dot{K}_t + \rho P_t \dot{S}_t = \rho(w_t \dot{K}_t + P_t \dot{S}_t) \qquad (19.42n)$$

From equation 19.42l, using $\dot{U}_C = 0$ and equation 19.42a,

$$(\text{d}/\text{d}t)\text{EDP}_t = \dot{H}_t^* / U_C = \dot{H}_t^* / w_t \qquad (19.42o)$$

Combining equations 19.42n, 19.42o and 19.42l then gives

$$(\text{d}/\text{d}t)\text{EDP}_t = \rho[\dot{K}_t + (P_t / w_t)\dot{S}_t] = \rho(I_t - Q_R R_t)$$
$$= \rho(\text{EDP}_t - C_t) \qquad (19.42p)$$

Using equation 19.42i the solution of this differential equation in EDP$_t$ can be shown to be

$$\text{EDP}_t = \rho W_t = Q_K W_t \qquad (19.42q)$$

where W_t is the economy's wealth at time t, as defined by the present discounted value of consumption from time t onwards:

$$W_t = \int_t^\infty C_\tau e^{\rho(\tau-t)} d\tau \qquad (19.42r)$$

This is a rewritten version of a famous result due to Weitzman (1976). Since the marginal product of capital Q_K is the interest rate in a competitive economy, this is the basis for the interpretation of EDP_t, which is properly measured national income, as the 'return' (at the going rate of interest) on the economy's total stock of wealth. If, moreover, there are constant returns to scale in the economy's production function $Q(K_t, R_t)$, then wealth could be interpreted not just as the present discounted value of future consumption, but also as the value today in consumption units of the economy's productive assets:

$$W_t = K_t + Q_R S_t \qquad (19.42s)$$

Hartwick's rule and sustainable income

There is a powerful appeal in the idea that income is the interest earned on wealth, and that consuming exactly one's income – no more and no less – should be sustainable for ever. Is that what equation 19.42q above is saying for an economy? That is, are there circumstances in which EDP is *sustainable* national income? The answer is 'yes', but only in a case of severely restricted practical value, which unfortunately is often misunderstood in the literature, creating much confusion on this topic. What can be said is the following. *If* optimal consumption happens to equal EDP *always*, and *if* constant consumption is physically feasible – note the 'if' and 'always' caveats – then both consumption and EDP will be constant for ever; or in other words, sustainable. The proof of this is as follows. We start from the first 'if', by assuming

$$C_t = Q(K_t, R_t) - \dot{K}_t = EDP_t \qquad (19.43a)$$

always, which from equation 19.42l means that

$$\dot{K}_t = Q_R R_t \qquad (19.43b)$$

always. The rule in equation 19.43b, which says 'investment in reproducible capital is always equal to resource rents', is *Hartwick's rule* (after John Hartwick who discovered it in 1977, see Hartwick, 1977). Taking the time derivative of consumption from equation 19.43a then gives

$$\dot{C}_t = Q_K \dot{K}_t + Q_R \dot{R}_t - \ddot{K}_t$$
$$= Q_K \dot{K}_t + Q_R \dot{R}_t - (\dot{R}_R R_t + Q_R \dot{R}_t)$$

using Hartwick's rule. Note that without the 'always', we could not have taken and used the time derivative of $\dot{K} = Q_R R_t$ to substitute for $\ddot{K}$. Using Hotelling's rule written as equation 19.42j then gives

$$\dot{C} = Q_K \dot{K}_t - Q_R Q_K R_t$$

which using Hartwick's rule again is

$$\dot{C} = 0$$

that is, constant consumption.

However, *there is no reason why optimal consumption should equal EDP*, and hence why Hartwick's rule (and hence constant consumption) should hold on an optimal path. Indeed, constant consumption may not even be feasible. In general, optimal consumption will rise or fall over time, and will be more or less than EDP at any point in time; and hence capital investment will be more or less than resource rents at any time.

However again, what happens if the economy is constrained to follow Hartwick's rule? (We will not show how this constraint might be achieved, but one way would be to introduce a macroeconomically significant policy of tax incentives to invest more.) It turns out that consumption will indeed be constant, but the constraint policy will force the economy off the optimal path: equation 19.41a will no longer be maximised. As a result, both prices and quantities on a constant-consumption path will generally be different from their optimal values. Nevertheless, some sort of present-value function, using a different utility discount factor (say $\lambda(t)$ instead of $e^{-\rho t}$ in equation 19.41a) will still be maximised on the highest possible constant consumption path. ρ will be replaced throughout by $-\dot{\lambda}/\lambda$, but (as the reader can readily check) the form of Hotelling's rule as equation 19.42j, used above in the proof of constant consumption, will be unchanged.

At any point in time, aggregate investment, defined as $\dot{K}_t - Q_R R_t$, is therefore an unreliable indicator of an economy's sustainability. The optimal path of an economy may be unsustainable at time t, and yet aggregate investment may be positive then. Or, if there is technical progress in production (which we have ignored above), it turns out that the economy can be sustainable at t even though aggregate investment is negative then. And the problem remains even if one tries to use the 'right' price, Q_R, which would apply on the constant-consumption path, because the quantities of investment $\dot{K}_t$ and resource depletion R_t will still be wrong. Trying to use Hartwick's rule ('invest resource rents') as either a policy prescription to achieve sustainability, or as the basis for 'sustainability accounting', therefore faces a fundamental chicken-and-egg problem. The rule works only if sustainability, in the form of constant consumption, and hence both sustainability prices and quantities, have already been achieved! Moreover, achieving constant consumption when it is not the optimal path raises an awkward political question: which matters more, sustainability or optimality?

Another frequent misunderstanding in the literature is that keeping consumption constant means keeping wealth constant. The trouble is that wealth can be defined in different ways. If wealth is defined as the time integral of aggregate investment, then obviously it remains constant on a constant-consumption path, thanks to Hartwick's rule. But if wealth is defined as earlier, as the present value of future consumption or the aggregate value of current assets, then wealth need not be constant. Indeed, in the best-known example of constant consumption with non-renewable resources, discovered in 1974 by Robert Solow (Solow, 1974a), wealth must be *rising* for ever to keep consumption constant. Intuitively, what is happening is that in the Cobb–Douglas production function Solow uses, $Q(K_t, R_t) = K_t^\alpha R_t^\beta$, the marginal product of capital investment Q_K is falling because an ever-rising stock of capital K_t has to be combined with an ever-shrinking resource flow R_t. So, by equation 19.42q, wealth W_t must be rising if the product $Q_K W_t = \text{EDP}_t = C_t$ is to be constant.

Appendix 19.2 Adjusting national income measurement to account for the environment

In this appendix we explore further the approach to national income measurement developed in Appendix 19.1, by applying it to models which capture other dimensions of the economy–environment interrelations that underlie an interest in environmental accounting. The caveats of Appendix 19.1 regarding the interpretation of the results as measures of sustainable income in the sense generally understood also apply here. We will, however, concentrate here on deriving the adjustments, rather than pursuing those issues in more general contexts.

Consider first a non-renewable resource-using model economy, which is that of Appendix 19.1 modified such that resource extraction is costly and there is exploration activity. The optimisation problem is

$$\text{Max} \int_0^\infty U(C_t)e^{-\rho t}dt \text{ subject to } \dot{S}_t = -R_t + N_t$$

$$\text{and } \dot{K}_t = Q(K_t, R_t) - C_t - G(R_t, S_t) - F(N_t, S_t)$$

where N_t is new discoveries brought about by exploration activity with the cost function $F(N_t, S_t)$, such that costs rise with the level of exploration activity,

$F_N = \partial F_t / \partial N_t > 0$, and as the stock of resources is depleted, $F_S = \partial F_t / \partial S_t < 0$. The costs of extraction are given by $G(R_t, S_t)$, as in Appendix 15.3. For this problem the current-value Hamiltonian is

$$H_t = U(C_t) + P_t(-R_t + N_t) + w_t(Q\{K_t, R_t\} - C_t - G\{R_t, S_t\} - F\{N_t, S_t\})$$

with necessary conditions which include

$$\partial H_t / \partial C_t = U_C - w_t = 0 \tag{19.44a}$$

$$\partial H_t / \partial R_t = -P_t + w_t Q_R - w_t G_R = 0 \tag{19.44b}$$

$$\partial H_t / \partial N_t = P_t - w_t F_N = 0 \tag{19.44c}$$

Note from equations 19.44b and 19.44c that

$$P_t / w_t = Q_R - G_R = F_N$$

so that marginal discovery cost, F_N, is equal to marginal rent, $Q_R - G_R$.

The maximised Hamiltonian can be written as

$$H_t^* = U(C_t) + w_t \dot{K}_t + P_t \dot{S}_t$$

and using $U = U_C C$ and $U_C = w_t$ we can write

$$\text{EDP}_t = H_t^* / U_C = C_t + \dot{K}_t + (P_t / w_t)\dot{S}_t$$

which is

$$EDP_t = C_t + I_t - (P_t/w_t)(R_t - N_t)$$
$$= NDP_t - (Q_R - G_R)(R_t - N_t)$$
$$= NDP_t - (Q_R - G_R)R_t + (Q_R - G_R)N_t$$
$$= NDP_t - (Q_R - G_R)R_t + F_N N_t$$

so that EDP_t for this economy is NDP_t less the depreciation of the non-renewable-resource stock, which is the total Hotelling rent; that is, marginal rent multiplied by extraction net of new discoveries.

Now consider the use of renewable resources in production, so that the current-value Hamiltonian is

$$H_t = U(C_t) + P_t(F\{S_t\} - R_t) + w_t(Q\{K_t, R_t\} - C_t - G\{R_t, S_t\})$$

where R_t is resource use again and $F(S_t)$ is the intrinsic growth function. In Chapter 17 we used $G(S_t)$ for this function, but here we retain $G(\cdot)$ for the cost function so as to make the results now to be derived readily comparable with those for the non-renewable resource model just considered. Note that harvest cost depends on the size of the harvest and the stock size. The necessary conditions here include

$$\partial H_t/\partial C_t = U_C - w_t = 0 \qquad (19.45a)$$

$$\partial H_t/\partial R_t = -P_t + w_t Q_R - w_t G_R = 0 \qquad (19.45b)$$

where equation 19.45b implies

$$P_t = w_t(Q_R - G_R)$$

The maximised Hamiltonian can again be written

$$H_t^* = U(C_t) + w_t \dot{K}_t + P_t \dot{S}_t$$

and, proceeding as previously, we get

$$EDP_t = C_t + I_t + (P_t/w_t)\dot{S}_t$$
$$= NDP_t - (Q_R - G_R)(R_t - F\{S_t\}) \qquad (19.45c)$$

which is the direct analogue to the result for a non-renewable resource. Here the marginal rent is multiplied by the harvest net of intrinsic growth. Note that if there is sustainable yield harvesting, $R_t = F(S_t)$ and no adjustment to NDP_t is required.

Suppose now that the renewable resource is not an input to the production of the consumption/capital good, but is an argument in the utility function. The production input case might be thought of as the way timber gets used, the utility function argument case as the way fish get used – whereas timber gets used

to produce commodities for consumption, fish gets directly eaten. For this latter case,

$$H_t = U(C_t, R_t) + P_t(F\{S_t\} - R_t) + w_t(Q\{K_t\} - C_t - G\{R_t, S_t\})$$

with necessary conditions which include

$$\partial H_t/\partial C_t = U_C - w_t = 0 \qquad (19.46a)$$

$$\partial H_t/\partial R_t = U_R - P_t - w_t G_R = 0 \qquad (19.46b)$$

which imply

$$U_R/U_C = (P_t/w_t) + G_R \qquad (19.46c)$$

for the price of caught fish available for consumption; that is, the consumption price of fish is marginal rent plus marginal cost. Using $U(C_t, R_t) = U_C C_t + U_R R_t$ and proceeding as before,

$$EDP_t = H_t^*/U_C = C_t + (U_R/U_C)R_t + \dot{K}_t + (P_t/w_t)\dot{S}_t$$
$$= (C_t + \{U_R/U_C\}R_t) + I_t + (P_t/w_t)(F\{S_t\} - R_t)$$

which by equation 19.46c and using C_t^* for aggregate consumption is

$$EDP_t = C_t^* + I_t - (P_t/w_t)(R_t - F\{S_t\})$$
$$= NDP_t - (P_t/w_t)(R_t - F\{S_t\})$$
$$= NDP_t - (\{U_R/U_C\} - G_R)(R_t - F\{S_t\}) \qquad (19.46d)$$

This has the same structure as equation 19.45c in that EDP_t is NDP_t less depreciation, but note that P_t/w_t, used to value the change in stock size, is different in this case.

A third plausible specification for a model of an economy exploiting renewable resources has the harvest as an input to production and the stock size as an argument in the utility function. Thus, for example, harvested timber is used in production, while standing timber is a source of aesthetic pleasure and recreation. In such a case, the Hamiltonian is

$$H_t = U(C_t, S_t) + P_t(F\{S_t\} - R_t) + w_t(Q\{K_t, R_t\} - C_t - G\{R_t, S_t\})$$

and the necessary conditions include

$$\partial H_t/\partial C_t = U_C - w_t = 0 \qquad (19.47a)$$

$$\partial H_t/\partial R_t = -P_t + w_t Q_R - w_t G_R = 0 \qquad (19.47b)$$

where equation 19.47b implies

$$P_t = w_t(Q_R - G_R) \qquad (19.47c)$$

Then using $U(C_t, S_t) = U_C C_t + U_S S_t$

$$H_t^*/U_t = C_t + (U_S/U_C)S_t + \dot{K}_t + (P_t/w_t)\dot{S}_t$$

and

$$EDP_t = NDP_t + (U_S/U_C)S_t$$
$$- (Q_R - G_R)(R_t - F\{S_t\}) \qquad (19.47d)$$

As compared with equation 19.45c there is a structural difference here. As well as subtracting depreciation from NPD_t, it is now necessary to add the value of the stock of the renewable resource, where the valuation uses U_S/U_C. Note further that in this case, we would generally assume that there was no market in the consumption of the amenity services provided by the stock, so that this 'price' could not be revealed in fully competitive markets, but would have to be ascertained by the sorts of methods discussed in Chapter 12.

The point being made here in looking at these three renewable resource models is that what we think we have to do to go from NDP to EDP, in terms of the nature of the adjustments and the valuations used with them, depends on the model that is used to analyse the problem. Since reasonable people may reasonably disagree about the specification of the model that captures the stylised facts of the way economic activity uses environmental services, it follows that there is no single correct answer to the question of how to get from NDP to EDP. Also, the answer may imply the need for non-market valuation, even if we are prepared to assume fully competitive markets where markets operate. The same point arises if we consider the matter of pollution and arising environmental degradation.

To illustrate this consider the model from Chapter 16, which has an index of environmental quality affecting both utility and production, where that index is a function of the current flow of residuals and the accumulated stock, where the production function recognises the materials balance principle, and where clean-up is undertaken. The optimisation problem is

$$\text{Max} \int_0^\infty U(C_t, E\{R_t, A_t\})e^{-\rho t} \text{ subject to } \dot{S}_t = -R_t$$

$$\dot{K}_t = Q(K_t, R_t, E\{R_t, A_t\}) - C_t - G(R_t, S_t) - V_t$$

$$\dot{A}_t = M(R_t) - \alpha A_t - F(V_t)$$

Here $G(\cdot)$ is extraction cost. V_t is clean-up expenditure and $F(V_t)$ is the effect of that expenditure. The current-value Hamiltonian is

$$H_t = U(C_t, E\{R_t, A_t\}) + P_t(-R_t)$$
$$+ w_t(Q\{K_t, R_t, E(R_t, A_t)\} - C_t - G_t(R_t, S_t) - V_t)$$
$$+ \lambda_t(M\{R_t\} - \alpha_t A_t - F\{V_t\})$$

with necessary conditions including

$$\partial H_t/\partial C_t = U_C - w_t = 0 \qquad (19.48a)$$

$$\partial H_t/\partial R_t = U_E E_R - P_t + w_t Q_R + w_t Q_E E_R$$
$$- w_t G_R + \lambda_t M_R = 0 \qquad (19.48b)$$

$$\partial H_t/\partial V_t = -w_t - \lambda_t F_V = 0 \qquad (19.48c)$$

From equation 19.48c

$$\lambda_t/w_t = -1/F_V \qquad (19.48d)$$

and using this and equation 19.48a in equation 19.48b gives

$$P_t/w_t = (U_E E_R/U_C) + Q_R + Q_E E_R - G_R - (1/F_V)M_R$$
$$= (Q_R - G_R) + (\{U_E/U_C\} + Q_E)E_R - (1/F_V)M_R$$
$$(19.48e)$$

The maximised value of the Hamiltonian can be written

$$H_t^* = U(C_t, E\{R_t, A_t\}) + P_t\dot{S}_t + w_t\dot{K}_t + \lambda_t\dot{A}_t$$

and using $U(\cdot) = U_C C_t + U_E E_t$ and dividing by $U_C = w_t$

$$EDP_t = H_t^*/U_C$$
$$= C_t + (U_E/U_C)E_t + \dot{K}_t + (P_t/w_t)\dot{S}_t + (\lambda_t/w_t)\dot{A}_t$$

or

$$EDP_t = NDP_t + (U_E/U_C)E_t - (P_t/w_t)R_t$$
$$+ (\lambda_t/w_t)(M\{R_t\} - \alpha A_t - F\{V_t\})$$

which on substituting for P_t/w_t from equation 19.48e and rearranging can be written as

$$EDP_t = NDP_t + (U_E/U_C)E_t - (Q_R - G_R)R_t$$
$$- (\{(U_E/U_C) + Q_E\}E_R - (1/F_V)M_R)R_t$$
$$- (1/F_V)(M\{R_t\} - \alpha A_t - F\{V_t\}) \quad (19.48f)$$

So, going from NDP to EDP now involves four adjustments. While the first two are easy to interpret (the second is just depreciation of the resource stock) an intuitive interpretation of the latter two is complicated. For our purposes there are two important points. The first is that implementing these adjustments would require non-market valuation.

The second is that if the environmental quality does not affect utility, $U_E = 0$ so that the first adjustment in equation 19.48f is not required and the third is modified. For any particular pollutant, whether $U_E = 0$ should be assumed or not is an empirical question, which would have to be decided by non-market valuation.

As another example of the dependency of the adjustment prescription on model specification, suppose that $M(R_t) = \beta R_t$ and E_t is a function only of A_t. Then the model might represent carbon dioxide emissions and the climate change problem, where gross emissions are a fixed proportion of the mass of fossil fuel, R, burned, and where it is only the concentration in the atmosphere that is relevant to climate change, which affects utility and production. In this case, clean-up can be thought of as tree planting. Then, with $E_R = 0$ equation 19.48e becomes

$$P_t/w_t = Q_R - G_R - (\beta/F_V)$$

and equation 19.48f becomes

$$\begin{aligned} EDP_t = {} &NDP_t + (U_C/U_E)E_t - (Q_R - G_R)R_t \\ &+ (\alpha A_t)/F_V + F(V_t)/F_V \end{aligned} \tag{19.49}$$

which again illustrates the dependence of the necessary adjustments on model structure and assumptions.

Appendix 19.3 The UNSTAT proposals

The recent version of the international System of National Accounts (SNA), published in 1993 by the United Nations Statistical Division (UN, 1993b), addressed for the first time the possible incorporation of environmental costs and assets into the SNA. However, the report does not recommend the integration of environmental accounts into the central or core SNA. Instead it proposes, for those countries interested in and capable of compiling environmental accounts, a system of satellite accounts. These take the standard SNA as a starting point, showing how they might be complemented or modified by the inclusion of stocks and flows arising from the interaction between the economy and the environment. The section of the report dealing with this is more of a review of the current state of the art, and a guide to national accounts practitioners who may wish to experiment with environmental accounting, than a firm proposal for a particular design and methodology.

The discussion and presentation are closely modelled on the System of Environmental Economic Accounts (SEEA) proposed in the UN handbook *Integrated Environmental and Economic Accounting* (UN, 1992). The SEEA focuses on (i) accounting adequately for the depletion of scarce natural resources and (ii) measuring the costs of environmental degradation and its prevention. The basic structure of the SEEA and its links with the SNA is illustrated in Table 19.11, which can also be used to explain the derivation of the main aggregates of the satellite environmental accounts.

The shaded part of Table 19.11 covers the conventional SNA aggregates. Row i records opening assets, **K0$_{p.ec}$** being the value of stocks of human-made (produced) capital, and **K0$_{np.ec}$** the value of stocks of natural resources (oil and gas, cultivated forests, and so on) regarded as economic assets by the SNA.[13] Row ii records total supply, comprising domestic production (**P**) and imports (**M**).

Row iii shows how total supply is used. A proportion of supply is used in further production (**Ci**); the balance is either exported (**X**), consumed by households or government (**C**), or invested (**Ig**).

Column 1 shows the cost structure of domestic production **P**, comprising the cost of goods and services used in production (**Ci**), the cost of consumption of fixed (human-made) capital (**CFC**), and the balancing value-added, or net domestic product (**NDP**). Note that **NDP** + **CFC** = Gross Domestic Product. Consumption of fixed capital also appears as a negative item in Column 4; gross investment **Ig** **less** capital consumption **CFC** = net investment **I**.

Row v yields the familiar national accounts identity

---

13 We retain the somewhat cumbersome notation used in the UN text, for ease of cross-reference.

Table 19.11 Basic structure of the SEEA

		Economic activities				Economic assets	Environment
							Other
		Production	Rest of world	Final consumption	Produced assets	Non-produced natural assets	non-produced natural assets
		1	2	3	4	5	6
Opening stock of assets	i				$K0_{p.ec}$	$K0_{np.ec}$	
Supply	ii	P	M				
Economic uses	iii	Ci	X	C	Ig		
Consumption of fixed capital	iv	CFC			−CFC		
Net domestic product	v	NDP	X−M	C	I		
Use of non-produced natural assets	vi	Use_{np}				$-Use_{np.ec}$	$-Use_{np.env}$
Other accumulation of non-produced natural assets	vii					$I_{np.ec}$	$-I_{np.env}$
Environmentally adjusted aggregates in monetary environmental accounting	viii	EDP	X−M	C	$A_{p.ec}$	$A_{np.ec}$	$-A_{np.env}$
Holding gains/losses	ix				$Rev_{p.ec}$	$Rev_{np.ec}$	
Other changes in volume of assets	x				$Vol_{p.ec}$	$Vol_{np.ec}$	
Closing stock of assets	xi				$K1_{p.ec}$	$K1_{np.ec}$	

Source: UN (1993b)

$$NDP = (X - M) + C + I$$

Rows ix and x include various adjustments to the stock of produced and non-produced assets, including adjustments to account for changes in prices of assets, destruction of assets due to natural disaster, and certain other changes which affect the level of stocks of assets. For produced economic assets, opening stocks $K0_{p.ec}$ plus net investment I, plus or minus adjustments $Rev_{p.ec}$ and $Vol_{p.ec}$, gives closing stocks $K1_{p.ec}$ (or opening stocks in the next accounting period). For non-produced economic assets, the entries $Rev_{np.ec}$ and $Vol_{np.ec}$ denote corresponding adjustments to opening stocks $K0_{np.ec}$, resulting in closing stocks $K1_{np.ec}$. The 'Other changes in volume of assets', $Vol_{np.ec}$, include changes in known economic reserves of natural assets.

The non-shaded part of the table shows how the system can be extended to incorporate other environmental accounts, which may be expressed in physical or monetary units, or both. Expressed in physical units, these additional flows can be viewed as supplementary to the SNA: expressed in monetary units, they could be used to obtain environmentally adjusted measures of domestic product, as discussed in the chapter.

The additional column 6 covers natural capital not classified as economic (because their usage does not involve market or quasi-market transactions), such as air, uncultivated land, particular ecosystems, virgin forest, and most forms of surface water. The additional row vi records the use or consumption of non-produced natural assets, Use_{np} – that is, the depletion/degradation of natural capital, analogous to CFC for human-made capital. Use_{np} itself comprises $Use_{np.ec}$ – the depletion of economic natural assets such as subsoil minerals, commercially exploited forests, and so on – and $Use_{np.env}$ – the degradation of other natural assets caused by human activities, such as air, water and soil pollution, extinction of species, and so on. These are entered as negative elements in columns 5 and 6, hence reducing the stocks of natural assets.

Row vii – 'Other accumulation of non-produced natural assets' – records the transfer of assets from the non-economic to the economic category. For example, improved techniques of extraction have enhanced reserves of economically recoverable oil; the quantity or value of the increase in reserves would appear as a positive entry in column 5, and as an equal but negative entry in column 6. By construction, the entries in this row will sum to zero.

The addition of rows vi and vii to the table will affect one of the entries in the SNA part of the table, namely 'Other changes in the volume of (non-produced) assets', $Vol_{np.ec}$. In the SNA, this item includes changes in stocks of economic natural assets, whether through depletion/degradation, or the transfer of assets from the non-economic to the economic category. In the SEEA, these components of $\mathbf{Vol_{np.ec}}$ will be recorded in rows vi and vii of column 5. If the entries in the additional rows and columns are expressed in physical units, this completes the table. The SNA monetary aggregates remain unchanged.

The environmental data supplement the monetary accounts by linking levels of economic activity with changes in the environment. However, if these environmental changes can be monetised, the conventional SNA aggregates can be modified to reflect the use of environmental assets.

Row viii records the modified data. In column 1, the consumption of natural capital ($\mathbf{Use_{np}}$) is deducted from **NDP** (net domestic product) to give **EDP** – environmentally adjusted domestic product, which approaches the concept of sustainable income. Columns 2 and 3 remain unchanged. Columns 4–6 introduce the concept of net accumulation in place of net capital formation in the SNA. In fact, for produced assets, net accumulation is the same as net capital formation, so that $\mathbf{A_{p.ec}} = \mathbf{I}$. For non-produced economic assets, net accumulation is the sum of depletion/degradation $\mathbf{Use_{np.ec}}$ (negative) and additions to economic reserves $\mathbf{I_{np.ec}}$ (positive), hence $\mathbf{A_{np.ec}}$ can be positive or negative. Net accumulation of other non-produced natural assets ($\mathbf{A_{np.env}}$) is always negative.

The accounting identity between net production and expenditure noted in the equation above now becomes

$$\mathbf{EDP} = (\mathbf{X} - \mathbf{M}) + \mathbf{C} + \mathbf{A_{p.ec}} + (\mathbf{A_{np.ec}} - \mathbf{A_{np.env}})$$

Since $\mathbf{A_{p.ec}} = \mathbf{I}$, and $\mathbf{I_{np.ec}}$ and $-\mathbf{I_{np.env}}$ cancel out, the term inside the brackets is equal to $-\mathbf{Use_{np}}$, which is also the difference between NDP and EDP, hence the identity is maintained.

Presented as a satellite account, the SEEA has a number of obvious merits. It integrates environmental and economic accounts while maintaining continuity and consistency in time series of national accounts by retaining the conventional SNA definitions and aggregates. As satellite accounts, it is less important to attempt to achieve comprehensive coverage of environmental assets before compiling integrated accounts. For certain environmental assets, for example oil and gas, scarce subsoil minerals and

Table 19.12 Two-digit ISIC categories that identify environmental protection services

Code	Category
37	Recycling
90	Sewage and refuse disposal, sanitation and similar activities
90.1[a]	Collection, transport, treatment and disposal of waste
90.2[a]	Collection and treatment of waste water
90.3[a]	Cleaning of exhaust gases
90.4[a]	Noise abatement
90.5[a]	Other environmental protection services n.e.c.
90.6[a]	Sanitation and similar services

[a] Proposed SEEA breakdown
Source: UN (1993b)

commercial forestry, there are sufficient data on stocks, flows and market values to include them in a set of integrated accounts. However, as discussed in the text, even where such data are available it may be of doubtful value for the purposes of measuring sustainable income. In other cases, for example emissions of industrial pollutants, data on physical quantities may be adequate, but valuation may be difficult. As additional data become available, or acceptable methods of valuation are developed, the coverage of the satellite accounts can be extended.

The SEEA also proposes a more transparent treatment of expenditures on environmental protection (referred to in the chapter as defensive expenditures), by proposing a finer breakdown of the ISIC codes which relate to environmental protection, and by transferring protective expenditures which are undertaken as ancillary activities from their industries of origin to the relevant subsector of environmental protection services. A possible subsectoral breakdown suggested in the SEEA is shown in Table 19.12. Thus, for example, if a paper plant collects and treats waste water from its manufacturing process, the expenditures associated with that activity should be transferred from paper manufacturing to subsector 90.2 – collection and treatment of waste water. This would make it possible to identify more exactly the levels of expenditure on environmental protection (and, as some environmentalists have proposed, to adjust the measure of domestic product to exclude such defensive expenditures). However, as remarked in the text of the chapter, it is often difficult to separately identify these ancillary expenditures. For example, the cost of catalytic converters in vehicles is included in the vehicle price and it may not be feasible to separately identify the cost of the exhaust system, and more particularly the part of the vehicle running expenses attributable to exhaust gas cleaning. Nevertheless, environmental protection services, like other services, are growing in importance in relation to overall economic activity, and this in itself supports the case for a greater degree of detail in classification.

Appendix 19.4 El Serafy's method for the estimation of the depreciation of natural capital

The principle underlying El Serafy's rule for the calculation of a user cost measure of depreciation for a non-renewable resource is as follows. From the net receipts from sales a certain proportion is assumed to be set aside and invested at a constant rate of return in order to yield a constant level of income indefinitely. User cost is then defined as the difference between net receipts and that constant income, which is regarded as the true, or sustainable, income from resource depletion. Given some specialising assumptions, this principle leads to a very simple rule for calculating depreciation for non-renewable resources as user cost, and the corresponding true income from resource extraction.

Assuming that receipts accrue at the end of the period, and using the same notation as in the text, the value of a resource deposit at the start of the period is given by:

$$V_0 = \{R_1(P_1 - C_1)/(1 + r)\} + \{R_2(P_2 - C_2)/(1 + r)^2\} + \ldots + \{R_T(P_T - C_T)/(1 + r)^T\}$$

$$= \sum_{t=1}^{T} R_t(P_t - C_t)/(1 + r)^t \qquad (19.50)$$

If we use X for a constant perpetual income stream, the present value of that stream at the start of the period is given by:

$$W_0 = X/(1 + r) + X/(1 + r)^2 + X/(1 + r)^3 + \ldots$$

$$= \sum_{t=1}^{\infty} X/(1 + r)^t \qquad (19.51)$$

Now assume $R_t = R$, $P_t = P$ and $C_t = C$ for all t, and use $N = R(P - C)$ for net receipts and $d = 1/(1 + r)$ so that equation 19.50 can be written as

$$V_0 = N[d + d^2 + \ldots + d^T] \qquad (19.52)$$

and equation 19.51 as

$$W_0 = X[d + d^2 + d^3 + \ldots] \qquad (19.53)$$

where the term inside the brackets on the right-hand side of equation 19.53 is an infinite series. Note that $d < 1$ for $r > 0$.

Multiplying both sides of equation 19.52 by d gives

$$dV_0 = N[d^2 + d^3 + \ldots + d^{T+1}] \qquad (19.54)$$

and subtracting equation 19.54 from equation 19.52 gives

$$V_0 - dV_0 = N[d - d^{T+1}]$$

so that

$$V_0 = N[d - d^{T+1}]/[1 - d] \qquad (19.55)$$

Rewrite equation 19.53 for a finite time horizon, n, as

$$W_0' = X[d + d^2 + \ldots + d^n]$$

where n is some finite number, and proceeding as we did above we get

$$W_0' = X[d - d^{n+1}]/[1 - d]$$

where letting $n \to \infty$ makes d^{n+1} vanish in the limit, so that we have

$$W_C = \mathop{\mathrm{Lim}}_{n \to \infty}(W_0') = dX/[1 - d] \qquad (19.56)$$

for the present value of the perpetual income stream.

Now, if this perpetual income stream is to be solely based on the ownership of the resource deposit, assuming a fully competitive economy, we must have $V_0 = W_0$; that is, the value of the mine at the start of the period must be equal to the present value of the perpetual income stream. Using equations 19.55 and 19.56 this gives

$$N[d - d^{T+1}]/[1 - d] = dX/[1 - d]$$

which on collecting terms and substituting $1/(1 + r)$ for d is

$$X = N[1 - \{1/(1 + r)^T\}]$$

or

$$N - X = N/(1 + r)^T$$

where substituting for $N = R(P - C)$ we get

$$R(P - C) - X = R(P - C)/(1 + r)^T$$

for user cost, so that for this measure of depreciation we have

$$D_N = R(P - C)/(1 + r)^T \tag{19.57}$$

as in the text of the chapter.

User cost/depreciation as a proportion of net receipts is

$$\{R(P - C) - X\}/\{R(P - C)\} = 1/(1 + r)^T \tag{19.58}$$

and depends only on the lifetime of the resource stock and the interest rate. Sustainable or true income as a share of net receipts is simply one minus the share of user cost. Table 19.13 gives the user cost share for different values for resource lifetime and the interest rate. With low interest rates and short lifetimes, user cost is nearly 100% of net receipts (the income share is close to zero). With long lifetimes and high interest rates, nearly all net receipts count as income. For any given asset lifetime, notice the importance of the choice of interest rate.

Table 19.13 User cost share of receipts from sales of non-renewable natural resources

Lifetime of resource at current extraction rates (years)	Discount rate (%)				
	1	3	5	7	10
1	99	97	95	93	91
5	95	86	78	71	62
10	91	74	61	51	39
25	78	48	30	18	9
50	61	23	9	3	1
100	37	5	1	0	0

References

ABS (1995) *National Balance Sheets for Australia: Issues and Experimental Estimates 1989 to 1992.* Australian Bureau of Statistics, Canberra.

Ackerman, B.A. and Hassler, W.T. (1981) *Clean Coal and Dirty Air.* Yale University Press, New Haven, CT.

Adamowicz, W., Louviere, J. and Williams, M. (1994) Combining revealed and stated preference methods for valuing environmental amenities. *Journal of Environmental Economics and Management* **26**, 271–292.

Adams, D.D. and Page, W.P. (1985) *Acid Deposition: Environmental, Economic and Policy Issues.* Plenum Press, New York.

Adar, Z. and Griffin, J.M. (1976) Uncertainty and the choice of pollution control instruments. *Journal of Environmental Economics and Management* **3**, 178–188.

Adelman, M.A. (1990) Mineral depletion, with special reference to petroleum. *Review of Economics and Statistics* **72**(1), 1–10.

Adelman, M.A. (1995) *The Genie out of the Bottle: World Oil since 1970.* MIT Press, Cambridge, MA.

Adger, W.N., Pettenella, D. and Whitby, M.C. (eds) (1997) *Climate Change Mitigation and European Land Use Policies.* CAB International Publishing, Wallingford, Oxon, United Kingdom.

Ahmad, Y., El Serafy, S. and Lutz, E. (eds) (1989) *Environmental Accounting for Sustainable Development: A UNDP–World Bank Symposium.* World Bank, Washington, DC

Alexandratos, N. (ed.) (1995) *World Agriculture: Towards 2010, An FAO Study.* John Wiley, Chichester, and FAO, Rome.

Amundsen, E.S., Bjorndal, T. and Conrad, J.B. (1995) Optimal harvesting of the Northeast Atlantic minke whale. *Environmental and Resource Economics* **6**, 167–185.

Anderson, D. and Bird, C.D. (1990a) *The Carbon Accumulation Problem and Technical Progress.* University College, London and Balliol College, Oxford.

Anderson, D. and Bird, C.D. (1990b) *The Carbon Accumulation Problem and Technical Progress: A Simulation Study of the Costs.* University College, London and Balliol College, Oxford.

Anderson, F.J. (1985) *Natural Resources in Canada: Economic Theory and Policy.* Methuen, Agincourt, Ontario.

Anderson, F.J. (1991) *Natural Resources in Canada: Economic Theory and Policy,* 2nd edition. Nelson, Scarborough, Ontario.

Anderson, K. (1992a) The standard welfare economics of policies affecting trade and the environment. Chapter 2 in Anderson, K. and Blackhurst, R. (eds) *The Greening of World Trade Issues.* Harvester Wheatsheaf, Hemel Hempstead.

Anderson, K. (1992b) Effects on the environment and welfare of liberalising world trade: the cases of coal and food, in Anderson, K. and Blackhurst, R. (eds) *The Greening of World Trade Issues.* Harvester Wheatsheaf, Hemel Hempstead.

Anderson, L.G. (ed.) (1977) *Economic Impacts of Extended Fisheries Jurisdiction.* Ann Arbor Science Publishers, Ann Arbor, MI.

Anderson, L.G. (1981) *Economic Analysis for Fisheries Management Plans.* Ann Arbor Science Publishers, Ann Arbor, MI.

Anderson, L. (1986) *The Economics of Fisheries Management.* Johns Hopkins University Press, Delaware, MD.

Anderson, L.G. (1995) Privatising open access fisheries: individual transferable quotas. Chapter 20 (pp. 453–74) in Bromley, D.W. (ed.) *The Handbook of Environmental Economics.* Blackwell, Oxford.

Anderson, R.C., Lohof, A.Q. and Carlin, A. (1997) *The United States Experience with Economic Incentives in Pollution Control Policy.* Environmental Law Institute for the US EPA, Washington, DC.

Andreasson, I.-M. (1990) Costs for reducing farmer's use of nitrogen in Gotland, Sweden. *Ecological Economics* **2**(4), 287–300.

Antweiller, W., Copeland, B.R. and Taylor, M.S. (2001) Is free trade good for the environment? *American Economic Review* **91**(4), 877–908.

Arndt, H.W. (1978) *The Rise and Fall of Economic Growth: A Study in Contemporary Thought.* Longman Cheshire, Sydney.

Arrow, K. (1951) *Social Choice and Individual Values.* Yale University Press, New Haven, CT.

Arrow, K. and Fisher, A.C. (1974) Environmental preservation, uncertainty and irreversibility. *Quarterly Journal of Economics* **88**, 313–319.

Arrow, K. and Lind, R. (1970) Uncertainty and the evaluation of public investment decisions. *American Economic Review,* 60, June.

Arrow, K., Bolin, B., Costanza, R., Dasgupta, P., Folke, C., Holling, C. S., Jansson, B-O., Levin, S., Mäler, K.-G., Perrings, C. and Pimental, D. (1995) Economic growth, carrying capacity and the environment. *Science* **268**, 520–521.

Arrow, K., Cline, W.R., Mäler, K.-G., Manasinghe, M., Squitieri, R. and Stiglitz, J.E. (1996) Intertemporal equity, discounting and economic efficiency, in Bruce, J.F., Lee, H. and Haites, E.F. (eds) *Climate Change 1995: Economic and Social Dimensions of Climate Change.* Cambridge University Press, Cambridge.

Asheim, G.B. (1986) Hartwick's rule in open economies. *Canadian Journal of Economics* **19**, 395–402.

Atkinson, G. and Pearce, D.W. (1993) Measuring sustainable development. *The Globe,* No. 13, June 1993, UK Global Environment Research Office, Swindon.

Axelrod, R. (1984) *The Evolution of Cooperation.* Basic Books, New York.

Ayres, R.U. (1999) Industrial metabolism and the grand nutrient cycles. in van den Bergh, J.C.J.M. (ed.) *Handbook of Environmental and Resource Economics.* Edward Elgar, Cheltenham.

Ayres, R.U. and Kneese, A.V. (1969) Production, consumption and externalities. *American Economic Review* **59**(3), 282–297.

Azar, C., Holmberg, J. and Lingren, K. (1996) Socio-ecological indicators for sustainability. *Ecological Economics* **18**, 89–112.

Bailey, M.J. (1982) Risks, costs and benefits of fluorocarbon regulations. *American Economic Review* **72**, 247–250.

Baland, J. and Platteau, J.P. (1996) *Halting Degradation of Natural Resources.* Clarendon Press, Oxford.

Barber, W.J. (1967) *A History of Economic Thought.* Penguin, London.

Barbier, E.B. (1989a) *Economics, Natural Resources Scarcity and Development: Conventional and Alternative Views.* Earthscan, London.

Barbier, E.B. (1989b) The global greenhouse effect: economic impacts and policy considerations. *Natural Resources Forum* **13**(1).

Barbier, E.B. and Burgess, J.C. (1997) The economics of tropical forest land use options. *Land Economics* **73**(2), 174–195.

Barbier, E.B. and Markandya, A. (1990) The conditions for achieving environmentally sustainable development. *European Economic Review* **34**, 659–669.

Barbier, E.B. and Pearce, D.W. (1990) Thinking economically about climate change. *Energy Policy* **18**(1), 11–18.

Barbier, E.B., Burgess, J.C. and Pearce, D.W. (1990a) *Slowing Global Warming: Options for Greenhouse Gas Substitution*. London Environmental Economics Centre.

Barbier, E.B., Burgess, J.C., Swanson, T.M. and Pearce, D.W. (1990b) *Elephants, Economics and Ivory*. Earthscan, London.

Barbier, E.B., Burgess, J.C. and Folke, C. (1994) *Paradise Lost? The Ecological Economics of Biodiversity*. Earthscan, London.

Barker, T. (1990) *Review of Existing Models and Data in the United Kingdom for Environment–Economy Linkage*. Cambridge Econometrics, Department of Applied Economics, University of Cambridge.

Barker, T. (1997) Taxing pollution instead of jobs: towards more employment without more inflation through fiscal reform in the UK, in O'Riordan, T. (ed.) (1997) *Ecotaxation*. Earthscan, London.

Barnett, H.J. (1979) Scarcity and growth revisited, in V. Kerry Smith (ed.) *Scarcity and Growth Reconsidered*. Johns Hopkins University Press, Baltimore, MD.

Barnett, H.J. and Morse, C. (1963) *Scarcity and Growth: The Economics of Natural Resource Availability*. Johns Hopkins University Press, for Resources for the Future, Baltimore, MD.

Barney, G.O. (Study Director) (1980) *The Global 2000 Report to the President of the United States*, 3 vols. Pergamon Press, New York.

Barrett, S. (1990) *Pricing the Environment: The Economic and Environmental Consequences of a Carbon Tax*. Briefing Paper, London Business School.

Barrett, S. (1994a) Self-enforcing international environmental agreements. *Oxford Economic Papers* **46**, 874–894.

Barrett, S. (1994b) The biodiversity supergame. *Environmental and Resource Economics* **4**(1), 111–122.

Barrett, S. (1995) The problem of global environmental protection. *Oxford Review of Economic Policy* **6**, 68–79.

Barrett, S. (1998) Political economy of the Kyoto Protocol. *Oxford Review of Economic Policy* **14**(4), 20–39.

Bartelmus, P. (1994) *Environment Growth and Development: The Concepts and Strategies of Sustainability*. Routledge, London.

Bartelmus, P., Stahmer, C. and van Tongeren, J. (1993) Integrated environmental and economic accounting – a framework for an SNA satellite system, in Lutz, E. (ed.) *Toward Improved Accounting for the Environment*. An UNSTAT–World Bank Symposium, The World Bank, Washington, DC.

Bator, F.M. (1957) The simple analytics of welfare maximisation. *American Economic Review* **47**, 22–59.

Baumol, W.J. (1977) *Economic Theory and Operations Analysis*, 4th edition. Prentice Hall, London.

Baumol, W.J. and Oates, W.E. (1971) The use of standards and prices for the protection of the environment. *Swedish Journal of Economics* **73**, 42–54.

Baumol, W.J. and Oates, W.E. (1979) *Economics, Environmental Policy and the Quality of Life*. Prentice-Hall, Englewood Cliffs, NJ.

Baumol, W.J. and Oates, W.E. (1988) *The Theory of Environmental Policy: Externalities, Public Outlays and the Quality of Life*, 2nd edition. Prentice-Hall, Englewood Cliffs, NJ.

Beauchamp, T.L. and Bowie, N.E. (1988) *Ethical Theory and Business*, 3rd edition. Prentice-Hall, Englewood Cliffs, NJ.

Becker, G. (1960) An economic analysis of fertility, in Coale, A.J. *et al.* (eds) *Demographic and Economic Changes in Developed Countries*. Princeton University Press, Princeton, NJ, pp. 209–231.

Beckerman, W. (1972) Economists, scientists and environmental catastrophe. *Oxford Economic Papers* **24**, 237–244.

Beckerman, W. (1974) *In Defence of Economic Growth*. Jonathan Cape, London.

Beckerman, W. (1980) *Introduction to National Income Analysis*, 3rd edition. Weidenfeld and Nicholson, London.

Beckerman, W. (1992) Economic growth and the environment: whose growth? Whose environment? *World Development* **20**, 481–496.

Beckerman, W. (1994) 'Sustainable development'. Is it a useful concept? *Environmental Values* **3**, 191–209.

Bell, F. and Leeworthy, V. (1990) Recreational demand by tourists for saltwater beach days. *Journal of Environmental Economics and Management* **18**(3), 189–205.

Benkovic, S. and Kruger, J. (2001) To trade or not to trade? Criteria for applying cap and trade. *The Scientific World*, No. 1.

Bennett, J. and Adamowicz, V. (2001) Some fundamentals of environmental economics modelling, in Bennett, J. and Blamey, R. (eds) *The Choice Modelling Approach to Environmental Valuation*. Edward Elgar, Cheltenham.

Bennett, J. and Blamey, R. (eds) (2001) *The Choice Modelling Approach to Environmental Valuation*. Edward Elgar, Cheltenham.

Benson, J. and Willis, K. (1991) *The Demand for Forests for Recreation*. University of Newcastle, Newcastle.

Bentham, J. (1789) *An Introduction to the Principles of Morals and Legislation*. L.J. LaFleur, New York, 1948 edition.

Berck, P. (1979) The economics of timber: a renewable resource in the long run. *Bell Journal of Economics* **10**, 447–462.

Berck, P. (1995) Empirical consequences of the Hotelling principle, in Bromley, D.W. (ed.) *The Handbook of Environmental Economics*. Blackwell, Oxford.

Berck, P. and Roberts, M. (1996) Natural resource prices: will they ever turn up? *Journal of Environmental Economics and Management* **31**(1), 65–78.

Berndt, E. and Field, B. (eds) (1981) *Measuring and Modelling Natural Resource Substitution*. MIT Press, Cambridge, MA.

Bernstam, M.S. (1991) *The Wealth of Nations and the Environment*. Institute of Economic Affairs, London.

Bertram, I.G., Stephens, R.J. and Wallace, C.C. (1989) *The Relevance of Economic Instruments for Tackling the Greenhouse Effect*. Economics Department, Victoria University, New Zealand, Report to the New Zealand Ministry of the Environment.

Biancardi, C., Tiezzi, E. and Ulgiati, S. (1993) Complete recycling of matter in the frameworks of physics, biology and ecological economics. *Ecological Economics* **8**, 1–5.

Bishop, R.C. (1978) Endangered species and uncertainty: the economics of a safe minimum standard. *American Journal of Agricultural Economics* **60**, 10–18.

Bishop, R.C. (1982) Option value: an exposition and extension. *Land Economics* **58**, 1–15.

Bishop, R.C. and Heberlein, T.A. (1979) Measuring values of extramarket goods: are indirect measures biased? *American Journal of Agricultural Economics* **61**(5), 926–930.

Bishop, R.C. and Welsh, M.P. (1992) Existence value in benefit-cost analysis. *Land Economics* **68**, 405–417.

Bishop, R.C. and Woodward, R.T. (1995) Valuation of environmental quality under certainty, in Bromley, D.W. (ed.) *The Handbook of Environmental Economics*. Blackwell, Oxford.

Bishop, R.C., Champ, P.A. and Mullarkey, D.J. (1995) Contingent valuation, in Bromley, D.W. (ed.) *The Handbook of Environmental Economics*. Blackwell, Oxford.

Bjorndal, T. (1988) The optimal management of North Sea herring. *Journal of Environmental Economics and Management* **15**, 9–29.

Bjorndal, T. and Conrad, J.M. (1987) The dynamics of an open-access fishery. *Canadian Journal of Economics* **20**, 74–85.

Blackman, A. and Harrington, W. (1999) *The Use of Economic Incentives in Developing Countries: Lessons from International Experience with Industrial Air Pollution*. RFF Discussion Paper 99-39, May.

Blamey, R.K. (1996) Citizens, consumers and contingent valuation: clarification and the expression of citizen values and issue-opinions, in Adamowicz, W.L., Boxall, P., Luckert, M.K., Phillips, W.E. and White, W.A. (eds) *Forestry, Economics and the Environment*. CAB International, Wallingford, pp. 103–133.

Blamey, R.K. (1998) Decisiveness, attitude expression and symbolic responses in contingent valuation surveys. *Journal of Economic Behavior and Organization* **34**, 577–601.

Blamey, R.K. and Common, M. (1994) Sustainability and the limits to pseudo market valuation, in van den Bergh, J.C.J.M. and van der Straaten, J. (eds) *Concepts and Methods for Sustainable Development: Critique and New Approaches*. Island Press, Washington, DC.

Blamey, R.K. and Common, M.S. (1999) Valuation and ethics in environmental economics, in van den Bergh, J.C.J.M. (ed.) *Handbook of Environmental and Resource Economics*. Edward Elgar, Cheltenham.

Blamey, R.K., Common, M. and Quiggin, J. (1995) Respondents to contingent valuation surveys: consumers or citizens? *Australian Journal of Agricultural Economics* **39**, 263–288.

Blaug, M. (1985) *Economic Theory in Retrospect*, 4th edition. Cambridge University Press, Cambridge.

Boardman, A.E., Greenberg, D.H., Vining, A.R. and Weimer, D.L. (2001) *Cost-Benefit Analysis: Concept and Practice*, 2nd edition. Prentice-Hall, New York.

Bockstael, N.E. (1995) Travel cost models, in Bromley, D.W. (ed.) *The Handbook of Environmental Economics*. Blackwell, Oxford.

Bockstael, N.E. and McConnell, K.E. (1993) Public goods as characteristics of non-market commodities. *Economic Journal* **103**, 1244.

Bockstael, N.E., Hanemann, W.M. and Strand, I.E. (1987a) *Measuring the Benefits of Water Quality Improvements using Recreational Demand Models*. Environmental Protection Agency Co-operative Agreement CR-811043-01-0.

Bockstael, N.E., Strand, I.E. and Hanemann, W.M. (1987b) Time and the recreational demand model. *American Journal of Agricultural Economics* **69**, 293–302.

Boero, G., Clarke, R. and Winters, L.A. (1991) *The Macroeconomic Consequences of Controlling Greenhouse Gases: A Survey*. UK Department of the Environment.

Böhm, P. (1981) *Deposit-refund Systems: Theory and Applications to Environmental, Conservation, and Consumer Policy*. Johns Hopkins University Press, Baltimore, MD.

Böhm, P. and Russell, C.S. (1985) Comparative analysis of alternative policy instruments, in Kneese, A.V. and Sweeney J.L. (eds) *Handbook of Natural Resource and Energy Economics*, Vol. I. North-Holland, Amsterdam.

Booth, D.E. (1994) Ethics and the limits of environmental economics. *Ecological Economics* **9**, 241–252.

Bose, R.K., Srinivas, D., Mathur, R., Dass, A. and Alur, M. (1997) *Environmental Aspects of Energy Use in Large Indian Metropolises*. Tata Energy Research Institute, Report number 94EM53. [Online at www.teriin.org/reports/rep06/rep06.htm]

Bose, R.K., Vasudeva, G., Gupta, S. and Sinha, C. (1998) *India's Environment Pollution and Protection*. Tata Energy Research Institute, Report number 97ED57. [Online at www.teriin.org/reports/rep01/rep01.htm]

Boulding, K.E. (1966) The economics of the coming spaceship earth, in H. Jarrett (ed.) *Environmental Quality in a Growing Economy*. Resources for the Future/Johns Hopkins University Press, Baltimore, MD, pp. 3–14.

Bovenberg, A.L. (1997) Environmental policy, distortionary labour taxation and employment: pollution taxes and the double dividend. Chapter 4 (pp. 68–104) in Carraro, C. and Siniscalco, D. (eds) *New Directions in the Economic Theory of the Environment*. Cambridge University Press, Cambridge.

Bowes, M.D. and Krutilla, J.V. (1985) Multiple use management of public forest lands, in Kneese, A.V. and Sweeney, J.L. (eds) *Handbook of Natural Resource and Energy Economics*, Vol. II. North-Holland, Amsterdam.

Bowes, M.D. and Krutilla, J.V. (1989) *Multiple-use Management: The Economics of Public Forestlands*. Resources for the Future, Washington, DC.

Bowler, P.J. (1992) *The Fontana History of the Environmental Sciences*. Fontana, London.

Boxall, P.C., Adamowicz, W., Swait, J., Williams, M. and Louviere, J. (1996) A comparison of stated preference methods for environmental valuation. *Ecological Economics* **18**. 243–253.

Boyden, S. (1987) *Western Civilization in Biological Perspective: Patterns in Biohistory*. Oxford University Press, Oxford.

Boyer, M. and Laffont, J-J. (1999) Towards a political theory of the emergence of environmental incentive regulation. *RAND Journal of Economics*, **30**(1) Spring, 137–157.

Boyle, K.J. and Bishop, R.C. (1987) Valuing wildlife in benefit-cost analysis: a case study involving endangered species. *Water Resources Research* **23**, 942–950.

Braden, J.B. and Segerson, K. (1993) Information problems in the design of nonpoint-source pollution policy, pp. 1–36, in Russell, C.S. and Shogren, J.F. (eds) *Theory, Modeling and Experience in the Management of Nonpoint-Source Pollution*. Kluwer Academic Publishers, Boston, MA.

Brekke, K.A. (1997) Hicksian income from resource extraction in an open economy. *Land Economics* **73**, 516–527.

Brennan, G. and Lomasky, L. (1993) *Democracy and Decision: The Pure Theory of Electoral Preference*. Cambridge University Press, Cambridge.

Bromley, D.W. (ed.) (1995) *The Handbook of Environmental Economics*. Blackwell, Oxford.

Bromley, D.W. (1999) *Sustaining Development. Environmental Resources in Developing Countries*. Edward Elgar, Cheltenham.

Brookshire, D.S., Thayer, M.A., Schulze, W.D. and D'Arge, R.C. (1982) Valuing public goods: a comparison of survey and hedonic approaches. *American Economic Review* **71**, 165–177.

Brookshire, D., Eubanks, L. and Randall, A. (1983) Estimating option price and existence values for wildlife resources. *Land Economics* **59**(1), 1–15.

Brookshire, D., Thayer, M., Tschirhart, J. and Schulze, W. (1985) A test of the expected utility model: evidence from earthquake risks. *Journal of Political Economy* **93**(2), 369–389.

Broome, J. (1992) *Counting the Cost of Global Warming*. White Horse Press, Cambridge.

Browder, J.O. (ed.) (1988) *Fragile Lands of Latin America: Strategies for Sustainable Development*. Westfield Press, Boulder, CO.

Brown, G.M. and Field, B.C. (1978) Implications of alternative measures of natural resource scarcity. *Journal of Political Economy* **86**, 229–244.

Brown, G.M. and Field, B.C. (1979) The adequacy of measures for signalling natural resource scarcity, in Smith, V.K. (ed.) *Scarcity and Growth Reconsidered*. Johns Hopkins University Press/Resources for the Future, Baltimore, MD.

Brown, G. and McGuire, C.B. (1967) A socially optimal pricing policy for a public water agency. *Water Resources Research* **3**, 33–44.

Brown, I. (1989) Energy subsidies in the United States, in *Energy Pricing: Regulation Subsidies and Distortion*. Surrey Energy Economics Centre Discussion Paper No. 38, University of Surrey, UK, March.

Brown, K. and Pearce, D.W. (1994) *The Causes of Tropical Deforestation*. UCL Press, London.

Brown, L.R. (1981) *Building a Sustainable Society*. W.W. Norton, New York.

Brown, L.R. and Kane, H. (1994) *Full House: Re-assessing the Earth's Population Carrying Capacity*. W.W. Norton, New York.

Bruce, J.P., Lee, H. and Haites, E.F. (1996) *Climate Change 1995: Economic and Social Dimensions of Climate Change*. Cambridge University Press, Cambridge.

Bryant, C. and Cook, P. (1992) Environmental issues and the national accounts. *Economic Trends* No. 469, HMSO, London.

Buchanan, J. and Tullock, G. (1962) *The Calculus of Consent: Logical Foundations of Constitutional Democracy*. The University of Michigan Press, Ann Arbor.

Buchanan, J.M. and Tullock, G. (1980) *Toward a Theory of the Rent Seeking Society*. Texas A & M University Press, College Station, TX.

Burniaux, J-M., Martin, J.P., Nicoletti, G. and Martins, J.Q. (1991a) *GREEN – A Multi Region Dynamic General Equilibrium Model for Quantifying the Costs of Curbing CO_2 Emissions: A Technical Manual*. OECD, Department of Economics and Statistics Working Paper No. 104, OECD/GD(91)119, Resource Allocation Division, OECD, June.

Burniaux, J-M., Martin, J.P., Nicoletti, G. and Martins, J.Q. (1991b) *The Costs of Policies to Reduce Global Emissions of CO_2: Initial Simulation Results with GREEN*. OECD, Department of Economics and Statistics Working Paper No. 103, OCDE/GD(91)115, Resource Allocation Division, OECD, June.

Burniaux, J-M., Martin, J.P., Nicoletti, G. and Martins, J.Q. (1992) The costs of international agreements to reduce CO_2 emissions, in *European Economy: The economics of Limiting CO_2 Emissions*, Special Edition No. 1. Commission of the European Communities, Brussels.

Burniaux, J-M., Martin, J.P., Oliveira-Martins, J. and van der Mensbrugghe, D. (1994) Carbon abatement transfers and energy efficiency' in Goldin, I. and Winters, L.A. (eds) *The Economics of Sustainable Development*. Cambridge University Press, Cambridge.

Burrows, P. (1979) *The Economic Theory of Pollution Control*. Martin Robertson, Oxford.

Burrows, P. (1995) Nonconvexities and the theory of external costs, in Bromley D.W. (ed.) *The Handbook of Environmental Economics*. Blackwell, Oxford.

Business Week (1991) Saving the planet: environmentally advantaged technologies for economic growth. Special supplement, 30 December.

Cairncross, F. (1992) *Costing the Earth: The Challenge for Governments, the Opportunities for Business*. Harvard Business School, Boston, MA.

Cairns, R.D. (2002) Green accounting using current imperfect prices, *Environment and Development Economics*, **7**(2), 207–215.

Calish, S., Fight, R.D. and Teeguarden, D.E. (1978) How do nontimber values affect Douglas-fir rotations? *Journal of Forestry* **76**, 217–221.

Cameron, J. and Aboucher, J. (1991) The precautionary principle: a fundamental principle of law and policy for the protection of the global environment. *Boston College International and Comparative Law Review* **14**, 1–27.

Carraro, C. and Siniscalco, D. (eds) (1993) *The European Carbon Tax: An Economic Assessment*. Kluwer, Dordrecht.

Carraro, C. and Siniscalco, D. (eds) (1997) *New Directions in the Economic Theory of the Environment*. Cambridge University Press, Cambridge.

Carruthers, I. (1994) Going, going, gone! Tropical agriculture as we knew it. *Tropical Agriculture Newsletter* **13**(3), 1–5.

Carson, R.T. (1995) *Contingent Valuation Surveys and Tests of Insensitivity to Scope*. Mimeo, Department of Economics, University of California, San Diego.

Carson, R.T., Mitchell, R.C., Hanemann, M., Kopp, R.J., Presser, S. and Rudd, P.A. (1995a) *Contingent Valuation and Lost Passive Use: Damages from the Exxon Valdez*. Department of Economics, University of California, San Diego, Discussion Paper 95-02, January.

Carson, R.T., Wright, J., Carson, N., Alberni, A. and Flores, N. (1995b) *A Bibliography of Contingent Valuation Studies and Papers*. Natural Resource Damage Assessment Inc, La Jolla, CA.

CEC (Commission of the European Communities) (1983) *Acid Rain: A Review of the Phenomenon in the EEC and Europe*. Graham and Trotman, London.

CGIAR (1994) (Consultative Group on International Agricultural Research Secretariat.) *Current CGIAR Research Efforts and Their Expected Impact on Food, Agriculture, and National Development*. Draft paper (CGIAR, Washington, DC, March).

Chiang, A.C. (1984) *Fundamental Methods of Mathematical Economics*, 3rd edition. McGraw-Hill, New York.

Chiang, A.C. (1992) *Elements of Dynamic Optimization*. McGraw-Hill, New York.

Chichilnisky, G. and Heal, G.M. (2000) *Environmental Markets: Equity and Efficiency*. Columbia University Press, New York.

Cicchetti, C.V. and Freeman, A.M. (1971) Option demand and consumer surplus, further comment. *Quarterly Journal of Economics* **85**, 528–539.

Cipolla, C.M. (1962) *The Economic History of World Population*. Penguin, Harmondsworth.

Ciriacy-Wantrup, S. von (1968) *Resource Conservation: Economics and Politics*, 2nd edition. University of California Press, Berkeley and Los Angeles.

Clark, C.W. (1985) *Bioeconomic Modelling and Fisheries Management*. John Wiley, New York.

Clark, C.W. (1990) *Mathematical Bioeconomics: The Optimal Management of Renewable Resources*, 2nd edition. John Wiley, New York.

Clark, C.W., Clark, F.H. and Munro, G.R. (1979) The optimal exploitation of renewable resource stocks: problems of irreversible investment. *Econometrica* **47**, 25–47.

Clawson, M. (1959) *Methods of Measuring the Demand for and Value of Outdoor Recreation*. Reprint Number 10, Resources for the Future, Washington, DC.

Clawson, M. (1977) *Decision Making in Timber Production, Harvest, and Marketing*. Research Paper R-4, Resources for the Future, Washington, DC.

Clawson, M. and Knetsch, J. (1966) *Economics of Outdoor Recreation*. Johns Hopkins University Press, Baltimore, MD.

Cleveland, C.J. (1993) An exploration of alternative measures of resource scarcity: the case of petroleum resources. *Ecological Economics* **7**, 123–157.

Cline, W.R. (1989) *Political Economy of the Greenhouse Effect*. Mimeo, Institute for International Economics, Washington, DC.

Cline, W.R. (1991) Scientific basis for the greenhouse effect. *Economic Journal* **101**, 904–919.

Cline, W.R. (1992) *The Economics of Global Warming*. Institute for International Economics, Washington, DC.

Clunies Ross, A. (1990) *Transfers versus Licences as Incentives to Governments for Environmental Correctives*. Paper submitted to the Development Studies Association Annual Conference 1990, University of Strathclyde, Department of Economics, Glasgow.

Coase, R. (1960) The problem of social cost. *Journal of Law and Economics* **3**, 1–44.

Cobbing, P. and Slee, W. (1993) A contingent valuation of the Mar Lodge Estate. *Journal of Environmental Planning and Management* **36**(1), 65–72.

Coggins, J.S. and Ramezani, C.A. (1998) An arbitrage-free approach to quasi-option value, *Journal of Environmental Economics and Management*, **35**, 103–125.

Cohen, M.A. (1986) The costs and benefits of oil spill prevention and enforcement. *Journal of Environmental Economics and Management* **13**, 167–188.

Cole, H.S.D., Freeman, C., Jahoda, M. and Pavitt, K.L.R. (eds) (1973) *Thinking about the Future: A Critique of the Limits to Growth*. Chatto and Windus, London, for Sussex University Press.

Common, M.S. (1985) The distributional implications of higher energy prices in the UK. *Applied Economics* **17**, 421–436.

Common, M.S. (1989) The choice of pollution control instruments: why is so little notice taken of economists' recommendations? *Environment and Planning A* **21**, 1297–1314.

Common, M. (1995) *Sustainability and Policy: Limits to Economics*. Cambridge University Press, Melbourne.

Common, M.S. (1996) *Environmental and Resource Economics: An Introduction*, 2nd edition. Longman, Harlow.

Common, M.S. (2004) *Ecological Economics: An Introduction to the Study of Sustainability*. Cambridge University Press, Cambridge.

Common, M.S. and Hamilton, C. (1996) The economic consequences of carbon taxation in Australia, in Bouma, W.J., Pearman, G.I. and Manning, M.R. (eds) *Greenhouse: Coping with Climate Change*. CSIRO Publishing, Collingwood.

Common, M.S. and McPherson, P. (1982) A note on energy requirements calculations using the 1968 and 1974 input output tables. *Energy Policy* **10**, 42–49.

Common, M.S. and Norton, T.W. (1992) Biodiversity: its conservation in Australia. *Ambio* **21**, 258–265.

Common, M.S. and Perrings, S.C. (1992) Towards an ecological economics of sustainability. *Ecological Economics* **6**(1), 7–34.

Common, M.S. and Salma, U. (1992a) Economic modelling and Australian carbon dioxide emissions. *Mathematics and Computers in Simulation* **33**, 581–96.

Common, M.S. and Salma, U. (1992b) *An Economic Analysis of Australian Carbon Dioxide Emissions and Energy Use: Report to the Energy Research and Development Corporation*. Canberra: Centre for Resource and Environmental Studies, Australian National University, Canberra.

Common, M. and Salma, U. (1992c) Accounting for Australian carbon dioxide emissions. *Economic Record* **68**, 31–42.

Common, M. and Sanyal, K. (1998) Measuring the depreciation of Australia's non-renewable resources: a cautionary tale. *Ecological Economics* **26**, 23–30.

Common, M.S., Reid, I. and Blamey, R. (1997) Do existence values for cost benefit analysis exist? *Environmental and Resource Economics* **9**, 225–238.

Common, M.S., Stoeckl, N. and Bull, T. (1999) The travel cost method: an empirical investigation of Randall's difficulty. *Australian Journal of Agricultural Economics*, forthcoming.

Commoner, B. (1963) *Science and Survival*. Ballantine, New York.

Commoner, B. (1972) *The Closing Circle*. Jonathan Cape, London.

Connor, S. (1993) Ozone depletion linked in rise to harmful radiation. *The Independent*, 23 April.

Conrad, J.M. (1995) Bioeconomic models of the fishery, in Bromley, D.W. (ed.) *The Handbook of Environmental Economics*. Blackwell, Oxford, UK.

Conrad, J.M. (1999) *Resource Economics*. Cambridge University Press, Cambridge.

Conrad, J.M. and Clark, C.W. (1987) *Natural Resource Economics: Notes and Problems*. Cambridge University Press, Cambridge.

Conrad, J.M. and Olson, L.J. (1992) The economics of a stock pollutant: aldicarb on Long Island. *Environmental and Resource Economics* **2**, 245–258.

Conway, G.R. (1985) Agroecosystem analysis. *Agricultural Administration* **20**, 31–55.

Conway, G.R. (1992) Sustainability in agricultural development: trade-offs with productivity, stability and equitability. *Journal for Farming Systems Research and Extension*.

Coote, A. and Lenaghan, J. (1997) *Citizens' Juries: Theory and Practice*. Institute for Public Policy Research, London.

Cornes, R. and Sandler, T. (1996) *The Theory of Externalities, Public Goods and Club Goods*, 2nd edition. Cambridge University Press, Cambridge.

Costanza, R. (1989) What is ecological economics? *Ecological Economics* **1**, 1–17.

Costanza, R. (ed.) (1991) *Ecological Economics: The Science and Management of Sustainability*. Columbia University Press, New York.

Costanza, R. and Perrings, C. (1990) A flexible assurance bonding system for improved environmental management. *Ecological Economics* **2**, 57–75.

Costanza, R., Daly, H.E. and Bartholomew, J.A. (1991) Goals, agenda and policy recommendations for ecological economics, in Costanza, R. (ed.) (1991) *Ecological Economics*. Columbia University Press, NY.

Costanza, R., d'Arge, R., de Groot, R., Farber, S., Grasso, M., Hannon, B., Limburg, K., Naeem, S., O'Neill, R., Paruelo, J., Raskin, R., Sutton, P. and van den Belt, M. (1997) The value of the world's ecosystem services and natural capital. *Nature* **387**, 253–260.

Cowan, S. (1998) Water pollution and abstraction and economic instruments. *Oxford Review of Economic Policy* **14**(4), 40–49.

Crandall, R. (1992) Policy watch: corporate average fuel economy standards. *Journal of Economic Perspectives* **6**, Spring, 171–180.

Cremer, H. and Gahvani, F. (2001) Second-best taxation of emissions and polluting goods. *Journal of Public Economics* **80**, 169–197.

Crocker, T.D. (1999) A short history of environmental and resource economics, in van den Bergh, J.C.J.M. (ed.) *Handbook of Environmental and Resource Economics*. Edward Elgar, Cheltenham.

Cropper, M.L. and Oates, W.E. (1992) Environmental economics: a survey. *Journal of Economic Literature* **30**, 675–740.

Crosson, P.R. and Brubaker, S. (1982) *Resource and Environmental Effects of US Agriculture*. Johns Hopkins University Press for Resources for the Future, Baltimore, MD.

Cummings, R., Brookshire, D. and Schulze, W. (eds) (1986) *Valuing Environmental Goods: An Assessment of the Contingent Valuation Method*. Rowman and Allenheld, Lanham, MD.

Cunningham, S., Dunn, M. and Whitmarsh, D. (1985) *Fisheries Economics: An Introduction*. St. Martin's Press, New York.

Dajoz, R. (1977) *Introduction to Ecology*. Translated by A. South. Hodder and Stoughton, London.

Dales, J.H. (1968) *Pollution Property and Prices*. Toronto University Press, Toronto.

Daly, H.E. (1968) On economics as a life science. *Journal of Political Economy* **76**, 392–406.

Daly, H.E. (1973) The steady state economy: toward a political economy of biophysical equilibrium and moral growth, in Daly, H.E. (ed.) (1973) *Toward a Steady State Economy*. W.H. Freeman, San Francisco.

Daly, H.E. (1974) The economics of the steady state. *American Economic Review* **64**(2), 15–21.

Daly, H.E. (1977) *Steady State Economics*. W.H. Freeman, San Francisco.

Daly, H.E. (1987) The economic growth debate: what some economists have learned but many have not. *Journal of Environmental Economics and Management* **14**(4).

Daly, H.E. (1999) Steady-state economics: avoiding uneconomic growth, in van den Bergh, J.C.J.M. (ed.) *Handbook of Environmental and Resource Economics*. Edward Elgar, Cheltenham.

Daly, H.E. and Cobb, J.B. (1989) *For the Common Good: Redirecting the Economy Toward Community, the Environment and a Sustainable Future*. Beacon Press, Boston.

D'Arge, R.C. and Kogiku, K.C. (1972) Economic growth and the environment. *Review of Economic Studies* **40**, 61–78.

Dasgupta, P. (1982) *The Control of Resources*. Basil Blackwell, Oxford.

Dasgupta, P. (1990) The environment as a commodity. *Oxford Review of Economic Policy* **6**(1), 51–67.

Dasgupta, P. (1992) *The Population Problem*. Manuscript, Faculty of Economics and Politics, University of Cambridge.

Dasgupta, P. (1993) Natural resources in an age of substitutability. Chapter 23 in Kneese, A.V. and Sweeney, J.L. (eds) *Handbook of Natural Resource and Energy Economics*, Volume 3. Elsevier Science, Amsterdam.

Dasgupta, P. (1994) Exhaustible resources: resource depletion, research and development and the social rate of discount, in Layard, R. and Glaister, S. (eds) *Cost Benefit Analysis*, 2nd edition. Cambridge University Press, Cambridge.

Dasgupta, P. (1995) Optimal development and the idea of net national product, in Goldin, I. and Winters, L.A. (eds) *The Economics of Sustainable Development*. Cambridge University Press, Cambridge.

Dasgupta, P. (2001) *Human Well-being and the Natural Environment*. Oxford University Press, Oxford.

Dasgupta, P. and Heal, G.M. (1974) The optimal depletion of exhaustible resources, *Review of Economic Studies*, Symposium, May, 3–28.

Dasgupta, P. and Heal, G.M. (1979) *Economic Theory and Exhaustible Resources*. Cambridge University Press, Cambridge.

Dasgupta, S. and Mitra, T. (1983) Intergenerational equity and efficient allocation of resources, *International Economic Review* **24**, 133–53.

Deaton, A. and Muellbauer, J. (1980) *Economics and Consumer Behaviour*. Cambridge University Press, Cambridge.

de Bruyn, S.M. and Heintz, R.J. (1999) The environmental Kuznets curve hypothesis, in van den Bergh, J.C.J.M. (ed.) *Handbook of Environmental and Resource Economics*. Edward Elgar, Cheltenham.

DeCanio, S.J., Howarth, R.B., Sanstad, A.H., Schneider, S.H. and Thompson, S.L. (2000) *New Directions in the Economics and Integrated Assessment of Global Climate Change*. Pew Center on Global Climate Change, Arlington, Virginia, USA. [Online at www.pewclimate.org/projects/directions.cfm].

de Graaf, H.J., Musters. C.J.M. and ter Keurs, W.J. (1996) Sustainable development: looking for new strategies. *Ecological Economics* **16**, 205–216.

Department of Energy (1984) *Digest of United Kingdom Energy Statistics 1983*. HMSO, London.

Department of Energy (1989) *An Evaluation of Energy Related Greenhouse Gas Emissions and Measures to Ameliorate Them*. Energy Paper No. 58, January, HMSO, London.

Desvousges, W., Smith. V. and Fisher, A. (1987) Option price estimates for water quality improvements. *Journal of Environmental Economics and Management* **14**, 248–267.

Deverajan, S. and Fisher, A.C. (1980) Exploration and scarcity. *Journal of Political Economy* **90**, 1279–1290.

Deverajan, S. and Fisher, A.C. (1982) Measures of resource scarcity under uncertainty, in Smith, V.K. and Krutilla, J.V. (eds) *Explorations in Natural Resource Economics*. Johns Hopkins University Press/Resources for the Future, Baltimore, MD.

Diamond, J. (1993) *The Rise and Fall of the Third Chimpanzee*. Vintage Press, London.

Diamond, J. (1998) *Guns, Germs and Steel: A Short History of Everybody for the Last 13000 Years*. Vintage Press, London.

Diamond, P.A., Hausman, J.A., Leonard, G.K. and Denning, M.A. (1993) Does contingent valuation measure preferences? Experimental evidence, in Hausman, J.A. (ed.) *Contingent Valuation: A Critical Assessment*, 31–85. North-Holland, Amsterdam.

Dietz, F.J., Simonis, U.E. and van der Straaten, J. (eds) (1993) *Sustainability and Environmental Policy: Restraints and Advances*. Edition Sigma, Berlin.

Dinar, A. (ed.) (2000) *Political Economy of Water Pricing Reforms*. Oxford University Press, for the World Bank, Washington, DC.

Dinwiddy, C.L. and Teale, F.J. (1988) *The Two-Sector General Equilibrium Model: A New Approach*. Philip Allan, Oxford.

Dixit, A.K. and Nalebuff, B. (1991) *Thinking Strategically*. W.W. Norton, New York.

Dixit, A.K. and Pindyck, R.S. (1994) *Investment under Uncertainty*. Princeton University Press, Princeton, NJ.

Dorfman, R. (1985) An economist's view of natural resource and environmental problems. Chapter 4 in Repetto, R. (ed.) *The Global Possible*. Yale University Press, New Haven, CT.

Dosi, C. and Tomasi, T. (eds) (1994) *Nonpoint Source Pollution Regulation: Issues and Analysis*, Kluwer Academic, Dordrecht.

Dovers, S. (1994) Historical and current patterns of energy use, in Dovers. S. (ed.) *Sustainable Energy Systems: Pathways for Australian Energy Reform*. Cambridge University Press, Cambridge.

Downing, P. (1981) A political economy model of implementing pollution laws. *Journal of Environmental Economics and Management* **8**, 255–71.

DTLR (2001) *Multi Criteria Analysis: A Manual*. Department for Transport, Local Government and the Regions, London.

Durning, A.B. (1989) *Poverty and the Environment: Reversing the Downward Spiral.* Paper No. 92, Worldwatch Institute, Washington, DC.

Easterlin, R.A. (1978) The economics and sociology of fertility: a synthesis, in C. Tilley (ed.) *Historical Studies of Changing Fertility.* Princeton University Press, Princeton, NJ.

Easterlin, R.A. (ed.) (1980) *Population and Economic Change in Developing Countries.* University of Chicago Press, Chicago.

Ecstein, O. (1958) *Water Resources Development: The Economics of Project Evaluation.* Harvard University Press, Cambridge, MA.

Edmonds, J. and Barns, D.W. (1990a) *Estimating the Marginal Cost of Reducing Global Fossil Fuel CO_2 Emissions.* PNL-SA-18361, Pacific Northwest Laboratory, Washington, DC.

Edmonds, J. and Barns, D.W. (1990b) *Factors Affecting the Long Term Cost of Global Fossil Fuel CO_2 Emissions Reductions.* Global Environmental Change Programme, Pacific Northwest Laboratory, Washington, DC.

Edmonds, J. and Reilly, J.M. (1985) *Global Energy: Assessing the Future.* Oxford University Press, New York.

Edmonds, J., Scott, M.J., Roop, J.M. and MacCracken, C.N. (1999) *International Emissions Trading and Global Climate Change: Impacts on the Costs of Greenhouse Gas Mitigation.* Pew Center on Global Climate Change, Arlington, VA. [Online at www.pewclimate.org/projects/econ\emissions.cfm].

Edwards, S.F. (1986) Ethical preferences and the assessment of existence values: does the neoclassical model fit? *Northeastern Journal of Agricultural Economics* **15**, 145–59.

Edwards, S.F. (1992) Rethinking existence values. *Land Economics* **68**, 120–122.

Edwards-Jones, G., Davies, B. and Hussain, S. (2000) *Ecological Economics: An Introduction.* Blackwell, Oxford.

EEA (2000) *Environmental Taxes: Recent Developments in Tools for Integration.* Environmental Issue series, No 18, November. European Environmental Agency, Copenhagen. Available online from www.eea.eu.int.

EEA (2001) *Reporting on Environmental Measures: Are we Being Effective?* Environmental Issue series, No. 25, November. European Environmental Agency, Copenhagen. Available online from www.eea.eu.int.

Ehrenfeld, D. (1988) Why put a value on biodiversity? in E.O. Wilson (ed.) *Biodiversity*, pp. 212–216, National Academy of Science Press, Washington, DC.

Ehrlich, P.R. and Ehrlich, A.E. (1981) *Extinction: The Causes and Consequences of the Disappearance of Species.* Random House, New York.

Ehrlich, P.R. and Ehrlich, A.E. (1990) *The Population Explosion.* Hutchinson, London.

Ehrlich, P.R. and Ehrlich, A.E. (1992) The value of biodiversity. *Ambio* **21**, 219–226.

Ehrlich, P.R. and Holdren, J.P. (1971) Impact of population growth, *Science*, 171, 1212–1217.

Ekins, P. and Simon, S. (1998) Determining the sustainability gap – national accounting for environmental sustainability, in Vaze, P. (ed.) *UK Environmental Accounts 1998.* The Stationery Office, London.

Ellerman, D.A. (2001) *Considerations for Designing a Tradable Permit System to Control SO_2 Emissions in China.* MIT Center for Energy and Environmental Policy Research. Report 2001–009.

Ellis, G.M. and Fisher, A.C. (1987) Valuing the environment as input. *Journal of Environmental Management* **25**, 149–56.

El Serafy, S. (1989) The proper calculation of income from depletable natural resources, in Ahmad, Y.J., El Serafy, S. and Lutz, P. (eds) *Environmental Accounting for Sustainable Development.* World Bank, Washington, DC.

El-Swaify, S.A. and Yakowitz, D.S. (eds)(1998) *Multiple Objective Decision Making for Land, Water and Environmental Management.* Lewis, Boca Raton, FL.

ENDS Report. Various issues (e.g. ENDS Report 312, January 2001: Preparing for the Emissions trading Game) Environmental Data Services at www.ends.co.uk.

Energy Information Administration (1995) US Department of Energy. *International Energy Outlook, 1995.* Report No. DOE/EIA-0484 (95), US Printing Office, Washington, DC.

EPA (1988) *The Potential Effects of Global Climate Change on the United States.* Edited by Smith, J.B. and Tirpak, D.A., in 3 volumes. US Environmental Protection Agency, Washington, DC.

EPA (1989) *Policy Options for Stabilizing Global Climate.* Draft Report to US Congress. Edited by Lashof, J.A. and Tirpak, D.A., in 2 volumes. US Environmental Protection Agency, Washington, DC.

EPA (1991) *Final Regulating Impact Analysis of National Primary Drinking Water Regulations for Lead and Copper.* US Office of Drinking Water, US Environmental Protection Agency, Washington, DC.

EPA (1993) United States Environmental Protection Agency 33/50 Program: Third Progress Update, EPA Report No. 745-R-93-001. US Environmental Protection Agency, Washington, DC.

EPA (1999) *Economic Incentives for Pollution Control.* US Environmental Protection Agency, Washington, DC. Online at http://yosemite1.epa.gov/ee/epalib/incent.nsf

EPA (2001) *The United States Experience with Economic Incentives for Protecting the Environment.* US Environmental Protection Agency, Washington, DC. Online at www.epa.gov.

Esty, D.C. (1994) *Greening the GATT: Trade, Environment and the Future.* Institute for International Economics, Washington, DC.

Everest, D. (1988) *The Greenhouse Effect, Issues for Policy Makers.* Joint Energy Programme, Royal Institute of International Affairs, London.

ExternE (1995) *Externalities of Energy.* Vol. 4: Oil and Gas. EUR 16523 EN. The European Commission, Luxembourg.

Fankhauser, S., Smith, J.B. and Tol, R.S.J. (1999). Weathering climate change: some simple rules to guide adaptation decisions. *Ecological Economics* **30**(1), 67–78.

FAO (1992) *Marine Fisheries and the Law of the Sea: A Decade of Change.* The Food and Agriculture Organisation of the United Nations, Rome.

FAO (1994) *The State of Food and Agriculture.* The Food and Agriculture Organisation of the United Nations, Rome.

FAO (1995) *Forest Resource Assessment 1990: Global Synthesis.* The Food and Agriculture Organisation of the United Nations, Rome.

FAO (2001) *Global Forest Resources Assessment 2000,* The Food and Agriculture Organisation of the United Nations, Rome. Available in printed form as FAO Forestry Paper 140 and also available online by searching from the forestry section of the FAO web site at www.fao.org/forestry/index.jsp.

FAO (2002) *The State of World Fisheries and Aquaculture.* Available online at www.fao.org. The Food and Agriculture Organisation of the United Nations, Rome.

Farmer, M.C. and Randall, A. (1997) Policies for sustainability: lessons from an overlapping generations model. *Land Economics* **73**(4), 608–622.

Farrow, S. (1985) Testing the efficiency of extraction from a stock resource. *Journal of Political Economy* **93**(3), 452–487.

Faucheux, S. and Froger, G. (1995) Decision making under environmental uncertainty. *Ecological Economics* **15**, 29–42.

Faucheux, S., Pearce, D. and Proops, J. (eds) 1996. *Models of Sustainable Development.* Edward Elgar, Cheltenham.

Faucheux, S., Muir, E. and O'Connor, M. (1997) Neoclassical natural capital theory and 'weak' indicators for sustainability. *Land Economics* **73**, 528–52.

Faustmann, M. (1968) Calculation of the value which forest land and immature stands possess for forestry, in M. Gane (ed.) and W. Linnard (trans.) *Martin Faustmann and the Evolution of Discounted Cash Flow: Two Articles from the Original German of 1849.* Institute Paper No. 42, Commonwealth Forestry Institute, University of Oxford.

Feldman, S.L. and Raufer, R.K. (1982) *Emissions Trading and Acid Rain: Implementing a Market Approach to Pollution Control.* Rowman and Littlefield, Totowa, NJ.

Field, C.B. (2001) Sharing the garden, *Science* **294**, 21 December, 2490–2491.

Fisher, A.C. (1979) Measurements of natural resource scarcity, in Smith, V.K. (ed.) *Scarcity and Growth Reconsidered.* Johns Hopkins University Press, Baltimore, MD.

Fisher, A.C. (1981) *Resource and Environmental Economics.* Cambridge University Press, Cambridge.

Fisher, A.C. and Hanemann, W.M. (1986) Environmental damages and option values. *Natural Resources Modeling* **1**, 111–24.

Fisher, A.C. and Hanemann, M. (1987) Quasi option-value: some misconceptions dispelled. *Journal of Environmental Economics and Management* **14**, 183–190.

Fisher, A.C. and Krutilla, J.V. (1974) Valuing long run ecological consequences and irreversibilities. *Journal of Environmental Economics and Management* **1**, 96–108.

Fisher, A.C. and Peterson, F. (1976) The environment in economics: a survey. *Journal of Economic Literature* **14**, 1–33.

Fisher, A.C. and Rothkopf, M.H. (1989) Market failure and energy olicy. *Energy Policy* **17**(4), 397–406.

Fishkin, J.S. (1997) *Voice of the People.* Yale University Press, New Haven, CT.

Folke, C. (1999) Ecological principles and environmental economic analysis, in van den Bergh, J.C.J.M. (ed.) *Handbook of Environmental and Resource Economics.* Edward Elgar, Cheltenham.

Forrester, J.W. (1971) *World Dynamics.* Wright-Allen Press, Cambridge, MA.

Forster, B.A. (1975) Optimal pollution control with a non-constant exponential decay rate. *Journal of Environmental Economics and Management* **2**(1), 1–6.

Foster, J. (ed.) (1997) *Valuing Nature? Ethics, Economics and the Environment.* Routledge, London.

Freeman, A.M. (1979) *The Benefits of Environmental Improvement: Theory and Practice.* Johns Hopkins University Press, Baltimore, MD.

Freeman, A.M. (1985) Supply uncertainty, option price and option value. *Land Economics* **61**(2), 176–181.

Freeman, A.M. (1993) *The Measurement of Environmental and Resource Values.* Resources for the Future, Washington, DC.

Freeman, A.M. (1995) Hedonic pricing models, in Bromley, D.W. (ed.) *The Handbook of Environmental Economics.* Blackwell, Oxford.

French, H. (1990) Clearing the air, in Brown, L.R. (ed.) *State of the World, 1990.* Norton, New York.

Frey, B.S., Schneider, F. and Pommerehne, W.W. (1985) Economists' opinions on environmental policy instruments: analysis of a survey. *Journal of Environmental Economics and Management* **12**, 62–71.

Funtowicz, S.O. and Ravetz, J.R. (1991) A new scientific methodology for global environmental issues, in Costanza, R. (ed.) *Ecological Economics: The Science and Management of Sustainability.* Columbia University Press, New York.

Garcia, S.M. and de Leiva Moreno, I. (2001) *Global Overview of Marine Fisheries. Paper presented at the Reykjavik Conference on Responsible Fisheries in the Marine Ecosystem,* Reykjavik, Iceland, 1–4 October. Fisheries Department, United Nations Food and Agriculture Organisation.

Garcia, S.M. and Staples, D. (2000) Sustainability reference systems and indicators for responsible marine capture fisheries: a review of concepts and elements for a set of guidelines. In: Sustainability Indicators in Marine Capture Fisheries. Special Issue. *Marine Fisheries Research* **51**, 384–426.

Georgescu-Roegen, N. (1971) *The Entropy Law and the Economic Process.* Harvard University Press, Cambridge, MA.

Georgescu-Roegen, N. (1976) Energy and economic myths, in Georgescu-Roegen, N.E. *Energy and Economic Myths: Institutional and Analytical Economic Essays.* Pergamon, New York.

Georgescu-Roegen, N. (1979) Energy analysis and economic valuation. *Southern Economic Journal* **45**, 1023–1058.

Gintis, H. (2000) *Game Theory Evolving.* Princeton University Press, Princeton, NJ.

Glasser, H. (1999) Ethical perspectives and environmental policy analysis, in van den Bergh, J.C.J.M. (ed.) *Handbook of Environmental and Resource Economics.* Edward Elgar, Cheltenham.

Glasson, J., Therivel, R. and Chadwick, A. (1994) *Introduction to Environmental Impact Assessment. Principles and Procedures, Process, Practice and Prospects.* UCL Press, London.

Goldin, I. and Winters, L.A. (eds) (1995) *The Economics of Sustainable Development.* Cambridge University Press, Cambridge.

Goodland, R. (1999) The biophysical basis of environmental sustainability, in van den Bergh, J.C.J.M. (ed.) *Handbook of Environmental and Resource Economics.* Edward Elgar, Cheltenham.

Goodpaster, K.E. (1978) On being morally considerable. *Journal of Philosophy* **75**, 168–176.

Goodstein, E.S. (1992) Saturday effects in tanker oil spills. *Journal of Environmental Economics and Management* **23**, 276–288.

Goodstein, E.S. (1995) *Economics and the Environment.* Prentice-Hall, Englewood Cliffs, NJ.

Goodstein, E.S. (1999) *Economics and the Environment,* 2nd edition. Prentice-Hall, Englewood Cliffs, NJ.

Gordon, H.S. (1954) The economic theory of a common-property resource: the fishery. *Journal of Political Economy* **62**, 124–142.

Goulder, L.H. and Mathai, K. (2000) Optimal CO_2 abatement in the presence of induced technological change. *Journal of Environmental Economics and Management* **39**(1), 1–38.

Graham-Tomasi, T. (1995) Quasi-option value, in Bromley, D.W. (ed.) *The Handbook of Environmental Economics.* Blackwell, Oxford.

Gravelle, H. and Rees, R. (1981) *Microeconomics.* Longman, London.

Graves, P.E., Sexton, R.L., Lee, D.R. and Jackstadt, S. (1994) Alternative fishery management policies: monitoring costs versus catch limits. *Environmental and Resource Economics* **4**, 595–8.

Gray, L.C. (1914) Rent under the assumption of exhaustibility. *Quarterly Journal of Economics* **28**, 466–489.

Gray, R.H. (1994) Corporate reporting for sustainable development: accounting for sustainability in 2000 AD. *Environmental Values* **3**, 17–45.

Green, C. (2000) Potential scale-related problems in estimating the costs of CO_2 mitigation policies. *Climatic Change* **44**(3), 331–349.

Greenaway, D., Leybourne, S.J., Reed, G.V. and Whalley, J. (1993) *Applied General Equilibrium Modelling: Applications, Limitations and Future Development.* HMSO, London.

Greene, W.H. (1993) *Econometric Analysis,* 2nd edition. Macmillan, New York.

Gregory, R. and Wellman, K. (2001) Bringing stakeholder values into environmental policy choices:

a community-based estuary case study, *Ecological Economics,* **39**, 37–52.

Groombridge, B. (ed.) (1992) *Global Biodiversity. Status of the Earth's Living Resources.* Chapman and Hall, London.

Grossman, G.M. and Krueger, A.B. (1995) Economic growth and the environment, *Quarterly Journal of Economics* **112**, 353–377.

Grubb, M. (1989a) *The Greenhouse Effect: Negotiating Targets.* Royal Institute of International Affairs, London.

Grubb, M. (1989b) *On Coefficients for Determining Greenhouse Gas Emissions from Fossil Fuels.* IEA Expert Seminar on technologies to reduce greenhouse gas emissions, Paris, March (IEA/OECD).

Grubb, M. (2000) Economic dimensions of technological and global responses to the Kyoto Protocol. *Journal of Economic Studies,* **27**(1–2), 111–125.

Gulland, J.A. (1971) *The Fish Resources of the Ocean.* Fishing News Books, Oxford.

Hackett, S. (1995) Pollution-controlling innovation in oligopolistic industries: some comparisons between patent races and research joint ventures. *Journal of Environmental Economics and Management* **29**, 339–56.

Hahn, R.W. (1984) Market power and transferable property rights. *Quarterly Journal of Economics* **99**, 763–765.

Hahn, R.W. (1989) Economic prescriptions for environmental problems: how the patient followed the doctor's orders. *The Journal of Economic Perspectives* **3**, 95–114.

Hahn, R.W. (1995) Economic prescriptions for environmental problems: lessons from the United States and continental Europe, in Eckersley, R. (ed.) *Markets, the State and the Environment.* Macmillan, Melbourne.

Hahn, R.W. and Hester, G.L. (1989a) Where did all the markets go? An analysis of the EPA's emission trading program. *Yale Journal of Regulation* **6**, 109–53.

Hahn, R.W. and Hester, G.L. (1989b) Marketable permits: lessons for theory and practice. *Ecology Law Quarterly* **16**, 361–406.

Halkos, G. and Hutton, J. (1993) *Acid Rain Games in Europe.* Discussion Papers in Economics No. 93/12, University of York, UK.

Hall, C., Cleveland, C. and Kaufmann, R. (1986) *The Ecology of the Economic Process: Energy and Resource Quality.* Wiley-Interscience, New York.

Hall, D.C. and Hall, J.V. (1984) Concepts and measures of natural resource scarcity with a summary of recent trends. *Journal of Environmental Economics and Management* **11**, 363–379.

Hall, D.C. and Howarth, R.B. (2001) *The Long-Term Economics of Climate Change: Beyond a Doubling of Greenhouse Gas Concentrations.* Advances in the Economics of Environmental Resources. JAI Press Inc./ Elsevier Science, Amsterdam / New York.

Hall, D.C. et al. (1989) Organic food and sustainable agriculture. *Contemporary Policy Issues,* **7**, October.

Halvorsen, R. and Smith, T.R. (1991) A test of the theory of exhaustible resources. *Quarterly Journal of Economics* **106**(1), 123–140.

Hamilton, C. (1997) *The Genuine Progress Indicator: A New Index of Changes in Well-being in Australia*. The Australia Institute, Canberra.

Hamilton, K. (1994) Green adjustments to GDP. *Resources Policy* **20**, 155–168.

Hamilton, K. (2000) *Genuine Saving as a Sustainability Indicator*. Environmental Economics Series Paper No. 77, World Bank, Washington, DC.

Hamilton, K., Pearce, D.W., Atkinson, G., Gomez-Lobo, A. and Young, C. (1994) *The Policy Implications of Natural Resource and Environmental Accounting*. CSERGE Working Paper GEC 94-18. University College, London.

Hammack, J. and Brown, G. (1974) *Waterfowl and Wetlands: Towards Bioeconomic Analysis*. Johns Hopkins University Press, Baltimore, MD.

Hanemann, M. (1991) Willingness to pay and willingness to accept: how much can they differ? *American Economic Review* **81**(3), 635–647.

Hanley, N. (1988) Using contingent valuation to value environmental improvements. *Applied Economics* **20**, 541–549.

Hanley, N. (1989a) Valuing rural recreation benefits: an empirical comparison of two approaches, *Journal of Agricultural Economics* **40**, 361–74.

Hanley, N. (1989b) *Problems in Valuing Environmental Improvements from Agricultural Policy Changes: The Case of Nitrate Pollution*. Discussion Paper No. 89/1, Economics Department, University of Stirling.

Hanley, N. and Spash, C. (1993) *Cost–Benefit Analysis and the Environment*. Edward Elgar, Aldershot.

Hannesson, R. (1993) *Economics of Fisheries*. Columbia University Press, New York.

Hansen, J. (1990) *Greenhouse and Developing Countries*. Paper presented at the symposium 'Environment and Economics in the Developing Countries', Association of the Bar of the City of New York, 23 May.

Hansen, J. *et al.* (1988) Global climate changes as forecast by Goddard Institute for Space Studies three dimensional model. *Journal of Geophysical Research* **93**(D8), 9341–9364.

Harberger, A.C. (1971) Three basic postulates for applied welfare economics: an interpretative essay. *Journal of Economic Literature* **9**, 785–797.

Hardin, G. (1986) The tragedy of the commons. *Science* **162**, 1243–1248.

Hardin, G. (1993) *Living within Limits: Ecology, Economics and Population Taboos*. Oxford University Press, New York.

Hardin, G. and Baden, J. (1977) *Managing the Commons*. W.H. Freeman, San Francisco.

Harris, C.C. and Brown, G. (1992) Gain, loss and personal responsibility: the role of motivation in resource valuation decision-making. *Ecological Economics* **5**, 73–92.

Harris, D.P. (1993) Mineral resource stocks and information. Chapter 21 in Kneese, A.V. and Sweeney, J.L. (eds) *Handbook of Natural Resource and Energy Economics. Volume 3*, Elsevier Science Publishers, Amsterdam.

Harris, M. (1998) *Lament for an Ocean*. McClelland & Stewart, Toronto.

Harris, M. and Ross, E.B. (1987) *Death, Sex and Fertility: Population Regulation in Preindustrial and Developing Societies*. Columbia University Press, New York.

Harrison, G.W. (1992) Valuing public goods with the contingent valuation method: a critique of Kahneman and Knetsch. *Journal of Environmental Economics and Management* **23**, 248–57.

Harrod, R.F. (1948) *Towards a Dynamic Economy*. St Martins Press, London.

Hartman, R. (1976) The harvesting decision when a standing forest has value. *Economic Inquiry* **14**, 52–58.

Hartwick, J.M. (1977) Intergenerational equity and the investing of rents from exhaustible resources. *American Economic Review* **67**, 972–974.

Hartwick, J.M. (1978) Substitution among exhaustible resources and intergenerational equity. *Review of Economic Studies* **45**, 347–354.

Hartwick, J.M. (1990) Natural resource accounting and economic depreciation. *Journal of Public Economics* **43**, 291–304.

Hartwick, J.M. (1992) Deforestation and national accounting. *Environmental and Resource Economics* **2**, 513–521.

Hartwick, J.M. and Hageman, A.P. (1993) Economic depreciation of mineral stocks and the contribution of El Serafy, in Lutz, E. (ed.) *Toward Improved Accounting for the Environment: An UNSTAT–World Bank Symposium*. World Bank, Washington, DC.

Hartwick, J.M. and Olewiler, N.D. (1986) *The Economics of Natural Resource Use*. Harper and Row, New York.

Hartwick, J.M. and Olewiler, N.D. (1998) *The Economics of Natural Resource Use*, 2nd edition. Harper and Row, New York.

Harvey, A.C. (1989) *Forecasting, Structural Time-Series Models and the Kalman Filter*. Cambridge University Press, Cambridge.

Hausman, J.A. (ed.) (1993) *Contingent Valuation: A Critical Assessment*. Elsevier, New York.

Hawksworth, D.L. (ed.) (1995) *Biodiversity: Measurement and Estimation*. Chapman and Hall, London.

Heal, G.M. (1981) Economics and resources, in Butlin, R. (ed.) *Economics of the Environment and Natural Resource Policy*. Westview Press, Boulder, CO.

Heijman, W. (1990) *Natural Resource Depletion and Market Forms*. Wageningen Economic Papers, Wageningen Agricultural University, The Netherlands.

Heilbronner, R.L. (1991) *The Worldly Philosophers: The Lives, Times and Ideas of the Great Economic Thinkers*. Penguin, London.

Helm, D. (1993) The assessment: reforming environmental regulation in the UK. *Oxford Review of Economic Policy* **9**(4), 1–13.

Helm, D. (1998) The assessment: environmental policy – objectives, instruments and institutions. *Oxford Review of Economic Policy* **14**(4), 1–19.

Henderson, J.V. and Tugwell, M. (1979) Exploitation of the lobster fishery: some empirical results. *Journal of Environmental Economics and Management* **6**, 287–96.

Henry, C. (1974) Investment decisions under uncertainty: the 'irreversibility effect'. *American Economic Review* **64**, 1006–1012.

Herfindahl, O.C. and Kneese, A.V. (1974) *Economic Theory of Natural Resources*. C.E. Merrill, Columbus, OH.

Heyes, A.G. (1998) Making things stick: enforcement and compliance. *Oxford Review of Economic Policy* **14**(4), 50–63.

Heywood, V.H. (1995) *Global Biodiversity Assessment*. Cambridge University Press, for UNEP, Cambridge.

Hicks, J.R. (1939) *Value and Capital*. Oxford University Press, Oxford.

Hicks, J.R. (1941) The rehabilitation of consumers' surplus. *Review of Economic Studies* **8**, February, 108–116.

Hilborn, R., Walters, C.J. and Ludwig, D. (1995) Sustainable exploitation of renewable resources. *Annual Review of Ecological Systems* **26**, 45–67.

Hirsch, F. (1977) *Social Limits to Growth*. Routledge & Kegan Paul, London.

Hirschborn, J. (1991) Technological potential in pollution prevention. *Pollution Prevention* **1**(2), 21–24.

Hirshleifer, J. (1980) *Price Theory and Applications*, 2nd edition. Prentice-Hall, Englewood Cliffs, NJ.

Hoel, M. (1989) *Global Environmental Problems: The Effects of Unilateral Action Taken by One Country*. Working Paper No. 11, Department of Economics, University of Oslo.

Hogan, W.H. and Manne, A.S. (1979) Energy–economy interactions: the fable of the elephant and the rabbit? in Pindyck, R.S. (ed.) *Advances in the Economics of Energy and Resources*. Vol. 1. JAI Press, Greenwich, CT.

Hohmeyer, O. (1988) *Social Costs of Energy Consumption*. Springer, Heidelberg.

Hohmeyer, O. and Rennings, K. (eds) (1999) *Man-made Climate Change: Economic Aspects and Policy Options*. Proceedings of an International Conference held at Mannheim, Germany, March 6–7, 1997. Physica-Verlag, Heidelberg, Germany.

Holling, C.S. (1973) Resilience and stability of ecological systems. *Annual Review of Ecological Systems* **4**, 1–24.

Holling, C.S. (1986) The resilience of terrestrial ecosystems: local surprise and global change, in Clark, W.C. and Munn, R.E. (eds) *Sustainable Development in the Biosphere*. Cambridge University Press, Cambridge.

Hotelling, H. (1931) The economics of exhaustible resources. *Journal of Political Economy* **39**, 137–175.

Houghton, J.T. (1997) *Global Warming: The Complete Briefing*, 2nd edition. Cambridge University Press, Cambridge.

Houghton, J.T., Jenkins, G.J. and Ephrams, J.J. (1990) *Climate Change: The IPCC Scientific Assessment*. Cambridge University Press, Cambridge.

Houghton, J.T., Callander, B.A. and Varney, S.K. (eds) (1992) *Climate Change 1992: The Supplementary Report to the IPCC Scientific Assessment*. Cambridge University Press, Cambridge.

Houghton, J.T., Meira Filho, L.G., Callander, B.A., Harris, N., Karenberg, A. and Maskell, K. (1996) *Climate Change 1995: The Science of Climate Change*. Cambridge University Press, for the IPCC, Cambridge.

Hufschmidt, M.M., James, D.E., Meister, A.D., Bower, B.T. and Dixon, J.A. (1983) *Environment, Natural Systems and Development: An Economic Valuation Guide*. Johns Hopkins University Press, Baltimore, MD.

Hume, D. (1739) A Treatise on Human Nature, in *Hume's Moral and Political Philosophy*. 1968, Hafner, New York.

Hume, D. (1751) An Enquiry Concerning the Principle of Morals, in *Hume s Moral and Political Philosophy*, 1968, Hafner, New York.

Hunt, W.M. (1980) Are 'mere things' morally considerable? *Environmental Ethics* **2**(1).

Huppert, D.H. (1990) *Managing Alaska's Groundfish Fisheries: History and Prospects*. University of Washington Institute for Marine Resources Working Paper, May.

IEA (1990) *Energy and the Environment: Policy Overview*. International Energy Agency, Organisation for Economic Co-operation and Development, Paris.

IEA (1995) *World Energy Outlook*. International Energy Agency, Organisation for Economic Co-operation and Development, Paris.

Ingham, A. and Ulph, A. (1990) *Market-based Instruments for Reducing CO_2 Emissions – The Case of UK Manufacturing*. Discussion Paper in Economics and Econometrics, No. 9004, University of Southampton, UK, November.

International Union for Conservation of Nature and Natural Resources (1980) *World Conservation Strategy*. IUCN/UNEP/WWF, Gland, Switzerland.

IPCC (1990) *Second Draft Reports of the Intergovernmental Panel On Climate Change (Climate, Impact and Policy Groups)*, April 1990. The report of the first group (Climate) has been published as: Houghton, R., Jenkins, G.J., and Ephraums, E. (1990) *Climate Change: the IPCC Scientific Assessment*. Cambridge University Press, Cambridge.

IPCC (1992) (Intergovernmental Panel on Climate Change, United Nations). *1992 Supplement: Scientific Assessment of Climate Change*. World Meteorological Organisation/United Nations Environment Programme, Geneva.

IPCC (1994) (Intergovernmental Panel on Climate Change, United Nations). *Radiative Forcing of Climate Change: The 1994 Report of the Scientific Assessment Working Group of IPCC*. World Meteorological Organisation/United Nations Environment Programme, Geneva, 1994.

IPCC (1995a) (Intergovernmental Panel on Climate Change, United Nations). *IPCC Synthesis Report, July 29, 1995 draft*. World Meteorological Organisation/United Nations Environment Programme, Geneva, 1995.

IPCC (1995b) (Intergovernmental Panel on Climate Change, United Nations). *A Review of Mitigation Cost Studies*, in IPCC Synthesis Report. WMO/UN, Geneva, chapter 9

IPCC (1995c) (Intergovernmental Panel on Climate Change, United Nations). *The Social Costs of Climate Change: Greenhouse Damage and the Benefits of Control*. Chapter 6 in Second Assessment Report, Working Group III, April 1995 Draft. World Meteorological Organisation/United Nations Environment Programme, Geneva, 1995.

IPCC(1) (2001) *Climate Change 2001: The Scientific Basis. Third Assessment Report of Working Group I of the IPCC*. Published by Cambridge University Press, Cambridge for the World Meteorological Organization – IPCC Secretariat, Geneva.

IPCC(2) (2001) *Climate Change 2001: Impacts, Adaptation and Vulnerability. Third Assessment Report of Working Group II of the IPCC*. Cambridge University Press, Cambridge.

IPCC(3) (2001) *Climate Change 2001: Mitigation. Third Assessment Report of Working Group III of the IPCC*. Cambridge University Press, Cambridge.

Iudicello, S., Weber, M. and Wieland, R. (1999) *Fish, Markets, and Fishermen: The Economics of Overfishing*. Island Press, Washington DC.

Jackson, A.R.W. and Jackson, J.M. (2000) *Environmental Science*, 2nd edition. Pearson, Harlow.

Jackson, T. and Marks, N. (1994) *Measuring Sustainable Development – A Pilot Index: 1950–1990*. Stockholm Environment Institute and New Economic Foundation, London & Stockholm.

Jacobs, M. (1997) Environmental valuation, deliberative democracy and public decision-making institutions, in Foster, J. (ed.) *Valuing Nature? Ethics, Economics and the Environment*. Routledge, London.

Jaffe, A.B. and Stavins, R.N. (1994) The energy-efficiency gap: What does it mean? *Energy Policy* **22**(1), 504–10.

Jaffe, A.B., Peterson, S.R., Portuey, P.R. and Stavins R. (1995) Environmental regulation and the competitiveness of US manufacturing, *Journal of Economic Literature* **33**, 132–163.

Janssen, R. (1992) *Multiobjective Decision Support for Environmental Management*. Kluwer Academic, Dordrecht.

Janssen, R. and Munda, G. (1999) Multi-criteria methods for quantitative, qualitative and fuzzy evaluation problems, in van den Bergh, J.C.J.M. (ed.) *Handbook of Environmental and Resource Economics*. Edward Elgar, Cheltenham.

Jansson, A.M., Hammer, M., Folke, C. and Costanza, R. (eds) (1994) *Investing in Natural Capital: The Ecological Economics Approach to Sustainability*. Island Press, Washington, DC.

Jeffries, M.J. (1997) *Biodiversity and Conservation*. Routledge, London.

Jevons, W.S. (1865) *The Coal Question: An Inquiry Concerning the Progress of the Nation and the Probable Exhaustion of our Coal Mines*. Flux, A.W. (ed.) (rev. 3rd edition 1965). A.M. Kelly, New York.

Jevons, W.S. (1871) *The Theory of Political Economy*. Macmillan, London.

Johansson, P-O. (1987) *The Economic Theory and Measurement of Environmental Benefits*. Cambridge University Press, Cambridge.

Johansson, P. and Löfgren, K. (1985) *The Economics of Forestry and Natural Resources*. Basil Blackwell, Oxford.

Johnson, D.G. (1984) In Simon, J.L. and Kahn, H., *The Resourceful Earth*, Basil Blackwell, Oxford.

Johnson, M.G.M. (1989) *Leading Issues in Economic Development*, 5th edition, Oxford University Press, New York.

Johnson, R.W. and Brown, G.M. Jnr. (1976) *Cleaning up Europe's Waters: Economics, Management and Policy*. Praeger, New York.

Jorgensen, D. and Griliches, Z. (1967) The explanation of productivity change. *Review of Economics and Statistics* **34**, 250–282.

Jorgensen, D.W. and Wilcoxen, P.J. (1990a) *The Costs of Controlling US Carbon Dioxide Emissions*. Paper presented at Workshop on Economic/Energy/Environmental Modelling for Climate Policy Analysis, Washington, DC, USA, 22–23 October.

Jorgensen, D.W. and Wilcoxen, P.J. (1990b) *Global Change, Energy Prices, and US Economic Growth*. Paper presented for the Energy Pricing Hearing, US Department of Energy, Washington, DC, USA, 20 July.

Jorgensen, D.W. and Wilcoxen, P.J. (1990c) Environmental regulation and US economic growth. *RAND Journal of Economics* **21**(2), 314–341.

Joskow, P.L. and Schmalensee, R. (2000) The political economy of market-based environmental policy: the US acid rain program, pp. 603–45, in Stavins, R.N. (ed.) *Economics of the Environment: Selected Readings*, 4th edition. W.W. Norton, New York.

Just, R.E., Hueth, D.L. and Schnitz, A. (1982) *Applied Welfare Economics and Public Policy*. Prentice-Hall, Englewood Cliffs, NJ.

Kahneman, D. and Knetsch, J.L. (1992a) Valuing public goods: the purchase of moral satisfaction. *Journal of Environmental Economics and Management* **22**, 57–70.

Kahneman, D. and Knetsch, J.L. (1992b) Contingent valuation and the value of public goods: reply. *Journal of Environmental Economics and Management* **22**, 90–94.

Kamien, M.I. and Schwartz, N.L. (1991) *The Calculus of Variations and Optimal Control in Economics and Management*, 2nd edition. Elsevier, New York.

Kant, I. *Groundwork of the Metaphysic of Morals*. Section II, Various translations and editions.

Keepin, B and Kats, G. (1988) Greenhouse warming: comparative analysis of nuclear and efficiency abatement strategies *Energy Policy* **16**(6), 538–561.

Kemp, D.D. (1990) *Global Environmental Issues: A Climatological Approach*. Routledge, London.

Kemp, M.A. and Maxwell, C. (1993) Exploring a budget context for contingent valuation estimates in Hausman, J.A. (ed.) *Contingent Valuation: A Critical Assessment*. North-Holland Press, Amsterdam, pp. 218–265.

Keynes, J.M. (1931) Economic possibilities for our grandchildren, in *Essays in Persuasion*. Macmillan, London.

Keynes, J.M. (1936) *The General Theory of Employment, Interest and Money*. Macmillan, London.

Klassen, G.A.J. and Opschoor, J.B. (1991) Economics of sustainability or the sustainability of economics: different paradigms. *Ecological Economics* **4**, 93–115.

Kling, C.L. and Crooker, J.R. (1999) Recreation demand models for environmental valuation, in van den Bergh, J.C.J.M. (ed.) *Handbook of Environmental and Resource Economics.* Edward Elgar, Cheltenham.

Kneese, A.V. (1984) *Measuring the Benefits of Clean Air and Water.* Resources for the Future, Washington, DC.

Kneese, A.V. and Bower, B.T. (1968) *Managing Water Quality: economics technology and institutions.* Johns Hopkins University Press, Baltimore, MD.

Kneese, A.V. and Schulze, W.D. (1985) Ethics and environmental economics, Chapter 5 in Kneese, A.V. and Sweeney, J.L. (eds) *Handbook of Natural Resource and Energy Economics*, Vol. 1. Elsevier Science Publishers, Amsterdam.

Kneese, A.V. and Sweeney, J.L. (1985a) *Handbook of Natural Resource and Energy Economics.* Vol. 1. Elsevier Science Publishers, Amsterdam.

Kneese, A.V. and Sweeney, J.L. (1985b) *Handbook of Natural Resource and Energy Economics.* Vol. 2. Elsevier Science Publishers, Amsterdam.

Kneese, A.V. and Sweeney, J.L. (1993) *Handbook of Natural Resource and Energy Economics.* Vol. 3. Elsevier Science Publishers, Amsterdam.

Kneese, A.V., Ayres, R.V. and D'Arge, R.C. (1970) *Economics and the Environment: A Materials Balance Approach.* Johns Hopkins University Press, Baltimore, MD.

Knetsch, J. (1990) Environmental policy implications of disparities between willingness to pay and compensation demanded. *Journal of Environmental Economics and Management* **18**, 227–237.

Knight, F.H. (1921) *Risk, Uncertainty and Profit.* Houghton Mifflin, New York.

Köhn, J., Gowdy, J., Hinterberger, F. and van der Straaten, J. (eds) (1999) *Sustainability in Question: The Search for a Conceptual Framework.* Edward Elgar, Cheltenham.

Kolstad, C.D. (1987) Uniformity versus differentiation in regulating externalities. *Journal of Environmental Economics and Management* **14**, 386–399.

Kolstad, C.D. (1996) Learning and stock effects in environmental regulation: the case of greenhouse gas emissions. *Journal of Environmental Economics and Management* **31**, 1–18.

Kolstad, C.D. (2000) *Environmental Economics.* Oxford University Press, New York.

Kolstad, C.D. and Krautkraemer, J.A. (1993) Natural resource use and the environment, in Kneese, A.V. and Sweeney, J.L. (eds) *Handbook of Natural Resource and Energy Economics*, Vol. 3. Elsevier Science Publishers, Amsterdam.

Kosmo, M. (1989) *Money to Burn? The High Price of Energy Subsidies.* World Resources Institute, Washington, DC.

Kramer, R.A. and Mercer, D.E. (1997) Valuing a global environmental good: US resident's willingness to pay to protect tropical rain forests. *Land Economics* **73**(2), 196–210.

Krebs, C.J. (1972) *Ecology: The Experimental Analysis of Distribution and Abundance.* Harper and Row, New York.

Krebs, C.J. (1985) *Ecology.* Harper and Row, New York.

Krebs, C.J. (2001) *Ecology: The Experimental Analysis of Distribution and Abundance*, 5th edition. Harper and Row, New York.

Kreps, D.M. (1990) *A Course in Microeconomic Theory.* Harvester Wheatsheaf, New York.

Kriström, B. (1999) Contingent valuation, in van den Bergh, J.C.J.M. (ed.) *Handbook of Environmental and Resource Economics.* Edward Elgar, Cheltenham.

Krupnick, A.J. (1986) Costs of alternative policies for the control of nitrogen dioxide in Baltimore, Maryland. *Journal of Environmental Economics and Management* **13**, 189–197.

Krutilla, J.V. (1967) Conservation reconsidered. *American Economic Review* **54**(4), 777–786.

Krutilla, J.V. and Fisher, A.C. (1975) *The Economics of Natural Environments: Studies in the Valuation of Commodity and Amenity Resources.* The Johns Hopkins University Press, Baltimore, MD.

Kuznets, S. (1955) Economic growth and income inequality. *American Economic Review* **49**, 1–28.

Kwerel, E. (1977) To tell the truth: imperfect information and optimal pollution control. *Review of Economic Studies* **44**(3), 595–601.

Laffont, J-J. (1994): Regulation of pollution with asymmetric information, pp. 39–66 in Dosi, C. and T. Tomasi (eds) *Nonpoint Source Pollution Regulation: Issues and Analysis*, Kluwer Academic, Dordrecht.

Laffont, J-J. and Tirole, J. (1993) *A Theory of Incentives in Procurement and Regulation.* MIT Press, Cambridge, MA.

Laffont, J-J. and Tirole, J. (1996) Pollution permits and environmental innovation. *Journal of Public Economics* **62**, 127–40.

Lancaster, K. (1966) A new approach to consumer theory. *Journal of Political Economy* **74**, 132–157.

Lande, R., Engen, S. and Saether, B. (1994) Optimal harvesting, economic discounting and extinction risk in fluctuating populations. *Nature* **372**, 88–90.

Laplante, B. and Rilstone, P. (1996) Environmental inspections and emissions of the pulp and paper industry in Quebec. *Journal of Environmental Economics and Management* **31**, 19–36.

Lashof, D. and Ahuja, D.R. (1990) Relative contributions of greenhouse gas emissions to global warming. *Nature* **334**, 529–531.

Layard, P.R.G. and Glaister, S. (eds) (1994) *Cost–Benefit Analysis*, 2nd edition. Cambridge University Press, Cambridge.

Layard, P.R.G. and Walters, A.A. (1978) *Microeconomic Theory.* McGraw-Hill, Maidenhead.

Leach, G. (1975) *Energy and Food Production.* International Institute for Environment and Development, London.

Lecomber, R. (1975) *Economic Growth versus the Environment.* Macmillan, London.

Lederberg, J., Shope, R.E. and Oaks, S.C. Jnr. (1992) *Emerging Infections: Microbial Threats to Health in the United States.* National Academy Press, Washington, DC.

Lee, N. and Kirkpatrick, C. (2000) *Sustainable Development and Integrated Appraisal in a Developing World.* Edward Elgar, Cheltenham.

Lee, W.R. (1979) *European Demography and Economic Growth.* St. Martins Press, New York.

Lele, S.M. (1991) Sustainable development: a critical view. *World Development* **19**, 607–621.

Leopold, A. (1970) A Sand County Almanac, in *Essays on Conservation*, Round River, New York, first published 1949.

Leontief, W. (1966) *Input–Output Economics.* Oxford University Press, Oxford.

Leontief, W. (1970a) Environmental repercussions and the economic structure: an input–output approach. *Review of Economics and Statistics* **52**, 262–277.

Leontief, W. (1970b) The dynamic inverse, in Carter, A.P. and Brody, A. (eds) *Contributions to Input–Output Analysis.* North-Holland, Amsterdam.

Leontief, W. and Ford, D. (1972) Air pollution and economic structure: empirical results of input output computations, in Brody, A. and Carter, A. (eds) *Input Output Techniques.* North-Holland, Amsterdam.

Leontief, W. *et al.* (1977) *The Future of the World Economy.* Oxford University Press, New York.

Lind, R. (ed.) (1982) *Discounting for Time and Risk in Energy Policy.* Johns Hopkins University Press, Baltimore, MD.

Locke, J. (1960) *Second Treatise on Civil Government.* Cambridge University Press, New York (Laslett Edition).

Lomborg, B. (2001) *The Skeptical Environmentalist: Measuring the Real State of the World.* Cambridge University Press, Cambridge.

Lotka, A.J. (1925) *Elements of Physical Biology.* Williams and Wilkins, Baltimore, MD.

Lovelock, J. (1989) *The Ages of Gaia: A Biography of Our Living Earth.* Oxford University Press, Oxford.

Lovins, L.H., Hawken, P. and Lovins, A.B. (2000) *Natural Capital: The Next Industrial Revolution.* Earthscan, London.

Ludwig, D., Hilborn, R. and Walters, C. (1993) Uncertainty, resource exploitation and conservation: lessons from history. *Science* **260**, 17–36.

Ludwig, D., Walker, B. and Holling, C.S. (1997) Sustainability, stability and resilience. *Conservation Ecology* [online] 1(1): 7. URL www.consecol.org/vol1/iss1/art7.

Lutz, E. (ed.) (1993) *Toward Improved Accounting for the Environment: An UNSTAT–World Bank Symposium.* World Bank, Washington, DC.

Maass, A., Hufschmidt, M., Dorfman, R., Thomas, H.A., Marglin, S. and Fair, G. (1962) *Design of Water Resource Systems.* Harvard University Press, Cambridge, MA.

MacArthur, R. and Wilson, E.O. (1967) *The Theory of Island Biogeography.* Princeton University Press, Princeton, NJ.

McCormick, J. (1989) *The Global Environmental Movement: Reclaiming Paradise.* Bellhaven, London.

MacGillivray, A. (1994) *Environmental Measures.* Environmental Challenge Group, London.

McInerney, J. (1976) The simple analytics of natural resource economics. *Journal of Agricultural Economics* **27**, 31–52.

McKinsey (1989) *Protecting the Global Environment.* McKinsey and Company, Report to Ministerial Conference on Atmospheric Pollution and Climatic Change, Noordwijk. The Netherlands, November.

McNeely, J.A. (1988) *Economics and Biological Diversity.* IUCN, Gland.

McNicoll, I.H. and Blackmore, D. (1993) *A Pilot Study on the Construction of a Scottish Environmental Input–Output System.* Report to Scottish Enterprise, Department of Economics, University of Strathclyde, Glasgow.

Maddison, A. (1995) *Monitoring the World Economy.* OECD, Paris.

Magat, W.A., Krupnik, A.J. and Harrington, W. (1986) *Rules in the Making: A Statistical Analysis of Regulatory Agency Behavior.* Resources for the Future, Washington, DC.

Mäler, K-G. (1974) *Environmental Economics: A Theoretical Inquiry.* John Hopkins University Press, Baltimore, MD.

Mäler, K.G. (1985) Welfare economics and the environment. Chapter 1 in Vol. 1, Kneese, A.V. and Sweeney, J.L. (eds) *Handbook of Natural Resource and Energy Economics.* Elsevier Science Publishers, Amsterdam.

Mäler, K-G. (1990) International environmental problems. *Oxford Review of Economic Policy* **6**(1), 80–107.

Mäler, K-G. (1991) National accounting and environmental resources. *Environmental and Resource Economics* **1**, 1–15

Malthus, T.R. (1798) *An Essay on the Principle of Population as it Affects the Future Improvement of Society.* Ward Lock, London. (Also available edited by Flew, A. 1970, Pelican.)

Manne, A.S. (1979) ETA Macro, in R.S. Pindyck (ed.) *Advances in the Economics of Energy and Resources,* Vol. 2. JAI Press, Greenwich, CT.

Manne, A.S. and Richels, R.G. (1989) *CO$_2$ Emission Limits: An Economic Analysis for the USA.* Mimeo, Stanford University and Electric Power Research Institute, Paolo Alto, CA, November. (Also Published in *The Energy Journal* **11**(2), 51–74).

Manne, A.S. and Richels, R.G. (1990) CO$_2$ emission limits: a global economic cost analysis. Paper presented at the workshop on Energy/CO$_2$ Data, International Institute for Applied System Analysis, Laxenburg, Austria, 22–23 January. Published in *The Energy Journal* (1991), **12**(1).

Marglin, S. (1963) The social rate of discount and the optimal rate of investment. *Quarterly Journal of Economics* **77**, 95–111.

Marin, A. and Psacharopoulos, G. (1982) The reward for risk in the labour market: evidence from the United Kingdom and a reconciliation with other studies. *Journal of Political Economy* **90**.

Markandya, A. (1992) The value of the environment: a state of the art survey, in Markandya, A. and Richardson, J. (eds) *The Earthscan Reader in Environmental Economics.* Earthscan, London.

Markandya, A. and Richardson, J. (eds) (1992) *The Earthscan Reader ia Environmental Economics.* Earthscan, London.

Marshall, A. (1890) *Principles of Economics.* Macmillan, London.

Martinez-Alier, J. (1987) *Ecological Economics.* Basil Blackwell, Oxford.

Marx, K. (1960 edition) *Capital* (in 3 volumes). Foreign Languages Publishing House, Moscow.

Maxwell, J., Lyon, T. and Hackett, S. (1996) *Self-regulation and Social Welfare: The Political Economy of Corporate Environmentalism.* Working Paper. Humboldt State University, Arcata, CA.

May, R.M. (1988) How many species are there on earth? *Science* **241**, 1441–1449.

May, R.M. (1994) The economics of extinction. *Nature* **372**, 42–43.

Meadows, D.H., Meadows, D.L., Randers, J. and Behrens, W.W. (1972) *The Limits to Growth: A Report for The Club of Rome's project on the Predicament of Mankind.* Earth Island, Universe Books, New York. (Also known as Club of Rome Report.)

Meadows, D.H., Meadows, D.L. and Randers, J. (1992) *Beyond the Limits: Global Collapse or a Sustainable Future.* Earthscan, London.

Mendelsohn, R. (ed.) (2001) *Global Warming and the American Economy. A Regional Assessment of Climate Change Impacts.* New Horizons in Environmental Economics Series. Edward Elgar, Cheltenham / Northampton, MA.

Menger, K. (1950) *Principles of Economics.* Free Press, New York.

Mikesell, R. (1977) *The Rate of Discount for Evaluating Public Projects.* American Enterprise for Public Policy Research, Washington, DC.

Mill, J.S. (1857) *Principles of Political Economy.* J.W. Parker and Son. (6th edition, 1865, Augustus M. Kelly, New York.)

Mill, J.S. (1863) *Utilitarianism.* Fontana Library edition, Collins, London.

Miller, M.H. and Upton, C.W. (1985) A test of the Hotelling valuation principle. *Journal of Political Economy* **93**(1), 1–25.

Miller, R.E. and Blair P.D. (1985) *Input–Output Analysis; Foundations and Extensions.* Prentice-Hall, Englewood Cliffs, NJ.

Milliman, M. and Prince R. (1989) Firm incentives to promote technological change in pollution control. *Journal of Environmental Economics and Management* **17**, 247–65.

Millock, K.D., Sunding, D. and Zilberman, D. (1997) *An Information-revealing Incentive Mechanism for Nonpoint Source Pollution.* Manuscript, Department of Agricultural and Resource Economics, University of California, Berkeley, CA.

Mills, E.S. (1978) *The Economics of Environmental Quality.* Norton, New York.

Mintzer, I.M. (1987) *A Matter of Degrees: The Potential for Controlling the Greenhouse Effect.* Research Report 5, World Resources Institute, Washington, DC.

Mishan, E.J. (1967) *The Costs of Economic Growth.* Staples Press, London.

Mishan, E.J. (1977) *The Economic Growth Debate: An Assessment.* George Allen and Unwin, London.

Mitchell, R. and Carson, R. (1984) *A Contingent Valuation Estimate of National Freshwater Benefits.* Technical Report to the United States Environmental Protection Agency. Resources for the Future, Washington, DC.

Mitchell, R. and Carson, R. (1989) *Using Surveys to Value Public Goods: The Contingent Valuation Method.* Resources for the Future, Washington, DC.

Montero, J-P., Sánchez, J.M. and Katz, R. (2000) *A Market-based Environmental Policy Experiment in Chile.* MIT Center for Energy and Environmental Policy Research. Report 2000-005.

Montgomery, C.A. and Adams, D.M. (1995) Optimal timber management policies, in Bromley, D.W. (ed.) *The Handbook of Environmental Economics.* Blackwell, Oxford.

Montgomery, C.A., Pollak, R.A., Freemark, K. and White, D. (1999) Pricing Biodiversity. *Journal of Environmental Economics and Management* **38**, 1–19.

Montgomery, D.W. (1972) Markets in licences and efficient pollution control programs. *Journal of Economic Theory* **5**. 395–418.

Munda, G., Nijkamp, P. and Rietveld, P. (1994) Qualitative multicriteria evaluation for environmental management. *Ecological Economics* **10**, 97–112.

Munro, G. (1981) The economics of fishing: an introduction, in Butlin, J.A. (ed.) *The Economics of Environmental and Natural Resources Policy.* Westfield Press, Boulder, CO.

Munro, G. (1982) Fisheries, extended jurisdiction and the economics of common property resources. *The Canadian Journal of Economics* **15**, 405–425.

Myers, N. (1979) *The Sinking Ark.* Pergamon, New York.

Naess, A. (1972) The shallow and the deep, long-range ecology movement. A summary. *Inquiry* **16**, 95–100.

NAPAP (1990) *National Acid Precipitation Assessment Program. 1989 Annual Report to the President and Congress.* Washington, DC.

Neher, P.A. (1990) *Natural Resource Economics: Conservation and Exploitation.* Cambridge University Press, Cambridge.

Nelson, J.P. (1982) Highway noise and property values: a survey of recent evidence. *Journal of Transport Economics and Policy* **XIC**, 37–52.

Neumayer, E. (1999) *Weak versus Strong Sustainability: Exploring the Limits of Two Opposing Paradigms.* Edward Elgar, Cheltenham.

Nicoletti, G. and Oliveira-Martins, J. (1993) Global effects of a European carbon tax, in Carraro, C. and Siniscalco, D. (eds) *The European Carbon Tax: An Economic Assessment.* Kluwer, Dordrecht.

Nordhaus, W.D. (1972) *World Dynamics: Measurement without Data.* Cowles Foundation Discussion Paper. Reprinted in *The Economic Journal,* December 1973, 1156–1183.

Nordhaus, W.D. (1973) The allocation of energy resources. *Brookings Papers on Economic Activity* **3**, 529–576.

Nordhaus, W.D. (1977) The demand for energy: an international perspective, in Nordhaus, W.D. (ed.) *International Studies in the Demand for Energy*. North Holland, Amsterdam.

Nordhaus, W. (1982) How fast should we graze the global commons? *American Economic Review*, Papers and Proceedings **72**, 242–246.

Nordhaus, W. (1989) *The Economics of the Greenhouse Effect*. Mimeo, Department of Economics, Yale University, New Haven, CT.

Nordhaus, W. (1990a) Greenhouse economics. *The Economist*, 7 July.

Nordhaus, W. (1990b) *An Intertemporal General Equilibrium Model of Economic Growth and Climate Change*. Yale University. Paper presented at Workshop on Economic/Energy/Environmental Modelling for Climate Policy Analysis, Washington, DC, 22–23 October.

Nordhaus, W. (1991a) To slow or not to slow: the economics of the greenhouse effect. *The Economic Journal* **101**, 920–937.

Nordhaus, W. (1991b) The cost of slowing climate: a survey. *The Energy Journal* **12**, 37–65.

Nordhaus, W.D. (1994) *Managing the Global Commons: The Economics of Climate Change*. The MIT Press, Cambridge, MA.

Nordhaus, W.D. (2001) Global warming economics. *Science* **294**(5545): 1283–1284.

Nordhaus, W.D. and Boyer, J. (1999) Roll the DICE again: economic models of global warming. Electronic Manuscript version DICE v.101599, 25 October. Internet availability at: www.econ.yale.edu/~nordhaus/homepage/homepage.htm

Norgaard, R.B. (1975) Resource scarcity and new technology in US petroleum development. *Natural Resources Journal* **15**, 265–295.

Norgaard, R.B. (1984) Coevolutionary development potential. *Land Economics* **60**, 160–173.

Norgaard, R.B. (1988) The rise of the global economy and the loss of biological diversity, in Wilson, E.O. (ed.) *Biodiversity*. National Academy of Science Press, Washington, DC.

Norton, B.G. (1994) Economists' preferences and the preferences of economists, *Environmental Values* **3**, 311–32.

Nozick, R. (1974) *Anarchy, State and Utopia*. Johns Hopkins University Press, Baltimore, MD.

O'Connor, M. (1993) Entropy structure and organisational change, *Ecological Economics* **8**, 95–122.

O'Connor, R. and Henry, E.W. (1975) *Input–Output Analysis and its Applications*. Charles Griffin, London.

Odum, H.T. (1995) *Environmental Accounting: Emergy and Environmental Decision Making*, John Wiley, New York.

OECD (1975) *The Polluter Pays Principle: Definition Analysis Implementation*. OECD, Paris.

OECD (1989) *Economic Instruments for Environmental Protection*. OECD, Paris.

OECD (1994a) *Environmental Indicators: OECD Core Set*. OECD, Paris.

OECD (1994b) *Project and Policy Appraisal: Integrating Economics and Environment*. OECD, Paris.

OECD (1995) *Environmental Taxation in OECD Countries*. OECD, Paris.

OECD (1996a) *Implementation Strategies for Environmental Taxes*. OECD, Paris.

OECD (1996b) *Subsidies and Environment: Exploring the Linkages*. OECD, Paris.

OECD (1996c) *Saving Biological Diversity*. OECD, Paris.

OECD (1997a) *Energy Policies and Employment*. OECD, Paris.

OECD (1997b) *Environmental Taxes and Green Tax Reform*. OECD, Paris.

OECD (1997c) *Towards Sustainable Fisheries: Economic Aspects of the Management of Living Marine Resources*. OECD, Paris.

OECD (1997d) *Evaluating Economic Instruments for Environmental Policy*. OECD, Paris.

OECD (1998) *Improving the Environment through Reducing Subsidies*. Part I, Summary and Policy Conclusions. OECD, Paris.

OECD (1999) *Economic Instruments for Pollution Control and Natural Resources Management in OECD Countries: A Survey*. (ENV/EPOC/GEEI(98)35/REV1/FINAL, 8 October. Available online via www.oecd.org.) OECD, Paris.

Office of Air and Radiation, US Environmental Protection Agency (EPA) and the World Resources Institute (1995) *Protection of the Ozone Layer*. EPA Environmental Indicators, EPA 230-N-95-002 (EPA, Washington, DC, June).

Office of Technology Assessment (1984) *Acid Rain and Transported Air Pollutants: Implications for Public Policy*. US GPO, Washington, DC.

Olson, M. (1965) *The Logic of Collective Action*. Harvard University Press, Cambridge, MA.

Opschoor, J.B. and Vos, H.B. (1989) *The Application of Economic Instruments for Environmental Protection in OECD Member Countries*. OECD, Paris.

O'Riordan, T. (ed.) (1997) *Ecotaxation*. Earthscan, London.

Ostrom, E. (1998) A behavioral approach to the rational-choice theory of collective action. *American Political Science Review* **92**, 1–22.

Ostrom, E., Dietz, T., Dolsak, N., Stern, P.C., Stonich, S. and Weber, E.U. (eds) (2002) *The Drama of the Commons*. Committee on the Human Dimensions of Global Change, National Research Council (US), National Academy Press.

Page, T. (1973) The non-renewable resources subsystem, in Cole, H.S.D., Freeman, C., Jahoda, M. and Pavitt, K.L.R. (eds) *Thinking about the Future: A Critique of the Limits to Growth*. Sussex University Press, London.

Page, T. (1977) *Conservation and Economic Efficiency: An Approach to Materials Policy*. Johns Hopkins University Press, Baltimore, MD.

Page, T. (1982) Intergenerational justice as opportunity, in MacLean, D. and Brown, P. (eds) *Energy and the Future*. Rowman and Littlefield, London, MD.

Page, T. (1997) On the problem of achieving efficiency and equity, intergenerationally. *Land Economics* **73**(4), 580–596.

Palmquist, R.B. (1999) Hedonic models, in van den Bergh, J.C.J.M. (ed.) *Handbook of Environmental and Resource Economics*. Edward Elgar, Cheltenham.

Panayotou, T. (1993) *Empirical Tests and Policy Analysis of Environmental Degradation at Different Stages of Economic Development*. Working Paper WP238, Technology and Employment Programme, International Labor Office, Geneva.

Pareto, V. (1897) *Cours d'Economie Politique*. Lausanne.

Park, C. (2001) *The Environment: Principles and Applications*, 2nd edition, London: Routledge.

Parry, I.W.H., Williams, R.C. and Goulder, L.H. (1999) When can carbon abatement policies increase welfare? The fundamental role of distorted factor markets. *Journal of Environmental Economics and Management* **37**, 52–84.

Payne, J.W., Bettman, J.R. and Johnson, E.J. (1992) Behavioural decision research: a constructive processing perspective. *Annual Review of Psychology* **43**, 87–131.

Pearce, D.W. (ed.) (1991a) *Blueprint 2: Greening the World Economy*. Earthscan, London.

Pearce, D.W. (1991b) The role of carbon taxes in adjusting to global warming. *The Economic Journal* **101**, 938–948.

Pearce, D.W. (1994) The environment: assessing the social rate of return from investment in temperate zone forestry, in R. Layard and S. Glaister (eds) *Cost–Benefit Analysis*, 2nd edition. Cambridge University Press, Cambridge, pp. 464–490.

Pearce, D.W. and Atkinson, G.D. (1993) Capital theory and the measurement of sustainable development: an indicator of 'weak' sustainability. *Ecological Economics* **8**, 103–108.

Pearce, D.W. and Atkinson, G. (1995) Measuring sustainable development, in Bromley, D.W. (ed.) *The Handbook of Environmental Economics*. Blackwell, Oxford.

Pearce, D.W. and Brisson, I. (1993) BATNEEC: the economics of technology-based environmental standards, with a UK case illustration. *Oxford Review of Economic Policy* **9**(4), 24–40.

Pearce, D.W. and Markandya, A. (1989) *Environmental Policy Benefits: Monetary Valuation*. OECD, Paris.

Pearce, D.W. and Moran, D. (1994) *The Economic Value of Biodiversity*. Earthscan, London.

Pearce, D.W. and Nash, C.A. (1981) *The Social Appraisal of Projects: A Text in Cost Benefit Analysis*. Macmillan, London.

Pearce, D.W. and Turner, R.K. (1990) *Economics of Natural Resources and the Environment*. Harvester Wheatsheaf, Hemel Hempstead.

Pearce, D.W., Markandya, A. and Barbier, E.B. (1989) *Blueprint for a Green Economy*. Earthscan, London.

Pearce, D.W., Barbier, E. and Markandya, A. (1990) *Sustainable Development: Economics and Environment in the Third World*. Edward Elgar, Aldershot.

Pearce, F. (1987) *Acid Rain*. Penguin, Harmondsworth.

Pearse, P.H. (1990) *Introduction to Forest Economics*. University of British Columbia Press, Vancouver.

Pearson, M. and Smith, S. (1990) Taxation and environmental policy: some initial evidence. *Institute of Fiscal Studies Commentary* 19.

Peet, J. (1992) *Energy and the ecological economics of sustainability*. Island Press, Washington, DC.

Peltzman, S. (1976) Towards a more general theory of regulation. *Journal of Law and Economics* 19, 211–248.

Penz, C.P. (1986) *Consumer Sovereignty and Human Interests*. Cambridge University Press, Cambridge.

Perlman, M. (1984) The role of population projections for the year 2000, in Simon, J.L. and Kahn, H., *The Resourceful Earth*. Basil Blackwell, Oxford.

Perman, R. (1994) The economics of the greenhouse effect. *Journal of Economic Surveys* 8(2), June.

Perrings, C. (1987) *Economy and Environment: A Theoretical Essay on the Interdependence of Economic and Environmental Systems*. Cambridge University Press, Cambridge.

Perrings, C. (1989) Environmental bonds and environmental research in innovative activities. *Ecological Economics* 1, 95–115.

Perrings, C. (1991) Reserved rationality and the precautionary principle: technological change, time and uncertainty in environmental decision making, in Costanza, R. (ed.) *Ecological Economics: The Science and Management of Sustainability*. Columbia University Press, New York.

Perrings, C. (1995) Ecology, economics and ecological economics. *Ambio* 24(1).

Perrings, C.A., Mäler, K-G., Folke, C., Holling, C.S. and Jansson, B-O. (1995) *Biodiversity Loss. Economic and Ecological Issues*. Cambridge University Press, Cambridge.

Peskin, H. with Lutz, E. (1990) *A Survey of Resource and Environmental Accounting in Industrialized Countries*. World Bank, Washington DC. Environmental Working Paper 37.

Peterson, F.M. and Fisher, A.C. (1977) The exploitation of extractive resources: a survey. *Economic Journal* 87, 681–721.

Peterson, G.L. (1992) New horizons in economic valuation: integrating economics and psychology, in M. Lockwood and T. DeLacey (eds) *Valuing Natural Areas*, Johnstone Centre of Parks Recreation and Heritage, Charles Sturt University, Albury, NSW.

Peterson, G.L., Brown, T.C., McCallum, D.W., Bell, P.A., Birjulin, A.A. and Clarke, A. (1996) Moral responsibility effects in valuation of WTA for public and private goods by the method of paired comparison, in Adamowicz, W.L., Boxall, P., Luckert, M.K., Phillips, E.E. and White, W.A. (eds) *Forestry Economics and the Environment*. CAB International Publishing, Wallingford, Oxon.

Petsonk, A., Dudek, D.J. and Goffman, J. (1999) *Market Mechanisms and Global Climate Change: An Analysis of Policy Instruments*. Pew Center on Global Climate Change, Arlington, VA, [Online at www.pewclimate.org/projects/polwmarket.html]

Pezzey J.C.V. (1992) Sustainability: an interdisciplinary guide *Environmental Values* 1, 321–362.

Pezzey, J.C.V. (1996) *An Analysis of Scientific and Economic Studies of Pollution Assimilation*. Working paper 1996/97, Centre for Resource and Environmental Studies, Australian National University, Canberra.

Pezzey, J. (1997) Sustainability constraints versus optimality versus intertemporal concern, and axioms versus data. *Land Economics* 73(4), 448–466.

Pezzey, J.C.V. and Toman, M.A. (2002) *The Economics of Sustainability: A Review of Journal Articles*, Discussion Paper 02-03, Resources for the Future, Washington, DC.

Pigou, A.C. (1920) *The Economics of Welfare*. Macmillan, London.

Pimental, D. *et al.* (1995) Environmental and economic costs of soil erosion and conservation benefits. *Science* 267(5201), 1117–1122.

Pindyck, R.S. (1978) *The Structure of World Energy Demand*. MIT Press, Cambridge, MA.

Plott, C.R. (1993) Contingent valuation: a view of the conference and associated research, in Hausman, J.A. (ed.) *Contingent Valuation: A Critical Assessment*. North Holland, Amsterdam, pp. 468–478.

Plourde, C.G. (1972) A model of waste accumulation and disposal. *Canadian Journal of Economics* 5, 199–225.

Plummer, M.L. and Hartman, R.C. (1986) Option value: a general approach. *Economic Inquiry* 24 (July), 455–471.

Pollock Shea, C. (1988) Shifting to Renewable Energy, in Starke, L. (ed.) *State of the World 1988*. Worldwatch Institute, Washington, DC, 62–82.

Ponting, C. (1992) *A Green History of the World*. Penguin, Harmondsworth.

Porter, M. (1990) *The Competitive Advantage of Nations*. Free Press, New York.

Porter, M. (1991) America's green strategy. *Scientific American* 168.

Porter, R.C. (1982) The new approach to wilderness preservation through cost benefit analysis. *Journal of Environmental Economics and Management* 9, 59–80.

Portes, R.D. (1970) The search for efficiency in the presence of externalities, in Streeten, P. (ed.) *Unfashionable Economics: Essays in Honour of Lord Balogh*. Weidenfeld and Nicholson, London, pp. 343–361.

Portney, P.R. (1989) Policy watch: economics and the Clean Air Act. *Journal of Economic Perspectives* 4(4), 173–182.

Portney, P.R. (1990) Air pollution policy, in Portney, P. (ed.) *Public Policies for Environmental Protection*. Resources for the Future, Washington, DC.

Prell, M.A. (1996) Backstop technology and growth: doomsday or steady-state? *Journal of Environmental Economics and Management* 30(2), 252–264.

Price, C. (1993) *Time, Discounting and Value*. Blackwell, Oxford.

Proops, J.L.R. and Atkinson, G. (1996) A practical sustainability criterion when there is international

trade, in Fauchez, S., O'Connor, M. and van der Straaten, J. (eds) *Sustainable Development: Analysis and Public Policy*. Kluwer, Amsterdam.

Proops, J.L.R., Faber, M. and Wagenhals, G. (1993) *Reducing CO₂ Emissions: A Comparative Input–Output Study for Germany and the UK*. Springer-Verlag, Berlin.

Proost, S. (1999) Public economics and environmental policy, in van den Bergh, J.C.J.M. (ed.) *Handbook of Environmental and Resource Economics*. Edward Elgar, Cheltenham.

Quinn, E.A. (1986) *Projected Use, Emission and Banks of Potential Ozone Depleting Substances*. Rand Corporation Report, No. 2282, EPA, Washington, DC.

Ramage, J. (1983) *Energy: A Guidebook*. Oxford University Press, Oxford.

Ramsey, F. (1928) A mathematical theory of savings. *Economic Journal* 38.

Randall, A. (1986) Human preferences, economics and the preservation of species, in Norton, B.G. (ed.) *The Preservation of Species*. Princeton University Press, Princeton, NJ.

Randall, A. (1991) The value of biodiversity. *Ambio* 20, 64–68.

Randall, A. (1994) A difficulty with the travel cost method. *Land Economics* 70, 88–96.

Randall, A. and Farmer, M.C. (1995) Benefits, costs, and the safe minimum standard of conservation, in D.W. Bromley (ed.) *The Handbook of Environmental Economics*, Blackwell, Oxford.

Randall, A. and Stoll, J.R. (1980) Consumer's surplus in commodity space. *American Economic Review* 70, 449–455.

Randall, A., Ives, B. and Eastman, C. (1974) Bidding games for valuation or aesthetic environmental improvements. *Journal of Environmental Economics and Management* 1, 132–149.

Rao, P.K. (2000) *The Economics of Global Climatic Change*. M.E. Sharpe, Armonk, NY.

Rasmusen, E. (2001) *Games and Information: An Introduction to Game Theory*, 3rd edition. Blackwell, Oxford.

Rawls, J. (1971) *A Theory of Justice*. Oxford University Press, Cambridge, MA.

Ready, R.C. (1995) Environmental valuation under uncertainty, in Bromley, D.W. (ed.) *The Handbook of Environmental Economics*. Blackwell, Oxford.

Reaka-Kudla, M.L., Wilson, D.E. and Wilson, E.O. (eds) (1996) *Biodiversity II*. National Academy Press, Washington, DC.

Redclift, M. (1992) The meaning of sustainable development. *Geoforum* 23(3), 395–403.

Regan, T. (1981) On the nature and possibility of an environmental ethic. *Environmental Ethics* 3, 19–34.

Reilly, J.M., Edmonds, J.A., Gardner, R.H. and Brenkert, A.L. (1987) Uncertainty analysis of the IEA/ORAU CO₂ emissions model. *Energy Journal* 8(3), 1–30.

Renner, A. (1999) Some methodological reflections: a plea for a constitutional ecological economics, in Köhn, J., Gowdy, J., Hinterberger, F. and van der Straaten, J. (eds) *Sustainability in Question: The Search for a Conceptual Framework*. Edward Elgar, Cheltenham.

Rennings, K. and Wiggering, H. (1997) Steps toward indicators of sustainable development: linking economic and ecological concepts. *Ecological Economics* **20**, 25–36.

Repetto, R. (ed.) (1985) *The Global Possible*. Yale University Press, New Haven, CT.

Repetto, R. and Gillis, M. (1988) *Public Policies and the Misuse of Forest Resources*. Cambridge University Press, Cambridge.

Repetto, R., Wells, M., Beer, C. and Rossini, F. (1987) *Natural Resource Accounting for Indonesia*. World Resources Institute, Washington, DC.

Repetto, R., Magrath, W., Wells, M., Beer, C. and Rossini, F. (1989) *Wasting Assets: Natural Resources in the National Income Accounts*. World Resources Institute, Washington, DC.

Resource Assessment Commission (1991) *Kakadu Conservation Zone Inquiry: Final Report*. Australian Government Publishing Service, Canberra.

Rettig, R.B. (1995) Management regimes in ocean fisheries, in Bromley, D.W. (ed.) *The Handbook of Environmental Economics*. Blackwell, Oxford.

Ribaudo, M.O., Horan, R.D. and Smith, M.E. (1999) *Economics of Water Quality Protection from Nonpoint Sources*. Agricultural Economic Report number 782, Economic Research Service, United States Department of Agriculture, Washington, DC.

Ricardo, D. (1817) *Principles of Political Economy and Taxation*. Reprint, 1926, Everyman, London.

Ritu, K., Robins, N., Chaturvedi, A.K., Srinivasan, R. and Gupta, J. (1996) *Incentives for Eco-efficiency Lessons from an Evaluation of Policy Alternatives: A Case Study of the Steel Sector in India*. Collaborative Research in the Economics of Environment and Development, Working Paper No. 11.

Robbins, L. (1935) *An Essay on the Nature and Significance of Economic Science*. Macmillan, London.

Rogers, J.J.W. and Feiss, P.G. (1998) *People and the Earth: Basic Issues in the Sustainability of Resources and Environment*. Cambridge University Press, Cambridge.

Rojstaczer, S., Sterling, S.M. and Moore, N.J. (2001) Human appropriation of photosynthesis products, *Science* **294**, 21 December, 2549–2552.

Romstad, E., Simonsen, J.W. and Vatn, A. (eds) (1997) *Controlling Mineral Emissions in European Agriculture: Economics, Policies and the Environment*. CAB International Publishing, Wallingford Oxon, UK.

Rose-Ackerman, S. (1973) Effluent charges: a critique. *Canadian Journal of Economics* **6**(4), 512–528.

Royal Commission on Environmental Pollution (1994) *Transport and the Environment*. Eighteenth Report, HMSO, London.

RSPB (1994) *Environmental Measures: Indicators for the UK Environment*. Royal Society for the Protection of Birds, Sandy, Bedfordshire.

Runge, C.F. (1995) Trade pollution and environmental protection, in Bromley, D.W. (ed.) *The Handbook of Environmental Economics*. Blackwell, Oxford.

Russell, C.S. and Shogren, J.F. (eds) (1993) *Theory, Modeling and Experience in the Management of Nonpoint-Source Pollution*, Kluwer Academic, Boston.

Ruth, M. (1999) Physical principles and environmental economic analysis, in van den Bergh, J.C.J.M. (ed.) *Handbook of Environmental and Resource Economics*. Edward Elgar, Cheltenham.

Sagar, A.D. and Najam, A. (1998) The human development index: a critical review. *Ecological Economics* **25**, 249–64.

Sagoff, M. (1988) *The Economy of the Earth*. Cambridge University Press, Cambridge.

Sagoff, M. (1994) Should preferences count? *Land Economics* **70**, 127–44.

Sagoff, M. (1998) Aggregation and deliberation in valuing environmental public goods: a look beyond contingent pricing. *Ecological Economics* **24**, 213–230.

Salop, S., Scheffman, D. and Schwartz, W. (1984) A bidding analysis of special interest regulation: raising rivals' costs in a rent seeking society, in *The Political Economy of Regulation: Private Interests in the Regulatory Process*, Rogowsky, R. and Yandle, B. (eds) Federal Trade Commission, Washington, DC.

Salvanes, K.G. and Squires, D. (1995) Transferable quotas, enforcement costs and typical firms: an empirical application to the Norwegian trawler fleet. *Environmental and Resource Economics* **6**, 1–21.

Sandler, T. (1993) Tropical deforestation: markets and market failure. *Land Economics* **69**, 225–233.

Sandler, T. (1997) *Global Challenges: An Approach to Environmental, Political and Economic Problems*. Cambridge University Press, Cambridge.

Sanjour, W. (1992) *What EPA Is Like And What Can Be Done About It*. Environmental Research Foundation, Washington, DC.

Sarokin, D. (1992) *Toxic Releases from Multinational Corporations*. The Public Data Project, Washington, DC.

Schaefer, M.B. (1954) Some aspects of the dynamics of populations important to the management of commercial marine fisheries. *Bulletin of the Inter-American Tropical Tuna Commission* **1**, 25–26.

Schaefer, M.B. (1957) Some consideration of population dynamics and economics in relation to the management of marine fisheries. *Journal of the Fisheries Research Board of Canada* **14**, 669–681.

Schaeffer, D.J., Herricks, E. and Kerster, H. (1988) Ecosystem health. I. Measuring ecosystem health. *Environmental Management* **12**(4), 445–455.

Schkade, D.A. and Payne, J.W. (1993) Where do the numbers come from? How people respond to contingent valuation questions, in Hausman, J.A. (ed.) *Contingent Valuation: A Critical Assessment*. North-Holland, Amsterdam, pp. 271–293.

Schkade, D.A. and Payne, J.W. (1994) How people respond to contingent valuation questions: a verbal protocol analysis of willingness to pay for an environmental regulation. *Journal of Environmental Economics and Management* **26**, 88–109.

Schmalensee, R., Joskow, P.L., Ellerman, A.D., Montero, J.P. and Bailey, E.M. (1998) An interim evaluation of sulfur dioxide emission trading. *Journal of Economic Perspectives* **12**(3), 53–68.

Schmidheiny, S. (1992) *Changing Course: A Global Perspective on Development and the Environment*. MIT Press, Cambridge, MA.

Schneider, S.H. (1989) The greenhouse effect: science and policy. *Science* **243**, February, 771–781.

Schulze, W.D., Brookshire, D. and Saddler, T. (1981a) The social rate of discount for nuclear waste storage. *Natural Resources Journal* **21**(4), 811–832.

Schulze, W., D'Arge, R. and Brookshire, D. (1981b) Valuing environmental commodities: some recent experiments. *Land Economics* **57**, 151–72.

Scitovsky, T. (1986) *Human Desire and Economic Satisfaction: Essays in the Frontiers of Economics*. Wheatsheaf, Brighton.

Segerson, K. (1988) Uncertainty and incentives for non-point pollution control. *Journal of Environmental Economics and Management* **15**(1), 87–98.

Segerson, K. (1990) Liability for groundwater contamination from pesticides. *Journal of Environmental Economics and Management* **19**(3), 227–243.

Selden, T.M. and Song, D. (1992) *Environmental Quality and Development: Is There a Kuznets Curve for Air Pollution?* Department of Economics, Syracuse University, Syracuse, New York.

Sen, A.K. (1977) Rational fools: a critique of the behavioural foundations of economic theory. *Philosophy and Public Affairs* **16**, 317–44.

Sen, A.K. (1981) *Poverty and Famines: An Essay on Entitlement and Deprivation*. Clarendon Press, Oxford.

Sen, A. (1987) *On Ethics and Economics*. Blackwell, Oxford.

Seskin, E.P., Anderson, R. Jr. and Reid, R.O. (1983) An empirical analysis of economic strategies for controlling air pollution. *Journal of Environmental Economics and Management* **10**, 112–124.

Sethi, R. and Somanathan, E. (1996) The evolution of social norms in common property resource use. *American Economic Review* **86**, 766–88.

Shafik, N. and Bandyopadhyay, S. (1992) *Economic Growth and Environmental Quality: Time Series and Cross-Country Evidence*. Background Paper for the World Development Report 1992, The World Bank, Washington, DC.

Shogren, J.F. (1993) Reforming nonpoint pollution policy, in Russell, C.S. and Shogren, J.F. (eds) *Theory, Modelling and Experience in the Management of Nonpoint-Source Pollution*. Kluwer Academic, Dordrecht, pp. 329–345.

Shogren, J.F., Herriges, J.A. and Govindasamy, R. (1993) Limits to environmental bonds. *Ecological Economics* **8**, 109–133.

Shone, R. (1997) *Economic Dynamics*. Cambridge University Press, Cambridge.

Simon, J.L. (1981) *The Ultimate Resource*. Princeton University Press, Princeton, NJ.

Simon, J.L. and Kahn, H. (1984) *The Resourceful Earth*. Basil Blackwell, Oxford.

Simon, J.L. and Wildavsky, A. (1993) *Assessing the Empirical Basis of the 'Biodiversity Crisis'.* Competitive Enterprise Foundation, Washington, DC.

Singer, P. (1979) Not for humans only: the place of non-humans in environmental issues, in Goodpaster, K.E. and Sayes, K.M. (eds) *Ethics and Problems of the Twenty First Century.* University of Notre Dame Press, Notre Dame, IN.

Singer, P. (1993) *Practical Ethics*, 2nd edition. Cambridge University Press, Cambridge.

Siniscalco, D. (eds) (1993) *The European Carbon Tax: An Economic Assessment.* Kluwer, Dordrecht.

Slade, M.E. (1982) Trends in natural-resource commodity prices: an analysis of the time domain. *Journal of Environmental Economics and Management* 9, 122–137.

Smart, B. (1992) *Beyond Compliance: A New Industry View of the Environment.* World Resources Institute, Washington, DC.

Smith, A. (1776) *The Wealth of Nations* (Cannan, E. ed., 1961). Methuen, London.

Smith, F.D.M., Daily, G.C. and Ehrlich, P.R. (1995) Human population dynamics and biodiversity loss, in Swanson, T.M. (ed.) *The Economics and Ecology of Biodiversity Decline.* Cambridge University Press, Cambridge.

Smith, S. (1993) Distributional implications of a European carbon tax, in Carraro, C. and Siniscalco, D. (eds) *The European Carbon Tax: An Economic Assessment.* Kluwer, Dordrecht.

Smith, S. (1998) Environmental and public finance aspects of the taxation of energy. *Oxford Review of Economic Policy* 14(4), 64–83.

Smith, V.K. (ed.) (1979) *Scarcity and Growth Reconsidered.* Johns Hopkins University Press, for Resources for the Future, Baltimore, MD.

Smith, V.K. (1992) Arbitrary values, good causes and premature verdicts. *Journal of Environmental Economics and Management* 22, 71–89.

Smith, V.K. (2000) JEEM and non-market valuation, *Journal of Environmental Economics and Management* 39(3), 351–374.

Smith, V.K. and Desvousges, W.H. (1986) *Measuring Water Quality Benefits.* Kluwer Nijhoff, Boston.

Smith, V.K. and Kaoru, Y. (1990) Signals or noise? Explaining the variation in recreation benefit estimates. *American Journal of Agricultural Economics* 72, 419–433.

Smith, V.K. and Krutilla, J.V. (1979) The economics of natural resource scarcity: an interpretive introduction, in Smith V.K. (ed.) *Scarcity and Growth Reconsidered.* Johns Hopkins University Press, Baltimore, MD.

Smith, V.K., Desvousges, W.H. and McGivney, M.P. (1983) The opportunity cost of travel time in recreational demand models. *Land Economics* 59, 259–278.

Smith, V.L. (1972) Dynamics of waste accumulation versus recycling. *Quarterly Journal of Economics* 86, 600–616.

Söderbaum, P. (2000) *Ecological Economics: A Political Economics Approach to Environment and Development.* Earthscan, London.

Solow, R.M. (1956) A contribution to the theory of economic growth. *Quarterly Journal of Economics* 70, 65–94.

Solow, R.M. (1974a) Intergenerational equity and exhaustible resources. *Review of Economic Studies*, Symposium, May, 29–46.

Solow, R.M. (1974b) The economics of resources and the resources of economics. *American Economic Review* 64, 1–14.

Solow, R. (1986) On the intergenerational allocation of natural resources. *Scandanavian Journal of Economics* 88(1), 141–149.

Solow, R.M. (1991) *Sustainability: An Economist's Perspective.* Paper presented at Woods Hole Oceanic Institution, MA, 14 June and reprinted in Dorfman, R. and Dorfman, N. (1993) *Economics of the Environment: Selected Readings*, 3rd edition. W.W. Norton, New York.

Solow, R. (1992) *An Amost Practical Step toward Sustainability.* Resources for the Future, Washington, DC.

Solow, R. (1993) An almost practical step toward sustainability. *Resources Policy*, September 1993, 162–172.

Spash, C.L. and Hanley, N.D. (1995). Preferences information and biodiversity preservation. *Ecological Economics* 12, 191–208.

Spofford, W.O. Jr. (1984) *Efficiency Properties of Alternative Source Control Policies for Meeting Ambient Air Quality Standards: An Empirical Application to the Lower Delaware Valley.* Discussion Paper D-118, November, Resources for the Future. Washington, DC.

Stavins, R.N. (1995) Transactions costs and tradeable permits. *Journal of Environmental Economics and Management* 29, 133–48.

Stavins, R.N. (1997) *Private Options to Use Public Goods: The Demand for Fishing Licenses and the Benefits of Recreational Fishing.* John F. Kennedy School of Government, Harvard University and Resources for the Future. Prepared for presentation at the 1997 Allied Social Science Associations meeting in New Orleans, LA, 4–6 January, 1997.

Stavins, R.N. (1998) What can we learn from the grand policy experiment? Lessons from SO_2 allowance trading. *Journal of Economic Perspectives* 12(3), 69–88.

Stebbing, A.R.D. (1992) Environmental capacity and the precautionary principle. *Marine Pollution Bulletin* 24(6), 287–295.

Stern, D.I. and Common, M.S. (2001) Is there an environmental Kuznets curve for sulfur? *Journal of Environmental Economics and Management* 41, 162–178.

Stern, D.I., Common, M.S. and Barbier, E.B. (1994) *Economic Growth and Environmental Degradation: A Critique of the Environmental Kuznets Curve.* Discussion Papers in Environmental Economics and Environmental Management, No. 9409, The University of York, August.

Stern, D.I., Common, M. and Barbier, E.B. (1996) Economic growth and environmental degradation: the environmental Kuznets curve and sustainable development. *World Development* 24, 1151–1160.

Stevens, T.H., Echeverria, J., Glass, R.J., Hager, T. and More, T.A. (1991) Measuring the existence value of wildlife: what do CVM estimates really show? *Land Economics* 67, 390–400.

Stigler, G. (1971) The economic theory of regulation. *Bell Journal of Economics and Management Science* 2, 3–21.

Stiglitz, J.E. (1974) Growth with exhaustible resources: efficient and optimal growth paths. *Review of Economic Studies*, Symposium, May, 139–152.

Stiglitz, J.E. (1994) Discount rates: the rate of discount for benefit–cost analysis and the theory of second-best, in R. Layard and S. Glaister (eds) *Cost–Benefit Analysis*, 2nd edition. Cambridge University Press, Cambridge, pp. 116–159.

Stirling, A. (1997) Multi-criteria mapping: mitigating the problems of environmental valuation?, in Foster, J. (ed.) *Valuing Nature? Ethics, Economics and the Environment.* Routledge, London.

Stockhammer, E., Hochreiter, H., Obermayr, B. and Steiner, K. (1997) The index of sustainable economic welfare (ISEW) as an alternative to GDP in measuring economic welfare: the results of the Austrian (revised) ISEW calculation 1955–1992. *Ecological Economics* 21, 19–34.

Stollery, K.R. (1983) Mineral depletion with cost as the extraction limit: a model applied to the behaviour of prices in the nickel industry. *Journal of Environmental Economics and Management* 10, 151–165.

Streeten, P. (1987) *What Price Food? Agricultural Policies in Developing Countries.* St Martin's Press, New York.

Sutinen, J. and Anderson, P. (1985) The economics of fisheries law enforcement. *Land Economics* 61, 387–97.

Swallow, S.K. and Wear, D.N. (1993) Spatial interactions in multiple use forestry and substitution and wealth effects for the single stand. *Journal of Environmental Economics and Management* 25, 103–120.

Swallow, S.K., Parks, P.J. and Wear, D.N. (1990) Policy-relevant nonconvexities in the production of multiple forest benefits. *Journal of Environmental Economics and Management* 19, 264–280.

Swanson, T.M. (1995a) (ed.) *Intellectual Property Rights and Biodiversity Conservation.* Cambridge University Press, Cambridge.

Swanson, T.M. (1995) (eds) *The Economics and Ecology of Biodiversity Decline.* Cambridge University Press, Cambridge.

Symons, E.J., Proops, J. and Gay, P.W. (1991) Carbon taxes, consumer demand and carbon dioxide emissions: a simulation analysis for the UK. *Fiscal Studies* 15 19–43.

Symons, E.J., Proops, J.L.R. and Gay, P.W. (1993) Carbon taxes, consumer demand and carbon dioxide emission: a simulation analysis for the UK. Mimeo, Department of Economics, University of Manchester, Manchester, UK.

Tahvonen, O. (1995) Dynamics of pollution control when damage is sensitive to the rate of pollution accumulation. *Environmental and Resource Economics* 5, 9–27.

Tahvonen, O. and Kuuluvainen, J. (1995) The economics of natural resource utilisation, in *Principles of Environmental and Resource Economics: A Guide for Students and Decision Makers*, Folmer, H., Gabel, H.L. and Opschoor, H. (eds). Edward Elgar, Aldershot.

Tahvonen, O. and Salo, S. (1999) Optimal forest rotation with in situ preferences. *Journal of Environmental Economics and Management* **37**, 106–128.

Tietenberg, T.H. (1980) Transferable discharge permits and the control of stationary source air pollution: a survey and synthesis. *Land Economics* **56**, 391–415.

Tietenberg, T.H. (1984) *Marketable Emission Permits in Theory and Practice*. Paper presented at the Conference, Economics of energy and Environmental Problems, Yxtaholm, Sweden, 6–10 August.

Tietenberg, T.H. (1989) Acid rain reduction credits. *Challenge* **32**, March/April.

Tietenberg, T.H. (1990) Economic instruments for environmental regulation. *Oxford Review of Economic Policy* **6**(1), 17–34.

Tietenberg, T. (1992) *Environmental and Natural Resource Economics*, 3rd edition. HarperCollins, New York.

Tietenberg, T.H. (1995) Transferable discharge permits and global warming, in Bromley, D.W. (ed.) *The Handbook of Environmental Economics*. Blackwell, Oxford.

Tietenberg, T.H. (2000) *Environmental and Natural Resource Economics*, 5th edition. HarperCollins, New York.

Tobey, J.A. (1990) The effects of domestic environmental policies on patterns of world trade: an empirical test. *Kyklos* **43**, 191–209.

Todaro, M.P. (1989) *Economic Development in the Third World*, 4th edition. Longman, New York.

Toman, M.A. (ed.) (2001) *Climate Change Economics and Policy: An RFF Anthology*. Resources for the Future Press, Washington, DC.

Toman, M.A., Pezzey, J. and Krautkraemer, J. (1993) *Economic Theory and 'Sustainability'*. Department of Economics, University College London, Discussion Paper in Economics No. 93-15, August.

Toman, M.A., Pezzey, J. and Krautkraemer, J. (1995) Neoclassical economic growth theory and 'sustainability', in Bromley, D.W. (ed.) *The Handbook of Environmental Economics*. Blackwell, Oxford.

Tomasi, T., Segerson, K. and Braden, J. (1994) Issues in the design of incentive schemes for nonpoint source pollution control, pp. 1–37 in Dosi, C. and Tomasi, T. (eds) *Nonpoint Source Pollution Regulation: Issues and Analysis*, Kluwer Academic, Dordrecht.

Turner, R.K. and Bateman, I. (1990) *A Critical Review of Monetary Assessment Methods and Techniques*. Environmental Appraisal Group, University of East Anglia.

Ulph, D. (1997) Environmental policy and technological innovation, Chapter 3 (pp. 43–68) in Carraro, C. and Siniscalco, D. (eds) *New Directions in the Economic Theory of the Environment*. Cambridge University Press, Cambridge.

UN (1989a) *World Population Prospects 1988*. Population Studies No. 106, United Nations Department of International Economic and Social Affairs, New York.

UN (1989b) *Levels and Trends of Contraceptive Use as Assessed in 1988*. Population Studies No. 110, United Nations Department of International Economic and Social Affairs, New York.

UN (1990) *Demographic Yearbook 1988*. United Nations Department of International Economic and Social Affairs, New York.

UN (1992) *Integrated Environmental and Economic Accounting*. United Nations, New York.

UN (1993a) *Earth Summit: Agenda 21, the United Nations Programme of Action*. United Nations Department of Public Information, New York.

UN (1993b). Handbook of National Accounting: Integrated Environmental and Economic Accounting. Studies in Method (Series F, No. 61), Department for Economic and Social Information and Policy Analysis, Statistical Division, United Nations, New York.

UN (1996) United Nations Population Division, *World Population Prospects 1950–2050* (The 1996 Revision), on diskette, United Nations, New York.

UN (1997) *Critical Trends: Global Change and Sustainable Development*. United Nations, New York.

UN (2000) *Integrated Environmental and Economic Accounting: An Operational Manual*. United Nations Statistical Division Studies in Methods, Series F, No. 78, United Nations, New York.

UNCTC (United Nations Centre for Transnational Corporations) (1992) *International Accounting*. UNCTC, New York.

UNDP (1990) United Nations Development Programme, *Human Development Report 1990*. Oxford University Press, New York.

UNDP (1995) United Nations Development Programme, *Human Development Report 1995*. Oxford University Press, New York.

UNDP (1996) United Nations Development Programme, *Human Development Report 1996*. Oxford University Press, New York.

UNDP (1997) United Nations Development Programme, *Human Development Report 1997*. Oxford University Press, New York.

UNDP (1998) United Nations Development Programme, *Human Development Report 1998*. Oxford University Press, New York.

UNDP 2000. *Human Development Report 2000*. Oxford University Press for United Nations Development Programme, New York.

UNDP 2001. *Human Development Report 2001*. Oxford University Press for United Nations Development Programme, New York.

UNEP (1987) United Nations Environment Programme, *Environmental Data Report*, 1st edition 1987/88, Basil Blackwell, Oxford.

UNEP (1989) United Nations Environment Programme, *Environmental Data Report*, 2nd edition 1989/90, Basil Blackwell, Oxford.

UNEP (1991) United Nations Environment Programme, *Environmental Data Report*, 3rd edition, Basil Blackwell, Oxford.

UNEP (1995) *Global Biodiversity Assessment*. Cambridge University Press, Cambridge.

UN FAO (Food and Agriculture Organisation) *The State of Food and Agriculture* (1979, 1981, 1985, 1989, 1994, 1995), United Nations, Rome.

UNFPA (1995) *The State of World Population 1995*. United Nations Population Fund, New York.

UNPD (1998) *World Population Projections to 2150*. United Nations Department of Economic and Social Affairs, Population Division. United Nations Publications, New York.

UN Statistical Division (1992) *Handbook of the International Comparison Programme*. Department of Economic and Social Development, Studies in Methods, Series F, No. 62. United Nations, New York.

US Department of Commerce National Oceanic and Atmospheric Administration (1993) *Natural Resource Damage Assessments under the Oil Pollution Act of 1990. Federal Register* **58**(10), 4601–4614.

Usher, D. (1980) *The Measurement of Economic Growth*. Blackwell, Oxford.

van den Bergh, J.C.J.M. and Hofkes, M.W. (1999) Economic models of sustainable development, in van den Bergh, J.C.J.M. (ed.) *Handbook of Environmental and Resource Economics*. Edward Elgar, Cheltenham.

van den Bergh, J.C.J.M. and van der Straaten, J. (eds) (1994) *Concepts, Methods and Policy for Sustainable Development: Critique and New Approaches*. Island Press, Washington, DC.

van Houtven, G. and Cropper, M.L. (1996) When is a life too costly to save? The evidence from US environmental regulations. *Journal of Environmental Economics and Management* **30**, 348–368.

Van Kooten, G.C. and Bulte, E.H. (2000) *The Economics of Nature: Managing Biological Assets*. Blackwell, Malden, MA.

Van Pelt, M.J.F. (1993) Ecologically sustainable development and project appraisal in developing countries. *Ecological Economics* **7**, 19–42.

Varian, H.R. (1987) *Intermediate Microeconomics*, 2nd edition. W.W. Norton, New York. (First edition, 1980.)

Vatn, A. and Bromley, D. (1995) Choices without prices without apologies, in Bromley, D.W. (ed.), *The Handbook of Environmental Economics*. Blackwell, Oxford.

Vatn, A., Bakken, L.R., Botterweg, P., Lundeby, H., Romstad, E., Rørstad, P.K. and Vold, A. (1997) Regulating nonpoint source pollution from agriculture: an integrated modelling analysis, *European Review of Agricultural Economics* **24**(2), 207–229.

Vaze, P. (1998a) Environmental accounts – valuing the depletion of oil and gas reserves, in Vaze, P. (ed.) *UK Environmental Accounts 1998*. The Stationery Office, London.

Vaze, P. (ed.) (1998b) *UK Environmental Accounts 1998*. The Stationery Office, London.

Vaze, P. (1998c) Environmental input–output tables for the United Kingdom, in Vaze, P. (ed.) *UK Environmental Accounts 1998*. The Stationery Office, London.

Verhoef, E.T. (1999) Externalities, in van den Bergh, J.C.J.M (ed.) *Handbook of Environmental and Resource Economics*. Edward Elgar, Cheltenham.

Victor, D.G., Rautsiala, K. and Skolnikoff, A. (eds) (1998) *The Implementation and Effectiveness of International Environmental Commitments*. MIT Press, Cambridge, MA.

Victor, P. (1972) *Pollution: Economy and Environment*. Toronto University Press, Toronto.

Vincent, J.R. (1992) The tropical timber trade and sustainable development. *Science* **256**, 19 June, 1651–1655.

Vincent, J.R. and Blinkley, C.S. (1993) Efficient multiple-use forestry may require land-use specialisation. *Land Economics* **69**, 370–376.

Viscusi, W.K. (1992) *Fatal Tradeoffs. Public and Private Responsibilities for Risk*. Oxford University Press, Oxford.

Viscusi, W.K. (1993) The value of risks to life and health. *Journal of Economic Literature* **31**, 1912–1946.

Viscusi, W.K. (1996) Economic foundations of the current regulatory reform efforts. *Journal of Economic Perspectives* **10**(3), 119–134.

Vitousek, P.M., Ehrlich, P.R., Ehrlich, A.H. and Matson, P.A. (1986) Human appropriation of the products of photosynthesis. *Bioscience* **36**, 368–373.

Vitousek, P.M., Mooney, H.A., Lubchenco, J. and Melillo, J.M. (1997) Human domination of earth's ecosystems, *Science* **277**, 494–499.

Volterra, V. (1931) *Leçons sur la théorie mathématique de la lutte pur la vie*. Gauthier-Villars, Paris.

Wackernagel, M. and Rees, W. (1996) *Our Ecological Footprint: Reducing the Human Impact on the Earth*. New Society Publishers, Gabriola Island, British Columbia.

Wackernagel, M. and Rees, W.E. (1997) Perceptual and structural barriers to investing in natural capital: economics from an ecological footprint perspective. *Ecological Economics* **2**, 3–24.

Wackernagel, M., Schulz, N.B., Deumling, D., Linares, A.C., Jenkins, M., Kapos, V., Monfreda, C., Loh, J., Meyers, N., Norgaard, R. and Randers, J. (2002) Tracking the ecological overshoot of the human economy. *Proceedings of the National Academy of Sciences* **99**, No. 14, 9266–9271.

Walras, L. (1954) *Elements of Pure Economics*. Richard D. Irwin, Homewood, IL.

Warnock, G.J. (1971) *The Object of Morality*. Methuen, New York.

Watson, R.A. (1979) Self-consciousness and the rights of non-human animals. *Environmental Ethics* **1**(2), 99.

Watt, K.E.F. (1973) *Principles of Environmental Science*. McGraw-Hill, New York.

WCED (World Commission on Environment and Development) (1987) *Our Common Future*. Oxford University Press, and United Nations, New York.

WCU (World Conservation Union) (1990) *Environmental Issues in Eastern Europe: Setting an Agenda*. The Royal Institute of Environmental Affairs, Energy and Environment Programme, London.

Weimer, D.L. and Vining, A.R. (1992) Welfare economics as the foundation for public policy analysis: incomplete and flawed but nevertheless desirable. *Journal of Socio-Economics* **21**(1), 25–39.

Weisbrod, B.A. (1964) Collective consumption services of individual consumption goods. *Quarterly Journal of Economics* **78**(3), 471–477.

Weitzman, M.L. (1976) On the welfare significance of national product in a dynamic economy. *Quarterly Journal of Economics* **90**, 156–162.

Weitzman, M.L. (1997) Sustainability and technical progress. *Scandanavian Journal of Economics* **99**, 1–13.

Weizsäcker, E.U. von (1989) *Global Warming and Environmental Taxes*. International Conference on Atmosphere, Climate and Man, Turin, January.

Weizsäcker, E.U. von and Jesinghaus, J. (1992) *Ecological Tax Reform: a Policy Proposal for Sustainable Development*. Zed Books, London.

Weizsäcker, E.U. von, Lovins, A.B. and Lovins, L.H. (1997) *Factor Four: Doubling Wealth, Halving Resource Use*. Earthscan, London.

Weyant, J.P. (2000) *An Introduction to the Economics of Climate Change Policy*. Pew Center on Global Climate Change, Arlington, VA. [Online at www.pewclimate.org/projects/econ/introduction.cfm].

Weyant, J.P. and Hill, J.N. (1999) Introduction and overview. *The Energy Journal*, Special Issue (The Costs of the Kyoto Protocol: A Multi-Model Evaluation), vi–xiiv.

Whalley, J. and Wigle, R.M. (1989) *Cutting CO_2 Emissions: The Effect of Alternative Policy Approaches*. Paper presented at the NBER conference on AGE modelling, San Diego, CA.

Whalley, J. and Wigle, R.M. (1990) *The International Incidence of Carbon Taxes*. Paper presented at conference on 'Economic Policy Responses to Global Warming', Rome, 4–6 October, October 1990 revision. National Bureau of Economic Research, Cambridge, MA; and Wilfrid Laurier University, Waterloo, Canada. Published in *Energy Journal* (1991) **11**(4).

Whalley, J. and Wigle, R. (1991) The international incidence of carbon taxes, in Dornbusch, R. and Poterba, J. (eds) *Economic Policy Responses to Global Warming*. MIT Press, Cambridge, MA.

White, K.S., Manning, M. and Nobre, C.A. (eds) (2001) *Climate Change 2001: Impacts, Adaptation, and Vulnerability: A Report of Working Group II of the Intergovernmental Panel on Climate Change*. World Meteorological Organization – IPCC Secretariat, Geneva.

WHO (1995) *The World Health Report 1995: Bridging the Gaps*. The United Nations World Health Organisation (WHO), Geneva.

Wilen, J.E. (1976) *Common Property Resources and Dynamics of Overexploitation: The Case of the North-Pacific Fur Seal*. Resource Paper No. 3, University of British Columbia, Vancouver.

Wilen, J.E. (1985) Bioeconomics of renewable resource use, Chapter 2 in Kneese, A.V. and Sweeney, J.L. (eds) *Handbook of Natural Resource and Energy Economics*. Volume 1. Elsevier Science Publishers, Amsterdam.

Williams, R.H. (1990a) Low-cost strategy for coping with CO_2 emission limits (A critique of CO_2 Emission Limits: an Economic Cost Analysis for the USA by Alan Manne and Richard Richels), Center for Energy and Environmental Studies, Princeton University, Princeton, US. Published in *Energy Journal*, 1990, **11**(4).

Williams, R.H. (1990b) *Will Constraining Fossil Fuel Carbon Dioxide Emissions Cost so Much?* Center for Energy and Environmental Studies, Princeton University, Princeton, NJ.

Willig, R.D. (1976) Consumer's surplus without apology. *American Economic Review* **66**, 589–597.

Willis, K. and Garrod, G. (1991a) An individual travel cost method of evaluating forest recreation, *Journal of Agricultural Economics* **42**, 33–42.

Willis, K.G. and Garrod, G.D. (1991b) *The Hedonic Price Method and the Valuation of Countryside Characteristics*. ESRC Countryside Change Initiative Working Paper 14, University of Newcastle

Wilson, E.O. (1980) Extract from article published in *Harvard Magazine*, January–February.

Wilson, E.O. (ed.) (1988) *BioDiversity*. National Academy of Science Press, Washington, DC.

Wilson, E.O. (1992) *The Diversity of Life*. Harvard University Press, Cambridge, MA.

Winpenny (1991) *Policy appraisal and the Environment. A Guide for Government Departments*. HMSO, London.

Winter, I.A. (1992) The trade and welfare effects of greenhouse gas abatement: a survey of empirical estimates, in Anderson, K. and Blackhurst, R. (eds) *The Greening of World Trade Issues*. Harvester Wheatsheaf, New York.

WMO (World Meteorological Organisation and United Nations Environment Programme) (1991) *Scientific Assessment of Stratospheric Ozone, 1991*. Executive Summary, 22 October.

World Bank (1992) *World Development Report 1992*. International Bank for Reconstruction and Development, Washington, DC.

World Bank (1993) (Mitchell, D.O. and Ingco, M.D.) *The World Food Outlook*. The World Bank, Washington, DC.

World Bank (1995) *Monitoring Environmental Progress: A Report on Work in Progress*. International Bank for Reconstruction and Development, Washington, DC.

World Bank (1996) *Monitoring Environmental Progress: Expanding the Measure of Wealth*. International Bank for Reconstruction and Development, Washington, DC.

World Commission on Dams (2000) *Dams and Development: A New Framework for Decision Making*. Earthscan, London.

World Commission on Environment and Development. (Brundtland Commission) (1987) *Our Common Future*. Oxford University Press, Oxford.

World Energy Council (1993) *Energy for Tomorrow's World: The Realities, the Real Options, and the Agenda for Achievement*. Kogan Page, London, and St. Martin's Press, New York.

WR (1990) *World Resources 1990–91*. World Resources Institute, Oxford University Press, Oxford.

WR (1992) *World Resources 1992–93*. World Resources Institute, Oxford University Press, Oxford.

WR (1994) *World Resources 1994–95*. World Resources Institute, Oxford University Press, Oxford.

WR (1996) *World Resources 1996–97*. World Resources Institute, Oxford University Press, New York.

WR (1998) *World Resources 1998–99*. World Resources Institute, Oxford University Press, New York.

WRI (2000) *World Resources 2000–2001: People and Ecosystems; the Fraying Web of Life.* World Resources Institute, Washington, DC.

WWF (1993) *The Right to Know: The Promise of Low-cost Public Inventories of Toxic Chemicals.* The World Wildlife Fund, Washington, DC.

Xie, J. (1996) *Environmental Policy Analysis: A General Equilibrium Approach.* Avebury, Aldershot.

Young, J.T. (1991) Is the entropy law relevant to the economics of natural resource scarcity? *Journal of Environmental Economics and Management* **21**(2), 169–179.

Young, M.D. (1990) Natural resource accounting, in Common, M.S. and Dovers, S. (eds) *Moving toward Global Sustainability: Policies and Implications for Australia.* Centre for Continuing Education, Australian National University, Canberra.

Young, M.D. (1992) *Sustainable Investment and Natural Resource Use: Equity, Environmental Integrity and Economic Efficiency.* United Nations Scientific and Cultural Organisation, Paris.

Young, R.A. (2001) *Uncertainty and the Environment: Implications for Decision Making and Environmental Policy.* Edward Elgar, Cheltenham.

Name Index

Subject Index